# Whole Cloth

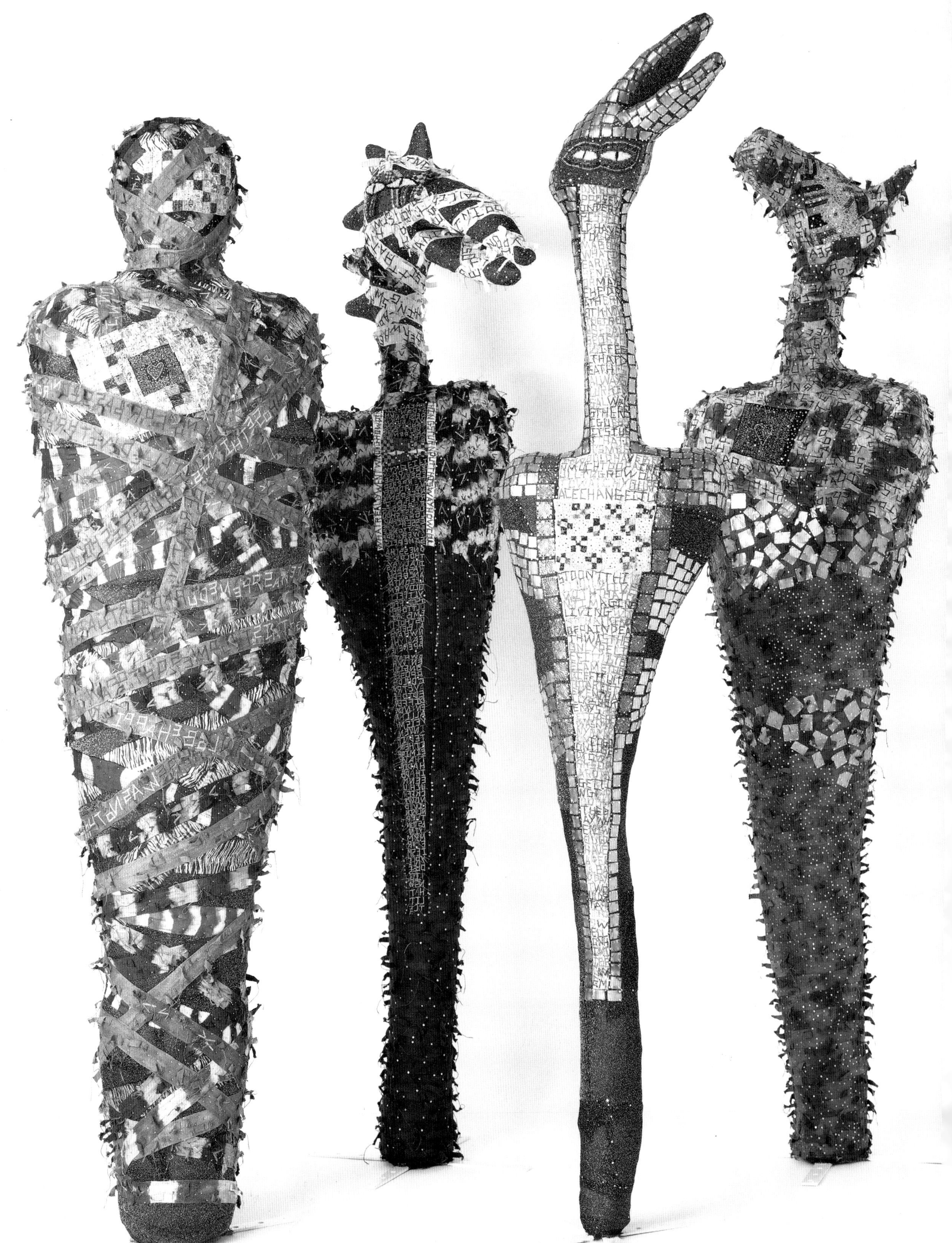

David Lewis-Baker Bath Oct 2007

Mildred Constantine
and Laurel Reuter

# Whole Cloth

The Monacelli Press

First published in the United States of America in 1997 by
The Monacelli Press, Inc.
10 East 92nd Street, New York, New York 10128.



Library of Congress Cataloging-in-Publication Data
Constantine, Mildred.
Whole cloth / Mildred Constantine and Laurel Reuter.
p. cm.
Includes bibliographical references.
ISBN 1-885254-75-X
1. Textile fabrics in art. 2. Art, Modern—20th century. I. Reuter, Laurel. II. Title.
N8251.T4C66 1997
709'.04—dc21 97-28737

Frontispiece: Janet Markarian, Creature Torso series (see fig. 90).

Printed in Hong Kong

Designed by Fahrenheit

# Contents

We dedicate this book to Ralph W. Bettelheim, Mildred Constantine's late husband, for his years of unwavering belief in our work on *Whole Cloth*.

We thank those artists of our own time who took pieces of cloth and transformed them into art. They, along with their dealers, gave generously of their time and information over the long gestation of this book. We thank Walter Scheuer, Elizabeth and Pirie MacDonald, Marilyn Fundingsland, and the late Elaine McKenzie for their kind and active support of Laurel Reuter, who embarked upon this work while simultaneously founding an art museum. We also thank Louise Irizarry, long-time private secretary of Mildred Constantine, who spent endless hours working alongside us during the research and writing. Finally, we thank our publisher, Gianfranco Monacelli, for his sustained interest in the book; our designer, Paul Montie, for his elegant graphic treatments; and our editor, Andrea Monfried, for her diligence and wisdom as she shepherded *Whole Cloth* through its final stages.

—Mildred Constantine and Laurel Reuter

Back in the fifteenth century, "whole cloth" was used synonymously with "broad cloth," that is, cloth that ran the full width of the loom. The term dropped into disuse along in the eighteenth century, except in the figurative sense. In early use, the phrase retained much of the literal meaning, a thing was fabricated out of the full amount or extent of that which composed it . . . But by the nineteenth century it would appear that tailors or others who made garments were pulling the wool over the eyes of their customers, for, especially in the United States, the expression came to have just the opposite meaning. Instead of using whole material, as they advertised, they were really using patched or pieced goods, or, it might be, cloth which had been falsely stretched to appear to be of full width.

Charles Earle Funk, *A Hog on Ice and Other Curious Expressions*

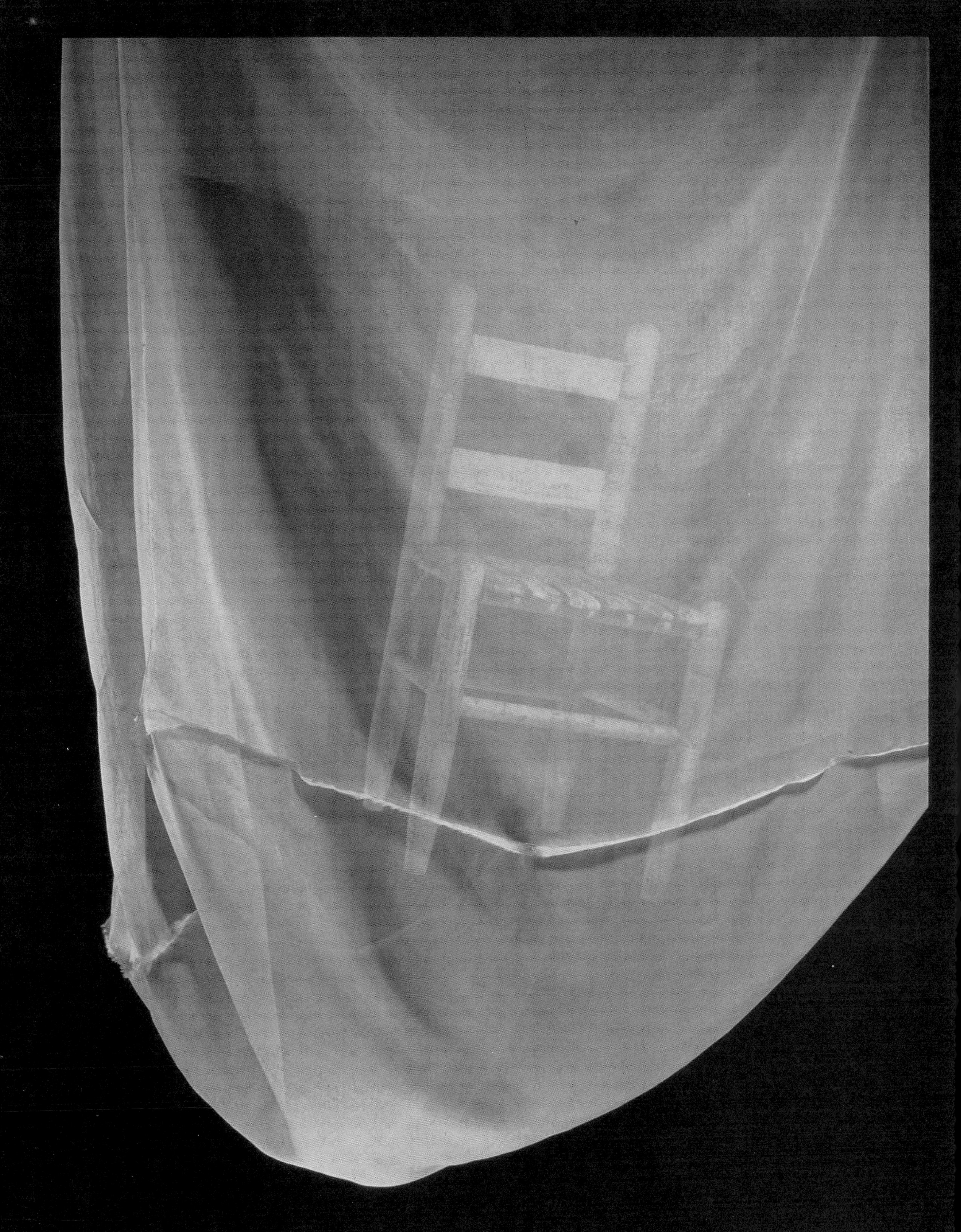

# Introduction

*Whole cloth,* wrote John Ruskin, is "wool of sheep, thread of flax, bark of tree—there exists no matrix. It can be shaped beyond the boundaries of origin. It shifts from the potential to an actuality that has a myriad of shapes and a myriad of ways of moving, responding to the action of the individual who manipulates it. It possesses the mysterious sense of unaccountable life in things themselves."

*Whole cloth* is planar and pliable; it can be given volume. One can animate cloth: drape, crumple, and fold it; compress, pleat, and tuck it; festoon, swag, and swaddle it; bunt it and cut it; tear, sew, and furl it; appliqué, quilt, and fabricate it. Cloth is ductile; it expands and contracts. Cloth can be embellished with stitches, dyes, or print. Cloth can be burned or scored. It is for each generation to expand the vocabulary of approaches to cloth.

*Whole cloth* is a fabricated product obtained by a basic immutable process: yarns are divided into at least two elements, warp and weft, and then interwoven at right angles.

*Whole cloth* has different widths, weights, surfaces, textures, dimensions, and densities and varying degrees of opacity or transparency.

*Whole cloth* demands total design knowledge in its creation. The designer must understand the limitations and capabilities of the production process.

*Whole cloth* is a fabrication or fictitious statement or forgery.

Cloth. What an elegant substance it is, at play with the breeze, in combat with the wind, protecting and wrapping and shielding and comforting. Like a seductive woman, sometimes it is bold and sometimes it is barely there. Cloth is the stuff of mystery for making costumes and stage sets, wedding veils and death shrouds. Even children use lengths of cloth when they first begin to play dress-up. Cloth, that old silent companion of the human race, has always kept very special company with artists. This is a book about cloth and the magic artists make of it.

Lenore Tawney, *In Utero I* (see figure 78).

For hundreds of years painters used cloth strictly as support for their pigments. Cloth was the unobtrusive partner in the relationship. Then, beginning around 1912 with Pablo Picasso and Georges Braque, cloth assumed an unprecedented role in art—it moved from behind the picture plane. Those two artists were the first to make collages with cloth. Later others made assemblages, environments, and three-dimensional sculpture. Such creative innovators as Christo, Robert Rauschenberg, Salvador Dalí, Claes Oldenburg, Mariano Fortuny, and Henri Cartier-Bresson independently gravitated to cloth because it allowed them great freedom; they cared little that they had broken ranks with traditional art materials. Rapidly, as the twentieth century progressed, cloth became the medium, the material, the aesthetic, and the substance of much of contemporary art. Scholars, critics, museums, and art schools were forced to reassess the range of materials acceptable for making "high art." This radical change, pioneered by the likes of Rauschenberg, is reflected in all aspects of the contemporary art world, where a multimedia approach to materials has become standard.

Artists working in cloth come from many disciplines, diverse philosophies, and no specific geographical place. They create in no particular art form or style. Collectively they constitute no movement. Rather, they work in the established fields of photography and set design, painting and sculpture, architecture and fashion. However, by having released themselves from traditional ideas about the use of materials, they are free to create new ways of making sculpture, of creating costumes. In this way these artists redefine traditional art forms. Painting changed totally when cloth became more than a surface for holding paint. The chapters of this book trace the effect that cloth has had upon a broad swath of artists working throughout the Western world.

The chapter ". . . And Then Came Whole Cloth" traces the history of cloth as it was invented and utilized by humans from prerecorded times into the present day. Although first used for clothing and shelter, cloth soon became essential in the making of art. With the advent of the twentieth century, the use of cloth by artists exploded. That explosion, outlined in this chapter, lays the foundation for the rest of the book.

"Metaphor and Symbol" brings together artists from many disciplines intent upon exploring the social dimensions of life through works of art. Early on, Joseph Beuys led in the exploration of the complicated relationships between humans and the cloth they weave. Important artists followed him, including Louise Bourgeois and Michael Tracy. Their work enters the consciousness as both symbol and message. This art is cumulative. Objects pile on top of objects. Bits of information gradually mount into larger truths. The work of these artists has close affinities with the rise of anthropology as a field of study during the modern era, and with the strong influence that archaeology has had upon mass culture in the 1960s and 1970s. Simultaneously politics became an equally vital influence on mass culture, and since then Western art has evolved along parallel lines as it developed a political dimension, especially in the waning years of the twentieth century.

"Unframed, Unstretched, and Unbound" charts the course art took as cloth came off the stretcher, as the vertical and horizontal lost their dominance. Sam Gilliam, by hanging his canvas aloft and unfettered, and Rauschenberg, by using a variety of cloths in various positions, redefined what constitutes a painting. Their seminal visual statements, made in the 1950s and 1960s, have become landmarks of art history. Another generation of artists, including Eva Hesse and Lenore Tawney, took the freed cloth and created new forms that exist in space between the floor and the wall, and that are neither painting nor sculpture. For a while people feared that painting was dead. Today we know that painting just encompasses more definitions and more possibilities.

"Bits and Pieces" explores how collage and quilt making have traditionally reflected the fragmentation of contemporary society. From Kurt Schwitters to Faith Ringgold, artists have cut and reassembled bits of cloth in order to build a cohesive world. Some works are narrative, others abstract. The bits and pieces might be anything: labels, scraps from the wastebasket, ribbons, treasured fragments of cloth—whatever is at hand.

"Sculpted Forms" is not specifically about soft sculpture, although certainly that is included. Instead, it is about the pliable made rigid, and the rigid made pliable. The work is figurative, it is narrative, and it is abstract. The artists are as varied as their methods; Magdalena Abakanowicz, Lee Bontecou, Lloyd Hamrol, Tadeusz Kantor, and Claes Oldenburg all use cloth to sculpt monumental forms.

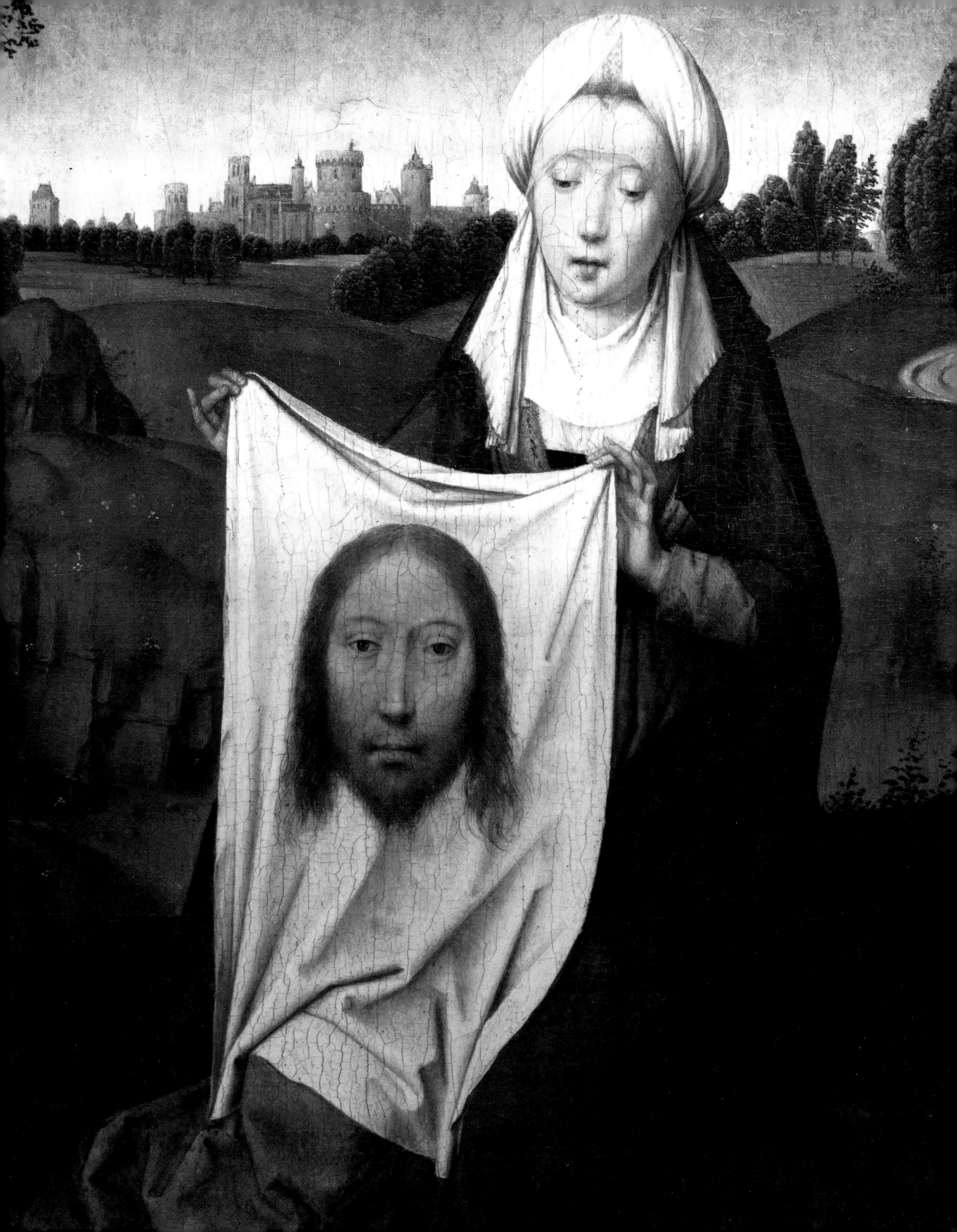

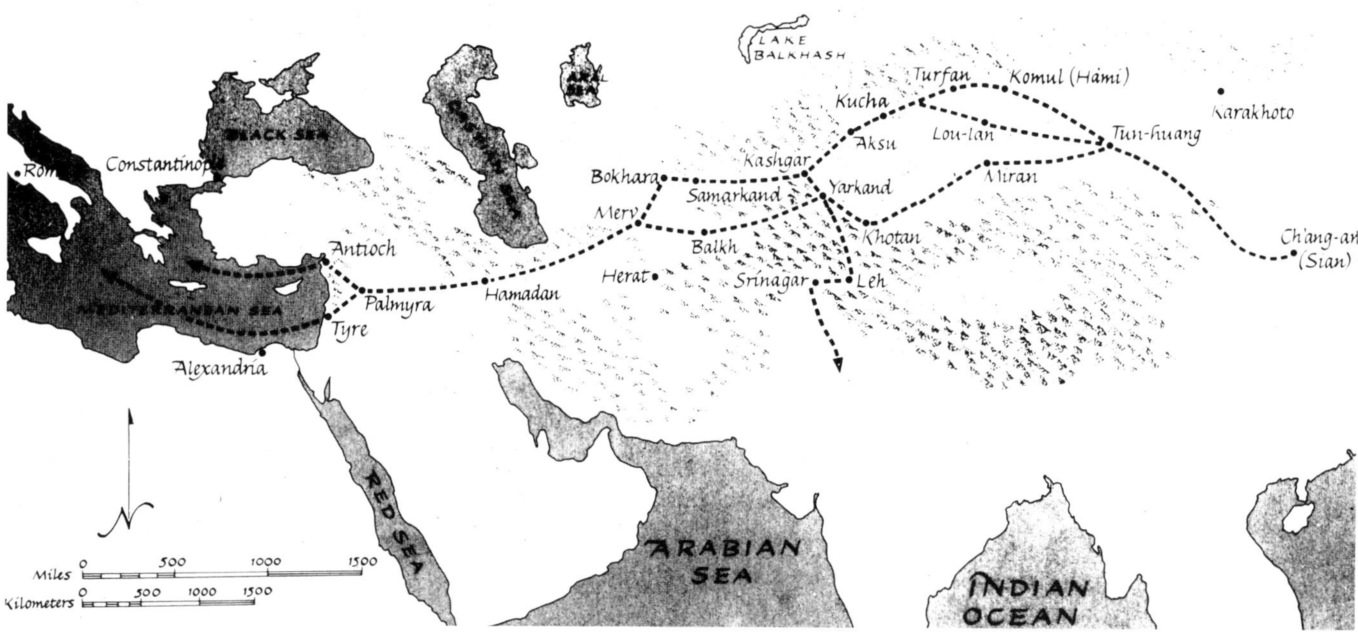


7. Map of the Silk Road.

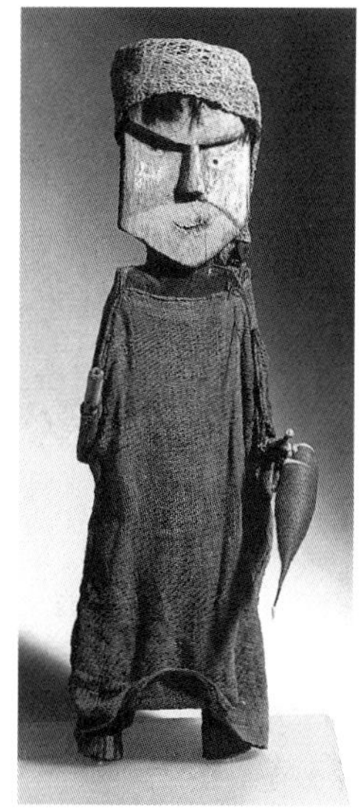

8. Spinner, Chancay, Peru, c. twelfth century. Wood, fabric, thread, human hair, and paint. Collection Israel Museum, Jerusalem.

Woven vegetable fibers in the pre-Columbian culture of northern Peru date back to 8500 B.C. But cordage has been found from as early as 10,000 B.C. in Japan. The late Junius Bird, the eminent scholar from the American Museum of Natural History, stated that, in the main, and throughout all of Peru, cotton was used except in the highlands where it could not be cultivated.[3] Bird further speculated that cloth made of cotton, sometimes smeared with a red pigment, was the first medium of artistic expression on the South American continent (figs. 8, 9).

Researchers wonder about both the beginnings of knowledge and the movement of that knowledge from one culture to another. For instance, scholars believe that sometime after wool came into use in India cotton cultivation began. Because of the humid climate, and because wool decomposes more readily than either flax or cotton, little evidence remains. The earliest cotton fragment now in existence dates from around 1750 B.C. It was found at Mohenjo-Daro in the Indus Valley. This scrap of cloth proves that dyeing with mordants was already an advanced skill in that part of the world. Scholars also assume that trade in cotton cloth existed between India and Babylonia from before the time of Buddha.[4] Fine muslin and calicoes, made in India as early as the eighth century B.C., were brought to the West by traders from the Middle East. Consequently, early Egyptologists assumed that cotton was the material used by the Egyptians to shroud their dead. It was not until 1830 that an Englishman, James Thompson, looked at mummy cloth through the microscope and identified it as having been woven from flax. Since then, researchers have found evidence of processed flax in Egypt as long ago as Neolithic and pre-Dynastic times. Made of the finest linen, mummy cloth has been found with woven widths of over five feet and lengths in excess of sixty feet. It is now known that linen was preferred over wool, the by-product of unclean animals, because it came green from the fields and, through sophisticated processing techniques, emerged as a bleached white thread that could be finely woven. Thus it alone could be worn by visitors to the temples of Egypt; it alone was fit for sacred burials. It was not until the twelfth century A.D. that Egyptians began to produce the cotton cloth they had long imported from India and its more easterly neighbors.

The cultivation of domesticated silk began in China and was already recorded in the written language by 2600 B.C. However, it was not until the beginning of the Han dynasty that China began to export silk. That date, around 202 B.C., marks the dawn of the legendary Silk Road, the great connecting route between East and West, China and Rome. Having two branches, a Northern Route and a Southern Route, the road crossed deserts and high plateaus before finally reaching the Mediterranean. Silk centers sprang up along these routes in the oasis cities—the garrison towns and stopovers. Each came to concentrate on a different stage of silk manufacture; for example, one city might specialize in dyeing, another in unraveling the cloth in order to reweave the threads into cloth of the local taste (fig. 7).

Whereas economic factors forged the Silk Road, it was the transport of ideas, art, and artifacts that altered the course of early civilizations. The plain silks, damasks, gauze, and painted and printed silks, as they moved westward, were most often accompanied by other commodities, such as the medicinal Chinese rhubarb and cinnamon. But in all this traffic, perhaps the most significant and lasting treasure transmitted along the Silk Road was Buddhism, which gradually wound its way eastward from Gandhara to Xi'an, the ancient capital of Cathay—tied up in a bundle of cloth.

The appearance of silk was not confined to China and its export on the Silk Road. For example, there is evidence that the Zapotec Indians from the mountains near Oaxaca, Mexico, gathered a fine, short-fiber silk from the branches of oak trees found in the wild, which they spun and wove into thin crepe, possibly before the Spaniards arrived. This tradition continues today (figs. 10, 11). There is also evidence that silk appeared in northern Europe in the latter half of the sixth century B.C. According to H. J. Hundt, this was indeed cultivated silk.[5] Intriguing questions remain. Did knowledge of the cultivation

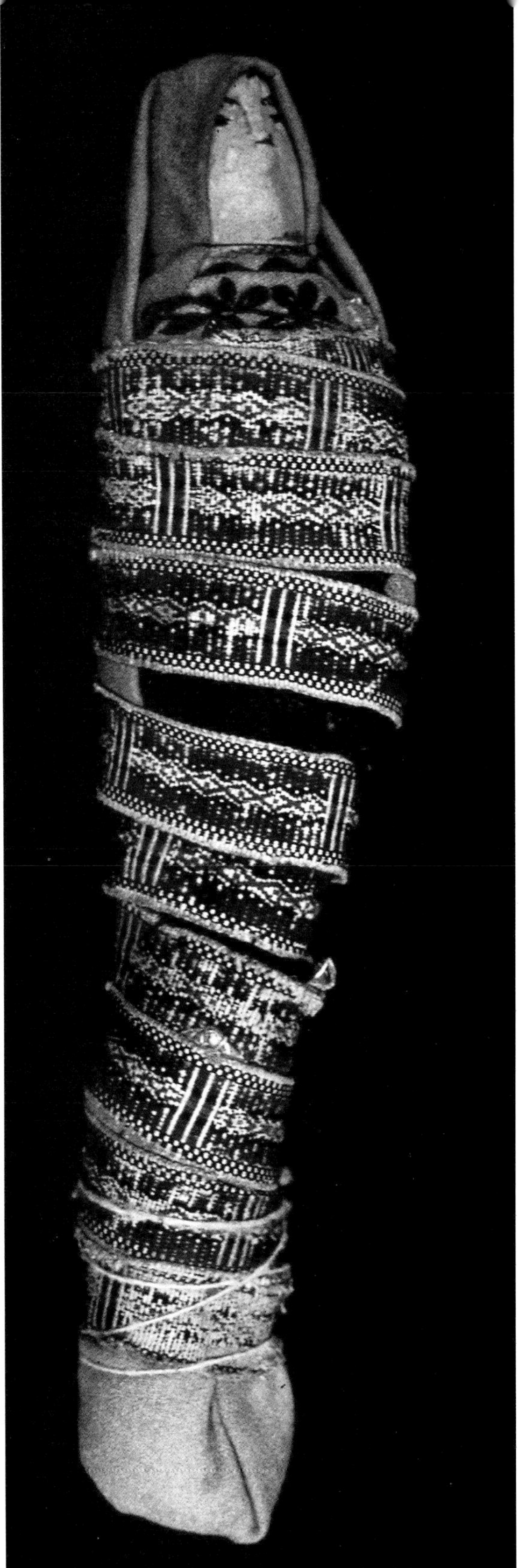

9. Doll, Ecuador, 1982. 17½ x 4 x 3″. Collection Janet Markarian.

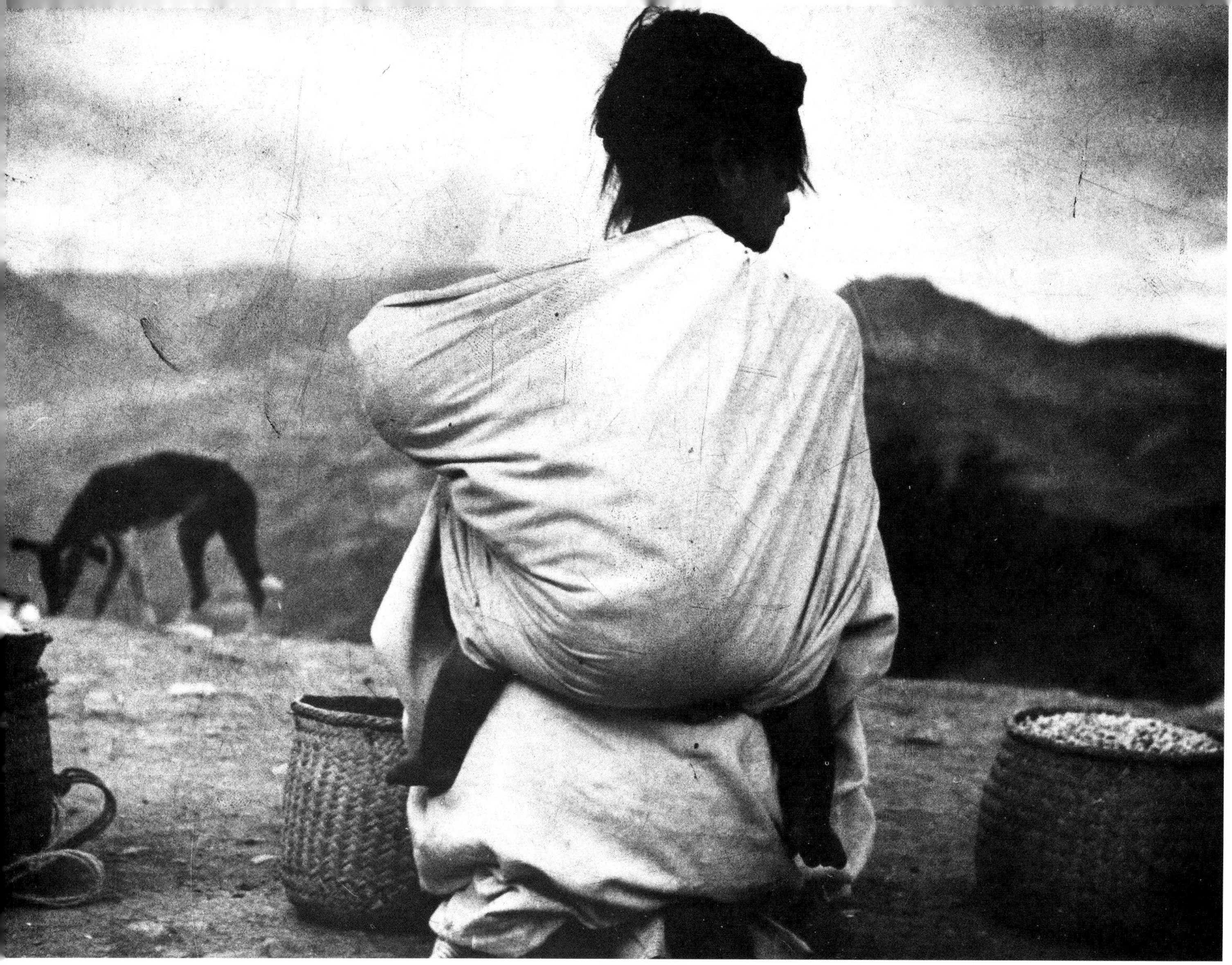

10. Julio Fuentes, *Zapotec Woman*, Oaxaca, Mexico, 1938. Collection Mildred Constantine, New York.

of silk seep out of China before A.D. 550, supposedly the date when missionaries to China smuggled the eggs of silkworms and seeds of mulberry trees out of the country to take to Byzantium in order to encourage the spread of the industry?

Finally, one is left to speculate. Cording and thread making were universal in prehistoric cultures, but the weaving of cloth was not. Why did the weaving of flax and cloth made of bast and wool appear among the early lake dwellers of what is now Switzerland? Why does weaving seem to have evolved independently in India, in Indonesia, and the lands surrounding the Mediterranean, but not in Africa and Australia? These questions remain.

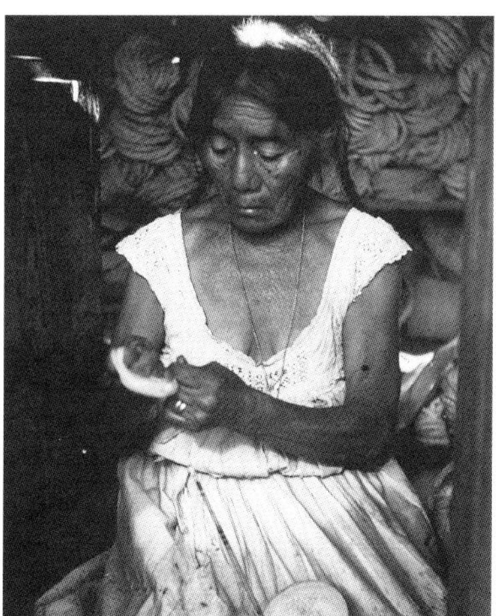

11. James Bassler, *Zapotec Woman Spinning Local Wild Silk*, Oaxaca, Mexico, 1970.

# The Emergence of Cloth in Europe

Swiss archaeologists have proven that prehistoric cloth did exist on continental Europe. It was the trade of cloth, however, that helped shape Europe's history. Before the time of Christ, merchants from the Near East brought fine cottons to Greece, Italy, and Spain. In turn, in the early sixteenth century Portuguese traders passed the cottons on to the Spice Islands, to England and France, and to Mediterranean sites inaccessible to Near Eastern traders. The cities at the hub of that trade were destined to become centers for industries devoted to the production of cloth, including the preparation of fibers, spinning, weaving, bleaching, and dyeing. As these production centers sprang up, associations of cloth merchants developed—first in the Byzantine Empire and later in Greece. By the twelfth century, craft guilds had come to dominate the industry in France, Italy, Belgium, England, Spain, and Germany. Long before the end of the Middle Ages in Europe, the weaving of cloth had become vigorous and well organized. Historian Barbara Tuchman has suggested that the manufacture of textiles was to the Middle Ages what the automobile industry became to the twentieth century.[6]

John Hunisak has written about the guild system in Florence, crediting cloth itself with helping give birth to Renaissance sculpture. According to him, by 1400:

> More than a third of the Florentine population earned its living in the cloth industry, and two of the three most powerful guilds in the city represented that industry—the Lana, who were the wool manufacturers, and the Calimala, who finished imported cloth. So powerful, rich and influential were these two guilds that they were charged by the city government with construction and embellishment of the two most important buildings in Florence. The Lana was entrusted with the cathedral and its bell tower, the Calimala with the baptistery. It was however the lesser known, but wealthy Linauali guild, the manufacturers of linen, who commissioned Donatello to create a statue of its patron Saint Mark for the external niche at Or San Michele. Scholars agree that this work is a revolutionary sculpture.[7]

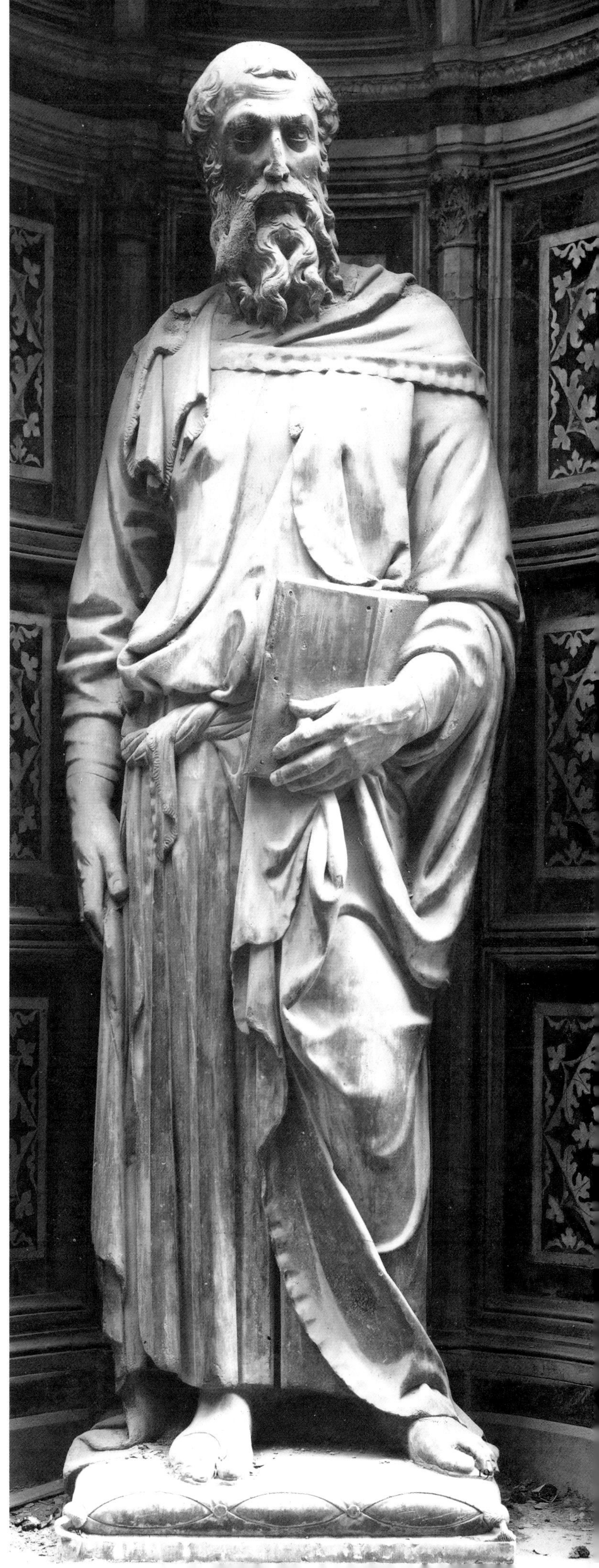

12. Donatello, *Saint Mark*, 1411–13. Marble, 7′9″ high. Collection Church of Or San Michele, Florence, Italy.

When looking at *Saint Mark*, one sees the plasticity of figure and drapery exquisitely revealed by Donatello through the contrasting effects of rhythm. The body is an articulated structure; the drapery is a separate, secondary element determined by the shape underneath. The stone drapery behaves like real cloth in its active dialogue with the body, revealing its shape. The convincing figure looks as if he could remove his clothing if he chose (fig. 12).

Thus, by the end of the Middle Ages, Donatello had created, for the first time, a sculpture in marble where cloth served its natural function of covering yet revealing the body underneath. Draped figures had certainly appeared in art prior to this time. The drapery, however, always concealed the structure of the body, allowing the head, feet, and hands to protrude from the mass of clothing. By his handling of the stone drapery, Donatello redefined the function of cloth as a supple and dynamic entity. He succeeded to such an extent that the viewer senses through sight alone the tactile richness of the stone garments.

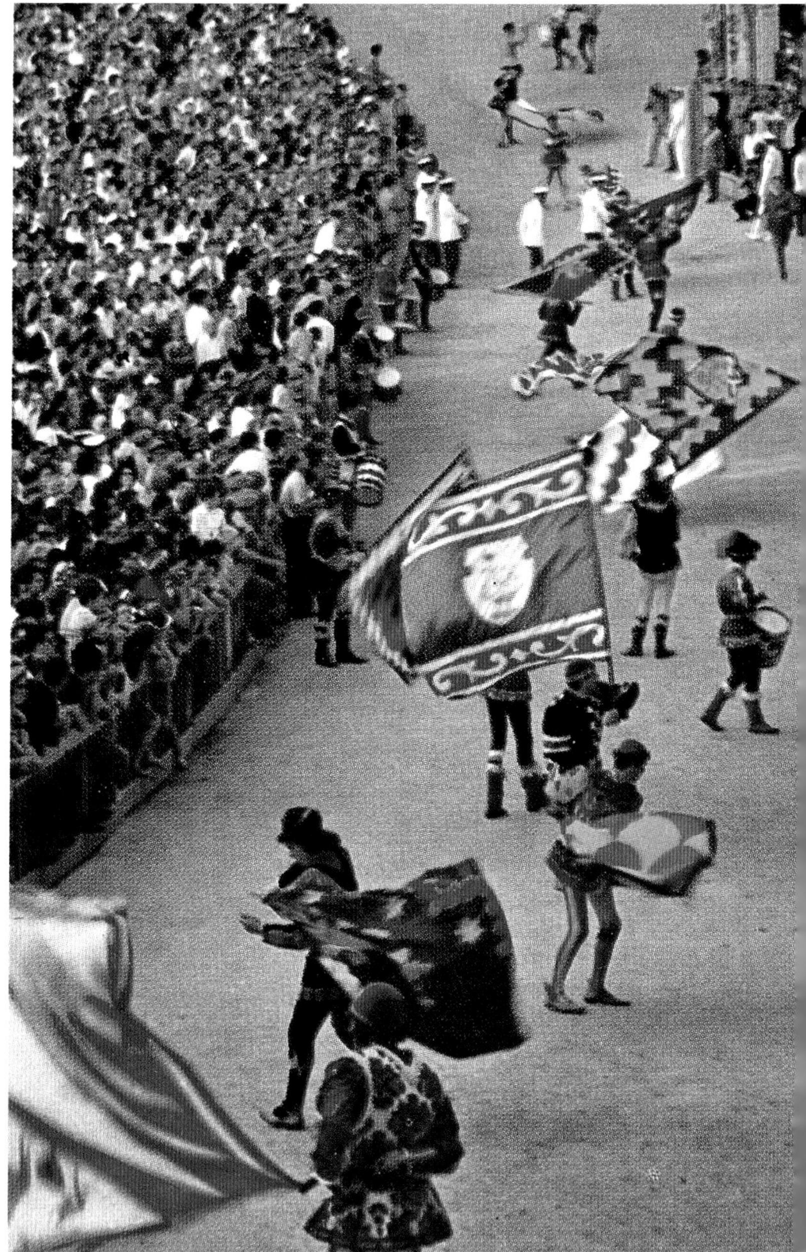

13. Siena flags, Siena, Italy.

# The Artist and Cloth: Historical Precedents

Technically, every painting on canvas or cloth is a painted textile. Artists began using cloth as a support system for their paintings centuries ago. Fabric as support for painting can be traced back at least as far as the Twelfth Dynasty in Egypt (c. 2000–1786 B.C.), and the practice must have preceded that by many centuries.[8]

In 1971 Chinese archaeologists discovered three tombs two miles east of Ch'ang-sha. Known as the Mawangdui Tombs, they have been identified as the burial chamber of the Da family of the Western Han period (206 B.C.–A.D. 9). Two of the three tombs had not been touched for 2,100 years. The remarkably preserved contents included more than twenty ancient Chinese books written on silk (paper was not to be invented until the following, Eastern Han period). The tombs also contained the earliest complete paintings known in China, all executed on silk. Obviously, the technique of painting on silk was highly developed by the time the Da family was buried, between 160 and 150 B.C. Thus it can be assumed that painting on cloth was already an old art form in China. It can also be assumed from the fragments unearthed elsewhere that the tradition of painting on cloth had its impetus in painted temple banners of both silk and ramie.

Another find along the Silk Road is equally important to artists of the latter half of the twentieth century as a historical precedent in the use of cloth for art. In the Silk Road city of Serindia, a walled-up chapel in the Caves of a Thousand Buddhas produced a great cache of textiles, among them the oldest patchwork in existence today. This mosaic-like work was made prior to A.D. 900, whereas the earliest surviving patchwork in England dates to around 1700—a set of bedcovers with matching bed hangings, now housed at Levens Hall in Cumbria.

Cloth became important to artists in Europe at a much later date than in the rest of the world. European artists created in mosaic, in fresco, and in stained glass, all forms tied to architecture. They also illuminated manuscripts and painted in egg tempera on wood. The icon, the altarpiece, the windows and walls of the churches did not indicate the use of cloth, except for the Lenten veil and the silk or linen banner that seemed to crop up everywhere, but especially among the Sienese in the thirteenth and fourteenth centuries (fig. 13).

There was also a wonderful development in England. From the eleventh to the fourteenth centuries the English made superb embroideries on cloth, almost all of which were created for the church. The embellishment of cloth with surface threads certainly was not invented by the English, but they, more than any, put their personal mark upon it. The most remarkable of English embroideries to have survived is the Bayeux Tapestry, made between 1066 and 1082. This splendid work is not a tapestry, although it relates to the wall in the manner of tapestry, but an embroidery, 120 yards long and 20 inches high, worked with wool-worsted thread on coarse linen. The embroidery, which is thought to be commissioned for William the Conqueror's chapel by his half-brother, narrates the story of the Battle of Hastings and the events leading up to the battle.

It was not until the discovery of the artistic possibilities of oil-based paint by the Master of Flémalle and his contemporaries that artists began to paint on canvas instead of wood panels. This coincided with a general desire for lighter, more portable works of art, paintings less tied to architecture, for example Botticelli's *Birth of Venus,* completed in oil on canvas in the 1480s. By the late 1490s a new fashion for thinly painted oil colors on canvas had superseded tempera in much of Europe. By 1509 Giorgione had painted *The Tempest* on canvas. Soon it was the preferred material of both Giorgione and Titian, the painters credited with inaugurating the Venetian High Renaissance. Thus was born the tradition of painting with oil on canvas, which would be unchallenged for the next four hundred years.

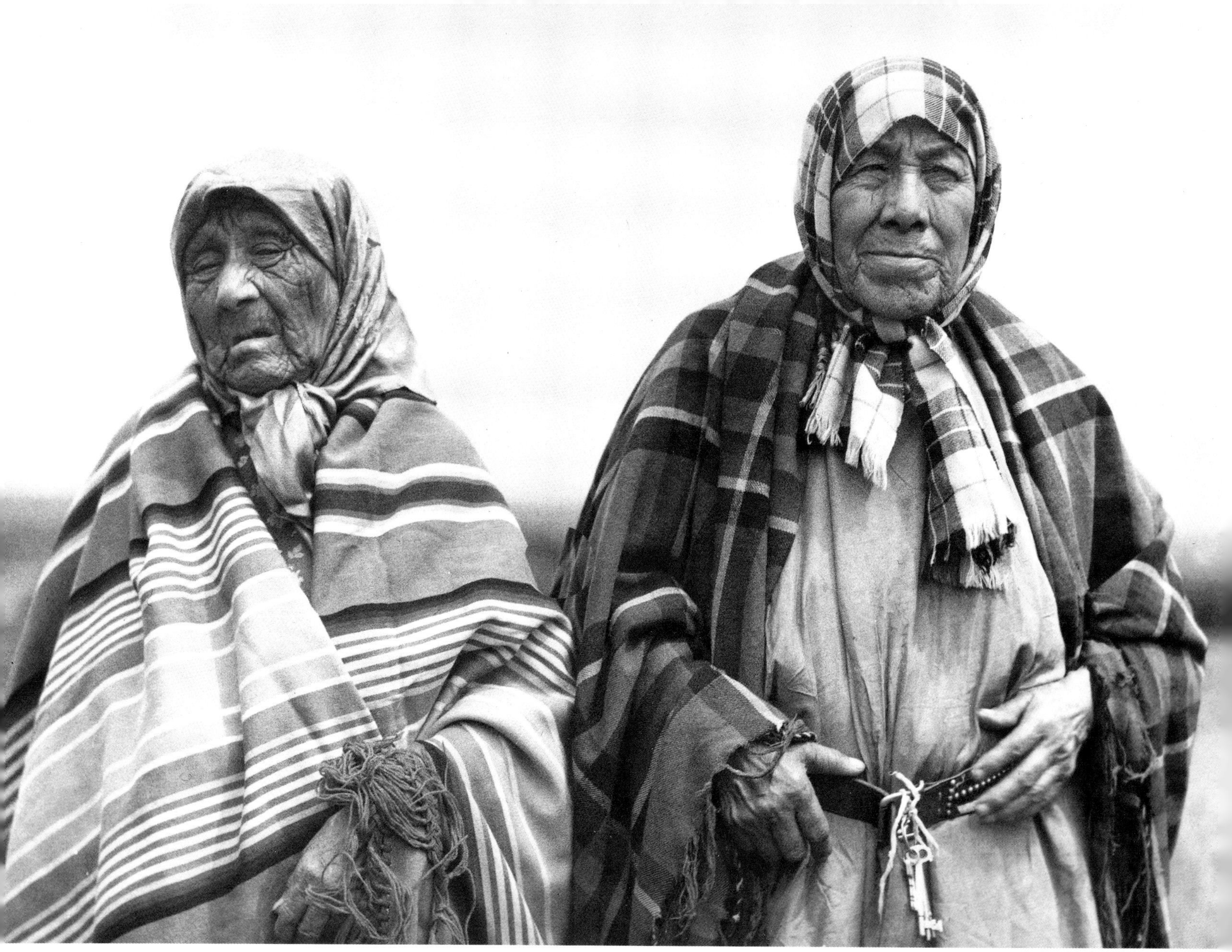

14. Antelope Woman and Sitting Crow (Mandan Indians), June 1942, Ft. Berthold Reservation, North Dakota. Collection State Historical Society of North Dakota, Bismarck.

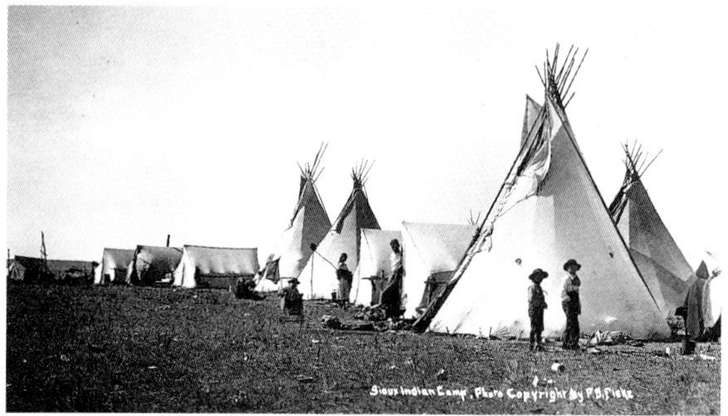

15. Frank B. Fiske, *Sioux Indian Camp,* Standing Rock Indian Reservation, North Dakota, c. 1910–20. Collection State Historical Society of North Dakota, Bismarck.

# Cloth in the New World

In the New World the textile arts began very early and developed to a high level, both aesthetically and technically. By A.D. 1200 weavers in the Andean region were producing some of the finest and most complicated woven fabrics the world has ever known. Long before Europeans stepped ashore, native cotton, supplemented by other vegetable fibers, was being woven into cloth on both continents. In addition, Andean weavers had learned to harvest the glossy wool of the llama and the alpaca and the silky wool of the vicuña.

It was much later, around 1600, that the Spanish introduced sheep to the Pueblo peoples of North America. Because the Navajo, taught by their Pueblo neighbors, did not begin to weave until a hundred years later, they based their whole textile tradition on wool. The Hopi, alone among the North American tribes, have an ancient and continuous textile tradition that goes back to their Anasazi ancestors, who wove cotton cloth from at least the beginning of the Christian era.

Cloth itself had many uses. The Incas and Mayas made objects as diverse as ceremonial masks and children's toys from cloth. The indigenous people of North America used cloth for everything from the inner wrappings of their sacred bundles to clothing and shelter. They fashioned cotton, woven on upright looms, into shawls, robes, breechcloths, sashes, kilts, headbands, garters, leggings, and blankets—especially blankets (figs. 14–16).

Women's dress centered on the blanket in the Southwest, whereas on the Northern Plains, where Native Americans traditionally dressed in hides, the white man's cloth was little used until the Indian's traditional materials became scarce. Thus the wool trade blanket, introduced along with such coveted objects as shiny beads, iron knives, and steel axes as barter for favors or furs, replaced the buffalo robe as an article of clothing sometime in the first half of the nineteenth century on the Eastern Plains. Within the communal life of the Plains Indian, the blanket gradually assumed a very special role. It came to define the private space reserved for courtship. For instance, a Crow man might offer to wrap a desired woman in his blanket, and she had the choice to accept or to reject his offer. If she acquiesced, it indicated the potential acceptance of a more permanent relationship. If the two chose to marry, the people they visited would give them blankets in recognition of their commitment to each other.

By the late nineteenth century, weaving had become a commercial enterprise for Native Americans. The handwoven blanket evolved into the collector's rug. Yet, at the end of the twentieth century, the "store-bought" cloth blanket still plays a powerful role in native societies. In the Southwest, the Blanket Indian, swathed in commercially made sheets or blankets, is the epitome of the "traditional Indian," gracing the communal squares of the pueblos. On the Northern Plains the inexpensive, thermal blanket bought at the local general store has become, along with the star quilt, a traditional gift at a feast or "giveaway."

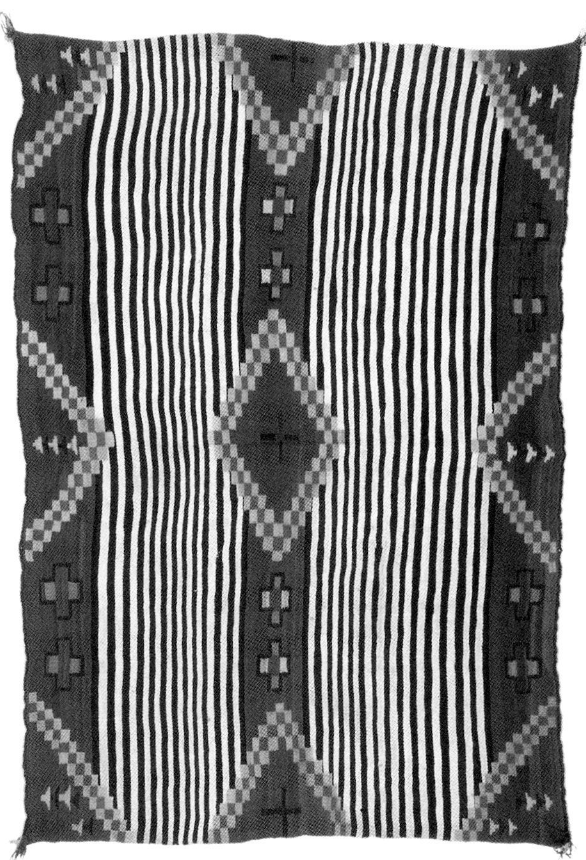

16. Navajo chief's blanket, nineteenth century.

Cloth had other attractions in the New World. Stroud cloth, which came from the small English mill town of Stroud in Gloucestershire, was made as early as 1683 specifically as a blanket manufactured for barter or sale in trading with the North American Indians. This dark blue, red, or sometimes green woolen material was traded to tribes across the continent, but was especially valued on the plains and the prairies, and in the woodlands. Stroud was constructed into whole garments; it was attached to objects such as shields; and it became the streamer needed to adorn the dance costume. Silk ribbons were coveted for similar purposes.

*Bayeta,* the Spanish word for baize, was a coarse woolen stuff, also manufactured in England, traded to Spain, and then sent to Mexico. It finally entered the Southwest around 1800 in the form of yardage or in the uniforms of Spanish soldiers. The Navajo, especially, prized cochineal-dyed *bayeta,* not as a material for constructing articles of clothing but to unravel and

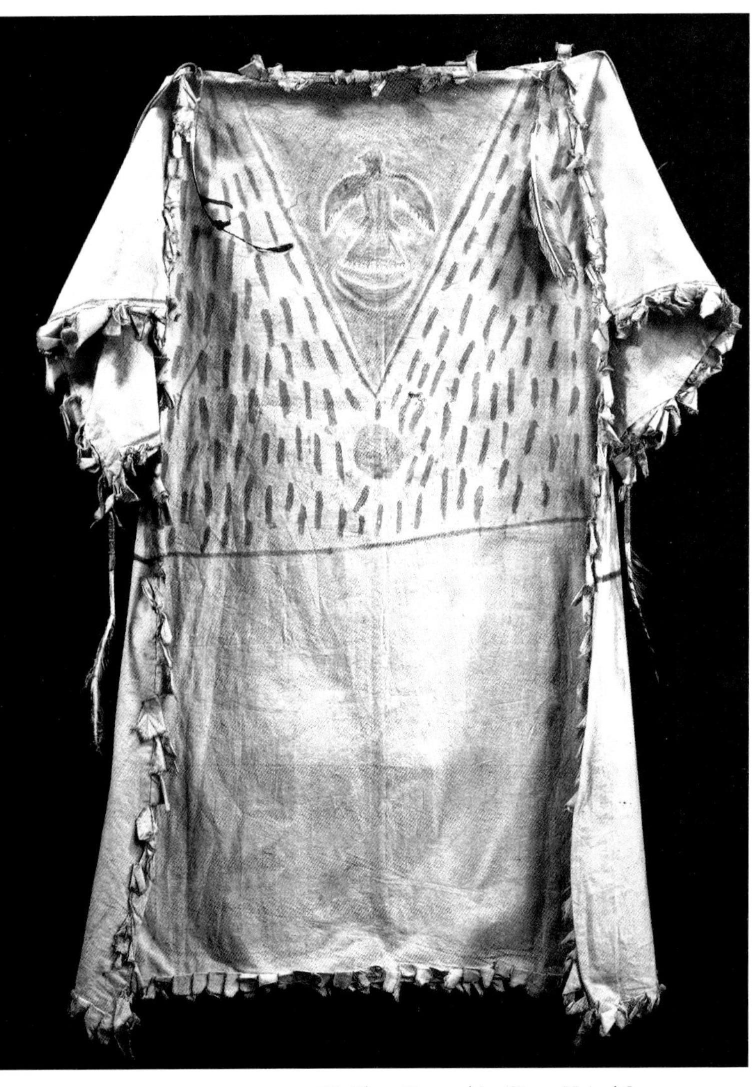

17. Ghost Dance shirt, Sioux, United States, c. nineteenth century. Collection Peabody Museum of Archeology and Ethnology, Harvard University, Cambridge, Massachusetts.

reweave into their blankets. Thus the Navajo abandoned the advantage of ready-made fabric in order to supplement the colors available for their own weaving. When the coveted *bayeta* was unavailable, they resorted to red trade blankets, red flannel underwear, or just red flannel, all to be unraveled and rewoven on their own looms. Little did those Navajo weavers know they were participating in an ancient tradition. For example, when the heavy Chinese silks first arrived in Rome over a thousand years earlier, wealthy women had them unraveled and rewoven into revealing gauze or tapestries, a few of which still survive. Likewise, the city of Palmyra, a stage on the Silk Road, became known as a center for unraveling. Here in that ancient Syrian city, reputedly built by King Solomon, silks were unpicked and rewoven to the local preference. In all of these instances complete unraveling was done for reasons of taste. In Africa, the Kalabari women of Nigeria devised a unique process of altering the pattern of cloth imported from India and England. They cut and removed threads to create a new design in the cloth, that is, cloth by abstraction. The Kalabari still wear such *pelete bite* textiles.

Other forms of cloth became important in the New World in the nineteenth century. As the buffalo became scarce, canvas-covered tepees replaced buffalo-skin tepees. After 1821, factory-made calicoes and coarse muslin invaded the entire North American continent, via Persia, India, England, and then New England. Muslin, along with paper, replaced hide as a foundation for record keeping, winter counts, and painting. And finally, by the late 1880s, the Ghost Dance movement had swept across the Plains, stimulating an outpouring of vision-inspired art on clothing. The coarse muslin shirts and dresses were painted with images believed capable of stripping the white man's bullets of their power, of bringing back the buffalo (fig. 17).

It is thus no surprise that contemporary Native American artists, coming from this strong tradition of soft materials, continue to incorporate cloth into their art. Nor is it surprising that many non-Indian artists have found the indigenous textile traditions of the Americas both powerful and immediate. This influence will be seen over and over in the chapters that follow.

Innovation in the use of cloth was not limited to the native peoples of the New World. For example, patchwork, an ancient method of extending the life of cloth by binding fragments into

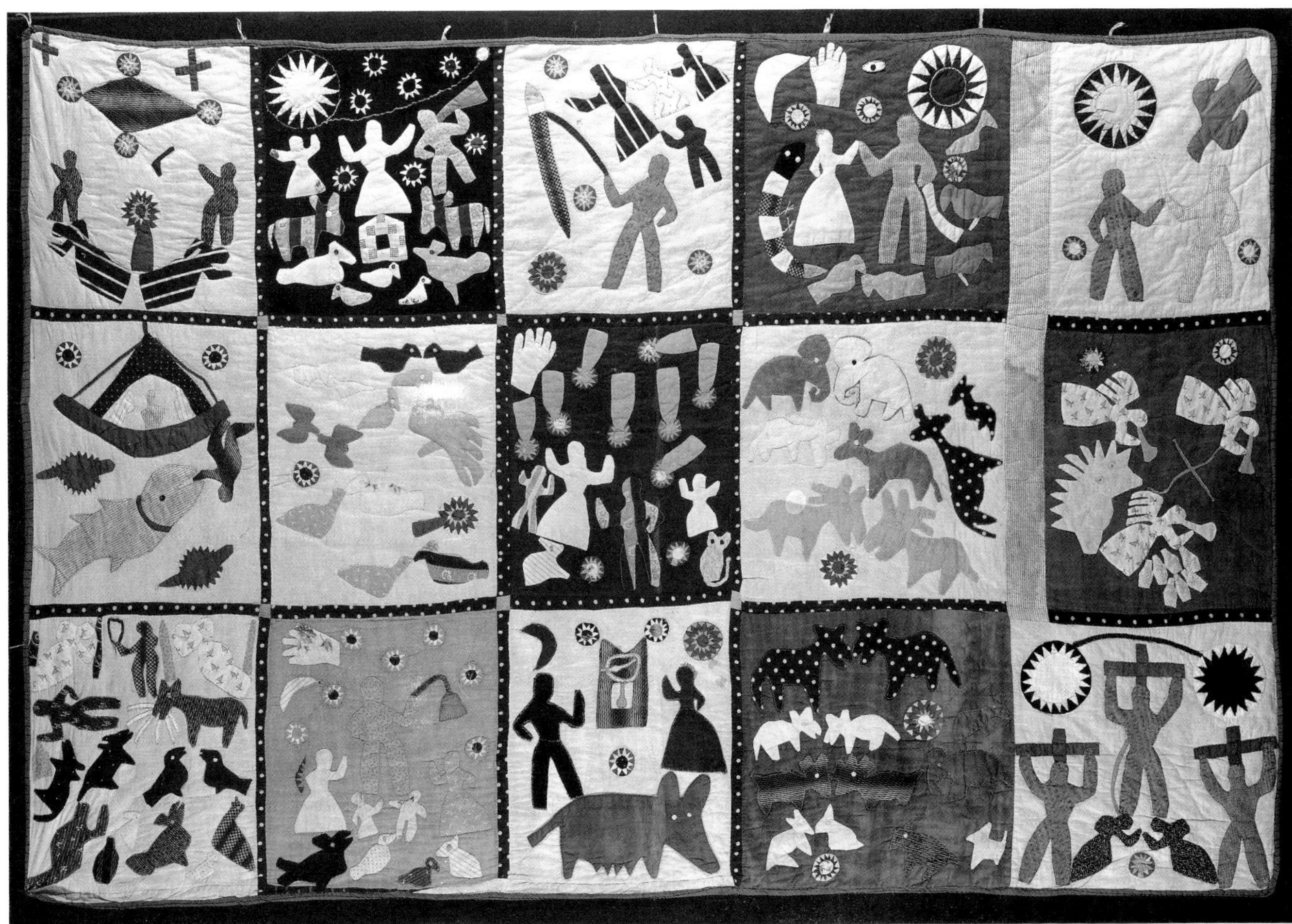

18. Harriet Powers, *The Creation of the Animals*, 1895–98. Pieced and appliquéd cotton with plain and metallic yarns, 105⅛ x 68⅞". Made in Athens, Georgia. Collection Museum of Fine Arts, Boston, Collection: M. and M. Karolik.

a whole, flourished in the United States during the nineteenth century, brought on by two economic forces. Poverty-stricken women mended and patched their way into making pieced quilts to be used as blankets; or more eloquently stated, "A woman made utility quilts as fast as she could so her family wouldn't freeze, and she made them as beautiful as she could so her heart wouldn't break."[9]

At the same time, growing wealth in the United States resulted in a leisure class of women. Sewing bees filled up their afternoons with conversation and quilt making. Through the making of quilts, women were continuing the tradition of English embroidered and appliquéd coverlets. At the same time, quilts were being made by an important third group—African-American women. When quilting for their white owners or employers, they worked in the Anglo-Saxon tradition. However, when making quilts for their own families, they drew on their African traditions (fig. 18; see chapter 4, "Bits and Pieces," for further discussion).

As blankets became commonplace, quilts fell out of favor. It was not until the 1970s that the women's movement rediscovered quilting and brought about a renaissance in the craft, which resulted in quilts becoming accepted today as fine art.

# Cloth and the Industrial Revolution

Cloth was the first material to be industrialized on a massive scale, probably due to the urgent need to clothe a rapidly expanding population. Two inventions facilitated this: the first was the invention, by an Englishman, Edmund Cartwright, of the patterned power loom in 1785. This made it practical to weave wide cloth in quantity. Then in 1793 Eli Whitney developed the famous cotton gin, the first mechanical means to separate fiber from the cotton seed, thus clearing the way for the mass production of cloth.

Meanwhile, the most significant domestic appliance to come out of the nineteenth century was the sewing machine, first designed in 1833 by an American, Walter Hund; improved and patented by Elias Howe Jr. in 1846; and perfected by Isaac Singer in 1851.[10] The sewing machine did more than any other product or invention of the time to liberate women from domestic drudgery. In the decades following industrialization, good ready-made clothing became more and more available to everyone at a cost of one-sixth of the time and energy required by hand sewing. Once clothes were less costly, the public was willing to exchange durability and service for style and fashion. This increased the demand for new clothing, encouraged further industrialization, and stimulated the distribution, promotion, and merchandising of the newly designed fashions created for each coming season. This same system of supply and demand continues into contemporary times.

However, it was not long before people began to react against the uniformly mundane cloth coming out of factories. They yearned for handcrafted materials and goods. England, as the chief innovator of the eighteenth-century Industrial Revolution, had a particularly long road to travel to develop a viable modern craft movement. This dissatisfaction with the low level of design brought about by industrialization eventually spawned the Arts and Crafts movement in 1888. The leaders of the movement urged a unification of all the arts and crafts to bring about important reforms in such areas as architecture, interior design, furniture, fabric, carpets, wallpapers, and typography. It succeeded, however, in producing products that were essentially for the elite. Time had become money, and handcrafted items were expensive. There was a dissident group within the Arts and Crafts movement that still felt the need to reconcile art and society by creating objects of honest design and production. However, the general population could no longer look to handmade, one-of-a-kind, crafted items to meet their utilitarian needs but rather had to choose from the wide array of industrial goods that was coming out of factories. Cottage crafts continued to decline. Nowhere was this more evident than in England, where flourishing textile factories had made manufactured cloth the most accessible of materials.

Although the Arts and Crafts movement was transplanted to the Continent, by the 1900s it had been succeeded by Art Nouveau, claimed by its champions to be the new art of the new times. Unlike the Arts and Crafts movement, the essential thrust of Art Nouveau was the acceptance of technology and the machine as the means of creating a new style of art. This movement swept Europe. Historically, Art Nouveau fulfilled a liberating function by discarding old, outworn conventions, thus setting the stage for the developments that followed in the twentieth century.

# The Twentieth Century: Industry and Design Join Hands

Historians claim that William Morris started the Arts and Crafts movement "by reviving handicraft as an art worthy of the best of men's effort; [however,] the pioneers of the turn of the century went further by discovering the immense untried possibilities of machine art. The synthesis, in creation as well as in theory, is the work of Walter Gropius."[11]

In 1919 Gropius, one of the leading German architects of the time, formed the Staatliches Bauhaus in Weimar, Germany. At the inaugural ceremonies he said: "We seek to form a new body of craftsmen who will no longer know that pride of class that erects a high wall between artisans and artists." For the first time in the Western world, fiber arts were taught right beside painting and architecture—the high arts. The work ranged from pictorial weaving to the exploration of new materials (cellophane and rayon). In addition, the Bauhaus established a laboratory for students to experiment with machines capable of producing for the broadening mass market.

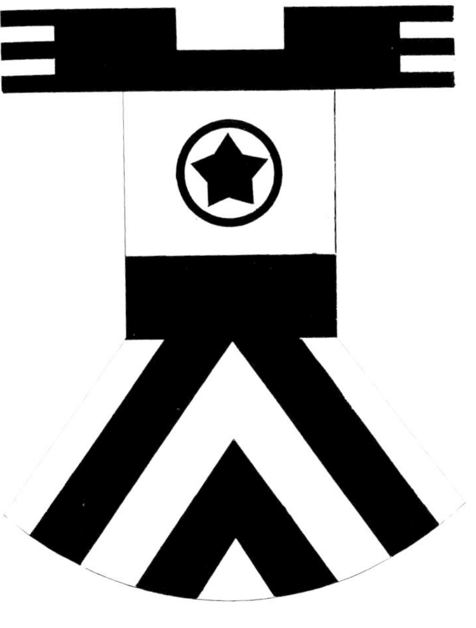

19. Varvara Stepanova, *Design for Sports Costume*, early 1920s.

As the Bauhaus developed in Germany, a second design revolution began in the Soviet Union. Radical Russian artists sought a national renewal in art. Their ideas were as active, creative, and progressive as were Soviet political and social reforms. This extended to such views as those expressed by Vladimir Tatlin, the great Soviet Constructivist, who said: "Artistic creation is a way to find exemplary solutions to society's economic and practical problems."

Varvara Stepanova, impelled by the social views expressed by Tatlin, considered textile production to be significant. Thus it is not surprising that in the 1920s, Stepanova and Lyubov' Popova designed stage costumes as a first step in the systematic work done for textile production, and importantly, they did it without compromising their design principles. They also worked in the design department of the First State Textile Factory (1921). *Design for Sports Costume* reflects Stepanova's use of her talents toward this purpose (fig. 19).

The ideas of high art and commercial design were intermingled by this time. Two major exhibitions best represented this phenomenon, while predicting what would follow in the next decade: the "Exposition internationale des arts décoratifs et industriels modernes," which took place in Paris in 1925, and the "International Exhibition of Contemporary Industrial Art," which was held in New York in 1930.

The Paris exposition clearly indicated a synthesis of two styles into a new, third style, Art Deco, an amalgam of late Art Nouveau with some aspects of Bauhaus style. In addition, it showed that Art Deco incorporated subject material inspired by Aztec and Mayan temples, Native American motifs, Egyptian symbols, and the streamlining of "modernistic" industrial design.

As the Paris exposition testified, new fabric designs were abundant. Artists like Sonia Delaunay created designs for scarves, coats, blankets, vests, and ballet costumes. Delaunay conceived of fabric as a method of working toward modern sensibility. She went on to design several thousand fabrics, having them printed in Lyons, France, and in Holland (fig. 20).

The New York exhibition, held at the Metropolitan Museum of Art, focused on metalwork and cotton textiles, particularly those designed expressly for machine production. It was dominated by Europeans and illustrated the influences of the machine itself, to which all methods of hand production

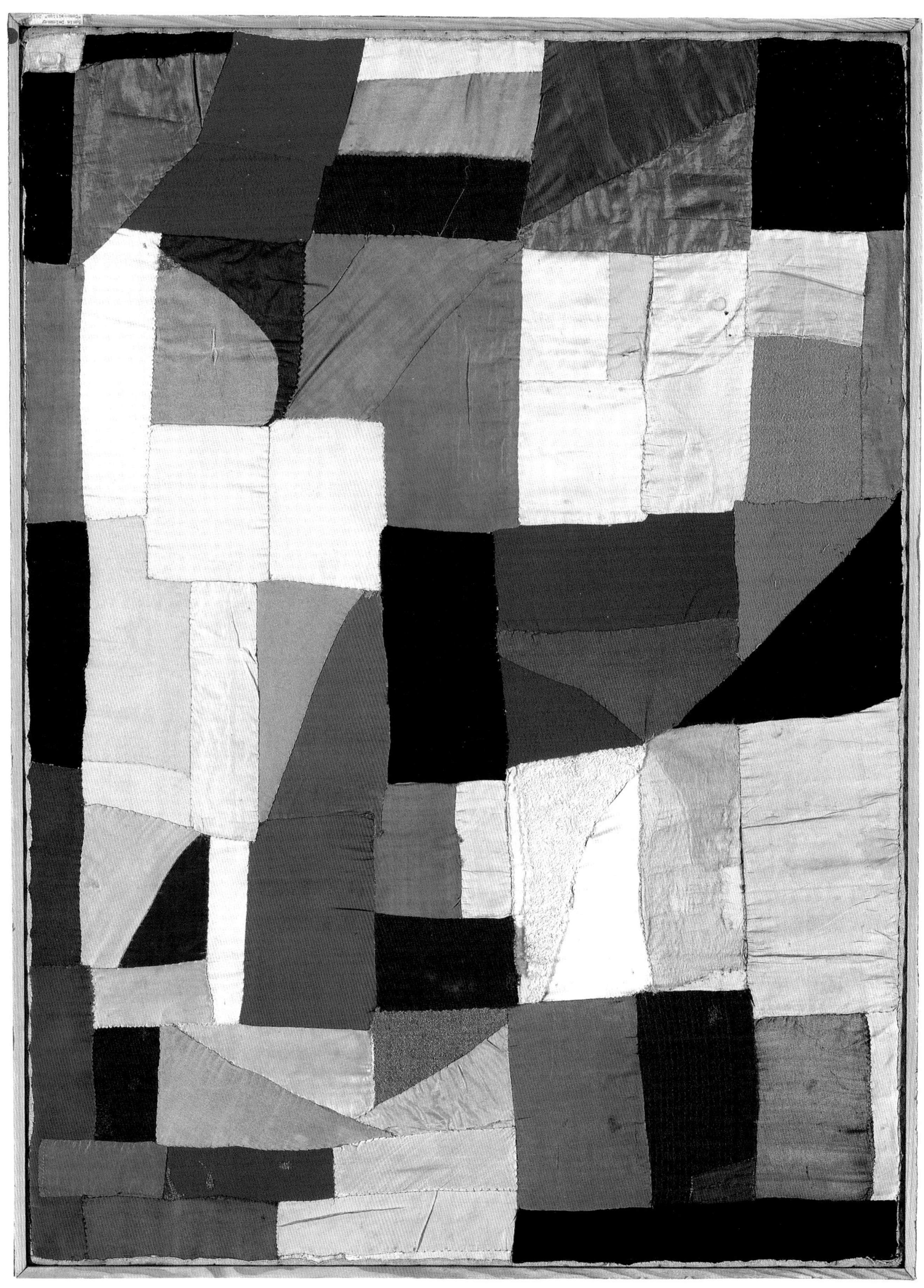

20. Sonia Delaunay, *Blanket*, 1911. Appliquéd fabric, 42⅞ x 31⅞″. Collection Musée National d'Art Moderne, Paris, gift of the artist.

became subordinate. This was the strongest concept to emerge from the exhibition, and it marks the 1920s as a period of transition to the mature industrial age.

"Industrial design" began its undisputed reign in the 1930s. The term was applied to the design of all objects and machines used in an industrialized society. Modern design principles, such as visual coherence, integrated forms, and fit of product to user, determined the streamlined look of everything from gasoline pumps to cigarette lighters, from radios to airplanes.

World War II prompted phenomenal change in industrial design. Even cloth, a natural material, did not escape. The global war disrupted supplies of raw materials, such as silk and rubber, causing the explosion of the synthetics industry in the United States. Nylon, the first truly human-made fiber, was developed in the Du Pont laboratories in 1939 for use in hot-air balloons and parachutes. The United States government heavily subsidized the synthetics industry during the war. Oil became readily available and inexpensive once the war was over. Thus the petrochemical-based, synthetic fiber industry, fueled by the war, went on to dominate the world of cloth well into the 1970s (fig. 21).

The postwar period saw the textile industry accelerate the production of fabrics as it switched to an expanding home market. By this time, immense, complex looms had been introduced, which could produce any textile structure. When the landmark exhibition "Textiles USA" was shown at New York's Museum of Modern Art in 1956, it included well-designed, useful, handcrafted fabrics, as well as manufactured mill cloth and industrial fabrics, such as rayon tire cord fused with synthetic rubber, another by-product of the Second World War.

Challenged by foreign competition, especially by production in Asia, the industry moved into a healthy time. Mass manufacture, low cost, great variety, and controlled improvement in production created a new ideal of quality. With the development of synthetic fiber for domestic use after the war, a wider variety of fabrics than ever became available. In the 1960s, cloth production accelerated, spearheaded by the introduction of innovations such as double knits for apparel and blends for no-iron sheets and shirts. Polyester, first commercially produced in 1953, became king. Its percentage of the fiber market grew from 1960 to 1973 by a phenomenal rate of 27 percent each year. But the synthetic textile industry turned its back on good design. Not until 1980 did it become apparent that the lack of style and the lack of comfort, essential elements in good design, coupled with overproduction, almost killed the synthetic textile industry.

The fabric designer Jack Lenor Larsen has called the 1970s the "beige decade," a time when a vanguard of designers returned to natural materials and colors. Larsen had already industrialized and internationalized his production during the 1960s, so he was ready to lead this movement. He believed that "the future of textile production is here in the United States, where we have the variety, the skills, and revived processes. While technical feats and volume of production are no longer a challenge, we are behooved to keep an open dialogue among artists, craftspeople, and the industry."

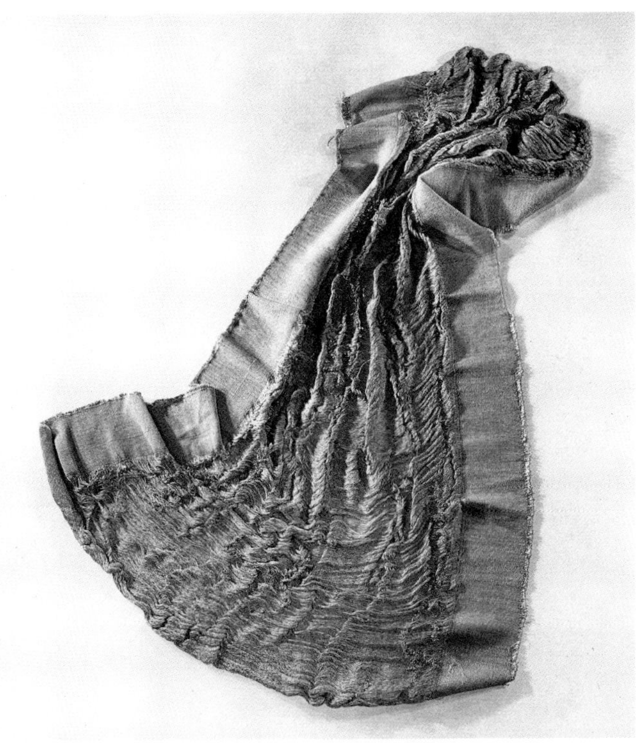

21. Tyron tire cord fabric. Rayon from the Industrial Rayon Corporation, Cleveland, Ohio.

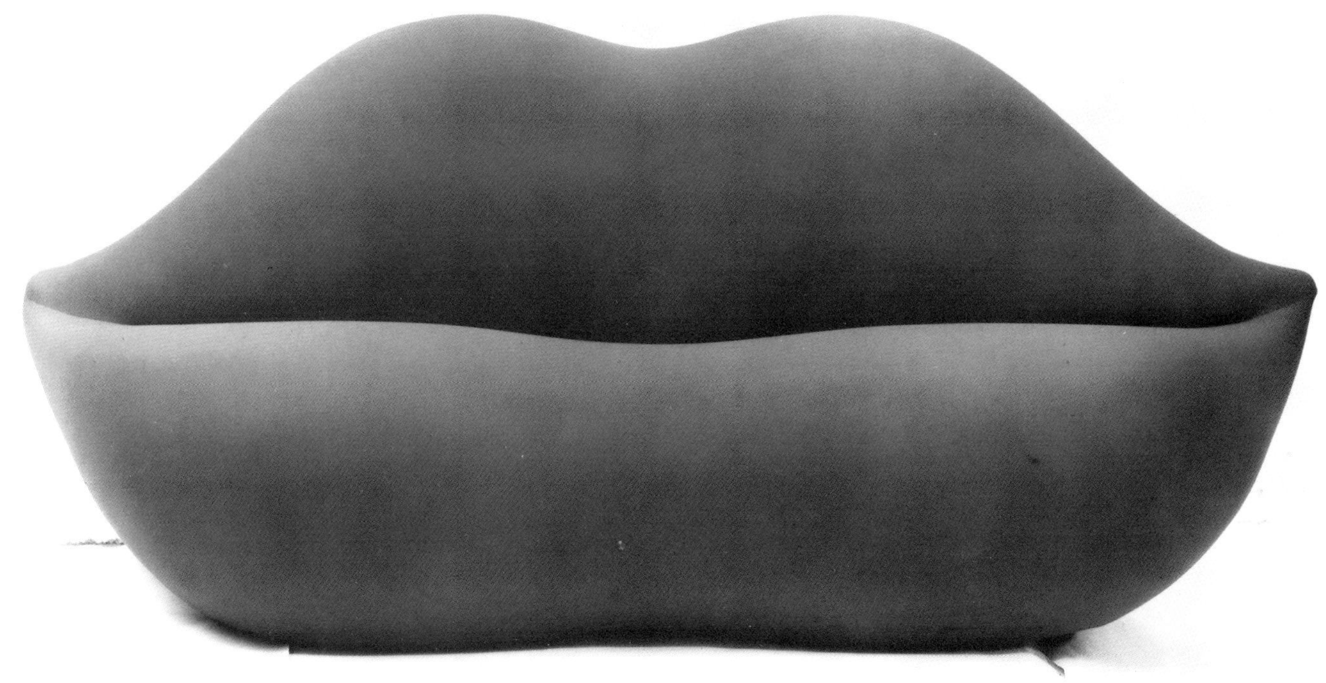

22. Salvador Dalí, *Mae West's Lips,* 1936 copy. Synthetic fabric, 22⅛ x 82⅝ x 31½″. Private collection, Switzerland.

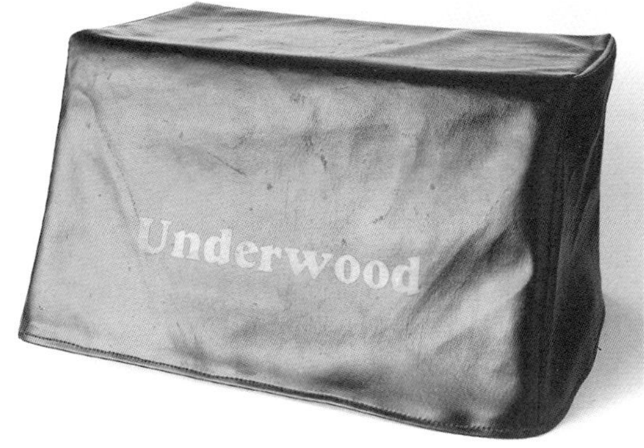


23. Marcel Duchamp, *Traveler's Folding Item,* 1964, third version. Ready-made, black plastic Underwood typewriter cover, 16 x 9⁵⁄₁₆ x 11½″. Collection Ringling Museum of Art, Sarasota, Florida, gift of Mary Sisler Foundation, Mrs. William T. Sisler, 1978 (MF 78.6).

# Cloth and the Fine Arts in the Early Twentieth Century

While the pre-1920s industrial world was producing masses of cloth for general use, artists were appropriating it for their own, other uses. Wrapped, compressed, and not utilitarian, cloth began to play an early and important role in twentieth-century art. By 1912, Georges Braque and Pablo Picasso had begun to make "paste-ups" or collages. This has remained a viable art form right into present times and seems to naturally encompass cloth (figs. 22, 23, 25).

Kurt Schwitters, Man Ray, and Marcel Duchamp, all considered Dadaists in 1920, made important pieces with cloth. In 1920 Man Ray produced a sewing machine wrapped and tied with string on a wheelbarrow—the form smothered in its wrapping. In 1938 Duchamp installed 1,200 coal sacks on the ceiling as an installation piece in the "Exposition internationale du surréalisme" in Paris, thus sowing the seeds for installation art. On the use of cloth by artists of the Surrealist movement, Whitney Chadwick remarked:

> Draped Cloth—gauzy, torn or frayed, thickly folded or stretched taut—surely becomes one of Surrealism's most potent signs that we are at the threshold of an altered consciousness, at the moment when the world of reality fuses imperceptibly with unconscious fear and desire to reveal the surreal. The shroud-like cloths that drape the architectural scaffolding in Kay Sage's paintings or the white cloth that covers the heads of the lovers in [René] Magritte's (recalling his childhood experience of seeing his drowned mother's body with her nightgown drawn around her head hiding her face) carry intimations of death into the world of the living, as I think does the torn fabric that often appears in [Léonor] Fini's paintings in conjunction with bones, skulls, etc. In [Dorothea] Tanning's painting cloth becomes the carrier of unspecified ecstatic emotion and almost always accompanies her prepubescent female figures. In Tanning and in Magritte cloth is often literally drawn back (the curtains in Magritte, for example) to allow us to see into another realm or state of consciousness. And, finally, cloth has a very important function in the work of the women artists when it becomes part of the whole theme of masquerade—of self-consciously created sexual identities based on costuming and display.[12]

Chadwick's observations certainly foretold the fiber installations that were to emerge in the 1960s. However, the formal Surrealist movement came to an end in the early 1940s with the beginning of the Second World War. Art, like life, was subsumed by the war (fig. 24).

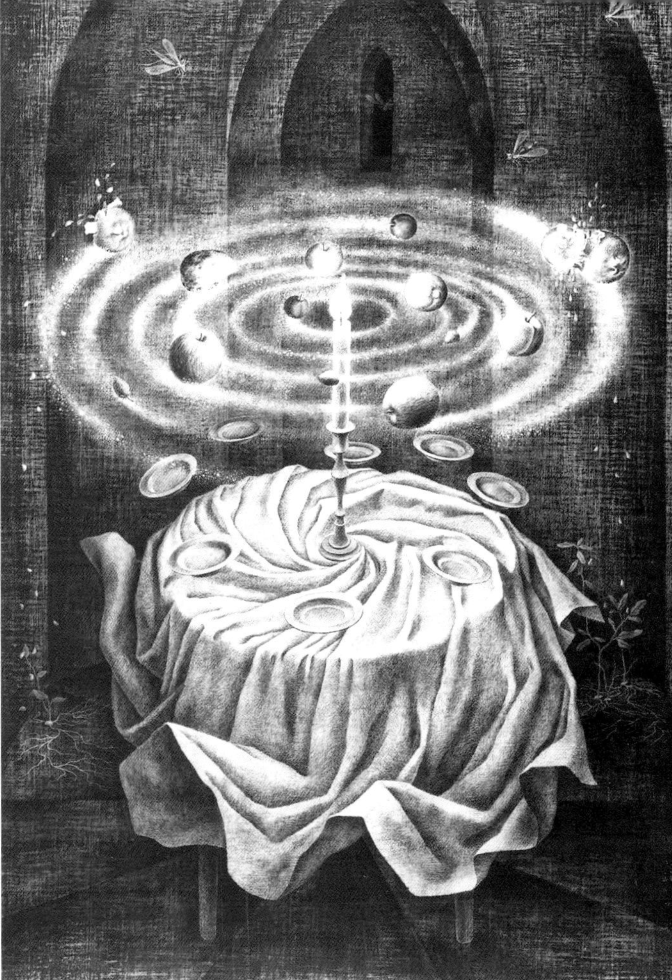

24. Remedios Varo, *Resurrected Still Life*, 1963. Oil on canvas, 43⅜ x 31½". Collection Sra. Alejandra Varsoviano de Gruen, Mexico.

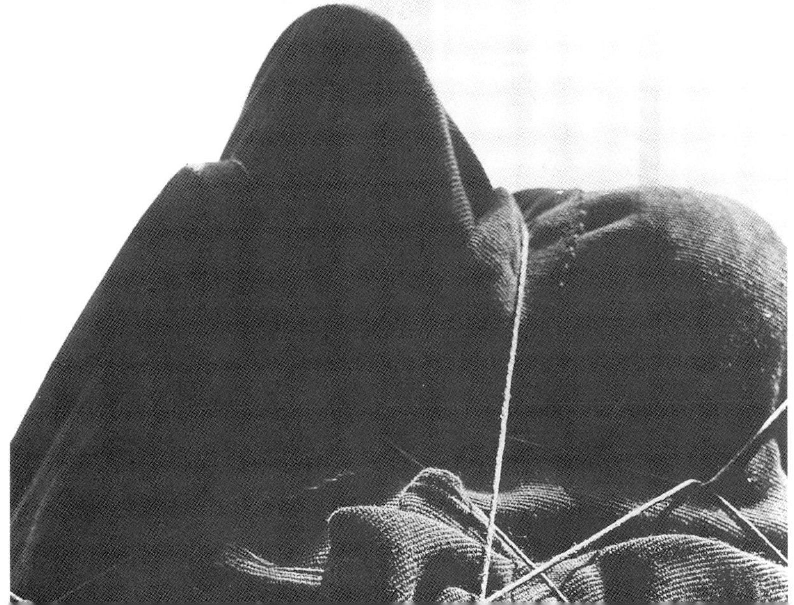

25. Man Ray, *Enigma of Isidore Ducasse*, 1920. Mixed media, 17¾ x 22⅞ x 9". Collection Lucien Treillard, Paris.

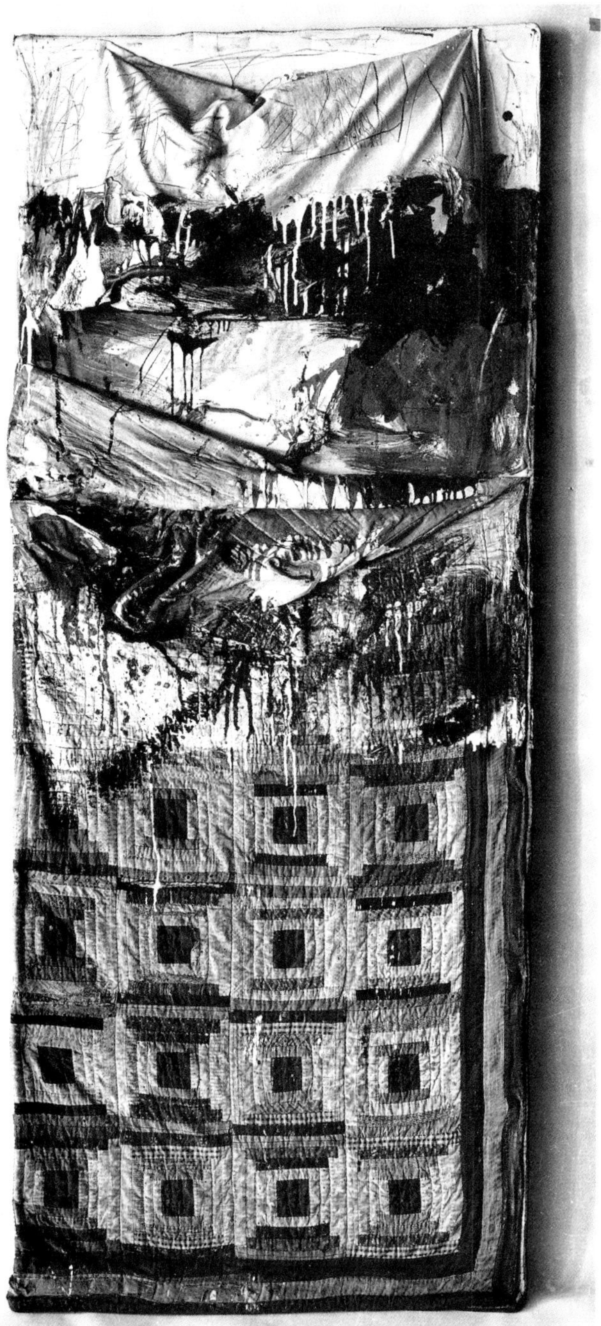

26. Robert Rauschenberg, *Bed*, 1955. Mixed media, 75¼ x 31½ x 6½″. Collection Museum of Modern Art, New York.

# Cloth and Contemporary Art

The Abstract Expressionist movement, centered in New York in the late 1940s and 1950s, changed the definitions of painting and sculpture for the rest of the century. When Jackson Pollock abandoned the conventions of easel, canvas, oil, and brush, painting became an adventure, often chaotic, free from all restraints. In sculpture, as old antagonisms toward abstraction began to break down, the human figure all but disappeared. During these years sculptors assembled rather than modeled or carved. Diverse materials including found objects were welded and glued to produce works that were visually compelling.

As Abstract Expressionism revolutionized the "high arts" of painting and sculpture, it also opened the way for a diversity of artistic expression never before possible. Fiber, ceramics, industrial design, dance and music, performance, theater, film, and poetry were finally affected by the ideas of Abstract Expressionists.

By the late 1950s the art world was adrift. How were artists to follow Jackson Pollock and Abstract Expressionism? Could the figure be returned to painting without making a de Kooning? How could artists create art that was closer to ordinary life? As early as 1952 Robert Rauschenberg had begun to make art that confronted these questions. He belonged to no school, although his work echoed Duchamp and Man Ray. In 1952 he wrapped mud in cloth, placed the bundles in a painted box, and called it *Soles*. By 1955 he was making art out of everything from garbage to grass to his own bedclothes, including the now famous quilt that once wrapped the daughter of artist Dorothea Rockburne at Black Mountain College (fig. 26). Rauschenberg coined the word *combine* for his paintings, which incorporated objects in and onto his support to a degree far greater than that of traditional collage. When in 1959 he was included in the "Sixteen Americans" exhibition at the Museum of Modern Art in New York, he stated: "A pair of socks is not less suitable to make a painting than wood, nails, turpentine, oil and fabric." His ideas—along with those of the painter Jasper Johns, the composer John Cage, the choreographer

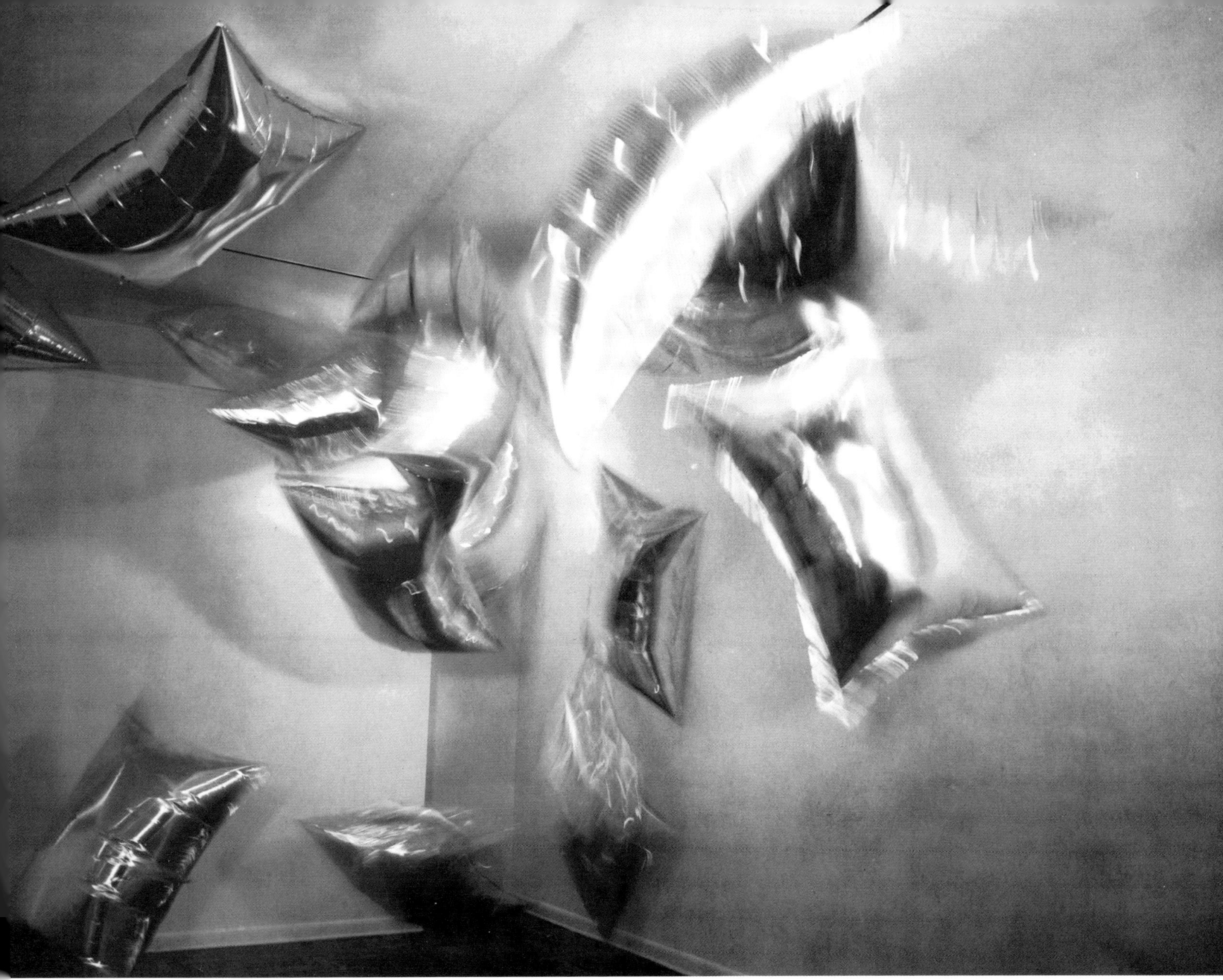

27. Andy Warhol, *Clouds*, set for *Rain Forest*, Merce Cunningham Dance Company, 1968. Mylar filled with helium.

Merce Cunningham, and others—began to ferment within the larger art world, especially after he won the grand prize for painting at the Venice Biennale in 1964. Ultimately his work became the intellectual food for the next decade of artists. Rauschenberg continues to use cloth today.

What Rauschenberg began with his combines culminated in the Museum of Modern Art's 1961 exhibition "The Art of Assemblage." Assemblage, formed by the additive process, is a three-dimensional extension of collage. By the mid-1960s another spin-off was in full swing on the West Coast, Funk art. This object-oriented movement transformed the ideas that had been fermenting since the germinal days of Black Mountain College through a West Coast sensibility. The term *funk* was borrowed from jazz, and in important ways the art resembled the music. "Funk art is hot rather than cool; it is committed rather than disengaged; it is bizarre rather than formal; it is sensuous; and frequently it is quite ugly and ungainly . . . It is symbolic in content and evocative in feeling."[13] Primarily males participated and few of them used cloth, drawn instead to harder materials.

Conversely, on the East Coast, artists seemed to be moving away from the object. If Assemblage is art that moves away from the flat plane and actively intrudes into the space of the spectator, then the next step was art that could be walked into,

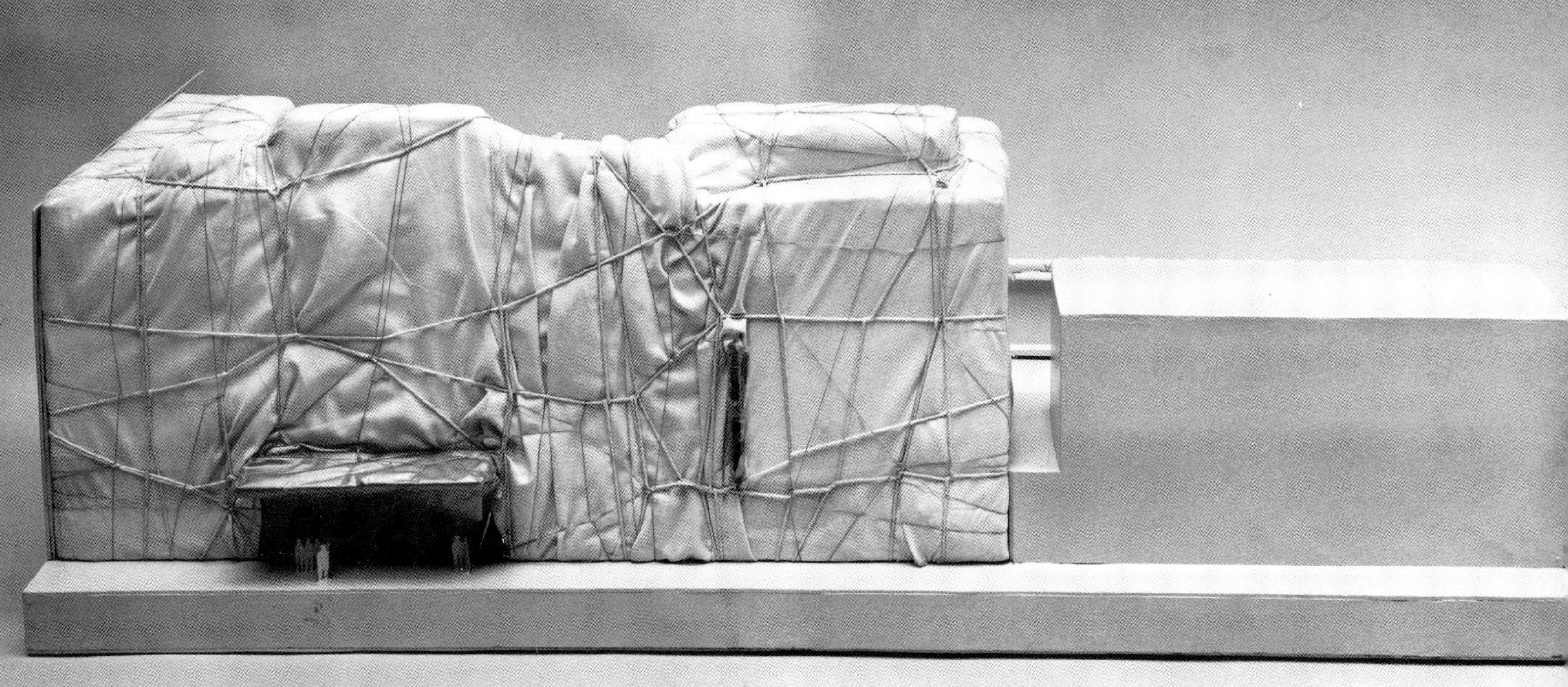

28. Christo, *The Museum of Modern Art Packaged*, 1968. Scale model: painted wood, cloth, twine, and polyethylene, 16 x 48⅛ x 24⅛″ (including two painted wood bases). Collection Museum of Modern Art, New York, gift of D. & J. de Menil.

that would envelop the viewer, or environmental site-specific art. Cloth became more important in environmental art than it had been in either Assemblage or Funk art because it allowed the artist to extend the scale, to build big and cheaply, to create illusion as it is created in theater. Only one step further from environments was environments where events took place, or Happenings. Because these were created by visual artists most often in galleries, they were not considered theater. But they borrowed freely from the ideas of dance and theater (fig. 27).

Most of the young artists of the time participated in one or another of these events. For example, in the autumn of 1959 Rauschenberg was publicly joined in making his kind of art by Allan Kaprow, who directed his first Happenings at the Reuben Gallery in New York. Among those participating were Claes Oldenburg and Lucas Samaras. Kaprow's concern was for an art that "must become preoccupied with and even dazzled by the space and objects of our everyday life, either our bodies, clothes, rooms, or if need be, the vastness of 42nd Street."[14]

Oldenburg may have articulated it best when he stated that one of the fundamental premises of his art, and a part of his democratic intention, was to give the public some foothold in his art, to reach an audience thus far untouched by visual art. While adhering to the ideas of modernism, he wanted his art to remain accessible to everyone on some level.

The early Happenings drew from Abstract Expressionism a sense of performance and risk. Oldenburg's art shows a long-standing interest in theater, which drew him to Happenings, environments, and performance. But he and his contemporaries looked to Cubist collage, to Schwitters, to Duchamp, and then to Johns and Rauschenberg for their attitudes toward materials. Instead of "sacred paint," they chose to use the materials at hand, from the household, from the street, from the hardware store, from memory, from the junkyard, from the artist's studio. Consistently they chose cloth. Oldenburg's everyday imagery, blown up in everyday materials, answered his demand for an art form that was accessible to the uninitiated. Oldenburg said of his attitudes toward materials:

> In fact, that is one way to view the history of art, in terms of material. For example, because my material is different from paint and canvas, or marble and bronze, it demands different images and it produces different results. To make my paint more concrete, to make it come out, I use plaster under it. When that doesn't satisfy me, I translate the plaster into vinyl, which enables me to push it around. The fact that I

> wanted to see something flying in the wind made me make a piece of clothing, or the fact that I wanted to make something flow made me make an ice cream cone.[15]

The materials in the early Happenings were fragile, as they were in much of Rauschenberg's work. Therefore, the art became impermanent, as impermanent or as permanent, that is, as a piece of cloth. The materials chosen by these artists were also materials capable of extension. For example, a piece of cloth could cover an object or encompass a whole room. An artist could expand an idea further and larger than at any time in history. Only practicality limited the artist's choice. Cloth, readily at hand, inexpensive, expandable, sometimes neutral and at other times charged with meaning and memory, was picked up by the artists again and again.

Christo, with his passionate involvement with cloth, pushed its capacity for expansiveness the furthest of all. He began with packages and wrapped objects. During his early days in Paris, having moved there from Bulgaria in 1958, he wrapped bottles and chairs, tables, oil barrels, and automobiles. Those were the days of transforming banal objects into art, the legacy of Man Ray and the Dadaists. Soon Christo shifted his work out of doors. He wrapped the Kunsthalle in Bern, Switzerland, in 1968 and the coast of Little Bay in Sydney, Australia, in 1969. Then came *Valley Curtain* (Rifle, Colorado, 1973), *Running Fence* (northern California, 1976), and *Wrapped Walk Ways* (Kansas City, 1978). All of these works, created in cloth for only a few days' duration, viewed by the masses through the media, exist for the future only on film (fig. 28).

Christo was not alone. By the end of the 1960s the whole out of doors became the environment, and true environmental art, sometimes relating to architecture, sometimes relating to nature, came into being. It was in this period that architect Frei Otto designed and built his tentlike structures in Germany. During the 1970s and 1980s such cloth structures proliferated throughout the world.

Beginning in the 1960s, the Art Fabric movement, although dominated at first by traditional handweaving, came to represent bold breakthroughs in the variety of materials and forms used by artists working with fiber. By the 1970s the artists working in fiber were functioning in the mainstream of contemporary art, sharing its artistic diversity. It was in this decade, when radical changes were afoot in the choice of materials, that cloth began to have more visibility. Fabric had become pervasive, both in the Art Fabric movement and among artists who had moved away from traditional fine-arts materials (figs. 29, 30).

Traditional painting was not discontinued, however, during those turbulent years. Pop art dominated, followed by the Minimalist school. The artists of those movements used cloth as artists had since 1500—simply as a support material for paint. It was not until the late 1960s that Ed Moses in Los Angeles, Alan Shields in New York, and Sam Gilliam in Washington, D.C., independently became interested in pushing abstract painting beyond the easel convention. Moses made unstretched, "soft" paintings, as did Shields. Shields also cut into his canvases and hung them freely within a room, allowing light to pass through. Gilliam, an African American and a leading member

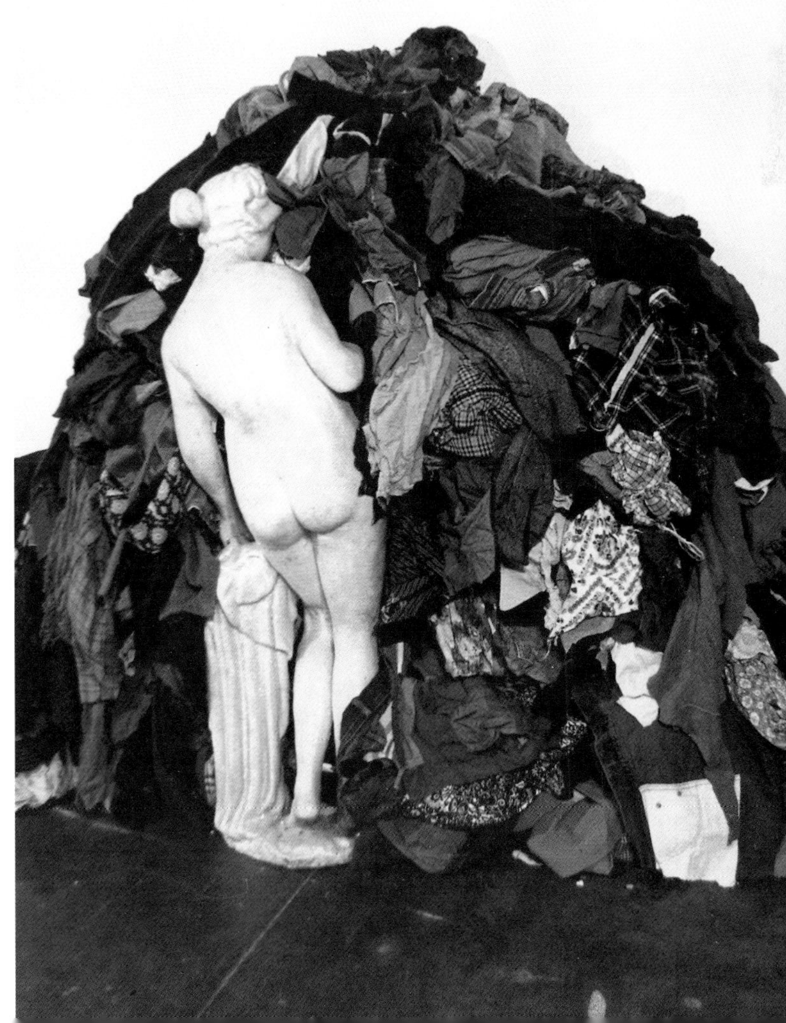

29. Michelangelo Pistoletto, *Venus of Rags*, 1967. Installation at the Institute for Contemporary Art, P.S. 1 Museum, Long Island City, New York.

of the Washington school of color painting, took his brilliantly spattered and tinted canvases off the stretcher and draped them informally on the wall or suspended them from the ceiling (fig. 31).

Gilliam's art had nothing to do with his race. But his success certainly inspired other black artists in the United States at that time. Many of them began to look to their African heritage for inspiration. The use of cloth has always been a source of great strength among African-American artists, which seems directly related to a very strong tradition of cloth in Africa. Commemorative masks, burial coverings, and embellished clothing, assets that both please aesthetically and enhance the owner's social standing in Africa, began to appear as motifs in the work of American blacks in the 1960s and 1970s.

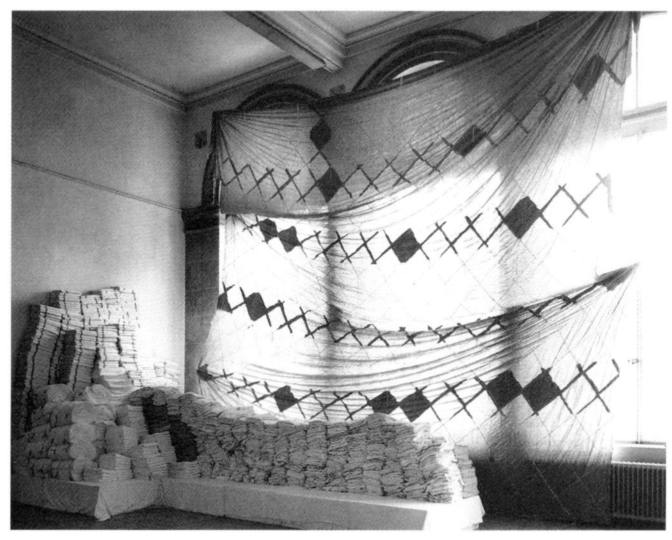

30. Sheila Hicks, *Le Démêloir*, 1977. Hand-mended sheets, folded hospital garments. Installation at the Lausanne Biennale, Switzerland.

31. Sam Gilliam, *Blue Extension*, 1969. Acrylic on canvas, 10 x 5′ (suspended and draped to 9½ x 32½′). Collection Middendorf Gallery, Washington, D.C.

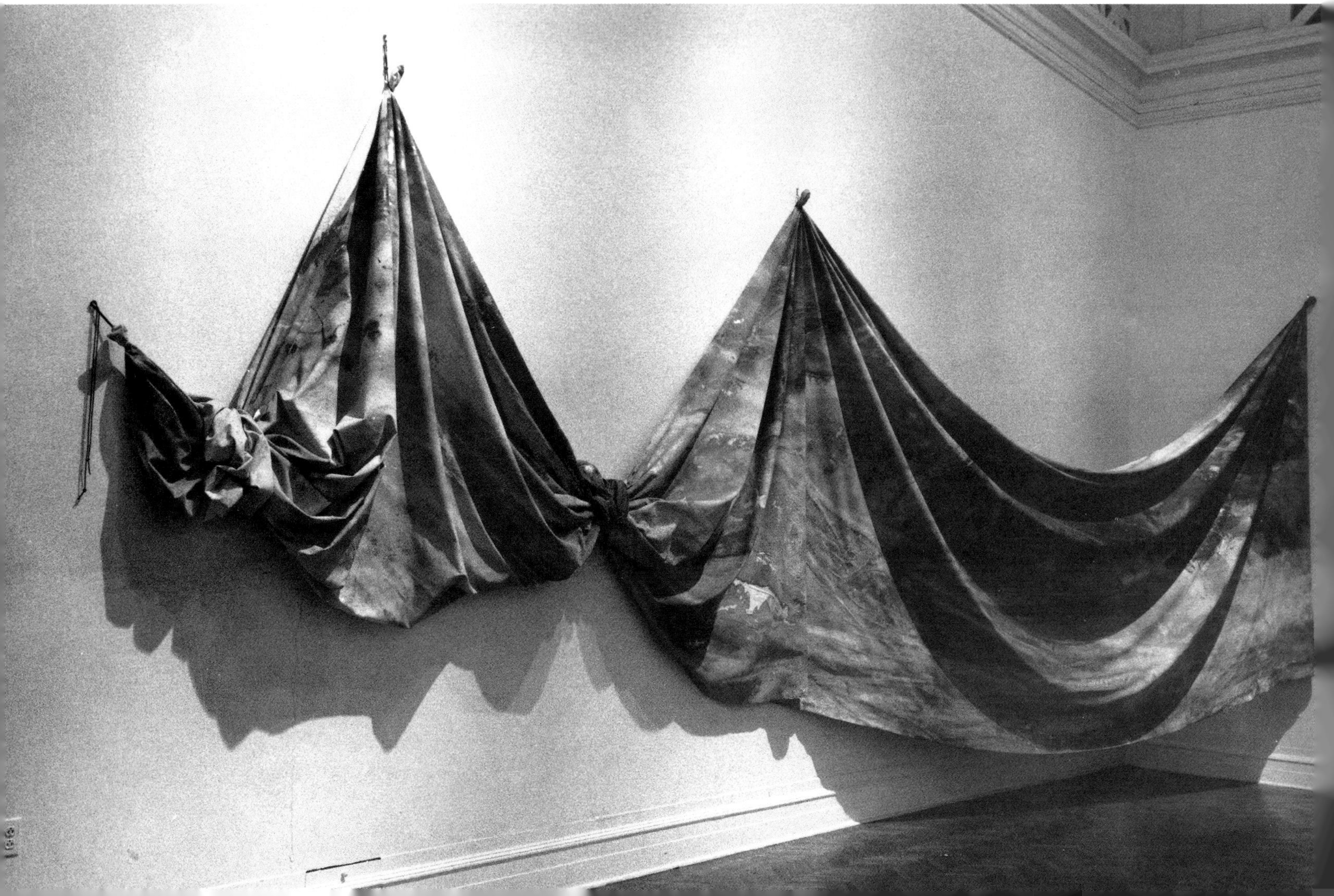

# The Sixties: A New Era

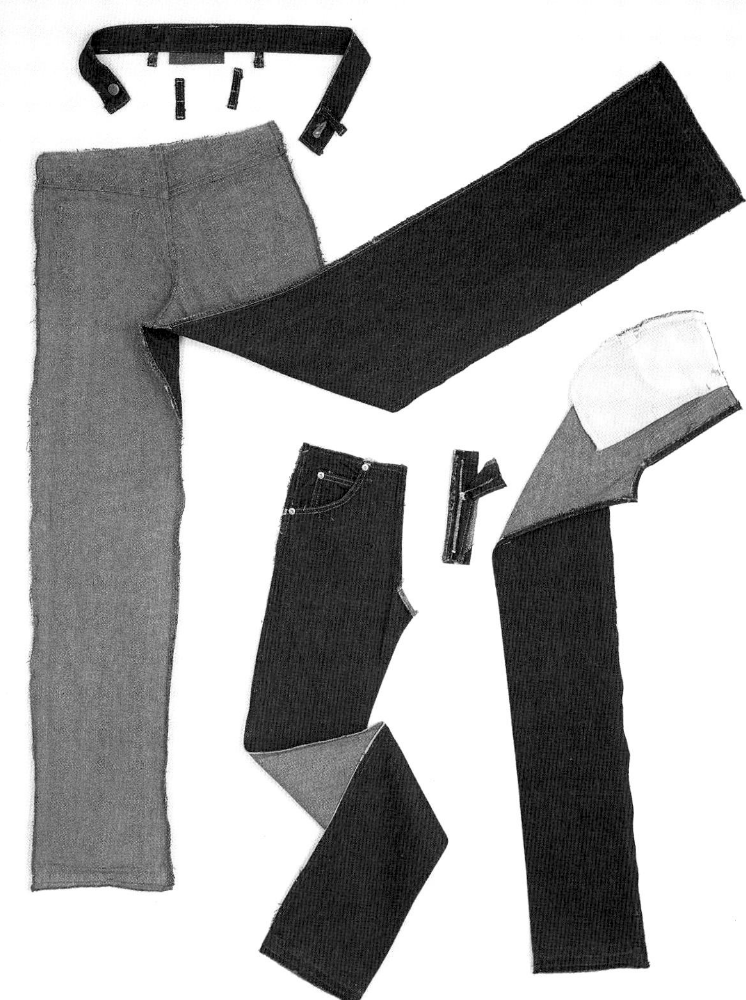

32. Parts of a pair of blue jeans.

The 1960s was a time of great unrest. America was waging its most unpopular war in history. Students protested against their teachers. Citizens protested against their government. The young went to war against their parents' lifestyles. The poet Allen Ginsberg hailed 1968 as a "crack in time." Revolution swept vigorously across the United States and Europe, expounding personalism and romanticism. It came at a time of transition, as the Western world moved from an industrial to a postindustrial age. In the postindustrial world the individual had few choices and little control of private destiny, or so it seemed to the young. Everything could be purchased, including one's value system. Not only did these young people want a more thoughtful and just world, they wanted to include all peoples—African Americans, women, Native Americans, Hispanics, Chinese . . .

As symbol of the revolt, the youth of the time simply refused to wear the uncomfortable and ugly polyester clothing of their parents. At first they adopted cotton jeans as their uniform, following the precedent of the Beat poets of the 1950s. Levi Strauss, a mid-nineteenth-century Bavarian immigrant to San Francisco, had taken it upon himself to clothe the working class of western America. To do so, he imported a strong cotton from France called *serge de Nîmes,* or denim. Soon every young boy in America, every miner and cowboy, was buying jeans from Levi Strauss (fig. 32).

It did not take long before the human need to embellish came upon the jeans-clad hippies. Jeans became studded, then embroidered, then beaded, then painted. Levi Strauss sponsored a juried exhibition in 1974 called "The Levi's Denim Art Contest." Ten thousand people entered.

Jeans finally proved too warm for hot climates. The young began to cast around for the cotton clothing they had seen in their travels abroad—for these were the children of affluence—but it was not on the United States market. The American cotton industry had been crippled by the consumer demand for carefree synthetics. It would be years before functional cotton clothing could come out of America. History repeated itself; India began to supply the Western world with cool, inexpensive, and colorful cotton clothing. Other developing countries joined India (fig. 33). It was a decade before America could compete, and then only because the industry accepted the challenge of aesthetically improving the product in response to the complaints of consumers. Secondly, textile producers began to blend natural fibers with synthetics for more comfortable clothing, to develop a wrinkle-free cotton, and to reduce cotton shrinkage from 5 percent to 1 percent—all in response to the complaints of mothers who had vowed they would never iron again.

Originating on the West Coast, the Wearable Art movement derived much of its vitality from the flower children of the denim culture. From the strong fiber-arts departments that were coming into being at universities everywhere, but especially in California, the movement took uncompromisingly high standards of workmanship and an insistence on the primacy of

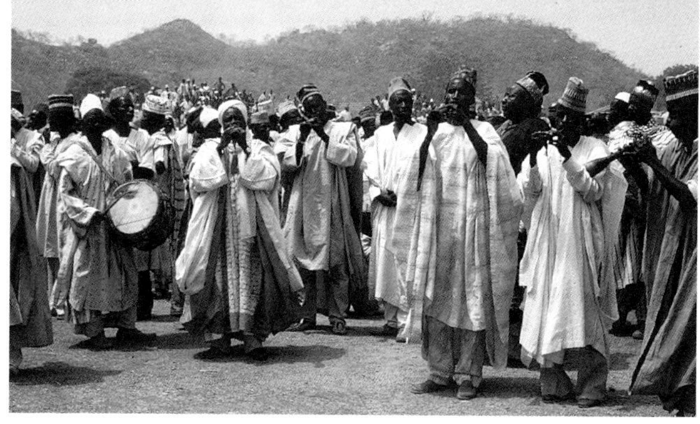

33. Hausa/Fulani musicians playing at the Gombi agriculture show, Northeastern Nigeria, February 1980.

the fabrics that were to be created or embellished. Inexpensive international travel, plus a boom in textile publications, gave these developing artists access to the world's textile history. Ideas flowed into the artists' studios from Japan, from Indonesia, from the great textile traditions of Africa and Indian South America. Artists were turned into craftspeople and craftspeople into artists. (See chapter 8, "Clothing the Body and the Spirit," for further discussion of this phenomenon.)

Thirty years after the Second World War, and for the first time in history, masses of people could choose how they wished to clothe themselves. Even the rich benefited, for one could argue that the Wearable Art movement, with its strong ethnic bent, coupled with a rash of extravagant exhibitions sponsored by the Costume Institute of the Metropolitan Museum of Art in New York, led Yves Saint Laurent to create his great 1976 Russian collection. That collection is often credited with reviving the couture industry. In the September 1976 U.S. *Vogue,* Pierre Schneider said, "What Yves Saint Laurent has done, with his latest collection is to remind us that fashion, in its radical form of haute couture, is costume . . . it strikingly illustrates the degree of sophistication attained by fashion's analysis of history . . . It's not nostalgia for the past, but for the eternal present which lies on the other side of the past."

Other influences entered the picture. By 1971 the women's movement was in full flower in the art world. Judy Chicago and Miriam Schapiro had begun the Feminist Art Program at the California Institute of Arts in Valencia, California, both hired by Schapiro's artist husband, Paul Brach, the school's dean. While there, Chicago and Schapiro created *Womanhouse,* the first all-female environment. Traditional women's arts, crafts, painting, collage, assemblage, weaving, sculpture, and performance were combined into an all-encompassing environment with women's experience as the dominant concern. Throughout the rest of the 1970s women artists often concentrated on collaboration with women, on discovering women artists of the past, and on celebrating the work of anonymous women, both past and present. These central concerns became the battlefield motivating the choice of subjects, materials, motifs, and themes in the art of many women.

Out of the unrest of the 1960s in America came a new awareness of subcultures. For example, the American Indian movement brought that group into public focus as never before—especially after the nationally televised shoot-out between the Sioux and the F.B.I. in Wounded Knee, South Dakota, in 1973. Americans were forced to examine the lives of a minority to whom they had previously paid little attention. One of the things they discovered was that these people traditionally had made great art. And it was art that was often made from soft materials.

In 1972 the Walker Art Center, the Minneapolis Institute of Art, and the Indian Art Association collaboratively sponsored a large exhibition in Minneapolis, "American Indian Art: Form and Tradition." "Sacred Circles: Two Thousand Years of American Indian Art" followed in London, and then came many others. These exhibitions contained an abundance of works on cloth: ledger paintings on muslin, shields with Stroud streamers, war clubs and arrows encased in beaded cloth or buckskin bags, dance shields of muslin, Hudson Bay blankets fashioned into simple binary clothing, and so on. Most of the objects were richly embellished and very beautiful to the twentieth-century eye. These exhibitions not only moved Native American creations out of the realm of anthropological artifact, but had great effect upon contemporary art. Many of the artists whose work appears in chapter 2, "Metaphor and Symbol," took their earliest inspiration from these great exhibitions.

# The Pervasive Life of Cloth

In the 1980s the art world became enormously diversified, a trend that has only intensified in the 1990s. Debates over multiculturalism and diversity swept through universities and museums. America the melting pot became the center of diaspora studies. Vast segments of the population began to define themselves in terms of ethnic ancestry. Exhibitions examining what might once have been arcane beliefs and practices became both vital and commonplace. For example, in 1984 the Caribbean Cultural Center in New York mounted an exhibition on the survival of African belief systems among Yoruba descendants in the Americas. Cloth purchased by the yard was fashioned into a spectacular throne for the initiation of a priest into the Santería religion, an Afro-Cuban religion of Yoruba origin. Usually found in private homes of Santería practitioners, this time the domestic throne was erected within the exhibition space (fig. 34). "The initiation throne consists of three basic elements: the canopy of cloth, which may be more or less elaborate; a sacred mortar where the initiate may sit, and a reed floor mat. Completed the night before the initiation, the throne stands

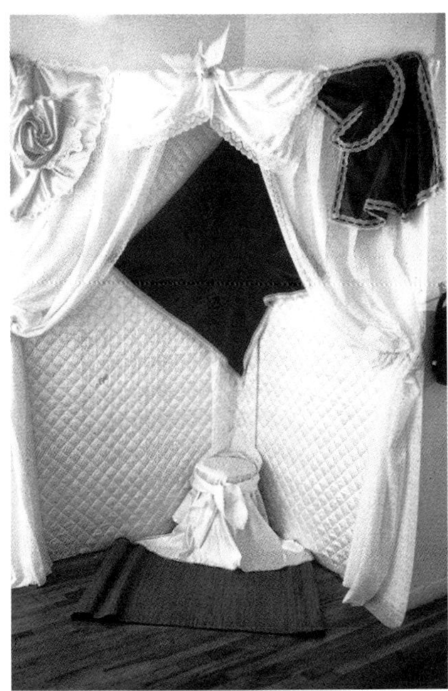

34 *(left)*. Antonio Queiro (priest), *Santería Initiation Throne*, 1984. Courtesy Caribbean Cultural Center, New York.

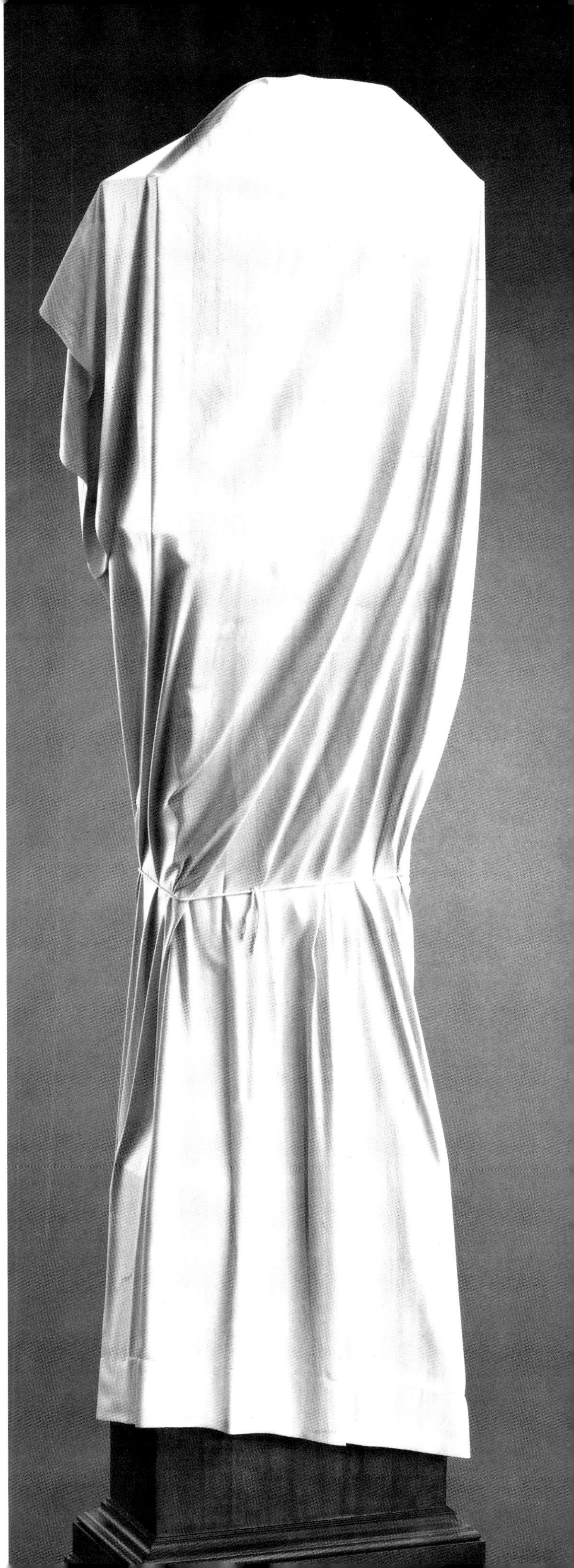

35 *(right)*. Wendell Castle, *Ghost Clock*, 1985. Bleached mahogany covered with cloth, 87½ x 24½ x 15″.

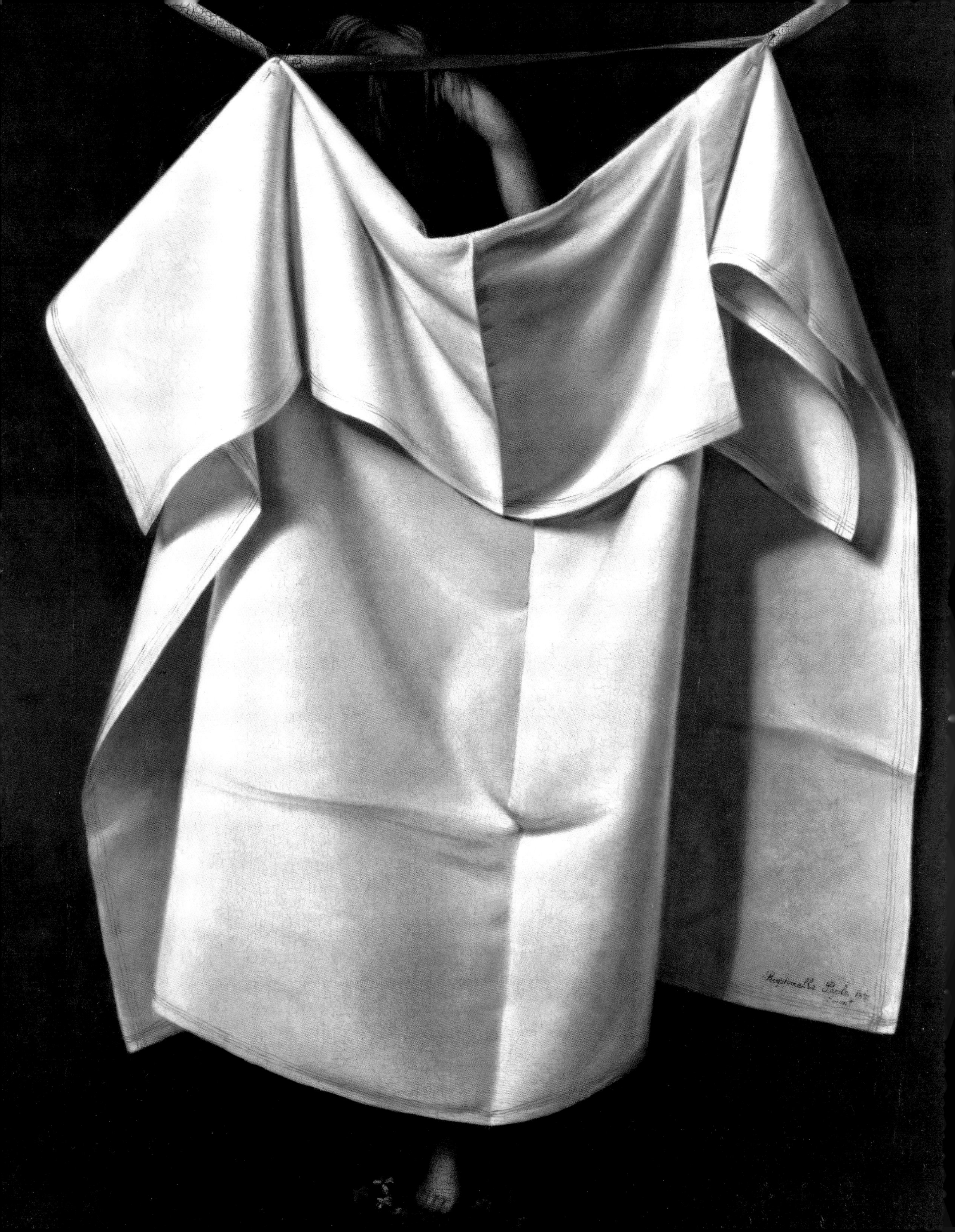

36 *(opposite).* Raphaelle Peale, *Venus Rising from the Sea—A Deception (After the Bath),* c. 1822. Oil on canvas, 29¼ x 24⅛″. Collection Nelson Atkins Museum, Kansas City, Missouri, purchase Nelson Trust.

for seven days (often Friday to Friday), and is taken down when the newly made priest leaves liminal seclusion for 'reincorporation' into the community on the 'Day of the Plaza' (Market Day)."[16]

Artists, while transforming their ideas into twentieth-century terms, produced original works that stressed the inherent properties of cloth (figs. 35–37). For both the wisdom and the freedom to create such works, they, like those to follow, became indebted to anonymous ancestors who for millennia have been commingling art and life. Today's artists are beholden:

- to those buried back in time who first twisted fibrous material into thread
- to the Chinese, who developed silk and then forged the international textile trade
- to the early people of Peru who took the weaving of cloth to a still-unmatched level of quality and beauty
- to the kings, rulers, and sultans from around the world and over the centuries who used cloth to mark their positions and announce their powers
- to the rise of the textile guilds in the Middle Ages
- to the Plains Indians of North America and all those other earlier nomadic peoples who developed cultures that used soft materials
- to the unknown and unnumbered women who have privately created works of art in cloth in order to grace their homes and nurture their souls
- to the English, for their factories in which cloth was the first material to be industrialized
- to the synthetics industry spawned by World War II
- to the social movements within the democratizing twentieth century
- to the artists from earlier decades of this century whose splendid leaps of artistic expression laid the groundwork for what would come later.

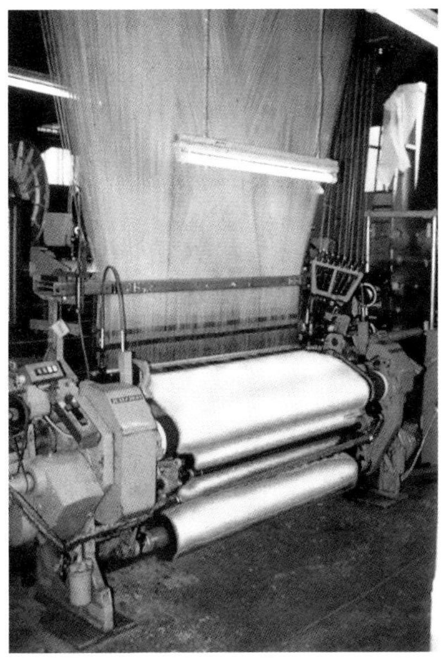

37. Mill cloth.

1. John Noble Wilford, "Site in Turkey Yields Oldest Cloth Ever Found," *New York Times,* July 13, 1993, B5.

2. Wilford, "Site in Turkey," B5.

3. Junius B. Bird, *Peruvian Paintings by Unknown Artists, 800 B.C. to 1700 A.D.* (New York: Center for InterAmerican Relations, 1973).

4. John Irwin, *Textiles and Ornaments of India* (New York: Museum of Modern Art, 1956), 26.

5. H. J. Hundt, "Uber vorgeschichtliche Seidenfunde," *Jahrbuch des Römisch-Germanischen Zentralmuseums* 16 (1969): 63.

6. Barbara Tuchman, *A Distant Mirror* (New York: Ballantine Books, 1978), 39.

7. John M. Hunisak, "The Revealing Cloth," *American Fabrics and Fashions.* 126 (1986): 47–48.

8. Rutherford J. Gettens and George L. Stout, *Painting Materials: A Short Encyclopedia* (New York: Dover Publications, 1980), 228.

9. Pattie Chase, "Quilting: Reclaiming Our Art," *Country Life,* Sept. 1976, 9.

10. Arthur J. Pulos, *American Design Ethic* (Cambridge, Mass: MIT Press, 1983).

11. Nikolaus Pevsner, *Pioneers of Modern Design* (New York: Museum of Modern Art, 1948).

12. Whitney Chadwick to Mildred Constantine, 1989.

13. Peter Selz, *Funk* (exhibition catalog, Berkeley: University of California, University Art Museum, 1967), 3.

14. Barbara Rose, *Oldenburg* (New York: Museum of Modern Art, 1970), 25.

15. "Claes Oldenburg, Roy Lichtenstein, Andy Warhol: A Discussion," moderated by Bruce Blaser and broadcast over radio station WBAI, New York, June 1964. Edited and published in *Artforum* 4, no. 6 (Feb. 1966): 22–23.

16. David H. Brown, "Thrones of the Orichas: Afro-Cuban Altars in New Jersey, New York, and Havana," *African Arts,* Oct. 1993, 46.

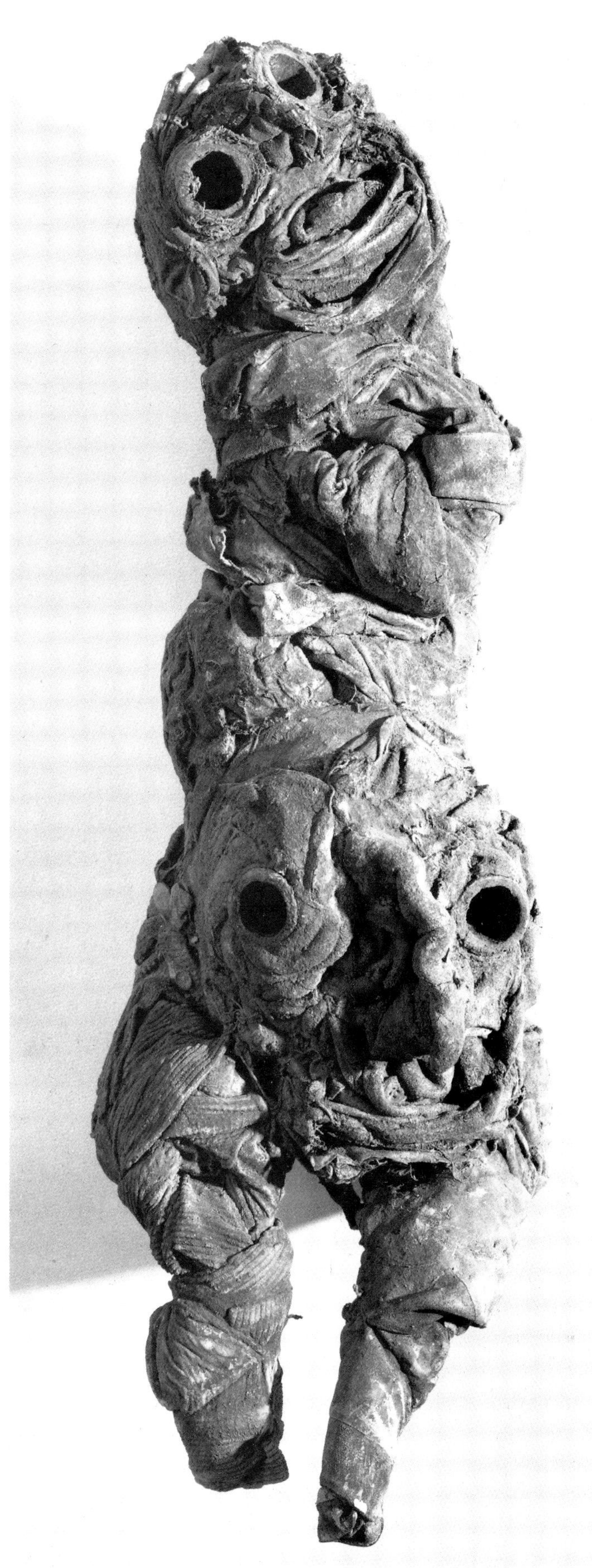

# Metaphor and Symbol

*The symbols of mythology are not manufactured; they cannot be ordered, invented or permanently suppressed. They are spontaneous productions of the psyche, and each bears within it, undamaged, the germ power of its source.*

Joseph Campbell,
*The Hero with a Thousand Faces*

Michel Nedjar is a maker of what he calls "dolls," although no one else would call them that. Actually, they are the antithesis of dolls—grotesque, their body parts undefined, their features lost, misplaced, or miscounted, and unnaturally creased and folded. They repel. Even in scale they are too large to fit the usual concept of doll. Instead, in Nedjar's hands, the human spirit seems to have wandered back into a primordial world (fig. 38).

Nedjar is best known as a French experimental film maker of the 1980s. In both his films and his dolls he gives substance to that old adage "Myth is the hidden part of every story." Like artists everywhere who create contemporary metaphorical work, his outsider art emerged from his outsider existence. Only by unraveling the myth of his own life has Nedjar placed himself, through his art, into the larger context of humankind.

His is an interesting story. The son of a professional tailor, the grandson of a Parisian ragpicker, Nedjar grew up envying his sister her dolls. But he was a male child, expected to follow his father. Yes, he wanted to sew, to make dolls, but not with the precision and skill of a tailor. Nevertheless, at fourteen he was apprenticed to a tailor. Frustrated and bored, he failed.

Scraping together meager funds, Nedjar set off to see the world, India and Mexico especially, drawn to the magic of their seemingly primitive societies. There he found cultures and objects imbued with ceremony. He later said about that time, "I have sketchbooks full of the mystical India, ashrams, colored images of Indian women, landscapes afloat on the imaginary, sunbursts . . . It was my first contact with High Magic, craftsmanship, the Baroque, death."[1]

By 1975 Nedjar was back in Paris and had begun to make his dolls. "It's grandmother for the fabrics and father for the needlework which pulls the pieces together. The ragpicker and

38 *(opposite)*. Michel Nedjar, *Poupée*, 1986. Cloth, 32 x 10 x 10″. Collection de l'Art Brut, Lausanne, Switzerland. Courtesy Rosa Esman Gallery, New York.

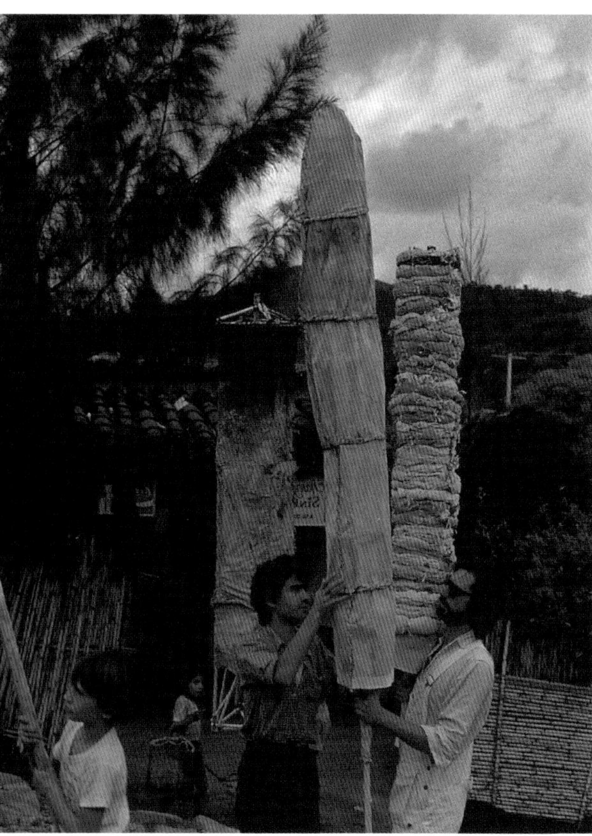

39. Frederic Amat, *Ceremonial Objects for Oaxaca Festival,* Mexico, 1978.

40 *(opposite).* Michael Tracy, *Cruz; la Pasiòn,* 1982–87. Latex and metallic pigment on plywood, wood, rope with horns, tin and brass milagros, needles, cloth braids, punched tin, 140 x 82 x 76″. The work was burned in *Sacrifice II,* April 4, 1990, at the River Pierce.

the tailor: it's strange how I combine these two things to give birth to a little creature."

These rag dolls, these creatures of the dark, these sophisticated sculptural works collected en masse by Jean Dubuffet for his Collection de l'Art Brut in Lausanne, Switzerland, are shrouded in the myth of Nedjar's personal history. But, like many of the artists discussed in this chapter, he needed to travel, to experience other cultures in order to see how myth could be transformed into objects and events, to understand how myth informs reality. Only then could he begin to tell his own story. He needed to expand his emotional and visual language, just as one achieves greater understanding of one's own language upon learning another. That Nedjar did not learn to read until he was eighteen years old may have accelerated his visual development.

Like Nedjar, Frederic Amat is also a child of old Europe, and like Nedjar, this Catalan from Barcelona was drawn at a young age to an ancient, more colorful, mythic world. First he studied set design and dance. Then, still just a youth, he set off to see the world. For him it was to be South America and later Mexico. Today he is a highly regarded painter, a set designer, and a performance artist. His art emerged through his acts of transforming ancient ceremonies into contemporary rituals, through creating modern theater from ancient rites, through rendering his perceptions of other cultures into performances of contemporary art. He made splendid artifacts of cloth, wood, and paper for his ceremonies, moving events that were to feed imagery into his painting for years to come (fig. 39).

Robert Graves, the eminent British scholar of historic and prehistoric uses of myth, defines true myth as "the reduction to narrative shorthand of ritual mime performed on public festivals and in many cases recorded pictorially on temple walls, vases, seals, bowls, mirrors, shields, tapestries, and the like."[2] Nedjar, Amat, and other artists are using cloth to create works of art that bridge the gap between twentieth-century life and the less accessible world of the poetic. To them it seems more possible to understand the magical or religious order of the world through primitive rites and ceremonial objects than through modern technology. These artists collect this experience through study, travel, or immersion in another physical or ritual place; then they transform a germinal human instinct to create, or to order, into a twentieth-century visual language, the narra-

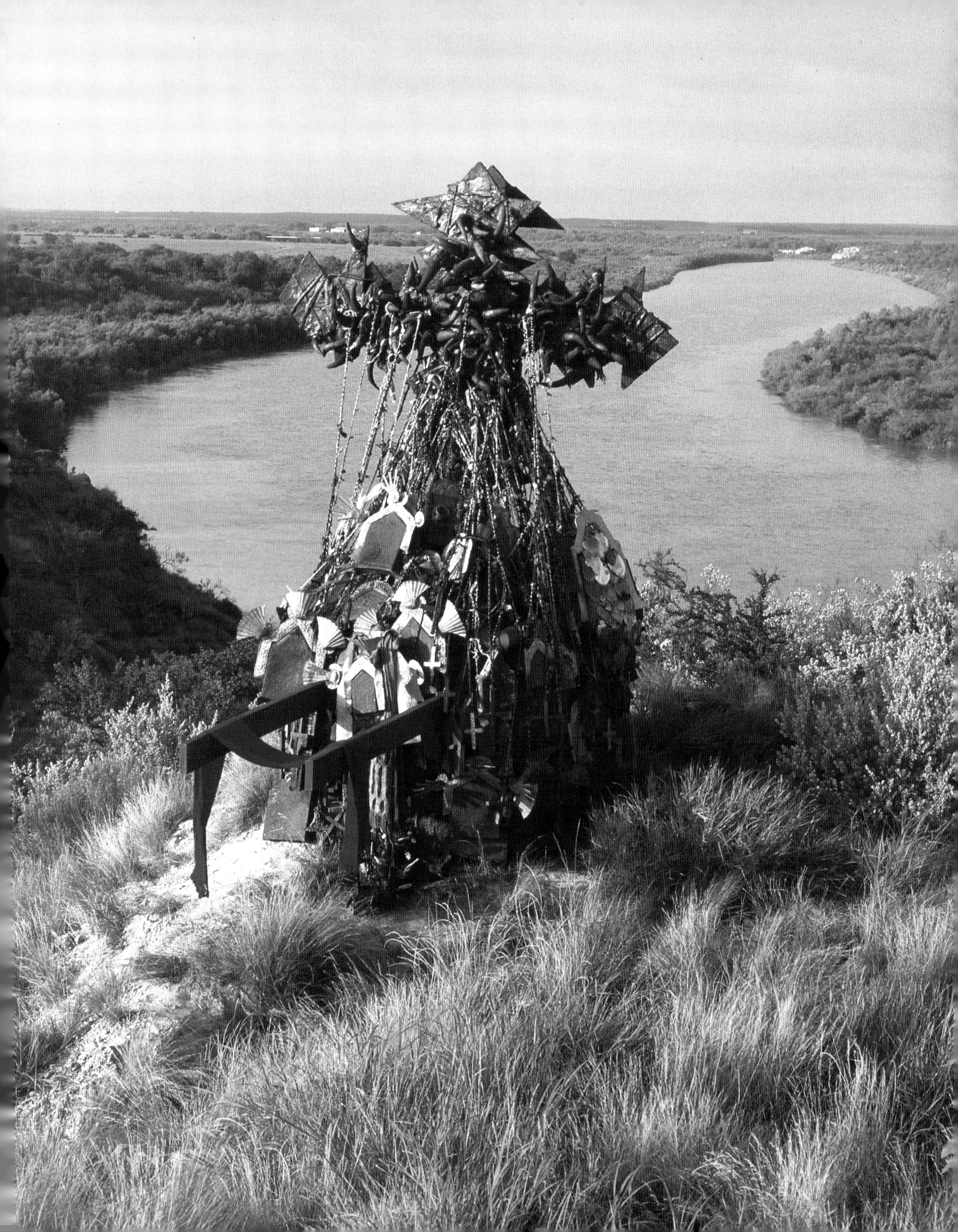

tive shorthand of their own times. Thus their new forms, resurrected from past connections, make the modern world more spiritually significant.

Michael Tracy's work, be it a chapel, an altar, or a monstrance, is the offspring of such a personal journey. He was born in Ohio but ultimately migrated to the poor Texas border town of San Ygnacio to establish his studio and to make his home. While an art student, he had haunted the Cleveland Museum of Art, absorbing the religious art of Italy, Byzantium, and the Orient. Upon graduation he began making annual pilgrimages to Italy. Then in 1972 he made his first trip to Mexico, the watershed event of his life. Never again would he dismiss it as "the country south of the border." For him "Mexico is Bruges, Flanders, when Hugo van der Goes lived in it . . . his Portinari altarpiece in Florence . . . Caravaggio's later paintings . . . Artaud, with particular reference to Mayan blood sacrifices and their current adulteration."[3] These became Tracy's Guadeloupes (sacred images).

Tracy, still working within the mainstream of contemporary aesthetic concerns, has gone on to create powerful images alive with religious and political content, wrought with rite and ritual. Unlike the contemporary "initiation thrones" of Santería practitioners (see fig. 34), these are Tracy's own inventions, intended solely as works of art. But like their predecessors and spiritual cousins, they very often incorporate cloth (fig. 40).

Because cloth is one of the oldest materials known to humans, having kept company with them from the beginning of organized life, and because it is malleable and given to swift transformations, it has served artists well as a bridge to the past and the present, a bridge that will continue into the future.

41. Joseph Beuys, *I Like America and America Likes Me*, 1974. Performance at René Block Gallery, New York. Courtesy Ronald Feldman Fine Arts, Inc.

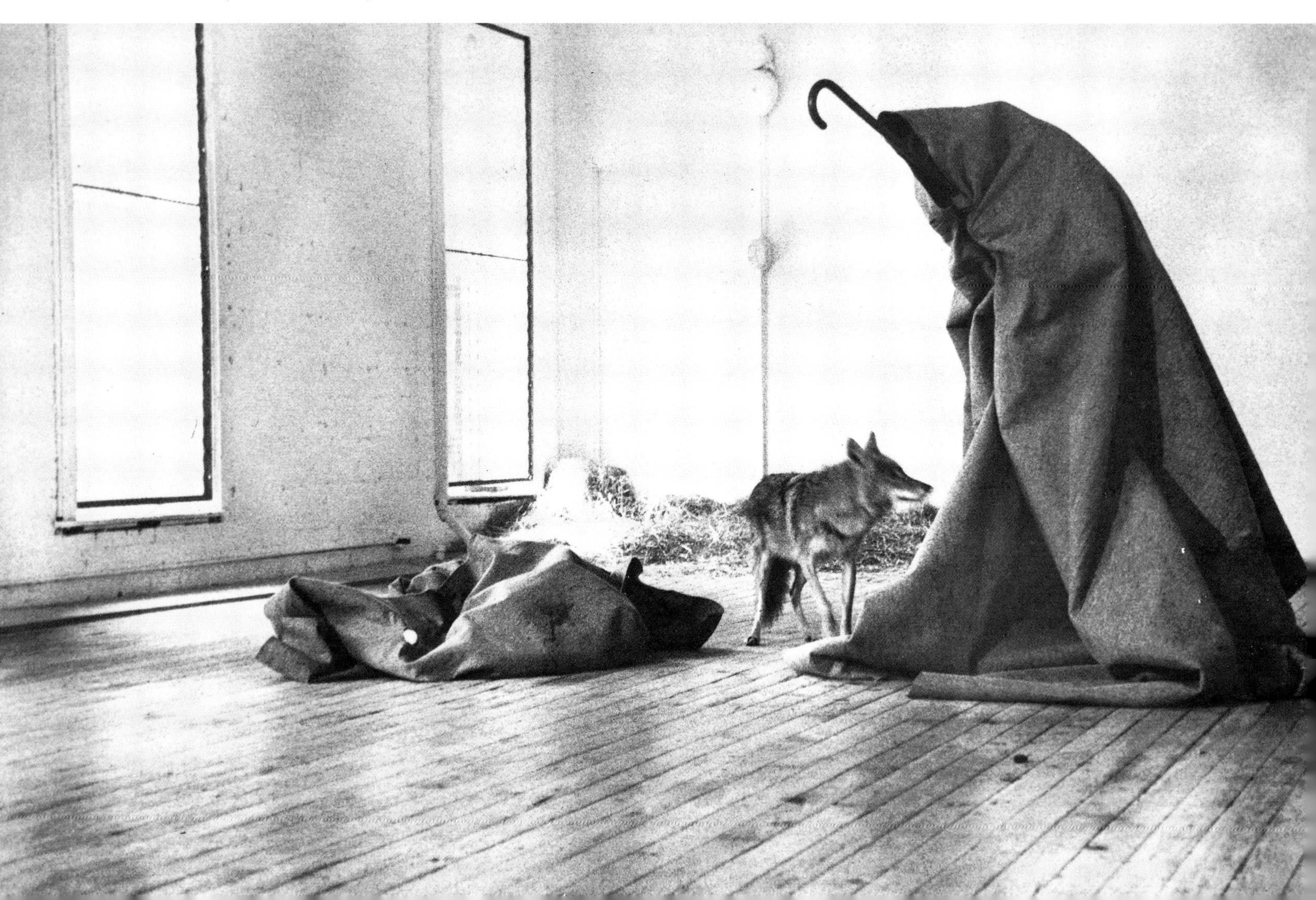

As Joseph Beuys said, "Effects are not descriptive but depend upon the cumulative meaning of the materials." And "The outward appearance of every object I make is the equivalent of some aspect of inner human life" (fig. 41).[4]

How Beuys discovered his materials is one of the great stories of twentieth-century art, and because Beuys is the ideological father of many of the artists discussed here, it is valuable to consider his work. Born in Germany in 1921, young Joseph spent an uneventful childhood—except for a stint in the traveling circus, his introduction to the powers of performance. Then at the age of nineteen he was drafted into the German army, destined to become a combat pilot and to spend nine months in a British prisoner-of-war camp. In 1943, while flying his JU-87 over the Crimea, he was hit by Russian flak and crashed in a snowstorm. Tartars rescued the unconscious young pilot from the wreckage, portaging him back to their camp. He later remembered:

> Had it not been for the Tartars I would not be alive today. They were the nomads of the Crimean, in what was then a no-man's land between the Russian and German fronts, and favored neither side. It was they who discovered me in the snow after the crash, when the German search parties had given up. I was still unconscious then and only came round completely after twelve days or so, and by then I was back in a German field hospital. So the memories I have of that time are images that penetrated my consciousness. The last thing I remember was that it was too late to jump, too late for the parachutes to open. That must have been a couple of seconds before I hit the ground . . . I remember voices saying "Voda" (water), then the felt of their tents, and the dense pungent smell of cheese, fat and milk. They covered my body in fat to help it regenerate warmth, and wrapped it in felt as an insulator to keep the warmth in.[5]

Felt and fat became Beuys's materials, yet in his work they are not used autobiographically but rather as expanding metaphors. Fat is his metaphor for spirituality, for the passage from one state to another. Felt is warmth, the harbor for energy. Felt is the insulator, a protective covering against other influences. Felt is a material that permits outside infiltration from outside influences. Felt is a deadened psychological world. Commercial felt is a material of the proletariat. A felt hat becomes more identifiable than the head wearing it, if it is worn often enough. Felt and fat finally evolved as germinal elements in the visual language that Joseph Beuys developed for pursuing larger questions.

Beuys believed that art results from creative thought rather than from the process of making art. Other artists discussed here arrived at the same conclusions but from different beginnings. They started out conventionally, painting and sculpting, practicing the high-art forms of the Western world. As they moved away from the art of their early education and into work that was more personal, and finally symbolic and metaphorical, they were often drawn to mixed media, to adding complexity and dimensionality to their work, whether it was sculpture, collage, or assemblage. Many began to make objects. Others, like Beuys, moved closer to performance. And because symbols are inherently abstract, much of this work is abstract in content if not in form. It seems to have evolved from private mythologies. The meanings are to be intuited rather than rationally understood. The themes, as in all of Beuys's art, are insinuated, not explicitly rendered.

Mike Kelley seems to have invented himself in order to interrupt Beuys's thinking for another generation. Nothing was more disconcerting to art audiences in the 1980s than to walk into their first Mike Kelley exhibition. It was as though a child, maybe a weird child with order/disorder deficiencies, had simply walked away from his or her room—the gender of the owner being indeterminate. Strewn around was a motley collection of cloth dolls and stuffed animals, crocheted or sewn, obviously dragged about and then abandoned by some dirty little kid. Or the room might house a collection of baby blankets carefully arranged in an order that meant nothing to anyone except the child bent upon establishing his or her own patterns of repetition. Unlike Nedjar's dolls, which hark back to a primordial human past, these dolls are too familiar. We know them intimately. Most of us received them as gifts in our own childhood. The artist seems bent upon making us uncomfortable. Kelley describes his choice of visual metaphor:

> Because dolls represent such an idealized notion of the child, when you see a dirty one, you think of a fouled child. And so you think of a dysfunctional family. In actuality, that's a

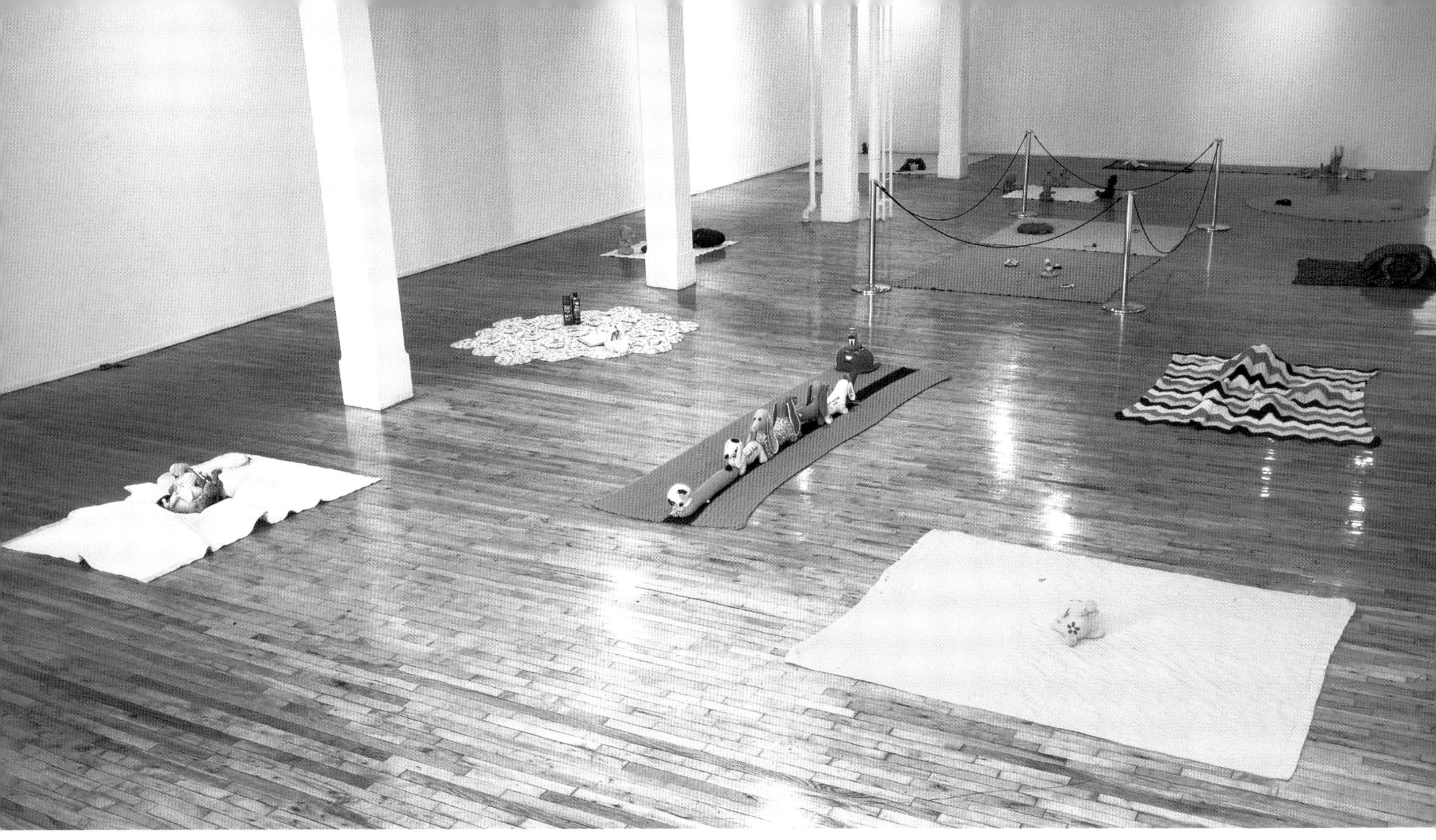

42. Mike Kelley, installation at Metro Pictures, 1990. Courtesy of the artist and Metro Pictures, New York.

> misreading because the doll itself is a dysfunctional picture of a child. It's a picture of a dead child, an impossible ideal produced by a corporate notion of the family. To parents, the doll represents a perfect picture of the child—it's clean, it's cuddly, it's sexless but as soon as the object is worn at all, it's dysfunctional. It begins to take on characteristics of the child itself—it smells like the child and becomes torn and dirty like real things do. It then becomes a frightening object because it starts to represent the human in a real way and that's when it's taken from the child and thrown away [fig. 42].[6]

Like Kelley, Maurizio Pellegrin amasses objects into an ambiguous whole. The work haunts the viewer, who is left to figure out what all these accumulated objects might mean. Pellegrin is an Italian from Venice, and it is Venice that haunts him. Each collection of objects, organized into a single work of art, seems to represent another portrait of that city of moving reflections. A work like *Inquieto Rosso (Agitated Red)* (fig. 43) is made up of thirteen elements. Each is treated like a treasure, an artifact of great concealed meaning. The object, clearly found by the artist just yesterday, speaks from the moment about a mythical past. Clothes hangers of various kinds, carefully stretched canvas cloth, the pressing pads of a tailor, unidentified objects sewn like brooches onto the carefully prepared cloth pillows: common objects given uncommon form. Each bears a number that seems to operate within a private and unbreakable code. Pellegrin makes art like Kelley's but unlike Kelley's—much too elegant—just as every city in the world is like Venice but unlike Venice.

Among those who choose to make symbol-laden, mythologically imbued objects, Frank Viner, like Beuys, is an influential, early force. Always drawn to art that was ambiguous, Viner created a powerful body of work that he called Spirit Catchers. Twenty years later, artists who have never heard of Frank Viner are still creating his kind of art from sticks and stones, from cloth and bones. Even back in the late 1960s and early 1970s, Viner's work was full and dense. It developed when painting and sculpture were becoming increasingly Minimalist. Unfashionably out of step with the times, created from humble and ephemeral materials, the work remains eerie and intelligent (fig. 44).

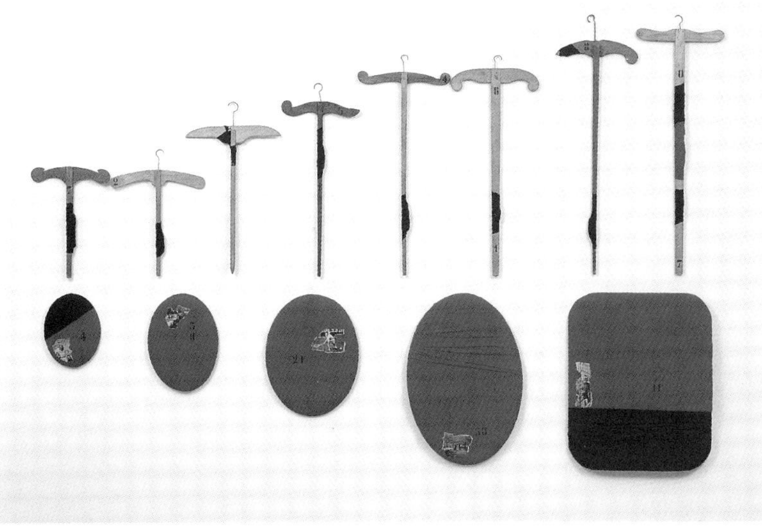

43. Maurizio Pellegrin, *Inquieto Rosso (Agitated Red)*, 1990. Thirteen elements, acrylic on padded canvas, paper, objects, 76 x 121″. Courtesy Feigen Inc., Chicago.

44. Frank Viner, *Spirit Traps*, 1974. Mixed media.

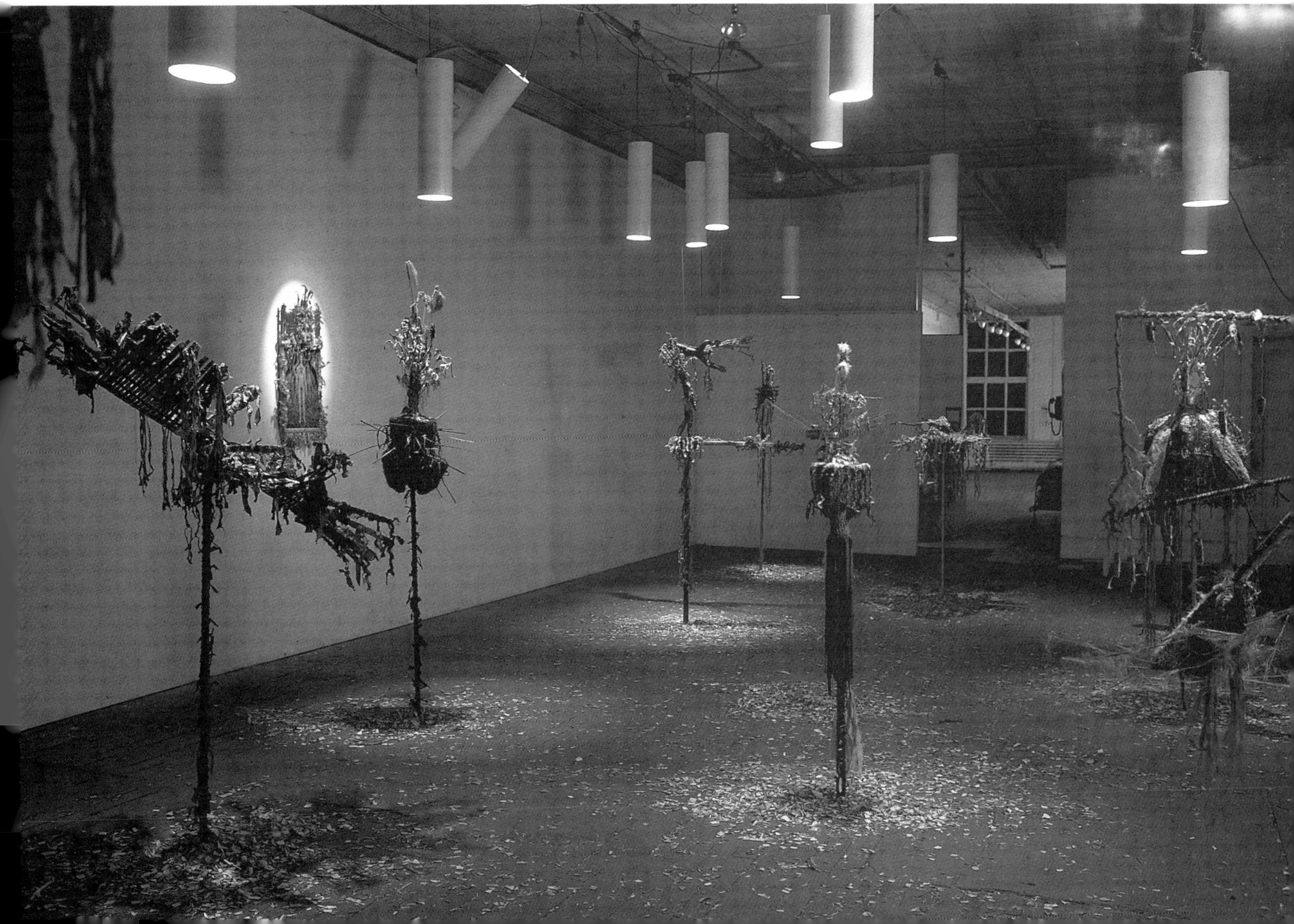

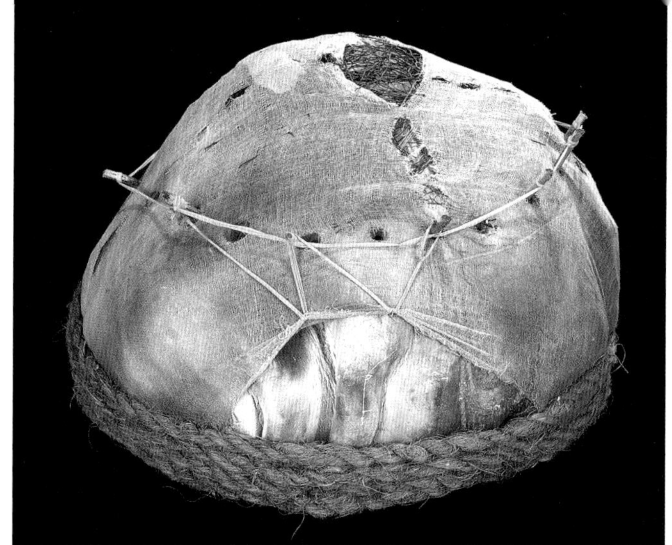

46. Bill Burke, *Mound #4,* 1979. Clay, gauze, ficus root, and lemon wood, 10 x 14″.

45. Donald Lipski, *Who's Afraid of Red, White, and Blue? #30,* 1990. Pear tree and cotton, 132 x 36 x 36″. Courtesy of the artist and Galerie Lelong, New York.

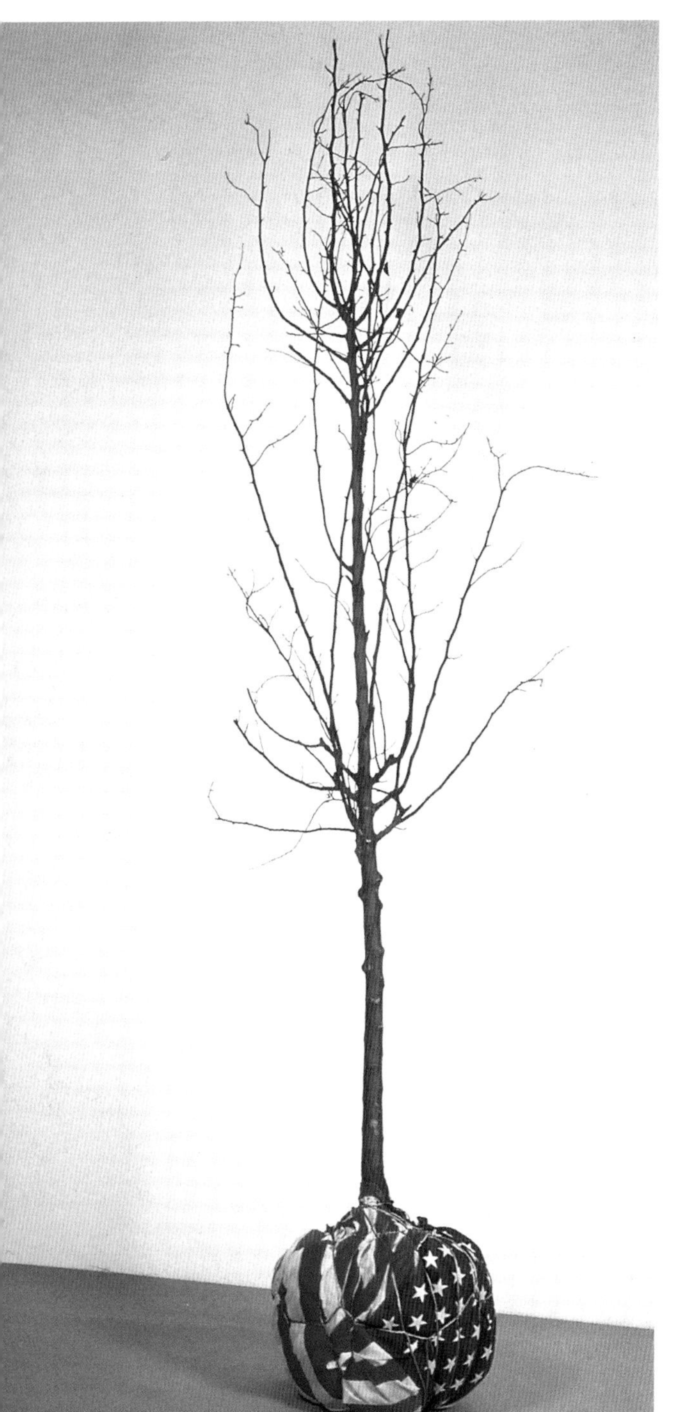

Cloth seemed to be a natural material for these object makers. Bill Burke's ceramic form is shrouded in cloth, whereas the clay surfaces of Michele Oka Doner's *Descending Torsos* suggests the cloaking of the ancient dead. Harmony Hammond wraps her *Swaddles* and builds her *Presences* with rags. Donald Lipski balls his bare root tree in an American flag and calls it *Who's Afraid of Red, White, and Blue?* at a time when the American red, white, and blue flag is one of the world's most charged images ever to be printed on mill cloth (figs. 45–48).

Other artists create objects but incorporate them into performances. Still others create performances that use cloth as costume, wherein the costume becomes metaphor for the artists' ideas. The most ambitious of these is Antoni Miralda, a Spaniard living in New York, who decided to create a new myth around New York's Statue of Liberty and the Columbus Column in Barcelona. The two monuments, both one hundred years old in 1986, face each other across the Atlantic. The artist decided to unite the Old World and the New World metaphorically by marrying the two statues in 1992 in Las Vegas. The first event in the six-year-long performance was the engagement party. This kick-off event was staged in the Jacob Javits Convention Center in the summer of 1986 as part of the summer festivities celebrating the refurbishment of the Statue of Liberty. Seamstresses worked for weeks turning 2,500 yards of nonflammable Dacron into the engagement gown. Titled *Sized for Liberty,* the pink-and-green dress is 100 feet long (fig. 49).

Miralda's performance piece, *Honeymoon,* had many acts. In 1988 he filled the Foundation Joan Miró in Barcelona with the bridal veil—23,000 feet of tulle. Thirty-five hundred Spanish citizens wrote love letters on behalf of Columbus to Lady Liberty. All were on display at the museum. That same

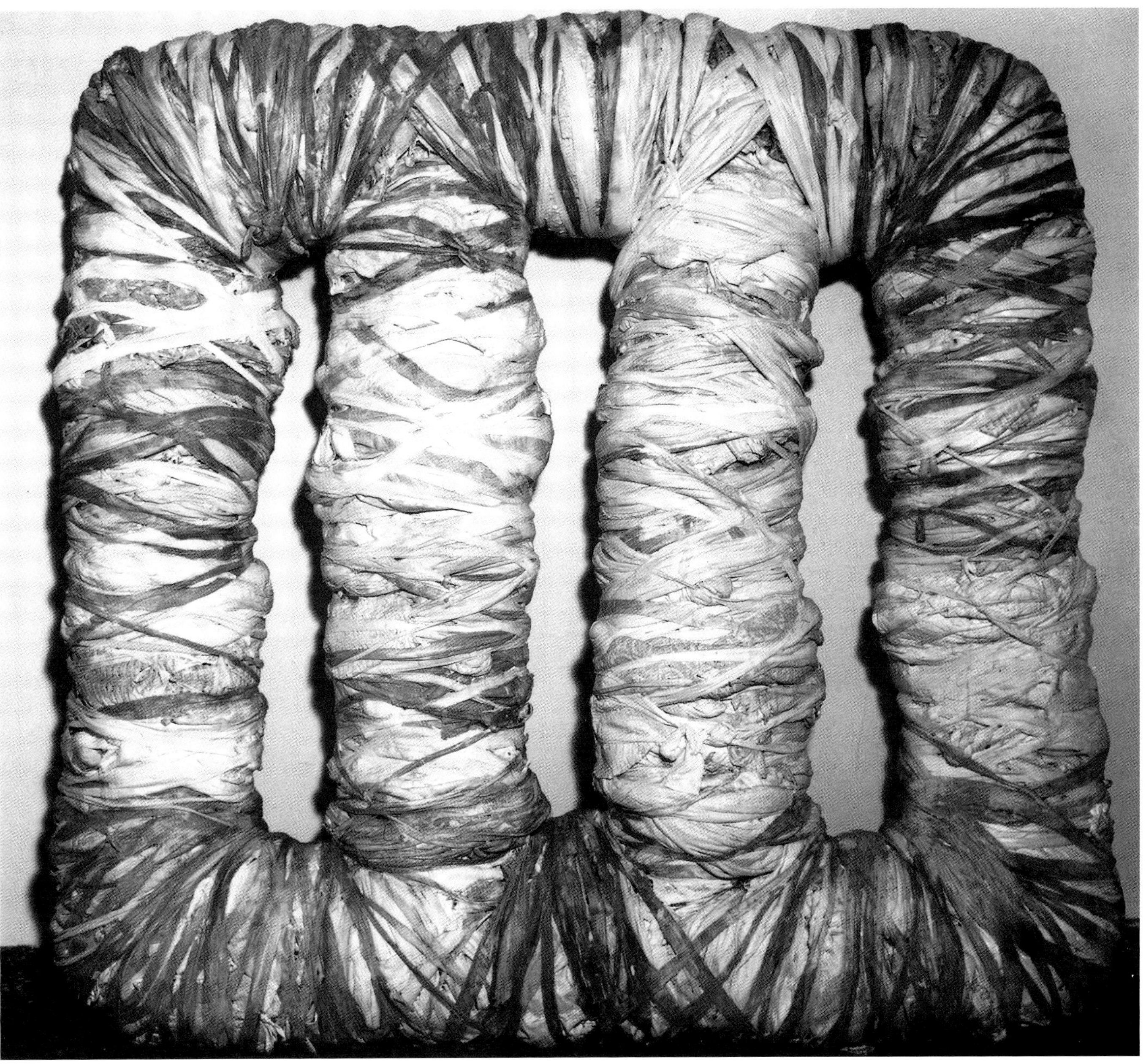

47. Harmony Hammond, *Swaddles*, 1979. Cloth, wood, gesso, liquid and foam rubber, 80 x 90 x 36″. Collection Denver Art Museum, Colorado.

year, *Liberty's Petticoat*, 20,000 feet of fabric, was unveiled at the Miami-Dade Community College in Florida. Other events unfolded at the Seibu Department Store in Tokyo; the International Jewelry Fair in Valencia, Spain; the Philadelphia Museum of Art; the Hispanic-American Columbus Day Parade on New York's Fifth Avenue; and on the banks of the Seine in Paris. Miralda's scale is enormous; his sense of play, unmatched. He truly understands how to make myth of art and art of myth, and to execute it grandly.

Throughout the history of art, artists have either depicted the myths of prehistory or applied mythic titles to their work as part of the process of forging new myths. It made little difference if the work was abstract or realistic. The Surrealists were the masters of this kind of mythmaking and the forebears of today's mythmakers. In the 1920s and 1930s artists such as Remedios Varo, René Magritte, and Salvador Dalí, all members of the Surrealist movement, engaged in weaving mythic symbolism. They fused ancient and classical myths into their own reali-

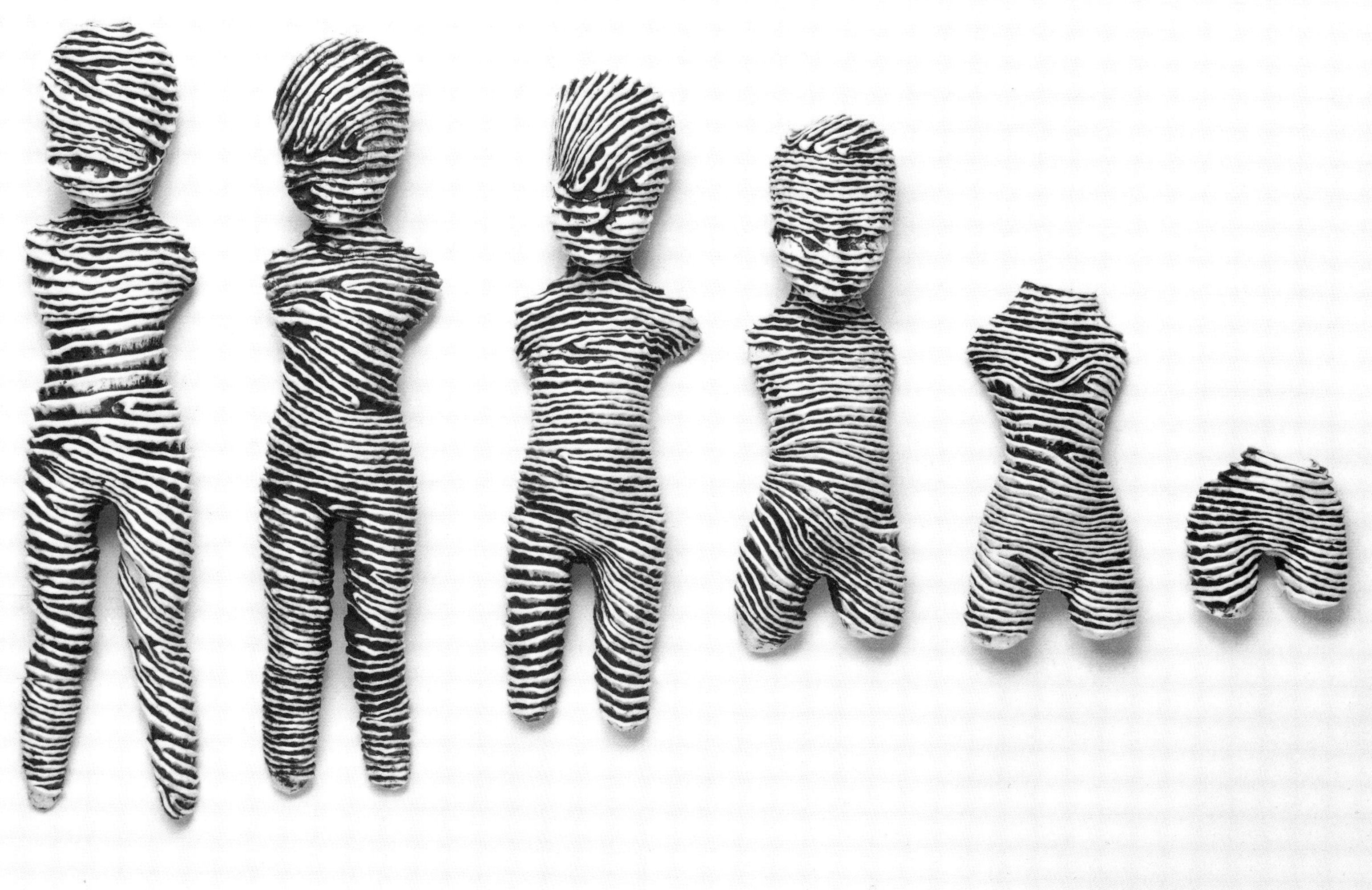

48. Michele Oka Doner, *Descending Torsos*, 1975–83. Clay, 3–16″. Collection Elizabeth M. Bank.

ties, dreams, and fantasies; they went in search of the marvelous. André Breton, in his *Surrealist Manifesto*, wrote:

> I believe in the future resolution of two states, dream and reality, which are seemingly contradictory, into a kind of absolute state of reality, a *surreality*, if one may so speak.
>
> Let us note the *hate of the marvelous* which rages in certain men. Let us not mince words: the marvelous is always beautiful, anything marvelous is beautiful, in fact only the marvelous is beautiful.[7]

In 1981, years after the Surrealist movement had formally ended, John Bernard Myers organized an exhibition for New York University's Grey Art Gallery that he called "Tracking the Marvelous," an exhibition starring the likes of Frank Viner and Eva Hesse. In the catalog Myers eloquently summarized the Surrealist legacy still alive among contemporary artists when he stated his own philosophy: "I had absorbed a Surrealist point of view: to keep myself open to wonder, to be endlessly curious, to revere the imagination, never to cease to desire more of life. And, above all, to track the marvelous. This quest is a search for one's self and the renewal of one's self."[8]

Louise Bourgeois was well schooled in the tradition that accepted the exploration of the unconscious as art's primary aim. She grew up in a Paris ruled by the ideas of Surrealism. She moved into the New York art world a year before the war broke out and the migration of Surrealist artists across the Atlantic began. The great themes of her artistic life soon emerged. She would explore the tense, often convoluted, surrealistic relationships between men and women, between inner sexuality and life in the outer world. Through autobiographical works such as *The Destruction of the Father*, she delved into her anxiety as a woman at war with her father (fig. 50).

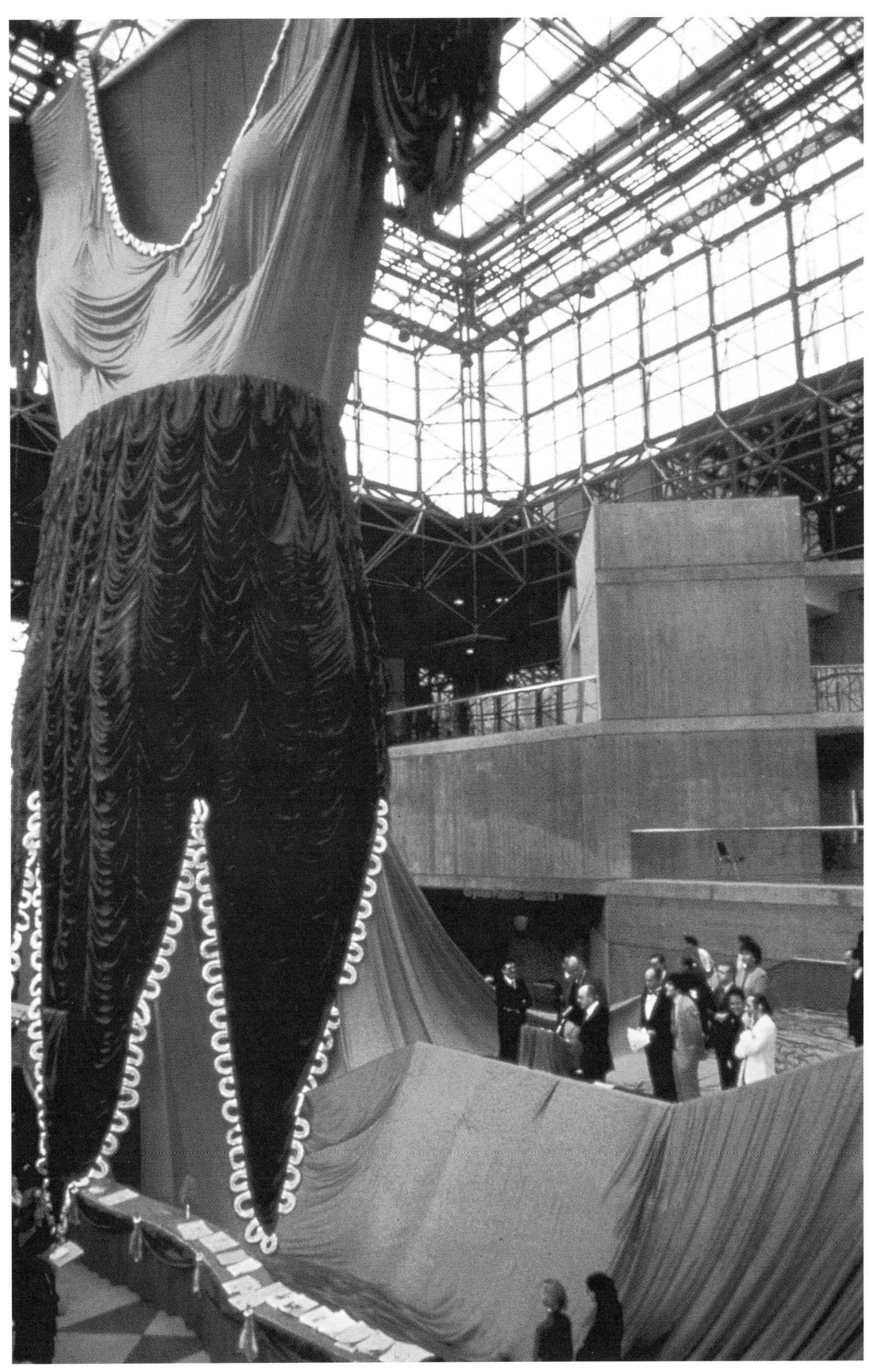

49. Antoni Miralda, *Sized for Liberty,* 1986. 2,500 yards of Dacron. Exhibited at the Jacob Javits Center, New York.

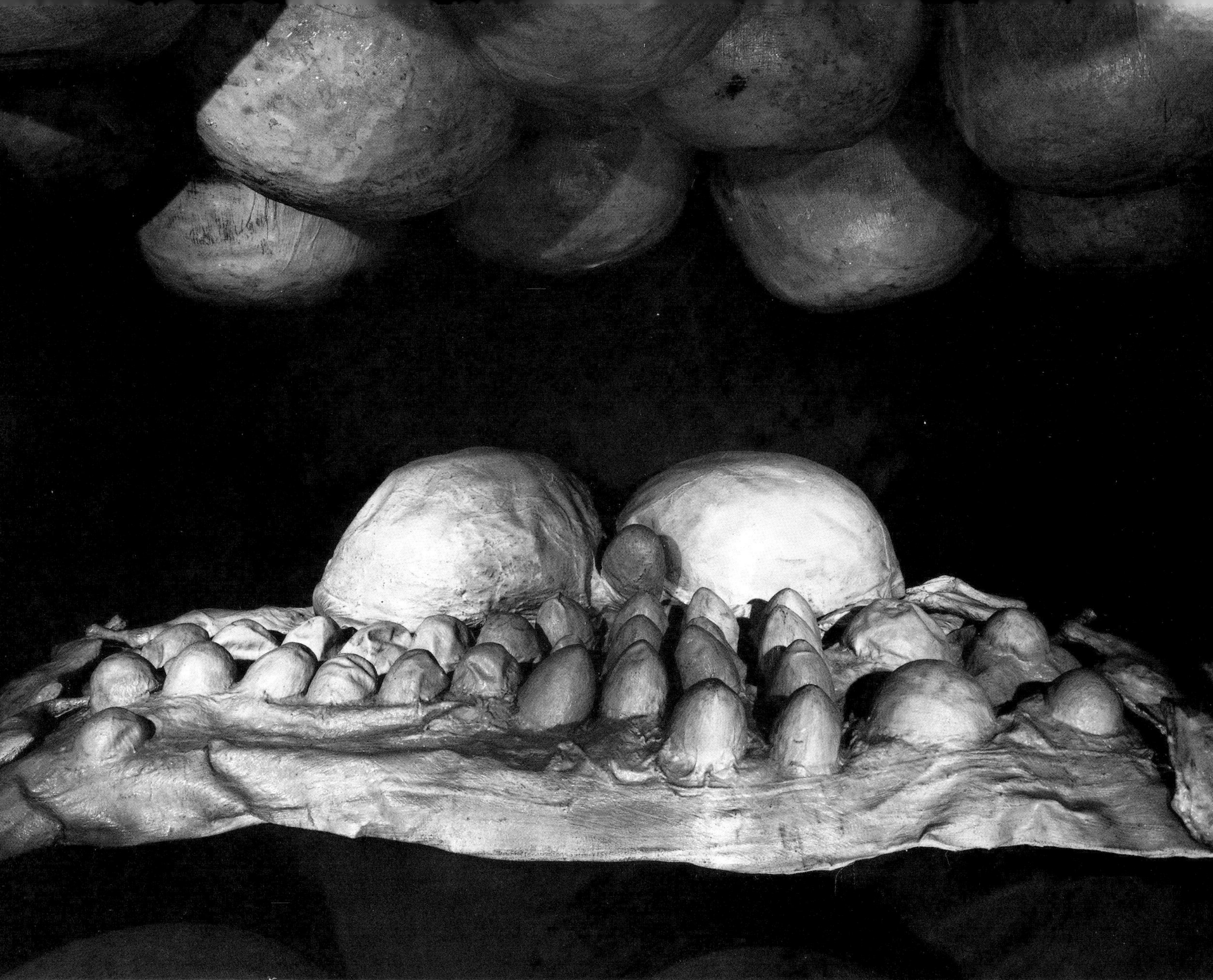

50. Louise Bourgeois, *The Destruction of the Father* (detail), 1974. Latex, latex over plaster, and mixed media, c. 9 x 11 x 9´. Courtesy Robert Miller Gallery, Inc., New York.

Barbara Zucker creates her *Dark Huts* out of similar bulbous shapes made of cloth and repeated over and over. They suggest breasts and bellies and the ancient lodging of the mound builders. By placing them in a field, she accentuates the relationship between women and nature, and the huts take on a timelessness that could not have been achieved in a gallery setting (fig. 51).

Few ceremonies exist without the presence of cloth in some form. Hermann Nitsch, Mary Beth Edelson, Donna Henes, and Betsy Damon create works of ceremony that are less personal and more social. In these ceremonies cloth is present almost as a silent partner. Nitsch, for example, has spent years tracking the dark side of the marvelous, pursuing in his work the primitive violence that exists in all societies, or in all humans. As intended, the viewer is repelled by his mystery theater performances, rituals that incorporate blood, gore, sex, and death, swathed, shrouded, and wrapped with cloth (fig. 52).

Edelson and Damon are committed feminists, with a political point of view that propels their art as it has driven the work of Judy Chicago. Both Chicago's *Dinner Party* and her *Birth Project* drew power and ambiguity from traditionally embellished cloth designed by Chicago but executed by anonymous women.

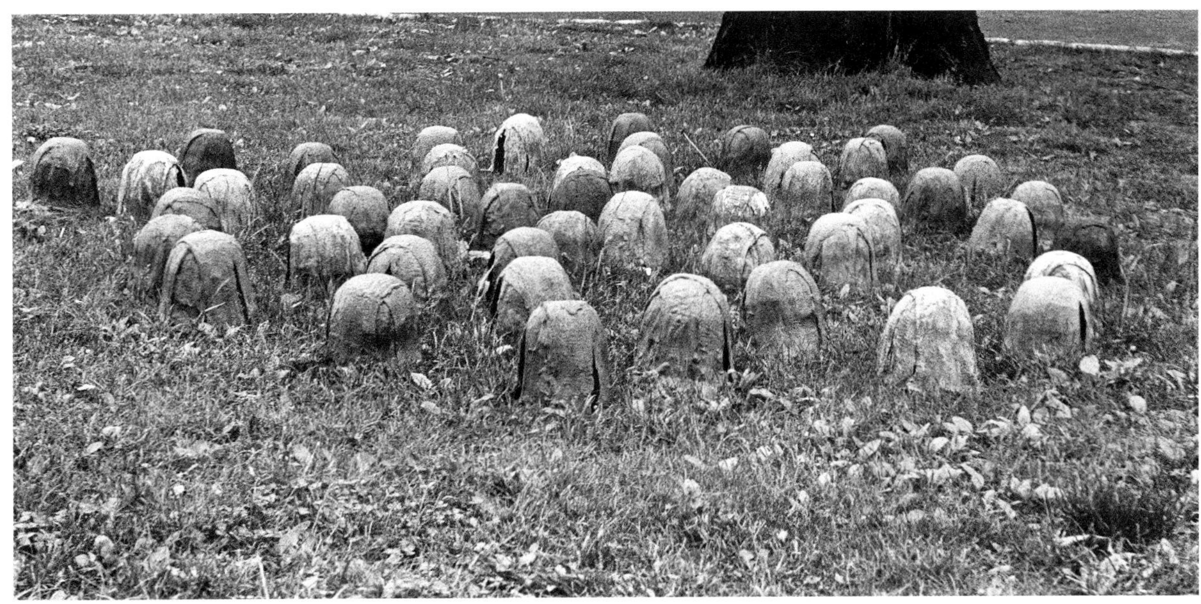

51. Barbara Zucker, *Dark Huts*, 1973. Hydrocal, cheesecloth, pigment, fifty units. Outdoor installation at Sarah Lawrence College, Bronxville, New York. Courtesy Pam Alder Inc., New York.

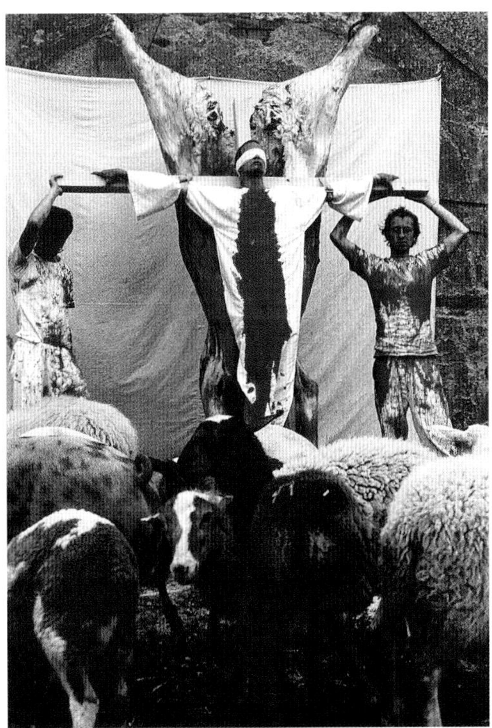

52. Hermann Nitsch, *Aktion* (from sunrise July 27 until sunrise July 30, 1984). Das Origien Mysterien Theatre.

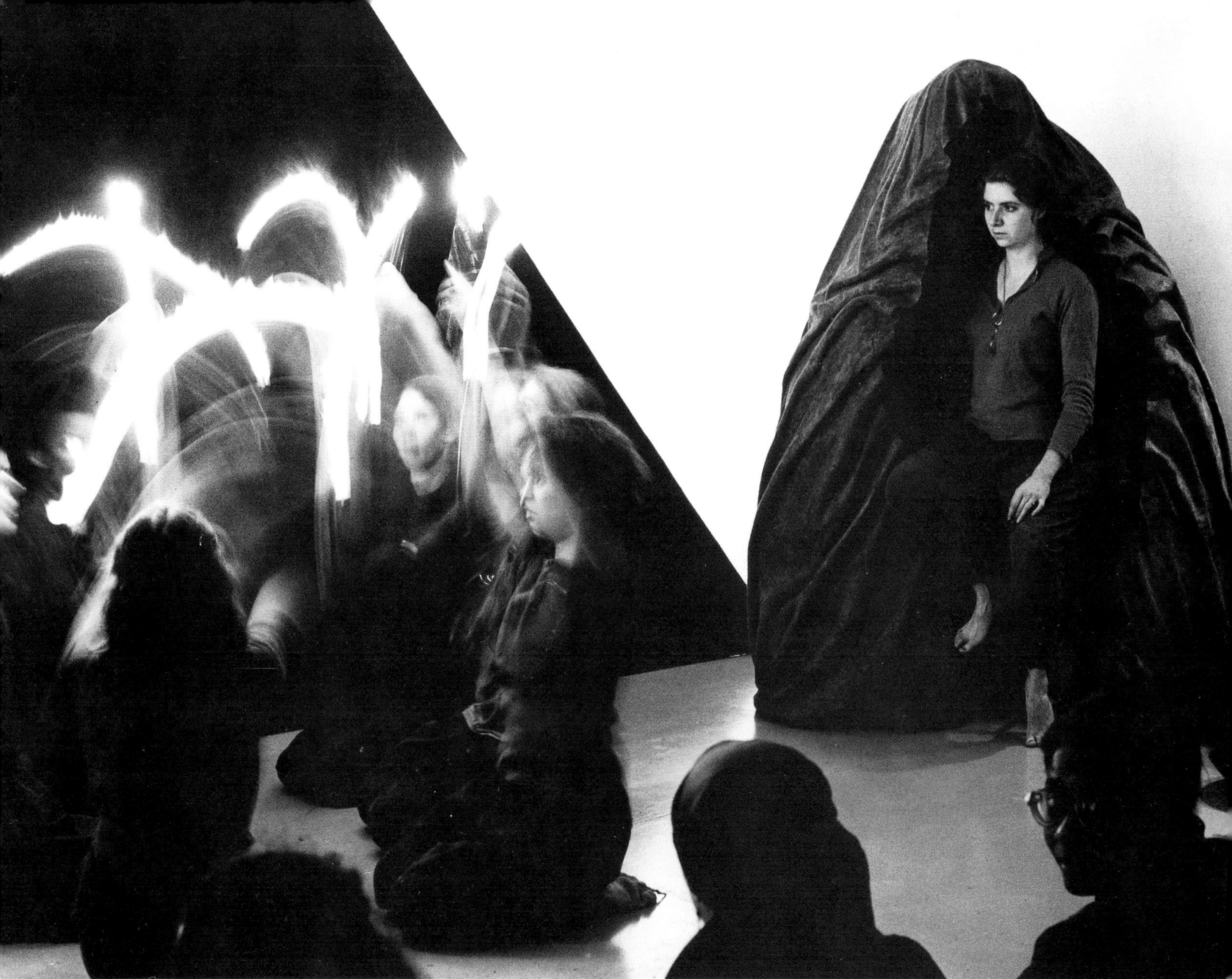

53. Mary Beth Edelson, *Toothless*, 1977. From the performance *The Nature of Balancing*, 1979.

For fifteen years Mary Beth Edelson has explored the Great Goddess theme, experimenting with collective creativity, researching the nature of goddess worship, and developing rituals and performances that unearth the core of female experience. The resulting body of work is large and consistent. During the 1970s she created a large cycle of work, *Memorials to 9,000,000 Women Burned as Witches in the Christian Era*, which reflected her research into the stamping out of goddess worship in the Middle Ages. *Toothless*, a cavelike sculpture in the form of a woman, was used as a prop in the 1979 performance *The Nature of Balancing*. According to the artist, *Toothless* referred to Sheela-na-gig, the Celtic goddess of creation and destruction whose open vagina symbolized male fears of the *vagina dentata*, the toothed vagina. Much of Edelson's mature work relates to cloth as she folds it, hangs it, expands it, or limits it. Even when she paints on canvas the images are often of flowing cloth. The artist seems unable to separate her intrinsically female ideas from a female presence that she finds in the cloth (fig. 53).

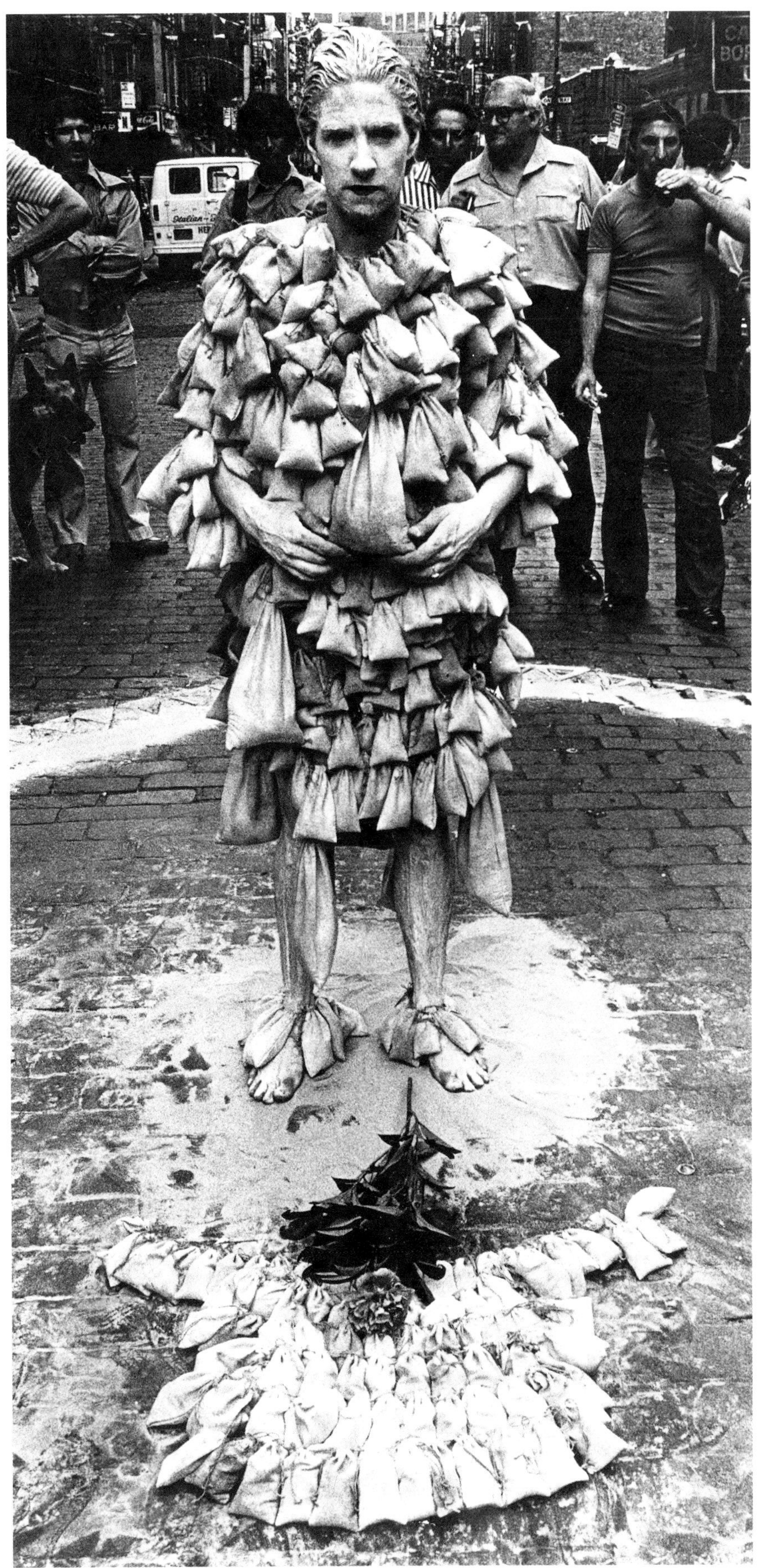

54. Betsy Damon, *7,000-Year-Old Woman,* 1977. Street performance.

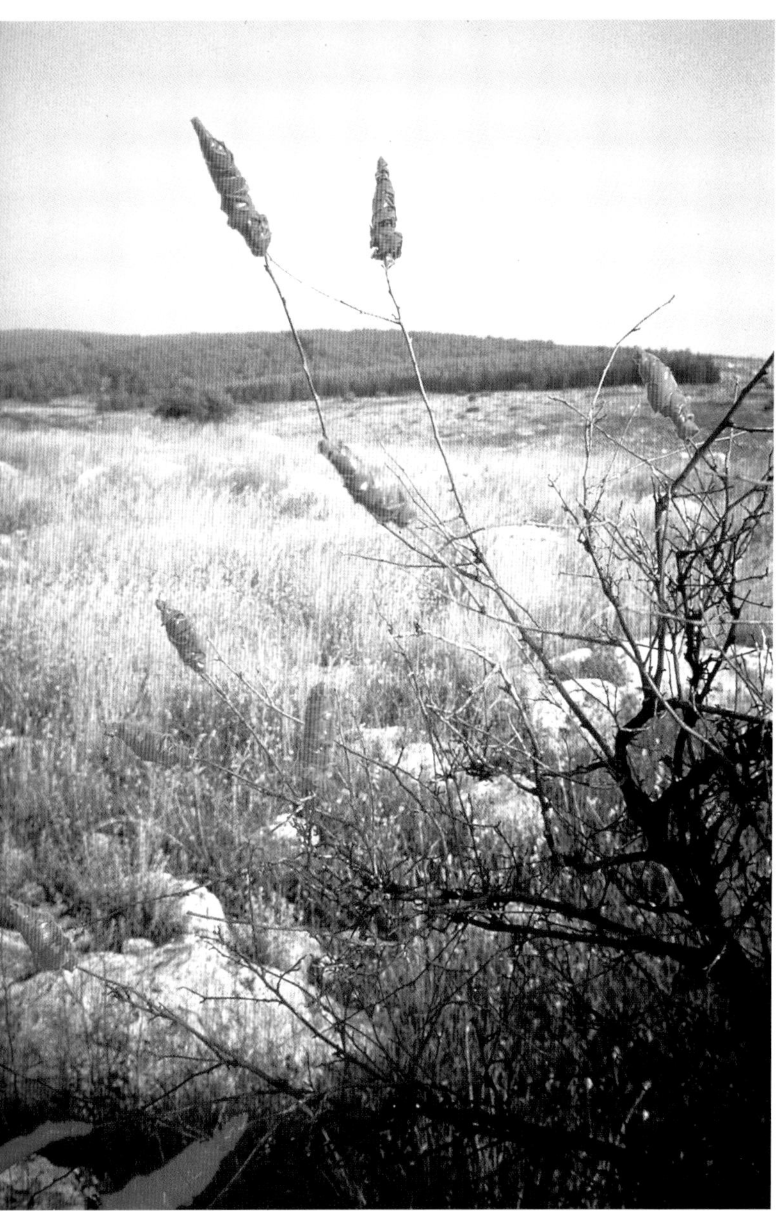

55. Donna Henes, *Spontaneous Site Celebration, Spider Woman Series,* 1984.

Betsy Damon's *7,000-Year-Old Woman* was a street performance enacted in 1977 in New York as a feminist ceremonial giveaway. Dressed in her costume of detachable bags, Damon went into the street and drew a circle around herself with dry pigment, seeking "to define a female space in the hostile city." She proceeded to give away her pigment-filled bags. Through this remarkable piece of street theater, Damon sought to confront the idea of time. With slow and deliberate motions she handed out the bags, one by one, "divesting herself of the burden of time." Her intention was to give each willing passerby a moment of time in which to create something new. (The artist wryly commented afterward that some things do not change. Primarily children took the offered gift. The little girls stashed the bags away, considering them treasures, while the little boys threw them at each other; fig. 54).

Damon chose to confront her public in its own territory. The spontaneous participation of an unsuspecting audience was essential to the wholeness of the piece. Conversely, Donna Henes needed the audience's full and knowing involvement in her participatory sculpture project *Dressing Our Wounds in Warm Clothes.* In New York on May 1, 1980, she left collection boxes at the Franklin Furnace (a public gallery space), at radio station WBAI, and at New York University. Henes, or Spider Woman as she calls herself, asked the public to contribute their favorite energy-endowed, energy-inducing items of old clothing. Thirty days later, on Memorial Day, she transported the charged clothing to the Manhattan Psychiatric Center on Ward's Island. Then she and the residents tore the clothing into strips. Beginning on the first of June and working through to the summer solstice, she and 4,159 patients, staff members, and visitors tied knots of clothing on trees, bushes, and fences. Cloth became the transmitter of powerful energy into the lives of the psychologically needy. Henes holds an anomalous position in the art world. Her resolutely unfashionable art is made even more so by its moral underpinnings, and by her belief that art can communicate with large groups of people and bring about positive change. She could not have created this work without a material as universally understood as cloth.

Henes founded her conceptual performance upon an old magical ceremony, the tying of knots at healing waters, a widespread custom practiced by women in countries as diverse as

Morocco, Scotland, and Armenia. Similarly, throughout the southern United States, there can be found various manifestations of the tradition of hanging bottles and bits of paper and cloth on trees in gardens and cemeteries. It is thought to have originated among the slaves from the ancient Kongo Kingdom (today Angola and Zaire). Like the prayer flags of Tibet, bits of cloth (or glass, or paper) fly in the wind as intermediaries with the unknowable (fig. 55). Henes evolved the piece out of her conviction that to tie knots at healing waters is as valid today as it was historically.

Other artists have drawn from supernatural concepts, from ancient religious ideas, from ceremonial objects, and from physical manifestations of spiritual power. Historically none are more powerful than those which look to the shroud or the veil, be it the Shroud of Christ, the Lenten Veil, or iconic paintings such as *Veronica's Veil* by Hans Memling (see fig. 6).

The veil, riddled with ancient symbolic meaning, was described by Homer as the "radiant white emblem of modesty." Veils reveal as they conceal. Veils tantalize. Veils make even the most ordinary mysterious. In 1980 Dorothee von Windheim produced *Salve Sancta Facies*, a series of gossamer shrouds, images of saints screened onto gauze or cheesecloth. Unframed, the pieces float on the wall, occasionally cascading onto the floor below. Sometimes the repeating faces shift from one von Windheim saint to another, finally becoming a frieze of the ancients. At other times the same face comes back again and again as von Windheim repeats the image over and over. Her shrouds are haunting; in their repetition they become almost unbearably haunting. Therein lies their power (fig. 56).

Eva Hesse once explained that she used repetition in her art because it recalled the absurdity of life. If something is absurd, it is much more exaggerated, more absurd if it is repeated. Had Donna Henes tied only a few knots on the grounds of the Manhattan Psychiatric Center, or had Betsy Damon given away only a few bags of dried pigment, neither would have made their point. Had Joseph Beuys worn his felt hat only now and then, no one would have noticed. A room full of von Windheim's shrouds takes the viewer's breath away. One hung somewhere on a gallery wall would go almost unnoticed.

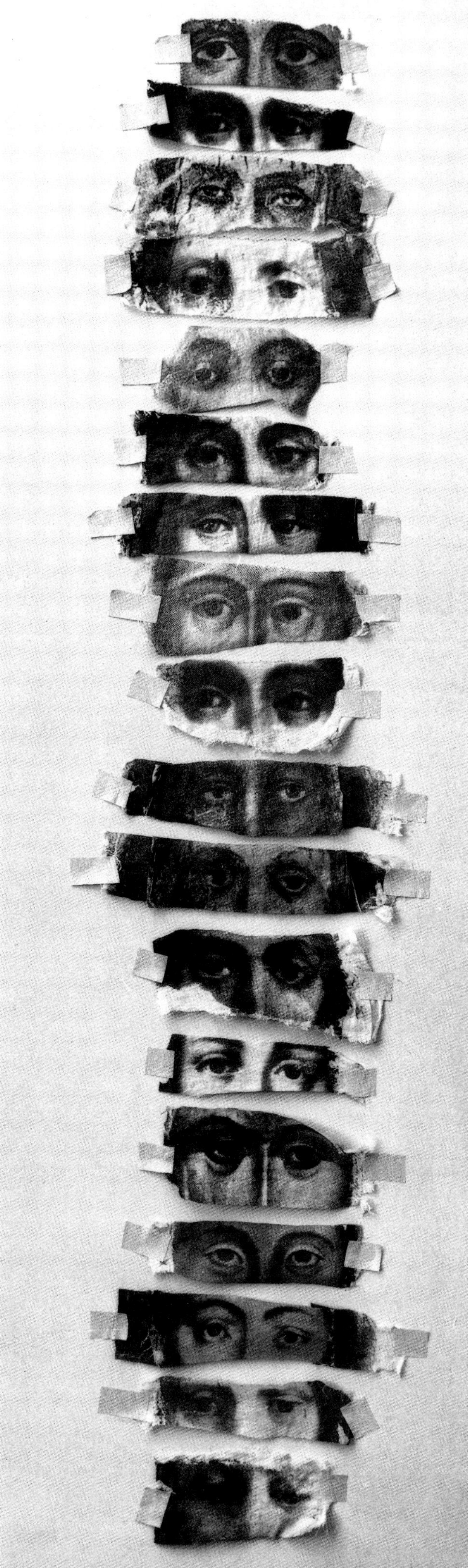

56. Dorothee von Windheim, *Salve Sancta Facies* (detail), 1980. Liquid light on baize. Courtesy D + C Mueller-Roth, Stuttgart, Germany.

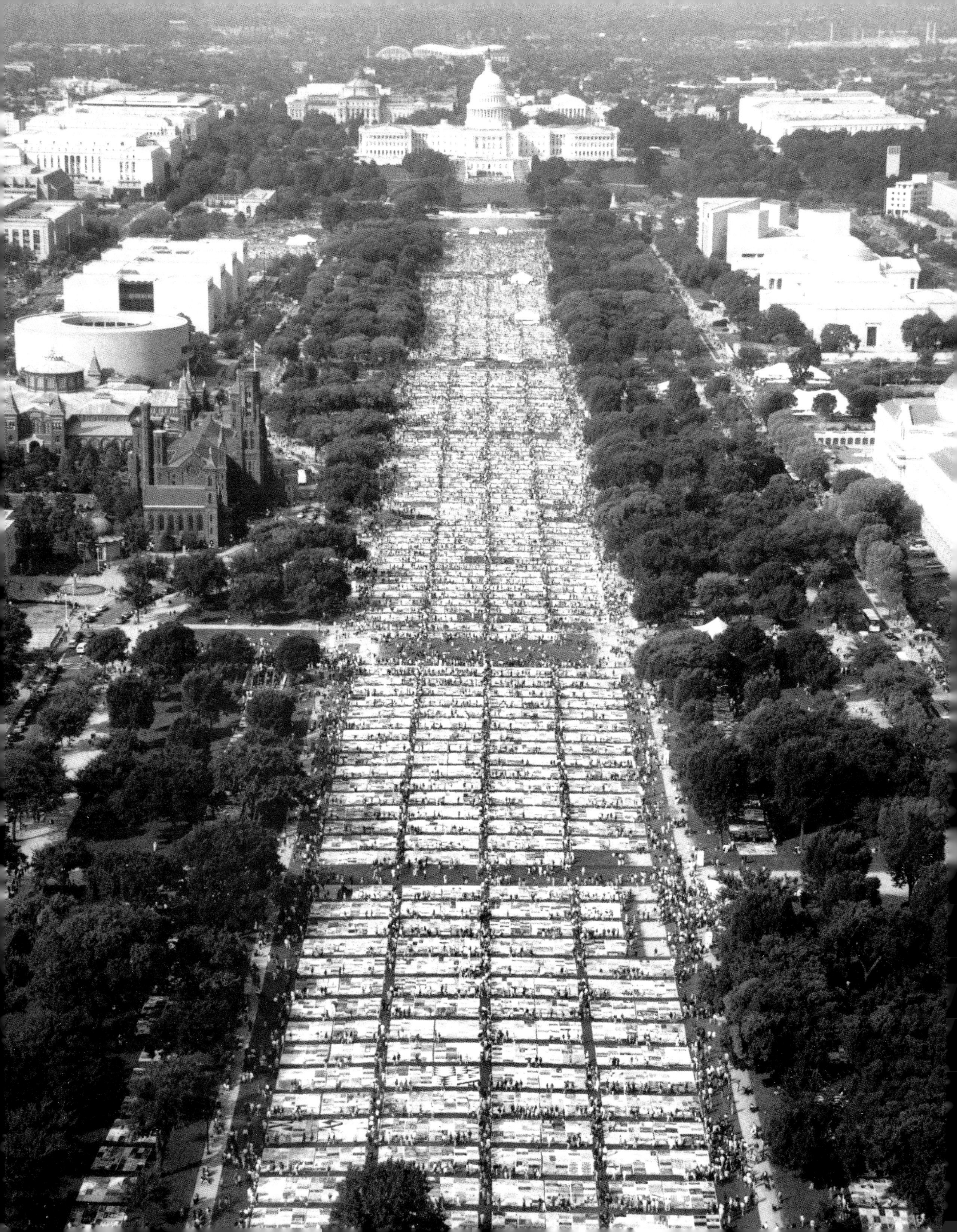

Likewise, repetition of an act of mourning implants a greater grief deeply in the collective heart. The most successful of war memorials, such as the Allied World War II Memorial in Manila or the Vietnam Memorial in Washington, D.C., succeed because the endless listing of individual names forces the viewer to confront the massive death that is all war. In the 1980s the mourning quilt was revived in San Francisco—but on a monumental scale. Sewing bees were organized first in the Bay Area and then across the United States as quilters joined together to make blocks in memory of friends and family members who had died of AIDS. In June 1987 the quilt was first shown. Forty blocks comprised the whole. By October 1989 the quilt had 10,848 blocks, weighed thirteen tons, and covered twenty-two acres when laid out on the Mall in Washington, D.C. As the epidemic continued into the 1990s the quilt doubled and tripled in size. The strength of the AIDS quilt is not in aesthetics, but in the powerful amassment of bits and pieces that stand in for human lives (fig. 57).

Cloth. Rolls and rolls of mill cloth piling up in warehouses all over the world. Miles and miles of camel trains bearing silk from the East to the West. Endless cloth binding the feet of endless Chinese women. Yards and yards of linen swaddling the Egyptian dead. Societies where the face of every woman is hidden behind a veil. Meanings expanded by metaphor upon metaphor. These are the inspirations underpinning the work of these artists intent upon creating modern myths and symbols from the substance of cloth.

1. Roger Cardinal, *Nedjar's High Magic* (exhibition brochure, New York: Rosa Esman Gallery, 1986).

2. Robert Graves, introduction to *The Greek Myths*, vol. 1 (New York: Penguin, 1955).

3. Lisa Liebmann, "Michael Tracy: A Full-Blown Geophysical Presence," *Artforum*, Feb. 1988, 40.

4. Caroline Tisdall, *Joseph Beuys* (New York: Solomon R. Guggenheim Museum, 1979).

5. Tisdall, *Joseph Beuys*, 16.

6. Ralph Rugoff, "Dirty Toys: Mike Kelley Interviewed," *XXIst century* 1, no. 1 (winter 1991–92): 4.

7. André Breton, *Manifeste du surréalisme* (Paris, 1924).

8. John Bernard Myers, *Tracking the Marvelous* (New York: New York University, 1981), 13.

57 *(opposite)*. The Names Project AIDS Memorial Quilt Washington, D. C. October 11-13, 1996. Courtesy The Names Project Foundation.

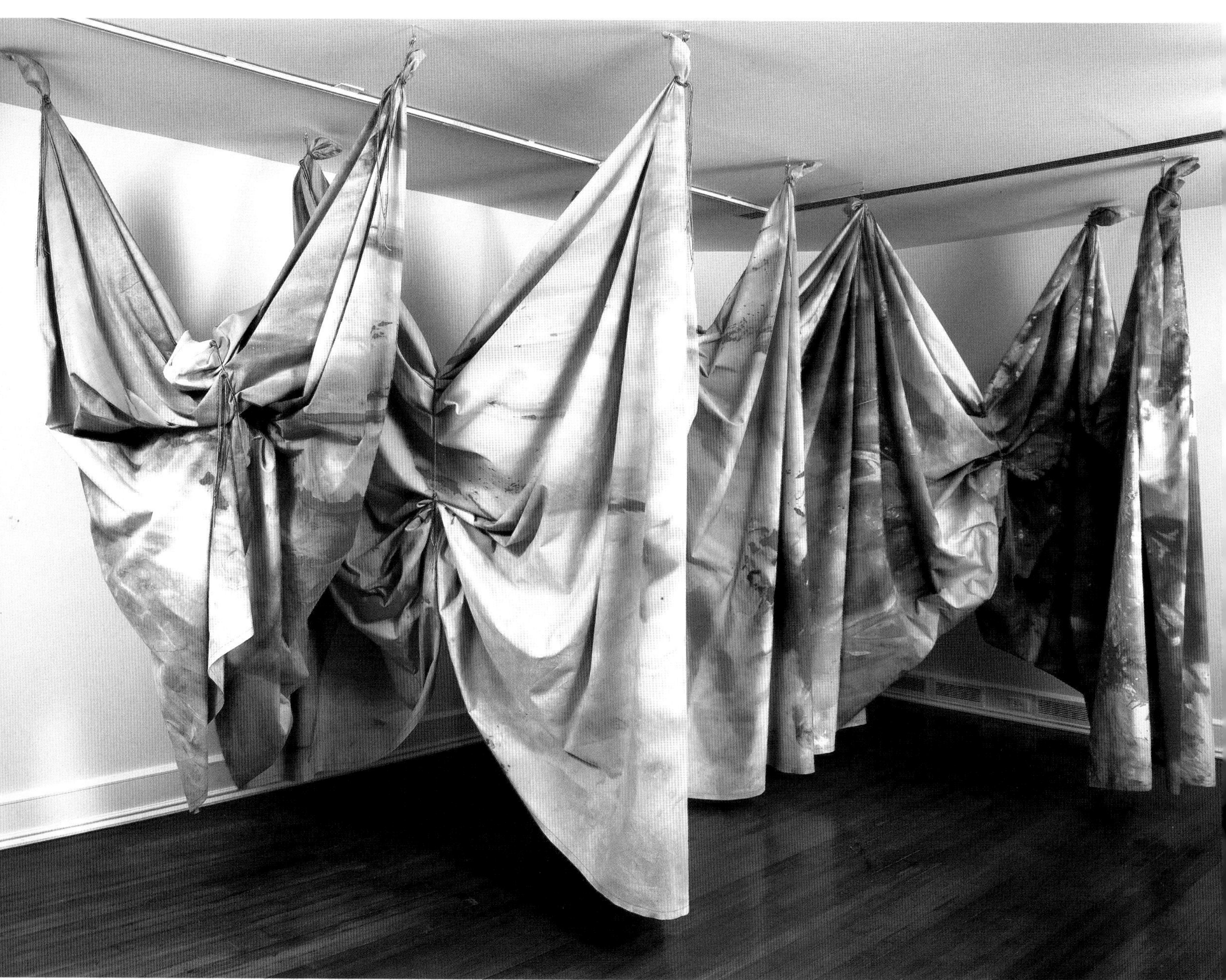

# Unframed, Unstretched, and Unbound

*My painting does not come from the easel. I hardly ever stretch my canvas before painting. I prefer to tack the unstretched canvas to the hard wall or floor. I need the resistance of a hard surface. On the floor I am more at ease. I feel nearer, more a part of the painting, since this way I can walk around it, work from the four sides and literally be in the painting.*

Jackson Pollock

58 *(opposite).* Sam Gilliam, installation of *Mandela* (left), 1970, 120 x 405″, and *Relative* (right), 1969, 120 x 538″. Both synthetic polymer paint on canvas.

## Painting: An American Movement

Jackson Pollock introduced into contemporary painting the idea of the unframed, unstretched, and unbound work of art. With his "drip" paintings of the late 1940s and early 1950s he sowed the idea of the unbound painting, although he continued to stretch and frame his canvases conventionally for the rest of his life. The general public might not have known the significance of those early, revolutionary paintings, but artists did. Pollock had deserted the Western tradition of easel painting. He had given up the brushstroke as the extension of the artist's hand. Instead he turned to unprimed and unstretched swaths of canvas that would absorb paint as dye rather than accept it as surface coating. In doing so, he was not only rejecting the accepted method of making a painting, he was grappling with a new idea of space. He wished to rid his paintings of the traditional idea of perspective that had dominated painting from the Renaissance until Cubism. He sought to work strictly within the two-dimensional space of his flat canvas, eschewing a figure-ground relationship and all hints of positive and negative space. Although he built up the surface with layers of textured paint, he insisted that the picture plane remain visually flat.

Helen Frankenthaler was among the first to understand that Pollock's paintings were most radical in technique, not content. By changing his technique, he was able to transform his content, thereby achieving the two-dimensional surface he sought. By 1952 Frankenthaler herself was staining diluted oil paint onto raw cotton duck. By treating canvas as cloth, and pigment as dye, she arrived at a new idea of the painted surface.

Morris Louis was later to say that Frankenthaler was a bridge "between Pollock and what was possible."[1] Louis, Kenneth Noland, and Jules Olitski, along with Frankenthaler, moved American painting in a direction that Pollock, the master of lights and darks, would not have imagined. They were interested in making paintings about light and color—pure, shimmering light and resonant, vibrant color. The goal was to create the transparent and reflective qualities of watercolor on a grand scale with oil paint. Cloth in its natural state freed these so-called color-field painters to emulate watercolor. Years before, between 1920 and 1953, John Marin had tried, but because he continued to prime his canvas in the old way, he failed. Only in his watercolors on paper did he achieve the vibrant, airy effect he sought.

As Frankenthaler discovered, the white of the unprimed canvas both reflected and absorbed light to a greater degree than prepared canvas. This was made most apparent in the 1986 Morris Louis retrospective at the Museum of Modern Art in New York. To be surrounded by those large, pulsating paintings was to be in a world of wondrous, translucent light. Although critic Barbara Rose did not equate the use of pigment with the dyeing process, she did pinpoint the revolutionary use of cloth in the paintings of these artists. As she observed,

> Frankenthaler often used bare canvas dramatically; and Louis and Noland were equally able to use unpainted areas as an expressive element. In his "unfurl" paintings, Louis apparently draped raw canvas over a trough, spilling rivulets of paint in diagonally spreading streams, leaving the center of the canvas dramatically bared. Because the naked, literally undressed, quality of the canvas as yielding fabric rather than hard ground is stressed, the viewer often has the acute physical sensation of being hurtled headlong through a space both mysteriously infinite and explicitly and concretely finite."[2]

But it was Sam Gilliam, a second-generation color-field painter from Washington, D.C., who was truly to elucidate the definition of the unframed, unstretched, and unbound abstract painting. By the late 1960s Gilliam was cutting large stretches of raw canvas, painting and dyeing on their thirsty surfaces, and placing them loosely within a space. He might drape the cloth casually over a sawhorse, pin it to a wall, or allow the material to cascade randomly from the ceiling into the center of the space. The work was large and visually potent, and unlike the work of his immediate predecessors, there was an intensity of darks that harked back to Pollock (fig. 58).

A breakthrough year for the unframed, unstretched, and unbound in the United States was 1968. It was a year of culmination, a year when labels such as Eccentric Abstraction, Anti-Form, Process art, and Anti-Illusionism became part of art jargon. Some artists, in revolt against Minimalism, were moving into art as idea, art as process, art as material. Cloth played a major role in this revolution, as illustrated by the works of Robert Rauschenberg.

In 1968 the "Anti-Form" exhibition was held at the John Gibson Gallery in New York. Richard Tuttle, Eva Hesse, Alan Saret, Keith Sonnier, and Richard Serra were among those in this pivotal show. Two months later, "Nine at Leo Castelli" (at the dealer's Upper West Side warehouse) was organized by painter Robert Morris and included several of the same artists. Frank Viner, Hesse, Tuttle, Sonnier, and Robert Morris himself were intent upon expanding the format and the materials of this "Process art." All of them were using soft materials. In an influential *Artforum* article Morris argued:

> The process of "making itself" has hardly been examined . . . Of the Abstract Expressionists only Pollock was able to recover process and hold on to it as part of the end form of the work . . . In object-type art process is not visible. Materials often are . . . Recently, materials other than rigid industrial ones have begun to show up. Oldenburg was one of the first to use such materials . . . A direct investigation of the properties of these materials is progress. This involves a reconsideration of the use of tools in relation to material. In some cases these investigations move from the making of things to the making of the material itself. Sometimes a direct manipulation of a given material without the use of any tool is made. In these cases considerations of gravity become as important as those of space. The focus on matter and gravity as means results in forms which were not projected in advance.[3]

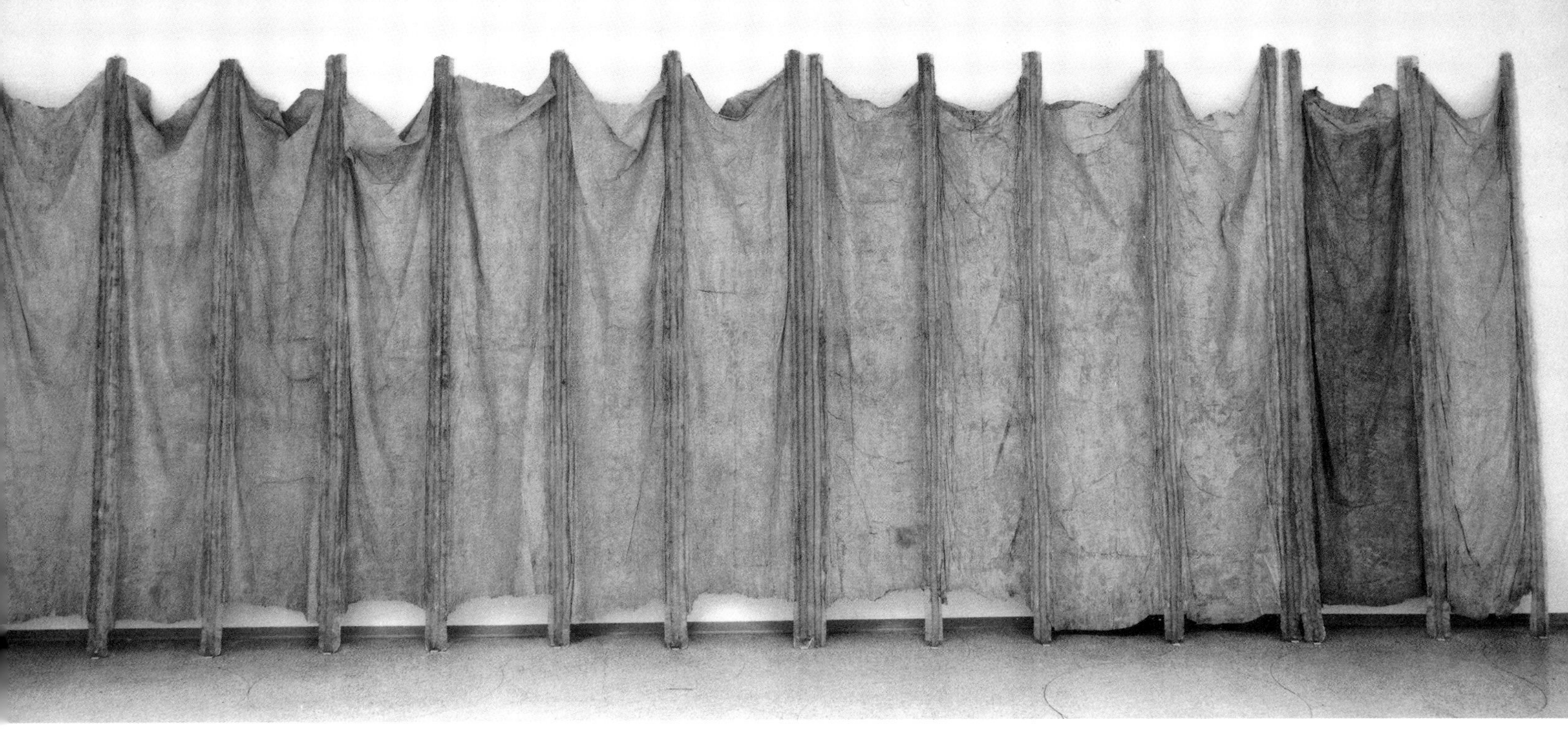

59. Eva Hesse, *Expanded Expansion*, 1969. Fiberglass and rubberized cheesecloth, three units of three, five, and seven poles, 120 x 180–240″ per unit. Collection Solomon R. Guggenheim Museum, New York.

Sam Gilliam's work, although removed from the New York scene that Morris was describing, exemplifies unstretched work that relies upon gravity for its form. Eve Hesse, however, relied upon both matter and gravity to delineate form.

Hesse was to emerge as one of the most idiosyncratic artists of her time; she would be far more influential than the art world of the late 1960s suspected. Hesse, like Viner, with whom she shared an appreciation for the fantastic, created works that were neither painting nor sculpture (see fig. 44). Both artists turned to soft materials to circumvent the prevailing formal Minimalism—although both continued to respect the more geometrically rigorous work. Seen from a vantage point twenty years later, the works of these two artists, and others like them, appear prophetic, visually fascinating, and solidly based in timeless formal attitudes.

By 1967 Hesse had become aware of liquid rubber, or latex. The material suited her well, for it allowed her to create a sensuous surface with her own hands. She was also attracted to the material as a conductor of light. The natural color of her underlying materials would not be changed by the latex and she would not be forced to bring additional color as pigment into her work. In pieces such as *Expanded Expansion* she applied latex and fiberglass to cheesecloth in order to make wall sheets. By May 1970, after three years of intense work, her rubberized fiberglass and cheesecloth *Contingent* was on the cover of *Artforum*. She lived a short time longer but made a solid body of work, much of it in unusual materials placed in unexpected contexts. Her use of latex to make the pliable rigid became common practice among artists in the 1980s; for instance, Lia Cook uses latex to stiffen her weavings into permanent forms.[4] The conservation problems that were to plague Hesse's work did not surface until years later (fig. 59).

Out in California, Ed Moses had discovered liquid resin. An Abstract Expressionist in the late 1950s and one of the first to show at the Ferus Gallery in Los Angeles, Moses was in a position to spearhead a movement of his own—soft painting. For his resin-backed, unstretched, softly hung paintings, he drew his imagery from his years of formal, repetitive, horizontal line work. Over the next decade many West Coast artists hung unstretched soft paintings on the walls of California galleries. Unfortunately, few of these innovative paintings migrated east into the New York gallery system.

Instead, it was a young man from Kansas who appropriated for his own use everything that had happened in soft painting, while sidestepping the materiality of a Viner or a Hesse. Alan Shields chose from the beginning to work in cloth. Actually, he

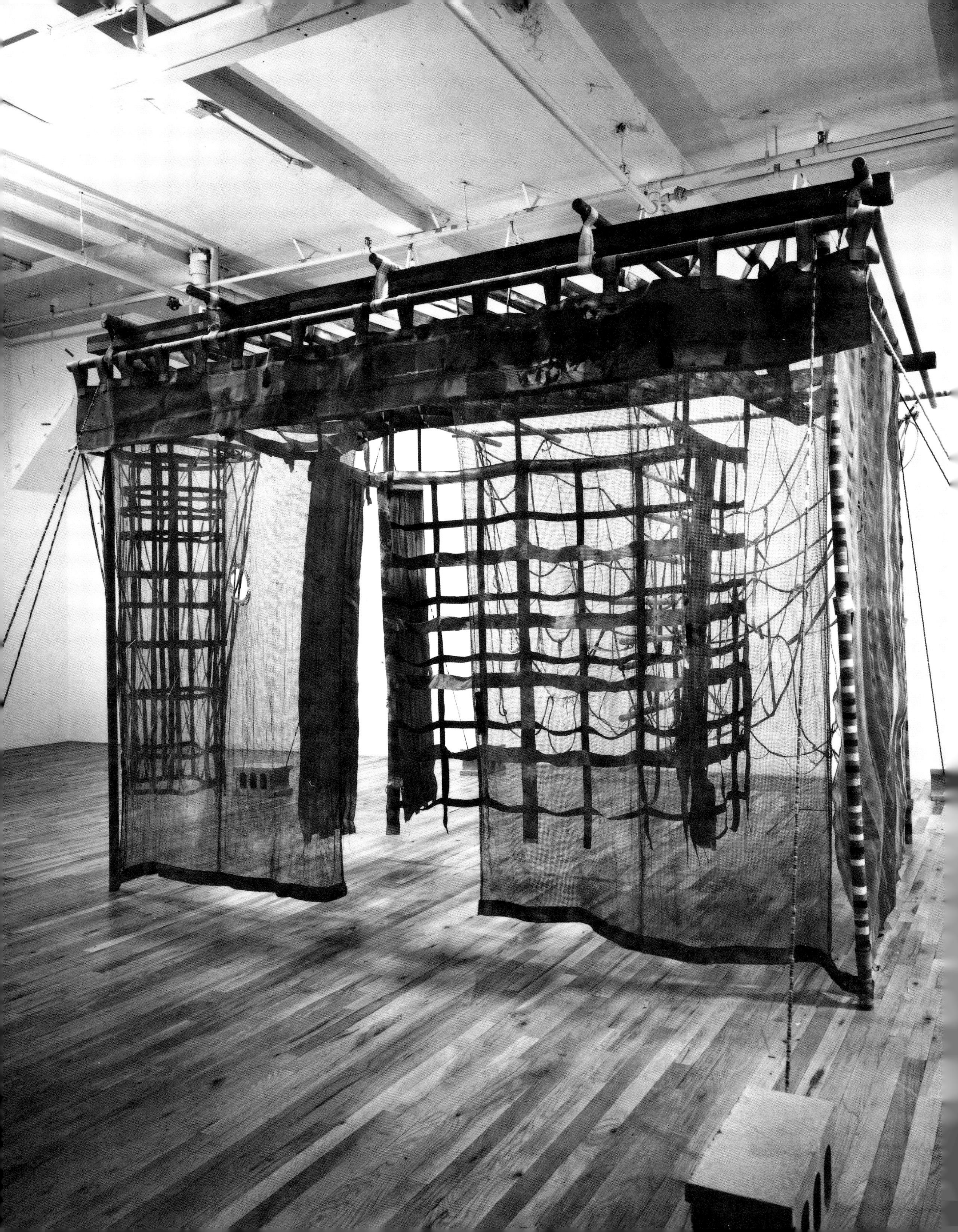

60 *(opposite)*. Alan Shields, *Ohio Blue Tip*, 1972–74.
Wood, canvas, rope, beads, concrete, and acrylic,
101 x 234 x 196″. Courtesy Paula Cooper Gallery, New York.

had begun as a child, when his mother taught him and his two sisters to sew. Shields went to Kansas State University to study civil engineering—a logical choice for a farm kid who did not want to become a farmer. Engineering, architecture, and art were in the same building, and it was not long before engineering succumbed to art. There were not many actual paintings in the life of a rural Kansas youngster; but there were some. In magazines he found Helen Frankenthaler, Larry Rivers, and Robert Rauschenberg. And even more importantly, he stumbled upon the 1956 Mark Rothko painting *Yellow Band* in the Sheldon Memorial Art Gallery in Lincoln, Nebraska. He was smitten.

In 1968 the twenty-four-year-old Shields moved to New York to see all of this new art for himself. He took with him a body of stitched canvases from his student days and images in his mind of artists using color and raw canvas to capture light. Before the year was out he had formed a professional alliance with the dealer Paula Cooper that has lasted into the present time.

Shields is an artist who found his own medium at the very beginning. He would paint, but not traditionally. He would sew in order to hold the parts together; but the sewn line would serve as his drawn line. He would paint loosely, abstractly, and sensuously as an antidote to spare Minimalism; he would dye cloth for the same reason. He would construct his works, building them with the grace and precision of the finest of engineers. Although he would take the formal grid from the Minimalists as his underlying structure, he would create works that were warm and passionate, relying upon his glowing palette to provide tension (fig. 60).

Although Shields was influenced by Pollock, through the work of Helen Frankenthaler, there was another influence that cannot be ignored. As a young student in Kansas he was particularly affected by Robert Rauschenberg. In fact, he credits Rauschenberg with being the greatest influence on most young student artists in the 1960s. There is almost no chapter in this book that could not include Rauschenberg, just as there seem to be few books on contemporary art that do not reproduce Rauschenberg's *Bed*, a seminal work of this century (see fig. 26).

From the beginning Rauschenberg's use of heterogeneous materials included cloth as a principle. He paralleled Pollock in that both introduced to painting revolutionary attitudes about cloth. But Pollock's usage grew out of traditional painting; Rauschenberg's came from collage. His early combines of 1953–55 sported the fabrics of rural America, those familiar to a young man from Galveston, Texas. In 1955 Rauschenberg made his strong and scruffy *Bed;* the art world was astonished by this combine about cloth. Only later would the artist turn to silks and fine gauzes, not because they were luxurious and he more worldly, but because he found that only natural fabrics, as opposed to cheaper synthetics, would take printer's ink—and Rauschenberg was always a printmaker. He also moved toward delicate fabrics as he became more interested in the phenomenon of light. He would deal in the transparency of light while layering his complex ideas. Through this layering of fluid material he gave coherence to what seemed like a hodgepodge of ideas and media. This early daring, this ability to create the poetic out of the mundane, which in the beginning was shocking, was his antidote to a tightly constructed art world. It was also the influence absorbed by artists in Europe and all over the United States, Alan Shields being only one.

As suggested above, Shields and Gilliam arrived at very personal art forms based upon their use of cloth. Although neither of them were to be closely associated with the Pattern and Decoration movement of the late 1970s, their use of cloth freed the canvas from its rectangular stretcher—an idea essential to the artists who followed. Shields and Gilliam also brought an exuberance to cloth that was rare in the art world of 1970.

Still, it was an art historian, Amy Goldin, who was the true catalyst for the Pattern and Decoration artist. As visiting professor at the University of California, San Diego, during the late 1960s and 1970s, she numbered among her students Robert Kushner and Kim MacConnel. Using Islamic art as a base, she taught them to question the role of decorative elements in traditional art forms, challenging her students to consider whether the decorative might also be valid in contemporary works of art. Together they formulated "criteria for judging the inherent decorativeness of works of art in all media." Briefly summarized, these included: "pattern must be the predominant sensation of the work as a whole; subject matter cannot be too forceful, i.e. meaning and/or content

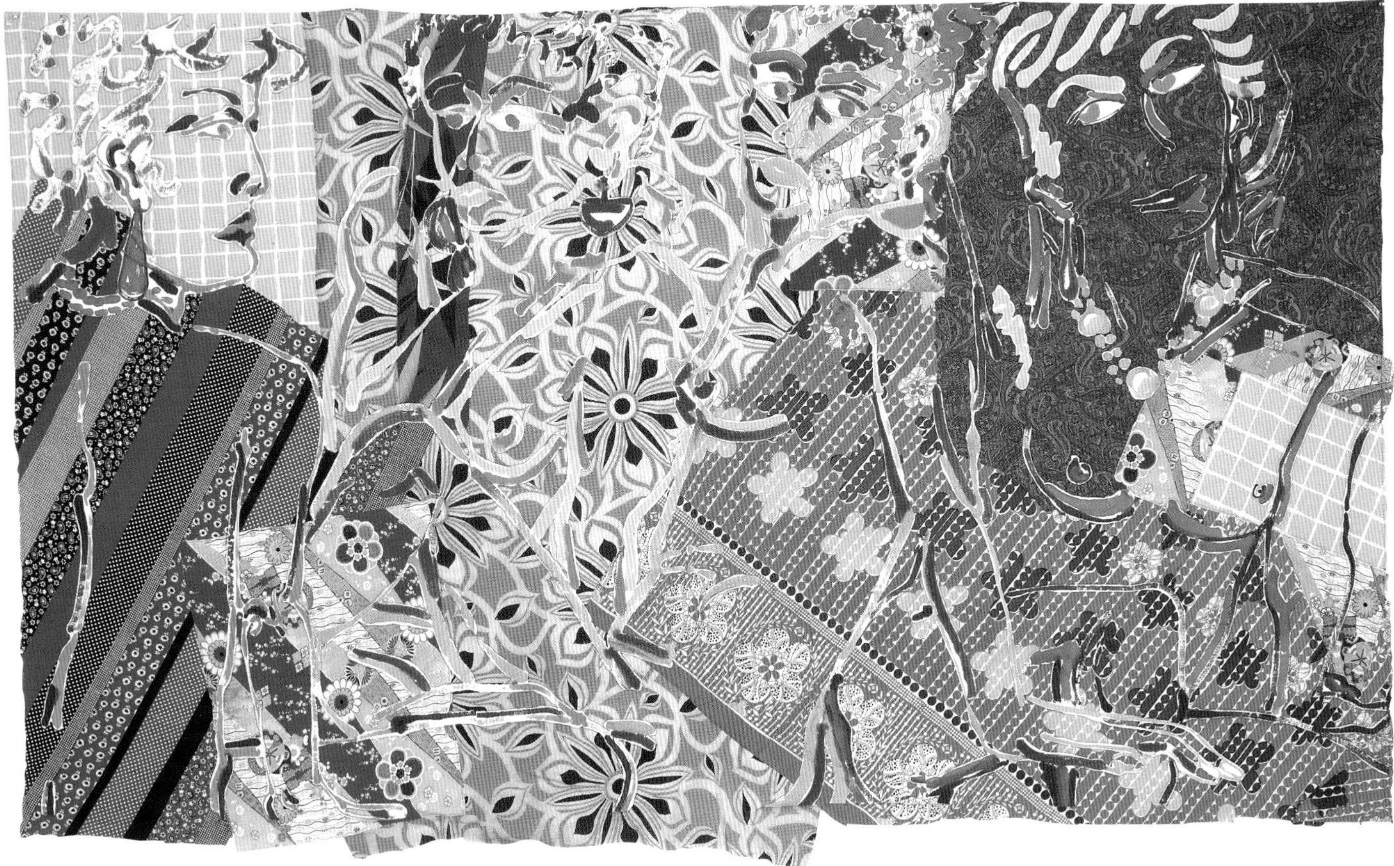

61. Robert Kushner, *Four Women,* 1983. Acrylic and various fabrics, 73 x 124¼″. Courtesy Holly Solomon Gallery, New York.

must be submerged; decorative forms will resist the incorporation of illusions of deep space; and in decorative art there must be the feeling of infinite sensory extensions beyond the object into the environment it commands."[5]

Cloth has always been the object of decoration. Hence it was not surprising that these artists, intent upon forging a new decorative art form, almost automatically reached for cloth. The work of MacConnel, Kushner, Lucas Samaras, and Miriam Schapiro all became identified with cloth. Of these, only Schapiro, who makes fabric collages (see fig. 93), chooses cloth for its sociological content. She entered the decorative movement not from the art historical perspective of the other male artists, but as a feminist incorporating the fabrics from women's lives into her work. Thus she added a rich dimension to the movement and she forced the art world at large to consider the inherent content of cloth within everyday life.

Robert Kushner's use of cloth has continued into the 1990s, both in costumes for performance and in mural-sized paintings. An early work such as *Four Women* is exuberant, noisy, and raw, reinforcing his intent to make anti-art or non-art. In reality, he has simply assisted in the twentieth-century drive to expand what is considered art (fig. 61).

# Europeans: Non-Mainstream Attitudes

The story of the development of the unframed, unstretched, and unbound painting, as told above, is an American story. This is not surprising, for following World War II, the Abstract Expressionists succeeded in shifting the center of the art world from Paris to New York. However, there were European artists making singularly significant works during these years that enriched the dialogue about the nature of the unstretched painting.

Almost universally, the Americans discussed in this chapter were moving toward light, toward airiness, toward an unfettered, flowing cloth. In Europe the opposite was true. Artists such as Antoni Tàpies, Lucio Fontana, and Alberto Burri were making art that was weighty, monumental, and somber. Whereas the Americans sought the qualities of watercolor in their paintings on cloth, the Europeans were involved with sculpture. It was as though the wars of the twentieth century, fought on their own ground, had clothed their spirits in heavier material.

Both Fontana, an Argentine who spent most of his life in Italy, and Tàpies, a Spaniard, arrived at their unconventional use of cloth because it illustrated their theories of art. Fontana wished to "destroy the conventional with its own weapons." So upon making a painting he would proceed to destroy it, to slash it, to puncture it, or to build up a thick impasto wound upon its surface. Even in reproduction, a work such as *Obietto Spaziale Attese* reveals the sculptural potential of painting. Fontana was fifty years old before he turned from sculpture to painting. That he should envision the traditional cloth canvas as a three-dimensional material is in keeping with his history (fig. 62).

Like Fontana, Tàpies was interested in the cloth itself. In 1952 he made a carefully considered, solitary resolution to associate himself with matter, with the very nature of material things, in order to penetrate their meaning and their fundamental significance.[6] He was interested in the sensual experience of art. He sought to provoke human, gut responses to sand, ashes, dust, paint, or cloth—all of which he built into his art. By provoking such a response, he hoped to gain some knowledge of the structure of reality.

More than all the other Europeans, Sigmar Polke sought in ordinary cloth another layer of meaning for his paintings. Polke simply removed the canvas and replaced it with trashy material. By 1967 he had completed *Lilac Form*, painted on cheaply printed fabric covered with sappy lilac flowers. "Although not the first time Polke utilized preprinted fabric as a ground for his paintings, it is perhaps the beginning of his use of such a backdrop to suggest the partly hallucinatory quality of what is painted on it . . . Polke discovered a way to depict several layers of consciousness at the same time by means of superimposing one or more figural motifs over a ground of printed fabric."[7]

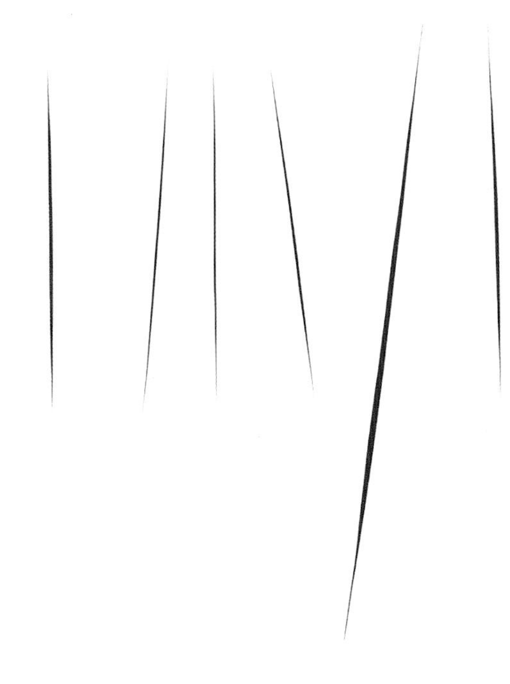

62. Lucio Fontana, *Obietto Spaziale Attese,* 1961. White cement on canvas with six slashes, 31 x 25″. Courtesy Pat Hearn Gallery, New York.

Polke found that he could paint hallucinatory experiences against a background of banality by choosing the most banal cloth for the background. Born in 1941 in what was to become East Germany, he managed to escape into West Germany by subway at the age of twelve. In 1982 he embarked upon a series of paintings that grappled with the reality of the Nazi concentration camp. The first of these, *Camp,* is painted on an ordinary purple bedspread fabric. Its color suggests dusk. Painted on its surface is a receding tunnel of wire fence over which are mounted the hated streetlights that turned all nights into day. The loosely splattered paint is echoed formally by the holes the artist has burned into the fabric. The cheesy fabric reinforces the banality of camp life, and of its oppressors, while the painting on the surface drips with fear.

Polke is a painter's painter, one who astonishes and influences other artists. His use of cloth, while only one of his many technical conventions, may be among the most powerful and influential in the post–World War II art world.

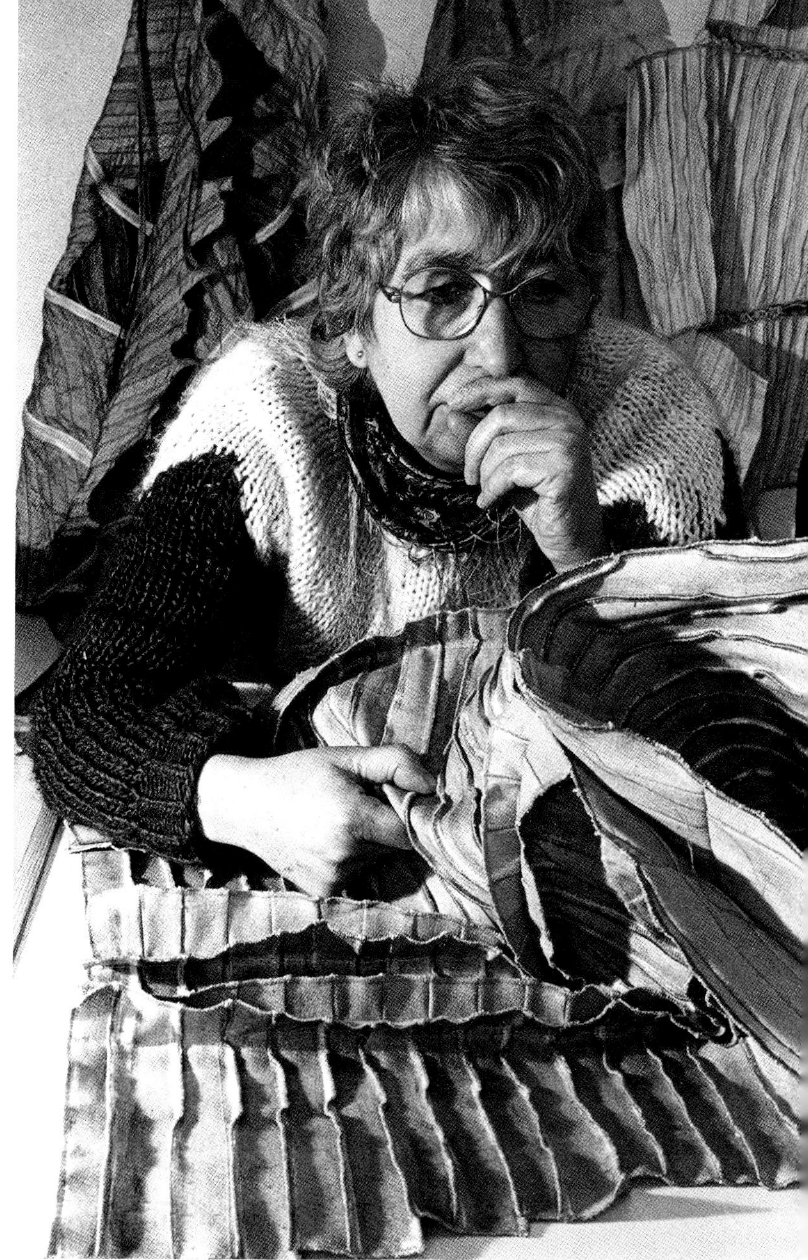

63. Mary Ball in her studio.

# The Impact of Traditional Needle Arts

To embroider is to decorate. To smock is to shape fabric to the body in a graceful, flexible fashion; to fold and tuck is to accomplish the same with less labor. To dye is to embellish and enrich cloth, to make it more beautiful. Confined to the realm of decorative arts by the Western world, these women's crafts have seldom crossed the invisible barrier into the fine arts. The notable exception is the eleventh-century Bayeux Tapestry—not a tapestry at all but an embroidery worked in worsted thread on linen (see page 21). Thought to be commissioned by the half-brother of the English king, William the Conqueror, it records the historical events of the Battle of Hastings.

The English have always valued the needle arts more than their neighbors (as have the Chinese halfway around the world). Like their gardens, English needle arts stem from a national, grass-roots passion that has developed into sophisticated art forms. In 1851 the English established the Victoria and Albert Museum in London, the first decorative arts museum in the world. Immediately important exhibitions of embroidery were mounted. In 1872 they founded the Royal School of Needlework, also in London, and again the first in the world. Here, women students were taught to approach their handiwork as an art form. A great renaissance in the needle arts followed, fired by William Morris and the Arts and Crafts movement. Crewelwork in particular flourished.

Then during the 1930s and 1940s manufactured goods invaded the home and English women set their needlework aside. It was not until the 1960s that they would pick it up again, inspired by the momentum of the Art Fabric movement, the escalating prestige of the Biennale International de la Tapisserie in Lausanne, Switzerland (Lausanne Biennale), and the international women's movement, which insisted upon a reassessment of traditional women's arts. New kinds of needleworkers were born of this new age. Educated in both the needle arts and the fine arts, they began to create a new hybrid art form from the two. In 1982 the National Museum of Modern Art in Kyoto mounted an important exhibition, "British Needlework," which identified the roots of the movement as peculiarly British. One hundred historical pieces of traditional embroideries, needle lace, beadwork, quilts, and smocks were included, selected as background for the new art. The work of twenty-four contemporary artists, two of whom were men, were showcased in the exhibition. These artists were deeply involved in visual issues. Mary Ball's abstract cloths, used to construct her walls, and Eng Tow's tucked marvels were among them (Tow, from Singapore, was included because she studied in England).

Ball and Tow, along with their counterparts throughout the West, were accepted as fine artists rather than handicraft makers because unframed, unstretched, and unbound works on cloth had become acceptable as art. Also, Minimalism had schooled the contemporary eye to appreciate the grid and to value the most subtle shifts of surface, color, or form—characteristics of much textile art (fig. 63).

Therefore, Eng Tow's 1978 *Chameleon*, the embodiment of subtlety and restraint, becomes a garden of delight if the viewer has come to value nuance (that is, the different graduations through which a color passes from its lightest to its darkest shade). Following the natural grid of the material, Tow tucks her fabric into a cloth relief. *Chameleon* is given more definite form by the application of satin stitches on the edges of the tucks. Tow often introduces color by spray-dyeing, printing, hand-printing, or embroidery. Her wall-hung works are large, filling the viewer's visual field. As the viewer moves from one side to the other in front of a work, the color field shifts. The light changes. The tucked material appears to harbor swells of moving light, waves of changing color brought to life by the movements of the viewer. As one stands to the right of the piece the cool colors dominate. Gradually, as one moves to the left, the complementary warm colors come into view. Like a wonderful and private garden, the work of art shifts with the light of day, revealing itself gradually to the participating viewer (figs. 65, 66).

Emilia Bohdziewicz of Poland won the Grand Prix at the 1987 International Textile Competition in Kyoto with a work called *256 Possible Combinations of the Sign Containing Eight Elements*. Working on white canvas, she made thousands of perfectly executed black lines with her sewing machine. The huge work (nearly twelve square feet) is a wonder of obsessive-compulsive sewing. Her art is cool and stunning as a visual statement; it is mind-boggling as an embroidery. Its minimalist statement is arrived at by the most "maximal" of techniques. The minimalist aesthetic in the hands of artists such as Bohdziewicz and Tow continues the idea of the grid, which is at the core of all textile construction. For that reason it remains alive within the cloth vocabulary long after the Minimalist movement in painting and sculpture has become a historical event (fig. 64).

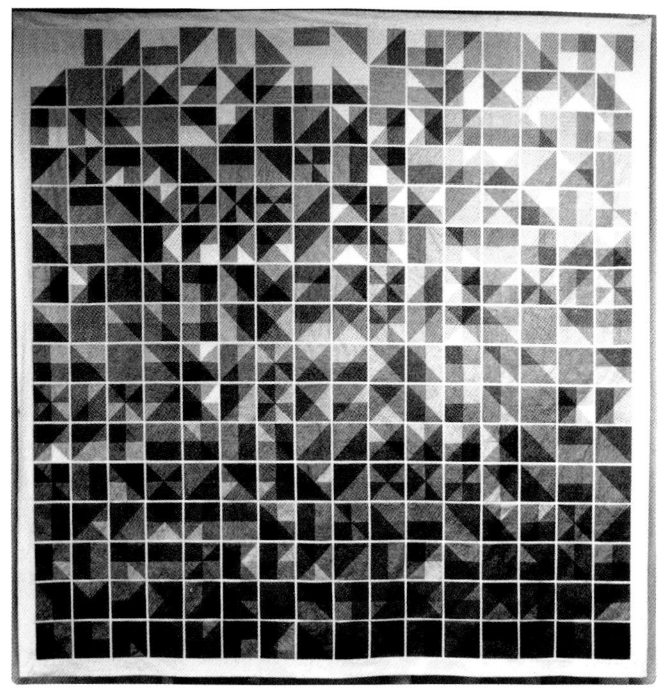

64. Emilia Bohdziewicz, *256 Possible Combinations of the Sign Containing Eight Elements*, 1987. White canvas, black thread, machine embroidery, 139⅝ x 139⅝″. Courtesy International Textile Fair 1987, Kyoto, Japan.

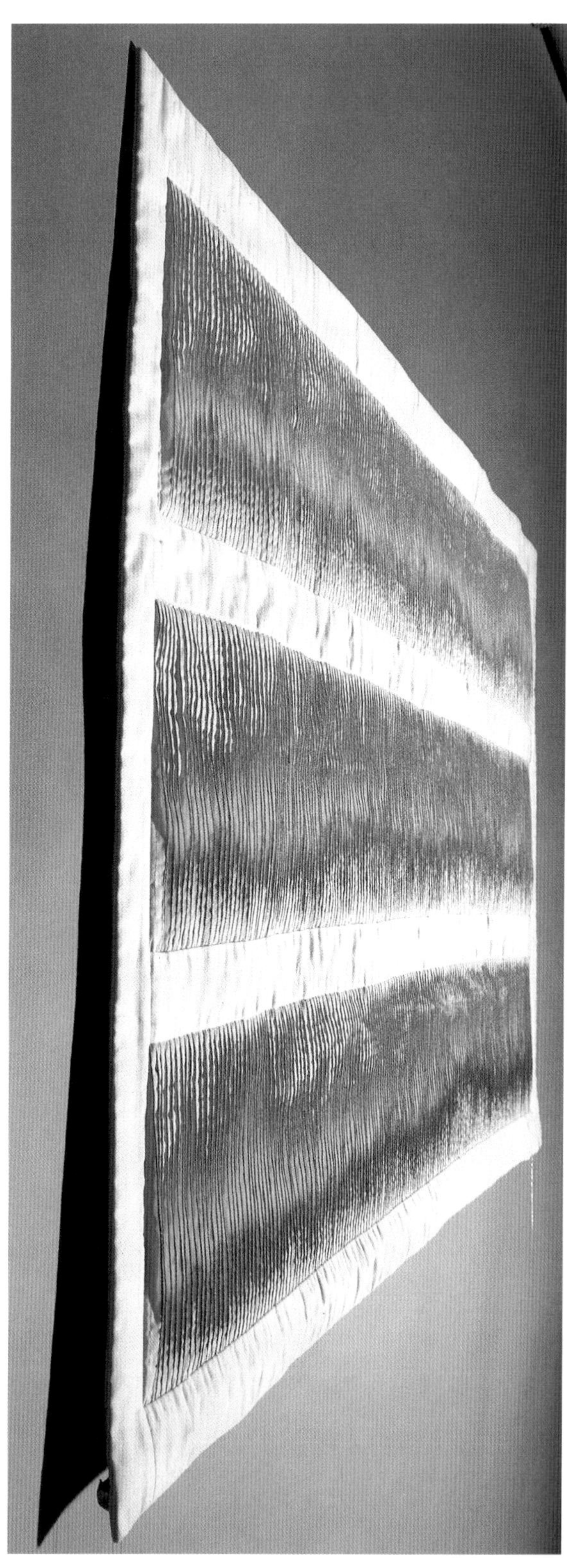

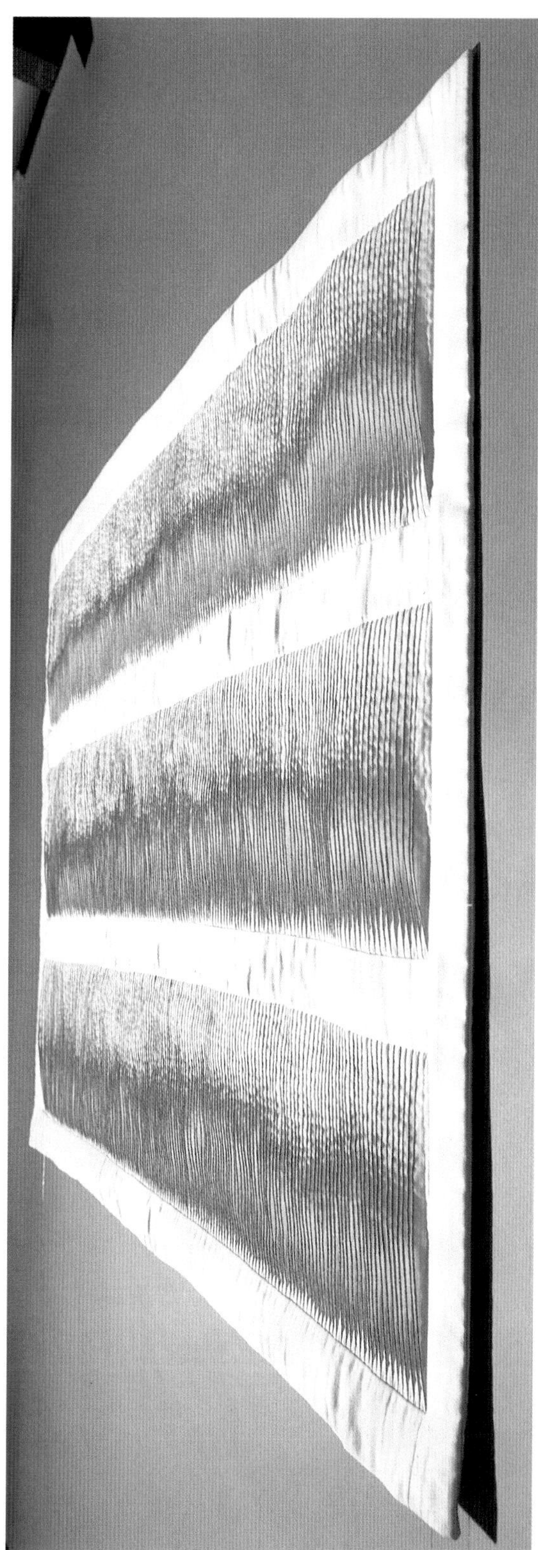

65, 66. Eng Tow, *Chameleon* (right and left views), 1978.
Cotton and cotton mixture, 75 x 40″. Permanent Art Collection,
Crown Wall Coverings, United Kingdom.

Kiki Smith learned to embroider as a child. It was one way her parents kept her entertained for hours on end as she hung out in her father Tony Smith's studio. As a mature artist she makes cast-bronze sculpture on a grand scale and prints that challenge the best technicians in the Western world. She also tie-dyes and embroiders. Woman's work is just as vital a means of expression as traditional men's work to this remarkable artist. In the mid-1980s she trained as an emergency medical technician and subsequently decided to study the human body from the inside out. She began a visual dissection of each bodily system through her art. In 1987 she embroidered nine biological systems onto oversize muslin sheets, which she named *Nervous Giant.* In 1991 she exhibited the embroideries at the Museum of Modern Art in New York. These gigantic figures on cloth, created through the most "ladylike" of techniques, embroidery, were without question the most important fiber works shown in New York that year. Smith redefined how the twentieth-century art world would have to view embroidery on cloth (fig. 67).

The contemporary art world is bursting with additional uses for cloth and fresh ways of employing traditional needlework techniques. For example, Colette, an American artist, stiffens satin and pushes it into shapes that reflect light. She confines the material within a rigid, framed space. Traditional smocking on cloth has served Francis Wilson well. His monumental Chalunga series consists of towering forms within space. Enigmatic, mysterious, neither human nor animal, the forms overpower their confinement. Smocked and painted, Wilson's cloth takes on its own life within the installation space determined by the artist. This American, a resident of Paris for twenty years, has arrived at an art form wherein the cloth and the pigment, the smocking and the painting, create the form. Abstract and vigorous, these soft, arched, three-dimensional forms are powerful as works of art. Barbara Ferguson, also American, uses traditional smocking on fabric to create a poetic cloth hanging, formal and yet surprisingly physical (figs. 68–70).

As stressed earlier, a principal impetus for drawing from traditional needlework was British (just as much historical needlework in the United States was British at some point of origin), but the practitioners came from all parts of the contemporary art world. Like cloth itself, the needle arts appear everywhere, in the most surprising guises—modified, changed, and

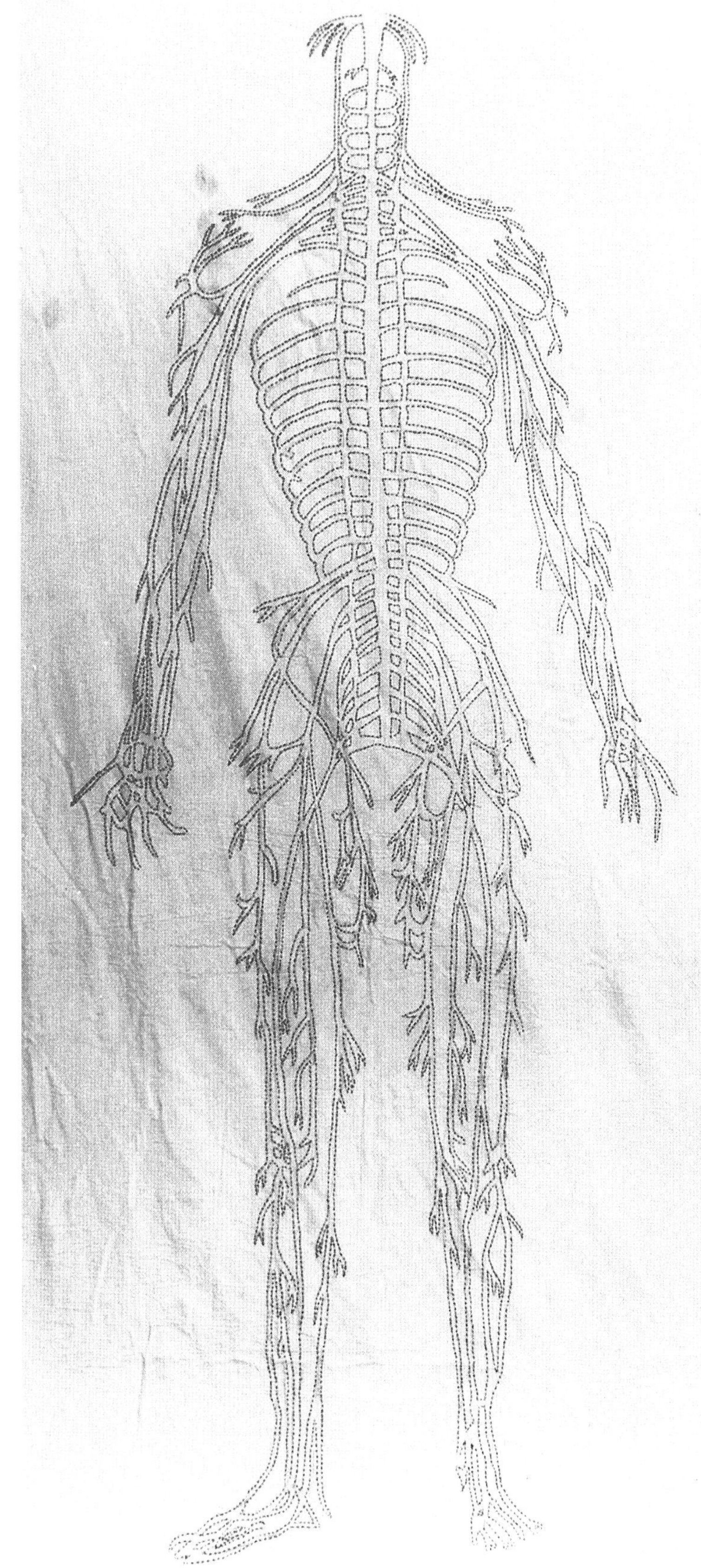

67. Kiki Smith, *Nervous Giant,* 1987. Embroidery thread on muslin, 12 x 48″.

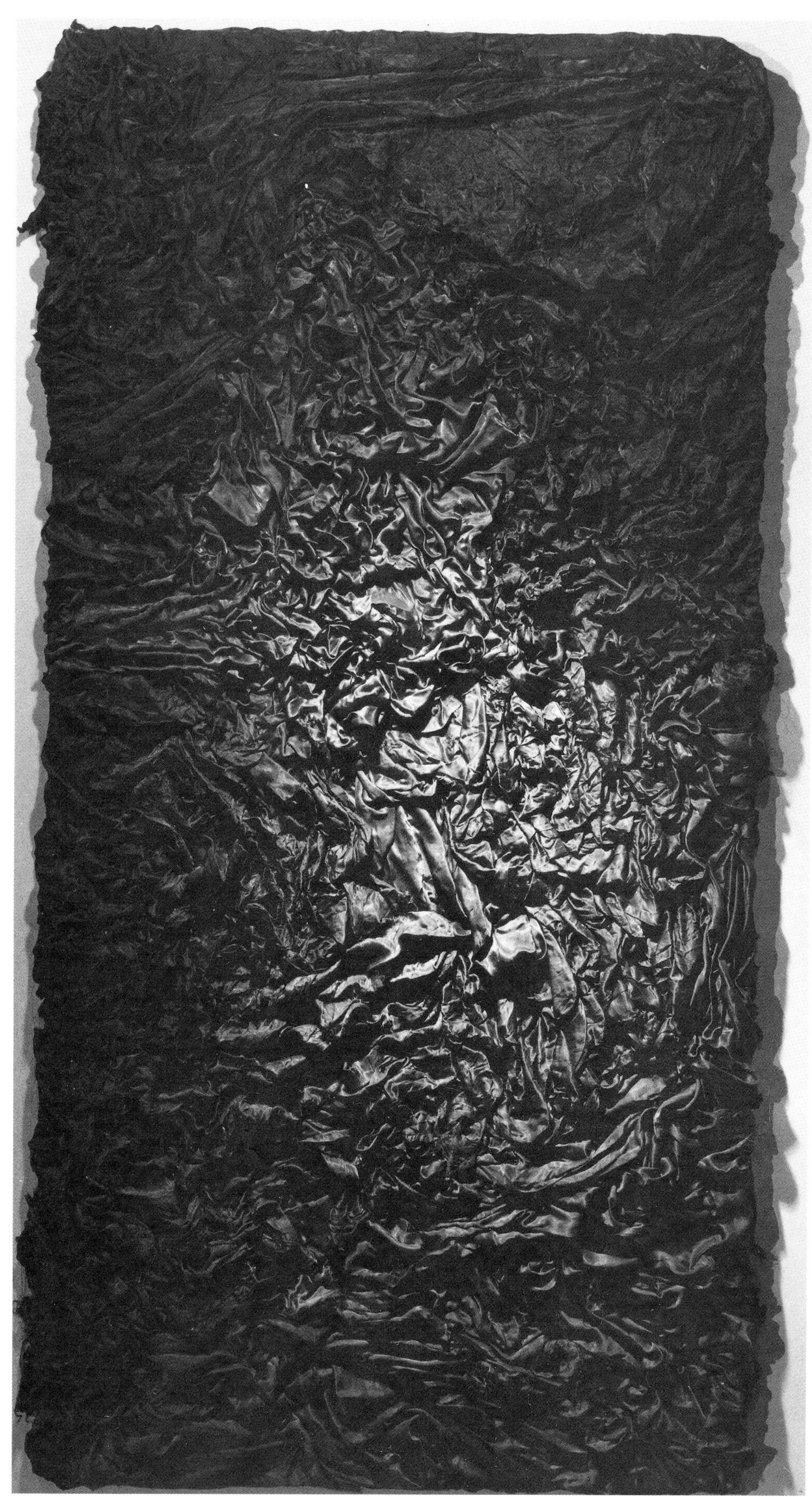

68. Colette, *Wall Panel*, 1978. Fabric painting of dyed black satin, 4 x 8′.

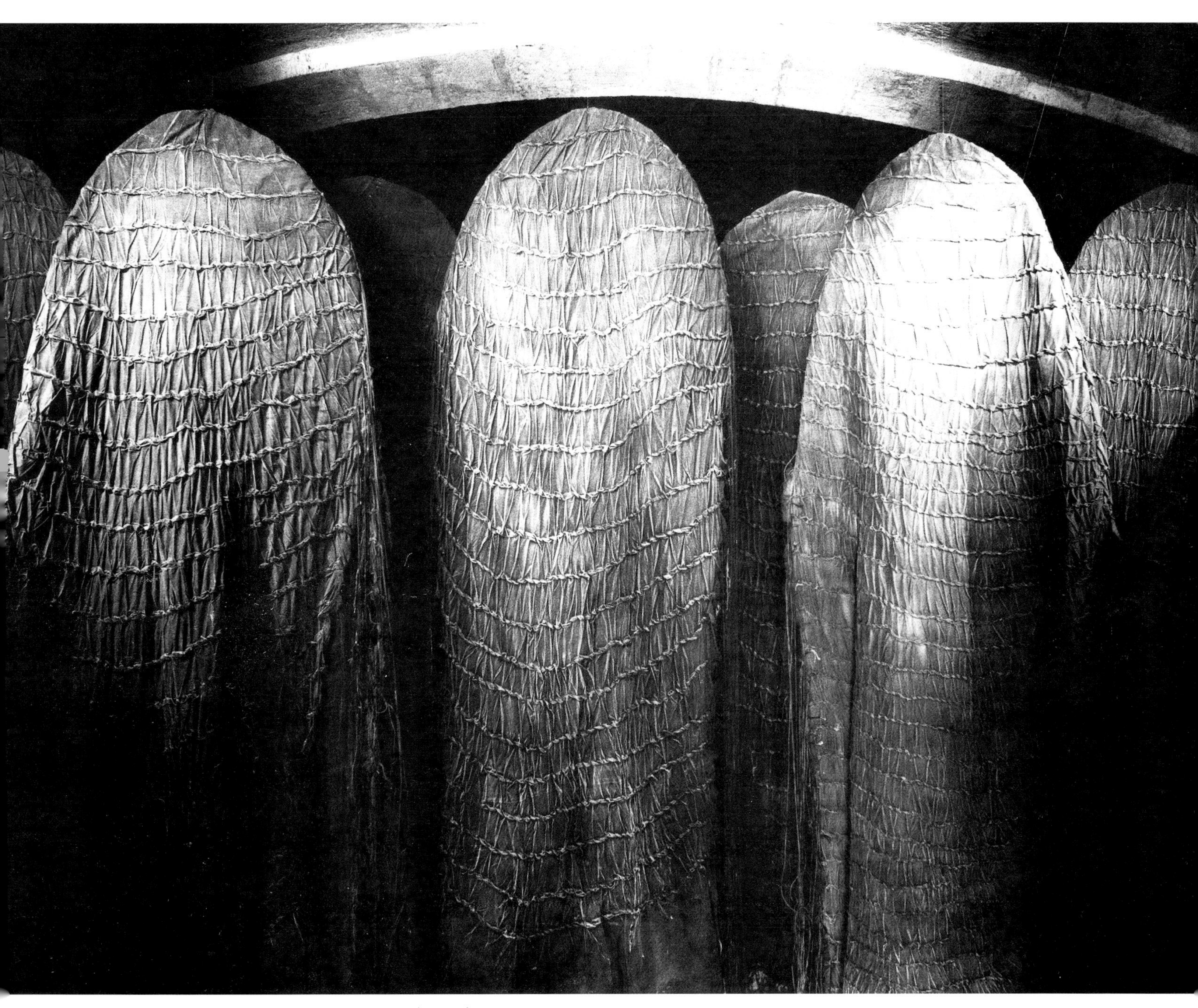

69. Francis Wilson, Chalunga series, 1982. Sewn and painted cotton canvas, stitched longotte (cotton broadcloth), twenty-one pieces, each 78¾ x 27⅝ x 1⅜″. Courtesy Mobilier National, France.

often unrecognizable until closely examined. Finally, an unstretched painting and an unstretched textile have much in common visually. They are united by certain vital ideas that surfaced in the art world in the middle decades of the twentieth century. First, no tradition of framing exists within the textile arts. It is recognized today that to frame a textile seems pretentious, an idea forced upon an art form by a commercial gallery system. (The exception is the practice of museums to frame fragile works for conservation purposes.) An unframed, unstretched, and unbound work of art is a natural form in an art world that has expanded its definitions to include ceramics and textiles as high art. Second, the Minimalist movement prepared the viewer to appreciate works of art that take their overall structure from the grid, the most basic structure of all woven textiles.

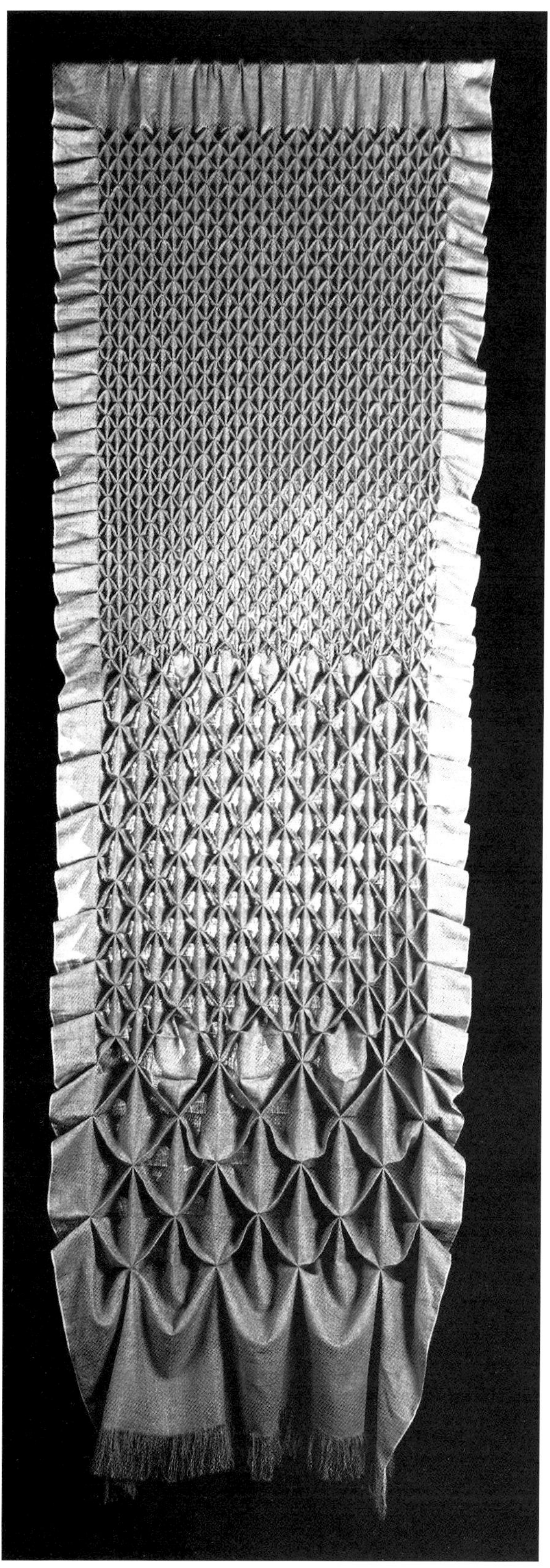

70. Barbara Ferguson, *Untitled.* Uncut linen, drawn threadwork, machine stitching, hemstitching, 9′ x 3′ x 4″. Collection Mr. and Mrs. Timothy Nissen, Basel, Switzerland.

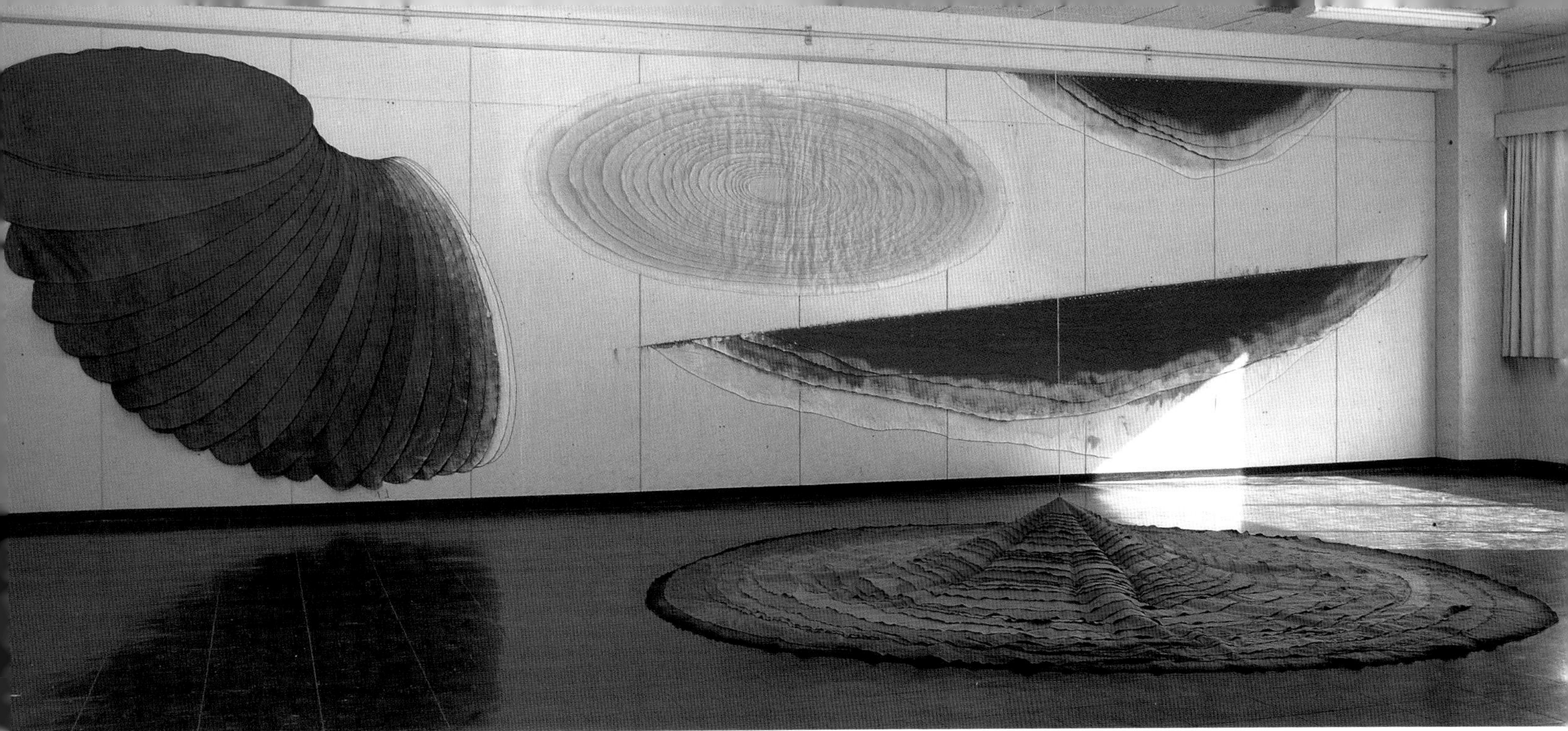

71. Hirotaka Nakagawa, *Disk Says*, 1988. Dyed, bleached, and sewn cotton, 195 x 390 x 195".

# Dyeing the Unframed, the Unstretched, and the Unbound

Jack Lenor Larsen based his book *The Dyer's Art* upon the premise that "in many cultures dyeing—especially patterned resist dyeing—is considered an art form, as weaving is elsewhere. Although Europeans have tended to focus on woven cloth, the great fabric traditions of India, Japan, Indonesia, Central Asia, and West Africa show as much—if not more—concern for resist dyeing than cloth making. In these cultures the cloth on which batik and plangi are executed, or the process that interlaces ikat yarns, is only as important as canvas is to a painter" (fig. 74).[8]

The freeing of canvas from its rigid stretcher was quickened and broadened by the influx of dyeing skills into the artist's studio. However, it could be argued that much of the first work made in Europe and the United States during the late 1960s and early 1970s, based upon the batik and tie-dye traditions of countries such as Indonesia and India, continued the tradition of the embellished surface. By and large, artists were initially drawn to intense dye colors as they learned the technical vocabulary of the dyeing process. Most often the finished work was too decorated and too precious to cross over into the world of the unstretched painting. The work was anchored in the idea of a brilliant surface; Western concerns of art seemed to play minor roles. The hand-dyed, cloth world of that era was simply awash with gaudy reds, yellows, and oranges, or mingled blues and greens, each demanding to be seen.

There are, of course, exceptions. An artist such as Daniel Graffin succeeds because he chooses to limit himself to a single dye: indigo. Consequently he forces himself to grapple with all of art's formal components—in addition to color. In *Trace Indigo No. 4* Graffin uses tritik, a Javanese technique of tie and dye. He stitches his design before putting the material into the dye vat. After dyeing, he pulls out the threads; only the traces where the needle punctured the cloth remain (fig. 73).

Once dyeing skills were widely learned, great works of art that were unframed, unstretched, and unbound, and that also were dyed, appeared in the contemporary art world. This happened most frequently in a culture that had an important dyeing tradition and an abundance of artists working with textiles: Japan. The Japanese tradition of scroll painting, rather than stretched canvas painting, only reinforced the emergence of dyeing the unstretched cloth as a functional technique for making works of art. For these artists color is specific and subservient to form, as illustrated by the installation work of Hirotaka Nakagawa that appeared in the 1989 Lausanne Biennale (fig. 71).

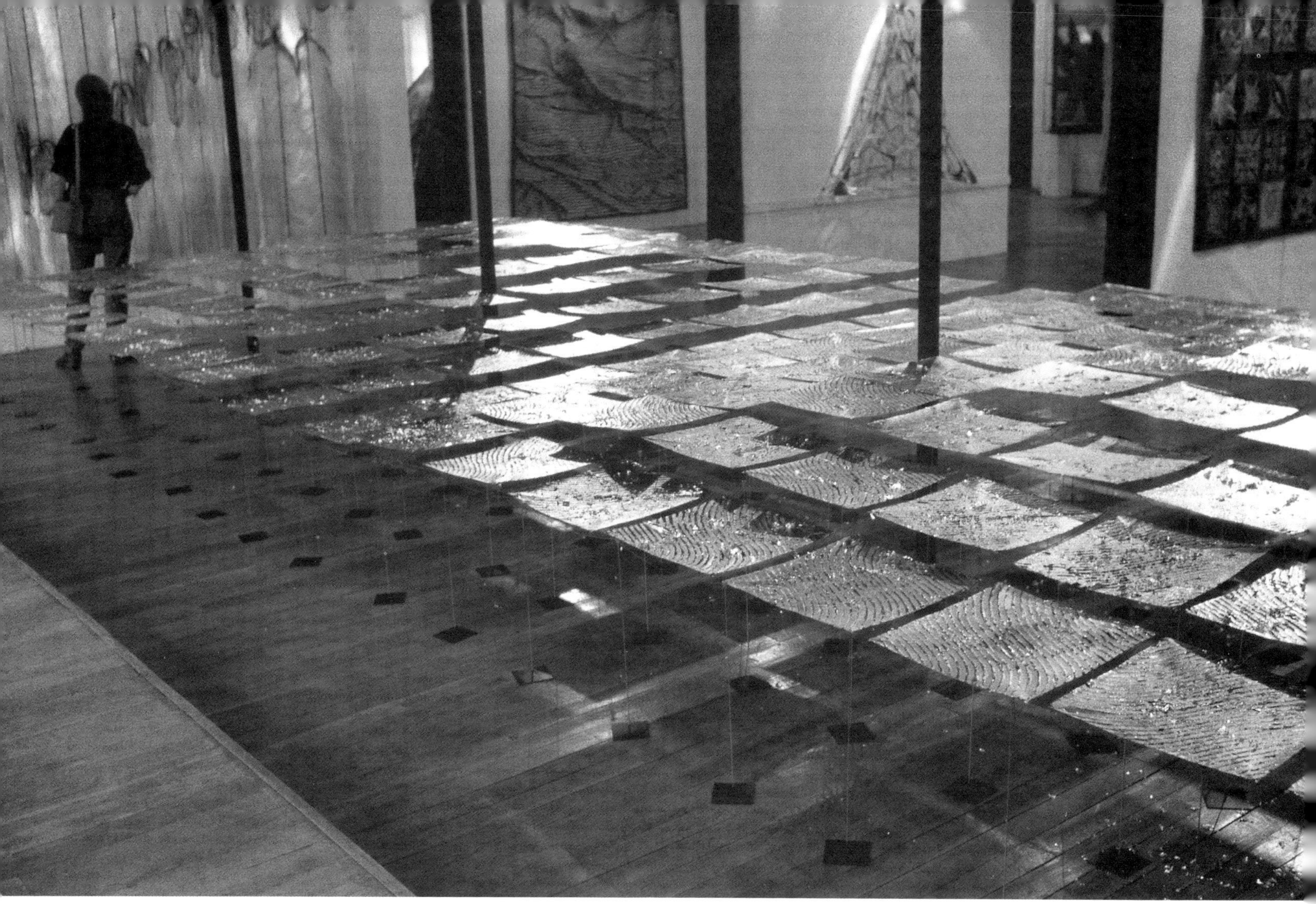

72. Teruyoshi (Tsuda) Yoshida, *Surface of the Lake,* 1985. Cotton cloth, gold leaf, iron stand, 49 x 26½ x 2´. Courtesy Central Museum of Textiles, Lodz, Poland.

*Surface of the Lake* by Teruyoshi Yoshida is dazzling gold. Yoshida limits himself to that gold, or so it seems, for his greater interest is in creating an untraditional landscape—and gold is the color of his landscape. By using the *kinsai-yuzen* technique of dyeing on cotton, which he augments with gold leaf, drawing, and screen-printing, Yoshida arrives at the luminescent surface he seeks. The viewer quickly forgets the complicated technique, so well does the artist communicate his visual goal. In the catalog for the 1987 Kyoto International Textile Competition, the work was described as follows:

> *The Surface of the Lake* speaks directly of the shimmering, light-reflective surface of a gently moving body of water at the time of the setting sun. Golden in color and intense in their reflections, the many fabric sections comprising this work appear to move independently in space, quite like the restless and random paths of movement observed in natural bodies of water. Each fabric square contains strips of intense color appearing from beneath the gold-leaf surface, contributing to the effect of undulating movement. The expansive scale of this work allows the viewer to almost float on the golden surface [fig. 72].[9]

In the fall of 1987 Hiroyuki Shindo created *Space Indigo* in a tiny gallery in Kyoto. His monumental hangings of indigo-dyed linen filled the otherwise empty room. The spiritual essence evoked by the repeated central images, by the spareness, and by the attention to light coalesced to recall similar rooms, such as John and Dominique de Menil's Chapel in Houston (1965–66) with Mark Rothko's paintings, where the missing light haunts in its absence, or Lenore Tawney's Circle in the Square series, installed in the galleries at the University of California, Fullerton, in 1975. Tawney suggests the powerful inner content of all of these works when she says of her own,

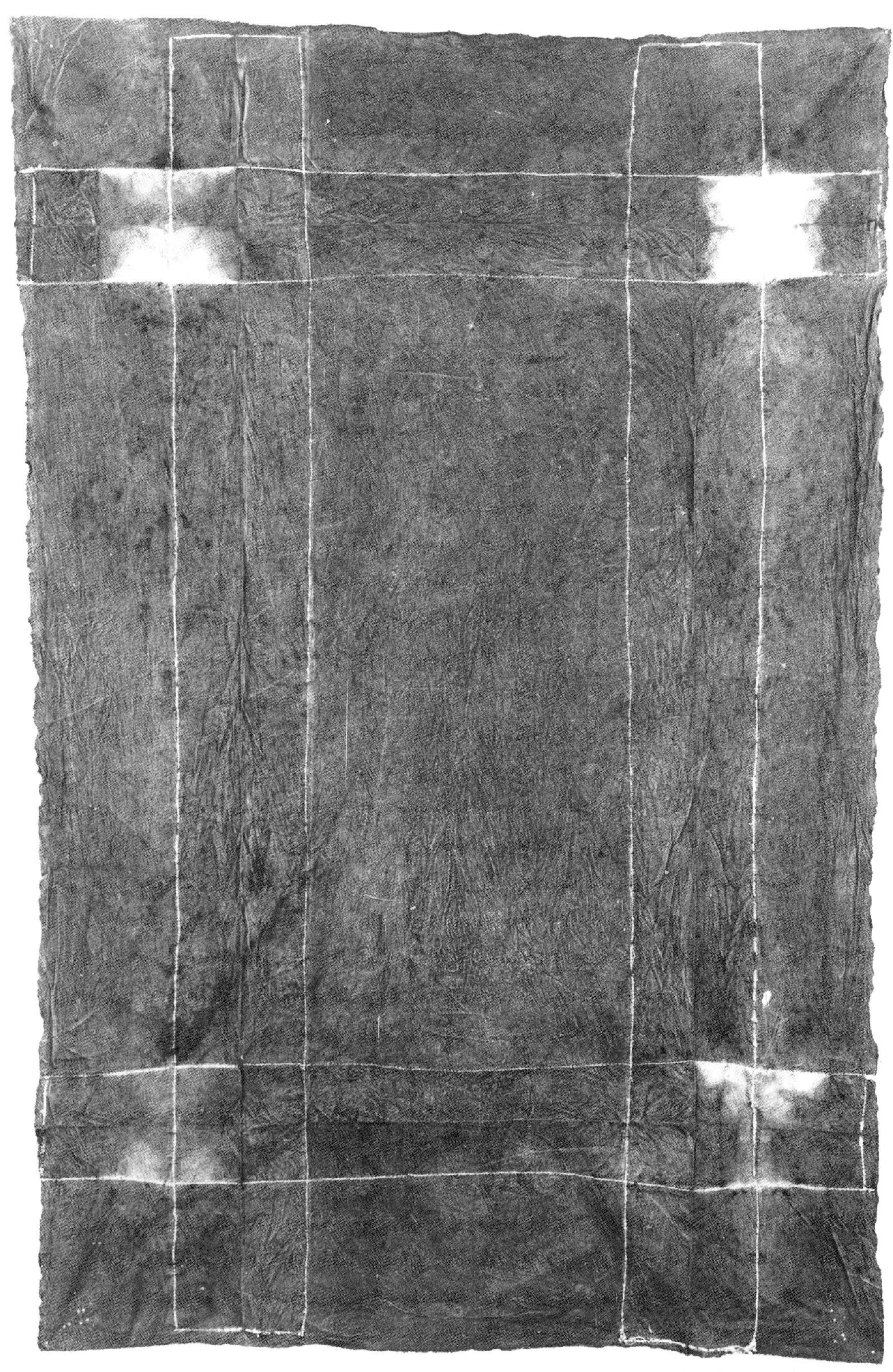

73. Daniel Graffin, *Trace Indigo No. 4,* 1978. Cotton, tie-and-dye technique (tritik), 25⅝ x 37⅜″.

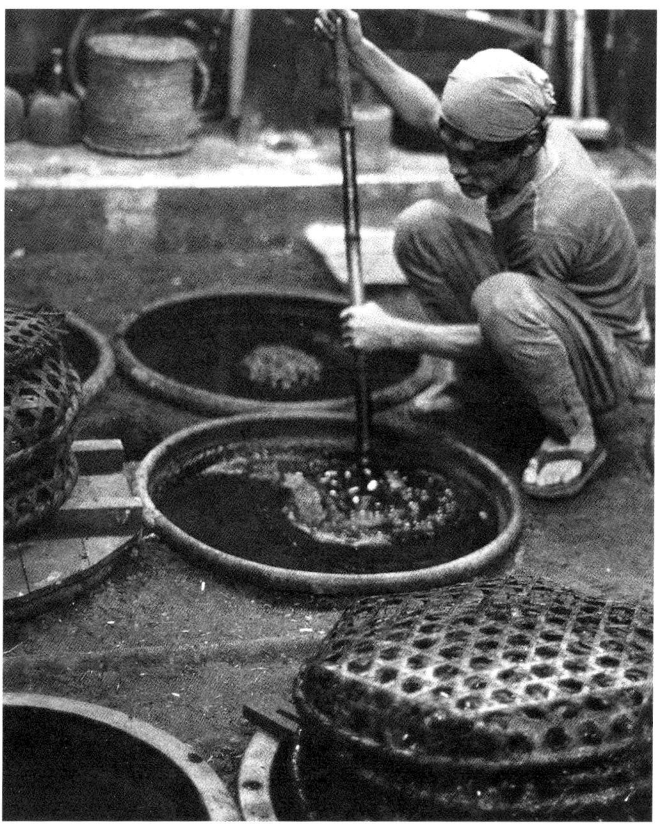

74. Hiroyuki Shindo in his studio.

"It's a circle in a square. These all have such significance in Jung for the Inner Self. The square means integration of the self—of course the circle means that too. So the circle in the square is *really* integration."[10]

Rothko painted his monolithic forms on stretched canvas; Tawney wove hers; Shindo dyes his with indigo. To walk into a room filled with Shindo's hangings is to encounter the human spirit in an abstract form. It is also to understand visually a timeless human bond with indigo—to many, the color of the human soul. Shindo uses dye to create; but in his hands the dye becomes a power unto itself (fig. 75).

In today's art world every technique from every culture is available to the contemporary artist. The resulting hybrid, often unrecognizable from its origins, is increasingly interesting. D'Arcie Beytebiere, an American from Seattle, uses a traditional Japanese dyeing process, *arashi shibori*, a form of plangi or tie-and-dye. She combines her resist-dye process with pleating as it was mastered by the Spanish designer Mariano Fortuny. The combination of pouring hot dye onto tightly wrapped pleats results in intense colors on the outer surface of the pleats and soft colors underneath. Her finished silk is a whirl of pleated fabric, which she fashions into clothing or mounts on the wall as a swirling, three-dimensional work of art (fig. 76).

Although dyes have played a major role in expanding the potential of unframed, unstretched, and unbound works of art, yet another demand must be made of conservators in the textile field. Knowledge of the preservation and conservation of textiles must be transferred to those artists just discovering the joys of "thirsty cloth." For example, the paintings of the Americans who first experimented with staining on unsized and unprimed canvas in the 1960s are conservation nightmares twenty-five years later. Those incandescent, glowing colors of the color-field paintings have quickly dimmed. Grime has accumulated on the unsized and unprimed, off-white canvas. And one cannot just send a valuable Helen Frankenthaler painting out to the dry cleaner.

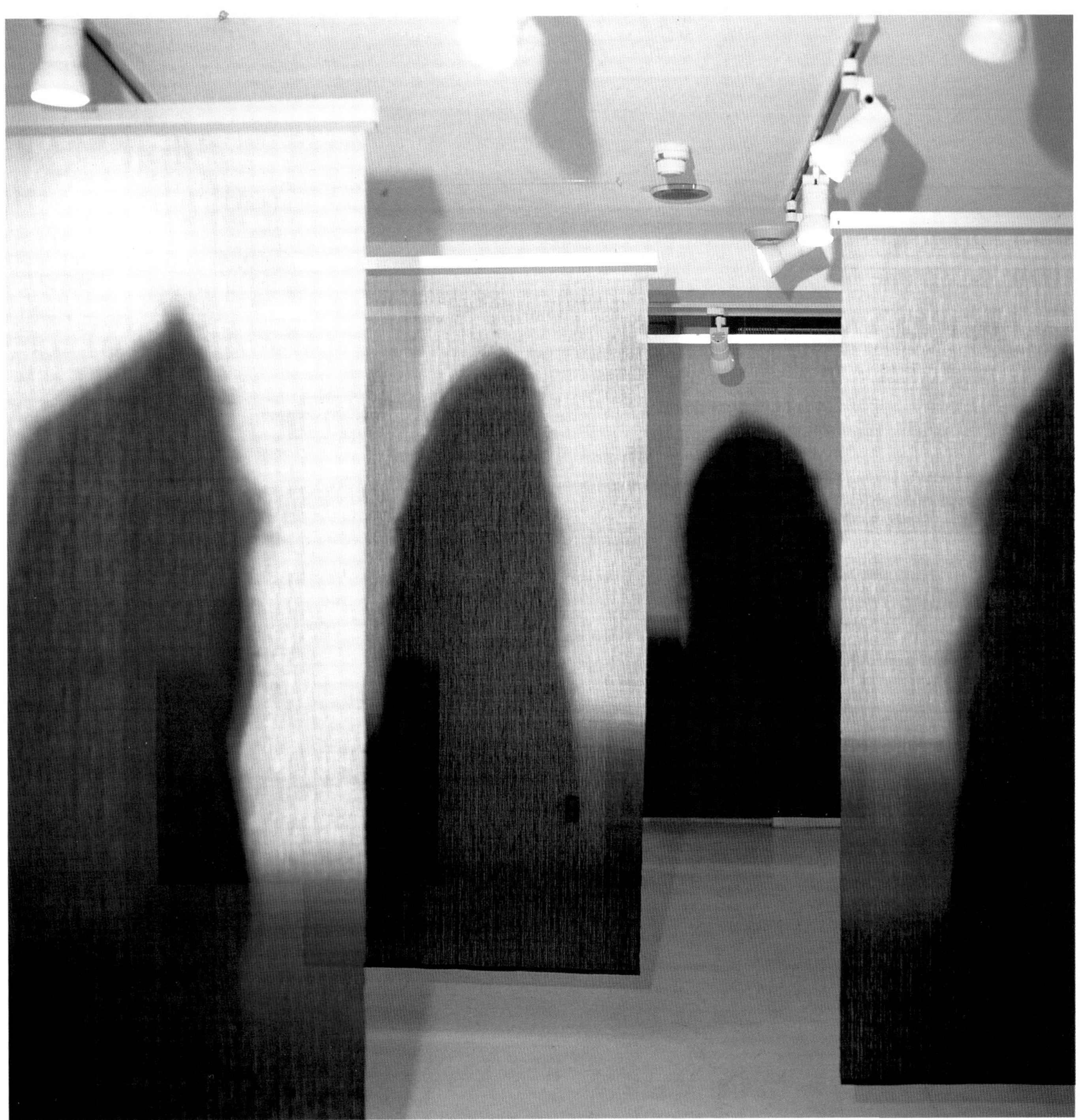

75. Hiroyuki Shindo, *Space Indigo*, 1988. Indigo on linen weave. Installation in Gallery Gallery, Kyoto, Japan, 1988.

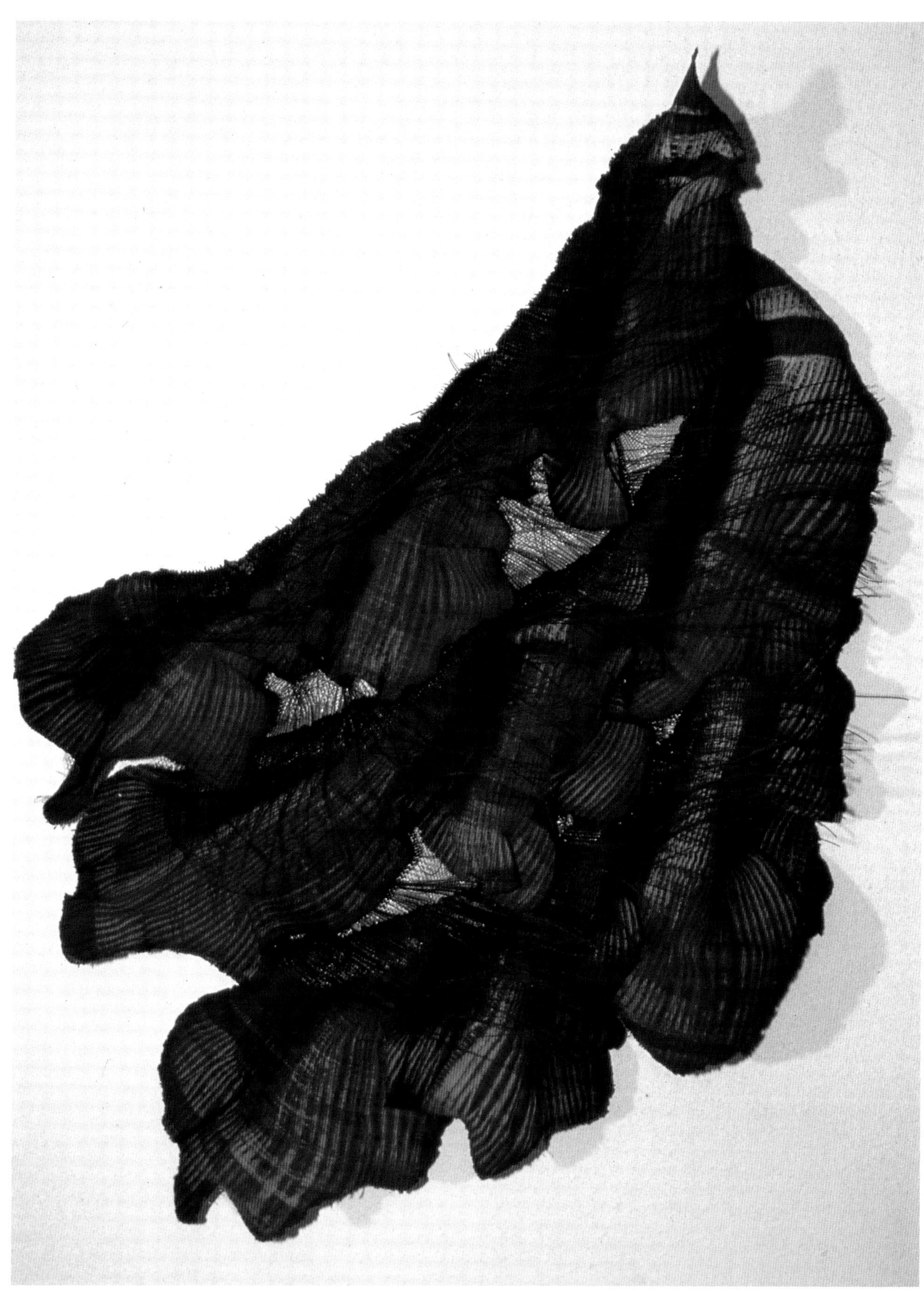

76. D'Arcie Beytebiere, *Untitled.* Pleated and dyed (*arashi shibori*) silk, 21 x 24″.

# The Legacy of Minimalism

To begin to speak of the Minimalists' legacy with a work by Robert Rauschenberg seems a travesty of language. Yet his *Franciscan II*, a restrained fabric assemblage, sets the precedent for an artistic ideal that is viable still—an ideal that is truly minimal in spirit and in vision. It is nothing more than cloth itself, with its inherent volatility of form, that holds the eye in the Rauschenberg work (fig. 77).

In *Franciscan II* Rauschenberg grapples with the fleeting nature or changeability of cloth. With weights, anchors, and tension lines, he brings mass and weight into a timeless and perfect balance. The vigor of the work comes from the realization that the dynamic cloth is only momentarily suspended. Its nature is to be endlessly flexible. It is tense against its restraints. At any moment the balance could change; the cloth could shift to a new form. That is the material nature of *Franciscan II*. Its poetic nature is far more subtle.

In naming the work, Rauschenberg alludes to an underlying religious intent. The Franciscans are a Roman Catholic order that was founded in Italy in 1209 by Saint Francis of Assisi. Its members have always devoted themselves to service: to missions, preaching, nursing, and so on. Historically they wore coarse gray or brown cloth robes, almost always cowled or hooded. Thus Rauschenberg's cloth, hung to suggest arms stretched wide, weighted with a skull-like stone, and suspended in an uneasy balance, could easily be interpreted as a twentieth-century religious work of art. The cloth in its paleness is only a ghost image of an earlier and rougher robe of service.

Masayaki Oda's equally symbolic work relies upon a similar tension between fluid cloth and its harnessing apparatus. He has actually driven rusty nails through his folded piece of cloth, thus attaching it to a rigid and anonymous surface. *Double Canvas*, like *Franciscan II*, is weighted at the center and then pulled taut by its tethers. Oda's *Double Canvas* succeeds openly as a religious work of art. This ambiguous image of a disembodied but nonetheless impaled loincloth becomes the symbol of the crucified Christ. And, like Rauschenberg, Oda has brought mass and weight into perfect balance (fig. 79).

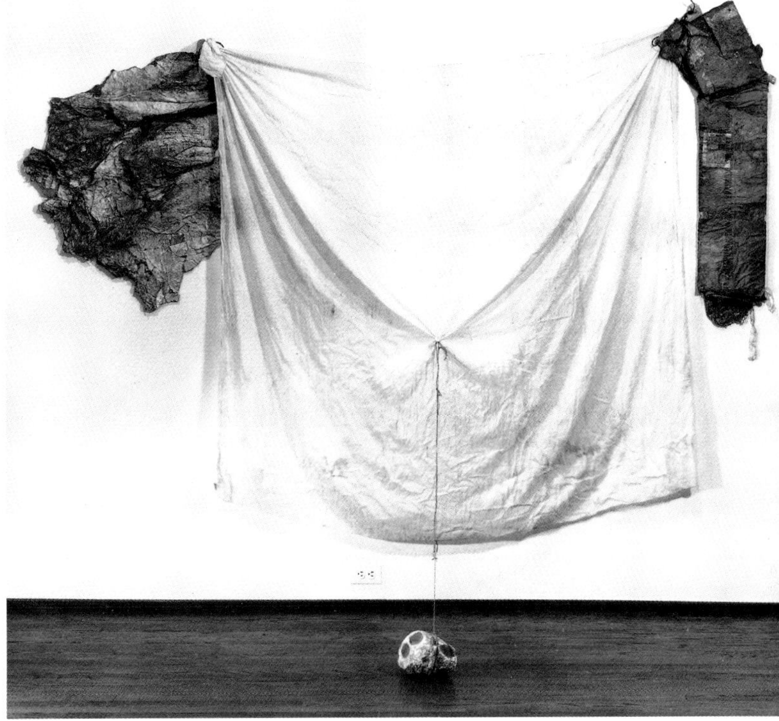

77. Robert Rauschenberg, *Franciscan II*, 1972. Cardboard, resin, cloth, string, and rock, 72 x 108 x 38″. Courtesy Museum of Modern Art, New York.

*In Utero I* by Lenore Tawney is a three-dimensional work in which the weight—this time a chair—is suspended within a womb of formless cloth. The chair, small, delicate, and covered with Persian poetry, floats weightless within a shell of transparent cloth. Poetic, mystical, it suggests an unnamed metaphor still unborn. This chair is unlike any other chair. Yet it is the cloth itself, by both withholding and disclosing, that enchants the viewer (fig. 78).

These three artists have chosen to use cloth poetically in its white and revealing state. Cloth in its dark and concealing mode is equally powerful, and equally capable of demanding center stage. Wojciech Sadley, a leading figure from the acclaimed Warsaw school of weaving, has taken a piece of dark cloth, shaped it to suggest the human torso, and gathered it together with a central knot located where one would find the pit of the stomach. The gesture is quick, the suggested figure spare, evoking a visceral response (fig. 80).

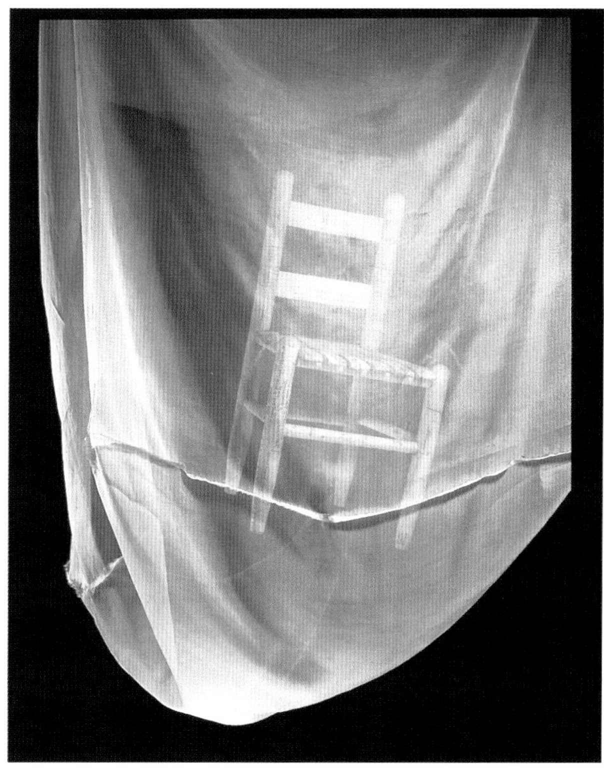

78 (see also page 8). Lenore Tawney, *In Utero I,* 1986. Cotton, chair with collage, 60 x 48 x 48″. Courtesy Mokotoff Gallery, New York.

79. Masayaki Oda, *Double Canvas,* 1983. Mixed media, 4 x 5′.

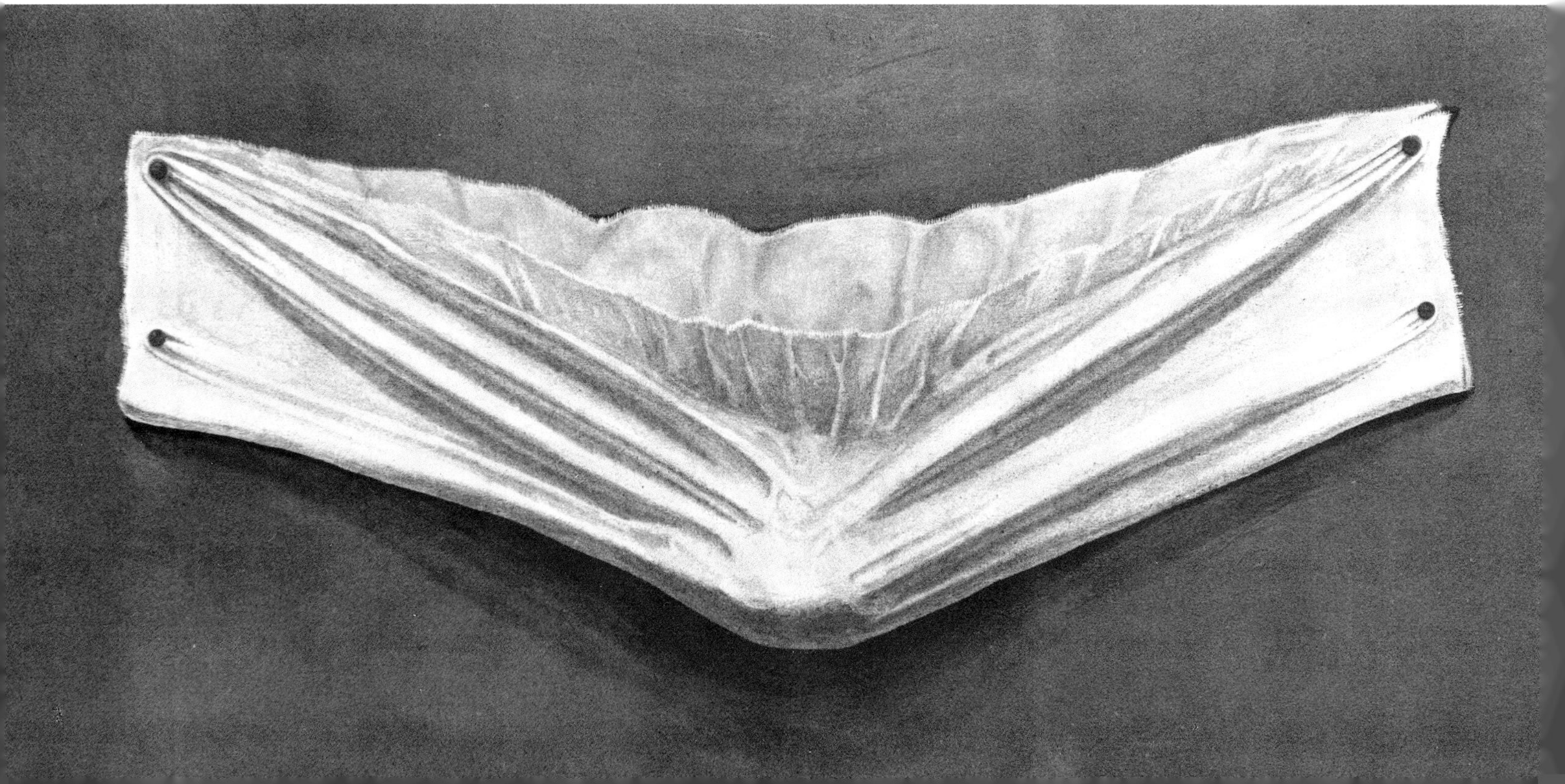

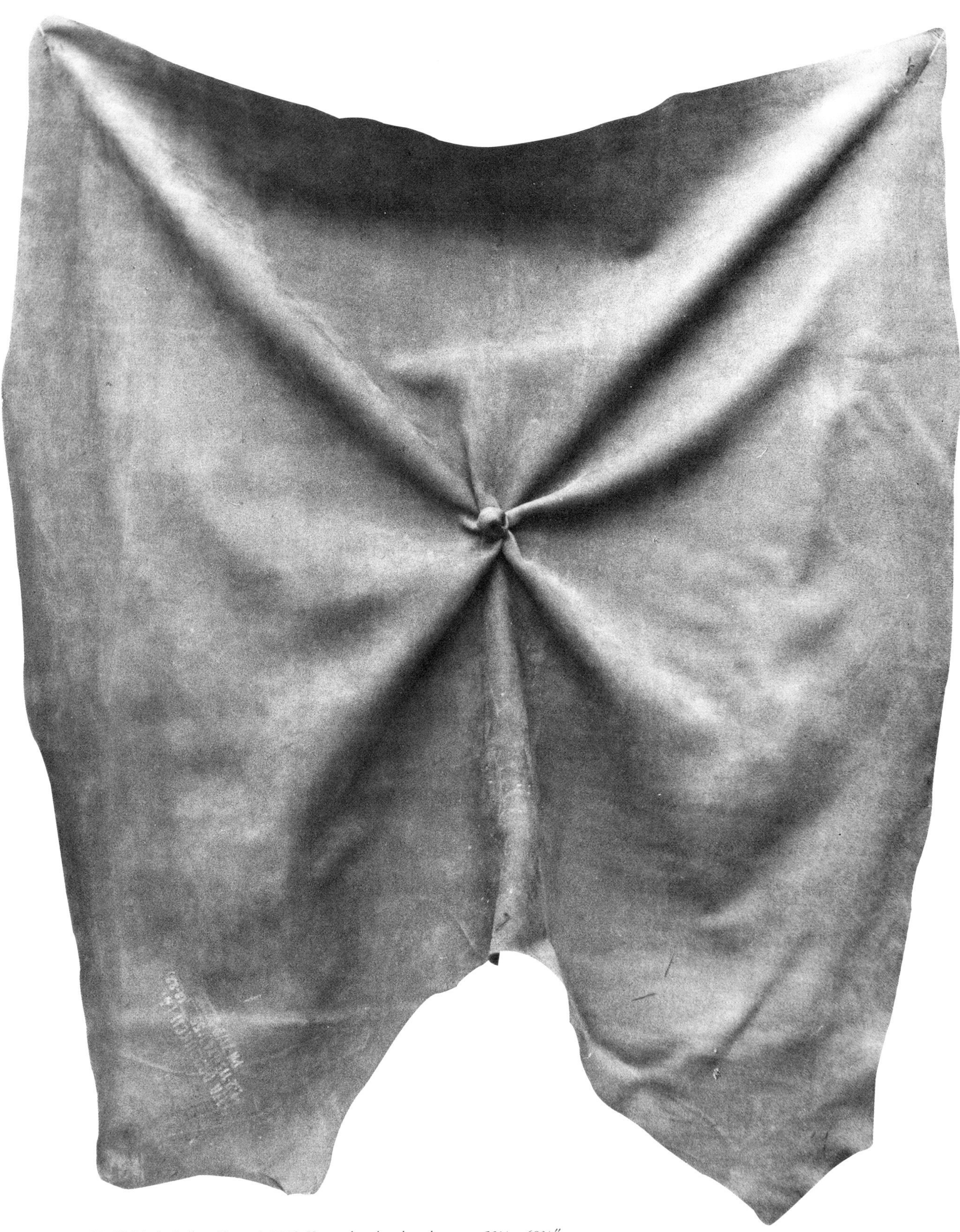

80. Wojciech Sadley, *Tatwazi,* 1976. Knotted and gathered cotton, 53⅛ x 68⅜".

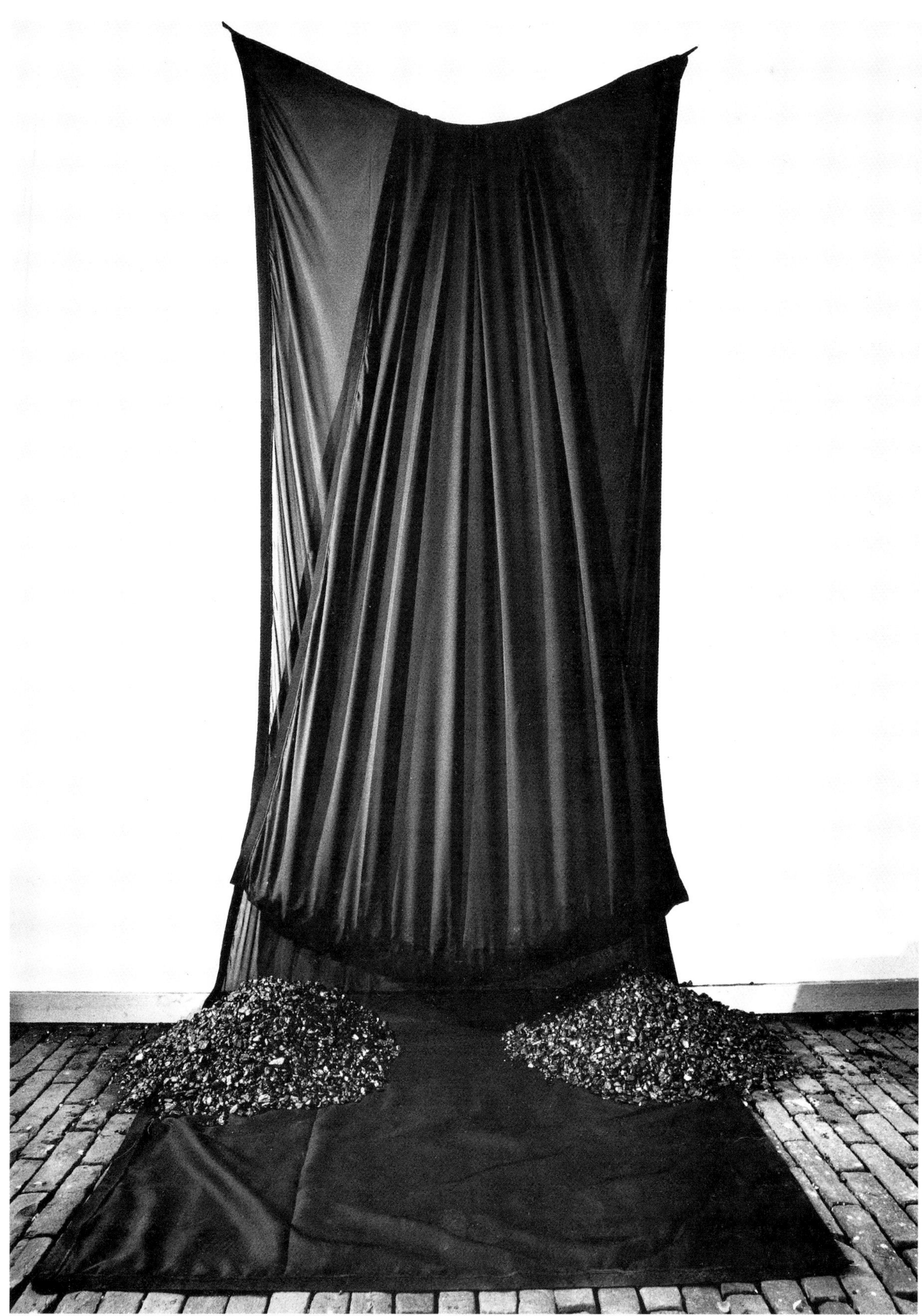

81. Harry Boom, *Untitled*, 1978. Acrylic paint on draped, tied, and twisted silk, 69⅜ x 43⅜″.

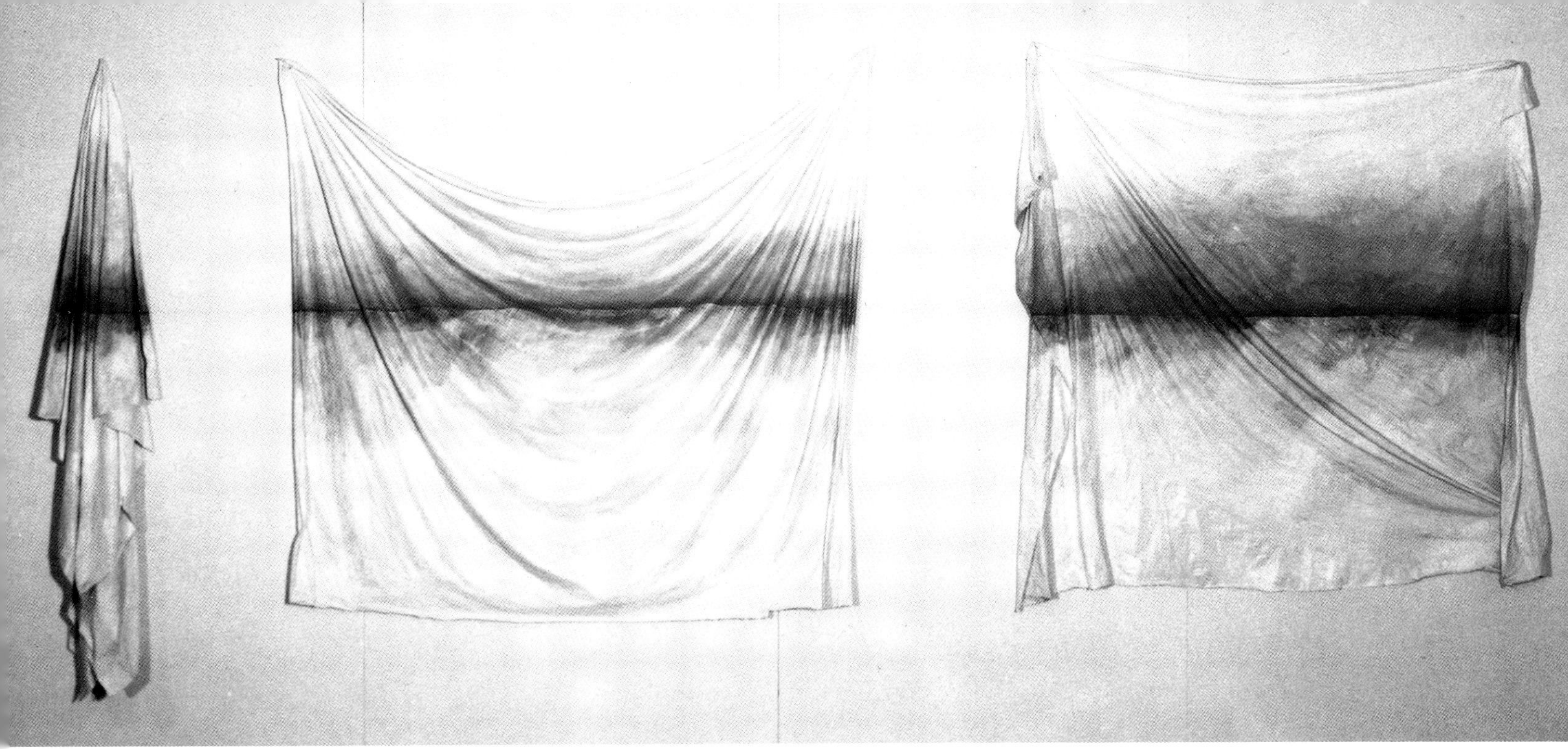

82. Susan Weil, *One Tack, Two Tack, Three Tack,* 1972. Acrylic on cotton, 6 x 13´.

Harry Boom, a student of Sadley's, came to share with his mentor a predilection for dark, ominous draped cloth. Whereas Sadley is faithful to the cloth, Boom transforms it into a symbolic garment held by tension and weights. The shiny black surface of the silk and the glittery surface of the coal add to the work's ambiguity (fig. 81).

Whole cloth, unframed, unstretched, and unbound, has evolved into a new category of art. It exists somewhere between the floor and the wall, often isolated in space. The materials used in these works of art comprise both the substance and the subject matter of the art. They are products of commerce. No mere piles of cloth, all are formally composed—witness the work *One Tack, Two Tack, Three Tack* by Susan Weil. Utilizing tacks and words to create a title, she banters with the ideas of formal composition even while imposing the most formal of horizon lines upon her ever-expanding pieces of cloth. Weil, along with her former husband, Rauschenberg, was in the vanguard of artists instinctively making art from cloth. One is left wondering if Weil wasn't a major influence in Rauschenberg's adoption of cloth in his art, because the two studied together in their formative years at Black Mountain College (fig. 82).

No single force has shaped this movement. Painters, needleworkers, dyers, sculptors, and traditional weavers all contributed to this transformation of old techniques into a modern-day art form. Artists from many parts of the world have dipped freely into seemingly unrelated traditions, intent upon expanding the boundless potential of cloth. Matt Mullican epitomizes the contemporary New York artist who has gone back to an ancient cloth form, the banner, in order to create both timely and timeless art. In his own words:

> By 1977 I had an overt kind of language that was very complicated and I was wondering what to do with it. Putting the signs on cloth and making a banner made sense. Just the word banner evokes so many different things.
>
> I began making banners using red, black, and white. I was creating a very complex structure with red as the color for the subject, and black and white the colors for language. I tried to make the banners as aggressive as I could. This color combination seemed to be the most aggressive that I could think of. I had a series of banners in front of the Museum of Contemporary Art in Los Angeles for a year and they were all slashed. They were placed in a space designed by Frank Gehry which is a sea of I-beams that are like teeth. It's extremely aggressive architecture so I came up with the most aggressive banners I could think of. I'm not a big fan of banners, per se. I use them because I'm interested in the relationship between banners and painting for instance [fig. 84].[11]

There are many ways that artists have expanded the idea of painting through the use of mill cloth. The Japanese artist Soiji Ida, in a work such as *Red Temple Dry Ruin,* seems to have created a summary work of art. The wall-mounted work draws

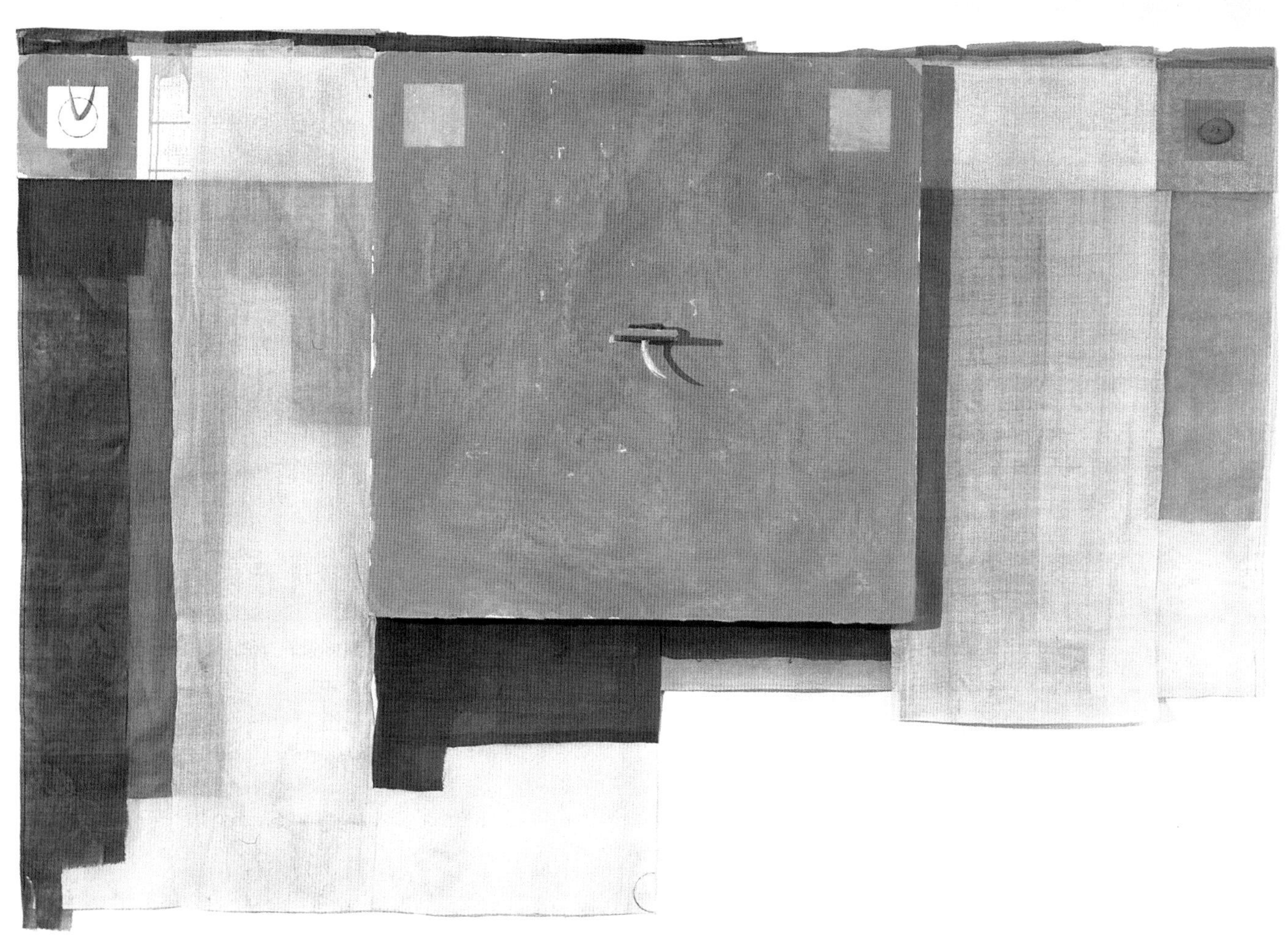

83. Soiji Ida, *Red Temple Dry Ruin, No. 20*, 1987. Mixed media including colored plastic on gold leaf, canvas with old kimono fabric, bronze, and stone, 26 x 30″.

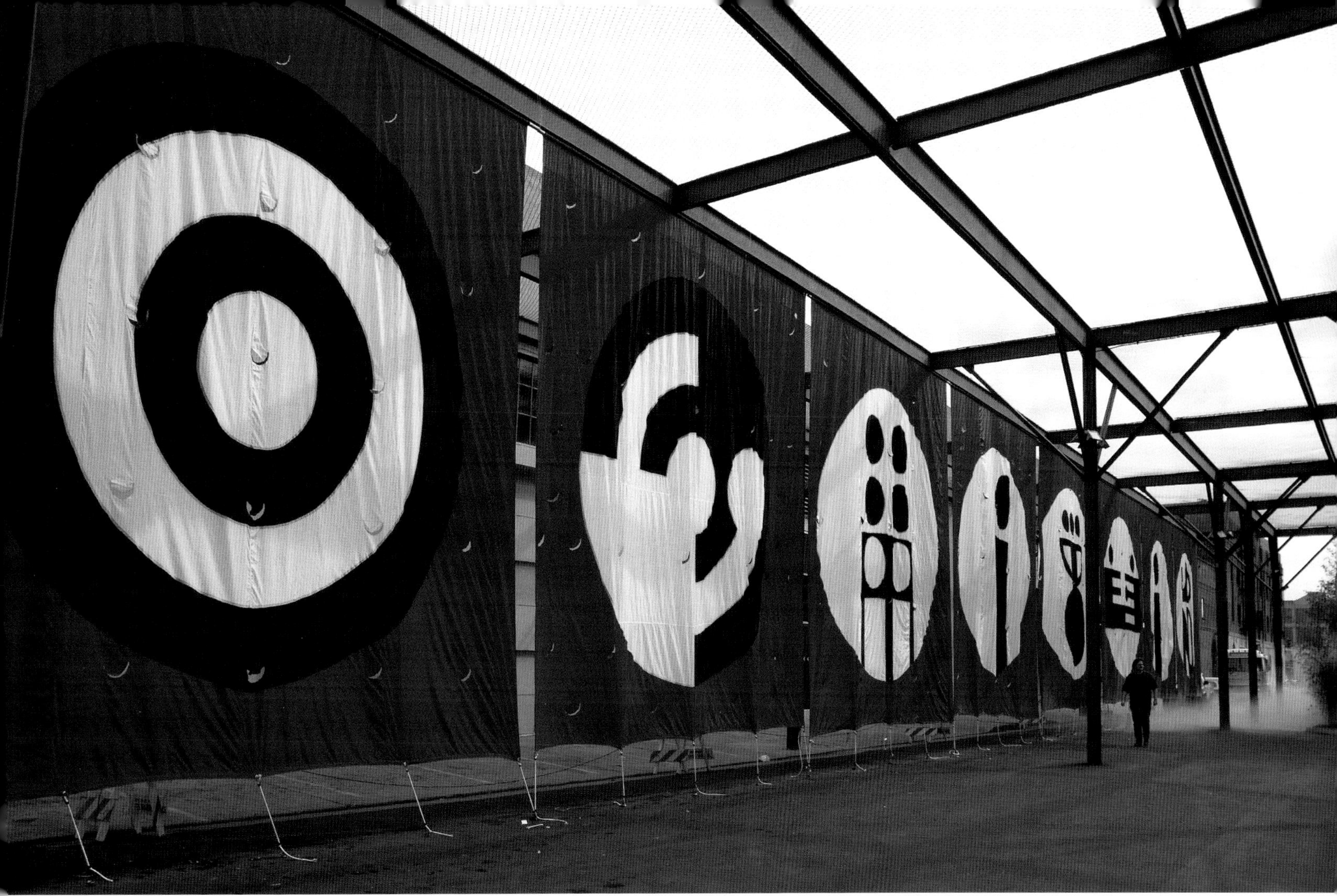

84. Matt Mullican, installation at the Museum of Contemporary Art, Los Angeles, 1986. Courtesy Michael Klein Inc., New York.

from the East for its sumptuous color and the West for its flat surface plane rooted in abstract painting (Ida lived and taught in the United States for almost a decade before returning to Japan). The delicate, transparent fabrics, vividly colored, echo the dyeing tradition of the Eastern world. This, however, is an illusion, as they are in reality commercial yard goods. Air and light and shadow are as much the subject of this work as the more usual formal concerns of art making—again a Japanese concept. Cloth alone would offer the artist such transparency, such floating loveliness. The acceptance of that loveliness, a totally uncontemporary idea, comes from Ida's roots in ancient Japanese art. This is a quality he shares with many of the Japanese artists in this book, and one that has pushed the boundaries of what constitutes serious art in the twentieth century, just as Kiki Smith's embroideries and Sigmar Polke's use of trashy cloth in lieu of canvas have redefined what art can be in our times (fig. 83).

1. Barbara Rose, *American Painting: The Twentieth Century* (New York: Rizzoli, 1980), 103.

2. Rose, *American Painting*, 105.

3. Robert Morris, "Anti-Form," *Artforum*, Apr. 1968.

4. Mildred Constantine and Laurel Reuter, *Frontiers in Fiber: The Americans* (exhibition catalog, Grand Forks, N.D. and Washington, D.C.: North Dakota Museum of Art/United States Information Agency, 1988).

5. Ruth K. Meyer, *Arabesque* (exhibition catalog, Cincinnati, Ohio: Contemporary Arts Center, 1978), 10.

6. Roland Penrose, *Tàpies* (New York: Rizzoli, 1978), 40.

7. John Caldwell, "Sigmar Polke," in *Sigmar Polke* (San Francisco: San Francisco Museum of Modern Art, 1990), 11.

8. Jack Lenor Larsen, *The Dyer's Art: ikat, plangi, batik* (New York: Van Nostrand Reinhold, 1976), 12.

9. International Textile Fair '87 Kyoto, Executive Committee, editors, *International Textile Competition '87 Kyoto* (exhibition catalog, Kyoto: International Textile Fair '87 Kyoto, 1987), work 4.

10. Lenore Tawney, *A Personal World* (exhibition catalog, Brookfield, Conn.: Brookfield Craft Center, 1978).

11. *Newsletter* (Independent Curators Incorporated, New York) 5, no. 4, (spring/summer 1990): 4.

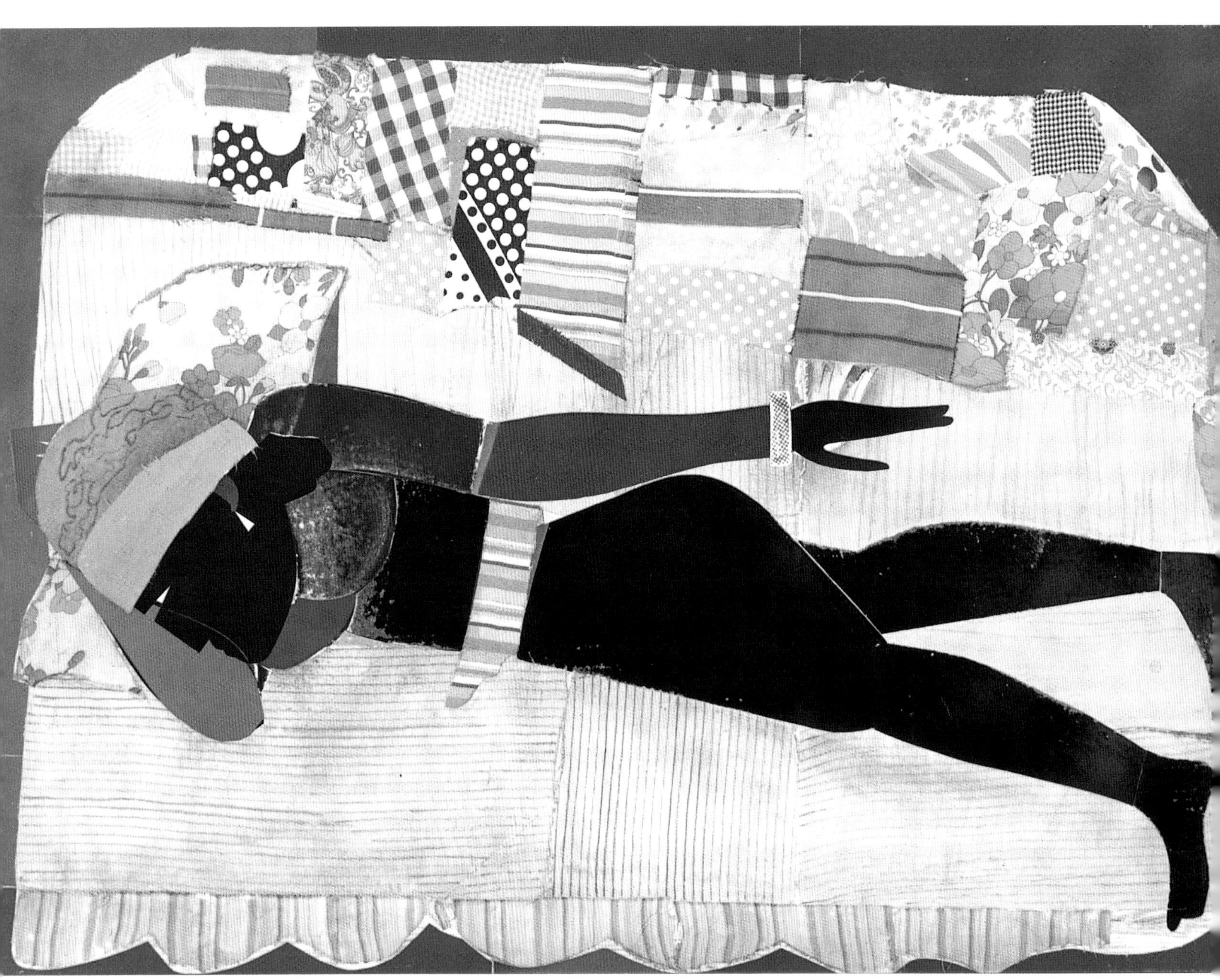

# Bits and Pieces

*The unlike is joined together and from the difference results the most beautiful harmony.*

Heraclitus

85 *(opposite).* Romare Bearden, *Patchwork Quilt,* 1970. Collage of cloth and paper with synthetic polymer paint on composition board, 35¾ x 47⅞″. Collection Museum of Modern Art, New York, Blanchette Rockefeller Fund.

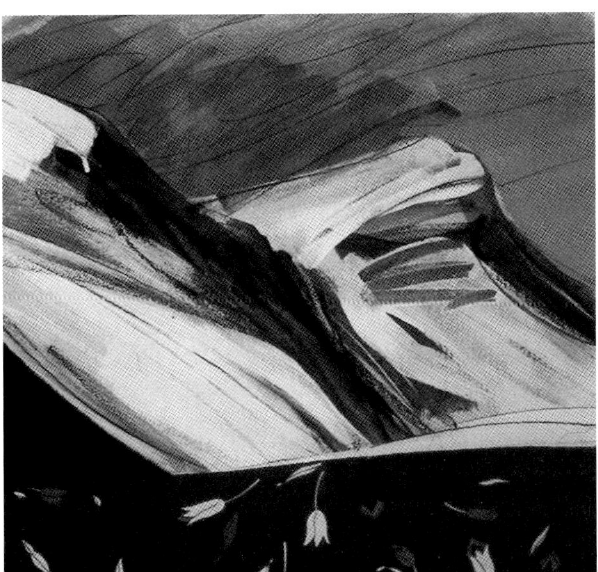

86. Neil Parsons, *Gunsight,* 1985. Mixed media, 20 x 20″. Collection North Dakota Museum of Art, Grand Forks.

Bits and pieces of cloth sewn or glued together curtain the world. Bits and pieces of knowledge skillfully intertwined make up the study of history. Every civilization has this tradition of squirreling away precious fragments until they are needed to construct a whole. Works of art, especially in the twentieth century, are often nothing more than ordered fragmentation—with each fragment carrying its own cultural load.

Quilting goes back to the beginnings of human occupation of the earth. Until the industrial revolution made cloth plentiful, every scrap was valuable, saved to be massed into a larger whole. Collage as it is known today developed after the mass manufacture of cloth began; thus it is based upon mill cloth, common cloth, ordinary cloth. Romare Bearden's collage *Patchwork Quilt* exemplifies this rich history of bits of cloth. Bearden uses the random pieces of mill cloth first as elements of bold design. That they form a patchwork quilt is secondary to the artist's formal use of the scraps of gaily colored cloth as foil for the powerful black body. The darkness of the body, the brilliance of the cloth swatches, and their geometric but asymmetrical arrangement allude to the earlier African-American quilt tradition. Slave women, still in touch with their African textile heritage, dug into the scrap bags of their white mistresses to make random-patterned patchwork quilts to warm the bodies of their own children. Today these slave quilts are among the most valued objects of early American art. The descendants of these quilts and the ideas they embody, like a Bearden work of art, are made by juxtaposing disparate textures and colors to achieve a pulsating, sophisticated whole (fig. 85).

Historically, collage began in Paris with Picasso and Braque who, from 1911 to 1913 under the banner of Cubism, cut scraps of material and pasted them onto their picture planes. Strips of imitation chair caning, part of a tobacco wrapper with contrasting stamps, half a masthead from a newspaper, a bit of newsprint made into a playing card, a hunk of cloth: these were the first bits and pieces to make their way into serious Western art. Little did Picasso and Braque know that collage would become a hallmark of twentieth-century art, echoing the fragmentation that is a hallmark of twentieth-century life.

By 1916 the Dada movement had begun, and almost immediately the Dadaists saw the advantage of working in collage. It was probably Kurt Schwitters, associated with the German Dadaists at the time, who became most identified with collage. He declared, "I could not, in fact, see the reason why old tickets, driftwood, cloakroom tabs, wires and parts of wheels, buttons, and old rubbish found in attics and refuse dumps should not be as suitable a material for painting as the paints made in factories." Almost fifty years later the idea was reiterated by Rauschenberg.

During the 1950s another European, Alberto Burri, devoted himself to the making of collages from cloth. As part of the Art Informel movement, he sought out everyday materials that were heavily textured. His material of choice became burlap. He was interested in the then prevalent idea of truth to materials, and would highlight a burlap collage with gold or red paint, or would slash the fabric, or stitch it, or pull it away from its underlying support. All this was done to draw attention to the nature of burlap itself, humble, unpretentious, rough but often quite beautiful. The strongly visual nature of the weave, or grain of the fabric, meant that strong formal elements could be achieved by cutting and piecing the burlap. Other fabrics were not necessary to Burri's art.

One of the important discoveries made by those first artists to work with collage was that space is different in a collage. It is not created by illusionistic means but by the actual overlapping of layers of pasted materials. The surface takes on particular importance. As the century progressed, artists began to speak of the integrity of the two-dimensional surface. It was not to be compromised by the third dimension. Collage was a forerunner of this attitude.

By the 1960s every art student in the United States routinely made collages. They came to serve a role not unlike that of drawings. The artist might work out ideas in collage, or make collages as finished works of art. It was within this new tradition that the Native American Neil Parsons came into artistic maturity.

In *Gunsight* Parsons demonstrates that he is fully aware of the conventions of modernism and the role of collage in their evolution. By pasting a flat expanse of cloth in the foreground of his deep-space landscape, he creates a dual reality and a dual visual space. His carefully chosen cloth not only abruptly arrests the eye with its flatness, it functions as a potent metaphor for the artist's private life. Parsons, a Blackfoot Indian, was born in 1938 and grew up in a reservation world where Indian children were deliberately schooled out of their "Indianness." They were forbidden to speak the language and learn the ways of their grandparents, sent instead along the path to "whiteness." Young Neil navigated that changing world successfully to become an artist, a painter of subtle, Minimalist canvases. He also became a professor of art in America's West and Southwest at a time when there were few American Indian professors of anything. But sometime after his fortieth birthday he left college teaching, Minimalist painting, and the deserts of the Southwest to return to his birthplace in Browning, Montana (fig. 86).

Always a thoughtful man, Parsons embarked upon a new life, or circled back to an older life. With the journey came a renewed vision of landscape and a powerful body of new work. Upon his return home Parsons gave vent to his earlier abstract tendencies, to a looser handling of the brush, and to the actual landscape. Gunsight, for instance, is only one of the great mountains that live in Parsons's memory and that appeared in his vision as he looked to the west from the family ranch in the foothills of the Rocky Mountains, on the edge of Glacier National Park. With pencil and wash the artist began to capture Gunsight, and the legendary mountains surrounding it, on paper, one at a time.

In reality, the soaring, icy peaks of the Rockies are foiled by gorgeous snowfields, which melt into springtime meadows. Because of their altitude, such meadows seem to know only two seasons: the dead of winter and the time of blossoming. For his meadows Parsons turned to cloth: the flower-covered calico of his Indian grandmother's dresses with their dark fields and gay sprinkling of delicate flowers. In *Gunsight*, cloth stands for the return to home, to the peace of a meadow hidden down below the fierce and stunning mountain, to his own Indianness.

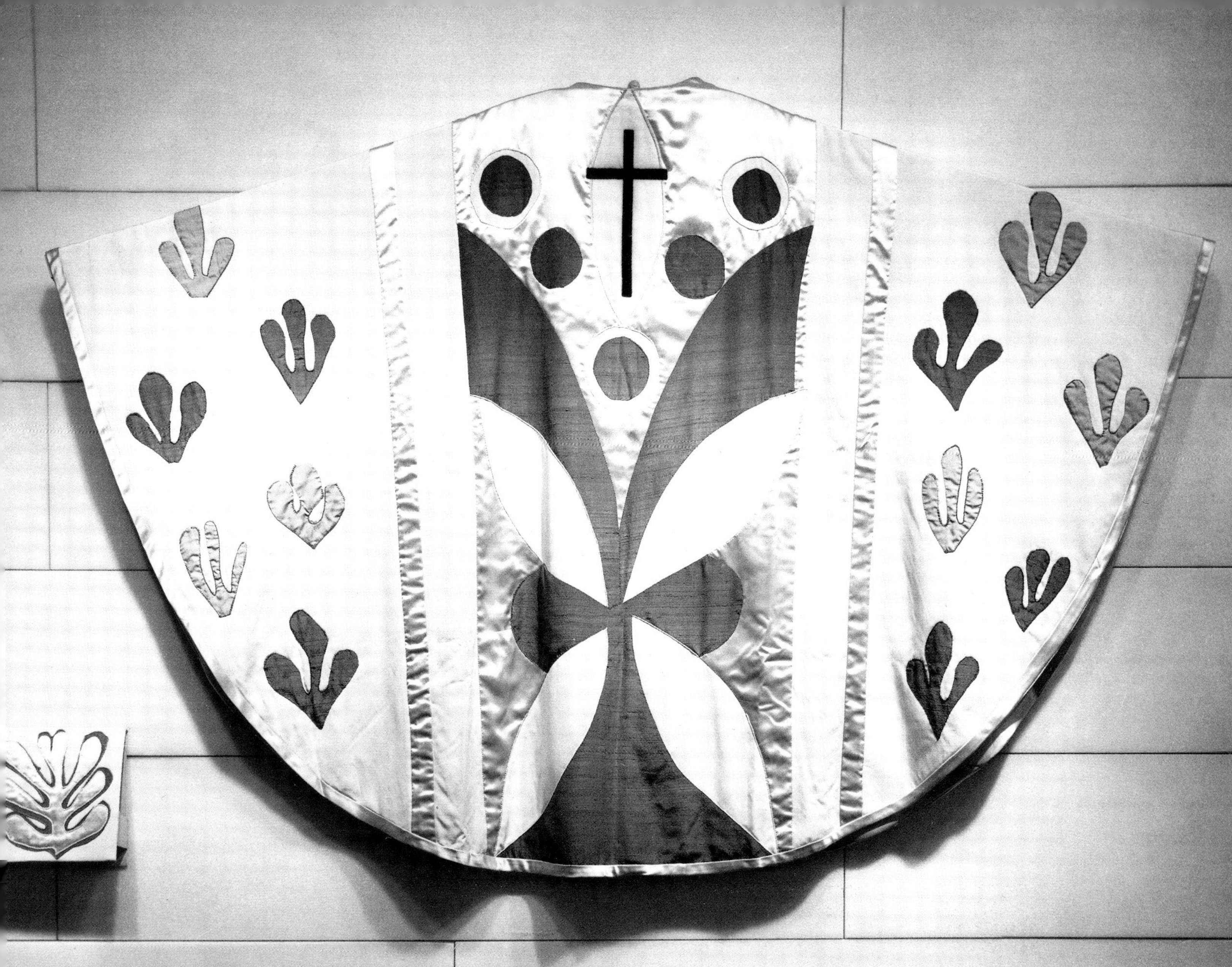

87. Henri Matisse, *Chasuble* (back), c. 1950. White silk with yellow and green satin appliqué. Collection Museum of Modern Art, New York, Lillie P. Bliss Bequest.

Ironically the cloth is also his toast to modernism, to the undeniably two-dimensional surface of a work of art in contemporary times.

Both Parsons and Bearden have chosen collage in order to enrich and intensify their vision. *Collage*, coming from the French word for "paste-up," is a central idea in the art of the twentieth century, be it film, poetry, the novel, or the visual arts. It seems to have developed concurrently with psychology's investigation into nonlinear learning. To learn by endlessly assimilating unrelated fragments is a twentieth-century concept. Ideas develop into amalgam.

The ingredients of a collage often play a double role. Although they have been shaped and combined, they do not lose their identity as scraps. Like random thoughts that gather into a human pattern of thinking, the parts of a collage both represent and present themselves. Whereas the Cubists and the Dadaists used mundane objects as artistic media, dismissing their cognitive meanings, artists such as Parsons select the elements of their collages for their inherent conceptual as well as formal qualities.

Along with claims for the modernism of collage, it is important to remember that this practice of making art from

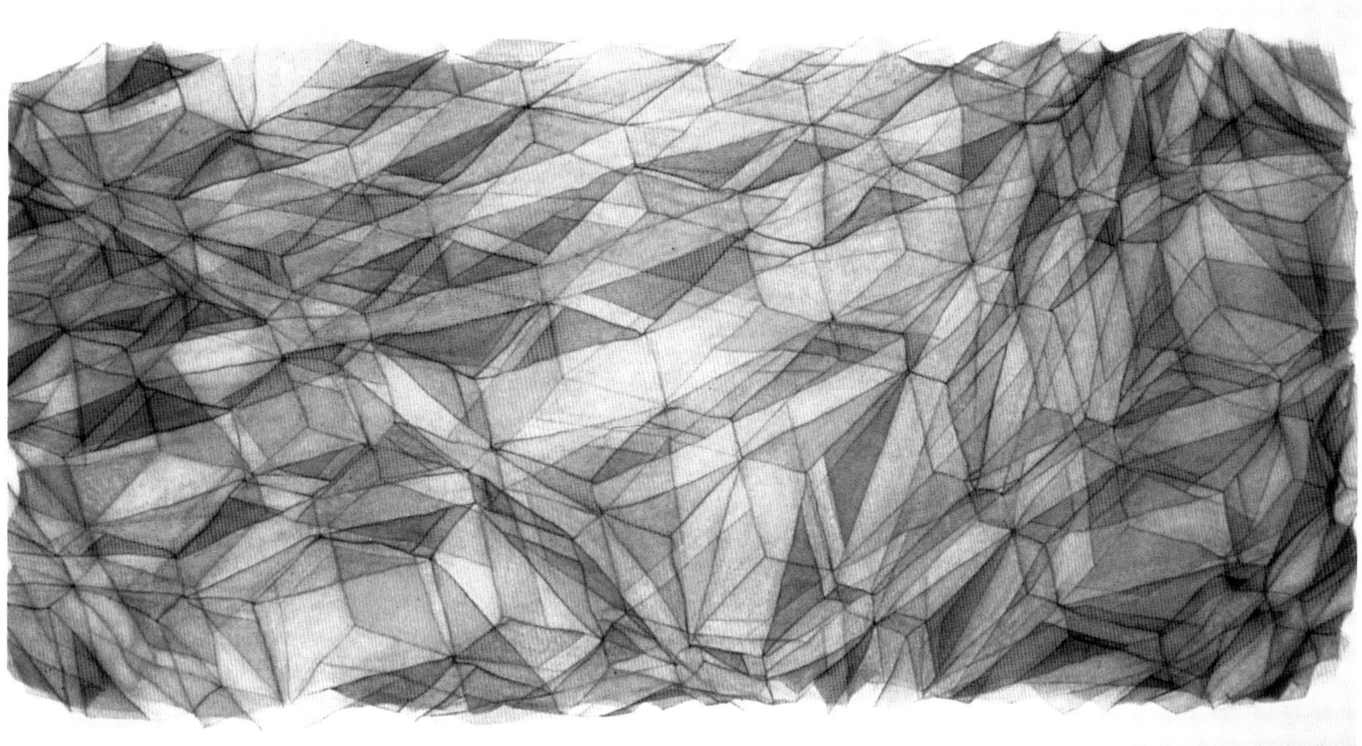

88. Connie Utterback, *Bandwave #13*, 1987. Nylon mesh, 39 x 78″.

bits and pieces is ancient. The gathering of fragments to make art is an activity as old as art history itself. Byzantine mosaics and stained-glass windows were collages. Folk artists in their scouring about for materials have always practiced collage. It is a universal art form that transcends race, class, time, and national boundaries. Contemporary artists continue to draw from these old traditions. For example, Henri Matisse, infirm in his old age, turned his artistic energy to cutting with scissors. His green and yellow *Chasuble* made in 1950 for the chapel at Vence in France continues in the time-honored tradition of appliqué. Although elegantly stitched on silk and velvet, the work is closely aligned in both design and technique with his cutouts (fig. 87).

The Byzantine mosaic and the stained-glass window are ultimately about fragmented light. Not surprisingly, fragmented light is also the issue for such contemporary artists as Connie Utterback, Janet Markarian, and Patricia Malarcher. Utterback's wall pieces are geometric wonders, clear, translucent, and beautiful, and being of the late twentieth century, they are made from industrial materials. Trained as a printmaker, she still begins her work with drawings. Using transparent papers, she builds up her sheets of geometric facets, first one layer, then another, and usually a third. The drawings, or cartoons, are enlarged; then each faceted shape is cut out of nylon monofilament material—the same factory-made nylon used to reinforce tires. Utterback buys it by the roll while it is still flexible, that is, before the tire company coats it with fiberglass. The colors come from fiberglass resin dyes. Little research has been done with these dyes, the tire companies having no concern with the color of the nylon embedded in their tires, so Utterback experiments, finding herself limited at this time to a pastel palate and unable to reproduce colors with any predictability from one dye bath to the next. Finally, the single facets of nylon fabric are fused together with a hot soldering iron, the joinings becoming the graphite lines of her initial drawings. They are then mounted on the wall, with each transparent layer of curtain placed in

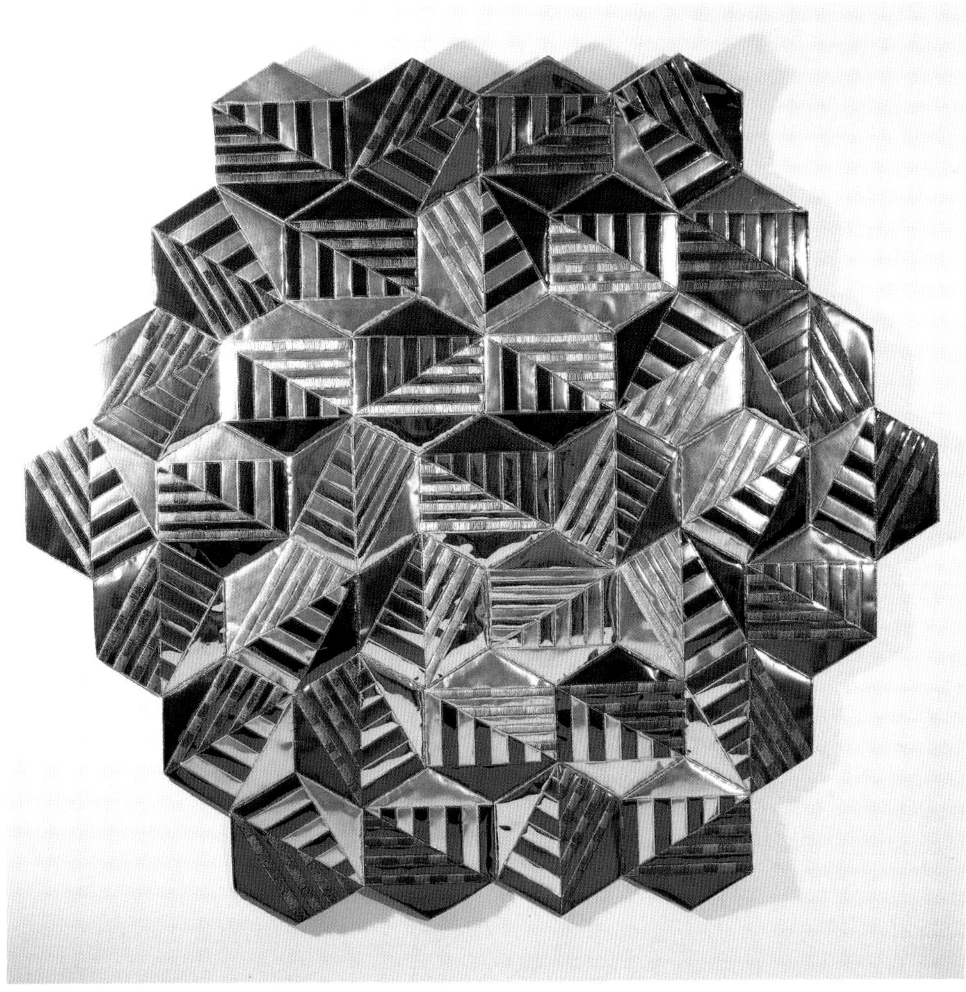

89. Patricia Malarcher, *Homage to Karl von Frisch,* 1982. Mylar appliqué, machine stitching, hand embroidery, 50 x 56″.

front of the next. Utterback's shimmering, pellucid mosaics of cloth owe their visual existence to all those works in glass and stone that preceded them by centuries (fig. 88).

Unlike Utterback, whose nylon materials read like fine gauze, Patricia Malarcher is interested in facets of material that reflect rather than transmit light. She quilts and appliqués plastic Mylar, as strong a metaphor as can be found for the marriage of contemporary industrial life and traditional crafts. Her references are diverse, ranging from folk art to geometric painting, from the quilter's craft to the current convention of creating large works, often in fiber, specifically designed to ameliorate immense and impersonal public spaces (fig. 89).

Another of these manipulators of light, Jarmilla Machova, relies upon the cutting and fusing of nonwoven materials, both opaque and transparent, in order to achieve translucency. Then she treats the surface, which may have evolved from layering five or six tiers of fabric, with dyes or with her implements of drawing—inks and dry pigments, including oil pastels. Her first priority is to create a rich textural composition. To achieve this she tries to control both the artificial and the natural lighting on each finished piece.

Utterback, Malarcher, and Machova are artists schooled in traditional textile arts. As they searched for a personal visual language they looked to the past and to the future, to the

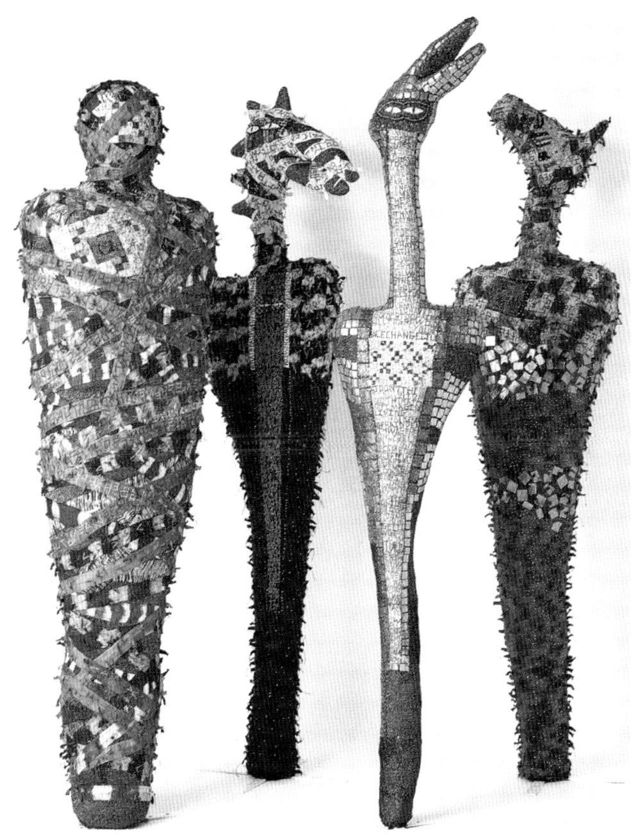

90 (see also page 2). Janet Markarian, Creature Torso series, 1987. Embellished fiber on armature, c. 75 x 17 x 7″. Collection North Dakota Museum of Art, Grand Forks, Helge Ederstrom Memorial Endowment.

historic textile world and to the mainstream of Western art. None has searched harder or further than their peer Janet Markarian. Like so many artists trained in the fiber departments of universities in the United States in the 1970s, she made a pilgrimage to Ecuador to study ancient weaving—funded by a Fulbright. She interned in the Textile Study Room of New York's Metropolitan Museum of Art. She taught at the fiber department of the School of the Chicago Art Institute.

Markarian's early interests were in surface design, the embellishment of cloth through a myriad of dyeing and related techniques. After years of studying historical textiles, she came into her own in the late 1980s with the creation of her Creature Torso series. Prior to this, surfaces had dominated her art; form had been subservient. Beginning with the first of these figures, *Mummy* (1987), she gradually created more intricate sculptural forms. Because Markarian was first of all an embellisher of cloth, she struggled to find form for her surfaces. Finally in her Creature Torso series, surface and form are in perfect balance. This is strong, enigmatic sculpture. The embellished, faceted areas of light and dark that define the form both absorb and reflect light, causing the figure to come alive, to dance. One is drawn; one is distanced. One comes back to the work again and again, seeking to know it from every angle. If she continues to make art, Markarian may well become one of the strongest artists to come out of the Art Fabric movement in the United States (fig. 90).

Few artists in the twentieth century are as identified with cloth as Robert Rauschenberg, and no one has investigated the interaction between cloth and light with such thoroughness. He has repeatedly said that his art is the result of a collaboration between himself and his materials, thus acknowledging "the reserve of possibilities built into the materials." As early as 1954 he was utilizing cloth as a rigid or fixed material in works such as *Red Interior*. By 1974–75, when he began both his Jammer series and his Hoarfrost series, Rauschenberg was allowing fabric to hang loosely. In the Jammer series the artist concentrated upon the natural properties of cloth whereas the Hoarfrosts are a series of unstretched paintings on fabric, which allowed Rauschenberg to investigate the embellishment potential of sundry transparent, opaque, and translucent natural fabrics.

Rauschenberg was the first artist to embrace cloth overwhelmingly as a material for making art, and to use it in a free, unpretentious, and varied manner—be it fine silk or cheap muslin. He was also already deeply involved with fragmented images as early as 1950. His work, more than any, predicted the splitting of ideas, the relationship of the unrelated, and the abandonment of linear thinking that would dominate the art of the latter decades of the twentieth century. The fragmentation that appeared in society in the 1960s prevailed in Rauschenberg's art from 1950 onward. An artist such as Joseph Cornell built his assemblages and collages from diverse and unrelated objects and images, but because they were contained by frame or box, they did not have the large, free-ranging scope of a Rauschenberg floating freely on cloth, or bridging painting and sculpture.

By 1980 fragmentation was the expected in art. Viewers had become used to the sculptural randomness of the Watts Towers, to the dislocated elements of a David Salle painting, to layered graphic design that would culminate a decade later in

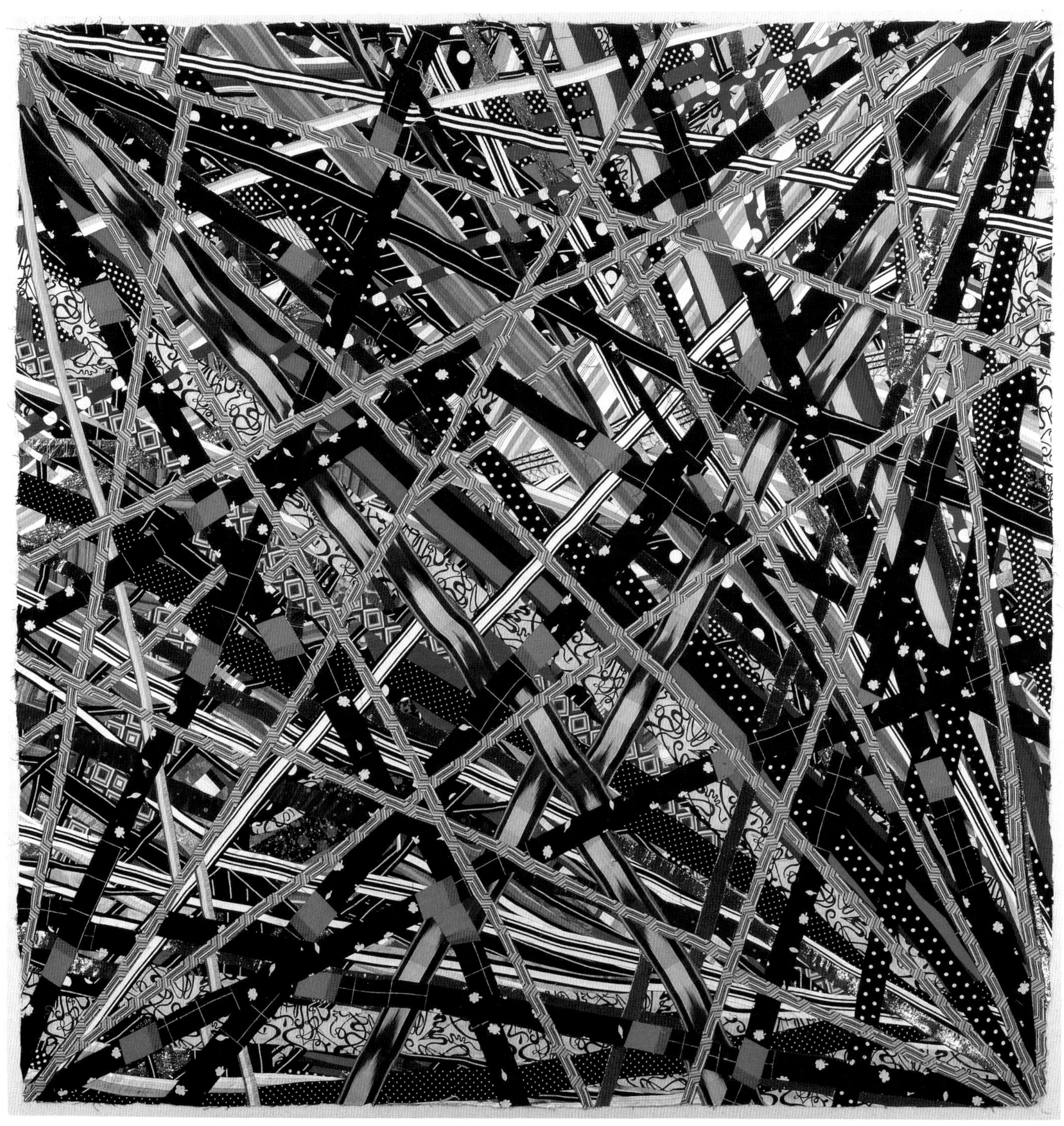

91. Lucas Samaras, *Reconstruction #26,* 1977. Cotton with sewing, 75½ x 77″. Collection Mr. and Mrs. Julius Davis, Minneapolis.

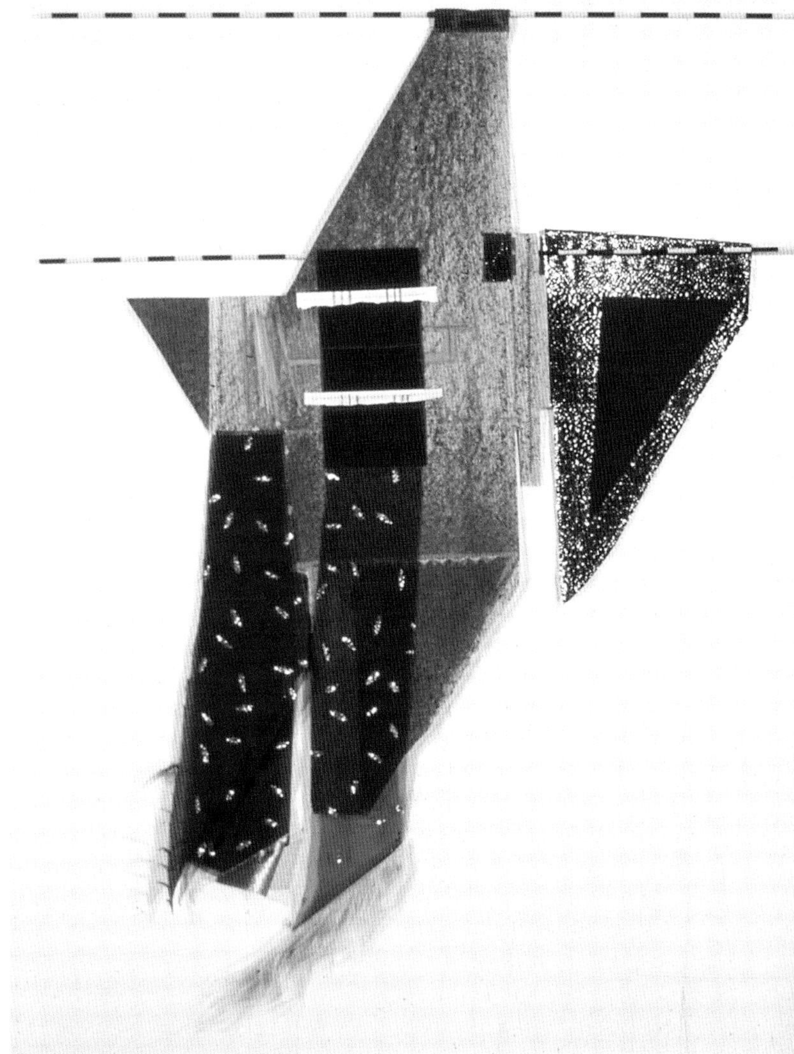

92. Martha Zelt, *Milagro para Angela,* 1986. Lithograph with added fabric and paper collage, machine stitching, 37¾ x 30¾". Collection North Dakota Museum of Art, Grand Forks.

the work of David Carson, to Frank Gehry's architecture with its disparate features that normally do not appear in architecture as conceived by modernism. Layering, a method of achieving fragmentation that was again practiced by Rauschenberg from his youngest days, was present everywhere in art by this decade. In photography, graphics, or painting, an unevenness of layering is intended to jar the viewer further, causing greater fragmentation. There are no national boundaries; fragmentation is universal in postindustrial society. Works of art made from bits and pieces totally reflect this new world.

Rauschenberg showed the way; artists such as Lucas Samaras followed. Samaras is a prolific artist, a painter and photographer who uses a variety of materials in his work. Best known for his Phototransformations, he was one of the first to experiment with altering the emulsion of a Polaroid photograph in order to create his own brand of surrealism. He also transforms actual objects. For example, he took a book and covered it with pins, nails, and a razor. Then he inserted a knife, a pair of scissors, and a broken pane of glass into its first pages. One of his principal series in cloth came into being in 1977. Called Reconstructions, they are flat surface compositions of cloth. Made of gaudily patterned fabrics such as Lurex, chiffon, and lamé, he cut the polka-dotted, patterned, and striped fabrics into strips and then sewed them into his compositions. These constructions are controlled and formal in spite of their wild graphic patterns, which provide both form and movement to the work. He uses machine stitching to help the eye travel over and under the various strips, thus causing the viewer to experience the insistent diagonal structure of the work (fig. 91).

What this work is about is barely suggested. Instead the viewer intuits Samaras's witty and charming allusions to contemporary life: that is the work's content. The poetic fabrication of the material, coupled with unusual spatial relationships, results in a sense of freedom, elegance, and vitality.

Martha Zelt is another of "Rauschenberg's children." With him she shares much: an inclination to combine materials such as wood, multifarious fabrics, and paper made to her specifications, if not by her own hand; great skill as a printmaker; her affinity for cloth. Whether she is making prints at Tamarind in New Mexico, or stitching together a multimedia piece on a sewing machine in her studio, this artist is constantly confronting the formal elements of making art. Trained as a muralist, she creates the monumental with a whisper. The most delicate of floating fabrics is anchored by the weight of an equally delicate wooden dowel. A bit of fur or a handful of sequins balances a complicated torn scrap of lithograph. Sometimes the viewer is confronted with a swatch of printed fabric echoed by a screen print of a fabric image. These masterful collages are as apt to be stitched together as they are to be pasted, for paste cannot become a formal element within the collage—stitching can and does. Like Rauschenberg, Zelt is comfortable working on a grand scale. And also like Rauschenberg, she is undaunted by small space. Critics speak of her work in terms of aerial views, kites, and landscapes. Such references may exist; but for Zelt the real subject of her print constructions is surface and light (fig. 92).

During the 1960s a third force, equal in power to collage and fragmentation, swept into the arena: the women's movement. Masses of women entered the art world as artists, curators, gallery owners, and power brokers. They brought with them a determination to investigate their own histories—personal accounts inextricably interwoven with cloth. Miriam Schapiro was among the first to insist that these were ingredients worthy of art making. Schapiro the feminist took the word *collage* and combined it with *female* to form *femmage:* an art form by which collage elements from women's lives (scraps of lace, labels, chintz, gingham, and other feminine paraphernalia) are made into works of art through the traditional craft techniques associated with women such as cutting, sewing, piecing, hooking, quilting, and appliqué. Women's culture is the framework for the creation of femmage. From 1971 on Schapiro created groundbreaking works of femmage that were literal and beautiful. Works from her Fan series are some of her most successful. Here she allows the framework of the fan to impose a formal composition upon her informal elements. Schapiro led with her work and she led with her teaching as she crisscrossed the country, endlessly meeting with young women. Twenty years later one hears mature women artists saying, "She gave me my first serious critique" (fig. 93).

Among the early and most momentous discoveries made by these pioneering women artists of the late 1960s and the 1970s were the lives of their own mothers and grandmothers, aunts and great-aunts. Betye Saar's work is a wonderful example of art that pays remarkable homage to those women from whom she came: her family as well as the wider world of African-American women. Born in 1926, young Betye had lost her father by the time she was six. She grew up with her mother, a seamstress, and her extended family of siblings, grandmother, aunts, and uncles. A southern Californian, the young girl often visited her grandmother in Watts. She learned to sew, to make things, to collect fascinating bits and pieces. Upon graduation from college, she worked as a costume designer, one of the only art-related fields open to African-American women at that time, given its roots in dressmaking. She married, raised children, and then, in the 1960s, at the height of both the black power movement and the feminist movement, she came into her own as an artist.

93. Miriam Schapiro, *Night Shade*, 1986. Fabric and acrylic on canvas, 48 x 96″.

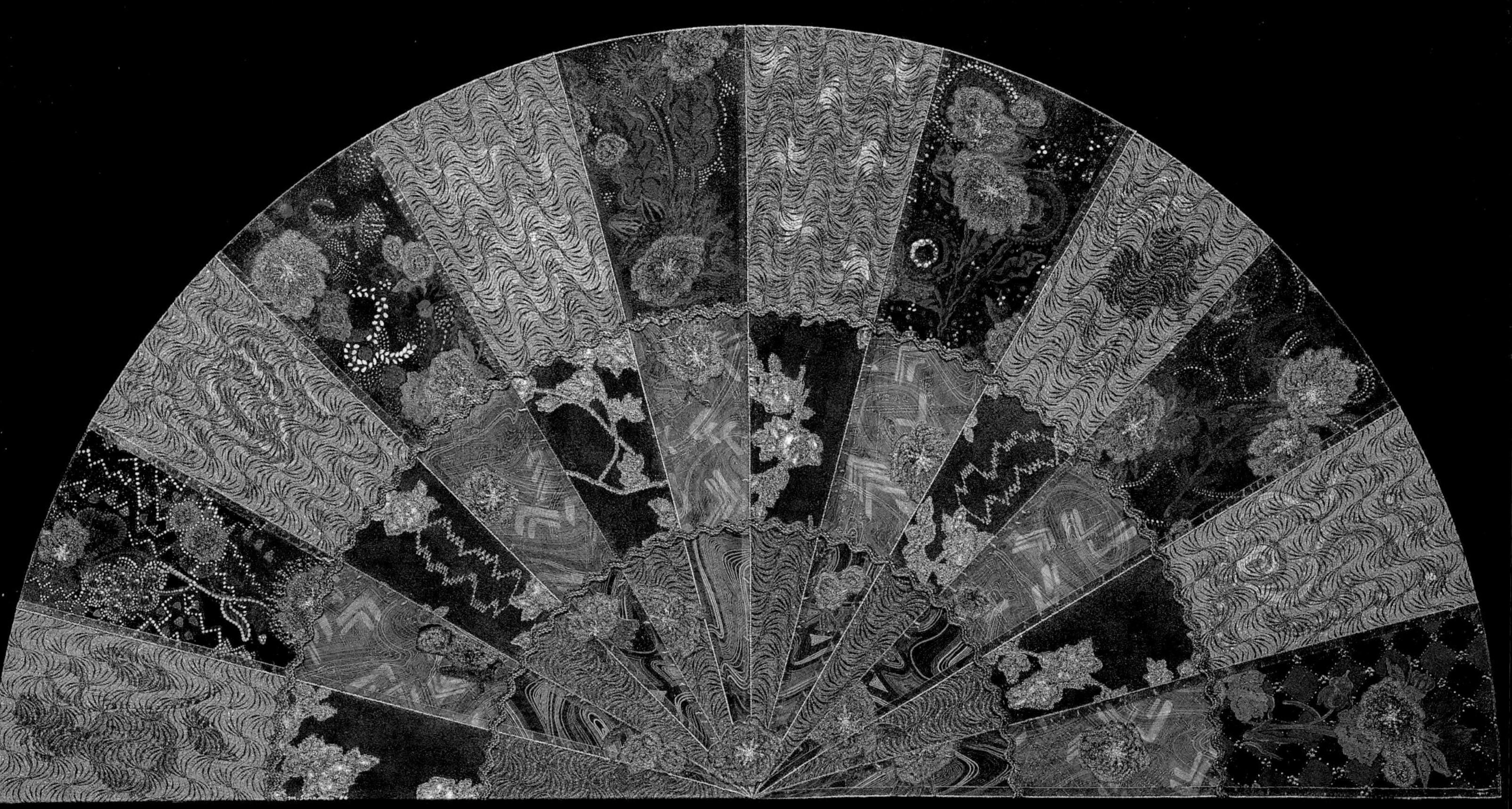

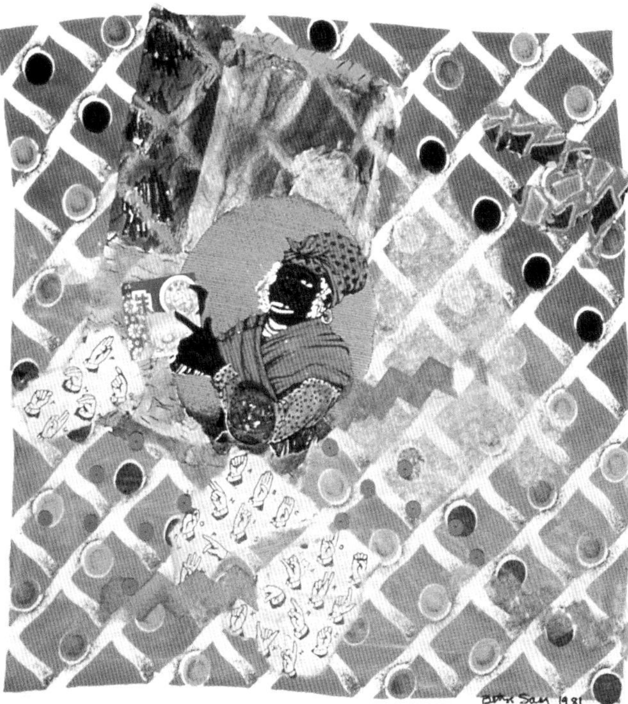

94. Betye Saar, *Dreams Dreams Come Play Your Dreams,* 1981. Collage of mixed media on silk handkerchief, 11¼ x 10½″.

Saar tells of the death of her great-aunt in Kansas City, Missouri, and the impact it had upon her art. The aunt had raised her mother; Betye considered her a grandmother. As the artist cleaned out the great-aunt's house she found the remains of a life she had little considered: boxes of pristine white gloves, lovely lace handkerchiefs, costume jewelry, autograph books, letters in fine old handwriting, faded photographs of genteel ladies. This became the material and the substance of a large body of work for Saar. She was to create assemblages contained in boxes; collages on transparent handkerchiefs; collages on pages from diaries, letters, and autograph books; and constructions of all kinds. Most included cloth (fig. 94).

Bonnie Lucas, like Saar, chooses to examine the lives of ordinary women; but unlike the reactions to Saar's work, those produced by Lucas's conclusions cause contemporary women to squirm. Lucas creates assemblages of domestic surrealism from soft, pastel fabrics—preferably sweet pinks highlighted by baby blues and gentle whites. With impeccable craftsmanship she stitches and glues baby clothes and frivolous female stuff, plastic and fabric ribbons, junk jewelry and doll parts into lovely, formal compositions. At first glance these handsome, framed works appear to be ads for baby powder. Ultimately, the viewer is struck by the dark irony of her statements about domestic life. According to Lucas her assemblages "change the context of the objects so that the resulting work is a nightmarish juxtaposition that makes the viewer uneasy" (fig. 95).

There was a second great discovery made by these women of the 1960s and 1970s. They learned that their grandmothers had made their own collage art form, the quilt.

The brilliant colors, abstract designs, sophisticated movement within the designs, and splendid craftsmanship riveted the attention of young women with fine-arts degrees. Patchwork quilts quickly became a burning issue within feminist circles. Some argued that "the existence of these colorful, stitched creations seemed to offer proof of women's ability to create a valid art form apart from the male-dominated institutions of high art." Indeed, one spokeswoman for the quilters, Patricia Mainardi, in a provocative article in *Feminist Art Journal,* asserted that women quilters anticipated recent developments in abstract art by more than a century.[1] Others viewed quilts more as tokens of women's traditional ability to triumph over adversity, to make the best of things in the face of continual oppression. Denied access to the official art world and its chosen art forms, women fulfilled their aesthetic potentials within the restricted and safely ahistorical areas of the decorative and the useful. They made things for their homes, their families, and themselves.

Today collectors by the scores fill their homes and coffers with both antique and contemporary quilts, with Amish quilts, slave quilts, and Native American star quilts. To chose from among the quilt makers is almost a random act. So many are so good. Of the older generation one might cite Mary Woodard Davis (1900–1989). She never became famous but she made a tremendous difference. The daughter of an Oklahoma tribal lawyer, she was sent to a convent in Kansas City for her early education. Here the nuns taught her the traditional skills needed by a "lady," including fine hand-sewing. In this cloistered life she learned to follow the advice of Thomas Jefferson to his daughter studying in Paris, "Don't neglect your needlework. It will get you through more long evenings and boring conversations than all your languages and fine arts combined."

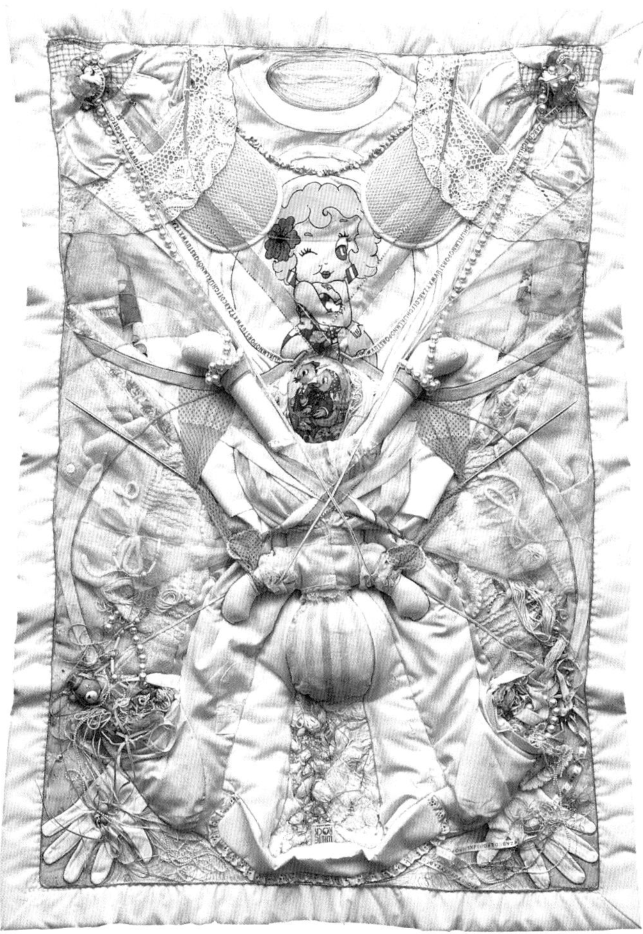

95. Bonnie Lucas, *White Rock*, 1986. Assemblage on fabric, 49 x 34 x 3″.

Davis always worked, as a teacher at Fordham University, as a costume designer on Broadway, in the W.P.A. theater in Washington. On the side she made things with her hands. In her mid-sixties she faced leaving her beloved Ankara, Turkey, her home for almost a decade. Following her finger as it traced the latitude of Ankara around the globe, she settled on Santa Fe, New Mexico. Once moved she invented a retirement job. In 1965 Davis began work to establish the Textile Workshops with the purpose of bringing the best artists and teachers to New Mexico. Certainly the level of the textile arts among both artists and craftspeople in the Southwest was enhanced by her teaching, her collecting, the exhibitions she organized, and the workshops she sponsored. When she was eighty years old she had her first New York exhibition in a mainstream art gallery: Craig Cornelius showed her quilts.

Davis created *Taos Quilt* from blocks of solid colors, hand pieced and hand quilted in the old traditional way. Like most contemporary quilts, this is intended as a wall textile. In 1984 Davis organized a painting exhibition, "Victor Higgins in New Mexico," for the Art Museum of South Texas in Corpus Christi. The catalog cover and exhibition poster both featured a small painting of a domestic interior, *Christmas Cactus*. It had been painted by the Taos school painter in the 1920s and featured a pot of flowering Christmas cactus set upon a table that was gaily spread with a patchwork textile. That geometric pastel table cover became the inspiration for *Taos Quilt*, which was to hang in her New York show, and which came to commemorate the last exhibition she was to organize. Appropriately named, the quilt calls to mind the adobe, brick-based architecture of the ancient Taos Pueblo apartment complex, bathed in the shimmering, pastel light of northern New Mexico (fig. 96).

Of the younger generation, one artist might be chosen to illustrate the work of thousands of quilt makers: Terrie Mangat. As a little girl she began to collect swatches of cloth. The artist remembers: "When I was six years old, my mom asked me what I wanted for Christmas. I said 'fabric.' She bought me six one-half-yard pieces and wrapped them up. They meant so much to me; I kept them in a box and took them out to enjoy. However, it wasn't until I graduated from art college in 1970 that I realized I could use fabric in my art instead of the 'approved' media."

Mangat's *Deer Dancers of San Ildefonso Pueblo* is an embellished quilt that records her interpretation of a historic event. While visiting in Santa Fe, she was taken to San Ildefonso Pueblo to watch the Deer Dance.

> Traditionally the dance takes place at the first light of dawn. I could appreciate the impact that daybreak would have. The dancers come down off the top of the hill outside the pueblo and into the square, while the sky changes color every few seconds. The deer costumes have been passed from generation to generation, and consist of hand-crocheted leggings, which I depict with my grandma's old lace; handwoven skirts; headdresses of antlers, sticks, and evergreens; and more sticks for leg extensions, decorated with feathers and bells. The faces are blackened and each dancer wears a shell bracelet on one arm and a black band on the other [fig. 97].

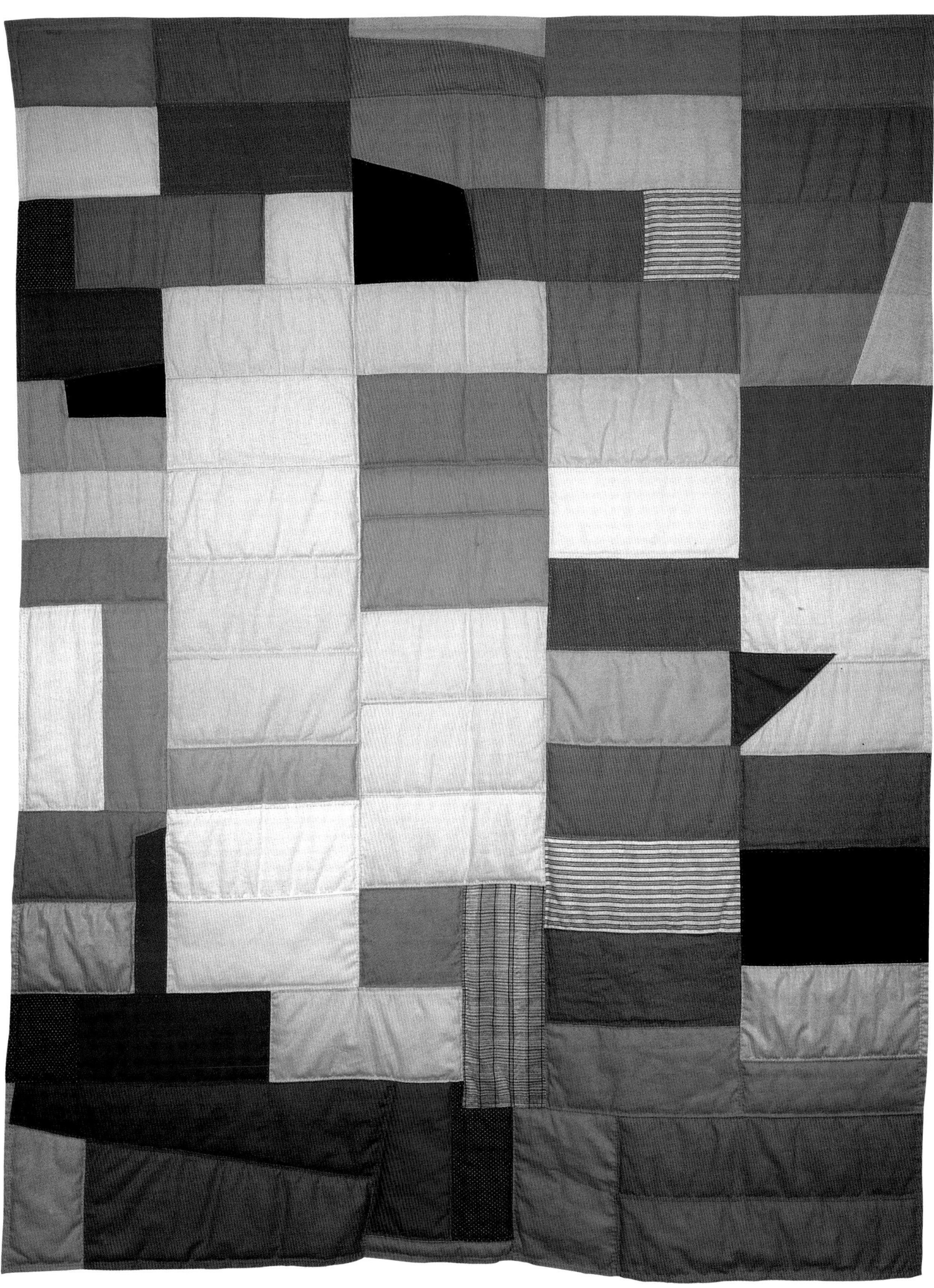

96. Mary Woodard Davis, *Taos Quilt,* 1984. Cotton, 42 x 54½″. Collection Laurel Reuter, Grand Forks, North Dakota.

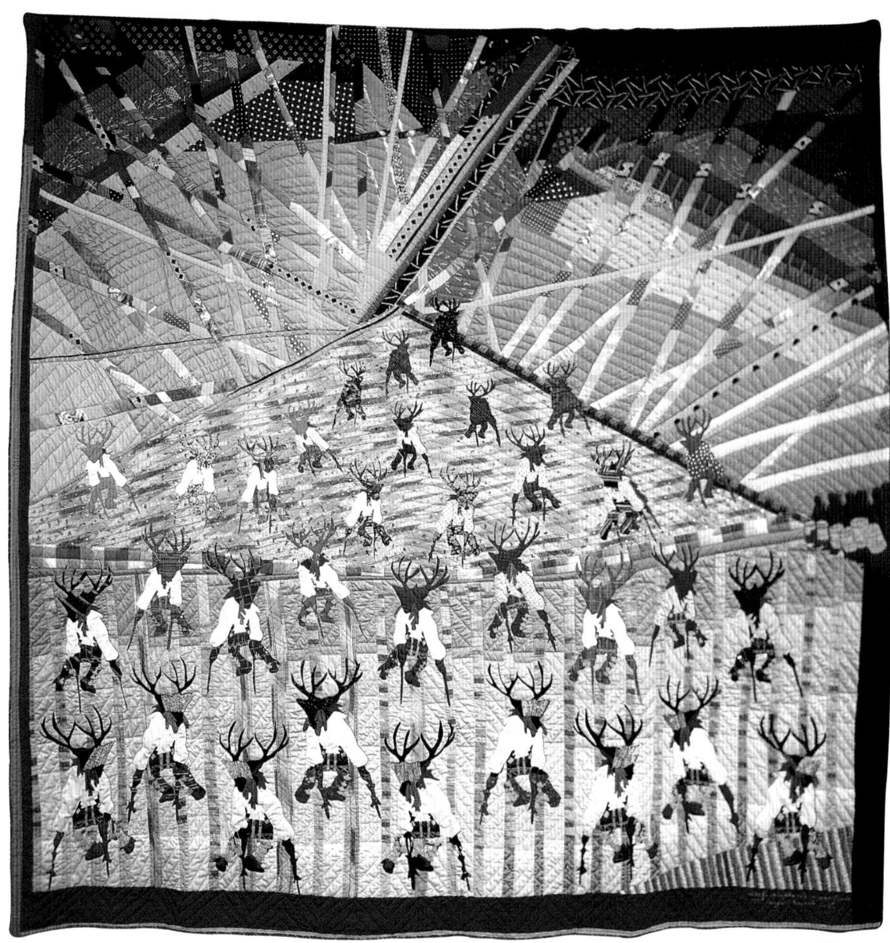

97. Terrie Mangat, *Deer Dancers of San Ildefonso Pueblo*, 1983. Quilt with embellishment, 105 x 105″.

Patterns appear and reappear in the lives of these women who use cloth to make art. Faith Ringgold, a quilt maker of the generation between Mangat and Davis, had a mother, Willie Posey, who, trained at the Fashion Institute of Technology in New York as a dress designer, "was always sewing." Ringgold says about her own art, "If I'd been left alone, I'd have done my own kind of thing based on sewing. As it was, it wasn't until the women's movement that I got the go-ahead to do that kind of work."

Ringgold is a politically active African-American artist who has spent the last thirty years making paintings, murals, soft sculptures, and performances that consider the lives of her family and community in New York's Harlem, where Ringgold was born and continues to live. Her work celebrates both being a woman and being African American.

She began as a conventional painter, but turned to soft sculpture because "it satisfied a tactile and spiritual need to work in textiles and to create tapestries, masks, and puppets similar to the objects women in primitive societies traditionally made." The switch to cloth came naturally to her because of her long relationship with sewing through her mother.

In 1970 she began collaborating on quilts with her mother. Later she moved from sewn quilts to quilts that she painted on. Ringgold has taken a gentle, traditional women's art form—quilting—and infused it with the vigor and spirit of a fabulous storyteller, for she quickly discovered that wall-hung quilts were perfect vehicles for telling stories. *The Wedding: Lover's Quilt #1* is characteristic of her printed, tie-dyed, and pieced fabric quilts. As in much of her work, one is struck by an immediate sense of cloth. *Lover's Quilt #1* is the first of a trilogy of large-

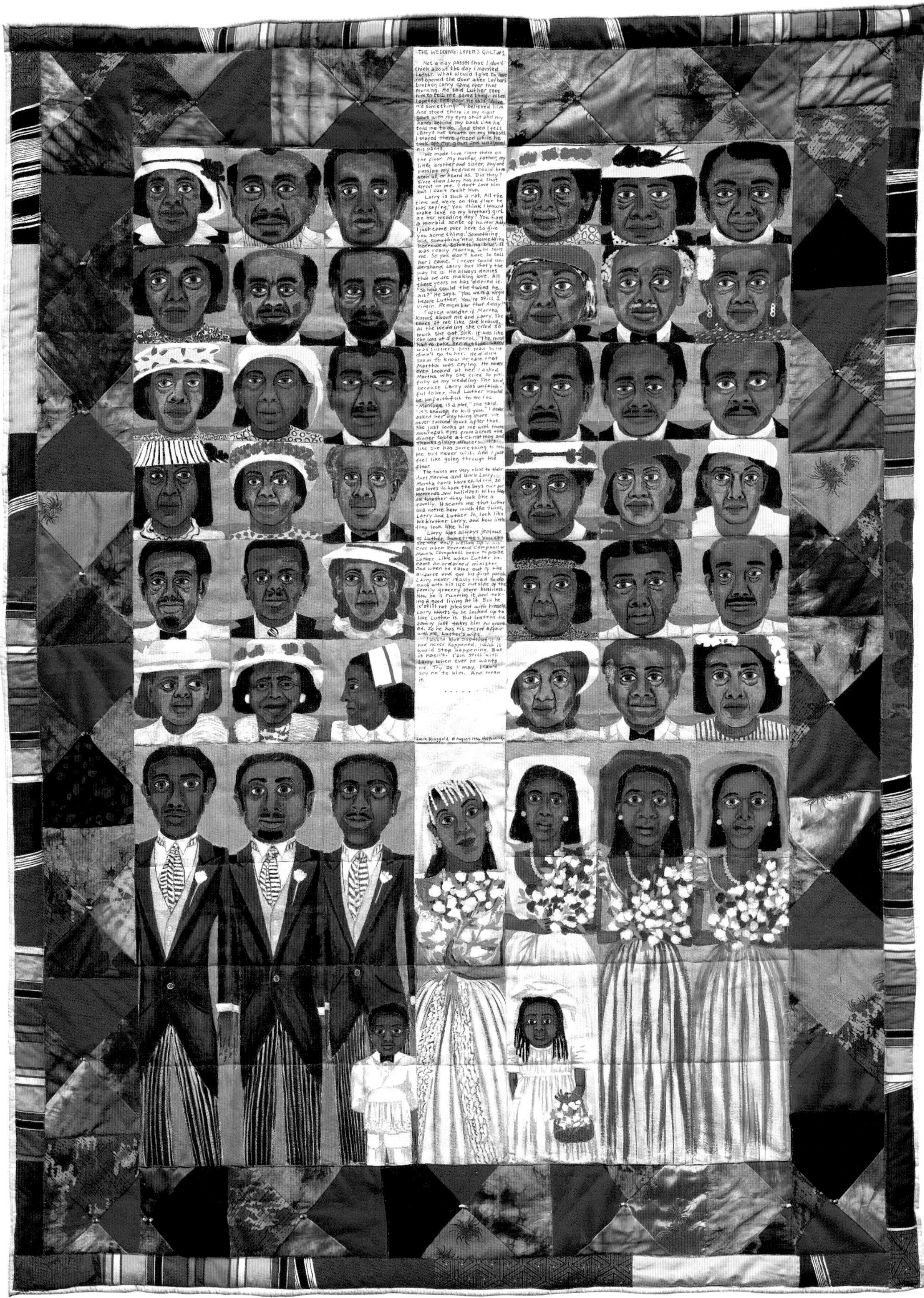

98. Faith Ringgold, *The Wedding: Lover's Quilt #1,* 1986. Acrylic on cotton canvas, tie-dyed, printed, and pieced fabric, 77½ x 58″. Courtesy Bernice Steinbaum Gallery, New York.

scale narrative quilts bound together by a continuous story told by Addy, the wife in the plot. The poignant tale, recalled in both words and images, is one of infidelity, of betrayal that is not unique to African-American experience but part of all experience (fig. 98).

There is an exuberance in Ringgold's quilts, a vitality that is not often found in quilts from the dominant American, white culture. One might speculate that Ringgold's work, like that of other African-American women artists, can be traced back to the appliqué work of the Congo, part of a long tradition of West African textiles. Maude Southwell Wahlman and Ellen King Torre point out that "quilts were produced by black women for utilitarian and decorative purposes in both white and black households. Quilts made for whites are hardly distinguishable from traditional Anglo-American ones. However, those quilts made for the personal use by blacks were designed and stitched in the African tradition."[2] Vertical stripes dominate, most often arranged to create large symmetrical and asymmetrical patterns. Robert Farris Thompson was the first to link the predilection of African-American quilters for color intensity to African origins, noting that African-American quilts display "high-affect" colors, in contrast to the pastel hues favored in Anglo-American quilts. While New Englanders preferred symmetry in their design, the preference among blacks was for asymmetry.[3] Romare Bearden's *Patchwork Quilt* collage, discussed at the beginning of this chapter, illustrates the same predilection.

Mary Woodard Davis, Faith Ringgold, and Terrie Mangat have made art from traditional quilt forms. Three additional artists illustrate the far-ranging influence of quilting on the greater art world. David Norstad cuts, pastes, and sews "rags" into charming pictures that straddle both old and new ways of looking at space. Trained as a painter, he works in cloth with a folk artist's sensibility. His *Airing Out* captures a moment in the lives of an old rural couple, the moment just as the wind is about to whisk their quilt away. Yet his sophisticated color sense, his skill at achieving wit by cutting, and his rich embellishment mark him as an artist in full control of his medium. These rag pictures hark back to exuberant storytelling quilts of an earlier time (fig. 99).

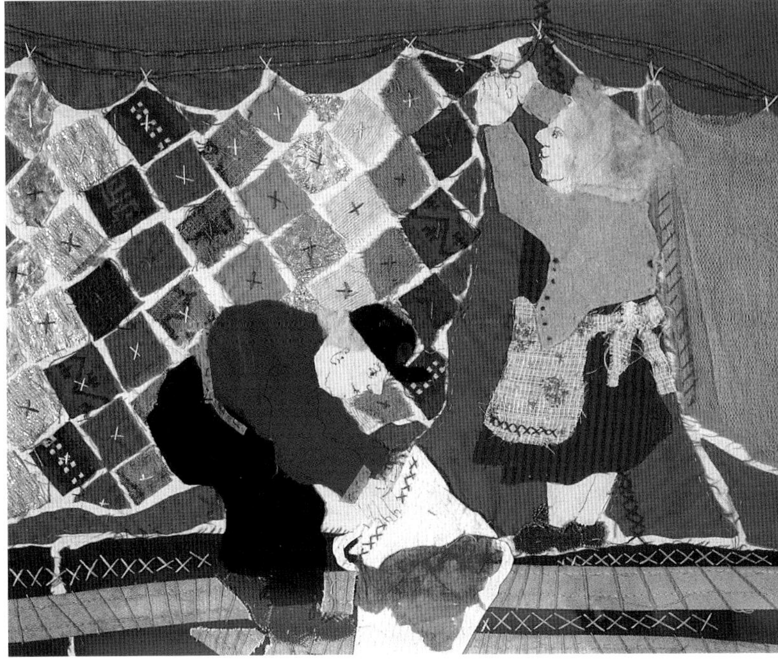

99. David Norstad, *Airing Out,* 1986. Fabric collage, 16 x 21". Collection William Goodall, Burns, Minnesota.

To be witty and charming a work need not be small in either scale or concept. Fifteen years ago Nek Chand began to build a rock garden in Le Corbusier's model city of Chandigarh, India. For years he worked secretly behind walls, afraid that the authorities would disapprove. Upon discovering the garden in 1972 the officials were not happy but finally agreed to let him stay and even gave him additional land and workers so he could continue. Chand was creating a fantasy world of recycled junk, acres and acres covered with over twenty thousand figures. Limiting himself to no particular scale, he made some figures larger than life, others only a foot high. He reused anything he could lay his hands upon, dressing his figures in the most wondrous of cloth fragments, making brightly colored patchworks because patches were what he found. These three-dimensional works of bits and pieces are full of humor and irony. They are conventional only in that they are put together with thread and needle.

Chand recently completed his first permanent installation outside of India. As part of the Festival of India he was invited to the United States to build an installation in the entrance to

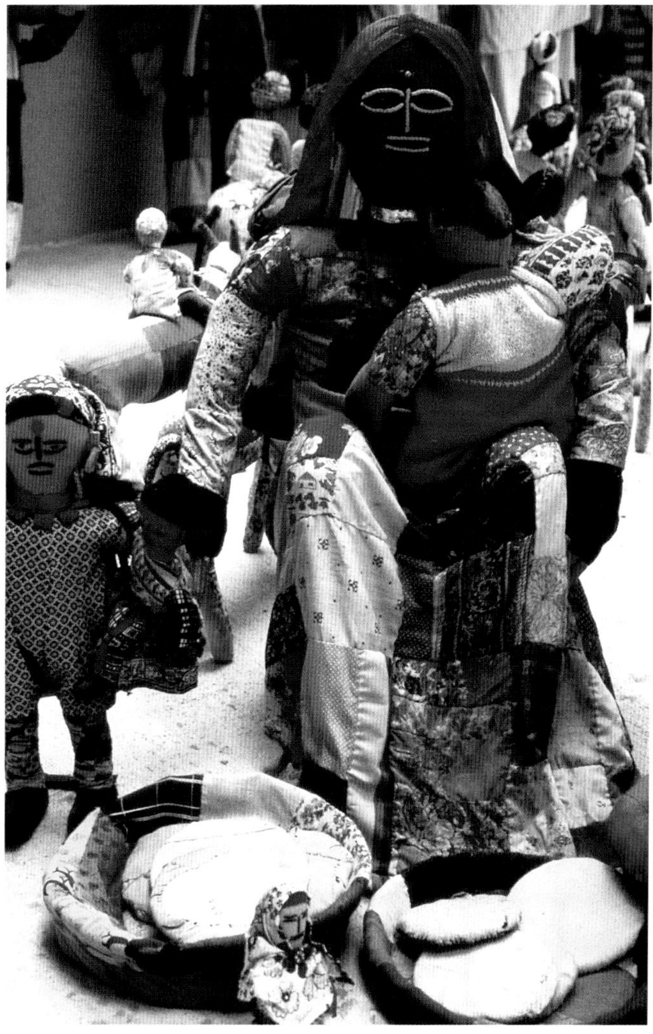

100. Nek Chand, *Fantasy Garden* (detail), 1985. Wrapping, pieced cloth, cast-off clothing.

the Capital Children's Museum in Washington, D.C., which opened on October 5, 1985. Here one can see bits and pieces of cloth handled with the same verve and skill that the legendary visionary artist Simon Rodia brought to fragments of crockery, glass, and tile in the building of his Watts Towers in Los Angeles (fig. 100).

Finally, Maggie S. Potter creates a modern rendition of an ancient friendship quilt, proving once again that the original content of the material assumes a second or overlying meaning as it is joined with other pieces. For instance, at one time Buddhist priests in Japan were supposed to dress in rags as a sign of humility. Many chose merely to affect humility and wore robes pieced together from forty-eight silken squares. Maggie Potter, a young American leading a vagabond life, decided that she had lost touch with too many of her friends and family members during her university years. She contacted everyone and had each send her labels for her garment *Label Jacket.* This friendship jacket is a near relative to the friendship quilts of her grandmother's generation. Through the sewing of the labels she reestablished contact with important people in her life. She was also able to read from the labels something of the paths traveled by the out-of-touch people during the intervening years. Thus the Buddhist robe and Potter's jacket resemble each other in that neither are what they seem; both carry the original context of the patches into the final work (fig. 101). The friendship quilt has reached its zenith in the AIDS Quilt, for which thousands of blocks have been created to honor those who have died of AIDS (see fig. 57).

Quilts and works of art made from bits and pieces seem synonymous. Yet seminal artists identified with the Art Fabric movement have drawn brilliantly from other historic textile forms. The great traditions are neither buried nor rejected, for they are the starting point for revolutionary contemporary work. Ed Rossbach, the dean, the mentor, the sage of the American fiber movement, is a scholar of the first order and a masterful teacher. From 1950 to 1989 he taught at the University of California, Berkeley, where he became recognized as a fearless innovator, always questing and questioning. He explains his tie to the past: "Research has been central to all my work for thirty years. I hope no one asks me what research means because there is a wide spectrum of interpretation today. For me it was reading, reconstruction, experimentation to achieve results I wanted. Some people don't want to be inhibited by what was done before they were born. They reject the past. They forget that technology builds on technology and art builds on art."[4]

Rossbach also believes that no matter how ancient the tradition, the artist must interpret it through his or her own time and materials. Therefore Rossbach long ago forsook precious materials for synthetics and junk, preferring the nonprecious, easily available "stuff" of his own time. *Montana Poncho* is a fine example of a work created from this point of view. In this flat collage of newspaper on canvas Rossbach has joined the unlike together, and "from the difference results the most beautiful harmony," in the words of Heraclitus. The resulting elegance belies the commonness of the materials. The stylized

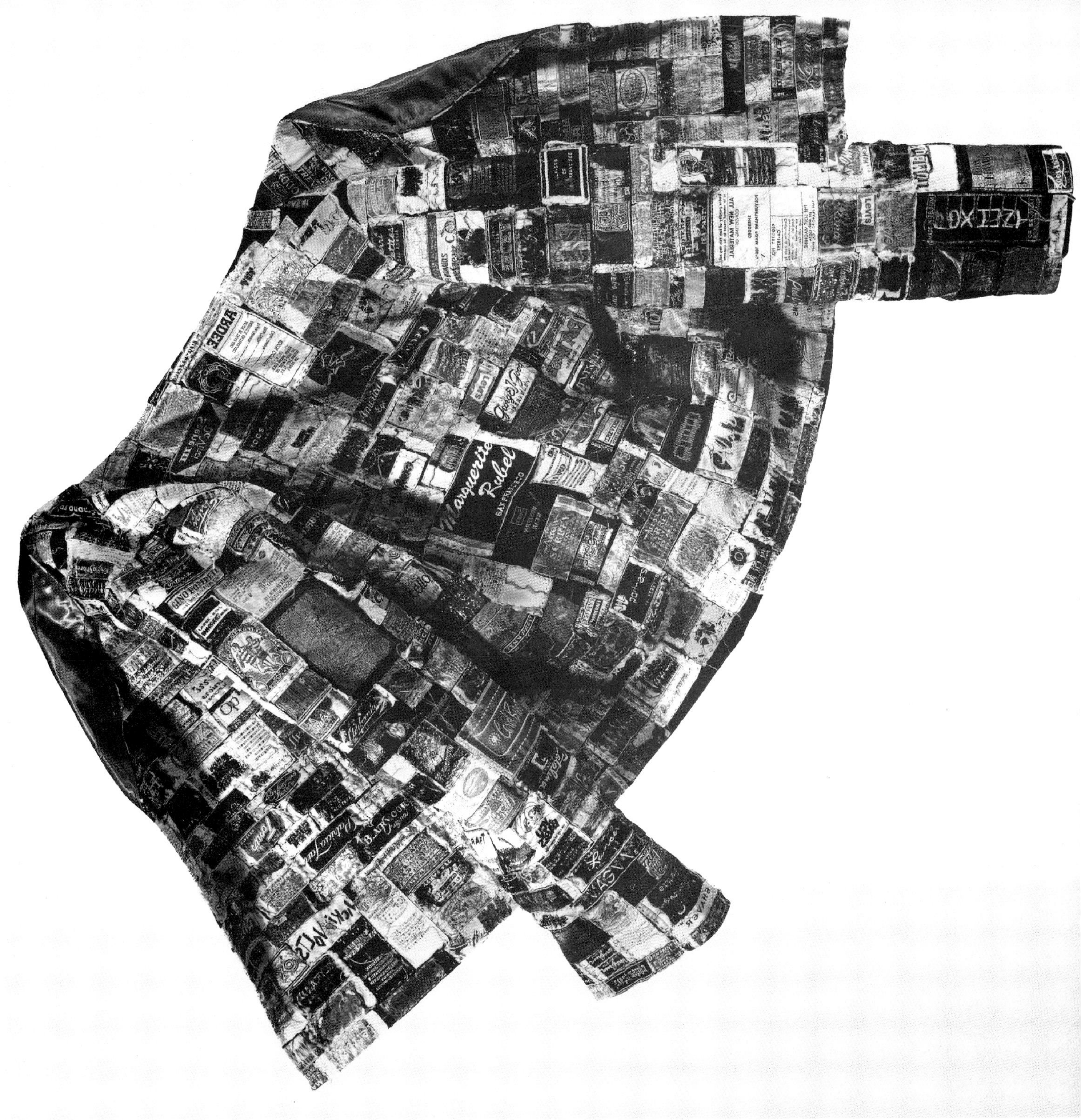


101. Maggie S. Potter, *Label Jacket,* 1978. Garment labels, patched and hand stitched, with machine- and hand-stitched synthetic fabric lining.

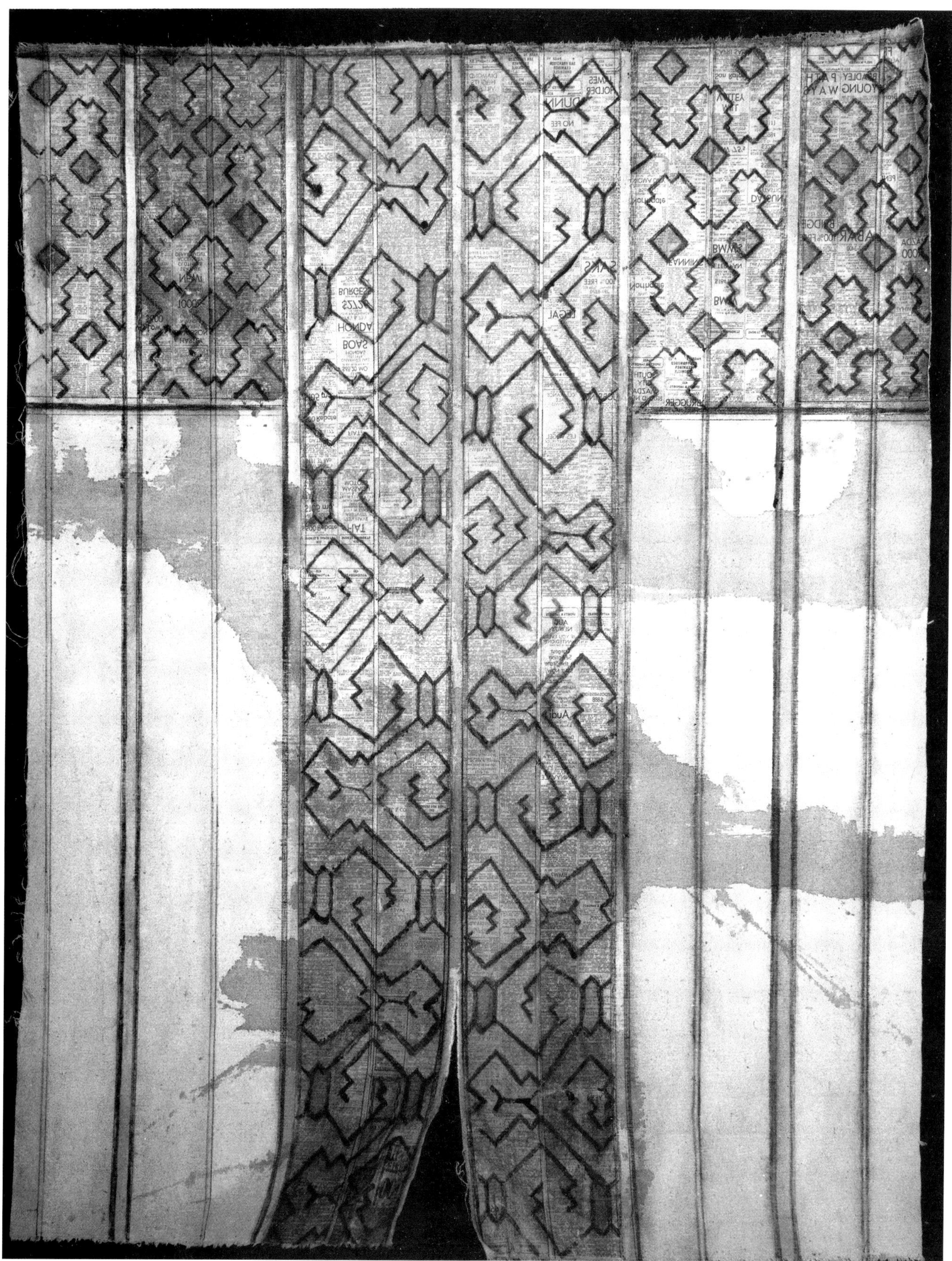

102. Ed Rossbach, *Montana Poncho*, 1975. Canvas, newspaper, 48 x 37″.

imagery is keenly counterpointed by the stripped references to a traditional, formal poncho (fig. 102).

In contrast to Rossbach's newsprint, Nancy Hemenway makes her collages of fine materials and traditional embroidery stitches. It is the scale of her work, and her reliance upon purely abstract forms, that gives power to her "bayatages," a word Hemenway coined to describe her collages of fiber and embroidery. The word is derived from the Spanish word *bayeta*—a densely packed, thick cloth—and from *collage.*

Not a weaver, Hemenway instead has collected handwoven and handspun wools—rare alpacas, delicate mohair, exquisite gossamer organdies, karakul, and choice yarns from many countries. Using full yardage, including the selvages, headings, and end fringes, she appliqués one cloth onto another. Layering, folding, and tucking techniques provide her with a path away from the flat, rectangular format so often associated with embroidery. Often the masses of cloth produce surprising, three-dimensional abstract shapes. Her skillful needlework goes far beyond the need for securing the fabric to its background. She draws with her embroidery needle in the same natural colors of her fabrics. Although each one of her embroidery stitches can be identified as belonging to a rich tradition, centuries old, she adapts them with great daring on a magnified scale (fig. 103).

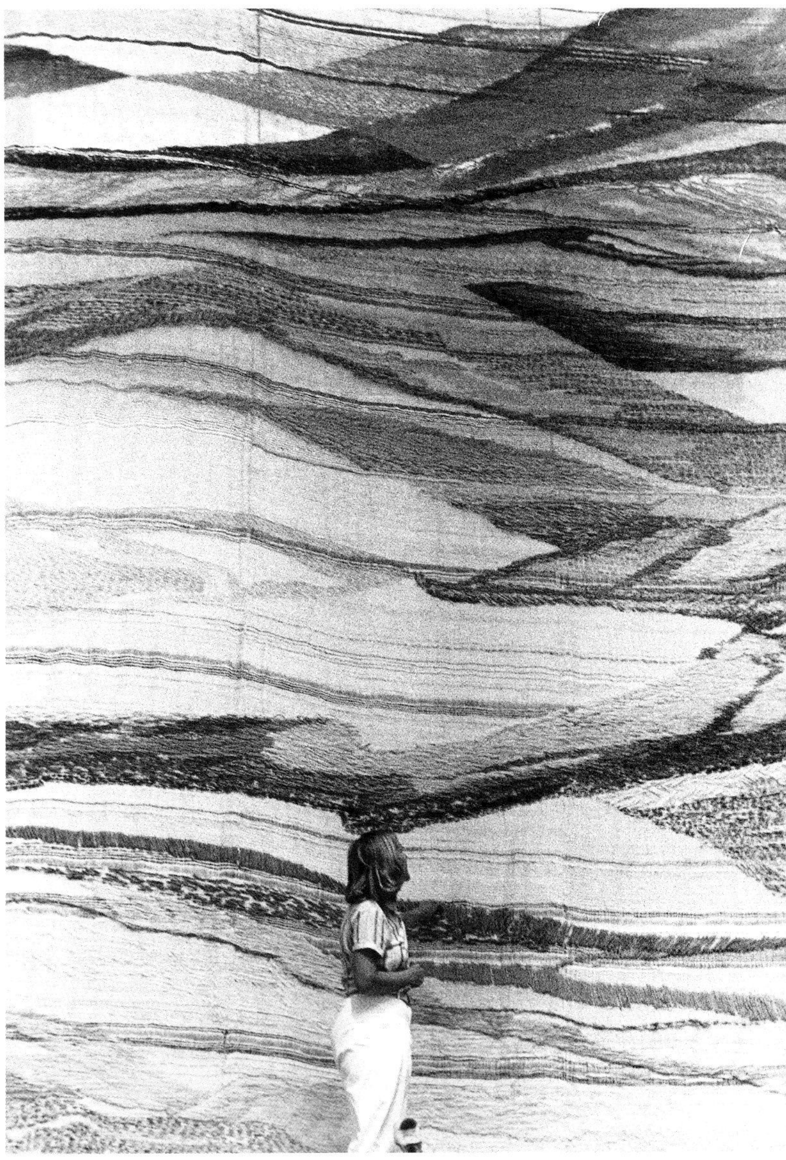

103. Nancy Hemenway with *Salt Shadow.* Studio installation, hand-embroidered mohair, karakul, alpaca, and lamb's wool on hand-spun mohair, 21′6″ x 18′4″.

James Bassler, a professor of fiber arts at the University of California, Los Angeles, is, like Ed Rossbach, known for his knowledge and love of historical textiles. Also like Rossbach he has sought to continue those traditions into twentieth-century art. Unlike most of the works in this book, he has not used mill cloth for his masterful work *Ribbed Shield.* Instead he wove his cloth in long, slender strips by a wedge weave technique, having first painted the warp. Only then did he treat it in the manner of mill cloth. After cutting his weaving into scraps, he reassembled the facets in a seemingly random fashion. The final work resembles a shield from an earlier Indian culture, or a nineteenth-century parfleche of an American Northern Plains tribe. As such, this contemporary wall piece, fragmented and stained, pays homage to all of those weavers of earlier times whose work is beloved by Bassler (fig. 104).

What finally makes the Bassler work so successful? The seemingly sumptuous surface that does not call attention to itself? The offhand, casual way that this highly structured work

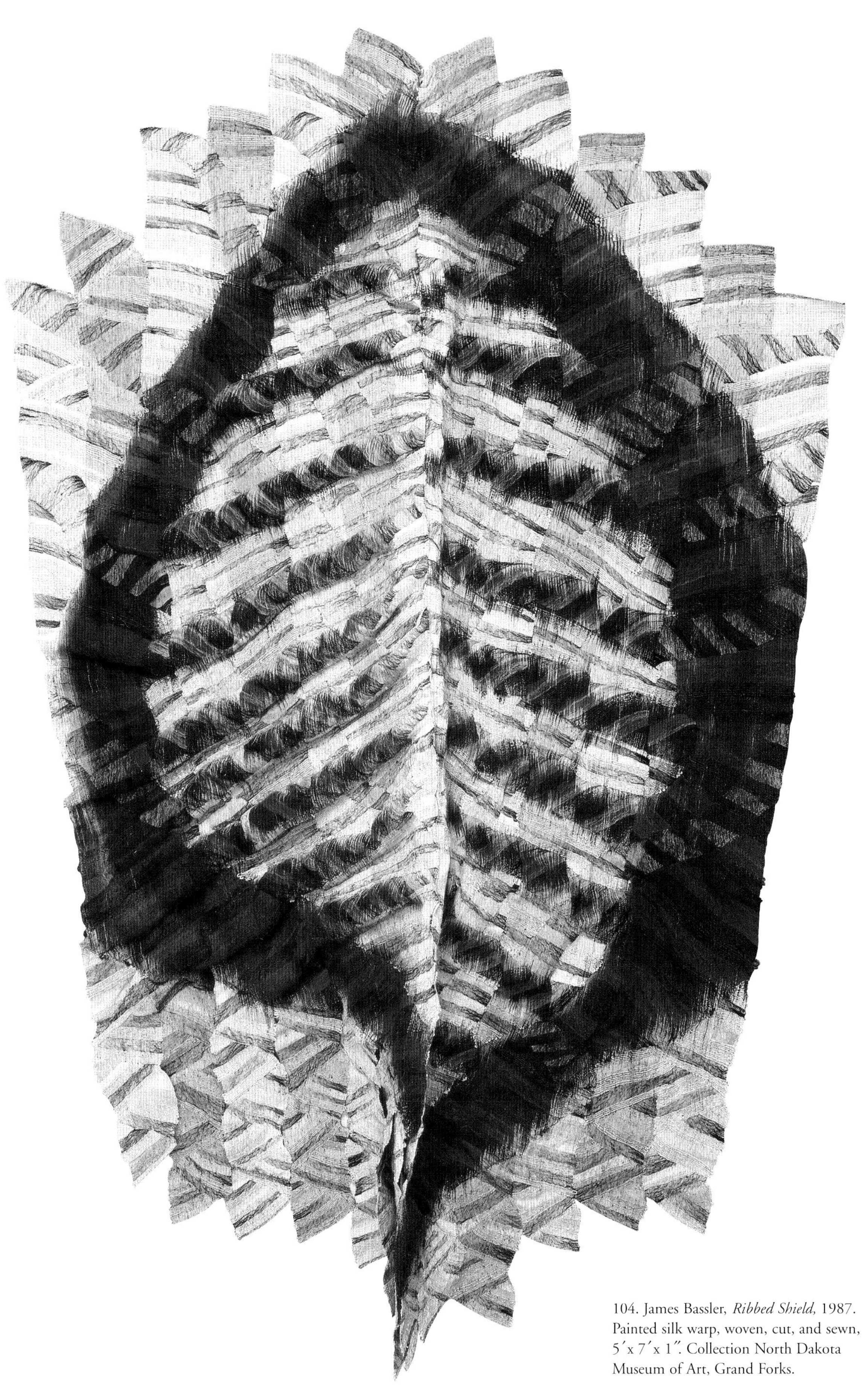

104. James Bassler, *Ribbed Shield,* 1987. Painted silk warp, woven, cut, and sewn, 5′x 7′x 1″. Collection North Dakota Museum of Art, Grand Forks.

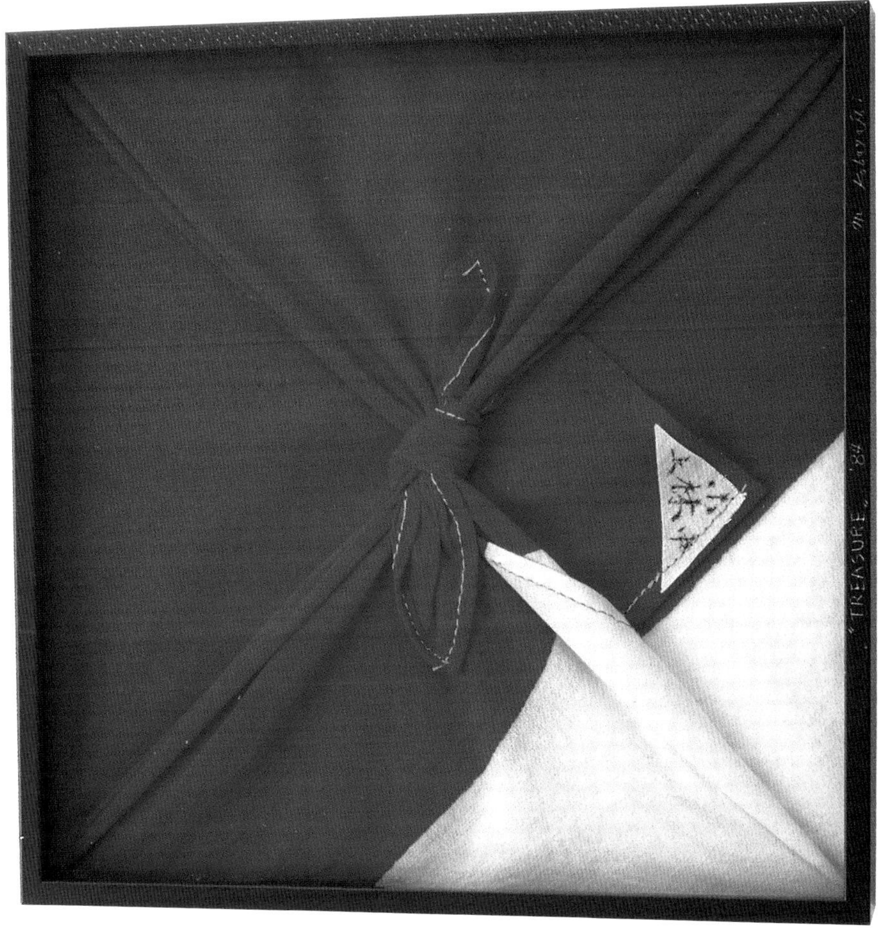


105. Masakazu Kobayashi, *Treasure*, 1984. Cotton, 8¾ x 8¾″. Collection Cleveland Museum of Art, gift of Mildred Constantine.

is put together? The strength of the overall image? How it graces the space it occupies? Or finally, could it be that by daring to cut the precious woven cloth into scraps Bassler has demolished its preciousness, reduced it as a textile, thus allowing the final work of art to transcend both material and technique?

Finally, in considering works of art made from bits and pieces, one is struck by the way the medium encourages artists both to be literal and to make sociological observations in a surprisingly witty way. For example, Masakazu Kobayashi is an established figure in the Japanese art world. His work is monumental, formal and elegant, and it appears in many important collections. Yet, in a small untitled collage he has created a marvelous takeoff on the *furoshiki*—the cloth used to wrap bundles in Japan. Simple in both color and composition, the work is held together literally and visually by a knot, tied dead center. On the underside of the wrapping, where one would usually find a label, the artist has placed his signature and turned it to the outside for the viewer to read. This playful offhanded work was created only to delight (fig. 105).

César's work *Jean* is created in exactly the same light spirit. He has simply compressed jeans, the symbol of youthful ideas and youthful rebellion in the late 1960s and early 1970s, into an almost unrecognizable mush. By crushing them into a pattern he has transformed them from a social statement into a work of art, just as the affluent of the next decade, with their

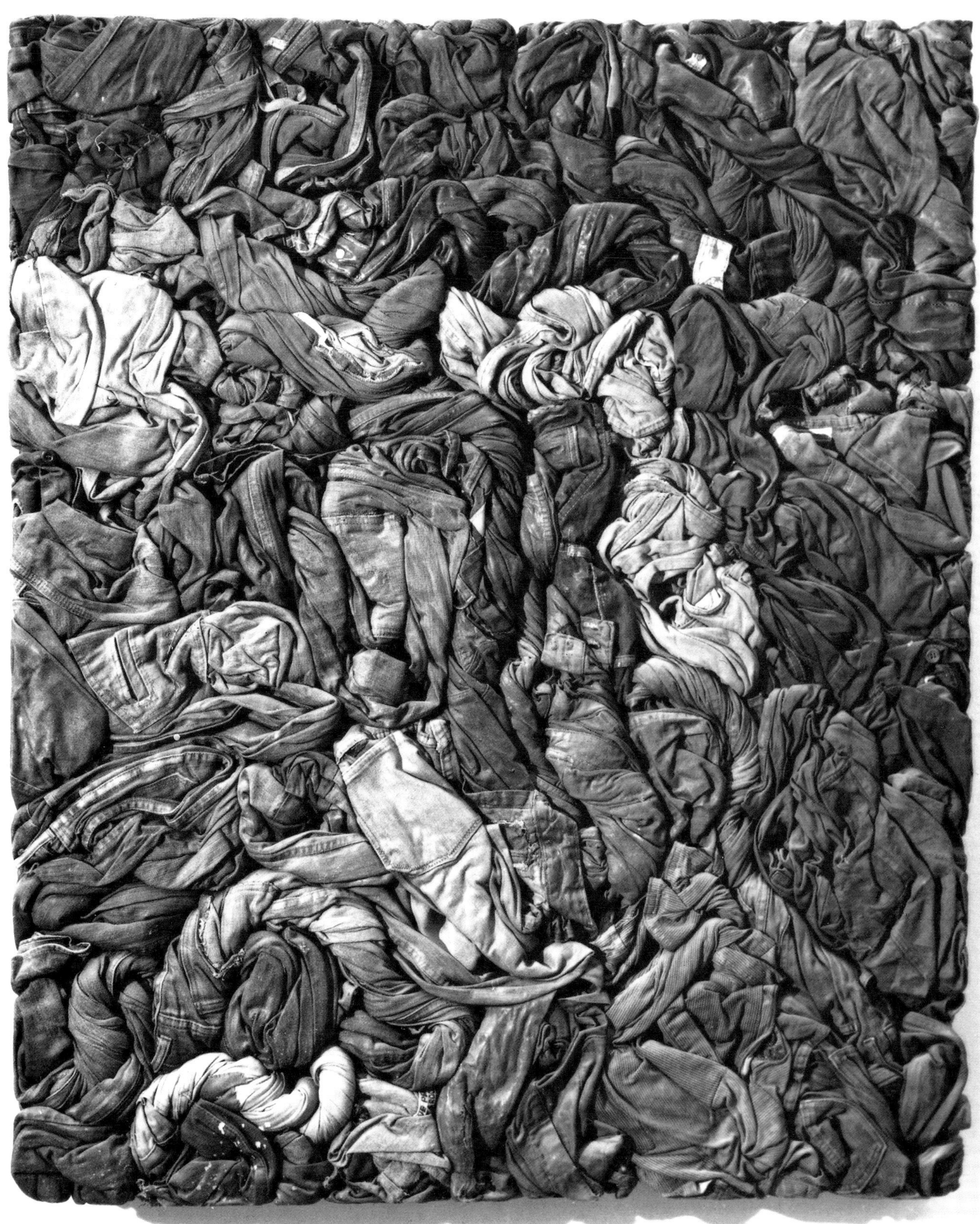

106. César (Baldaccini), *Jean*, 1975. Compressed cotton, 120 x 100 x 14″.

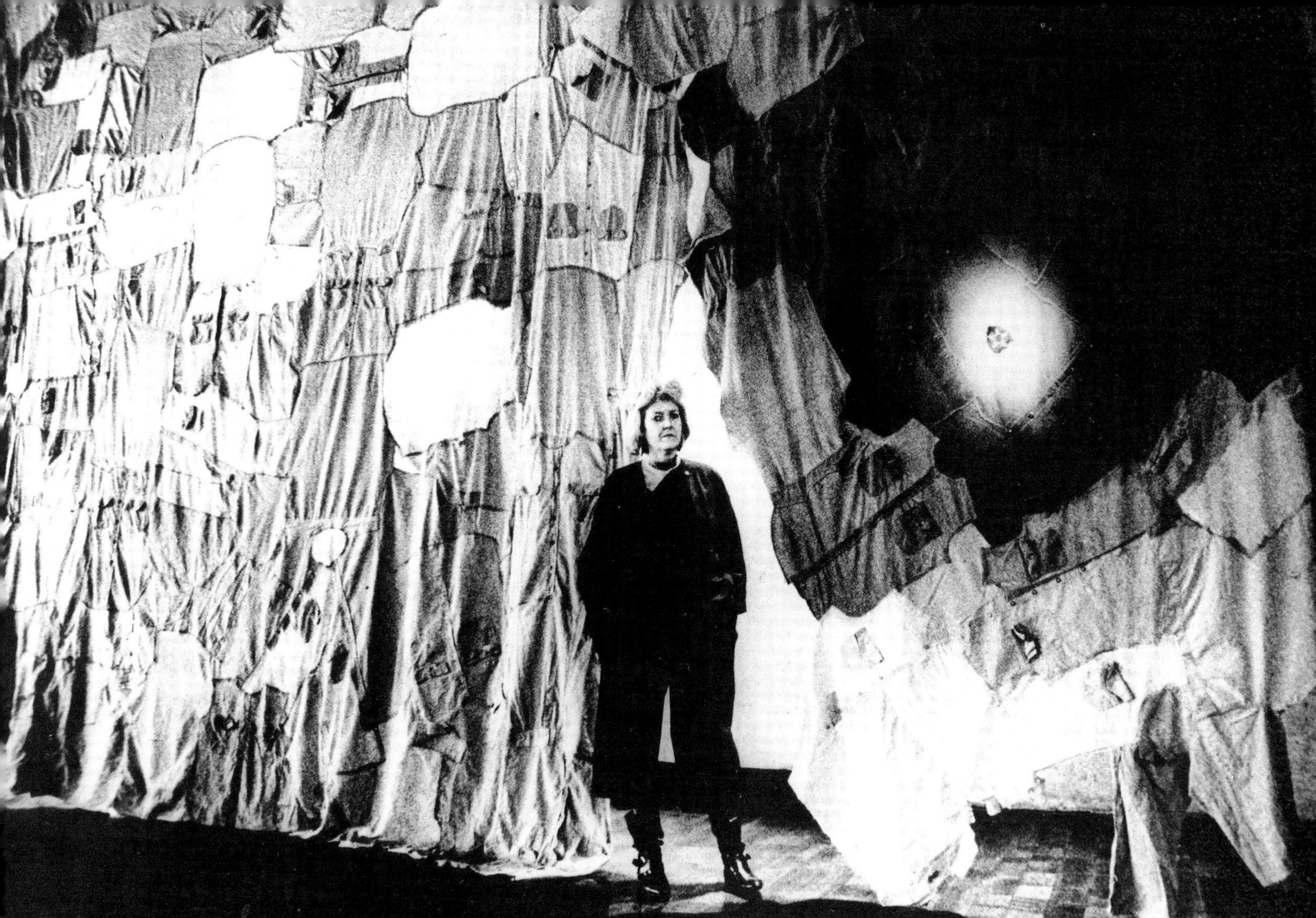

107. Sheila Hicks with *Khaki Uniforms Immobilized (United States, Europe, and Middle East),* 1985–86. Cotton army shirts, 252 x 252″. Installed at the Milwaukee Art Museum, Wisconsin.

designer jeans, would transform the symbol of rebellion into expensive, chic, fashionable dress. César could not have known that when he made the piece in 1975; he was only paying homage to the then-present power of jeans (fig. 106).

Both Kobayashi and César brought the original context of the cloth into their works of art. This is pointedly the object of Sheila Hicks's *Khaki Uniforms Immobilized (United States, Europe, and Middle East.)* For this twenty-one-foot-square room collage, she collected an array of army shirts and presented them as a protest of war. Like her installation in Montreuil, France (see fig. 169), this work demonstrates her interests in the use of recycled materials and in considering social issues through her art (fig. 107). Finally, collage in fabric has given artists of the twentieth century a fragmented means of dealing with a fragmented world. Somewhere down the tables of time in the recording of art history, the making of art with bits and pieces may become an important marker of the art of this century.

1. Patricia Mainardi, "Quilts: The Great American Art Form," *Feminist Art Journal* 2, no. 1 (winter 1973): 18–23.

2. Maude Southwell Wahlman and Ellen King Torre, "The Art of Afro-American Quiltmaking: Origin, Development and Significance" (Ph.D. diss., Yale University, 1980).

3. Robert Farris Thompson, lectures, Yale University, 1977–80.

4. Virginia West, "Ed Rossbach: Embracing the Fabric of Art," *Fiberarts* 9, no. 1 (Jan.–Feb.): 31–33.

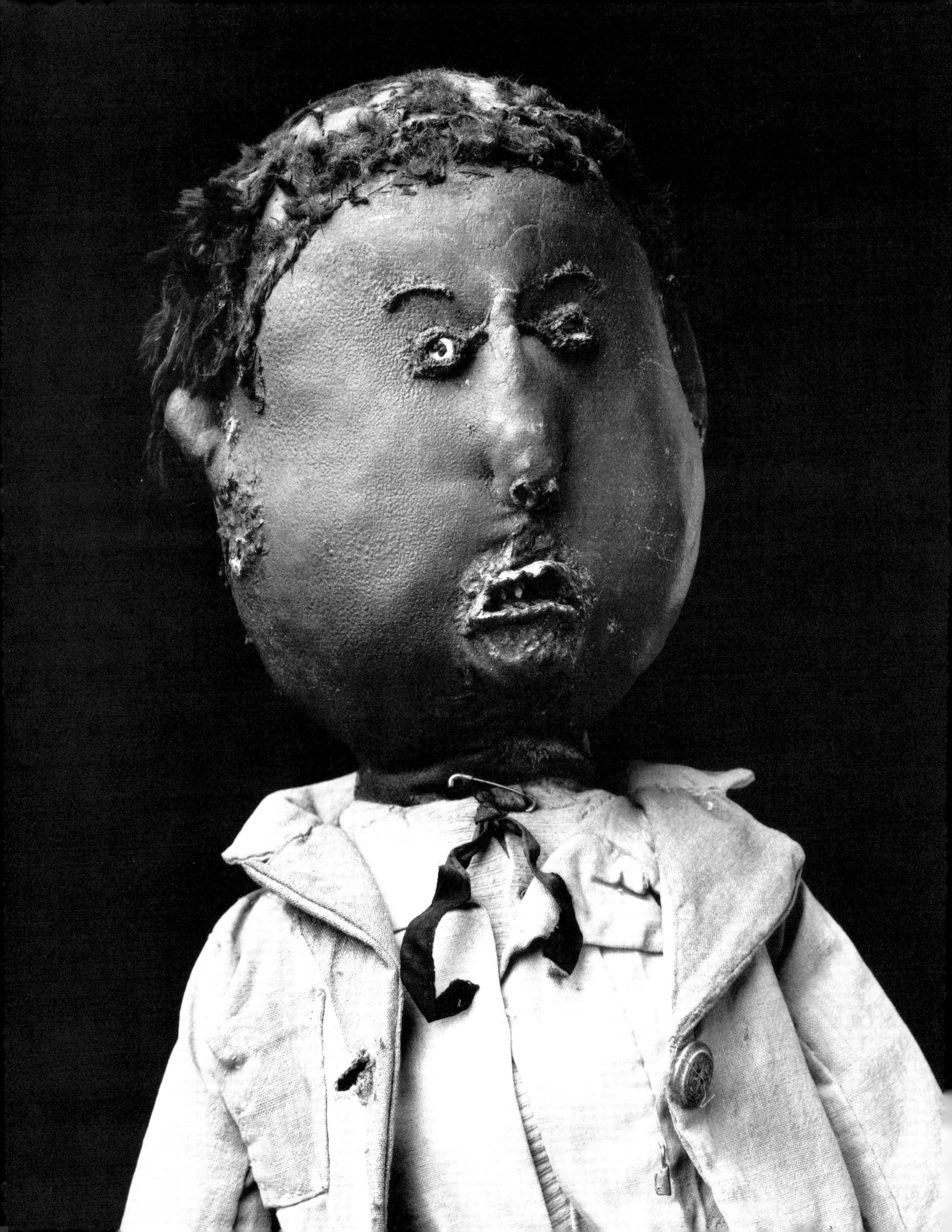

# Sculpted Forms

to scatter
to arrange
to repair
to discard
to pair
to distribute
to surfeit
to complement
to enclose
to surround
to encircle
to hide
to cover
to wrap
to dig
to tie
to bind
to weave
to join
to match
to laminate
to bond
to hinge
to mark
to expand
to dilute
to light

to roll
to crease
to fold
to store
to bend
to shorten
to twist
to dapple
to crumple
to shave
to tear
to chip
to split
to cut
to sever
to drop
to remove
to simplify
to differ
to disarrange
to open
to mix
to splash
to knot
to spill
to droop
to flow

to modulate
to distill
of waves
of electromagnetic
of inertia
of ionization
of polarization
of refraction
of simultaneity
of tides
of reflection
of equilibrium
of symmetry
of friction
to stretch
to bounce
to erase
to spray
to systematize
to refer
to force
of mapping
of location
of context
of time
of carbonization
to continue

to curve
to lift
to inlay
to impress
to fire
to flood
to smear
to rotate
to swirl
to support
to hook
to suspend
to spread
to hang
to collect
of tension
of gravity
of entropy
of nature
of grouping
of layering
of felting
to grasp
to tighten
to bundle
to heap
to gather

Richard Serra

108 *(opposite).* Unknown (Alabama), *Black Doll,* 1950s. Stitched and stuffed cloth, shell, bone, china paint, 38 x 13 x 7″. Collection Michael Hall, Bloomfield Hills, Michigan. Courtesy Contemporary Arts Center, Cincinnati, Ohio.

Sculpture has changed more dramatically in the twentieth century than at any other time in history. Furthermore, more than any other art form in the twentieth century, sculpture has changed in its techniques, its materials, and its concerns. Richard Serra's 1968 handwritten list of what sculptors do shows just how radically sculpture had evolved in the course of seventy years. For centuries, sculpture meant carving in stone. Casting in bronze, brass, or gold or carving in wood were almost the only alternatives.

Auguste Rodin is credited with pushing sculpture into the revolutionary twentieth century by toppling conventional statuary.[1] Picasso followed by dissecting Cubist space, and later by creating his collage sculptures, or assemblages. The Constructivists declared that "in constructive sculpture, space is not a part of the universal space surrounding the object; it is a material by itself, a structural part of the object—so much so that it has the faculty of conveying a volume as does any other rigid material."[2]

When the Dadaists began to make art from perishable materials they introduced time as an essential element of sculpture. This was reinforced by the Surrealists, with their shifting, curving, disparate images. It was a short step from using interpenetrating rather than displaceable spaces and shifting time to using cloth for making sculpture. Cloth, more than most materials, is transformable; it is fluid; and although it is temporary, it can also be made permanent. (Cloth, which is destroyed quickly when exposed to the elements, can be made rigid and permanent by chemical coatings.) Cloth transmutes light and it blocks light. Cloth

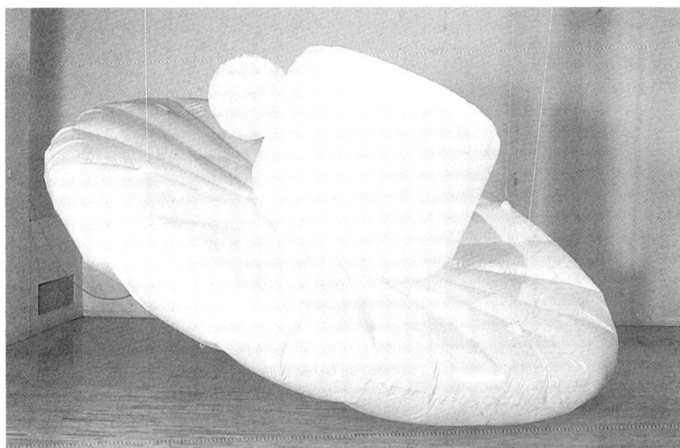

109. Claes Oldenburg and Coosje van Bruggen, *Expresso Cup Balloon*, 1986. Plastic, 75 x 15″. Props from *Il Corso del Coltello*, San Marco, Italy, 1985. Courtesy Leo Castelli Gallery, New York.

extends space further and with greater ease than any other material, which was to be aptly demonstrated by Christo in the years to follow. Sculptors quickly discovered the advantages of cheap factory cloth.

The 1913 Armory Show in New York introduced these radical ideas to American sculptors. Since they had no strong sculptural tradition of their own, they were primed to continue the revolution begun in Europe. They brought to it their own experiences as workers in the great industrial revolution, for American sculptors sprang from the common man. To support themselves as artists they became carpenters, welders, and mechanics. They handled heavy equipment and worked the assembly lines. Years later Meyer Schapiro marveled at what he observed: "Most astonishing of all were the open sculptures of metal without pedestals or frame, pure constructions like industrial objects, suspended from wall or ceiling; these first appeared shortly after the Armory Show and have transformed the character of sculpture in our time."[3] David Smith was the leading practitioner.

The materials and tools of industry did not rule alone. Ideas continued to emerge from every quarter. At the turn of the century Rodin had insisted that the whole of art history was his to mine. Picasso claimed African sculpture as part of his visual heritage. Sculptors discovered the primitive at about the same moment they discovered steel. The history of art shows that primitive cultures always prized soft, organic materials such as feathers, wool, bark, leaves, skins, hair, leather, and cloth—materials that helped to transmit the object's message. Folk artists around the world continue this tradition in the twentieth century (fig. 108). Magdalena Abakanowicz, the Polish sculptor whose work dominated the Lausanne Biennale during the 1960s and 1970s, wrote of her then revolutionary use of fiber:

> I see fiber as the basic element constructing the
> organic world on our planet,
> as the greatest mystery of our environment.
> It is from fiber that all living organisms are built—
> the tissues of plants, and ourselves.
> Our nerves, our genetic code,
> the canals of our veins, our muscles.
>
> We are fibrous structures.
> Our heart is surrounded by the coronary plexus,
> the plexus of most vital threads.
>
> Handling fiber, we handle mystery.
> A dry leaf has a network reminiscent of a dry mummy.
>
> What can become of fiber guided by the artist's hand and
> by his intuition?
>
> What is fabric?
> We weave it, sew it, we shape it into forms.
> When the biology of our body breaks down
> the skin has to be cut so as to give access to the inside.
> Later it has to be sewn, like fabric.
>
> Fabric is our covering and our attire. Made with our hands,
> it is a record of our souls.

Whereas Abakanowicz understood the intrinsic power of cloth, the Surrealists were closest to non-Western cultures in their expectations of materials. The Surrealists created art by endowing everyday objects with enchantment, sometimes perplexing, sometimes ironic. Marcel Duchamp conceived the readymade, "things" as mundane as a soft Underwood typewriter cover fixed to a stem (see fig. 23). Meret Oppenheim transformed a teacup and a spoon with a fur lining. The Surrealist influence continued subtly to affect artists for decades. Out of it grew the whole soft sculpture movement.

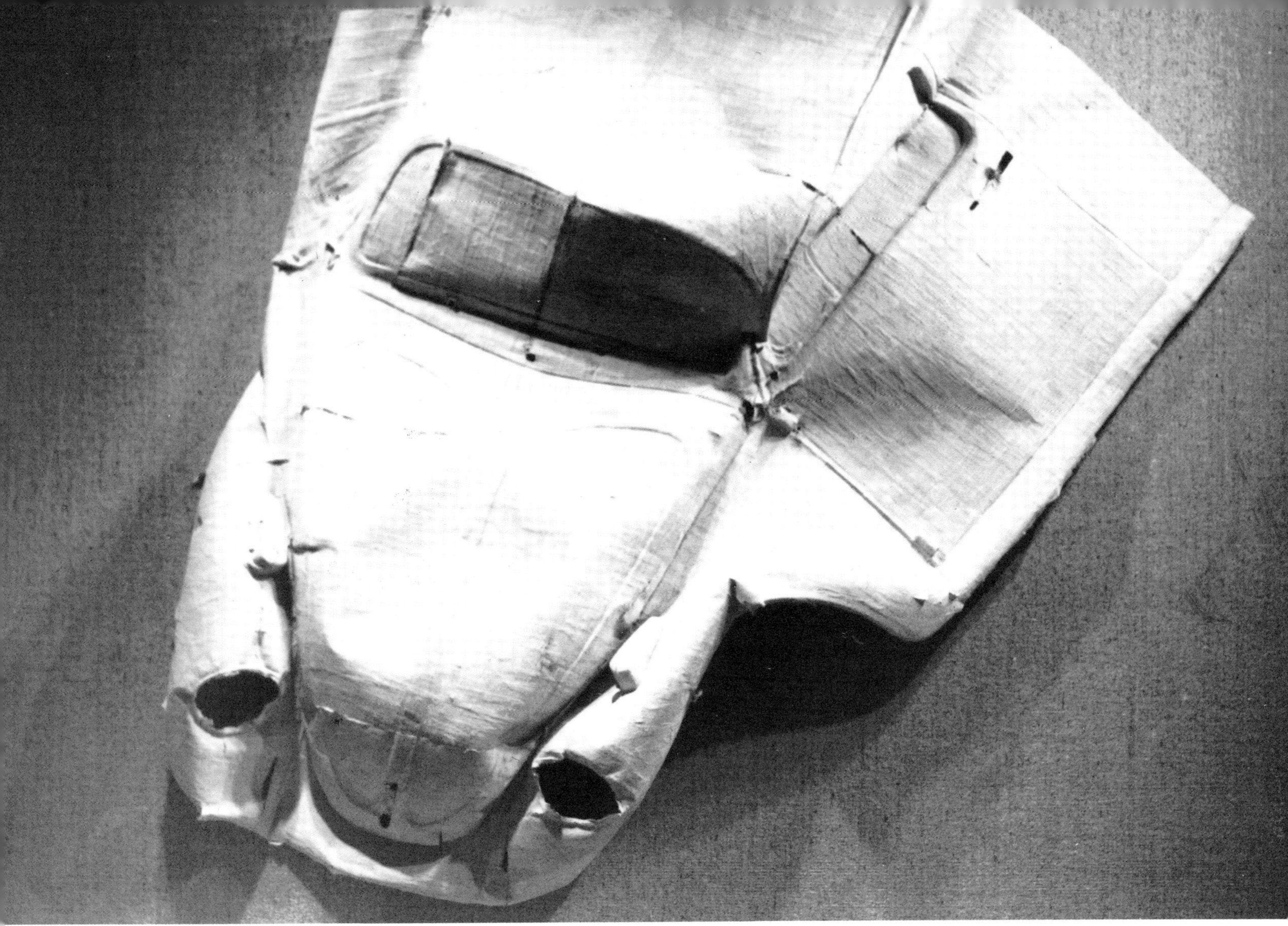

110. Badanna Zack, *Beetle Pelt #1*, 1981. Fabric, plaster, and glue, 9⅗ x 8 x 1′.

Its founder, Claes Oldenburg, made his first giant soft sculptures in 1962 for an exhibition at the Green Gallery in New York. These stuffed cloth sculptures, cut and sewn by his wife Pat, marked a new method and a new material for making sculpture. Although identified with Pop art, they paid homage to Oldenburg's Surrealist forefathers. In the years to follow he re-created numerous hard, everyday objects in soft materials: the fan, the telephone, the typewriter. In doing so he converted useful objects into gigantic parodies. For example, Oldenburg's *Expresso Cup Balloon* (1986), with Coosje van Bruggen, is a prop for *Il Corso del Coltello*, shown along the Canale di San Marco in Venice. The cup balloon is of plastic. This, like much of the artist's characteristic work, is an oversized spoof of familiar forms. Many works discussed in this chapter have evolved within the soft sculpture movement. Certainly Badanna Zack's stuffed *Volkswagen* is Oldenburg's stepchild (figs. 109, 110).

As the soft sculpture movement was gaining momentum in the galleries and studios of New York, West Coast artists were experimenting with environmental sculpture. Ed Kienholz, considered by many the father of the movement, was among the first to assemble sculpture as a complete environment. Sometimes he used cloth; sometimes he did not. Artists everywhere soon found that cloth, so malleable and available, allowed them to control the space that housed their forms both easily and cheaply.

Sculptors today fuse brilliant, modern technology with a well-developed, historically based craft sensibility. Sculptors also use every conceivable material to make their art. The field has become open-ended. One finds pliable materials made into pliable forms, pliable materials forced into astonishing rigidity, hard objects made soft, assemblages of related elements, assemblages of unrelated elements, simple forms, and complex constructions. Before considering the themes explored by these artists, one needs first to consider how they have used cloth.

Some works defy gravity; others are earthbound. Some are realistic while others are abstract or metaphoric. Many have continued the tradition of the figure, of the head, the torso, the portrait—formal themes of the past that seemed about to be abandoned during the 1960s and 1970s. Like marble and bronze, figurative imagery reappeared in the early 1980s.

The formal relationships by which sculpture was judged in the past have given way to a new aesthetic. Formerly one evaluated such things as the volume created by the balance of the figure, the negative and positive spaces, the theme, the appropriateness of the material to the theme, the visual impact in terms of scale, the craftsmanship or technical execution, and the eloquence of expression. Today, while some of these criteria still might apply, one is more often struck by how the soaring imagination of the artist has been freed by the vast technology of a new time.

# Pliable Material into Pliable Form

Cloth in its natural state is soft and pliable. Yayoi Kusama, a Japanese artist who became ensconced in the New York art scene during the 1960s, was certainly one of the first to sew cloth into soft sculpture. Her work at that time was outrageously sexual, as is suggested by *Couch and Canvas*, a sculpture covered with stuffed and sewn cloth phalluses. She worked cumulatively, forming visual statements through obsession, repetition, and accumulation. This same obsessive repetition appears over and over among artists creating sculpture from cloth (fig. 111).

In 1961 Kusama first showed her phallus-ridden sculpture. Twenty-five years later, and half a world away, Kyung-Youn Chung takes a single cloth form, stuffs great numbers of them, and builds them into a larger whole. Her unit is the white

111. Yayoi Kusama, *Couch and Canvas*, 1962. Assemblage of cotton, c. 35 x 83 x 35″. Collection Hood Museum of Art, Dartmouth College, Hanover, New Hampshire.

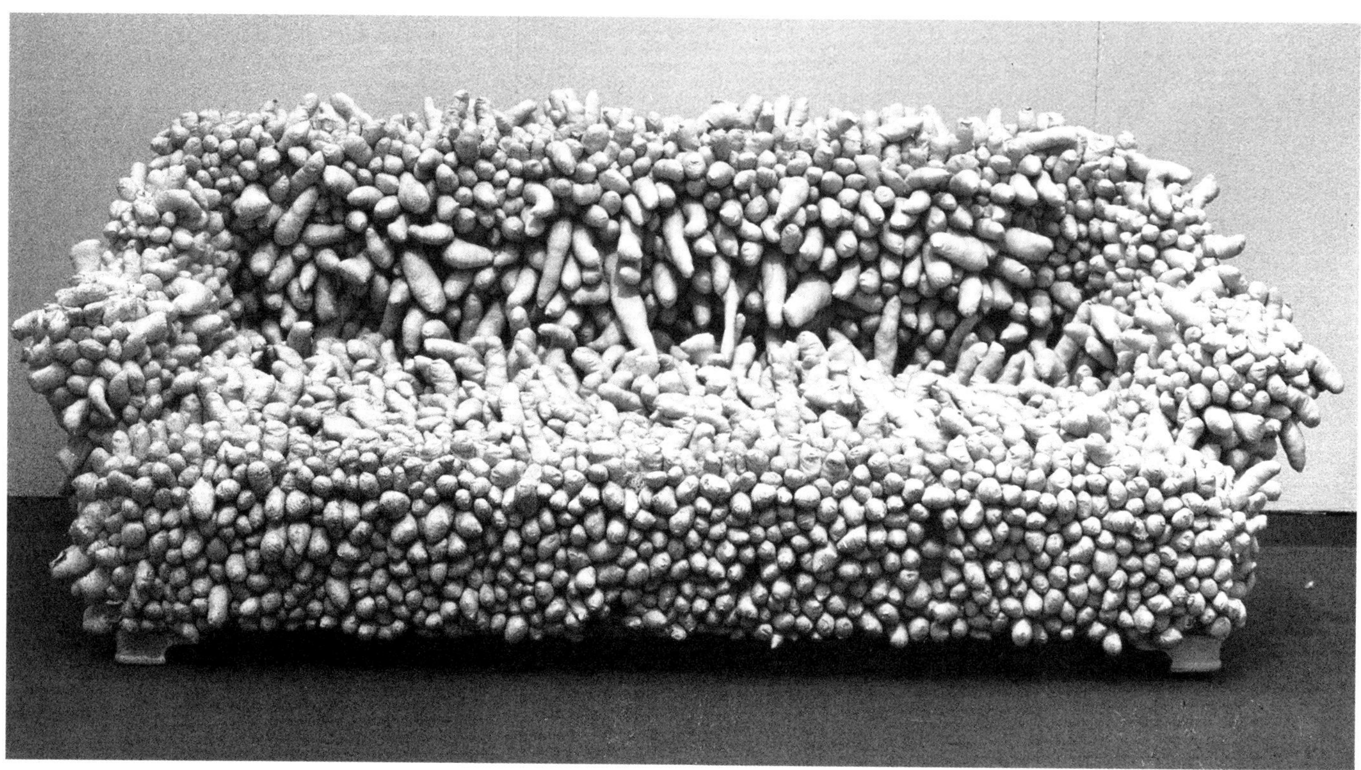

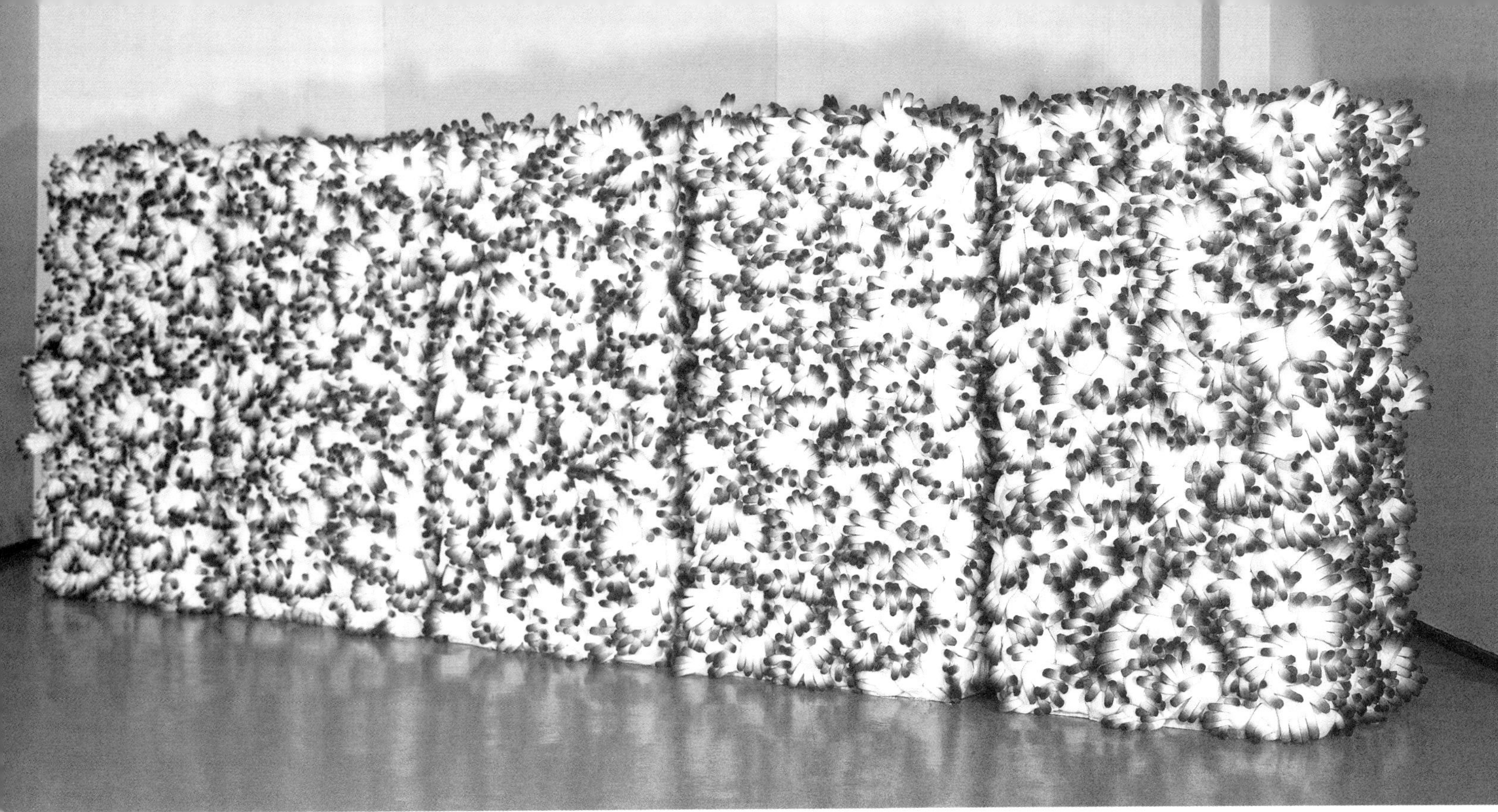

112. Kyung-Youn Chung, *Untitled*, 1986. Cotton gloves, three units, each 81 x 33½ x 31½". Collection National Museum of Contemporary Art, Seoul, Korea.

cotton glove of the Asian worker. Chung, one of South Korea's most venturesome young artists, studied art in the United States. She returned home to see with fresh eyes the symbolic power in both Japan and South Korea of the simple white glove. Today she orders them from the factory by the thousands. Once she has dyed them in her studio she masses them into humorous, whimsical sculpture. Hundreds of soft, stuffed hands, their fingers dyed the same color, grope from the center, poignant yet funny as humanity seen en masse can be both poignant and funny (fig. 112).

Like Kusama with her phalluses and Chung with her gloves, Lloyd Hamrol filled 1,763 cotton bags with 11,500 pounds of sand in order to build the 55-foot-long, 55-ton *Soft Wall for Artpark* in Lewiston, New York, in 1976. Those statistics added up to a remarkable piece, installed with a bricklayer's skill, which was as sensuous as a soft bag and as powerful as a restraining brick wall. The success of the work lay in its ambiguity. The viewer was forced to wonder, did the wall restrain or protect? Does a dike keep out the water or does the bunker hole in the people? Hamrol bade his viewer to enter the work physically. Yet his insistent geometry turned it into a contemplative experience. Had the sand been housed in anything but cloth it would not have projected the eloquence of the mundane as it does (fig. 115).

Cloth is remarkably adaptable to figurative work, as the history of dollmaking attests. However, very few dolls ever become art. When they do, the results are often witty and always unexpected. For example, Sharron Quasius has created a tableau of astonishing reality. In this tour de force she has reverted to a famous painting by Emanuel Leutze, *Washington Crossing the Delaware*. With simple cotton duck she has deftly sculpted her figures as though they were part of a carved marble frieze on a Neoclassical building. This wry use of cloth results in a humorous, unsettling work of art (fig. 114).

Lois Johnson, a printmaker from Philadelphia, certainly considered the classical frieze and its uses when she was asked to collaborate with Phillips Simkin on a site-specific installation for the thirteenth Olympic Winter Games at Lake Placid, New York, in 1980. Simkin was building a large installation, *Rosebud II: Seven Self-Propelled Earthly Parodies*, a series of seven ripstop-nylon houses based upon the seven stages of life. The houses were to be installed on the ice (see fig. 144). As a companion work Johnson created *Audience Frieze*, her frozen tribute to the spectator. The figures in her "audience" were also intended to serve as shills to attract the crowd onto the ice—an age-old use of the frieze. She decided upon one hundred figures and invited one hundred friends to send her their photographs. She then enlarged the faces to life size and silk-screened each onto a cutout head. She made the figures matching sets of silk-screened mittens, cowboy boots, and mufflers. Then she sewed all the parts onto identical cotton bodies. The bodies were to be soaked in water and allowed to freeze as freestanding figures. However, there was an unseasonable thaw at the Olympics that January and the figures were hung by clothespins on a line. A year later she repeated the piece in North Dakota in February. Again the weather turned warm. Johnson good-humoredly renamed *Audience Frieze;* it became *Friends on a Clothesline* (fig. 113).

A decade later Kiki Smith silk-screened her own set of figures onto cloth. Smith's ongoing exploration of the biological systems of the human body expanded to a parallel interest in the evolution of the human body. Out of this came works of art based upon Lucy, the three-million-year-old *Australopithecus afarensis* female skeleton found in 1974 by Donald Johanson at Hadar, northeast of Addis Ababa in Ethiopia. Smith imagined Lucy's progeny through different mediums, including the stuffed cloth figures of *Lucy's Daughters* (fig. 116).

Fabric certainly lends itself to lightness of mood and grace of statement. William King's *Irish Poet* is both witty and light-handed. Since the early 1950s King has been creating wry and quietly cynical three-dimensional sketches of members of the human race. In the beginning he carved them from wood. Later he saw the advantage of draping cloth over an armature: cloth took form quickly. It proved a more suitable method of executing a quick "sketch" whereby he could elicit the essential features while ignoring the details (fig. 117).

113. Lois Johnson, *Audience Frieze/Friends on a Clothesline*, 1980. Life-size cotton bodies with silk-screened boots, scarves, mittens, and faces. Installed at the North Dakota Museum of Art, Grand Forks.

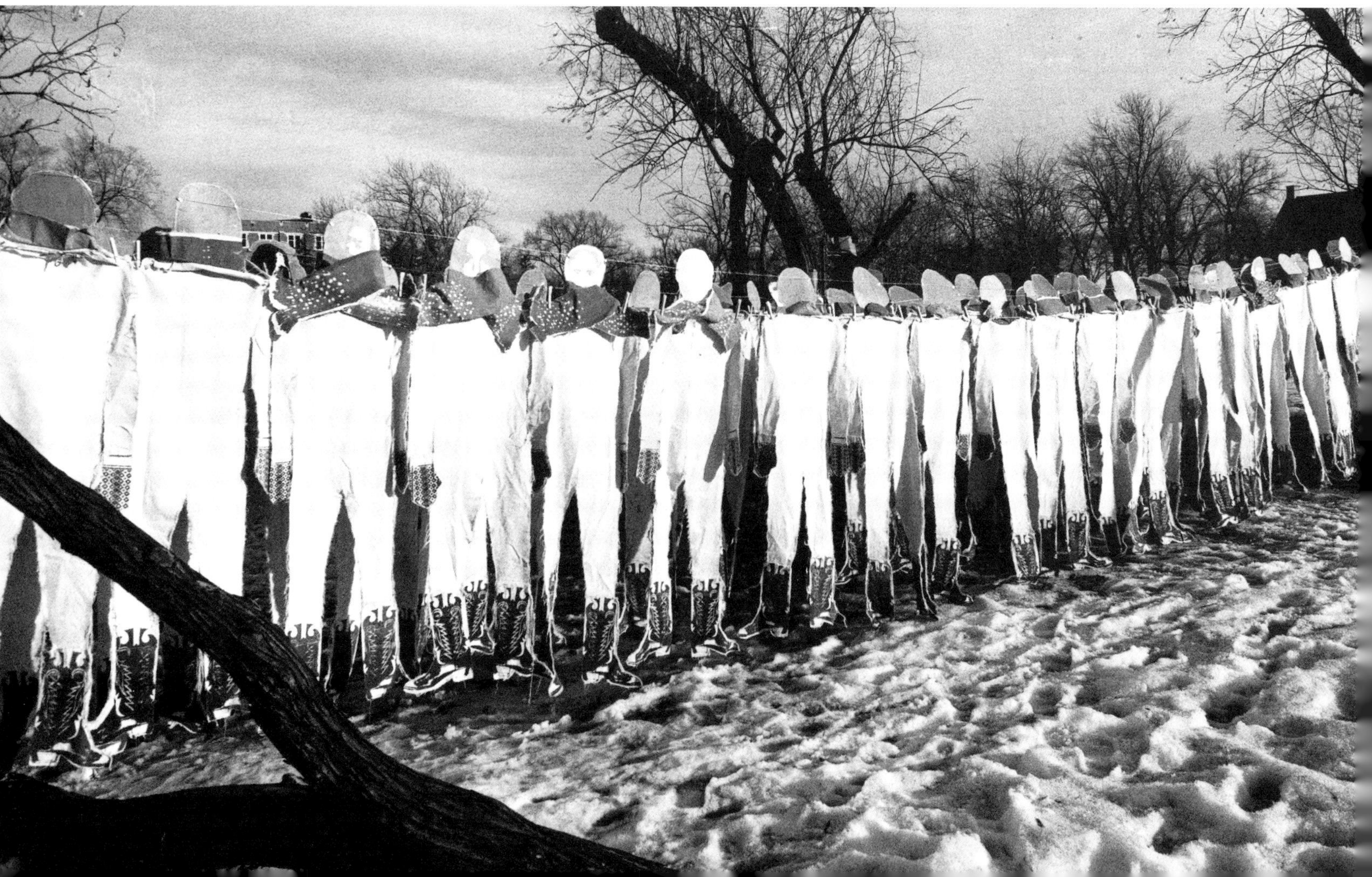

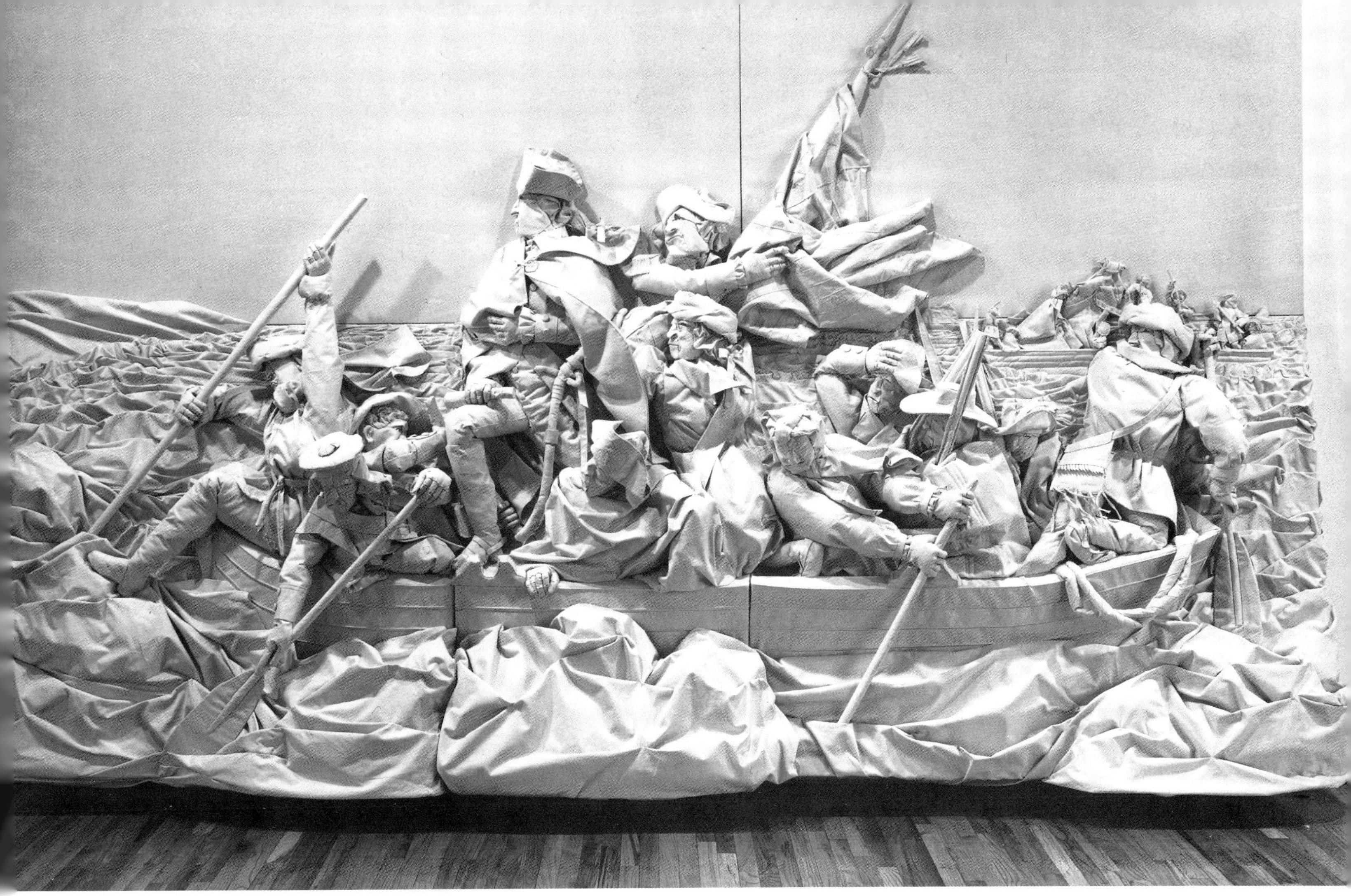

114. Sharron Quasius, *Washington Crossing the Delaware,* 1982. Cotton duck on wood, 8 x 14 x 2′. Courtesy O. K. Harris Works of Art, New York.

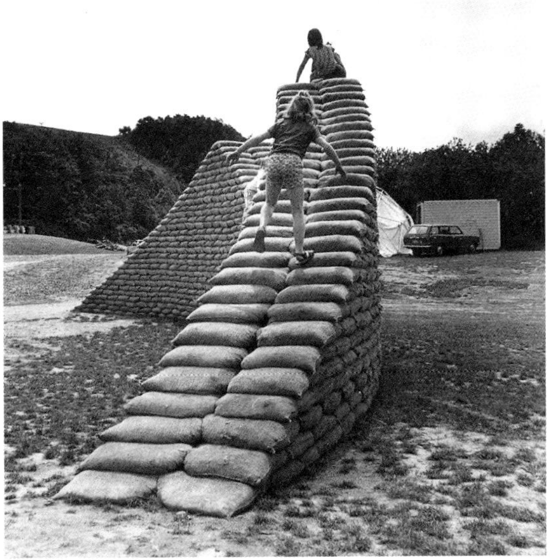

115. Lloyd Hamrol, *Soft Wall for Artpark,* 1976. Burlap sandbags, 117 x 721 x 36″.

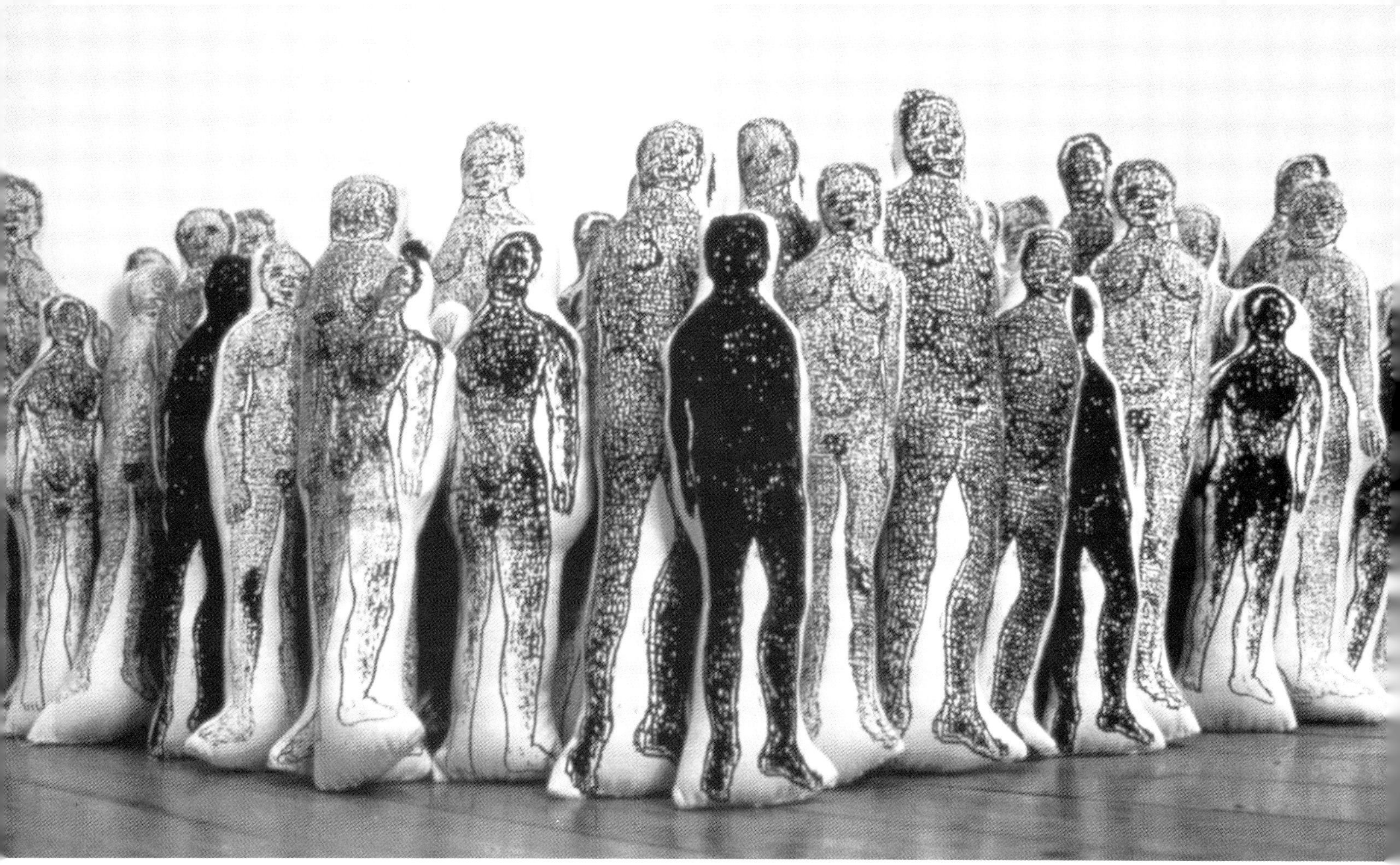

116. Kiki Smith, *Lucy's Daughters*, 1990. Life-size silk-screen-on-cloth figures. Collection Rena Rosenwasser and Penny Coober, Berkeley.

In the sculpture of Robert Knight cloth takes on far darker connotations. This work is figurative and realistic but succeeds in its otherness. Cloth is clothing in this British sculptor's work, but clothing that suggests far more than covering. In these works clothing is social class; clothing is despair; clothing is being inadequate to the dreams of the body beneath. Knight creates his life-size, tableau-like sculptures from fiberglass. He truncates the body, leaving only a relief of the core, or the most vulnerable area of the figure. He then swaddles the body in the clothing that represents the discomfiture of its existence (fig. 118).

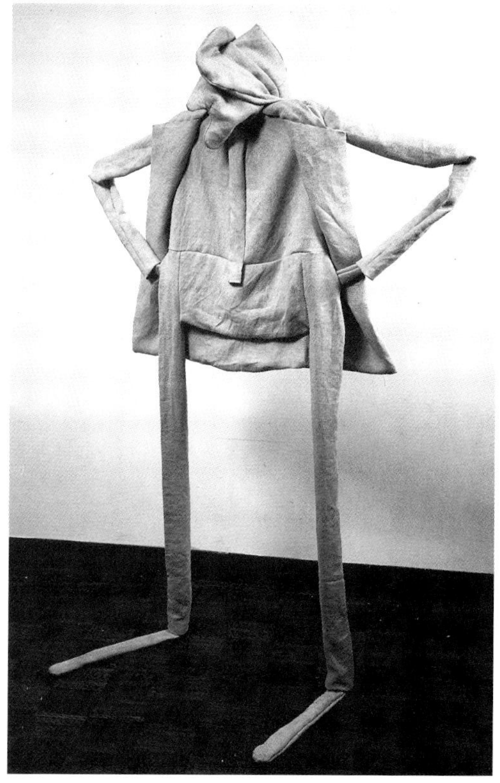

117. William King, *Irish Poet,* 1980. Linen, 59″ high. Courtesy Terry Dintenfass, Inc., New York.

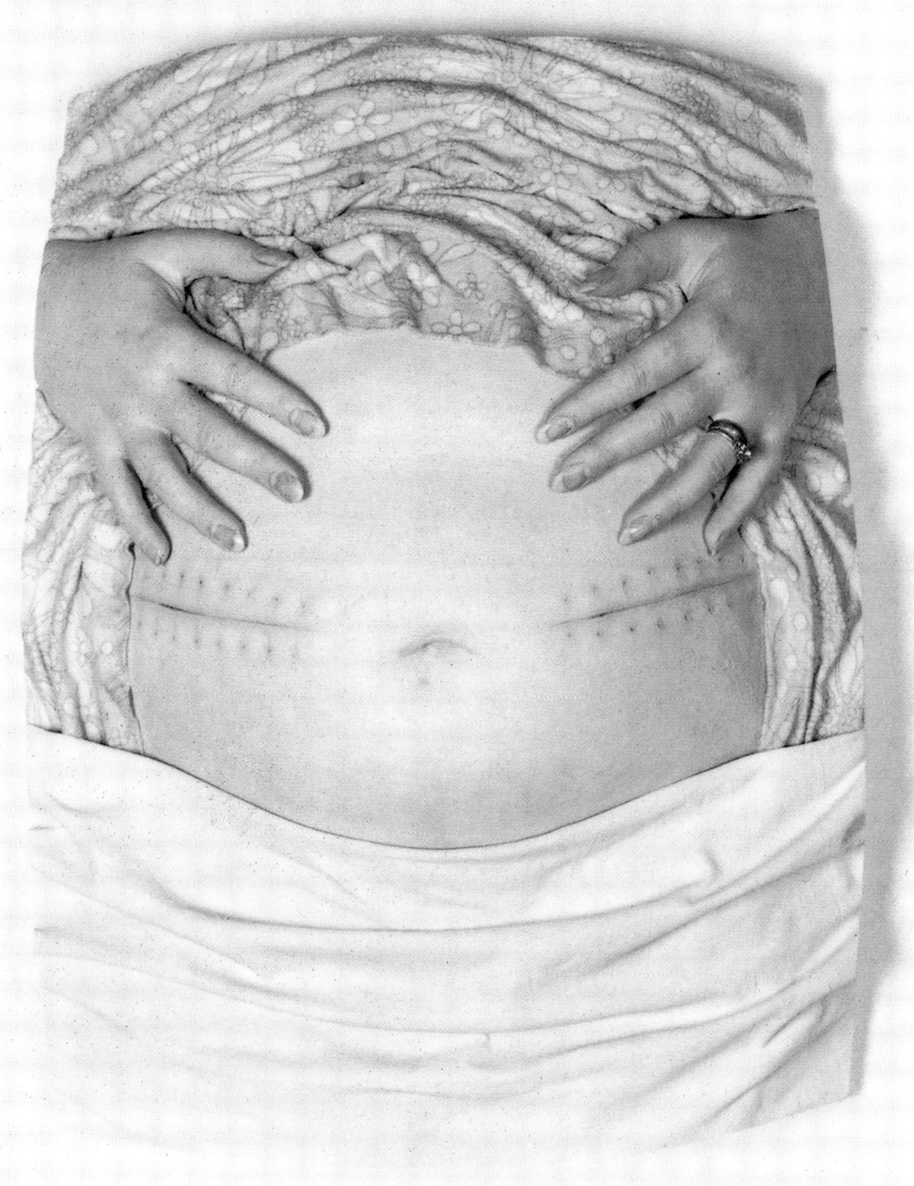

POOR FLORA

[SYMPAT HECTOMIES]

118. Robert Knight, *Poor Flora (Sympat Hectomies)*, 1981. Fiberglass, cloth, and mixed media, 43 x 31 x 6″.

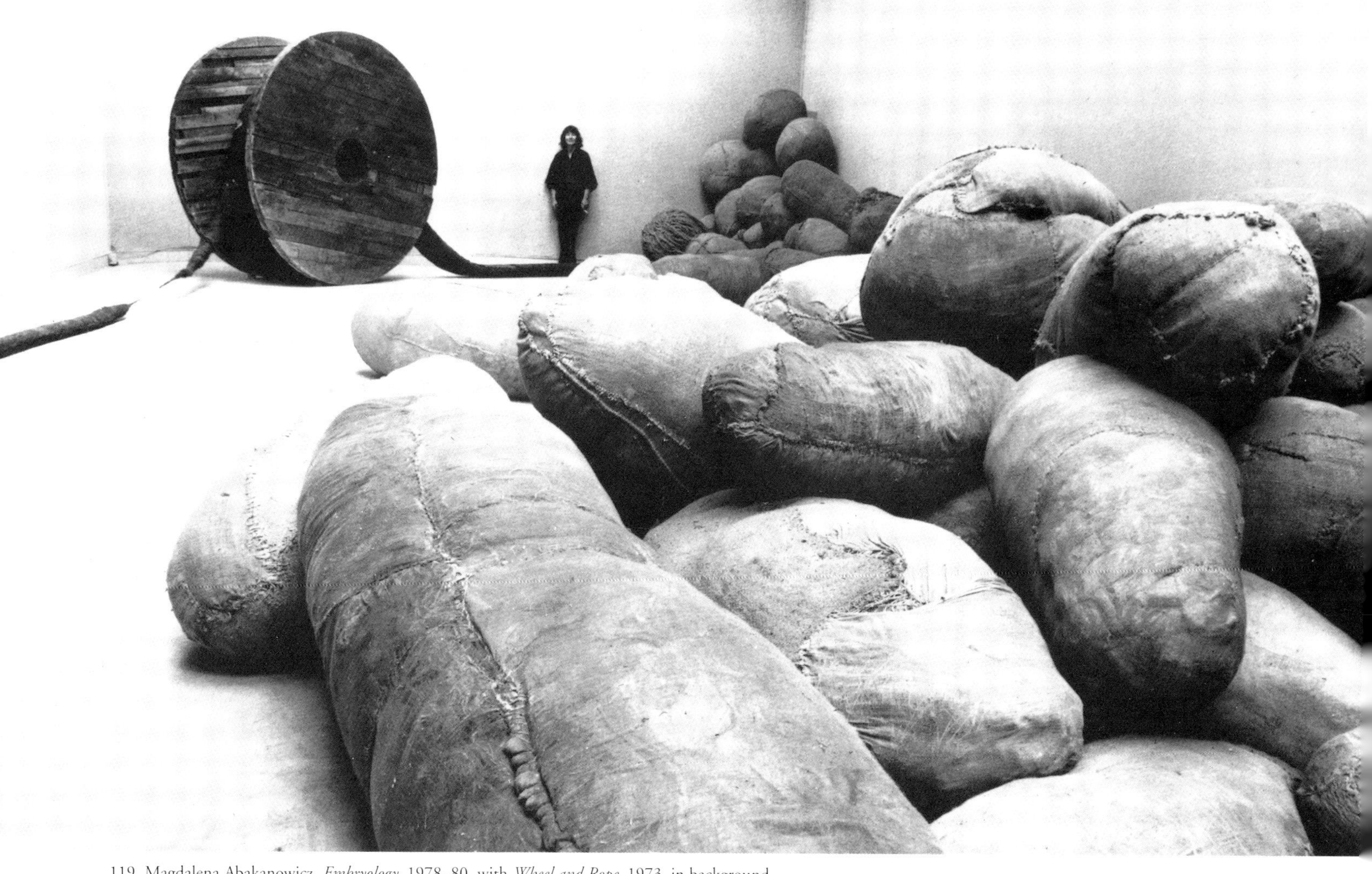

119. Magdalena Abakanowicz, *Embryology*, 1978–80, with *Wheel and Rope*, 1973, in background. Installation at the Venice Biennale, 1980.

# Pliable Materials Made Rigid

Cloth in its natural state is pliable and soft. Modern technology has given twentieth-century artists remarkable means for making cloth rigid. Poland's Magdalena Abakanowicz has consistently used soft, organic materials to create both figurative and abstract forms. In the statement at the beginning of this chapter she said: "I see fiber as the basic element constructing the organic world on our planet, as the greatest mystery of our environment." This proposition is developed in the abstract forms of her works on the embryology theme. Erasmus Darwin, eminent botanist and grandfather of Charles Darwin, wrote in *Zoonomia* (1794–96) that he viewed embryology as a tool of continuous progress to greater size and complexity. Abakanowicz's embryological forms have great weight and volume. In their differing shapes, and in their "skins" of wrapped and sewn jute sacking, they suggest the endless diversity of all embryology. This is part of a large, ongoing body of work called the Alteration Cycle, which the artist has been developing since 1978 (fig. 119).

Abakanowicz's *Embryology* embodies the figure in its most abstract form, whereas Muriel Castanis's cloth figures, frozen by epoxy, evoke full-bodied classical sculptures complete with enveloping drapery. The hardened cloth, however, encloses empty space. In keeping with her classical parody, she sometimes restores the pedestals to her figures. At other times the figures float against the wall (fig. 121).

Castanis was inspired by classical sculpture, while Margaretha Dubach seeks the commanding presence so often found in Egyptian sculpture. The quality of rigidness dominates her work. With this rigidity she suggests the awesome power of an ancient Egyptian statue, not the presence of a living animal. The cloth binding the animal, or the skin of the sculpture, hides the firm musculature underneath. The wrapped bundles under the animal suggest offerings. All of this is light-

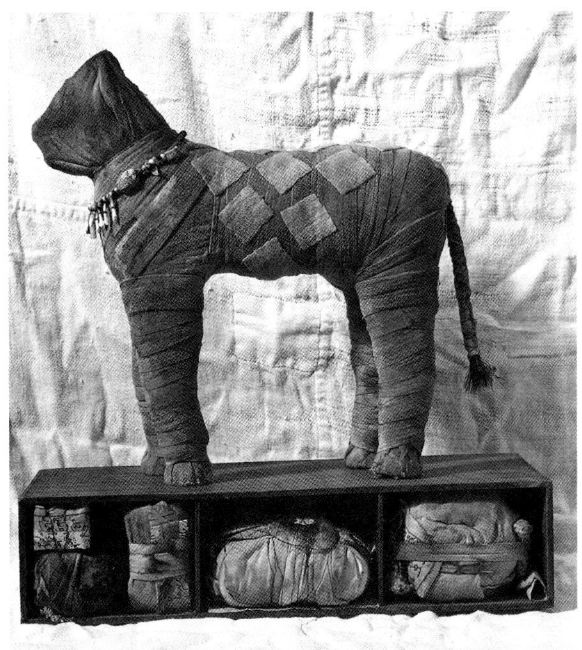

120. Margaretha Dubach, *Grabbeigaben,* 1978. Cloth and wood, 16 x 15½ x 5⅞″.

121. Muriel Castanis, *Wall Piece,* 1986. Cloth and epoxy, 56 x 84 x 15½″. Courtesy O. K. Harris Works of Art, New York.

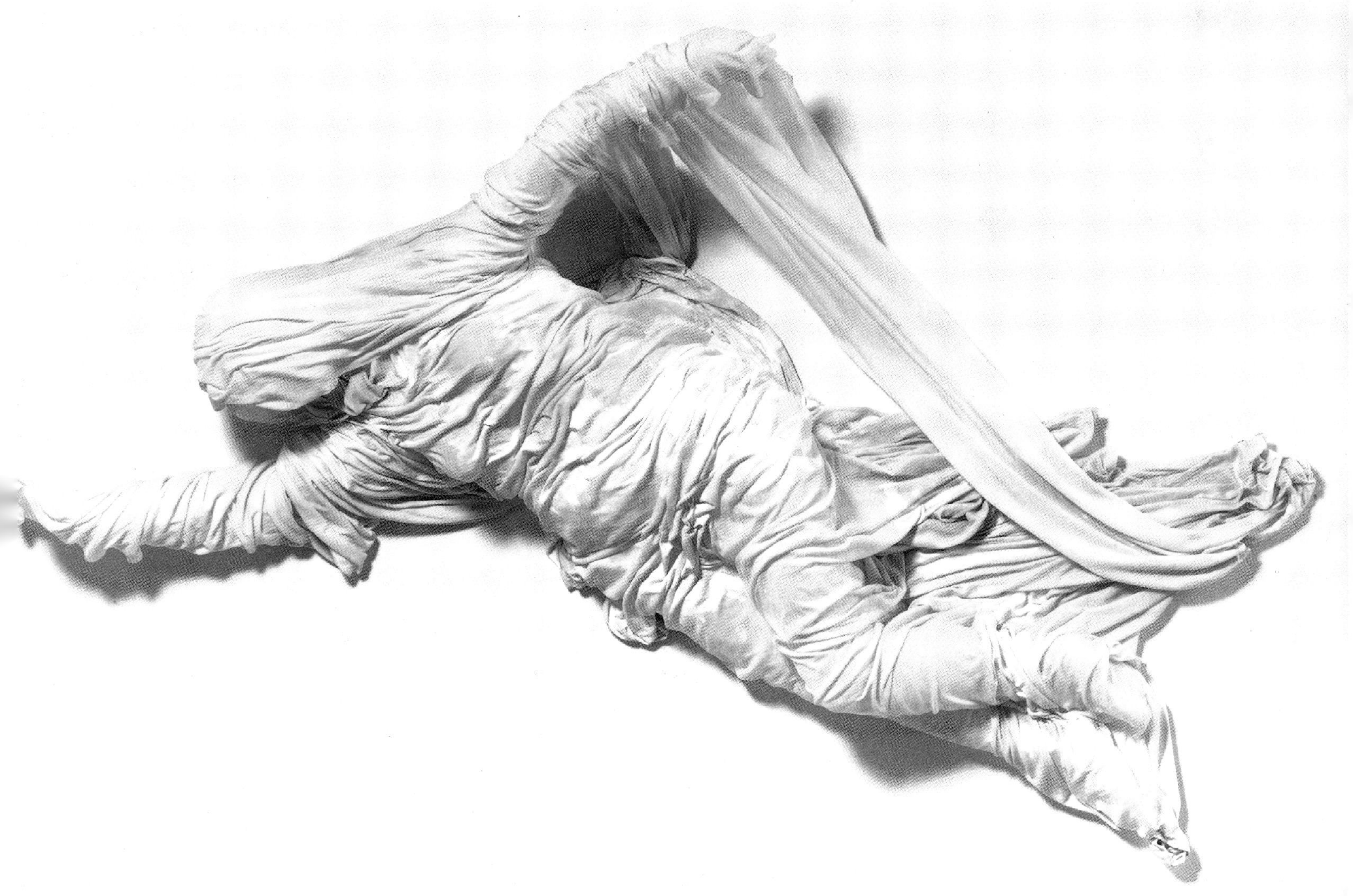

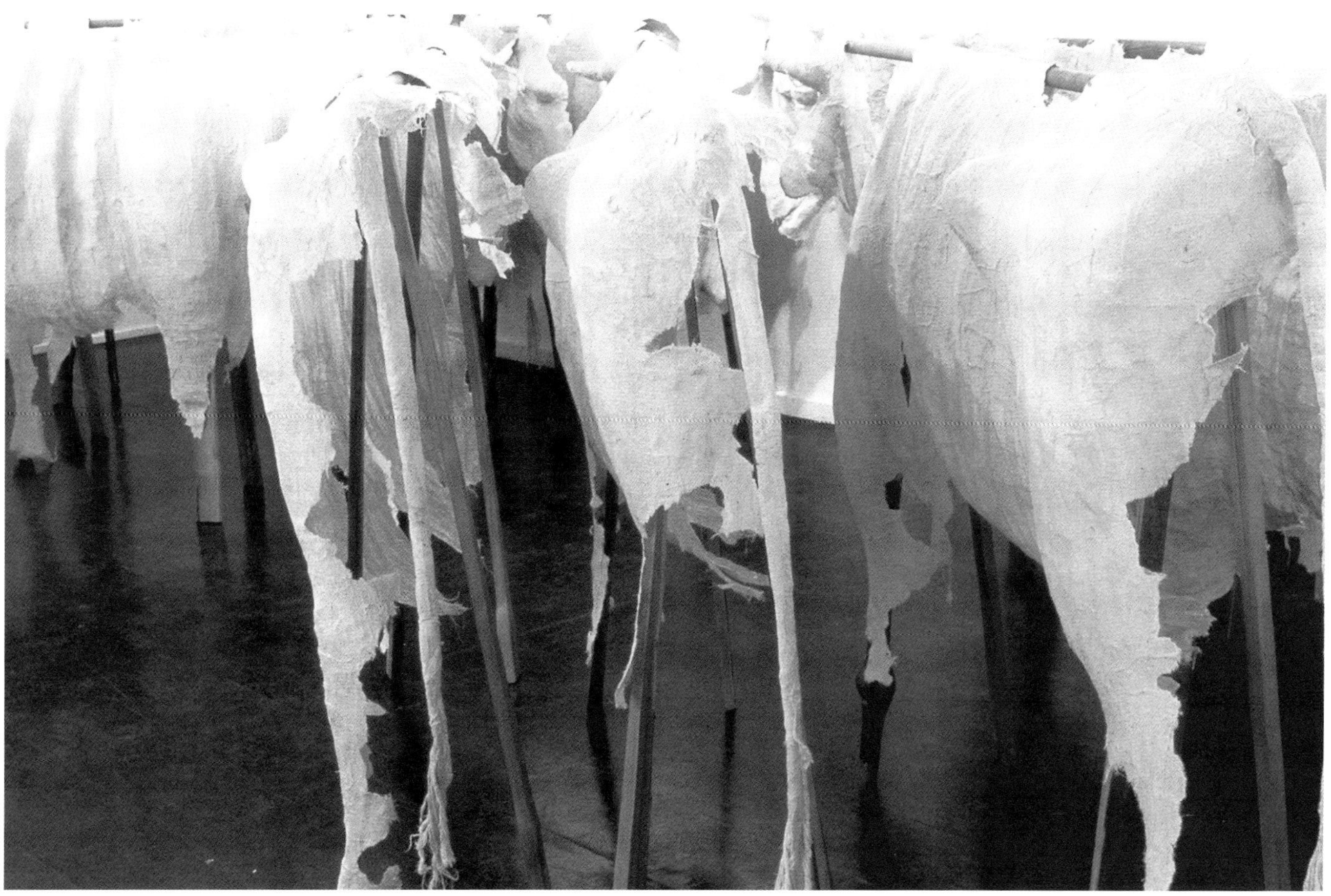

122. Camrose Ducote, *Celestial Sanctuary*, 1983. Twelve life-size fragmented cows, unbleached gauze, water-and-glue paste, lacquer sanding sealer, dowel, 4 x 24 x 24´.

ened by the patchwork spots on the animal, a touch of pure whimsy (fig. 120).

Camrose Ducote's *Celestial Sanctuary* is a herd of cows—in truth, hollow shapes made of gauze stiffened with paste. The brittle and translucent membrane suggests the appearance of parched rawhide. The pigmented, incomplete, almost ephemeral bodies are faithful in their physical structure, yet they are present more in spirit than in flesh. Surprisingly, they still project a characteristic animal heaviness and imply an instinct to herd (fig. 122).

Maureen Connor's figures are not figures at all. They are huge napkins, audacious in scale. Her folding techniques are typical of those used in nineteenth-century homes. Here the rigid organdy constructions defy gravity. They never lose their identity, but like much surrealist work in which scale is exaggerated out of context, the napery takes on a sculptural presence (fig. 124).

All of this figurative work has an ethereal quality resulting from artists using cloth in its undyed state. By dying the cloth, and increasing the scale, Inese Mailitis and Ivars Mailitis succeed in creating advancing, ominous human figures. These Soviet collaborators echo in cloth the spirit of the gigantic, menacing, ax-wielding men for which Jonathan Borofsky became famous (fig. 123).

Sometimes the presence of the figure is only suggested. Tomoko Ishida created a grid of freestanding poles upon which she hung white shirts for an installation at the Taipei Museum of Fine Arts. Upon walking into the piece, the viewer feels a swarm of white-colored men approaching as if a traffic light has changed on any street in the center of the financial district of

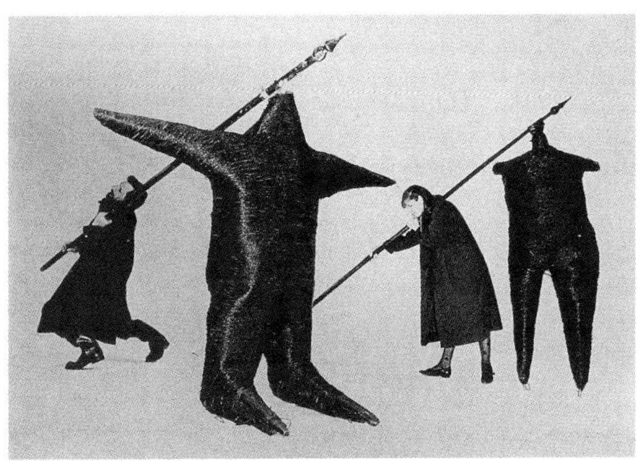

123. Inese Mailitis and Ivars Mailitis, *People as Banners,* 1988. Wood, fabric, and rope, 118 x 78¾ x 59″.

124. Maureen Connor, *Linens,* 1980. Starched, folded, ironed, and tucked organdy, 3–8′ high. Installation at the Acquavella Gallery, Inc., New York.

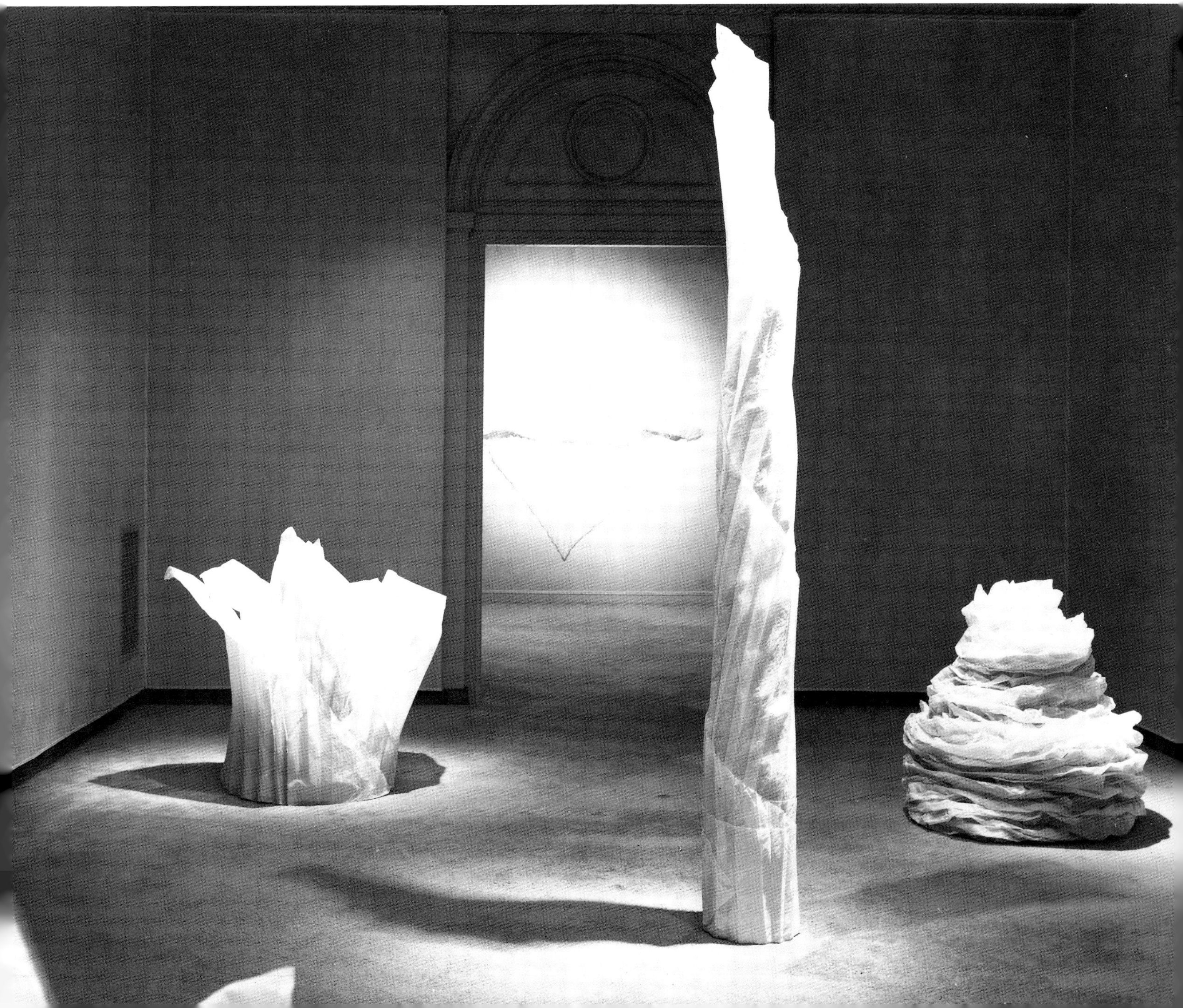

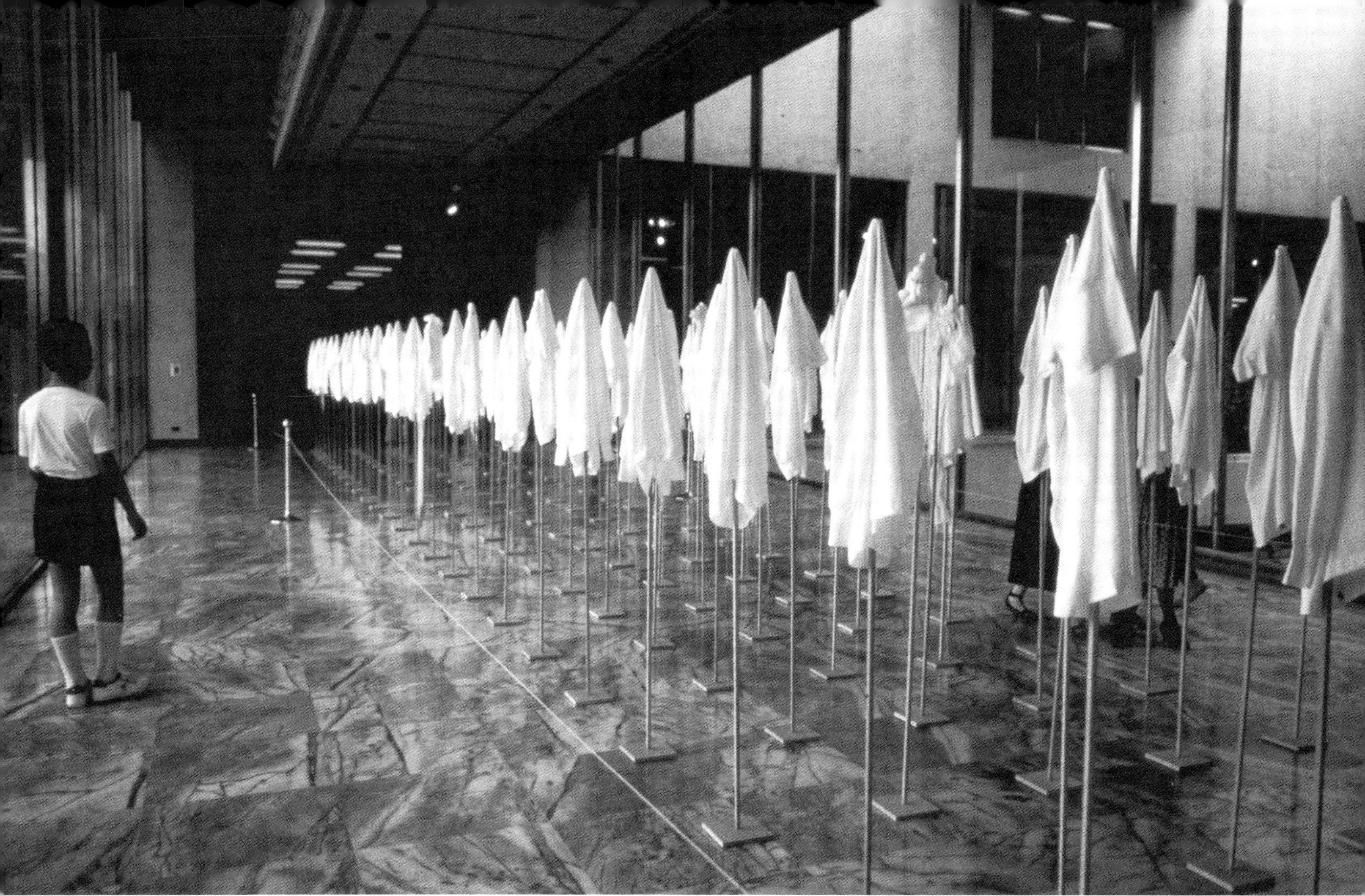

125. Tomoko Ishida, *Undershirt,* 1986. Shirts with stands, c. 34¾ x 77½ x 3½´. Installed at the Taipei Museum of Fine Arts, Taiwan.

any postindustrial city. Ishida did not stiffen the shirts; she allowed them to hang still, effigies for the missing men who normally stuff them (fig. 125).

Other objects imply the human figure, objects as mundane and as surprisingly potent as a chair. From the beginning of recorded history the chair has been transformed, cushioned, covered, and camouflaged by cloth. Many grandmothers covered their furniture to protect it from the sun. White slipcovers announced summer. Chairs were shrouded in cloth to hide worn spots, or to make the room something other than it seemed. Architects and designers have paid particular attention to the chair. So have artists. The chair stands in for the figure in the same way Joseph Beuys's felt hat came to represent him.

Gaetano Pesce drapes fiberglass filled with Dacron, then soaked in resin, into the shape of the chair. This sculpture is in sharp contrast to those of Antoni Tàpies and Ewa Kuryluk. The former uses the chair as a prop, relying upon the softness of the cloth for appeal. Kuryluk, too, sees the chair as a prop, but her cloth covering on the chair supports a figure, as chairs should. However, the figure is drawn in red (figs. 127–29).

The figure and all its extensions is a common theme among artists making pliable materials rigid. Kiyomi Iwata, a Japanese American who chooses to draw from both cultures, stands apart as an artist making small visual poems, reminiscent of haiku. Her transparent boxes of organza fit no categories. These lyrical objects are limited in scale. Unlike most of the artists who stiffen cloth by mechanical means, Iwata determines the final size of each work by the capacity of the material to support itself. Each delicate little box must stand on its own physically, just as all of these works of art must transcend the materials and methods by which they are made and be judged solely by the visual language of objects (fig. 126).

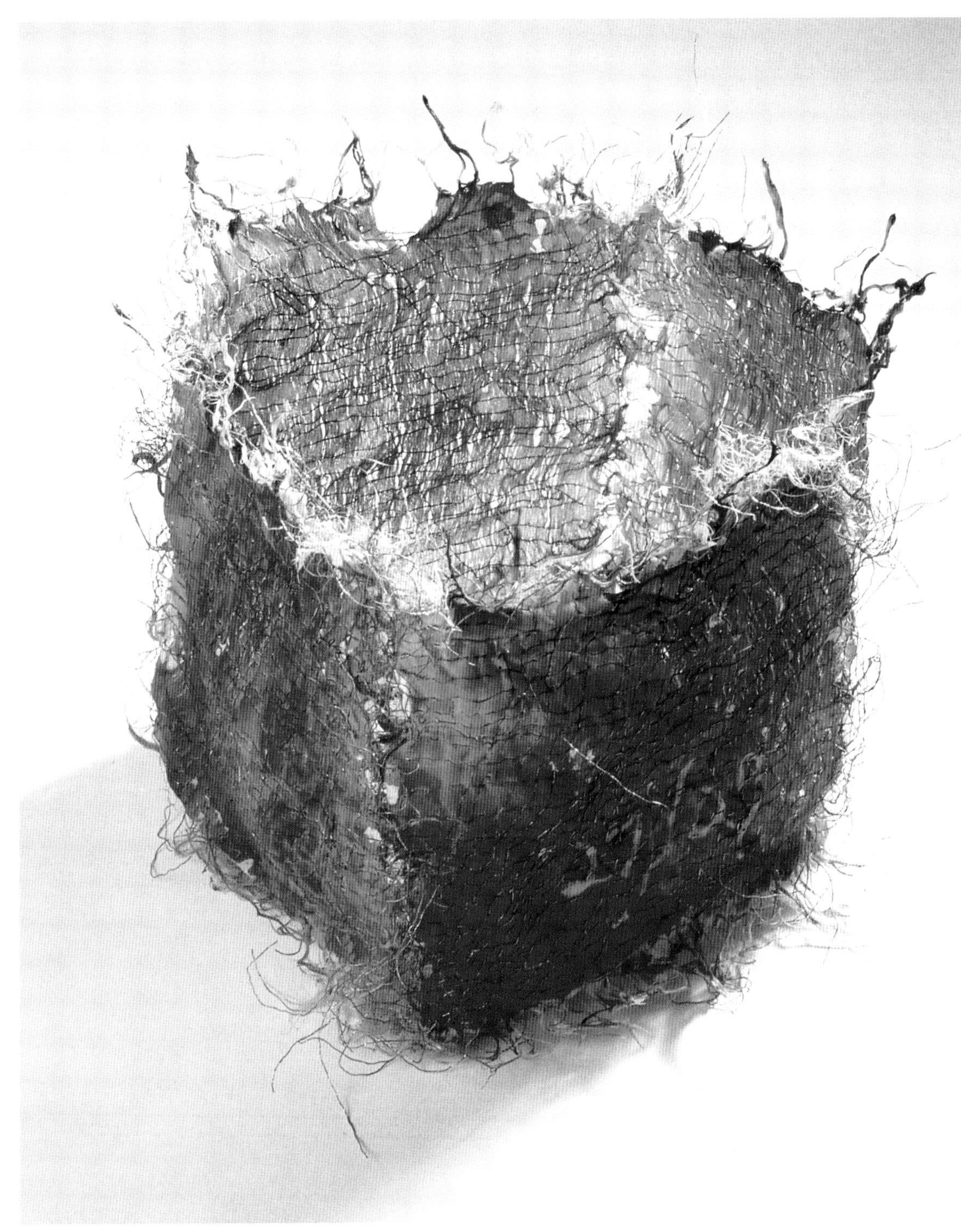

126. Kiyomi Iwata, *Pomegranate Box*, 1987. Silk organza, 7 x 7 x 7″.

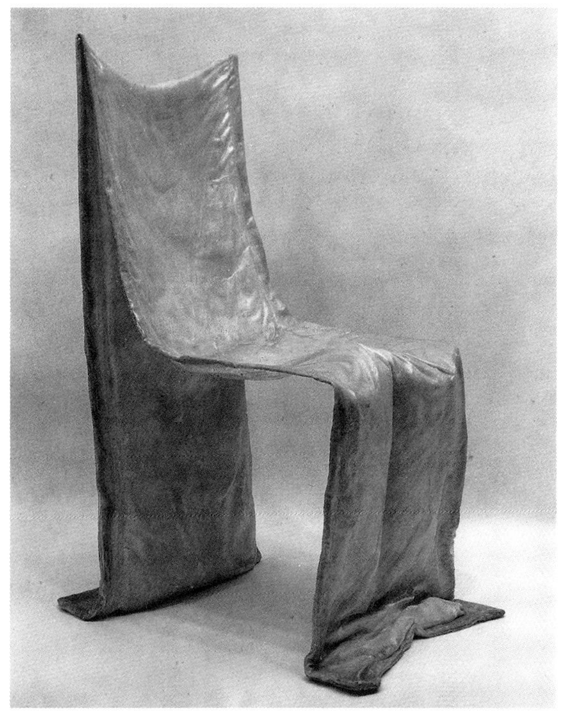

127. Gaetano Pesce, *Golgatha Chair*, 1974. Molded fiberglass, cloth, and resin, 39 x 25 x 16¼″. Collection Museum of Modern Art, New York, Estée and Joseph Lauder Design Fund.

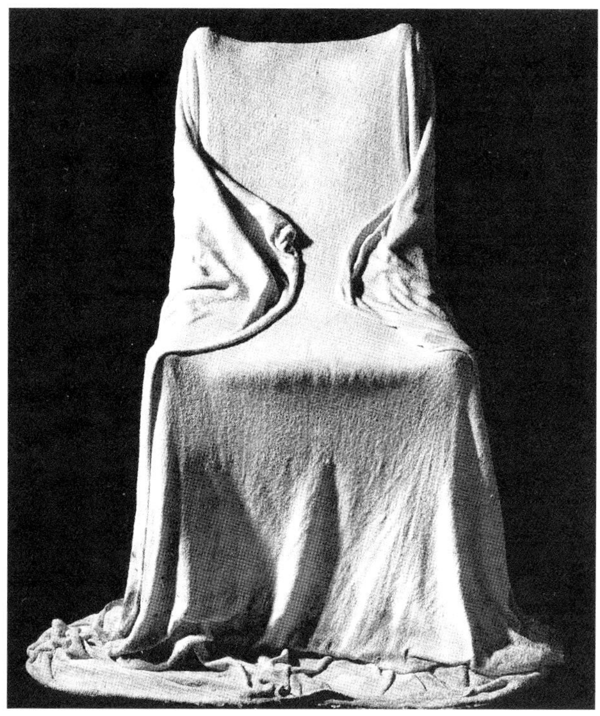

128. Antoni Tàpies, *Chaise couverte*, 1970. Chair with cloth, 30¾ x 28⅜ x 20⅞″. Collection Wilheim-Lehmbruck-Museum, Duisburg, Germany. Courtesy Galerie Maeght Lelong, Zurich, Switzerland.

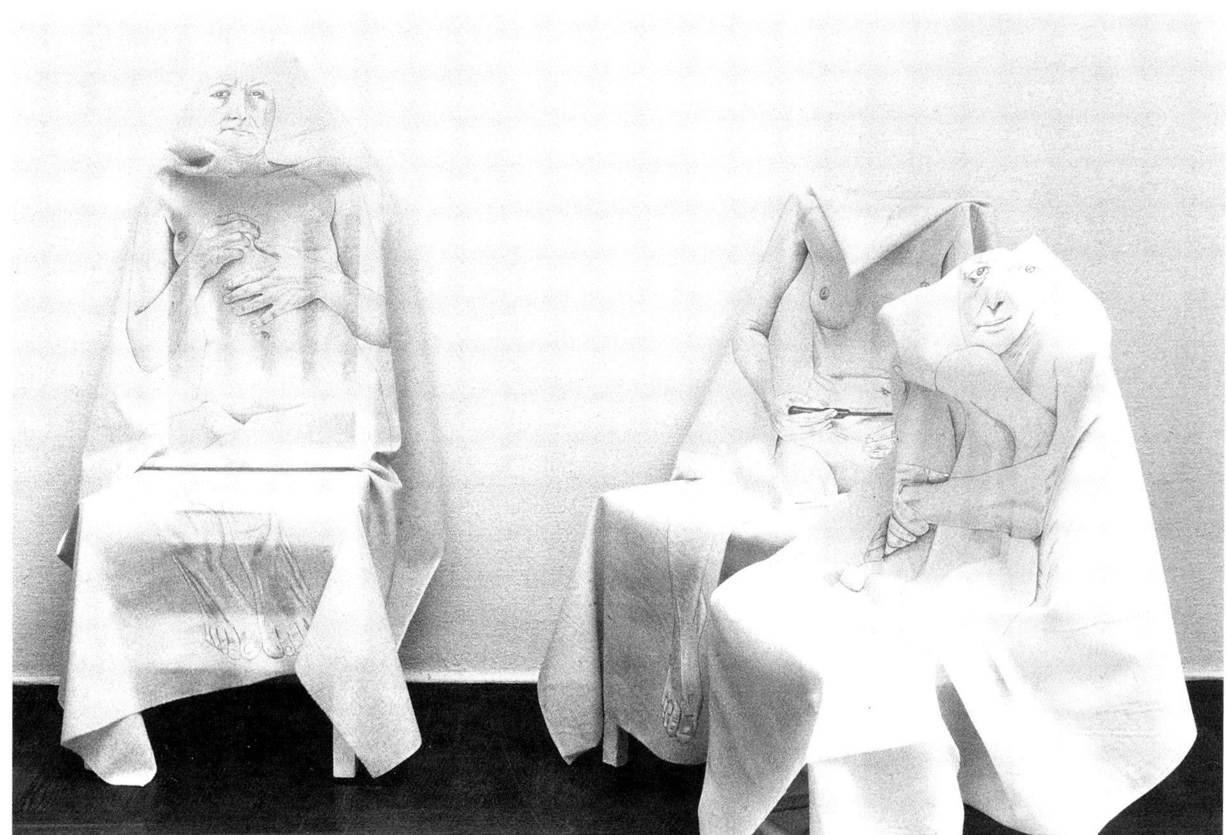

129. Ewa Kuryluk, *Three Chairs*, 1982. Acrylic and felt pen on cotton draped over wooden chairs, each chair 34 x 19 x 19″.

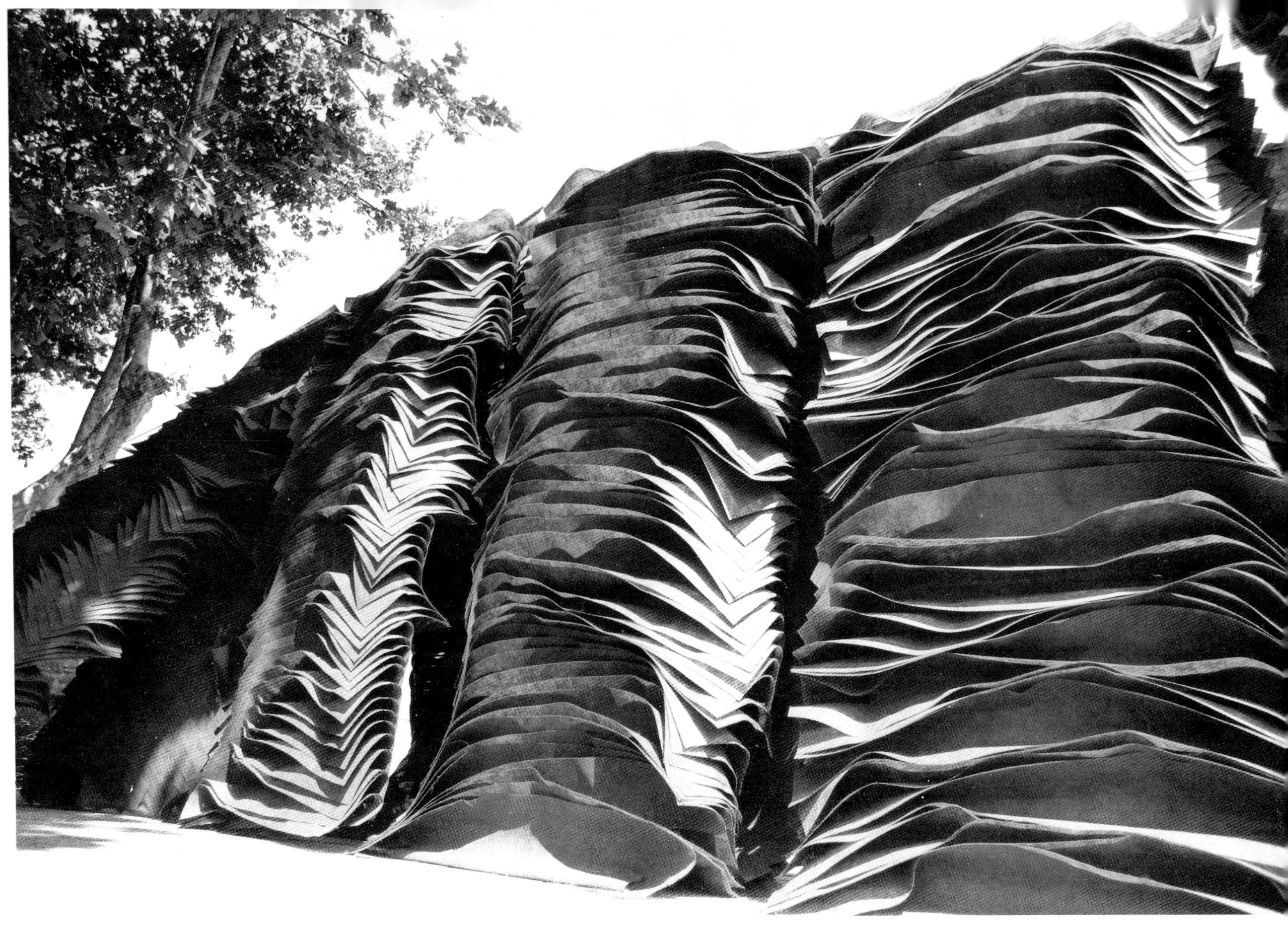

130. Jagoda Buić, *Black Rhythm,* 1984. Lutrival fiber (spun fleece), 98⅜ x 236¼ x 110¼″.

# Constructions

To assemble disparate parts into a unified, aesthetic whole is to create an assemblage. To build a system, be it visible or invisible, that supports its outer sheath is to build a construction. A persistently recurring theme in contemporary sculpture is the exploration of architectural elements—doors and windows, tents, houses, temples. Artists construct and reconstruct. Sculptors working in cloth are not exempt.

Jagoda Buić has turned her attention to wall-like structures. Her wall for the 1985 Lausanne Biennale, constructed out of a spun fleece called Lutrival, is an "ancient, weathered wall." It resulted from her desire to explore the "rough austerity of materials" within her memories of the landscape of her homeland, Yugoslavia (fig. 130).

Lee Bontecou's untitled wall relief is more complex in intention. It is sewn together from pieces of burlap scraps stretched taut over a hidden, skeletal frame. The tension in the piece results from its rigidity, which shifts the emphasis from form to mass and line. Unlike works discussed earlier in this chapter, line is achieved by the actual sewing of the cloth rather than by an armature or support structure. The surface is arrestingly smooth. Because the work projects from the wall, the viewer finds it discomforting, not knowing exactly what the artist intends. Its presence is physically menacing (fig. 131).

Masafumi Maita was born in Manchuria in 1944. At the age of three he was taken to Japan, there to remain. Although he has become known internationally for his monumental works in stone, he has a parallel artistic life working in fragile, fibrous materials. The artist begins by constructing from rope elemental forms such as circles, triangles, and squares, which he

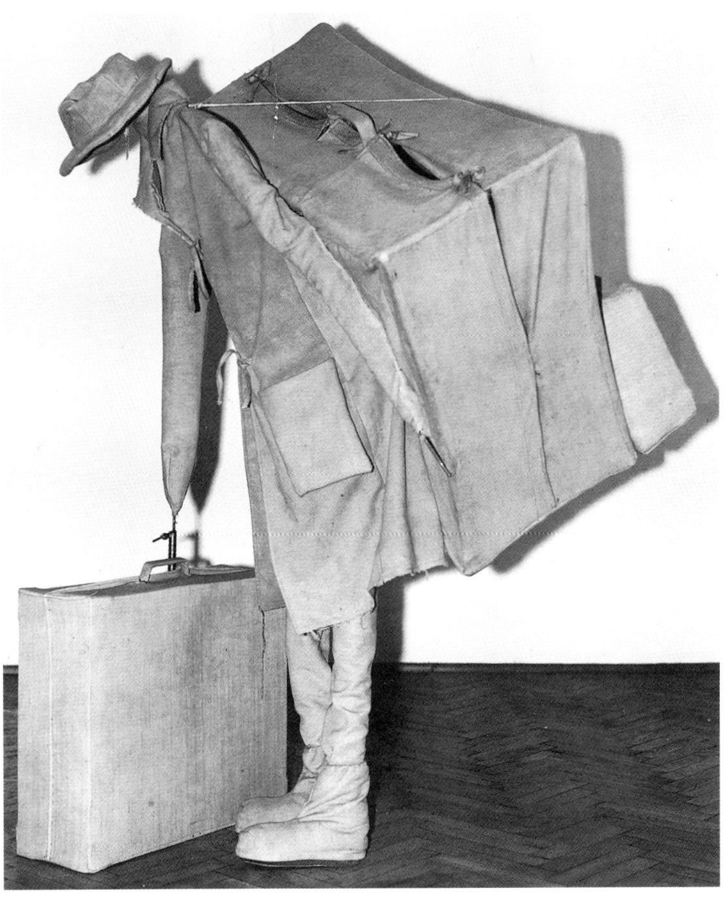

133. Tadeusz Kantor, *Edgar Warpol: Man with Suitcases*, 1968. Mannequin from production of *The Water Hen* by Stanislaw Ignacy Witkiewicz (1921), 66⅞ x 39⅜ x 39⅜". Collection Museum Sztuki, Lodz, Poland.

larger love of both nature and the world constructed by humans. Rodney O'Brien, an Australian journalist, describes Maita's love of cloth:

> Among Maita's memories of childhood are the beautiful threads of kimono silk with which his mother worked. He inherited her appreciation for old fabric and particularly the way it was once cherished. Now he travels through Japan in search of it, to tiny tucked-away antique shops and to isolated farmhouses. These pieces of left-over fabric, he realizes, are from an age when there could be no waste and even the smallest scraps were treasured. Because of his deep affection for the material he rarely uses the fabric he collects but stores it, not because it is unsuitable, but because he does not wish to destroy the history it represents.[4]

Still, snatches of history-laden cloth make their way into his contemporary bound works, there to provide the bridge between generations and centuries. Maita, with restraint and reverence, succeeds in creating a marriage between the centuries that is both seamless and peaceful. It is these ancient pieces of cloth that serve as his most transcendent material.

# Assemblage

Only a few works in cloth are assembled rather than constructed or built. Those that exist rely upon the aesthetic of juxtaposition and seem most powerful when the disparate elements retain marks of their previous form and history. This is difficult to achieve when using mill cloth, already anonymous in content if not in form.

A mannequin by Tadeusz Kantor is one of the few known assemblages in cloth. Kantor, artist, actor, animator, and founder of theatrical movements, was also one of Poland's most important directors. In this capacity as director and stage designer he created assemblages as characters in plays. Because his work developed parallel to the great European art movements of this century, he drew his vocabulary from them. His theatrical work was closely allied with the "autonomous theater," that is, theater that obeys its own laws as opposed to the theater of reproduction. Kantor created the mannequin *Edgar Warpol: Man with Suitcases* for his 1968 production of Stanislaw Ignacy

Witkiewicz's 1921 play *The Water Hen.* He did not consider it a production but rather a happening in which Witkiewicz's text was a partner. Kantor said, "We do not play Witkiewicz but along with Witkiewicz." Kantor explained his use of mannequins in his "Manifesto: The Theatre of Death" (1975):

> The mannequin I used in *The Water Hen* was a successor to the "Eternal Wanderer" and "Human Ambellages," one which appeared naturally in my "Collections" as yet another phenomenon consistent with my long-held conviction that only the reality of the lowest order, the poorest and least prestigious objects are capable of revealing their full objectivity in a work of art.
>
> Mannequins and wax figures have always existed on the peripheries of sanctioned Culture. They are not admitted further; they occupied places in Fair Booths, suspicious Magicians' Chambers, far from the splendid shrines of art, treated condescendingly as Curiosities intended for the tastes of the masses. For precisely this reason it was they, and not academic museum creations, which caused the curtain to move at the blink of an eye.[5]

From the most common material, cloth, Kantor assembled his parts to establish an emotional whole, the projection of an actor's character. In a country under censorship, as Poland was during much of Kantor's career, criticism and social comment clearly had to be subtly implicit. Therefore Polish directors, working in a world of compromised words, relied on the visual to speak. Kantor succeeded in making the audience feel the weight of the suitcase, the patchwork of the character's soul, by assembling pieces of cloth (fig. 133).

But why create sculpture out of cloth? As the 1980s drew to a close the Walker Art Center in Minneapolis opened its highly acclaimed sculpture garden. Impressive and permanent works of sculpture are carefully placed throughout old-fashioned garden rooms bereft of plants. Later a large, informal park section was added—again intended to house permanent installations of sculpture. Missing, by and large, are many of the ideas germinal to the radical revolution in sculpture that continued from the first half of the century into the second. There is little evidence of impermanence, mixed media, installations that force sculpture and environment to become equal players, and sculpture from unimportant materials. For example, the sculptor Deborah Butterfield first captured the art world's attention with her life-size horses made from found wood and scrap metal. The Walker was one of the first museums to acquire an important outdoor Butterfield horse. However, this was one of the artist's later horses, scaled larger than life, and cast in bronze. While important as a public monument, the bronze horses lack the vitality and absolutely stunning marriage of image and material that characterized Butterfield's early horses. Likewise, the gigantic Claes Oldenburg and Coosje van Bruggen *Spoonbridge and Cherry* (1985–88), made of stainless steel and painted aluminum and installed at the foot of the Walker garden, does not delight in the way a similar work in cloth pleases and surprises the viewer—despite its role as the signature work of the garden. Only half the story of twentieth-century sculpture is told at the Walker—the half that was created from timeless, permanent materials and placed in formal gallery settings. The other half is being invented by more unorthodox artists such as the ones represented here who work in cloth.

1. Dore Ashton, *Modern American Sculpture* (New York: Harry N. Abrams, n.d.), 6.

2. Naum Gabo, *Of Divers Arts*, Bollingen Series XXXV.8 (New York: Pantheon, 1962).

3. Meyer Schapiro, *Modern Art: 19th and 20th Centuries* (New York: George Braziller, 1978), 149.

4. Rodney O'Brien, "Homage to the Seasons: Masafumi Maita," *Intersect* 1, no. 5 (May 1985): 39.

5. Tadeusz Kantor, "Manifesto: The Theatre of Death," ed. Catherine Itzen, in Bohdan Drozdowski, ed., *Twentieth Century Polish Theatre* (London: John Calder, 1979).

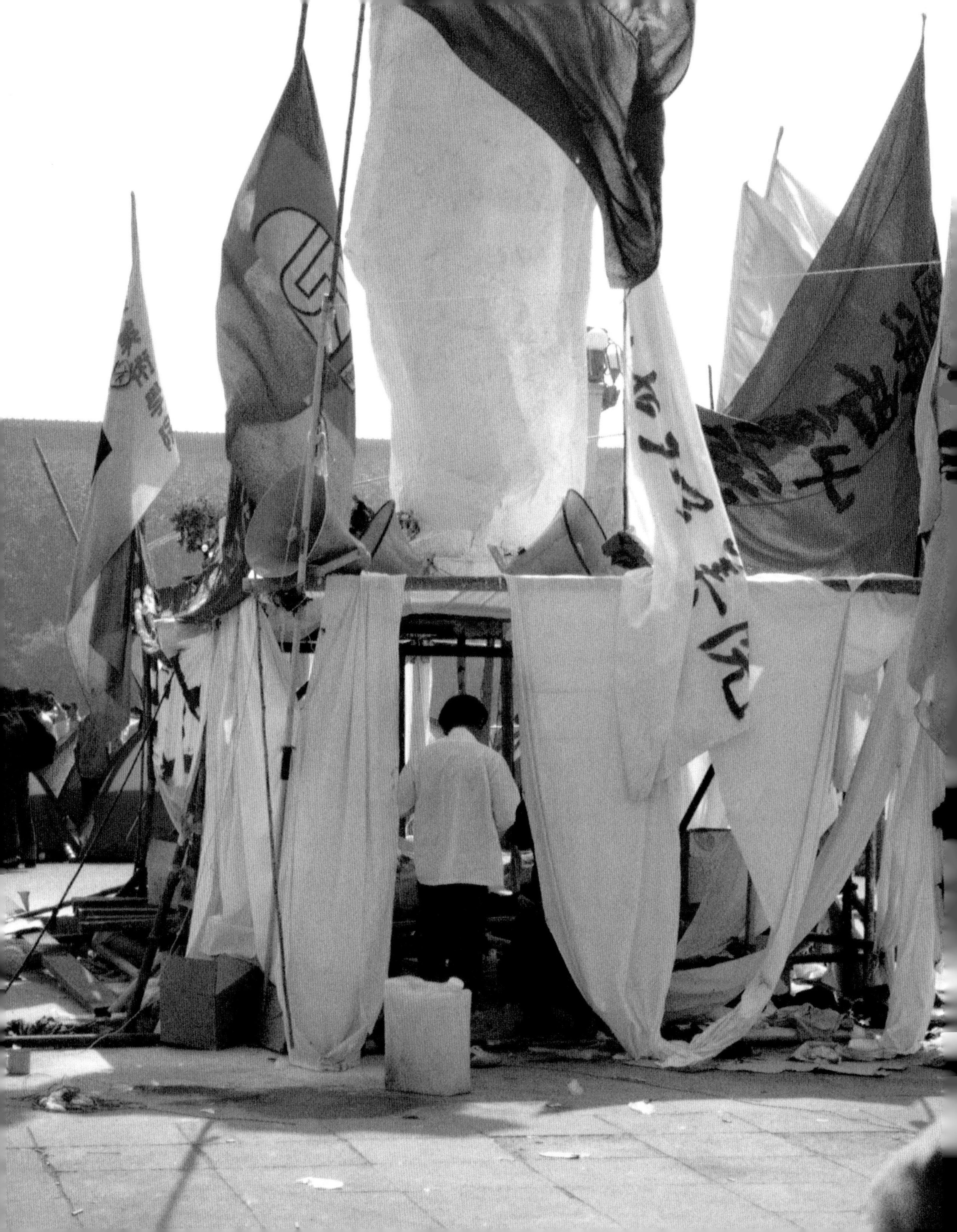

# In the Realm of Space

*The work is not about wrapping as much as it is about the use of fabric, in the city or in a landscape, to bring about transformation . . . What intrigues me is the way nomadic tribes, like those in Tibet, can create, overnight, a giant city of tents—and then it vanishes. I attempt to relay in my work that same idea of transience and passing.*

Christo

## A Tented World

Humans first sought shelter in nature's architecture, in the found volume of the cave or the honeycomb grotto. Later, humans, the builders, created volume by carving into snow to make igloos, by forming heaps of earth and stone into mounds, by twining twigs and vines into protective roofing. Nomadic peoples, always at the mercy of the vagaries of nature, needed portable, reliable shelter. They needed cloth. So sometime still before recorded history, humans, the fabricators, learned to make cloth, and then to make tents.

Christo speaks of the magic of the tented city. He echoes a broader human experience, for many tented images haunt the contemporary psyche. During biblical times the original tent of meeting was pitched in the Sinai Desert. Centuries later, and half a world away, the tented tabernacle evolved into the revival-meeting tents of American fundamentalist Christians. And who can forget the television images beamed by satellite from Beijing to the world in the spring of 1989? This was the tented city erected by Chinese students in Tiananmen Square. The world watched, spellbound, as the young people sat out their confrontation with their government in pop-up tents and canvas army tents, in emergency medical tents and makeshift cloth shelters. Nor will the world forget the night the army tore them down (fig. 134).

Other tents live in the human mind. Among the earliest were the special tents of black goat hair that the Bedouins

134 *(opposite). Eight Went In, One Came Out,* June 3, 1989. Medical tent, Tiananmen Square, Beijing, China.

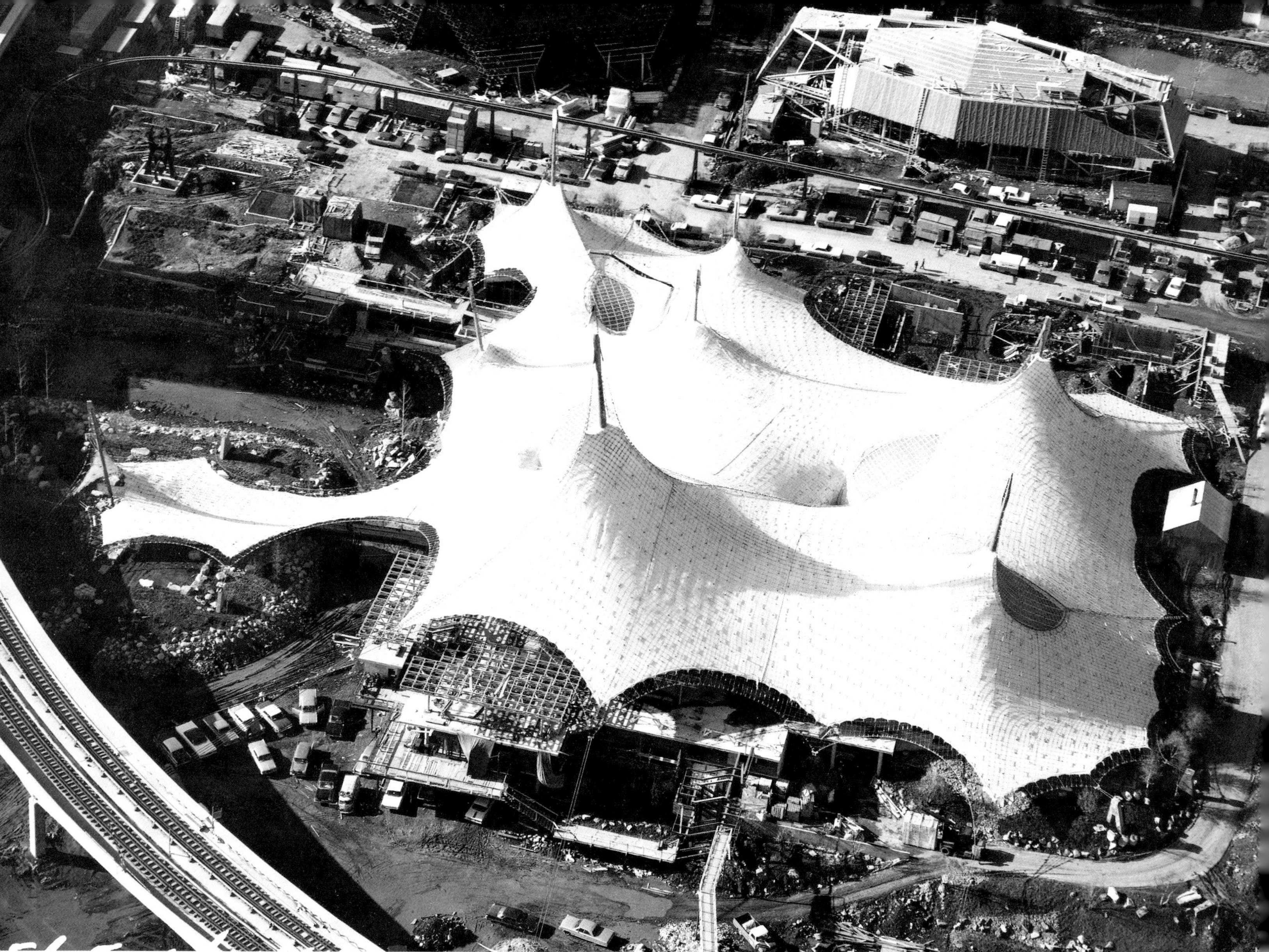

135. Frei Otto (with Rolf Gutbrod, O. Tarnowski, and George F. Eber), pavilion of the Federal Republic of Germany, Expo '67, Montreal, Canada. Translucent synthetic fabric over net wire ropes, edge, eye, and ridge wire, ropes, turnbuckle hangers, 46–125 x 345 x 427´.

erected on the Ajdir Plateau of the Atlas Mountains during the Middle Ages for holiday encampments. Although huge in size, costly to produce, and carefully planned with defined spaces for specific uses, they were still envisioned as temporary shelter. In ancient Persia the palaces of the shah were surrounded by royal encampments (see fig. 2). The vast tented city that the last shah of Iran erected to harbor his international guests for his coronation remains memorable.

As that fated shah demonstrated, the modern world, steeped in technology, still finds in tents the perfect shelter. Hundreds of permanent buildings are constructed with fabric roofs on the great Sahara Desert in response to the need to make conditions tolerable for vast numbers of people working in intense heat. These structures provide ample proof that rugged fabrics, scientifically developed to withstand weather, are viable in today's building industry. Since the 1950s tents have evolved rapidly, becoming light in weight, colorful, easy to install, and astonishingly portable. The current era must be considered the golden age of tent design.

Tents have many manifestations: the portable ceremonial canopy, the canvas storefront awning that shelters pedestrians, the timeless umbrella, the army tent, the circus tent, the boy-scout tent, the oxygen tent, the wedding tent, and the sports dome. The whole human race seems to have lodged in tents, or at least encamped in them, at one time or another. Also, the tent evolved into a ball; its airtight skin was inflated; the ball became a balloon.

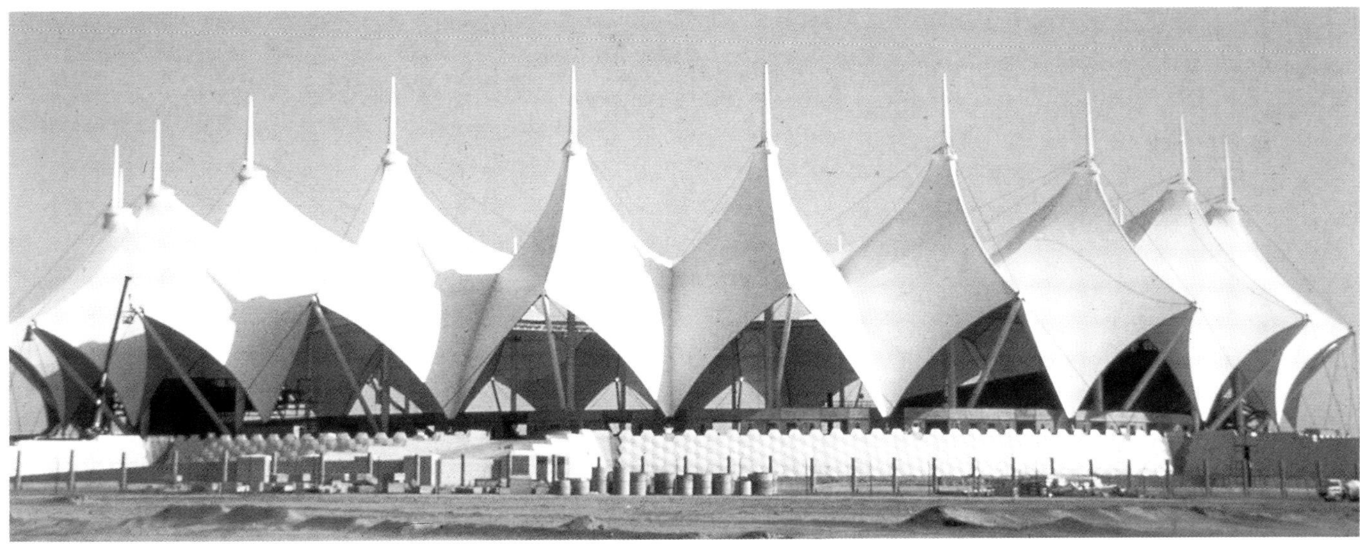

136. Horst Berger, Riyadh International Stadium, Saudi Arabia, 1985.
Tensile roof design, 945´ in diameter. Architects: Ian Fraser, John Roberts and Partners.

Around 1850 the engineering of tents became experimental; iron struts designed to support sheets of glass began to appear as tentlike forms. The most important of these, the Crystal Palace in London, was built in 1851, and from that time forward the interrelationship between the architect and the engineer became the nexus of tent design. Over the next hundred years the shell or membrane structure of the cloth tent metamorphosed into a remarkable architectural presence—truly minimal and yet completely efficacious. In 1954 Sigfried Giedion wrote in *Architectural Record* that the new shell structures were capable of not only roofing enormous assembly halls but also of expressing the emotional aspirations of modern civilization.

Over the next three decades such tensile forms were to come into wide use. Frei Otto is an architect who wrote his doctoral thesis on suspended roofs. His concern was with the fundamentals of structure—how to achieve more with less, how to elevate the traditional cloth tent to a modern building capable of exceptionally large spans. His solution was to introduce synthetic fabrics characterized by extreme lightness and great strength. He and Rolf Gutbrod together created the Pavilion of the Federal Republic of Germany at the World Exposition in Montreal in 1967. The saddlelike curvatures, and the thin membranes stretched over light frames designed to provide the required tension, resulted in a functional pavilion that was unusually poetic as architecture. It was a human-made landscape. Its entire area was covered by a single prestressed membrane of irregular plan and varying height. The translucent skin of cloth hung from its own wire net (fig. 135).

Using cotton canvas or synthetic fabrics—sometimes translucent, sometimes coated with plastics, sometimes colored—Otto built a myriad of structures: shelters and exhibition pavilions, hangar tents, a bandstand, structures for an open theater, roofs for stadiums, skating rinks, water towers, silos, and projection screens.

Like Frei Otto, engineer Horst Berger became convinced that the possibility of fabric structures could and would change architecture. He foresaw the possibility of permanent cloth structures and proved it by building the Haj Terminal at the Jedda Airport and the Riyadh International Stadium, both in Saudi Arabia. The air terminal is spanned by a 105-acre cloth roof. The sports stadium has a roof, 945 feet in diameter, that covers sixty thousand spectators, leaving a hole to the sky in the center, required to meet international regulations for open-field play (fig. 136).

Berger has settled upon loom-woven material because he finds it durable, it can be made noncombustible, and it is

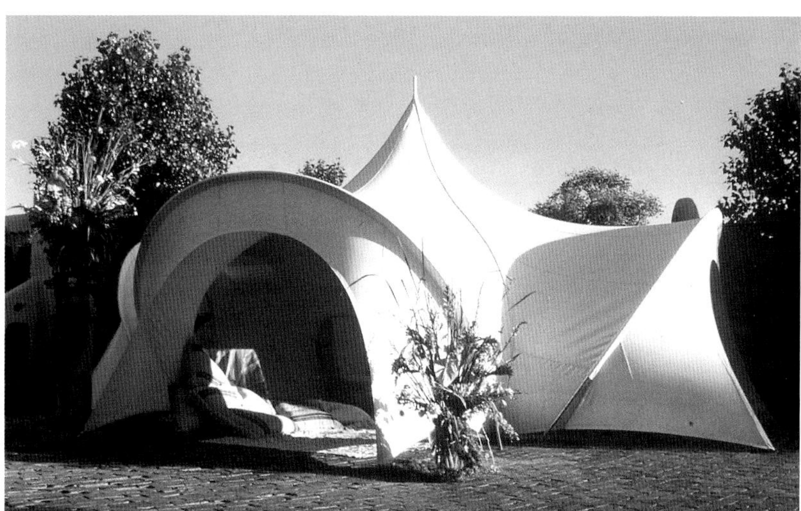

137. Bill Moss, *Optimum 350,* 1979. Cotton, 350´ of floor space, 12´ high, 25´ square.

highly translucent. Previously he had experimented with many fabric treatments, including Teflon, and later, silicone-coated fiberglass.

One marvels at the engineering of these tentlike structures, at the grace of the rigging of mast and cable. No sailing ship ever demanded as much of its masters. But finally it is the sheer beauty of the cloth structures that commands the imagination. The human race has found an even more spectacular way of tenting. French pilot and writer Antoine de Saint-Exupéry summed it up wonderfully in his book *Wind, Sand and Stars:*

> Have you ever thought—that all of man's industrial efforts, all his computations and calculations, all the nights spent over working draughts and blueprints, invariably culminate in the production of a thing whose sole and guiding principle is the ultimate principle of simplicity? It is as if there were a natural law which ordained that to achieve this end, to refine the curve of a piece of furniture, or a ship's keel, or the fuselage of an airplane, until gradually it partakes of the elementary purity of the curve of a human breast or shoulder, there must be the experimentation of several generations of craftsmen. In anything at all, perfection is finally attained not when there is no longer anything to add, but when there is no longer anything to take away, when a body has been stripped down to its nakedness.

Otto and Berger were interested in expanding architectural space by developing tent technology. Bill Moss, a painter who came to consider himself a fabric sculptor, envisioned space made sculptural on the human scale. It is he who in the late 1960s invented the pop-up tent, that highly portable, small pup tent that revolutionized the world of camping, hiking, exploring, mountaineering, and even protesting.

It all started accidentally, when Moss tired of making traditional paintings. As an experiment he removed his painting from the wall, seeking to create a three-dimensional, circular canvas. He found that by building a fabric dome, he could make a 360-degree painting. Once the kernel was wedged into his mind he could not be stopped. Again, useful spaces emerged out of the original idea, this time the pop-up tent—cloth given form by a lightweight curvilinear frame made of aluminum and fiberglass rods.

Moss quickly became interested in designing tensioned-fabric housing, feeling that fabric, although generally overlooked as a building material, has endless application for enclosure of space. Subsequently, he created everything from display booths to emergency shelters. He made a proposal to the American Craft Museum in New York in 1980 for a portable museum. He used four thousand square feet of cotton fabric, sandwiched in three layers for heat retention, for his tensioned-fabric structure, which he titled *Art You Can Live In.* That same year he received a National Endowment for the Arts award for a 350-square-foot living space that he called *Optimum 350.* The structure was twenty-five feet square and twelve feet high, with arched alcoves around a vaulted central space. It would function in either hot or cold weather, which suggested many uses: a domestic home in a temperate climate, a base camp in the Himalayas, a portable tent for the nomadic peoples of the Middle East. He created similar "space articulations," fabric shelters for urban plazas and housing developments. In all of this work, Moss never lost sight of fabric as material for sculpture (fig. 137).

The museum world also did not miss this tenting movement sweeping the architectural world. In May 1984 the exhibition "Temporary Space: The Contemporary Tent" opened under the canopy at the Temporary Contemporary, the most avant-garde art museum in Los Angeles. In the catalog essay curator Jacqueline Crist addressed the mountaineering tent as the essence of modern humanity's dream of freedom and independence:

> The ancient architecture of tensile structure and the evolution of form through function bring this compact and geometric shelter before us as a state of the art achievement in the design of temporary space. Providing a barrier between life and death these small cloth structures have seen the heights of the world's highest mountains and have traveled to far corners of the earth on the backs of not only explorers and scientists, but of ordinary men and women who yearn to set foot on new frontiers.
>
> The mountaineering tent is a simple architectural answer to complex design questions. Solving the need for a temporary shelter which must be lightweight, strong enough to withstand fierce winds, have the ability to breathe, thus preventing condensation but still be waterproof, has been a long and complicated process. The environment around the tent must not suffer so tents have been made in neutral colors, easy to look at and to live in. The tent must be in harmony with the world around it so we see smooth, flowing lines reminiscent of rolling hills and distant horizons. The mountaineering tent is architecture and design with function and balance with nature its highest priorities.

In 1989 the University of Northern Iowa found a remarkable solution to a shelter problem. Each year the *Des Moines Register* sponsors the "Ragbrai," the Great Bike Ride Across Iowa. Covering 479 miles, this is the oldest and largest touring bicycle ride in the world. Over 7,500 bikers and 2,500 support personnel would need to be housed on the night of July 27 on the Cedar Falls campus. Most importantly, given Iowa's hot and steamy weather, they would need shade and shelter from storms. The university established a $50,000 budget and commissioned Arizona sculptor James White to create a solution. White consulted with Bill Moss on tent structure before ordering 33,000 square feet of nylon fabric. White, the director of a commercial neon gallery in Tucson, hired the lighting designer from his gallery, Rick Holmes, as one project manager and Rico Eastman, an instructor at the Rhode Island School of Design, as the other (fig. 138).

Called *Square Wave—Aere Perennius*, the work incorporated 144 tentlike structures eighteen feet wide and eighteen feet deep. Three corners were staked to the ground. The fourth corner was stretched into the air and held with a twelve-foot-long steel support pole. Attached to each pole was a red-and-blue neon element. The neon lights were wired to a central control panel, allowing White to create a changing light show. The neon dimmed and brightened in a wave pattern across the square matrix of the pitched tents, which generated the first half of the title. *Aere perennius* is Latin for "more lasting than bronze." The artist believed, rightly, that the work of art would live in the minds of those who experienced it far longer than any conventional bronze sculpture—just as Deborah Butterfield's horses made of old wood live in the mind long after her monumental bronze renditions have faded from memory (see page 135).

Jim White, Frei Otto, Horst Berger, and Bill Moss create tented art out of physical need. Conversely, Nancy Hemenway creates sociological statements out of the tented form. In the early 1980s she began a series of sculptures based upon the tepee of the ancient Plains Indian. This prehistoric, cone-shaped, portable shelter was traditionally made of hide. Later, after European settlers introduced cloth into general usage on the North American continent (and buffalo were becoming scarce), Native Americans began to make summer tepees of heavy cotton canvas. Once the women had stitched them together, the men of the tribe covered the outer surfaces with painted scenes of battle and signs of good omen. But as the settlers swept across the Great Plains, forcing the nomadic peoples onto reservations, the tepee fell into general disuse. Today it mostly appears at summer powwow campgrounds, in the backyards

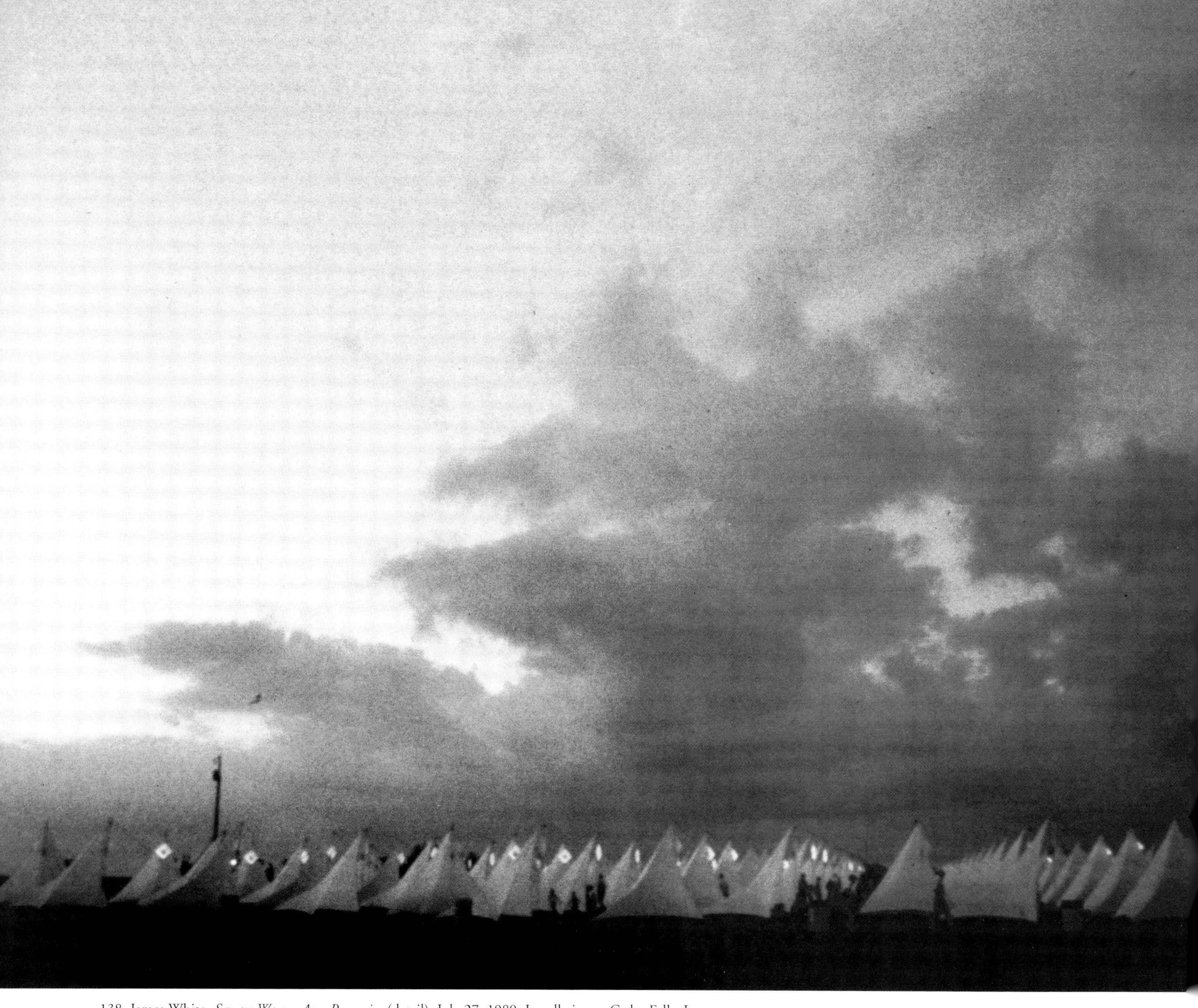

138. James White, *Square Wave—Aere Perennius* (detail), July 27, 1989. Installation at Cedar Falls, Iowa.

of children playing "Indian," in museums, and at special celebrations.

Embroidery is a craft redolent of another, more leisurely era. Ladies in genteel societies embroidered. European women migrating west were skilled with the needle, so they brought their fine fabrics and silken embroidery threads with them. Hemenway has embroidered for years, embellishing the surfaces of cloth with age-old stitches. However, unlike her predecessors who prided themselves on making tiny stitches, she embroiders on a grand scale. Instead of viewing stitching as lap work she envisions it as a means to create monumental works of art. To take the ancestral shelter of once august but now decimated tribes, and to cover it with a lady's embroidery stitches grown huge, is to make bitter comment on the fate of the first Americans. Chain stitches and French knots have replaced the painted exploits of warring braves. In this body of work Hemenway delineates the principle that form is important not as imitation but as metaphor for human experience (fig. 139).

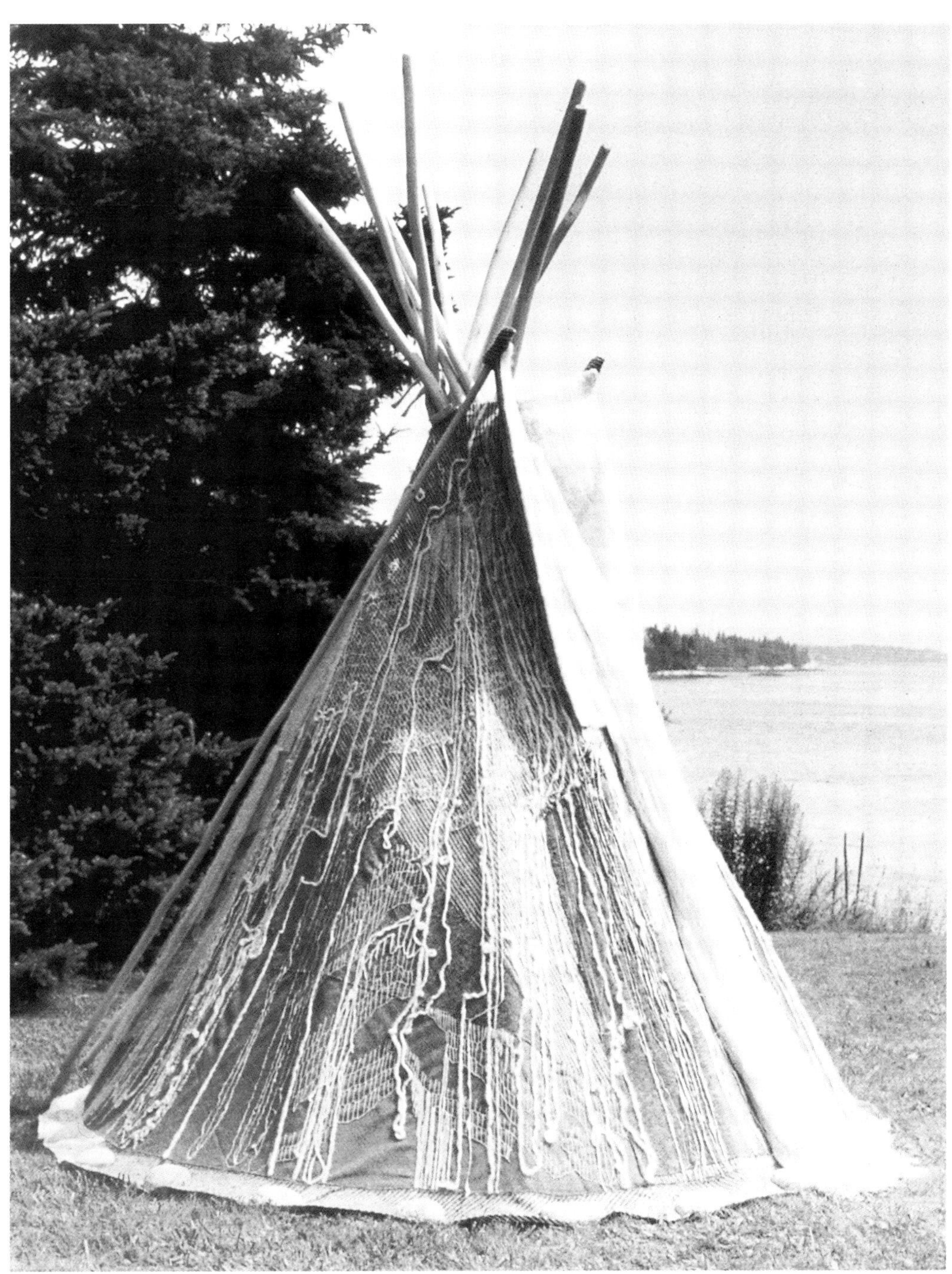

139. Nancy Hemenway, *Tipi Waterfall,* 1982. Embroidery, alpaca, wood, and stones, c. 156 x 312″.

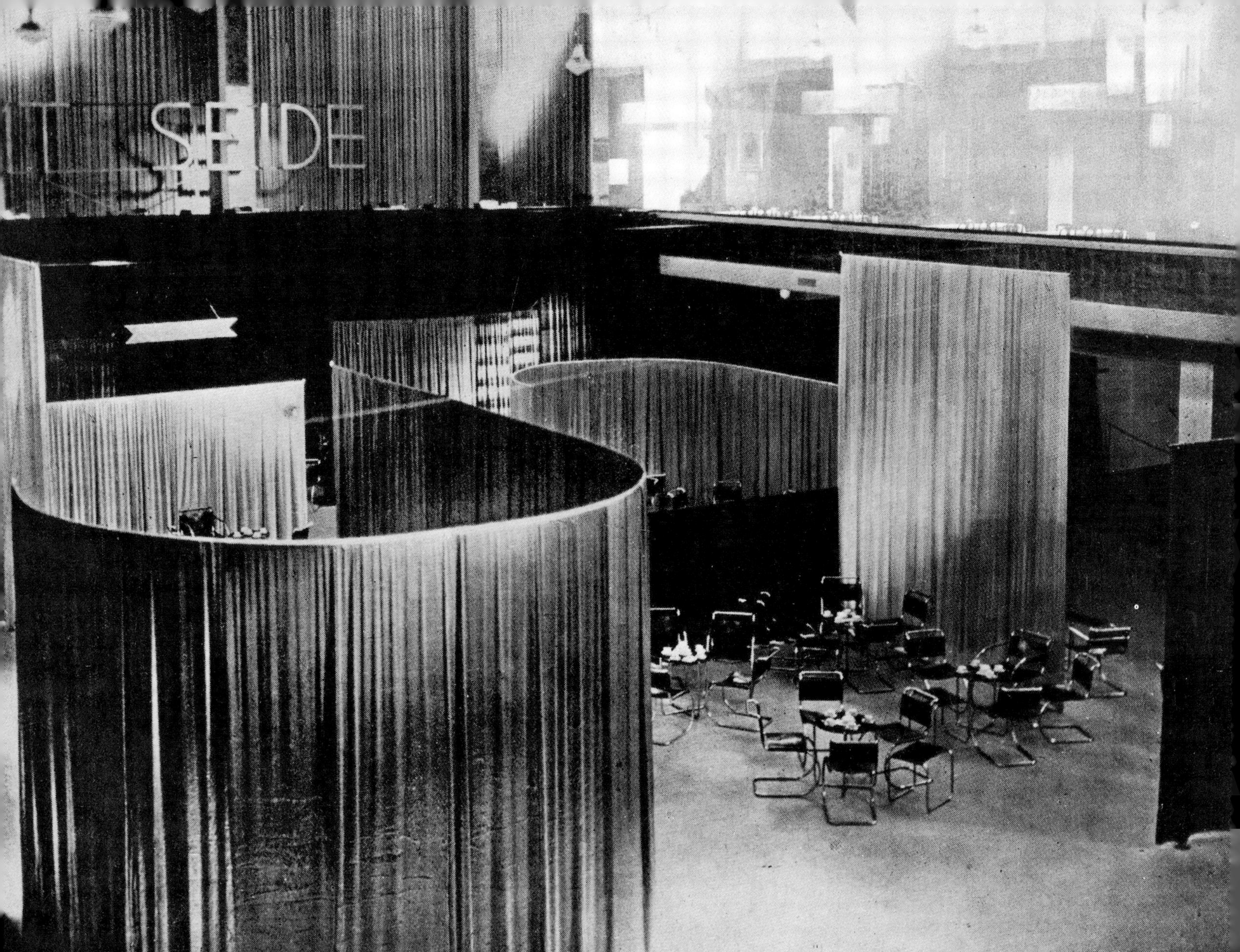


140. Lilly Reich and Ludwig Mies van der Rohe, *Café Samt und Seide (Velvet and Silk Café)*, 1927. Created for "Die Mode der Dame" ("Women's Fashion") exhibition of the Imperial Association of German Fashion Industry and the Berlin Fair office, fairgrounds, Berlin, September 21–October 16, 1927.

# Rooms Defined by Cloth

Lilly Reich, German designer and architect of the 1920s and 1930s, was always attracted to textiles. Most known for her contributions to exhibition design, and for her collaborations with Ludwig Mies van der Rohe, she often called upon cloth as the vehicle for her most important designs. In 1926 Reich designed, organized, and installed the exhibition "From Fiber to Textile" at the International Frankfurt Fair. A year later she was invited to collaborate with Mies in the creation of the *Café Samt und Seide (Velvet and Silk Café)* that was part of the exhibition "Die Mode der Dame" ("Women's Fashion"). Reich used hanging velvet draperies of black, orange, and red, plus black and lemon-yellow silks, to define a series of small spaces that flowed into each other. Hung from tubular rods in the manner of contemporary hospital room dividers, or simple shower curtains, the cloth served as an architectural element (fig. 140).

The French Conceptual artist Daniel Buren, like Reich, uses cloth to inscribe space, especially the space determined by architecture. Throughout his long career, the stripe has served as his motif. He applies it to everything from sails for boats to beach chairs to formal elements of architecture. By sheathing the outside of a building in cloth, he makes the viewer acutely aware of the shape and dimensions of the building. By clothing the inner confines of a building with striped cloth, he reconfigures the space, or he emphasizes the space already defined by architecture. Buren's stripes, assiduously applied either to the whole or to carefully chosen parts, command the viewer to see the formal attributes of both architecture and building. Cloth goes up and cloth comes back down. However, the sensibility and awareness of those who witness its short presence is forever altered. Buren has worked all over the world, from South Korea to the Caribbean, from across the United States to the whole of Europe. Universally, those who see his work respond with the same arrested attention (fig. 141).

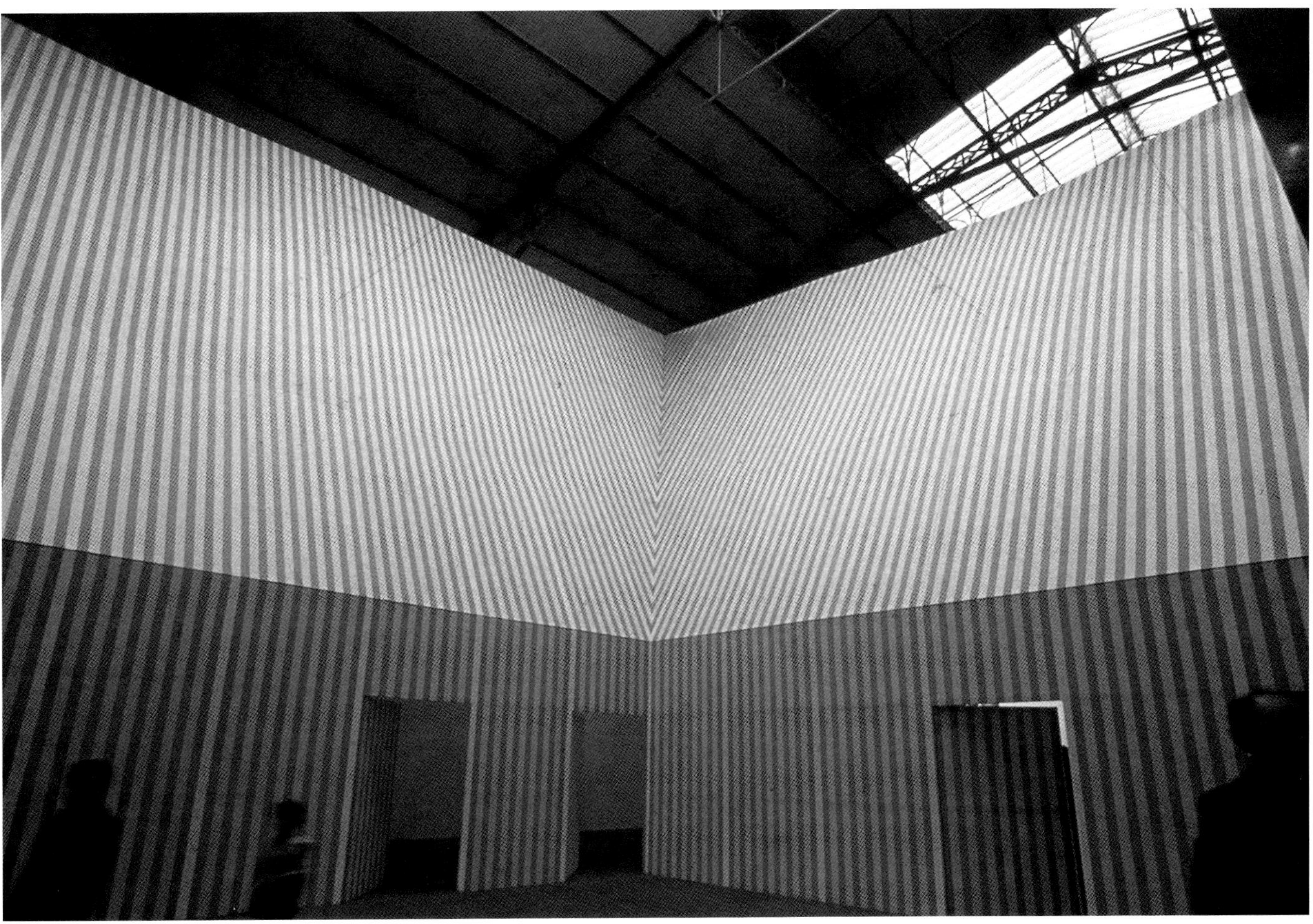

141. Daniel Buren, *La Rencontre des sites*, 1985. Shown at the Nouvelle Biennale, Paris. Courtesy John Weber Gallery, New York.

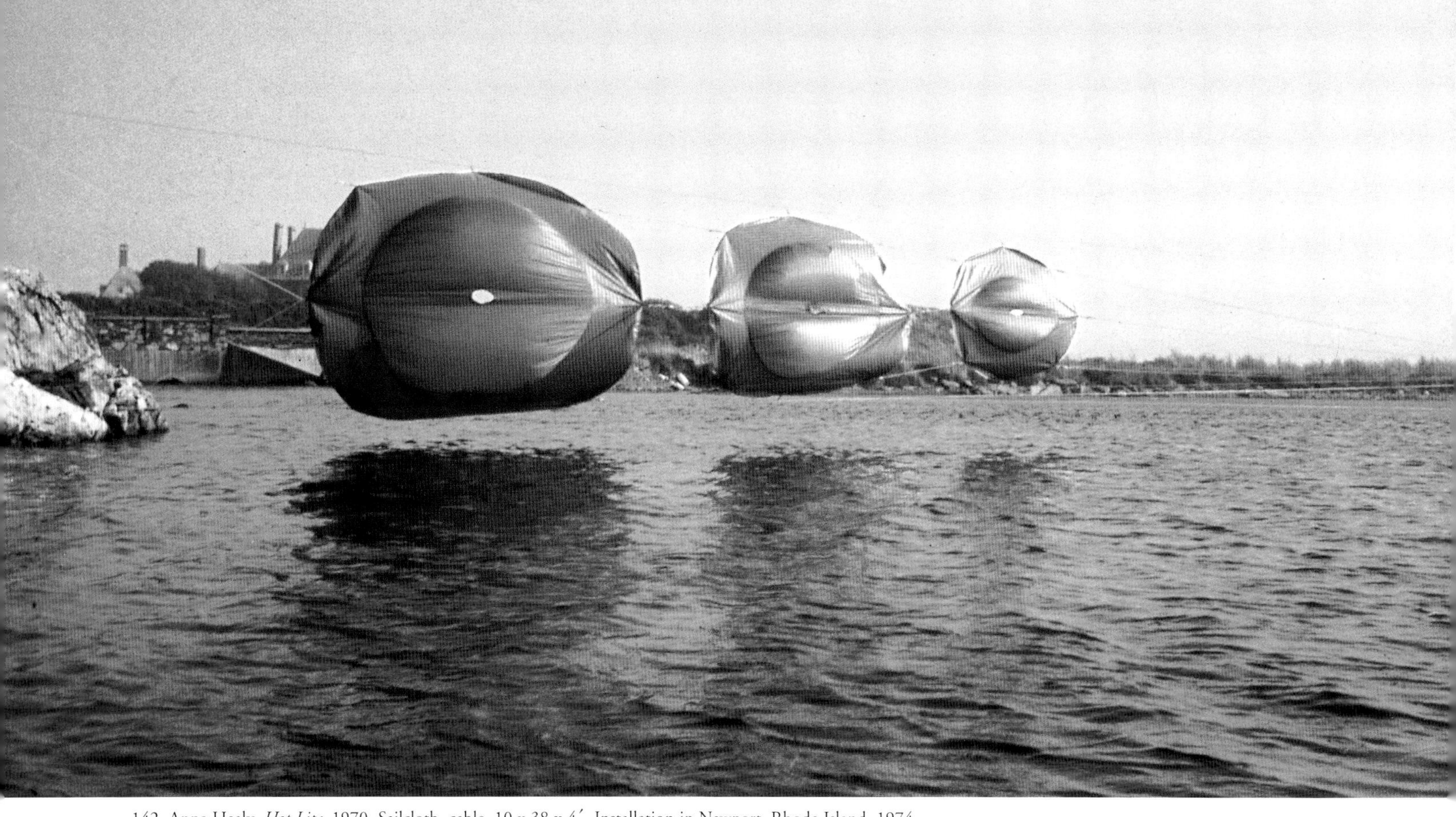

142. Anne Healy, *Hot Lips,* 1970. Sailcloth, cable, 10 x 38 x 4´. Installation in Newport, Rhode Island, 1974.

# Cloth in Space

Wind, water, light, and space: these are the earthly elements that artists who work out of doors depend on in making their works of art. To move into a space and to possess it is their immediate goal. If the work of art is successful, and only a handful have been, the artist transforms the viewers' relationship with the environment. For example, one cannot drive through the hills of Marin County north of San Francisco if one has seen Christo's *Running Fence*, or even the documentation of it, without vividly recalling it in the mind's eye.

Environmental works in cloth are temporary, but their existence is permanent in memory and through documentation. They go beyond Conceptual art because they have a powerful physical presence during their brief moments of being. It matters not whether they are in an urban setting, within a natural landscape, or tied to the sea. It only matters that the cloth be brought into contact with the essential elements. While many of these works are site specific, those that depend on transitory elements such as the wind are movable works of art capable of being installed in other places.

Among artists who first used cloth to make site-specific works are Phillips Simkin, Daniel Graffin, Magdalena Abakanowicz, Gerhardt Knodel, Ann Hamilton, and Leo Copers. Artists such as Anne Healy or Hideo Tanaka can create work anywhere as long as a particular integral natural element is present. Healy needs an expanse of water (fig. 142); Tanaka needs a wave-riddled strip of sand. Simkin needs a stretch of ice. But working with nature is risky business for artists, as well as athletes, as the 1980 Winter Olympics proved. Lois Johnson, Simkin's collaborator at Lake Placid, found her work crumbling when an unseasonable thaw descended upon the Olympics (see fig. 113 for Johnson's solution).

Simkin's *Rosebud II: Seven Self-Propelled Earthly Parodies* consisted of seven houses, ranging in height from twelve to over twenty feet. The artist made them from the same materials as ordinary winter parkas—quilted ripstop nylon stuffed with duck feathers. Each house contained a setting parodying one of the stages of life identified by Shakespeare in *As You Like It:*

bawling infant, whining schoolboy, sighing lover, quarrelsome soldier, bearded justice, spectacled geezer, and second childhood, "sans teeth, sans eyes, sans taste, sans everything." The viewer moved from infancy to old age, from a small house in the beginning to the largest house in the middle and back to a small house at the other end. Collectively, the houses formed an "ark" whose sides could be hauled up like sails. The ark sailed across the ice on the runners of 160 children's sleds, which according to Simkin, refer to both the universal vehicle of playing in the snow and the use of the sled named Rosebud in the film *Citizen Kane* as a metaphor for simultaneous joy and frustration (fig. 144).

Simkin's parka houses piece, doubling as life's sailing ship, is a complicated visual parody and one of the most recondite works of art in this book. Other artists look at the sail for its poetic, visual power. To capture the wind in art can become a life's work.

No one is more reliant upon the wind's play than Cindy Snodgrass. Her giant wind sculptures float from the stark, formal buildings of hard-edged, urban settings. The wind inflates and mobilizes these brightly colored, ripstop-nylon, free-form descendants of the kite. Fabric, which she always dyes herself, seems a natural medium for Snodgrass. Its lightness, its capacity for fullness, and its potential for infinite expansion allow her to create a public art that is both impermanent and ephemeral. She has launched these wind creations from buildings all over the United States (fig. 143).

Like Snodgrass, Daniel Graffin has made sails to catch the wind. For the 1995 Venice Biennale, General Commissioner Jean Clair invited Graffin to create a group of wind sculptures over the Grand Canal. The artist decided to base his work on the shapes of the coifs of the ambassadors in Piero della Francesca's Legend of the True Cross fresco cycle of about 1450 in the church of San Francesco in Arezzo. Graffin's goal was not

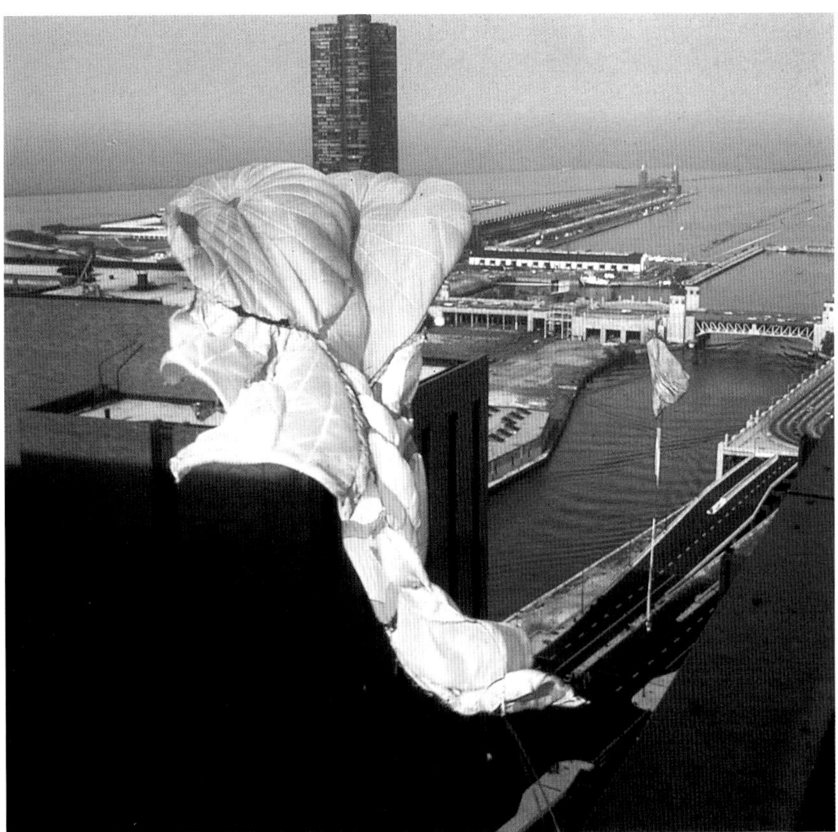

143. Cindy Snodgrass, *Wind Waves* (detail), 1975. Installed in Chicago. Ripstop nylon, 75 x 55 x 75´. Collection Herbert F. Johnson Museum of Art, Cornell University, Ithaca, New York.

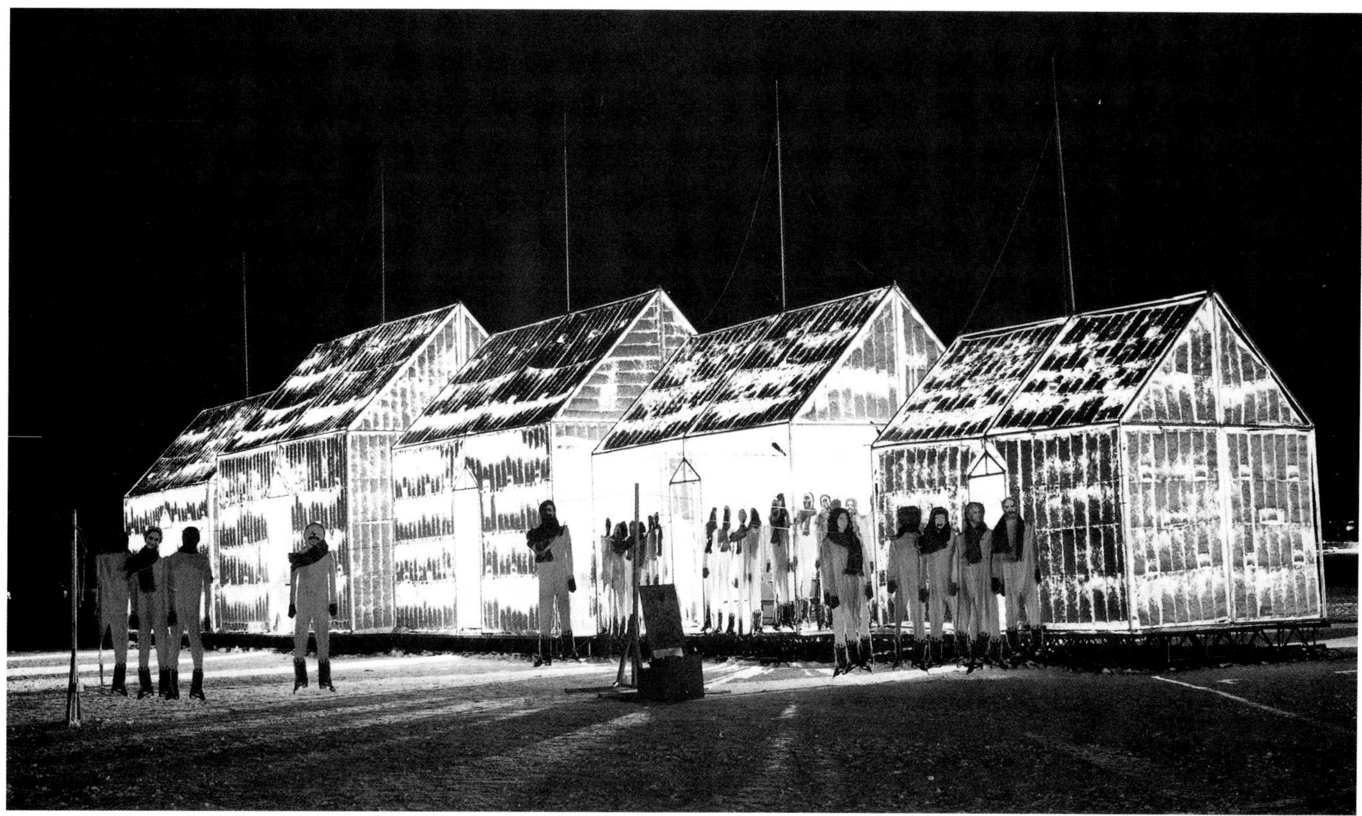

144. Phillips Simkin, *Rosebud II: Seven Self-Propelled Earthly Parodies,* 1980.
Installed on the lake at the thirteenth Winter Olympics, Lake Placid, New York.
Frame houses covered with quilted ripstop nylon filled with duck feathers, 12½–22 x 125′.
In the foreground is Lois Johnson's *Audience Frieze* (see fig. 113).

to create a figure in space by the usual method of outlining or contouring, but to build a cellular system of primary shapes that is made rigid by the wind rather than either an axle support or a still frame. The triangle, the square, and the pentagon made of sailcloth form the structural cells. They become three dimensional as the wind fills them, thus giving substance to these figures in space (figs. 145–47).

Other artists address the wind in its absence. For example, Vera Szekely's *Membrane* is an installation of twisting, curving, angling, sail-like forms that unfold in space. In the absolute rigidity forced upon them by a system of wood struts, they suggest endless movement—a mad, gyrating wind. Energy is crystallized in each cloth construction. Founded on the principle of reconciliation between opposites, the work is both terrestrial and aerial, moving in a circular motion—up, around, and back to the earth. Likewise Satoru Shoji incorporates the absent wind as an essential element in his Navigation series (figs. 148, 149).

The wind is long removed from the work of Machiko Agano. Only stillness remains. Air, space, and light permeate her composition of stirring shadows and depths. She takes the softest, most transparent silk organza and fashions it into diaphanous leaves. These gentle leaves breathe with a life all their own. The accumulation of delicate elements, unpretentiously installed, lends a spiritual presence to the place where the work resides (fig. 150).

In 1993 Mitsuo Toyazaki was invited by the North Dakota Museum of Art to participate in the exhibition "Light and Shadow: Japanese Artists in Space." The exhibition was held in

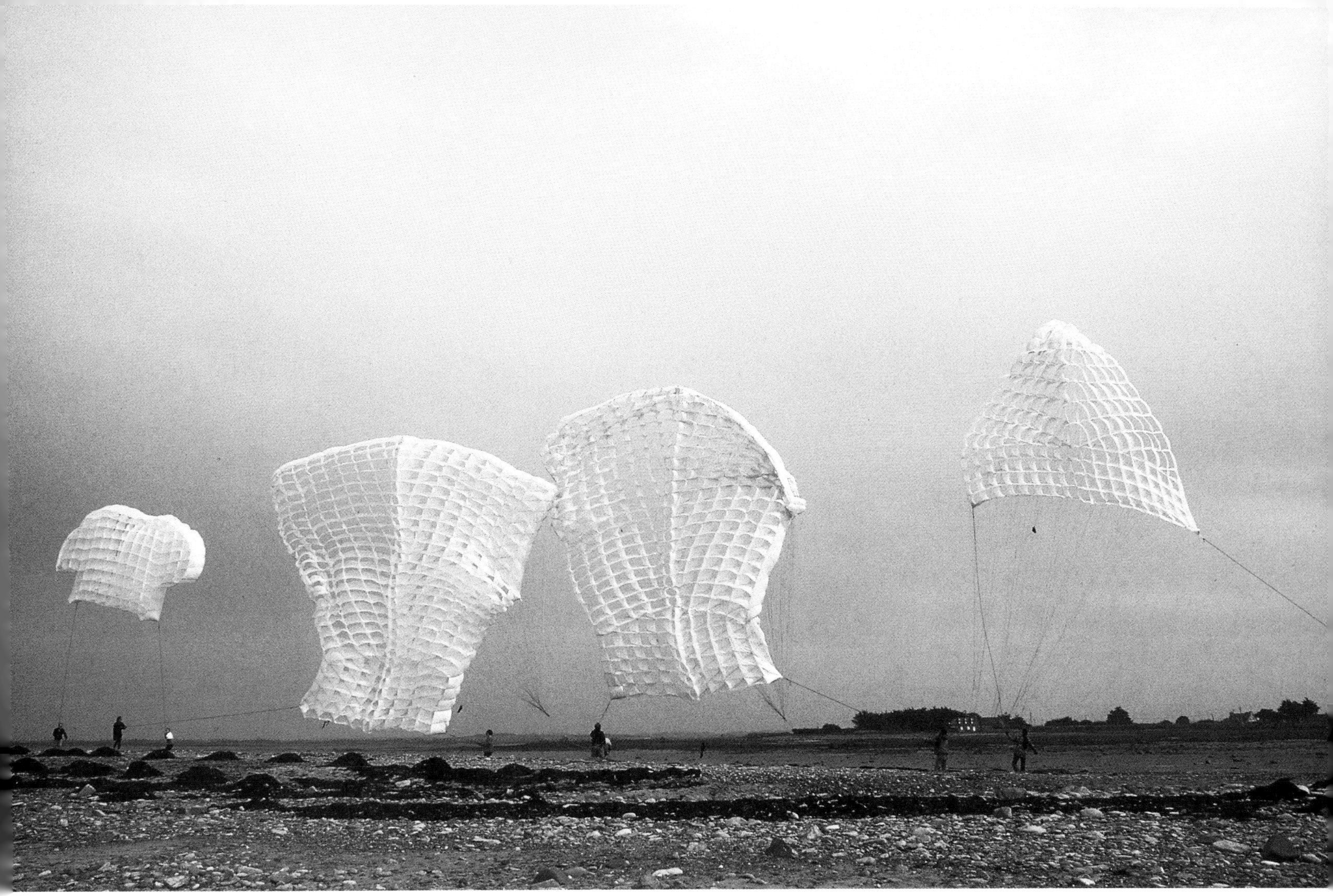

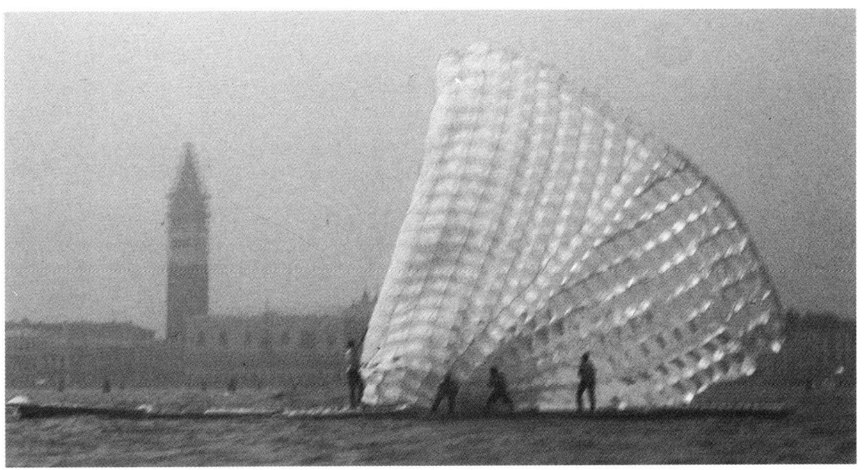

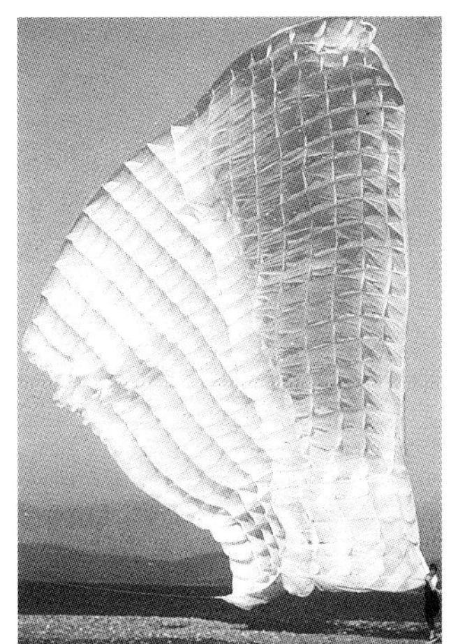

145–47. Daniel Graffin, *Wind Sculptures*, 1995. Sail cloth, c. 650 x 487 x 39′. Installed at the Venice Biennale, 1995.

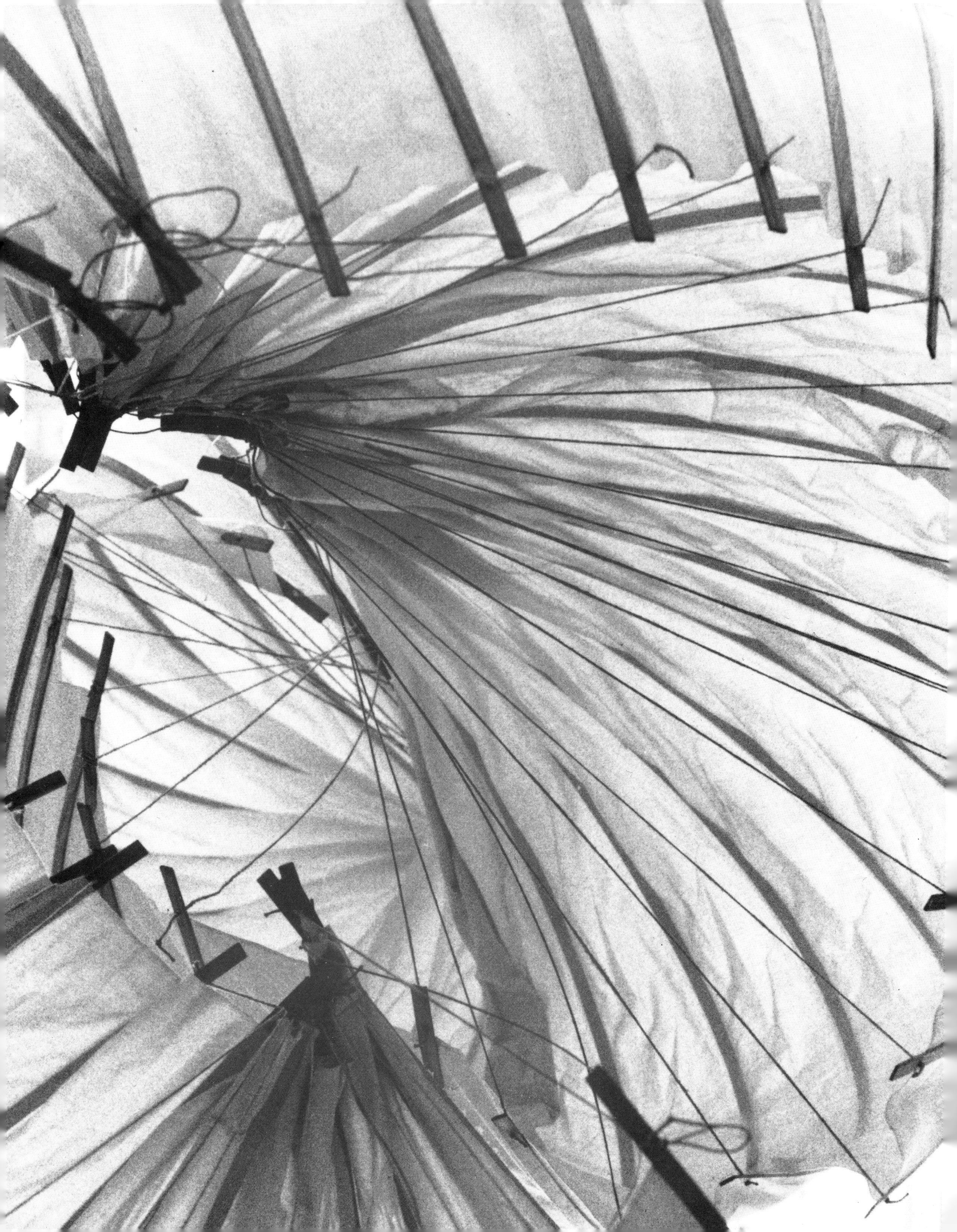

148 *(opposite).* Vera Szekely, *Membrane* (detail), 1982. Fabric, wood, and string.

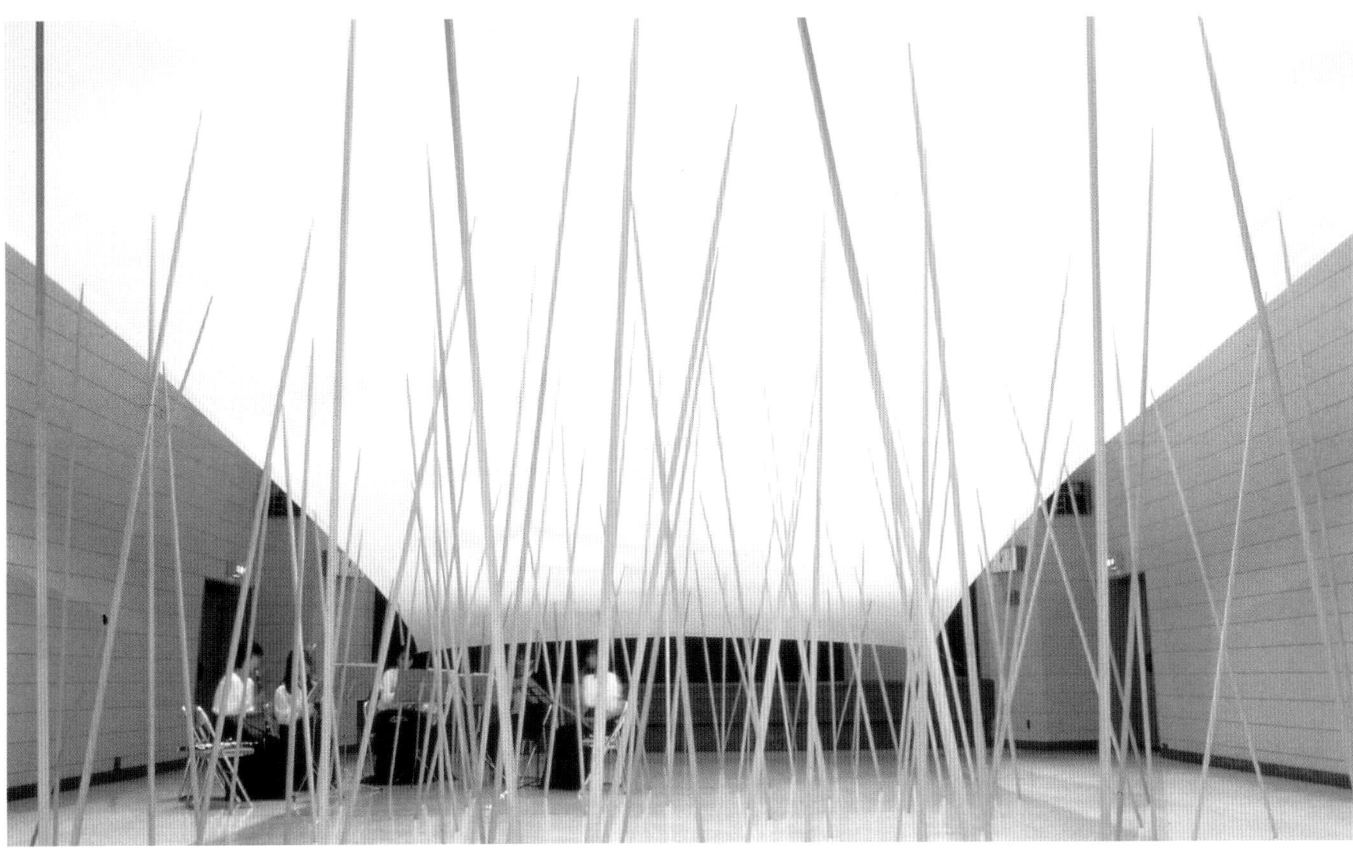

149. Satoru Shoji, *Navigation No. 4,* 1987. Cotton cloth, corded and painted wood poles, 39½ x 24⅗ x 11⅘′. Installed at the Mitsukoshi Yokohama Department Store.

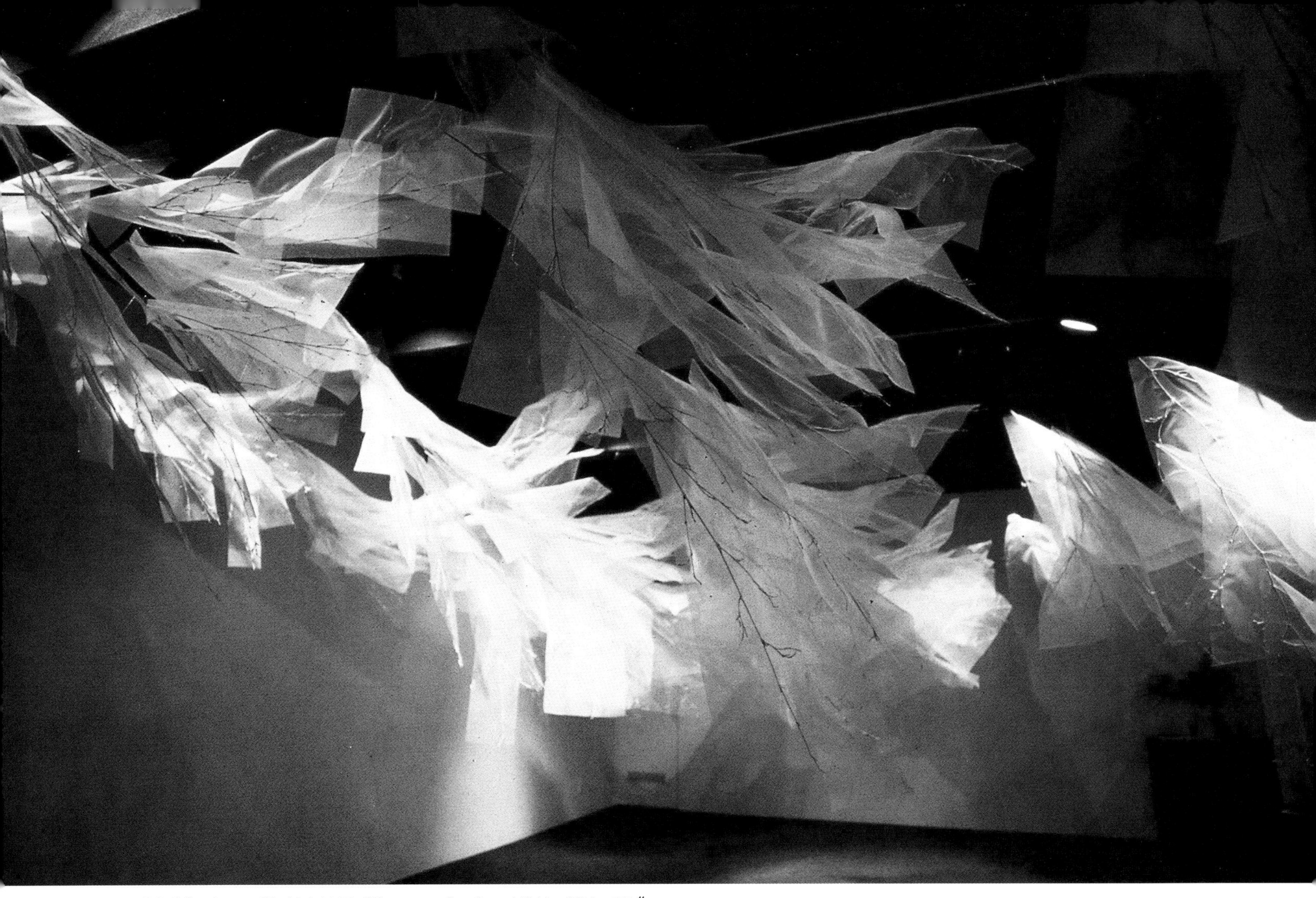

150. Machiko Agano, *Untitled,* 1987. Silk organza, bamboo, 161⅜ x 98⅛ x 3⅛″.

three parts over the course of a year and brought over a dozen artists from Japan to North Dakota to install work. Toyazaki's response did not parallel the work of the rest of the invited artists, who presented pieces in which light or its absence were formal elements. Instead Toyazaki thought about the United States and England, countries that, throughout their years of shared history, were always falling into either the light or the shadow of the other. He made two huge banners representing their respective national flags and hung them on the museum grounds in the direct path of the prevailing westerlies, the incessant winds of the northern High Plains. Side by side, the flags battled with the wind, sometimes in harmony, sometimes entangled, taking turns casting shadows one upon the other (fig. 153).

Hideo Tanaka, on the other hand, chooses the sea as his collaborator. Air, cloth, sand, water, and fire are the elements from which he makes grand abstractions. Composing his work over a period of days, he uses the camera to record its changes from construction to destruction, always subordinating his art to nature. Transformation and transition are at the heart of his aesthetic intentions. In the open-air installation at Hamamatsu Beach entitled *Vanishing (Season to Season),* the artist threaded cotton yardage with rope onto the surface of the sand. Eventually he set fire to the cloth, thus obliterating it. The effect of the fire was both creative and destructive. The imbedded, burned cloth resembles the frothy, broken tops of receding waves (figs. 151, 152).

Harne Takami, also in the "Light and Shadow: Japanese Artists in Space" exhibition, created a work in homage to her mother, a traditional Japanese geisha. In a labor-intensive act of meditation, she cut pounds of solid-colored cloth into small squares. She cast the precisely cut bits of red, yellow, green,

151. Hideo Tanaka on the beach installing *Vanishing (Season to Season)*, 1986.

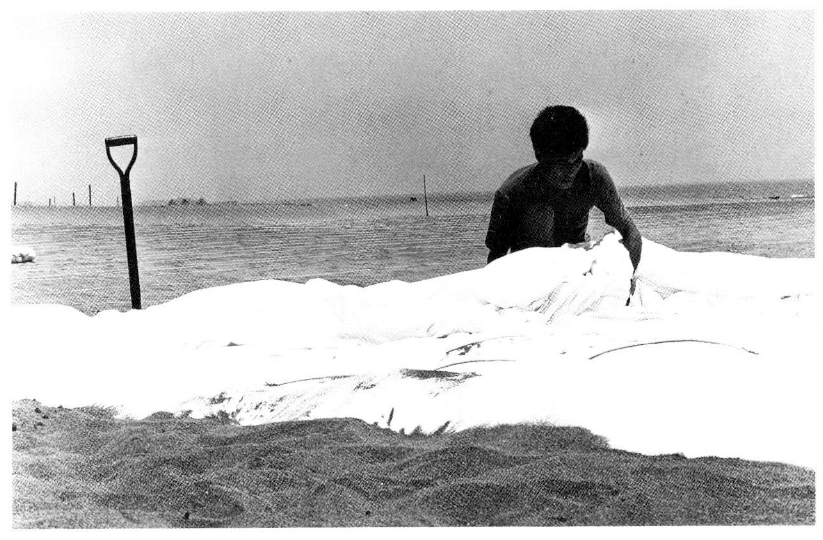

152. Hideo Tanaka, *Vanishing (Season to Season)*, 1986. Cotton cloth, sand, and fire, 58.2 x 50.6´. Open-air installation at Hamamatsu Beach, Japan.

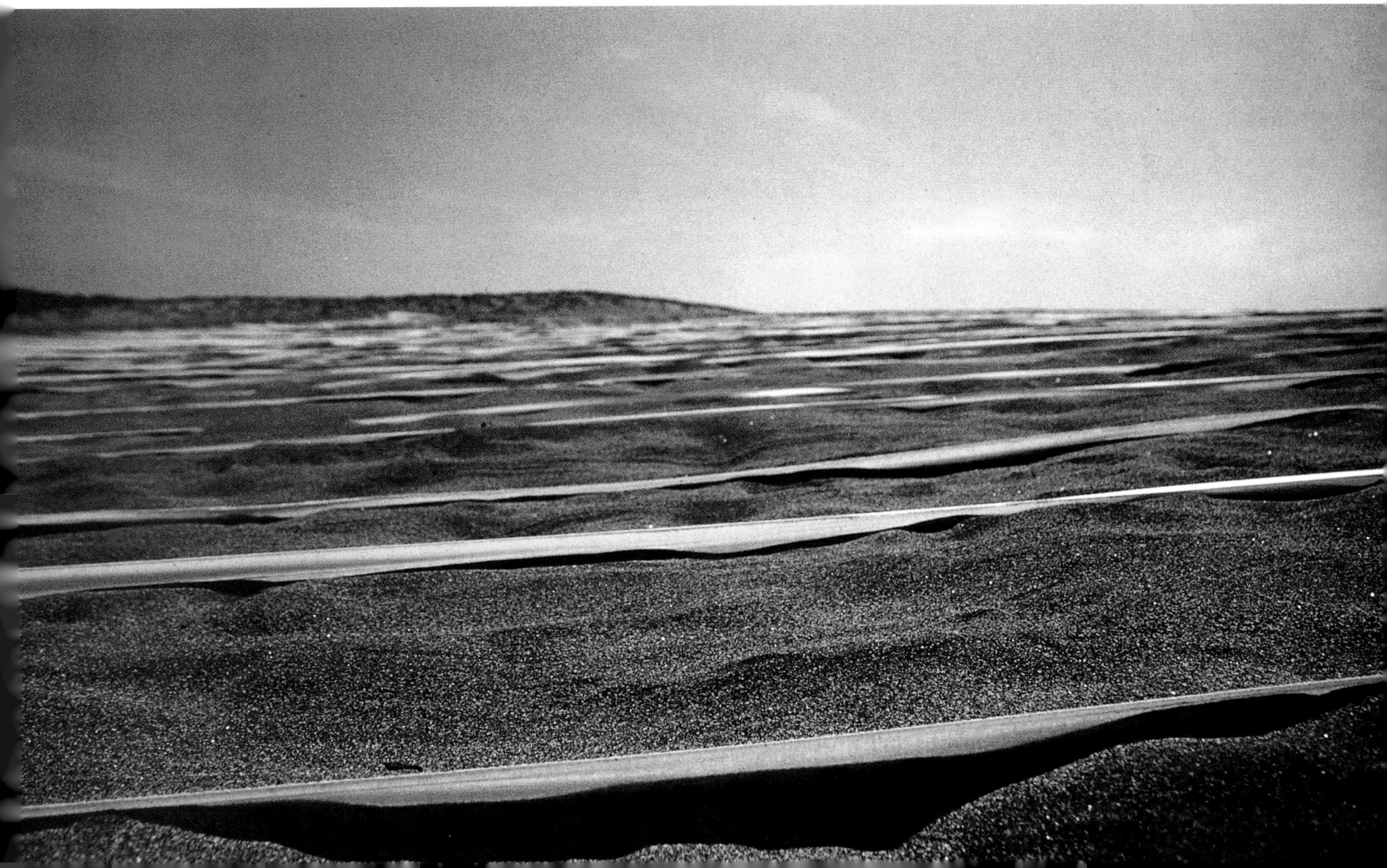

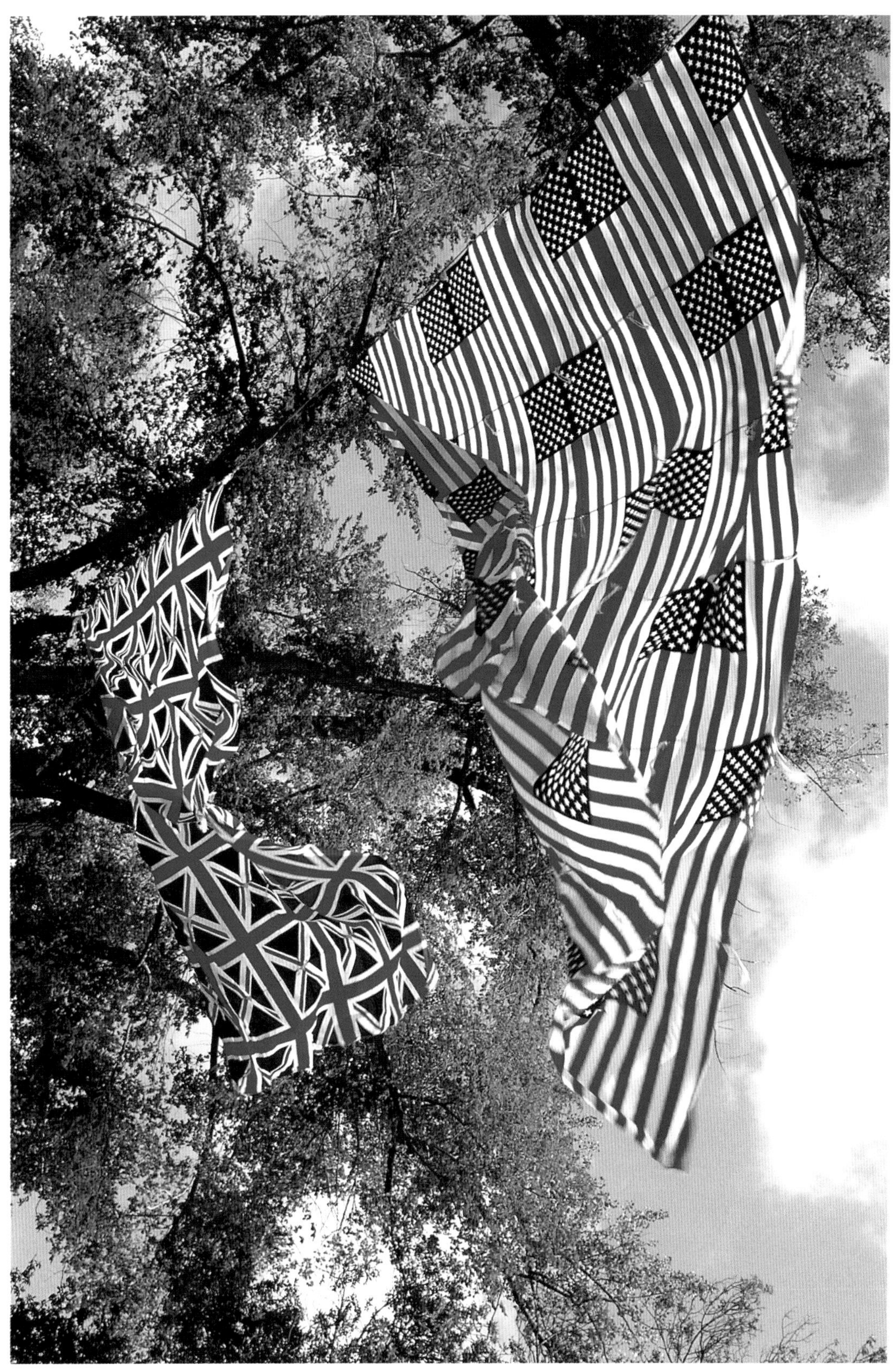

153. Mitsuo Toyazaki, *Stripes and Checks or the States and Great Britain,* 1994. Installed at the North Dakota Museum of Art, Grand Forks. Ready-made flags and grommets, two units, each 19′7″ x 13′9″.

154. Harne Takami, *River,* 1994. Cotton cloth and spotlight, 24′ x 33′ x 1″. Installed at the North Dakota Museum of Art, Grand Forks.

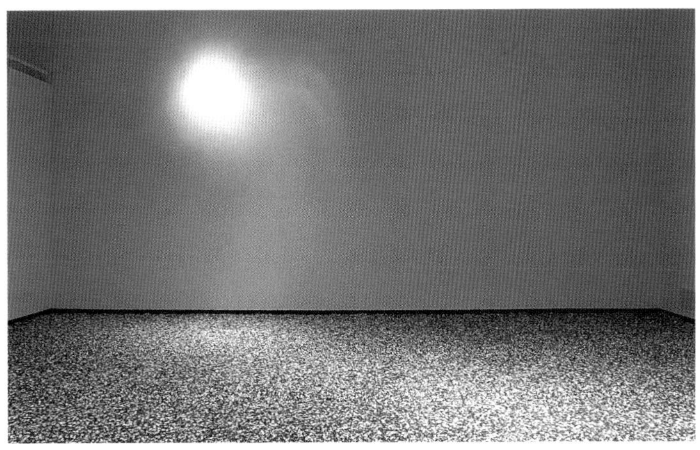

155. Christo and Jeanne-Claude, *The Pont Neuf Wrapped, Paris,* 1975–85. 440,000 square feet of woven polyamide fabric restrained by 42,900 feet of rope. Copyright Christo, 1985.

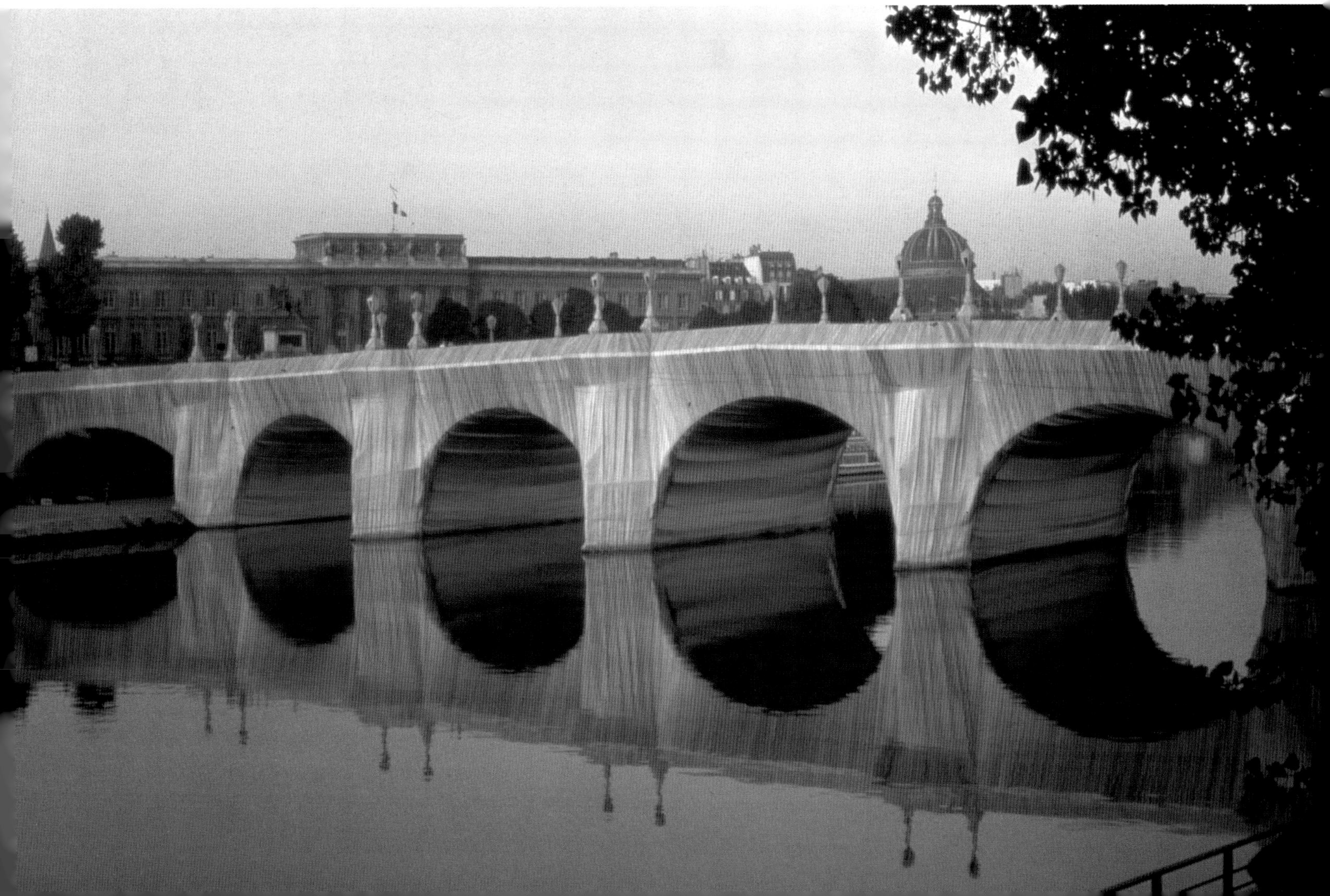

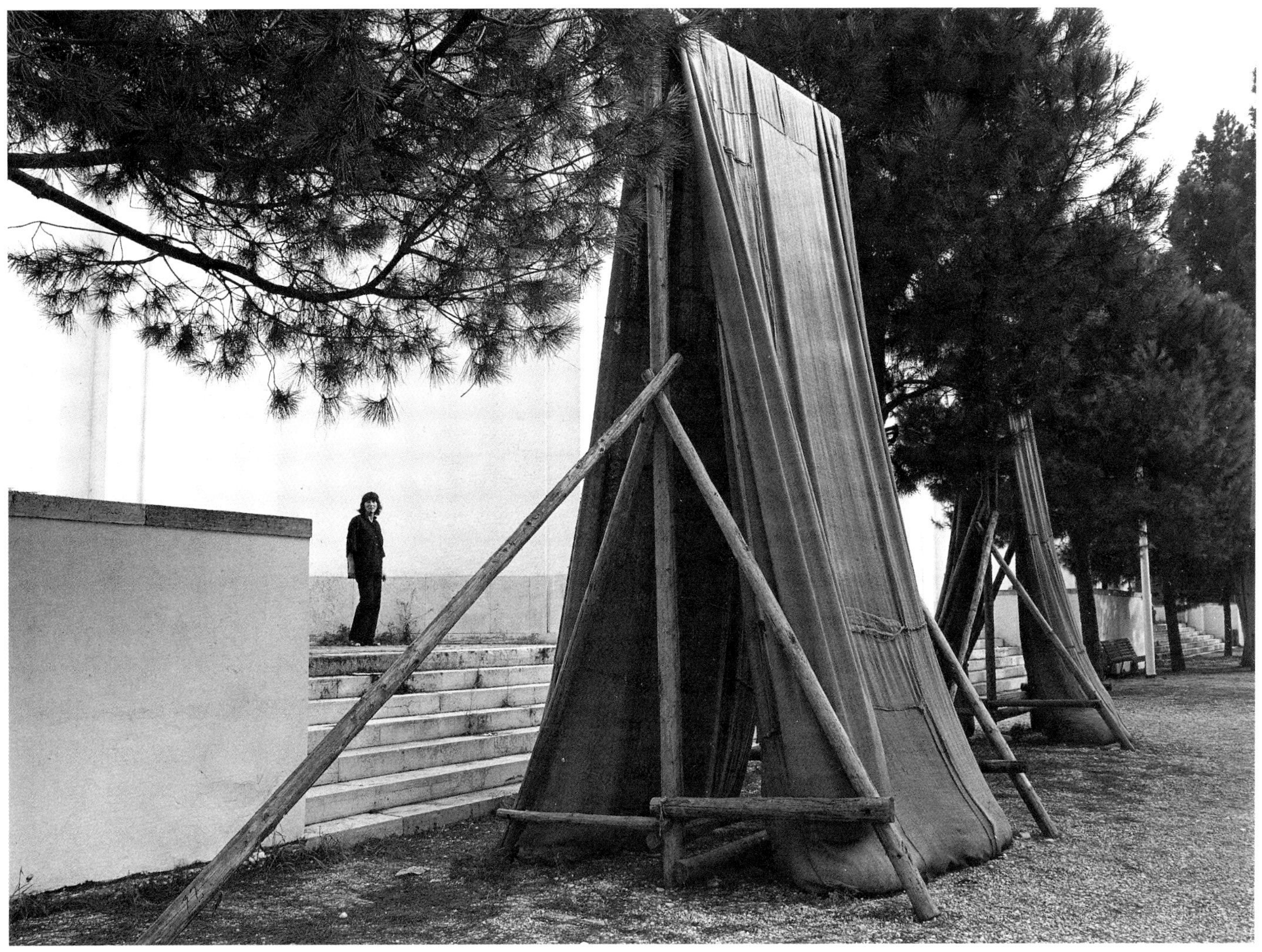

156. Magdalena Abakanowicz behind *Trzapeki* at the Polish Pavilion, Venice Biennale, 1980. Burlap and wood, two sections of variable dimensions.

white, and purple cloth across the gallery space in an act that emulated the motion of dropping cherry blossoms in a state of absolute ripeness. The artist stopped only when the space was fully covered to a one-inch thickness. She allowed the room to be filled with shifting natural light, and placed a single spotlight so that it would cast light across the space to evoke the presence of the spring moon. As in the real world, only evening visitors to the exhibition would experience the moonlight. This work of art succeeded because it was formally conceived, pared to absolute spareness, and rigorously enacted. The artist used cloth to define space as Daniel Buren might, used cloth to create the visual experience of walking under a cherry tree whose blossoms have fallen in windless conditions. But most importantly, she used cloth to honor her mother, a most traditional Japanese woman whose life is far removed from the contemporary art world. Takami's work, like that of Masafumi Maita, subtly but decisively bridges both the cultural and the aesthetic worlds of Japan's past and its present (fig. 154).

Poland's great twentieth-century artist Magdalena Abakanowicz maintains that although humans created for themselves an artificial world, they belong to an organic one. Nature comes first. Her art, like that of Takami, is about people within their larger existence, and it is never much removed from nature.

*Trzapeki* (named for the large wood frames on which Poles have traditionally beaten carpets) was Abakanowicz's installation at the Polish Pavilion at the Venice Biennale in 1980. It was an architectural fragment of cloth, a wood frame made to support hanging pieces of burlap sacking that had been sewn together, sail-like. The cloth form was partly stuffed to create visual bulges and to provide weight at the bottom. Installed against a white rectangular building, the burlap sacking became a part of the landscape, moving with the wind in concert with the nearby trees (fig. 156).

That work, with its casually hung cloth, anticipated Abakanowicz's installation at the Konsthall in the Swedish seaport of Malmö in 1981, only a year later. She gathered the paraphernalia of the pier—old fishing poles and used tarpaulins—and took it back to the exhibition space. The old canvas tarps, covered with rust, earth, and dust, were suspended from the ceiling and draped over a hole created by a removable floor: "It was dark. It could have been a bird, a fish, the bottom of a boat, or just a huge old rag."[1]

Christo treats nature's architecture and human architecture as though they were cut from the same cloth, be it the seacoast of Australia or a museum halfway around the world. He was quoted at the beginning of this chapter saying that "The work is not about wrapping as much as it is about the use of fabric, in the city or in a landscape, to bring about transformation."

*The Pont Neuf Wrapped, Paris* was a work of art that transformed a four-hundred-year-old Parisian bridge into a glowing cloth waterfall. Ten years in the planning, Christo and his partner Jeanne-Claude began the installation by preparing the cloth—440,000 square feet of woven polyamide fabric into which they had folds sewn every six inches. Their crew of five hundred engineers, construction workers, scuba divers, and rock climbers then stretched the fabric taut over the structure. The rock climbers were called upon to scale the monument for the final fitting. And finally, the fabric was bound into place with 42,900 feet of rope. No Parisian couturier ever fitted a dress with more care, and no contemporary artist can match Christo and Jeanne-Claude for creating theater on a grand scale. Still, what will be remembered is not the statistics but the image of the bridge, its contours pared to mass and line by cloth, its surface ever changing in the Paris light (fig. 155).

The artists' brilliance lies in their ability to define precisely both the natural and the architectural world in terms of modulating line. Whether they encompass a volume, such as the Pont Neuf, or define the rolling hills of California with their *Running Fence*, one is always struck by the elegance of the resulting line. Their predilection for working large, either in mass or in numbers of repetitions, only emphasizes their gorgeous sense of line in space. Nowhere did they achieve this more elegantly than with their *Umbrellas*. With the precision of engineers, Christo and Jeanne-Claude released the facts to the world press:

> —At sunrise, on October 9, 1991, Christo's 1,880 workers began to open the 3,100 umbrellas in Ibaraki and California, in the presence of the artist. The octagonal umbrellas, 6 meters high (19 feet 8 inches) and 8.69 meters in diameter (28 feet 6 inches), will meander in the landscape simultaneously. The 1,340 blue umbrellas in Ibaraki and the 1,760 yellow umbrellas in California will be placed sometimes in clusters, covering entire fields, or deployed in a line, or randomly spaced from each other, running alongside roads, villages and river banks.
>
> —This Japan-USA temporary work of art reflected the similarities and difference in the ways of life and the use of the land in two inland valleys, one 19 kilometers long (12 miles) in Japan, and the other 29 kilometers long (18 miles) in the United States.
>
> —In Japan, the valley is located north of Hitachiota and south of Satomi, 120 kilometers (75 miles) north of Tokyo, around Route 349 and the Sato river, in the Prefecture of Ibaraki, on the properties of 459 private landowners and governmental agencies.
>
> —In the United States, the valley is located 96 kilometers (60 miles) north of Los Angeles, along Interstate 5 and the Tejon pass, south of Gorman and Grapevine, on the property of Tejon Ranch, 25 private landowners as well as governmental agencies.
>
> —Eleven manufacturers in Japan, the United States, Germany and Canada prepared the various elements of the umbrellas: fabric, aluminum super-structure, steel frame bases, anchors, wooden base supports, bags and molded base covers.

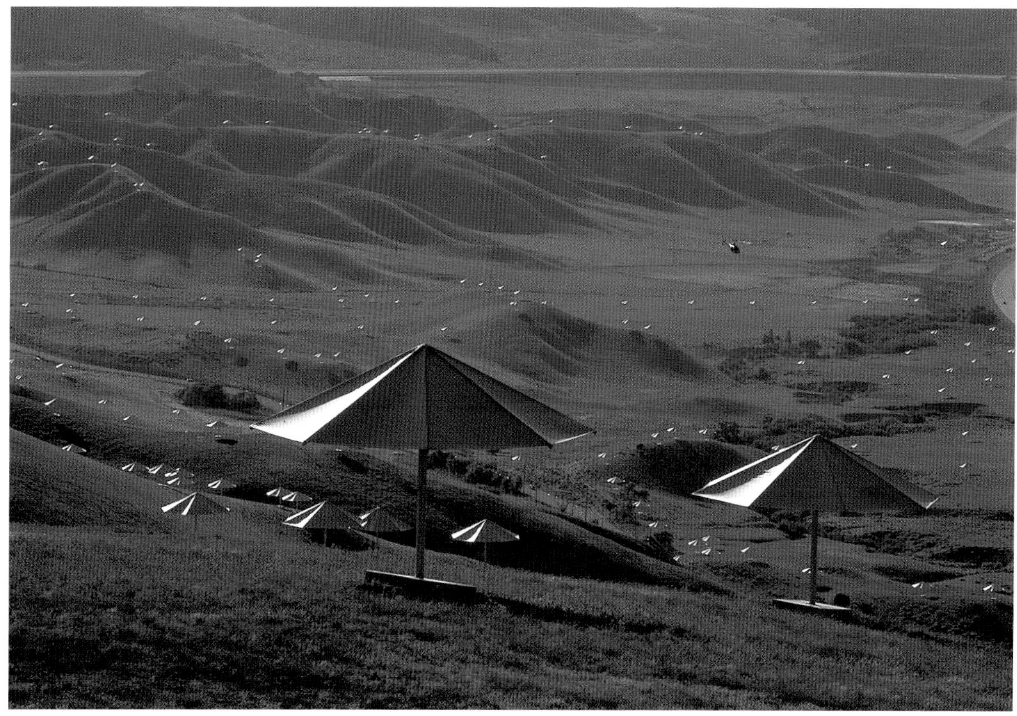

157, 158. Christo and Jeanne-Claude, *The Umbrellas, Japan-USA*, 1984–91, in Ibaraki, Japan, and California. 1,340 blue umbrellas in Japan and 1,760 yellow umbrellas in the United States. Fabric, aluminum superstructure, steel-frame bases, anchors, molded base covers. Each unit 19′8″ high and 28′6″ diameter. Copyright Christo, 1991.

—Each umbrella is numbered and filled recording the vertical and horizontal angles of the slope, the base condition, the bearing and distance to benchmarks and adjacent umbrellas. Several prototypes were built and tested in the field and at the wind tunnel of the National Research Council of Canada, in Ottawa, confirming that the umbrellas easily withstand winds of 104 km per hour (65 miles) in the opened position and 177 km (110 miles) when closed.

—For a period of 3 weeks in October 1991, *The Umbrellas* will be seen, approached and enjoyed by the public, either by car from a distance and closer as they border the roads, or on foot in a promenade route under *The Umbrellas* in their luminous shadows.

What could not be conveyed by the press release was the absolute visual power of *The Umbrellas* as a work of art. Certainly Christo and Jeanne-Claude knew, when they selected pigment-drenched blue and yellow, that the umbrellas would be seen across the world on international television, and seen they were. What the artists did not envision was the accidental death that resulted at the California site that would catapult *The Umbrellas* into headline news around the world. *The Umbrellas*, like *Running Fence*, will take its place as a masterpiece of late-twentieth-century art (figs. 157, 158).

When Christo and Jeanne-Claude create large works in public they cause the viewer to become more aware of how humans function in the natural world. For example, when they wrapped the walkways in Loose Park in Kansas City, Missouri, they caused the viewer to consider the idea of the park and how human beings create public spaces. Bernard Rudofsky has said that Christo's wrappings are Greek drapery transposed to contemporary idioms. If that is true, then Judith Morrill Hanes's *Door Frame* is the contemporary idiom transposed to Greek drapery. Both succeed because they make the viewer see the structures of ordinary life through "other glasses" (fig. 159).

To build architectural structures from cloth is a common practice from all times: witness the tent. To build cloth fragments of architecture as works of art is peculiar to the last two decades. Cornelius Rogge pretends to the first while actually being engaged in the latter. In 1976 Rogge installed six large tents in the sculpture garden of the Rijksmuseum Kröller-

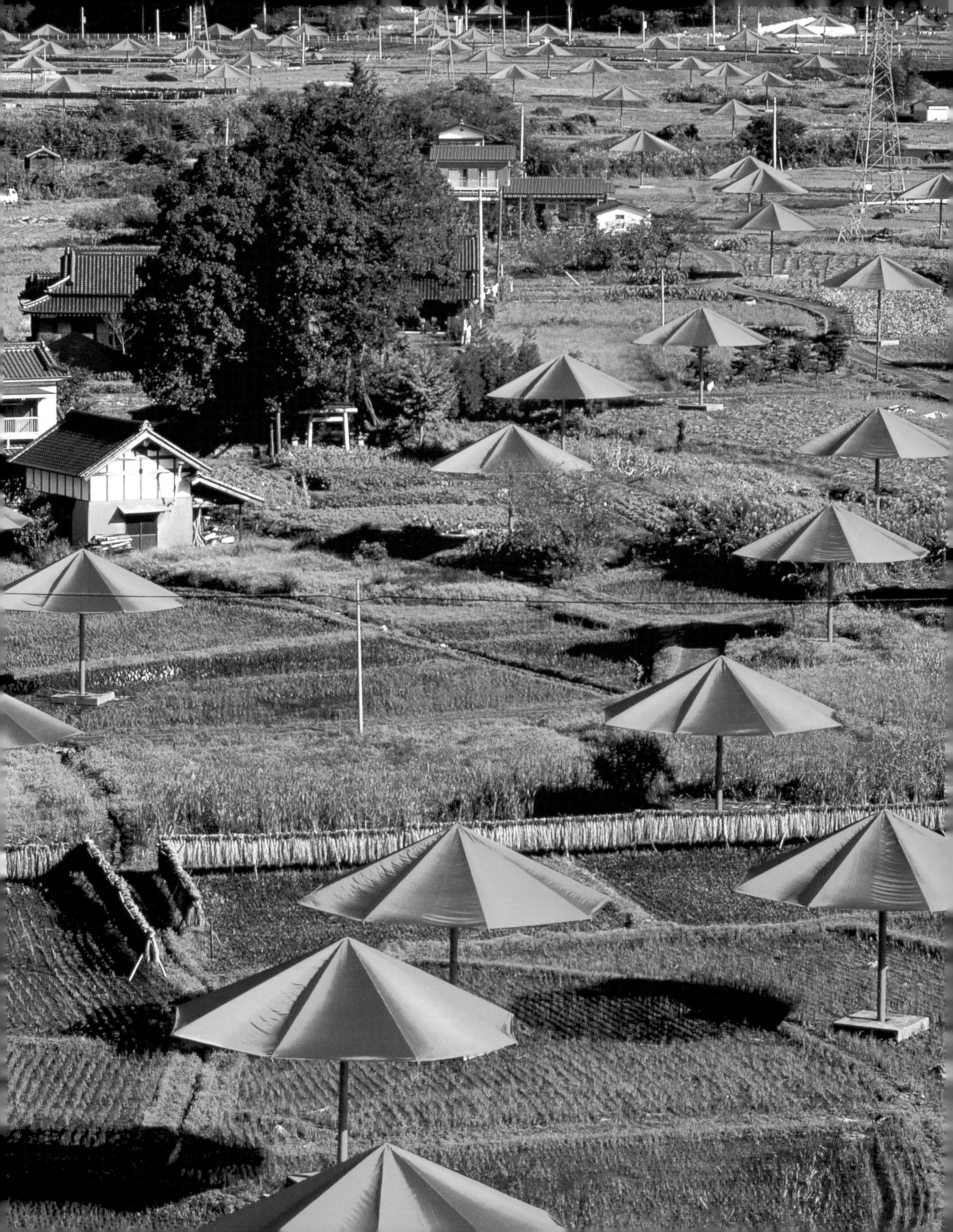

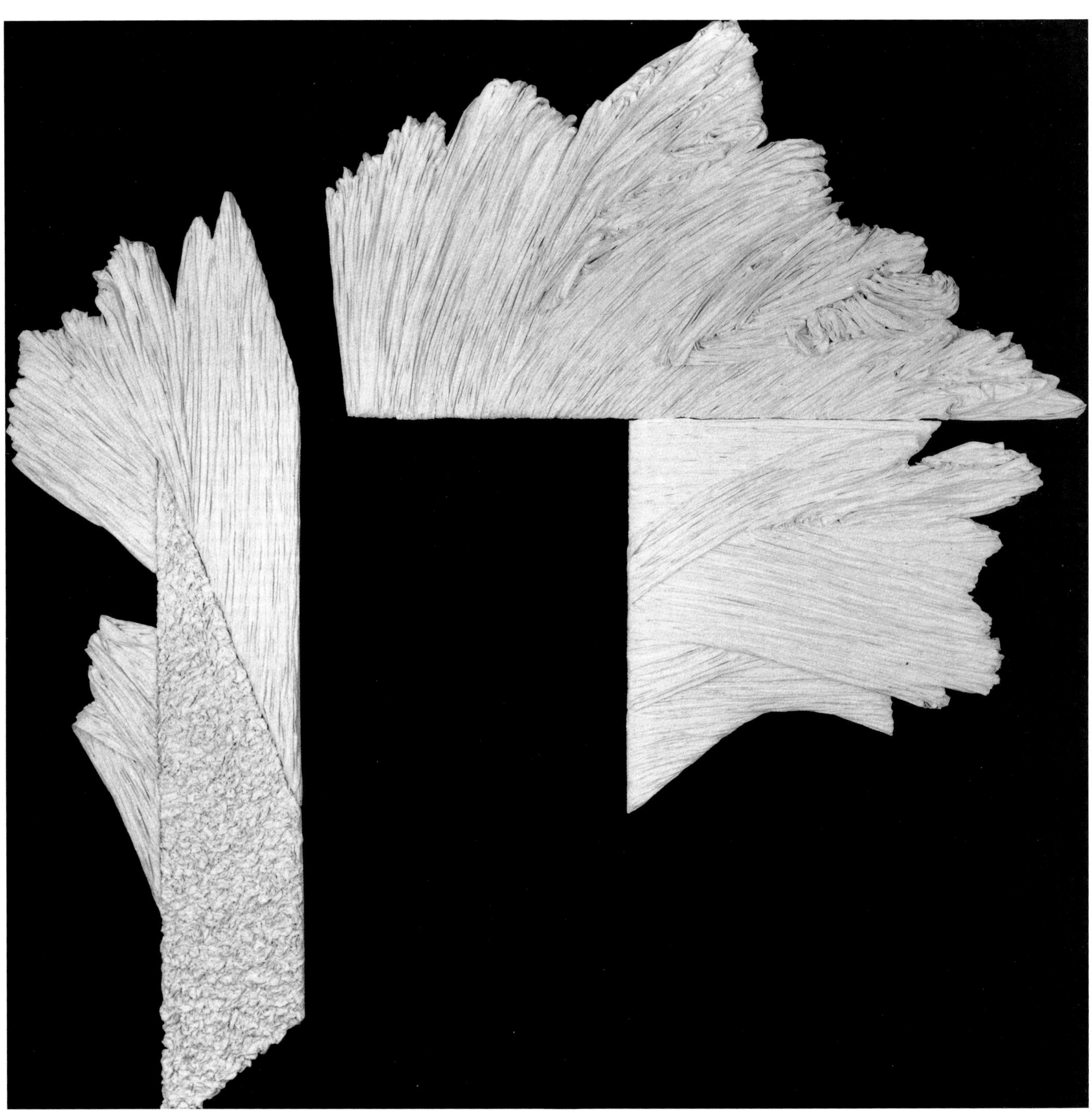

159. Judith Morrill Hanes, *Door Frame,* 1986. Muslin and gesso, 12′ x 12′ x 6″.

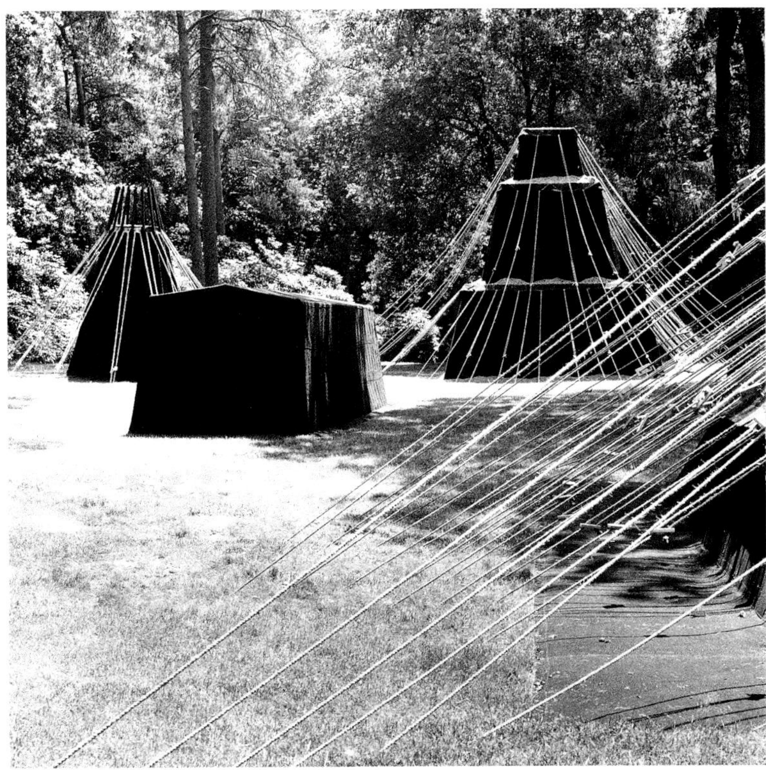

160. Cornelius Rogge, *Tent—Project 1976,* 1976. Installed at the Rijksmuseum Kröller-Müller, Otterlo, the Netherlands. Canvas over steel frame, c. 65 x 85′.

Müller in Otterlo, the Netherlands. The tents have the form of ziggurats, pyramidal with surrounding terraces. Some tents are cone-shaped, others are truncated pyramids. Heavy, dark brown canvas was placed over the steel frames and secured with guy ropes. Although the tents have a commonplace outer form, they have no entrances; one cannot go into them (fig. 160).

Like Rogge and Abakanowicz, Alan Saret, Hideo Mori, and Colette create architectural works. Of these, only Colette's are personal, that is, extensions of private life rather than public spaces. With the skill of a magician she combines art, design, theater, and architecture to create private chambers or boudoirs. Her lush, crushed and crinkled silks and satins smother her grotto of autobiographical fantasy: "I create my own landscape and then become one with it" (fig. 161).

Alan Saret's *Ghost House in Snow* is built of plastic and steel—and how efficiently, and with what imagination, he combines those incompatible materials. His self-supporting wire-fabric structural system results in a *Ghost House* that is both rigid and flexible. Its form is shaped by gravity and wind; it responds to touch like a leaf or a delicate membrane. And it undergoes seasonal changes. For example, in winter it wears a nylon coat. Lucy Lippard says of this shimmering, transparent, hollow mountain, "*Ghost House* was intended as an ethereal emblem of life where technology bows to the spirit of the natural world from which it derives its materials and inspiration" (fig. 162).

Hideo Mori has been working on a series called Rambling Home since 1977. Each work has a free organic form, or is made from a group of planar, geometric shapes. The interplay between the series and the landscape is vital to the success of this cloth architecture (fig. 165).

Building is a cellular activity. Beehives, human tissue, brick houses, and the work of Machiko Agano are examples of cellular construction. Daniel Graffin's monumental sails for the 1995

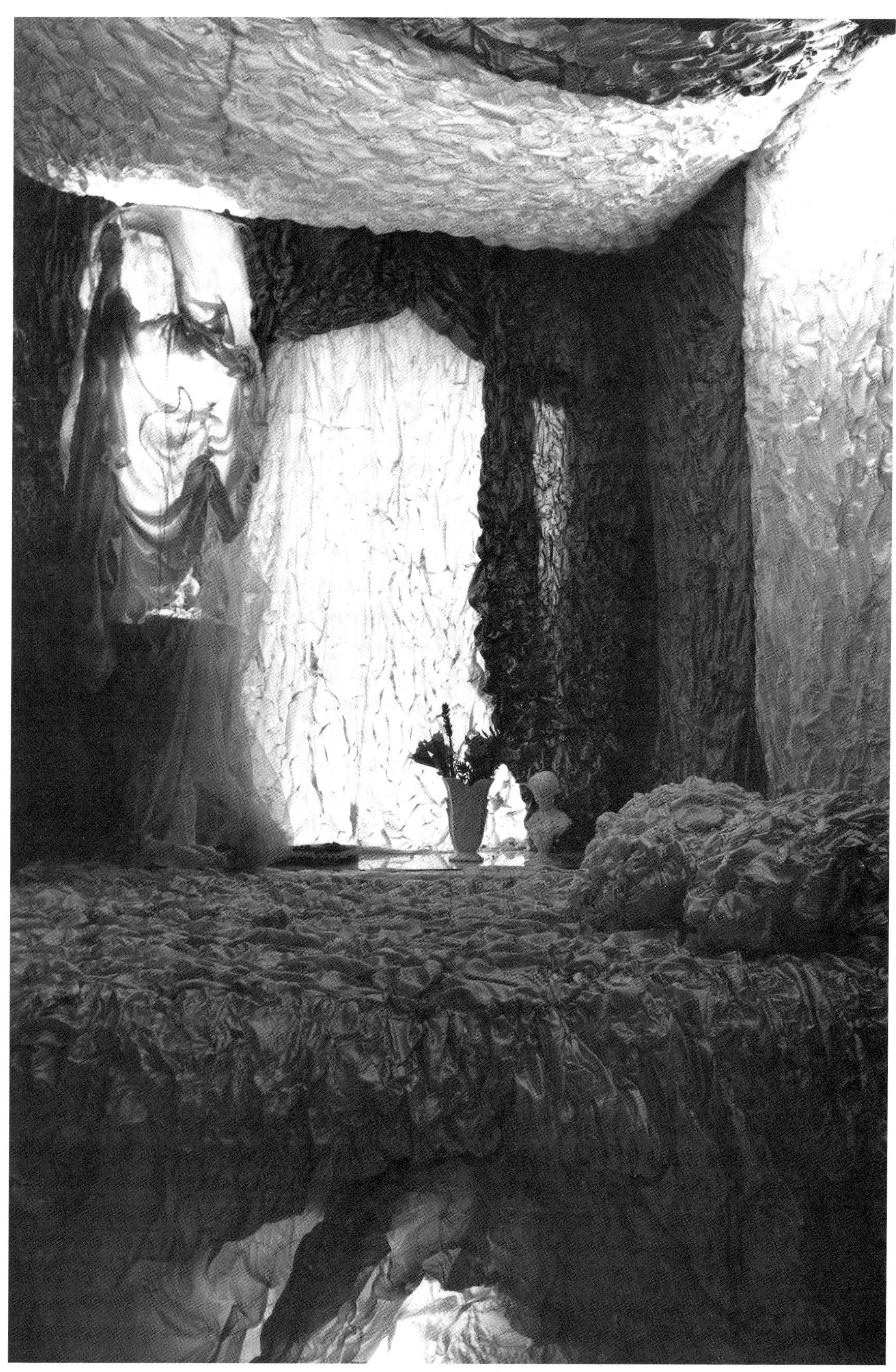

161. Colette, *One View of Beautiful Dreamer: Bed II,* 1980.

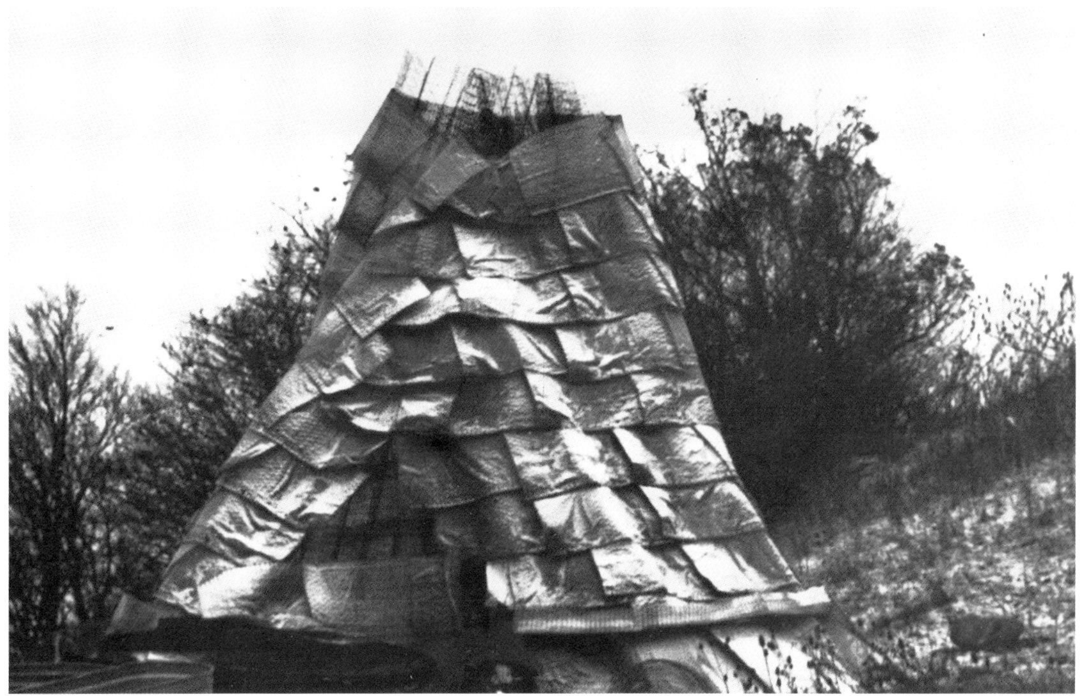

162. Alan Saret, *Ghost House in Snow,* 1975. Installed at Artpark, Lewiston, New York. Flexible steel and plastic skin.

Venice Biennale were also based upon a cellular construction. Similarly, Gerhardt Knodel's *Sounding* is made of U-shaped formations. The cellular nature is emphasized by the shadow image cast behind the "picture plane." Leo Copers uses cloth actually to transform the architectural space of the commanding cellar of the Romanesque abbey church of Saint Philibert in Tournus, France. His draped cloth takes on a cellular repetition that becomes startling only when one realizes that the drapes are formed by knives thrust through the cloth and into the stone wall of the abbey. The beautiful blue drapes suddenly become ominous. In the most elegant of settings the cloth harbors evil (figs. 163, 164).

Barbara Shawcroft's *Classical Ruins* is a sculpted wall made of rolled cloth bricks. She is concerned with how skeletal structures work in nature and, in common with these other artists, how cellular and modular construction implies infinitude. Shawcroft's wall promises renewal. Copers's installation alludes to destruction. Cloth is a material that lends to art a sense of immediacy and a sense of timelessness. For it is the inherent contradictions of cloth that make it vital material for art. *Living Space,* created by the architect Tadao Ando and the designer Shiro Kuramata for the exhibition "Tokyo: Form and Spirit" at the Walker Art Center in Minneapolis in 1985, illustrates this. The baroque drapery of white cloth appears to be very soft as it hangs on the wall and covers the floor. In fact, it is very hard, stiffened with a coat of FRP polymer (figs. 166, 167).

Other walls of cloth have had totally different purposes. In 1969 Robert Irwin was in Amsterdam installing a show at the Stedelijk Museum. While there, he discovered a whitish translucent material called scrim, a loosely woven yet strong cloth of cotton or linen. He remembers how it happened. "You walk down the streets and they're all lined with these terrific windows which they take incredible care of. And it seems like every lady in Holland makes curtains of the stuff." What fascinated him

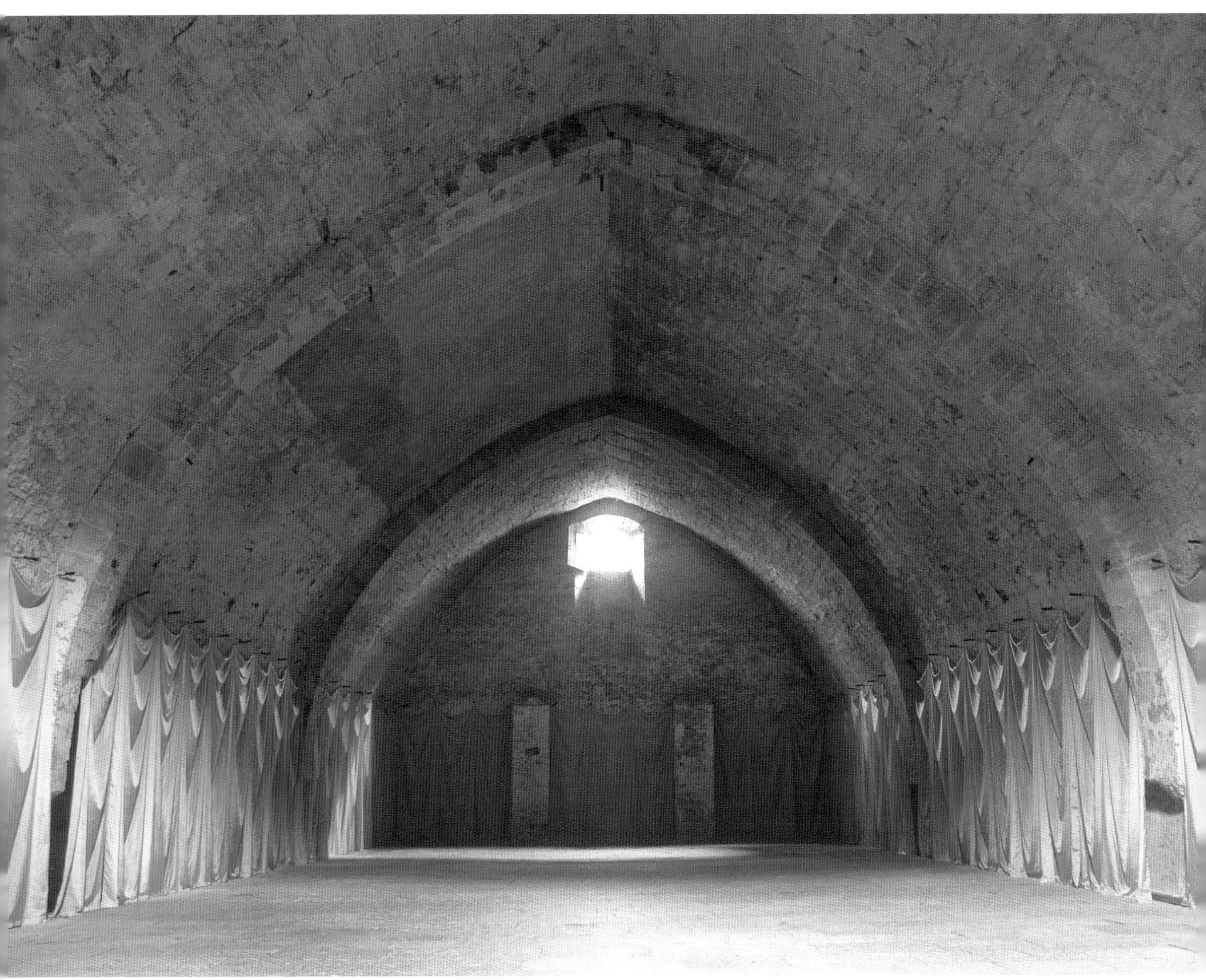

163. Leo Copers, *Untitled,* 1988. Installation in the cellar of the abbey church of Saint Philibert Tournus/Art Contemporain. Collection Musée Greuze, Tournus, France.

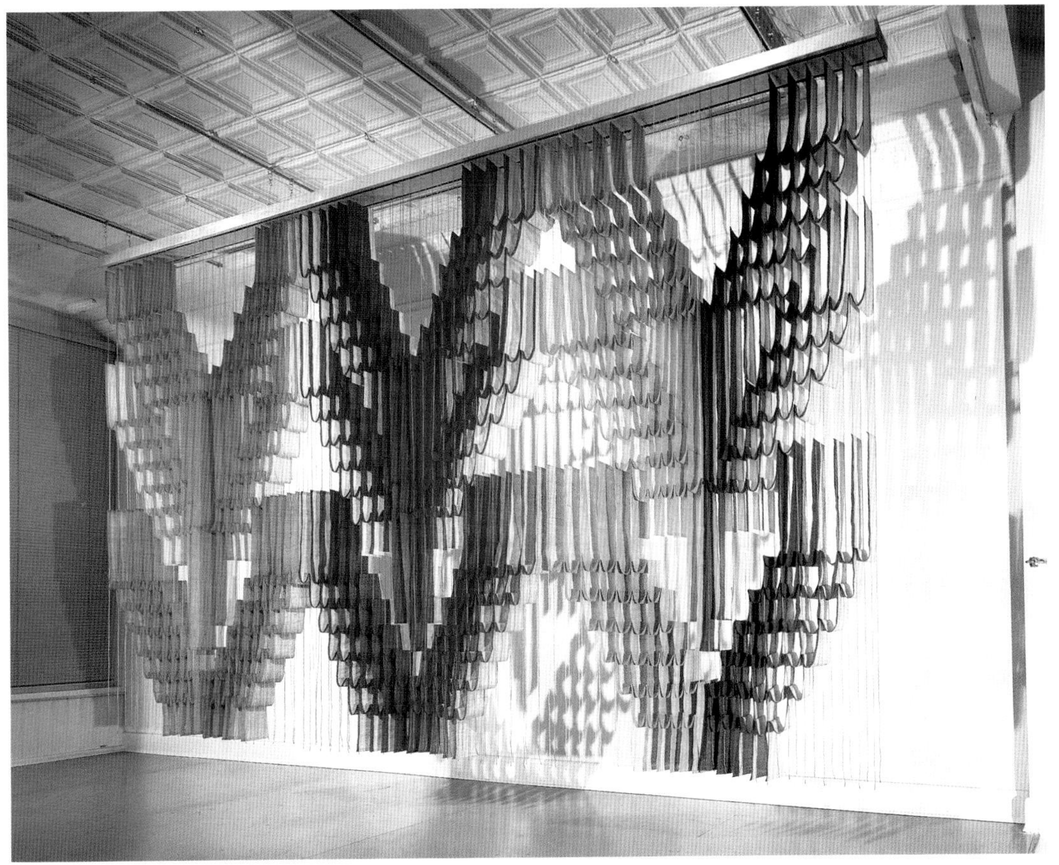

164. Gerhardt Knodel, *Sounding,* 1976. Tussah silk, nylon, and dye, 96 x 120″. Collection Maurice Cohen, South Field, Michigan.

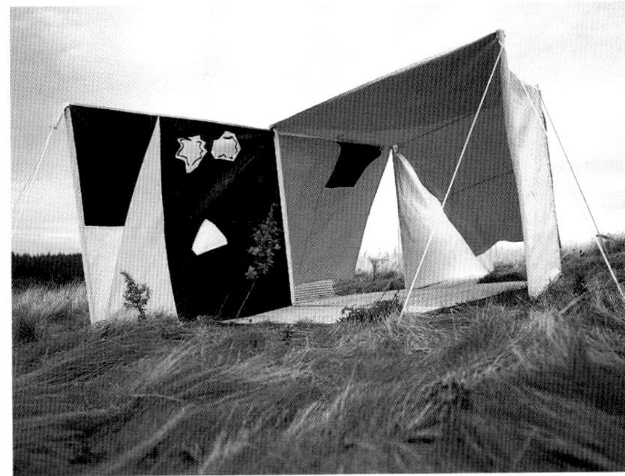

165. Hideo Mori, *Astar House,* 1983. Cloth and poles.

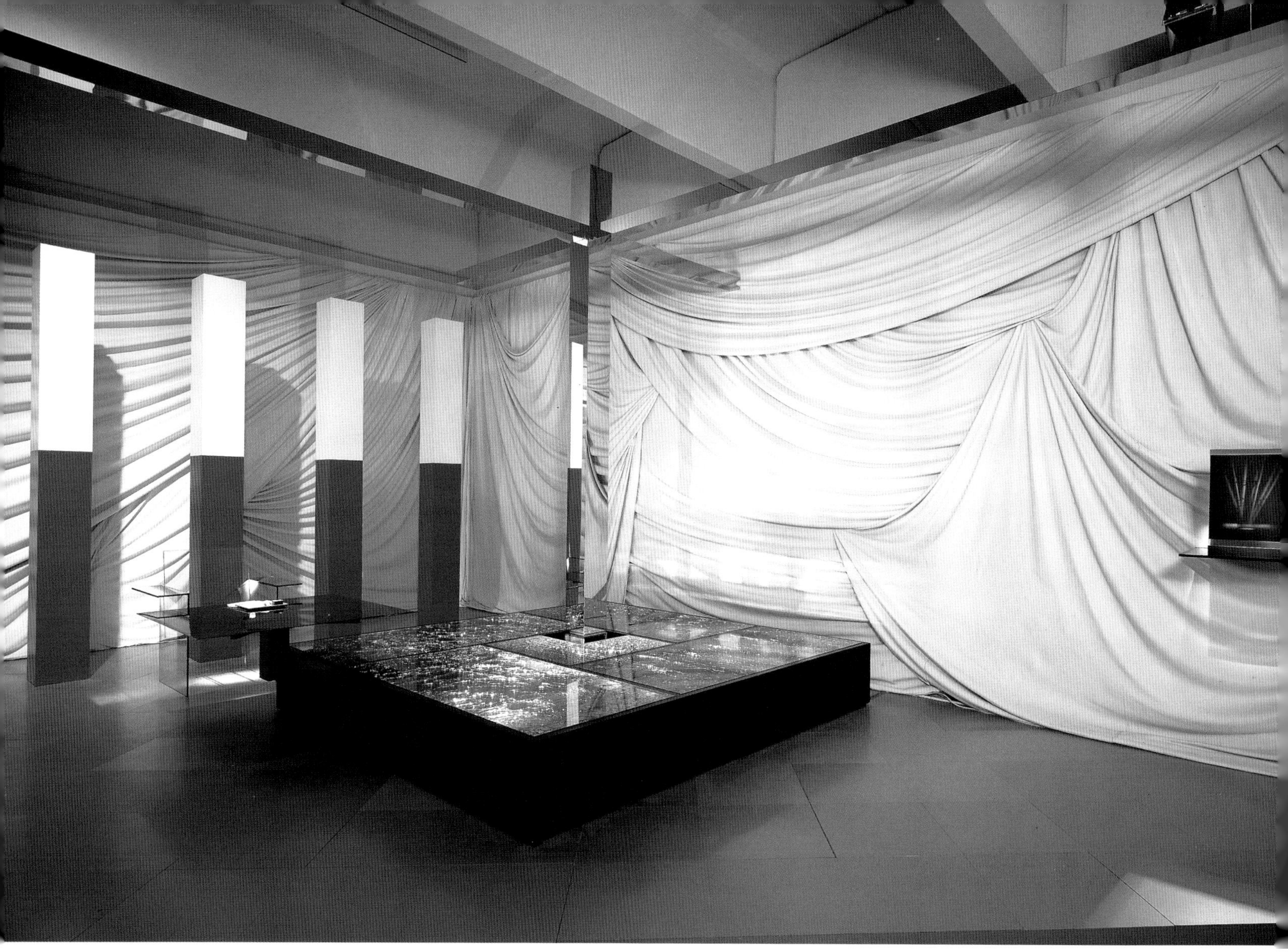

166. Tadao Ando and Shiro Kuramata, *Living Space,* 1985. Stainless steel, aluminum, wood, glass, and cloth stiffened with FRP polymer. Installed at the Walker Art Center, Minneapolis, Minnesota.

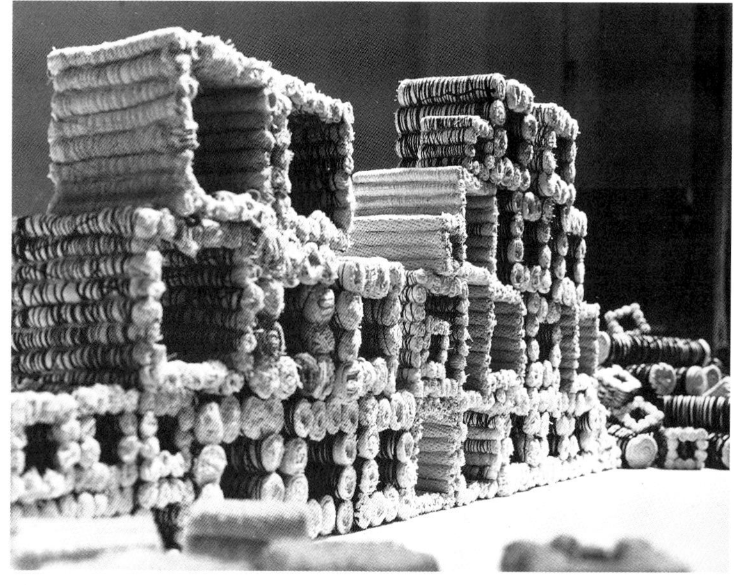

167. Barbara Shawcroft, *Classical Ruins*, 1986. Cloth brick wall construction, each module 2 x 2 x 5″.

was the "capacity of the scrim to give shape, as it were, to light. The material was transparent and yet not quite—light seemed to catch in the interstices, to catch and hold, to take on volume."[2]

Over the next ten years Irwin was to use countless bolts of scrim, building walls within gallery spaces that had the disquieting effect of somehow rendering light tangible. Irwin's installations of scrim are among the most sensuous art created in this century, and among the most difficult to photograph.

Masao Yoshimura, a Japanese artist born in Manchuria in 1946, has always preferred to work on a large, architectural scale. However, in the early 1990s family obligations caused him to move and his new studio was tiny. Working large became out of the question unless he could find a new solution. He arrived at one that was particularly Japanese: he would create tiny modules and extend scale by extending numbers of units. Working with silk organza and a sewing machine, he began to fabricate cubes of cloth, 5¼ inches in each dimension. He had made 1,012 boxes by the time he installed the work of the same name in the North Dakota Museum of Art in October 1993. Placed in a grid across the gallery floor, they created a shimmering sea of light, perfectly complemented by the scrim covering the gallery window and the shifting light coming in through the skylight, which changed constantly as clouds passed in front of the sun or as the sun rose and set. The individual cloth cubes became blocks of light, or facets to transmit light. They were without social content, intended as formal elements in a work about light (fig. 168).

There are social walls, invisible walls that cannot be crossed by different classes of society. And there are emotional walls and physical walls that separate both people and peoples. Unlike Yoshimura, Sheila Hicks amasses individual units to make social walls of cloth, that is, environmental installations of social commentary. That she chooses the wall as her format is important. She cements the meaning into her walls by the units of cloth she chooses as her building blocks.

Hicks began her environmental installations in 1974 using mended sheets and darned socks. She showed these in the window of the Amsterdam department store De Bijenkorf at the same time as a major exhibition of her work was on display in the Stedelijk Museum. This marked her transition from making single works of art to creating large environmental installations. Out of this evolved her submission to the 1977 Lausanne Biennale: darned sheets, hung together with eight tons of freshly washed and ironed laundry, all borrowed from the local hospital (see fig. 30). In that same year she installed *Reprisage Repertoire* in the "Fiberworks" exhibition at the Cleveland Museum of Art. It consisted of a wall of four linen drop cloths darned in diamond grids. In 1978 the Paris suburb of Montreuil invited her to create a work. She planned a street environment that would use appropriate everyday garments as repeating elements. She sought to make the exhibition about, and accessible to, all of those who lived and worked in Montreuil (fig. 169).

For her site-oriented installations Hicks chooses emotion-charged, ready-made items of daily use: hospital garments, cotton army shirts, old women's blouses. With these she creates accumulations, sometimes stacked and sometimes suspended. Certain works contain remnants, rags torn into strips, then sewn, meshed, and knotted back into a whole—recycled materials to suggest recycled lives. Her works are social treatises on the commonality of human experience. Her *Khaki Uniforms Immobilized* is made of military shirts from an array of armies, cut, reshaped, and pieced together. It is a forceful statement about men brought together in war (see fig. 107). Even when dealing with war, however, Hicks's walls of cloth never take on dark or somber overtones. Her linens are darned and patched, her sheets and hospital gowns come pressed and folded from the cleanest of laundries. Her military garb suggests the ordered world of multinational forces—or the world made orderly by multinational forces.

Hicks was one of the early artists to introduce the idea of masses of cloth standing in for human counterparts. That idea was absorbed by the mainstream, to be reenacted at other times in other places with new meanings. For instance, Ann Hamilton, who would have come upon Hicks's work during her years as a college student studying in a fiber department, began to make her own work based upon the massing of cloth fifteen years later. Hamilton's work is more ambiguous, and more intuited than Hicks's. One is never quite sure what it means, and that quality gives it a foreboding power.

*Indigo Blue* was a site-specific work created by Hamilton, in which she investigated the role of the laborer. The Spoleto

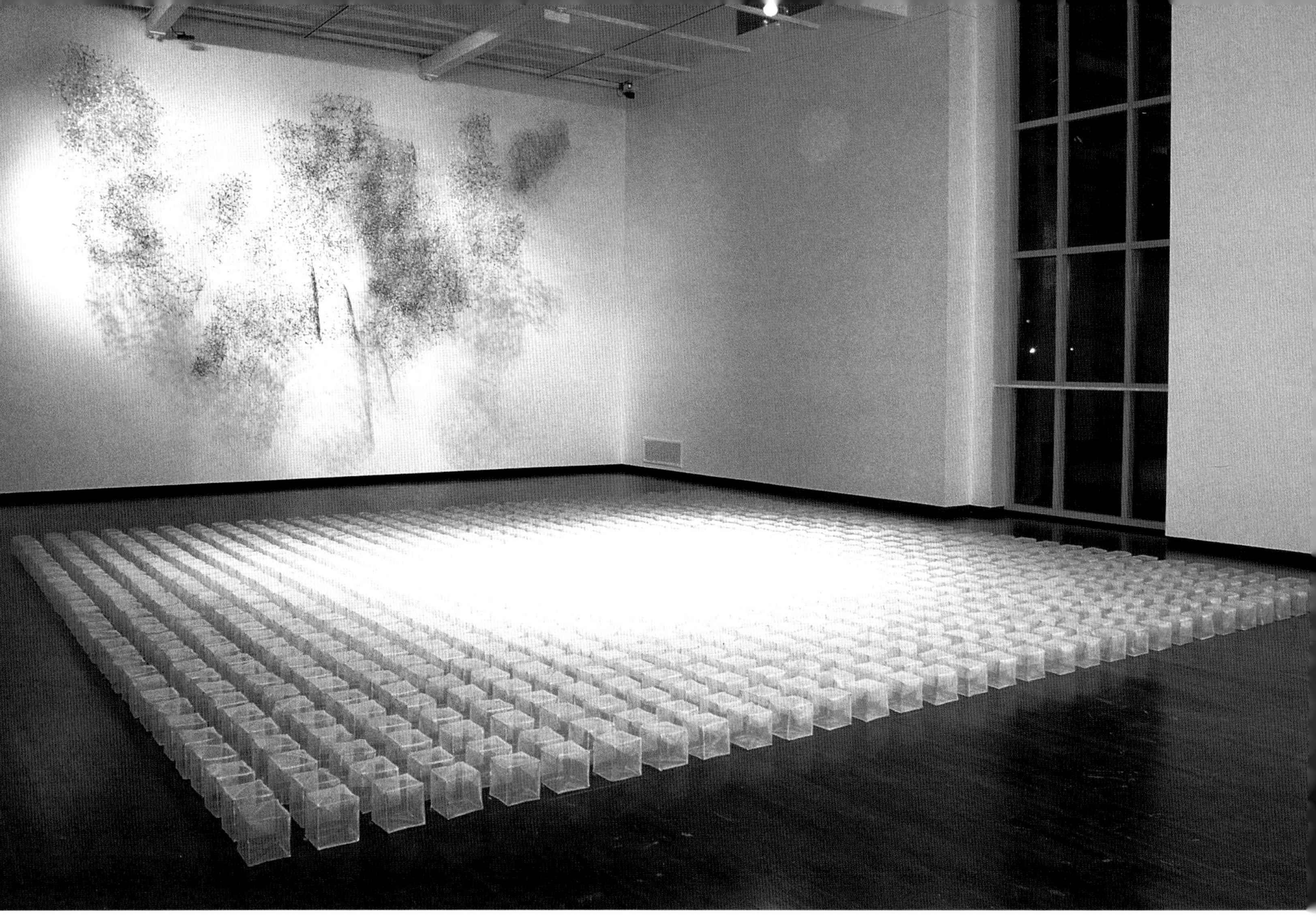

168. Masao Yoshimura, *One Thousand and Twelve Boxes*, 1993. Machine-stitched silk-organza boxes, one plastic bug, each box 5¼ x 5¼ x 5¼″. Installed at the North Dakota Museum of Art, Grand Forks. An installation by Tomoko Ishida is in the background.

Festival in Charleston, South Carolina, offered a choice of sites to invited artists, and Hamilton chose an old automotive garage. She, like Hicks before her, supervised the washing and folding of the clothes she would use, 14,000 pounds of blue men's work pants and shirts. And also like Hicks, she carefully laid them out in an ordered configuration. With the mound behind her (or the college student who sat in for her at times) she sat at a wooden table and methodically erased small blue history exam books with a pink pencil eraser and saliva. She extended her piece into the office space above; here she hung net bags filled with soybeans, which continued their life cycle, sprouting and then rotting in the humid summer air (fig. 170).

Hamilton creates site-specific works that involve tedious, repetitious actions. She accumulates individual units into larger statements. Because she believes that much of our true knowledge—not just information—comes to us through hearing, smelling, and touching, she incorporates these elements into her artworks, almost before she allows her viewer to see. She makes art about acts of labor, over which she and dozens of volunteers exert themselves. She underpins her creations with well-developed but subtle concepts that give a metaphoric complexion to her art seldom found in the contemporary art world. Given her background as a weaver, she often looks to fibrous materials, or cloth, for both her means and her metaphor.

Hamilton installed a two-room site-specific work, *Malediction*, in the Louver Gallery in New York in winter of 1991–92. Scatter art, or objects randomly distributed across the surface of a floor space, was happening all over the city at the time, and Hamilton contributed a fine example. The entrance room was covered with rags, sheets, and linens that had been

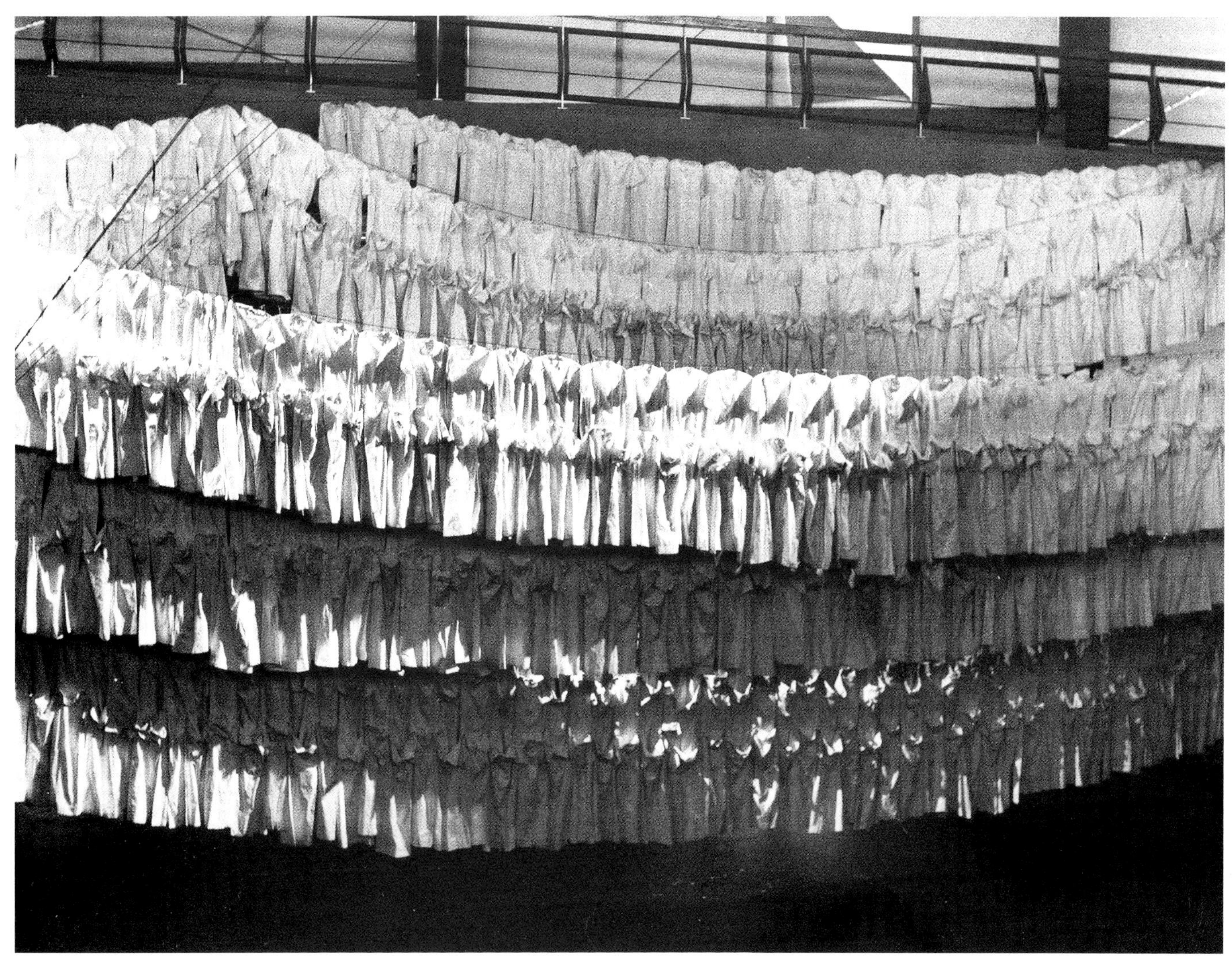

169. Sheila Hicks, *Street Environment,* 1978. Montreuil, France. Shirts and rope.

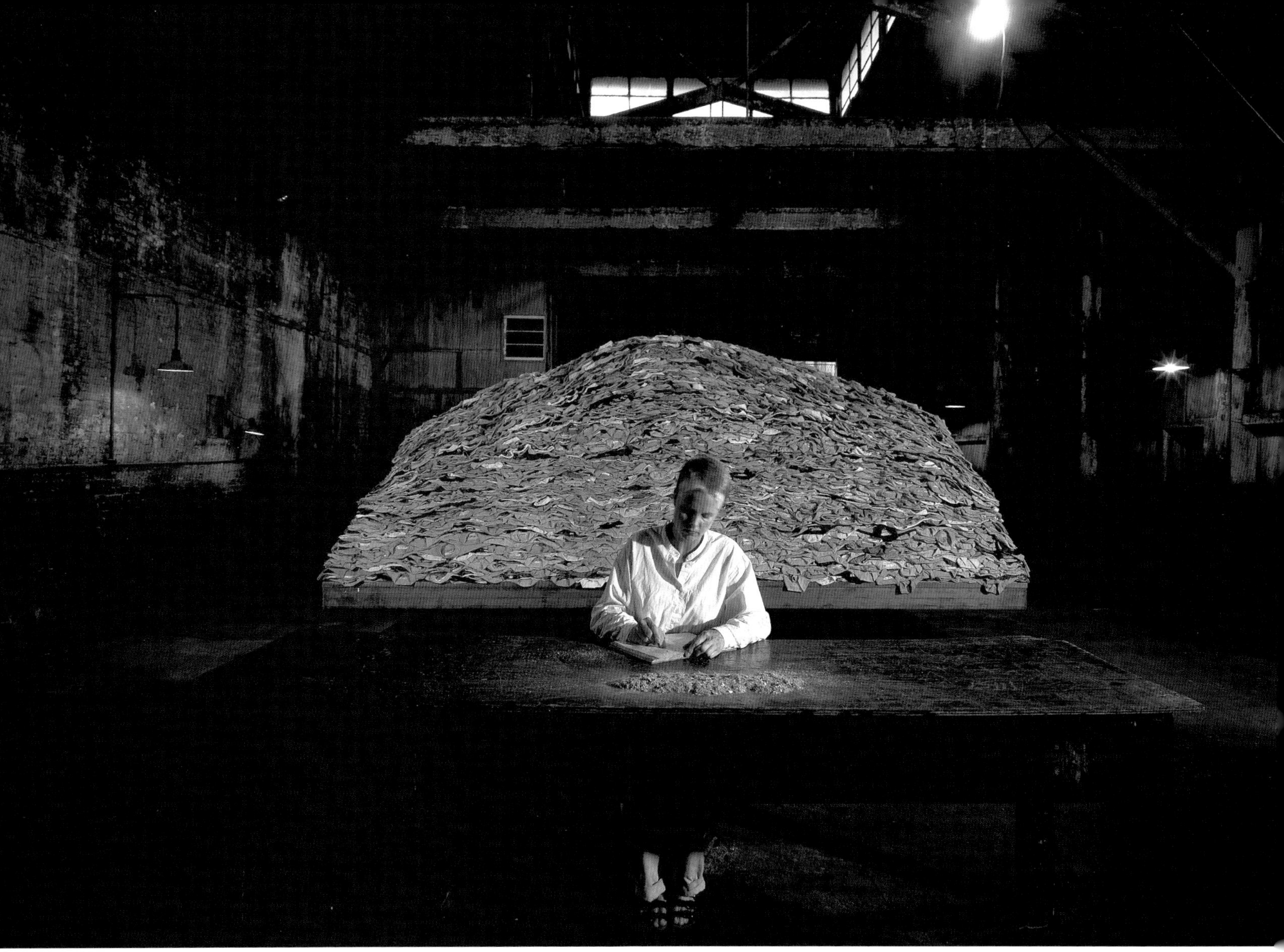

170. Ann Hamilton, *Indigo Blue,* 1991. Installation in conjunction with "Places with a Past," Spoleto Festival, Charleston, South Carolina. 14,000 pounds recycled work clothing (pants and shirts). Courtesy Sean Kelly, New York.

soaked in wine, wrung out, and tied in tightly twisted knots. To cross the room was itself a physical challenge. Gradually one became aware of sound, a voice, a woman's voice reciting snatches from Walt Whitman's *Song of Myself* and *I Sing the Body Electric.* Next to the entrance a felt hat had been placed upside down on a chair and filled with honey—honey to be tasted, smelled, and dipped into with the fingers in order to understand it as "honey." In the main room the artist was solemnly engaged in another of her seemingly unfathomable acts of repetitious labor. She sat with her back to the viewer at a refectory table. With quiet dignity she tore a piece of bread dough from a mound in a large bowl. She put it into her mouth, bit down to make an impression of her teeth, removed it, and carefully placed it beside her in a large wicker basket. She repeated this same action, over and over, throughout the whole of the day. She sat facing a wall stacked halfway to the ceiling with laundered sheets. The endless labor of women, and the hand-to-mouth existence of those same women, seems to be the core of the work. However, as with all of Hamilton's installations, the viewer ominously senses that more is going on than one can surmise. Why else would she have named the work *Malediction* (figs. 171, 172)?

Whereas both Hicks and Hamilton used mounds of cloth in an orderly way, the worlds of the French Conceptual artist Christian Boltanski are terribly disordered. His collections of used and shabby clothing are neither washed nor sorted. They

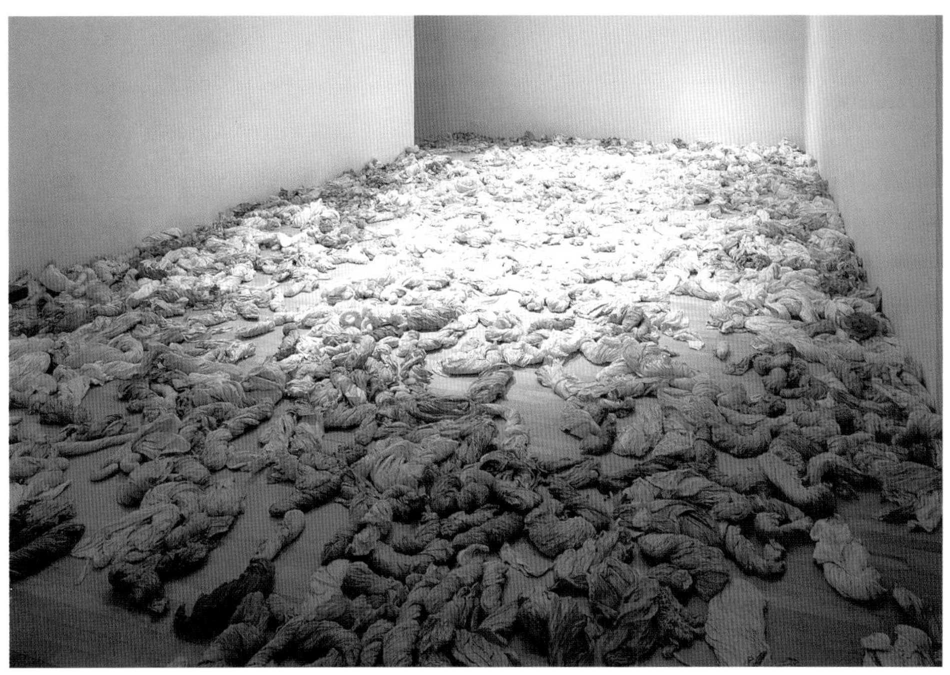

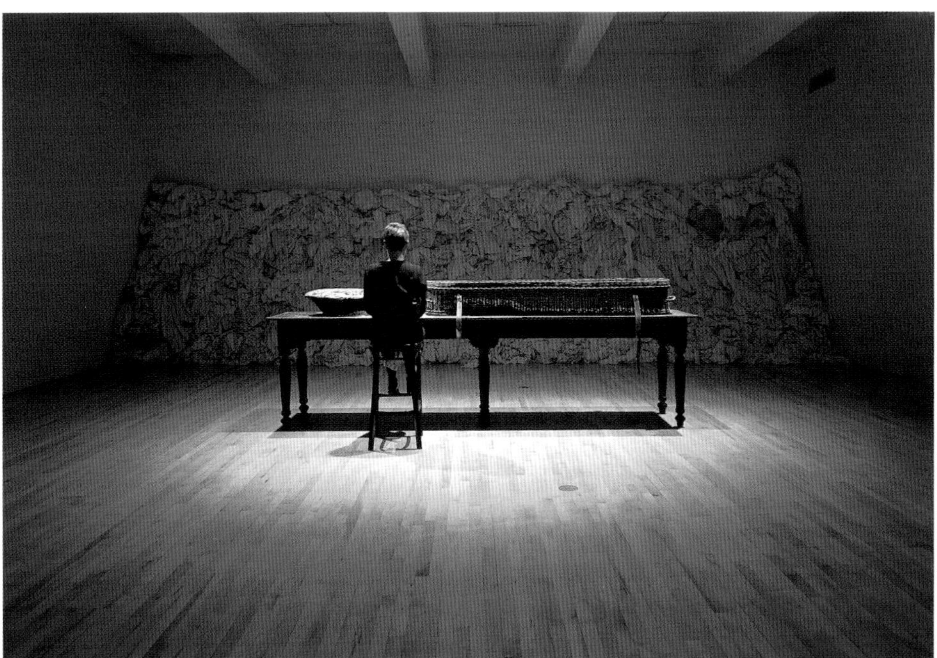

171, 172. Ann Hamilton, *Malediction,* December 7, 1991–January 4, 1992. Rags from sheets and linens (wine stained and wrung from washing), wall of piled bed linens, refectory table, bowl of bread dough, wicker basket, sound system. Exhibition installed in two rooms at the Louver Gallery, New York. Courtesy Sean Kelly, New York.

are added to already existing piles that overflow his studio and subsequently make their way into his work (in heaps reminiscent of Michelangelo Pistoletto; see fig. 29). In Boltanski's mind old clothes stand in for their missing owners. To walk on them is to tread on dead bodies. The garment is the abandoned outer skin; death has disposed of the inner occupant (fig. 173).

In 1988–89 Boltanski created a group of works that drew heavily on his piles of clothes. He called them Réserves. His *Réserve du musée des enfants* (1989) installed in the Musée d'Art Moderne de la Ville de Paris is one of the most unsettling works of recent times. Boltanski chose to install it in two dark and hapless basement rooms of the museum. In the first he mounted a wall of fifty-five blurred, enlarged photographs of middle-class European children. As is customary with this artist, the piece was dimly lit from above by bare lightbulbs. In the second room, separated from the first by a heavy iron door, were the children's clothes, shelved stacks of underwear, again dimly lit from above. Nothing explicitly told the viewer that these were the children lost to the Holocaust, but one sensed it from the heavy, oppressive, claustrophobic atmosphere that pervaded this work of art and from the age and time frame suggested by the photographs. Boltanski created a dark theater with his anonymous clothes, illuminated as they were by dime-store lamps and miles of makeshift extension cords. Frighteningly eerie, this was the stuff of uncertainty. The viewer who stumbled into this strangely placed installation quickly felt the urge to flee. About the piece Boltanski said:

> I believe that this work in particular was particularly significant in my oeuvre. Somehow, one has to make people feel insecure, make them feel that they have been touched, make something happen after all, at a time when all heads are filled with pictures from films, from magazines, from daily life. I like to exhibit in spaces that are not galleries in the traditional sense, because the unexpected creates an intensified sensitivity. Visitors feel insecure—they whisper or are afraid. The same holds true for my exhibition in candlelight where the dim light and the shadows create an unfamiliar ambiance. Then there is also the hypnotic effect of the garments, which one tries to touch. That also has something to do with the effect of a sacral object, perhaps of a fetish. Like the *Charged Objects* of Joseph Beuys, these clothes, too, are charged. Each individual garment has its history, its fate, its tragedy.[3]

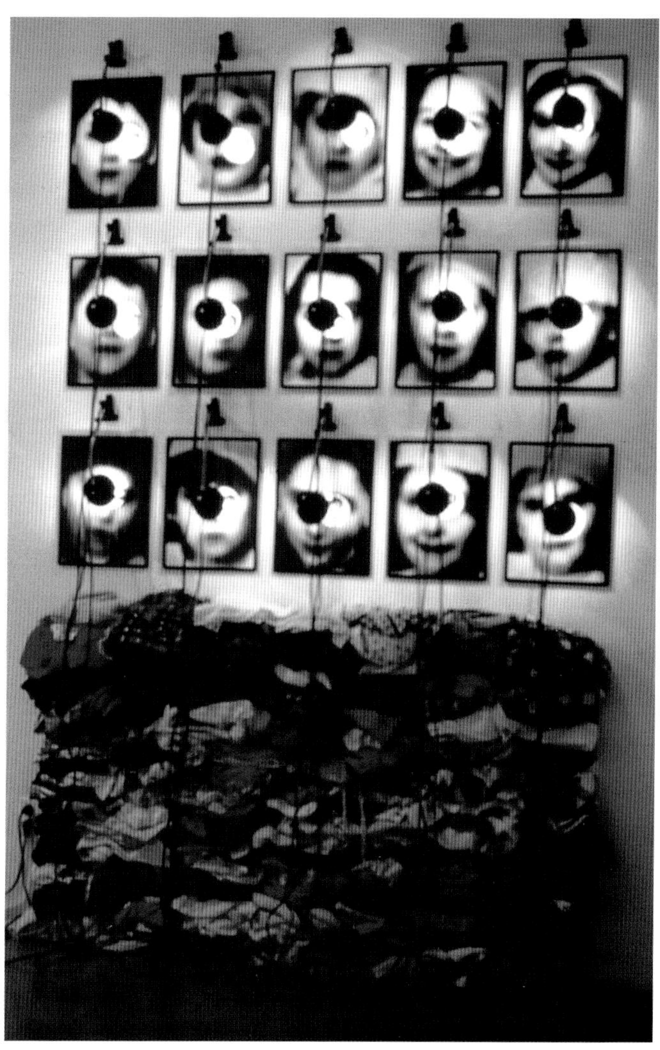

173. Christian Boltanski, *Monument Canada,* 1988. Clothes, fifteen lamps, fifteen black-and-white photographs, 110 x 70 x 7". Courtesy Marion Goodman Gallery, New York.

In the 1970s installation art was sensitive to landscape and architecture. Since then it has evolved into a means of addressing large human issues. The phenomenon of artists making installations grew out of the Happenings of the 1950s and 1960s, made sober by the Conceptual art of the decade that followed. The creation of an environment allows the artist to sandwich in layer upon layer of suggested meaning. Cloth gives an immediacy to this process, just as it provides the artist unparalleled opportunity to expand ideas spatially. One cannot cast in bronze what one can execute in cloth—especially if the artist integrates many forms of media into the work. Whereas Sheila Hicks explores sociological ideas in her installations, Boltanski addresses history and psychology in his mixed-media environments. Two other artists, Helen Escobedo and John Garrett, pursue equally unlikely areas of human experience: the larger world and the inner world.

Helen Escobedo is a Mexican artist who lives half the year in Mexico and half in Germany. All of her work confronts ecological issues. In 1990 she completed *La Muerte de la Ballena Gris,* in which she challenges the worldwide slaughter of whales. For the work she created four dead whales, each thirteen feet long, which lay side by side, skin torn open to reveal gaping wounds. The whales are made of bundled brushwood sprayed red and wrapped in plastic-coated cloth tied with jute. They lie on wooden trestles on a floor that has been covered with a deep layer of sawdust. The installation is built in a darkened chamber, reminiscent of a whaling ship. A stunning rendition of the ocean is painted on the screen at the end of the chamber. The viewer is attracted to the beauty of the whole piece, to the painting of the ocean, to the loveliness of the red bundles made even more striking by their cloak of black cloth. The installation is large; it is simple; it is arresting. Only after a moment does the dreadful state of the whales register in the viewer's consciousness (fig. 174).

*In Quest of the Last Dream* is John Garrett's psychological tour de force. The installation is a psychological place, a shimmering pastel dreamworld. In Garrett's vision the last dream is always the next psychological barrier that an individual must confront in the endless search for transformation. There may be rules in this game of life, but they must be discovered along the way. Ladders, metaphors for life's passage, are built from crutches. The steps of the ladders are not equidistant. Fragility

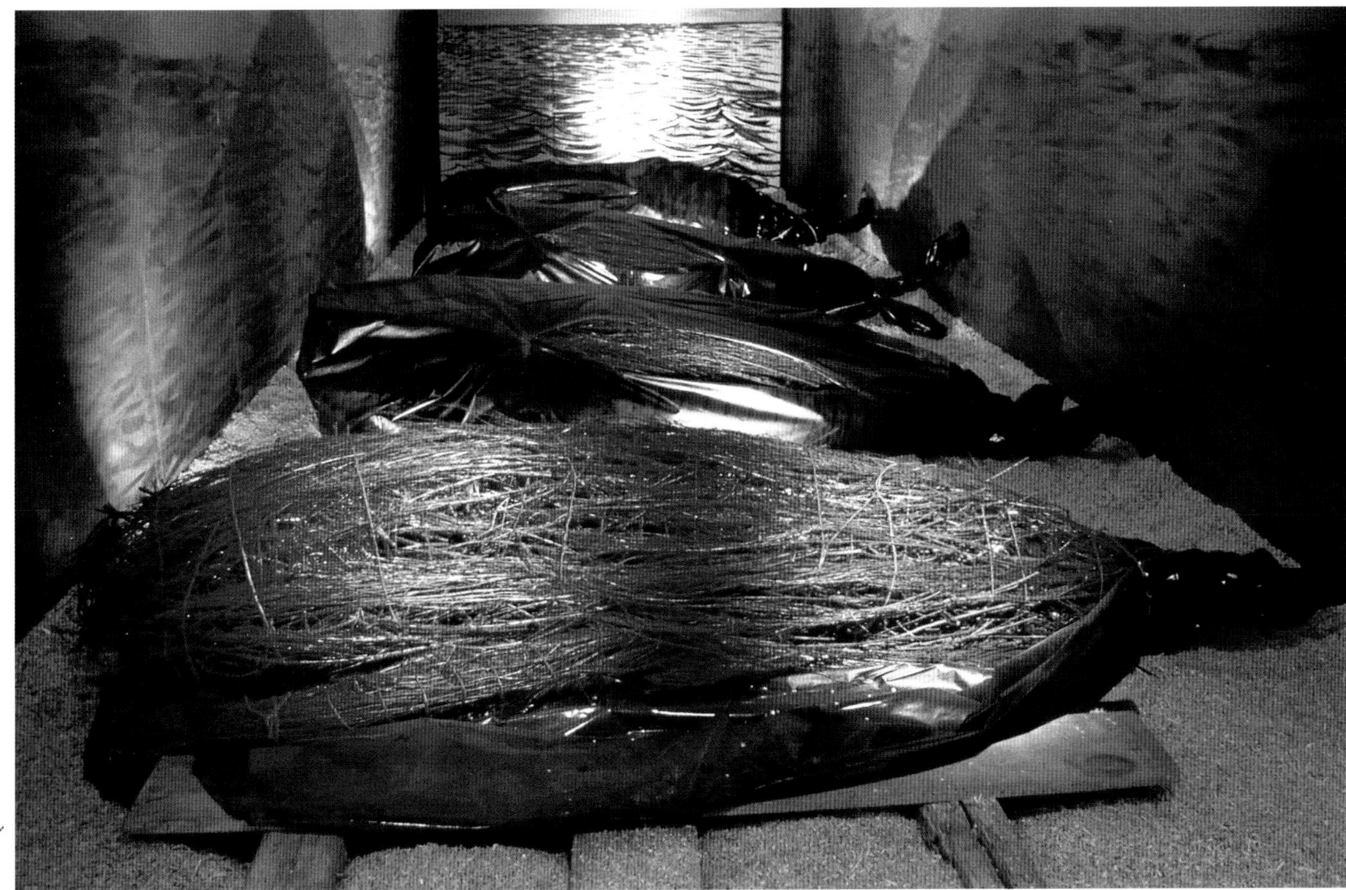

174. Helen Escobedo, *La Muerte de la Ballena Gris,* 1990. Brushwood wrapped in plasticized cloth tied with jute, each whale 13′ long.

may come in the middle or at either end: in midlife, childhood, or old age. Some steps are missing. The staff, a walking stick, is there to assist on this dangerous and difficult journey. The original shapes of all of these items are covered with layers of cloth and paint.

Like life, the dreamworld is radiantly lovely and offensively sleazy at the same time. Garrett conveys this visually by haphazardly sewing the cheapest, tackiest synthetic materials into drapes that become the backdrop for the whole piece. When lit, they glow. In contrast, he partially buries eighteen exquisite abstract paintings on paper, each eighteen inches square, under the mass of objects on the floor.

*In Quest of the Last Dream* was built, step by step, the way an oyster makes a pearl. A grain of sand is caught in the oyster shell. The presence of the unnatural body irritates the oyster, which responds by depositing layers and layers of mother-of-pearl from the lining of its shell around the offending kernel. The process goes on and on. Time passes and gradually a pearl comes into being. Garrett starts each element by building a wood or metal form. These are wrapped in cloth, then painted,

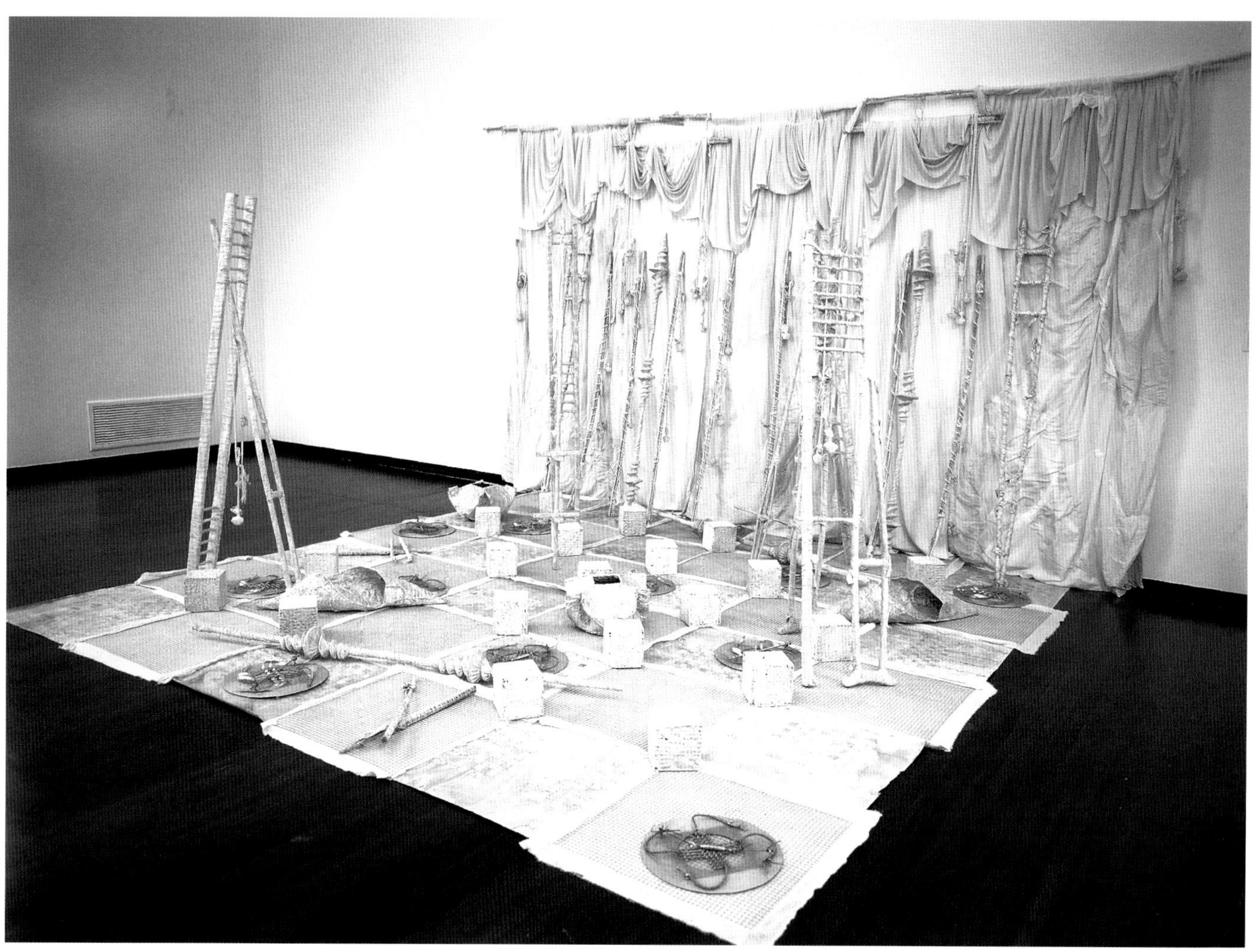

175. John Garrett, *In Quest of the Last Dream*, 1987. Painted fabric on wood and metal forms, paper, glue, and mixed-media surfaces, 8 x 12 x 12´. Installation traveled with "Frontiers in Fiber: The Americans" in China and Pacific Rim countries under the auspices of Arts America, United States Information Agency.

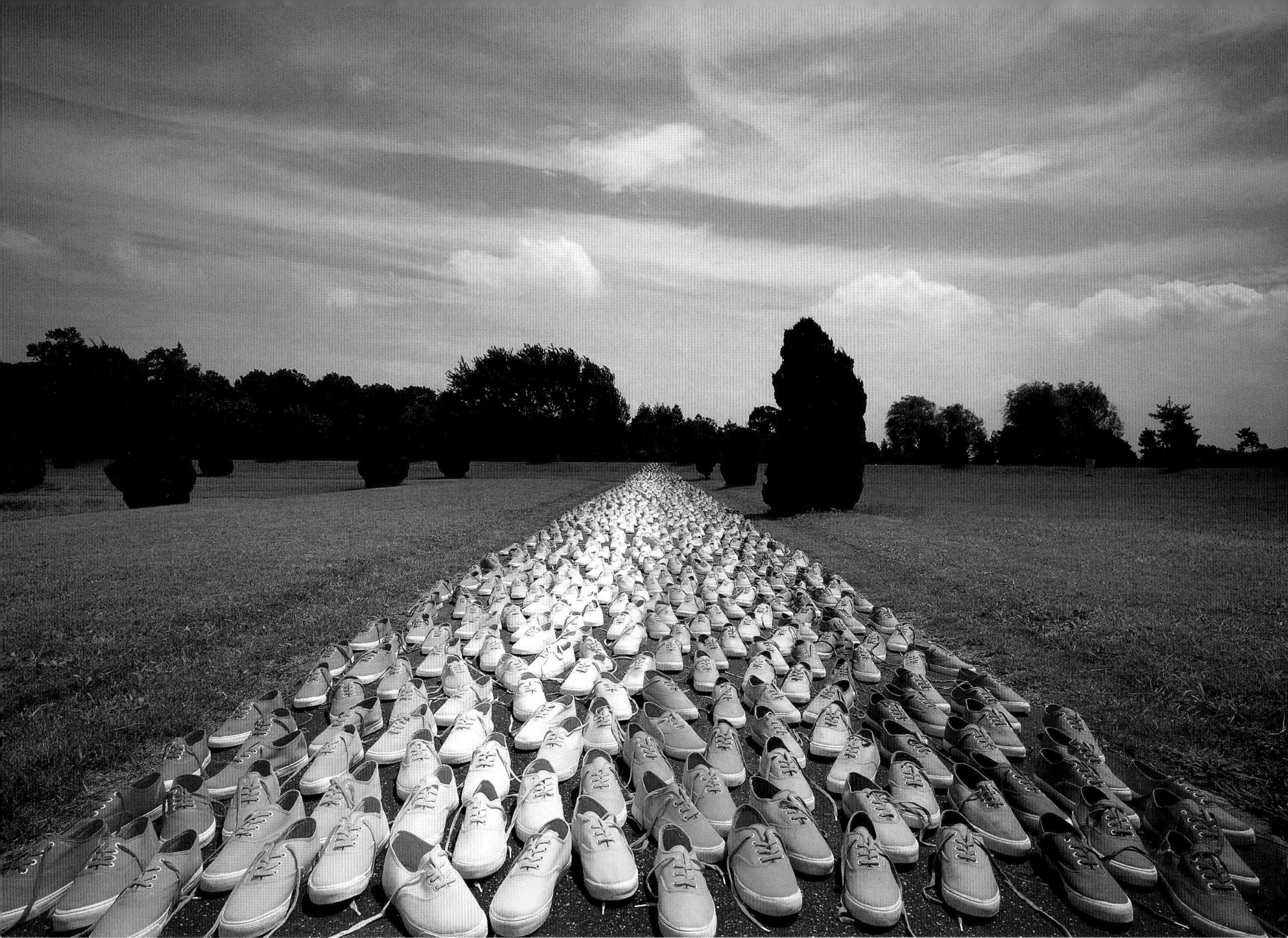

176. Mitsuo Toyazaki, *Over the Rainbow,* 1987. Installation of five hundred dyed sneakers.

then covered with glue. They dry; Garrett paints again. Gradually he builds up his layers. The cotton cloth holds and binds and supports and emerges. The whole installation is startlingly beautiful (fig. 175).

Finally, Mitsuo Toyazaki made one of the most memorial installations ever from the common, white, canvas tennis shoe. Like jeans, the tennis shoe represents the revolution of casual dress around the world. Masses of people wore inexpensive tennis shoes every day before Nike and Adidas invented a market for upscale running shoes. Toyazaki dyed five hundred shoes the colors of the rainbow, and then proceeded to turn them into a rainbow road disappearing into an elegant, pastoral, Japanese landscape (fig. 176).

1. *Magdalena Abakanowicz* (exhibition catalog, Museum of Contemporary Art, Chicago; New York: Abbeville Press, 1982), 110.

2. Lawrence Weschler, *Seeing Is Forgetting the Name of the Thing One Sees: A Life of Contemporary Artist Robert Irwin* (Berkeley and Los Angeles: University of California, 1982), 170.

3. Joachim Petersen, "Au Revoir les Enfants," *Contemporanea* (New York) 21 (Oct. 1990): 43.

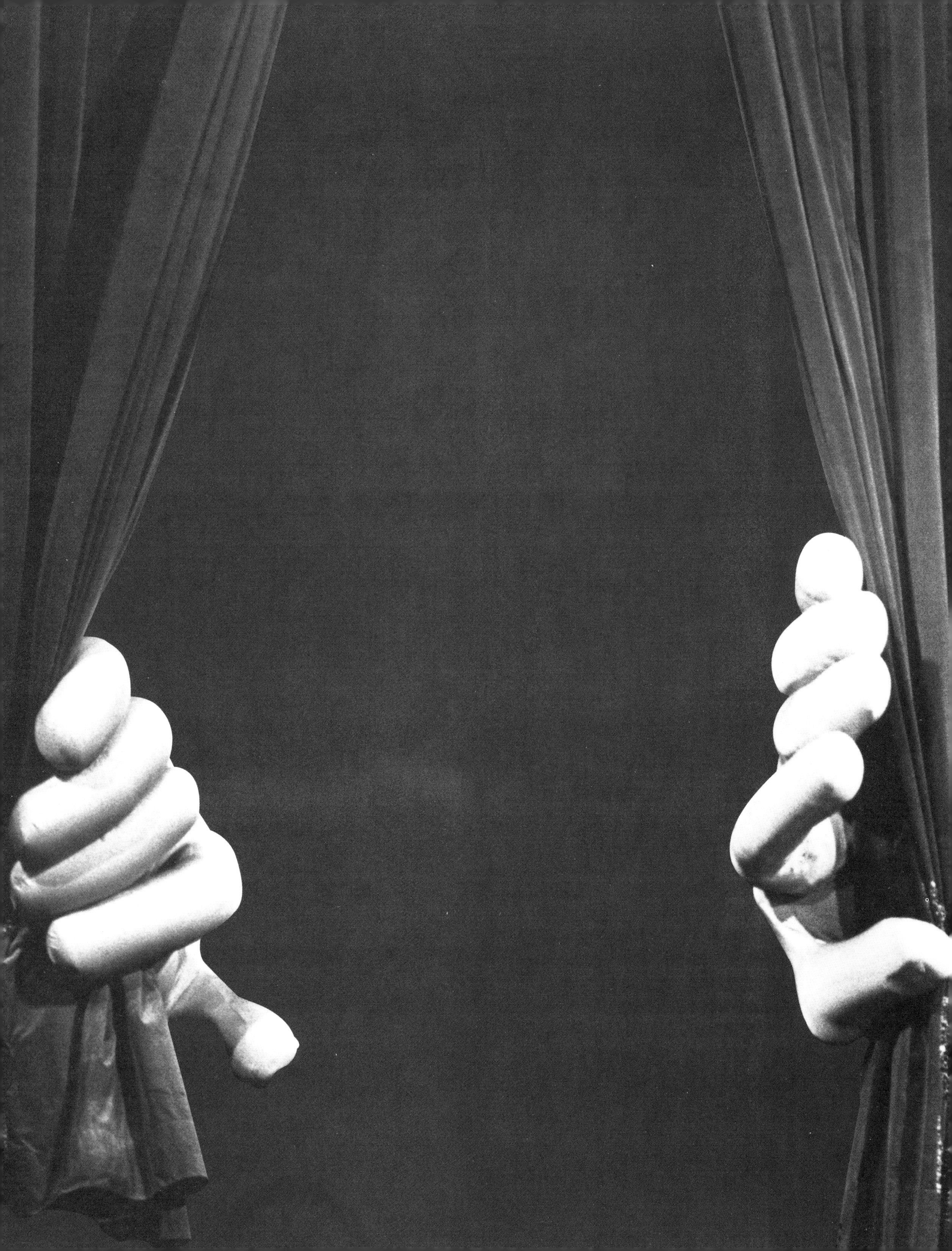

# From Swag to Scrim

*To all theatres of the world I demand the Merz Stage let veils waft, soft folds fall, let cotton wool drip and water sparkle.*

Kurt Schwitters

177 *(opposite).* Floriana Frassetto for Mummenschanz, *Hands.* Lycra, c. 39⅜ x 46⅛″. Performed at the Helen Hayes Theater, New York, 1986.

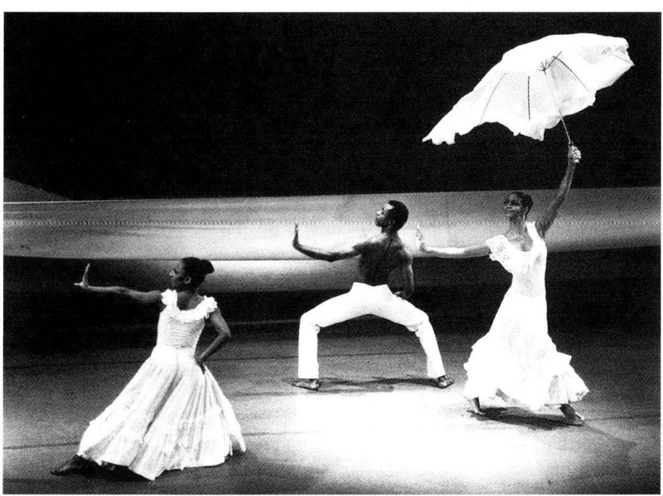

178. Alvin Ailey American Dance Theatre, New York, *Revelations: Wading in the Water.* Dancers: Sarita Allen, Melvin Jones, and Donna Wood.

"Let's pretend." Thus begins all theater. A mask, a piece of cloth, a word, a movement, an idea. These are the ingredients of life on the stage, the raw materials for imagining. Cloth, ubiquitous, ordinary, functional—but made extraordinary—has always been aligned with theater. *Cloth is theater.* The proscenium curtain introduces the performance. Closed, with its swags, pleats, folds, and color, it is mysterious. Then the side swags swing to the right and to the left, bewitching the audience with their swaying movements. Center stage emerges like the petals of a night flower. With anticipation and delight the audience accepts the beginning, prepared by the parting curtain. At this moment all disbelief has been suspended. In the past human hands parted the curtain; today the hands are electronic. Mummenschanz, a European mime group intent upon inventing their own visual language, understands the drama of the parting curtain, so they decided to begin their performance at the very beginning.

"Five minutes." The giant hands are brought onstage. Bernie and Andres pull down their cloth jersey helmets like racing drivers and mutter their last directives. "One minute." With the help of Elisabeth and Flo, they put on their costumes. Christian is given the signal that all is ready. Lights flicker on in front of the curtain, are turned off, light up again—the signal. Two giant hands reach for the curtain, begin to draw it open, slowly. The audience breaks out laughing (fig. 177).[1]

The members of this remarkable mime company not only create their own acts, they invent their masks and costumes as well. The contained figure has only movement and costume with which to communicate with the audience—and

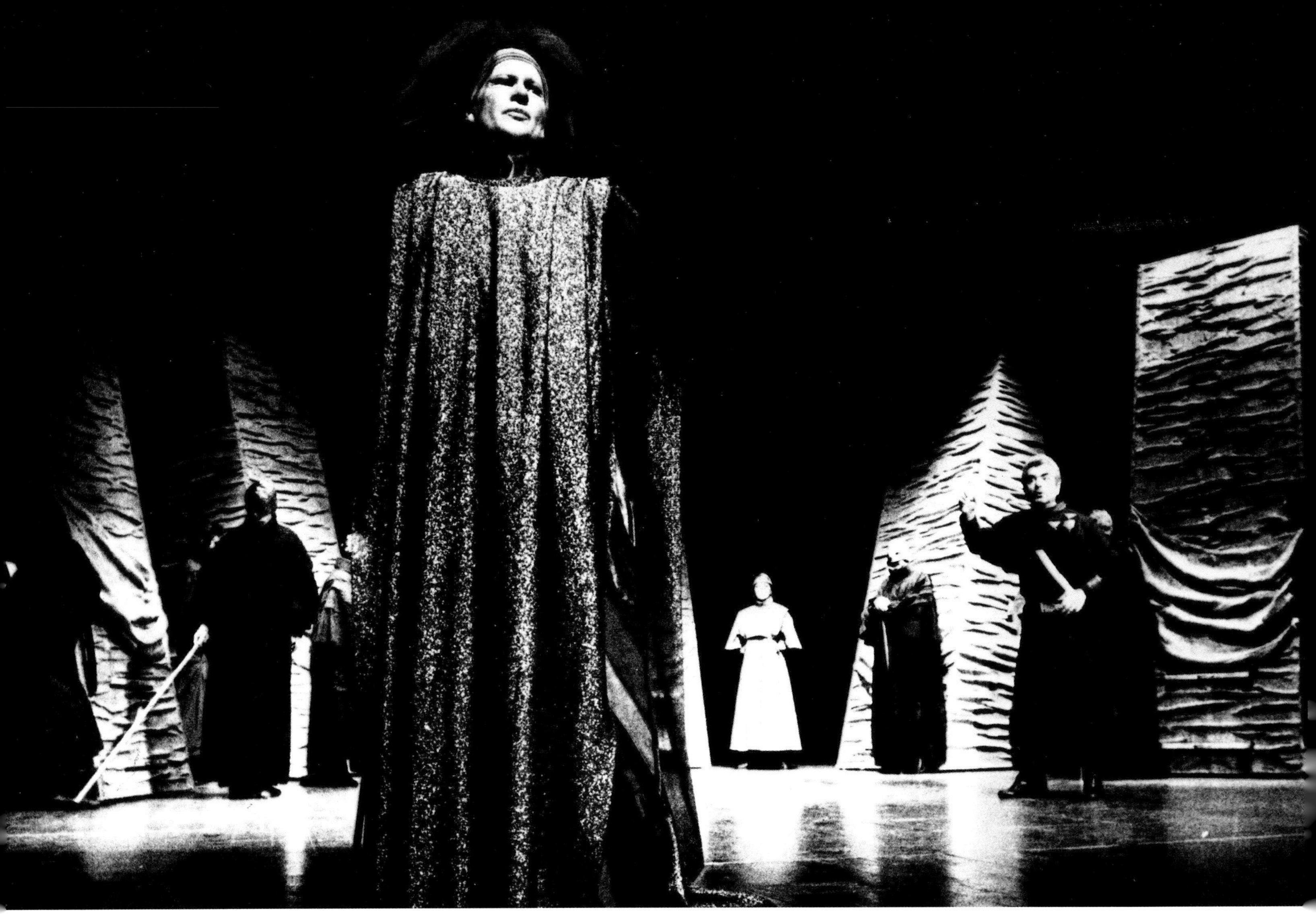

179. Jagoda Buić, set and costumes for T. Marojevic's *Antigona Today,* 1980. Jersey, jute, and clay.

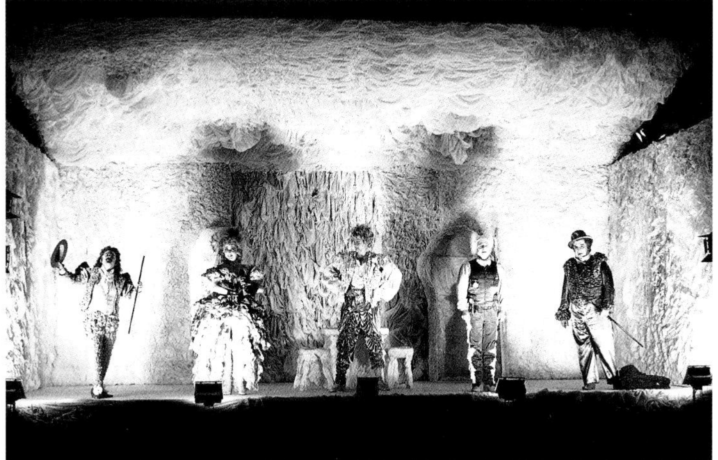

180. Colette, set for Ravel's *L'Heure Espagnole,* 1985. Berlin Deutsch Opera Productions.

Mummenschanz communicates brilliantly. Their themes are universal; their materials are just off the assembly line. They scrounge factory outlets and attend trade shows. They hunt the streets and browse department stores in search of the perfect synthetic cloth, the newest plastic, the weirdest toy. Then the American member of the Swiss troupe, Floriana Frassetto, with the help of her sewing machine, fashions a giant slinky, or full-body masks called Pizzas, or a UFO head, or an octopus. According to troupe member Andres Bossard, "Floriana has the advantage of being able to sit down at the sewing machine and do things that we are just thinking about. She has the ability to realize our theories, our scribbles." She replies, "I get fed up with discussion; I go get the fabrics, the materials, and do it." All members of Mummenschanz consider materials full-fledged partners in their work, enlarging their individual and collective imaginations with wit and fantasy.

Mummenschanz's gigantic stuffed gloves aptly demonstrate that cloth, fluid and chameleon-like, is easily formed into spectacular props. In 1960 Alvin Ailey choreographed his masterpiece *Revelations* as a tribute to his own African-American heritage. Judith Jamison with her huge and expressive hands and feet danced her heart out beside the endless river that flows through black life—represented on stage by a long, massive, undulating length of cloth. This may be the most remarkable use of cloth as cloth in the history of the performing arts in the twentieth century (fig. 178).

Visual artists have long participated in the performing arts. As historians have delighted in pointing out, Leonardo da Vinci and Bernini created pageants and performances based upon ideas they were already exploring in their drawing and architecture. In the twentieth century this became common practice, especially after 1940 when performance was finally recognized as an art form in its own right, thanks to the pioneering work of the Dadaists and the Futurists. For example, an artist like Colette, for whom cloth is the primary material, would naturally turn to cloth when creating for the stage. In her production of Maurice Ravel's *L'Heure Espagnole* at the Deutsch Opera in Berlin in May 1985, the entire set, as well as the singers, was covered with her familiar bunched, shredded, billowing, and cascading fabric, adapted ingeniously to emphasize the identity of each character. Likewise, Jagoda Buić's set and costume

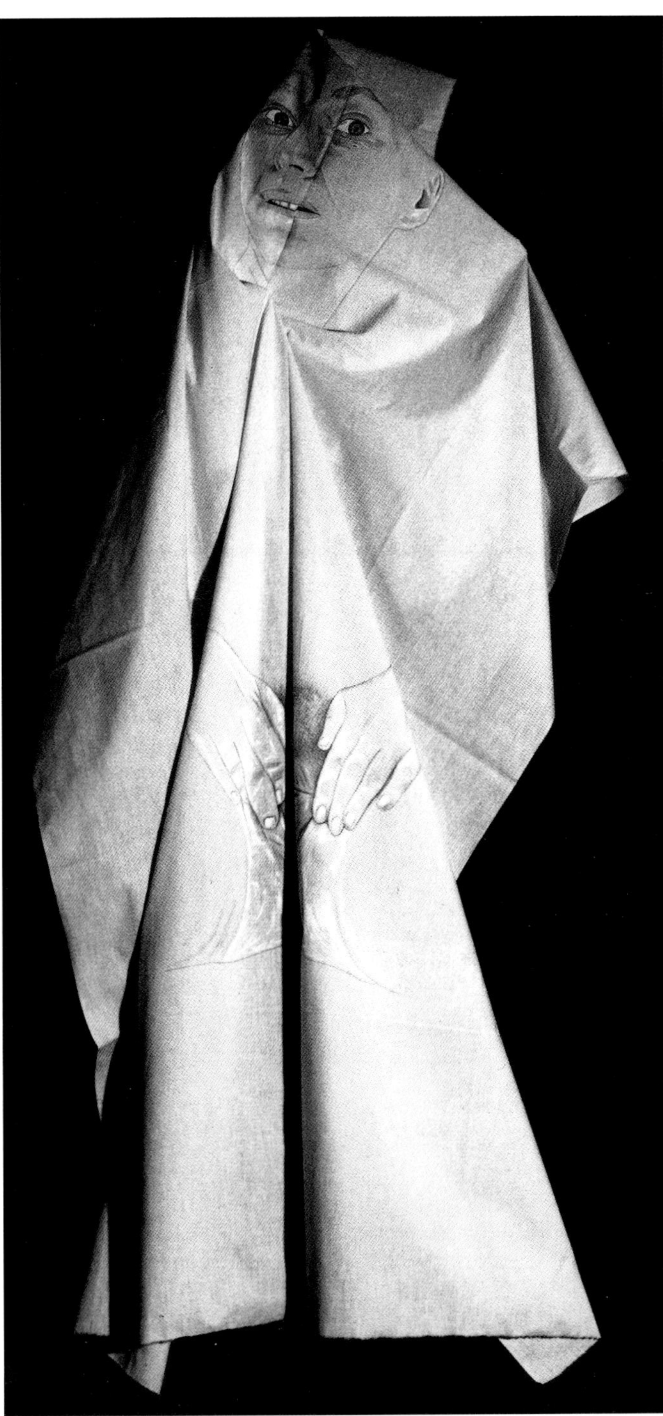

181. Ewa Kuryluk, costume for *Theatre of Love*, for the Mobius Performing Group, 1986–87. Embroidery on cloth.

design for *Antigona Today* recalls the sculpted tapestry walls for which this Yugoslavian artist became famous throughout the international Art Fabric world. Even when presented in exhibition as three-dimensional sculpture, Buić's weavings seem staged, as though they were created with the theater in mind (figs. 179, 180).

In the same vein, Ewa Kuryluk makes soft sculpture out of unbleached muslin (see fig. 129). When she was asked to create a large installation for the Mobius Performing Group's production of *Theatre of Love*, she used muslin for both the sets and the costumes. She explained her choice:

> I draw and paint on cotton and then I hang and fold and drape the material in different ways so that things acquire a third dimension. They become reliefs or even sculptures . . . I have always been interested in imprints, and in preserving memories, thus my drawings on the cotton. It is unbleached, so it is somehow evocative of skin. At the same time it reminds me of bed sheets, of the materials we wrap around our bodies. It becomes an intimate material, which makes me want to draw intimate images. The intimate moments of life become impressed into the cloth. The cloth is impregnated with them. I think of *Theatre of Love* consisting of old, faded drawings of erotic memories [fig. 181].

Artists work in traditional theater. They also create their own theater, collaborate with choreographers, invent happenings and performances. What places their work apart from traditional theater, or dance, or opera, is that it is visually and conceptually based. When artists approach the performing arts they not only bring their materials, as suggested above, but also their visual sensibilities. In 1905 Siegfried Jacobsohn wrote, "The task of the visual arts is not to reproduce reality, but by a profound refashioning of outward things, by the melodic weaving of perspective and distant vistas, to illustrate the inner weft of the drama."[2]

Jacobsohn foresaw the work of Isamu Noguchi nearly a half-century later. When Noguchi designed sets and costumes for the Martha Graham Dance Company he added a sculptural presence to the dance that no ordinary set designer could have imagined. When Martin Friedman organized the Noguchi retrospective for the Walker Art Center in 1978 he explained: "The movements of Graham's dancers were concise and authoritative but the atmosphere in which they moved was indeterminate. Therefore, she needed a designer who could reflect her symbolic views by creating mystical environments. To provide this unspecific quality of time and space, she invited the young sculptor, Isamu Noguchi, to work with her."[3]

In 1948 Noguchi created the set for *Diversion of Angels*, using opaque burlap scrim tautly stretched to reveal figures pressing into the scrim from behind—not unlike the work of the artist Lucio Fontana (see fig. 62). The forms on the scrim heralded the emerging earth forms that epitomized Noguchi's work from the 1960s until his death twenty-five years later. Friedman succinctly summarized the artist's perspective: "The stage in his view is a hypothetically perfect space where objects assume animate quality. His designs were intended to create atmosphere for rituals. He always conceived of theater as heightened reality, a process by which the audience could identify with the universal implications of the action" (fig. 182).

The spirit of Robert Rauschenberg looms over every chapter in this book. He, more than any other artist, made cloth an acceptable material for twentieth-century art. Although Claes Oldenburg created soft sculpture and Christo wrapped things with cloth, Rauschenberg created soft sculpture *and* wrapped things with cloth and did everything else as well. He learned the principles of collage as a child by watching his mother carefully arrange pattern pieces before cutting out his shirts. When he ran out of canvas, while broke and living in a cold-water flat in New York, he painted on Dorothea Rockburne's baby's quilt, thus creating one of the first unstretched paintings in the modern era and an icon of twentieth-century art (see fig. 26). He was equally inventive in the performing arts. The stage, in its broadest definition, became one more arena for his endless ingenuity.

Martha Graham's dance was psychologically based, the costumes and sets subservient to her desire to communicate inner emotion through movement. Merce Cunningham, on the other hand, saw the music, the choreography, the sets, and the costumes as independent forces unified by a specific duration of time. Noguchi and Graham made a perfect pairing; so did Robert Rauschenberg, with his free-for-all attitude toward art, and Merce Cunningham.

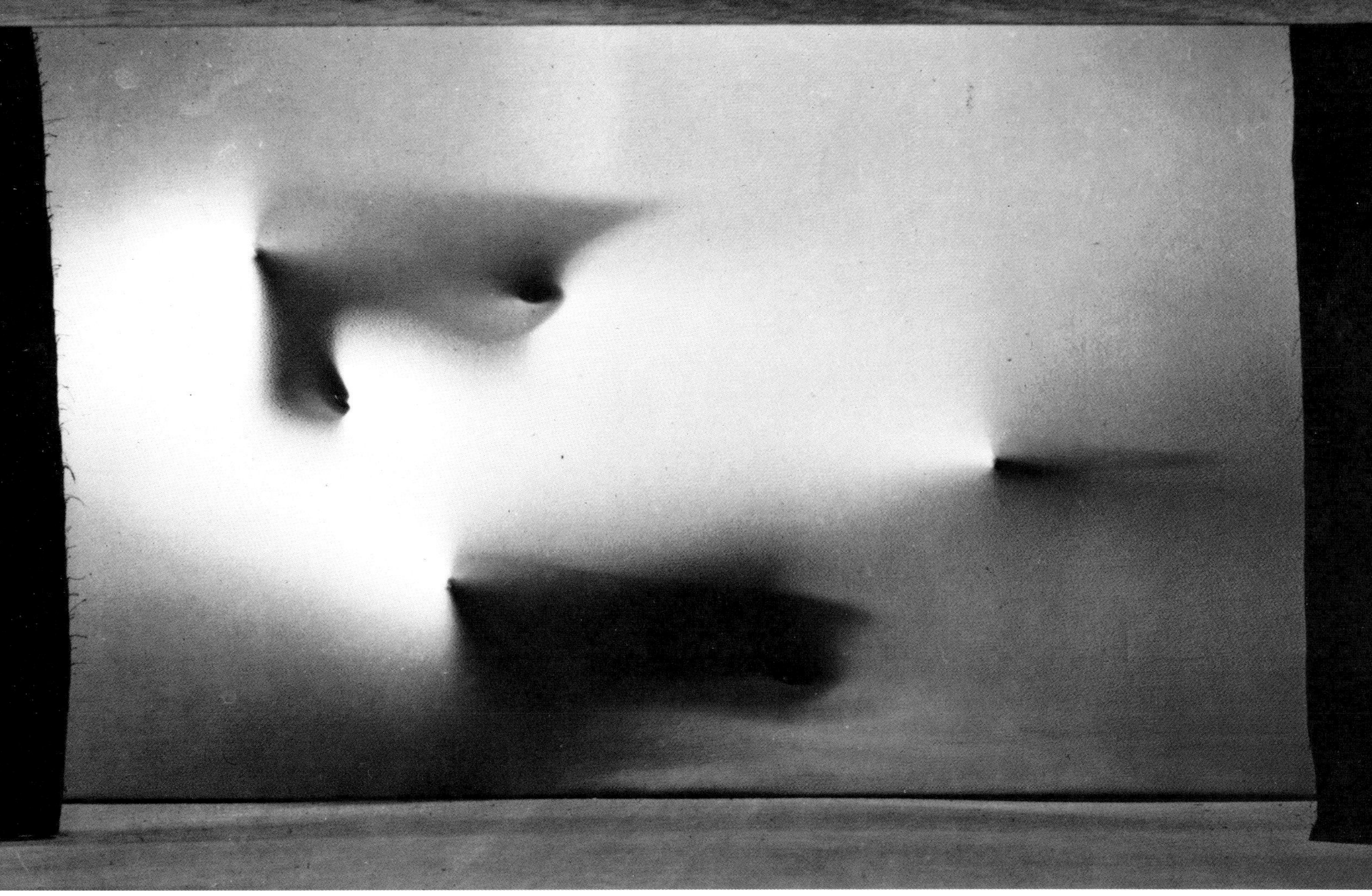

182. Isamu Noguchi, set for *Diversion of Angels*, Martha Graham Dance Company, New York, 1948. Burlap scrim. Choreography by Martha Graham.

In 1954 Rauschenberg created his first and possibly his most significant stage set, for the Cunningham production of *Minutiae*, for which contemporary composer John Cage wrote the music. One of his earliest combines, the *Minutiae* set consisted of the combination of paintings from his Red series and collages of cloth. The Red paintings came into being when the artist purchased cans of unlabeled house paint at a discount and they all turned out to be red (an early Happening?). The use of cloth seems to have come about because of the artist's inbred predilection for cloth, and because cloth is always at hand and Rauschenberg instinctively makes art from whatever is at hand. The sheen of floating red cloth, contrasted with the matte surface of the red paint, pieces of lace, and a shaving mirror, plus fluttering pink and blue cloth veils, gave the dancers a vibrating and beautiful set of screens with which to interact, and the dance premiered at the Brooklyn Academy of Music to rave reviews.

For ten years Rauschenberg collaborated with Cage and Cunningham, designing sets, costumes, and lighting. He formally resigned in 1964 but never gave up dance. He worked with other companies, including the Judson Dance Theater, the Paul Taylor Dance Company, and the Trisha Brown Company. During the 1960s he produced, choreographed, and performed nine of his own works, creating what were commonly called Happenings but that he preferred to call Theater Events. Later he rejoined Cunningham for specific productions, including *Travelogue* in 1977 (fig. 183).

*Minutiae* was visually dense; the surface of the set absorbed the light even though the shaving mirror was set spinning before curtain rise to reflect light, and cloth appendages wafted

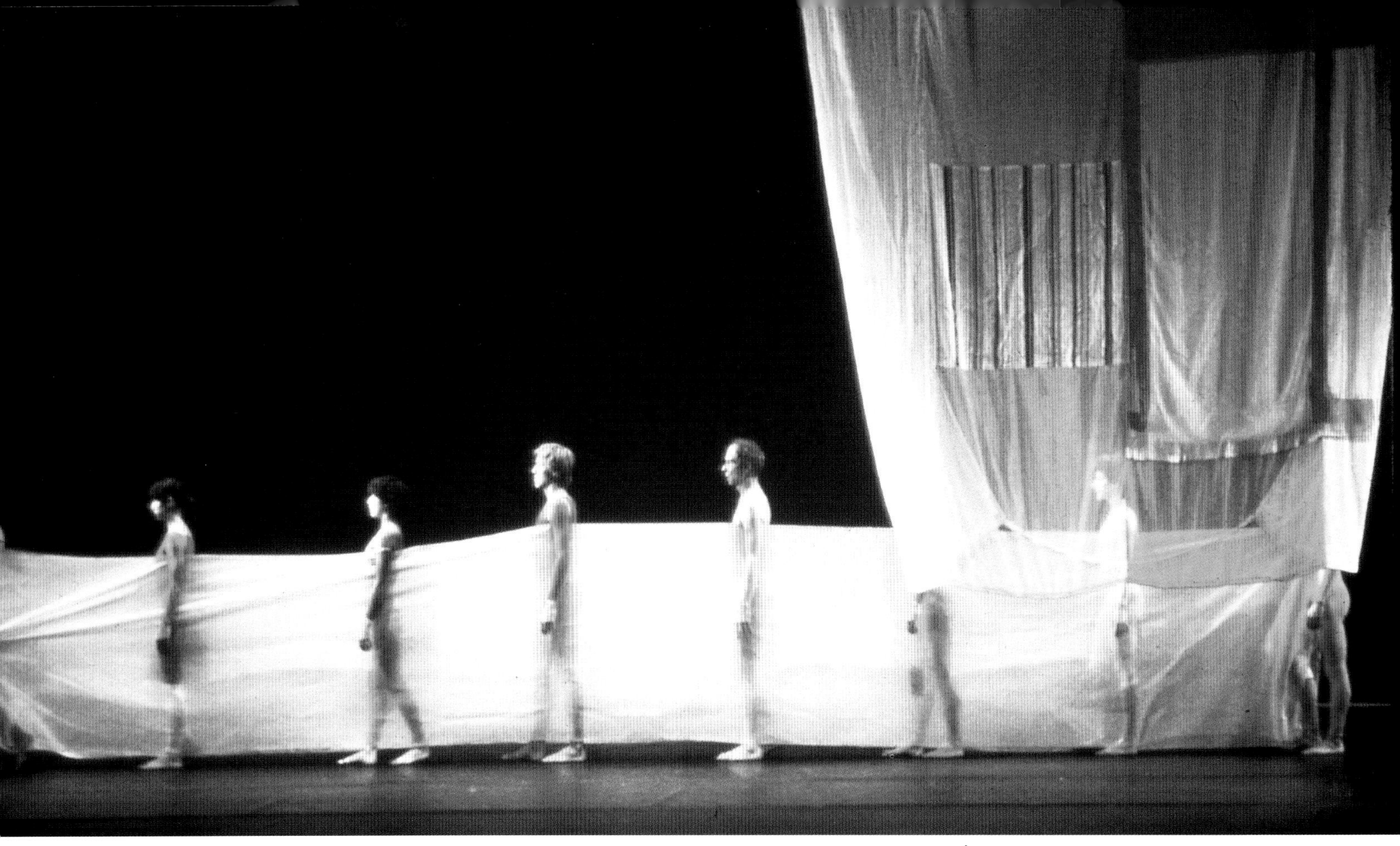

183. Robert Rauschenberg, set for *Travelogue,* for the Merce Cunningham Dance Company, New York, 1977. Music by John Cage (telephones and birds). Performance at the Minskoff Theatre, New York, January 18, 1977.

gently with the dancers' movements. The production was created during the height of Abstract Expressionism and the visual weight of that era marked the stage set. *Travelogue*, coming twenty-three years later, charts the artist's intervening search for light. First he made *Veils* (1974), a series of lithographs whose principle image was printmaker Tatyana Grosman's scarf. Rauschenberg was fascinated to discover that the image of a delicate piece of cloth was both luminous and transparent. This desired translucency led him further, to actually printing on cloth in the Hoarfrost series (see fig. 231). He was enamored with both the opacity and the translucency of cloth. Then in 1975 he traveled to India. According to Mary Lynn Kotz in her 1990 monograph *Rauschenberg: Art and Life:*

> Like other artists and writers before him, Rauschenberg was deeply affected by the sensual richness and color he saw in India. "For the first time, I wasn't embarrassed by the look of beauty, of elegance," he said. "Because when you see someone who has only one rag as their property, but it happens to be beautiful and pink and silk, beauty doesn't have to be separated." In India, Rauschenberg said he lost his fear "of something being beautiful. I've always said that you shouldn't have biases, you shouldn't have prejudices. But before that I'd never been able to use purple, because it was too beautiful."
>
> Rauschenberg took his son, a promising photographer, to shop for fabric. "He was very excited by what he saw there," recalled Christopher. "I can see him now, rolling out bolts and bolts of sari material, each one more beautiful than the last. He was feeling the texture, just amazed at the colors. A new sense of fabric came to him there" . . . the experience of India liberated him from his self-imposed restraint in the use of fabric.

In the ensuing years, Rauschenberg used shades of purple and pink and emerald green, turquoise blue, and other jewel-like colors in silks and brocades. This new sense of color was reflected, for example, in the Hoarfrost pieces Rauschenberg produced after his trip to India. In contrast to the earlier monochrome paintings on cheesecloth, later works in the series gave way to luxuriant, colorful fabrics.

The most direct result of this new sense of fabric came in 1975. Rauschenberg returned from India to begin his Jammers, a series of silk wall hangings. Choosing gorgeous, contrasting silks, he made panels, tied them together with string, and supported them with long poles leaning against the wall. Direct and unstudied, they are kin to the sail. *Travelogue* belongs with the Jammers. The spare angular simplicity of the set, props, and costumes commands the total stage space, made cohesive by the horizontal linear movement of cloth—again suggesting the sea. Here Rauschenberg gave free rein to his newly released instinct for the beauty and sumptuousness of cloth. The richness of cloth is the heart of his work for *Travelogue.*

Other dance companies and other artists use cloth in dance but few in the consummate way of Rauschenberg. Japanese artist Michie Yamaguchi constructed an enormous cloth pillow on the stage in the Osaka Bunka Joho Center in 1985 for the Sound Laboratory. In that most minimal of movement pieces, the performers, hidden under the pillow, rose and moved about before emerging from the cocoon. No material other than cloth could have produced this embryo effect (fig. 184).

To understand the body as one continuous moving form in space is often the starting point for costume designers (and set designers, as demonstrated by Yamaguchi). The sheer physicality of dance movement propels the dance: to skim, to pivot, to fly, to flow—to make patterns of movement is to dance. The properties of cloth and the way it is used in costume affect the audience's view of the body in motion. When Rudi Gernreich designed the costumes for Bella Lewitzky's 1976 production of *Inscape,* he created an altered human form. By incorporating wire ribs into the finials of both the sleeves and the skirt, Serena Richardson became something other than a human female dancer. Her movement was altered as well. Likewise, Frank Garcia, costume director for the Nikolais Dance Theatre since the 1950s, created the costumes for *Noumenon* in 1953 from stretch wool jersey. As the years progressed and the work stayed in the repertory, materials with increased elasticity became available—Jumboo, Millskin, and Spandex—which allowed even greater definition in shape and range motion. Still today the Nikolais/Louis Dance Theatre expands human form with cloth (figs. 185, 186).

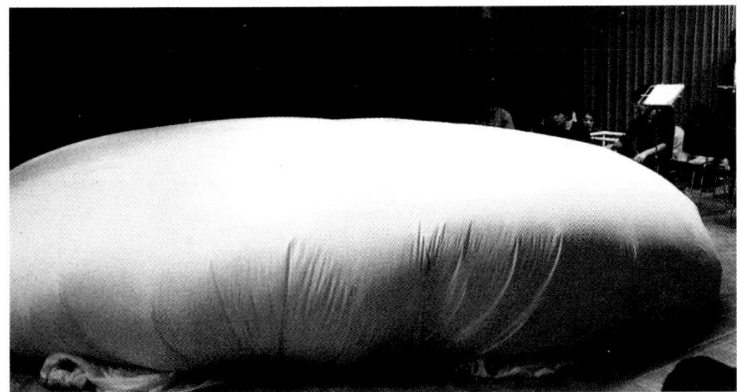

184. Michie Yamaguchi, set for the Sound Laboratory, Osaka Bunka Joho Center, 1985.

With Mummenschanz the human figure is subsumed by the costume. As Bernie Schurch, a member of the original troupe explained, "The human being disappears behind and in front of and between the things he lends his body to." Kindred to Mummenschanz is the abstract theater of Hanne Tierney—kindred in that the human actor is removed from the production. Tierney escaped Czechoslovakia at a young age to grow up in postwar Germany. She was apprenticed as a worker in a German spinning-wheel factory at thirteen but again escaped as quickly as possible, first to England where she began to write children's books, and later to New York. She spent the 1980s developing her own interpretation of the abstract theater that so interested Parisians a half-century earlier.

In a work such as her adaptation of Oscar Wilde's *Salome,* props replace human actors. Each prop is wired as a marionette. The strings reach to the ceiling and then across to one side to a playing board where Tierney conducts the performance, controlling the movements of each character while reciting their lines. Her voice, with its hard-to-identify accent, is as mesmerizing as the eerie, haunting, and strangely gorgeous presences on stage. Salome is represented by a headless apparition, an old green lace dress that was once in the wardrobe of Tierney's grandmother. Other characters might be plastic tubes, a pile of chains, and masks with ropes for bodies. Tierney's theater is magic symbolism, visually abstract but linear in script, or as linear as plays by Oscar Wilde or Gertrude Stein can be (fig. 187).

Clothing becomes character for Tierney. For other artists the clothed living figure becomes an abstraction. Performance artist Suzanne Lacy and the Danish performance group

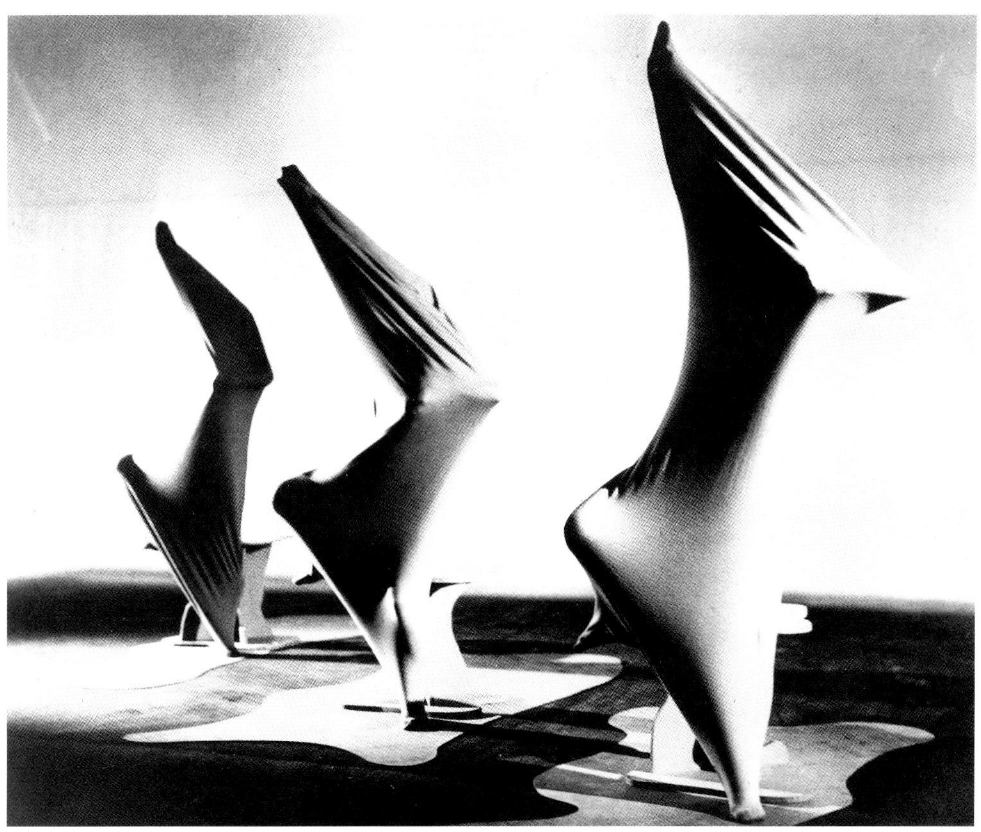

185. Frank Garcia, costumes for *Noumenon,* for the Nikolais Dance Theatre, New York, 1987 (first presented in 1953). Choreography by Alvin Nikolais.

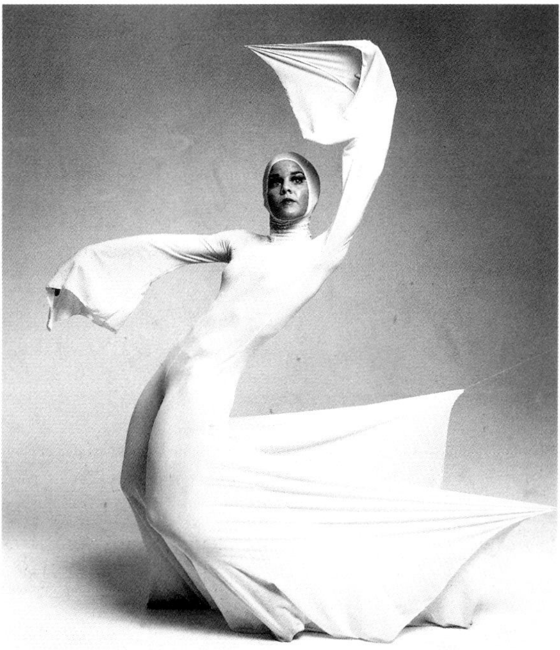

186. Rudi Gernreich, costume for *Inscape,* 1976.
Choreography by Bella Lewitzky. Dancer: Serena Richardson.

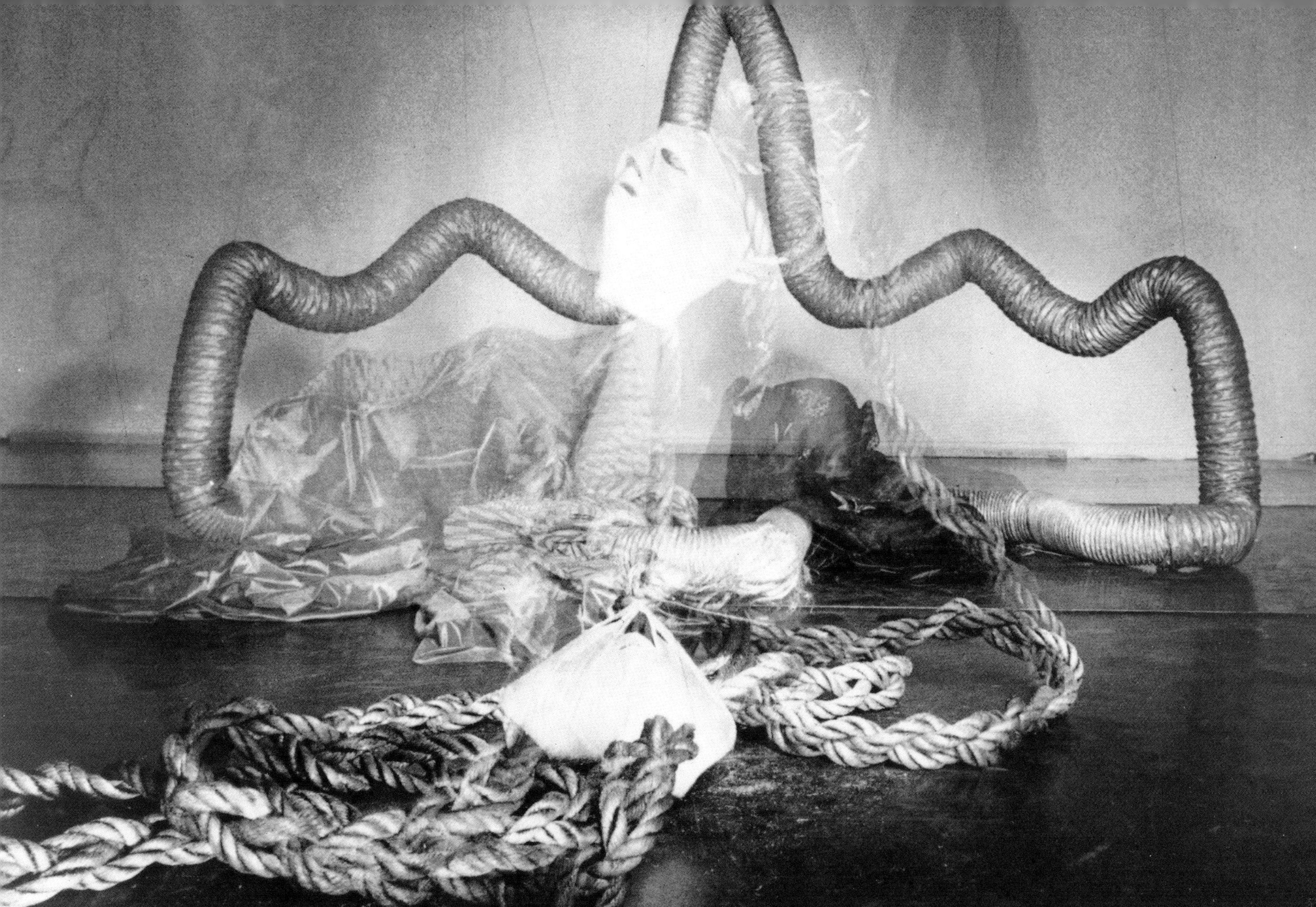

187. Hanne Tierney, *Salome*. Adapted by Tierney from Oscar Wilde's *Salome*. Performance at the North Dakota Museum of Art, Grand Forks, December 1986.

Billedstofteater both use the clothed human figure as the core of specific works: Lacy sometimes, Billedstofteater always.

Lacy, who is white, worked throughout the 1980s on collaborative projects with women of other races. She did this as a means of understanding the experience of being a minority in her own country. On May 31, 1986, Lacy arranged a living sculpture park on the campus of the University of California, Los Angeles, named *Dark Madonna*. Dark-skinned women of all ages and physical types were enveloped in white clothing and placed as statues throughout the lush green college campus. The figures took on a solid grandeur, a massiveness, an authority engendered by the whiteness of their costumes and the stillness of their poses (fig. 191).

Billedstofteater ("theater of image") was founded in 1977 by three artists, Else Fenger, Per Flink Basse, and Kirsten Dehlholm. The group sprung out of the Happenings and installation art of the 1960s. Happily, it has grown in the direction of truly avant-garde theater rooted in visual experience. Space, people, and costumes are the only elements. There are neither words nor professional actors. When the three principals settle upon an idea and a place, they put out a call for nonprofessional participants. Up to two hundred such people have taken part in a single performance. Through the costuming of off-the-street individuals, the group tries to uncover the authentic person. Sometimes Billedstofteater seeks out sites for performances; at other times museums invite them for specific occasions (figs. 188, 189).

In 1983 Billedstofteater was invited to create a series of works in conjunction with the opening of the Lausanne Biennale. Each work was based upon a different color: black, blue, or white. The performances took place in the galleries, the garden, the plaza in front of the museum, and the neighboring

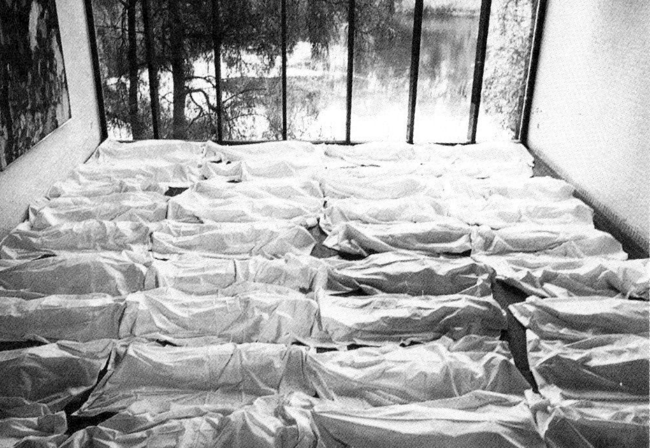

188. Billedstofteater, *Traek,* 1983. Performed at the Louisiana Museum of Modern Art, Humlebaeck, Denmark.

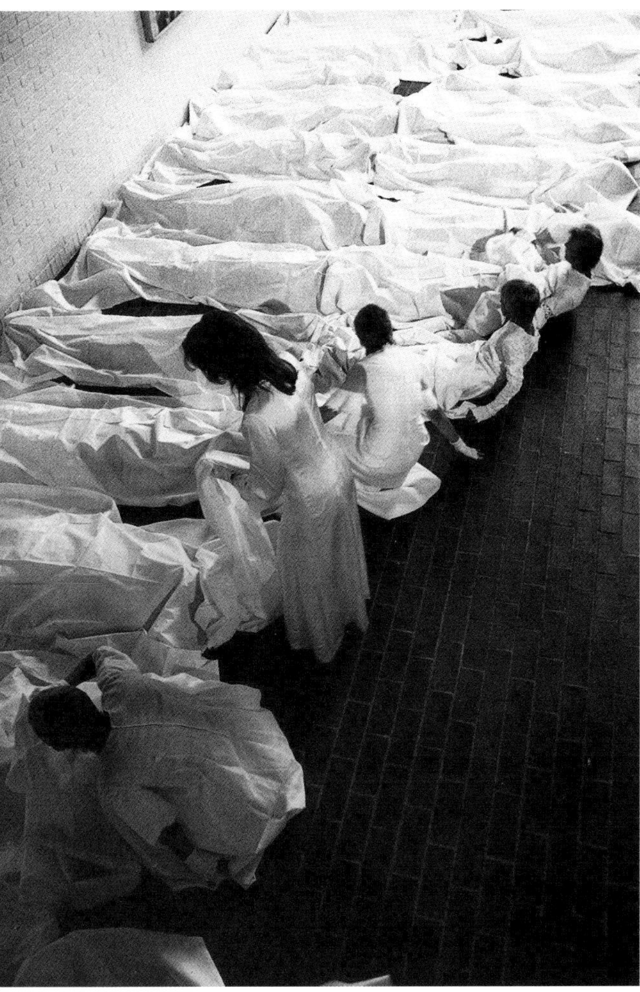

189. Billedstofteater, *Draft,* 1983. Performed at the Louisiana Museum of Modern Art, Humlebaeck, Denmark.

streets. On the day of the white performance the museum was packed. Avid fans of Billedstofteater, followers of the Art Fabric movement from around the world, participating artists, and regular museum visitors milled in the galleries, aware that a performance was scheduled but with no knowledge of where or what. Suddenly an unnoticed sheet of white cloth shifted in some part of a gallery. Very, very slowly, a white-clothed figure arose from under the sheet and began to walk toward the garden. Then another rose up from another space, and another, and another. Slowly, slowly, apparitions of all shapes, sizes, and ages came together. The museum audience remained silent. Nothing more happened. The performance was totally visual, an event locked in time and space and whiteness.

Frederic Amat created *Acció-Zero y Acció-1,* a performance in which he combined poetry and dance, in the same spirit of visual feast. It was performed in the Paulau de Congressos, Montjuic, Barcelona, between 1974 and 1976. Amat created his huge setting from simple forms. His sets and costumes were made of cloth, twigs, grasses, bones, skins of animals, and threads of many colors—an inventory of the markets and fiestas he finds magnetic. Fiber was a recurrent and dominant material. In one scene the head and limbs of a nude body were submerged into a sculptural package. The meanings of the work were to be intuited from the visual information provided by the artist (fig. 190).

Amat, Lacy, and Billedstofteater casually program or chart their performances. Chance events have much to do with the outcome, just as the reactions of the audience trigger Mummenschanz to improvise. This is an accepted ingredient in contemporary Western performance, entered into the canon by the early work of Cunningham, Cage, and Rauschenberg. This is not so in Asia, where performances are highly codified.
A dancer such as the Korean Kim Sook-Ja enthralled an audience of Western contemporary dancers at the American Dance Festival in Durham, North Carolina, in June 1986. She performed *Seung Moo,* which is said to have been created at the beginning of the twentieth century by the late Han Sun-Jun and is based upon a Buddhist ritual. The dance, including its fantastical cloth costume, is registered by the South Korean government as "Important Cultural Property Number Twenty-seven." Although highly ordered, works such as this interest and

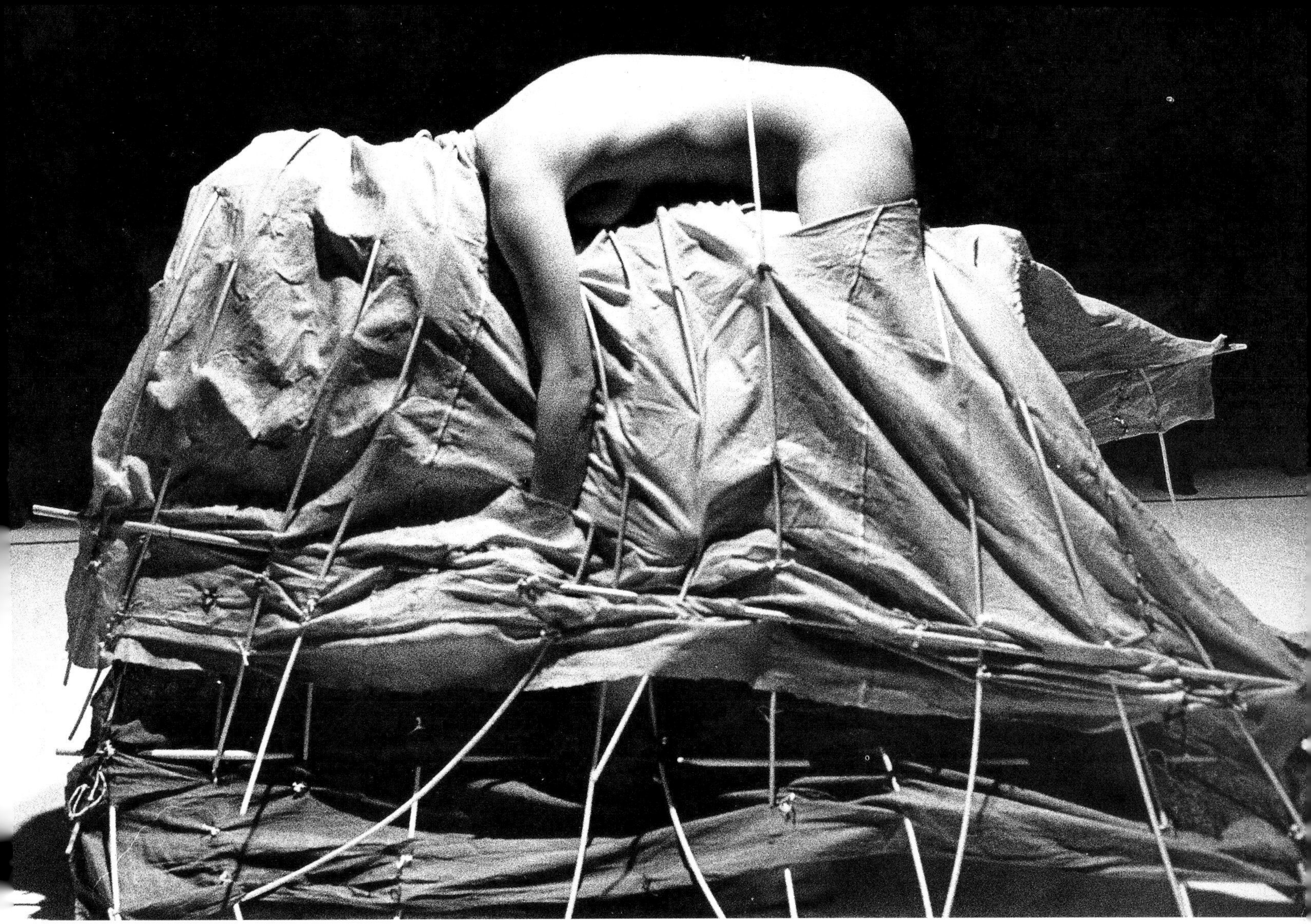

190. Frederic Amat, *Acció-Zero y Acció-1,* 1974–76.

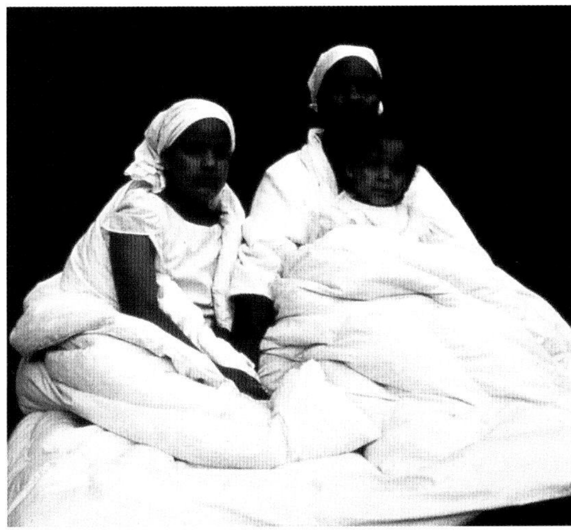

191. Suzanne Lacy, *The Dark Madonna.* Performance on the campus of the University of California, Los Angeles, May 31, 1986.

influence Western performers because they integrate theater, music, and dance. This work is also astonishing in that the costume is a great work of art in cloth—that is, the costume in motion (fig. 192).

Performance is an open arena. It incorporates everything from folk performances to third-world traditional dances to popular entertainments. When Pat Oleszko was attending the University of Michigan as an undergraduate studying in the department of fiber in the early 1970s, she needed a means of financial support. So she became a trained, professional stripper. In her art she combines her superb sewing skills with her equally good stripping skills to make outrageous, immoderate, flagrantly cynical performances that are great fun. Stripping honed her flare for making the audience connect with her. Her titles encapsulate her spirit: *Dots What's Happening!,* for the Metropolitan Museum of Art, New York (1980); *All the World's*

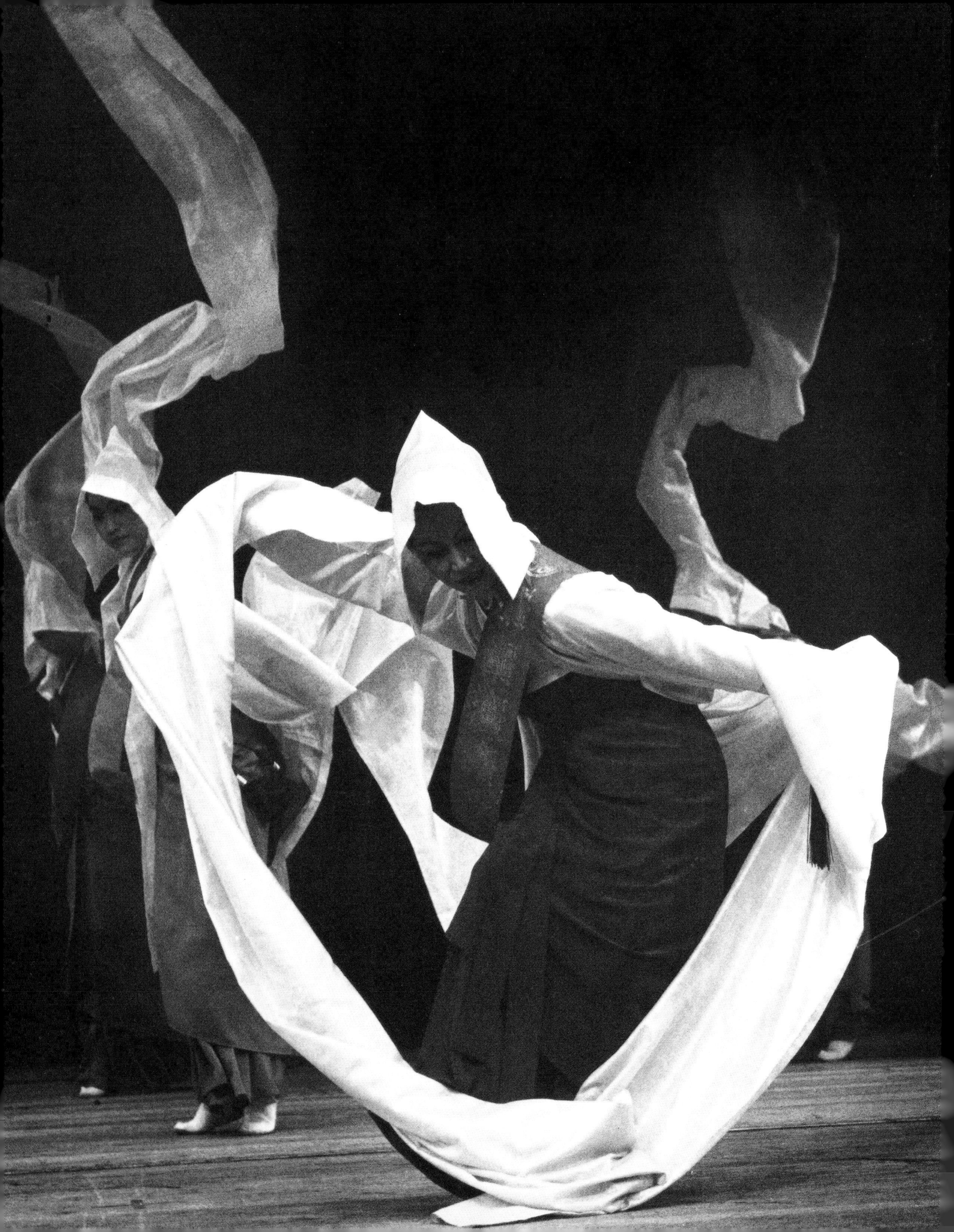

192 *(opposite)*. Kim Sook-Ja dancing in *Seung Moo*, c. 1985. This dance is said to be by the late Han Sun-Jun.

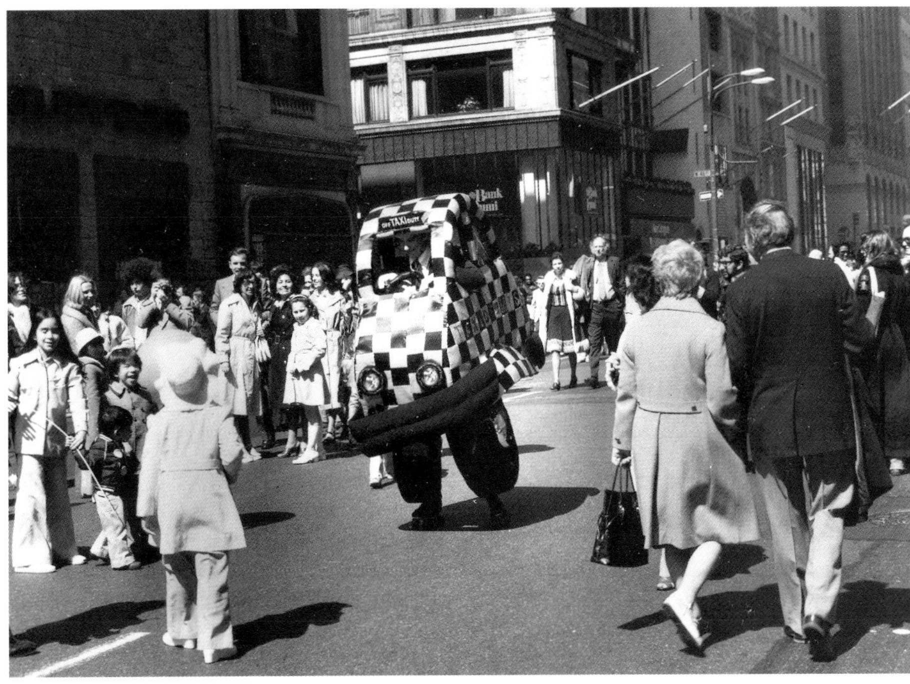

193. Pat Oleszko, *Taxidermiss*, 1976. Street performance in conjunction with the Museum of Modern Art's American bicentennial celebration.

*a Stooge*, for the downtown branch of the Whitney Museum of American Art, New York (1980); *The Pats to Suckcess*, for the Cooper-Hewitt National Museum of Design, Smithsonian Institution, New York (1977); and *The Soiree of 0: Let's Go*, for the New Performance Festival in Tokyo (1985). Egalitarian in art and nature, she has never confined herself to museums and high-art events but appears anywhere, including in the annual Macy's Thanksgiving Parade in New York as *Liberty is a Broad*, and in the city's annual Easter parade. Her witty frolicking is always underpinned by her own brilliant costuming. For her performance in connection with the Museum of Modern Art's American bicentennial celebration in 1976, *Taxidermiss*, Oleszko became her own New York taxi. She set her wearable Checker outfit of wood, foam, board, Dacron stuffing, and satin in motion with roller skates (fig. 193).

Throughout this century artists have made notable contributions to theater and dance and they have also developed performance art. Traditional theater, the opera, and the ballet have enriched the visual world in their own way. Perhaps no gift has been more useful than the simple cloth material scrim, which, for instance, Robert Irwin used extensively throughout the 1970s, as discussed in the previous chapter.

In the 1980s and 1990s cloth has become less important, as dance and theater have radically changed. Performers are sometimes nude, or almost so. Even more often they perform in the vernacular clothes of the everyday, in the clothes of the home and the street. But what if cloth did not exist? Could the performing arts have found their way without cloth? If children do not learn to play dress-up, to appropriate the props of adulthood, how do they learn to play "let's pretend"? A scarf, a cloak, a bedsheet, a hunk of fabric. These are the props of the imagination. Out of childhood games and their many props made of cloth comes each new generation in the performing arts. Before long, cloth will reassert itself in the imaginations of another wave of artists magnetized by the swag and the scrim.

1. Michael Buhrer, *Mummenschanz* (Switzerland: Panorama Verlag AG, 1984).

2. Henning Rischbieter, ed., *Art and the Stage in the 20th Century* (Greenwich, Conn.: New York Graphic Society, 1968), 9.

3. Martin Friedman, *Noguchi: Imaginary Landscapes* (Minneapolis: Walker Art Center, 1978), 25.

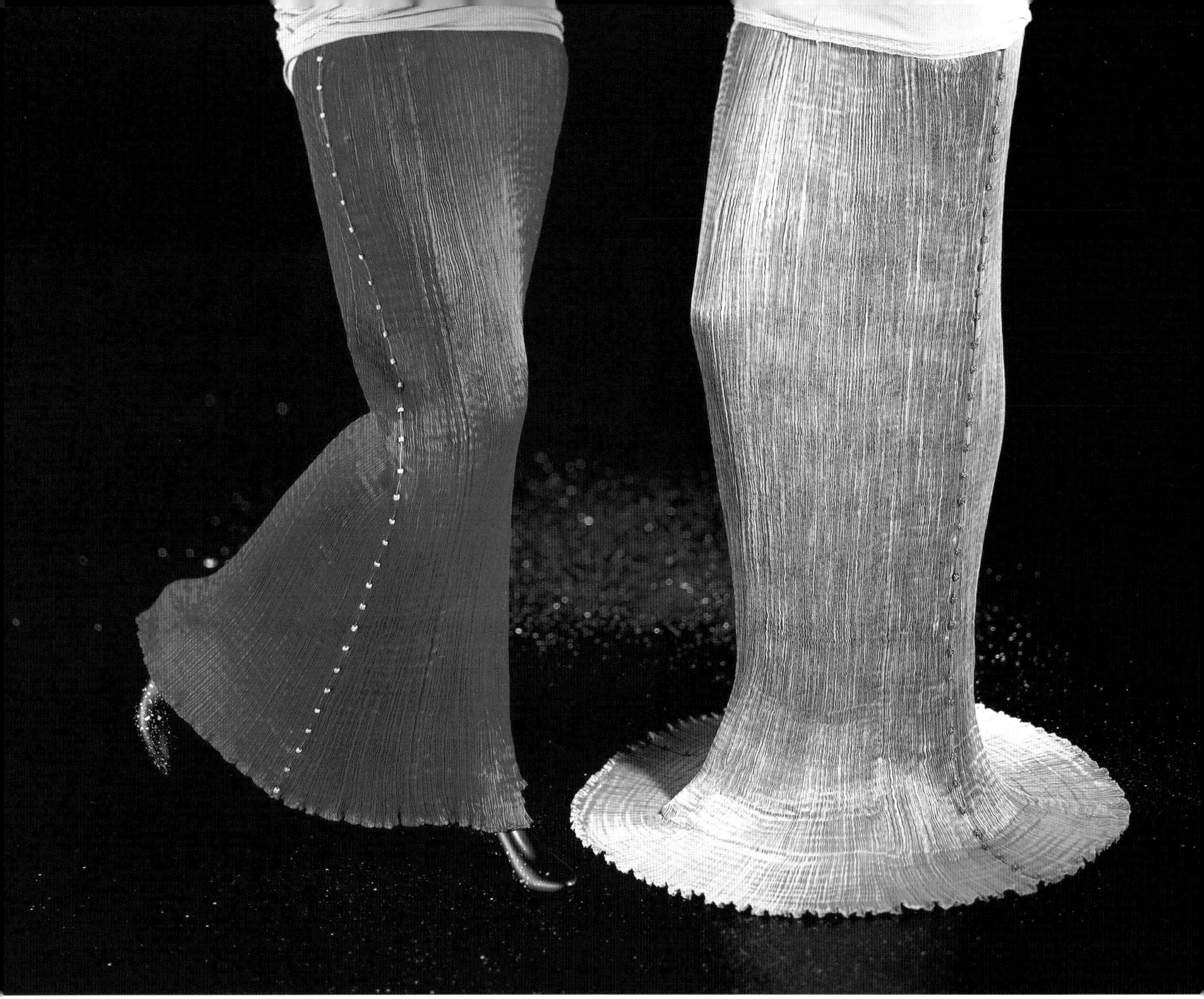

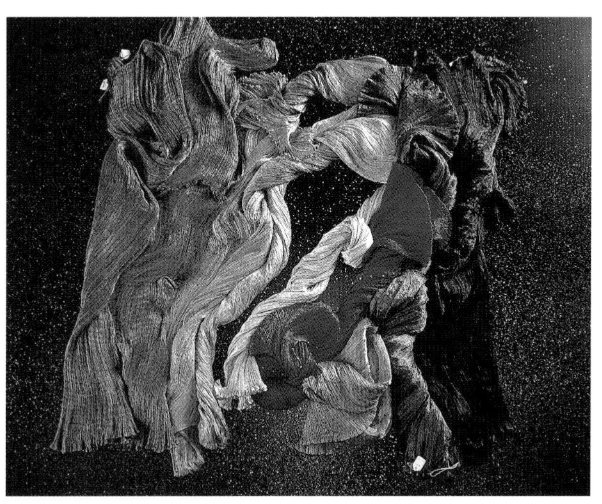

# Clothing the Body and the Spirit

*Body is to spirit*
*As cloth is to body*
*Grown to its own size:*
*Room in the air,*
*Air in the weave.*
*Waves in the breeze.*
*The earth spins and*
*Things come to an end.*
*So, day and night,*
*A body blooms*
*At its own hour.*
*Stretch the pause*
*Through the sky,*
*Or float—muted banner—*
*Signs, no designs.*

*Signs, no designs*
*Or float—muted banner—*
*Through the sky,*
*Stretch the pause*
*At its own hour.*
*A body blooms*
*So, day and night,*
*Things come to an end.*
*The earth spins and*
*Waves in the breeze.*
*Air in the weave.*
*Room in the air,*
*Grown to its own size:*
*As cloth is to body*
*Body is to spirit.*

Lawrence Wieder

194 *(opposite, top).* Mariano Fortuny, *Skirts on Mannequins,* silk. Courtesy of the Kyoto Costume Institute, Japan.

195 *(opposite, bottom).* Mariano Fortuny, *Tonal Range of Colors,* silk.

"Body is to spirit / as cloth is to body." Lawrence Wieder wrote this poem in response to the work of the Japanese designer Issey Miyake. This chapter is not about fashion; it is not about clothing. It is about artists who transcend, or set aside, both fashion and clothing in order to make their art—in order to address the spirit as well as the body. The twentieth century has seen an explosion of artists using clothing as a metaphor for the human spirit or the human figure. It has seen a homegrown Wearable Art movement influence the international haute couture industry, and then artists from that movement evolve into fashion designers in their own right. It has seen crossover in all directions, culminating in an international Florence Biennale, which opened in the fall of 1996 with the purpose of examining the relationship between art and fashion. Big names from the art world and big names from fashion were invited to Florence to collaborate: Roy Lichtenstein and Gianni Versace, Jenny Holzer and Helmut Lang, Mario Merz and Jil Sander, Damien Hirst and Miuccia Prada. The Florence Biennale did not spring from nowhere but evolved from decades of cross-pollination.

# The Historic Precedent

Historically, art and fashion have always kept company. Perhaps the first modern figure to make clothing—as an artist—was Mariano Fortuny de Madrazo, born in Granada, Spain, in 1871. His dresses are famous twentieth-century artifacts. He was not a couturier in the Parisian manner, and he lived a life far removed from the concerns of fashion. He began as a painter and an inventor. Even after establishing his atelier in his beloved Venice, he remained involved in photography, stage lighting, architecture, and theater design.

Fortuny's work is timeless, grasping the intangible with spirit and skill. From the beginning of his career until its end he consistently employed the same cut and fabrics. His garments required little shaping or sewing and allowed no embellishment. The vital essence of his art came from his resplendent, jewel-like colors, which were inspired by painters of the Venetian Renaissance, especially Carpaccio, coupled with his own method of permanent pleating. Fortuny's goal was to develop a natural dress that would reveal the female form underneath while allowing that woman complete freedom of movement—the precedent for which he found in Greek sculpture (figs. 194, 195). He succeeded in creating the sumptuous minimalism immortalized by Marcel Proust in *Remembrance of Things Past*:

> In matters of dress what appealed to her most at this time was everything that was made by Fortuny . . . Mme. de Guermantes seemed to me to carry to an even higher pitch the art of dressing . . . (her garments were not a casual decoration alterable at her pleasure, but a definite and poetical reality like that of the weather, or the light peculiar to a certain hour of the day.) Of all the outdoor and indoor gowns that Mme. de Guermantes wore, those which seemed most to respond to a definite intention, to be endowed with a special significance, were the garments made by Fortuny from old Venetian models, is it their historical character, is it rather the fact that each one of them is unique that gives them so special a significance that the pose of the woman who is wearing one while she waits for you to appear or while she talks to you assumes an exceptional importance, as though the costume had been the fruit of a long deliberation and your conversation was detached from the current of everyday life like a scene in a novel?

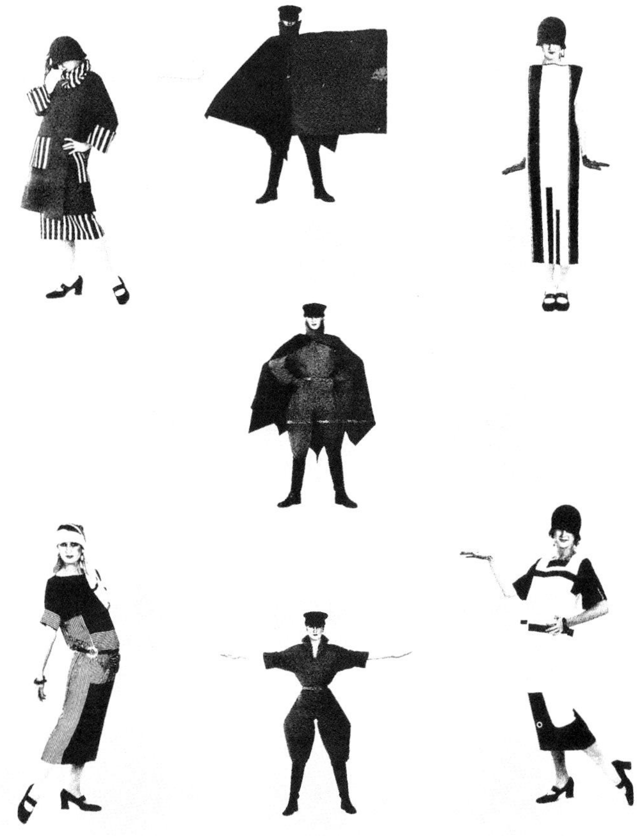

196. Models based on original designs by Alexandra Exter, Lyubov' Popova, Varvara Stepanova, and Nadezhda Lamova. Re-created by Erika Hoffman-Koenig for the exhibition "Russian Women—Artists of the Avant-Garde, 1910–1930," Galerie Gmurzynska, Cologne, 1979–80.

During the 1920s several artists turned their attention to clothing. Fired by the spirit of political, social, and economic revolution in the Soviet Union during that time, a group of influential artists, including Varvara Stepanova, Vladimir Tatlin, Alexander Rodchenko, and Lyubov' Popova, decreed that "under pressure from the revolutionary conditions of contemporaneousness we reject the pure forms of art. We recognize self-sufficient easel art as being outmoded and our activities as painters as being useless. We declare productivist art to be absolute and construction to be its only form of expression" (fig. 196).[1]

Clothing, be it for theater or mass production, was to be designed according to a system of formal elements. It was to be approached with the same expressive attitudes as the design of all other objects of daily use. Neither the human body nor movement was of prime importance. Abstract pattern was what mattered. For example, Rodchenko created his Constructivist clothing for the worker at the pattern stage. He saw the pieces as cut to shape, awaiting assembly into wearable garments.

Sonia Delaunay, an immigrant to Paris from Russia, introduced these radical ideas to the center of fashion. The influence of her abstract patterns, taken from Cubist paintings or from patchwork (see fig. 20) and used in clothing, is still felt today. She made her own fabrics, calling them "simultaneous materials" —collages of strongly colored, unlike materials such as taffeta, flannel, and organdy. This use of collage technique echoed what she was doing in her painting and printmaking. Delaunay effected a revolution in the fashion world of the 1920s stemming from her noninterest in fashion and her conviction that the Constructivist principles of painting were applicable to all art forms. By not being occupied with what was chic or glamorous, she was able to visualize clothing as a format for abstraction—an extreme point of view at that time. Forty years later, in 1964–65, André Courrèges began to create his optical clothing and Yves Saint Laurent brought out his Mondrian dress. Both fashion designers owed much to the art of Sonia Delaunay and the Russian Constructivists.

Coco Chanel became famous for her cubistic, box-suit jacket with its rectangular skirt. But her description of Elsa Schiaparelli as "that Italian artist who makes dresses" became the legend permanently inscribed upon Schiaparelli's image. Although meant disparagingly, Chanel accurately identified the one designer of this century most closely aligned with the art world, in particular with the Surrealist movement. Schiaparelli was friends with André Breton. Jean Cocteau and Christian Bérard collaborated with her. But even more than these, Salvador Dalí was both mentor and peer. In 1937 they collaborated on the Tear Illusion Dress. The tears were real on the veil and cape, illusive on the dress. (Some claim this to be the seed for the torn clothing of the punk rock movement of the 1970s, and for such Japanese designers of the early 1980s as Rei Kawakubo, for whom torn clothing was a recurring motif.) Dalí and Schiaparelli worked together for years, transforming the ideas of Surrealism into both fashionable and unfashionable clothing. Among their many joint ventures were the Shoe Hat; the Lobster Dress; the Mutton Chop Hat; and Schiaparelli's Desk Suit, based upon Dalí's drawing *The City of Drawers: Study for Anthropomorphic Cabinet* (fig. 197).

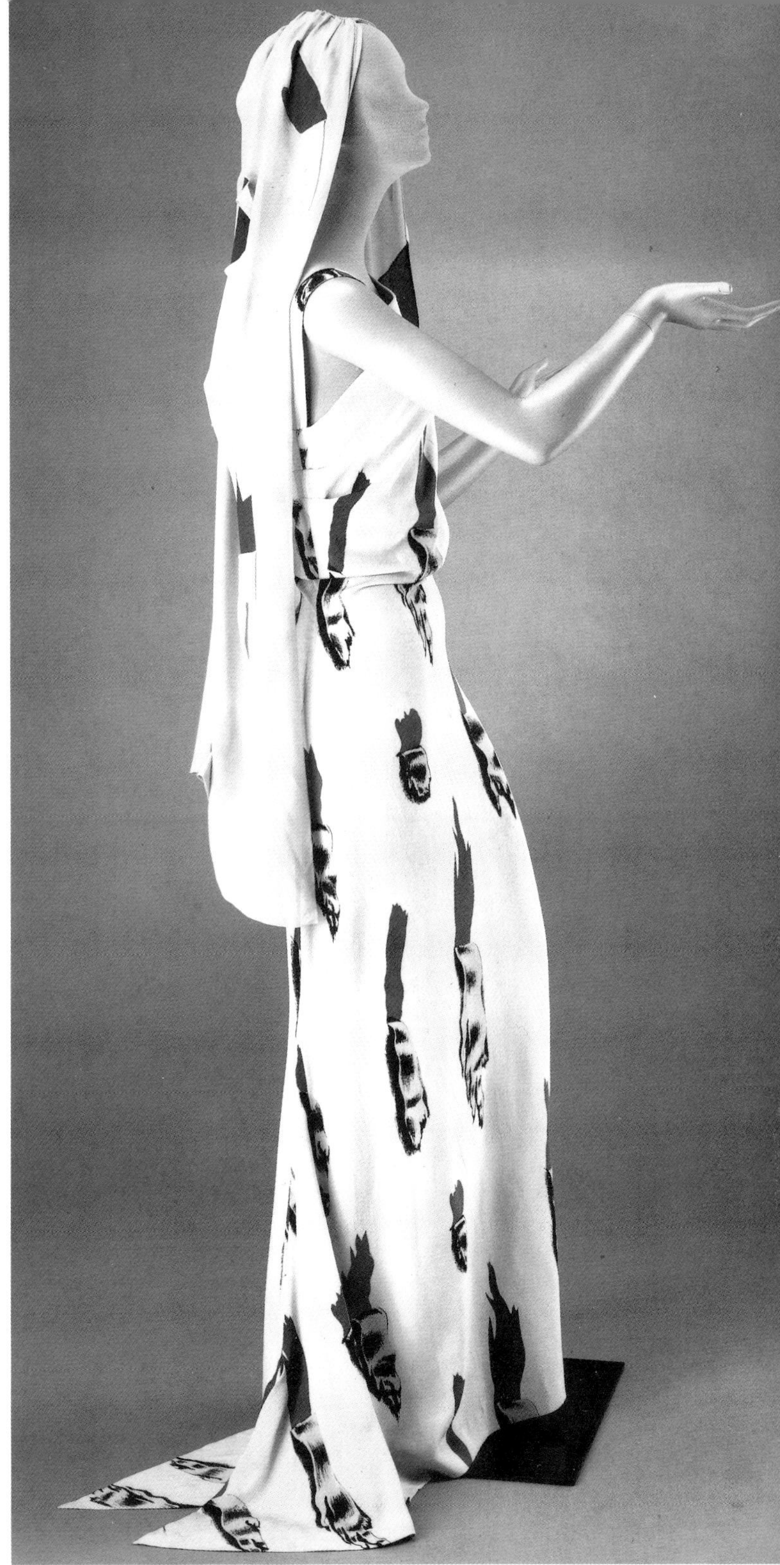

197. Elsa Schiaparelli, *Dress and Headscarf* (Tear Illusion Dress), 1937. Blue silk crepe, 57 x 41½". Courtesy Philadelphia Museum of Art, gift of Mme. Elsa Schiaparelli.

Schiaparelli brought wit, passion, and humor to a field bereft of them. Her influence is legendary: Yves Saint Laurent, Karl Lagerfeld, and Christian Lacroix, in addition to legions of artists who make wearable clothing and objects, claim direct ancestry. As important to twentieth-century fashion as Schiaparelli is, or Cristóbal Balenciaga, or even Fortuny, there is another, almost unknown to the general public, who stands head and shoulders with these greats. He is Charles James. When in 1983 curator Elizabeth Ann Coleman organized an exhibition of his work for the Brooklyn Museum, she wrote: "Line and cut, color and texture structure garments by Charles James. He went about constructing many of his fashion designs as an engineer builds a bridge. Mathematical principles served as a cornerstone and James created from his unerring eye for color and texture works of art, not from unyielding stone or metal, but fluid fabric . . . The Genius of Charles James cuts through cloth with a lunge of the shears."[2]

James was born in England in 1906 and lived there until the age of nineteen when he moved to his mother's hometown, Chicago, to become a milliner under the pseudonym Boucheron. In 1928 he moved to New York, and then a year later back to London, traveling between the two cities for the next decade. In 1940 James established his studio, Charles James Inc., in New York. He believed that works of fashion were like works of art and should endure for all seasons. His dresses would remain on the market for years even while he continued to work on them. In the course of his career, he developed two hundred thesis designs, or basic design modules, which could be varied in a thousand ways by interchanging parts. He is remembered for his grand, sculptural ball gowns, his Taxi dress with its spiral zipper (1933), and his experiments with new materials including rayon, Celenese, and Borgana—a plush Orlon and Dacron fur fabric for winter coats. He himself considered his Four Leaf Clover gown (1953) to be his masterpiece, a work of wearable sculpture in cloth.

In 1958 James, the self-taught fashion designer, retired from the couture industry and moved to a more private life, which included lecturing at the Rhode Island School of Design and the Pratt Institute in Brooklyn. As a historian of fashion he is remembered for saying that "Blue denim is America's greatest gift to the world."

# Jeans: A Worldwide Phenomenon

To leap from the great artist-designers of this century to jeans is to span a great distance. The designers were consumed with defining the body in space, with cloth as it could be draped and cut to create a work of art. Jeans came from the humblest of beginnings.

The Levi Strauss Company was founded during the 1840 gold rush in San Francisco in order to sell canvas tents to miners. But the miners needed pants even more, so the entrepreneurial, family-owned company cut up the tents and sewed them into sturdy "Levis." In 1873 Levi Strauss began to rivet their strong, denim, workingmen's pants; the style was set (see fig. 32).

The Lee Company entered the field early on, selling mostly to cowboys. During the 1920s cattle ranches started to evolve into "dude ranches" for tourists. By 1946 the Lee Company was running full-page color advertisements for their jeans in *Life* magazine, instructing readers to "spread the romance of the West."

In the 1950s the Beat poets of San Francisco adopted jeans as their uniform, transforming the jeans into symbols of rebellion against middle-class life. The hippies of the 1960s quickly saw their power and turned them into a universal antifashion statement loaded with visceral impact. But nothing holds for long in the rapidly changing society of the twentieth century. In 1974 Levi Strauss sponsored the Levi's Denim Contest. Ten thousand entries of embellished jeans clothing were submitted to this landmark Wearable Art exhibition. Clearly, jeans had evolved from cult status to become widely accepted as standard American dress. By the end of the decade, designer jeans by Calvin Klein and Gloria Vanderbilt, and everyone else, were de rigueur in the fashion salons of the world.

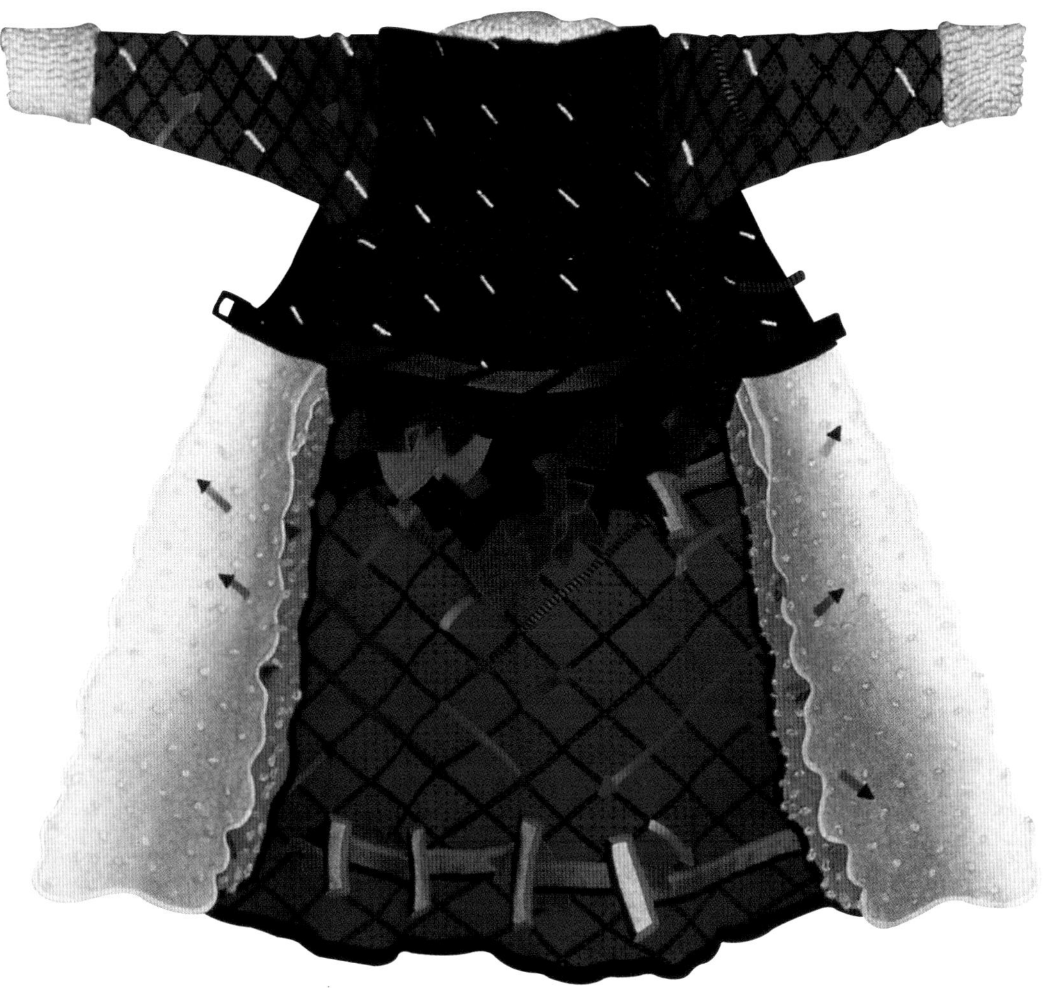

198. Jean Williams Cacicedo, *Chaps: A Cowboy Dedication,* 1983. Wool, jersey, and Dacron, 53 x 66″. Courtesy Julie: Artisan's Gallery, New York.

# Wearable Art Movement

With jeans came a break in how the Western world thought about clothes. Anyone could, and did, become a designer. The fashion industry, long centered in Paris, became democratic. London, New York, Tokyo, Milan, and artists' studios everywhere became potential centers for new ideas. Something called "wearable art," or "art to wear,"came into being.

Its roots go back to 1969, when five leaders of the movement graduated from Pratt Institute in Brooklyn: Sharron Hedges, Janet Lipkin, Jean Williams Cacicedo, Deanne Schwartz Knapp, and Marika Contompasis. Immediately others joined their ranks, including Marian Clayden and Ana Lisa Hedstrom. No movement was intended. At first these artists just made clothes for themselves and their friends. Because they were trained in art schools in either textiles or related fields of design, they approached clothing as artists. In the true sense they were interested in clothing both the body and the spirit. Because of their interest in ethnic clothing and in the history of textiles their work is highly referential. For example, the work of D'Arcie Beytebiere (see fig. 76) is informed by the earlier work of Fortuny and by the then-current international infatuation with pleating (stemming perhaps from the major exhibitions of Egyptian and Greek art shown in Europe and the United States in the 1970s). The kimono, ancient dyeing processes,

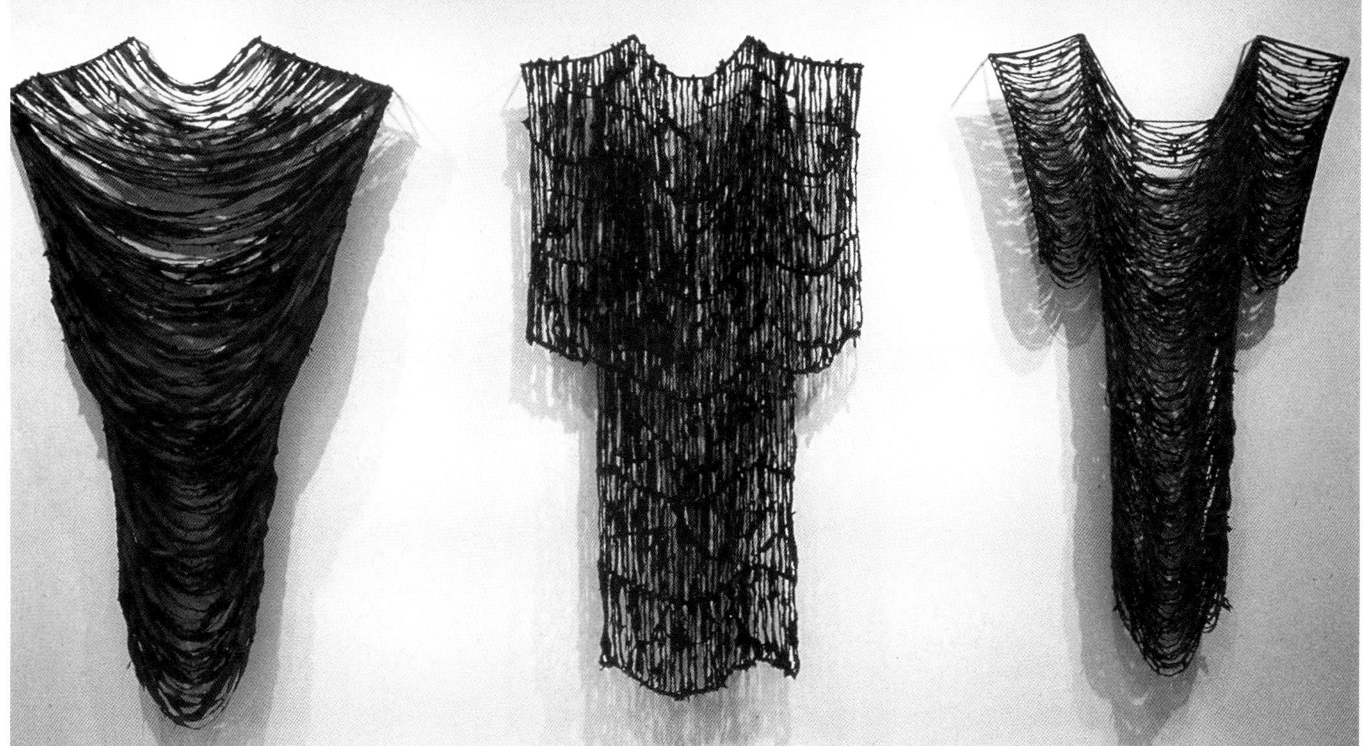

199. Tim Harding, *Shroud Triptych*, 1988. Silk, c. 92 x 42 x 3″.

handwoven and hand-constructed fabrics, unshaped dresses, knitting, and crocheting are only a few of the recurring elements of the Wearable Art movement.

Jean Williams Cacicedo's *Chaps: A Cowboy Dedication* celebrates the traditional costume of the cowboy from all over the world. It is a melody of textures and materials that incorporates hand-dyed wool, felting, knitting, crocheting, and appliqué. This strong work of art seems intended for the wall, or for temporary display upon a figure. The coat is less a thing to wear than a statement about the performance of wearing (fig. 198).

Tim Harding, another artist to come out of the Wearable Art movement, has always been interested in the individual's relationship with clothes:

> I went through a process of analyzing what clothing is about—its functions, how it has meaning about who we are and the kind of image we want to project. I was also looking at the special qualities of textiles that are used in people's daily lives. Fabrics are taken for granted; there are some exceptions, European tapestries during the Renaissance, for example, but mostly, fabrics have a mundane function, and are an intimate part of people's lives.
>
> That led me to the precious aspects of clothing. Good clothes shouldn't be stained, scorched or soiled; they need to be taken care of. The juxtaposition of preciousness and vulnerability was the basis for some of my early experiments.[3]

Harding's early experiments in scorching, burning, cutting, ripping, and actually shooting into the fabric with a rifle led him to the process for which he is internationally known—his dye-layer-quilt-slash-fray technique. The bottom layer of his sandwiched fabrics is usually left intact as the support. The sandwich is then quilted along predetermined lines, usually on the diagonal of the weave, and then cut along the quilted lines. The last step is to fray the fabric either by hand or by machine washing and drying. Harding ends up with a matte, pile surface when working with cottons, and a lighter, lustrous, and more elegant surface when using silks. The textiles are then cut into simple kimono shapes that are meant to hang on the wall when not being worn. By destroying, Harding creates a completely new cut of cloth (fig. 199).

In the early years of the Wearable Art movement, the 1970s, artists concentrated on the fabrication and embellishment of the material—the making of cloth. When the works fail they almost always fail in the cutting and draping—those strongholds of the couture masters. By the 1980s the Wearable Art movement had come to seem like a historic event. The original buyer of art-to-wear had joined the workforce and needed a different kind of clothing. One spectacular coat would no longer serve; whole working outfits were needed. A few of the early practitioners honed their skills and subsequently found ways of entering the fashion industry as designers of their own lines. They began to cross over from one-of-a-kind to manufacturing. The vitality they brought to the field dispersed across the whole industry. It was as though the Wearable Art movement had completed its work.

# The Japanese Enter the World Stage

In the early 1980s the Japanese moved onto center stage, capturing the attention of both the traditional couture world and the art world. And as it had been for the artists of the Wearable Art movement, the making of cloth was the basis of their art. Since the early 1970s, Kenzo, Hanae Mori, and Issey Miyake had worked in Paris within an occidental fashion matrix. But at the beginning of the next decade, specifically the 1982 fashion season, international attention shifted to Tokyo. The yen had become powerful; Japanese influence rose accordingly. A younger generation of designers, led by Kansai Yamamoto, Yohji Yamamoto, and Rei Kawakubo, introduced the world to a non-Western idea of clothing—one anchored in the premise that cloth comes first, and that shape is a given, based upon historical precedent.

Fabric design is the foundation of clothing design. Shape, as defined over the centuries by the evolving kimono, need not change from year to year. The figure is to be viewed as one looks at the landscape: horizontally, asymmetrically, and in the round. This is a radical departure from the traditional Western view of the figure as vertical and balanced, having a top and a bottom, a left and a right side. The Western-trained eye enters at the neckline and moves down, taking in the balanced elements to the left and the right, stopping where the designer specifies—the hemline. The Japanese-trained eye moves around the figure, taking in volume and space. Thus freed from constantly creating new shapes, or spaces, the Japanese designer is able to concentrate on scale and proportion (the challenges of cutting), and texture and color (the challenges of fabric design).[4]

Fifteen years later Rei Kawakubo of Comme des Garçons was to challenge the premise that the human shape is a given. Always in the vanguard of the avant-garde, she shocked the fashion world with her collection for the 1997 spring-summer season. Designed under the theme "Body Meets Dress. Body Becomes Dress. Dress Becomes Body," Kawakubo sent models onto the runway wearing down-filled pads inserted under-

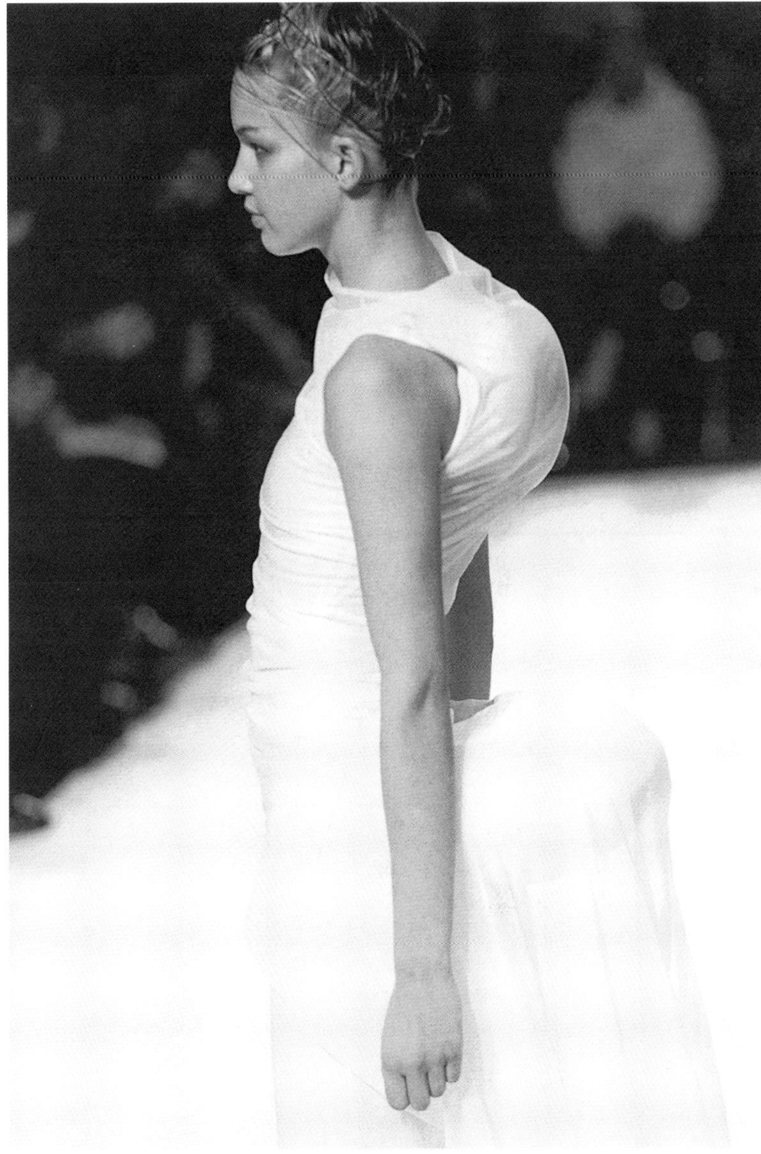

200. Rei Kawakubo, white dress from collection "Body Meets Dress. Body Becomes Dress. Dress Becomes Body," 1997. Collection Comme des Garçons.

neath stretch fabrics in order to sculpt unusual silhouettes. Continuing the tradition of asymmetry long associated with Japanese clothing, she placed her pads in different configurations around the figure. The female body had become sculpture; it had transformed into contorted shapes that echoed Louise Bourgeois's installation for the 1996 São Paulo Biennale with its bulbous, cloth-stuffed, hanging figures reminiscent of metamorphosing human forms. For both Bourgeois and Kawakubo, "Fashion is content . . . Fashion is the language

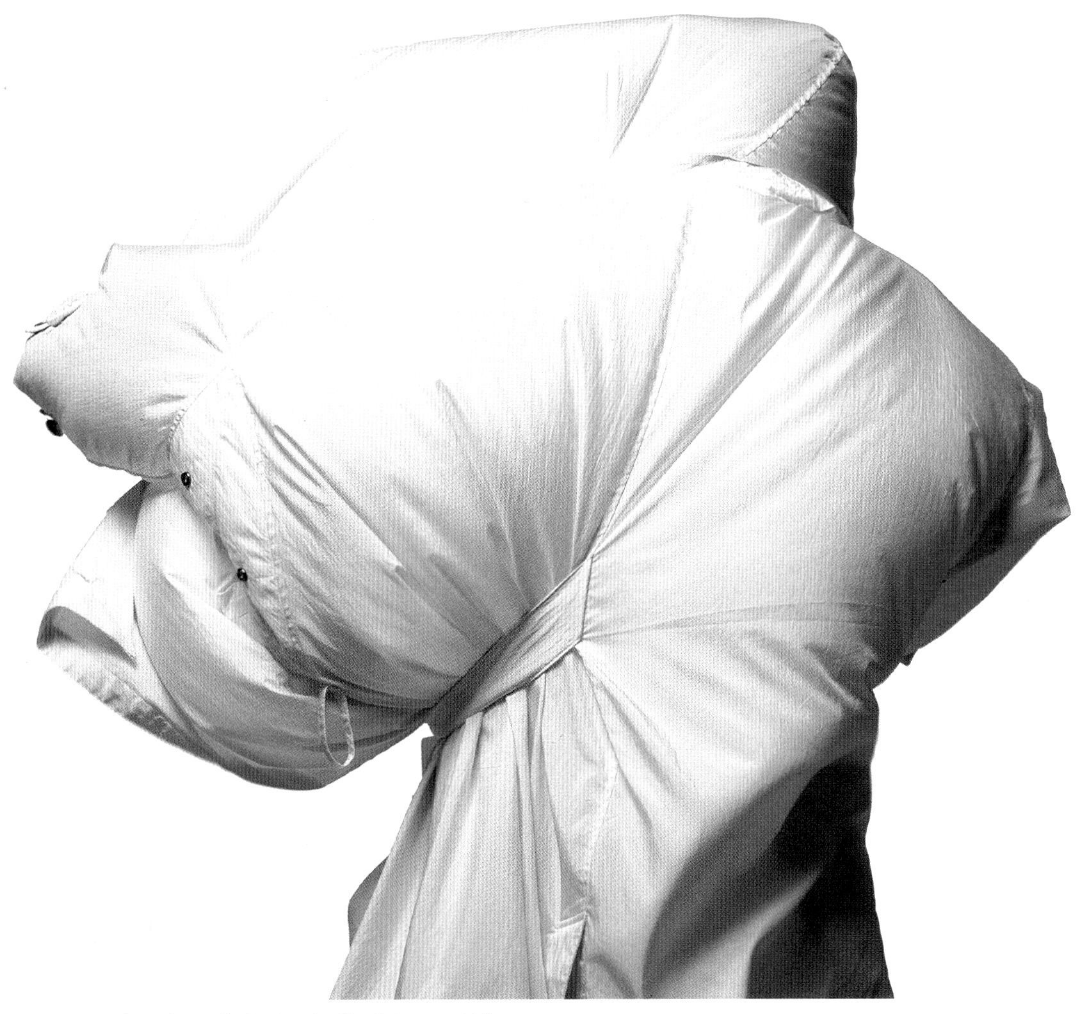

201. Issey Miyake and Miyake Design Studio, *Raincoat,* 1984.

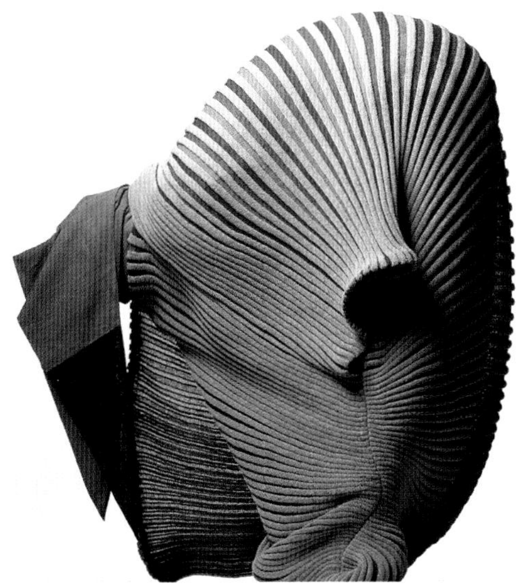

202. Issey Miyake and Miyake Design Studio, *Knit Shell Coat,* 1984.

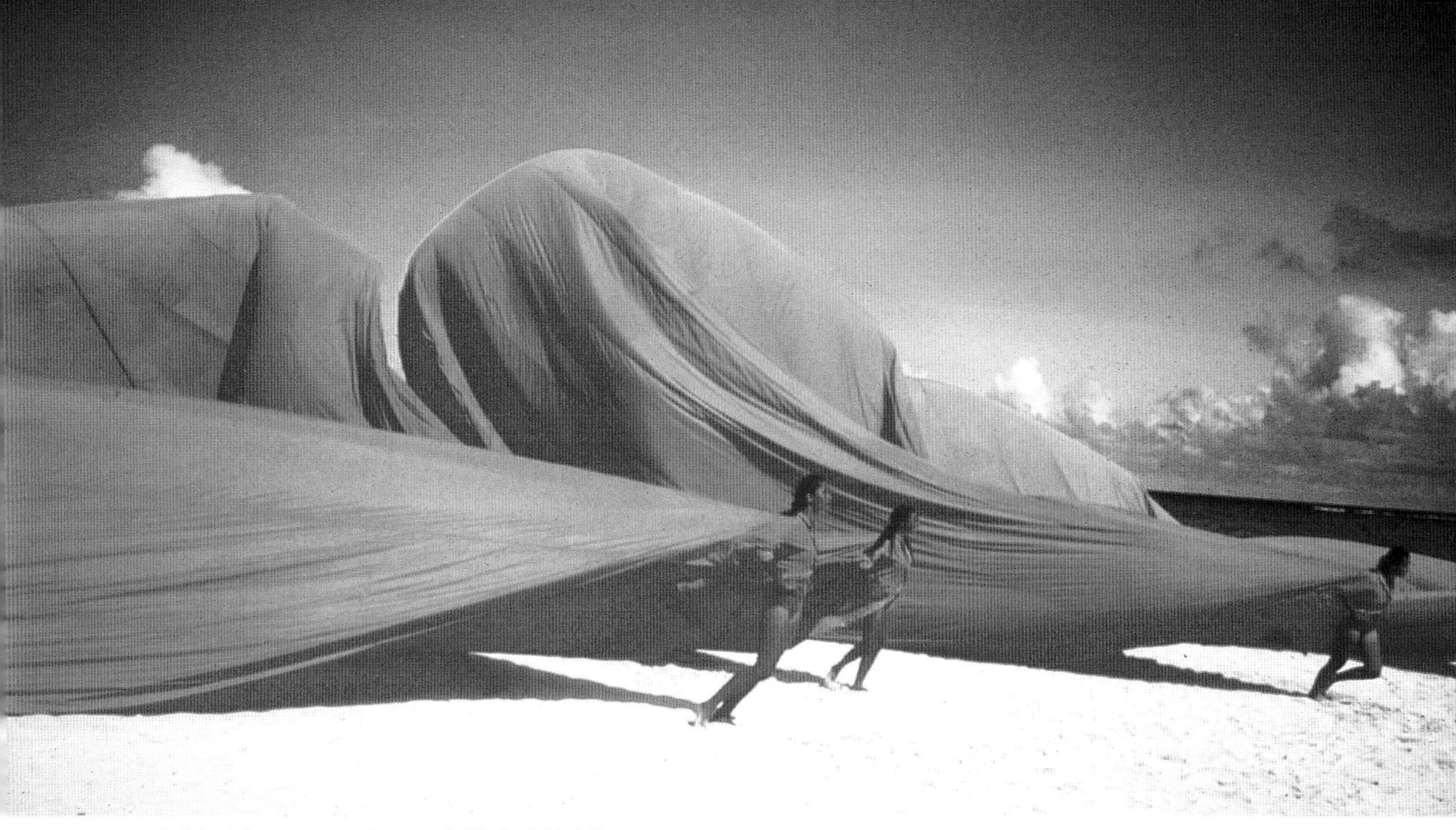

203. Yoshiki Hishinuma, *Divine Essence in the Wind* and *Black Horse.*

of the body, clothing is not a second skin, but rather the body itself, as well as a fantasmatic work."[5] Neither creates work that is beautiful or pretty, both being more interested in the visceral form that radiates out from the center of the human being (fig. 200). Both Kawakubo and Bourgeois echo the vision of the French artist Michel Nedjar (see fig. 38) whose dolls are actually the grotesque antithesis of dolls.

Issey Miyake has continued over the years to address an international audience, while leading the movement toward a more Japanese concept of clothing. For him, "cloth is clothing." In his own words, "The most important part in making clothing is to start to design the fabrics." In this he echoes his compatriots Kansai Yamamoto, who spends as much as three-quarters of his time on textiles, and Hanae Mori, who uses all her own fabrics, woven, printed, and dyed for her in Kyoto.

The essence of Miyake's art lies in the subtle flexibility of his thinking, and in his unmistakable sense of life. His goal is not to release the human body "from the confines of society, but to release one's body from one's self." Miyake attempts not to change form but to go beyond form. His exploratory drive, together with the ambiguity of his vision, is expressed by his words "Shape without shape, form without form." This is what causes the metamorphosis, as cloth reacts and animates each movement of the body (figs. 201, 202).

Neither function nor practicality nor logic enter into the thinking of Yoshiki Hishinuma, a former student of Miyake's. His clothes are the essence of exuberance and performance. They are emotional and spontaneous expressions, and always, the whirling possibilities of cloth energize the maker, the wearer, and the viewer (fig. 203).

Obviously these are not works intended for the street, although both Miyake and Hishinuma create street clothes. Rather they are works of art akin to the nonfunctional clothing of Nick Vaughn, or the conceptual clothing from Marian Schoettle's Clothing Enigma series (fig. 204).

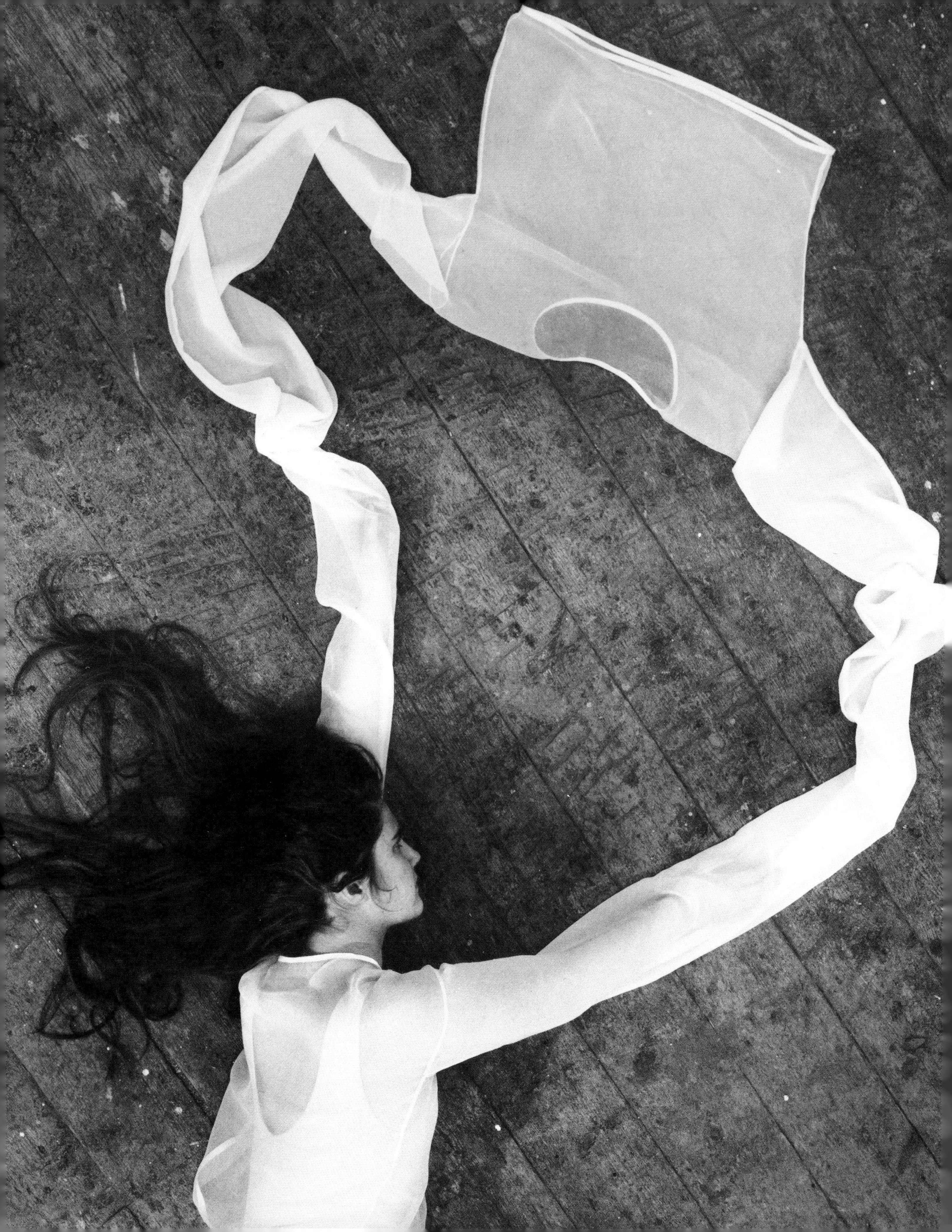

204 *(opposite).* Marian Schoettle, *Double Shirt,* 1987. Silk mousseline. Performed at Unit 7 Studios, London.

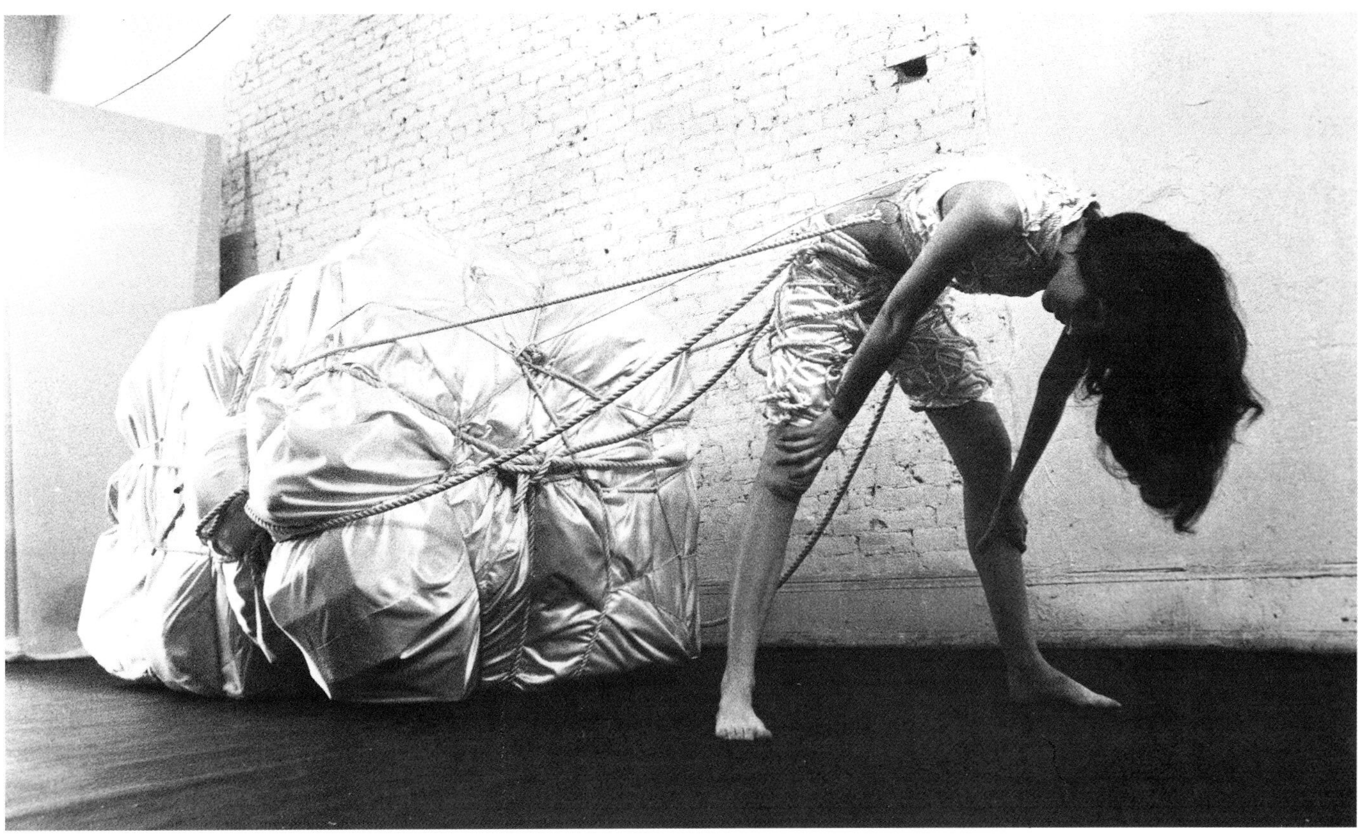

205. Christo, *Wedding Dress (as worn by Wendy),* 1967. Satin fabric and silk rope, 48 x 38 x 65″.

# Contemporary Artists Transform Clothes

Parallel to the development of art within the fashion world, and to the flourishing of a Wearable Art movement, was a third and even more pervasive force: artists who made art through the vehicle of clothes. In 1961 the sculptor-turned-painter Lucio Fontana produced a series of slit dresses that must be viewed as sculpture. Clothing in the hands of an artist of Christo's stature becomes material for dark and pungent social commentary. As enigmatic and surreal as Duchamp's *The Bride Stripped Bare by Her Bachelors, Even,* Christo's *Wedding Dress* of 1967 is a package of four hundred square feet of white satin pulled by a young woman harnessed with two hundred feet of silk rope. The vulnerable and deluded young girl has willingly, and with unquestioned hope, taken up a great weight of metaphorical baggage wrapped up in the bundles of life. Attired in the miniskirt of the times, she looks as betrayed by fashion as by the conventions of the middle-class life promised to a young bride (fig. 205).

Nick Vaughn creates "sculptures" or performance pieces that at first glance appear to be everyday clothes gone a little mad. Vaughn says he chooses clothes for his medium because everyone is literate in cloth and he wants to make art that can be understood by the masses. In 1983 someone gave Vaughn a fifty-foot bolt of purple polyester fabric. He used the entire piece, creating an ordinary, long-sleeved shirt. But the left side of the shirt flows on and on, to the end of the bolt of cloth. Either he or a friend might wear the shirt to an appropriate event—that is, an occasion such as a dinner party where one would wear a purple shirt—"carrying his tail along with him." The shirt becomes a wonderful metaphor for the burdens and excesses of fashion, convention, and uniformity. Humorous,

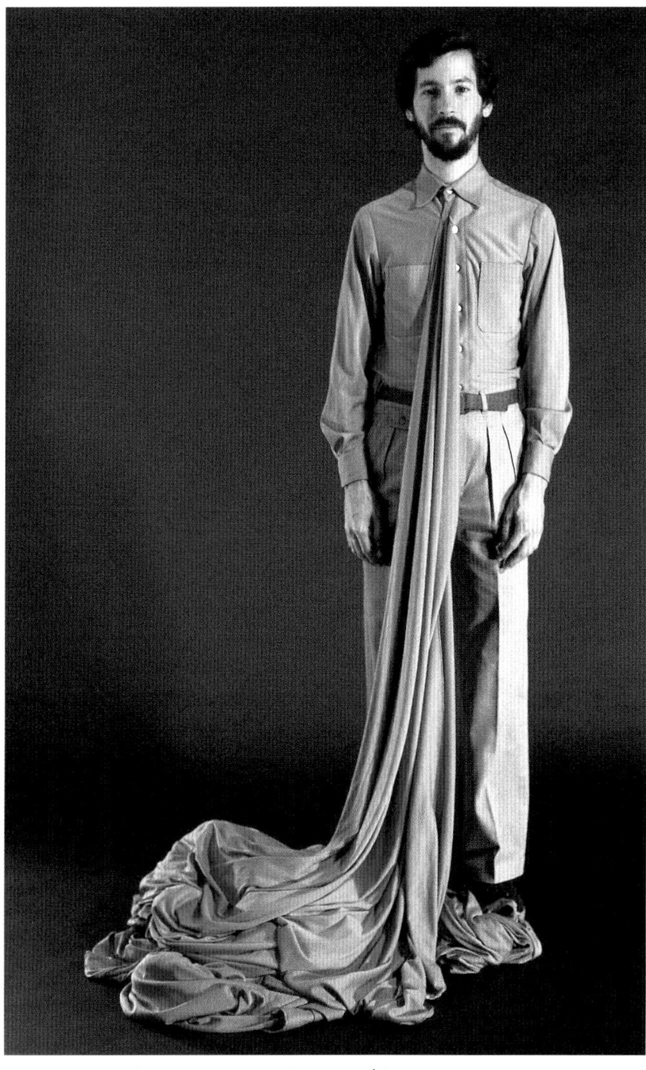

206. Nick Vaughn, *Shirt,* 1983. Polyester, 50´ long. Worn by Jon Wieder.

indeed, and certainly nonfunctional, to which he responds: "Humor is something I never think about when I'm working on my pieces. I'm always accused of it and it always seems I'm the last to get the joke . . . I want the wearer to look kind of clumsy" (fig. 206).

Judith Shea, who had a two-person exhibition with Vaughn at the Walker Art Center in Minneapolis in 1984, is a sculptor who was trained as a fashion designer. Her interest in the history of clothing has led her to a preoccupation with the structure of garments. Working in a variety of media—painted canvas, felt, cast iron, and bronze—she visualizes clothing as pure geometric shapes. Cones, darts, and cylinders, the basic vocabulary of women's clothing construction, become the elements of her sculpture (fig. 207).

A decade later, Beverly Semmes continues the tradition begun by Vaughn, that of exaggerating the dimensions of a piece of clothing to the point of absurdity. Be it a dress twelve feet long, or oversized but much too short little-girl's dresses, they allude to the nature of attraction and dismissal, of allure and repulsion. Her cascading dresses can be read as waterfalls within a landscape. Twin clothing units—two matching dresses hung side by side—might be more about the missing heads than the present objects of clothing. Almost always Semmes's work speaks to the difficulty of real human beings choosing clothes that will signal to the world who they are at the moment (fig. 210).

Clothing, as Vaughn correctly surmised, is a powerful metaphor for the human being, capable of standing in for the real person. For example, Jim Dine has used the image of the bathrobe in his art for years as an autobiographical icon. The printmaker Allegra Ockler actually embeds pieces of used clothing into her handmade paper works, allowing the garments to suggest their larger life, or the lives of their former owners (fig. 211). During the 1980s the German painter Anselm Kiefer was doing the same thing, embedding pieces of clothing, along with various other found materials, in his oil paintings. Throughout this book one finds the pervasive use of clothing as metaphor. The artists range from Antoni Miralda, with his gigantic wedding dress for the imagined marriage between Barcelona and New York (see fig. 49), to Maureen Connor, with her gigantic folded napkins suggesting the figure and its dress (see fig. 124), to Christian Boltanski, who uses the clothing of absent children to suggest their loss to the gas chambers of the concentration camps (see fig. 173). Colette, whose work always borders on autobiography, explains, "My art (fragments of my living environment, curtains, bed spreads, tablecloths) is turned into fashion. And then my fashions are recycled into art."

Sometime in the early 1980s Rei Kawakubo declared, "I only work in three shades of black." She is credited with starting the pervasive trend of black being the only acceptable color the sophisticate could wear for the next decade—especially those attached to the creative world, and even more so, those living in New York. In 1990 David Hammons made the work

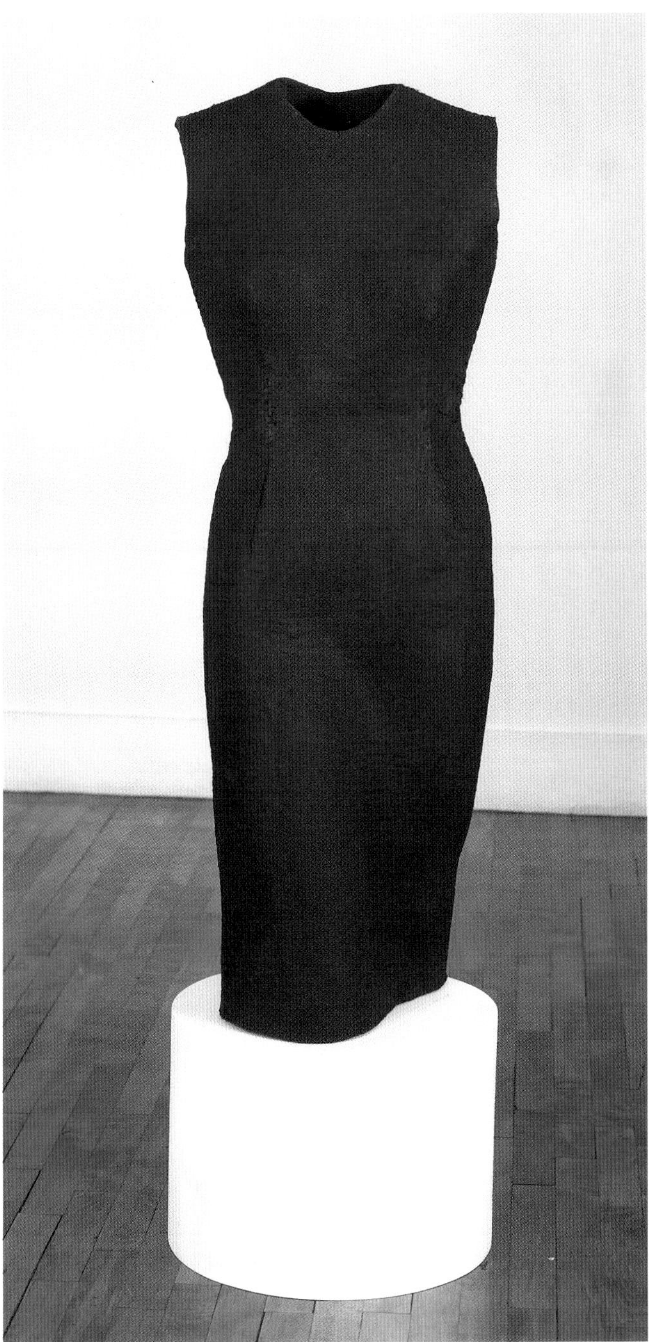

207. Judith Shea, *Black Dress,* 1983. Wool felt and India ink, 44½ x 15 x 12″. Courtesy Curt Marcus Gallery, New York.

*Death Fashion,* a theater piece with the walls and floor of the gallery put to use as a stage, and the actors represented by a rack of black clothes. His spoof on the fashionableness of nonfashion left self-conscious grins on the face of art world players. Hammons, an African-American artist who has long lived by choice on the fringes of the art world, does not buy his materials at the art supply store, preferring to pick up cast-off materials in Harlem where he lives. He says, "I am not interested in starting from nothing; all my material has a history on it. The history has to do with living and making do" (fig. 208).[6]

Like Hammons, Yong Soon Min uses pieces of clothing to represent larger social concerns. Born in a village in southern Korea during the Korean war, she began life immersed in Korean culture. However, her father, an officer with the South Korean armed forces and thus attached to the American military, had moved to the United States before her birth to teach the Korean language to American soldiers. It was several years later that she and her family were able to join him in the United States, which coincided with her first glimpse of him. She grew up in California, an Asian American who always felt slightly foreign. Much to her dismay, when she returned to South Korea as an adult she found she was also a foreigner on what she imagined was her home soil. Her work *Dwelling* encapsulates her bewilderment at her own identity. The gown is the traditional dress of the Korean woman, the *hanbok.* The artist borrows the words of poet Ko Won, himself a displaced Korean American, to incorporate into *Dwelling:* "To us . . . a birthplace is no longer our home. The place we were brought up is not either" (fig. 209).[7]

By the 1990s so many artists were making art involving some variation of clothing that exhibitions sprang up all over the United States and Europe. The Art Museum at Florida International University, Miami, presented "American Art Today: Clothing as Metaphor" in January 1993. The Aldrich Museum of Contemporary Art in Ridgefield, Connecticut, opened "Fall from Fashion" in May of that year. In September of the same year the Kohler Arts Center in Sheboygan, Wisconsin, offered "Discursive Dress." In 1994 Independent Curators Incorporated of New York sent their show "Empty Dress: Clothing as Surrogate in Recent Art" on the road. In 1995 the Winnipeg Art Gallery opened "A Dress: States of

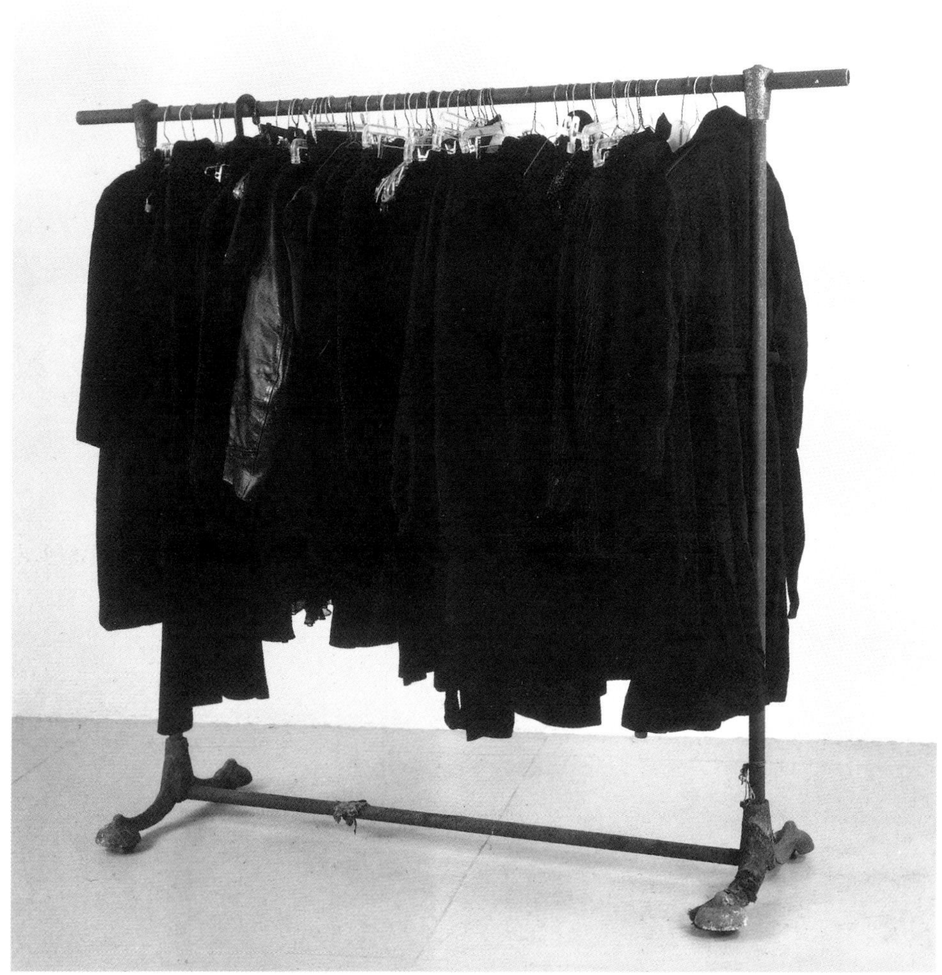

208. David Hammons, *Death Fashion,* 1990. Coat rack, black clothes, and hangers, 64 x 66 x 24″. Courtesy Jack Tilton Gallery, New York.

209 *(opposite).* Yong Soon Min, *Dwelling,* 1992. Mixed media, 72 x 42 x 28″.

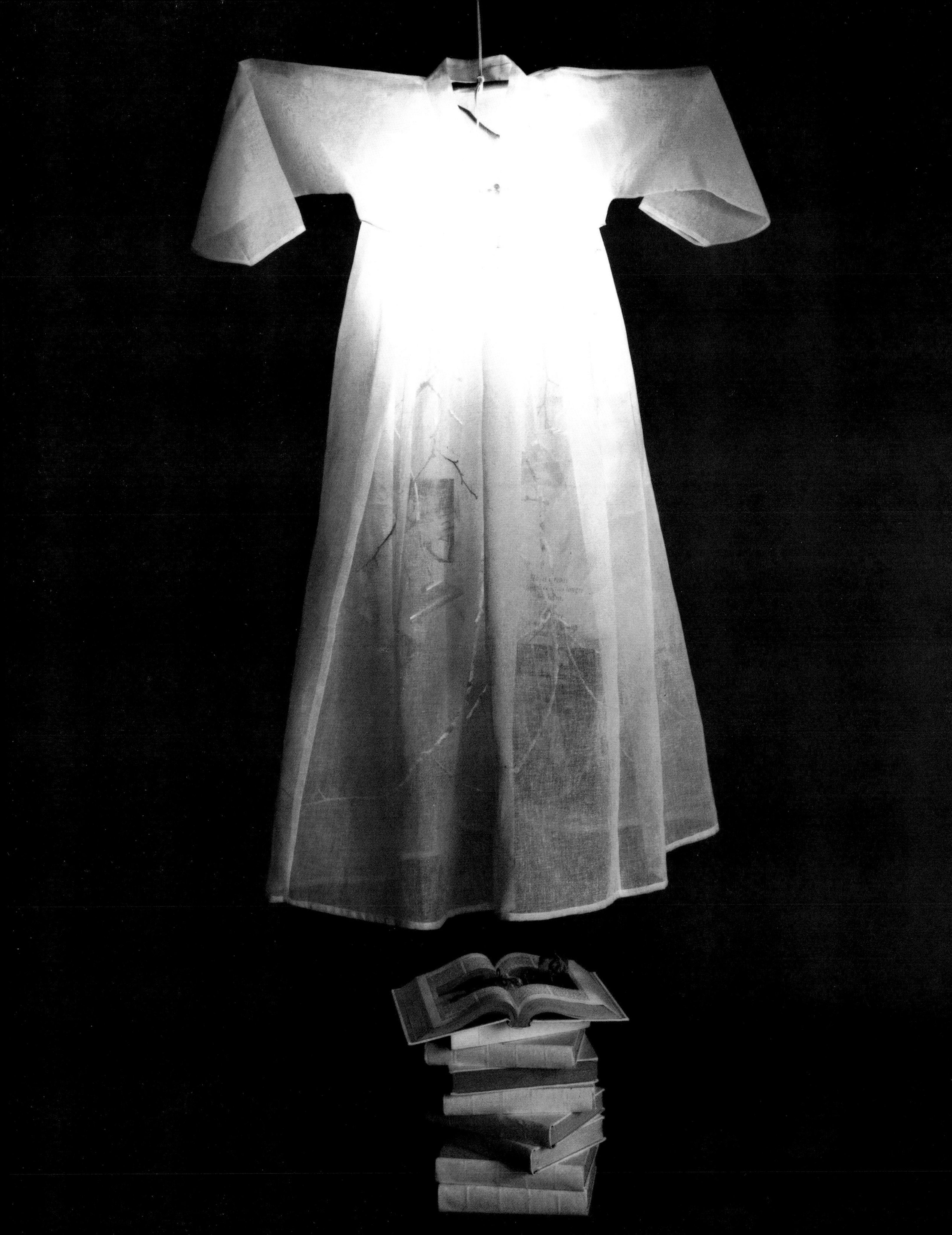

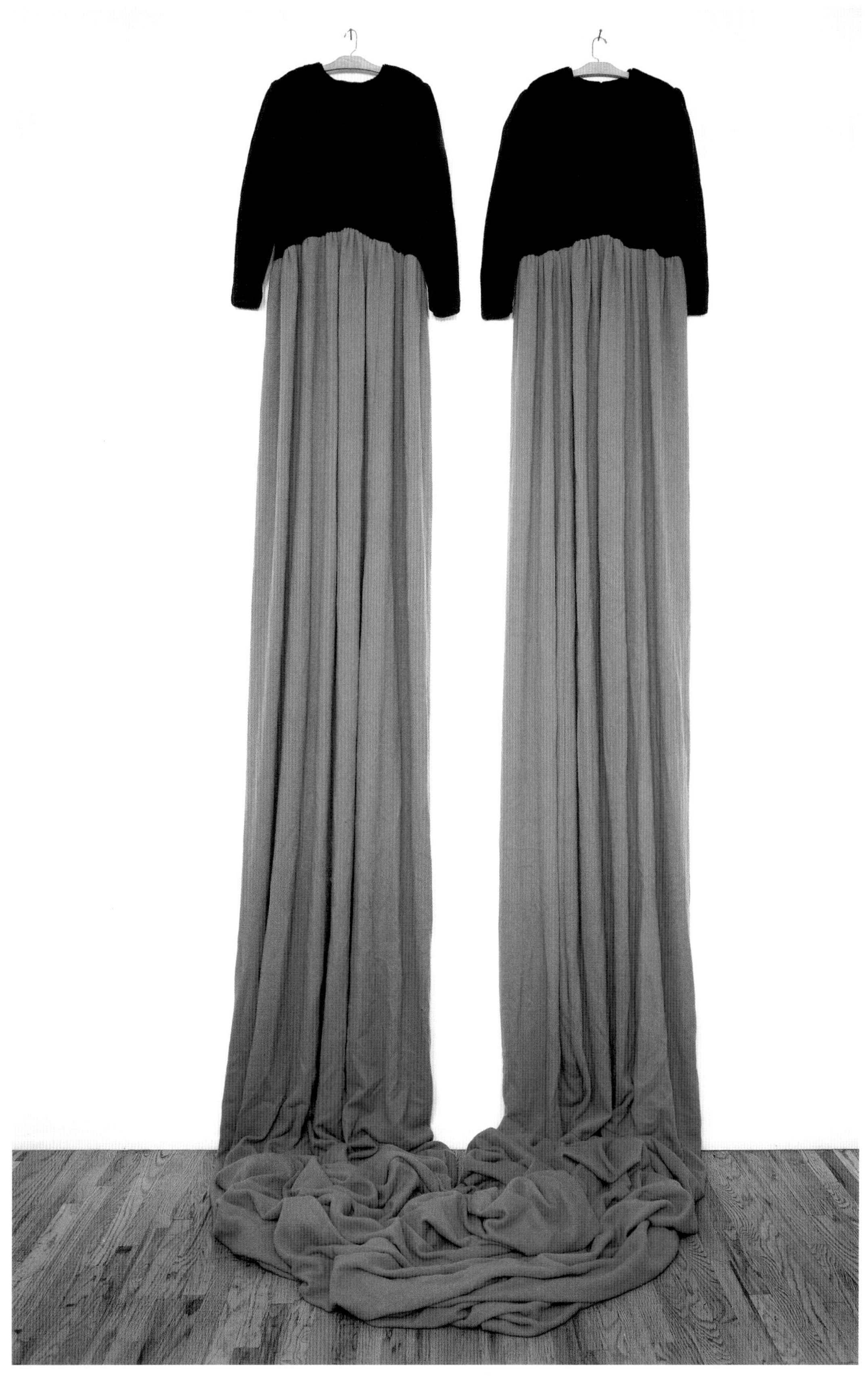

210. Beverly Semmes, *Water Coats*, 1991. Flannel and velvet, each 32 x 3′. Courtesy Michael Klein, New York.

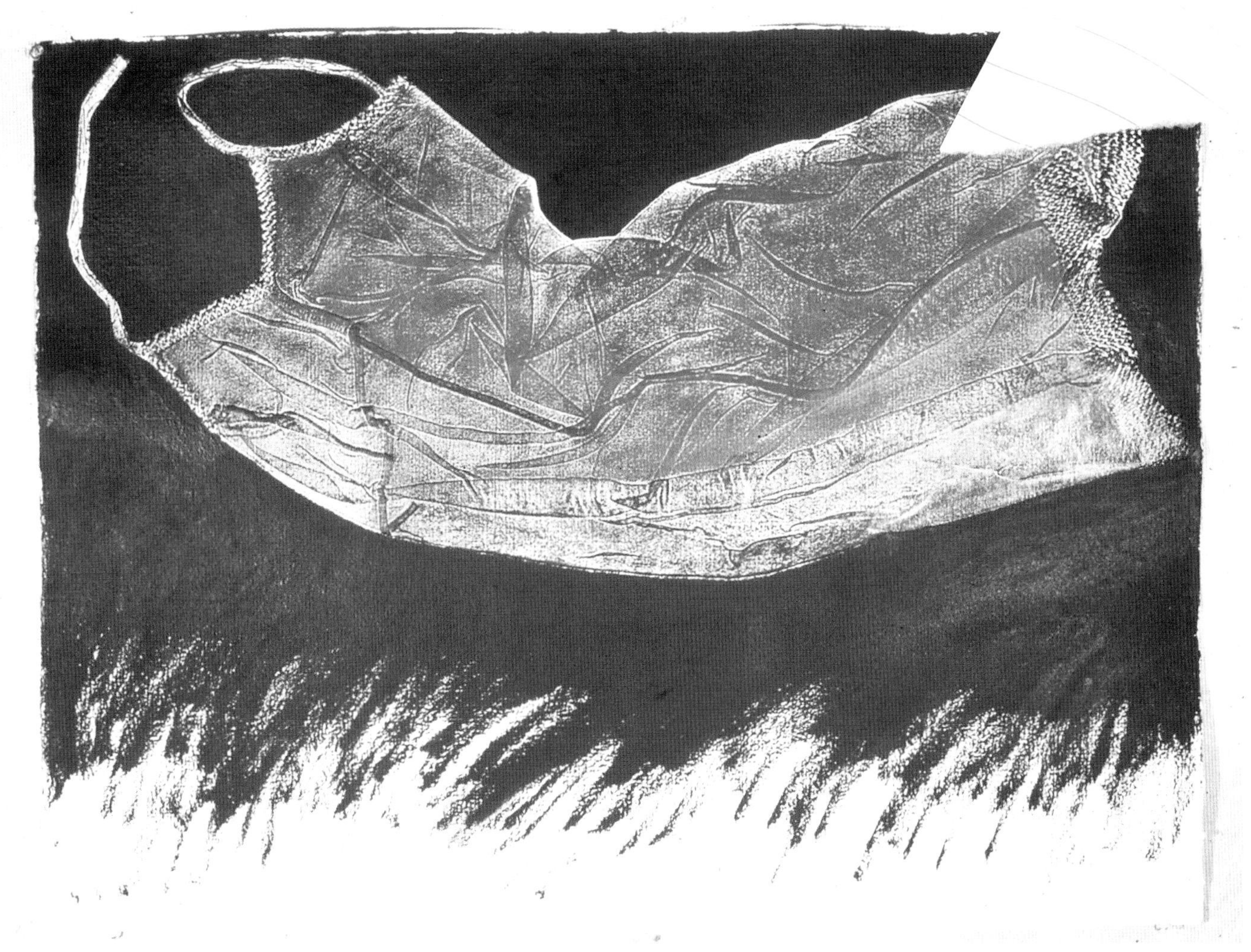

211. Allegra Ockler, *Silver Slip,* 1984. Garment laminated in handmade paper with painting, 30 x 38″.

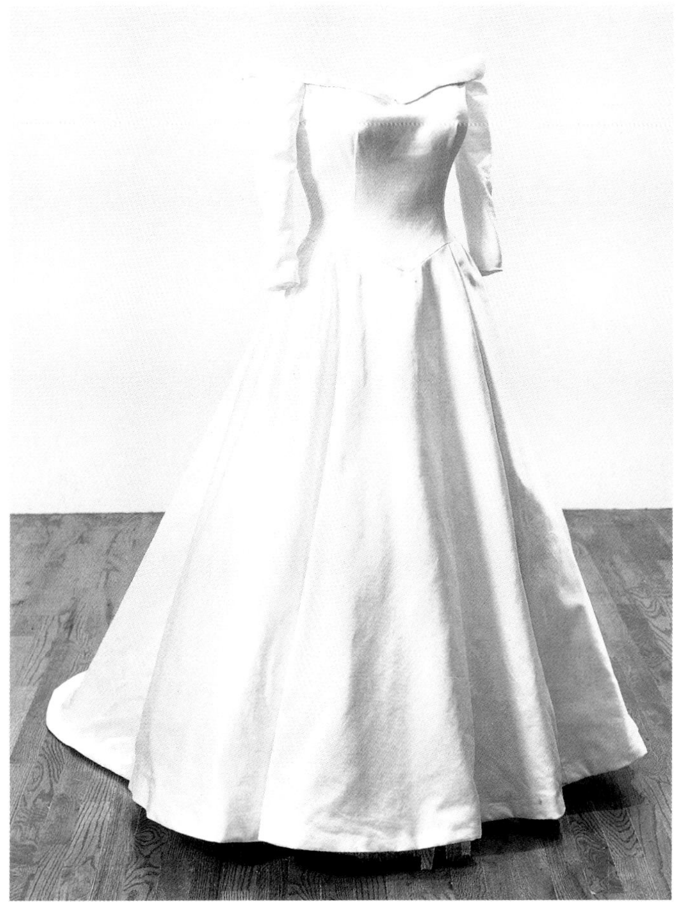

212. Robert Gober, *Wedding Gown*, 1989. Silk satin, muslin, linen, tulle, welded steel, 54¼ x 57 x 38½″.

Being." The September 18, 1994, issue of the *New York Times Magazine* published "A Fashion Gallery: Eight New York Artists Interpret the New York Fall Collections." The artists included Beverly Semmes, Pat Oleszko, Elaine Reichek, and Rob Wynne, all artists frequently included in the group exhibitions popping up everywhere.

Just as whole exhibitions mined clothing, certain pieces of clothing became potent images for art making, such as the wedding dress or the veil (see chapter 9, "The Camera View"). Christo may have made the first never-to-be-forgotten contemporary image of a bride, the one who has nothing to look forward to except labor. However, Robert Gober made his own contribution: the bride who waits. For a two-room installation at the Paula Cooper Gallery in New York, Gober placed an old empty wedding dress in the center of one room, backed by a wall that was papered with images of a sleeping white man and his dreams of a hanged black man. Desire exists; the bride is missing; the groom is impotent (fig. 212).

Sophie Calle is a French artist who combines photographs with text as the endgame of complicated, artist-as-detective adventures. She makes up her own rules and follows her own intricate routines. In her work *Autobiographical Stories*, Calle placed a photograph of a wedding dress next to a framed text that reads: "I always admired him, silently, since I was a child. On November 8th—I was thirty years old—he allowed me to pay him a visit. He lived several hundred kilometers from Paris. I had brought a wedding dress in my valise, white silk with a short train. I wore it on our first night together." Calle, for years the silent voyeur shadowing randomly chosen strangers to make them unwitting participants in her art, has reversed roles in her autobiographical series. The visitor to the gallery is now the voyeur in Calle's life, the wedding dress her stand-in (fig. 213).

Duane Michals is a storyteller, a photographer who years before it was either acceptable or fashionable made art that challenged racism and sexism, and alienation between children and adults. He made art that told the story of what it means to be

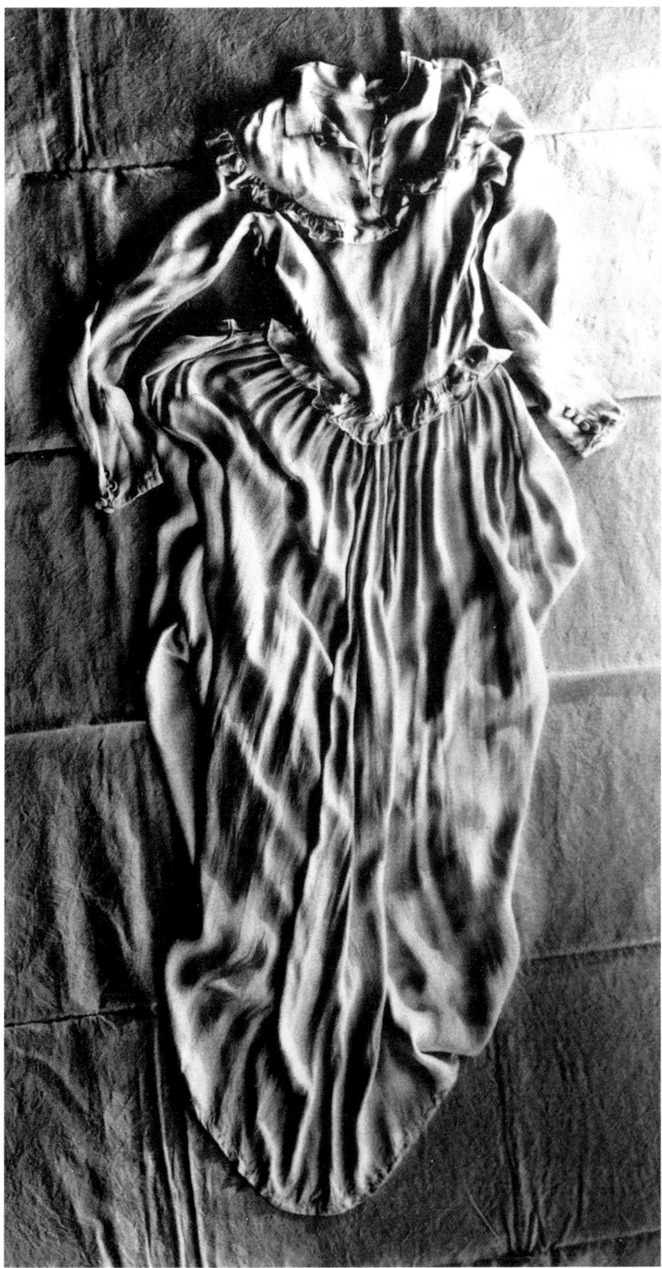

213. Sophie Calle, *Autobiographical Stories,* 1988–89. Wedding dress and gelatin silver print, 38⅞ x 64⅞″. Courtesy Fred Hoffman Gallery, Santa Monica, California.

gay in a straight world, what it means to be black in a white world. Such art was not worth much as a commodity when he started, so he carved out a second career for himself as fashion photographer. This, of course, put him in constant touch with cloth, with its usefulness in creating make-believe. Michals developed a way of telling his story through pictures, in a series, that, like animation, make slight changes from frame to frame. In his famous sequence *Bogeyman,* he used a hunk of cloth draped like a figure to suggest the bogeyman. This is exactly what children do to represent the bogeyman, the one who scares you in the dark, just as the black man and the gay man were scary to people when Michals began making his art. Underlying all of Michals's work is a sweetness that has endeared him to his large audience. One thinks, If this man says so, I had better listen. What a wonderful role for an artist, and how useful bits of cloth have been to him in making up his truth-telling fairy tales (fig. 214).

Regina Frank chose to take a dress and magnify its meaning. For the 1995–96 Winnipeg Art Gallery exhibition she created a tent in the form of a silk dress, anchored it with several dozen combat boots, all facing inward, and placed a computer inside the dress/tent that was hooked to the Internet. The artist communicated from Germany with viewers to the gallery. The output from her electronic-mail messages was posted on the gallery walls at the edge of the installation. Clearly the dress had become "address." The dress is where one resides; it contains the whole being. The presence of the combat boots anchoring the fine silk suggested the traditional roles of male and female within the house, one to encompass, the other to protect or, more ominously, to encase (fig. 215).

Barton Lidice Beneš, on the other hand, took an object of adornment and in anger transformed it from cloth into a final, permanent memorial to a young woman who died of AIDS. Whereas Michele Oka Doner (see fig. 48) chose to create a work of art from clay in the image of cloth, Beneš takes an object that is already made of cloth, the AIDS ribbon traditionally made of red silk, and transforms it into a tombstone.

Death and its bedmate, memory of the life that was, begot the work *Brenda.* Brenda was a real person who grew up with real parents. She had a brother, Christopher. She was a lesbian and a mother. Her life unraveled. She started using drugs, and

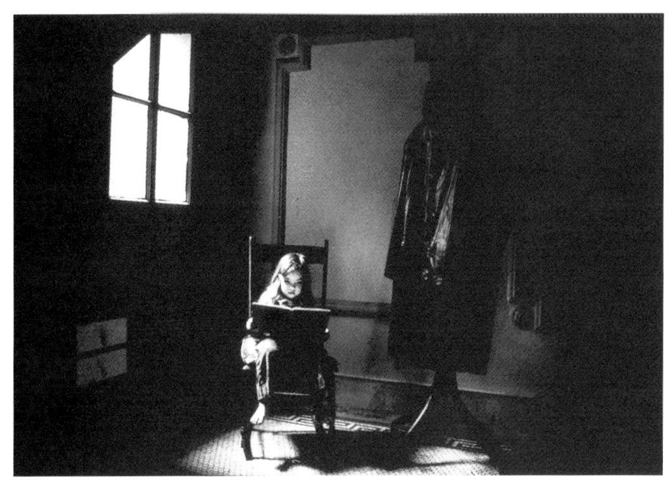
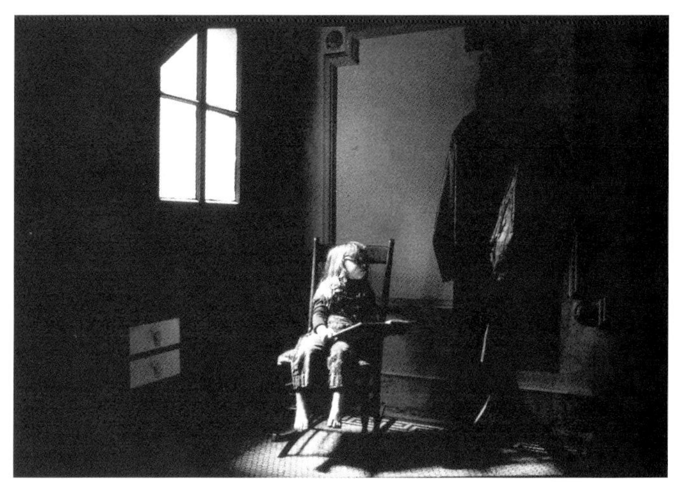
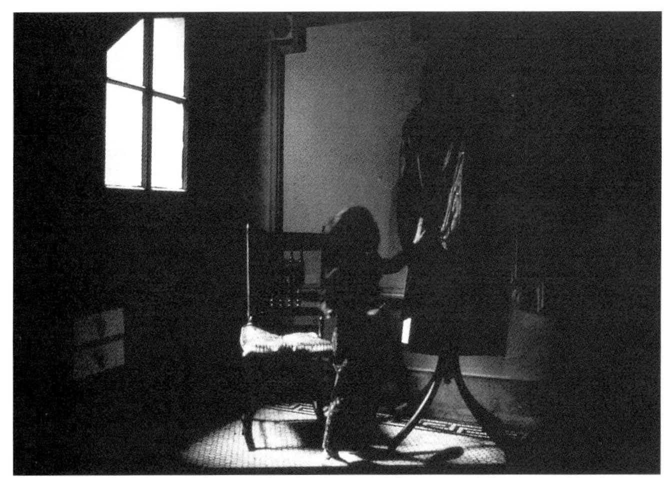
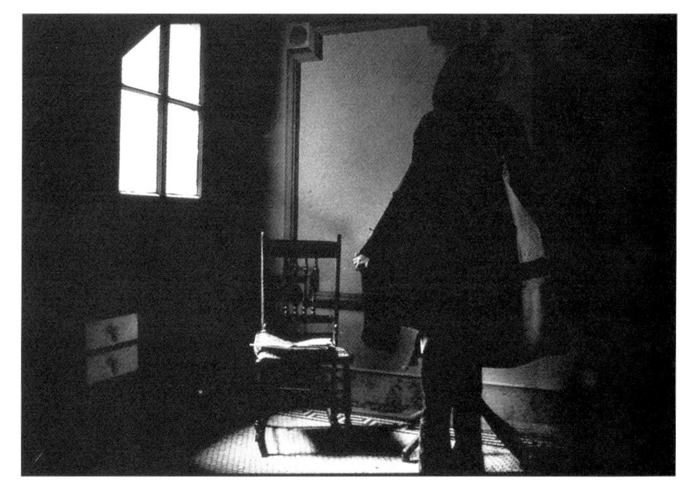
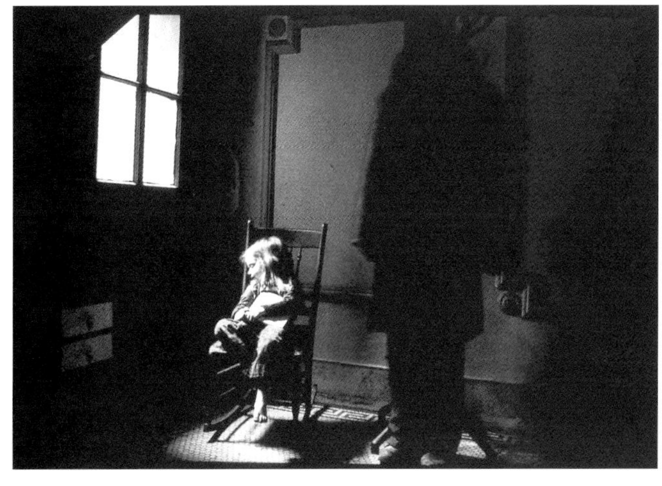
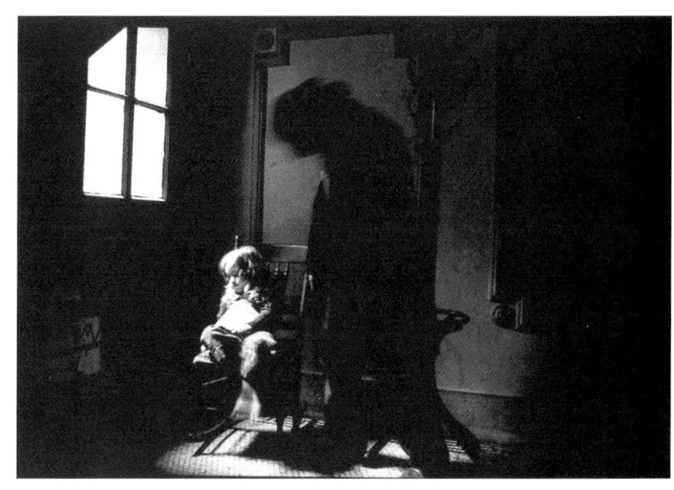

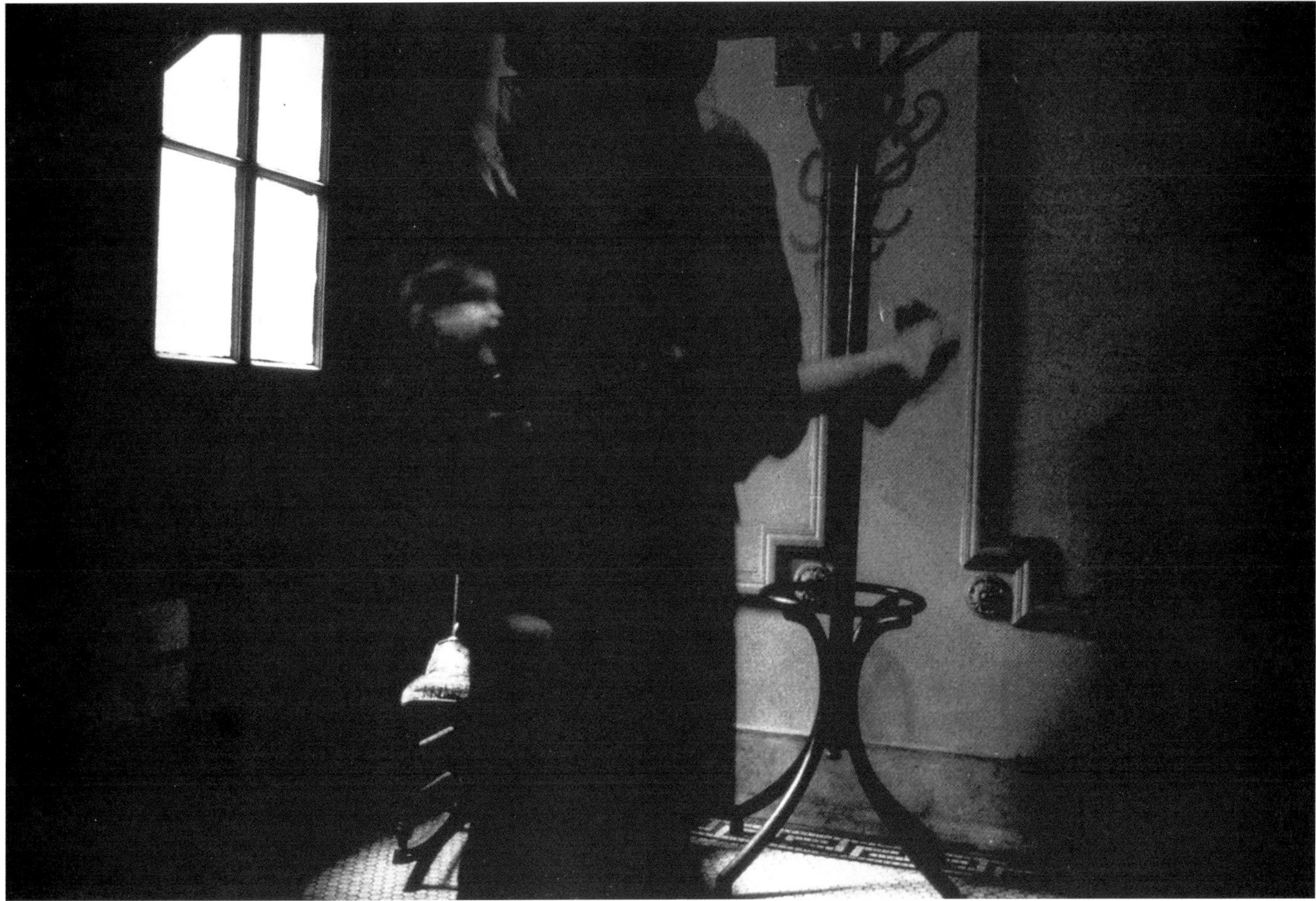

214. Duane Michals, *The Bogeyman,* 1973. Gelatin silver prints. Series 5, seven images, each 5 x 7″ (image 7 enlarged). Courtesy Sidney Janis Gallery, New York.

through some shared needle somewhere along the way, she contracted the AIDS virus. Soon she lost her family. The children became street kids. Only Christopher stayed in touch. Brenda became one of life's lost people to whom no one paid much attention. A few days after she died, Christopher sought out his friend Beneš. Tucked under his arm was a Tiffany cardboard box, the container for Brenda's ashes. No one wanted them. Would Beneš turn the cremated remains into a memorial? The artist accepted with one condition: Christopher would have to approve the concept for the work before Beneš would actually begin.

The artist mulled it over. He wanted to create a work that would bring Brenda more acknowledgment in death than she had ever found in life, more dignity in death than she had known in life. He cast about for a metaphor to symbolize Brenda—and he found one. Beneš, himself HIV positive, had come to hate AIDS ribbons. He saw them as nothing more than politically correct fashion items. Everyone had one pinned on for the Academy Awards ceremony; one could buy them inset with diamonds in fancy jewelry stores. Repulsed, Beneš maintained that "If you want to do something about AIDS, contribute to research, or make dinner for a sick friend.

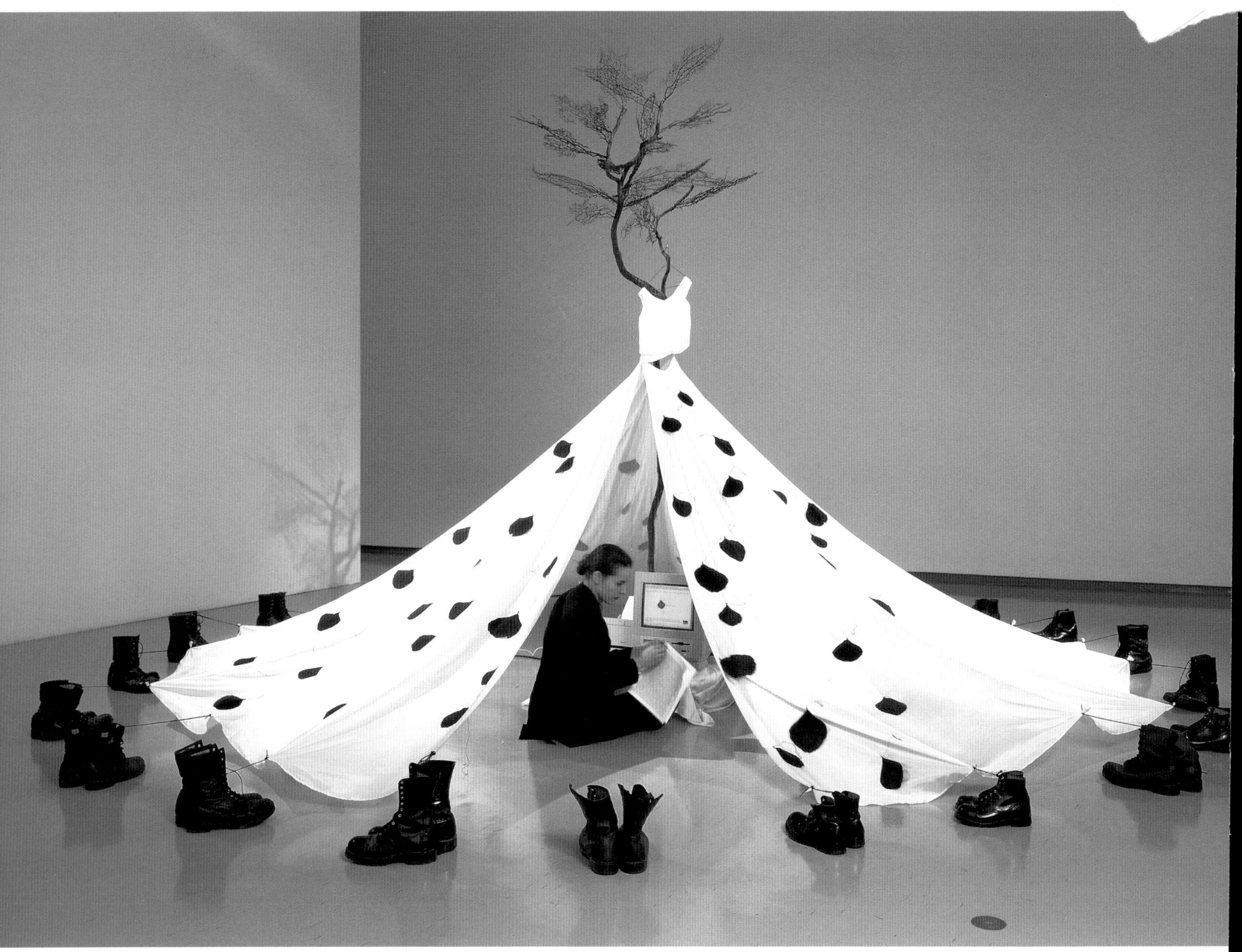

215. Regina Frank (The Artist is Present), *As long as the river flows, the grass grows, the sun shines . . .* , 1995. Silk dress, power PC (Performa), handmade coral tree, combat workboots, altered leaves, and computer printouts. Installed at the Winnipeg Art Gallery, Canada, as part of the exhibition "A-Dress: States of Being," November 1995–March 1996.

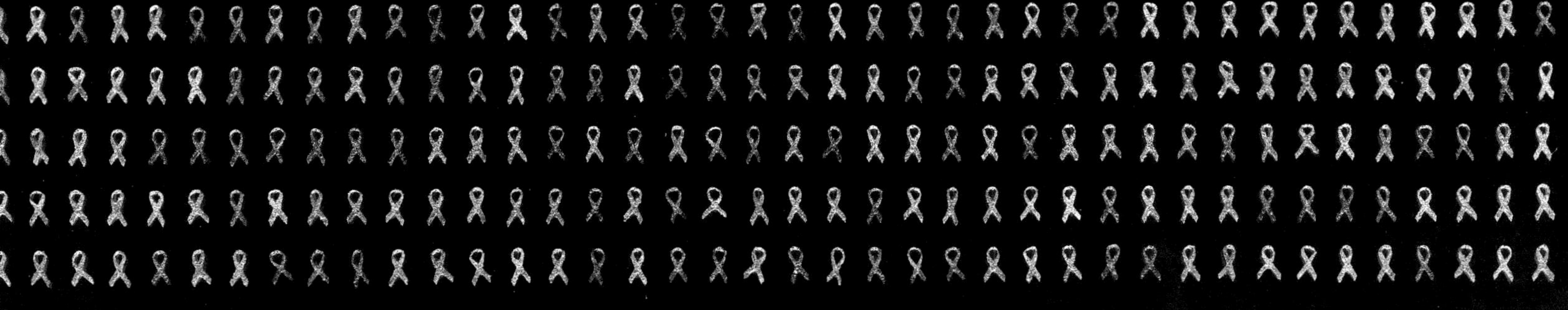
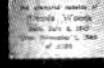

216. Barton Lidice Beneš, *Brenda*, 1993. Two hundred ribbons, paper, cremation ashes, and brass plaque, each ribbon 3½ x 1½ x ½″. Courtesy North Dakota Museum of Art, Grand Forks.

Don't wear one of those awful red ribbons." He decided to take the visual metaphor of the red ribbon and give it a potency it never had.

The artist set to work fashioning two hundred AIDS ribbons out of heavy paper. He coated them with glue and breaded them with Brenda's ashes. They were to be installed on a museum wall, row upon row, in pristine order, one after another. Their elegant shapes, dressed with that refined, ash-gray, textured surface, would be set off by an engraved bronze plaque centered below:

The Cremated Remains of Brenda Woods
Born July 5, 1947
Died November 1, 1989
of AIDS

The work, glimpsed on a distant wall, embodies serenity and beauty. Only when the viewer steps close and realizes that these exquisite objects are made from the ashes of a real-life Brenda does the piece take on its discomforting power. In death Brenda achieves a potency she never had in life (fig. 216). Clearly clothing as metaphor has reached a culmination in the waning years of the twentieth century. Then again, humans and the clothes they wear will always remain of keen interest to artists.

1. John Bowlt, "From Pictures to Textile Prints," *Print Collectors Newsletter*, March 1976, 16.

2. Elizabeth Ann Coleman, "Charles James," *American Fabrics and Fashions* 128 (1983): 21.

3. Karen Searle, "Tim Harding," *Ornament* 13, no. 1 (autumn 1989): 38–45.

4. For further discussion see Colin McDowell, *McDowell's Directory of Twentieth Century Fashion* (Englewood Cliffs, N.J.: Prentice-Hall, 1958), 178–79.

5. Paulo Herkenhogg, "Louise Bourgeois Architecture and High Heels," *23. Bienal Internacional de São Paulo: Salas Especiais* (São Paulo, Brazil: Fundacão Bienal de São Paulo), 255.

6. Amei Wallach, *New York Newsday*, Dec. 23, 1990.

7. Ko Won, "Home," *AmerAsia Journal* 16, no. 1 (1990): 132.

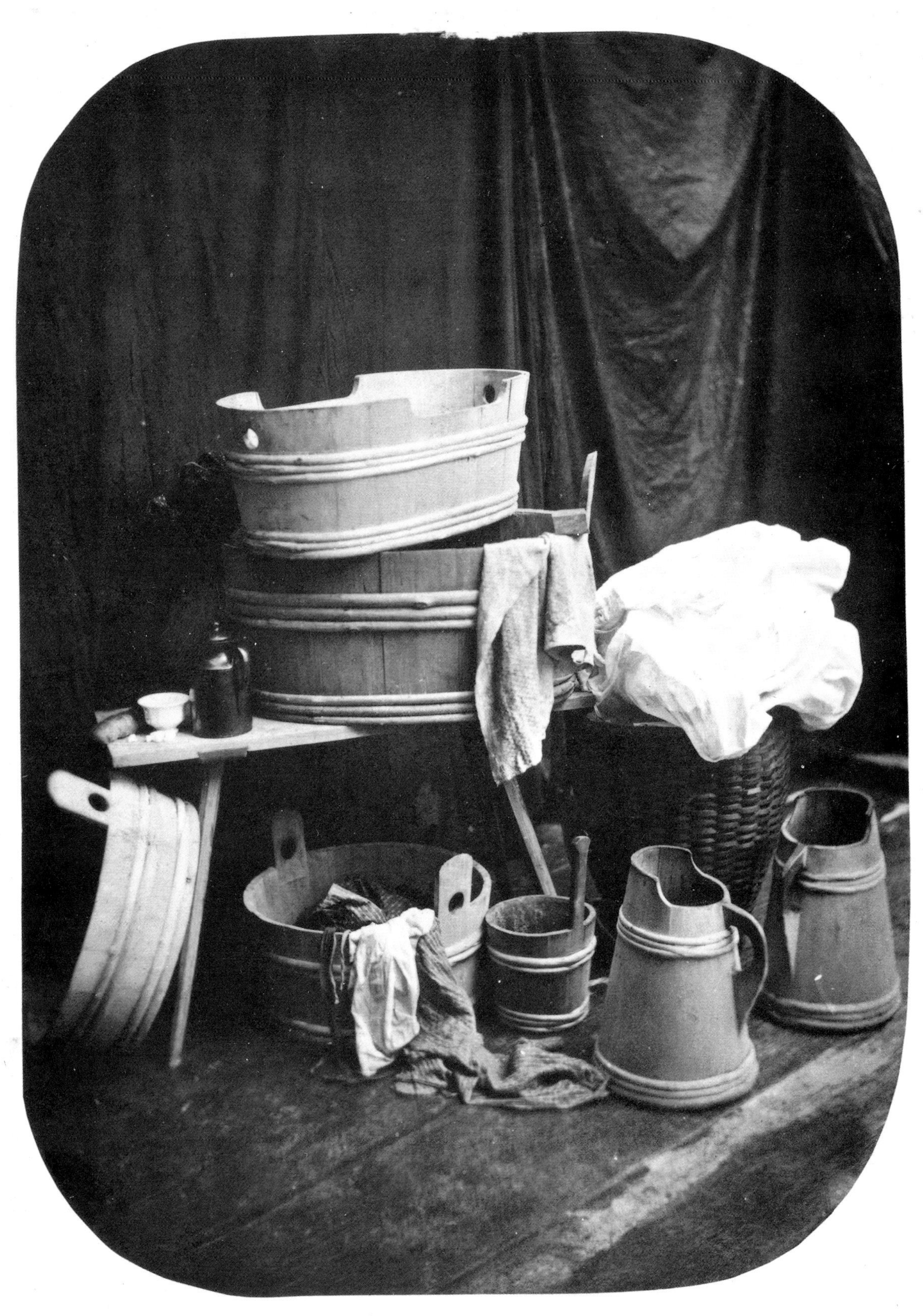

*Collod.-Phot. v. H. Krone, 1853.*

# The Camera View

*The facts of our homes and times, shown surgically, without the intrusion of the poet's or painter's comment or necessary distortion, are the unique contemporary field of the photographer . . . it is for him to fix and to show the whole aspect of our society, the sober portrait of its stratifications, their background and embattled contrasts. The facts sing for themselves.*

Lincoln Kirstein

In 1938 Lincoln Kirstein made that statement about the photographs of Walker Evans. How the civilized world wanted it to be true. Finally a medium had been found that would reveal the unquestionable truth—no philosophy, no subjectivity, no interpretation, no art—just truth. Kirstein's assessment of photography was brilliantly debunked by José Arcadio Buendía, the gentle madman in Gabriel García Márquez's 1967 masterpiece *One Hundred Years of Solitude.*

José Arcadio Buendía lived out his life in the most remote of tropical villages, driven mad by his desire to understand life's biggest questions. Each season a shutter to the outside world flicked open for the tiny village with the arrival of Melquíades, a wandering gypsy. Without fail, each visit brought another great invention: ice, the sextant, the Pianola, and most astonishingly of all, the camera. Wildly hopeful, José Arcadio Buendía seized the daguerreotype. "When he saw himself and his whole family fastened onto a sheet of iridescent metal for an eternity, he was mute with stupefaction. He resolved to use it to obtain scientific proof of the existence of God. Through a complicated process of superimposed exposures taken in different parts of the house, he was sure that sooner or later he would get a daguerreotype of God, if He existed, or put an end once and for all to the supposition of His existence."

José Arcadio Buendía failed to surprise Divine Providence, and the modern world finally accepted that no truth could be manipulated more than photographic truth. The photographer Frederick Sommer aptly summed it up: "Life itself is not the reality. We are the ones who put life into stones and pebbles."

217 *(opposite).* Hermann Krone, *Still Life,* 1853. Albumen print. Collection Deutsches Museum, Munich, Germany.

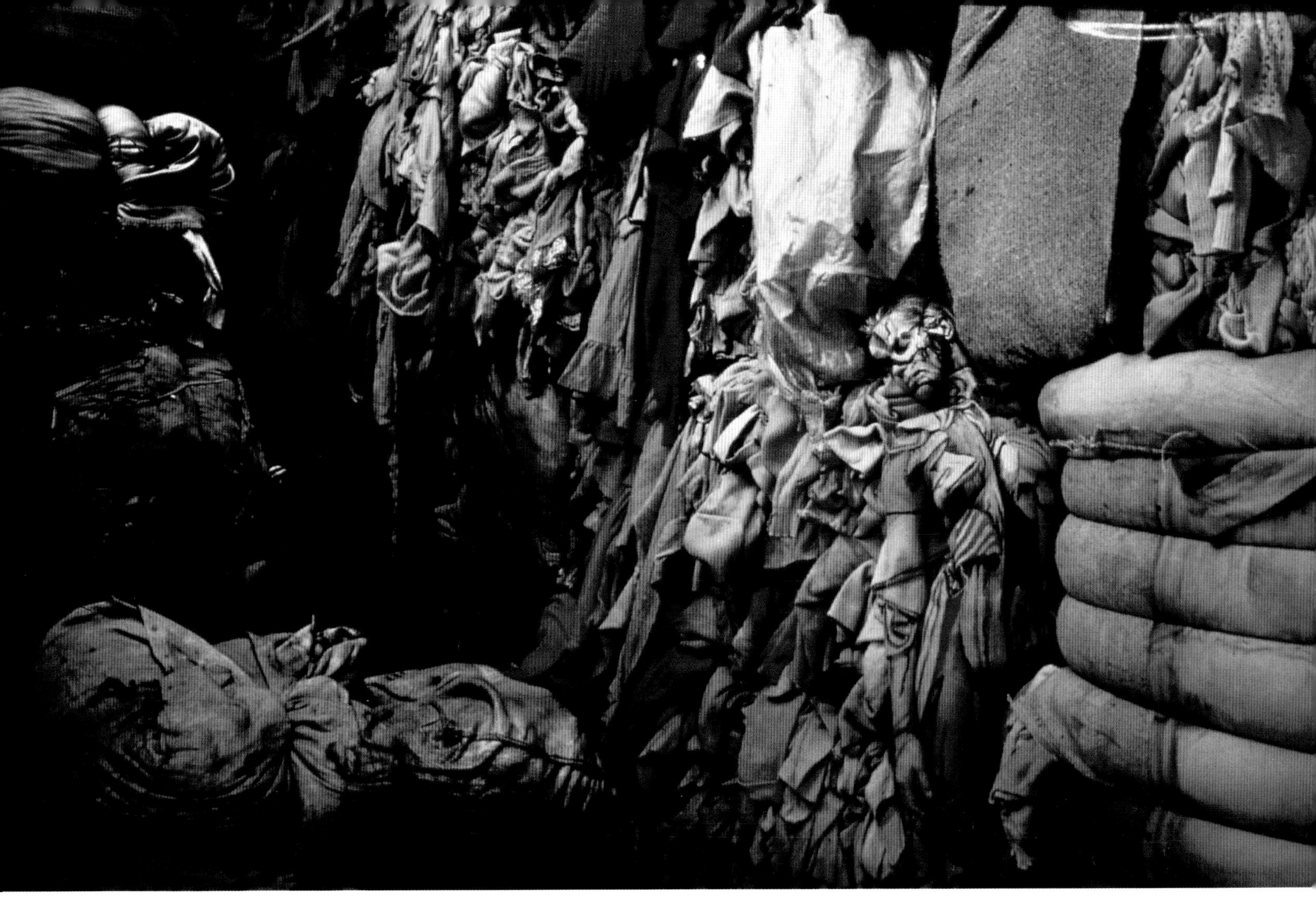

218. Vera Lehndorff and Holger Trülzsch, *Pink 51/11, Prato,* 1985.
Unique Polaroid polacolor print. Courtesy Scott Hanson Gallery.

Photographers of cloth tell convoluted truths. Cloth, sometimes humble, sometimes sumptuous, comes fresh from the mill steeped in exotic, sensuous, and romantic suggestion. Thus it is almost impossible to photograph cloth as a neutral object—it never was a neutral object. Cloth has its own living presence. As early as 1853 Hermann Krone captured the humble nature of mill cloth in his quietly romantic photograph *Still Life.* Over a century later Vera Lehndorff and Holger Trülzsch flaunt the exotic and sensuous aspects of mill cloth in their photographs. Trülzsch is a painter and photographer; Lehndorff became famous in the 1960s as the extravagantly beautiful actress and model Veruschka. As collaborators, he is the painter, and she is the canvas. He is the photographer; she is the subject. Together they create wildly romantic photographs of transfiguration (figs. 217, 218).

*Pink 51/11, Prato* is from Lehndorff and Trülzsch's series of haunting, subject-oriented images in which cloth plays the dominant role. There is something melancholy about the body as it is metamorphosed into a statue, as it consciously disintegrates into the wall of cloth. The work of these two artists traffics in decay, in transformed surfaces. This is art made solemn. It reads like a silent performance—and that is how they intended it. Vera says, "My only interest is in fusing into a background." In these photographs reality is transformed so that it appears as it is, a perceptual phenomenon based on illusion. Robert Frank stated it more bluntly: "Realism is not enough—there has to be vision and the two together can make a good photograph." It is difficult to describe this thin line where matter ends and mind begins. Christian Vogt's Red Cloth series visually suggests that moment in time. He says, "The visible gives one's work its form, the non-visible its value." Had José Arcadio Buendía understood that this is the nature of photography, he might have captured God (fig. 219).

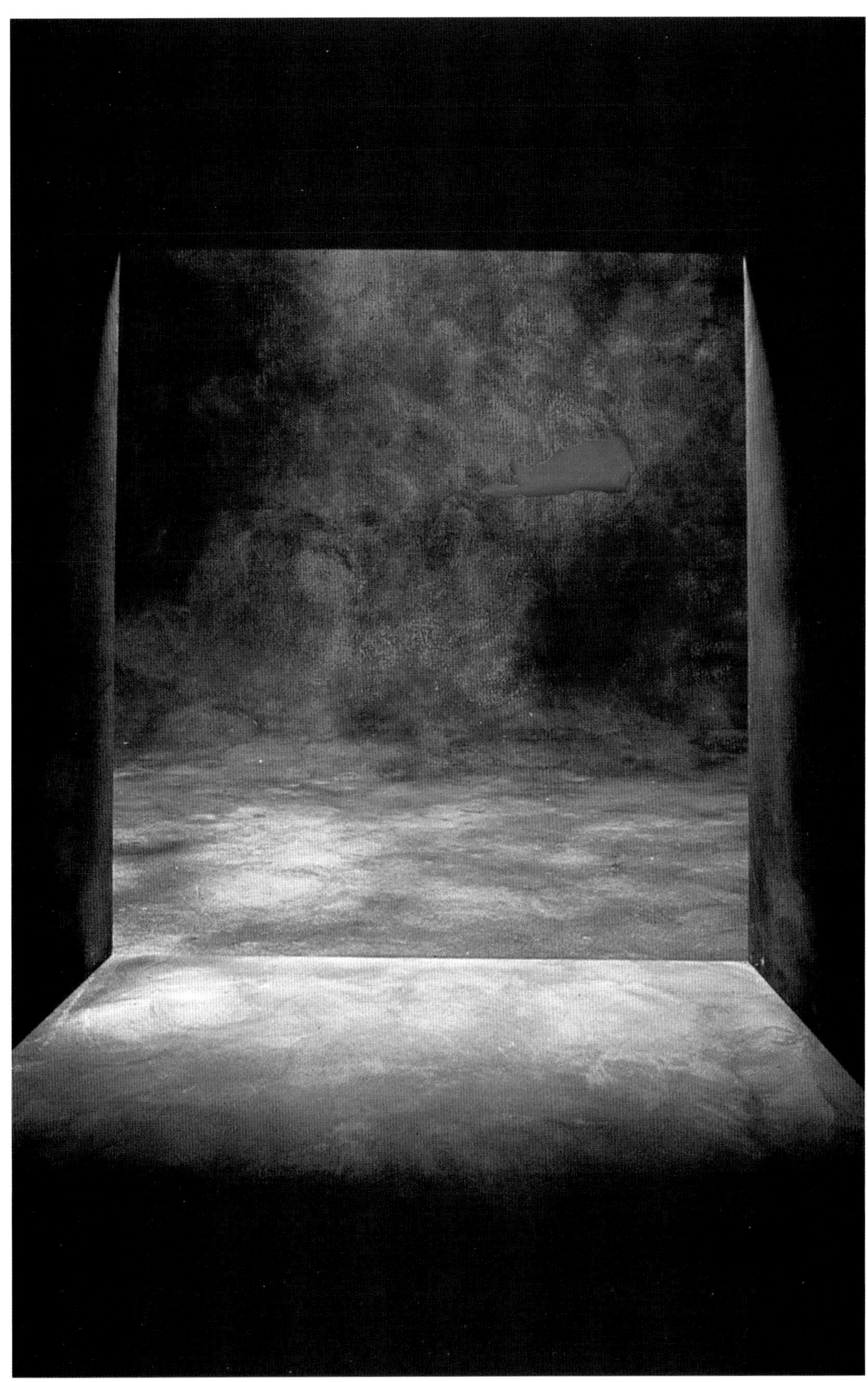

219. Christian Vogt, from Red Cloth series. Dye-transfer photograph, 10 x 7½″. Collection Laurel Reuter, Grand Forks, North Dakota.

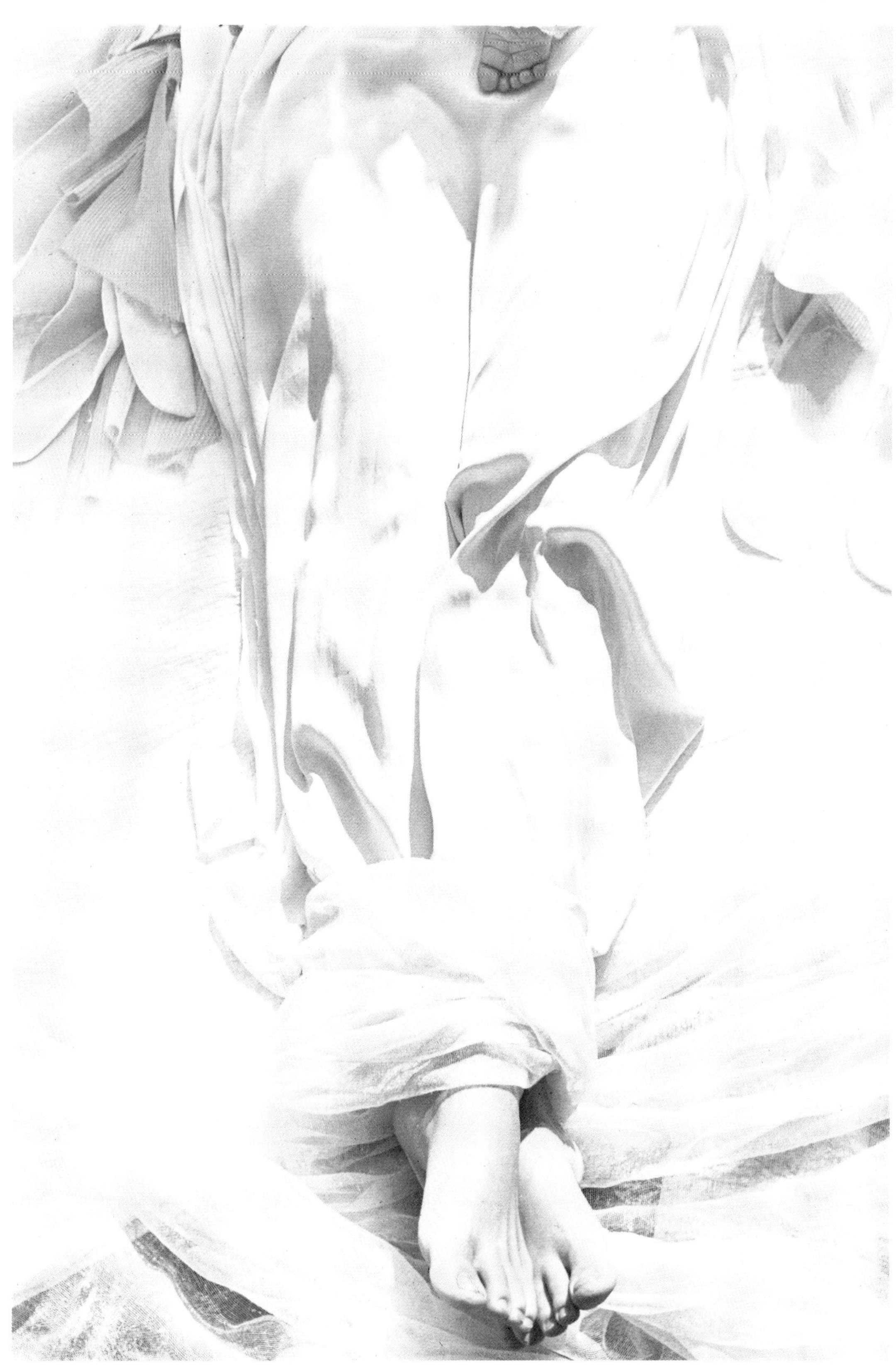

220. Joyce Tenneson, *Two Feet Plus One*, 1980.

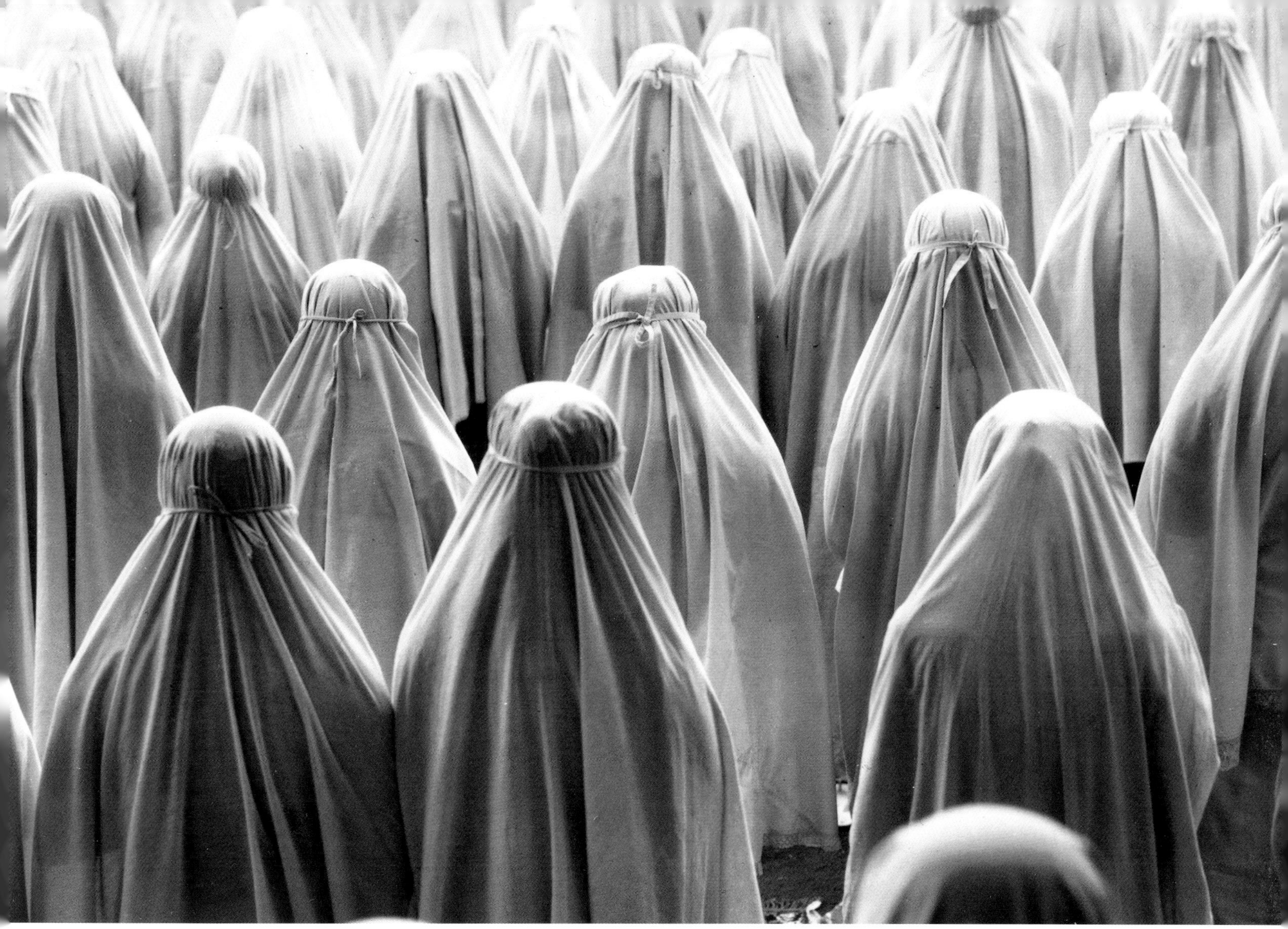

221. Charles O'Rear, *Prayer Vigil, Java, Indonesia,* 1984.

Tina Modotti, born in Italy in 1896, emigrated to the United States in her mid-twenties. In 1921, while in the midst of a brief career as a Hollywood actress, she began an influential relationship with the American photographer Edward Weston. Under his tutelage she learned photography. Her commitment to political reform, coupled with her opposition to Fascism, led her to a life in Mexico. Here she established the precedent of photographing cloth (fig. 222). Many photographers followed, including Manuel Alvarez Bravo. It was as though the sensuousness of the Mexican people was expressed through the daily contact with cloth, since cloth is elemental in Mexican culture. Photographers in Mexico have been repeatedly drawn to capturing cloth in the Mexican environment.

The combination of cloth and camera often produces pictures with a romantic edge. Joyce Tenneson seeks it in her own work. She says, "I like not to know the boundaries between

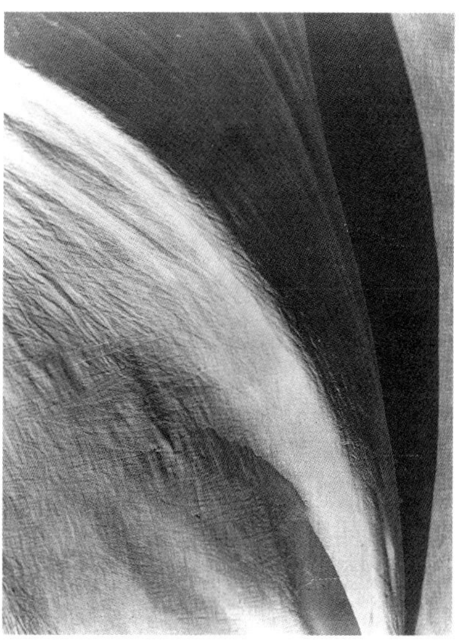

222 (see also page 232). Tina Modotti, *Cloth Folds,* c. 1926–30. Platinum-palladium print, 7⅛ x 9½″. Courtesy Museum of Modern Art, New York, anonymous gift.

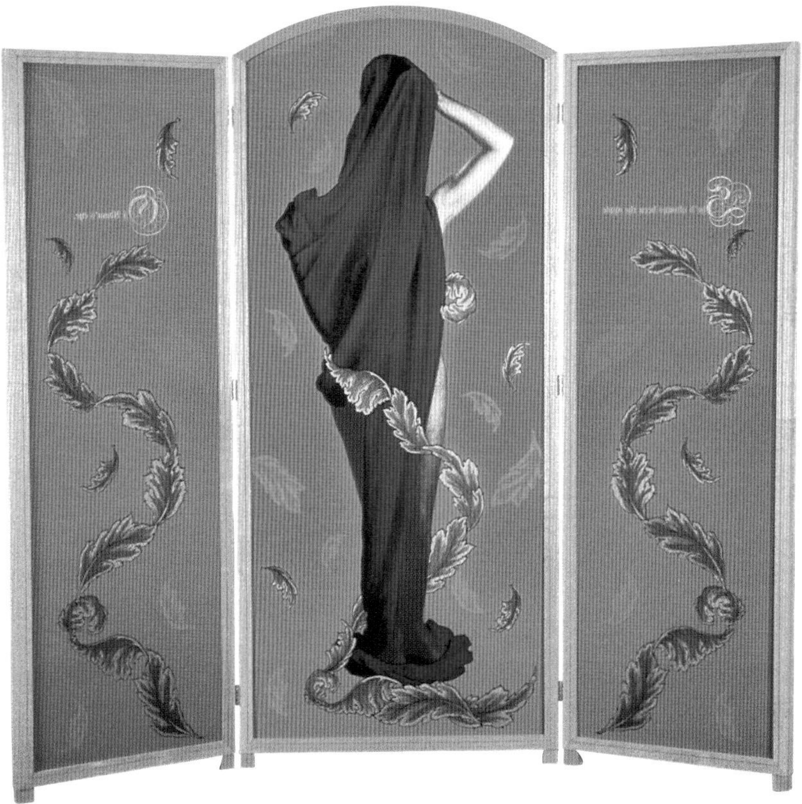

223. Carrie Mae Weems, *The Apple of Adam's Eye,* 1993. Monochromatic photographic image executed in pigment and silk embroidery on cotton sateen with Australian lacewood frame, 75 x 81½ x 1¾″. Edition of five plus artist's proof. Courtesy Fabric Workshop/Museum, Philadelphia.

cloth and skin and light and stone in whatever I am shooting." She achieves this with spectacular effect in both her black-and-white and her pale color photographs, where murmurous, diaphanous cloth floats over and through her ghostly figures. With the camera she seems to have captured the marblelike quality of a Renaissance sculpture by Desiderio. It is appropriate to liken a Tenneson photograph to a visual tone poem—a composition, though not in verse, that is characterized by great beauty of language or thought. More precisely, one might call the works of Joyce Tenneson tone poems in which cloth and skin, and stones and light are the only motifs (fig. 220).

One could speculate that neither the photographs of Tenneson nor those of Lehndorff and Trülzsch could have been made in America in the 1950s. The cultural climate was wrong. Cloth had lost its cachet. The textile industry was at an all-time aesthetic low, producing mile after mile of ugly synthetic yardage. It was not until the last half of the 1960s that the young in America led the return to cotton. The 1970s saw a burgeoning of demand for natural fibers of all kinds. Industry responded by finally producing quality fabrics, both natural and synthetic, that were beautiful as well as serviceable. Only after the rebuilding of the textile industry in the 1980s did it become possible for artists to formulate in their minds present-day images of vital, sensuous mill cloth. This restoration of cachet to mill cloth underpins both the Tenneson and the Lehndorff-Trülzsch photographs.

Cloth has another important role in photography; it becomes the human figure's equivalent. For example, nowhere has cloth provoked more ambiguous, metaphor-filled images than when Western photographers turn their cameras to the veiled woman of the East. Here there is absolutely no objectivity. One could argue that neither suffragettism nor feminism would allow the modern mind to view the veiled woman with objectivity—but one wonders if that was ever possible for the westerner. Consider Charles O'Rear's veiled Moslem women of Indonesia. What a magnetic and enigmatic world these hidden women inhabit. Like pawns in a chess game, each is exactly the same. Each is an unknowable woman; cloth is her stand-in. Cloth takes on the grace of her movement; she is swathed and finally swallowed by cloth. Woman and cloth become one. In 1948 Henri Cartier-Bresson photographed *Moslem Women on the Slopes of Hari Parba Hill, Srinager, India.* His cloth-enveloped women, poised like figures in an ancient stone frieze, are pitted against the village below and the mountains above—both the women and the landscape are timeless. Conversely, it is the contradiction in cultural time that provides the tension in

Jean-Philippe Charbonnier's 1955 photograph of a woman who has replaced her more traditional burden with a sewing machine, the tool of her trade in modern times. To Western eyes the early sewing machine was an anachronism. To Eastern eyes it was the exotic element when the photograph was taken in the mid-1950s (figs. 221, 225, 226).

Misha Gordin, a Latvian of Russian descent who immigrated to the United States in the early 1970s, brought with him a complicated view both of the world and of art making. Influenced by the European Surrealists in his early work, he went on to produce the remarkable Crowd series of dark, foreboding repeated images. Because the views are completely staged, the photographer allows his veiled women a self-awareness not present in the work of O'Rear, Cartier-Bresson, or Charbonnier. All eyes are closed in Gordin's photograph *Crowd #1* except those of one woman. With absolute intelligence and acute awareness she gazes at the viewer (fig. 227).

Carrie Mae Weems started with a black-and-white photograph of herself shrouded in a gauze veil and transformed it into a contemporary work of art that questions both gender and sexual power as traditionally possessed by men and women. Created at the Fabric Workshop/Museum in Philadelphia in 1993, this multipanel screen combines both text and imagery. The central figure of Eve is flanked by text that reads, "She'd always been the apple / Of Adam's eye." On the back side of the center panel it reads, "Temptation my ass, desire has its place, and besides, they were both doomed from the start." The lettering is finely embroidered in gold silk thread. The lush red surface of the work is set off by the green serpentine leaves that

224. Kenneth Josephson, *Bombay, India,* 1975.

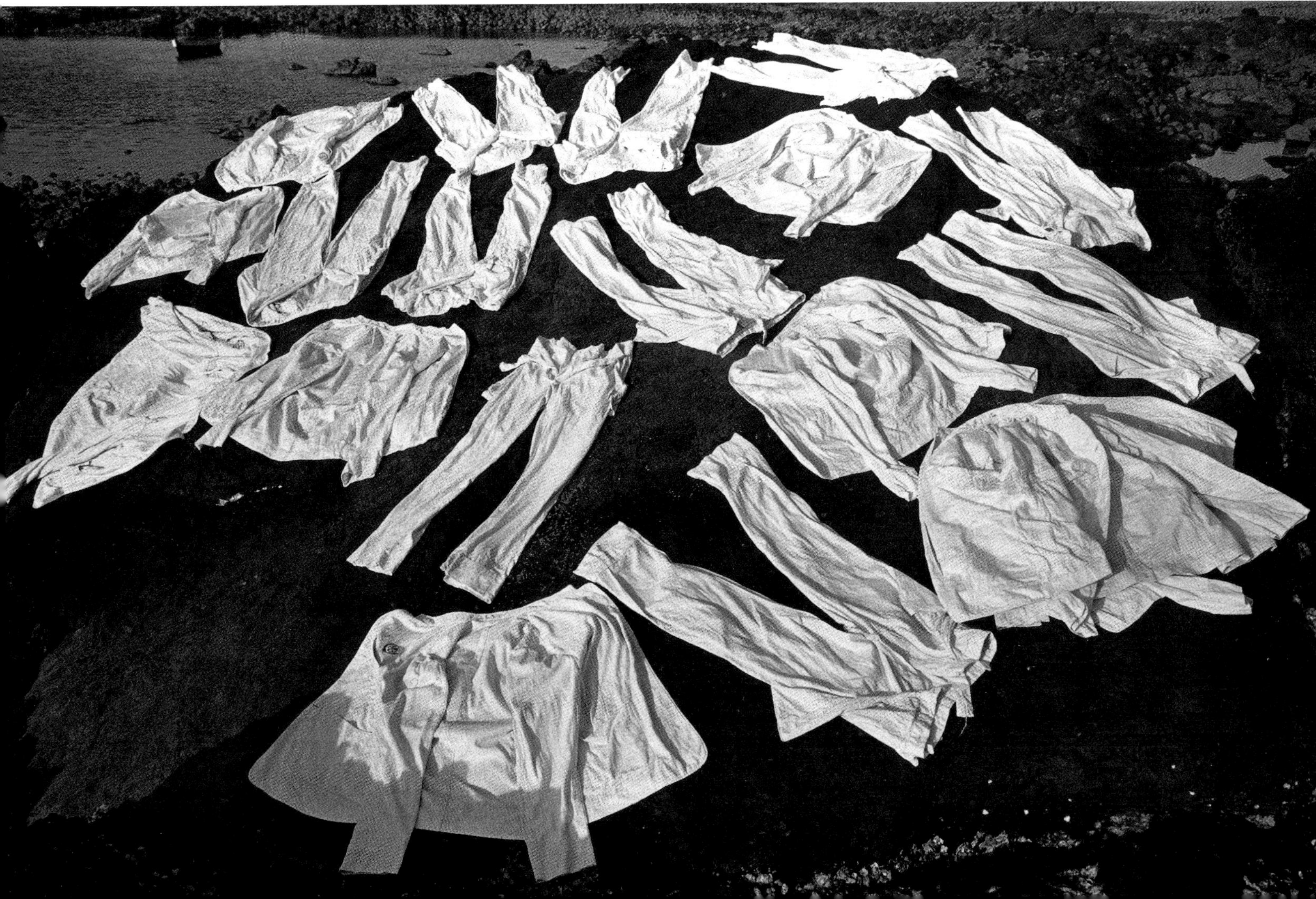

225. Jean-Philippe Charbonnier, *Kuwait Woman,* 1955. Courtesy Agence Top, Paris.

227 *(opposite).* Misha Gordin, *Crowd #1,* 1988. Silver gelatin print, edition of 7.

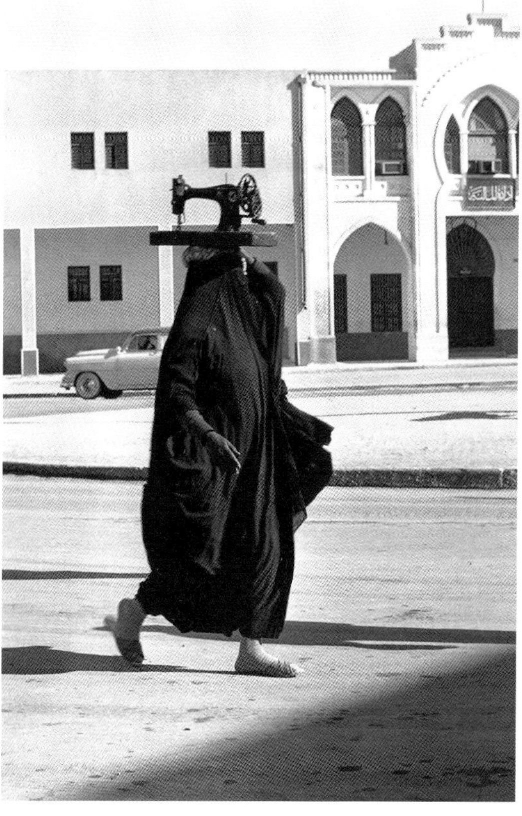

226. Henri Cartier-Bresson, *Moslem Women on the Slopes of Hari Parba Hill, Srinager, India,* 1948. Courtesy Magnum Photos, Inc.

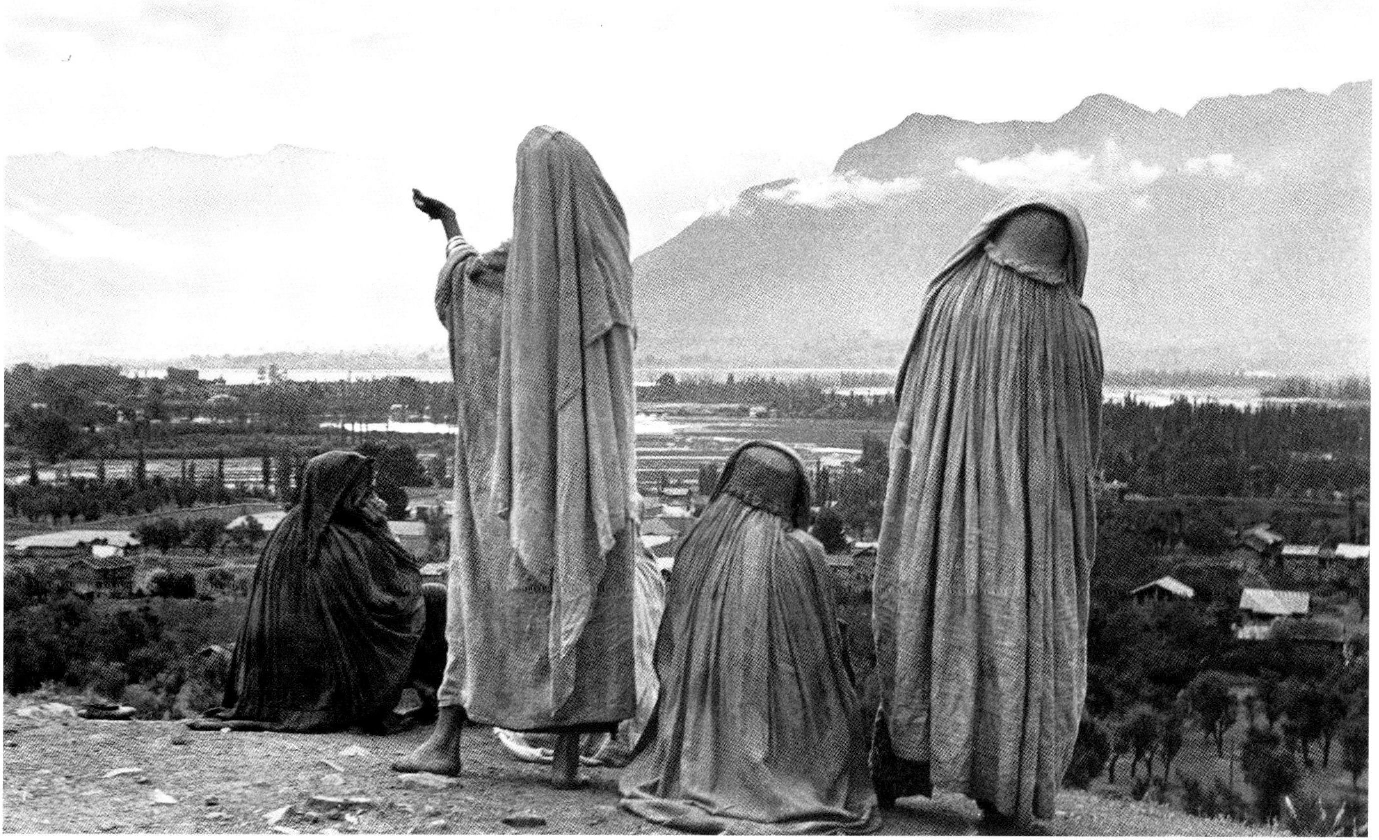

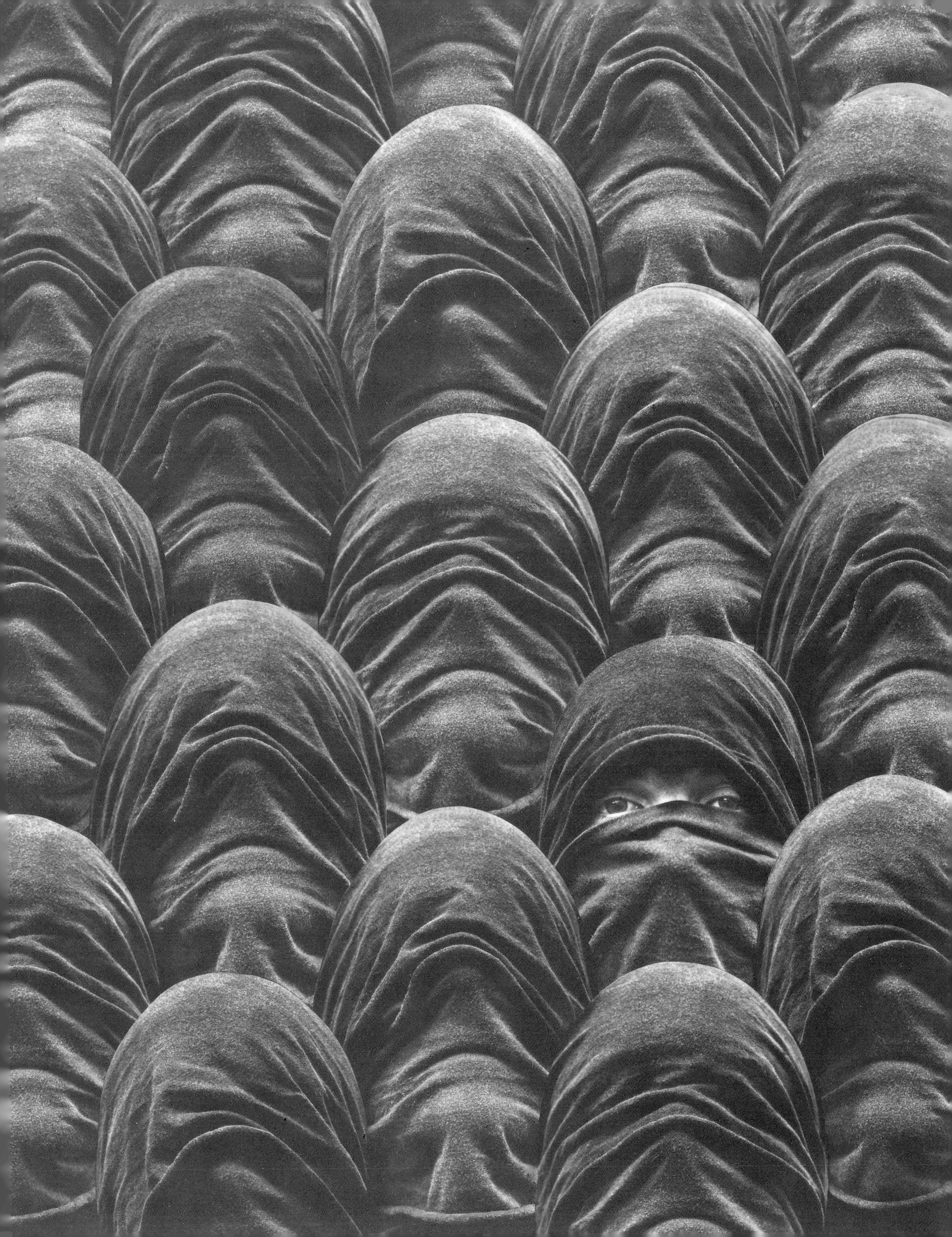

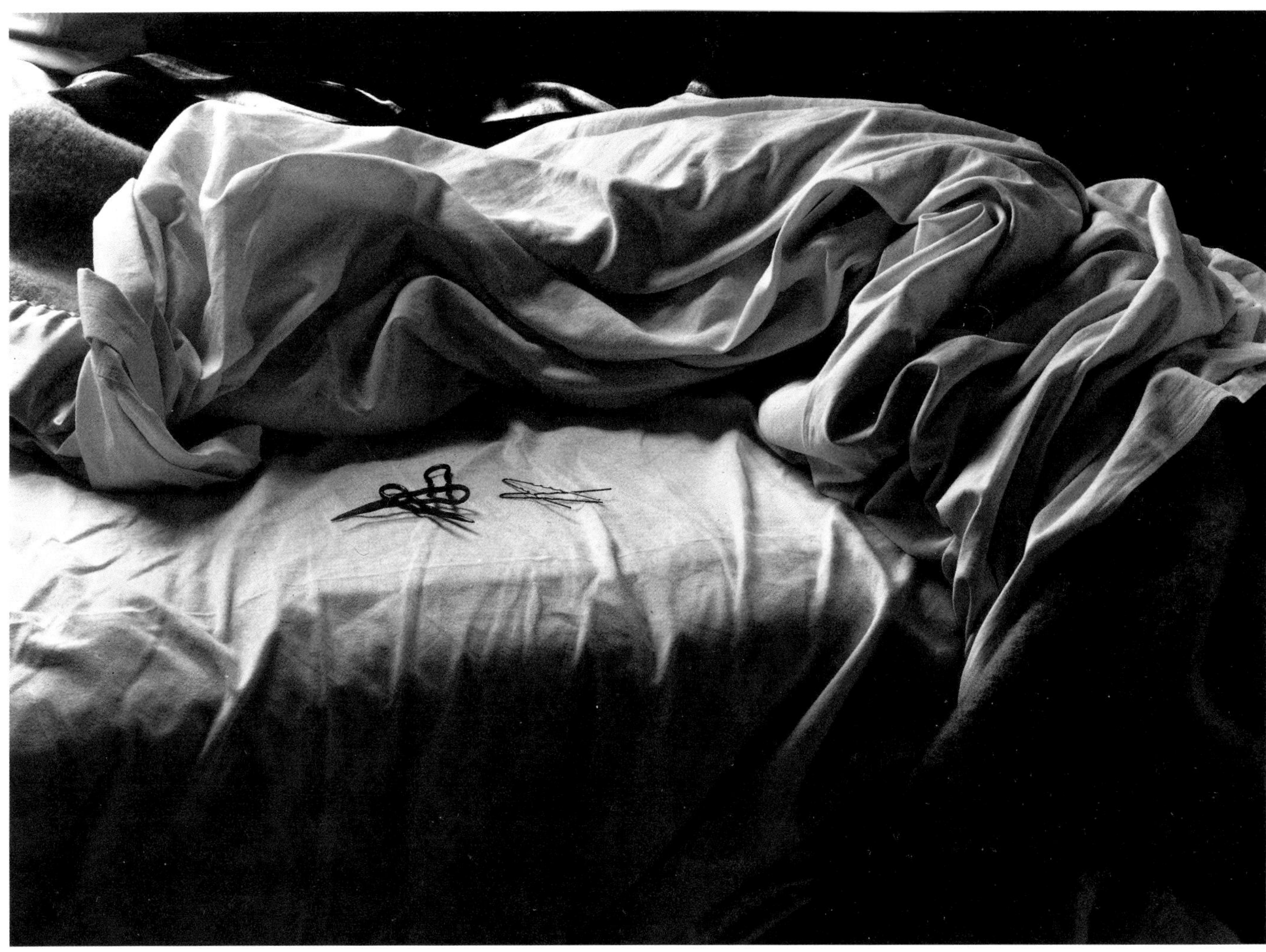

228. Imogen Cunningham, *The Unmade Bed,* 1957. Courtesy Imogen Cunningham Trust.

wind across both the front and back of the screen, reinforcing the essence of the Garden of Eden and original sin. While Misha Gordin's woman is aware of her veiled state and what it means to be a shrouded woman within the larger world, Weems's contemporary Eve is a full partner in the seduction (fig. 223).

Kenneth Josephson first traveled to India in 1975 to find a visual world awash with color and cloth. (In 1990 there were still 20 million handweavers working full time in India.) Josephson's black-and-white photographs from that trip are replete with cloth. This body of work is not surreal in the manner of much of his art; rather it is metaphorical. In his Bombay, India series, clothes are the metaphors for the people. Spread on the riverbank to dry, the clothes suggest the enormous number that is the population of India (fig. 224).

The bed, like the wedding dress or the veil of the East, is another metaphor for the human. Its narrative potency has always attracted photographers. The human is most often absent but his or her presence (most often hers) is almost palpable. Like the veil, the sheets subsume the hidden human form. In Imogen Cunningham's *Unmade Bed* a few scattered hairpins suggest the one who just left. The story is consigned to the viewer's experience, memory, or imagination. This is a straight, factual, and yet romantic image, which projects an intimacy often associated with cloth (fig. 228).

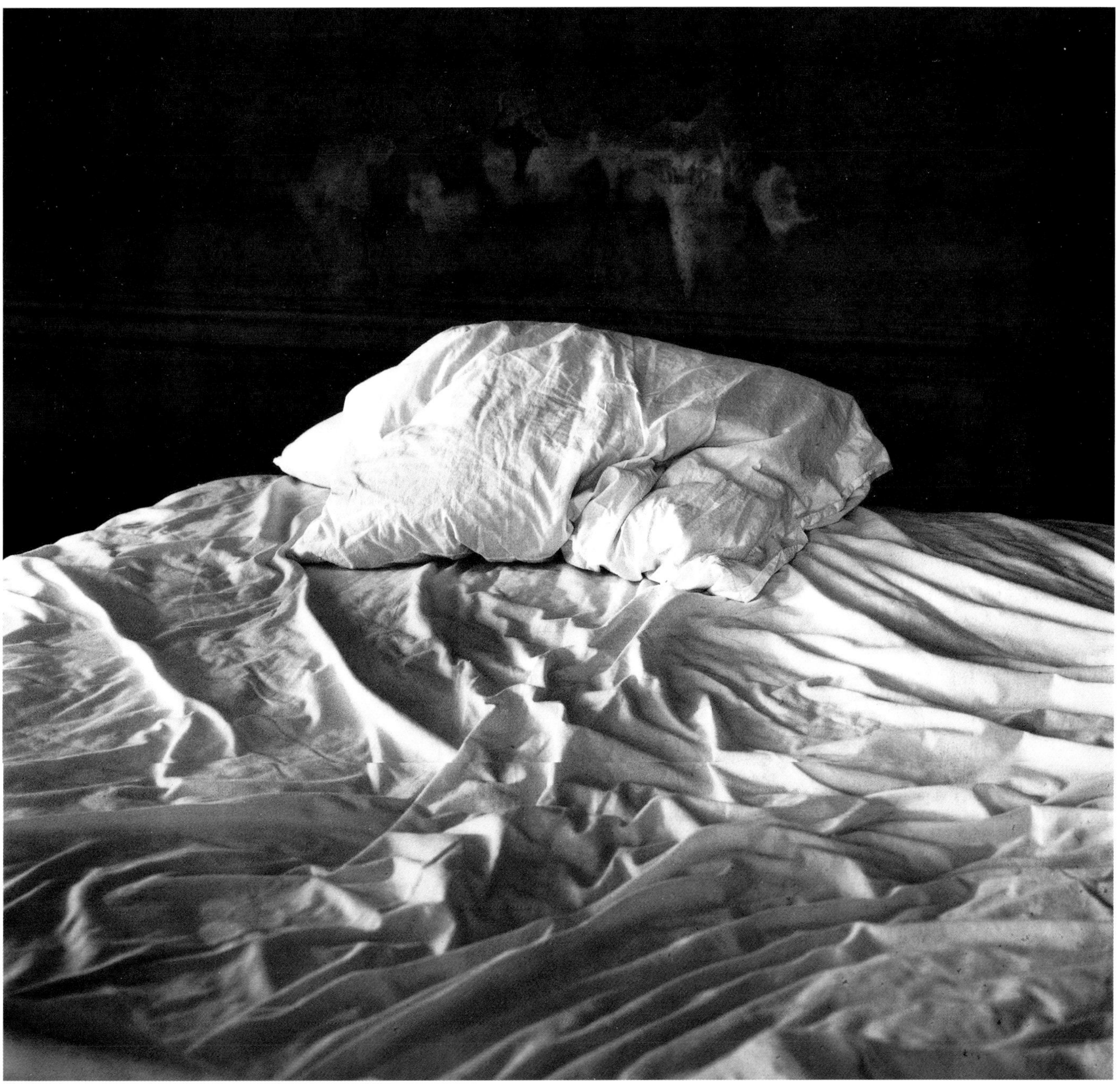

229. Diana Michener, *Bed #3,* 1981. Silverprint.

Whereas viewers are full participants in Cunningham's work, Diana Michener gives no quarter to the viewer intent on creating narrative. She uses space and pattern to draw the viewer into her faithful rendering of the scene she has put together for the camera. Her cloth has been manipulated into a still life; its draped forms appear unnatural. There is no missing human to haunt the viewer, just as no owner is ever suggested in historical still-life painting as it evolved in northern Europe (fig. 229).

Catherine Jansen, on the other hand, is vitally interested in the absent woman who might inhabit her *Softhouse: Sewing Space.* To Jansen, cloth and women have been inextricably bound together since the beginnings of time. A woman's rela-

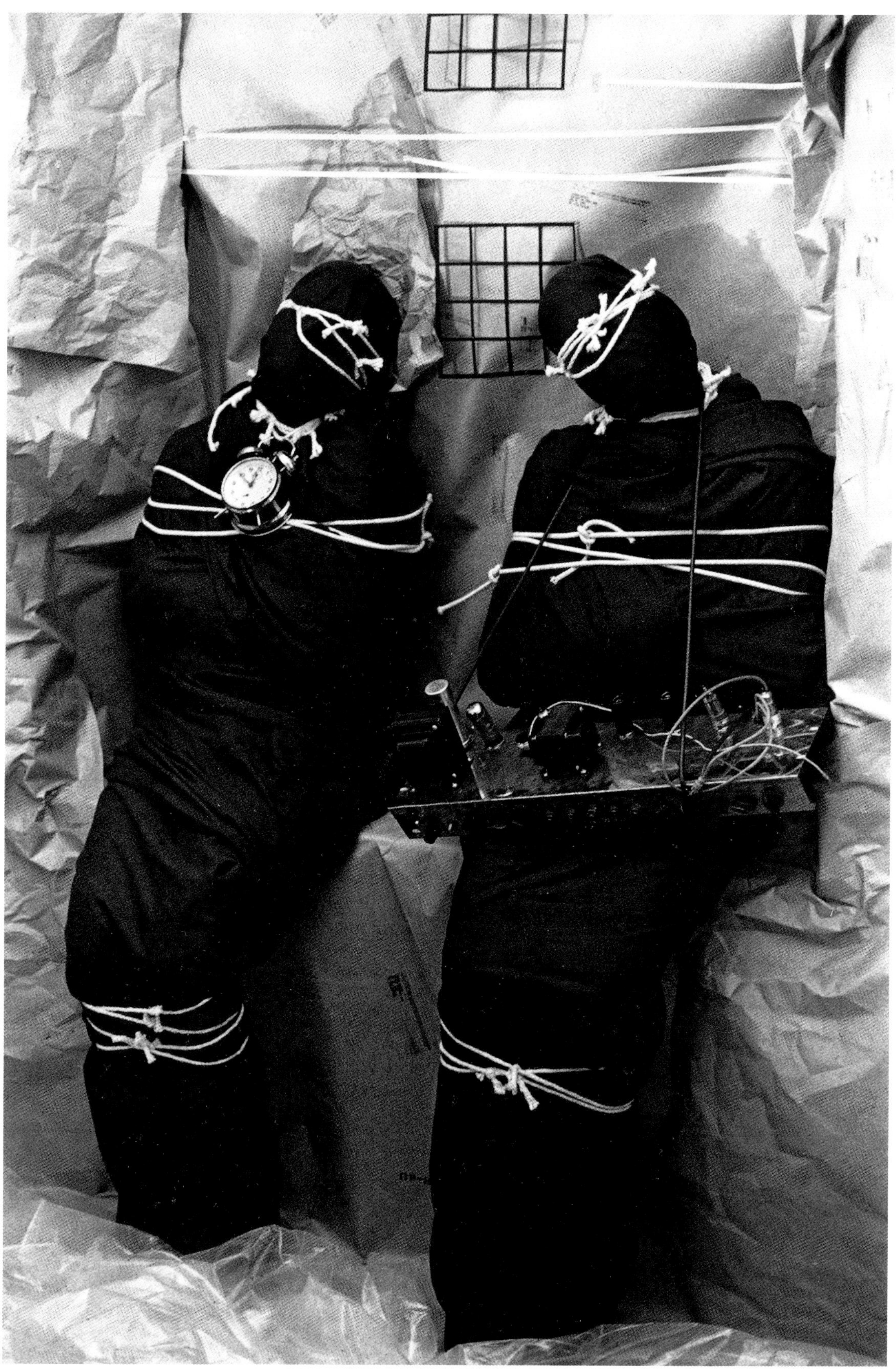

232. Ricardo Estanislao Zulueta, *Therapy II,* 1988. Photo Performance, 4 x 3´.

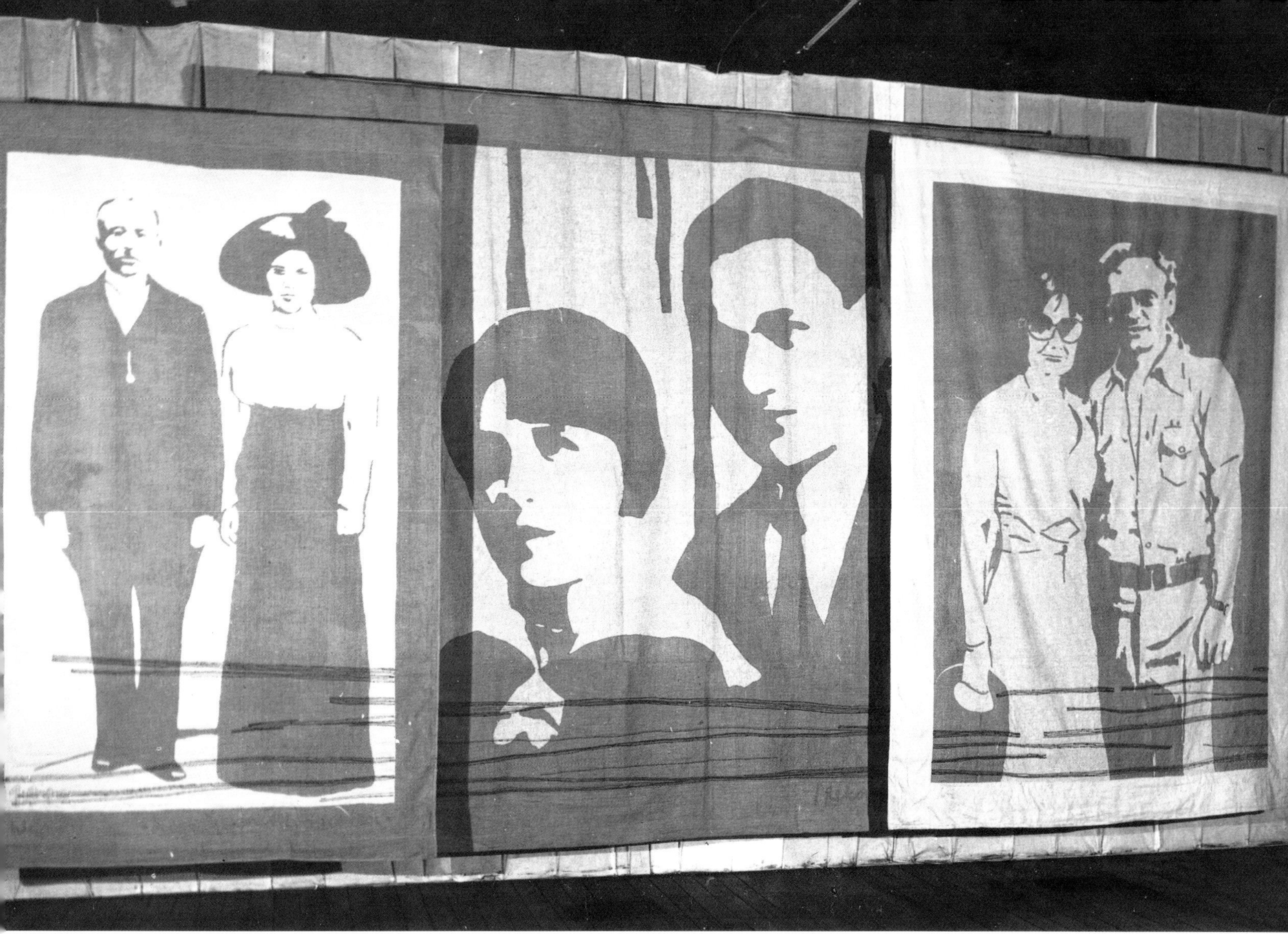

233. Stefan Poplawski, *Cardiogram of Generations, Vilna 1910, Michalowo 1935, Paris 1975 and 1978.* Photo on linen.

Where Rauschenberg wandered, many followed, expanding and pioneering new directions. Stefan Poplawski transferred his family album onto cloth using photolithography. By manipulating both the object and the process, he made it appear as though the image was woven into the fabric of the cloth. Ed Rossbach, on the other hand, used heat transfer to imprint his iconic image of pop star John Travolta onto silk organza (figs. 233, 234).

Cloth has been used photographically by other artists discussed in this book, especially those from printmaking backgrounds. Martha Zelt incorporates photo-based images into her collages (see fig. 92). Lois Johnson screened the photos of one hundred friends onto cloth for her *Audience Frieze* (see fig. 113). Both, like Rauschenberg, are technical virtuosos in the printmaking field and have exploited their technical skill to support their ideas.

If one were only to consider the photographs already discussed above, one might conclude that the combination of camera and cloth always produces romantic results. One might also conclude that cloth comes fresh from the mill steeped in exotic and sensuous suggestion, and that this seemingly inborn nature of cloth, however muted, is always present in the work of art. Often these two assumptions are proved true. But in their negation photographers produce remarkable art. John Batho's Tent series is a case in point.

Batho has chosen to photograph cloth because he feels it to be absolutely neutral. Cloth can take on pure shape, as in a beach umbrella, and pure color. The photographs in the Beach series are four-color carbon prints produced in a small atelier outside Paris by the printer Michel Fresson, whose father invented the process. They are printed with insoluble pigments similar to those used in paints. The process perfectly suits the

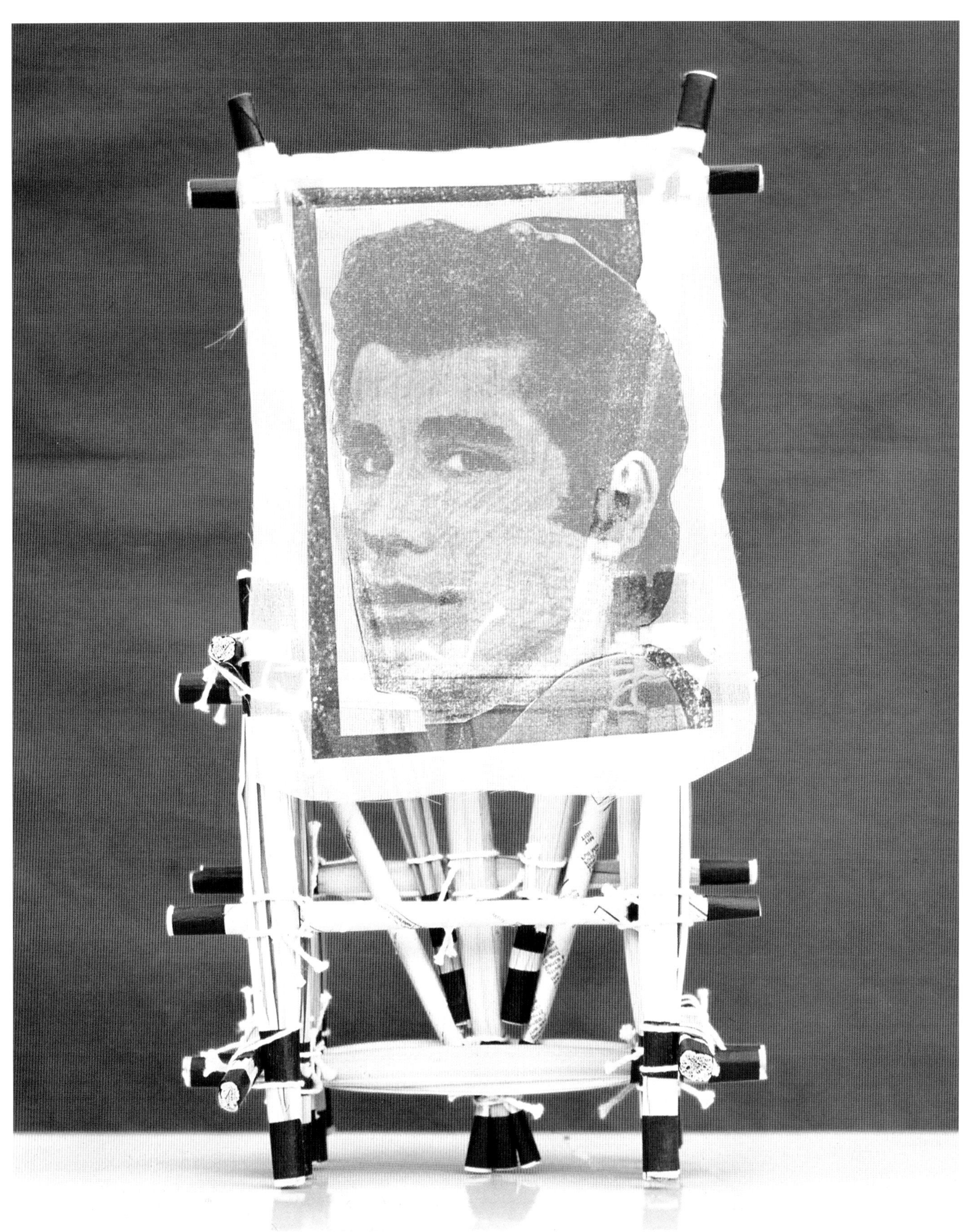

234. Ed Rossbach, *John Travolta,* 1978. Heat transfer, reeds, twine, silk organza, 17 x 9½ x 7½″.

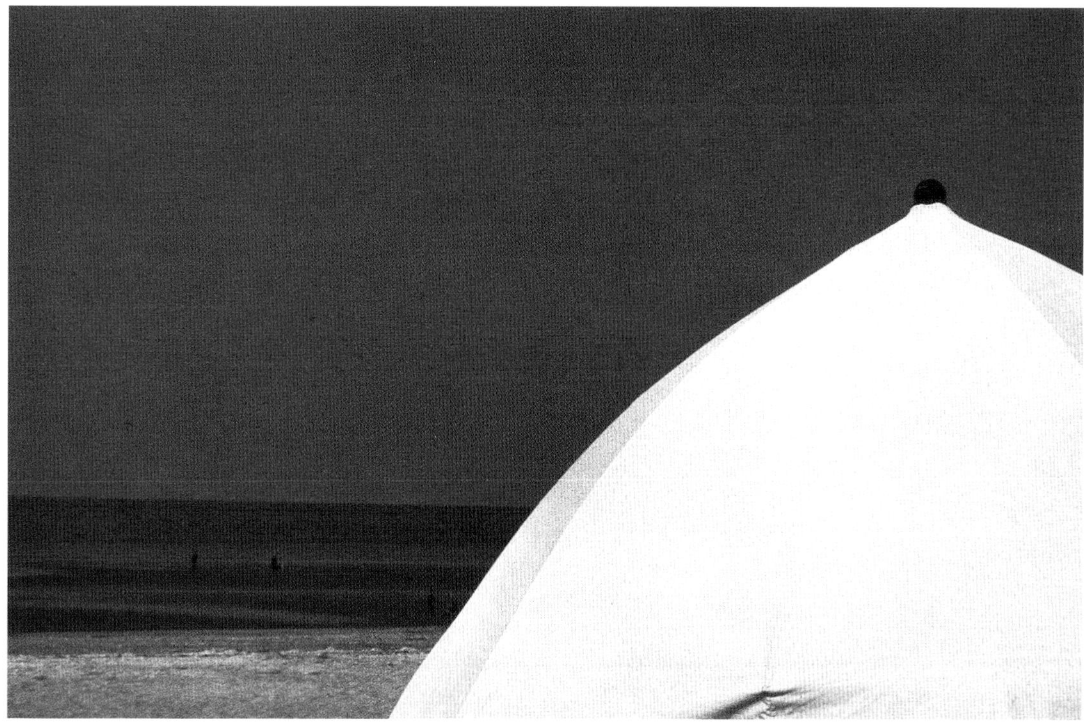

235. John Batho, *The Yellow Umbrella,* 1977. Four-color carbon process, 7¾ x 11¾″. Collection Laurel Reuter, Grand Forks, North Dakota.

artist's intention. He is interested in photographing color in and of itself, rather than photographing objects for their descriptive or informational value. Therefore Batho has placed the oldest of requirements upon cloth: that it absorb dye, or color (fig. 235).

Finally, photojournalists have scoured the world recording the plight of the oppressed, the war-embattled, and the hungry. The images enter into Western homes, originally through such magazines as *Life*, and today by satellite, to become seared into both private and public memory. Again and again cloth conveys the starvation and misery of those otherworldly inhabitants of lands not our own—filthy, worn, tortured cloth. For example, in the mid-1980s the Brazilian Sebastião Salgado traveled to West Africa, to what was once Lake Faguibine in Mali but has since been swallowed up by a consuming desert. For eighteen months Salgado worked with a French humanitarian aid group, photographing the famine-stricken world of the Sahel region of Africa. In his powerful body of photographs, "drought widows" and their starving children cross the sands of the dimly remembered lake bed, attempting to follow their long-gone men. Hanging from the shoulders and limbs of women such as these is tortured cloth. The starvation, the tension, the extreme angst of refugees everywhere are echoed by their tattered garments. Their unrest is reinforced by the unrest of angular, torn, wind-whipped cloth. Tormented souls receive neither protection nor comfort from equally tormented cloth. Had José Arcadio Buendía seen the images of the world's photojournalists he would have believed that the Christian God in his wrathful state certainly exists. Tortured cloth conveys his presence.

1. Joshua C. Taylor, Walter Hopps, and Lawrence Alloway, *Rauschenberg* (Washington, D.C.: Smithsonian Institution, National Collection of Fine Arts, 1977), 22.

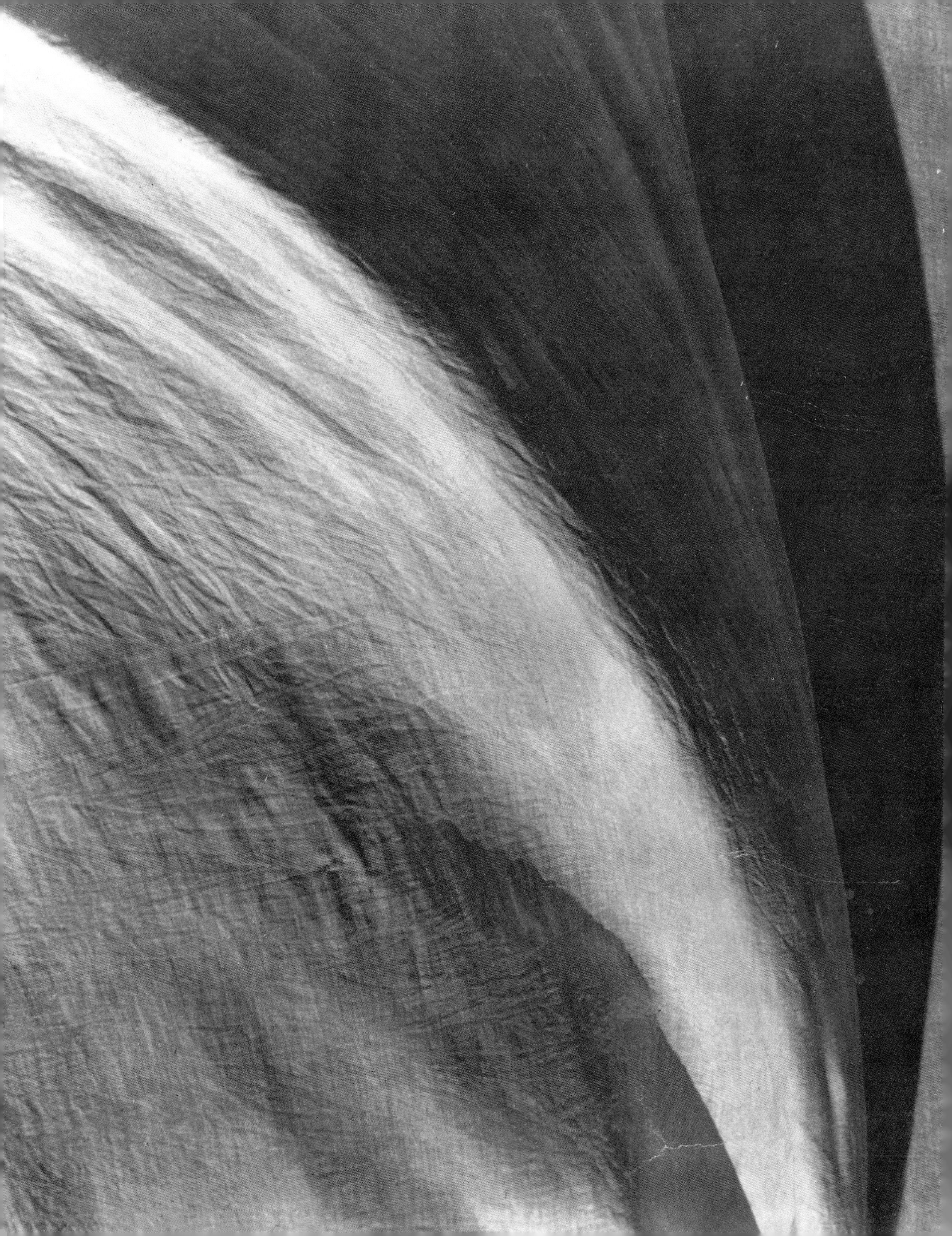

When we conceived this book over a decade ago we predicted that cloth would bind artists from the Art Fabric movement to those working in the more traditional fine arts. By publication time the book has become a historic record of the breaking down of all categories in art as mixed media and installation have invaded every aspect of contemporary art. Indeed, the use of cloth in works of art is not a movement but an all-pervasive trend adopted by artists of every cut and color. Sometimes cloth is the entire work of art, sometimes a component or a fragment. However, just as thread is assumed into material, cloth has been assumed into the fabric of twentieth-century art.

Tina Modotti, *Cloth Folds* (see figure 222).

# Biographies

The authors have made every effort to locate all of the artists whose work has been shown in this book; however, it has been impossible to trace some of them. The authors and the publisher would be grateful to receive any information not included herein and will include that information in subsequent editions.

**Magdalena Abakanowicz**, Poland, b. 1930.
Studied: Academy of Fine Arts in Warsaw, 1950–54.
Taught: Academy of Fine Arts, Poznan, Poland, 1965–90.
Solo Exhibitions: Since 1960 has had over ninety one-person exhibitions in museums and galleries in Europe, Canada, the Americas, Australia, and Japan including: Richard Gray Gallery, Chicago, 1990; Marlborough Fine Art, London, 1990; Galerie Pels-Leusden, Berlin, 1990; Sezon Museum of Art, Tokyo, 1991; Muzeum Sztuki, Lodz, Poland, 1991; Muzeum Narodowe, Wroclaw, Poland, 1991; Marlborough Gallery, New York, 1992; Walker Art Center, Minneapolis, Minn., 1992; Institute for Contemporary Art, P.S. 1 Museum, Long Island City, N.Y., 1993; Museum of Art, Rhode Island School of Design, Providence, 1993–94; Galerie des Polnischen Instituts, Düsseldorf, Germany, 1993–94; Mandeville Muzeum Sztuki, Lodz, Poland, 1994; Galeria Marlborough, Madrid, 1994; Fundació Pilar i Joan Miró, Palma, Mallorca, Spain, 1994; Yorkshire Sculpture Park, Wakefield, West Yorkshire, England, 1996; Galerie Marwan Hoss, Paris, 1996.
Collections: Muzeum Narodowe, Warsaw; Stedelijk Museum, Amsterdam; Centre Georges Pompidou, Paris; Museum of Modern Art, New York; Sezon Museum, Tokyo; Australian National Gallery, Canberra; National Museum of Modern Art, Seoul; Caracas Museum of Modern Art, Venezuela; Israel Museum, Jerusalem; Museo Rufino Tamayo, Mexico City; Art Institute of Chicago; Los Angeles County Museum of Art, Calif.; Metropolitan Museum of Art, New York; Storm King Art Center, Mountainville, N.Y.; and others.
Awards: Honoris Causa Doctorates, Royal College of Art, London, Honorary Doctorate of Fine Arts, Rhode Island School of Design; Grand Prize, São Paulo Biennale; Gottfried von Herder Prize, Vienna; Alfred Jurzykowski Prize, New York; Chevalier, Ordre des Arts et Lettres, Paris; Sculpture Center, New York, Award for Distinction.

**Machiko Agano**, Japan, b. 1953.
Studied: Kyoto University of Arts, B.A., 1977, M.A., 1979.
Solo Exhibitions: Galerie Iteza, Kyoto, 1978, 1980; Galerie Utsubo, Osaka, 1982, 1983, 1984; Esses Gallery, Tokyo, 1984; Gallery Maroni, Kyoto, 1987; Gallery Gallery, Kyoto, 1988; Kyoto Municipal Shijo Gallery, 1991.
Collections: National Museum of Art, Osaka; Kyoto Prefecture, Kyoto; Association Pierre Pauli, Switzerland.

**Alvin Ailey**, United States, 1931–89.
Founded the Alvin Ailey American Dance Theatre in 1958. *Revelations*, a classic in the Ailey repertoire, is one of numerous dances he created. Yves Harper designed the costumes and sets. Judith Jamison, the dancer upon whom Ailey set *Revelations*, succeeded him as artistic director of the company.
Awards: NAACP Springarn Medal; United Nations Peace Medal; Samuel H. Scripps American Dance Festival Award; Kennedy Center Honor; Handel Medallion; and others.

**Frederic Amat**, Spain, b. 1952.
Studied: Architecture and scenography.
Solo Exhibitions: Estudio Regueros, Madrid, 1990; Staller Center for the Arts, State University of New York, Stony Brook, 1991; Galeria Palace, Granada, 1991; Galeria Joan Prat, New York, 1992; Cartoixa de Valldemossa, Mallorca, 1992; Galeria Charpa, Valencia, 1992; Galeria Gamarra and Garrigues, Madrid, 1992; Villafranca del Penedes (Tarragona), Galeria Palma XII, 1993; Museo Rufino Tamayo, Mexico City, 1993; Fundació Joan Miró, Barcelona, 1994; Centro Cultural Tecla Sala, Barcelona, 1996.

**Tadao Ando**, Japan, b. 1941.
Studied: Basically self-taught although studied architecture in Europe and the United States from 1960 to 1969.
Taught: Yale University, New Haven, Conn., visiting professor, 1987; Columbia University, New York, 1988; Harvard University, Cambridge, Mass., 1990.
Professional Work: Practicing architect whose work includes: Azuma House, Sumiyoshi, Japan, 1976; Rokko Housing Project, Hyogo, Japan, 1984; Kobe Harbor, Japan, 1984; Festival Commercial Complex, Naha, Okinawa, 1984; Chapel on Mt. Rokko, Hyogo, Japan, 1985; Church-on-the-Water, Hokkaido, Japan, 1985–88; Children's Museum, Hyogo, Japan, 1987–88; Church of the Light, Osaka, Japan, 1988; Chikatsu-Asuka Tumuli Museum, Osaka, 1991; Japanese Pavilion at Seville World Exhibition, 1992.
Solo Exhibitions: Museum of Modern Art, New York, 1991; Sezon Museum of Art, Tokyo, 1992; Crystal Hall, Osaka, Japan, 1992; Centre Georges Pompidou, Paris, 1993.
Awards: Japanese Architectural Association prize in architecture for Azuma House; Mainichi Art Prize; Isoya Yoshido Award; Gold Medal of Architecture, French Academy of Architecture; Art Prize, Osaka Prefecture; Honorary Fellow, American Institute of Architects; Arnold W. Brunner Memorial Prize, American Academy and Institute of Arts and Letters; Carlsberg Architectural Prize, Denmark; Pritzker Prize for Architecture.

**Mary Ball**, England, b. 1922.
Studied: Goldsmiths' College 1942–44; Bath Academy of Art, 1951–52; Goldsmiths' College School of Art, 1972–73.
Solo Exhibitions: Newlyn Artists, Orion Gallery, Newlyn, England, 1995; Bakehouse Gallery, Penzance, England, 1996, 1997 (with Bob Berry); installation with Interartists, Lower Bakehouse Gallery, Penzance, England, 1997.

**James Bassler**, United States, b. 1933.
Studied: University of California, Los Angeles, M.A., 1968.
Taught: University of California, Los Angeles. Workshops at: Textile Workshops, Santa Fe, N. Mex., 1974, 1975, 1976; San Diego State University, Calif., 1974; Cranbrook Academy of Art, Bloomfield Hills, Mich., 1972; Los Angeles Handweavers Association, 1972; National Handweavers Association, Detroit, 1972.
Solo Exhibition: United States Embassy, Warsaw, 1995.
Collections: State of California, Sacramento, Calif.; *USA Today*, Corporate Office, Arlington, Va.; Oakland Museum, Calif.; Minneapolis Institute of Arts, Minn.; American Craft Museum, New York; Art Institute of Chicago; North Dakota Museum of Art, Grand Forks; Long House Museum, East Hampton, N.Y.
Awards: Silver Medal, Seventh International Triennale of Tapestry, Poland; Individual Fellowship Award, California Council for the Arts; National Endowment for the Arts Visual Artists Fellowship; Juror, Eighth International Triennale, Lodz, Poland.

**John Batho**, France, b. 1939.
Education: Self-taught.
Taught: Université de Paris, 1983–90; Ecole Nationale des Beaux-Arts, Dijon, 1992– .
Solo Exhibitions: Galeries Zabriskie, Paris and New York, 1978, 1980, 1982, 1984, 1985, 1986, 1992, 1995; Musée Montebello, Trouville-sur-Mer, 1990; "Floating Photos" installation, Municipal Swimming Pool of Trouville, 1990; Musée des Beaux-Arts, Alençon, France; C.A.C. la Quartier, Quimper, France, 1992; Hôtel de Ville, Rennes, France, 1994; Galerie Oniris, Bamoud, Dijon, France, 1995; and others.

**Romare Bearden**, United States, 1912–88.
Studied: New York University, B.S.; Art Students League, New York, 1937–38; Sorbonne, Paris, 1950–51.
Solo Exhibitions: Corcoran Gallery, Washington, D.C., 1966; Carnegie Institute, Pittsburgh, 1966; Fine Arts Building, Spelman College, Atlanta, 1967; Albany Museum, State University of New York, 1968; retrospective exhibition, Museum of Modern Art, New York, 1971; Pasadena Art Museum, Calif., 1971; High Museum of Art, Atlanta, 1972; North Carolina Museum of Art, Raleigh, N.C., 1972; Studio Museum in Harlem, New York, 1972; Everson Museum, Syracuse, N.Y., 1975; Baltimore Museum of Art, Md., 1981; Virginia Museum of Fine Arts, Richmond, 1981; Brooklyn Museum, N.Y., 1981.
Collections: Metropolitan Museum of Art, New York; Rochester Memorial Art Gallery, N.Y.; Whitney Museum of American Art, New York; Philadelphia Museum of Art; Museum of Fine Arts, Boston; Newark Museum, N.J.; Princeton University Art Museum, N.J.; Museum of Modern Art, New York; High Museum of Art, Atlanta; Madison Art Center, Wisc.; Flint Institute of Arts, Mich.; Saint Louis Art Museum; Akron Art Institute, Ohio; Mint Museum, Charlotte, N.C.; Studio Museum in Harlem, New York; Wadsworth Atheneum, Hartford, Conn.; Davidson College Museum of Art, N.C.; Honolulu Academy of Art.

**Barton Lidice Beneš**, United States, b. 1942.
Studied: Pratt Institute, Brooklyn, 1960–61; Ecole des Beaux-Arts, Avignon, France, 1968.
Solo Exhibitions: Hokin/Kaufman Gallery, Chicago, 1991; Bjorn Olsson Gallery, Stockholm, 1990; White Columns, New York, 1993; North Dakota Museum of Art, Grand Forks, 1993, 1994; Anders Tornberg Gallery, Lund, Sweden, 1994; Galleri Stefan Anderssen, Umea, Sweden, 1994, 1997; Galeria III, Lisbon, Portugal, 1995; RH Gallery, Liberec, Czech Republic, 1996; Novomestska Radnice (New Town Hall), Prague, Czech Republic, 1996; Coke Gallery, University of New Mexico Art Museum, Albuquerque, 1997.
Collections: Agnelli Collection, Turin, Italy; Albuquerque Museum of Art, N. Mex.; Bibliothèque Nationale, Paris; Charles A. Wustum Museum of Fine Arts, Racine, Wisc.; Chase Manhattan Bank, New York; Art Institute of Chicago; Delaware Art Museum, Wilmington; Federal Reserve Board, Washington, D.C.; Greenville Museum, S.C.; Kent State University, Ohio; Hofstra Museum, Hempstead, N.Y.; Malmo Museum, Sweden; McGill University, Rare Book Library, Montreal, Canada; Museum of Fine Arts, Racine, Wisc.; Museum of Modern Art, New York; North Dakota Museum of Art, Grand Forks; National Gallery, Canberra, Australia; National Museum of American Art, Washington, D.C.; New York Public Library; Newberry Library, Chicago; Princeton University, N.J.; Rutgers University, New Brunswick, N.J.; Ruth and Marvin Sackner Archive of Concrete and Visual Poetry, Miami; Sol Lewitt Collection, Chester, Conn.; University of Iowa Art Museum, Iowa City; University of New Mexico, Albuquerque; and others.
Awards: Invited Printmaker, Tamarind Institute, Albuquerque, N.M.; Pollock-Krasner Foundation Grant; Vorhees Grant for Printmaking, Rutgers University, N.J.; Grant for Mixed Media, Ariana Foundation for the Arts; C.A.P.S. Grant for Graphics, New York State Arts Council.

**Horst Berger**, United States, b. 1928 (Germany).
Studied: Architecture and social sciences, Iowa State University, Ames, 1949; Stuttgart University, Germany, Civil Engineering degree, 1954.
Professional Work: Affiliated with Severud Associates, New York, 1960–68; Geiger Berger Associates, New York, 1968; Horst Berger Partners, New York, 1983; fabric structures include: S.O.M.'s Haj Terminal, Jeddah, Saudi Arabia; Florida Festival; two Bullock's department stores; Canada Place, Vancouver; ceiling, Alexandra Palace, London; roof, San Diego Convention Center; roof, indoor practice facility, University of Wisconsin football team, Madison; retractable roof design, Phoenix Stadium, Ariz.

**Joseph Beuys**, Germany, 1921–86.
Taught: Professor of sculpture at Düsseldorf Academy of Art, Germany.
Solo Exhibitions: Fluxus, Düsseldorf Academy of Art, 1963; St. Stephan Gallery, Vienna, 1964; Documenta IV, Kassel, West Germany; Galerie René Block, Berlin, 1972; Ronald Feldman Fine Arts, New York, 1973; Galerie Klein, Bonn, 1973; Dartmouth College, Hanover, N.H., 1974; Konrad Fischer Gallery, Düsseldorf, 1976; Die National Galerie, Berlin; Solomon R. Guggenheim Museum, New York, 1979; "Das Kapital 1970–77 Joseph Beuys," Halle für Internationale Neue Kunst, Zurich,1981; Ulrich Museum of Art, Wichita State University, Kans., 1981; Victoria and Albert Museum, London, 1983; and others.

**D'Arcie Beytebiere**, United States, b. 1953.
Studied: Evergreen State College, Olympia, Wash., B.A., 1976; University of Washington, M.F.A., 1985.
Solo Exhibitions: Cerulean Blue Gallery, Seattle, Wash., 1985; numerous group exhibitions.
Collections: Numerous private and corporate collections.
Awards: Washington State Artist in the Schools; Imagination Celebration Visual Artist; Washington State Artist Trust Foundation Fellowship; Fashion Foundation International Textile Exhibition, Tokyo, Japan; Ideacomo Award, Como, Italy.

**Billedstofteater**, Denmark, 1977–86.
Flink Basse and Kirsten Dehlholm, Directors.
During the years of its existence this contemporary performance group brought out twenty-eight productions. The directors were responsible for the visual concept and the costumes. The performers were recruited from the streets.

**Emilia Bohdziewicz**, Poland, b. 1941.
Studied: Academy of Fine Arts in Warsaw, 1969.
Awards: Grand Prix, International Textile Competition in Kyoto, Japan.

**Christian Boltanski**, France, b. 1944.
Solo Exhibitions: Whitechapel Art Gallery, London, 1990; Institute of Contemporary Art, Nagoya, Japan, 1990; Palais des Beaux-Arts, Brussels, 1990; Marian Goodman Gallery, New York, 1991, 1995; Hamburger Kunsthalle, Hamburg, 1991; Galerie Ghislaine Hussenot, Paris, 1991; Musée de Grenoble, France, 1991; Stedelijk Van Abbe Museum, Eindhoven, the Netherlands, 1991; Galeria Foksals, Warsaw, 1992; Centro Cultural/Arte Contemperaneo, Mexico City, 1992; Karl Valentine Museum and Stadtmuseum, Munich, 1993; New York Public Library, 1993; Graphische Sammlung, Frankfurt, 1993; Oabla Art Center, Sarajevo, Bosnia and Herzegovina, 1994; Henry Moore Studio, Halifax, England; Center for Contemporary Art, Glasgow, 1994; Malmo Museum, Sweden, 1994; Cincinnati Art Museum, Ohio, 1994; DuPont Foundation for Contemporary Art, Tilburg, the Netherlands, 1995; Villa Medici, Rome, 1995; Kunsthalle Wien, Austria, 1995; Public Art Fund, New York, 1995; Centro Galego de Arte Contemporanea, Santiago de Compostela, Spain, 1996.
Collections: Numerous museums and private collections throughout the world.

**Lee Bontecou**, United States, b. 1931.
Studied: With William Zorach at the Art Students League, New York, 1952–55.
Collections: Hirshhorn Museum and Sculpture Garden, Smithsonian Institution, Washington, D.C.; Menil Collection, Houston, Tex.; Museum of Modern Art, New York; Whitney Museum of American Art, New York; Cleveland Museum of Art, Ohio.

**Harry Boom**, the Netherlands, b. 1945.
Studied: Academie Voor Beeldende Kunst, St. Joost, Breda, the Netherlands, 1963–68; Akademie Sztuk Pieknych, Warsaw, 1968–69.
Taught: Akademie Voor Beeldende Kunst, Enschede, the Netherlands; Academie Van Beeldende Vorming, Tilburg, the Netherlands, 1977. Since 1990: Cranbrook Academy of Art, Bloomfield Hills, Mich.; School of the Art Institute of Chicago; Art Institute, Cleveland, Ohio; Baltimore Art Institute, Md.; University of North Carolina, Chapel Hill; Ohio State University, Columbus; University of North Carolina, Raleigh.
Solo Exhibitions: Yaw Gallery, Birmingham, Mich., 1990; Manes Art Center, University of North Carolina, Chapel Hill, 1991; Galery Van Mourik, Rotterdam, 1991, 1993; Rijksmuseum, Amsterdam, 1992; Hopkins Hall Gallery, Ohio State University, Columbus, 1993.
Collections: Bankgirocentrale, Amsterdam; Frans Halsmuseum, Haarlem, the Netherlands; cities of Gouda, Hengelo, Rotterdam, and Utrecht; Nederlands Textielmuseum, Tilburg; Provinciehuis Zuid-Holland, The Hague; Rijksmuseum, Amsterdam.

**Louise Bourgeois**, United States, b. 1911 (France).
Studied: Sorbonne, Paris, 1932–35; Ecole du Louvre, 1936–37; Atelier Bissière, 1936–37; Ecole des Beaux-Arts, 1936–38; Academie de la Grande Chaumiere, 1937–38.
Solo Exhibitions: Parrish Art Museum, Southampton, N.Y., 1992; Milwaukee Art Museum, Wisc., 1992; Fabric Workshop/Museum, Philadelphia, 1992; Linda Cathcart Gallery, Santa Monica, Calif., 1993; Brooklyn Museum of Art, N.Y., 1994; Nelson-Atkins Museum of Art, Kansas City, Mo., 1994; Saint Louis Art Museum, 1994; Galeria Karsten Greve, Milan, 1994; Kestner-Gesellschaft, Hannover, Germany, 1994; Corcoran Gallery of Art, Washington, D.C., 1994–95; Musée d'Art Modern de la Ville de Paris, 1995; Musée d'Art Contemporain de Montréal, 1996; Musée National d'Art Modern, Centre Georges Pompidou, Paris, 1995; Helsinki City Art Museum, 1995; Galerie Karsten Greve, Cologne, 1995; National Gallery of Victoria, Melbourne, 1995; Museum of Contemporary Art, Sydney, 1996; Museo Marco, Monterrey, Mexico, 1996; University Art Museum, University of California, Berkeley, 1996; Art Gallery of Ontario, Toronto, 1996; Gallery Paule Anglim, San Francisco, Calif., 1996.
Collections: Albright-Knox Art Gallery, Buffalo, N.Y.; Australian National Gallery, Canberra; British Museum, London; Brooklyn Museum of Art, N.Y.; Carnegie Museum of Art, Pittsburgh; Denver Art Museum, Colo.: Graphische Sammlung Albertina, Vienna; Solomon R. Guggenheim Museum, New York; Kunstmuseum Bern, Switzerland; Hakone Open-Air Museum, Tokyo; Hirshhorn Museum and Sculpture Garden, Smithsonian Institution, Washington, D.C.; Metropolitan Museum of Art, New York; Museum of Fine Arts, Houston, Tex.; Museum of Modern Art, New York; Museé d'Art Contemporain de Montréal, Canada; Musée d'Art Modern de la Ville de Paris; Musée National d'Art Modern, Centre Georges Pompidou, Paris; National Gallery of Art, Washington, D.C.; Philadelphia Museum of Art; Rhode Island School of Design, Providence; Storm King Art Center, Mountainville, N.Y.; Tate Gallery, London; Uffizi Museum, Florence; Walker Art Center, Minneapolis, Minn.; Whitney Museum of American Art, New York.

Awards: Gold Medal of Honor, National Arts Club, New York; Fellow for Life at the Metropolitan Museum of Art, New York; Creative Arts Award Medal, Brandeis University, Mass.; Distinguished Artist Award for Lifetime Achievement, College Art Association; MacDowell Medalist, MacDowell Colony, Peterborough, N.H.; Lifetime Achievement Award, International Sculpture Center, Washington, D.C.; Grand Prix National de Sculpture, French Ministry of Culture; United States Official Representative at the Venice Biennale; Honorary Doctorate in Fine Arts, Pratt Institute, Brooklyn, N.Y.; Commission for Battery Park City Authority for the Robert F. Wagner Jr. Park, New York.

**Jagoda Buić**, Yugoslavia, b. 1930.
Studied: Zagreb, Rome, and Vienna.
Solo Exhibitions: Musée des Tapisseries, Aix-en-Provence, 1981; Atlantic Center for the Arts, Florida, 1983; Union des Banques Suisses, Zurich, 1988; Union des Banques Suisses, Tokyo, 1991; Chateau Chapelle Ducal, Abbaye du Ronceray, Angers, 1991; Musée des Beaux-Arts, Carcassonne, France, 1993; Kunsthalle, Darmstadt, Germany, 1995; Galerie Lelys, Paris, 1996; throughout Germany and Croatia, 1991–94.
Collections: Stedelijk Museum, Amsterdam; Musée d'Art Modern, Belgrade; Musée d'Art Modern, Dubrovnik; Musée des Arts Décoratifs, Lausanne; Metropolitan Museum of Art, New York; Dreyfus Foundation-General, New York; Musée d'Art Modern de la Ville de Paris; Museum Bellerive, Zurich; Rathaus, São Paulo; Cleveland Museum of Art, Ohio.
Awards: Triennale, Milan; Grand Prix, São Paulo Biennale; Prix Herder, University of Vienna; Medaille d'Honneur, International Triennale, Lodz, Poland; UNESCO Medal, Paris.

**Daniel Buren**, France, b. 1938.
Work: Since his involvement with the French group BMPT his work has become characterized by the systematic use of fabric or paper in 8.7-centimeter-wide vertical strips, applied to such surfaces as architectural structures, or left floating free. He creates his temporary works on site.
Installations: Columns of the Palais Royal, Paris; Museum of Modern Art, New York; Palais des Beaux-Arts, Brussels; Portland Center for the Visual Arts, Oregon; Israel Museum; Spoleto Festival, Italy; Musée Saint-Denis, Reims, France; Musée des Arts Décoratifs, Paris; Vancouver Art Gallery, Canada; Museum Van Hedendaagse Kunst, Grand, Belgium; Brooklyn Museum, N.Y.; Centre National d'Art Contemporain, Grenoble, France; French Pavilion, 1986 Venice Biennale; Malmo Museum, Sweden; Moderna Museet, Stockholm; Glenbow Museum, Calgary, Canada; Documenta VII, Kassel, West Germany.

**Bill Burke**, United States, b. 1948.
Studied: University of Georgia, Athens, B.S., 1968–72; State University College at New Paltz, N.Y., M.F.A., 1972–74.
Taught: State University College of New York, New Paltz, 1973–74; Florida International University, Miami, 1974– .
Solo Exhibitions: Barry University, Miami, 1990; Art Museum, Florida International University, Miami, 1992; Miami Dade Community College, North Campus Art Gallery, Miami, 1995; Ground Level Gallery, Lincoln Road, Miami Beach, 1996.
Collections: North Miami Museum of Contemporary Art; Art Museum, Florida International University, Miami; Appalachian Center for Crafts, Smithville, Tenn.; Art in Public Places, Miami; Daytona Beach Visual Arts Gallery, Fla.; Art Gallery, Lockhaven State College, Pa.; Art Gallery, Purdue University, West Lafayette, Ind.; Art Gallery, State University of New York, New Paltz; North Dakota State University, Fargo; Hollywood Art and Cultural Center, Fla.; and others.
Awards: Florida Craftman, Miami; Florida Visual Arts Fellowship, Four Arts Regional Award, Florida State University, Institute for Contemporary Art, Tallahassee, Fla.

**Jean Williams Cacicedo**, United States.
Studied: Pratt Institute, Brooklyn, N.Y., B.F.A., 1970.
Taught: Fiberworks Center for the Textile Arts, J.F.K. University, Berkeley, Calif., 1985–87; numerous workshops including Penland School of Crafts, N.C.; California College of Arts and Crafts, Oakland; University of Kansas, Lawrence.
Exhibitions: Julie: Artisan's Gallery, New York, 1973– ; Hand and the Spirits Crafts Gallery, Scottsdale, Ariz., 1984– ; Hibberd McGrath Gallery, Breckenridge, Colo., 1985– ; Obiko, San Francisco, 1985– ; and numerous national group exhibitions.
Collections: M. H. de Young Memorial Museum, San Francisco; American Craft Museum, New York; Coyote Point Museum, San Mateo, Calif.; Colorado Mountain College, Breckenridge; Julie: Artisan's Gallery, New York.
Awards: Artist of the Year, Contemporary Crafts Committee of the Art Guild of the Oakland Museum, Calif.; National Endowment for the Arts Craftsman Fellowship.

**Sophie Calle**, France, b. 1953.
Solo Exhibitions: Institute of Contemporary Art, Boston, 1990; Matrix Gallery, University of California, Berkeley, 1990; Galeria La Maquina Española, Madrid, 1991; Pat Hearn Gallery, New York, 1991; Musée d'Art Modern de la Ville de Paris, 1991; Donald Young Gallery, Seattle, 1992; Leo Castelli Gallery, New York, 1993; Fundacion Mendoza, Caracas, Venezuela, 1993; Hood Museum of Art, Dartmouth College, Hanover, N.H., 1993; Museum Boymans–van Beuningen, Rotterdam, 1994; Galerie Chantal Crousel, Paris, 1994; Musée Cantonal des Beaux-Arts, Lausanne, 1994; Fraenkel Gallery, San Francisco, 1994; Contemporary Arts Museum, Houston; University Art Museum, University of California, Santa Barbara; David Winton Bell Gallery, Brown University, Providence, R.I., 1995; High Museum of Art, Atlanta, 1995, 1996; Tel Aviv Museum of Art, Israel, 1996.

**Henri Cartier-Bresson**, France, b. 1908.
Studied: Painting with Andre Lhote in the late 1920s, then painting and literature at Cambridge University in 1928. Made a serious commitment to photography in 1931. Studied film with Paul Strand.
Founded: Cofounder of Magnum Photos, 1947.
Films: Assisted Jean Renoir on the films *La Vie est à nous,* 1936, and *La Règle du jeu,* 1939. Produced his own documentaries including *Le Retour,* 1945, with Richard Banks; one on the hospitals of Republican Spain with Herbert Kline, 1937; and *The Europeans,* 1955.
Solo Exhibitions: Julien Levy Gallery, New York, 1932; Museum of Modern Art, New York, 1946, 1987; Grand Palais, Paris, 1969.
Collections: Menil Foundation, Houston, Tex.; Bibliothèque Nationale, Paris; Victoria and Albert Museum, London; Museum of Modern Art, New York; Fine Arts University, Osaka, Japan; and others.

**Muriel Castanis**, United States, b. 1926.
Solo Exhibitions: Robert Moses Plaza, Fordham University at Lincoln Center, New York, 1990; Hokin Gallery, Palm Beach, Fla., 1991; Robert Kidd Gallery, Birmingham, Mich., 1992; O.K. Harris Works of Art, New York, 1993; MTA Flatbush Avenue Station, New York, 1996–97.
Collections: Norton Gallery of Art, West Palm Beach, Fla.; New School for Social Research, New York; Sydney and Frances Lewis Foundation, Richmond, Va.; Palais Mendoub, Morocco; Martin Margulies, Coconut Grove, Fla.; David Bermant, Rye, N.Y.; Technimetrics Inc., New York; Peretz & Marks Inc., New York; Virlane Foundation, New Orleans, La.; Butler Institute of American Art, Youngstown, Ohio; Hanes Family Collection, Winston-Salem, N.C.; Art South Inc., Philadelphia.
Awards: Sculpture Grant Award, Tiffany Foundation, New York; Creative Artists Public Service (CAPS) Grant; Award of Distinction, Virginia Museum of Fine Arts Biennale, Richmond.

**Wendell Castle**, United States, b. 1932.
Studied: University of Kansas, B.F.A., 1958, M.F.A., 1961.
Solo Exhibitions: Detroit Institute of Arts, Mich., 1989–91; American Craft Museum, New York, 1989–91; Peter Joseph Gallery, New York, 1991, 1993, 1995; Edwin A. Ulrich Museum of Art, Wichita State University, Kans., 1994; Carleton College Art Gallery, Northfield, Mich., 1994; Anne Reed Gallery, Ketchum, Idaho, 1995; College of Architecture and Design, Kansas State University, Manhattan, 1995.
Collections: Addison Gallery of American Art, Andover, Mass.; American Craft Museum, New York; Art Institute of Chicago; Brooklyn Museum, N.Y.; Detroit Institute of Arts, Mich.; Lannan Foundation Collection; Metropolitan Museum of Art, New York; Museum of Decorative Arts, Montreal, Canada; Philadelphia Museum of Art; Renwick Gallery of the National Museum of American Art, Smithsonian Institution, Washington, D.C.; White House, Washington, D.C.; Wolfsonian Foundation, Miami Beach, Fla.
Awards: Honorary Doctorate of Humane Letters, St. John Fisher College, Rochester, N.Y.; National Endowment for the Arts Visual Artists Fellowship; Visionaries of the American Craft Movement, American Craft Museum; Artist in Residence, Rochester Institute of Technology, School for American Crafts, N.Y.

**César** (Baldaccini), France, b. 1924.
Studied: Ecole des Beaux-Arts, Marseilles.
Exhibits: Throughout the United States, South America, and Japan.

**Nek Chand**, India.
Studied: Self-taught.
Work: A folk artist, Chand began his life-long work creating the Rock Garden, or Kingdom of Gods and Goddesses, in Chandigarh, India, in 1958. He was assisted by his wife, Kamala. When the garden was discovered by government officials in 1972, it already occupied several acres. After a great official uproar, the government decided to sanction the work, pay the artist an official salary, and assign sixty acres and hundreds of workers to the project. Other permanent installations include the entrance to the Capitol Children's Museum, Washington, D.C. In 1980 Chand installed a temporary exhibit of sculpture that he gave to the children of France at the Centre Georges Pompidou in Paris.

**Jean-Philippe Charbonnier**, France, b. 1921.
Taught: College d'Art et Technologie, Derby, France, 1976–83.
Solo Exhibitions: Maison de la Culture, Le Havre, France, 1972; Photographers Gallery, London, 1972; Cultural Center, Brussels, 1974; French Institute, Stockholm, 1974; Cultural Center, Berlin, 1976; Agathe Gaillard Galerie, Paris, 1976, 1978; Galerie Nagel, Berlin, 1976, 1978; Galerie Penning, Eindhoven, the Netherlands, 1980; retrospective exhibition, Musée d'Art Modern de la Ville de Paris, 1983; Cultural Center, Chicago, 1983; Musée de l'Elysee, Lausanne, 1984; Centre Photographique, Stockholm, 1984.

**Christo** (Christo Javacheff), Bulgaria, b. 1935. Resides in United States.
Studied: Fine Arts Academy, Sofia, Bulgaria, 1955–56.
**Jeanne-Claude** (de Guillebon), Morocco, b. 1935. Resides in United States.
Studied: University of Tunis, 1952.
Selected Joint Projects: *The Pont-Neuf Wrapped,* Paris, 1985; *The Umbrellas,* Japan–United States, 1991; *Wrapped Reichstag,* Berlin, 1995.
Joint Exhibitions: Throughout Europe, Australia, Argentina, Japan, Canada, United Arab Emirates, Brazil, Korea.
Awards: Medaille des Arts Plastiques, Fondation d'Academie d'Architecture, Paris; National Arts Club Gold Medal of Honor, New York; Establishment of the Jeanne-Claude and Christo Visual Arts Scholarship by the College of Saint Rose, Albany, N.Y.; Doctorates in the Arts, Manhattanville College, Purchase, N.Y.; Doctorates of Fine Arts, Pratt Institute, Brooklyn, N.Y.; Doctorates Philosophiae Honoris Causa, Humboldt University, Berlin; Crystal Award, World Economic Forum, Davos, Switzerland; Bambi Award for Culture, Munich; Praemium Imperiale Award for Outstanding Achievements in the Arts, Tokyo; Doctorates of Fine Arts, Connecticut College, New London.

**Kyung-Youn Chung**, Korea, b. 1955.
Studied: Hong-Ik University, Seoul, 1973–75; Massachusetts College of Art, B.F.A., 1978; Rhode Island School of Design, M.A.E., 1979.
Taught: Hong-Ik University, Seoul.
Solo Exhibitions: Gallery Hyundai, Seoul, 1990; Lynn City Museum, Mass., 1992; Museum of Fine Arts, Boston, 1993; Moscow Industrial and Applied Arts Institute Exhibition Hall, 1995; Gallery Hankuk, Seoul, 1995.
Collections: National Museum of Contemporary Art, Seoul, and others.
Awards: Bronze Award, Baghdad International Festival of Art; Prize of '88 Korea Reporters' Association; Prize at the First International Suk-Ju of Art; Special Award, Osaka Triennale 90.

**Colette**, Tunisia, b. 1947. Resides in United States.
Solo Exhibitions: Carol Johnssen, Munich, 1990; Kunsthalle, Remchingen, Germany, 1994; Gallery Lok, New York, 1994; Beatrice Wasserman Gallery, Cologne, 1994; Uptown Downtown Gallery, New York, 1995; Eugenia Cucalon Gallery, New York.
Collections: Aldrich Museum of Contemporary Art, Ridgefield, Conn.; Brooklyn Museum, N.Y.; Ludwig Museum, Cologne, Germany; Solomon R. Guggenheim Museum, New York; Newport Harbor Art Museum, Los Angeles; Weatherspoon Art Museum, N.C.; Museum of Contemporary Art, Los Angeles; Florida International University Museum, Miami.

**Maureen Connor**, United States, b. 1947.
Studied: Pratt Institute, New York, M.F.A. 1973.
Professional Work: Visiting sculptor, School of the Museum of Fine Arts, Boston.
Solo Exhibitions: Simon Watson Gallery, 1992; Germans van Eck, New York, 1992; Alternative Museum, New York, 1994–95; P.P.O.W. New York, 1995; Baxter Gallery, Maine College of Art, Portland, 1995; William F. Brush Gallery, St. Lawrence University, Canton, N.Y., 1996; Galerie Sima, Nuremberg, Germany, 1996; Kunstraum Munich, Germany, 1997.
Collections: Best Products, Virginia; Bellevue Hospital, New York.
Awards: New York Experimental Glass Workshop; P.S.C. CUNY Grant, Research Foundation, City University of New York; John Simon Guggenheim Memorial Foundation Fellowship; National Endowment for the Arts Visual Artists Fellowship.

**Leo Copers**, Belgium, b. 1947.
Solo Exhibitions: Kunstforum, Munich, 1990; Museum van Hedendaagse Kunst, Antwerp, 1990; Galerie Bellamy 19, Vlissingen, the Netherlands, 1990; Galerie Six Friedrich, Munich, 1990, 1993; Galerie Ric Urmel, Ghent, Belgium, 1991, 1992; Jack Tilton Gallery, New York, 1991, 1997; Galerie Carstans, Berlin, 1992; Provinciaal Museum, Hasselt, Belgium, 1993; Galerie Isy Brachot, Brussels, 1994; De Watertoren, Vlissingen, the Netherlands, 1994; Vera Van Laar Galerij, Antwerp, Belgium, 1997.

**Imogen Cunningham**, United States, 1883–1976.
Studied: University of Washington, Seattle; received the national Pi Beta Phi Scholarship to Technische Hochschule, Dresden.
Solo Exhibitions: Brooklyn Institute of Arts and Sciences, N.Y., 1912; Los Angeles County Museum, Calif., 1932; M. H. de Young Memorial Museum, San Francisco, Calif., 1932, 1970; Dallas Art Museum, Tex., 1935; E. B. Crocker Art Gallery, Sacramento, Calif., 1936; San Francisco Museum of Art, Calif., 1951, 1954, 1964; Mills College, Oakland, Calif., 1953; Cincinnati Museum of Art, Ohio, 1956; Oakland Museum, Calif., 1957; George Eastman House, Rochester, N.Y., 1961; Art Institute of Chicago, 1964; Henry Gallery, University of Washington, Seattle, 1965, 1974; Stanford Art Gallery, Stanford University, Palo Alto, Calif., 1967, 1976; California College of Arts and Crafts Gallery, Oakland, Calif., 1968; Focus Gallery, San Francisco, 1968; Museum of History and Technology, Smithsonian Institution, Washington, D.C., 1968–69; Friends of Photography Gallery, Carmel, Calif., 1971; Witkin Gallery, New York; Metropolitan Museum of Art, New York, 1973; Grapestake Gallery, San Francisco, 1976; Japan, Sweden, Finland, England, Denmark, 1981–96; and others.
Traveling Solo Exhibitions: throughout Japan with cooperation of Shadai Gallery, Tokyo, and U.S. Information Service, 1977–78; throughout Europe by the Western Association of Art Museums, 1977–78; throughout the United States by the American Federation of Arts, 1983–86; Arts America Exhibition in Europe, 1987–90.
Collections: major holdings in George Eastman House, Rochester, N.Y.; Museum of Modern Art, New York; and others.
Awards: Honorary Member of American Society of Magazine Photographers; establishment of Imogen Cunningham Trust to Reproduce and Preserve Work; Honorary Doctorate of Fine Arts, California College of Arts and Crafts, Oakland.

**Salvador Dalí**, Spain, 1904–89.
A painter, printmaker, and filmmaker associated with the Surrealist movement. His meticulously rendered paintings of dreamlike images influenced the Magic Realists who followed. Dalí collaborated with Luis Buñuel on two films, *Un Chien andalou* (1928) and *L'Age d'or* (1931). In the last fifty years of his life Dalí concentrated on creating his own public image, based upon his outrageous depictions of his own face, which became his strongest professional signature. He produced numerous editions of prints that he signed before the image was placed on the paper, an affront to many but a Surrealist act to others. His paintings are in the collections of major museums across the Western world.

**Betsy Damon**, United States, b. 1940.
Studied: Skidmore College, Sarasota Springs, N.Y., B.A., 1963; Columbia University, New York, M.F.A., 1966.
Taught: Minneapolis College of Art and Design, Minn., 1990; University of Minnesota, 1991; Hubert Humphrey Institute, Minneapolis, Minn., 1991, 1992; "Keepers of the Waters" Workshop for Anoka Citizens, Minn., 1992; Trinity University, San Antonio, Tex., 1993; Humboldt State University, Arcata, Calif., 1993.
Solo Exhibitions: Blue Star Gallery, San Antonio, Tex., 1991; Hubert Humphrey Institute for Public Policy and Walker Arts Center, Minneapolis, 1991–92; Trinity University Gallery, San Antonio, Tex., 1993.
Public Works: "Keepers of the Waters" collaboration with Hubert Humphrey Institute for Public Policy, Minnesota Extension Service, and Water Resource Research Center, 1991; Northern Waters Network, Wisc., 1994; Swede Hollow Park and Community, St. Paul, Minn., 1995; art and science collaborations in high schools in Chengdu, China, 1995; four

parks in Chengdu, China, 1996; Lhasa, Tibet, 1996.
Awards: Artist Grant, Artists Space; Threshold Foundation Grant; Ruth Chenven Foundation Grant; New York Foundation for the Arts Fellowship; Mid-Life Career Award, Women's Caucus for Art, San Francisco; National Endowment for the Arts Visual Artists Fellowship; Jerome Foundation Grant for workshops for artists and scientists; Arts Midwest Grant; Jerome Foundation Travel Grant to China; Bush Fellowship.

**Mary Woodard Davis**, United States, 1900–1990.
Studied: University of Oklahoma; Royal College of Needlework, London.
Taught: Fordham University, New York. Founded the Textile Workshops, Santa Fe, N.M., 1967.
Work: Costume designer for Broadway shows, New York; designer of children's clothing line; worked with the W.P.A. Washington Theater Project, Washington, D.C.; worked in Ankara, Turkey, developing cottage industry for silk-screened fabrics.
Solo Exhibitions: Craig Cornelius Gallery, New York, 1984; North Dakota Museum of Art, Grand Forks, 1985.

**Sonia Delaunay**, Russia, 1885–1979.
Studied: Academy, Karlsruhe, Germany, 1903–4; Academie de la Palette, Paris, 1905.
Solo Exhibitions: first solo exhibition, Galerie Notre-Dame-des-Champs, 1908; Italy, Israel, England; major retrospectives at Gimpel Fils, London, 1966; Musée National d'Art Modern, Paris, 1967; Corcoran Gallery, Washington, D.C., 1971.

**Donatello**, Italy, c.1386–1466.

**Michele Oka Doner**, United States, b. 1945.
Studied: University of Michigan, Ann Arbor, M.F.A., 1968.
Solo Exhibitions: Art et Industrie, New York, 1989, 1990; Meadow Brook Art Gallery, Oakland University, Rochester, Mich., 1990; Alice Simsar Gallery, Ann Arbor, Mich., 1990; Pewabic Society, Detroit, Mich., 1990; Feigenson/Preston Gallery, Detroit, Mich., 1991.
Public Installations: Hayden Planetarium, American Museum of Natural History, New York; Woodstock Artists' Cemetery, N.Y.; Children's Museum of Manhattan, New York; Herald Square Subway Complex, New York; Venice, Italy, Project; City of Santa Monica, Calif.; Feldpausch, Zurich; Criminal Justice Center, Philadelphia; Miami International Airport, Fla.; School of Physics, University of Michigan, Ann Arbor, 1996; Washington National Airport, Alexandria, Va.
Collections: Art Institute of Chicago; Cooper-Hewitt National Design Museum, Smithsonian Institution, New York; Detroit Institute of Arts, Mich.; Philip Morris Collection, New York; John and Mable Ringling Museum, Sarasota, Fla.; Lannan Foundation, Lake Worth, Fla.; University of Michigan Museum of Art, Ann Arbor; American Craft Museum, New York; Kellogg Foundation, Battle Creek, Mich.; Syz Collection, Geneva; Chateau Menetou, France; Tampa Museum of Science and Industry, Fla.; Michigan Botanical Gardens, Grand Rapids.

**Margaretha Dubach**, Switzerland, b. 1938.
Studied: Kunstgewerbeschule, Lucerne, 1955–60.
Solo Exhibitions: Galerie Krebs, Bern, 1990, 1995; Galerie zur blauen Schnecke, Zurich, 1991; Zyt Galerie, Sempach, 1991, 1993; Galerie Farel, Aigle, 1991, 1996; Museum Bellerive, 1993; Galerie Esther Hufschmid, Zurich, 1993, 1996; Galerie Zimmermannhaus, Bruges, Belgium, 1994; Galerie Falkengasse, Bruges, Belgium, 1994; Medizinhistorisches Museum der Universität Zurich, 1994–95, 1996; Kornschutte Rathaus, Lucerne, 1995; Stadtmuseum Lindau, Germany, 1995; Galerie Marianne Brand, Geneva, 1995.
Awards: Prize of the City of Geneva; Swiss Center, London.

**Marcel Duchamp**, France, 1887–1968. Became U.S. citizen in 1947.
Studied: Painting at Academie Julian, 1904–5.
Exhibited in France and United States from 1909 until his death. Lived in the United States for several years starting in 1915, leaving briefly to live in Argentina, and revisited Europe until his return to New York in 1920. Cofounder with Katherine Dreier and Man Ray of the Société Anonyme, 1920. First puns published in 1921. "Ready-mades" shown in Paris, 1936. Participated in the organization of the International Exhibition of Surrealism, 1938. First painting sold to Museum of Modern Art, New York, 1945. Lectured and participated in exhibitions throughout the U.S. In 1964 Galleria Schwarz in Milan produced thirteen Ready-mades in editions of eight signed and numbered copies.

**Camrose Ducote**, United States, b. 1952.
Education: Self-taught.

**Mary Beth Edelson**, United States.
Studied: School of the Art Institute of Chicago; DePauw University, Ind., B.A.; New York University, New York, M.A.
Solo Exhibitions: Solan/Maxwell, New York, 1990; A/C Project Room, New York, 1993; Nicole Klagsbrun Gallery, New York, 1993; Creative Time, New York, 1994–95; Nicolain Wallner Gallery, Copenhagen, 1996.
Collections: Solomon R. Guggenheim Museum, New York; Walker Art Center, Minneapolis, Minn.; National Museum of American Art, Smithsonian Institution, Washington, D.C.; National Museum of Women in the Arts, Washington, D.C.; Museum of Contemporary Art, Chicago; Corcoran Gallery of Art, Washington, D.C.; Indianapolis Museum of Art, Ind.; Detroit Institute of Art, Mich.; Museum of Modern Art, New York.
Awards: Honorary Doctorate of Fine Arts, DePauw University, Ind.

**Helen Escobedo**, Mexico, b. 1934.
Studied: Royal College of Art, London.
Solo Exhibitions: Galeria Sloane, Mexico City, 1990; Ordrup Samlung Museum, Copenhagen, 1990; Musée de Quebec, Canada, 1992; Exconvento de Sta. Teresa, Mexico City, 1993; Universities Field Staff International–Institute of World Affairs, Antwerp, Belgium, 1993; Museo de Arte Contemporaneo Sofia Imber, Caracas, Venezuela, 1995; Winnipeg Art Gallery, Canada, 1996.
Installations: Faculty of Political Science, Universidad Nacional Autonoma de Mexico, Mexico City, 1991; Bosque de Chapultepec, Mexico City, 1991; Helsingin Kaupungin Taidemuseo, Helsinki, 1991; Balliol St. John's and University College, Museum of Modern Art, Oxford, England, 1992; Parque de la Paz, San Jose, Costa Rica, 1993; Tel Aviv, Israel, 1993; Cuba Biennale, Havana, 1994; Longueuil Park, Montreal, Canada, 1995; Museum Wurth and Kunsthalle, Düsseldorf, Germany, 1995; Foundation Derovin, Val David, Quebec, Canada, 1996.
Awards: Tlatlico Prize for Sculpture, Palace of Fine Arts, Mexico City; Competition Award, National University of Mexico; finalist, International Water Competition for New Orleans World Exhibition; Elected Associate Member, Academie Royale de Sciences, Lettres, et Beaux-Arts de Belgique; John Simon Guggenheim Memorial Foundation Fellowship; second prize, Centro Cultural Tijuana, Mexico.

**Barbara Ferguson** (Burns), United States, b. 1958.
Studied: Virginia Polytechnic Institute and State University, B.A. in Architecture, 1982; M.A. in Architecture, 1983.
Work: Became a registered architect in 1992 and established her own practice.
Exhibitions: As a quilt maker she exhibits in the Arlington, Va., area, especially with the Alexandria Quilters.

**Lucio Fontana**, Italy, 1899 (Argentina)–1968.
Studied: Accademia di Brera, Milan, 1928.
Solo Exhibitions: Galleria del Milione, Milan, 1930; Martha Jackson Gallery, New York, 1960; retrospective exhibition, Walker Art Center, Minneapolis, Minn., 1966; Marlborough-Gerson Gallery, New York, 1967; Stedelijk Museum, Amsterdam, 1967; retrospective exhibition, Solomon R. Guggenheim Museum, New York, 1977; retrospective exhibition, Centre Georges Pompidou, Paris, 1988.
Other Exhibitions: Museum of Modern Art, New York, 1949; Documenta, Kassel, Germany, 1959; Fifth São Paulo Biennale, 1959; Palazzo Grassi, Venice, 1960.

**Mariano Fortuny de Madrazo**, Spain, 1871–1949. Resided in Italy.
Fortuny was a painter and inventor who revolutionized fashion. From Art Nouveau he developed the idea of a natural uncorseted dress that flowed over the body, allowing freedom of movement to the wearer. His interest in light led him to invent new ways of handling fabric and dying cloth. In 1909 in Paris he patented his Delphos dress and his method of pleating. After perfecting pleated silk he turned his attention to printed velvet. Again he patented his method of stenciling the velvet. In his studio at the Palazzo Orfei in Venice he both created and oversaw all aspects of his designs, from developing his unique vegetable-based colors to his own dying methods, from the making of screen blocks to pattern designs. Today his clothing and fabrics are collected by museums all over the world.

**Regina Frank** (The Artist is Present), Germany.
Studied: Hochschule der Kunste, Berlin, M.A.
Solo Exhibitions: Leuschnerdamn 37b, Berlin, 1990; Wallgrabentheater, Freiburg, Germany, 1990; Rathaus, Freiburg, Germany, 1990; Bundesrat, Bonn, Germany, 1991; Gallery Wilfriede Maab, Berlin, 1992; Gallery Wewerka, Berlin, 1994.
Performance Installations: *Natura Viva* (in the pond), Akademie der Kunste, Elanseatenweg, Berlin; *Searching for Babata,* Window in City–Center in Desert–Kibbutz Mizpe Ramon, Israel; *Hermes' Mistress,* Bronx Museum, N.Y.; Museum of Contemporary Art, Los Angeles; Performance Index throughout Basel, Switzerland; Winnipeg Art Gallery, Canada.

**Floriana Frassetto**, United States, b. 1950.
Created Mummenschanz with collaborators Andres Bossard and Bernie Schurch.

**Julio Fuentes**, Mexico, b. c.1914.

**Frank Garcia**, United States, b. 1931.
Studied: Textile Institute, New York, 1950s.
Professional work: Costume Director for Nikolais Dance Theatre and Murray Louis Dance Company.

**John Garrett**, United States, b. 1950.
Studied: Claremont McKenna College, Calif., B.A., 1972; University of California, Los Angeles, M.A., 1976.
Taught: University of California, Los Angeles.
Solo Exhibitions: Art Store Gallery, Los Angeles, 1987; Crain/Wolov Gallery, Tulsa, Okla., 1989; Suzanne Brown Gallery, Scottsdale, Ariz., 1991; Schneider-Bluhm-Loeb Gallery, Chicago, 1992; Worth Gallery, Taos, N. Mex., 1992, 1994, 1995, 1996; Brown-Grotta Gallery, Conn., 1995.
Collections: American Craft Museum, New York; Erie Art Museum, Pa.; High Museum of Art, Atlanta; Oakland Museum, Calif.; Albuquerque Museum, N. Mex.; Craft and Folk Art Museum, Los Angeles; Harvard University, Cambridge, Mass.
Awards: National Endowment for the Arts Visual Artists Fellowship.

**Sam Gilliam**, United States, b. 1933.
Studied: University of Louisville, Ky., B.A., 1955, M.A., 1961.
Taught: Carnegie Mellon University, Pittsburgh, 1985–89.
Solo Exhibitions: Galerie Darthea Speyer, Paris, 1991; Walker Hill Arts Center, Seoul, 1991; American Craft Museum, New York, 1991; United States Information Agency exhibition in Helsinki, 1992; Whitney Museum of American Art at Philip Morris, New York, 1994–95; J. B. Speed Art Museum, Louisville, Ky., 1996; Baumgartner Galleries, Washington, D.C., 1996.
Collections: Art Institute of Chicago; Baltimore Museum of Art, Md.; Boymans–van Beuningen Museum, Rotterdam, the Netherlands; Museum of Art, Carnegie Institute, Pittsburgh; Cincinnati Museum of Art, Ohio; Corcoran Gallery of Art, Washington, D.C.; Detroit Institute of Art, Mich.; Greenville Museum of Art, S.C.; High Museum of Art, Atlanta; Hirshhorn Museum and Sculpture Garden, Smithsonian Institution, Washington, D.C.; Howard University, Washington, D.C.; Menil Collection, Houston, Tex.; Metropolitan Museum of Art, New York; Musée d'Art Modern de la Ville de Paris; Museum of African Art, Smithsonian Institution, Washington, D.C.; Museum of Modern Art, New York; National Gallery of Art, Washington, D.C.; Art Museum, Princeton University, N.J.; Studio Museum in Harlem, New York; Tate Gallery, London; Walker Art Center, Minneapolis, Minn.; Whitney Museum of American Art, New York.
Awards: Order of Merit Award, Alumni Association, University of Louisville, Ky.; Honorary Doctorate, Atlanta College of Art; National Endowment for the Arts Visual Artists Fellowship; Honorary Doctorate of Arts and Letters, Northwestern University, Evanston, Ill.; Fellow of the University, University of Louisville, Ky.; Honorary Doctorate, Corcoran Gallery and School of Art, Washington, D.C.

**Robert Gober**, United States, b. 1954.
Studied: Tyler School of Art, Rome, 1973–74; Middlebury College, Vt., B.A., 1976.
Solo Exhibitions: Paula Cooper Gallery, New York, 1990; Tyler School of Art, Philadelphia, 1990; Galleria Marga Paz, Madrid, 1990; Boymans–van Beuningen Museum, Rotterdam, the Netherlands, 1990; Kunsthalle Bern, 1990; Galerie Nationale du Jeu de Paume, Paris, 1991; Museo Nacional Centro de Arte Reina Sofia, Madrid, 1992; Dia Center for the Arts, New York, 1993; Serpentine Gallery, London, 1993; Tate Gallery Liverpool, England, 1993; Galerie Samia Saouma, Paris, 1994; Galerija Dante Marino Cettina, Umag, Croatia, 1995; Museum für Gegenwartskunst, Basel, Switzerland, 1995–96; Max Hetzler Gallery, Berlin, 1996; Museum of Contemporary Art, Los Angeles, 1997.

**Misha Gordin**, United States, b. 1946 (Latvia).
Solo Exhibitions: New Gallery, Bemis Project, Omaha, Nebr., 1990; Mark Masouka Gallery, Las Vegas, Nev., 1990, 1991; Klein Art Works, Chicago, 1991, 1994; Bentley-Tomlinson Gallery, Scottsdale, Ariz., 1992; Dennas Museum Center, Northwestern Michigan University, Traverse City, 1993; Morgan Gallery, Kansas City, Mo., 1994; North Dakota Museum of Art, Grand Forks, 1994; Bentley Gallery, Scottsdale, Ariz., 1995; Thomson Gallery, Minneapolis, Minn., 1995; Cedar Rapids Museum of Art, Iowa, 1996.
Collections: Art Institute of Chicago; Everson Museum of Art, Syracuse, N.Y.; International Museum of Photography, Rochester, N.Y.; Jesse Besser Museum, Alpena, Mich.; Musée National d'Art Modern, Centre Georges Pompidou, Paris; National Museum of Modern Art, Kyoto; North Dakota Museum of Art, Grand Forks; Toledo Museum of Art, Ohio.
Awards: Gold Medal, Salon International d'Art Photographique, Demain, France; National Endowment for the Arts Visual Artists Fellowship.

**Daniel Graffin**, France, b. 1938.
Studied: Polytechnic School of Art, London, 1956; Ecole des Metiers d'Art, Paris, 1957; with the architect Ramses Wissa Wassal in Cairo, 1962.
Solo Exhibitions: Kahlemberg Gallery, Santa Fe, N. Mex., 1990; Centre d'Art Contemporain, Meru, France, 1990; Centre d'Art Contemporain, Redu, Belgium, 1990; Configura, Erfurt, Germany, 1991; Cultural Services, Consulate General of France, New York, 1992; AB Galerie, Paris, 1993; Gallery Shapiro, Mexico, 1995; Venice Biennale, Italy, 1995; Museo Marco, Monterrey, Mexico, 1996.
Sculpture Installations: AT&T, Basking Ridge, N.J.; Hotel Camino Real, Cancun, Mexico; International House System, Brussels; Hotel Intercontinental Riyadh, Saudi Arabia; Northwestern National Bank, St. Paul, Minn.; B.O.A.D., Lome, Togo; Hyatt Hotel, Woodfield, Ill.; Graybar Corp., Clayton, Mo.; Kimberly Clark Corp., Neenah, Wisc.; PIC Corp., Dallas; King Saud University, Riyadh, Saudi Arabia; Marriott Marquis Hotel, Atlanta; Marina Center Hotel, Singapore; Société des Autoroutes Paris-Rhin-Rhône (SAPRR), France; Adaron Group Headquarters, Southern Life Center, Greensboro, N.C.; Central Diagnostic Laboratory, Los Angeles; Tour AGF, Paris; Homart Development, Sacramento; Société ESCOTA, Alpes de Hautes-Provence, Sistern; Fuqua School of Business, Duke University, Durham, N.C.; Sears, Chicago; "100 Reaumur," Paris; Hotel des Impôts, Antibes, France.
Awards: Mention Speciale du Jury for film *Faces AU vent,* Beaubourg Art Film Festival, France.

**Ann Hamilton**, United States, b. 1956.
Studied: St. Lawrence University, Canton, N.Y., 1974–76; University of Kansas, B.F.A., 1979; Yale School of Art, M.F.A., 1985.
Taught: University of California, Santa Barbara, 1985–91.
Solo Exhibitions: San Diego Museum of Contemporary Art, La Jolla, 1990; Louver Gallery, New York, 1991; Twenty-First International São Paulo Biennale, Brazil, 1991; List Visual Art Center, Massachusetts Institute of Technology, Cambridge, Mass., 1992; Walker Art Center, Minneapolis, Minn., 1992; Dia Center for the Arts, New York, 1993; Museum of Modern Art, New York, 1994; Tate Gallery Liverpool, England, 1994; Institute of Contemporary Art, Philadelphia, 1995; Stedelijk Van Abbe Museum, Eindhoven, the Netherlands, 1996; Wexner Center for the Arts, Columbus, Ohio, 1996.
Awards: Louis Comfort Tiffany Foundation Award; Skowhegan Medal for Sculpture; College Art Association Artist Award; National Endowment for the Arts Visual Arts Fellowship; MacArthur Foundation Fellowship.

**Harmony Hammond**, United States, b. 1944.
Collections: Phoenix Art Museum, Ariz.; Metropolitan Museum of Art, New York; Art Institute of Chicago; Fine Arts Museum of New Mexico, Santa Fe; Wadsworth Atheneum, Hartford, Conn.; Museum of Contemporary Art, Chicago; Brooklyn Museum of Art, N.Y.; Philip Morris Company, New York; General Mills Corporation, Minneapolis, Minn.; Notre Dame University, Ind.; St. Thomas Aquinas Church, St. Paul, Minn.; Chemical Bank, New York.
Awards: MacDowell Colony Fellowship; Yaddo Fellowship; National Endowment for the Arts Visual Artists Fellowship; Creative Artists Public Service (CAPS) Grant, New York State Council on the Arts; Money For Women Fund Grant.

**David Hammons**, United States, b. 1943.
Studied: Chouinard Art Institute, Los Angeles, 1968; Otis Art Institute of Parsons School of Design, Los Angeles, 1968–72.
Solo Exhibitions: Institute for Contemporary Art, P.S. 1 Museum, Long Island City, N.Y., 1990; Jack Tilton Gallery, New York, 1990, 1991; Institute of Contemporary Art, Philadelphia, 1991; San Diego Museum of Contemporary Art, La Jolla, Calif., 1991; American Academy in Rome, 1992; Illinois State Museum, Springfield, 1993; Williams College Art Center, Williamstown, Mass., 1993; Museum of Modern Art, San Francisco, 1993; Veravitagioia, Milan, 1994; Sara Penn/Knobkerry, New York, 1994; Salzberger Kunstverein, Austria, 1995.
Awards: National Endowment for the Arts Visual Artists Fellowship; New York State Council on the Arts Artist Grant; John Simon Guggenheim Memorial Foundation Fellowship; Art Matters, New York; Foundation for the Arts; Rome Prize, American Academy in Rome; Tiffany Grant; Brendan Gill Award, Municipal Art Society; MacArthur Foundation Fellowship; D.A.A.D., Berlin.

**Lloyd Hamrol**, United States, b. 1937.
Studied: University of California, Los Angeles, B.A., 1959, M.A. 1963.
Collections: Smithsonian Institution, Washington, D.C.; Los Angeles County Museum of Art, Calif.; Pasadena Museum of Modern Art, Calif.; Lannan Foundation, Palm Beach, Fla.
Awards: National Endowment for the Arts Visual Artists Fellowship.

**Judith Morrill Hanes**, United States, b. 1950.
Studied: Wellesley College, Mass., B.A., 1971.

**Tim Harding**, United States.
Studied: Hamline University, St. Paul, Minn., B.A.; Minneapolis College of Art and Design, Minn.
Solo Exhibitions: Center for Tapestry Arts, New York, 1991; Art Complex Museum, Duxbury, Mass., 1992; American Craft Museum, New York, 1992.
Collections: U.S. Embassy, Bangkok, Thailand; University of St. Thomas Museum, St. Paul, Minn.; American Craft Museum, New York; Minnesota Museum of Art, St. Paul; Cooper-Hewitt National Design Museum, Smithsonian Institution, New York; Neutrogena Corporation, Los Angeles.
Awards: IGEDO, International Textile Foundation, Tokyo; National Endowment for the Arts Visual Artists Fellowship.

**Anne Healy**, United States, b. 1939.
Studied: Queens College, City University of New York, B.A., 1962.
Taught: University of California, Berkeley, 1993; Art Commissioner, San Francisco Arts Commission, 1992– .
Solo Exhibitions: Art Institute of Southern California, Laguna Beach, 1989; Saint Peter's Church, New York, 1990.
Collections: State of Washington Arts Commission, Olympia; City of Oakland, Calif.; Litton Industries, Los Colinas, Tex.; Stanford University, Palo Alto, Calif.; State of Washington Arts Commission, Olympia.
Awards: Travel Grant, University of California, Berkeley, 1987, 1992, 1995; Academic Senate Committee on Research Grant in Aid of Research, University of California, Berkeley, 1988–89; Academic Senate Committee on Teaching Grant, University of California, Berkeley, 1988–89; Humanities Research Fellowship, University of California, Berkeley, 1988–89, 1994–95.

**Nancy Hemenway**, United States, b. 1920.
Studied: Wheaton College, Mass., B.A.; Graduate School of Music, Harvard University, 1941–42; Art Students League, New York, 1961–64; Graduate School of Arts and Sciences, Columbia University, New York, 1961–64.
Solo Exhibitions: Carpenter Center for the Visual Arts, Harvard University, Cambridge, Mass., 1991; DePauw University, Emison Art Center, Greencastle, Ind., 1994; Boothbay Region Art Foundation, Boothbay Harbor, Maine, 1995; Maine College of Art, Baxter Gallery, Portland, 1995; Bates College Museum of Art, Olin Art Center, Lewiston, Maine, 1996; Portland School of Art, Maine, 1995–96.
Awards: Deborah Morton Award, Westbrook College, Portland, Maine; National Endowment for the Arts Visual Artists Fellowship; Honorary Doctorate of Fine Arts, Wheaton College, Norton, Mass.

**Donna Henes**, United States, b. 1945.
Solo Exhibitions: Connemara Nature Conservancy, Dallas, 1991; Islip Art Museum, East Islip, N.Y., 1993, 1995.
Performances: Since 1972 has created installations and produced public participatory events in museums, universities, parks, plazas, and institutes in more than fifty cities in nine countries.
Books: Author of *Celestial Auspicious Occasions: Seasons, Cycles, and Celebrations; Dressing Our Wounds in Warm Clothes;* and *Noting the Process of Noting the Process.*
Awards: New York Foundation for the Arts Fellowship; National Endowment for the Arts Visual Artists Fellowship; National Endowment for the Arts Interarts Grant.

**Eva Hesse**, United States, 1936 (Germany)–1970.
Studied: Cooper Union, New York, 1954–57; Yale University, New Haven, Conn., 1959.
Solo Exhibitions: Robert Miller Gallery, New York, 1991 (traveled to Galerie Renos Xippas, Paris, 1991); Yale University Art Gallery, New Haven, Conn., 1992 (traveled to Hirshhorn Museum and Sculpture Garden, Smithsonian Institution, Washington, D.C., 1992–93).
Collections: Kunsthalle, Düsseldorf, Germany; Museum of Modern Art, New York; Art Institute of Chicago; Whitney Museum of American Art, New York, Krefeld Museum, Germany; Allen Memorial Art Museum, Oberlin College, Ohio; Weatherspoon Gallery, University of North Carolina, Greensboro; Aldrich Museum of Contemporary Art, Ridgefield, Conn.; Rijksmuseum Kröller–Müller, Otterlo, the Netherlands; Wexner Center for the Visual Arts, Ohio State University, Columbus; Milwaukee Art Center, Wisc.; Wallraf Richartz Museum, Cologne; Tate Gallery, London; Moderna Museet, Stockholm; National Museum of Women in the Arts, Washington, D.C.; Israel Museum, Jerusalem; University Art Museum, University of California, Berkeley; Solomon R. Guggenheim Museum, New York; National Gallery of Australia, Canberra; Albright–Knox Art Gallery, Buffalo, N.Y.; Musée National d'Art Modern, Centre Georges Pompidou, Paris.

**Sheila Hicks**, United States, b. 1934.
Studied: Yale University School of Art, New Haven, Conn., B.F.A., 1957, M.F.A., 1959.
Solo Exhibitions: Matsuya Ginza, Tokyo, 1990; Seoul Art Center, 1991; Kajima, Tokyo, 1991; National Museum of Decorative Arts, Prague, Czech Republic, 1992; Perimeter Gallery, Chicago, 1995; Museum of Nebraska Art, Kearney, 1996; Century Association, New York, 1997.
Collections: Metropolitan Museum of Art, New York; Museum of Modern Art, New York; Art Institute of Chicago; Stedelijk Museum, Amsterdam; Museums of Modern Art, Tokyo and Kyoto; Centre Georges Pompidou, Paris; Philadelphia Museum of Art; Minneapolis Institute of Art, Minn.; Musée des Arts Decoratifs, Paris; Musée des Arts Decoratifs, Prague; Saint Louis Art Museum; Museo de Bellas Artes, Chile; Museum of Fine Arts, Boston.
Awards: Gold Medal, American Institute of Architects; Medal of Fine Art, French Academy of Architecture; decorated by the French Government, Officier des Arts et Lettres, 1996.

**Yoshiki Hishinuma**, Japan, b. 1958.
Worked at the Miyake Design Studio in Tokyo and as a free-lance designer since 1978. Has exhibited since 1980.

**Soiji Ida**, Japan, b. 1941.
Studied: Kyoto Municipal University of Art, 1965.
Solo Exhibitions: Cincinnati-Chidlaw Gallery, Ohio, 1990; Holly Solomon Gallery, New York, 1990; Sheehan Gallery, Whitman College, Washington, D.C., 1990; Ceramic Art Gallery, Tokyo, 1990; Gallery/K's Studio "Parade," Tokyo, 1996.
Collections: Kyoto Municipal Museum of Art; Victoria and Albert Museum, London; National Museum of Modern Art, Kyoto; National Museum of Modern Art, Tokyo; Museum of Modern Art, New York; Japan Society, New York; Museum of Modern Art, Krakow, Poland; San Francisco Museum of Modern Art, Calif.; Warszawa National Museum, Poland; Walker Art Center, Minneapolis, Minn.; National Museum of Modern Art, Ljubljana, Slovenia; National Museum of Art, Osaka; Los Angeles County Museum of Art, Calif.; British Museum, London; Smithsonian Institution, Washington, D.C.
Awards: Suntory Prize; Grand Prix; Yamaguchi General Prize.

**Tomoko Ishida**, Japan, b. 1958.
Studied: Kyoto Seika University, B.F.A., 1982.

**Kiyomi Iwata**, United States, b. 1941 (Japan).
Studied: Penland School of Crafts, N.C., 1967–68; Virginia Museum of Fine Arts, Richmond, 1967–68; Haystack Mountain School of Crafts, Deer Isle, Maine, 1970, 1973, 1976; New School of Social Research, New York, 1971, 1974–75.
Solo Exhibitions: Contemporary Crafts Gallery, Portland, Ore., 1992; Bellas Artes Gallery, New York, 1992; Newark Museum, N.J., 1994; Perimeter Gallery, Chicago, 1994; Kiang Gallery, Atlanta, 1996; Georgia Museum of Art, Athens, 1996.
Collections: American Craft Museum, New York; Cleveland Museum of Art, Ohio; Newark Museum, N.J.; Georgia Museum of Art, Athens; Rhode Island School of Design Museum of Art, Providence; Charles A. Wustum Museum of Fine Arts, Racine, Wisc.; Erie Art Museum, Pa.; Savaria Museum, Szombathely, Hungary; Long House Foundation, East Hampton, N.Y.; and others.
Awards: National Endowment for the Arts Visual Artists Fellowship; New York Foundation for the Arts Artist Fellowship.

**Catherine Jansen**, United States.
Studied: Cranbrook Academy of Art, Bloomfield Hills, Mich., B.F.A., 1971; Tyler School of Art, Philadelphia, M.F.A., 1976.
Taught: Bucks County Community College, Newtown, Pa.
Solo Exhibitions: Moore College of Art, Philadelphia, 1991; James A. Michener Museum of Art, Doylestown, Pa., 1994; Owen Patrick Gallery, Philadelphia, 1995.
Collections: Philadelphia Museum of Art; Photographic Resource Center, Tucson, Ariz.; High Museum of Art, Atlanta; Honolulu Academy of Arts, Hawaii; John Michael Kohler Art Center, Sheboygen, Wisc.; James A. Michener Museum of Art, Doylestown, Pa.; Smith Klein and Beckman; AARP Corporation; Delaware Bank.
Grants: Individual Artist Grant, Pennsylvania Council of the Arts; Cultural Incentive Grant.

**Lois Johnson**, United States, b. 1942.
Studied: University of North Dakota, Grand Forks, B.S., 1964; University of Wisconsin, Madison, M.F.A., 1966.
Taught: University of the Arts, Philadelphia College of Art and Design, 1967– ; visiting artist and lecturer, Penland School, N.C.; Carnegie Mellon University, Pittsburgh; Arts Center of Alaska, Anchorage; University of Wisconsin, Madison.
Solo Exhibitions: North Dakota Museum of Art, Grand Forks, 1990; Print Club, Philadelphia, 1994.
Collections: National Museum of American Art, Smithsonian Institution, Washington, D.C.; Fogg Art Museum, Harvard University, Cambridge, Mass.; Elvehjem Museum of Art, University of Wisconsin, Madison; North Dakota Museum of Art, Grand Forks; Adolph Dehn Memorial Collection, New York Public Library; Fleming Museum, Burlington, Vt.; Philadelphia Museum of Art; University of Wisconsin Memorial Union Collection, Madison; University of Lethbridge, Alberta, Canada; Metropolitan Museum of Art, New York; University of Tampa, Fla.
Awards: Percent for Art Commission for the City of Philadelphia; University of North Dakota Sioux Alumni Award; Pennsylvania State Council on the Arts Individual Artist Grant.

**Kenneth Josephson**, United States, b. 1932.
Studied: Rochester Institute of Technology, N.Y., B.F.A., 1957; Institute of Design of the Illinois Institute of Technology, Chicago, M.S., 1960.
Taught: School of the Art Institute of Chicago.
Solo Exhibitions: Museum of Contemporary Art, Chicago; Art Institute of Chicago; Rhona Hoffman Gallery, Chicago, 1991; La Serre Gallery, Beaux-Arts de Saint-Etienne, France, 1996.
Collections: Museum of Modern Art, New York; Art Institute of Chicago; Bibliothèque Nationale, Paris; Center for Creative Photography, University of Arizona, Tucson; Fogg Art Museum, Harvard University, Cambridge, Mass.; Fotograficka Museet, Stockholm; Metropolitan Museum of Art, New York; Museum of Contemporary Art, Chicago; San Francisco Museum of Modern Art; National Museum of American Art, Smithsonian Institution, Washington, D.C.
Awards: John Simon Guggenheim Memorial Foundation Fellowship; National Endowment for the Arts Visual Artists Fellowship; Ruttenberg Arts Foundation, Chicago.

**Tadeusz Kantor**, Poland, 1915–90.
Studied: Krakow Academy of Fine Art, 1939.
Work: Founder of the Theatre of Death. Brought to New York by Ellen Stewart, he appeared at La Mama in 1979.
Awards: Obie.

**Rei Kawakubo**, Japan, b. 1942.
Studied: Aesthetics at Keio University, Tokyo.
Work: Following graduation, worked in advertising for Asahi Kasei Textiles, leaving them to become a free-lance photographer's stylist. Unable to find the clothes she wanted for her ads, she created them herself, which led her to start her own company in 1973, of which she is both designer and president. Comme des Garçons Co. now contains several divisions in addition to the women's division, "Homme" for men, "Robe de Chambre," a collection of linens and at-home wear, and "Tricot" knitwear.

**Mike Kelley**, United States, b. 1954.
Studied: University of Michigan, Ann Arbor, B.F.A., 1976; California Institute of the Arts, Valencia, M.F.A., 1978.
Solo Exhibitions: Galerie Ghislaine Hussenot, Paris, 1990; Metro Pictures, New York, 1990, 1992; Hirshhorn Museum and Sculpture Garden, Smithsonian Institution, Washington, D.C., 1991; Jablonka Galerie, Cologne, 1991; Galerie Peter Pakesch, Vienna, 1991; Galeria Juana de Aizpura, Madrid, Spain, 1991, 1995; Institute of Contemporary Art, London, 1992; CAPC Musée d'Art Contemporain, Bordeaux, France, 1992; Portikus, Frankfurt, 1992; Rosamund Felsen Gallery, Los Angeles, Calif., 1992, 1994; Whitney Museum of American Art, New York, 1993; Los Angeles County Museum of Art, Calif., 1993; Kestner-Gesellschaft, Hannover, Germany, 1995; Wako Works of Art, Tokyo, 1996; Museu d'Arte Contemporani, Barcelona, 1997; Center for Contemporary Art, Malmo, Sweden, 1997; Stedelijk Van Abbe Museum, Eindhoven, the Netherlands, 1997.
Collections: CAPC Musée d'Art Contemporain, Bordeaux, France; Eli Broad Family Foundation, Los Angeles; Lannan Foundation, Los Angeles; Los Angeles County Museum; Museum Boymans–van Beuningen, Rotterdam; Museum Moderner Kunst, Vienna; Museum of Contemporary Art, Los Angeles; Museum of Fine Arts, Boston; Museum of Modern Art, New York; Museum van Hedendaagse Kunst, Ghent, Belgium; Whitney Museum of American Art, New York.
Awards: Louis Comfort Tiffany Foundation Award; National Endowment for the Arts Visual Artists Fellowship.

**William King**, United States, b. 1925.
Studied: University of Florida, Tallahassee, 1942–44; Cooper Union Art School, New York, 1945–48; Brooklyn Museum Art School, N.Y., 1949; Academia dei Belle Arti, Rome, 1949–50; Central School, London, 1952.
Taught: Brooklyn Museum Art School, 1952–55; Art Students League, New York, 1968–69; University of Pennsylvania, Philadelphia, 1972–73.
Solo Exhibitions: Terry Dintenfass Gallery, New York, 1990, 1992, 1994, 1996; Simmons Visual Arts Center, Brenau College, Gainsville, Ga., 1992; Pitt Program Council, University of Pittsburgh, 1995; Seacon Square, Bangkok, Thailand, 1996.
Collections: Hirshhorn Museum and Sculpture Garden, Smithsonian Institution, Washington, D.C.; Rose Art Museum, Brandeis University, Waltham, Mass.; Hopkins Art Center, Dartmouth College, Hanover, N.H.; University of California, Berkeley; Guild Hall, East Hampton, N.Y.; Weatherspoon Art Gallery, University of North Carolina, Greensboro; Sara Roby Foundation; Metropolitan Museum of Art, New York; Whitney Museum of American Art, New York; Solomon R. Guggenheim Museum, New York; Los Angeles County Museum; First National Bank of Chicago; Temple University, Philadelphia.
Awards: Cooper Union Art School, Sculpture Prize; Fulbright Grant; Margaret Tiffany Blake Fresco Award; Augustus St.-Gaudens Medal, Cooper Union; Creative Artists Public Service Award and Grant; Distinction Prize, Hakone Open-Air Museum, Japan; Gold Medal, National Academy of Design, New York; Louis Nevelson Award, National Academy of Design, New York.

**Robert Knight**, England, 1921–88.
Studied: Leicester College at Art, 1936–37; Royal Academy of Arts, sporadically, 1950–70.
Solo Exhibitions: Newcastle Polytechnic Gallery, Newcastle-upon-Tyne, England, 1981; Nicholas Treadwell Gallery, London, 1970, 1972, 1974 (London and Düsseldorf), 1981.
Other Exhibitions: Various venues including a 1968 exhibition with the London Group; "Realistic Art in Our Time," Recklinghausen Museum, Germany, and São Paulo Biennale, 1973; "Mythologies Quotidiennes," Musée d'Art Modern de la Ville de Paris, 1980.

**Gerhardt Knodel**, United States, b. 1940.
Studied: University of California, Los Angeles, B.A., 1959–62; California State University at Long Beach, M.A., 1968–70.
Taught: Cranbrook Academy of Art, Bloomfield Hills, Mich., 1970–96, director, 1996– .
Solo Exhibitions: Textile Arts International, Minneapolis, Minn., 1990; Bellas Artes, Santa Fe, N. Mex., 1990; Bellas Artes, New York, 1990; Seattle Pacific University, Wash., 1991; Walker's Point Art Center, Milwaukee, Wisc., 1993; Katie Gingrass Gallery, Milwaukee, Wisc., 1993; Dennos Museum of Art, Traverse City, Mich., 1993; Sybaris Gallery, Royal Oak, Mich., 1993, 1995.
Collections: National Museum of Fine Arts, Washington, D.C.; Cranbrook Academy of Art, Bloomfield Hills, Mich.; Minneapolis Institute of Art, Minn.; Milwaukee Museum of Art, Wisc.; Detroit Institute of Art, Mich.; Rhode Island School of Design, Providence; Wadsworth Atheneum, Hartford, Conn.
Grants: National Endowment for the Arts Visual Artists Fellowship; Michigan Foundation for the Arts Award; Matrix: Midland Award for Excellence in the Arts, Midland Center for the Arts, Mich.; U.S./Japan Fellowship (co-sponsored by the National Endowment for the Arts and the Japanese Cultural Commission); Fellow, American Craft Museum, New York.

**Masakazu Kobayashi**, Japan, b. 1944.
Studied: Kyoto Municipal University of Arts, B.F.A., 1966.
Solo Exhibitions: Gallery Gallery, Kyoto, 1981, 1982, 1984, 1985, 1986, 1987; Gallery UEDA, Tokyo, 1988.
Two-Person Exhibitions: Art Museum of Santa Cruz County, Calif., 1989; Municipal Shijo Gallery, Kyoto, 1990; Komatu Art Space, Tokyo, 1991.
Collections: City of Lausanne, Switzerland; Central Museum of Textiles, Lodz, Poland; National Museum of Modern Art, Kyoto; Philadelphia Museum of Art.
Awards: International Textile Competition Kyoto '87; First Takashimaya Culture Foundation, 1991.

**Hermann Krone**, Germany, 1827–1916.
Acclaimed for portrait daguerreotypes, nude studies, and still lifes, this native of Dresden valued the potential of photography for art and documentation. He was director of the Photographisches Institut in Dresden. In 1872 he published *King's Album of Saxon Cities* to celebrate the golden wedding anniversary of the rulers of Saxony.

**Shiro Kuramata**, Japan, 1934–91.
Studied: Kurasawa Design Institute, 1965.
Work: Established Kuramata Design Office in 1965.
Awards: Ordre des Arts et Lettres, Paris.

**Ewa Kuryluk**, France, b. 1946 (Poland).
Studied: Academy of Fine Arts, Warsaw, M.F.A., 1964–70; Jagiellonian University, Krakow, Ph.D., 1970–73.
Taught: Graduate faculty, adjunct, New School for Social Research, New York, 1988– ; University of California, San Diego, 1991–92; New York University, New York, 1995.
Solo Exhibitions: Art in General, New York, 1990; University of California, San Diego, 1992; Gerlesborgsskolan, Sweden, 1996.
Collections: Bibliothèque Nationale, Paris; Graphische Sammlung Albertina, Vienna; National Humanities Center, Research Triangle Park, N.C.; Bass Museum of Art, Miami Beach, Fla.; National Museum, Warsaw, Poland; National Museum, Wroclaw, Poland; National Museum, Krakow, Poland; National Museum, Poznan, Poland; Museum of Modern Art, Lodz, Poland.
Awards: Fellow of the Italian Government, University of Urbino; Fellow of the European Exchange Program, New York University; Fellow, Institute for the Humanities at New York University; Rockefeller Fellow, National Humanities Center, N.C.; Hodder Fellow, Princeton University, N.J.; Fund for Free Expression Award; General Electric Foundation Award for Younger Writers; Honorary Award, Fourth International Drawing Triennale, Wroclaw, Poland; Rockefeller Fellowship; Asia Cultural Council Fellowship in Japan; Polish Cultural Foundation Award.

**Yayoi Kusama**, Japan, b. 1929.
Studied: Municipal School of Arts and Crafts, Kyoto, Japan, 1948; Art Students League, New York, 1957.
Solo Exhibitions: Nabis Gallery, Tokyo, 1991; Tokyo Art Expo, 1991; Sogetsu Museum of Art, Tokyo, 1992; Japanese Pavilion, Venice Biennale, 1993; Gallerie Valentina Moncada, Rome, 1993; Gallerie d'Arte del Naviglio, Venice, 1993; Fukuoka Art Museum, Japan, 1993; Komagane Kogen Art Museum, Nagano, Japan, 1994; Fuji Television Gallery, Tokyo, 1994; Ota Fine Arts, Tokyo, 1995, 1996; Media of Modern Art Contemporary Gallery, Fukuoka, Japan, 1996; Paula Cooper Gallery, New York, 1996; Robert Miller Gallery, New York, 1996.
Collections: Museum Ludwig, Cologne; Dartmouth College Museum, Hanover, N.H.

**Robert Kushner**, United States, b. 1949.
Studied: University of California, San Diego, B.A., 1971.
Solo Exhibitions: Gloria Luria Gallery, Bar Harbor Islands, Fla., 1990; Gallery Basque, Fukuoka, Japan; Crown Point Press, New York, 1990–91; American Craft Museum, New York, 1991; Holly Solomon Gallery, New York, 1991, 1993; Kunsthallen Brandts Klaedefabrik, Odense, Denmark, 1992; Midtown Payson Galleries, New York, 1992, 1995; Montclair Art Museum, N.J., 1993; Yoshiaki Inoue Gallery, Osaka, 1993, 1996; Gallery APA, Nagoya, Japan, 1994; Crown Point Press, San Francisco, Calif., 1994; Barbara Scott Gallery, Miami Beach, Fla., 1995.
Collections: Albright-Knox Art Gallery, Buffalo, N.Y.; Australian National Gallery, Canberra; Baltimore Museum of Art, Md.; Brooklyn Museum of Art, N.Y.; Denver Art Museum, Colo.; J. Paul Getty Trust, Malibu, Calif.; Library of Congress, Washington, D.C.; Metropolitan Museum of Art, New York; Minneapolis Institute of Arts, Minn.; Museum Moderner Kunst, Palais Lichtenstein, Vienna; Museum of Modern Art, New York; Neue Galerie-Sammlung Ludwig, Aachen, Germany; Oakland Museum, Calif.; Philadelphia Museum of Art; San Francisco Museum of Modern Art, Calif.; Tate Gallery, London; Whitney Museum of American Art, New York.
Awards: American Institute of Architects Award for Excellence in Design, Rockefeller Center, New York.

**Suzanne Lacy**, United States, b. 1945.
Studied: University of California, Santa Barbara, B.A., 1968; Fresno State College, Calif., 1969–71; California Institute of the Arts, Los Angeles, M.F.A., 1993.
Taught: Dean, School of Fine Arts, California College of Art and Crafts, 1987– .
Solo Exhibitions: Municipal Art Society, New York, 1990; Women's Building, Los Angeles, 1990; Pennsylvania State University, Pittsburgh, 1990; Whyte Gallery, Banff, Alberta, Canada, 1991; West Gallery, California State, Fullerton, 1992; Whitney Museum of American Art, New York, 1993; Artpark, Niagara Falls, N.Y., 1993; Cleveland Center for Contemporary Art, Ohio, 1994; University Art Museum, Berkeley, Calif., 1995; Snug Harbor Cultural Center, Staten Island, N.Y., 1995.
Awards: National Endowment for the Arts Visual Artists Fellowship; McKnight Fellowship, Minneapolis, Minn.; Film in the Cities Film Fellowship, Minneapolis–St. Paul, Minn.; Minnesota State Arts Board Fellowship; California Arts Council Individual Artist Fellowship; Distinguished Alumni, California Institute of the Arts; Planning Grant, Artpark, New York State Parks Department; Lila Acheson Wallace Reader's Digest Arts International Fellowship; John Simon Guggenheim Memorial Foundation Fellowship; National Endowment for the Arts Individual Artist Fellowship; Women in Film Finishing Grant, Minneapolis, Minn.; National Endowment for the Arts Media-Arts Grant; Alliance of Arts Organizations Artists Grant; National Alliance of Arts Organizations Artists Grant.

**Vera Lehndorff**, Germany.
Studied: Painting and design at Fachschule für Gestaltung, Hamburg, and in Florence for two years.
Work: Became known as Veruschka while learning to act with Lee Strasberg in New York, and has appeared in many films including *Blow-Up* (Michelangelo Antonioni, 1967), *Salome* (Carmelo Bene, 1971), and *Dorian Gray im Spiegel des Boulevard-Presse* (Ulrike Ottinger, 1983). First body painting in 1966. Over the years collaborated with the photographer Holger Trülzsch, which resulted in the book *"Veruschka" Trans-Figurations,* for which Susan Sontag wrote the introduction. (See Holger Trülzsch for a listing of their collaborative work.)

**Donald Lipski**, United States, b. 1947.
Studied: University of Wisconsin, Madison, B.A., 1970; Cranbrook Academy of Art, Bloomfield Hills, Mich., M.F.A., 1973.
Solo Exhibitions: Hudson River Museum, Yonkers, N.Y., 1990; Cleveland Center for Contemporary Art, 1990; Fabric Workshop, Philadelphia College of Art and Beaver College, Philadelphia, 1990; Galerie Lelong, New York, 1992; Brooklyn Museum of Art, N.Y., 1993; Galerie Lelong, Paris, 1995; Galleria Il Ponte, Rome, 1995; Parrish Art Museum, Southampton, N.Y., 1996.
Collections: Commission for installation in Grand Central Station, New York, 1997; Chase Manhattan Bank, New York; Brooklyn Museum of Art, N.Y.; Corcoran Gallery of Art, Washington, D.C.; Denver Art Museum, Colo.; Indianapolis Museum of Art, Ind.; Jewish Museum, New York; Menil Collection, Houston, Tex.; Metropolitan Museum of Art, New York; Museum of Contemporary Art, Chicago; Museum of Fine Arts, Boston; Panza Collection, Italy; Walker Art Center, Minneapolis, Minn.; Whitney Museum of American Art, New York.
Awards: National Endowment for the Arts Visual Artists Fellowship; New York Foundation on the Arts Fellowship; John Simon Guggenheim Memorial Foundation Fellowship; Award, American Academy of Arts and Letters.

**Bonnie Lucas**, United States, b. 1950.
Studied: Wellesley College, Mass., B.A., 1972; Rutgers University, New Brunswick, N.J., M.F.A., 1979.
Taught: Parsons School of Design, New York, 1988–94; Maryland Institute College of Art, Baltimore, 1992; College of the Atlantic, Bar Harbor, Maine, 1994; City College of New York, 1996.
Solo Exhibitions: Avenue B Gallery, New York, 1985, 1986, 1987; Souyun Yi Gallery, New York, 1991; Edith Blum Gallery, College of the Atlantic, Bar Harbor, Maine, 1994.
Collections: Rutgers University Art Gallery, N.J.; New York Public Library.
Grants: Art Matters; Mary Elvira Stevens Traveling Fellowship, Wellesley College; Visiting Artist, American Academy in Rome.

**Inese Mailitis**, Russia, b. 1959.
**Ivars Mailitis**, Russia, b. 1956.
Exhibition: Joint work in the Fourteenth Lausanne Biennale, 1990, and others.

**Masafumi Maita**, Japan, b. 1944 (Manchuria).
Solo Exhibitions: Gallery Caption, Gifu Prefecture, Japan, 1990; Kamakura Gallery, Tokyo, 1991; Gallery Yamaguchi, Tokyo, 1992; SOKO, Tokyo, 1992.
Collections: Musée d'Arte Modern de Paris; Musée d'Art Modern, Strasbourg, France; Utsukushigahara Open Air Museum, Japan; Museum of Modern Art, Toyama, Japan; Japan Cultural Forum.
Awards: Universiad Kobe Memorial Grand Prize, Ninth Contemporary Sculpture Exhibition at Kobe; Special Prize, Fourth Henry Moore Grand Prize Exhibition; Special Prize, Aomori Expo '88 Memorial Contemporary Sculpture Exhibition; Kobe Educational Committee Grand Prize, Eleventh Contemporary Sculpture Exhibition at Kobe.

**Patricia Malarcher**, United States, b. 1930.
Studied: Upsala College, East Orange, N.J., B.A., 1952; Catholic University of America, Washington, D.C., M.F.A., 1958; doctoral studies, New York University, 1985.
Taught: Peters Valley Craft Center, Layton, N.J., 1988–89; guest critic, Cleveland Institute of Art, 1990; workshop, Pittsburgh Fiberarts Guild, 1990; Creativity Workshop for Maine Craft Association, Haystack Mountain School of Crafts, Deer Isle, Maine, 1991; sabbatical replacement, Montclair State College, N.J., 1992.
Solo Exhibitions: Interchurch Center, New York, 1990; Newark Museum, N.J., 1991; Target Gallery, Torpedo Factory, Art Center, Alexandria, Va., 1991; Rider College, Lawrence, N.J., 1993; Macy Gallery, Teachers College, Columbia University, New York, 1994; Atlantic Community College, Mays Landing, N.J., 1996.
Collections: United States State Department, Bangkok; St. Peter's Medical Center, New Brunswick, N.J.; Cleveland Museum of Art; Bristol Myers Squibb, Lawrenceville, N.J.; United States Embassy of Oman; Caldwell College, N.J.; Mercy Catholic Medical Center, Upper Darby, Pa.; Hackensack Medical Center, N.J.
Awards: James Renwick Fellowship, Smithsonian Institution Craft Fellowship; New Jersey State Council on the Arts; Lifetime Award for Achievement in Crafts, National Museum of Women, Washington, D.C.; Merit Award, *Surface Design* Journal Writing Competition, 1990.

**Terrie Hancock Mangat**, United States, b. 1948.
Studied: University of Kentucky, Lexington, B.A., 1966–70; Penland School of Crafts, N.C., 1968, 1969, 1978.
Solo Exhibitions: Morlan Gallery, Transylvania College, Lexington, Ky., 1979; Cincinnati Commission for the Arts Gallery, Ohio, 1980; Carl Solway Gallery, Cincinnati, Ohio, 1982, 1988; Bernice Steinbaum Gallery, New York, 1990.
Collections: Chase Manhattan Bank; Ponderosa Collection, St. Louis, Mo.
Awards: Ohio Council on the Arts.

**Janet Markarian**, United States, b. 1953.
Studied: California College of Arts and Crafts, Oakland, 1972–75; Rochester Institute of Technology, N.Y., B.F.A., 1975; University of Georgia, Athens, M.F.A., 1981.
Work: Textile conservation at the Victoria and Albert Museum, London; Metropolitan Museum of Art, New York.
Collections: North Dakota Museum of Art, Grand Forks.
Awards: Fulbright-Hays Research Grant.

**Henri Matisse**, France, 1869–1954.
The oldest of the founding fathers of twentieth-century painting, Matisse first studied law in Paris, from 1887 to 1889, and practiced briefly. He began to paint in 1989 while convalescing from an illness. Deciding to study art formally, he trained first at the Académie Julian in Paris from 1891 to 1892, and then under Gustave Moreau at the Ecole des Beaux-Arts from 1892 to 1897. Respected for his drawing skills, Matisse became famous for his use of shocking strong colors. In 1905 he participated in the landmark exhibition at the Salon d'Automne and the Salon des Indépendants, the inaugural exhibition of Les Fauves (the Wild Beasts), which included Georges Braque, André Derain, Maurice de Vlaminck, and Raoul Dufy. Whereas Cézanne pioneered the integration of surface ornament into the design of the picture, Matisse made it, along with color that is expressive rather than allusive, the mainstay of his paintings. His work was influenced by frequent travels to Morocco and by seeing exhibitions of Islamic art. In 1905–6 he exhibited what many consider his most important painting, *Joy of Life,* at the Barnes Foundation in Pennsylvania. In 1908 he began to show at the Stieglitz Photo-Secession "291" Gallery in New York, and he was included in the Armory Show in 1910. By this time Matisse had become internationally famous and was exhibiting extensively in Europe and the United States. From 1916 on he lived in the south of France. In his last years he worked on *papiers découpés,* paper cutouts in which he used geometrical abstractions and floral plant patterns to express his endless fascination with color and exotic decorative forms.

**Hans Memling**, Flanders, c.1430–94.

**Duane Michals**, United States, b. 1932.
Studied: University of Denver, B.A., 1953.
Solo Exhibitions: San Francisco Museum of Modern Art, 1990; North Dakota Museum of Art, Grand Forks, 1990; Espace Photographique de Paris, 1992; Beam Gallery, Tokyo, 1992; Galeria USVU, Bratislava, Slovakia, 1993; Braunschweig Photomuseum, Germany, 1995; Sidney Janis Gallery, New York, 1976– .
Collections: Art Institute of Chicago; Museum of Fine Arts, Boston; High Museum of Art, Atlanta; Honolulu Academy of Art; Metropolitan Museum of Art, New York; Museum of Modern Art, New York; Philadelphia Museum of Art; San Francisco Museum of Modern Art; Bibliothèque Nationale, Paris; Hamburg Museum of Arts and Crafts, Germany; Israel Museum, Jerusalem; Musée d'Art Modern de la Ville de Paris; National Museum of Canada, Ottawa; Vancouver Art Gallery, British Columbia, Canada; North Dakota Museum of Art, Grand Forks.
Awards: Creative Artists Public Service (CAPS) Grant, New York State Arts Council; National Endowment for the Arts Visual Artists Fellowship; Pennsylvania Council of the Arts; Cooper Union, New York; Carnegie Foundation Photography Fellow; Medaille de Vermeil de la Ville de Paris; Southern Methodist University, Dallas; Meadows Distinguished Visiting Professor; Infinity Award for Art and Nissan International Fellow, International Center of Photography, New York; Honorary Fellowship, Royal Photographic Society, Bath, England; Officier, Ordre des Arts et Lettres, Paris; Century Award, Museum of Photographic Arts, San Diego; Youth Friends Award, School Art League of New York City; Honorary Doctorate of Fine Arts, Art Institute of Boston; Gold Medal for Photography, National Arts Club, New York.

**Yong Soon Min**, Korea, b. 1953. Resides in United States.
Studied: University of California, Berkeley, B.A., 1975, M.A., 1977, M.F.A., 1979; Whitney Museum Independent Study Program, New York, 1981.
Taught: Visiting Artist in Residence, University of Southern Maine, Portland, 1992; Visiting Faculty, Rhode Island School of Design, Providence, 1992; Assistant Professor, University of California, Irvine, 1993– .
Solo Exhibitions: Public Art Fund, New York, 1988; 911 Contemporary Arts Center, Seattle, 1990; Bronx Museum of the Arts, N.Y., 1991; University of Southern Maine, 1992; Hartford Civic Center and University of Connecticut at Storrs, 1994; Smith College Museum of Art, Northampton, Mass., 1994.
Awards: Yaddo Fellowship; Artist in Residence Grant, New York State Council on the Arts; National Endowment for the Arts Visual Artists Fellowship; Institute for Contemporary Art, P.S. 1 Museum, Long Island City, N.Y.; National Endowment for the Arts and Arts International; Percent for Art Commission for Queens Regional Public Library, N.Y.; Fine Arts Faculty Research Grant and Career Development Award, University of California, Irvine; City of Los Angeles Cultural Affairs Department Grant.

**Antoni Miralda**, Spain, b. 1942.
Studied: School of Textile Engineers, Tarrasa, 1956–61; Cours de Methode Comparée des Arts Plastiques; Centre International d'Etudes Pedagogiques, Sovres, France, 1962–64.
Collections: Moderna Museet, Stockholm; Centre Georges Pompidou, Paris; Musée Cantini, Marseilles, France; Art Gallery of New South Wales, Australia; and others.
Awards: Barcelona Bursary; Laureate, Fifth Biennale de Paris.

**Issey Miyake**, Japan, b. 1938.
Studied: Tama Art University, Tokyo, 1964.
Work: Presented first fashion collection in Tokyo, 1963; established Miyake Design Studio in Tokyo, 1970; established Issey Miyake International, Inc., 1971.
Solo Exhibitions: Fashion Institute of Technology, New York, 1987; Musée des Arts Décoratifs, Paris, 1988; Tokyo Museum of Contemporary Art, Tokyo, 1990; Naoshima Contemporary Art Museum, Kagawa, Japan, 1992.
Awards: Mainichi Design Prize; First Hiroshima Art Prize; Commandeur des Arts et Lettres, French Government; Asahi Prize; Honorary Doctorate, Royal College of Art, London, 1993; Fifteenth Aguja De Oro Award, Madrid, 1995.

**Tina Modotti**, Italy, 1896–1942.
Although remembered as an actress, a model for artists, a fighter for the cause of humanity, and a companion of artists and revolutionaries, Tina Modotti was most importantly a photographer. She came to the United States from her home in Udine, Italy, in 1913 and settled with her family in San Francisco. She married Roubaix de l'Abrie Richéy and moved with him to Los Angeles, where in 1920 she was featured in several Hollywood films. Her husband, known as Robo, died in 1922, a year after she had met Edward Weston, with whom she began to study photography. Modotti and Weston lived together in Mexico from 1923 until 1926, during which time Modotti modeled for Weston and also began to exhibit with him. During this time she modeled for Diego Rivera's murals in the chapel at the Chapingo Agricultural School as well. She was expelled from Mexico in 1930 for her political involvements. Subsequently she spent 1935–39 in Spain working as a nurse in the Spanish Civil War. She returned to Mexico in 1939 and remained there until her death three years later. Modotti showed extensively in Mexico. The Museum of Modern Art in New York mounted the first important international exhibition of her photographs in 1977. The Philadelphia Museum organized a retrospective in 1995 that traveled to the Museum of Fine Arts, Houston, and to the San Francisco Museum of Modern Art. The most recent show of her work was at the University of California at San Diego, and her work is in most of the major public photography collections in the Western world.

**Hideo Mori**, Japan, b. 1940.
Studied: Musashino Art University of Tokyo, 1962.
Taught: Professor of stage design, exhibitions, and fashion at Musashino Art University of Tokyo.

**Bill Moss**, United States, 1933–94.
Studied: University of Michigan, Ann Arbor, 1941–43; Cranbrook Academy of Art, Bloomfield Hills, Mich., 1946–48.
Taught: Arizona State University, Tempe, 1983–85; Haystack Mountain School of Crafts, Deer Isle, Maine, 1985, 1986.
Solo Exhibitions: Park-McCullough House Association, Bennington, Vt., 1980; Guild Hall, Easthampton, N.Y., 1980; Maine Coast Artists Gallery, Rockport, 1981; Boston Architectural Center, Mass., 1983.
Awards: National Endowment for the Arts Crafts Fellowship; International Fabric Design Awards; New England Treasure Artist, University of Massachusetts.

**Matt Mullican**, United States, b. 1951.
Studied: California Institute of the Arts, Valencia, B.F.A, 1974.
Solo Exhibitions: List Visual Arts Center, Massachusetts Institute of Technology, Cambridge, 1990; Rijksmuseum Kröller-Müller, Otterlo, the Netherlands, 1991; Brooke Alexander Gallery, New York, 1991; Barbara Gladstone Gallery, New York, 1992; Museum of Contemporary Art, La Jolla, Calif., 1992; Kunstmuseum Luzern, Lucerne, Switzerland, 1993; Wiener Secession, Vienna, Austria, 1994; Nationalgalerie, Berlin, 1995; IVAM Centre del Carme, Valencia, Spain, 1995; Daniel Blau, Munich, Germany, 1995; Centre for Contemporary Art, Ujazdowski Castle, Warsaw, Poland, 1996; Janice Guy, New York, 1996; Stedelijk Van Abbe Museum, Eindhoven, the Netherlands, 1997; Kunstverein Arnsberg, Germany, 1997.
Collections: Los Angeles County Museum of Art, Calif.; Newport Harbor Museum, Calif.; Museum of Contemporary Art, Los Angeles, Calif.; Santa Barbara Museum of Art, Calif.; Tate Gallery, London; Haags Gemeentemuseum, The Hague; Metropolitan Museum of Art, New York; University of Southern Florida Art Museum, Tampa; FRAC Nord-Pays-de-Calais, Lille, France; Paine Webber, New York; Chase Manhattan Bank, New York; Progressive Corporation, Cleveland, Ohio; Walt Disney Corporation, Los Angeles; Interpublic Group of Companies, Inc., New York; Nordstern Allgemeine Insurance Co., Cologne, Germany.
Grants: National Endowment for the Arts Visual Artists Fellowship; John Simon Guggenheim Memorial Foundation Fellowship; Deutsche Akademische Austauschdienst Fellowship, Berlin Program, Germany.

**Hirotaka Nakagawa**, Japan, b. 1962.
Studied: Musashino Art University of Tokyo, M.A., 1988.
Solo Exhibitions: Gallery Tamura, Tokyo, 1990.

**Michel Nedjar**, France, b. 1947.
Education: Self-taught; became a tailor's apprentice at age fourteen; later traveled to India and Mexico.
Work: First made rag dolls in 1975; in 1980 began to draw; later began to make films.

**Hermann Nitsch**, Austria, b. 1938.
Studied: Graphic design.
Work: Conceived the Orgies Mysteries Theater (O. M. Theater) in 1957; published first book on the subject in 1969.
Exhibitions and Performances: First exhibition of action paintings in Vienna, 1960; theater pieces performed in Vienna, 1963–66; performs in New York at the Judson Church and Cinemathèque, 1968; purchases Prinzendorf Castle in northern Austria to use as the center for the O. M. Theater, 1971; performances and exhibitions continue in Italy, France, the United States, and Germany (Nitsch composes music for performances); participates in Documenta V, Kassel, Germany, and at Mercer Center, Everson Museum, U.S., 1971; performance lasting three days and nights at Prinzendorf, 1985; set design and codirectorship of the opera *Herodiade* by Jules Massenet at the Vienna State Opera, 1994–95; action in the wine yards of San Martino, Naples, 1996.
Collections: Museum of Modern Art, New York; Solomon R. Guggenheim Museum, New York; Metropolitan Museum of Art, New York; Yale University Art Gallery, New Haven, Conn.; Art Gallery of Ontario, Toronto; Tate Gallery, London; Centre Georges Pompidou, Paris; Stedelijk van Abbe Museum, Eindhoven, the Netherlands; Castello di Rivoli, Turin, Italy; Sammlung Nordrhein-Westfalen, Düsseldorf, Germany; Museum Ludwig, Cologne, Germany; Staatliche Graphische Sammlung, Munich, Germany; Lenbachhaus, Munich, Germany; Nationalgalerie, Munich, Germany; Staatsgalerie Stuttgart; Kunsthalle Hamburg; Museum Neue Galerie, Saarbrücken, Germany; Schloss Moorsbroich, Leverkusen, Germany; Museo Capodimonte, Naples; Kunstmuseum Bern; Kunstmuseum Winterthur, Germany; Museum Moderner Kunst Stiftung Ludwig, Vienna; Wolfgang Gurlitt Museum, Linz, Austria; Rupertinum, Salzburg; Ferdinandeum Innsbruck, Austria; Sammlung Schömer, Klostermeuberg, Germany.

**Isamu Noguchi**, United States, 1904–88.
Studied: In Japan and the United States.
Solo Exhibitions: Eugene Schoen Gallery, 1929; Marie Sterner Gallery, New York, 1930; John Becker and Demotte Galleries, New York, 1932; Marie Harriman Gallery, New York, 1935; Museum of Modern Art, New York, 1946; Egan Gallery, New York, 1949; Stable Gallery, New York, 1954, 1959; Cordier and Warren Gallery, New York, 1961; Gallery Claude Bernard, New York, 1964; Whitney Museum of American Art, New York, 1968; Walker Art Center, Minneapolis, Minn., 1978.
Awards: John Simon Guggenheim Memorial Foundation Fellowship; Bollingen Foundation Fellowship.
Set Design: Martha Graham Dance Company, 1935–66.
Public Projects: gardens for UNESCO in Paris, 1956–58; garden for Beinecke Library at Yale University, New Haven, Conn.; Israel Museum, Jerusalem; outdoor sculpture for Pepsico, Purchase, N.Y.; Federal Building, Seattle, Wash.; Seattle Art Museum, Wash.; Marine Midland Bank Building, New York; John Hancock Life Insurance Company, New Orleans, La.; and others.

**David Norstad**, United States, b. 1947.
Studied: North Dakota State University, Fargo, B.A., 1974.
Solo Exhibitions: Art Connection, Fargo, N. Dak., 1993, 1994, 1995; Edgewood Orchard, Door County, Wisc., 1994; Fergus Falls Community College, Minn., 1995; Center for the Arts, Fergus Falls, Minn., 1996.
Awards: Washington and Jefferson Juried Show, Gold Medallion, Washington, Pa., 1996, and others.

**Allegra Ockler** (Marquart), United States, b. 1943.
Studied: State University of New York at Buffalo, B.F.A., 1966–69; Ohio University, Athens, M.F.A., 1969–72.
Taught: Western Michigan University, Kalamazoo, 1972–76; Maryland Institute, College of Art, Baltimore, 1976– ; numerous workshops and residencies, including Ohio University, Athens, 1993; Château de Lesvault, Onlay, France, 1995; Ecole Regional des Beaux-Arts, Caen, France.
Exhibitions: Gallery 500, Elkins Park, Pa., 1990; numerous group exhibitions in the printmaking field.
Collections: Baltimore Museum of Art, Md.; Philadelphia Museum of Art; Château de Lesvault, Onlay, France; Huntsville Museum of Art, Ala.; Alma College, Mich.; Kanagawa Prefecture Government, Japan; Hyatt Regency, Baltimore, Md.; Federal Reserve Bank of Richmond, Va.; Citicorp, Baltimore, Md.
Awards: Ford Foundation; United Independent Colleges of Art; Maryland Arts Council; Mellon Foundation; MacDowell Fellowship.

**Masayaki Oda**, Japan, b. 1950. Resides in United States.
Studied: Cranbrook Academy of Art, Bloomfield Hills, Mich., 1976; University of California, Los Angeles, M.A., 1978, M.F.A., 1979.
Taught: Lo Studio delle Giglio, Tokyo, 1970–71; Haystack Mountain School of Crafts, Deer Isle, Maine, 1975; University of California, Los Angeles, 1976–79, 1982.
Solo Exhibitions: Virginia Beach Center for the Arts, Calif., 1990; Galerie Hubertus Wunschik, Düsseldorf, Germany, 1993; Kunstpalast im Ehrenhof Museum, Düsseldorf, Germany, 1993; Hunsaker/Schlesinger Fine Art, Santa Monica, Calif., 1996.
Commissions and Collections: Sculpture Plaza, Mazda Motors, Flat Rock, Mich.; Sculpture Plaza, Virginia Beach Center for the Arts, Calif.; International Garden and Greenery Exposition, Osaka, Japan; Art-in-Architecture Program, Landart Project, Tecate, Calif.; Citizen Corporation, Santa Monica, Calif.; Detroit Art Institute, Mich.; Cranbrook Academy of Art, Bloomfield Hills, Mich.; Yasuda Bank and Trust, Los Angeles, Calif.; Kajima International, Los Angeles, Calif.: Security Pacific Bank, Los Angeles, Calif.; and others.
Awards: Ford Foundation Grant; National Endowment for the Arts Visual Artists Fellowship; First Prize, International Environmental Art Competition, Osaka, Japan; German Award, Osaka Triennale.

**Claes Oldenburg**, Sweden, b. 1929. Resides in United States.
Studied: Yale University, New Haven, Conn., B.A., 1946–50; School of the Art Institute of Chicago, 1952–54.
Solo Exhibitions: Leo Castelli Galleries, New York, 1990; Castelli Graphics, New York, 1990; Galleria Christian Stein, Milan, 1990; Brooke Alexander Editions, New York, 1990; Mayor Gallery, London, 1990; Seagram Plaza, New York, 1991; Portikus, Frankfurt, 1992; Cleveland Center for Contemporary Art, Ohio, 1992; Museum für Gegenwartskunst, Basel, 1992; Walker Art Center, Minneapolis, Minn., 1992; Pace Gallery, New York, 1992; Hochschule für Angewandte Kunst, Vienna, 1992; Musée Municipal La Roche-sur-Yon, France, 1993; Musée d'Art Modern Saint-Etienne, France, 1993; Solomon R. Guggenheim Museum, New York, 1994; Kunst- und Ausstellungshalle der Bundesrepublik Deutschland, Bonn, 1994.
Collections: Art Institute of Chicago; Solomon R. Guggenheim Museum, New York; Hirshhorn Museum and Sculpture Garden, Smithsonian Institution, Washington, D.C.; Israel Museum, Jerusalem; Kunstmuseum Basel; Musée National d'Art Modern, Centre Georges Pompidou, Paris; Museum of Contemporary Art, Los Angeles; Museum of Modern Art, New York; National Gallery of Art, Washington; Philadelphia Museum of Art; Tate Gallery, London; Walker Art Center, Minneapolis, Minn.; Whitney Museum of American Art, New York.
Awards: Brandeis Award for Sculpture; Skowhegan Medal for Sculpture; Art Institute of Chicago; Medal of the American Institute of Architects; Wilhelm-Lehmbruck Sculpture Award, Duisburg, Germany; Wolf Foundation Prize, Israel.

**Pat Oleszko**, United States, b. 1947.
Studied: University of Michigan, B.F.A., 1970.
Performances and Events: Miami-Dade Community College, Miami, Fla., 1990; Lincoln Center, New York, 1990; Earth Day Parade, New York, 1990; Banff Centre for the Arts, Alberta, Canada, 1991; Center for Contemporary Art, Santa Fe, N. Mex., 1991; Aspen Design Conference, Colo., 1991; International Theater Festival, Tulsa, Okla., 1991; National Museum of Women in the Arts, Washington, D.C., 1992; Bass Museum of Art, Miami Beach, Fla., 1993; Neuberger Museum of Art, Purchase, N.Y., 1993; Textile Museum, Antwerp, Belgium, 1993; Nexus, Atlanta, 1994; and others.
Exhibitions: American Craft Museum, New York, 1990.
Awards: Creative Artists Public Service (CAPS) Grant, New York State Council on the Arts; National Endowment for the Arts Visual Artists Fellowship; Jim Hensen Foundation; Massachusetts Council on the Arts, New Works; John Simon Guggenheim Memorial Foundation Fellowship; New York Foundation of the Arts Fellowship, 1991; First Prize, Fourth of July Parade, Aspen, Colo., 1993.

**Charles O'Rear**, United States, b. 1941.
Studied: Journalism; turned to photojournalism.
Awards: American Society of Magazine Photographers; National Press Photographers Association.
Published in *National Geographic, Communication Arts Magazine*, and others.
Books: *High Tech: Silicon Valley*, 1985.

**Frei Otto**, Germany, b. 1925.
Studied: Technological University, Berlin, 1952.
Taught: Yale University, New Haven, Conn., 1960; Technological University, Berlin, 1962; University of California, Berkeley, 1962; Technological University, Stuttgart, Germany, 1964.

**Neil Parsons**, United States, b. 1938.
Studied: Montana State College, B.S., 1961; Montana State University, M.A., 1964; post-graduate study, University of Washington, 1967.
Taught: Institute of American Indian Arts, Santa Fe, N. Mex., 1964–67; Western State College of Colorado, Gunnison, 1967–70; University of Montana, Missoula, 1970–72; Blackfeet Community School, Browning, Mont., 1972–77; Museum of the Plains Indian, Evergreen State College, Olympia, Wash., 1988–93.
Work: Consultant, Museum of the Plains Indian, Browning, Mont., 1975–77; Consultant, Montana Arts Council, 1977–80; Director, New Visions Gallery, Billings, Mont., 1980–87.
Exhibitions: "Pintura Amerindia Contemporanea," Chile, Peru, Bolivia, Colombia, and Ecuador; Contemporary Native American Painters, Edinburgh Festival, Scotland; "The Spirit of the Earth," Buscaglia-Castellani Gallery, Niagara Falls, N.Y.; "Submuloc—Contemporary Native American Artists Recall Columbus" (traveling); "Our Land/Ourselves," University of New York, Albany (traveling); and others.
Collections: Throughout the Western United States.

**Raphaelle Peale**, United States, 1774–1825.
Son of the famous painter Charles Willson Peale, who established an important school of realist painting in Philadelphia. Raphaelle and his brothers joined their father in establishing in Philadelphia the Museum of Natural History, which became the prototype for later similar museums. Brother Rembrandt Peale, the most gifted of the sons in portraiture and miniatures, and Raphaelle, noted for still lifes, worked closely with their father and each other throughout their artistic careers.

**Maurizio Pellegrin**, Italy, b. 1956.
Studied: University of Venice; Academy of Fine Arts, Venice.
Solo Exhibitions: San Diego Museum of Contemporary Art, La Jolla, Calif., 1990; Jack Shainman Gallery, New York, 1990, 1992, 1995; Galleria Tommaseo, Trieste, Italy, 1990, 1994; Feigen, Inc., Chicago, 1991; Corcoran Gallery of Art, Washington, D.C., 1992; Galleria Andreas Binder, Munich, 1992; Mark Moore Gallery, Santa Monica, Calif., 1993; Miami Dade Community College, Fla., 1993; Galleria Il Ponte Contemporanea, Rome, 1994; John C. Stoller Gallery, Minneapolis, Minn., 1994; Center for Fine Arts, Miami, 1995.

**Gaetano Pesce**, Italy, b. 1939. Resides in New York and Paris.
Studied: Faculty of Architecture, University of Venice, Italy, 1958–65; experimental school, New Venice College of Industrial Design.
Taught: Institute of Architecture and Urban Studies, Strasbourg, France, 1975– ; Visiting Professor, Carnegie Mellon University, Paris, 1980; Cooper Union, New York.
Exhibitions: Musée des Arts Décoratifs, Paris, 1990; Musée d'Art Modern, Strasbourg, 1991; Gallery Ma, Tokyo, 1991; Tel Aviv Museum of Art, 1991; Peter Joseph Gallery, New York, 1991; retrospective exhibition, Centre Georges Pompidou, Paris, 1996.
Awards: "Design Distinction" award, *I.D.* Magazine Annual Award Competition, 1996.
Collections: Museum of Modern Art, New York; Metropolitan Museum of Art, New York; Musée des Arts Décoratifs, Paris; Centre Georges Pompidou, Paris; Museo d'Arte Moderna, Turin; Canadian Centre for Architecture, Montreal; and others.

**Michelangelo Pistoletto**, Italy, b. 1933.
Work: Painter and sculptor close to the Arte Povera movement. As a child worked with his father, a painting restorer in Italy. In 1963 began to exhibit full-scale figures painted on shiny metallic surfaces. Since the 1980s has been working in sculpture that pursues the dialectic of opposites between heaviness and lightness, working great blocks of marble as if they were polyurethane, and vice versa.

**Stefan Poplawski**, Poland, b. 1945.
Studied: Higher School of Fine Arts, Poznan, Poland.
Exhibitions: Nationally and internationally since 1972.
Collections: Central Museum of Textiles, Lodz, Poland; National Museum in Warsaw and Poznan; Peggy Guggenheim Collection, Venice; Center for Art and Culture, Brussels.

**Lyubov' Sergeevna Popova**, Russia, 1899–1924.
Worked in Paris and Russia, 1912–13; worked with Vladimir Tatlin, Nedezhda Udaltsova, and Alexandr Vesnin; traveled in France and Italy, 1914; contributed to "Jack of Diamonds" (Moscow, 1914 and 1916); painted in non-objective style, 1915–21; painted architectonic compositions, 1916–18; painted painterly constructions, 1919–21; professor at Svomas/Vkhutemas, 1918; contributed to Tenth State Exhibition, "Non-Objective Creation and Suprematism," and other exhibitions, 1919; member of Inkhuk, 1920; took part in "5x5=25," 1921; rejected studio painting and experimented with design in various fields including book design, porcelain, textiles, and clothing; created set and costume designs for Meierkhold's production of Crommelynck's farce *The Magnanimous Cuckold*, 1922; contributed to the Erste Russische Kunstaustellung in Berlin; designed sets and costumes for Sergei Tretiakov's *Earth on End*, 1923; worked on dresses and textile designs for the First State Textile Factory, Moscow, 1923–24; posthumous exhibition in Moscow, 1924.

**Harriet Powers**, United States, 1837–unknown.

**Sharron Quasius**, United States, b. 1948.
Studied: University of Wisconsin, Oshkosh, B.F.A., 1967–72; University of Oklahoma, Norman, M.F.A., 1973–75.
Solo Exhibitions: Florida Gallery, Center for the Arts, Vero Beach, 1990; Hopkins Gallery, Palm Beach, Fla., 1991; Palm Beach Community College, Palm Beach Gardens, Fla., 1995.
Collections: Metropolitan Museum of Art, New York; Tampa Museum of Art, Fla.; Metropolitan Bank of Addison, Ill.; Housatonic Museum of Art, Bridgeport, Conn.; Norton Center for the Arts, Danville, Ky.
Grants: Individual Visual Artists Fellowship, Wisconsin Arts Board; National Endowment for the Arts Crafts Fellowship.

**Robert Rauschenberg**, United States, b. 1925.
Studied: Kansas City Art Institute; Academie Julien, Paris; Black Mountain College, N.C.; Art Students League, New York.
Solo Exhibitions: Leo Castelli Gallery, New York; Neue Berliner Galerie, Alten Museum, Berlin; Galerie Montaigne, Paris; National Art Gallery, Kuala Lumpur; Knoedler and Company, New York; Pyo Gallery, Seoul; Nippon Convention Center, Makauhari Messe, Japan; Gemini G.E.L., Los Angeles, Calif.; Whitney Museum of American Art, New York; Galerie Jamileh Weber, Zurich; Corcoran Gallery of Art, National Gallery of Art, Washington, D.C.; and others.
Collections: Museum of Modern Art, New York; Whitney Museum of American Art, New York; Moderna Museet, Stockholm; Kunstsammlung Nordrhein-Westfalen, Düsseldorf; Stedelijk Museum, Amsterdam, the Netherlands; Philadelphia Museum of Art; Albright-Knox Art Gallery, Buffalo, N.Y.; Tate Gallery, London; Pasadena Art Museum, Calif.; Baltimore Museum of Art, Md.; Museum of Contemporary Art, Chicago; Wadsworth Atheneum, Hartford, Conn.: Peter Ludwig, Wallraf-Richartz Museum, Cologne, Germany; Neue Galerie, Aachen, Germany; Minneapolis Institute of Arts, Minn.; Hirshhorn Museum and Sculpture Garden, Smithsonian Institution, Washington, D.C.; and others.
Awards: Grand Prize, Venice Biennale; Golden Plate Award, Twenty-Fifth Anniversary Salute to Excellence, American Academy of Achievement; International Center of Photography Art Award; Gold Medal of Honor, National Arts Club, New York; Grand Prix d'Honneur, Thirteenth International Exhibition of Graphic Art, Ljubljana, Slovenia; Gold Medal, Oslo, Norway; Officier, Ordre des Arts et Lettres, Culture and Communication Ministry, France; and others.

**Man Ray**, United States, 1890–1978. Resided in France.
Studied: National Academy of Design and Ferrer Center, New York.
Work: In 1921 settled in Paris; worked in rayograms, photography, and film. Embraced Surrealism. Shown world-wide since 1915.

**Lilly Reich**, Germany, 1985–1947.
Studied: With Josef Hoffman, Wiener Werkstatte, 1908; Hohere Fachschule für Dekorationskunst, Berlin, 1910.
Work: Starting in 1911 exhibited clothing displays and interiors and designed exhibitions. Collaborated with the architect Ludwig Mies van der Rohe, working with him on the design and organization of exhibitions as well as model apartments.

**Faith Ringgold**, United States, b. 1930.
Studied: City College, New York, B.S., 1955, M.A., 1959.
Solo Exhibitions: High Museum of Art, Atlanta, 1990; Arizona State University Art Museum, Tempe, 1990; Sawhill Art Gallery, James Madison University, Harrisonburg, Va., 1990; Southwest Craft Center, San Antonio, Tex., 1990; Museum of African-American Art, Los Angeles, 1991; Albright-Knox Art Gallery, Buffalo, N.Y., 1991; Miami University Art Museum, Oxford, Ohio, 1991; Textile Museum, Washington, D.C., 1993; Children's Museum of Manhattan, New York, 1993–95; Saint Louis Art Museum, 1994; Athenaeum Music and Arts Library, La Jolla, Calif., 1995; A.C.A. Gallery, New York, 1995; Indiana University of Pennsylvania, 1995; Bowling Green State University, Ind., 1996.
Collections: Solomon R. Guggenheim Museum, New York; Museum of Modern Art, New York; Studio Museum in Harlem, New York; Newark Museum, N.J.; High Museum of Art, Atlanta; Spencer Museum, University of Kansas, Lawrence; Harold Washington Library Center, Chicago; Women's House of Detention, Riker's Island, New York; Brooklyn Children's Museum, N.Y.; Williams College Museum of Art, Williamstown, Mass.
Awards: National Endowment for the Arts Award for Sculpture; Dryfus-MacDowell Fellowship, Petersborough, N.H.; Honorary Doctorate of Fine Art, Moore College of Art, Philadelphia; Honorary Doctorate of Fine Art, College of Wooster, Ohio; John Simon Guggenheim Memorial Foundation Fellowship; Public Art Fund, Port Authority of New York and New Jersey and Carter G. Woodson Foundation, New York; New York Foundation for the Arts Award; National Endowment for the Arts Visual Artists Award; Mid-Atlantic Arts Foundation Award, Baltimore, Md.; La Napouli Foundation Award, France; Artist of the Year Award, Studio Museum in Harlem; Honorary Doctorate of Fine Arts, Massachusetts College of Art, Boston; Honorary Doctorate of Fine Arts, City College

of New York; Artist of the Year Award, Department of Art Education, School of the Art League of New York; Honorary Doctorate, California College of Arts and Crafts; Fifteenth Annual, Queens Museum of Art, Flushing, N.Y.; Key to the City, Lake Charles, La.

**Cornelius Rogge**, the Netherlands, b. 1932.
Studied: Rietveldakademie, 1950–52; Rijksakademie, 1955–57.
Taught: L'Academie Royale de 's-Hertogenbosch, 1972–83.
Solo Exhibitions: Galerie Ram, Rotterdam, 1988, 1992, 1993; Aleph. Hedendaagse Kunst Almere, 1990; Kunstvereiniging Diepenheim, 1990; Stedelijk Musea Gouda, 1992; Kunst Rai, Galerie Ram, 1993.
Collections: Peter Stuyvesant Stichting, Amsterdam; Stedelijk Museum, Amsterdam; Centraal Museum der Gemeente Utrecht; Rijksmuseum Kröller-Müller, Otterlo; Collections der Etat.
Awards: American Cassandra Award; David Roell-Prijs Government Award.

**Ed Rossbach**, United States, b. 1914.
Studied: University of Washington, Seattle; Columbia University, New York; Cranbrook Academy of Art, Bloomfield Hills, Mich.
Taught: Professor Emeritus, University of California, Berkeley.
Solo Exhibition: Textile Museum, Washington, D.C., 1990.
Collections: Women's College, University of North Carolina, Greensboro; California State Fair, Sacramento; University of Indiana, Bloomington; University of Illinois, Urbana; Mansfield State College, Mass.; Museum of Modern Art, New York; Art Institute of Chicago; Brooklyn Museum of Art, N.Y.; Detroit Institute of Arts, Mich.; Oakland Museum, Calif.; Metropolitan Museum of Art, New York; Milwaukee Art Museum, Wisc.; Musée des Arts Décoratifs de Montréal, Canada; National Museum of American Art, Renwick Gallery, Smithsonian Institution, Washington, D.C.; Stedelijk Museum, Amsterdam, the Netherlands; Trondheim Museum, Norway; University of Nebraska, Lincoln.
Awards: American Crafts Council Fellow; Living Treasure of California.

**Betye Saar**, United States, b. 1926.
Studied: University of California, Los Angeles, B.A., 1949; graduate studies, California State University, Long Beach; University of Southern California; California State University, Northridge.
Solo Exhibitions: Wellington City Art Gallery, New Zealand, 1989; Artspace Auckland, New Zealand, 1989; California State University, San Luis Obispo, 1989; Museum of Contemporary Art, Los Angeles, 1990; Objects Gallery, Chicago, 1991; Joseloff Gallery, University of Hartford, Conn., 1992; Hypo Square HypoBank, New York, 1992; Fresno Art Museum, Calif., 1993; Santa Monica Museum of Art, Calif., 1994; de Saisset Museum, Santa Clara, Calif., 1996; Palmer Museum of Art, Pennsylvania State College, 1996.
Collections: High Museum of Art, Atlanta; Hirshhorn Museum and Sculpture Garden, Smithsonian Institution, Washington, D.C.; Montclair Art Museum, N.J.; New Jersey State Museum, Newark; Oakland Museum, Calif.; Pennsylvania Academy of Fine Arts, Philadelphia; Philadelphia Museum of Art; San Francisco Museum of Modern Art; Museum of Fine Arts, Boston; California Community Foundation, Los Angeles; Kresge Art Museum, East Lansing, Mich.
Awards: National Endowment for the Arts Visual Artists Fellowship; J. Paul Getty Fund for the Visual Arts Fellowship; John Simon Guggenheim Memorial Foundation Fellowship.

**Wojciech Sadley**, Poland, b. 1932.
Studied: Academy of Fine Arts, Warsaw, 1949–59; Institute of Industrial Design, Warsaw, 1960–68.
Taught: Academy of Fine Arts, Warsaw.
Exhibitions: First, Second, Third, Fourth, Fifth, and Sixth Lausanne Biennales, Switzerland, and others.
Collections: National Museum, Warsaw; Museum of Sport, Warsaw; Wyczolkowski Museum, Bydgoszcz, Poland; Museum of Textile Industry History, Lodz, Poland; Museum Bellerive, Zurich; National Museum, Prague; National Museum of Modern Art, Osaka, Japan; Museum of Radio and Television, Chicago; Museo del Arte Moderno, Mexico City.
Awards: State Award, Poland; Special Prize, Exempla Exhibition, Munich.

**Lucas Samaras**, United States, b. 1936 (Greece).
Studied: Rutgers University, New Brunswick, N.J., 1955–59; Columbia University, New York, 1959.
Solo Exhibitions: Waddington Galleries, London, 1990; PaceMacGill Gallery, New York, 1991; Galerie Renos Xippas, Paris, 1991; Yokohama Museum of Art, Japan, 1991–92; Hiroshima City Museum of Contemporary Art, Japan, 1991–92; Museum of Modern Art, New York, 1992; Pace Gallery, New York, 1993; PaceWildenstein, 1994, 1996; Gallery Seomi, Seoul, 1995.
Collections: Albright-Knox Art Gallery, Buffalo, N.Y.; Aldrich Museum of Contemporary Art, Ridgefield, Conn.; Art Institute of Chicago; Art Museum, Princeton University, N.J.; Australian National Gallery, Canberra; Saint Louis Art Museum; Dallas Art Museum; Denver Art Museum; Fogg Art Museum, Harvard University, Cambridge, Mass.; Fort Worth Art Museum, Tex.; General Services Administration, Fine Arts Collection, Hale Boggs Federal Court House, New Orleans; Solomon R. Guggenheim Museum, New York; Hirshhorn Museum and Sculpture Garden, Smithsonian Institution, Washington, D.C.; Honolulu Academy of Art; Indiana University Art Museum, Bloomington; International Polaroid Collection, Polaroid Corporation, Cambridge, Mass.; Los Angeles County Museum of Art; Metropolitan Museum of Art, New York; Minneapolis Institute of Arts, Minn.; Museum of Art, Rhode Island School of Design, Providence; Museum of Contemporary Art, Chicago; Museum of Modern Art, New York; National Gallery of Art, Washington, D.C.; New Orleans Museum of Art; Philadelphia Museum of Art; Phoenix Art Museum, Ariz.; San Francisco Museum of Modern Art; Seattle Art Museum; Wadsworth Atheneum, Hartford, Conn.; Walker Art Center, Minneapolis, Minn.; Whitney Museum of American Art, New York; Hara Museum of Contemporary Art, Tokyo; Saint Louis Art Museum; Tate Gallery, London.
Awards: Woodrow Wilson Fellowship.

**Alan Saret**, United States, b. 1944.
Studied: Cornell University, Ithaca, N.Y., B.A., 1966; Hunter College, New York, 1967.
Solo Exhibitions: Institute for Contemporary Art, P.S. 1 Museum, Long Island City, N.Y., 1990; Greater Pittsburgh International Airport, 1992; Museum of Modern Art, New York, 1995.
Awards: John Simon Guggenheim Memorial Foundation Fellowship; National Endowment for the Arts Visual Artists Award.

**Miriam Schapiro**, United States, b. 1923 (Canada).
Studied: Hunter College, New York, 1943; University of Iowa, Iowa City, B.A., 1945, M.A., 1946, M.F.A., 1949.
Work: Founded the Feminist Art Program at California Institute of the Arts (with Judy Chicago), Valencia, 1971.
Solo Exhibitions: Bernice Steinbaum Gallery, New York, 1988, 1990; LewAllen/Butler Fine Art, Santa Fe, N. Mex., 1990; Phyllis Rothman Gallery, Fairleigh Dickinson University, Madison, N.J., 1990, 1991; Brevard Art Center and Museum, Melbourne, Fla., 1991; Colorado State University, Fort Collins, 1992; Fullerton College Art Gallery, Calif., 1992; Guild Hall Museum, East Hampton, N.Y., 1992; A.R.C. Gallery, Chicago, 1993; Steinbaum Krauss Gallery, New York, 1994; West Virginia University, College of Creative Arts, Morgantown, 1994; James Madison University, Harrisonburg, Va., 1996.
Collections: Allen Memorial Art Museum, Oberlin, Ohio; Art Gallery of New South Wales, Sydney, Australia; Brooklyn Museum of Art, N.Y.; Guild Hall Museum, East Hampton, N.Y.; Fogg Art Museum, Harvard University, Cambridge, Mass.; Hirshhorn Museum and Sculpture Garden, Smithsonian Institution, Washington, D.C.; Israel Museum, Tel Aviv; Jewish Museum, New York; Metropolitan Museum of Art, New York; Mills College, Oakland, Calif.; Museum of Fine Arts, Boston; Museum of Modern Art, New York; National Gallery of Art, Washington, D.C.; Peter Ludwig Collection, Aachen, Germany; Saint Louis Art Museum; University Art Museum, Berkeley, Calif.; Whitney Museum of American Art, New York; Worcester Art Museum, Mass.
Awards: John Simon Guggenheim Memorial Foundation Fellowship; Honors Award, Women's Caucus for Art; Doctorate of Fine Arts, California College of Arts and Crafts, Oakland, Calif.; Rockefeller Foundation Grant, Bellagio Study and Conference Center, Italy; Honorary Doctorate, Moore College of Art, Philadelphia; Honorary Doctorate, Miami University, Oxford, Ohio.

**Elsa Schiaparelli**, Italy, 1890–1973. Resided in France.
Studied: Philosophy.
Work: Married and moved to New York. In 1920 returned to Paris and began to design. By 1930 employed two thousand knitters. In 1935 opened her first couture boutique at the Place Vendôme. Perhaps her greatest contribution to couture was to involve artists in fashion, a trend that continues into the present. Became heralded as the fashion designer most

closely associated with the Surrealist movement. In 1933 created the pagoda sleeve, which resulted in wide padded shoulders, reminiscent of those on a guard's greatcoat; this remained the dominant fashion shape until Dior's New Look. In 1940 received the Neiman-Marcus Award and in 1954 published her autobiography, *Shocking Life.*

**Marian I. Schoettle**, United States, b. 1954.
Studied: Colgate University, N.Y., B.A., 1972–76.
Solo Exhibitions: Couman's Gallery, Utrecht, 1990; de Flint, Amersfort, 1991; Suzanne Biederberg Gallery, Amsterdam, 1992; Time Based Arts, Amsterdam, 1992; Textile Museum of the Netherlands, Tilburg, 1993; Galerie Marzee, Nijmegen, 1996.
Collections: Victoria and Albert Museum, London; Nederlands Textielmuseum, Tilburg; Municipal Museum of The Hague.
Awards: Best of Show Award, "Artworks" exhibition, Helen Drutt Gallery, Philadelphia; American Craft Council Fellow.

**Beverly Semmes**, United States.
Studied: Skowhegan School of Painting and Sculpture, Maine, 1982; Boston Museum School; Tufts University, Medford, Mass., B.A., 1980, B.F.A., 1982; Yale School of Art, New Haven, Conn., M.F.A., 1987.
Solo Exhibitions: Institute of Contemporary Art, Philadelphia, 1993; Southeastern Center for Contemporary Art, Winston-Salem, N.C., 1993; Camden Arts Centre, London, 1994; James Hockey Gallery, Farnham, England, 1994; Southampton City Art Gallery, England, 1994; Gallerie Ghislaine Hussenot, Paris, 1994; Michael Klein Gallery, New York, 1994; Baxter Gallery, Maine College of Art, Portland, 1995; Museum of Contemporary Art, Chicago, 1995; Kemper Museum for Contemporary Art and Design, Kansas City, Mo., 1995; Hirshhorn Museum and Sculpture Garden, Smithsonian Institution, Washington, D.C., 1996; Smith College Museum of Art, Northampton, Mass., 1996; Norton Museum of Art, West Palm Beach, Fla., 1996; Virginia Museum of Fine Arts, Richmond, 1996.
Awards: Yale School of Art Fellowship; Alice Kimball English Traveling Fellowship; Art Matters Grant; Artists Space Grant; Mid-Atlantic Foundation Fellowship, Sculpture; National Endowment for the Arts Visual Artists Fellowship.

**Barbara Shawcroft**, United States, b. 1930 (England).
Studied: Central School of Arts and Crafts, London, 1952–53; Ontario College of Art, Toronto, 1957–58; North Carolina State University, Raleigh, 1960–61; California College of Arts and Crafts, Oakland, M.F.A., 1973.
Taught: University of California, Davis, 1982– . Visiting Artist to Austria, Centre Raiffeisenhoff, Graz, Austria; Visiting Artist to Switzerland, City of Bern; Visiting Artist to Finland, Finnish Ministry of Culture.
Exhibition: California Crafts Museum, San Francisco, 1993.
Collections: J. Patrick Lannan Foundation, West Palm Beach, Fla.; Three Embarcadero Center, San Francisco; National Museum of American History, Smithsonian Institution, Washington, D.C.; BART Embarcadero Station, San Francisco; School of Design, North Carolina State University, Raleigh; Water Resources Building/GSA, Sacramento, Calif.; Philip Frucht Associates, San Francisco; Fondazione Arte Della Seta Lisio, Florence; M. H. de Young Memorial Museum, San Francisco; Long House Foundation, East Hampton, N.Y.; National Museum of American History, Smithsonian Institution, Washington, D.C.
Awards: Faculty Research Award, University of California, Davis; National Endowment for the Arts Apprenticeship Fellowship Grant; Gold Medal, Sixth International Lace Biennale, Civic Museum, Sansepolcro, Italy.

**Judith Shea**, United States, b. 1948.
Studied: Parsons School of Design, New York, A.A., 1969, B.F.A., 1975.
Solo Exhibitions: Max Protetch Gallery, New York, 1991, 1993, 1994; Laumeier Sculpture Park, St. Louis, Mo., 1992; John Berggruen Gallery, San Francisco, 1992, 1996; Saint-Gaudens National Historic Site, Cornish, N.H., 1994; University of the Arts, Philadelphia, 1994–95; Doris C. Freedman Plaza, New York, 1995.
Awards: National Endowment for the Arts Visual Artists Fellowship; Solomon R. Guggenheim Sculptor in Residence, Chesterwood, Mass.

**Alan Shields**, United States, b. 1944.
Studied: Kansas State University, Manhattan, 1963–66; Theater Workshop, University of Maine, 1966–67.
Solo Exhibitions: Paula Cooper Gallery, New York, 1991; Pruijs and Ratalowicz, Amsterdam, 1994; Renee Fotouhi Fine Arts, East Hampton, N.Y., 1995; Ann Harper Gallery, Amagansett, New York, 1995, 1996; Avero Holding Company, 1995–96; Art Powerhouse, Cleveland, Ohio, 1996; Belles Artes, Santa Fe, N. Mex., 1996.
Collections: High Museum of Art, Atlanta; Staatliche Museum, Berlin; Museum of Fine Arts, Boston; Massachusetts Institute of Technology, Cambridge, Mass.; Cleveland Museum of Art; Indianapolis Museum of Art; Walker Art Center, Minneapolis, Minn.; Storm King Art Center, Mountainville, N.Y.; Museum of Modern Art, New York; Metropolitan Museum of Art, New York; New York University; Whitney Museum of American Art, New York; Vassar College Museum of Art, Poughkeepsie, N.Y.; National Gallery of Art, Washington, D.C.; Corcoran Gallery of Art, Washington, D.C.; Hirshhorn Museum and Sculpture Garden, Smithsonian Institution, Washington, D.C.; National Gallery of New Zealand, Wellington.
Awards: John Simon Guggenheim Memorial Foundation Fellowship.

**Hiroyuki Shindo**, Japan, b. 1941.
Studied: Kyoto City University of Art, B.F.A., 1965, M.F.A., 1967.
Work: Traditional indigo dyer and kimono maker.
Solo Exhibitions: Gallery Yu, Tokyo, 1990; Gallery Thukasa, Kyoto, 1990; Gallery Gallery, Kyoto, 1992; North Dakota Museum of Art, Grand Forks, 1993.
Collections: Museo de Arte Carrillo Gil, Mexico; Cleveland Museum of Art; Stedelijk Museum, Amsterdam; Art Institute of Chicago; Textile Museum, Toronto, Canada; North Dakota Museum of Art, Grand Forks.

**Satoru Shoji**, Japan, b. 1939.
Studied: Kyoto Fine Art College, Sculpture Special Course, 1964.
Solo Exhibitions: National Gallery, Bangkok, 1990; Gallery NW-House, Tokyo, 1991; Sakura Gallery, Nagoya, 1991, 1992; Kirin Plaza, Osaka, 1992; NHK Nagoya Broadcasting Corporation Center, 1992; Oribe-Tei, Ichinomiya, 1992; Galerie 16, Kyoto, 1992, 1994; Soko Tokyo Gallery, 1993; North Dakota Museum of Art, Grand Forks, 1994; Niigata City Art Museum, 1995.
Collections: Museum Bellerive, Zurich; Wakamiya Street Park-Sculpture Plaza, Nagoya; National Gallery, Bangkok; Niigata City Art Museum.

**Phillips M. Simkin**, United States, b. 1944.
Studied: Tyler Art School, Temple University, Philadelphia, B.F.A., 1961–65; Cornell University, Ithaca, N.Y., M.F.A., 1965–67; University of Pennsylvania, postgraduate fellowship, 1968.
Taught: York College, City University of New York, 1973– .
Solo Exhibitions: Snug Harbor Cultural Center, Staten Island, N.Y., 1991–92; Bi-State Development Agency, St. Louis, Mo., 1991–92; Curran-Fromhold Detention Center and Philadelphia Criminal Justice Center, Pa., 1993–95.
Awards: National Endowment for the Arts Visual Artists Fellowship; Commission Award, Curran-Fromhold Prison, Philadelphia; Commission Award, New Philadelphia Criminal Justice Center.

**Kiki Smith**, United States, b. 1954 (West Germany).
Solo Exhibitions: Museum of Modern Art, New York, 1990; Centre d'Art Contemporain, Geneva, 1990; Institute for Contemporary Art, Clocktower, Long Island City, N.Y., 1990; Tyler Gallery, Tyler School of Art, Philadelphia, 1990; Fawbush Gallery, New York, 1990, 1992, 1993; Institute of Contemporary Art, Amsterdam, 1991; University Art Museum, Berkeley, Calif., 1991; Corcoran Gallery of Art, Washington, D.C., 1991; Greg Kucera Gallery, Seattle, Wash., 1991; Rose Art Museum, Brandeis University, Waltham, Mass., 1992; Osterreichisches Museum für Angewandte Kunst, Vienna, 1992; Moderna Museet, Stockholm, 1992; Bonner Kunstverein, Bonn, 1992; Shoshana Wayne Gallery, Santa Monica, Calif., 1992; Galerie Fricke, Düsseldorf, 1992; Williams College Museum of Art, Williamstown, Mass., 1992; Wexner Center for the Arts, Columbus, Ohio, 1993; Phoenix Art Museum, Ariz., 1993; Shoshana Wayne Gallery, Los Angeles, 1993; Anthony d'Offay Gallery, London, 1993, 1995, 1997; University Art Museum, Santa Barbara, Calif., 1994; Louisiana Museum of Modern Art, Humlebaek, Denmark, 1994; Galerie René Blouin, Montreal, 1994; Israel Museum, Jerusalem, 1994; Barbara Gross Galerie, Munich, 1994; Laura Carpenter Fine Art, Santa Fe, N. Mex., 1994; Pace Drawings, New York, 1994; Power Plant, Toronto, 1994–95; Barbara Krakow Gallery, Boston, 1994, 1996; North Dakota Museum of Art, Grand Forks, 1995; Whitechapel Art Gallery, London, 1995; PaceWildensteinMacGill, Los Angeles, 1995; PaceWildenstein, New York, 1995, 1996; Art Museum, Michigan State University, East Lansing, 1996; St. Petri-Kuratorium, Lübeck, Germany, 1996; Huntington Gallery, Massachusetts College of Art, Boston, 1996; Musée

des Beaux-Arts, Montreal, 1996; Museum of Contemporary Art, Los Angeles, 1996–97; Modern Art Museum, Fort Worth, Tex., 1997; A/D Gallery, New York, 1997.
Collections: Art Institute of Chicago; Corcoran Gallery of Art, Washington, D.C.; High Museum of Art, Atlanta; Israel Museum, Jerusalem; Louisiana Museum of Modern Art, Humlebaek, Denmark; Metropolitan Museum of Art, New York; Moderna Museet, Stockholm; Museum of Fine Arts, Houston, Tex.; Museum of Modern Art, New York; Tate Gallery, London; Victoria and Albert Museum, London; Whitney Museum of American Art, New York; North Dakota Museum of Art, Grand Forks; Yale University Art Gallery, New Haven, Conn.; and others.

**Cindy Snodgrass**, United States, b. 1952.
Studied: Kansas City Art Institute, B.F.A., 1970–73; School of the Art Institute of Chicago, M.F.A., 1974–75.
Taught: Syracuse University, N.Y., 1980; Artist in Residence, Warren County Elementary Schools, Pa., 1992.
Projects and Exhibitions: Dakar, 1990; Carnegie Mellon University, Pittsburgh; Manchester Craftsmen's Guild, Pittsburgh, 1991–94; Carnegie Science Center, Pittsburgh, 1994; Ohio State Multicultural Center, Columbus, 1994; Tayamentasachta, Greencastle, Pa., 1995.
Awards: Heinz Endowment Grant.

**Varvara Fedorovna Stepanova**, Russia, 1894–1958; pseudonyms: Agrarykh, Varst.
Studied: Kazan Art School (where she met Alexander Rodchenko), 1911; studied under Ilia Mashkov and Konstantin Yuon, Moscow; Stroganov Art School, 1913–14.
Taught: Gave private lessons; professor, Textile Department of Vkhuterras, 1924–25.
Work: contributed to Moscow Salon, 1914; closely involved with IZO NKP, 1918 on; member of Inkhuk, 1920; designed sets and costumes for Meierkhold's production of *The Death of Tarelkin,* 1922; worked at First State Textile Factory, Moscow, as a designer, with Lyubov' Popova, Rodchenko et al., 1923; closely associated with "Lef" and "Navyi lef," 1923–28; typography, posters, and stage designs, mid-1920s on; worked on propaganda magazine *USSR in Construction,* 1930s.
Exhibitions: V and X State Exhibitions, 1918, 1919; "5x5=25," 1921; "Exposition internationale des arts décoratifs et industriels modernes," Paris, 1925; "Russian Xylography of the Past Ten Years," Leningrad, 1927; Erste Russische Kunstausstellung, Berlin.

**Vera Szekely**, Hungary, b. 1922. Resides in France.
Studied: Graphics in Budapest and Paris.
Solo exhibitions: Paris; Orleans, France; Caen, France; Amiens, France; Nice, France; The Hague; Amsterdam; Budapest.

**Harne Takami**, Japan, b. 1959.
Studied: Kyoto Seika University, 1982.
Solo Exhibitions: Gallery Gallery, Kyoto, 1990; Sakura Step Gallery, Kyoto, 1991; Kichizyoji Palco Gallery, Tokyo, 1991; La Fence, Osaka, 1993.

**Hideo Tanaka**, Japan, b. 1942.
Studied: Musashino Art University, Tokyo, B.A., 1965; research, Jack Lenor Larsen Design Studio, New York, 1978; Fashion Institute of Technology, New York, 1978.
Solo Exhibitions: Nuno, Kokura, 1991; Gallery Gallery, Kyoto, 1991; La Chambre Blanch, Quebec, Canada, 1992; Gallery Sennbikiya, Tokyo, 1992, 1996; Kobou, Ginza, Tokyo, 1994; Long House Gallery, East Hampton, N.Y., 1995.
Collections: Museum of Contemporary Art of Moreria, Mexico; Erie Art Museum, Pa.; American Craft Museum, New York; Cleveland Museum of Art, Ohio.

**Antoni Tàpies**, Spain, b. 1923.
Studied: Law.
Work: Along with other painters and poets founded the Surrealist-inspired movement Dau al Set in Barcelona in 1948, which published a periodical of the same name. The group drew attention to the accomplishments of such Catalunyan artists as Joan Miró, heralded the medieval masterpieces of Catalan art, and lauded such important modern masters as Paul Klee. It remained the most influential movement in Spain for the next decade. Tàpies came into prominence as a painter during the 1950s. Known for his interest in using surprising materials such as marble dust and sand to create unusual surfaces, and for his sculptures and collages as well as paintings. Continues to exert great influence on young Spanish artists.
Exhibitions: First exhibited in New York at the Martha Jackson Gallery in the 1970s; continues to exhibit worldwide in galleries and museums including a solo exhibition at PaceWildenstein, New York, 1996.

**Lenore Tawney**, United States, b. 1907.
Studied: University of Illinois, Champaign-Urbana; weaving with Marli Ehrman, sculpture with Archipenko, tapestry with Marta Taipale, Institute of Design, Chicago.
Solo Exhibitions: American Craft Museum, New York, 1990; Delaware Arts Center Gallery, Narrowsburg, N.Y., 1991; Maryland Institute College of Art, Baltimore, 1992; Tenri Gallery, New York, 1994; Society for Contemporary Crafts, Pittsburgh, 1995; Perimeter Gallery, Chicago, 1995; Contemporary Museum, Honolulu, 1996; Skidmore College, Saratoga Springs, N.Y., 1996; Stedelijk Museum, Amsterdam, 1996; E. M. Donohue Gallery, New York, 1996.
Collections: Kunstgewerbemuseum, Zurich; Museum Bellerive, Zurich; First National Bank of Chicago; University of Southern Illinois, Edwardsville; Brooklyn Museum of Art, N.Y.; Cooper-Hewitt National Design Museum, Smithsonian Institution, New York; Museum of Contemporary Crafts, New York; Museum of Modern Art, New York; Cleveland Museum of Art; American Craft Museum, New York; Art Institute of Chicago; Cleveland State Office Building; Philip Morris Collection.
Awards: Fellow of American Crafts Council.

**Joyce Tenneson**, United States, b. 1945.
Studied: George Washington University, Washington, D.C., M.A., 1969; Union Graduate School, Antioch College, Yellow Springs, Ohio, Ph.D., 1978.
Taught: Northern Virginia Community College, Alexandria, 1978–80; Washington School of Psychiatry, 1978–80; Corcoran School of Art, Washington, D.C., 1979–83.
Work: Photographs have appeared in many magazines including *Time, Life, Premier, Esquire,* and *New York Times Magazine.* Has published five books of photography.
Solo Exhibitions: Over one hundred worldwide.
Collections: Library of Congress, Washington, D.C.; Smithsonian Institution, Washington, D.C.; Bibliothèque Nationale, Paris; Corcoran Gallery of Art, Washington, D.C.; Rufino Tamayo Museum of Contemporary Art, Mexico; City of Paris Collection; Musée Reatu, Arles, France; Women's Interart Center, New York.
Awards: Prix Jasmin, French *Vogue;* Infinity Award, International Center of Photography, New York; Photographer of the Year, Women in Photography organization.

**Hanne Tierney**, United States, b. 1940 (Germany).
Studied: Self-taught.
Performances: Construction and Process, Lodz, Poland, 1990; Institute for Contemporary Art, P.S. 1 Museum, Long Island City, N.Y., 1991; Lincoln Center, New York, 1992; Flynn Gallery, New York, 1992; North Dakota Museum of Art, Grand Forks, 1993; Puppentheater Festival, Bielsko, Poland, 1994; Figurentheater Festival, Braunschweig, Germany, 1994; Public Theater, New York, 1994; Sculpture Center, New York, 1995, 1997; Art International, Wanas, Sweden, 1996; University of Maryland, Baltimore, 1996; New Wave Festival, Brooklyn Academy of Music, N.Y., 1996.
Awards: National Endowment for the Arts Performance Fellowship.

**Eng Tow**, Singapore, b. 1947.
Studied: Coventry College of Art, Warwickshire, England, 1968–69; Winchester School of Art, Hampshire, England, B.A., 1969–72; Royal College of Art, London, M.A., 1972–74.
Solo Exhibitions: Deutsche Bank, Singapore, 1991; Erica Underwood Gallery, Perth, Australia, 1991; Fort Canning Centre, Singapore, 1992; Takashimaya Gallery, Singapore, 1993; Singapore Museum, 1996.
Collections: Crafts Council, England; National Museum Art Gallery, Singapore; Dynasty Hotel, Singapore; Pan Pacific Hotel, Marina Square, Singapore; Fukuoka Museum, Japan; Japan Economic Development Board, New York; Singapore Embassy, Washington, D.C.; Leeds City Art Gallery, England; Citibank National, New York; Changi International Airport II, VIP Complex, Singapore; Curtin University of Technology, Australia; Banyan Tree Resorts, Phuket, Thailand.
Awards: Asian Cultural Council, John D. Rockefeller III Fund; Japan Foundation Fellowship; Artist in Residence, Curtin University, Australia.

**Mitsuo Toyazaki**, Japan, b. 1955.
Studied: Tokyo University of Art, B.F.A., 1979, M.F.A., 1981.
Exhibitions: "Light and Shadow: Japanese Artists in Space," North Dakota Museum of Art, Grand Forks, and others.
Awards: Japan Contemporary Art and Crafts Exhibition.

**Michael Tracy**, United States, b. 1943.
Studied: St. Edwards University, Austin, Texas, B.A., 1964; Cleveland Institute of Art, 1964–67; University of Texas, Austin, M.F.A., 1969.
Solo Exhibitions: Artspace, San Francisco, 1990; Raab Gallery, Berlin, 1990; McNamee Gallery, St. Louis University, Mo., 1990; Zolla/Lieberman Gallery, Chicago, 1991; Daniel Weinberg Gallery, Santa Monica, Calif., 1991; Blue Star Art Space, San Antonio, Tex., 1992; Moody Gallery, Houston, Tex., 1993; Raab Gallery, London, 1993; St. Clemens Catholic Church, Hannover, Germany, 1993; Mattress Factory, Pittsburgh, 1994; Gallery Paule Anglim, San Francisco, Calif., 1994.
Permanent Installations: Sagrario de San Miguel Arc Angel, Our Lady of Guadeloupe Catholic Church, Alice, Tex.; Emmanuel Chapel, Corpus Christi Cathedral, Tex.; Chapel Altar Screen, St. Edwards University, Austin, Tex.

**Holger Trülzsch**, Germany.
Studied: Painting and sculpture at Akademie der Bildende Kunste, Munich.
Work: Has been involved with experimental music as a member of a group with whom he composed the music for Werner Herzog's film *Aguirre,* 1972, and has recorded several albums. Has collaborated with the model Vera Lehndorff, a.k.a. Veruschka.
Exhibitions: Fundatie Kunsthuis, Amsterdam, 1980; Palais des Beaux-Arts, Brussels, 1981; Musée Nationale d'Art Modern, Centre Georges Pompidou, Paris, 1982; Galerie de la Musée de la Photographie, Charleroi, Belgium, 1982; Palazzo Capponi, Florence, 1983; Galerie Springer, Berlin, 1983; Bette Stoler Gallery, New York, 1985, 1986; Four Arts Center, Tallahassee, Fla., 1985; Davis/McClain Gallery, Houston, Tex., 1986; Anne Berthoud Gallery, London, 1986; Art Institute of Chicago, 1987; Scott Hanson Gallery, New York, 1988.
Collections: Art Institute of Chicago; Bibliothèque Nationale, Paris; Heineken, Amsterdam; Musée d'Art Modern de la Ville de Paris; Museum für Kunst und Gewerbe, Hamburg; Musée National d'Art Modern, Centre Georges Pompidou, Paris; Polaroid Corporation, U.S.; Stedelijk Museum, Amsterdam.

**Connie Utterback**, United States, b. 1947.
Studied: Washington University, St. Louis, Mo., B.F.A., 1965–69; School of the Art Institute of Chicago, 1973–75; California State University, Long Beach, 1977–78; University of California, Los Angeles, M.F.A., 1978–81.
Taught: University of California, Los Angeles, 1981– .
Solo Exhibitions: Hearst Center for the Arts, Cedar Falls, Iowa, 1994.
Collections: Bank of Boston, New Bedford, Mass.; Beaumont Hospital, Bloomfield Hills, Mich.; Hillier Group, Princeton, N.J.; Ketchum Advertising, Los Angeles, Calif.; Touche Ross, Cincinnati, Ohio; Westin Hotel, Kansas City, Mo.
Awards: National Endowment for the Arts Visual Artists Fellowship.

**Remedios Varo**, Spain, 1908–63. Resided in Mexico.
Raised in a strict Spanish family and rigorously trained in academic art, Varo became involved in Barcelona's avant-garde. She fled the Spanish Civil War with the poet Benjamin Péret, later her husband, to join the inner circle of the Surrealists in Paris. Forced to flee again by the Nazis, Varo and Péret faced a year of mounting danger in Marseilles before securing passage to Mexico. She remained in Mexico City until she died, working as a painter.
Solo Exhibitions: Galería Diana, Mexico City, 1956; Galería Juan Martín, Mexico City, 1962; "La Obra de Remedios Varo," Instituto Nacional de Bellas Artes, Mexico City, 1964; "Obra de Remedios Varo," Museo de Arte Moderno, Mexico City, 1971; "Remedios Varo: 1913–1963," Museo de Arte Moderno, Mexico City, 1983; "Science in Surrealism: The Art of Remedios Varo," New York Academy of Sciences, National Academy of Sciences, Washington, D.C., 1986.

**Nick Vaughn**, United States, b. 1953.
Studied: Golden West College, Huntington Beach, Calif., A.A., 1974; California State University, Fullerton, B.A., 1976, M.A., 1978.
Exhibitions: Laguna Beach Museum of Art, Calif., 1982 (with Phyllis Green); Walker Art Center, Minneapolis, Minn., 1984 (with Judith Shea); Fine Arts Gallery, University of California, Irvine, 1987–88; University of Texas, San Antonio, 1988; Muckenthaler Cultural Center, Fullerton, Calif., 1992 (with Ellen Birrell).

**Frank Viner**, United States, b. 1937.
Studied: School of the Worcester Art Museum; Yale University, B.F.A., M.F.A.
Taught: School of Visual Arts, New York, 1964–74; Fairleigh Dickinson University, Madison, N.J., 1972–77.
Exhibitions: Numerous group exhibitions in the 1960s and 1970s.
Set/Costume Design: Scenic artist, New York.
Collections: Riverside Collection of the Rose Art Museum, Brandeis University, Waltham, Mass.; Milwaukee Art Center, Wisc.; Whitney Museum of American Art, New York; Brooklyn Museum of Art, N.Y.
Grants: National Endowment for the Arts Visual Artists Fellowship; Creative Artists Public Service Program.

**Christian Vogt**, Switzerland, b. 1946.
Work: Freelance photographer since 1969.
Solo Exhibitions: Photographer's Gallery, London; International Center of Photography, New York; Neikrug and Swiss Institute, New York; Swiss Institute, New York; Kunsthaus, Zurich; Yajima Gallery, Montreal, Quebec; Galerie Felix Handschin, Basel; Focus Gallery, San Francisco; Ray Hawkins Gallery, New York; Tel Aviv Museum; Rencontres Internationales de la Photographie, Arles, France; Galerie Watari, Tokyo; Preuss Museum, Norway; Edwynn Houk Gallery, Chicago; Galerie CCD, Düsseldorf; Kunstmuseum, Hannover; "Nostra Descrittive," Rimini, Italy; Museum für Gestaltung, Basel; Musée de l'Elysée, Lausanne; Museo del'Arte Moderna, Bologna; Espace Photographique de la Ville de Paris; Architekturmuseum, Basel; Galerie Littmann, Basel; Museo Ken Damy, Brescia, Milan; Cité Universitaire, Geneva; Galerie Littmann, Basel; and others.
Collections: Bibliothèque National, Paris; Swiss Foundation for Photography, Kunsthaus Zurich; Musée de l'Elysée, Lausanne; Moderna Museet, Stockholm; Tel Aviv Museum; Polaroid Collection, Cambridge, Mass.; J. Paul Getty Trust, Malibu, Calif.; Sammlung Ludwig, Frankfurt; Museum Ludwig, Cologne; and others.
Awards: Swiss Federal Grants; First Grand Prize, Triennale de Fribourg; Canada Council Grant; Art Director's Awards, Switzerland, Germany, New York, and Los Angeles; Clio Award, New York; Art Award of the City of Basel.

**Dorothee von Windheim**, Germany, b. 1945.
Studied: Hochschule für Bildende Kunste, Hamburg, 1965–71.
Taught: Kunsthochschule/Universität Kassel, 1989– .
Solo Exhibitions: Hamburger-Kunsthalle, 1987; Museum Wiesbaden, 1989; Stadtisches Museum Abteiberg Monchengladbach, 1991; Kunstverein Bochum, 1993; Kunstverein Schwerte, 1993; Galerie Boer, Hannover, 1993; Kunstraum Fleetinsel, Hamburg, 1994; Galerie Reckermann, Cologne, 1994; Stadtlische Galerie am Markt, Schwabisch-Hall, 1995.

**Andy Warhol**, United States, 1928–87.
Studied: Carnegie Institute of Technology.
Solo Exhibitions: Virginia Commonwealth University, Richmond, 1980; Lucio Amelio Gallery, Naples, 1980; Galerie Bischofberger, Zurich, 1980; Centre d'Art Contemporain, Geneva, 1980; Stedelijk Museum, Amsterdam, 1980; Jewish Museum, New York, 1980; Castelli Graphics, New York, 1981; Galerie Kammer, Hamburg, Germany, 1982; Dover Museum, England, 1982; Leo Castelli Gallery, New York, 1982, 1987; American Museum of Natural History, New York, 1983; Aldrich Museum of Contemporary Art, Ridgefield, Conn., 1983; State University of New York at Old Westbury, 1985; Marisa Del Re Gallery, New York, 1985; Fondazione Amelio Napoli Museo di Capodimonte, Naples, 1985; Texas Christian University, 1986; Dia Art Foundation, New York, 1986; Akira Ikeda Gallery, Tokyo, 1987; Galerie Beaubourg, Paris, 1987; Greenberg Gallery, St. Louis, 1987; Dia Art Foundation, Bridgehampton, N.Y., 1987; Cleveland Center for Contemporary Art, 1987.
Collections: Whitney Museum of American Art, New York; Los Angeles County Museum of Art; Museum of Modern Art, New York; Metropolitan Museum of Art, New York; Moderna Museet, Stockholm; Philadelphia Museum of Art; Walker Art Center, Minneapolis, Minn.; Detroit Institute of Arts, Mich.; Tate Gallery, London; Menil Foundation, Houston; Pasadena Art Museum, Calif.; Des Moines Art Center, Iowa; Art Institute of Chicago; Hirshhorn Museum and Sculpture Garden, Smithsonian Institution, Washington, D.C.; Teheran Museum of Contemporary Art, Iran.

**Carrie Mae Weems**, United States, b. 1953.
Studied: California Institute of the Arts, Valencia, B.A., 1981; University of California, San Diego, M.F.A., 1984; University of California, Berkeley, 1984–87.
Taught: California College of Arts and Crafts, Oakland, 1991.
Solo Exhibitions: Cepa Gallery, Buffalo, N.Y., 1990; P.P.O.W., New York, 1990, 1992; Institute of Contemporary Art, Boston, 1991; Trustman Gallery, Simmons College, Boston, 1991; New Museum of Contemporary Art, New York, 1991; Matrix Gallery, Wadsworth Atheneum, Hartford, Conn., 1991; Albright College, Reading, Pa., 1991; University of Southern California, Irvine, 1991; Art Complex Museum, Duxbury, Mass., 1991; Greenville County Museum of Art, S.C., 1992; Walter/McBean Gallery, San Francisco Art Institute, 1992; Linda Cathcart Gallery, Santa Monica, Calif., 1993; Rhona Hoffman Gallery, Chicago, 1993; New Langton Arts, San Francisco, 1993; Fabric Workshop and Museum, Philadelphia, 1993; National Museum of Women in the Arts, Washington, D.C., 1993–94; San Francisco Museum of Modern Art, 1993–94; Afro-American Museum, Los Angeles, 1993–94; Walker Art Center, Minneapolis, Minn., 1993–94; Institute of Contemporary Art, Philadelphia, 1993–94; Hood Museum of Art, Dartmouth College, Hanover, N.H., 1994; Contemporary Arts Center, Cincinnati, Ohio, 1995; J. Paul Getty Museum, Malibu, Calif., 1995; Biennial Exhibition, Seoul, 1995; Museum of Modern Art, New York, 1996.

**Susan Weil**, United States.
Studied: Academie Julian, Paris; Black Mountain College, N.C.
Solo Exhibitions: Queens Museum, N.Y., 1990; Nine Gallery, Portland, Ore., 1990; Anders Tornberg Gallery, Lund, Sweden, 1990, 1997; Galerie Aronowitsch, Stockholm, 1992; Museum Astley, Uttersberg, Sweden, 1992; Printmaking Workshop, New York, 1992; Gallery Astley, Seattle, 1993; Galerie Simone Gognat, Basel, Switzerland, 1996; National Museum, Stockholm, 1997.
Collections: Museum of Modern Art, New York; Victoria and Albert Museum, London; J. Paul Getty Museum, Malibu, Calif.; Moderna Museet, Stockholm; Humanities Research Center, Texas; Graphische Sammlung, Munich; Harvard University, Cambridge, Mass.; National Museum, Stockholm; Milwaukee Art Museum, Wisc.; Saarland Museum, West Germany; Toledo Museum, Ohio.
Grants: National Endowment for the Arts Visual Artists Fellowship; John Simon Guggenheim Memorial Foundation Fellowship.

**James Richard White**, United States, b. 1950.
Studied: Ohio University, B.F.A., 1972, M.F.A., 1974.
Taught: Murray State University, Ky., 1974–81; Arizona State University, Tempe, 1981– .

**Francis Wilson**, United States, b. 1935. Resides in France.
Studied: University of Michigan, B.A., 1957; University of Paris, M.A., 1974.
Solo Exhibitions: Galerie La Main, Brussels, 1981, 1984; Pedjeshof Gallery, Grubbenvorst, the Netherlands, 1982, 1985; Galeries Nationales de la Tapisserie et d'Art Textile, Beauvais, France, 1984; Centre d'Art Contemporain Pablo Neruda, Corbeil, France, 1986; Galerie Keller, Paris, 1989, 1990; Espace Libergier, Reims, France, 1994.
Collections: North Dakota Museum of Art, Grand Forks; Musée d'Art Modern de la Ville de Paris; French National Collection of Contemporary Art; Musée des Arts Décoratifs, Paris; Raychem Corporation, France, Belgium, United States; Oce Company, Belgium.
Awards: Chevalier, Ordre des Arts et Lettres, Paris.

**Michie Yamaguchi**, Japan, b. 1950.
Studied: Seian Women's College, Kyoto, 1969–71; Ritsumeikan University, Kyoto, B.A., 1986–90.
Taught: Kyoto College of Art 1989– .
Solo Exhibitions: Kyoto College of Art, 1990; Wacoal Ginza Art Space, Tokyo, 1992; Gallery Maronie, Kyoto, 1992, 1993; Gallery Space 21, Tokyo, 1993; Takamatsu Municipal Museum of Art, 1993.
Collections: Daimatsu Company, Kyoto; National Museum of Art, Osaka.
Award: Fourth Itami Craft Exhibition Award, Itami City Craft Center, Hyogo, Japan.

**Teruyoshi (Tsuda) Yoshida**, Japan, b. 1943.
Studied: Kyoto City University of Fine Art, B.F.A., 1969, M.F.A., 1971.
Taught: Seian Women's College of Kyoto, 1974– .
Solo Exhibitions: Gallery Maronie, Kyoto, 1990, 1991, 1992; Wacoal Ginza Art Space, Tokyo, 1990, 1992, 1996.
Collections: Museo de Arts Moderano de Barcelona, Spain; Institute of Contemporary Arts, Kunsan National University, Korea.
Awards: Supreme Prize, Contemporary Japanese Painters for Canada; Grand Prize, Exposisio de Pintura Contemporania a Barcelona; Bronze Prize, Fifth International Triennale of Tapestry, Lodz; Bronze Prize, Contemporary Japanese Painters for Mexico; Outstanding Award, International Textile Competition Kyoto '87.

**Masao Yoshimura**, Japan, b. 1946.
Studied: Kyoto City University of Arts, B.F.A., 1970, M.F.A., 1972.
Solo Exhibitions: Wacoal Ginza Art Space, Tokyo, 1990; Gallery Maronie, Kyoto, 1990, 1995; Galerie 16, Kyoto, 1991; Gallery Space 21, Tokyo, 1993.

**Badanna Zack**, Canada, b. 1933.
Studied: University of Concordia, Montreal; Rutgers University, New Brunswick, N.J.

**Martha Zelt**, United States, b. 1930.
Studied: Temple University, Pa., B.A., 1968.
Taught: Philadelphia College of Art; University of North Carolina, Chapel Hill; Distinguished Visiting Professor, University of Delaware; Pennsylvania Academy of the Fine Arts; Virginia Intermont College; and others.
Solo Exhibitions: Hodges-Taylor Gallery, Charlotte, N.C., 1990; Hickory Museum of Art, N.C., 1992; Taiwan Museum of Art, 1993; Xalapa, Veracruz, Mexico, 1994; Civic Center, Roswell, N. Mex., 1996; Pembroke University, N.C., 1996.
Collections: Brooklyn Museum of Art, N.Y.; Carnegie Institute; Philadelphia Museum of Art; Princeton University, N.J.; Pennsylvania Academy of the Fine Arts; Roswell Museum, N. Mex.; Rhode Island School of Design, Providence; Yale University, New Haven, Conn.; University of New Mexico; and others.
Awards: Pennsylvania Academy Fellowship.

**Barbara Zucker**, United States, b. 1940.
Studied: University of Michigan, B.S., 1962; Hunter College, New York, M.A., 1977.
Taught: University of Vermont, Burlington.
Solo Exhibitions: Sculpture Center, New York, 1989; Haenah-Kent Gallery, New York, 1990; Artists Space, New York, 1994; Goldie Paley Gallery, Moore College of Art and Design, Philadelphia, 1996; One Great Jones, New York, 1997.
Awards: Public Sculpture Commission, Greenwich Library, Conn.; Yaddo Fellowship; Purchase Prize, Ulster County Council on the Arts; National Endowment for the Arts Visual Artists Fellowship; Giverny Fellowship, France; Ucross Foundation, Wyoming.

**Ricardo Estanislao Zulueta**, United States, b. 1962 (Cuba).
Solo Exhibitions: Artists Space, New York, 1992; Humane Society, Western Front, Vancouver, 1993; Center for the Fine Arts, Metro-Dade Art in Public Places, National Foundation for Advancement in the Arts, Miami, 1993; Information Stands, School 33, Baltimore, Md., 1993; San Francisco Art Commission (eight BART and MUNI stations), 1994.
Collections: Cintas Foundation Art Collection; Florida International University Permanent Art Collection, Miami; International Center of Photography, New York; J. I. Kislak Corporate Art Collection; Lehigh University Art Collection; Miami-Dade Public Library Permanent Art Collection; Metro-Dade Art in Public Places; Museum of Art, Fort Lauderdale, Fla.
Awards: San Francisco Art Commission Public Art Grant; Art Matters Fellowship; Mid-Atlantic Artists Residency, National Endowment for the Arts, Baltimore, Md.; National Foundation for the Advancement of the Arts; New York Foundation for the Arts Artists' Fellowship; Cintas Foundation Fellowship; Igor Foundation Artists Grant; Artist in Residence Grant, New York Foundation for the Arts; Artists Space Artists Grant; New York State Council on the Arts Installation Grant; Ludwig Vogelstein Foundation.

# Bibliography

In addition to the notes in each chapter, which include many of the most important books and articles, the following references have been invaluable. The authors' work on their earlier books (*Beyond Craft: The Art Fabric* by Mildred Constantine and Jack Lenor Larsen [New York: Van Nostrand Reinhold, 1973]; *The Art Fabric: Mainstream* by Constantine and Larsen [New York: Van Nostrand Reinhold, 1980]; *Frontiers in Fiber: The Americans* by Mildred Constantine and Laurel Reuter [Grand Forks: North Dakota Museum of Art, 1988]; *Lethal Weapons* by Laurel Reuter [Grand Forks: North Dakota Museum of Art, 1993]) has also informed the text.


Baal-Teshura, Jacob. *Christo & Jeanne-Claude.* Cologne: Benedikt Taschen Verlag, 1995.

Barber, Elizabeth J. W. *Prehistoric Textiles: The Development of Cloth in the Neolithic and Bronze Ages.* Princeton, N.J.: Princeton University Press, 1991.

Barber, Elizabeth Wayland. *Women's Work: The First 20,000 Years.* New York: W. W. Norton & Company, 1994.

Biennale Internationale de la Tapisserie, later known as the Biennale Internationale de Lausanne, Musée Cantonal des Beaux-Arts, Lausanne, Switzerland. Catalogs. Lausanne: CITAM.

Billeter, Erika. *Mythos und Ritual in der Kunst der 70er Jahre.* Zurich: Kunsthaus Zürich, 1981.

Billeter, Erika, ed. *Die Maler und das Theater im 20. Jahrhundert.* Bern, Switzerland: Benteli, 1986.

Bruce, Chris, Rebecca Solnit, and Buzz Spector. *Ann Hamilton São Paulo/Seattle.* Seattle: Henry Art Gallery, University of Washington, 1992.

Colchester, Chloë. *The New Textiles: Trends and Traditions.* London: Thames and Hudson, 1991.

Cooke, Lynne, Marina Warner, and Dave Hickey. *Ann Hamilton: Tropos.* New York: Dia Center for the Arts, 1993.

Emery, Irene. *Archeological Textiles.* Roundtable proceedings. Washington, D.C.: Textile Museum, 1975.

———. *The Primary Structures of Fabrics: An Illustrated Classification.* Washington, D.C.: Textile Museum, 1966.

Felshin, Nina. *Empty Dress: Clothing as Surrogate in Recent Art.* Exhibition catalog. New York: Independent Curators, 1993.

Ferris, Alison. *Discursive Dress.* Sheboygan, Wisc.: John Michael Kohler Arts Center.

Forsha, Lynda, Susan Stewart, and Hugh M. Davies. *Ann Hamilton.* San Diego: San Diego Museum of Contemporary Art.

Geijer, Agnes. *The History of Textile Art.* New York: Pasold Research Fund/Sotheby Parke Bernet Publications, 1979.

Goldberg, RoseLee. *Performance: Live Art 1909 to the Present.* New York: Harry N. Abrams, 1979.

Hishinuma, Yoshiki. *Clothes.* Tokyo: Yobisha Co., 1986.

Hollander, Anne. *Seeing Through Clothes.* London: Viking Penguin, 1978.

Janis, Harriet, and Rudi Blesh. *Collage: Personalities, Concepts and Techniques.* Philadelphia: Chilton Company, 1962.

Kent, Kate Peck. *Prehistoric Textiles of the Southwest.* Santa Fe: School of American Research; Albuquerque: University of New Mexico Press, 1983.

Kotz, Mary Lynn. *Rauschenberg/Art and Life.* New York: Harry N. Abrams, 1990.

Kuryluk, Ewa. *Veronica and Her Cloth.* Cambridge, Mass.: Basil Blackwell, 1991.

Larson, Kay. *American Art Today: Clothing as Metaphor.* Miami: Art Museum at Florida International University, 1993.

Liebmann, Lisa. "A Fashion Gallery." *New York Times Magazine,* Sept. 18, 1994, 72–81.

Lippard, Lucy R. *Overlay: Contemporary Art and the Art of Prehistory.* New York: Pantheon, 1983.

Lonier, Terri L., and Julie Schafler. *Maximum Coverage: Wearables by Contemporary American Artists.* Sheboygan, Wisc.: John Michael Kohler Arts Center, 1980.

*Looking at Fashion.* Florence: Biennale di Firenze, Skira Editore, 1996.

Martin, Richard. *Fall From Fashion.* Ridgefield, Conn.: Aldrich Museum of Contemporary Art, 1993.

Metcalf, Eugene, and Michael Hall. *The Ties That Bind: Folk Art in Contemporary American Culture.* Cincinnati: Contemporary Art Center, 1986.

Miyake Design Studio. *Issey Miyake East Meets West.* Tokyo: Kunihiko Shimonaka, 1978.

Restany, Pierre. *Miralda! "Une vie d'artiste."* Barcelona: Ambit, 1982.

Rosenblum, Naomi. *A World History of Photography.* New York: Abbeville Press, 1984.

Rowe, Ann Polard, and Rebecca A. T. Stevens. *Ed Rossbach: 40 Years of Exploration and Innovation in Fiber Art.* Exhibition catalog (Textile Museum, Washington, D.C.). Asheville, North Carolina: Lark Books, 1990.

Rudofsky, Bernard. *The Unfashionable Human Body.* New York: Doubleday & Company, 1971.

Schwabsky, Barry, Lynne Tillman, and Lynne Cooke. *Jessica Stockholder.* London: Phaidon Press, 1995.

Seitz, William C. *The Art of Assemblage.* New York: Museum of Modern Art, 1961.

Serra, Richard. *Richard Serra/Sculpture.* Exhibition brochure. New York: Museum of Modern Art, 1986.

Stroud, Marion Bauton. *An Industrious Art: Innovation in Pattern and Print at the Fabric Workshop.* Philadelphia: Fabric Workshop; New York: W. W. Norton & Company, 1991.

Thomas, Michel, Christine Mainguy, and Sophie Pommier. *Textile Art.* Geneva: Editions d'Art Albert Skira, 1985.

Tsuji, Kiyoji. *Fiber Art Japan.* Tokyo: Shinshindo Publishing Co., 1994.

Waldman, Diane. *Collage, Assemblage, and the Found Object.* New York: Harry N. Abrams, 1992.

Weiner, Annette, and Jane Schneider, eds. *Cloth and the Human Experience.* Washington, D.C.: Smithsonian Press, 1989.

Wye, Deborah. *Louise Bourgeois.* New York: Museum of Modern Art, 1982.

# Index of Names

Numbers in **bold** refer to figure numbers.

## Photography Credits

Numbers refer to figure numbers.

2. Antoine Sevruguin
5. UPI/Bettman Newsphotos, New York
11. James Bassler
12. Alinari, Italy
14. Lloyd Hamrol
16. John Garrigan
17. Hillel Burger
21. Courtesy Museum of Modern Art, New York
24. Janet Kaplan
26. Rudolph Burckhardt
27. Courtesy Leo Castelli Gallery
29. Edward Leffingwell
30. Jacques Bétant
31. John Gossage
32. Taunton Press, *Threads,* Feb.-Mar. 1986
33. Marla C. Berns
34. David H. Brown
35. Bruce Miller
36. Robert Newcombe
39. Guillermo Olguin Montse Altes
40. Hickey-Robertson
41. Caroline Tisdall
47. John Kasparian
48. Dirk Bakker
50. Peter Moore
52. Richard Monas
54. Su Friedman
55. Sarah Jenkins
56. D. V. Windheim
57. Paul Margolies
59. David Heald
60. Edva-Inker
61. D. James Dee
62. Phillips/Schwab
63. Sarah Wyld/Photo-Copy
68. Al Mozell
69. F. Wilson
70. Vincent LiSanti
71. Takashi Hatakeyama
77. Eric Pollitzer
78. John Bigelow Taylor
83. Ric Sferra, Minneapolis, Minn.
89. Kay Ritta
91. Courtesy Pace Gallery, New York
95. D. James Dee
100. Pok Chi Lau
101. Bayens Photo Company
103. Stephen Rubicam
104. Susan Einstein
106. Walter Drayer
108. Ron Forth
111. Walter Drayer
114. D. James Dee
115. Lloyd Hamrol
117. Edva-Inker
119. Jan Nordahl, Södertälje, Sweden
120. Walter Drayer
121. D. James Dee
123. Valts Kleins
128. Courtesy Galerie Maeght Lelong, Zurich, Switzerland
133. Jolanta Sadowska
134. Laurel Reuter
135. Courtesy Museum of Modern Art, New York
140. Courtesy Museum of Modern Art, New York, Mies van der Rohe Archive
148. Tadasu Yamamoto
149. Per Bergstrom, Stockholm, Sweden
153. Ric Sferra, Minneapolis, Minn.
154. Ric Sferra, Minneapolis, Minn.
155. Wolfgang Volz
156. Jan Nordahl
157. Wolfgang Volz
158. Wolfgang Volz
161. Coco Klinholz
163. Marielys Lorthios
165. Hisano Ino
166. Courtesy Walker Art Center
168. Ric Sferra, Minneapolis, Minn.
170. Ann Hamilton
171. D. James Dee
172. D. James Dee
178. Lois Greenfield
180. Kranichphoto
183. Charles Atlas
185. P. Berthelot
186. Dan Esgro
187. Jim Staebler
188. Torben Voigt, Denmark
189. Torben Voigt, Denmark
190. Colifa, Barcelona
192. Lee Eun-joo
193. Neil Selkirk
194. Minsei Tominaga
198. Bob Hansson
201. Gilles Tapie
202. Gilles Tapie
203. Yutaka Sakano
205. Jeanne-Claude
209. Erik Landsberg, New York
213. Courtesy Fred Hoffman Gallery, Santa Monica, Calif.
216. Ric Sferra, Minneapolis, Minn.

## About the Authors

Mildred Constantine is an art historian, curator, and educator. She was curator at the Museum of Modern Art for over twenty years and has organized exhibitions for that museum and for the Smithsonian Institution. Her books include *Tina Modotti: A Fragile Life, Beyond Craft: The Art Fabric* (with Jack Lenor Larsen), and *The Art Fabric: Mainstream* (with Larsen), and she has written and edited many publications for the Museum of Modern Art. She lives and works in New York.

Laurel Reuter is the director of the North Dakota Museum of Art, which she founded in the late 1970s as the state's first art museum. She has curated over one hundred exhibitions of contemporary art, toured exhibitions throughout the Pacific Rim and China, and published extensively in the field of contemporary art. Most recently she has written the exhibition catalog *Autobiography: Words and Images from Life* about the work of three Canadian artists, as well as monographs on South African artist Georgie Papageorge and Uruguayan painter Ignacio Iturria.

# From International Waters

# From International Waters

## 60 Years of Offshore Broadcasting

*Mike Leonard*

FOREST PRESS (HESWALL)

*ISBN 0 9527684 0 2*



*First published 1996*

*Reprinted (with minor amendments) 1997*



*Printed in Great Britain by*

*Alphagraphics Ltd., Pall Mall House, Mercury Court, Tithebarn Street, Liverpool L2 2QP*

*Published by*

*Forest Press (Heswall), P O Box 1, Heswall, Wirral, L60 3TH, England.*

*British Library Cataloguing-in-Publication Data*

*A catalogue record for this book is available from the British Library.*

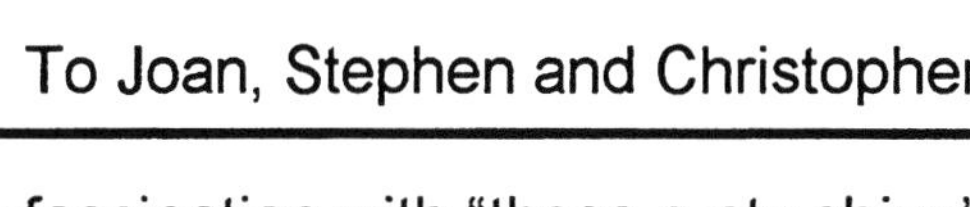

To Joan, Stephen and Christopher

for patiently tolerating my fascination with "those rusty ships"

# Acknowledgements

Many people and organisations have provided help and assistance to me in researching information for this book.

I would particularly like to thank the following who have assisted greatly with various research details:- Geoff Baldwin of *Radio Review*, Chris Edwards and Francois Lhote of *Offshore Echo's,* DFDS Seaways, the *Daily Mail* Research Library and Mike Kerslake of *Playback Radio Works*. My thanks also to Ted Allbeury for contributing a foreword and to Bill Armstrong and Andy Horner for their invaluable assistance and technical advice on matters associated with production aspects. Without all this help such a comprehensive record would not have been possible.

Thousands of source documents were studied during the course of my research and I thank all those un-named people who produced contemporary publications and records chronicling events surrounding offshore radio. I would particularly like to record my thanks to the late Roland 'Buster' Pearson whose *Monitor Magazine* proved an invaluable source of extremely detailed and accurate information covering some of the most active and volatile years of offshore broadcasting history.

I have acknowledged separately all individual sources of photographs used in this book - where these are known. Unfortunately although extensive efforts have been made to trace the originators of others I have sometimes been unsuccessful, nevertheless I also offer my thanks to them, whoever they are.

Finally, but most importantly, I would like to thank all those who owned, operated and worked on offshore broadcasting stations providing entertainment pleasure for millions of people and without whose efforts this book would not have been possible at all.

Picture Acknowledgements

I thank the following people and organisations for kindly supplying photographs used in this book. Every effort has been made to trace copyright of others, but sometimes this has proved unsuccessful. Any further information about the source of photographs will be incorporated in possible future editions.

Geoff Baldwin (Pages 346, 354, 356, 357, 374, 388, 398, 399, 420); Caroline Sales (pages 490 and 540); Danish State Archive/DFDS Seaways (page 63); Stuart Dobson (page 469); the former Free Radio Association (pages 48, 50, 66, 84,90, 98, 112-114, 118, 129, 133, 197, 206, 225, 229, 231, 235 and 250); Lion Keezer (page 288); Mike Kerslake (pages 461 and 465); Keystone (page 83) *Offshore Echos* Magazine (pages 23, 91, 309, 385, 452, 472, 484, 511, 515, 518 and, 522); Pye of Cambridge (page 81); Paul Rusling (page 519).

# Contents

# Introduction

If you ask anybody over the age of about 35 to name an offshore or 'pirate' radio station most will probably answer "Radio Caroline".

For over three decades the name of Radio Caroline has been synonymous with the whole concept of floating radio stations broadcasting from international waters, outside territorial limits and outside government regulation or control.

During the 1960s Radio Caroline was the first of a flotilla of such stations off the British coast whose collective activities influenced public and official thinking on the range and choice of radio services available at that time. Changes and developments in the structure of British radio broadcasting since then can still be traced back to the influence of those 60s offshore broadcasters.

However, the story of offshore broadcasting is much older even than Radio Caroline and far more widespread than those stations which broadcast from off the British coast. Similar stations have been located off Scandinavia, Holland, Belgium, Israel, New Zealand, Africa and even the USA.

In writing this book I have attempted to chronicle the complete worldwide story of offshore broadcasting and to place all relevant incidents in their historical context. It has not always been easy to achieve this objective because by their very nature offshore stations were organised in a clandestine manner and within this secretive atmosphere rumours and counter-rumours abounded. Firm information often became distorted, either deliberately or through the dissemination of gossip disguised as 'news'.

However, very many facts are known for certain and, wherever possible, the information contained in this book has been verified from more than one source. Where doubt remains (and in some cases the real truth may never be known) this is made clear or alternative versions are provided, so you can draw your own conclusions.

I hope this book is one which everyone interested in this phenomenon of 20th Century social and broadcasting history will find interesting, informative and useful. No doubt many readers who have knowledge or personal experience of working on offshore stations will have details to expand information or to fill in any gaps and I would welcome that feedback for inclusion in any possible future editions.

*Mike Leonard*

December 1996

# Foreword

When Mike Leonard asked me to write a foreword to this book he sent me a copy of something that I wrote nearly 30 years ago and I felt that, in fact, it shows not much has altered since those days:-

*Red Sands Rendezvous*

*One of the problems of discussing anything new in Great Britain is the difficulties induced by our strong sense of national hypocrisy and this, when coupled with a natural resistance to any kind of change, clouds most issues in our public life.*

*For many years we had BBC radio and it was a much valued part of our lives for both information and entertainment. Catch-words and jokes were based on radio programmes and the interpretation of the world news was based on the BBC news. We were very proud of what we got and the world-wide acceptance of our radio station with its impartial reporting of the news from all parts of the world seemed to justify our pride.*

*When BBC Television first started it was for a few hours a day and for the very small audience who could afford television sets. One of the strongest arguments against television was that it would stop people reading books. However, I fail to see that reading a book has any more virtue to it than looking at television.*

*Not only was this initial argument against television proved quite wrong because television has done much to increase the reading of books, but it was wrong in its basic thought - that reading a book was a virtue and looking at television was either a lesser virtue or an actual vice. People say "Ah yes but a lot of what appears on television is just twaddle", but there is an even greater proportion of twaddle in books and like many other people I read that too because we are not always in a mood either with books or television to be educated or improved. We sometimes just want to relax.*

*When independent television came along it is interesting to note that it was felt necessary to refer to it as 'independent' rather than 'commercial'. The great argument against it was that the public would not like the advertisements and that the programmes would appeal to the lowest level of taste. It was inferred that the good British citizen would much prefer the higher standards of BBC Television, but like so many preconceived ideas all this was soon proved to be wrong.*

*The argument then used by the defenders of the state monopolies that ITV only succeeds because of the low intellectual level of its programmes. This may of course be so. Nevertheless the other side of this argument is that ITV does provide the public with what it wants and if the intellectual level of what the public wants is low that must be blamed on our educational system, not on those who provide our entertainment.*

*The audience listening to pirate radio stations had to be measured in millions. Again the criticism comes up that the millions only listen because of the low intellectual level of the programmes. Now, the programmes provided by the pirates were virtually entirely music and some stations played pop and some stations played sweet music. I wonder who are the people who decide that both of these are low on the intellectual scale? Much as I like classical music I cannot see why at the same time I cannot like Jerome Kern and Ivor Novello or The Beatles. These intellectual classifications seem to me a proof of narrow mindedness.*

*The most interesting fact is that the views which I am expressing in this small magazine, Breakthrough, are held by large numbers of people, but they have to be expressed in this small magazine because no newspaper would give space to airing them. Why? Simply the newspapers do not want competition from commercial radio for their advertising. They are afraid that just as television was shown as a rival for the available advertising money, commercial radio would be yet another. So, although brief reports will be given on meetings and rallies for commercial radio they are always slanted and frequently misreported and the general impression given that the people concerned are a bunch of cranks.*

*Even politicians who support commercial radio talk about protecting newspapers and the great tragedy it would be if a newspaper ceased to publish. However, the British being what they are I am sure there must have been lots of protest at the passing of the town criers when newspapers were first published.*

*In ten years time I think there will only be two or three newspapers because our news and commentary on the news will come to us each day through the television receivers. At the pressing of a button the news will be pumped out of the television set on a long sheet of paper like a teleprinter works now. Equally our television and radio will come to us via satellites from all over the world, but this will only happen when we accept that all forms of communication should be completely independent and that the listener and viewer in any country in the world should be able to see and hear anything he chooses.*

(*Breakthrough Magazine,* October 1969)

I feel that one of the great mistakes made was to lump radio and television together in the BBC. They are two entirely different media and because the new arrangements meant that there was no radio licence, it also meant that there was no independent funding of BBC radio. With the advent of more and more satellite receivers it is only a matter of years before some government has to recognise that it is quite unfair for people to pay a TV licence to fund an organisation that no longer provides the main part of their entertainment.

I read now that we have our first "women's" radio station, Viva!, which reminds me of how we started off the days of Radio 390's broadcasting with "Eve - Women's Magazine of the Air". As a matter of interest I still get letters from many Radio 390 listeners.

It all seems a long time ago now, but there is no doubt that one still hears echoes from those very happy days.

*Ted Allbeury*

*Ted Allbeury has been successful in many professional spheres both before and since his association with offshore radio during the mid-1960s.*

*Leaving school at 16 to work in a foundry he later qualified as a pilot and eventually joined the Army Intelligence Corps. He served in Africa, Italy and Germany, where he was involved in rounding up Nazi intelligence personnel and seeking out last ditch underground movements - experience he was to put to good use in his later writings.*

*After the War he held various sales management posts and became an advertising and public relations consultant. It was during this time that he became successfully involved in offshore radio as Managing Director of easy listening station Radio 390, and later Radios 355 and 227. Following the demise of offshore broadcasting he became a farmer, but returned to the world of public relations in the mid-1970s.*

*His first espionage thriller, "A Choice of Enemies", was published in 1973 and has since been followed by over 20 titles, making him one of Britain's top-selling authors.*

## Chapter 1

# Why Offshore ?

Before beginning to trace the detailed history of offshore radio and television it is worth taking some time to explore why this broadcasting phenomenon ever came to exist in the first place.

Establishing a radio or television station which transmits its programmes from a ship or sea-bed structure in sometimes dangerous and inhospitable conditions miles out at sea is not everyone's idea of a sensible business venture. So why did anybody do it and why did the stations have to be located away from all the comforts and convenience of a land-base?

There are many reasons why entrepreneurs and enthusiasts alike set up offshore stations to challenge or compete with established broadcasters. Apart from the profit motive, which applied to nearly all offshore ventures, some people had identified gaps or shortcomings in the existing services, which were generally state monopolies, and sought to fill them. Others saw a station, over which they had complete control, as the ideal vehicle to promote the output of their own record labels or recording artists. A few, attempting to emulate the perceived success of the larger, well organised offshore broadcasters, simply hoped to make a quick profit, but the reality for them was often a loss making venture.

For whatever 'business' reason the stations were established, one feature common to all was that they had to operate outside the jurisdiction of the country or countries to which they broadcast and the reasons for having to do so can be traced back to the beginning of broadcasting history.

### Government Regulations

Almost from the outset regulatory controls were imposed by governments of all political shades over the use of airwaves, usually permitting only a state-owned or state-operated service to broadcast within a specific country. Alternatively some governments issued a limited number of licences, franchises or concessions to 'independent' operators granting them, in effect, monopoly rights to provide a particular service.

A classic example of this type of governmental control was to be found in Britain where Marconi's invention of wireless telegraphy had been patented in 1896. The following year Marconi's Wireless Telegraph Company Ltd. was formed and started to commercially exploit this new means of communication, primarily in maritime transmissions using Morse Code. However, by 1904 the British parliament had introduced the Wireless Telegraphy Act prohibiting the establishment of any new wireless telegraph station, except under licence from the Postmaster General.

Severe restrictions were imposed on non-military uses of wireless telegraphy during the First World War, but when those were lifted in 1919 Marconi established a public broadcasting station at Writtle, near Chelmsford, transmitting for two and a half hours each day with a power of 6Kw.

#### FIRST OFFSHORE BROADCASTS

*Marconi used what might loosely be considered the first offshore radio station during his early experimental broadcasts. The yacht 'Electra' was purchased by the Marchese Marconi in 1919 and fitted out with what was then the latest radio equipment, or wireless apparatus, forming a unique floating laboratory. The 'Electra' was used by Marconi to investigate the possible use and application of radio transmissions as a navigational aid. The vessel also became involved in a broadcast of gramophone records to a meeting of the Imperial Press Union in Canada in July 1920 along with other Marconi stations in Chelmsford (Essex), Poldhu (Cornwall) and St. Johns (Newfoundland).*

By 1920 the Post Office, under pressure from the military authorities who had enjoyed exclusive rights during the War, prevented any further commercial development of wireless telegraphy until a system of public broadcasting and receiving licences had been introduced. These came in 1921 when 4,000 private individuals and 150 operators were officially licensed to receive or transmit radio broadcasts. Marconi was one of the 150 operators licensed by the Post Office and on 14th February 1922 his station - 2MT in Chelmsford started broadcasts while another experimental station was opened from Marconi House in central London.

The success of experimental broadcasts made by the Marconi Company led, in October 1922, to the formation by a number of radio manufacturers of the British Broadcasting Company Ltd. (BBC). On 18th January 1923 the BBC was licensed by the Postmaster General as the sole body authorised to "establish eight radio telegraphy stations and make transmissions from them of broadcast matter for general reception." The BBC, which obtained its income from half of the 10/- (50p) licence fee and a 10% royalty on all receiving sets sold, had a remit to broadcast "news, speeches, lectures, educational matter, weather reports, concerts and theatrical entertainment." The Company had thus been given monopoly rights over public broadcasting which it retained after becoming the British Broadcasting Corporation on 1st January 1927.

In addition to sound broadcasting the new Corporation took part in the early development of television, and as early as 1929 started experimental transmissions in that medium. In 1935 the Corporation was granted an additional licence by the Postmaster General to provide a public television service, which was introduced the following year. The BBC maintained its monopoly position in this medium for another 20 years but it was to be a lot longer before it relinquished that status in radio broadcasting. The story of how that position was challenged and broken is told in the chapters which follow.

This is one example of state control over the broadcasting systems but the situation was not unique to Britain and similar government licensing controls and restrictions were introduced by many other countries throughout the world.

## International Agreements

In addition to national government restrictions on who could provide broadcasting services the allocation of frequencies and transmitter powers were regulated by international agreement from quite early days. A number of such agreements were made at conferences of the Union Internationale de Radiophonie (UIR) in Geneva (1925), Brussels (1926), Prague (1929) Madrid (1932) and Lucerne (1933) and were designed initially to avoid technical chaos on the airwaves, particularly in Europe. Within a short time, however, the agreements were being broken or ignored -even by signatories to the original treaties, leading to the very chaos they were intended to prevent.

The 1948 Copenhagen Convention supposedly governed the use of radio frequencies after the Second World War and was most often quoted by governments and authorised broadcasters when accusing offshore stations of pirating frequencies and breaking international agreements. In fact when the Copenhagen Convention was signed seven countries (Austria, Iceland, Portugal, Spain, Luxembourg, Sweden and Turkey) refused to accept the frequencies which had been allocated to them. Further, by the time the first British offshore radio station arrived in 1964, seventeen countries who were signatories had still not fully ratified the agreement. The cumulative effect of this was that by the mid 1960s between 300 and 500 radio stations in Europe were using frequencies without authorisation under the 1948 Copenhagen Convention. In this context the relatively small number of frequencies used ('pirated') by the offshore stations pales into insignificance and many offshore broadcasters drew attention to this situation in justifying their own use of a frequency which had not been allocated to them under the international agreement.

Despite the repeated breaking of agreements all these controls made some sort of sense at the time they were introduced - radio is a very powerful medium, with the potential for a single station's broadcasts to reach many millions of listeners. The mere thought of anarchy on the airwaves was sufficient stimulus for most governments in the 1920s and 1930s to impose tight controls over who would be permitted to engage in the business of transmitting radio (and later television) programmes within their boundaries. Generally they opted to retain that right for themselves or for bodies over which they had overriding control.

In some countries the actual principle of having commercially funded programmes was repudiated by governments and state monopoly broadcasters alike. Radio was considered too powerful a medium to be controlled by private businessmen and it was feared that profits would be maximised at the expense of programme standards - as, according to critics, had apparently happened in the USA. Even in those countries which developed the hybrid of a state broadcasting service accepting commercial advertising spots or programme sponsorship the government-backed monopoly was usually protected from the introduction of a competitive private commercial system by restrictive rules and regulations.

## Breaking the monopolies

Over the years many state broadcasting systems became stale and insular, reluctant to experiment and slow to develop new programmes or services to meet the changing tastes of their listeners. Why should they try? They had a complete monopoly position with no worries about the output of competitors who may steal their audience. In many countries, particularly European ones, there was a latent demand amongst advertisers and listeners for alternative radio services, but before these could be provided loopholes in the various national and international regulations had to be identified.

In places with a state monopoly system such as Britain there simply was no opportunity for an entrepreneur to legally establish a private, commercially funded radio station broadcasting from within the country on a frequency which had been allocated to it by international agreement. Therefore, to put a station on the air within the limitations of the law, prospective operators were forced to look elsewhere for a base from which they could legitimately broadcast.

One loophole in the rules and regulations was found by enterprising British commercial broadcasters before the Second World War when the transmitters of various European stations were hired and used to beam programmes to audiences eager for a more varied and lively output than the BBC was offering at the time.

The first attempt at providing such an alternative to the fledgling BBC came in 1925 when the transmitter of Radio Paris was used to present an English language fashion programme sponsored by Selfridges, the London department store. Unfortunately due to the absence of almost any advance publicity for the programme the French station only received three letters from listeners saying they had heard the broadcast! Unsuccessful in audience terms it may have been, but this broadcast was to set a precedent for the future. The Radio Paris programme, and the sponsorship deal with Selfridges, had been arranged by Captain Leonard F Plugge, who having learnt from this experience re-emerged a few years later to arrange substantially more successful English language commercial broadcasts from transmitters across Europe.

Other entrepreneurs tried too. In 1927 Hilversum Radio in Holland broadcast a series of Sunday Concerts, sponsored by radio manufacturers Kolster Brandes Ltd., which were directed at listeners in Britain, while Radio Toulouse started English language broadcasts in 1929 with programmes sponsored by various British gramophone companies.

By the beginning of the 1930s Captain Plugge was back on the scene. A former consulting engineer on the London Underground, he was at that time running a business organising some of the earliest holiday package tours to France and his vehicle was equipped with one of the first ever car radios, manufactured by Philco. He realised as he toured France tuning in to various regional stations that they could be a possible outlet for further broadcasts to British audiences.

By 1930 five million radio sets had been sold in Britain and in May of that year, having learned many lessons from his initial experiences a few years earlier, Captain Plugge decided to form the International Broadcasting Company (IBC) and exploit this large potential audience. He managed to negotiate a deal with the head of the Benedictine distillery at Fecamp in northern France to hire airtime from his experimental station broadcasting under the call sign Radio Normandy.

The IBC started its transmissions in October 1931 using this transmitter on a wavelength of 269.5m. The broadcasts were initially transmitted at a power of 10Kw but this was later boosted to 20Kw when a new transmitter was installed at Louvetot in Normandy. Consequently the programmes were able to be received over a large part of southern England and the station soon attracted a large listenership.

The first employee of IBC and the station's first 'Disc Jockey' was Max Stanniforth who presented a three hour programme consisting largely of popular contemporary dance music. The station even invented the 'IBC Orchestra', leading listeners to believe that it could provide stiff competition for the BBC, which by then had its own range of successfully established orchestras. Although no such orchestra actually existed at IBC it served to give the distinct impression that the whole operation was much larger than it was in reality.

The International Broadcasting Company also later used the transmitters of other European stations to beam programmes to Britain - Poste Parisien on 312.8m with a power of 60Kw, Radio Lyons on 215m with a power of 25Kw, Radio Toulouse on 328.6m and Radio Mediterranne on 235.1m.

By the end of 1932 twenty one British advertisers were sponsoring English language programmes on European radio stations, including producers of cigarettes, foodstuffs, record and radio equipment and cars as well as film companies and various retail distributors. Advertising expenditure by British companies on these stations was estimated to be in the region of £400,000 per year in 1935 and by 1938 this figure had increased to £1.7 million, a very significant sum in those days.

### RADIO NORMANDY

*Radio Normandy's programmes, mainly sponsored 15 minute segments of music, were broadcast on Sundays from 7.00am-11.45am, 1.30pm -7.30pm and 10.00pm-1.00am and on weekdays from 7.00am-11.30am, 2.00pm-6.00pm and 12 midnight to 1.00am. The station's wavelength was changed to 212.6m in 1938 and again the following year to 274m. Early advertisers on the IBC programmes included Spinks (London jewellers) and Dunlop Tyres.*

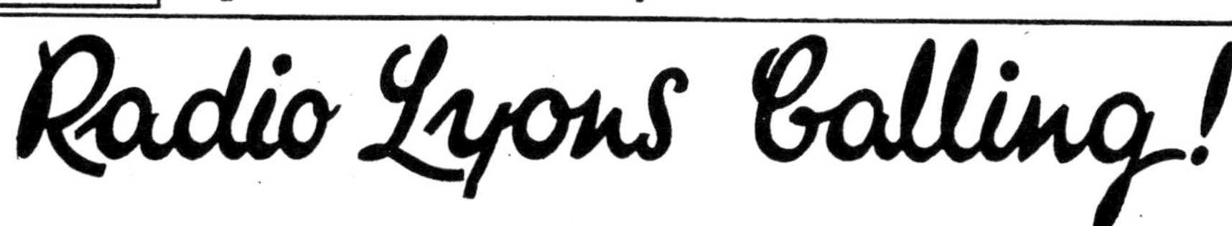


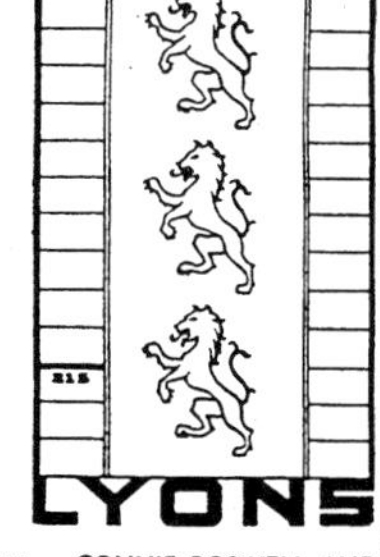


**Announcer: Gerald Carnes**

**Tune-in to 215 metres for never-failing entertainment—Variety, Dance Music, Music Hall, Organ Music, Humour, Song.**

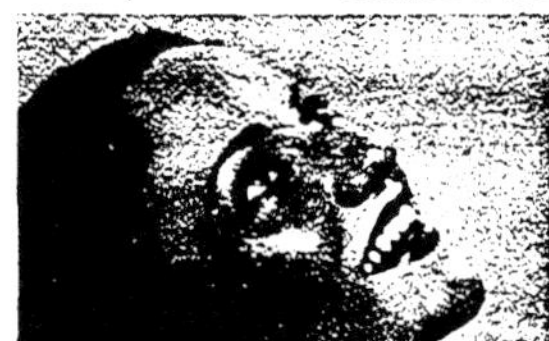

**9.15 p.m.** THE ZAM-BUK PROGRAMME A musical programme of interest to all.—*Sent to you by the makers of* Zam-Buk.

**9.30 p.m.** ALFREDO CAMPOLI AND HIS ORCHESTRA. A programme of light music, and an interesting talk by Nurse Johnson.—*Sent to you by courtesy of the makers of* California Syrup of Figs.

**9.45 p.m:** WALTZ TIME with Billy Bissett, Pat Hyde, Sam Costa and the Waltz Timers.—*Presented by* Phillips' Dental Magnesia

**10.0 p.m.** "SONGS AND SENTIMENT"

**10.30 p.m.** BENNY GOODMAN AND HIS ORCHESTRA. America's leading swing orchestra in a programme of gramophone records.

**10.45 p.m.** THE PALL MALL PARADE Another in the series of daily programmes, —*Presented by courtesy of the* House of Rothman.

**11.0 p.m.** "ON WITH THE DANCE" (Hot, Sweet and Swing). Dance music at its best.

**11.30 p.m.** "THE NIGHT WATCHMAN." Our daily patchwork of old ballads

**10.30 p.m.** CONNIE BOSWELL AND THE BOSWELL SISTERS. A Gramophone Record Programme. The Sisters Boswell (Connie, Martha and Vet) were born in New Orleans, Louisiana. When quite

## Rapid Expansion

By May of 1932 another European station, Radio Luxembourg had started test transmissions directed at Britain from its powerful transmitter in Junglinster and over the following months it continued to make these broadcasts on a number of wavelengths including 1250m, 1185m and 1191m. Regular English language programmes from this station were originally planned to commence on 4th June 1933, using a wavelength of 1191m in the long waveband. However, following complaints of interference and accusations (largely emanating from within the BBC) that it was pirating frequencies Radio Luxembourg delayed the introduction of its English language service. When the UIR Lucerne frequency allocation agreement came into effect on 1st January 1934 Radio Luxembourg changed its wavelength to 1304m and almost immediately began regular broadcasts to Britain. By the late 1930s Radio Luxembourg's popular English language programmes were being broadcast on Sundays from 8.15am-12midnight and at various times for up to eight hours each weekday.

Radio Luxembourg programmes were similar to those of the IBC affiliated stations in Europe and in the early years many were actually produced using IBC's London studio facilities. The IBC also obtained the concession to sell airtime on Radio Luxembourg's English service and early advertisers included national brands such as Bile Beans (a laxative), Zam Buck (a herbal based cream) and the Irish Hospitals Sweepstake. This concession was lost in 1936, however, when Radio Luxembourg decided to set up its own in-house sales organisation, Wireless Publicity Ltd.

Meanwhile in 1935 the IBC had formed its own production unit to record the growing number of sponsored programmes broadcast on various affiliated stations. The company's original studios were at 11 Hallam Street, London W1 and these soon expanded to adjacent properties at 8 and 9 Duchess Street. By 1937 the company had moved to larger premises on five floors at 37 Portland Place (near the BBC's then newly constructed headquarters, Broadcasting House) where it employed a staff of 180 people. It also had three outside broadcast vehicles which visited towns and seaside resorts throughout Britain recording programmes for later broadcast from the European transmitters. To deal with the vast interest in the Company's output the IBC Club was formed in 1932 and by the end of the decade it had achieved a membership of over 320,000.

As well as Radio Luxembourg and the IBC network a number of other European stations started broadcasts directed towards Britain including Radio Athlone (later Radio Eircann) in Ireland, Radio Cote de Azur in Spain and even Radio Ljubljana in Yugoslavia.

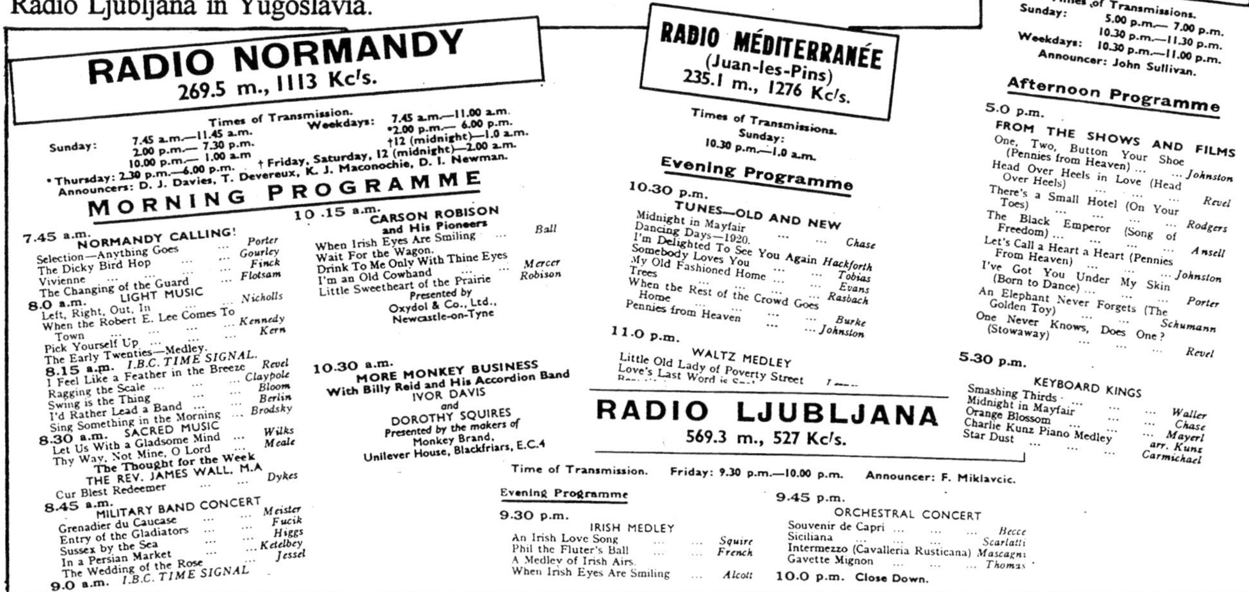

**RADIO NORMANDY**
269.5 m., 1113 Kc/s.

Times of Transmission.
Sunday: 7.45 a.m.—11.45 a.m. 2.00 p.m.— 7.30 p.m. 10.00 p.m.— 1.00 a.m
Weekdays: 7.45 a.m.—11.00 a.m. *2.00 p.m.— 6.00 p.m. †12 (midnight)—1.0 a.m.
* Thursday: 2.30 p.m.—6.00 p.m. † Friday, Saturday, 12 (midnight)—2.00 a.m.
Announcers: D. J. Davies, T. Devereux, K. J. Maconochie, D. I. Newman.

MORNING PROGRAMME

7.45 a.m. NORMANDY CALLING!
Selection—Anything Goes ... Porter
The Dicky Bird Hop ... Gourley
Vivienne ... Finck
The Changing of the Guard ... Flotsam

8.0 a.m. LIGHT MUSIC
Left, Right, Out, In ... Nicholls
When the Robert E. Lee Comes To Town ... Kennedy
Pick Yourself Up ... Kern
The Early Twenties—Medley.
I.B.C. TIME SIGNAL.

8.15 a.m.
I Feel Like a Feather in the Breeze ... Revel
Ragging the Scale ... Claypole
Swing is the Thing ... Bloom
I'd Rather Lead a Band ... Berlin
Sing Something in the Morning ... Brodsky

8.30 a.m. SACRED MUSIC
Let Us With a Gladsome Mind ... Wilks
Thy Way, Not Mine, O Lord ... Meale
The Thought for the Week
THE REV. JAMES WALL, M.A
Cur Blest Redeemer ... Dykes

8.45 a.m. MILITARY BAND CONCERT
Grenadier du Caucase ... Meister
Entry of the Gladiators ... Fucik
Sussex by the Sea ... Higgs
In a Persian Market ... Ketelbey
The Wedding of the Rose ... Jessel

9.0 a.m. I.B.C. TIME SIGNAL

10.15 a.m. CARSON ROBISON and His Pioneers
When Irish Eyes Are Smiling ... Ball
Wait For the Wagon.
Drink To Me Only With Thine Eyes
I'm an Old Cowhand ... Mercer
Little Sweetheart of the Prairie ... Robison
Presented by Oxydol & Co., Ltd., Newcastle-on-Tyne

10.30 a.m. MORE MONKEY BUSINESS
With Billy Reid and His Accordion Band
IVOR DAVIS
and
DOROTHY SQUIRES
Presented by the makers of Monkey Brand, Unilever House, Blackfriars, E.C.4

**RADIO MÉDITERRANÉE**
(Juan-les-Pins)
235.1 m., 1276 Kc/s.

Times of Transmissions.
Sunday:
10.30 p.m.—1.0 a.m.

Evening Programme

10.30 p.m. TUNES—OLD AND NEW
Midnight in Mayfair
Dancing Days—1920. ... Chase
I'm Delighted To See You Again ... Hackforth
Somebody Loves You
My Old Fashioned Home ... Tobias
Trees ... Evans
When the Rest of the Crowd Goes Home ... Rasbach
Pennies from Heaven ... Burke
... Johnston

11.0 p.m. WALTZ MEDLEY
Little Old Lady of Poverty Street
Love's Last Word is [illegible] [illegible]

**PARIS (Poste Parisien)**
312.8 m., 959 Kc/s.

Times of Transmissions.
Sunday: 5.00 p.m.— 7.00 p.m. 10.30 p.m.—11.30 p.m.
Weekdays: 10.30 p.m.—11.00 p.m.
Announcer: John Sullivan.

Afternoon Programme

5.0 p.m. FROM THE SHOWS AND FILMS
One, Two, Button Your Shoe (Pennies from Heaven) ... Johnston
Head Over Heels in Love (Head Over Heels) ... Revel
There's a Small Hotel (On Your Toes) ... Rodgers
The Black Emperor (Song of Freedom) ... Ansell
Let's Call a Heart a Heart (Pennies From Heaven) ... Johnston
I've Got You Under My Skin (Born to Dance) ... Porter
An Elephant Never Forgets (The Golden Toy) ... Schumann
One Never Knows, Does One? (Stowaway) ... Revel

5.30 p.m. KEYBOARD KINGS
Smashing Thirds ... Waller
Midnight in Mayfair ... Chase
Orange Blossom ... Mayerl
Charlie Kunz Piano Medley ... arr. Kunz
Star Dust ... Carmichael

**RADIO LJUBLJANA**
569.3 m., 527 Kc/s.

Time of Transmission. Friday: 9.30 p.m.—10.00 p.m. Announcer: F. Miklavcic.

Evening Programme

9.30 p.m. IRISH MEDLEY
An Irish Love Song ... Squire
Phil the Fluter's Ball ... French
A Medley of Irish Airs.
When Irish Eyes Are Smiling ... Alcott

9.45 p.m. ORCHESTRAL CONCERT
Souvenir de Capri ... Becce
Siciliana ... Scarlatti
Intermezzo (Cavalleria Rusticana) Mascagni
Gavette Mignon ... Thomas

10.0 p.m. Close Down.

All these commercially funded broadcasts from Europe, which consisted mainly of popular music of the day presented in a friendly and informal style, were extremely popular with British audiences who preferred them to the staid and dull BBC output. *The Survey of Listening to Sponsored Radio Programmes* published in 1938 by the Joint Committee of the Incorporated Society of British Advertisers and the Institute of Incorporated Practitioners in Advertising, showed that Radio Luxembourg alone had a Sunday audience rating of 45.7% in Britain compared with the BBC's 35%. However, despite this high audience level for Radio Luxembourg some of the other, smaller European stations were not so successful in attracting sufficient advertising income and subsequently discontinued their English language programming.

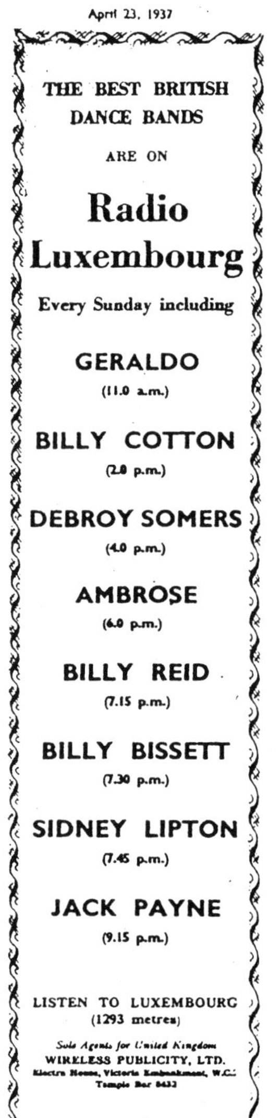


## Government Response

The British Government's response to the commercial radio broadcasts from Europe was hostile. It made a number of representations through the Union Internationale de Radiophonie (UIR) about the alleged 'pirating' of a frequency by Radio Luxembourg, but could do nothing about the IBC transmissions from Radio Normandy because that station broadcast quite legitimately on an authorised frequency. At the 1933 UIR Conference in Lucerne various countries, including Britain, tried to force Luxembourg to accept a medium wave frequency instead of its more powerful long wave one, but the tiny Principality refused to sign the agreement.

The only direct way that the authorities could strike at foreign based stations broadcasting to Britain was to refuse, through the General Post Office, to allow the use of telephone lines to relay programmes direct from London to the various transmitters in Europe. Consequently the stations had to record nearly all their programme material on large, 16 inch records (magnetic recording tape was not in general use in those days), which were then taken over to the Continent to be broadcast from the appropriate European transmitters. Later Radio Normandy installed two Western Electric 35mm cinema projectors and programmes were then recorded in London on the film soundtrack - giving superior sound quality and the ability to record full half hour shows on a single reel.

Another hostile reaction to the early commercial stations came in the form of a remarkable act of behind the scenes censorship by the British Government. It persuaded newspaper proprietors, mostly members of the Newspaper Publishers Association, not to publish information, especially programme schedules, about the broadcasts directed at Britain. Only one newspaper, the *Sunday Referee*, refused to comply with the Government's 'request' and continued to publish programme details for the European based commercial stations. For this defiance the paper was expelled from the Newspaper Publishers Association in February 1933. It was hoped that lack of information about programmes and wavelengths would prevent listeners tuning in, but the broadcasters hit back by publishing their own magazine, *Radio Pictorial*. This weekly magazine, sub titled "the all-family radio paper", was first published on 19th January 1934 and contained detailed programme listings for each station, including the titles of records to be played during various programmes.

LISTEN TO
LUXEMBOURG
EVERY DAY

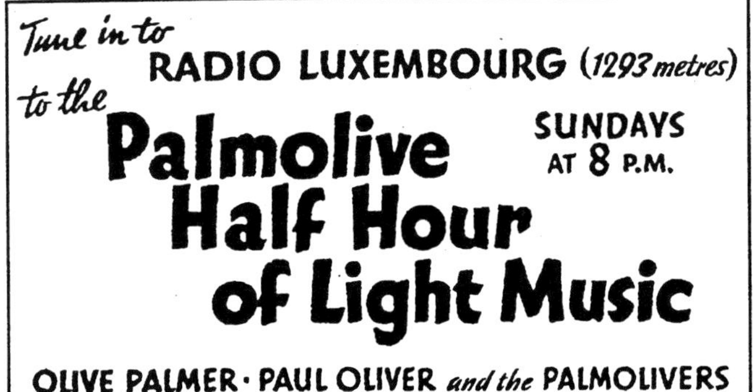

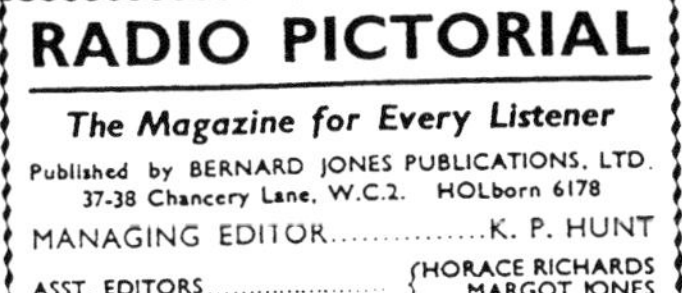
No. 174
RADIO PICTORIAL
The Magazine for Every Listener
Published by BERNARD JONES PUBLICATIONS, LTD. 37-38 Chancery Lane, W.C.2. HOLborn 6178
MANAGING EDITOR............... K. P. HUNT
ASST. EDITORS........................ HORACE RICHARDS, MARGOT JONES

THERE'S LAUGHTER IN THE AIR!

In November 1935 the *Sunday Referee* closed and (apart from *Radio Pictorial*) the communist party newspaper, the *Daily Worker*, became the only British publication carrying Radio Luxembourg's programme details. The paper proudly proclaimed "No other daily newspaper in Britain gives the Luxembourg programmes. The *Daily Worker* is now able to fill that gap."

The British Government also exerted further pressure against the European based stations by encouraging the BBC not to employ any artist or presenter who had worked for Radio Luxembourg and persuading the British Phonographic Industry (later the Performing Rights Society) to increase the fees it charged to Radio Luxembourg - effectively forcing that station to pay much higher rates than the BBC.

## The Ullswater Committee

The strength of feeling on both sides about the introduction of commercially funded broadcasting in Britain came the surface in evidence submitted to the Ullswater Committee in 1935. The Ullswater Committee had been established to examine various issues affecting broadcasting in Britain before the BBC's Charter became due for renewal in 1937.

In evidence to the Committee the IBC, together with radio manufacturers Philco, suggested that there should be limited hours of sponsored programmes on British radio, along the lines of the American model and that American programme practice and presentation styles should be introduced at peak listening times. The BBC refuted these suggestions and heavily criticised the introduction of American programme production standards. In its own evidence to the Committee the BBC said that, although it did not rule out sponsorship completely, it considered the suggestion "that in the compilation of sponsored programmes the final word, should rest with the sponsors is surely absurd."

Press and publishing interests, particularly national newspaper publishers, were also strongly against any suggested commercialisation of broadcasting in Britain. The example of American broadcasting practice was clearly not acceptable to the BBC or other vested interests at the time, although nobody took the trouble to ask listeners what they wanted to hear on their radios.

The Report of the Ullswater Committee, published in the spring of 1936, supported the view that British radio should not become commercially funded, although it did pose the possibility of using commercial sponsorship to help the development and launch of television broadcasting:-

*Direct advertising should continue to be banned ......Sponsored programmes, however, should not be banned provided they are used discretely. We hope that any increase in their use will be limited to the initial stages of television broadcasting.*

As for the alternative sources of radio programmes available to listeners in Britain from continental Europe, the Ullswater Committee was unequivocal in its condemnation of such stations:-

*Foreign commercial broadcasting should be discouraged by every available means, although it is obvious that co-operation with all foreign countries will be necessary to make this policy internationally effective.*

## The Bubble Bursts

Despite these Government actions the European commercial stations were extremely popular in Britain but just as they were becoming really successful the start of the Second World War put an end to alternative radio programmes for British audiences and advertisers as transmitters across Europe were closed or destroyed by the invading German Army. The IBC offered its entire facilities to the War Office to establish an entertainment station for troops and for use as a possible propaganda outlet for the Allies but this was refused. The British Government did, however, persuade the French authorities to use Radio Normandy's transmitters in 1940 to broadcast programmes under the call sign Radio International, but this outlet was itself forced to close in early 1941 when German troops arrived at Fecamp. Meanwhile, the IBC's premises in central London were severely bomb damaged during the Blitz and the organisation was never able to broadcast again after the War, although it did continue to produce some programmes for Radio Luxembourg.

Although Radio Luxembourg itself closed at 1.19pm on 21st September 1939 its powerful transmitter was retained and used by the Nazis throughout the war years for propaganda broadcasts to Britain by the infamous William Joyce, "Lord Haw-Haw". In September 1944 a special task force of the American 12th Army liberated the Luxembourg station which then became "the voice of the Supreme HQ of the Allied Expeditionary Force (SHAEF)" - a joint operation between America, Britain, France, Belgium and Luxembourg.

For a short time after this the American Office of War Information operated the station and during this period Winston Churchill had top secret plans for Radio Luxembourg's transmitter. The plan involved using the transmitter, backed by land-line facilities to the BBC studios in London, to beam propaganda programmes to the communist controlled countries of Eastern Europe - behind what Churchill had described as the 'Iron Curtain'. However, when Churchill lost the 1945 General Election this plan was dropped by the incoming Labour administration

In November 1945 the station was handed back to the Luxembourg Government and English language broadcasts from the Junglinster transmitter resumed in 1946. It was this outlet which, until the arrival of the offshore broadcasters in the mid 1960s, provided listeners in Britain with a regular nightly source of popular music programmes.

Many other newly liberated governments in Europe after the end of the Second World War decided to impose tight controls over radio broadcasting within their boundaries. The returning French Government announced in 1945 that it would not issue any private radio station licences at all. (Radio Normandy's premises and transmitters had in fact been destroyed in battles after the D-Day landings). Similarly the Belgian Government refused to allow any private radio stations to be established or re-opened after the War.

## Taking to Water

The effect of such tightly controlled national restrictions, as well as new post-war international agreements on frequency allocation, meant that by the early 1950's there was only one serious option available for prospective radio station owners who wished to challenge the established and authorised broadcasting systems. They would have to base their transmitters in the international waters of the high seas over which no government or state exercised direct control.

The framework of international law which allowed such a situation is quite complicated, but was the only option left to pursue. The concepts of 'national' and 'international' waters as well as the extent of territorial jurisdiction generally are laid down by international treaties and accepted by virtually every sovereign state throughout the world. These definitions, and rules for their application, are embodied in two International Conventions agreed at Geneva in 1958.

The extent of territorial jurisdiction beyond a state's own land mass is governed principally by the first treaty - the Convention on the Territorial Sea and the Contiguous Zone, which was agreed on 29th April 1958, coincidentally a few months before the first European offshore station was launched.

This Convention set down the principle that the sovereignty of a state can extend beyond its own land mass and defined specific areas of water including 'internal or national waters', 'territorial sea' and 'bays', all of which fall within the jurisdiction of the state. The Convention also went on to prescribe rules for determining the starting point from which territorial limits should be measured.

## Internal or National Waters

'Internal' or 'national' waters are those areas, including parts of the sea, which come under the full sovereignty of the territorial state. Such areas include inland waters (rivers, lakes, ports, harbours, anchorages, bays, gulfs and estuaries, areas of sea separated by islands and all waters to the landward side of baselines used as the starting point to measure the territorial sea.

The relevant state has jurisdiction over foreign merchant ships while they are in or travelling through these internal waters. Persons who have committed crimes on board foreign ships in internal waters may be arrested by the territorial state, which has jurisdiction concurrent with that of the vessel's flag state.

The 'territorial sea' is defined by the 1958 Convention as "the area to which the sovereignty of a state extends beyond its land territory and internal waters to include a belt of sea adjacent to the coast." This sovereignty also extends to airspace above the territorial sea as well as to its bed and subsoil.

At the time the Convention was agreed and for many years afterwards, (including the majority of the time offshore radio stations operated) the territorial sea was measured as a distance of three nautical miles from the coast. However, this distance was not itself fixed by international agreement. Indeed attempts to define a maximum breadth for territorial waters had failed at the Hague Codification Conference in 1930 and again at the United Nations Geneva Conferences in 1958.

The 1958 Convention did, however, fix an outer territorial limit of what is known as a 'contiguous zone'. This was determined as twelve miles from the baseline (usually a low water mark) from which territorial sea is measured and was the maximum distance to which any state could reasonably expect to extend its territorial claim.

In practice most coastal states at that time confined their territorial limits to three nautical miles and it was this relatively short claim that offshore radio stations were able to exploit so successfully for many years. Potential audiences were within easy reach of powerful (and sometimes not so powerful) transmitters and transporting regular supplies and personnel from land to the ships or other structures was relatively practical to achieve.

## High Seas or International Waters

The second Convention agreed at Geneva on 29th April 1958 dealt with the 'High Seas' - a term applied to all parts of the world's seas which are not included within the territorial sea or internal waters of any state. The agreements contained

**HOT PURSUIT AND BOARDING**

*'Hot pursuit' of a foreign ship on the high seas may be undertaken only when the authorities of a coastal state have a good reason to believe that the ship has violated the laws of that state. Pursuit must be commenced when the foreign ship, or one of its boats, is within either internal waters, territorial waters or the contiguous zone of the pursuing state. If the foreign ship is in the contiguous zone hot pursuit may only be undertaken if there has been a violation of one of the rights for which the zone was created i.e. customs, fiscal, immigration or sanitary regulations.*

*A warship which encounters a foreign merchant ship on the high seas is not justified in boarding her, except in one or more of the following circumstances:-*

*(a) with the consent of the state whose flag the ship is flying;*

*(b) where there is reasonable ground for suspecting the ship is engaged in piracy or the slave trade, or*

*(c) despite the flag it is flying the ship is in reality of the same nationality as the warship.*

*A warship may, however, interfere with a merchant ship which is either not flying a flag at all or is flying one of no recognised state - two very important provisions which were invoked at different times during the history of offshore broadcasting.*

in this Convention were fundamental to the ability of offshore broadcasters to operate, indeed without the freedom of the high seas there would never have been any offshore radio or television stations.

This Convention basically states that the high seas are open to all nations so that no one state may subject any part of them to its sovereignty. Freedom of the high seas is defined by the Convention as "freedom of navigation, freedom of fishing, freedom to lay submarine cables and pipelines and freedom to fly in the airspace above such waters." These freedoms are available to all states, coastal and non-coastal, but must be exercised subject to conditions laid down in the Convention and any other rules of international law. They also have to be exercised with reasonable regard to the interests of other states. In short the Convention makes all non-territorial waters available to any and all nations to exercise these specific freedoms without fear of restrictions imposed by any other sovereign states. They are simply waters over which no state can exercise control.

The general and most basic freedom of the high seas, as defined by the Convention, is the freedom of navigation. No state may interfere with ships of other states or exercise jurisdiction over them in times of peace, except inside the contiguous zone (i.e. the additional, usually nine miles, adjacent to the (three mile) territorial sea.) Even then inside this Contiguous Zone such interference can only be exercised to prevent infringement of a state's customs, fiscal, immigration or sanitary regulations or to pursue (under the doctrine of 'hot pursuit') infringements of those regulations which have already been committed inside its territory or territorial waters.

If a merchant ship is boarded under the conditions outlined above and it transpires that the suspect ship has not actually committed any violation justifying such action then the owners of that ship must be compensated for any loss or damage which may have been sustained.

A warship does, however, have the right to verify the ship's right to fly its flag - it may send a boat under the command of an officer to the suspected ship and if doubt remains after the ship's documents have been checked, it may proceed to undertake a further examination on board ship, but as the Convention states "this must be carried out with all possible consideration."

## Convention on the Continental Shelf

Another international convention with significance for offshore broadcasting was the Convention on the Continental Shelf, agreed at Geneva between April and October 1958. This Convention provided for coastal states to exercise sovereignty over the sea bed adjacent to their coastline for the purpose of exploring and exploiting its natural resources, particularly oil and gas deposits. In 1964 the Dutch Government became the first (and only) country to invoke the provisions of this Convention specifically for the purpose of outlawing an offshore broadcasting station and full details of how and why they did that will be discussed in Chapter 9. Coincidentally in the same year the British

Government gave effect to the Convention and introduced the Continental Shelf Act enabling it to exercise exploration rights in the North Sea for gas and oil deposits.

## Piracy

There is one further aspect of international law relevant to offshore broadcasting and that is the question of piracy. Pirate Radio is a title frequently attributed to offshore broadcasters, but for reasons different from those envisaged by the international legislators, nevertheless the issue has become confused over the years.

The offshore stations were originally given this title for two reasons - firstly because they 'pirated' the airwaves and did not broadcast on a frequency allocated under international agreements. Secondly they 'pirated' the material they broadcast and generally did not pay copyright or performance fees for the use of such pre-recorded music. In addition for newspaper headline writers the term 'pirate radio' successfully conjured up all the imagery of a group of swashbuckling, dare-devil people openly challenging the 'established' system and, being outside the law of a particular state, apparently remaining immune from prosecution.

This swashbuckling pirate image was at first accepted and even encouraged by the stations - it helped generate interest and media attention as well as cultivating a somewhat romanticised picture in the minds of listeners. However, once their future became threatened by the introduction of legislation and with allegations (largely unsubstantiated) of interference being caused by the unauthorised use of frequencies then the stations largely backed away from the use of the term 'pirate radio'. Unfortunately the label had stuck and the anarchic behaviour of some people involved in operating offshore stations only served to reinforce the relevance of the title. As various governments introduced or strengthened legislation to ban offshore radio newspaper headline writers had a field day with contrived pirate imagery.

However, away from the world of tabloid headline writers the meaning of real piracy is defined in international law by the Convention on the High Seas and has some very serious and specific offences attaching to it.

The Convention defines piracy as:-

"(a) any illegal act of violence, detention or depredation committed for private ends (i.e. acts done without authorisation from the government of any state), by the crew or passengers of a private ship (or aircraft) and directed on the high seas against another ship or aircraft or against persons or property on board such ship or aircraft or against a ship, aircraft, persons or property in a place outside the jurisdiction of any state;

(b) any act of voluntary participation in the operation of a ship or aircraft knowing it to be a pirate ship or aircraft (a ship or aircraft is considered a pirate if it is intended by the persons in control to be used for any of the acts which constitute piracy);

(c) any act of inciting or intentionally facilitating an act as described in paragraphs (a) or (b)."

The Convention also permits a state to seize a pirate ship or aircraft and the property on board using warships, military aircraft or other duly authorised vessels on government service.

It can clearly be seen from this that offshore radio broadcasting is not a pirate activity in the true sense of the international declaration - had it been then

### Flag States and Flags of Convenience

*A ship may sail in international waters only under the flag of one state and is subject to the exclusive jurisdiction of that state. This is the reason why almost all shipborne offshore radio stations flew the flag of a country which was nowhere near the area they were broadcasting to or from and they generally found a flag state whose rules of inspection were not as rigidly enforced as those of other nations. These so called Flag States (for example Panama, Honduras or Liberia) operated such lax rules in order to attract to their register as many ships as possible and consequently secure large incomes from the registration fees payable by ship owners. Offshore broadcasters generally had to ensure that their transmitting equipment was located in the hold of their ships so that, particularly in the case of Panama, they could be legally classed as cargo and not broadcasting equipment.*

stations would have been liable to boarding and seizure, even outside territorial waters, by warships of whatever state chose to act and the whole phenomenon of offshore broadcasting would probably have lasted just a few days.

## Exploiting the Loophole in International Law

To summarise, by the late 1950s, at the start of the main period of offshore broadcasting development, most countries maintained a territorial limit extending just three nautical miles from their coastline. The area beyond that limit was classified as international waters and as such outside the jurisdiction of any specific government. From a transmitter located in these international waters it was possible to beam broadcasts to a particular country, or group of countries, with their respective governments powerless to prevent it happening, except by the extreme and totalitarian measure of jamming the signal.

Therefore, it was not out of a desire, but from a legal and operational necessity that radio station operators wishing to challenge established broadcasters in the second half of the twentieth century did so from an offshore base. Operating in such a way was not illegal at the time since legislation did not exist to prevent it happening - it was merely outside the law of most, if not all, countries. A suitable loophole had been found and was exploited to the full.

The authorities clearly had to close the loophole, but they were also forced to deal with the matter in an entirely new and different way. It was a concept that had not been a serious problem before the late 1950s and over the years as the number and popularity of offshore stations grew governments of every political persuasion struggled to find a means of silencing them. These actions were taken ostensibly to comply with, and protect, international agreements, but in reality they had more to do with protecting the existing state monopoly broadcasting systems.

For the authorities the solution to the 'problem' of offshore broadcasters was far more complex than any government at first envisaged, involving a tangled web of international law and conventions which rendered them powerless to take direct, unilateral action. Within a framework of international agreements, which themselves carried no weight in law, most governments had to resort to introducing legislation which made it illegal for their own citizens to be involved in any way with the workings or promotion of an offshore broadcasting station. With a large number of countries passing such laws this ultimately had the effect of closing most stations, but some offshore broadcasters successfully defied and challenged the legislation designed to outlaw them. In the end, however, practical operating difficulties - directly or indirectly resulting from the legislation, lack of financial income or the ravages of the natural elements made them too, fall silent.

Having explained why and how the phenomenon of offshore broadcasting came about the remainder of this book traces its sixty year development and decline through all the dramas, crises, tragedies and successes. These incidents form a fascinating story in themselves, but together they are also a significant chapter in 20th Century social and broadcasting history.

## Chapter 2

# In The Beginning

Possibly the first plan for an offshore radio station came in the infant years of broadcasting itself when the owners of the London *Daily Mail* chartered a steam yacht, *Ceto,* as part of a promotional campaign. The newspaper planned to use the vessel to broadcast, from outside the three mile territorial limit, music and advertising announcements for itself and its sister publications the London *Evening News* and the *Sunday Dispatch.* The idea was conceived by the *Mail's* Director of Circulation and Publicity, Valentine Smith.

With a transmitter on board, the *Ceto* sailed from Dundee in Scotland for trials during the early summer of 1928. However, technical difficulties arose when the swell of the sea began to affect the broadcast signal, making reception on land virtually impossible. The slightest movement of the yacht, even in a calm sea, affected the primitive broadcasting equipment and finally the idea of transmitting programmes had to be abandoned.

Undaunted by this setback Valentine Smith then arranged for German sound equipment manufacturers, Siemens Halske, to supply four loudspeakers, each weighing six and a half hundredweight (330Kg), which were mounted on to the *Ceto's* superstructure. With this equipment in place the yacht sailed around Britain anchoring off holiday resorts and coastal towns 'broadcasting' gramophone records of popular music interspersed with advertisements for the three newspapers. Stephen Williams, who later worked for Radio Normandy and Radio Luxembourg, was in charge of presenting programmes and making the commercial announcements from on board the *Daily Mail* yacht.

The *Ceto* planned to leave Dundee on 25th June 1928 with a civic send off by the Lord Provost, Mr William High. However, due to technical adaptations needed to the on-board equipment the vessel did not actually leave port as planned, she simply sailed from the tidal basin to a berth in the harbour. Once the technical problems had been rectified a sample programme was 'broadcast' to the residents of Dundee, before the ship eventually left the Scottish port on 3rd July 1928.

On her outward journey the vessel sailed down the east coast, through the Channel, along the south coast and up the west coast as far as the Isle of Man. The return journey was used for the *Ceto* to revisit many resorts and towns where her original concerts had been a huge success.

At night the *Ceto* was illuminated by over 1,500 lightbulbs, spelling out the words *DAILY MAIL* in red and white, while two 1,000 candlepower searchlights were used to illuminate seaside promenades during concerts 'broadcast' from the ship. Local Mayors and other dignitaries also came on board at virtually every town or resort visited by the *Ceto* to welcome visitors and holidaymakers.

One of the local dignitaries was even responsible for the first 'live' performance from the *Ceto* on 19th July 1928. Councillor Robert Stokes (Chairman of Poole Borough Council's Parks Committee) came on board the vessel with other local councillors and sang two songs during one of the concert programmes.

### The *Ceto*

*The 'Ceto', under the command of Captain Frank T Rollo had a crew of 14 (including radio and marine engineers) and was equipped with a specially constructed studio, designed as an exact replica of a contemporary BBC studio.*

*The vessel was extremely popular and small boats visited her wherever she was anchored. Enterprising local boatmen at Ilfracombe were reported to be charging 1/- (5p) a head for taking sightseers out to the Ceto -a forerunner of similar trips out to view offshore radio ships made by local boatmen in the 60's, 70's and 80's!*

The *Ceto's* role as a broadcasting station ended on 1st September 1928, when after a final concert broadcast from a position near Tower Bridge on the River Thames, the ship was taken to Purfleet. Here all the broadcasting, studio and generating equipment was dismantled and the yacht returned to her former role as a pleasure vessel. Altogether during her ten week cruise the *Ceto* covered over 4,000 miles, visited 87 seaside resorts and coastal towns and 'broadcast' 300 concerts.

Although originally intended to be a broadcasting station, because of the technical difficulties experienced during the trials off Scotland, the *Ceto* really only 'shouted' programmes and commercial messages to audiences in relatively small areas along the coast. Valentine Smith's original concept, however, demonstrated that right from the beginning of radio broadcasting history the theoretical possibility of transmitting programmes, quite legally, from outside a nation's territorial limit had been identified. Only the lack of sufficiently sophisticated broadcasting equipment at the time prevented this pioneer from succeeding, but the principle Smith had identified was to remain fundamental to the operation of offshore radio stations for the next 63 years.

## The first true offshore broadcaster

It took some years before technical developments were sufficiently advanced for any further attempt was made to launch a radio station from on board a ship. When it did happen the development came about in an unlikely location.

Offshore radio is usually thought of in the context of providing an alternative to the established state monopoly broadcasting systems, but the world's first true commercial offshore station was, surprisingly, located off the west coast of the USA during the early 1930s. Surprisingly because the US Government and authorities had adopted a much less restrictive approach to the development of radio broadcasting than most of their European contemporaries. This was partly because of the geographical size of the country, but largely due to the fact that the USA then, as now, valued most highly the right of its citizens to freedom of speech - an entitlement enshrined in its constitution. As a result there were few restrictions on who was allowed to establish a broadcasting station and within a short time after the opening of station KDKA in Pittsburgh in 1920 hundreds of others had been launched across the country.

Initial reports of a planned offshore radio venture appeared in the *International Radio News* on 16th and 30th July 1932 indicating that a Los Angeles-based organisation planned to anchor its vessel 12 miles outside US territorial waters and broadcast programmes using a 16Kw transmitter. According to these press reports the station planned to take advertising for products not then permitted on federally licensed American radio stations and programming was to consist of "gramophone records, concerts from an orchestra, performances by solo artists, and horoscope predictions by the astrologer Zandra".

The organisers behind the project acquired a steamship, SS *City of Panama*, which had previously been fitted out as a casino and speakeasy. Such floating casinos were established in the 1920s and 30s to circumvent the anti-gambling and drinking laws in many states and operated on the same principle as offshore broadcasting -being located in international waters they were outside the territorial jurisdiction of, in this case, the USA. It was a small step from operating a floating casino to launching a floating radio station.

The vessel was registered in Panama, ostensibly to act as a showboat promoting the attractions of that country as a holiday destination for US tourists. A radio station licence, with the call sign RKXR was also granted to the organisation by the Panamanian Government in the belief that broadcasts would be used to promote tourism and industry in their country. Under this licence the station was authorised to broadcast experimental, non-commercial programmes on a frequency of 815kHz (368m) with a transmitter power of between 500 watts and 1Kw.

Reaction to the granting of the licence by Panama was not favourable in the United States - both the Government and owners of many authorised radio stations were seriously concerned that this new offshore station would interfere with existing broadcasting signals. The US State Department sent an urgent demand to the Panamanian Government requesting that both the registration of the *City of Panama* and the licence for station RKXR should be cancelled immediately. Panamanian response to the State Department's demands was dismissive. It considered that the US Government had no right to interfere with the activities of one of its legitimately registered vessels whilst in international waters. At the same time, however, Panamanian officials did indicate that the station would voluntarily adhere to the rules laid down by the US Federal Radio Commission (FRC) for licensed land-based stations.

Unfortunately these assurances from the Panamanian Government were soon discredited by the actions of the offshore station's owners who violated most, if not all, of their licence conditions when station RKXR eventually came on the air in May 1933.

Although authorised as a low power (500w-1Kw) non-commercial station RKXR immediately began broadcasting advertisements along with its popular music programmes and transmitted with a power more than five times in excess of the maximum permitted by the terms of its Panamanian licence.

Commercials were sold through an office established in Los Angeles and it was subsequently reported that advertisers were spending as much as $1,500 a month (1930s prices) in booking airtime on the offshore station. Advertisers were attracted to RKXR because of its enormous coverage area - achieved through use of the high power transmitter and clear channel frequency (no other station in that area was broadcasting on 815kHz).

While RKXR was able to benefit commercially from the use of this high powered transmitter, its strong signal badly affected transmissions by legal stations throughout the west coast of Southern California, particularly those broadcasting between 810kHz and 820kHz. Understandably these stations immediately lodged complaints with the Federal Radio Commission, but like many governments and official bodies over thirty years later, that agency was initially unwilling or unable to stop the activities of the offshore broadcaster. Reception of RKXR was also reported from places as far afield as the east coast of the United States, Hawaii and even north eastern Canada.

As the result of no action being taken on their behalf by the Federal Radio Commission some legal stations made direct contact with RKXR's backers, requesting that the offshore station move its transmissions from the 815kHz frequency. Amazingly the response from RKXR's management to these requests was that they would agree to change frequency only in return for substantial payments (amounting in some instances to many thousands of dollars) from the legal stations which claimed to be affected.

In June 1933 the US State Department, alarmed by reports of these extortion demands, again requested that the Panamanian Government revoke both the broadcasting licence for RKXR and the registration of the station's vessel *City of Panama*. This time the Panamanian Government's attitude was more positive. They were now fully aware that their 'tourism promotion' vessel and radio station were being wholly misused by the unscrupulous operators and agreed to the US Government request. Within a few days both the ship's registration and the radio station's licence had been withdrawn, but this did not deter the owners of the offshore station and RKXR continued broadcasting defiantly for several more weeks.

Meanwhile, both the US and Panamanian Governments discussed what action, if any, they could take to silence the now un-licensed station. Some initial confusion existed about its legal status on the high seas since the vessel was no longer registered by Panama, but eventually the US State Department was satisfied that it had grounds upon which to act. In August 1933 the *City of Panama* was seized at sea by officials from the State Department and the US Coastguard Service who towed the vessel into Los Angeles harbour.

The US Government's concern about RKXR was that if no action had been taken to silence the station then a fleet of similar offshore broadcasters would soon anchor off both the east and west coasts, causing interference to legal stations' transmissions. More seriously, as had been graphically demonstrated by the response from RKXR to requests for it to change frequency, an ugly situation could have quickly developed if other offshore broadcasters chose to behave in the same irresponsible manner and engage in similar extortion demands.

Following this belated, but in the end decisive, US Government action neither the owners of RKXR or the *City of Panama* were involved in further radio broadcasting, legal or otherwise, after August 1933. The action taken against this early offshore station and the demonstration of just what a threat it had posed to the established broadcasting system also helped shape future United States broadcasting laws, particularly those designed to prevent unauthorised transmissions. The impact of those laws became evident over half a century later when action was taken by the US authorities, this time rather more quickly than in 1933, to silence further offshore stations or even prevent ships involved with such projects leaving port. Details of these actions and their implications for offshore radio in America are fully discussed in Chapters 18 and 24.

## Other offshore broadcasting ventures

Although a number of other ship-borne radio stations were established in various parts of the world following the demise of RKXR these were mainly for propaganda and military broadcasts, or communications within fishing fleets and their programmes were not commercially funded.

An early example of this type of floating station was Radio Morue (Radio Cod) which accompanied French fishing fleets to the waters around Newfoundland in the late 1930s. The station, based on one of the trawlers, was operated by Rev. Yvon and broadcast religious messages and news items from home to fishermen on board other vessels in the fleet.

A propaganda offshore radio station operated between January and April 1938 from a small ship sailing along the European coast between France and Holland. The station - Radio Gegen das Dritten Reich (Radio Against the Third Reich) - had been secretly equipped in Britain by personnel from the BBC and the Dutch broadcasting organisation VARA. Programmes were intended to provide an uncensored and objective source of news and political commentary on events taking place at the time in Nazi Germany. The station broadcast on short wave and its target audience was listeners in Holland and inside Germany itself, where it was hoped to stimulate an anti-Nazi movement.

In 1941 Spanish Communists, who had been exiled by the right-wing Franco Regime after the Civil War, used a Russian trawler anchored in the Black Sea as a base from which to broadcast programmes to their home country. The station, Estacion Pyrenees, broadcast on shortwave and tried to make listeners believe that it was located somewhere in the Pyrenees Mountains on the French/Spanish border. Transmissions consisted, not surprisingly, of anti-Franco propaganda and although the ship-borne broadcasts ended after a short while the station's programmes continued to be relayed to Spain for some years from land-based transmitters in various sympathetic East European communist countries.

Another Spanish political group, this time separatists who claimed to be the Basque Government in exile, also used a trawler (anchored in the French port of Bayonne) to broadcast anti-Franco programmes under the call sign Radio Euzkad between 1950 and 1953.

The United States Government propaganda station Voice of America used a number of ships as offshore broadcasting bases, particularly during the 1940s and 1950s. In 1942 the *USS Texas* was anchored in the Mediterranean and equipped to broadcast Voice of America programmes as a counter to the many Nazi propaganda stations then on the air. These programmes, targeted at North Africa, were transmitted on 601kHz (498m) and commenced on 7th November 1942, coinciding with an Allied military advance in that area. However, some rapid Allied successes against the Nazi forces in North Africa meant that the station's mission became obsolete and transmissions were terminated after only a few weeks.

Three years later, in 1945, the Voice of America again used a ship, this time the *Phoenix*, anchored in the China Sea to broadcast propaganda programmes to the Far East on both shortwave and medium wave frequencies.

The most significant use of an offshore based transmitter by the Voice of America came in the early 1950s and was to serve as a role model for early European offshore commercial broadcasters. A merchant ship, *Doddridge* was converted, at a cost of $3.5million, into a floating radio station and renamed firstly *Coastal Messenger* and later *Courier*. The station was fitted out by US Coastguards who installed three on-board transmitters, one medium wave with a power of 150Kw, and two shortwave, each with an output of 35Kw.

Test broadcasts from this ship-borne station took place in the Caribbean during April 1952 on 1390kHz (215m) using an aerial held aloft by a helium filled balloon - a device tried again over 30 years later off the English coast by offshore station Laser 730 (see Chapter 22).

In August 1952, having successfully completed her test transmissions the *Courier* sailed to the Mediterranean and anchored off the Greek Island of Rhodes, commencing broadcasts as the Voice of America - Seabase Radio Station Dodecanese Islands - on 7th September 1952. The *Courier* remained broadcasting at this base until 1964 when she was converted for use in connection with early satellite communications, the Voice of America operation having being transferred to a landbased transmitter in Rhodes.

It was the successful operation of this ship-based Voice of America outlet and the experience of its US Navy radio engineers which helped some of the early European commercial offshore stations become established. Certainly the Swedish offshore station Radio Nord depended heavily on technical advice from US Navy radio experts who had been involved with the *Courier* and the concept of such a seaborne station was partly the inspiration for the launch of Radio Veronica off Holland and later Radio Caroline off the British coast.

## Commercial interest

While the practice of using ship-based radio stations for non-commercial military or political propaganda broadcasting had continued throughout the 1940's and 50's it was not until 25 years after the closure of RKXR that another commercial offshore radio station took to the airwaves. This time the location was northern Europe, but it is extremely doubtful that the people behind the venture knew anything about RKXR at the time they decided to set up their station. They had simply identified a legal loophole enabling them to operate from international waters and challenge an established state broadcasting system.

Despite numerous practical difficulties they succeeded in launching a pioneering radio station off the coast of Denmark in 1958 which itself went on to inspire the establishment of many similar stations throughout Europe and other parts of the world as the following chapters reveal.

# Chapter 3

# Scandinavia

The idea of launching this commercial offshore radio station was first considered in the unlikely setting of a silversmiths shop in Copenhagen during the winter of 1957.

One evening after the shop had closed its owner, Ib Fogh and his partner Peter Jansen were discussing the quality of radio in Denmark and the mundane programmes broadcast by the state network. During the conversation Ib Fogh suggested, perhaps not too seriously at that stage, that some private competition would be good for the state system.

As Danish law, like that of most other European countries, prohibited the establishment of a radio station without a government licence some means would have to be found of getting around this restriction. Broadcasting from a ship anchored outside Danish territorial waters was thought a possibility, but remained as no more than a fanciful idea on that winter's evening in Copenhagen.

## Turning a dream into reality

Ib Fogh kept in mind the notion of starting his own shipborne radio station to challenge the Danish state monopoly and during a visit to Switzerland early in 1958 he discussed the idea with some business associates. Fogh's proposal received enthusiastic support and together with Peter Jansen, he took steps to put into action what until then had only been a dream born out of a chance remark during that original conversation in 1957.

In great secrecy a suitable ship, the 107 ton German fishing vessel *Cheeta,* was located, purchased and taken to Stege, a small harbour south of Copenhagen, to be fitted out as a radio station.

To circumvent the laws and regulations designed to prevent unauthorised broadcasting stations in Denmark a complicated chain of foreign-registered companies was created. The *Cheeta* was purchased by a Swiss-based organisation which then leased her to an advertising agency whose registered office was in Liechtenstein. The ship herself was re-registered in Panama and flew that country's flag whilst at sea, as required by international maritime regulations.

While unlicensed broadcasting within Danish territory was illegal, the management of a radio station and recording of programme material for later transmission from a base outside the country was not against the law at that time. Consequently, the new station - to be known as Radio Mercur - established its offices and recording studios in the smart Copenhagen suburb of Gentofte in premises which accommodated over 30 people working in programme production and administration. The station also hired its own brass band to record a series of half hour programmes for broadcast each evening. Advertising time on the new station was sold through a separate, Danish registered, company Mercur Reklame, based in Roemersgade 9, Copenhagen.

Throughout the spring and early summer of 1958 work went ahead to install transmitting equipment on board the *Cheeta*. Because programmes were to be prerecorded on land and broadcast later from the ship no studios as such were constructed on board just a playback facility with two tape recorders and a small mixer unit.

## Radio Mercur's aerial

*Radio Mercur's aerial had a unique control device - an electrically powered rotator, mounted at the top of the mast, which enabled it to be turned and therefore always radiating the station's signal towards its target area, no matter which direction the Cheeta lay at anchor.*

It was not long before local press reporters became inquisitive about what was going on in the small port of Stege. Towards the end of June 1958 the station's (hitherto) secret activities were revealed in a local newspaper article and by early July detailed plans for the new station had been published by the Danish national press.

After fitting out had been completed the *Cheeta* left port on 11th July 1958 and anchored in a position in international waters south east of Copenhagen, but subsequently the ship was moved to a new anchorage south of the small island of Fyn in Oresund (The Sound). Further reports about the new station appeared on 15th July 1958 after the *Cheeta* had left port, announcing that regular programmes from Radio Mercur would begin on Saturday 19th July.

Test transmissions from the station's 1.5Kw transmitter started on 17th July 1958 on 93.12mHz in what was then known as the VHF band (now universally referred to as FM). As soon as these broadcasts began the Danish Post Office instructed the station to stop transmissions with immediate effect, but not surprisingly Radio Mercur ignored the order and continued broadcasting.

Only a few hours after the test transmissions had started Radio Mercur faced its first real crisis. During the night of 17th/18th July 1958 the *Cheeta's* anchor chain broke and the ship drifted helplessly towards the Swedish coast, eventually running aground near Malmo. Damage had been caused to the station's transmitting equipment and part of the aerial mast had also collapsed.

*The 'Cheeta' at anchor off Copenhagen*

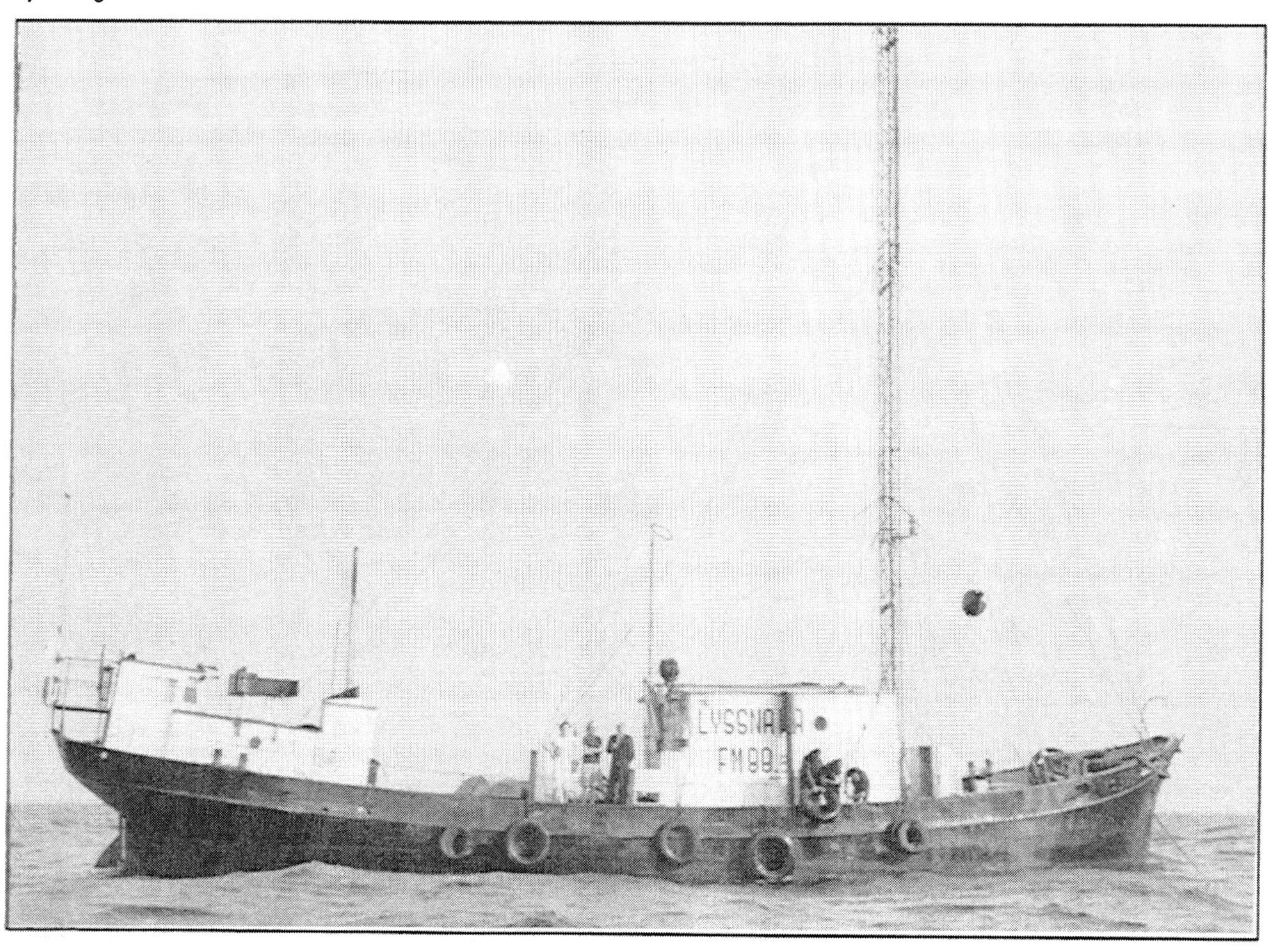

Unable to free herself the *Cheeta* had to be towed from her stranded position by a salvage tug, *Karl,* and was taken to the port of Limhamn in Sweden for repairs. Once these had been completed the radio ship returned to her anchorage on 25th July 1958 and test broadcasts resumed again on Thursday 31st July, this time without any further incident.

Radio Mercur began transmitting regular programmes from 6.00pm on Saturday 2nd August 1958. Europe's first commercial offshore radio station was on the air.

On 14th August 1958 the Panamanian authorities, acting on a request from the Danish government, gave Radio Mercur's owners an ultimatum that unless the station ceased transmissions, the *Cheeta* would loose her official registration and the right to fly that country's flag. Radio Mercur ignored the ultimatum and continued broadcasting so, on 25th August 1958, the Panamanian government carried out its threat and withdrew registration of the radio ship. Radio Mercur lodged an appeal with the Panamanian government, but subsequently claimed that the vessel had been re-registered in Honduras. However, some three years later events were to prove that this was not the case.

To the surprise of the Danish Government Radio Mercur became increasingly popular with listeners and advertisers. Broadcasting hours at this time were from 7.30am - 9.30am and 5.00pm - 12 midnight and programmes consisted mainly of 15 or 30 minute segments, many of which were sponsored by advertisers who quickly recognised the commercial potential of this new medium.

The station's frequency of 93.12mHz had been chosen as it lay conveniently between the Danish 1st and 2nd Networks, so listeners tuning their radios to either of these stations stood a good chance of unintentionally discovering Radio Mercur. The hope was that having discovered the new station they would stay tuned to its programmes. However, it quickly became apparent that Radio Mercur's transmissions on this strategically chosen frequency were causing interference to a station in Sweden, so to avoid upsetting listeners to that station and the possible threat of action from either the Danish or Swedish Post and Telegraph authorities, Radio Mercur changed to a new frequency of 89.55mHz at the beginning of September 1958.

## A Swedish dimension

Across The Sound in Sweden, businessman Nils-Eric Svensson, had been impressed by the immediate and widespread success of Radio Mercur's early broadcasts and thought about the possibility of establishing a similar station

### Radio Mercur's broadcasting hours

*At the beginning of 1959 broadcasting hours on Radio Mercur were:-*

*7.30am - 9.30am Radio Mercur (Danish)*

*11.00am - 2.00pm (weekdays) Skanes Radio Mercur*

*12noon -5.00pm (weekends) (Swedish)*

*5.00pm - 12 midnight Radio Mercur (Danish)*

*A public opinion survey taken to coincide with the station's first anniversary in August 1959 showed that 38% of the total population of Copenhagen regularly listened to Radio Mercur and to mark this success broadcasting hours were extended on both the Danish and Swedish services:-*

*6.00am - 9.00am Radio Mercur (Danish)*

*11.00am - 3.00pm Skanes Radio Mercur (Swedish)*

*4.00pm - 12 midnight Radio Mercur (Danish)*

exclusively for Swedish listeners. Without a ship and transmitter of his own he approached Radio Mercur to assess the possibility of hiring some of their vacant airtime during the day. The result was a deal which saw the opening of Skanes Radio Mercur (Swedish Radio Mercur) on 1st September 1958, with programmes exclusively in the Swedish language.

Skanes Radio Mercur recorded its programmes in Lanskrona, north of Malmo and in addition to the owner (Nils-Eric Svensson) employed a staff of just 2 DJs and 1 technician. In the early months of 1959 a former 1940s Swedish beauty queen, Britt Wadner, who had recorded some commercials for the station the previous year, joined Skanes Radio Mercur as sales manager, with responsibility for obtaining new advertising contracts. From this small beginning Britt Wadner was to become a major figure in the history of Scandinavian offshore radio.

## Rescue package and expansion

By February 1959, despite its initial popularity with advertisers, the Danish language Radio Mercur was discovered to be trading at a loss. The station had been severely underfunded from the outset and the high initial investment in transmitting equipment together with day-to-day running costs were not being recovered by sufficient advertising income.

Financial help for Radio Mercur came unexpectedly from a kindred spirit in the world of banking. In December 1958 Alex Thomsen had launched a new bank - Finance Banken - which challenged many of the existing practices and offered customers a higher rate of interest on their savings. Finance Banken was to the banking world what Radio Mercur was to the broadcasting world - an unconventional organisation mounting a challenge to the established system.

Alex Thomsen arranged to provide a large loan for Radio Mercur from the Finance Banken in return for an allocation of share capital in the station. With this substantial injection of capital Radio Mercur was able to improve both programme content and the technical quality of its transmissions. In addition Thomsen adopted a more aggressive marketing policy for the station and projected its huge commercial potential to prospective advertisers. The result was that Radio Mercur quickly succeeded in attracting more and more advertisers and programme sponsors and as a consequence became a viable commercial operation.

By August 1959 the co-founders of Radio Mercur, Ib Fogh and Peter Jansen, had withdrawn from day-to-day involvement with the station, but remained on the board of directors, while Production Manager, Benny Knusden, took over management responsibility from this time.

During the summer of 1959 an English language programme "Copenhagen Today" was introduced into Radio Mercur's programme schedules, with music and entertainment information aimed at tourists visiting Denmark. A weekly English language programme from London was also broadcast as were a number of English language commercials, notably a campaign for Roses Lime Juice.

## Official action

Meanwhile the Danish authorities were looking for a means by which they could take action against the popular offshore radio station anchored off their coast. They realised that unilateral action could only result in the station moving its centre of operations elsewhere, so they decided in 1959 to explore the idea of instigating concerted international action against offshore broadcasters. Coincidentally the International Telecommunications Union (ITU) had called a conference in Geneva to discuss issues affecting broadcasting in member states.

### ITU

*The International Telecommunications Union (ITU), based in Geneva, Switzerland is an international organisation set up to regulate and coordinate broadcasting and telecommunications in its member countries. Most, but not all, countries in the world are members oft he ITU.Representatives of the ITU member nations meet regularly at Conventions to review and draw up technical standards, radio regulation rules and frequency allocation policies. A subsidiary of the ITU, the International Frequency Regulation Board (IFRB) actually decides which countries are to be allocated specific frequencies and monitors the use of those allocations.*

At the Conference the Danish Telegraph Board proposed a recommendation, later adopted as Article 422, which prohibited, on an international scale, broadcasting from ships anchored in international waters. They also asked the Conference to authorise member states to investigate what specific action could be taken against the offshore stations then operating off the Scandinavian coasts.

The approval of Article 422 by the 1959 Convention, the full implications of which were only apparent at the time to countries served by offshore radio stations, became fundamental to providing the foundation for further action against such broadcasters. Member countries of the ITU now felt that they had an international obligation to act against any offshore broadcasters who appeared off their coasts and the Article gave significant backing and support to arguments put forward to outlaw such stations.

However, despite the Danish authorities forcing through this agreement at the Geneva Convention in 1959 no specific action was taken at that time against Radio Mercur. It was only after other offshore stations appeared off the coast of Sweden and Denmark that the Nordic Council, representing all Scandinavian countries , met to consider instigating some unified action.

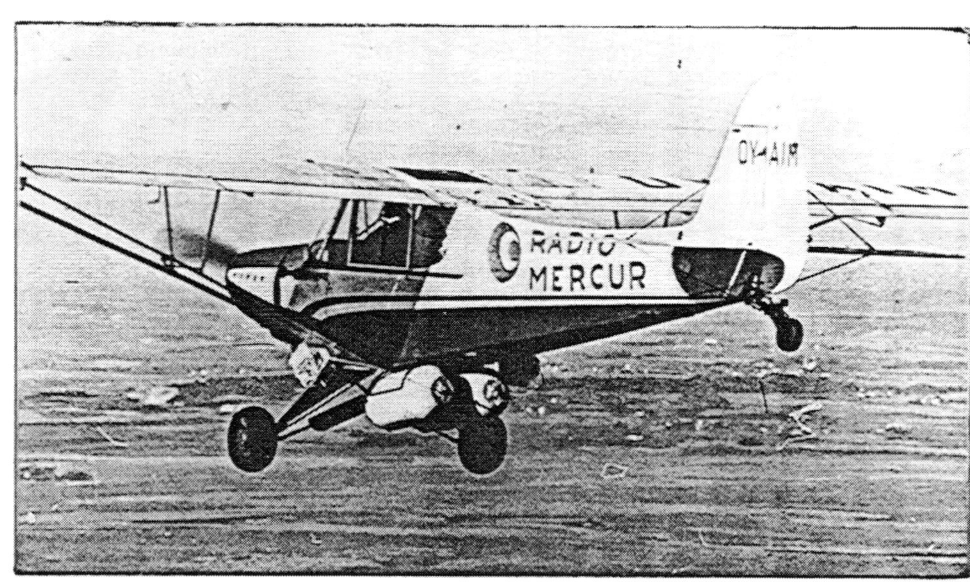


*The plane used by Radio Mercur to deliver supplies to the radio ship*

## Offshore radio expansion in Sweden

Meanwhile in November 1959 businessman, Jack Kotschack, inspired by the success and popularity of Radio Mercur off the Danish coast, decided to establish an offshore radio station to serve northern Sweden and in particular the capital city of Stockholm and its surrounding area. He was joined in this venture by two Americans, Gordon McLendon and Bob Thompson.

Jack Kotschack had no idea about starting a radio station when he agreed to act as host to the friend of a wartime American colleague visiting Stockholm. That friend, unknown to Jack Kotschack at the time, was Gordon McLendon, an American entrepreneur who amongst other business interests owned a chain of radio stations in the USA. The most well known of these was KLIF in Dallas, where in the mid 1950s McLendon had developed and introduced the Top 40 music and news format which is now so commonplace throughout the world.

It was during an after dinner conversation that Gordon McLendon asked Jack Kotschack if he could listen to some Swedish radio programmes. He could hardly believe his ears when he found both state channels broadcasting monotonous speech programmes and suggested that what Sweden needed was a music and news format station. Gordon McLendon was professionally aware of Radio Mercur's existence off the Danish coast and conversation soon turned to the possibility of establishing a similar offshore radio station broadcasting to Stockholm.

Jack Kotschack felt it essential that, unlike Radio Mercur, any station broadcasting to northern Sweden should use the medium waveband rather than VHF (FM), so preliminary technical advice was sought from one of McLendon's contacts, US Navy antenna expert John Mullaney.

Mullaney confirmed that experience with the Voice of America ship *Courier*, anchored off the Greek island of Rhodes showed that a so-called flat top antenna looped between two masts would provide a sufficiently strong signal for the northern Swedish target area. Having satisfied themselves that, technically, the project seemed feasible, Kotschack and McLendon set about sorting out the many practical problems which had to be resolved before their station could come on the air.

Because US Federal regulations prevented any one person from owning more than seven radio stations Gordon McLendon felt that he could not become financially involved in the Swedish station and he persuaded another Dallas businessman, Robert F (Bob) Thompson, to invest in the project.

An exploratory meeting was held with advertising agencies which showed that there would be positive support for a commercial radio station broadcasting to the Swedish capital. However, the station discovered later that this initial indication of support didn't fully materialise as the agencies withheld promised big contracts in the face of pressure from the Swedish Government.

Having met prospective advertisers it was not long before stories of the planned new Swedish offshore radio station reached the press. The Stockholm evening newspaper *Aftonbladt* first broke the story in late November 1959 under the dramatic if slightly inaccurate headline **DOLLAR MILLIONAIRE BACKS COMMERCIAL RADIO IN THE BALTIC.**

## Setting up the project

American financial backing for the project was not actually secured until January 1960 and at the same time Jack Kotschack was appointed General Manager of the planned new station. Gordon McLendon agreed to act as a consultant, strictly on a non-payment basis for fear of jeopardising his ownership of US radio stations, while fellow Dallas businessmen Jim Foster and Bob Thompson provided $400,000 to fund the station. A flag and registration for the station's ship (which at that stage had not even been obtained) were arranged as the result of various meetings in America and Nicaragua. President Samosa of Nicaragua personally agreed to register the station's ship and provide a flag for her to fly in return for the project's American backers completing some land purchases in Nicaragua.

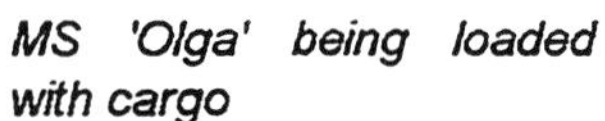

MS 'Olga' being loaded with cargo

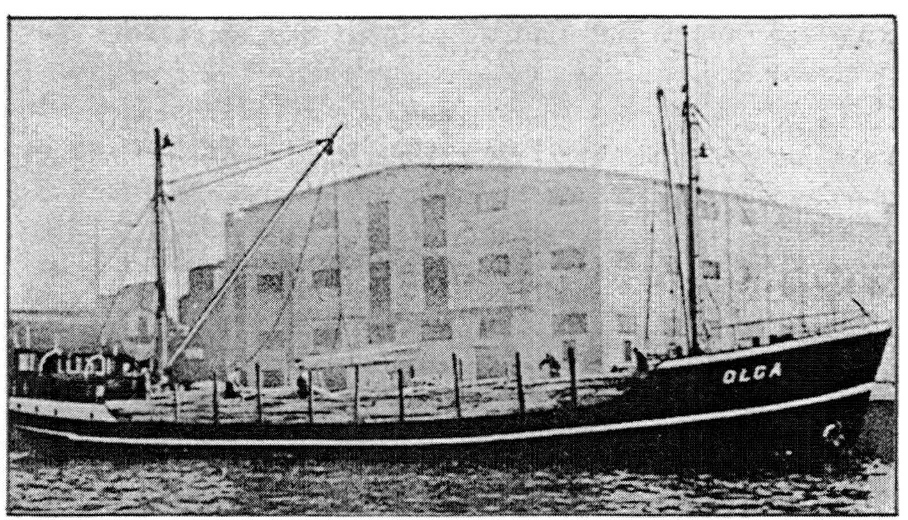


Three separate companies were established through which the planned offshore station - to be known as Radio Nord -

could operate. The Superior Shipping Co. (registered in Managua, Nicaragua) was to be the formal owner of the Radio Nord vessel. The main company, Nord Establishment, (registered in Vadez, Liechtenstein) would lease the ship from Superior Shipping, engage the marine crew and technicians, be responsible for programmes broadcast from the station and receive all advertising income. Airtime on the station was sold through a third company, Radio Reklam Productions AB, (registered in Sweden) which was also responsible for the actual production of programmes and the hire of on-air staff and radio technicians.

Obtaining and equipping a ship turned out to be a greater problem than at first anticipated, but with the help of another Texan, Jim Foster, the search began in February 1960. A seemingly suitable ship was located - the 500 ton salvage steamer *Herakles,* which had been built for the waters of the north Baltic Sea and was equipped with radar, echo sounder and a radio- telephone. However, Jim Foster rejected this vessel because he thought a larger ship was necessary, preferably one with diesel engines which could be started immediately in the event of an emergency. After inspecting and rejecting a great many other ships, Jim Foster eventually found what he was looking for in Keil, West Germany.

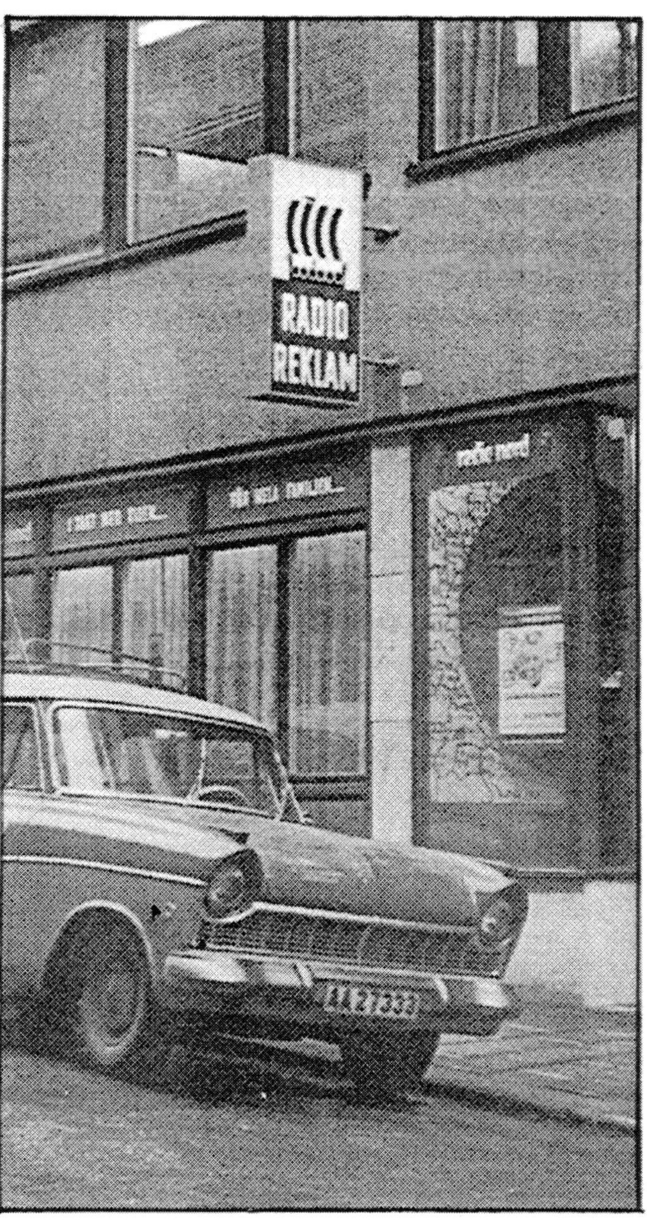

Radio Nord's offices in Copenhagen

Although no one could have known at that time the vessel he chose was destined to play a major role in offshore radio history for the next 20 years. The ship was a small cargo vessel which had been built in 1921 as a three masted steel schooner the SS *Margarethe.* In 1927 her length and weight had been increased, diesel engines installed and she was renamed MS *Olga,* after her then owner Olga Koppleman. The *Olga* spent 30 years in northern waters, plying cargoes of timber between Baltic and North Sea ports and was commandeered to serve in the German Navy by the landing tank squadron between June 1941 and November 1943. The Radio Nord owners renamed the ship *Bon Jour* and later *Magda Maria*, but after Radio Nord closed, she was renamed yet again as the *Mi Amigo*. With that name the vessel became a legend in offshore radio history as home to Radio Atlanta, Radio Caroline and many other offshore stations.

On 31st May 1960 the *Olga* entered the Norder Werft shipyard in Hamburg for conversion into a floating radio station. This yard was selected on advice from the Dutch offshore station Radio Veronica, whose vessel *Borkum Riff* had also been fitted out there earlier that year (see Chapter 4).

Work on the vessel took longer than expected and on 10th August 1960 the project suffered a serious and unexpected setback. Under pressure from the Swedish Telegraph Board the German authorities informed the shipyard that the provisions of a pre-war (Nazi) law, which was still in force, made it illegal to install, repair or operate a radio station on German territory without government permission. Accordingly in October 1960 the partly converted ship, now known as the *Bon Jour*, had to leave Hamburg and eventually she docked in the Nordhavs-Vaerftet yard in Langeline, near Copenhagen, where the aerial mast was erected and the transmitters installed.

The two 10Kw medium wave transmitters had been delivered to Copenhagen from America in 6000 loose parts requiring re-assembly - work which was carried out by KLIF's Chief Engineer Glen Callison and fellow American technician Archie Mesch who acted as consultant to Radio Nord.

Offices and land-based studios for Radio Nord were established in central Stockholm. Here two studios were constructed, one of which was capable of being divided so that facilities for three simultaneous recording sessions were available. This arrangement was later modified so the control room could also be used as a separate small studio, providing extra facilities for the vast volume of material which had to be recorded to keep the station supplied with programmes. In addition there was another studio located in separate premises in Stockholm which was used mainly for the production of commercials and in-house station promotions.

The studios were equipped with Ampex tape recorders and Spotmaster cassette machines for inserting jingles and commercials into programmes. The Spotmaster equipment from America gave Radio Nord the ability to provide a slick continuity of presentation which other stations, particularly the state network, lacked at that time.

By the time Radio Nord was ready to go on the air in December 1960 the station had a staff of 25, including announcers, technicians, administrative and sales personnel.

## More expansion in Denmark

Radio Mercur continued to steadily increase in popularity and maintain its challenge to the Danish and Swedish state radio networks throughout 1959 and 1960. By the end of 1960 however, it became apparent from operating experience that a larger ship would be needed for the station. To keep the operation outside the restrictions imposed by Danish law a London-based company, Baltic Panama Shipping Co. Ltd., purchased a 450 ton ship, *Habat,* and renamed her *Cheeta 2**. The vessel was then hired to another company, Internationale Radio Mercur Anstalt, based in Switzerland, which undertook the fitting of all the radio equipment, including a new 8Kw Siemens transmitter and a fully operational on-board studio.

Once completed the radio ship was then hired to Radio Mercur by the London-based company and test broadcasts from the new vessel started on 31st January 1961 on 88mHz. The following day, 1st February 1961 *Cheeta 2* took over Radio Mercur's broadcasts completely.

### RADIO NORD'S FIRST RATECARD

**The first advertising rate-card for Radio Nord initially quoted the following rates:-**

**10 seconds - 200Kr(£14)**

**30 seconds - 300Kr(£21)**

**60 seconds - 400Kr(£28)**

**Spot advertising at these rates was the main source of income, but sponsored programmes were also available on the station at the following rates:-**

**5 minutes - 1,200Kr(£84)**

**10 minutes - 1,800Kr(£126)**

**15 minutes - 2,500Kr(£175)**

**30 minutes - 5,000Kr(£350)**

**60 minutes - 10,000Kr(£700)**

**(*these figures reflect the January 1961 rate of exchange)**

**In order to assist with the sale of airtime to potential advertisers who were unfamiliar with commercial radio, a one hour pilot programme tape was made, to demonstrate just how the new station would sound.**

**The ship is commonly referred to in most offshore radio literature as Cheeta II, but Lloyds Register of Shipping, which is the officially recognised worldwide registration body for shipping, records her as Cheeta 2.*

The transmitter from the original *Cheeta* was later installed on *Cheeta 2* and used to broadcast the Swedish language programmes of Skanes Radio Mercur on the original frequency of 89.55mHz, making Radio Mercur the first offshore station to transmit separate programmes from the same ship simultaneously. Broadcasting hours now read:-

| | |
|---|---|
| 5.55am -10.00am | ) Radio Mercur (Danish) |
| 3.30pm - 12 midnight | ) on 88mHz |
| 7.00am - 8.00pm | ) Skanes Radio Mercur |
| 11.00pm - 12midnight | ) (Swedish) on 89.55mHz |

On 7th April 1961 more offshore broadcasting history was made by Radio Mercur when the station started experimental stereo transmissions. To achieve this the station used both transmitters on board the *Cheeta 2* , the left hand channel on 88mHz, the right hand on 89.55mHz, and consequently listeners needed two radios to receive these primitive stereo broadcasts.

Having been replaced by the new, larger ship the original *Cheeta* was taken to a Norwegian port in July 1961, but not for repairs and a refit as has often been reported. In fact she was leased to a Norwegian shipping company and used as a working vessel to transport cargoes of scrap iron between various Scandinavian ports.

## Frustrations for Radio Nord

The Radio Nord ship *Bon Jour* was finally fitted out by mid December 1960 and she left Copenhagen at 6.00pm on Tuesday 20th December for her anchorage near Almagrundet Lighthouse off Stockholm. The station intended to be on the air for Christmas and an advertisement appeared in one Stockholm newspaper, *Expressen,* publicising the start of transmissions. However, because of press antipathy towards the station the advertisement was not placed directly by Radio Nord, but through a music publishing house - Metronome Corporation. The copy read " Metronome Corporation congratulates Radio Nord on their start on 494m". Apart from *Expressen* all other Stockholm newspapers refused to accept the advertisement.

A series of unexpected incidents frustrated the station's well laid plans to be on the air for Christmas. Only two and a half hours after leaving Copenhagen the Captain of the *Bon Jour* decided to drop anchor for a few hours as the weather was becoming extremely foggy. The voyage resumed the following day, 21st December, but at 5.00pm, just over half way through the journey to the *Bon Jour's* intended anchorage, the Captain again dropped anchor off the island of Gotska Sandon. The problem this time was that the stays on the mast had worked loose during severe gales and it was thought necessary to repair the damage before sailing on. At 11.00am on 23rd December the *Bon Jour* set sail again, anchoring a few hours later at what the Captain thought was the correct position. Engineers switched on the transmitter but the aerial short-circuited and everything went dead.

### Radio Nord's wavelength

*Radio Nord's test transmissions were initially on 606kHz (495m) medium wave, but were moved to 602kHz (498m) to avoid night-time interference from a French station in Lyon. However, as all publicity material and jingles had already been prepared for the station to broadcast on 495m this continued to be the announced wavelength for Radio Nord throughout its time on the air.*

Radio Nord's owners had sent special Christmas programme tapes on board a fishing boat, the *Dannette* which had instructions to rendezvous with the *Bon Jour* when she arrived at the prearranged anchorage position. Because the Captain had anchored the *Bon Jour* in the wrong location the *Dannette* spent two days searching for the radio ship, eventually finding her on Christmas Eve 1960.

On Christmas Day, instead of the planned opening of Radio Nord the crew actually abandoned ship, thinking that the mast was about to collapse on the deck. They were taken to Sandhamn by a pilot vessel, leaving the *Bon Jour* riding at her anchorage unmanned. The following day they were persuaded to return to the radio ship and on 27th December 1960 the *Bon Jour* herself was towed into Sandhamn by a salvage tug, the *Neptun.*

The radio ship was later taken to Lidingo for repairs, but on arrival there the crew discovered that the shipyard had closed down six months earlier! Amidst this fiasco and with press demands for the Swedish authorities to declare the *Bon Jour* unseaworthy, the vessel briefly visited Stockholm before leaving hurriedly for Abo in Finland to avoid being impounded by Swedish government marine inspectors.

After entering the Crichton-Fulcan shipyard in Abo for repair a new Captain was engaged by Jack Kotschack to take command of the radio ship. However, the Finnish Government, at the request of their Swedish counterparts, pressurised the shipyard into refusing a repair berth for the vessel so once again the *Bon Jour* was forced to set sail, anchoring in nearby Chalk Harbour. Despite this setback the shipyard owner, who was personally very sympathetic towards the station, arranged for a party of workers to travel to the ship and carry out repairs at sea, a task which was completed on 4th February 1961.

The radio ship anchored off Orno on 6th February 1961 , but just as final engineering checks were being carried out a crack was heard from the mast. This time the insulators had fractured and yet again the *Bon Jour* was forced to go into port, arriving at the Finnboda shipyard in Stockholm on 7th February 1961. Here new insulators were installed, all equipment checked and, despite the transmitters having been sealed by the Swedish authorities, a number of test transmissions were made from the ship while she was still anchored in central Stockholm. The crew had discovered a way to bypass the Swedish Telegraph Service's seals which they insisted had to be placed on the transmitters every time the ship entered Swedish waters!

Having completed the repairs and technical overhaul the *Bon Jour* was able to leave port on 21st February 1961 and sailed once again for her anchorage off Stockholm. Shortly afterwards the first test transmissions were made, but after a day or two the condensers started causing problems and the ship returned yet again to the Finnboda shipyard.

## On the air at last

By 1st March 1961 the ship was back at her anchorage and had resumed test transmissions. The repairs at the Stockholm shipyard had been completed just before the Swedish Government passed a law (which actually came into effect on 1st April 1961) stating that any radio ship entering their territorial waters would have its transmitting equipment removed and confiscated.

After two and a half months of frustrating delays and frequent visits to port for repairs to the ship and transmitting equipment, Radio Nord was finally able to begin official programmes at 10.00am on 8th March 1961. On that opening day the station ended its transmissions at 6.00pm in the evening, but the following day programmes started again at 6.00am and within a very short time Radio Nord was broadcasting 24 hours a day.

Once regular transmissions had started the Swedish Government put pressure on Nicaragua to withdraw registration from the *Bon Jour*. The station managed to arrange alternative registration with Panama, but to do this had to change the ship's name yet again, this time to *Magda Maria*. The registration was carried out through the Panamanian Consul in Hamburg who, hearing of the station's urgent necessity to have legal documentation for the ship, charged a large fee for his services. It was later discovered that he had also made provision for further

## A DAY IN THE LIFE OF A RADIO NORD NEWSMAN

| | |
|---|---|
| ***5.00am*** | *Wake-up, start collecting and editing news for the first bulletin at 6.00am* |
| ***6.00am-9.00am*** | *Present the live programme "Nordnorgon", record news programmes from other stations and edit for use by Radio Nord ,present hourly bulletins* |
| ***9.00am*** | *After breakfast continue with news collection and editing of stories for hourly bulletins* |
| ***10.00, 11.00am*** | *Present live news bulletins* |
| ***12 noon*** | *The plane usually arrived with early editions of the evening papers containing local news items which had to be rewritten or the 1.00pm bulletin* |
| ***1.00pm-2.00pm*** | *Present the live programme "Siesta on Board" and news bulletins.* |
| ***2.00pm-3.00pm*** | *Log new commercials received in the plane drop and sometimes produce inserts and commercials on tape, present hourly bulletins* |
| ***3.00pm-5.00pm*** | *Prepare and write two special daily news reports- "Around the World with Radio Nord", a three minute item containing 'light' news and "Business News", a similar length item about events in the world of commerce* |
| ***5.00pm--7.00pm*** | *Present updated news bulletins* |
| ***8.00pm-9.00pm*** | *Occasionally present another live programme; present hourly bulletins* |
| ***9.00pm-2.00am*** | *Live news bulletins every hour* |

*This schedule was shared between two on-board news staff and was arranged so that each had 12 (not continuous) hours rest a day. Newsreaders normally worked 4 days on the ship with 2 rest days off, the day in between being spent at the landbased studios recording commercials etc.*

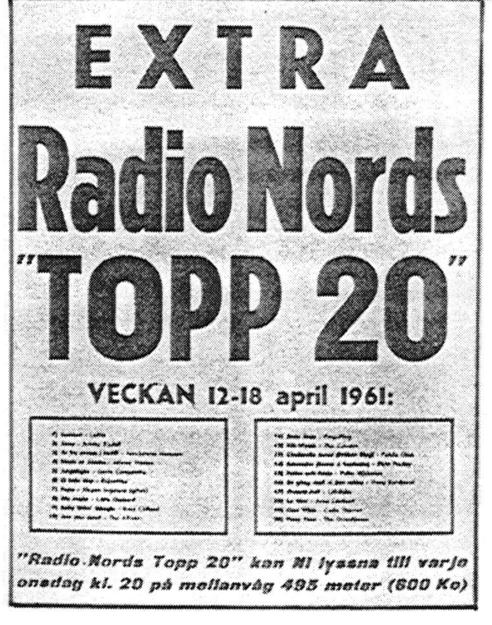


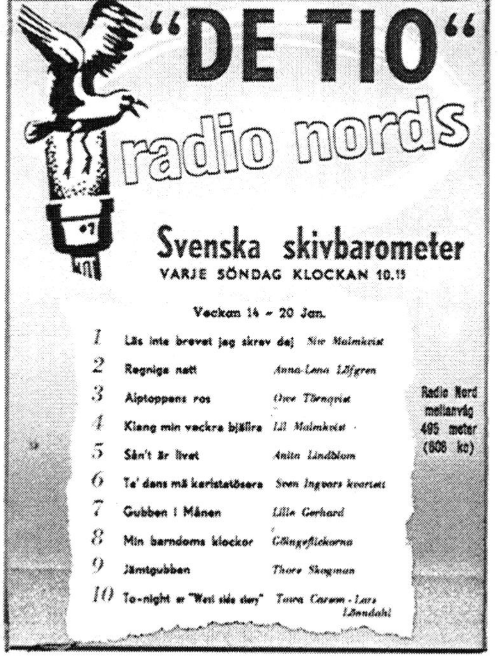

large fees by time-limiting the papers and by limiting registration to the ship's place of operation, which caused problems when the *Magda Maria* subsequently had to move from her anchorage in international waters.

Although the vessel had been renamed *Magda Maria* to comply with Panamanian re-registration requirements she was still generally referred to by her former name, *Bon Jour*. This name was erroneously used by the owner of the station, Jack Kotschack, throughout his official history of Radio Nord published in 1963 and has appeared in most other documentation since then. However, the name *Magda Maria* was clearly painted on the ship's stern during the majority of her time as home to Radio Nord and as this was the vessel's registered name from March 1961 it has been used throughout the remainder of this account of Radio Nord's history.

## Revolutionary format

Radio Nord's programmes were a mixture of live broadcasts from the ship and pre-recorded tapes from the Stockholm studios. Usually 16 news bulletins a day were broadcast between 6.00am and 2.00am, although this number could vary slightly depending on staff availability and weather conditions. The on-board newscasters were also responsible for presenting live programmes, such as "Nordnorgon" between 6.00am and 9.00am and "Siesta on Board" between 1.00pm and 2.00pm.

The format Radio Nord offered its listeners was something completely new to Europe. Even the other contemporary offshore radio stations off the coasts of Denmark and Holland did not produce their programmes in the American-influenced Top 40 Format. Most other commercial popular music stations of the time, including Radio Luxembourg as well as those offshore, presented quarter, half or hour long programmes (each usually sponsored by a different advertiser) with specific types of music - dance followed by rock, followed by Latin American etc., but Radio Nord's radically different approach to programming style was guided by two main principles:-

- no listener tuning into the station should have to switch off because the kind of music they preferred would not be heard within a reasonable time
- everyone should be able to turn programmes on and off when they pleased, without being tied to particular programme times.

From the start too, the maximum time between each record - both for commercials and DJ announcements - was limited to one minute (a policy adopted again by another offshore station, Laser 558, over 25 years later), while the hourly newscasts were given a maximum of three minutes airtime. Another time limit, although rarely achieved in practice, was that a maximum of 12 minutes each hour was allocated for commercials.

The guiding light behind this programme policy was, of course, Gordon McLendon, whose station in Dallas, KLIF, had successfully pioneered such a format. KLIF was particularly strong on news with the slogan "Tomorrow's Newspaper Today". News was broadcast every hour, with headlines every half hour and no item was allowed to be presented in the same style twice. If nothing had happened to update a story since the previous newscast then it was rewritten so that it sounded fresh to the listener. KLIF also employed mobile units to gather news around Dallas and for on-the-scene reports.

The use of this latter facility was obviously impossible for an offshore station, but Radio Nord nevertheless managed to develop a very efficient news operation, possibly the most sophisticated of any offshore station. Negotiations with news agencies such as Associated Press and United Press International for a direct teleprinter feed to the radio ship came to nothing, but undaunted by this setback an ingenious news-gathering system was developed by the station.

The Radio Nord offices in Stockholm obtained early editions of the morning newspapers at 3.00am and edited stories from them for use on radio bulletins. They also monitored the Swedish State Radio news for more up-to-date information and made regular checks with control centres of the various emergency services.

The edited stories were then fed to the ship via the ship-to-shore telephone link. News staff on board the *Magda Maria* also monitored foreign news broadcasts, including those of the BBC World Service and Voice of America for additional material and background information. Sports results were obtained by station staff phoning the various arenas while horse racing results from the track at Solvalla were broadcast shortly after each race. This amazing feat was achieved by correspondents at the track phoning details of results, odds and cancellations to Radio Nord's Stockholm News Department, who then relayed the information out to the ship.

The system of using ship-to-shore telephone facility to relay news in this way was eventually stopped in the autumn of 1961 when the Swedish Telegraph Board ordered the Stockholm Radio station at Stafsnos to handle only emergency calls to the *Magda Maria.* The ship-based news staff were then forced to gather stories themselves from foreign station's hourly news bulletins. This meant that Radio Nord news bulletins had to be broadcast at a quarter past the hour and as a consequence the station suffered many jibes from the Swedish press about "presenting the latest news - 15 minutes later". By the beginning of 1962, however, a radio telephone link had been established on board the *Magda Maria* and Radio Nord was once again able to present up-to-date news on the hour.

## Tendering arrangements for Radio Nord

Radio Nord was at first serviced by a fishing boat tender, *Listerlind,* which took crew and equipment out to the *Magda Maria.* However, the *Listerlind* was soon found to be too small and uncomfortable for the three hour journey from ship to shore and was replaced by a larger tender, the *Bellana.* Bulk supplies of oil and water were delivered by the Grogg Co. of Stockholm using one of their ships, *Fredsgrogg.* All journeys

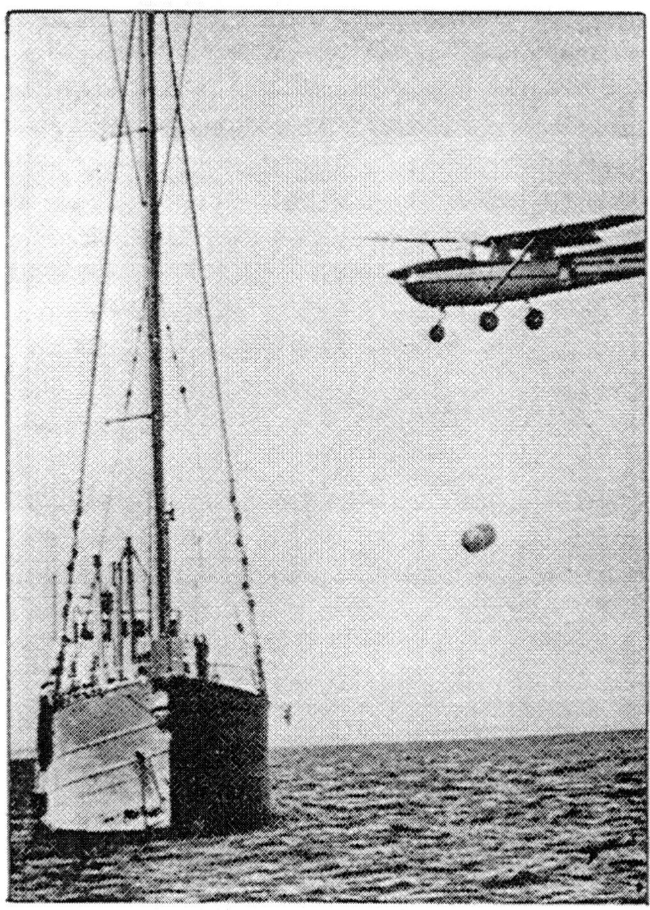

*Radio Nord's daily delivery of supplies and programme tapes by plane*

to the ship were cleared through customs and Swedish Government export licences had to be obtained for certain items of specialist technical equipment.

The station also used a Cessna light aircraft, similar to that used by the Danish offshore station Radio Mercur, to drop canisters containing programme tapes, commercials, mail, newspapers and messages on an almost daily basis. The canisters, with a line attached to them, were thrown from the aircraft so that they would land in the sea across another line which trailed from the stern of the ship and was secured to floats. The ropes attached to the canister would catch in the floats and it was then hauled on board by the crew using a rope and pulley mechanism. So effective was this delivery system that during the life of the station only two canisters were not retrieved from the sea.

The curtailment of the ship-to-shore telephone service also had an effect on the station's supply operation. 'Domestic' messages from the *Magda Maria* to the Stockholm office about supplies now had to be transmitted over the air at a set time (12.30pm) each day during normal programming. This system was eventually modified so that a tape containing the messages was recorded at slow speed and replayed over the air at fast speed (and sometimes, to maintain confidentiality, backwards) at 4.00am each morning when the audience levels were at their lowest.

## Radio Nord's commercial development and success

Radio Nord's programme format of music and regular news bulletins proved immensely popular with Swedish listeners. In response to this offshore competition Swedish State Radio introduced an easy listening service - Melodi Radio on 5th May 1961, just six weeks after Radio Nord had come on the air.

An opinion poll taken in June 1961 by the Institute for Market Inquiries (IMU) showed that, even after the introduction of Melodi Radio, more listeners consistently tuned into Radio Nord for their musical entertainment. The following results from that poll show the percentage of households in Radio Nord's reception area which regularly tuned to the station at the peak listening times on weekdays:-

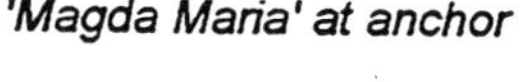
*'Magda Maria' at anchor*

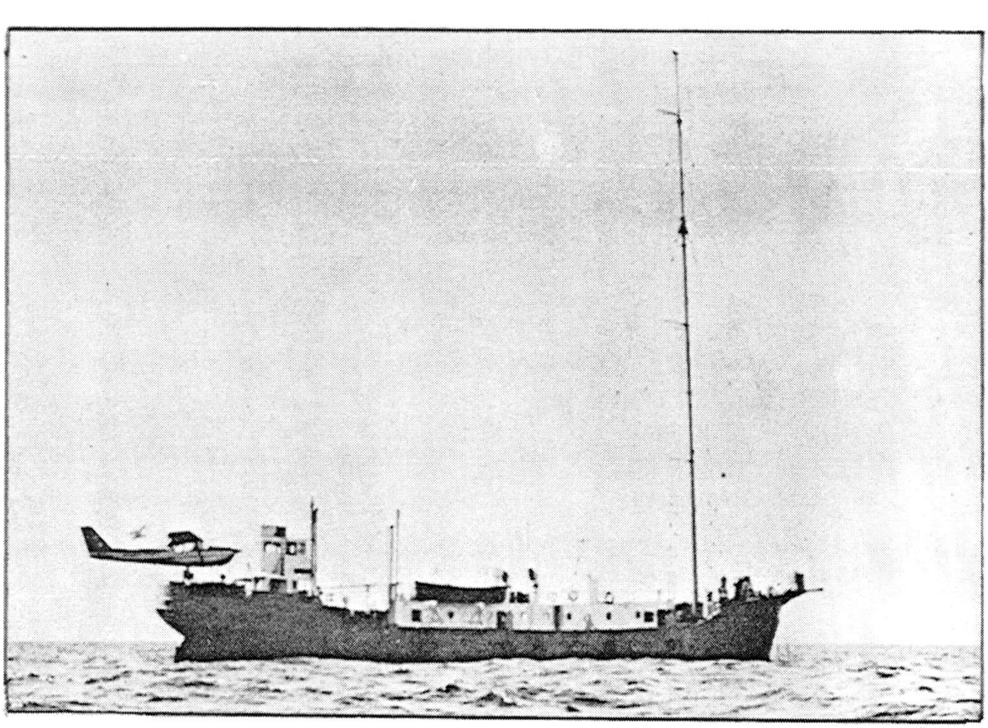

| | RADIO NORD % | MELODI RADIO % |
|---|---|---|
| 6.00am | 3.2 | 2.2 |
| 7.00am | 7.4 | 4.4 |
| 7.30am | 8.2 | 4.8 |
| 12 noon | 7.6 | 7.7 |
| 1.30pm | 7.0 | 8.2 |
| 2.00pm | 7.4 | 9.2 |
| 3.00pm | 7.6 | 7.6 |
| 5.00pm | 11.6 | 7.8 |
| 5.30pm | 11.4 | 7.6 |
| 6.00pm | 10.4 | 7.2 |
| 6.30pm | 10.2 | 5.2 |
| 7.00pm* | 10.6 | 3.6 |

(* at this time Melodi Radio relayed the programmes of Swedish Radio's Programme 2)

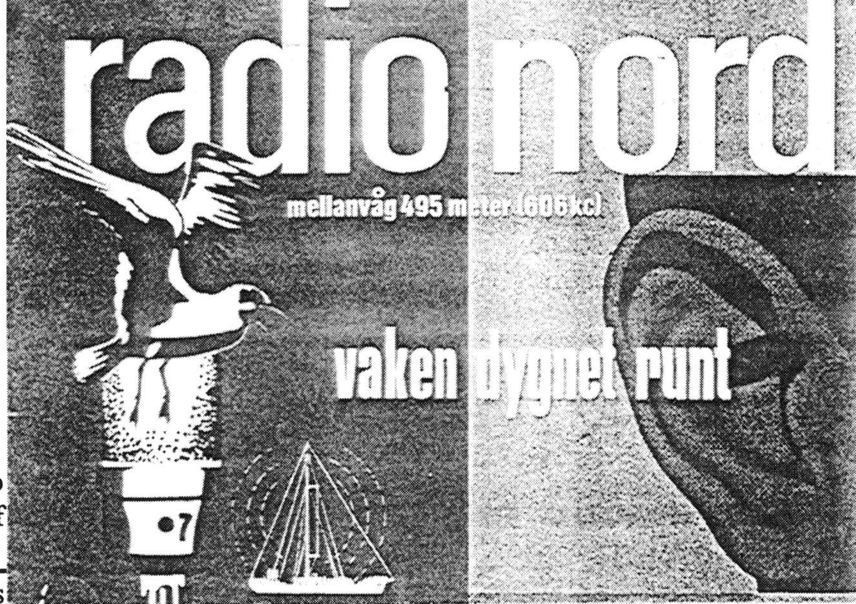


It is clear that Radio Nord was most popular in the breakfast and early evening 'drivetime' periods, comparing unfavourably only around lunchtime. Radio Nord's management quickly took action to improve programme presentation at lunchtime in order to rectify the situation revealed by this survey.

At first Radio Nord only had one advertiser - the Westinghouse Corporation, but a number of 'friendly' organisations were given free 'meal ticket' spots in return for goods and services they had supplied so the on-air effect was that the station sounded commercially successful from day one. Gradually businessmen began to realise the benefits of using the station in their advertising campaigns and some amazing sales results were achieved following promotion on Radio Nord.- Duralex glass manufacturers claimed to have increased sales of their products by 300% as a direct result of advertising on Radio Nord while Westinghouse sold its entire Swedish stock of dishwashers in a matter of days following a series of commercials on the station. However, some large advertisers (and their agencies) who had initially expressed interest and support became reluctant to use Radio Nord after having been 'advised' that if they did so lucrative government supply contracts would be cancelled.

## Discontent and breakaway in Denmark

Returning to Denmark in mid 1961, despite Radio Mercur's success the owners' overriding desire to maximise profits was beginning to cause programme standards to fall to a level thought unacceptable by some senior staff. A number of attempts were made by three senior personnel - Production Manager Benny Knusden, Legal Adviser Bero Aegac and Sales Director of Radio Mercur Reklam, Vaar Jensen to achieve what would have amounted to a management buy-out, but without success. Ib Fogh, by now resident in Spain, refused to sell his shareholding in the station he had founded, so the disillusioned staff decided to leave Radio Mercur and start another offshore station of their own.

Using the same smokescreen of ownership a new company was registered in Liechtenstein - Etablissement Technique Int. and with finance from Itablise Mark Technique in Switzerland, a 240 ton Lebanese freighter *Nijmah Al Hazz* was acquired, renamed and re-registered in Libya as the *Lucky Star*. The ship was fitted out as a radio station in Belgium with German transmitting equipment and an American-made aerial system. The new station - known as DCR (Danmarks Commercielle Radio) started broadcasting on 15th September 1961 on 93.94mHz (announced as 94mHz) with a power of 20Kw - significantly more than Radio Mercur.

As with Radio Mercur, DCR's programmes were pre-recorded in landbased studios in Copenhagen and taken out to the ship for later transmission. DCR was on the air on weekdays from 3.30pm to 11.00pm and on Sundays from 9.00am to 12 midnight, covering all of Zeeland and part of Funen with its powerful transmitter. The new station's style and content of programmes differed significantly from those of Radio Mercur, with more classical music, operas, plays and discussions being broadcast.

In the face of competition from the new offshore station Radio Mercur immediately increased its Danish language broadcasting hours to 6.00am to 11.00am and 2.00pm to 12 midnight. At about the same time Radio Mercur also acquired a theatre in central Copenhagen, which it renamed Radio Mercur City, and transferred its studio and administrative operations to this new headquarters.

With two radio ships now broadcasting from off its coast, but no legislation as yet to outlaw them, the Danish authorities felt they needed to take some action to make life as difficult as possible for the stations. On 29th September 1961 the Danish Post Office instructed coastal radio stations not to accept communications to or from the radio ships, except in emergency situations.

As well as making practical difficulties for the operators this ban also had programming implications, particularly for Radio Mercur which had previously used Lyngby Radio to transmit interviews and reports to their ship for re-broadcast later during daily programmes. One irony of this new situation was that the then Danish Prime Minister, Viggo Kampmann, had himself been interviewed during a Radio Mercur programme using the ship-to-shore radio link shortly before the authorities imposed the ban.

The Danish authorities were also engaged in talks with their Swedish counterparts to find a way of jointly tackling the growing number of offshore radio stations. By this time, October 1961, Sweden also had two stations beaming programmes to its population - Skanes Radio Mercur in the south and Radio Nord anchored in the north off Stockholm.

## More expansion

In November 1961 the *Cheeta* returned from Norwegian waters to a new anchorage at Elefantgrunden, between Fyns Hoved, Funen and Reersa, Zeeland and resumed her role as a radio ship enabling Radio Mercur to achieve wider coverage of Denmark by the introduction of a second service. Transmissions of Radio Mercur (West) started from this anchorage on 25th November 1961, using two directional aerials to beam programmes to Aarhus and Ordense.

A few weeks later, during a storm on 14th December 1961, the *Cheeta's* new aerial mast collapsed and Radio Mercur (West) was temporarily put off the air. It was then decided that the two ships in the Radio Mercur network should change places -the larger *Cheeta 2* being better able to cope with the rough seas at the Zeeland anchorage, while the *Cheeta* could ride at anchor in the calmer waters of The Sound off Copenhagen. This exchange of anchorages took place on 16th December 1961.

Radio Mercur programmes were still recorded in the Copenhagen studios but now two copies of tapes were made, one for each ship. The same pre-recorded programmes were broadcast simultaneously from both ships, apart from two and a half hours a day when each station (Radio Mercur (East) off Copenhagen and Radio Mercur (West) off Funen) provided listeners in their respective areas with local programming.

## Drama at Radio Nord

After nine months on the air without any real problems, trouble came for Radio Nord on 6th December 1961, when during a 70mph gale the *Magda Maria* began dragging her anchor and started to drift from her mooring at about 11.00am. Although no one could have imagined it at the time this was to be the first of many such storm dramas which would affect the ship during its offshore radio life.

The storm had actually started on 2nd December 1961 when a steadily increasing wind and rough seas made the *Magda Maria* roll dramatically at her anchorage. Twelve people were on board at the time, but the only marine crew were the Captain, one sailor, a 16 year old deck-boy and a young engineer.

Everybody on board grew increasingly tired and physically exhausted as the storm continued day after day - sleeping was impossible in such conditions with furniture, fittings and the contents of cabins being thrown around as the ship tossed violently in the heavy seas.

By the early morning of 6th December the storm had intensified and with waves towering above the ship, causing her to keel, at times over to 45 degrees, the anchor chain broke and the *Magda Maria* started to drift. In the studio broadcasting staff fought to keep the taped programmes on the air, but with the constant movement of the ship tapes and cartridges were flung from their racks and strewn across the floor.

Having confirmed that the *Magda Maria* was actually drifting, the Captain ordered the engines to be started, but pressure in the air tanks had dropped from the required level of 18 kilos to just 3 kilos. Without sufficient air pressure the diesel engines could not be started and the on-board compressor, which could have been used to raise the pressure was also found to be out of action. The Captain, by now up to his waist in water on the deck, ordered the crew to pump up the pressure using the only means left available - the hand pump. Everyone on board had to assist with this exercise because it was impossible for one man to work for long in the cramped conditions of the engine room where the pump handle was located.

After several hours pumping the pressure reached 18 kilos and a few attempts were made to start the engine, but without success. With the pressure dropping once more further attempts to start the engines were useless so everyone had to return to the hand pump and begin the operation all over again.

At this stage in the drama the Captain contacted Stockholm Radio asking them to notify the station's office of the situation. In making this call he was invoking the emergency clause the Telegraph Board had allowed for when they banned the normal ship-to-shore radio link a few months earlier.

Incredibly Radio Nord's programmes were transmitted as normal throughout this drama until 5.00pm when the news service had to be discontinued. This was because the on-board newsreader had to take the rudder of the ship after the engines had eventually been started. There were two problems associated with steering the *Magda Maria* - firstly she was a 'direct steered' vessel, which means the rudder cables went straight from the wheelhouse to the rudder with no servo engine, so the full weight of the ship could be felt at the wheel. Secondly, the weight of the tall mast at the front of the ship had the effect of making the bow dip into the sea, forcing the rudder at the stern out of the water, reducing its effectiveness in steering the ship

With the engines now running, but only at a quarter power because of problems with the water cooler, a decision had to be made about where the ship should head. The Captain, aware that the law forbade offshore radio ships to enter Swedish territorial waters except in an emergency nevertheless, sought, and was given, permission from the Radio Nord office to head for the Swedish port of Sandhamn because of the critical situation facing the *Magda Maria* at that time.

Throughout this drama Radio Nord's programmes had been kept on the air, but by midnight on 6th/7th December 1961 it was estimated that the ship must be inside Swedish territorial waters and so transmissions were suspended.

The ship was guided into port at Sandhamn by pilots and docked for repairs. Fortunately for Radio Nord the authorities did not enforce the law relating to confiscation of broadcasting equipment and merely sealed the station's transmitters. This decision was made on humanitarian grounds as it was thought the *Magda Maria* would have been wrecked had she stayed at sea in the severe storm conditions, with consequent danger to the lives of those on board.

Repairs to the engine and aerial mast stays were completed and a new anchor installed by 8th December 1961. The *Magda Maria* left port hurriedly in case the authorities changed their minds about confiscation of equipment and sailed, through thick fog, back to her anchorage from where broadcasts recommenced later the same day. The seals, which had been placed on the transmitter by the Swedish Telegraph Board when the *Magda Maria* entered port, had not been removed and once again the crew managed to find a way of bypassing them to put Radio Nord back on the air. Broadcasts continued for a further three weeks with this arrangement before the seals were eventually taken off by the station's engineers!

Apart from some hours in the early days of the station's broadcasts this short break in transmissions was the only time Radio Nord went off the air during its 15 month life.

## Danish merger

After less than three months on the air the programming format of the second Danish offshore broadcaster, DCR, had become very similar to that of the state radio network and the station failed to achieve real popularity either with listeners or advertisers. By contrast the first offshore station, Radio Mercur, was reported to have had a turnover of 6 million Kr.(£420,000) during 1961 and with two ships on the air was attracting large audiences and advertising revenue.

In December 1961 talks started between representatives of DCR and Radio Mercur, with a view to a merger of the rival stations, under the Radio Mercur call-sign. One obstacle to the plan was the refusal of joint Managing Director and co-founder of Radio Mercur, Ib Fogh to resign from the management board, but by January 1962 he had accepted that for the future good of the station his resignation was the only way forward and he agreed to leave. With his departure negotiations were completed quite quickly and at the end of January 1962 the two stations finally merged. The share capital of the new company was divided between the remaining original Radio Mercur owners (60%) and the owners of DCR (40%).

Following the merger DCR ceased separate transmissions on 29th January 1962 and Radio Mercur (East) programmes were then relayed from the *Lucky Star* on 93.94mHz. *Cheeta 2* meanwhile continued to broadcast Radio Mercur (West) programmes to Funen and East Jutland.

With three ships ( *Cheeta, Cheeta 2* and *Lucky Star* ) at its disposal Radio Mercur now had the potential to achieve complete coverage of Denmark and become a truly national station. However, shortly after the merger with DCR the *Cheeta* (then still anchored off Copenhagen) found herself in difficulties during a gale on 12th February 1962 and put out a distress call. The ship was assisted to Langeline Quay in Copenhagen by a tug and once in port she was immediately detained by police. Investigations subsequently revealed that after Panama withdrew its registration (in August 1958) the ship had remained stateless, although the station's owners had always claimed the vessel was legally registered in Honduras.

Fortunately, because of the recent merger, the station had the former DCR ship *Lucky Star* available which was now able to fully take over the broadcasts of Radio Mercur (East) on 88mHz instead of just relaying the *Cheeta's* output.

## Breakaway

Early in 1962 the owners of Skanes Radio Mercur sold their interest in the station to the Sales Manager, Mrs. Britt Wadner. Mrs. Wadner intended to keep the Swedish language programmes on the air, but wanted to break away from hiring airtime from the Danish Radio Mercur and planned to start her own full time Swedish language offshore radio station directed at Malmo in southern Sweden.

At the beginning of March 1962 the former Radio Mercur vessel *Cheeta* was put up for sale by the salvage company and was purchased by Britt Wadner. After having resolved ownership and legal formalities with the various authorities Mrs. Wadner returned the radio ship to sea in March 1962, anchoring outside Swedish territorial limits off Malmo

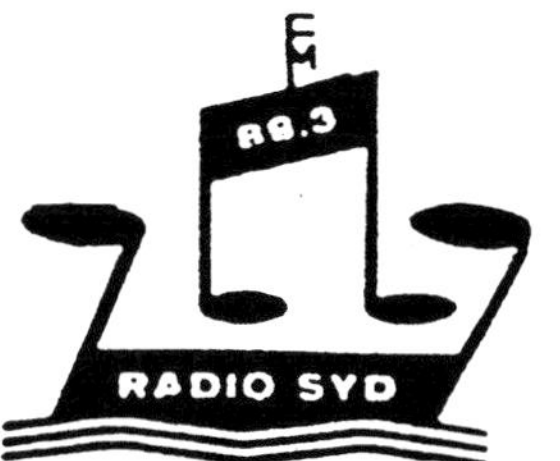


On 1st April 1962 the first broadcasts from a new Swedish offshore station - Radio Syd -were heard on 89.62mHz, broadcasting popular music programmes 21 hours a day using a 5Kw transmitter. Radio Syd which at that time had a staff of 33 mainly operating from offices and landbased studios in Malmo had been launched at a crucial time just as legislation was being enacted by four Scandinavian governments to ban offshore broadcasting.

## Government action

Radio Mercur, Skanes Radio Mercur, Radio Nord and to a lesser extent, DCR, had proved themselves to be enormously popular with listeners and advertisers. However, the Scandinavian authorities were not so pleased about the growing number of radio stations anchoring off their coasts and the threat they posed to the established state monopoly services.

Following a recommendation by a special committee of the Nordic Council in February 1962 a concerted approach was agreed by four Scandinavian governments to deal with the 'problem' of offshore radio stations. The four governments in question - Denmark, Sweden, Norway and Finland - started to progress through their respective parliaments domestic legislation making it an offence for their nationals to supply, broadcast from, advertise on or assist an offshore station in any way.

The Danish legislation was introduced into parliament on 3rd April 1962 and was finally approved on 14th July 1962 (83 members voting in favour and 38 against with 23 abstentions). The Swedish Bill - Lex Radio Nord - was

### 'JAMMING' SIGNAL

*In March 1962 an unidentified signal appeared at the same time each evening jamming Radio Nord's broadcasts during the very popular and highly lucrative sponsored Top 20 programme. Protests were lodged with the Swedish Telegraph Board, who denied responsibility, but mysteriously the jamming signal stopped a few days later.*

introduced on 29th March 1962 and passed by Parliament on 6th June. Norway and Finland, although neither was served by an offshore station, also introduced similar laws which were passed on 22nd June and 27th July 1962 respectively.

With each country having put in place its domestic legislation a meeting of ministers representing the four governments took place in Stockholm on 3rd July 1962 and agreement was reached that all anti-offshore broadcasting laws would come into effect at midnight on 31st July 1962.

## Ambitious plans halted

During the summer of 1962 plans were made by Radio Nord to start an easy-listening service on FM to complement the Top 40 Format on 495m, with the same commercials being broadcast on both stations. Work on installing the FM transmitter to launch the service was completed on board the *Magda Maria* early in June 1962.

An even more ambitious plan, involving co-operation with another offshore broadcaster, was also in the pipeline during the summer of 1962. Jack Kotschack and the other owners of Radio Nord had long cherished the idea of doing for television what they were already achieving with their radio station - breaking the state monopoly and giving audiences the sort of programmes they really wanted.

The problem with television transmissions from a ship is that when the vessel pitches and tosses in rough seas, the transmitted signal is badly distorted and satisfactory reception is virtually impossible on land. It was only when the Radio Nord directors heard about a technical development in America that the idea of an offshore television station became more than just a dream. The US Navy had managed to develop an aerial system which could be used on board ships anchored at sea to transmit television signals. Exactly how this device solved the 'rolling picture' problem was, of course, top secret, but through various contacts in the American Navy Radio Nord were convinced that they could acquire one of the units for use in their project.

As the Stockholm Archipelago (where the Radio Nord vessel, *Magda Maria* was anchored) was considered too wide to achieve satisfactory transmissions into the Stockholm city area it was decided that the project would have to be based in the south of the country with programmes beamed to Sweden's next largest centre of population, Malmo, from a vessel anchored in The Sound.

Across The Sound is Denmark and its capital city, Copenhagen, which was already served by an offshore station, Radio Mercur. Initial discussions took place between the two stations (both of whom were keen on establishing a television service) and a joint venture was officially entered into by Radio Nord and Radio Mercur. A new company - Mercur Television Anstalt - was formed under the joint ownership of both stations. Nord Establishment was to be responsible for the acquisition and installation of the transmitting equipment on the Radio Mercur vessel and for the purchase of programme material from the USA, while Radio Mercur would provide the ship-borne base and handle local programme production from its landbased studios. The service was planned to operate for 18 hours a day beaming entertainment and news programmes to an audience of over 3 million people in Denmark and southern Sweden.

The easy -listening FM service of Radio Nord and the joint television service with Radio Mercur were planned to start in July 1962, but the introduction of pan-Scandinavian legislation outlawing offshore broadcasting meant that both stations had to close before either new service could be launched.

## Closures

Radio Mercur, the first European station to start broadcasting from the high seas closed its 'West' station from the *Cheeta 2* on 10th July 1962 and the ship sailed to Elensburg in West Germany amidst rumours of plans that she would become an offshore station anchored off Greece. However, the vessel was subsequently sold to Mrs. Britt Wadner, owner of Radio Syd, which had decided to stay on the air in defiance of the new legislation. Although there is some uncertainty as to whether the *Cheeta 2* was used immediately by Radio Syd (it may have been kept as a 'reserve' vessel in case *Cheeta* was forcibly boarded by the authorities) it is known that some equipment was transferred to the *Cheeta* in 1962 to replace that ship's less sophisticated facilities.

Radio Mercur (East), on board the *Lucky Star* anchored off Copenhagen continued to broadcast for a further three weeks, closing only when the new law came into effect at midnight on 31st July 1962. The final hour was a nostalgic look back at the history of the station with programme excerpts and 'good luck' messages from former announcers. Earlier the same day the entire Radio Mercur record library had been sold at an auction in Copenhagen.

That was not the end of the story for Radio Mercur, however. After the station had closed the *Lucky Star* remained at sea and at 5.00pm on 13th August 1962 transmissions were once again started using some of the station's old programme tapes. The original Radio Mercur owners denied any responsibility for these transmissions and stated that during the life of the station they had only ever hired the ship, through an associate company, from the vessel's actual owner, Senor Louis Artura Delboso of Guatemala.

Two days later, on 15th August 1962 armed Danish police boarded the *Lucky Star* amidst reports that there had been a murder on board. As the ship apparently had no official registration (the Lebanese flag flying from the stern was a fake) a customs vessel escorted her into port at Tuborg. The former radio ship was impounded until her owners appeared and the registration irregularities had been cleared up, but the crew of the *Lucky Star* were not detained, even though they refused to disclose the name of the vessel's owner.

A court subsequently ruled that the boarding and seizure of the *Lucky Star* in international waters had been legal because she was stateless. It was suggested that the ship would be released only if its transmitting equipment was removed, but subsequently a further court ruling said that the ship could remain fitted out as a broadcasting station pending the outcome of legal proceedings. Unfortunately the ultimate fate of the *Lucky Star* is unknown.

Three months after the closure of Radio Mercur the Danish state radio system, Danmarks Radio, started Programme 3, with a format remarkably similar to Mercur's, but of course without any commercials. Many of the former Radio Mercur staff were, however, taken on by Danmarks Radio to present Programme 3.

In the face of the Scandinavian anti-offshore legislation coming into effect Radio Nord closed on 30th June 1962, with a final hour of nostalgic music and station jingles. Most programmes during the last few days of broadcasting were transmitted live from the ship and Jack Kotschack went on air during the final day to thank listeners and advertisers for their support during the previous 15 months.

It had been decided to close Radio Nord a month ahead of the new legislation coming into effect because prospective purchasers had been found for the fully equipped radio ship. The purchasers, Project Atlanta, had plans to use the *Magda Maria* as the base from which to launch the first offshore radio station off the British coast.

A few days after Radio Nord closed the *Magda Maria* sailed for Spain to be overhauled as part of the sale agreement, arriving at El Ferrol on 2nd August 1962. It should come as no surprise, however, to find that was not the final port of call for the ship which was destined to become a legend in offshore radio history (see Chapter 6).

Whilst Radio Mercur and Radio Nord had both ceased transmissions one station decided to defy the new Scandinavian laws - Radio Syd - broadcasting to southern Sweden from a position outside territorial waters off Malmo.

Following Mrs. Wadner's announcement that she would defy the new law and keep Radio Syd on the air after midnight on 31st July 1962, the Swedish Government tried to interfere with the station's broadcasts by changing the FM frequency of the much more powerful state station, Radio Halsinborg. However, two days before the change was due to take place Radio Syd itself moved frequency from 89.62mHz to 88.3mHz and so avoided a potential jamming situation.

Radio Syd continued to grow in popularity and, despite the station being outlawed after 1st August 1962 a Club Radio Syd was formed for listeners, achieving an almost immediate membership of over 10,000. In October 1962 Mrs. Wadner was prosecuted under the provisions of the anti-offshore broadcasting laws and fined for continuing with Radio Syd's broadcasts, but despite her prosecution the station remained on the air.

Now is an opportune time to leave Radio Syd defiantly broadcasting its programmes to southern Sweden and look at events which had been happening elsewhere in Europe during the early 1960s.

## Chapter 4

# Dreams Fulfilled and Shattered

While all this activity was taking place in Scandinavia there had also been offshore radio developments elsewhere. In Holland a meeting of a group of radio dealers, convened by Lambertus Marie (Bep) Slootmans, was held in the Krasnapolsky Hotel in Amsterdam on 15th October 1959. The purpose of this meeting was to try and obtain agreement on a policy towards the import of foreign made radios, which could be sold at higher profit than the home-produced Phillips Group products then dominating the Dutch market.

But something more radical and exciting came out of the meeting that evening. Also present was another radio dealer, Max Lewin, who had long nurtured the idea of setting up a political radio station outside Dutch territory, and Hendricus (Henk) Oswald, a plastics manufacturer who had watched the development of Radio Mercur in Denmark and saw the commercial possibilities for a similar station being established to serve Holland.

## The VRON Project

These three businessmen proposed to their fellow dealers at the Krasnapolsky Hotel meeting the idea of establishing an offshore station serving Holland. There was a lukewarm response at first, but the meeting eventually agreed in principle to investigate the legal position and commercial viability of such a proposal. A further meeting was convened a few days later when more details about the scheme were presented, resulting in 19 businessmen agreeing to invest money in the project, now known formally as Vrije Radio Omroep Nederland (VRON).

With about £10,000 of financial backing pledged from this meeting Slootmans, Lewin and Oswald started to develop the project. Although these three were taking the lead at this stage two other people, later to play significant roles in offshore radio history, were on the sidelines of the embryonic VRON. Kees Manders, an Amsterdam night club owner, was for two weeks, 'artistic director' to the project - his quick departure being due to what he alleged to be the incompetence of Oswald, Slootmans and Lewin. Another businessman present at the 19th October meeting was Dirk Verweij, a textile manufacturer from Hilversum, who although enthusiastic about the commercial possibilities of the VRON project had not agreed at that stage to invest any money. He and his brothers were, however, later to play very significant roles in the fortunes of VRON.

Early signs of the problems ahead became evident after only three weeks when Max Lewin pulled out of the project because of disagreements with his original partners, leaving Slootmans and Oswald to progress matters on behalf of investors. A further meeting of VRON shareholders was called on 16th November 1959, again at the Krasnapolsky Hotel, supposedly to enable those present to hear a 'test broadcast' of VRON from the North Sea. Shareholders, on hearing what they understood to be the test transmission were impressed that such rapid progress had apparently been made with the project and immediately agreed to continue providing further financial backing.

The whole event, however, was a sham, stage managed by Slootmans and Oswald and designed to secure that all important additional financial support. The transmission had in fact come, not from a ship in the North Sea, but from Oswald's office less than 200 yards from the Krasnapolsky Hotel!

As with so many 'new' ideas the backers of VRON were not the only people to have thought of establishing a radio station at sea off the coast of Holland. Two Hague advertising agents, Will J Hoordijk and Jan Beeuwkes had also started making plans for an offshore radio station, but they lacked financial resources to successfully launch their idea. They did, however, know of a suitable vessel - a former German lightship the *Borkum Riff* - lying in Emden harbour, West Germany which was for sale and which would make ideal base for an offshore radio station. Frustrated financially Hoordijk and Beeuwkes decided to approach the VRON organisation with a view to pooling their respective knowledge and resources into one project.

For VRON Slootmans and Oswald favoured the idea of co-operating with the two advertising men, mainly because they knew about the availability of a suitable ship but also their experience in the world of advertising was likely to be beneficial to the commercial success of the proposed radio station. After initial discussions the two groups agreed to co-operate and Hoordijk and Beeuwkes were appointed advertising managers for VRON. A few days later Slootmans, with fellow shareholder Phil Krant, drove to Emden and on 9th December 1959 they purchased the *Borkum Riff* for £7,000. A crew was engaged to man the ship and work started almost immediately to convert the vessel for her new role.

While the *Borkum Riff* was being fitted out another shareholder in VRON, Norbert Jurgens, together with Hendrik A 'Bul' Verweij (brother of Dirk Verweij, the Hilversum textile manufacturer present at the original VRON meeting), searched for a country of registration which would provide a flag for the radio ship to fly once at sea. They eventually succeeded in obtaining registration for the *Borkum Riff* from the Panamanian Embassy in London.

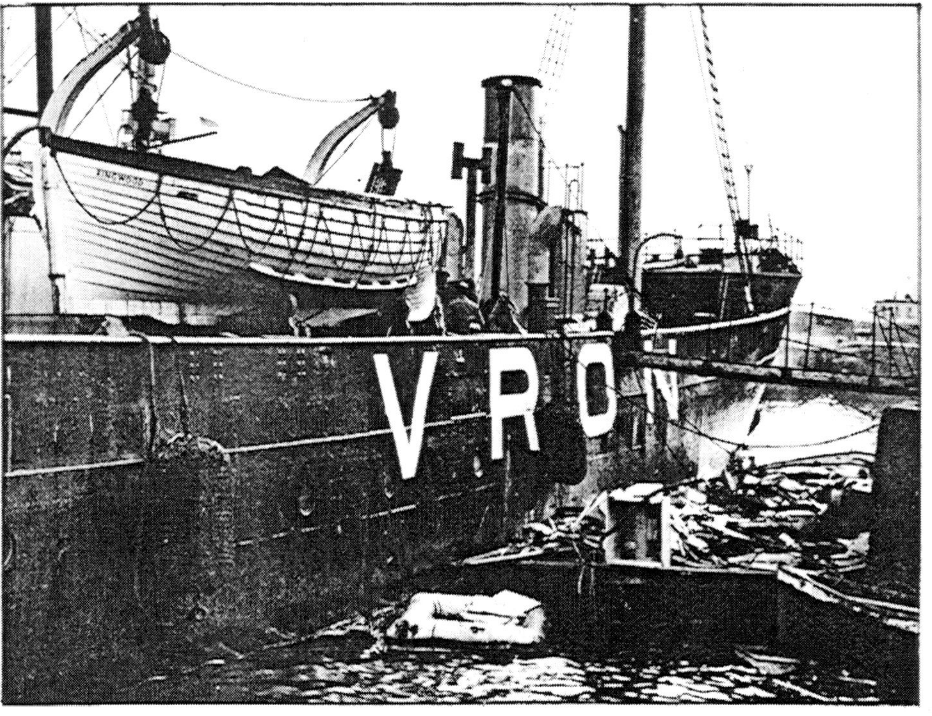


*The 'Borkum Riff' being converted to a radio ship in Emden*

In order to conduct all this business the VRON Project was put on a more formal footing with the registration of a holding company Anstalt Veronica -in Leichtenstein. The name 'Veronica' had been derived from the expansion of the acronym of the project's title.

## More deception

By December 1959 technical director Hendricus Oswald announced that the transmitter he had built was ready for installation on the *Borkum Riff*, but before this could happen his premises were raided by police and Dutch Post and Telegraph Board (PTT) officials who confiscated certain items of equipment.

Just why this raid took place only became clear some time later when it transpired that again the whole event had been stage managed to fool investors into providing yet more financial support. After the 'raid' Oswald appealed to VRON's backers and succeeded in obtaining further funding to build another transmitter to replace the one 'seized' by the authorities. In fact Oswald, having run out of money before completing work on the transmitter had himself arranged for the authorities to be told that such equipment was under construction at his premises. The only items seized were some defunct spare parts.

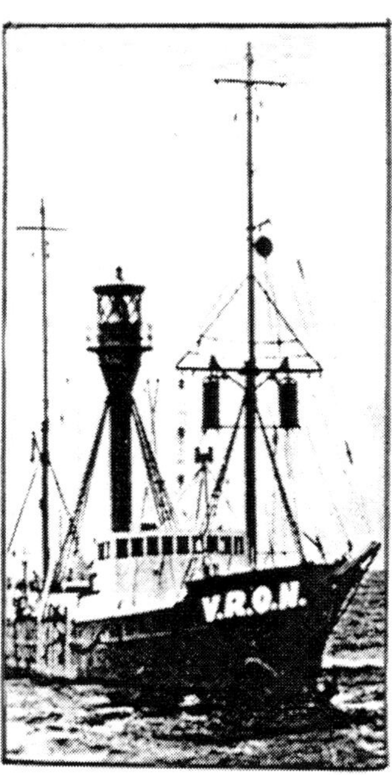

The fake radio ship photograph to mislead VRON shareholders

A transmitter was eventually constructed by Oswald and on 9th February 1960 it was taken across the border into Germany for installation on the *Borkum Riff* in Emden Harbour. However, police stopped the van carrying the transmitter just inside the German border and ordered the driver to return to Holland where Dutch PTT officials were waiting and once again confiscated the equipment.

By now VRON shareholders were becoming uneasy about the delay in getting their station on the air so the ever resourceful Oswald, this time in collaboration with Norbert Jurgens, arranged another 'test transmission', supposedly from a vessel in the North Sea. This time the transmission actually came from a deserted island on Lake Loosdrecht, near to where Jurgens lived, but to complete the illusion that the Project's ship was at sea photographs of a German lightship, similar to the *Borkum Riff*, were produced. The photographs had been doctored to show the initials 'VRON' overpainted on the bow of the lightship. Yet again shareholders were duped into believing that the radio station was further advanced than it really was, in fact from the fake photographs circulated at the meeting it must have appeared almost ready to go on the air.

It was another two months, however, before things really started to happen when, after receiving technical advice from engineers of the Danish offshore pioneer Radio Mercur, Oswald eventually succeeded in constructing a suitable transmitter. Despite a warning letter from the German Post Office, about the illegality of installing radio transmitting equipment on board a ship in a German port, work continued and fitting out of the *Borkum Riff* for her future role was completed by mid-April 1960. (The VRON organisation had simply ignored the German warning and continued with the installation of radio equipment, unlike the Swedish offshore station Radio Nord later that year, which actually moved its vessel from Emden to Denmark in the face of similar warnings from the authorities (see Chapter 3).

Just as the *Borkum Riff* was about to be towed from Emden by the English tug *Guardsman* in mid-April 1960 the authorities refused to release her until certain customs documentation had been put in order. A further delay was experienced when the Emden Harbour Master chained up the ship, acting on instructions from the Dutch Consul in West Germany. The Dutch authorities had incorrectly and somewhat naively, assumed that the *Borkum Riff* was Dutch owned and would be flying the Netherlands flag, but when informed in a strong official protest by the Panamanian Embassy in London that she was in fact registered in Panama and owned by a Liechtenstein company, the German authorities no longer had reason to detain the vessel. However, even after being released the *Borkum Riff* was shadowed by a Dutch police launch from the harbour entrance until she reached her anchorage in international waters.

## Radio Veronica on the air

The *Borkum Riff* had finally left harbour on Wednesday 20th April 1960 and the following day she anchored off Katwijk aan Zee on the Dutch coast. The first test transmissions from the new station - Radio Veronica - were made the same day on 1620kHz (185m) with a transmitter power of just 1Kw. This time the test transmissions were not a hoax, they really did come from the VRON Project's ship at anchor in the international waters of the North Sea.

Programme tapes made in the station's Amsterdam studio were taken out to the *Borkum Riff* by a small fishing vessel for the first few days until Dutch customs authorities refused to allow any further such deliveries. With this lifeline cut the station resorted to using a light aircraft (as Radio Mercur had done in Scandinavia) to drop daily supplies and programme tapes to the ship.

Further obstacles were also placed in the way of Radio Veronica by the authorities once broadcasts had started - registration of the station as a limited company (NV) in Holland was refused, Hendricus Oswald's passport was withdrawn, directors' telephones were tapped and ship-to-shore communications with the *Borkum Riff* were blocked.

Complaints of interference to coastal maritime radio stations began almost as soon as the Veronica test transmissions had started and when regular programmes commenced on 6th May 1960 the PTT jammed Radio Veronica's signal from a Naval station at Nordeich. Radio Veronica moved frequency to 1640kHz (182m) but this proved unsatisfactory, causing even more interference and being unobtainable on many domestic radio receivers. Consequently after just seven days on the air the station ceased transmissions on 13th May 1960 to adjust its equipment, returning two days later on 1562kHz (192m). This new frequency proved far more satisfactory, with a stronger signal being achieved in the primary target area despite transmitter power remaining at only 1Kw.

The Panamanian Government withdrew registration from the *Borkum Riff* in June 1960, but the owners were able to re-register the ship in Guatemala. However, after the Verweij brothers took control of Radio Veronica in late 1960 the ship was quietly re-registered yet again, this time in East Germany where the brothers had many business connections, although this information was not revealed until many years later, after the offshore station had closed.

Programming on Radio Veronica was amateurish at first. Programmes were pre-recorded, initially using a domestic tape recorder on a kitchen table with a microphone suspended from the ceiling, while presenters played records from their own personal collections because music companies were unwilling to supply new releases to the station and money was not available to purchase a regular supply of discs.

By mid-summer 1960 the quality and professionalism of the station had improved slightly and gradually it became more and more popular with listeners. The offshore station's growing popularity was not due to the professional quality of its programmes but was largely attributable to the fact that it catered for the musical tastes of young people, something the state radio services of both Holland or Belgium failed to do at that time.

The first advertisers to purchase airtime on Radio Veronica were Van Nelle tobacco and Lexington cigarettes. Radio Veronica also heavily promoted the 'Nur Die' brand of nylon stockings, manufactured by a company in which the Verweij brothers had an interest, as well as 'Berdi' suede and leather clothing, whose directors also had a financial involvement with the station at that time.

These early advertisers could testify to the popularity of Radio Veronica from some amazing sales successes. For example as a result of advertising on the station Nur Die stockings claimed to have achieved sales of over one million Guilders and later the Verweij brothers used their own textile manufacturing facilities to produce what became known as 'Veronica Stockings'.

Unfortunately despite these apparent successes many of the early advertisers were companies in which Radio Veronica directors also had interests and they actually brought the offshore station very little hard revenue, the consequences of which were felt after only six months on the air.

## Rescue Package

An audience of 5 million was claimed by Radio Veronica following a listenership survey published in November 1960, but despite this popularity advertisers were still largely reluctant to buy airtime on the station. With high operating costs and little commercial income Radio Veronica quickly began to accumulate substantial debts. By the end of November 1960 a rescue package had been mounted by the three textile manufacturers from Hilversum, brothers Dirk, Jaap and 'Bul' Verweij, who took over responsibility for the management of the floundering station and injected much needed financial support.

Having established themselves as managers of the station and firmly in control of the financial situation the Verweijs soon dismissed Oswald together with advertising managers Hoordijk and Beeuwkes. Another of the original co-founders of Radio Veronica ,'Bep ' Slootmans was also by now no longer concerned with the day-to-day management of the organisation so with complete management and financial control in their hands the Verweij brothers set about improving Radio Veronica in every way possible. They worked hard at creating and cultivating a respectable business-like image for the station, including the payment of all taxes and copyright fees to the appropriate authorities and within a few months of their takeover the station was employing a total staff of 40 both at sea and in the land-based studios and offices. Early in 1961 the station's land-based operations were moved to a small studio at Zeedijk 27a in Hilversum, Holland's broadcasting 'capital'.

Throughout 1961 improvements were made in many areas by the new management of Radio Veronica. The station's format was revamped with regular programmes such as "Jukebox" and "Coffeetime" being introduced. As a direct result of these changes increasing interest was shown by advertisers who began to realise the advantages of using the station to promote their products. As a consequence commercial income soared and operational improvements were made as a result of this increased revenue - the land-based studio facilities were gradually upgraded and a small fishing boat, *Ger Anna,* was acquired by the station to provide a regular tender service to the *Borkum Riff.*

### VERONICA RADIOS

*During 1961Radio Veronica produced and started to market its own brand of transistor radio - Model VR608 - which kept listeners tuned to the station because it was designed to only receive programmes broadcast on 192m (1562kHz)!*

## English language broadcasts

Towards the end of January and in February 1961 test transmissions took place from the *Borkum Riff* for an English language service - known as CNBC (Commercial Neutral Broadcasting Company). This company which hired airtime and landbased facilities from Radio Veronica operated from offices at Royalty House, Dean Street, London.

The English language station's announcers recorded programmes at Radio Veronica's Hilversum studios for later transmission from the *Borkum Riff,* while advertising sales for the station were handled by Ross Radio Productions Ltd. of 23 Upper Wimpole Street London W1, a company which at that time also produced sponsored programmes for Radio Luxembourg.

## Questions

*Questions were asked in the House of Commons about CNBC's broadcasts directed at Britain. The Lord Privy Seal, Edward Heath, was asked whether representations had been made to the Guatemalan Government over the registration of the radio ship, Borkum Riff, in apparent contravention of the 1958 Convention of the High Seas. Mr. Heath said the Guatemalan Government had assured the British authorities that the vessel was not registered with them and he informed the House that it was not at all clear what was the country of registration of the vessel.*

*The BBC meanwhile monitored the offshore station's broadcasts and a spokesman said: We shall watch developments with interest and we shall certainly take action if it interferes with BBC broadcasts or reception of other people's broadcasts. We would have something to say to the Postmaster General. However, the Postmaster General's office said it was difficult to know what could be done if the vessel were lying outside British territorial waters.*

It has generally been reported that the first CNBC test transmissions took place in February 1961. However, documentary evidence in the form of programmes tapes and correspondence from the station's manager to a listener in Britain exist which both quote dates in November 1960 as being the start of test transmissions for CNBC. Whether these test tapes were in fact actually transmitted in November 1960 is difficult to confirm now, but it would appear from the evidence available that they may have been. It is certain, however, that two hours of test broadcasts from CNBC started at 5.00am on 16th February 1961. After a few days CNBC's on-air time changed to 8.00am - 1.00pm and broadcasts under this call-sign continued for some weeks. CNBC programmes consisted of light music presented by English and Canadian announcers Bob Fletcher, Paul Hollingdale (later to appear on the BBC Light Programme and Radio 2) and Doug Stanley.

It was planned that when the station came on the air with regular programmes it would broadcast between 6.00am and 12 noon, and 11.00pm -2.00am on Mondays to Fridays, with a weekend service between 8.00am and 2.00pm and 11.00pm - 2.00am.

However, because of Radio Veronica's low power transmitter reception of the CNBC signal in England was weak and mainly confined to areas along the east and south east coasts, with the important commercial target area of London not being reached. Because of this and the increasing popularity of Radio Veronica itself in Holland, CNBC broadcasts were discontinued on 22nd March 1961. The few hours a day allocated to the English language station could now be more profitably filled by Radio Veronica's Dutch programming and advertising.

CNBC, although only short-lived as a radio station and never really progressing beyond the test transmission stage, did have the distinction of being the first offshore radio station whose programmes were directed at a British audience. The low power of the transmitter on the *Borkum Riff* and its distance from the English coast hampered CNBC's chance of success, but the potential of this English language offshore station had not gone unnoticed. Before long plans were being made by a number of British businessmen to set up offshore stations with sufficient transmitter power and ships anchored in positions which would ensure a strong signal did reach the commercially important areas of London, south east England and the Midlands. More details of these various plans will be discussed in Chapter 5.

CNBC

„Your Friendly Host on the Dutch Coast"

Represented by:
Ross Radio Productions Ltd.

ROYALTY HOUSE, DEAN STREET, LONDON, W.1 TELEPHONE: GERRARD 6065

CNBC

Your Friendly Host on the Dutch Coast"

P.O. BOX 344, HILVERSUM (HOLLAND) TELEPHONE 12345

COVERING SOUTHERN ENGLAND AND THE NETHERLANDS - CNBC - 192 M

## Radio Veronica

Meanwhile, Dutc language Radio Veronica had itself benefited from the short-lived test transmissions of CNBC. The requirements of the English-language station meant that extra studio facilities had been built to record programmes and the professionalism of the more experienced English and Canadian announcers had had a positive influence on their Dutch counterparts.

One interesting event occurred in mid 1961, which although dismissed at the time was to be of considerable significance a few years later. The Verweij brothers received an approach from Rotterdam shipbuilder and businessman Cor Verolme offering to construct an artificial island in the North Sea for Radio Veronica to use as a base instead of the *Borkum Riff*. At that time the Radio Veronica organisation turned down the offer because of uncertainty about the international and maritime legal status of such a structure - a decision that was to be proved correct a few years later.

The positive financial and management input of the Verweij brothers also began to show improved results and by the beginning of 1962 Radio Veronica, after a shaky start, had become as popular and profitable in Holland (perhaps even more so) as her contemporaries Radio Mercur and Radio Nord had in Scandinavia.

Programming too had settled down to a recognisable format with half hour segments using titles such as "A Minute's Rest with Veronica", "Shopping with Veronica" and " Having a Meal with Veronica". By late 1962 Radio Veronica had an estimated audience in excess of 5 million listeners with advertising turnover of 12 million Guilders (£1.2m).

A listener's club - Vrienden van Veronica (Friends of Veronica) - was established in July 1962 with members each paying one Dutch Guilder to join. An indication of just how popular the station had become can be gauged from the fact that within three months over 50,000 Guilders (£5,000) was donated to charity using money raised from these subscriptions, although one organisation, the Queen Wilhelmina Fund, refused a 10,000 Guilders (£1,000) donation from the station.

Radio Veronica also seemed to be under no apparent threat at this time from the government in Holland, unlike her Scandinavian contemporaries. During the first half of 1962 while Radio Veronica had been growing in strength four Scandinavian governments had been debating and enacting new legislation to close the stations off their coasts. However, despite setting up a Commission in July 1962 to draft a Bill outlawing offshore radio the Dutch Government, partly because of its own instability and partly because of the immense popularity of Radio Veronica, did not actively pursue the introduction of any legislation to close the station.

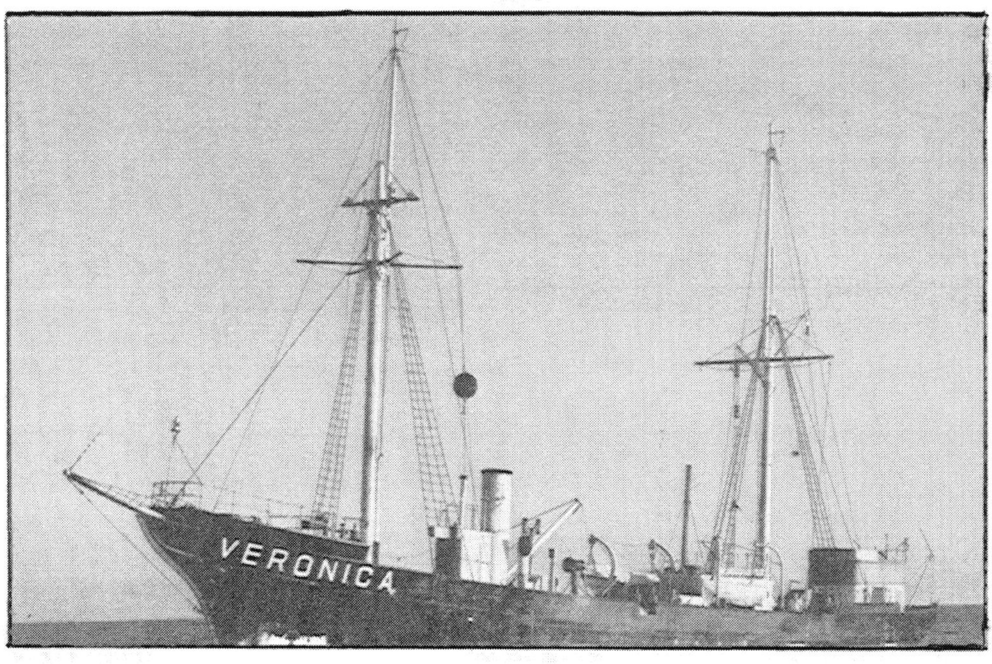


*The 'Borkum Riff' at anchor.*

## Belgium

Further down the coast, however, events were not so fortunate for an offshore broadcaster during 1962. Georges de Caluwe, inspired by the success of offshore radio in Scandinavia and neighbouring Holland, decided to re-launch his previously land-based station, Radio Antwerpen, from a ship anchored off the Belgian coast.

Georges de Caluwe was an Antwerp radio engineer who in 1922 had been granted a licence to establish the first local commercial radio station in Belgium. That station was Radio Antwerpen (with the call-sign ON4ED) but it became popularly known as Radio Kerkske (Radio Little Church) because its transmitter was located on a church tower.

Early in 1940, with the Nazi war machine threatening his country de Caluwe's station was forced by the Belgian Government to relay the programmes of NIR, the then state radio service. In May of that year, as Nazi forces were about to overrun Belgium, de Caluwe decided that he must destroy the transmitter to prevent it being used for propaganda broadcasts by the invading army. He literally took a hammer and smashed the transmitter until all that remained were pieces of scrap metal. However, during the years Belgium was occupied he secretly built another transmitter so that in 1945 with the end of hostilities Radio Antwerpen would be able to return to the air. This secretly constructed radio equipment was in such a state of readiness that station ON4ED was able to recommence broadcasting the day after British tanks passed the transmitter site in Edegem.

However, the Belgian Government on its return from wartime exile in London decided that all radio stations would in future be state controlled and , despite putting up a fight to regain his former licence, de Caluwe was forced to close Radio Antwerpen on 31st August 1948 when all his broadcasting equipment was confiscated. He appealed many times to have his licence reissued, but without success.

At the 1954 Belgian Parliamentary Elections de Caluwe launched his own party, campaigning for the right to be able to reopen Radio Antwerpen again. Although his party received over 10,000 votes, the authorities in Brussels remained unmoved and no new licence was issued .The following year de Caluwe took matters into his own hands and started broadcasting without a licence - effectively a landbased pirate - but after five days the authorities closed the station and seized his transmitting equipment. He was subsequently prosecuted but acquitted when the case came to court.

**MAANDAG**

**19 november**

**VOORMIDDAG**

UILENSPIEGEL. — 7.00 : Morgengroet. — 7.05 : Muziek bij de koffie, door Pit Jager. — 8.30 : Uit de oude doos. — 9.00 : Varia. — 9.30 : Roulette. — 10.00 : Klank en ritme, met Kurt Edelhagen en Los Espanolex. — 10.30 : Varia. — 11.00 : Werken met muziek, door Mini Huybrechts.
VERONICA. — 8.00 : Ook goeiemorgen, gewenst door Fred van Amstel. — 9.00 : Gevar. platen. — 10.00 : Koffietijd met Tineke. — 11.00 : Non-stop.

**12 UUR**

UILENSPIEGEL. — 12.00 : Groeten van Uilenspiegel. — 12.30 : Zacharias Express.
VERONICA. — 12.00 : Non-stop. — 12.30 : « Eet smakelijk », Tony Vos draait plaatjes. — 12.45 : Dansend door 't leven.

**13 UUR (1 U.)**

UILENSPIEGEL. — 13.00 : Varia. — 13.30 : Sterren van bij ons.
VERONICA. — 13.00 : Non-stop. — 13.30 : Combo-shirt. — 13.45 : Non-stop.

**14 UUR (2 U.)**

UILENSPIEGEL. — 14.00 : Cineradio. — 14.30 : Koncertwerken.
VERONICA. — 14.00 : Gevar. progr. — 14.15 : Alles draait om... — 14.30 : Muzikale zonnestralen.

**15 UUR (3 U.)**

UILENSPIEGEL. — 15.00 : Operette : « Czardasvorstin » (Kalman). — 15.30 : En nu... Will Ferdy.

VERONICA. — 15.00 : Muzikale zonnestralen (vv.). — 15.30 : Nonstop.

**16 UUR (4 U.)**

UILENSPIEGEL. — 16.00 : Het orkest Leo Martin. — 16.30 : « Y'a de la musique ».
VERONICA. — 16.00 : Joost weet nog niet wat hij mag weten.

**17 UUR (5 U.)**

UILENSPIEGEL. — 17.00 : Muziek bij de tee, met Roger Williams en Tony Bennet. — 17.30 : « Een mop, een plaat », door Fred Steyn.
VERONICA. — 17.00 : De Teenbeatclub, gepresenteerd door Wim Croupier. — 17.15 : Populaire pl. — 17.45 : Welkom in het land van Cuyk.

*Programme schedules published during the short time that Radio Veronica and Radio Antwerpen were both broadcasting*

## The Owl Mirror

In 1962, frustrated by the years of bureaucratic delays and refusals to grant him a licence de Caluwe, although by then 73 years old, decided to resurrect his beloved Radio Antwerpen, this time from a ship off the Belgian coast. The example of the Scandinavian and Dutch offshore stations had given him renewed hope and, he thought, the ideal solution for his desire to return Radio Antwerpen to the airwaves.

He purchased a concrete built ex-French Navy stores vessel, the *Crocodile,* which was re-registered in Panama under the name of a legendary Flemish folk hero *Uilenspiegel* (Owl Mirror). A smaller vessel was also acquired for use as a tender and renamed *Nelle* after the folk hero's wife. The *Uilenspiegel* was fitted out with radio equipment, including a 10Kw transmitter, in Antwerp Harbour, while land-based studios for pre-recording programmes were established in Neviersstraat in another part of the city.

The *Uilenspiegel* was finally equipped by October 1962 and she left Antwerp Harbour to anchor outside Belgian territorial waters off Zeebrugge. The ship's crew consisted of a captain, a navigating officer and first, second and third engineers, of whom two were always on board. There was also a cook and second cook, three sailors, two 'music engineers' and two programme producers, plus respective relief staff.

In common with all other contemporary offshore radio stations most of Radio Antwerpen's programmes were pre-recorded on tape in the land-based studios for later transmission from sea, although occasional live programmes were broadcast often by Georges de Caluwe who regularly spent time on board the radio ship.

Test transmissions started at 2.25pm on 12th October 1962 on 1492kHz (201.7m) with regular programmes commencing on 15th October 1962. During the week before transmissions officially started Georges de Caluwe bought airtime on Dutch offshore neighbour, Radio Veronica, to mount a promotional campaign for Radio Antwerpen. The Dutch owners of Radio Veronica accepted these advertisements because they provided commercial revenue and the Dutch station considered that Radio Antwerpen's signal and programming posed no real threat of competition for its own audience.

Radio Antwerpen broadcast continuously from 7.00am - 12 midnight and proved so popular with listeners that Belgian state radio, BRT, soon extended its own on-air hours to close at midnight as well. The format included classical as well as popular music and all programmes were broadcast in Flemish, apart from a half hour French language programme ("Il Y'a de la Misique") aired daily between 4.30pm and 5.00pm. Another regular programme was the lunchtime (12noon - 1.00pm) request show "Greetings from *Uilenspiegel* ",which was often hosted live from on board the ship by Georges de Caluwe himself.

In November 1962 Radio Antwerpen also began transmitting its programmes on 7600kHz in the 41m short waveband and reception reports for these broadcasts were received from as far away as Canada. Later that same month (November 1962) the station encountered its first storm at sea and was forced to leave the air after putting out a distress call. The aerial had collapsed during the storm, but engineers managed to carry out emergency repairs and transmissions were able to resume the following day.

## Disaster

Darker clouds were on the horizon for Radio Antwerpen as the Belgian Government decided to follow the Scandinavian example and introduce legislation early in December 1962 to outlaw offshore radio stations. The Belgian Marine Offences Act was passed on 13th December 1962 and became effective five days later. By a tragic coincidence on the same day that the legislation was passed Georges de Caluwe died in an Antwerp hospital following an operation.

During the night of 15th/16th December 1962 the *Uilenspiegel* was battered by strong winds and heavy seas. The crew discovered that part of the ship had become flooded and the shortwave aerial had fallen on the medium wave mast causing damage to both transmission facilities. The *Uilenspiegel* herself began to drift just before noon on 16th December 1962 and at 1.12pm the alarm was raised by the cross-channel ferry, *Suffolk Ferry* that the radio ship was in desperate need of assistance. The crew of the *Uilenspiegel* were in contact with the ferry and at 1.14pm she broadcast another message, this time an SOS reporting that the radio vessel was sinking and requested lifeboat assistance.

At 2.23pm Zeebrugge lifeboat drew alongside the *Uilenspiegel,* together with the salvage tug *Burgemeester Vandamme.* By 3.30pm the damaged radio ship had drifted to within a mile of Zeebrugge and six of the ten crew were taken off by the lifeboat. Unfortunately during this operation a lifeboatman was crushed between the two ships and later died of his injuries.

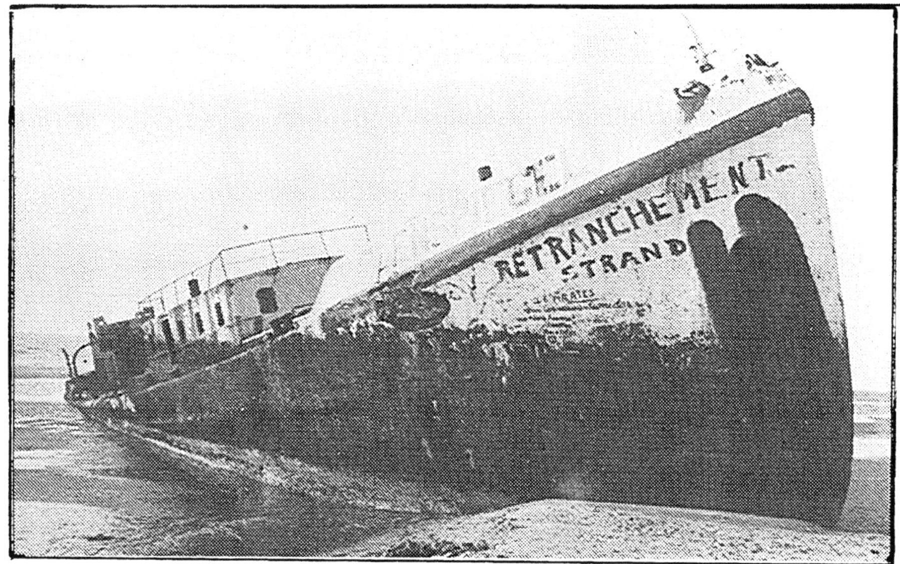


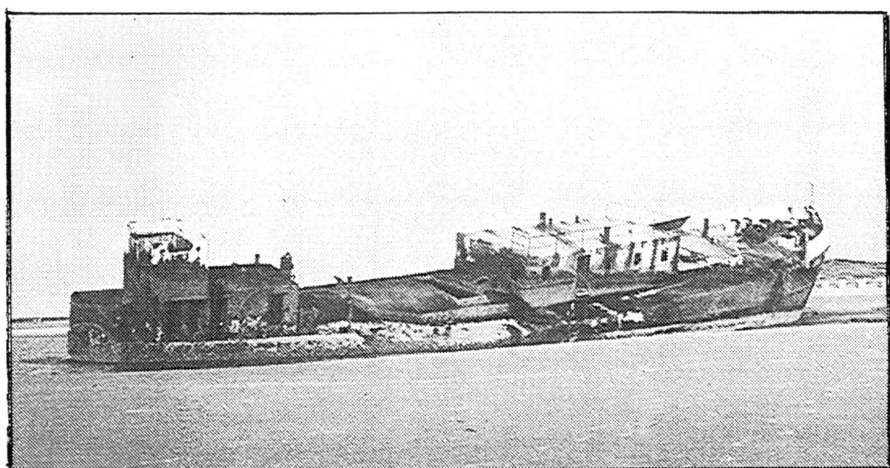

The wreck of the 'Uilenspiegel'

Four crew members remained on board the *Uilenspiegel* as the tug started to tow her towards Flushing, but by 4.30pm, when the vessel was a mile off Knocke, the weather had deteriorated so much that the lifeboat made an attempt to take aboard the remaining crew of the radio ship. However, because of engine trouble the lifeboat itself was forced to return to port and shortly afterwards the salvage tug's tow rope snapped. Despite this setback the tug managed to rescue the remaining four crew from the *Uilenspiegel* shortly before the radio ship ran aground at Cadzand, just 500 yards inside the Dutch border.

With the radio station outlawed by the new Belgian legislation and the owner, Georges de Caluwe having died, Radio Antwerpen's ship was abandoned on the beach where she had run aground. No attempt was made to salvage her and eventually, stripped of all equipment by vandals, she gradually sank into the sand. The wreck of the *Uilenspiegel* remained on Cadzand beach for nine years before being blown up in 1971 by the authorities who considered it had become a safety hazard. However, the lower part of the wreckage was never fully removed and it was to be another 22 years before the local council, concerned that holidaymakers were injuring themselves on the remaining parts of the ship, decided to fence off the area where the *Uilenspiegel* had run ashore. An inauspicious end to one man's dream of resurrecting the radio station he had once owned and successfully operated, quite legally, from land.

So by the end of 1962 only two offshore radio stations were still broadcasting - Radio Syd off Sweden and Radio Veronica off Holland .

Radio Syd had decided to defy the new Scandinavian law which had closed Radio Mercur and Radio Nord while in Holland the enormous popularity of Radio Veronica and the delicate political balance of the Dutch parliament combined to stall any positive action being taken against the station by the authorities.

# Chapter 5

# Almost There

During late 1961 and early 1962 in Britain - the largest potential market in Europe for commercial radio - there were a number of people who were devising projects to launch offshore radio stations.

At that time in Britain the BBC was still operating a policy of broadcasting live music by its own orchestras and dance bands rather than recorded material by well known artists. This resulted in very little opportunity for listeners to hear any of the hundreds of singles released by record companies each week. The only other source of broadcast music, for listeners and record companies, was Radio Luxembourg. This station had itself undergone a transition in the mid 1950s when its evening broadcasts of light entertainment programmes had been threatened by the launch of commercial television in Britain.

At that time Radio Luxembourg's output was based on sponsored shows, with programme content being dictated by the sponsor, for example a typical evening schedule would contain a number of 15 or 30 minute programmes such as "The Cliff Richard Show" (music), "The Sporting Challenge" (in which listener's questions about sporting achievements and records were put to Memory Man Leslie Welch), "Italy Sings" (Italian music), "Record Crop" (music), "Bringing Christ to the Nations" (religious broadcast) and "Spin With the Stars" (music).

In 1959 the station changed its output to target the newly identified 'teenage market' and dispensed with these light entertainment programmes, replacing them with pop music shows. One serious side effect of this change in policy was that sponsors became more difficult to find and in any event many of the larger advertisers had deserted to commercial television, taking with them programmes such as "Opportunity Knocks" and "Take Your Pick". This void in sponsors was filled by Radio Luxembourg negotiating package deals with various record companies to buy large amounts of airtime on the station. The result was over 50 hours a week of chart music being broadcast to Britain in programme segments sponsored and produced by the major record companies. However, Radio Luxembourg's programmes could only be received during the evenings when the station faced severe competition from commercial television.

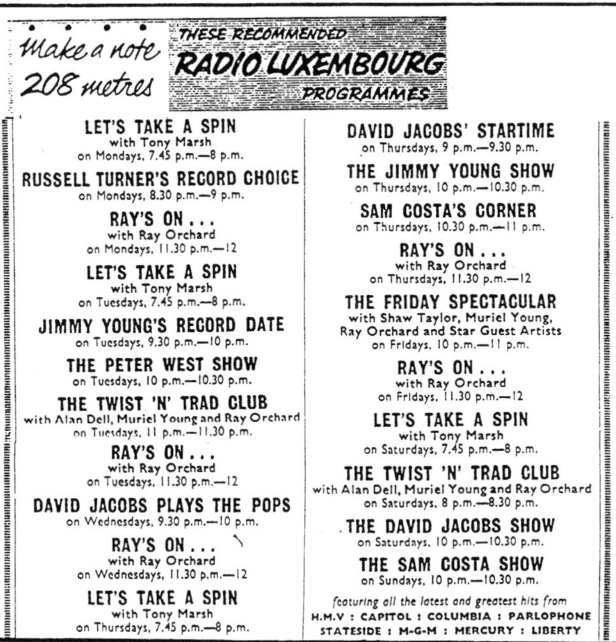


*A typical Radio Luxembourg programme schedule in 1962*

The emergence of a strong British music industry in the early 1960's forced the pace for the more widespread provision of pop music programmes on radio. The BBC did very little, if anything, to respond to this growth, relying on its outdated agreement with the Musicians Union which restricted the amount of 'needle time' (time allocated to playing records during broadcasts) to 24 hours a week, spread over its three national networks. Radio Luxembourg tried to respond, but had its own problems - its agreements with record companies effectively tied up most of its airtime, it was geographically isolated from the source of the new music revolution, still having no direct landline facilities between its London studios and the transmitters in Europe, and it only broadcast during the evenings.

Into this scenario came a number of businessmen who saw a potential market for an all day pop music station and who had witnessed the success of similar projects in Scandinavia and Holland. The time seemed ripe to launch an offshore radio station to serve Britain.

## The Voice of Slough

The first public announcement of such a project appeared in an article in *The Times* on 10th October 1961. John Thompson, a 42 year old journalist from Slough, and co-director Robert Collier, a wholesale newsagent, were the driving force behind the scheme. Together they had formed a radio broadcasting company - The Voice of Slough Ltd. with a nominal share capital of £3,000 and registered offices at 35 Beechwood Gardens, Slough. Technical adviser to the project was Arnold Swanson, a 56 year old Canadian millionaire who had made his fortune from the invention and manufacture of car safety belts.

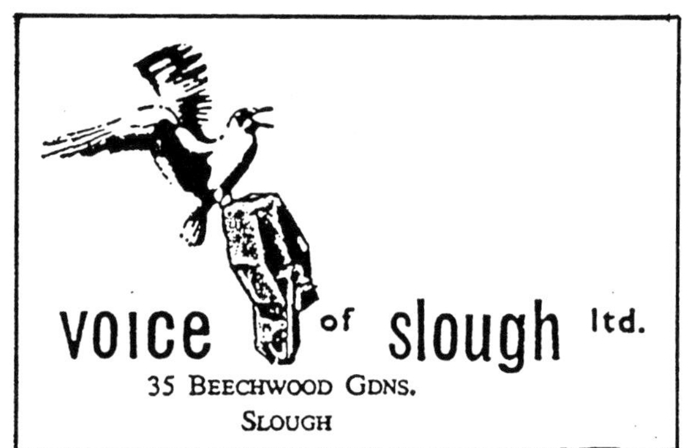


Thompson originally came from Yorkshire but after the end of the Second World War he had emigrated to Canada becoming a reporter on a local newspaper and eventually an announcer and DJ on a Vancouver radio station. In the late 1950s he returned to England working as a journalist for the local newspaper in Slough.

A 70 ton motor fishing vessel, *Ellen* was said to have been purchased and fitted out at a secret location in Scotland with an on-air date for the station planned for 1st December 1961. Although registered as the Voice of Slough the station had a number of other proposed call-signs including Radio LN (Ellen), Radio ELB and finally GBLN (Great Britain, Ellen or Great Britain, London).

The project's radio ship was to be anchored not far from the Nore lightship off the Essex coast near Southend and broadcasts were to be on 980kHz (306m) with a transmitter power of between 1Kw and 5Kw. All programmes were to be pre-recorded either in 'studios' located in two wooden huts at the rear of a cottage in Aylesbury or in a 30' caravan which had been equipped as a mobile studio facility.

The 24 hour format was, according to the station's publicity material, to be "musical and directed mainly at the young, with regular news commentaries and current affairs programmes throughout the day." Peak-time advertising rates were quoted at a simple £3-18-0d (£3.90) for 25 words, with six minutes per hour being devoted to commercial announcements. Thompson also hinted that broadcasting facilities could be used to provide a local community station directed at Southend and claimed to have support from the Mayor of the town for such a venture. He did however, indicate that the

The Voice of Slough has it taped

Disc jockeys (radio) plan pirate ship

THEY ARE TO RUN 24-HOUR SHOWS

First time

station would not take up the offer of a civic send off by the Mayor for fear of action the Postmaster General might take against them.

Keith Martin, an announcer who had worked with Paul Hollingdale and Doug Stanley at the short- lived Radio Veronica English service, CNBC and who later went on to become involved with Radio Atlanta and Radio Caroline, recorded some programmes for the proposed station in the Aylesbury studios.

Despite initial press publicity in October 1961 the proposed starting date for the station - 1st December 1961- came and went with nothing being heard on the airwaves. The project reportedly floundered when record companies refused to allow the station to infringe copyright restrictions by tape recording discs for later broadcast. However, correspondence from John Thompson exists which indicates that as late as September 1962 he was still pursuing plans to launch his offshore station, under the call-sign GBLN. In that correspondence he claimed the ship was being held up by British Customs authorities on a technicality, but that he was trying to free her from "red tape" and put the station on air by mid-October 1962.

## GBOK

At about the same time that the Voice of Slough (or GBLN) was first due to come on air, December 1961, the project lost its technical adviser, Arnold Swanson. Reportedly Swanson had been offered a 59% share in the Voice of Slough in return for his financial support estimated to be in the region of £100,000. However, he had now decided instead to launch his own station - GBOK (Great Britain OK) - from an 84 year old former lightship, which he claimed to have purchased. This wooden vessel, the *Lady Dixon*, which he re-registered in Liberia, had been built in 1878 to serve as a lightship off the north west coast of Ireland.

ADANAC BROADCASTING AGENCY

(Managing Executive:- R. G. DUNLOP)

*Telephone:* Thame 3

A. J. SWANSON
M. E. SWANSON

NOTLEY ABBEY,
LONG CRENDON,
BUCKINGHAMSHIRE.

The Amalgamated Broadcasting Company was formed to front the project with registered offices and studios at Swanson's home, Notley Abbey, Thame, Buckinghamshire. Swanson converted the stables of this grand house, which had previously been owned by Sir Laurence Olivier, into recording studios. A London office for the Amalgamated Broadcasting Co. was also established at 151 Fleet Street, EC4, but commercial airtime on the planned station was to be sold through another company, Adanac Broadcasting Agency, which also operated from the same two addresses.

Announcer Ed Moreno (who was later to work for several offshore radio stations) spent four days a week for several months recording GBOK programmes at the Notley Abbey studios and was paid £50 per week by Swanson, quite a substantial sum in the early 1960s. American Evangelist Ted Armstrong (whose programmes were heard on many later British offshore stations) bought airtime on GBOK and even publicised the station's forthcoming launch in some of his literature.

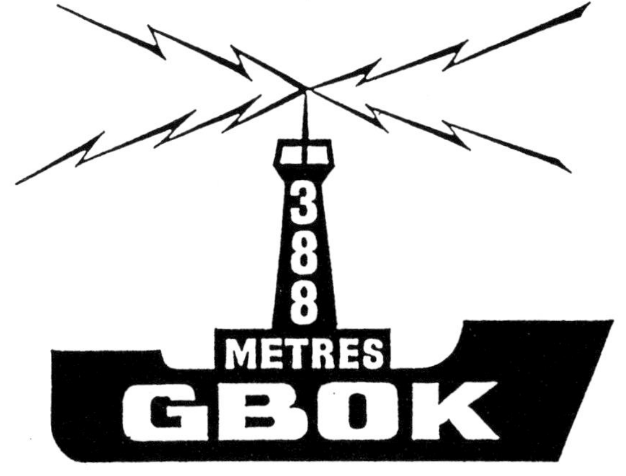


First actual press reports of GBOK appeared in the *Southend Standard* on 15th February 1962, indicating that the station would be broadcasting music, features and advertising 24 hours a day from a former lightship anchored near The Nore, the same location as had been planned for the Voice of Slough's broadcasting vessel, starting on 28th February 1962.

The station planned to broadcast on 773kHz (388m) with a power of 5Kw and hoped to reach a potential audience of 11 million listeners within a 150 mile radius covering the south east and Midlands. Places as far away as Nottingham, Leicester, Coventry, Birmingham and Bristol were planned to be within the station's primary coverage area and a "bonus French audience" across the English Channel was also offered for the benefit of advertisers .

## American format

GBOK was promoted in a glossy 12 page brochure published in January 1962, which attempted to explain in some detail to listeners and potential advertisers (who were accustomed only to the BBC's style of programming) just how a 24 hour American format music station would sound.

Programmes were to be of popular music with five minute news broadcasts on the hour every hour - a completely new experience for British listeners who were used to the BBC's diet of early morning, lunchtime and evening set piece news bulletins. GBOK planned to make the claim "First with the Important News" for this service.

After the early morning "Wake-up Show" ended at 9.00am another new concept of programming was proposed. Known as the "Bandwheel", this show (an internationally copyrighted programme to which GBOK had exclusive British rights) was scheduled to run for 10 hours each day. It would be interrupted only by news on the hour and a two hour "Motorway Special" between 4.00pm and 6.00pm each evening, recognising the then new and growing market for drive-time listeners- commuters with car radios.

According to the station's promotional literature the Bandwheel was an actual wheel, 9' in diameter with room in the centre for the announcer's desk and microphone. The wheel was divided into quarters, each allocated to particular artists or performers which were changed regularly throughout the day. An inner circle on the wheel was divided into thirty three 15 minute segments and eleven 10 minute segments - "Bandwheel" One to Forty Four. Exactly which artist entertained during a particular segment was determined by the announcer spinning the Bandwheel and wherever the pointer stopped the named artist's record would be played.

These segments were available for sponsors to purchase and the announcer would then mention their name and product frequently during that part of the programme.

In association with the "Bandwheel" programme the station also planned to run a Jackpot Competition for listeners to predict (from a list printed on an entry form) which artists would perform in each of the 44 daily segments for the forthcoming two weeks! Entry forms were to be distributed through sponsors' retail outlets and Jackpot winners would be drawn by the announcer in the middle of each 10 or 15 minute segment.

Between the hours of 10.00pm and 6.30am GBOK planned the "All Night Dance Party", with sponsors being sought for each hourly segment or even the complete night's programme. Prime time advertising rates ranged from £16 for 20 seconds to £90 for a 15 minute segment, with discounts for multiple bookings. Sponsorship of the nightly "Dance Party" was to be by negotiation while newscasts could also be sponsored at the 5 minute rate plus a 33% premium. By March 1962 Arnold Swanson was claiming to have already sold enough airtime to finance a complete year's programming on GBOK.

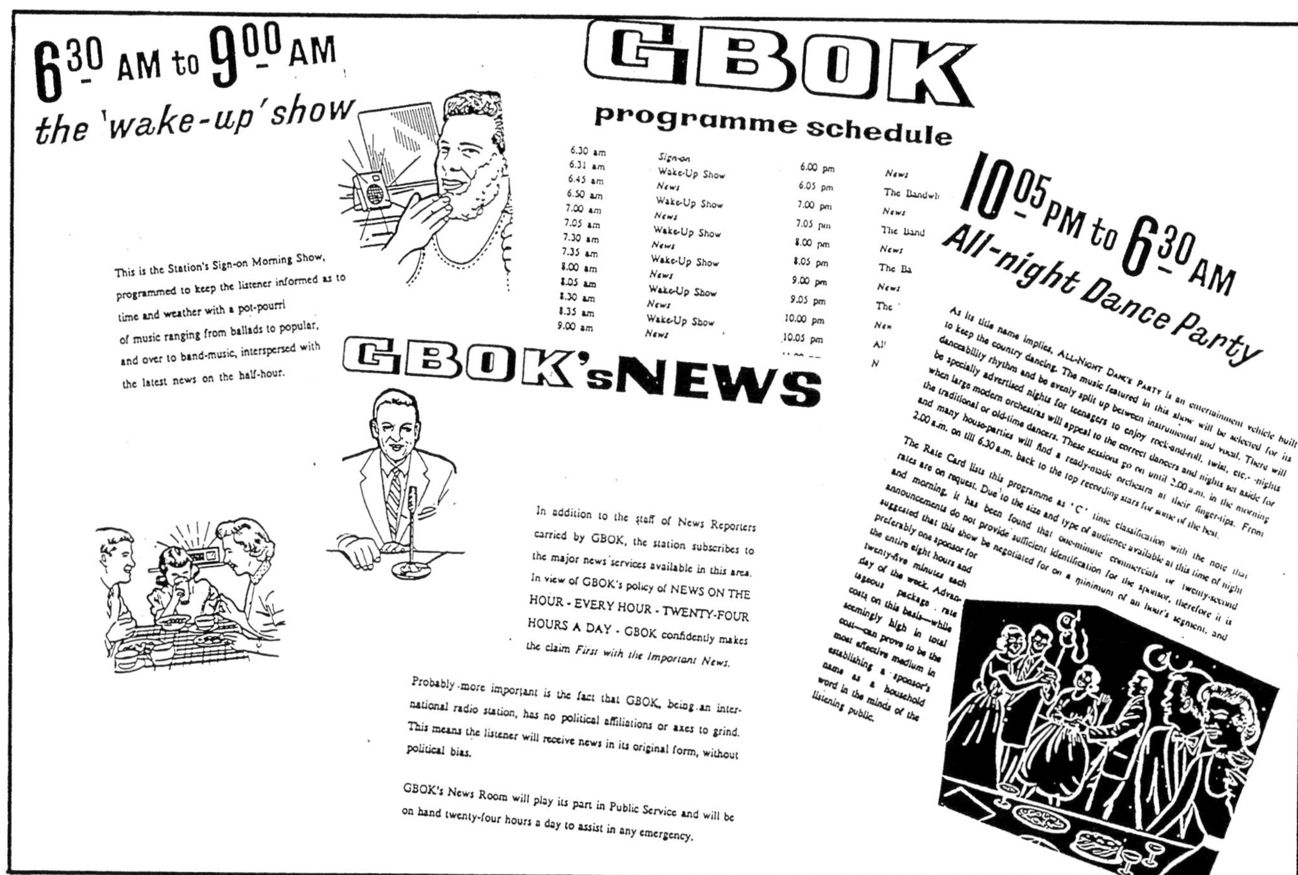

6.30 AM to 9.00 AM

the 'wake-up' show

This is the Station's Sign-on Morning Show, programmed to keep the listener informed as to time and weather with a pot-pourri of music ranging from ballads to popular, and over to band-music, interspersed with the latest news on the half-hour.

GBOK

programme schedule

| | | | |
|---|---|---|---|
| 6.30 am | *Sign-on* | 6.00 pm | *News* |
| 6.31 am | Wake-Up Show | 6.05 pm | The Bandwh |
| 6.45 am | *News* | 7.00 pm | *News* |
| 6.50 am | Wake-Up Show | 7.05 pm | The Band |
| 7.00 am | *News* | 8.00 pm | *News* |
| 7.05 am | Wake-Up Show | 8.05 pm | The Ba |
| 7.30 am | *News* | 9.00 pm | *News* |
| 7.35 am | Wake-Up Show | 9.05 pm | The |
| 8.00 am | *News* | 10.00 pm | *Nev* |
| 8.05 am | Wake-Up Show | 10.05 pm | All |
| 8.30 am | *News* | | *N* |
| 8.35 am | Wake-Up Show | | |
| 9.00 am | *News* | | |

GBOK'sNEWS

In addition to the staff of News Reporters carried by GBOK, the station subscribes to the major news services available in this area. In view of GBOK's policy of NEWS ON THE HOUR - EVERY HOUR - TWENTY-FOUR HOURS A DAY - GBOK confidently makes the claim *First with the Important News.*

Probably more important is the fact that GBOK, being an international radio station, has no political affiliations or axes to grind. This means the listener will receive news in its original form, without political bias.

GBOK's News Room will play its part in Public Service and will be on hand twenty-four hours a day to assist in any emergency.

10.05 PM to 6.30 AM

All-night Dance Party

As its title name implies, ALL-NIGHT DANCE PARTY is an entertainment vehicle built to keep the country dancing. The music featured in this show will be selected for its danceability rhythm and be evenly split up between instrumental and vocal. There will be specially advertised nights for teenagers to enjoy rock-and-roll, twist, etc.- nights when large modern orchestras will appeal to the correct dancers and nights set aside for the traditional or old-time dancers. These sessions go on until 2.00 a.m. in the morning and many house-parties will find a ready-made orchestra at their finger-tips. From 2.00 a.m. on till 6.30 a.m. back to the top recording stars for some of the best.

The Rate Card lists this programme as 'C' time classification with the note that rates are on request. Due to the size and type of audience available at this time of night and morning, it has been found that one-minute commercials or twenty-second announcements do not provide sufficient identification for the sponsor, therefore it is suggested that this show be negotiated for on a minimum of an hour's segment, and preferably one sponsor for the entire eight hours and twenty-five minutes each day of the week. Advantageous package rate costs on this basis—while seemingly high in total cost—can prove to be the most effective medium in establishing a sponsor's name as a household word in the minds of the listening public.

*Pages from a brochure published to explain GBOK's programming style*

## Problems and failure

At the beginning of March 1962 the station encountered an unexpected problem, the *Lady Dixon* (which some press reports suggested had been renamed *The Bucaneer*) was moored at a wharf in a muddy Essex creek at Pitsea in the Thames Estuary. Sailing the vessel from this mooring depended on high spring tides reaching Pitsea and flooding the creek. Unfortunately for GBOK the first spring tide did not prove to be high enough to float the *Lady Dixon*, which became stuck on a mudbank. Attempts by two tugs to release the ship failed because only one end could be raised from what was fast becoming a mud cradle around the ex-lightship's wooden hull. It was decided therefore to wait for the next high tide on 6th March 1962 and the station's on-air date was postponed.

It was not until 9th March 1962 that the *Lady Dixon* was successfully refloated by the tug *Bold Pioneer* and towed to Sheerness for final fitting out. National publicity for the proposed station appeared in an article in *The Times* on 10th March 1962 which reported that once machinery and transmitting equipment had been installed the vessel would be towed to her position in international waters and broadcasting would commence "within two weeks". The vessel did indeed arrive at Sheerness on 12th March 1962 for fitting out as a floating radio station, however, it is unclear whether this was ever achieved although there are reports of an unofficial test transmission having been made from the *Lady Dixon* whilst in port, resulting in a raid by Post Office officials.

PIRATE RADIO SHIP GETS TRAPPED IN THE MUD

BRITISH BROADCASTS HAVE TO BE POSTPONED

***RADIO 'PIRATES' SIGN UP LONG JOHN SILVER***

RADIO GBOK WAITS FOR TIDE

Broadcasts may start on March 6

By July 1962 Arnold Swanson announced that work on the *Lady Dixon* was to be abandoned as she was no longer considered sufficiently seaworthy for her role as a radio ship. Altogether over £15,000 had been lost on work associated with fitting out the ageing vessel. Undaunted by this setback Swanson also announced that he had now acquired a 2,200 ton ex-Tank Landing Craft which would be converted into a radio ship at a cost of £30,000. The new craft was to have a stronger transmitter giving thc station a projected coverage area as far north as Manchester. Swanson claimed that GBOK would start broadcasts from its new vessel by September 1962, but the station never appeared on the air.

## Other plans

Despite the non-appearance of either GBLN or GBOK the idea of operating an English language offshore radio station had not been lost completely.

In 1960 an Australian ex-wartime bomber pilot and music publisher, Allan Crawford, had established a business in London managing minor artists and producing cover versions of hit songs on his own record labels.

Crawford had, until 1959, worked both in Britain and Australia as Managing Director of a music publishing company - Southern Music - before leaving to establish his own business, Merit Music Publishing Ltd. which produced records on three subsidiary labels - Rocket, Sabre and Carnival.

The music industry in the late 1950's and early 1960's was very different to what it is now. In those days the industry still in the transitional stage from basing 'hit' records and chart listings on sales of sheet music to basing them on record sales. Even so the bulk of record releases were taken from films or stage productions and two, three or more versions of the same song were often released by different artists and record companies. Therefore it was the song, not the particular artist which made it into the charts. It was not uncommon for those listings to contain two or three versions of the same song, but by different artists on different record labels. Record companies employed their own artists to produce cover versions of hit songs and of any titles which had already been hits in America, often after a time gap of up to twelve months.

It was into this environment that Allan Crawford launched his own music publishing business. Crawford's business philosophy was simple if a little naive, he thought that increased record sales, and consequently Top 20 chart listings, could best be achieved by repeatedly promoting artists and labels to the largest possible audience

## Project Atlanta

In 1961 Crawford rented some new office accommodation, which by coincidence was in the building vacated by the recently defunct CNBC project. Reputedly it was whilst clearing out papers and promotional material left by the previous occupants that Crawford realised the potential for starting an offshore radio station broadcasting to an English speaking audience. Frustrated by the monopoly controls exercised by the established broadcasters Allan Crawford decided, in keeping with his own business philosophy, that if he started a radio station of his own he would have the means to endlessly promote his record labels and artists to a large audience.

Crawford set about convincing a number of wealthy and influential backers of the commercial potential for launching a radio station to challenge the BBC monopoly. The result was the formation of Project Atlanta Ltd., which initially had 38 separate investors each holding anything between just 50 and 10,000 of the company's 150,000 £1 shares. Some of the initial shareholders listed in the company registration documents were:-

- Frank Victor Broadribb (a City financier) - 10,000 shares
- Major Cecil Lomax (Publisher and Lloyds underwriter) - 4,000 shares
- William Wells (an accountant ) - 1,250 shares
- Sir Robert and Lady Barlow (Sir Robert was Chairman of Metal Box Ltd.) -1,000 shares
- Major Oliver Smedley (a former Vice-Chairman of the Liberal Party) - 1,250 shares
- Kitty Black ( a theatrical impresario) 1,250 shares

Both of the latter shareholders arranged for other companies of which they were also directors to acquire substantial numbers of Project Atlanta shares. Two of Smedley's companies - Investment and General Management Services Ltd. and Misse-en-Scene Ltd. held 30,000 shares, while Kitty Black's CBC (Plys) Ltd. held 36,000 shares. In addition a number of respectable City trust funds and investment companies held over 40,000 shares in Project Atlanta Ltd.

## Scandinavian connection

The date was early summer 1962 and Allan Crawford was aware that the Scandinavian offshore stations (with the exception of Radio Syd) were about to close because of new legislation coming into effect at the beginning of August to outlaw them. Crawford had closely followed events surrounding these Scandinavian stations and he negotiated a deal with the American backers of Radio Nord to purchase that station's vessel, *Magda Maria,* complete and ready to broadcast, together with the entire contents of the fully equipped land-based studios in Stockholm. In addition Crawford was interested in taking on some of the Radio Nord technical staff and marine crew to continue running the *Magda Maria* and all its equipment. The prospect of this sale to Project Atlanta had, in part, led to the early closure of Radio Nord - in June 1962 rather than at the end of July when the Scandinavian legislation came into effect.

As a result of this deal providing a ready-made, fully equipped ship-borne radio station the backers of Project Atlanta could dispense with the original plan to fit out their own ship which, it had always been recognised from the Scandinavian and Dutch stations' experience, would be fraught with legal difficulties and technical problems.

Bob Thompson (one of the American backers of Radio Nord) and Allan Crawford reached a preliminary agreement for the purchase by Project Atlanta of the *Magda Maria* and all the associated radio equipment and even agreed a delivery date for the ship to drop anchor in the Thames Estuary. But before anchoring off the British coast it was agreed that the *Magda Maria* would go into port for a complete technical and marine overhaul.

Even before Radio Nord had closed rumours of the sale of the *Magda Maria* started to circulate in Sweden during the early part of June 1962 and the station's owners became very nervous that the authorities would attempt in some way to seize the vessel, possibly if she sailed through the narrow channel between Sweden and Denmark. These fears proved unfounded, however, because after lying at anchor for a few days following Radio Nord's closure, the *Magda Maria* successfully slipped away from Scandinavian waters sailing quietly through The Oresund and into the international waters of the North Sea.

The *Magda Maria* docked at El Ferrol in northern Spain on 2nd August 1962 where a complete overhaul of the vessel took place as part of the agreement with Project Atlanta. The renovated ship left El Ferrol on 14th September 1962, giving her destination as Dover, England and a few days later she dropped anchor, as agreed, in the Thames Estuary.

Unfortunately during the time that the *Magda Maria* had been docked in El Ferrol the Danish authorities had boarded and seized the former Radio Mercur vessel *Lucky Star*. This seizure took place on 15th August 1962 and, although it was subsequently discovered that the *Lucky Star* was in fact stateless this was not clear at the time of the boarding. The vessel then was anchored in international waters, apparently flying the Lebanese flag which only later proved to be a fake.

This deliberate flouting of international maritime law by the Danish authorities in forcibly boarding what at the time appeared to be a foreign registered ship outside their territorial limits frightened off some of Allan Crawford's financial backers. They feared that the British authorities may well do the same to the vessel in the Thames Estuary and withdrew their funding from Project Atlanta.

With the *Magda Maria* now in position off the British coast, fully equipped and ready to broadcast, Crawford tried to renegotiate the deal with Bob Thompson in an effort to keep Project Atlanta alive. Allan Crawford suggested that Thompson should give him what amounted to a credit arrangement so that Project Atlanta would not have to pay in full for the *Magda Maria* until the station had been broadcasting for some time and the attitude of the British authorities had become clear. This way, if the ship had been seized and confiscated, Project Atlanta would only have incurred minimal financial losses in leasing the ship.

Thompson, on the other hand, wanted the refurbished ship paid for in full before broadcasting began so that if the vessel were seized by the British authorities he and the former Radio Nord organisation would not lose financially or be responsible in any way for the detained vessel. Unable to agree a compromise both parties stood their ground and finally the deal between Radio Nord and Project Atlanta was called off.

## Confusion and uncertainty

In early October 1962 the *Magda Maria*, with a Polish captain and crew, together with one Swedish radio technician on board sailed from the Thames Estuary and dropped anchor off the coast of Holland, near the Radio Veronica ship *Borkum Riff*.

Although the deal with Project Atlanta had fallen through Bob Thompson was willing to wait a short while for Allan Crawford to try and secure alternative

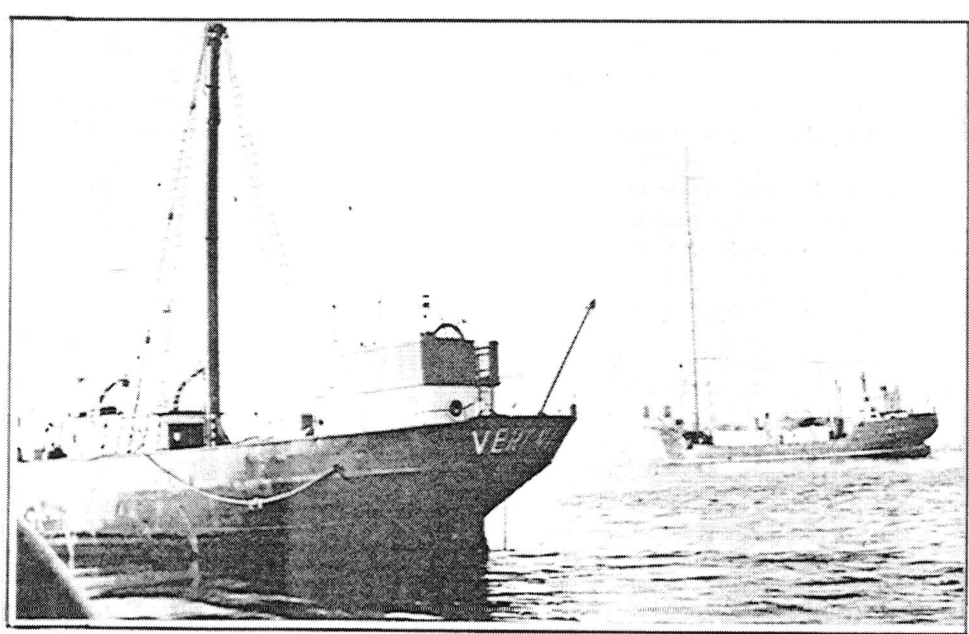

*The former Radio Nord ship, 'Magda Maria' anchored near Radio Veronica' vessel 'Borkum Riff' in 1962*

sources of funding. However, at the same time other possible purchasers were being sought - after all Thompson had a former radio ship to dispose of and it was a 'hot' property, unwelcome in many European ports, the subject of constant attention from various authorities and with the ever present threat of seizure or even sabotage attacks.

The Dutch and Belgian press at the time speculated about various plans for the ship, including a claim by a Dutch businessman that he would purchase her either to launch a second Dutch offshore station (to compete with Radio Veronica) or to establish a station off the British coast. There were also suggestions that the vessel would be used to house a television station beaming programmes to Belgium.

Another rumour circulating was that the ship had been sold to the Cuban Government for use as a propaganda station anchored off the United States coast. This particular story had some credibility because it circulated at the time of the Cuban Missile Crisis, which posed the first real threat to world peace since the end of the Second World War. US President John F Kennedy was involved in a standoff with Premier Kruschev of the USSR over the build-up of Soviet missiles on the island of Cuba, all provocatively directed towards America. It is quite conceivable that, at that particular time, the Communist Government of Cuba, backed by the USSR, would have wished to use an offshore radio station as a base from which pump propaganda into America.

After about three weeks lying at anchor near Radio Veronica the *Magda Maria* entered Ostend Harbour in late October 1962. The Polish Captain hurriedly left the ship after she docked amidst persistent rumours that the Swedish Government was about to launch a raid on the vessel. He was soon replaced by another captain and the ship remained closely guarded to prevent sabotage attacks against it and the radio equipment on board.

While the *Magda Maria* was in Ostend rumours continued to be published in the European press about her future. The Belgian television station rumour continued to flourish with a report in October 1962 that broadcasts would start in February 1963. On 15th November 1962 one Dutch newspaper reported that a Belgian radio and television station was planned from the ship, with the radio station transmitting on FM as well as 605m medium wave. In early December 1962 a Belgian newspaper even published a specific starting date of 18th December 1962 for a radio station based on the *Magda Maria*. This time the vessel was reportedly to be anchored off the French coast because the Belgian Government was in the process of introducing legislation outlawing offshore radio stations (see Chapter 4).

After this series of rumours in late 1962 all came to nothing speculation surrounding the future of the *Magda Maria* seemed to die down for a while and nothing more was heard of plans for either the Belgian radio and television station, nor of the proposed competition for Radio Veronica.

What is certain though is that throughout this period the *Magda Maria* was still in the ownership of the Radio Nord organisation and Bob Thompson was still handling the sale of the vessel through a series of agents and companies based in various central European countries. On 11th January 1963 the vessel, which by now had been renamed *Mi Amigo,* was recorded as entering Flushing Harbour for bunkering. Details supplied to the harbour authorities at the time show that she was then owned by a company called Amatara, whose address was given as PO Box 34605, Vaduz, Liechtenstein. After the bunkering had been completed the *Mi Amigo* left Flushing on 15th January 1963, but put into Brest four days later reportedly to have damaged steering gear repaired.

At about the same time Bob Thompson, having been unable to sell the ship as a fully equipped radio station, decided to sail the *Mi Amigo* across the Atlantic to Texas where it was planned to remove all the radio equipment and convert her into a fishing cruiser for recreational use by members of the former Radio Nord consortium.

Accordingly the *Mi Amigo* set sail from Brest on 26th January 1963, calling at Las Palmas en route before arriving in Galveston, Texas on 9th March 1963. There are some unsubstantiated reports that the ship was used briefly at this time to broadcast programmes from the Gulf of Mexico before finally having her transmitting mast removed.

## Project Atlanta succeeds

Meanwhile, Allan Crawford had not given up his plan to launch a British offshore radio station and throughout 1963 he sought to obtain new sources of finance for Project Atlanta. By December of that year he had succeeded and the *Mi Amigo* was finally acquired by Project Atlanta from Bob Thompson and the former Radio Nord consortium. Luckily that consortium's plans to strip all radio equipment from the vessel and fit her out as a luxury cruiser had not been completed (only the transmitting mast and rigging had been removed) so with the transfer of ownership finalised, the *Mi Amigo* set sail from Galveston on 28th December 1963, heading once again towards the British coast.

The *Mi Amigo* arrived in Las Palmas just over one month later, on 30th January 1964, after encountering heavy Atlantic storms during which she nearly sank. On 5th February 1964 the vessel entered El Ferrol in Spain for repairs, ballasting and strengthening of her hull. These works were completed within 10 days and the ship sailed once again calling at Corunna between 28th February and 3rd March 1964, while Crawford desperately made arrangements to try and find a quiet port in which the *Mi Amigo* could be fitted with a new transmitter mast for her continuing role as a floating radio station.

# Chapter 6

# Your All Day Music Station

During his efforts to raise financial backing throughout 1962 and 1963 Allan Crawford had discussed his planned radio station with many people, amongst whom was a young Irish club-owner and pop group manager, Ronan O'Rahilly.

At the same time as Crawford was seeking financial backing for Project Atlanta O'Rahilly himself was working, without much success, to try and promote one of his artists, Georgie Fame, on the established radio stations - Radio Luxembourg and the BBC Light Programme.

Then 23 years old, O'Rahilly was the rebellious son of a wealthy Irish businessman. His father, Aodhogan O'Rahilly had operated, amongst other ventures, the Preston-Greenore ferry service on behalf of British Railways and subsequently purchased the port of Greenore when that service was discontinued. O'Rahilly's grandfather had been killed while charging a British machine-gun post in Dublin during the 1916 Easter uprising, an event in Irish history commemorated in a poem by W B Yeats. Ronan himself had come to London in the late 1950s and joined an acting school- Studio 57. In the early 1960s he had also become involved in running the Scene Club in Great Windmill Street at the heart of London's Soho district promoting records for the Ric Gunnel Agency and managing groups such as Blues Incorporated, which at that time included Mick Jagger and Charlie Watts, later of the Rolling Stones.

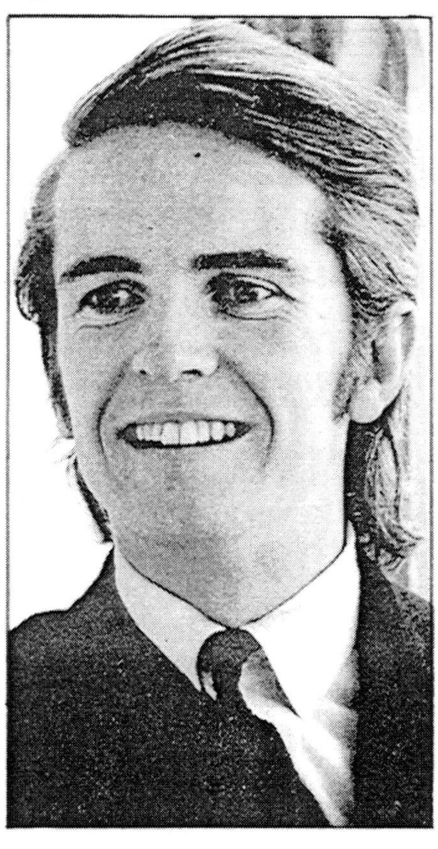
*Ronan O'Rahilly in 1964*

The Scene Club was patronised mainly by enthusiasts of rhythm and blues and jazz music with artists such as Georgie Fame and the Rolling Stones regularly booked to perform there long before they became popular household names. The club's resident DJ - Guy Stevens - was also a partner in Britain's first independent record label, Sue Records, which catered for fans of soul and blues music.

It has become an offshore radio legend that after a fruitless meeting in 1962 with senior executives of Radio Luxembourg in London O'Rahilly concluded that the only way to secure airtime for artists who were not signed up by the major record companies, was to start his own radio station.

## Raising backing

Having explored and rejected for various reasons the possibility of hiring the transmitters of a foreign based broadcaster to launch his own radio station the idea of offshore radio appealed to him as a possible solution. Ronan O'Rahilly was aware of the concept of offshore radio stations - he had learned about the Voice of America ship *Courier* operating off the Greek coast and the hugely successful Dutch offshore station, Radio Veronica.

Allan Crawford knew O'Rahilly through a group of mutual acquaintances living in the then ultra-fashionable Kings Road area of Chelsea. It was during a meeting in a bar along the Kings Road that the offshore radio station idea was first discussed by the two men. At that point O'Rahilly himself could not provide financial backing for Crawford, but took him to Ireland where he introduced the Australian to his father and showed him the port of Greenore. During the course of this meeting with O'Rahilly's father Crawford made available the results of research he had carried out into the feasibility of operating an offshore radio project off the British coast.

Ronan O'Rahilly led Crawford to believe that both of them could cooperate and launch two offshore radio stations - one to serve the south east of England (operated by Crawford) and the other to serve northern England and Ireland (operated by O'Rahilly). However, O'Rahilly maintained a hidden agenda. Using the information in Crawford's market research material he set about raising funding to launch his station first and steal the lucrative London and south east England market from Crawford's Project Atlanta.

Project Atlanta had commissioned technical research documents and marketing profiles which showed the expected reception area and anticipated audience levels for a radio station anchored off the Essex coast. Armed with a copy of these documents O'Rahilly approached likely backers, conveying the impression that the research had been carried out for his own station.

Eventually he managed to raise more than £250,000 of capital from English, Irish and Swiss sources to get the project started, using a holding company, Planet Productions Ltd., which he had already registered some time previously for another purpose.

One of O'Rahilly's Kings Road acquaintances, Ian Ross, persuaded his father, a venture capital broker in the City of London to back the station and, together with a business colleague, John Sheffield (Chairman of Norcros), these two men owned over 80% of Planet Production's original shares.

Another backer, although not himself a major shareholder, was Jocelyn Stevens (who also happened to be John Sheffield's son-in-law), then editor of the influential glossy magazine *Queen,* whose offices in London's Fetter Lane were used as a temporary headquarters by Planet Productions Ltd.

Once sufficient funding had been arranged Ronan O'Rahilly engaged shipbrokers to find a suitable ship on which he could house the new radio station. Eventually, in Rotterdam they discovered a suitable vessel, an ex-Danish passenger ferry, *Fredericia.* However, part way through the negotiations the ship's owners, DFDS Ferries, became suspicious that the ship was to be used to house an offshore radio station. Because of the Danish anti-offshore broadcasting laws they then insisted on clauses being included in the contract to the effect that it would not be used as an offshore radio station.

Ronan O'Rahilly then discontinued negotiations through these brokers and set about engaging another broking company to purchase the vessel. To avoid any similar setbacks he drew up a cover story that the ship was to be used to transport cattle from Ireland and, despite some misgivings on the part of the brokers about using an ex-passenger ferry for this purpose, the deal was concluded satisfactorily.

Planet Productions leased the vessel from a Swiss registered company - Alruane - and she sailed from Rotterdam on 13th February 1964 heading for Greenore in Ireland, the port owned by O'Rahilly's father. Because of the O'Rahilly family's control over the port work to equip the *Fredericia* for her new role could be carried out there in great secrecy.

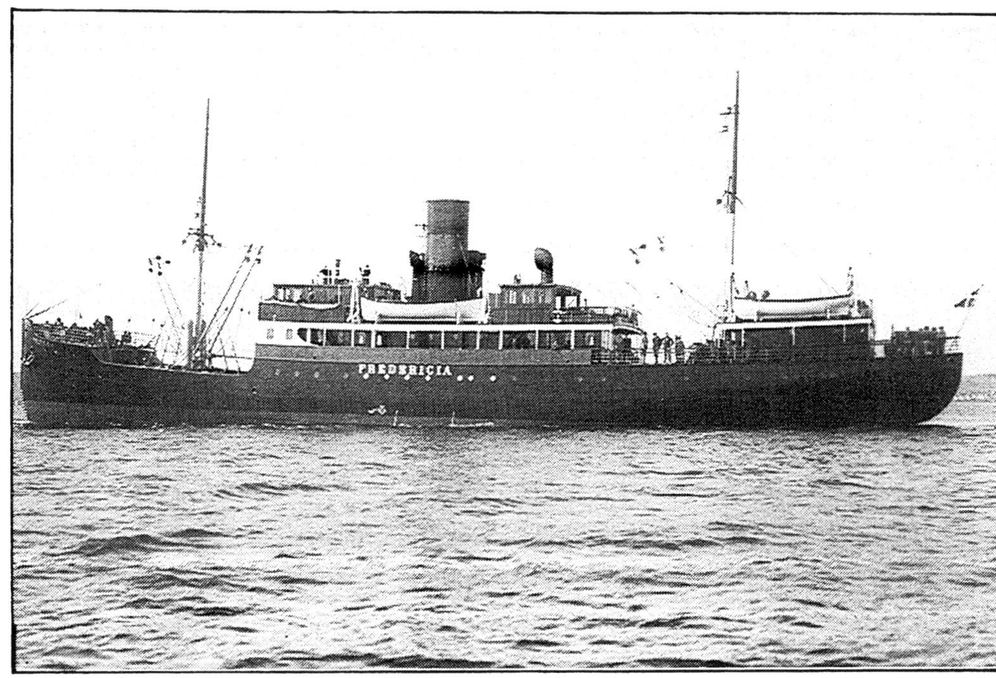

The 'Fredericia' in service as a DFDS passenger ferry

## Project Atlanta

At this precise time the Project Atlanta ship *Mi Amigo* was in El Ferrol, Spain undergoing strengthening repairs and Allan Crawford did not have a port to which he could take the vessel to fit her with a new transmitter mast. He presented a proposal to Ronan O'Rahilly - if he could persuade his father to allow the *Mi Amigo* to be fitted out at Greenore (alongside the *Fredericia*) then Crawford would allow O'Rahilly to use his London studios to pre-record programmes and also provide technical 'experts' to assist with the fitting out of the *Fredericia.*

Allan Crawford's understanding was still that Ronan O'Rahilly's station would be serving the north of England, Scotland and Ireland from an anchorage in the Irish Sea so the offer of technical assistance did not conflict with his own plans for a station serving London and south east England. In addition, Crawford's ship, having already been equipped as an offshore radio station (Radio Nord), needed much less work doing to it than the *Fredericia* which had to be completely fitted out by O'Rahilly and his team.

The deal was agreed and the *Mi Amigo* sailed from Corunna on 3rd March 1964 arriving in Greenore about 10 days later. The *Fredericia,* which by now had been renamed *Caroline,* was already in the small Irish port being fitted out with broadcasting equipment including a 168' aerial mast and two 10Kw Continental Electronics transmitters.

## Why 'Caroline'?

The story of how Ronan O'Rahilly's vessel and radio station came to be named 'Caroline' reveals an impetuosity which was to become a hallmark of the whole project. No market research was undertaken, not even a short-list of possible names was compiled for the station. The name 'Caroline' was reputedly decided on by O'Rahilly whilst reading a magazine during a flight to New York to purchase equipment for his station.

Like so many of his generation O'Rahilly had been captivated by the charismatic figure of John F Kennedy as he rose through the political ranks to become President of the United States. The fact that Kennedy also happened to be of Irish descent added a further dimension to the cultural empathy felt for him by the young O'Rahilly. Kennedy, with his charm, energy and young family had won the hearts and minds of a whole generation in America and throughout the world. When he was assassinated in Dallas in November 1963 the world was stunned and united in sharing the grief of his bereaved family.

It was a photograph in *Time-Life* magazine of Kennedy's young daughter Caroline interrupting a meeting of Presidential advisers at the White House which, according to O'Rahilly himself, encapsulated just the right spirit - combination of youth, vibrance and lack of regard for the 'establishment' way of doing things. This was exactly the spirit he wanted to convey through his offshore radio station. Radio Caroline it was to be.

## Preparations begin

Back to Greenore where the installation of radio and other equipment on board the MV *Caroline* was progressing under the supervision of a former BBC engineer, Arthur Carrington, who had pioneered aerial and undersea television transmissions and also been involved in radar research and development for the Government. Although the port's workforce kept silent about the nature of the ship's conversion it was not long before the town's residents noticed the huge aerial mast growing to its 168' height and the local newspaper sent a reporter down to Greenore to investigate the mystery ship.

With natural Irish charm the O'Rahilly family circulated a story that the ship was a marine research vessel and needed the tall mast to help it search for deep sea sponges! Satisfied that he had obtained an explanation for the unusual work being carried out on the ship the reporter left Greenore and his paper printed the story.

So convincingly was this cover story put across that there was little further speculation about the true nature of the activity surrounding *Caroline* or of her future role. The later arrival of Crawford's *Mi Amigo* to have a similar tall mast installed consequently raised few enquiries from local residents or the media, although once Radio Caroline had actually come on the air interest in the *Mi Amigo* at Greenore became more intense.

Other activities, in particular enquiries made of potential advertisers, led to rumours and speculation about the planned offshore station. The Postmaster General was even asked about the Government's attitude to the plans for an offshore station to anchor off the British coast on 6th February 1964, nearly two months before Radio Caroline went on the air. The Postmaster General, Mr. Reginald Bevins informed the House of Commons in his reply:-

*Yes I am aware of these plans. Such broadcasting would contravene international regulations and endanger international agreements on the sharing of radio frequencies. It would almost certainly cause serious interference to radio communications in this and other countries. The Council of Europe has under consideration a Convention aimed at preventing broadcasting from ships on the high seas. This may point to the need for new legislation in due course. Meanwhile I am glad to say that I have very encouraging indications that responsible interests in this country have no intention of supporting any such venture. I am keeping a close watch on the problem.*

With both radio ships being fitted out in the same port, which itself was owned by the family relatives of a person planning to launch one of the offshore stations, it was not surprising to hear stories of delaying tactics being employed against the rival station.

At one stage the Project Atlanta crew were ordered to anchor the *Mi Amigo* outside Greenore harbour for a few days, which meant no work was done on the ship whilst *Caroline* received the undivided attention of the workforce. Also, throughout those few days at anchor in Dundalk Bay the *Mi Amigo* had to ride out a severe storm during which she very nearly ran aground.

In retaliation for these delaying tactics the Atlanta organisation recommended to Caroline some radio technicians, who it turned out were totally inexperienced. Their inept installation of equipment on the MV *Caroline* later resulted in severe interference being caused to television broadcasts over a large part of Ireland during test transmission made from the ship while she was still in port.

A' boarding party' was subsequently sent by Radio Caroline to the *Mi Amigo* resulting in the disappearance of two Spotmaster tape machines from the Atlanta ship. Needless to say these useful items of equipment subsequently reappeared aboard the MV *Caroline*. Years later Project Atlanta's Allan Crawford was able to talk light-heartedly about the 'skulduggery' that had gone on between the two rival groups, but at the time it was all carried out with a very serious objective - to be the first British offshore radio station on the air.

## Caroline hits the airwaves

Eventually conversion and installation work was completed on the MV *Caroline* and she set sail from Greenore at 7.30pm on Monday 23rd March 1964. It was then that Allan Crawford fully realised the Caroline station was not destined to serve the north of England, Scotland and Ireland, but instead it was to snatch his own lucrative target area of London and the south east.

*Caroline* anchored briefly off the Isle of Man to ride out a storm before sailing south through the Irish Sea, giving her destination as Spain. However, on Wednesday 25th March 1964, when the vessel reached Lands End and changed course entering the English Channel, coastguards all along the south coast of England began to take even greater interest in her, repeatedly asking the Captain for his destination. Captain Baeker, in command of the vessel at the time, would only reply that he was sailing under sealed orders from the owners and refused to reveal any destination.

The authorities were so concerned by the mystery ship that for a short while *Caroline* was shadowed by a Royal Navy destroyer from Plymouth as she sailed through the Channel. By 7.00pm on Friday 27th March 1964 (which also happened to be Good Friday) *Caroline* had reached her destination and she dropped anchor three and a half miles off Harwich on the Essex coast.

It has been widely accepted that the first test transmissions took place at about 11.55pm that evening on a frequency of 1495kHz (201m), the first record played being Jimmy McGriff's "Around Midnight", although some reports suggest that tests were aired earlier that evening.

The test broadcasts continued the following morning, now using a frequency of 1520kHz (197m) with a transmitter power of 10Kw and at 12 noon on Easter Saturday, 28th March 1964, Radio Caroline officially started broadcasting. The opening announcement was made by Simon Dee -

*This is Radio Caroline on 199m your all day music station. We are on the air every day from 6.00 in the morning until 6.00 at night.*

Following this live opening announcement the first programme (which was pre-recorded on tape) was a

### *Rival radio opens up at sea*

BRITAIN'S first commercial radio station was launched yesterday— at sea, in international waters, five miles off Harwich on the East Coast.

Test programmes — first tune was the Beatles' latest hit *Can't Buy Me Love* — were heard in London, the Home Counties and East Anglia.

I heard them loud and clear on a transistor radio in Fleet-street.

#### *Not pirates*

But yesterday the man behind radio Caroline, 23-year-old Ronan O'Rahilly, said: "We are not contravening any regulations. I know of no reason to prevent us broadcasting. We are not pirates."

rudimentary Top 20 show, introduced by Chris Moore, with the first record being "Not Fade Away" by the Rolling Stones (not, as has been inaccurately reported for many years, "Can't Buy Me Love" by The Beatles).

On land Ronan O'Rahilly had made preparations for a press conference in London, where it was planned that reporters from all national newspapers and press agencies would witness the start of broadcasts from Radio Caroline. As noon approached, however, O'Rahilly was becoming increasingly anxious about the whole credibility of his project because the radio he had with him in the press conference was merely making a series of crackling noises. In desperation he picked up the radio and beckoned the reporters to follow him outside. They were just in time to hear, with amazing clarity, the opening announcement by Simon Dee. It later transpired that O'Rahilly had chosen for the press conference premises whose construction had the effect of completely blocking out incoming radio signals.

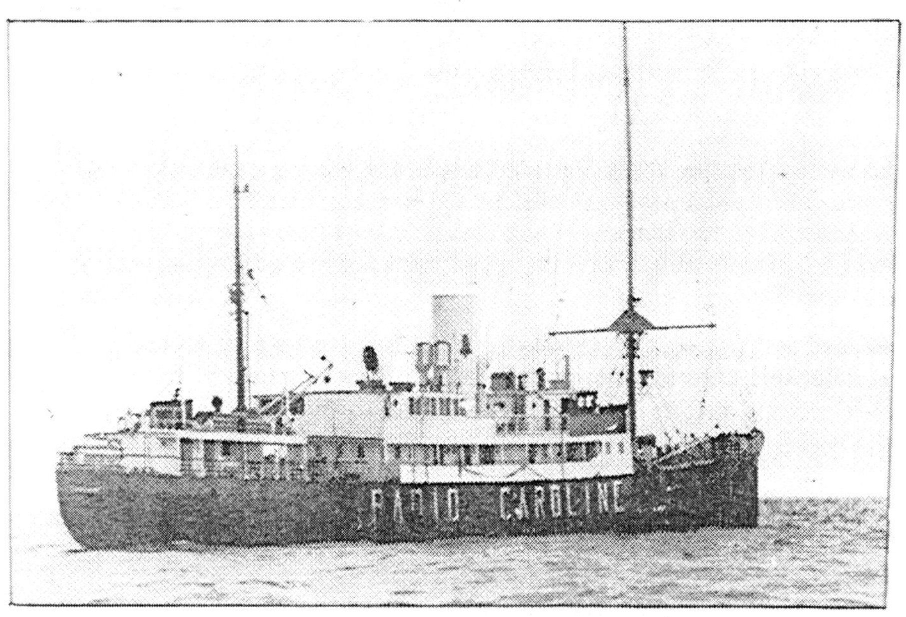


The MV 'Caroline'

Those on board the MV *Caroline* were uncertain about official reaction to the new station. Initially it was far from clear how the authorities would respond and the biggest concern to the Radio Caroline staff was that the ship would be forcibly boarded and seized whilst at sea. When the time had finally come to put the new station on the air DJs, Simon Dee and Chris Moore on board the MV *Caroline* experienced a sense o uncertainty about what they were doing - daring eachother to actually flick the switch and make the live opening announcement. For the first few weeks there was a nervous atmosphere amongst the crew and DJs, who lived with the constant fear that at any time they could be arrested, taken back to land and prosecuted for illegal broadcasting.

## Popular and not so popular

Following its official opening Radio Caroline received enormous publicity in the press and on television news bulletins and word quickly spread about the new all-day music station. Regular transmissions initially took place between 6.00am and 6.00pm and audience figures grew rapidly.

Within four days of the Easter Saturday opening thousands of letters were received at the station's London office and over 300 others arrived at the shipping agent's address in Harwich. On the following Wednesday, 1st April 1964, the first tender delivered nine mail sacks full of letters and requests to the radio ship. As well as letters DJs were sent gifts including sweets, cigarettes, chocolates and clothes by enthusiastic listeners wishing to provide them with some home comforts during their long stay at sea. By 9th April press reports indicated that in the station's first 10 days on the air over 20,000 letters had been received from enthusiastic listeners.

The station was not popular with everybody however. After Radio Caroline had been on the air for just two days complaints were received about the station causing interference to communications with lightships and the lifeboat service.

The General Post Office asked the International Telecommunications Union (ITU) on 1st April 1964 to help stop the unauthorised broadcasts. Two days later the ITU replied that it would request Panama, under whose flag the radio ship was registered, to investigate the situation. Radio-telephone ship-to-shore facilities were also withdrawn by the Post Office, cutting the station off from direct contact with its landbased offices.

Hostile reaction in the House of Commons to the start of Radio Caroline's broadcasts came almost immediately in March 1964, when Postmaster General, Reginald Bevins, promised "action soon" to deal with this and any other offshore radio station. Initial questions had been raised about Radio Caroline because of fears its signal would affect the emergency services' transmissions. Some other MPs, however, spoke of more sinister matters including the dangers of subversive propaganda or publicity for obscene material being broadcast by the offshore station.

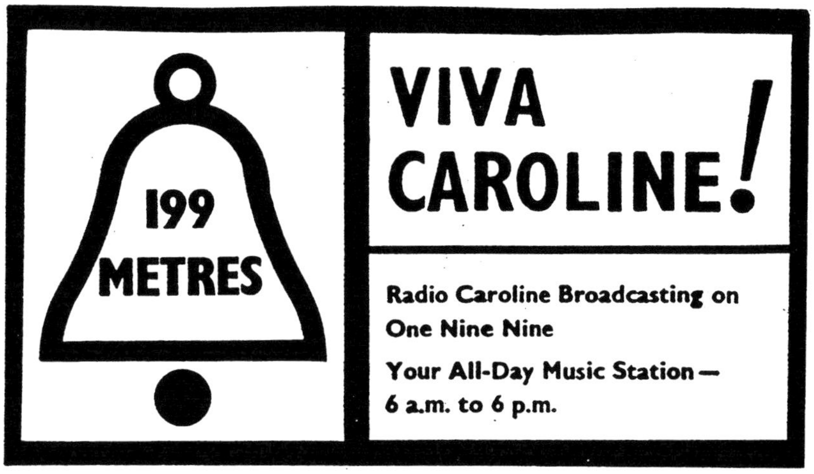

On 7th April 1964 the Panamanian authorities were reported to have withdrawn the ship's official registration and on the same day the MV *Caroline* sailed a mile up the coast to a new anchorage off Felixstowe, further away from the main shipping lanes.



*One of Radio Caroline's first items of publicity material, a forerunner to later car stickers*

Coincidentally also on 7th April Postmaster General Reginald Bevins told the House of Commons that a number of actions were being planned by the Government against Radio Caroline, including if necessary jamming the station's signal. He also assured the House that advertisers had agreed to boycott Radio Caroline, that the respective record and music industry associations were co-operating with the Government in taking action against the station and also confirmed that Panama had withdrawn the radio ship's registration.

Mr. Paul Williams (Conservative) asked the Postmaster General to tell the House who the station was hurting. Mr. Bevins replied that Radio Caroline was causing interference to a Belgian maritime station and to British maritime services. He went on to state:-

*Broadcasting on the High Seas is specifically forbidden by the international radio regulations, to which nearly all countries of the world belong. We have co-operated with the International Telecommunications Union in reporting and publicising the measures taken by individual members of the Union to implement this prohibition. An agreement on this subject is being considered by the Council of Europe. My officials have taken an active part in the framing of this agreement and I expect the text to be settled soon.*

Although the possibility of jamming Radio Caroline's signal was subsequently dismissed by the Government as an unacceptable option, direct action against the ship at that time could have succeeded in early closure of the station and probably would have frightened off any other proposed offshore broadcasters. The Danish authorities' forcible boarding of the Radio Mercur ship *Lucky Star* in August 1962 had already had just that effect on some of Project Atlanta's original financial backers (see Chapter 5).

Various authorities made life as difficult as possible for those operating Radio Caroline and subsequent offshore radio stations. Crew and supplies travelling to and from the radio ships were required to undergo Customs clearance and inspections by water, immigration, Trinity House, port health authorities, the Board of Trade and local harbour authorities.

## Official visit

However, the nearest any official body came to attempting direct intervention in the early maritime operation of Radio Caroline occurred on 6th May 1964 when, at 12.20pm the Royal Navy vessel HMS *Venturous* came alongside the MV *Caroline* and requested permission to board the ship to inspect her bonded stores.

Permission was refused by the Captain of the *Caroline* on the basis that it was a foreign-registered ship anchored in international waters. As a gesture of goodwill he did offer to allow one man aboard, via a lifeboat, but this offer was refused by the Customs officials who had come out with the Royal Navy on board *Venturous*. Eventually the *Venturous* sailed away from the MV *Caroline* at 12.33pm without having succeeded in putting a man on board the radio ship.

Listeners to Radio Caroline were kept fully informed of this incident by DJ Simon Dee through live newsflashes interrupting normal programmes. This high profile publicity probably deterred the Navy and HM Customs from taking any action to board the *Caroline* by force. The effect of this lack of direct action at the outset of the station's life gave offshore broadcasters and listeners alike the clear message that the authorities accepted the lawful status of foreign-registered ships anchored in international waters and were unwilling to take confrontational action against them and their crews.

In fact both the outgoing Conservative and the incoming Labour Governments of 1964 procrastinated so much over what action to take against the early stations that offshore radio came to be seen as a relatively safe proposition by other aspiring operators, and it was only a matter of time until an armarda of stations appeared around the coast of Britain.

## Hostile reaction

In June 1964 Jeremy Thorpe MP (Liberal) introduced a Bill in Parliament requiring all commercial radio stations to be registered with the Government. In introducing his Bill Mr. Thorpe stated that the withdrawal of registration from the *Caroline* by Panama meant that the offshore station had no legal protection, was liable to seizure, and those working on board could be arrested. He went on to accuse the Postmaster General of condoning law breaking by not withdrawing the radio receiving licences of those people who listened to the offshore station (estimated to be over 7 million at that time!). The Bill received its formal first reading , but without Government backing it got no further through the parliamentary process.

The Government preferred to await international action to outlaw offshore broadcasters as the Postmaster General again informed the House of Commons on 2nd June 1964:-

*The Council of Europe has been studying this problem and a draft Convention is now in an advanced stage of preparation. What is required to deal with the problem is concerted international action. The Government therefore proposes to await the conclusion of this Convention and then to consider legislating on lines proposed by the Convention.*

Outside the Government various organisations and authorities also made threatening noises against Radio Caroline and other offshore broadcasters particularly as the number of stations began to increase. In April 1964 Phonographic Performances Ltd. (who collected copyright fees for any public performances of their members' recorded works) threatened to issue a writ against Radio Caroline to prevent the station 'stealing' copyright material. In a statement made at the time of this announcement Phonographic Performances Ltd. said: "Indiscriminate broadcasting of records is detrimental to the interests of the industry, musicians and artists." Although nothing definite came of this threat, Radio Caroline and some later stations did offer to pay copyright fees, placing Phonographic Performances in a difficult position. On the one hand the organisation vociferously criticised offshore radio stations for not paying fees, but at the same time it did not want to be seen to accept any monies from what, in its opinion, amounted to illegal business activities.

In another case of dual standards, major record companies adopted both a public and a private attitude to the offshore broadcasters. Publicly they refused to co-operate with the stations, but behind the scenes all companies or their representatives made great efforts to ensure that copies of the latest releases were made available unofficially for the offshore stations to play.

**I WANT MY CAROLINE**

*Radio Caroline's first car sticker, 1964*

The Musicians Union too vetoed any of its members taking part in live recording sessions for offshore radio programmes and, despite some early television appearances by offshore DJs such as Simon Dee and Tony Blackburn, entertainment unions and the BBC later refused to allow such personal appearances on television or BBC radio pop music programmes.

On the other hand Radio Caroline's own publicity material, issued in June 1964, stated that during the previous month an agreement had been made to pay a percentage of any income earned by the station to another organisation, Performing Rights Society, which looks after the interests of composers and publishers of music.

Other media organisations provided a mixed response to the arrival of the offshore radio stations off the British coast. Popular national newspapers were, in general, favourably disposed to the stations - the *News of the World, Daily Sketch* and *The People* bought advertising time as soon as Radio Caroline started broadcasting commercials. The quality press, however, were less supportive with both *The Times* and *The Guardian* publishing a number of articles roundly condemning the activities of the offshore broadcasters.

During the early months of Radio Caroline's transmissions the station's programmes consisted of DJs announcements and, of course, music all day - which was the great novelty and attraction for listeners. Many (but not all) of the early programmes were from the pre-recorded stock which had been made by Simon Dee, Chris Moore and Carl Conway in London studios while the station was still in the planning stage. Tapes were often broadcast more than once and after a few weeks on the air Simon Dee and Chris Moore resorted to editing the recordings by cutting and splicing tapes to vary the order of records!

## COPYRIGHT

The rights of record manufacturers to receive copyright payments is contained in the Copyright Act 1956 and there are two entitlements to such payments:-

(a) for the recording itself and the artist making the recording - collection and protection of this copyright is handled by Phonographic Performances Ltd.

(b) for the music and words of a song, the copyright for which is handled by the Performing Right Society.

Copying, re-recording and unauthorised use of records for public performance is an infringement of copyright and this was one of the major allegations levied against the offshore stations.

## PHONOGRAPHIC PERFORMANCES LTD (PPL)

This organisation was established in 1934 to protect its members from the threat posed by the unauthorised use of their work for public performances.

PPL saw the unlimited use of records by the offshore radio stations as a threat to the livelihood of their members because in their view it would almost certainly mean a decrease in the demand for live performances. Such over exposure of recorded music by offshore stations was also perceived by PPL as a threat to the sales of records, again producing an adverse effect on musicians' livelihoods.

The organisation collects all fees on behalf of its members for the broadcasting and public performances of recordings for which licences have been issued. After deduction of administrative costs the balance is shared between the Musicians Union, the artist who made the record and the record manufacturer.

## PERFORMING RIGHTS SOCIETY LTD (PRS)

PRS was formed to protect the performing rights of composers, lyric writers and publishers. The Society accepts assignments of the public performance and broadcasting rights of the work of its members and negotiates, collects and distributes the resulting fees. Although the Society received a number of payments from certain offshore radio stations its official policy was to oppose their existence and as a member of the British Copyright Council it joined in representations being made to the Government to outlaw the offshore broadcasters. The Society did this on the basis that the stations were operating outside the national legal system and by doing so were evading a number of legal liabilities and responsibilities. The Society sought to justify its apparent contradictory stance on this issue in the following statement provided to the author of "Radio Caroline", John Venmore-Rowland in 1967:-

"The Society is not in a position either to grant an offshore broadcaster a licence, or to withhold its licence. Any obligation which is felt to fall on an offshore broadcaster to pay something corresponding to a royalty for the music which he broadcasts is therefore purely a moral one and, if in recognition of such a moral obligation a particular offshore broadcaster is prepared to pay to the Society sums calculated on a basis regarded as reasonable by the Society, then there does not appear to be any motive of principle for the refusal by the Society to accept such payments. It should not be a consequence of such acceptance, however, that the Society renounces its attitude to the general question of offshore broadcasting."

The question of the impact of offshore radio on record sales was a controversial one and an argument which lasted throughout the lifetime of the stations.

Statistics show that in the first six months of 1965 sales of singles declined by 23% - which record companies attributed directly to the offshore stations. Bill Townsey, a spokesman for Decca Records said:-

*People are not buying [records] because of over exposure on the 'pirates'. A record has been played on one station as often as 14 times a day. Being in international waters the pirates needn't pay us a penny and we have no control over what they play.*

Record companies failed to acknowledge in making these allegations that sales of LPs (albums) had increased during this period. The offshore stations also opened up the market for smaller record companies - the reason Radio Caroline had been conceived in the first place - and this undoubtedly irritated the larger companies who hitherto effectively had a cartel arrangement in place and controlled the airtime on Radio Luxembourg

The impact of the offshore stations in this direction can be demonstrated by the fact that in 1961 EMI and Decca alone accounted for 84 of all Top Ten singles records produced in Britain. By 1966 their share had dropped to 57% with the explosion of smaller labels and their promotion on the offshore stations.

Advertisers were at first reluctant to buy airtime, preferring to wait and see what the station sounded like, the size of audience it attracted and more importantly, what, if any, official action would be taken against it or anyone who was seen to be supporting it commercially.

## Programme content

Listening to recordings of those very early Radio Caroline programmes today, 30 years later, it is hard to believe that the station took off with such immense and immediate popularity. At first the DJs only announced record titles and artists names, although some informal banter did develop later, together with comments about what was happening on and around the ship. In fact to begin with the DJs didn't even operate their own turntables, resorting to the then industry standard system of relying on a sound engineer - who sat on the opposite side of a studio, separated from the presenter by a soundproof glass panel.

The programme content in those early days was a blend of pop music by artists such as The Beatles, Cliff Richard and others, mixed with established ' middle of the road' material from performers such as Ray Conniff, Mantovani and Frank Sinatra. This initial blend of widely varying musical styles reflected, to a certain extent, the backgrounds of the early Radio Caroline staff. They had come, not from the world of pop music or light entertainment, but from Ronan O'Rahilly's theatrical circle and the avant-garde of the early 60s 'Chelsea Set' and the station's early record library, which contained many discs from their own personal collections, reflected this diversity.

Even though many of the early programmes were pre-recorded and contained music which was not pop or chart material, audiences in their millions, young and old alike, loved the informality of the station and most of all the unique phenomenon of music broadcasts being available all day, every day. Part of the explanation for this can be found by examining what else was available in musical entertainment on British radio in 1964.

Until the arrival of Radio Caroline the availability of popular music programmes on British radio was extremely limited. Radio Luxembourg, transmitted its English language service during the evenings, but this suffered from a signal which was often badly distorted and regularly faded, due to atmospheric conditions and the distance of the station's under powered transmitter from the target audience. The station claimed to be a leader of the musical revolution, but most of its shows were 15 or 30 minute segments sponsored by major record companies and contained only short extracts from current releases. For example in a 15 minute programme DJs were often expected to include up to 14 titles - as well as introductions and commercial announcements!

The other source of musical entertainment, the BBC Light Programme, provided listeners with a total of less than four hours a week of pop music with "Saturday Club" and the Sunday afternoon chart programme "Pick of the Pops". There were a number of other music based programmes on the BBC at the time -"The Jack Jackson Show", "Housewive's Choice", "Two Way Family Favourites", "Midday Spin" or of course "Uncle

### Radio Caroline Programme Schedule April 1964

**6.00am** **The Early Show**, *Simon Dee/Tom Lodge*
**9.00am** **On the Air**, *Carl Conway*
**11.00am** **Top Deck**, *Chris Moore/Jerry Leighton*
**12noon** **Music Around Lunchtime**, *Chris Moore/Tom Lodge*
**2.00pm** **Soundtrack**, *Simon Dee*
**4.00pm** **The Big Line-Up**, *Chris Moore/Tom Lodge*
**6.00pm** **Downbeat**
**10.00pm** **Closedown**
**12midnight** **The Late Late Show**
**3.00am** **Closedown**

Mac's Children's Favourites". All these programmes contained either live cover versions by session musicians or many 'hardy annual' records which cropped up again and again in listener's requests. Only occasionally did a current or recent chart hit feature in one of these BBC programmes. "Skiffle Club", which later became "Saturday Club", provided the only real outlet for new artists or material, but opportunity for exposure was very limited.

In response to growing audience demand Radio Caroline soon increased its airtime from the initial twelve hours a day and continued broadcasting until 10.00pm each night. This was subsequently modified to 8.00pm because of poor night time reception caused by interference from continental stations. Later Radio Caroline started to reopen again on Saturday and Sunday mornings at five minutes past midnight (when the continental stations had closed) and stayed on the air until 3.00am with late night party music.

A Gallup poll published in April 1964, after the station had been on the air for just one month, revealed that out of a potential audience of 20 million listeners aged 17 and above an estimated 7 million had tuned to Radio Caroline's broadcasts at one time or another.

What is really astounding about this achievement of such a high audience figure is that Radio Caroline arrived unannounced, in fact veiled in great secrecy unlike today's sophisticated marketing and promotion of any new product or service. Even after transmissions had started the station did not promote itself in any other medium (press or poster advertising for example), relying solely on self-generated 'news value' publicity and word of mouth recommendation. The immediate and overwhelming popularity of Radio Caroline programmes demonstrated the public demand which existed at that time for an all-day music station, a demand which established broadcasters had singularly failed to appreciate let alone tried to provide.

## First Ratecard

*Radio Caroline's first advertising ratecard showed the following charges which were based on estimated audience levels inside a primary reception area of 100 miles radius from the ship:-*

**6.00-7.00am**
*£70 per minute*
**7.00-9.00am**
*£110 per minute*
**9.00am-12noon**
*£80 per minute*
**12noon-3.00pm**
*£100 per minute*
**3.00-4.30pm**
*£70 per minute*
**4.30-6.00pm**
*£100 per minute*

*There were pro-rata rates for 45, 30 and 15 seconds, with series discounts ranging from 5% for 13 spots to 15% for 52 spots.*

## Commercials arrive

By the end of April 1964 advertisers, realising the huge size of Radio Caroline's audience and the apparent absence of any official action against the station were beginning to loose their initial inhibitions about buying airtime.

The very first commercial on the station, aired on 1st May 1964, was for Woburn Abbey, a stately home opened to the public by its owner, the Duke of Bedford. Increased attendances were reported by the Duke in the days immediately after transmission of this commercial and soon afterwards other advertisers also began booking airtime. Amongst early Radio Caroline advertisers were national clients such as Harp Larger, *News of the World,* William Hill's Turf Accountants, Ecko Radios, Bulgarian Holidays, Peter Evans Eating Houses and Kraft Dairylea Cheese.

The biggest boost of commercial confidence for the fledgling station came on 13th May 1964 when, in that single day, bookings for £30,000 worth of advertising were received. This surge of interest followed a written statement to the House of Commons the previous day by Postmaster General Reginald Bevins indicating that, although Radio Caroline had allegedly been responsible for interference to British and Belgian maritime communications during its first few days on the air, interference since then had been negligible and, for the time being at least, the Government had put off taking any unilateral action against offshore broadcasters pending the formulation of a concerted approach by all European countries.

## Concerted Action

The concerted European action hinted at by the Postmaster General on 12th May 1964 moved a step nearer the following day when a committee of the 17 member states of the Council of Europe adopted a draft agreement to outlaw offshore broadcasting. This agreement was to make it illegal to broadcast, to member countries from a base, either at sea or in the air, which was outside territorial limits or to cause interference to the authorised radio services of those countries. The agreement also contained a provision to make it an offence to supply, service, advertise on or assist an offshore broadcaster in any way. The draft agreement went forward as a recommendation from the Ministerial Committee for adoption by the Council of Europe at a Convention to be held later in the year. Once adopted as a 'statement of intent' it would then be up to member countries to implement its provisions through the individual enactment of domestic legislation.

The Postmaster General told the House of Commons on 2nd June 1964 that concerted European action, along the lines of the Council of Europe recommendation, was needed because any unilateral British law could be evaded if parallel provisions were not embodied in legislation passed by other countries. In the same statement he also rejected a suggestion that because of the popularity of the offshore stations the Government should introduce local radio to Britain (either commercially funded or via the BBC), but hinted that following the General Election due later that year, a Conservative Government, if returned, would undertake a comprehensive review of the demand for local radio broadcasting. That demand had already been identified (along with a recommended course of action to provide local radio in Britain) by the Pilkington Committee in its 1962 Report. However, the Government had chosen to take no action on these recommendations at that time.

By-mid May 1964, after six weeks on the air, Radio Caroline had firmly established itself with listeners and a growing number of advertisers. The station had also succeeded in establishing beyond doubt that there was a substantial demand for the service and style of programming it broadcast.

It is interesting to note that this demand had been identified and fulfilled, not by the BBC with its vast resources and audience research facilities, but by a group of entrepreneurs who were willing to go outside the established system, unsure at first what action, if any, would be taken against them, in order to provide listeners with the type of radio programmes they wanted to hear rather than what the 'establishment' broadcasters thought they ought to hear.

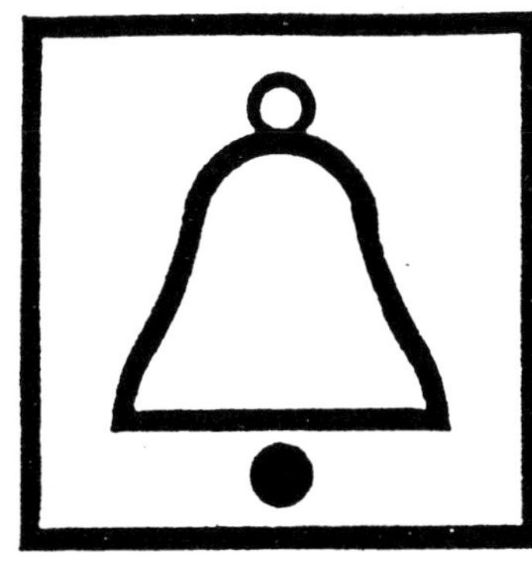

RADIO CAROLINE

199 metres

Planet Productions Limited, 54-62 Regent Street London W1. Regent 7616-7

# Chapter 7

# Radio Rivals

Meanwhile in Greenore the *Mi Amigo* was still being fitted out with her new aerial mast. By the middle of the month this work had been completed and the ship was able to leave port on 17th April 1964, giving her destination as El Ferrol in Spain. The *Mi Amigo* sailed through the Irish Sea, keeping outside territorial waters, but as she approached Lands End at 12.30am on 21st April 1964 the 168' mast began swaying dangerously. Part of the rigging had become loose and the swaying action seriously affected the ship's steering. There was nothing else the Captain could do but enter British territorial waters to find a calm anchorage off Falmouth while the damage was repaired. However, during that morning a Force 8 gale blew up along the English Channel and at 3.00pm the *Mi Amigo* was forced to leave her anchorage and actually enter Falmouth harbour.

The Captain tried to send a message to Project Atlanta's London office via Lands End Radio asking for riggers, who had previously worked on the MV *Caroline,* to come to Falmouth and undertake the essential repairs. However, Lands End Radio refused to handle the message from the *Mi Amigo* and it had to be transmitted via a continental station.

The riggers were eventually brought to Falmouth to carry out the repairs and once this work had been completed, the *Mi Amigo* set sail again on 23rd April 1964. Although the ship had received no official attention whilst in port she immediately sailed outside British territorial waters and anchored at a position 10 miles south east of Falmouth, staying there for 24 hours before resuming her voyage.

By 27th April 1964 the *Mi Amigo* had arrived at her destination and anchored in international waters off Frinton-on-Sea on the Essex coast, approximately 14 miles from the MV *Caroline,* but the planned test transmissions for Radio Atlanta did not take place immediately. Rough weather prevented radio technicians getting aboard the ship and it was not until 30th April 1964 that a small motor barge, the *Peterna,* was able to draw alongside and transfer technical personnel to the *Mi Amigo.*

*Radio Atlanta fails to come on the air*

WITH a massive publicity build-up lying behind him, Mr. Allan Crawford, managing director, pressed the remote control button in London that was to switch on Radio Atlanta, Britain's second pirate radio station, anchored off Frinton. But the station did not come on the air because

Mr. Crawford, 42-year-old music publisher, was to have launched the new radio station which he describes as a "worthy alternative for B.B.C.", in a fashionable London hotel at 11 a.m. on Tuesday.

The technical trouble was complicated by the fact that technicians were unable to reach the radio ship, Mi Amigo, because of bad weather.

Walton coastguards expressed anxiety this week, after the announcement that Radio Atlanta was to transmit on 197 metres, close to their distress wavelength.

But at a Press conference, Mr. Crawford pointed out that the station was only provisionally transmitting on 197 metres. He stressed that his firm, Project Atlanta Ltd., were taking great care in their final choice of the wavelength.

24 HOURS A DAY

When the station does start broadcasting it will be on the air for 24 hours a day. "The programmes will be of the light entertainment type and specially designed for family listening." Mr. Crawford said.

Advertising will start as soon as possible and will be limited six minutes each hour.

## Second offshore station

Radio Atlanta eventually commenced test transmissions on 9th May 1964 using the same frequency as Radio Caroline - 1520kHz (197m) - after that station had ended its days broadcasting. This first transmission was presented by Australian DJ Colin Nicol, but the broadcast was something more than just a technical test, it was also a listener awareness exercise, attracting Radio Caroline's audience just as that station had closed for the day.

Regular programmes from Radio Atlanta eventually started at 6.00pm on 12th May 1964 on a slightly different frequency -1495kHz (201m), using a transmitter power of 10Kw. This frequency was a mere whisker away from Radio Caroline's

1520kHz (197m) and it is certain that many people happened on Radio Atlanta's early broadcasts whilst intending to tune their radios to Caroline. The station's opening day was punctuated with "Good Luck" messages from contemporary pop stars such as Frank Ifield, Cliff Richard and the Shadows, Harry Seacombe and Rolf Harris. Allan Crawford launched his long awaited station, which had been almost four years in the planning, at a press conference held in London's Waldorf Hotel. Radio Atlanta's initial broadcasting hours were from 6.00am-6.00pm, but this was quickly extended to 6.00am-8.00pm in line with Caroline's similar extension in late May 1964.

**RADIO ATLANTA**

**REQUIRE THE FOLLOWING STAFF**

| | |
|---|---|
| **Sales Executives:** | Media selling experience a distinct advantage. Must, however, be conversant with functions of advertising media. Advertising agency experience useful. |
| **Traffic Controller:** | To manage various procedures surrounding scheduling of airtime bookings. Must have experience. Chance for a frustrated number two. |
| **Sales Co-ordinator: (female)** | To deal with enquiries (telephone and letter) and generally to liase with media department of advertising agencies. A sort of "Girl Friday." |
| **Secretary (1):** | This position calls for a person conversant with advertising procedures. Ideal type is probably at present employed in media or an advertising agency. Initiative and down to earth common sense essential. |
| **Secretary (2):** | A personality conscious publicity girl with experience of Public Relations, who can use initiative and who needs little supervision. |
| **Copy Typists:** | Must be accurate. Work involves contracts, invoices and programme airtime schedules. |

Salaries for all above positions subject to negotiation.

*All applications addressed to:*

LESLIE T. PARISH, PROJECT ATLANTA LTD., 47 Dean St., W.1. Telephone: REGent 7451

Following the same pattern as the Scandinavian and Dutch offshore stations Radio Atlanta's programmes were taped on land for later re-broadcast from the *Mi Amigo*. Presentation was slicker than the initial Radio Caroline programmes (which were also largely pre-recorded) but lacked the spontaneity of live broadcasting which by mid-May filled almost all of Caroline's daily output. This spontaneity and informality was one major feature of offshore broadcasting which appealed to audiences - DJs talking about life on board the ship, weather conditions, passing shipping and other snippets of information made listeners feel they were sharing in part of the station's day-to-day life.

As well as presentation style the format of Radio Atlanta also differed significantly from that of Radio Caroline. The station programmed different types of music in individual time segments throughout the day - Rhythm and Blues, Latin American, Film Music etc., rather than the general mix played all day-long by Radio Caroline, whose programme changes, usually every two or three hours, were really only a change of DJ or announcer.

## Merger

With the history of close links between Radio Caroline and Radio Atlanta since their inception and the fact that they were both targeting the same audience in the south and east of England it is not surprising that by early June 1964 rumours began to circulate about a merger between the two rivals. At that time Radio Caroline had been on the air for two months and Radio Atlanta for just three weeks, but it took nearly another month of negotiations before the directors of both stations agreed to a formal merger and a joint press release was issued on Thursday 2nd July 1964:-

*The directors of Project Atlanta and Planet Productions today issued a joint statement announcing a merger between Radio Atlanta and Radio Caroline. The companies are responsible for the advertising and selling of time on the two offshore commercial radio stations.*

### Radio Atlanta Programme Schedule, May 1964

*(Compare to Radio Caroline's first programme schedule on page71)*

*Monday-Friday*

**6.00am Early Call,** *Bob Scott*

**6.15am Country and Western Style,** *Johnnie Jackson*

**6.45am Early Call,** *Bob Scott*

**7.30am Breakfast Club,** *Ted King*

**8.45am Musical Mailbag,** *Richard Harris*

**10.00am Work Along,** *Clive Burrell*

**11.15am Morning Star,** *Tony Withers*

**11.30am Spin Around,** *Clive Burrell*

**1.00pm Headline Hits,** *Tony Withers*

**2.00pm Music the Wide World Over,** *Richard Harris*

**4.00pm Sounds of the Sixties,** *Tony Withers*

**6.00pm All Systems Go,** *Mike Raven*

**6.30pm Music of the Moment,** *Neil Spence*

**8.00pm Closedown**

## NEWS RELEASE

COMMERCIAL RADIO MERGER

*Mr. Allan Crawford, Managing Director of Project Atlanta, and Mr. Ronan O'Rahilly,Managing Director of Planet Productions will become joint managing directors of the new operation.*

*The ship broadcasting the present Radio Caroline programmes, MV Caroline, will sail to the Isle of Man tomorrow morning (Friday) to a position five miles from Ramsey, Isle of Man. It will continue to broadcast Radio Caroline programmes on its way to its destination and will remain on 199 metres medium wave.*

*The ship MV Atlanta (sic) will continue broadcasting from its present position to the Greater London area and south east England under the national call sign,Radio Caroline.*

*In their joint statement Mr. Crawford and Mr. O'Rahilly said:*

*' The decision to merge was taken in view of the enormous interest from the public and advertisers in other parts of England outside the original broadcasting area. This network will cover the most populous areas of Great Britain.*

*It will specifically meet the demands from advertisers in the north and Midlands and from existing advertisers who are already taking time on the two stations.*

*All departments will merge to operate from one office. The Caroline Club and other land-based operations will continue and be extended to cover the new broadcasting area.'*

### ATLANTA NOW CAROLINE —AND CAROLINE LEAVES

RADIO Atlanta, off Frinton, becomes Caroline this morning. And Radio Caroline is leaving her moorings off Harwich to take up a new position off the Isle of Man.

There has been much talk of a merger between the two radio ships but it was confirmed this week that negotiations had now been clinched.

From this morning onwards Radio Atlanta will broadcast Caroline's programmes, but an Atlanta spokesman stressed, "The name Atlanta will not be totally submerged—there are plans afoot for its future use."

The official explained that the disc jockeys aboard the Mi Amigo, the Atlanta ship, would be "half ours and half Caroline's."

"It was inevitable that the two companies should merge," he commented. "After all, they started off hand-in-hand."

He added that with a ship off Frinton and another in the Irish Sea, Radio Caroline would have almost complete coverage of the country.

## "World in Action" Granada TV

*The same day that Radio Atlanta commenced broadcasts Granada Television screened the first British documentary about offshore radio in its weekly current affairs programme, "World in Action".*

*The programme dealt with the success of Radio Caroline since its launch at the end of March 1964 and featured interviews with the station's founder, Ronan O'Rahilly who, together with Jocelyn Stevens, Chris Moore (Programme Director) and Ian Ross (Sales Director) were filmed in the offices of Queen magazine, the original Caroline headquarters.*

*The then Postmaster General, Reginald Bevins (Conservative) and opposition spokesman Roy Mason (Labour) also appeared in the programme presenting their respective cases. Reginald Bevins stated, not for the first or last time, that the Government was waiting for the Council of Europe to take action internationally before deciding to introduce any domestic legislation to outlaw the offshore radio stations. However, claimed Mr. Bevins, the Post Office had put its point of view about offshore radio to the advertising industry as far back as November 1963 and he was sure that, as a result, the stations would not be able to sell any commercial airtime which they needed to do in order to survive for any length of time.*

*For the opposition Roy Mason warned that the Government was storing up trouble for itself by delaying to take any action against the stations and stated that there was a threat that the offshore broadcasters would start promoting products which were not permitted to be advertised on British television.*

*Exclusive footage of the Radio Atlanta vessel Mi Amigo being fitted out in the small Irish port of Greenore and of its voyage south around the coast of Britain (including having to put into Falmouth with a storm damaged mast) was featured in the programme as were shots of Radio Atlanta programmes being recorded in a 'secret' London studio. Radio Atlanta's founder, Allan Crawford, was also interviewed about his station and talked of the rivalry with Radio Caroline.*

*The programme included extracts from cinema films featuring replica 17th Century pirate ships, conjuring up the imagery which was to stay for ever with the offshore stations. It ended with speculation (strongly rebutted by Jocelyn Stevens) that the stations, and in particular Radio Caroline, were financed by a sinister European-based 'Mr. Big', who had vague and undisclosed plans for the future of British broadcasting.*

As part of the merger agreement Radio Caroline took over responsibility for Radio Atlanta's debts and the original directors of the company were to receive one third of any profits made after 2nd July 1964.

Without any ceremony Radio Atlanta ceased broadcasting from the *Mi Amigo* at 8.00pm that evening (2nd July 1964) and, after Radio Caroline had also closed for the day, the MV *Caroline* sailed to within a mile of the former Atlanta vessel, *Mi Amigo.*

Arrangements were then made to enable Radio Caroline to commence transmissions at 6.00am the next morning as scheduled, not from the MV *Caroline* as it had since the end of March, but from the former Radio Atlanta ship, *Mi Amigo.* The intention was that it should not have been obvious for Radio Caroline's listeners that overnight the station had completely transferred operations to what had formerly been a rival radio ship.

Because Radio Atlanta's programmes were mostly taped on land the *Mi Amigo* had no DJ crew and no on-board record library, although there were turntables and a microphone in the studio which had been used in the days of Radio Nord. In order to retain some programme continuity and familiar voices for Radio Caroline's listeners in London and the south east, DJs Simon Dee and Doug Kerr, together with a small supply of records and tapes, were taken in a tender from the MV *Caroline* across to the *Mi Amigo* to prepare for the next days broadcasting under the new call sign, Radio Caroline South.

Once on board, the *Mi Amigo* the Radio Caroline staff met some slight resistance from the Dutch Captain who, because of language differences had not fully understood the merger arrangements and anyway did not welcome the prospect of having English DJs on board his ship. He had been happy with the Radio Atlanta arrangement were the only on-board personnel were the Dutch crew and some radio technicians.

In an effort to thwart the new arrangements, of which he did not approve, the Captain hid vital parts of studio equipment, including styluses for the turntable pick-up arms. Without these the Caroline DJs could not play their records and the planned live programmes of Caroline South from the *Mi Amigo* would be impossible. It was only after hours of persuasion and eventually by getting the Captain drunk that the DJs were able to elicit from him where the missing components had been hidden. By the time everything had been found it was 2.00am and, with essential wiring work not completed until about 5.40am, Radio Caroline South only just made it on air as scheduled at 6.00am on Friday 3rd July 1964.

## Caroline North

Meanwhile the original Radio Caroline ship MV *Caroline,* after having transferred two of her DJs and a supply of records to the *Mi Amigo* remained at anchor near the former Radio Atlanta ship for most of Friday 3rd July 1964. She eventually set sail just after 12.30a.m. on Saturday 4th July 1964, under the command of Captain Hengeveld, heading for a new anchorage in the Irish Sea. The ship kept outside territorial waters and the DJs left on board, Tom Lodge, Jerry Leighton and Alan Turner continued broadcasting as normal during the voyage through the English Channel and northwards up the Irish Sea.

**Radio Caroline North's first Programme Schedule, July 1964**

| | |
|---|---|
| 6.00am | The Early Show, *Tom Lodge* |
| 9.00am | The Sound of Music, Part 1, *Tom Lodge* |
| 10.00am | The Sound of Music, Part 2, *Jerry Leighton* |
| 11.00am | Top Deck, *Jerry Leighton* |
| 12noon | Date with Caroline, *Alan Turner* |
| 1.00pm | Spinaround, *Tom Lodge* |
| 2.00pm | Soundtrack, *Jerry Leighton* |
| 4.00pm | The Big Line Up, *Tom Lodge* |
| 6.00pm | Sunset Spin, *Alan Turner* |
| 9.00pm | Closedown |
| 12.05am | The Late Late Show, *Alan Turner* |
| 3.00am | Closedown |

**Caroline North**

*Radio Caroline North broadcast on the original Caroline frequency of 1520kHz (197m) with a power of 20Kw, while Caroline South retained the former Radio Atlanta frequency of 1495kHz (201m), with a power of 10Kw. However, nationally the announced wavelength of both stations was "Caroline on 199m".*

Captain Hengeveld regularly came on the air to keep listeners up to date with the ship's progress and announce approximate times of arrival off specific coastal towns. The MV *Caroline* created a lot of interest, with listeners flashing their car headlights at the ship from various vantage points and a local boat owner in Cornwall even took a supply of newspapers out to the ship as she sailed past Padstow.

By 8.00am on Monday 6th July 1964 the MV *Caroline* had reached Anglesey off the North Wales coast. She then moved to a position off Dublin for a few days before finally heading to what was to be her anchorage position for almost four years - Ramsey Bay off the northern coast of the Isle of Man, where she arrived on 13th July 1964. From this position the station, now using the call sign Radio Caroline North, could reach the north and Midlands of England, most of Wales, south west Scotland and much of the north and east of Ireland.

## United but separate

With the two sister stations Radio Caroline was now able to offer audiences and advertisers what was, in theory, a national daytime commercial radio station. However, the North and South stations each broadcast their own independent programmes and developed quite separate identities. This was in contrast to the former Radio Mercur arrangement in Denmark where those sister stations (Mercur East and West) broadcast the same pre-recorded programmes simultaneously, except for two hours a day of local output (see Chapter 3)

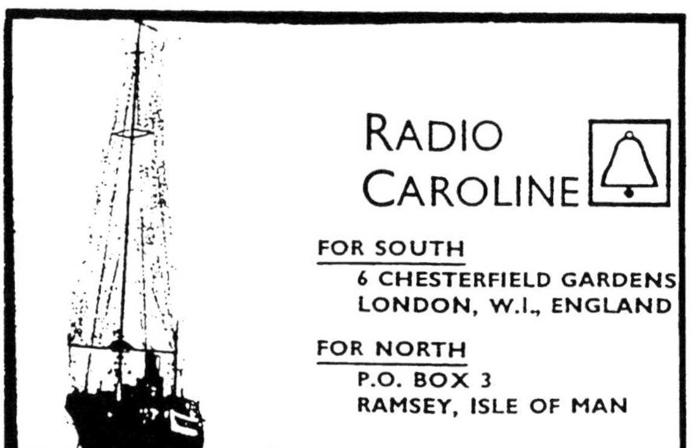


Transmission hours for Radio Caroline North remained as 6.00am-8.00pm and, initially the 12.05am-3.00am weekend broadcasts, which had been started while the ship was off the Essex coast, were also continued. However, these late night programmes were soon discontinued due to staff shortages.

On Caroline South the former Radio Atlanta transmission hours of 6.00am-8.00pm were retained at first, even though listeners in that station's reception area had been used to the late night weekend programmes now being enjoyed by audiences in the north.

Although the outlook appeared promising for the new 'national' offshore station some unexpected problems arose from the merger of Radio Caroline and Radio Atlanta. Several Atlanta DJs refused to join the new Caroline network and Radio Atlanta General Manager, Leslie Parrish, resigned over a difference of opinion on policy matters.

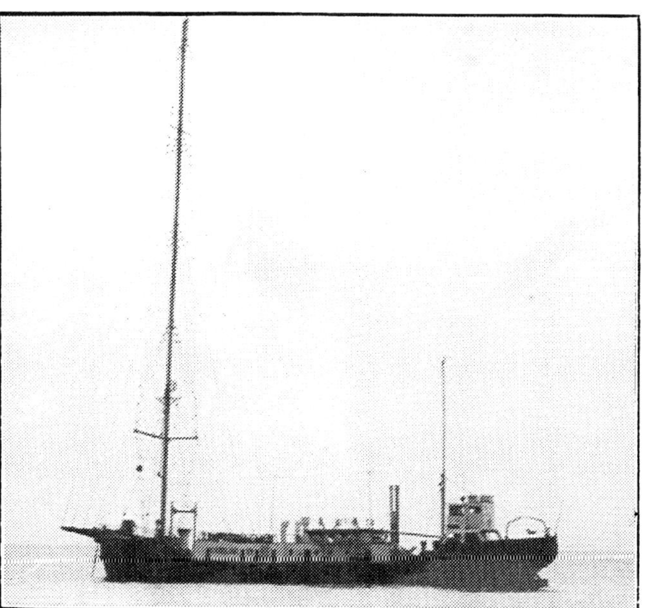

*The 'Mi Amigo' at anchor off the Essex coast*

On Caroline South, over which Allan Crawford retained a significant degree of control, DJs were continually being instructed to play his record company's cover versions of hit singles - as had been the policy on Radio Atlanta. These included such titles as

"Please Please Me" by the Bell Boys and "Needles and Pins" byTony Steven, rather than the more popular chart hits by The Beatles and The Searchers which listeners preferred. This policy caused resentment from the former Radio Caroline DJs, who previously experienced freedom of choice over which music they played, and this undoubtedly had a detrimental effect on the programming output of Caroline South.

Meanwhile, Radio Caroline North, under Ronan O'Rahilly's direct control, programmed very differently and was able to reflect more accurately audience demand for the new, vibrant beat music, itself largely emanating from groups based in Liverpool and the north west of England.

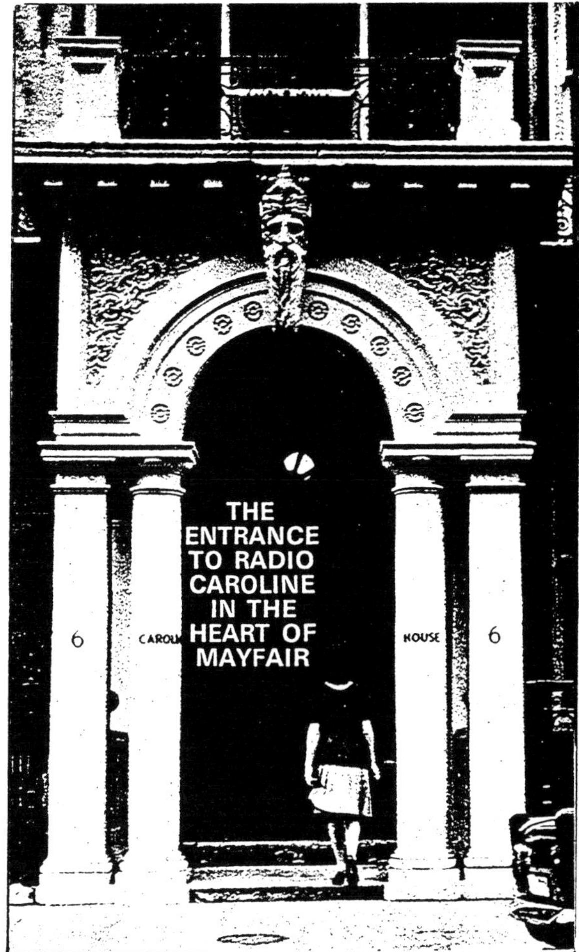


*Caroline House, 6 Chesterfield Gardens, London*

As well as programming differences crewing of the radio ships also caused unexpected friction after the merger. Originally the MV *Caroline* had been crewed by the Wijsmuller Supply and Tendering Co. of Soest, Holland under the command of one of their captains, Captain Bakker. Captain Bakker was what is known in maritime circles as a 'runner', responsible for bringing ships from one port to another, then leaving to do the same thing with another vessel. Once the MV *Caroline* had been anchored in position off the Essex coast at the end of March 1964 Ronan O'Rahilly engaged his own Captain and crew. Scotsman Captain George Mackay was signed up by O'Rahilly to command the MV *Caroline* while Captain Bakker was taken, in a wooden rowing boat under cover of darkness to Clacton beach and left to make his own way to his next command. This unusual way of relieving a Captain of his command was due to the fact that the radio ship could not enter British territorial waters because Radio Caroline was by then on the air!

After the merger Wijsmuller, which had supplied the Captain and crew for the former Radio Atlanta ship *Mi Amigo,* insisted on also providing a full compliment of crew and a Captain for the MV *Caroline.* Captain Abraham Hengeveld from Wijsmullers took command of the MV *Caroline* during her voyage to the Isle of Man and stayed with the ship for about six weeks in Ramsey Bay. There was also considerable dissatisfaction amongst the crew of the MV *Caroline,* who had not been paid or given shore leave for two months, so gradually O'Rahilly's staff were replaced or absorbed onto the Dutch tendering company's payroll.

With two stations on the air the Radio Caroline organisation had to also set about solving some practical and logistic problems to supply and staff both ships, to sell commercial airtime nationally and locally and to deal with a vast number of letters and enquiries from listeners.

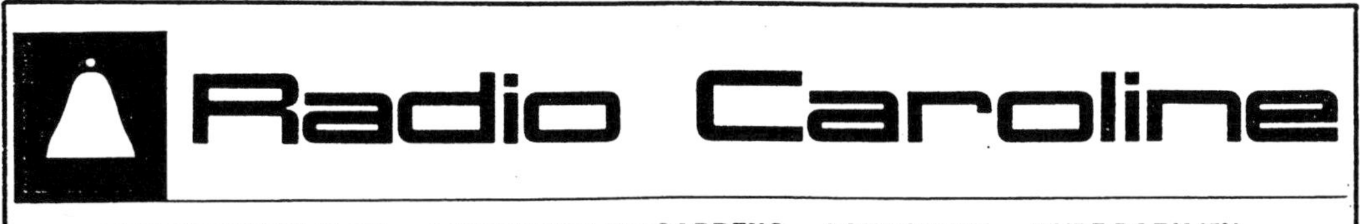

**Live music**

*On 5th May 1964 the first attempt to broadcast live music from a radio ship was made by Radio Caroline. This came about as the result of a chance meeting between Ronan O'Rahilly and Jimmy Smith at the 21 Club.*

*A few days later Jimmy Smith, Tony Crombie and Tony Thorpe, together with Hammond Organ, guitar set and drums were taken aboard the 'Mi Amigo'.*

*The live performance took place on deck because the Hammond Organ could not be taken down the companion way to the studio. However the practical difficulties encountered in this episode meant that no further attempts were made to broadcast live music from the radio ship.*

Shortly after the merger Radio Caroline moved its administrative headquarters- from the *Queen* magazine building in Fetter Lane to a large three storey building at 6 Chesterfield Gardens - renamed Caroline House - in the heart of London's Mayfair.

Here, housed on separate floors of this excessively spacious, but most impressive building, were the station's advertising sales team, the administration offices, press and public relations staff and the listener enquiries and promotions department. Studio facilities were also built in the basement to record commercials and promotions on tape for later transmission from the two ships. Following the merger Caroline headquarters also absorbed Radio Atlanta's land-based servicing and advertising sales facilities

The Post Office installed telephone facilities in Caroline House, but refused to list the station by name in the London directory. Not until the end of November 1964 did they reluctantly agree to a listing, but then only as "Caroline Sales". Although the Post Office could not bring itself to acknowledge the existence of Radio Caroline by listing its number in the directory they earned substantial revenue from telephone traffic to and from Caroline House - estimated to be over 2,000 calls each day, an average of one every 15 seconds.

In order to deal with the vast number of enquiries from listeners for information about the station and for items of publicity material such as badges and car stickers, the Caroline Club had been launched shortly before the merger with Radio Atlanta. For 10/6d (55p) listeners could join the Club and received in return an information booklet about the ship and the DJs, a pin badge, car sticker and details of various promotional offers - Caroline T- shirts, fashion accessories etc. After the merger with Atlanta on 2nd July, the Caroline Club was immediately extended to offer membership to listeners on a nationwide basis. The first "Caroline Club Requests" programme was aired on Radio Caroline South on 11th July 1964.

Because of the volume of mail generated as a result of the huge national audience, increased interest from advertisers and the logistical problems of supplying and staffing two ships, Radio Caroline soon opened a second office, at 61 Lord Street, Liverpool, to service the needs of the northern station. At the same time listeners to Radio Caroline North were invited to send record requests and mail for the DJs direct to an address in the Isle of Man - PO Box 3, Ramsey - from where it could be taken out to the ship on the weekly tender.

The Liverpool office also established a northern sales team who sold airtime to 'local' advertisers in the reception area of Caroline North. At first a small coaster from Douglas in the Isle of Man, was also hired through the Dutch servicing and salvage company Wijsmuller to tender the northern ship. This temporary arrangement later changed when one of Wijsmuller's own vessels was brought to the Island and based in the Manx fishing port and holiday resort of Ramsey, from where it took over the transfer of crew, and supplies to the MV *Caroline.*

## Manx opposition

The arrival off the Isle of Man of the MV *Caroline* with her powerful 20Kw transmitter upset the Island's recently opened (legal) local commercial radio station, Manx Radio. This station, then broadcasting on VHF (FM) only with a power of just 50 watts, complained to the Post Office about interference to its transmissions allegedly caused by Caroline North's powerful medium wave transmitter.

Manx Radio was Britain's first licensed commercial radio station and had started experimental broadcasts, on 5th June 1964 as the result of a prolonged pressure campaign by local businessmen on the Isle of Man which enjoys a certain amount of independence from the British Government in the conduct of its internal affairs. Ironically the practical extent of this independence was to be acrimoniously tested a few years later, precisely because of Radio Caroline's presence off the Island's coast (see Chapter 12).

The Isle of Man relies on the British Government for the conduct of its external affairs such as defence, foreign policy and international agreements, but it legislates for its own domestic affairs and has its own judicial and monetary system, all administered through Tynwald, one of the oldest democratically elected parliaments in the world. The Island's domestic laws in fact closely follow those of mainland Britain although sometimes important differences are agreed by Tynwald and it was one of these which resulted in the establishment of Manx Radio.

In 1959 Tynwald had authorised the establishment of a 100Kw medium wave radio transmitter on the Isle of Man to boost the Island's economy and tourist trade and to provide a base for advertisers wishing to reach a large audience on the British mainland. The service would have been a competitor for the BBC and in many ways paralleled the pre-war commercial broadcasts to Britain from continental Europe. However, because the Island's Government had also adopted the provisions of the Wireless Telegraphy Act of 1949 a licence from the British Government's Postmaster General was required before any such radio station could be established. The British Government not surprisingly refused to issue a licence for a high power medium wave transmitter but did, somewhat reluctantly, offer a licence for a local station, provided its signal was transmitted on such a low power that it could not be heard on the mainland.

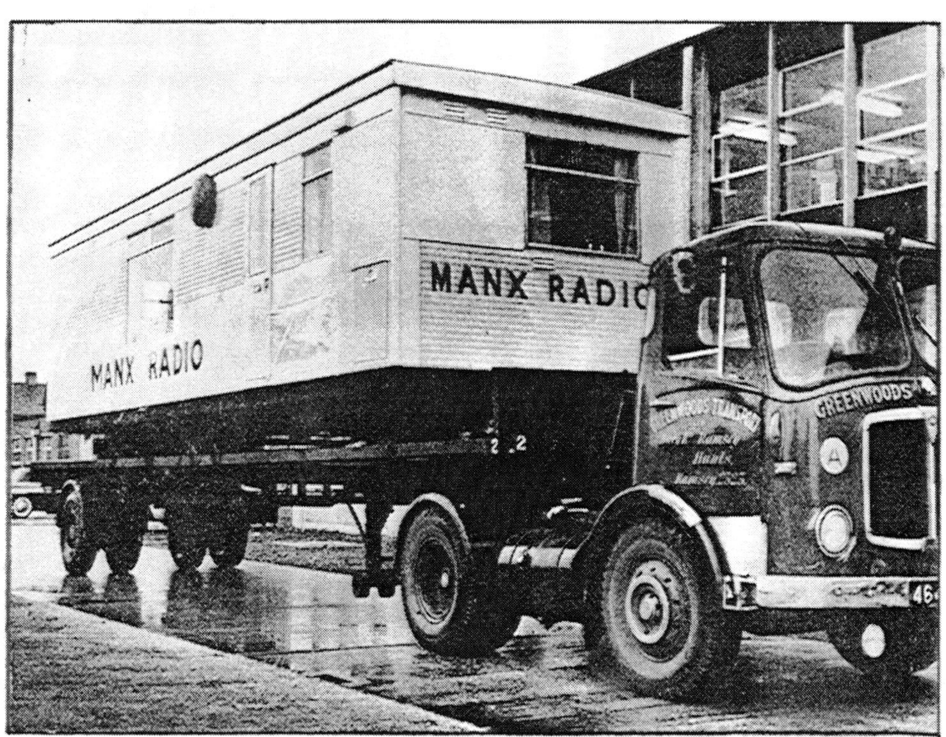


This proposition for a low powered station was not thought to be commercially viable at the time and nothing more happened until 1964 when two businessmen, Richard L Meyer and T H Colbourn, together with the communications conglomerate Pye Ltd., formed a new company - the Isle of Man Broadcasting Co. Ltd. - to establish and operate a local commercial radio station on the Island.

*Manx Radio's first studio leaving the Pye factory in Cambridge where it had been custom built*

Mr. T H Colbourn was a local radio and television retailer and as a member of the Manx Parliament had for some years promoted the idea of the Island having its own commercial radio station. Richard L Meyer had been involved in commercial radio during the 1930s as General Manager of Captain Plugge's International Broadcasting Company, which had beamed programmes to Britain from various European land-based transmitters (see Chapter 1).

In May 1964 the British Post Office issued a temporary licence to the new company authorising it to make experimental broadcasts on VHF (FM) only, from a temporary studio housed in a caravan. The first broadcast, under the call sign Manx Radio, took place on 5th June 1964 and consisted of a commentary on the world famous TT motorcycle races.

Experimental transmissions by the new local station, consisting of four hours a day of music programmes, then continued throughout the summer of 1964 on VHF (FM). However, this signal was only effectively covering about half the Island and the number of listeners then owning radio sets capable of receiving VHF (FM) broadcasts was estimated at just 2,500. The company operating the new local station complained about the frequency and power limitations allocated to them in the light of Radio Caroline's arrival off the Island. They pleaded in a telegram to the Prime Minister and the Postmaster General "If you are unable to check Caroline please give us a chance to compete by allocation of comparable medium wave lengths and power." Consequently in October 1964 the Post Office issued Manx Radio with a further licence to broadcast on 1594kHz (188m) in the medium wave band using a power of just 50 watts, and transmissions on this frequency started on 23rd November 1964.

With this background of a long-running dispute between the Island Government and the British Post Office over the issue of a high power medium wave broadcasting licence it is easy to understand the initial feeling of antipathy towards Radio Caroline when its powerful northern transmitter was positioned off the Manx coast.

Radio Caroline North, however, soon became accepted by the Isle of Man Government and the Manx people in general. Constant on-air references by the DJs to the "wonderful" or "beautiful" Isle of Man together with, at one stage, free promotions for the Manx Tourist Board undoubtedly boosted the Island's tourism figures for the three and a half years the station was anchored in Ramsey Bay.

The Island and its people did not forget this when the British Government tried to impose legislation on the Manx statute book outlawing Radio Caroline and a bitter constitutional dispute ensued (see Chapter 12).

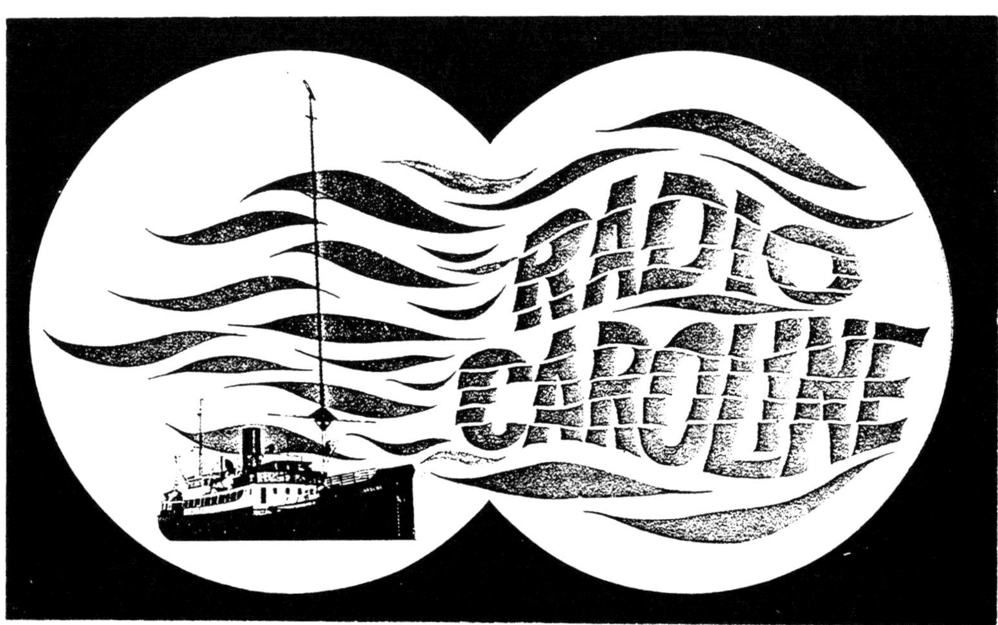


*The cover of an early information booklet published by Radio Caroline for Caroline Club members*

# Chapter 8

# Rapid Expansion

During the spring and early summer of 1964 while Radio Caroline and Radio Atlanta had been establishing themselves independently and then merging to form an almost national station another development was taking place in the Thames Estuary which, although relatively low key at first, was later to be of considerable significance for British offshore radio. This was the use of semi-derelict wartime structures which had been abandoned by the Government during the late 1950s.

In May 1964 David Sutch, an outrageously extrovert pop singer, better known as Screaming 'Lord' Sutch, decided to establish his own offshore radio station. He had been inspired by the success of Radios Caroline and Atlanta, but his station was largely to be a publicity and promotional exercise for himself and other, then unknown, artists.

Sutch had been a rock and roll singer for many years, touring dance halls and gaining notoriety through his outrageous stage act. He first achieved national fame in 1963 when he stood as a candidate in the Parliamentary by-election at Stratford-upon-Avon on behalf of the National Teenage Party. The by-election was attracting national interest because it had been brought about through the resignation of John Profumo, then a minister of state, who had been involved in a sex/spy scandal which rocked and ultimately brought down the Conservative Government. Sutch failed to win the parliamentary seat at Stratford and lost his deposit, but went on to become a national folk-hero and earn an entry in the *Guinness Book of Records* for standing as a candidate in over 33 parliamentary by-elections as well as a number of general election contests, representing first the National Teenage Party and more recently the Monster Raving Loony Party.

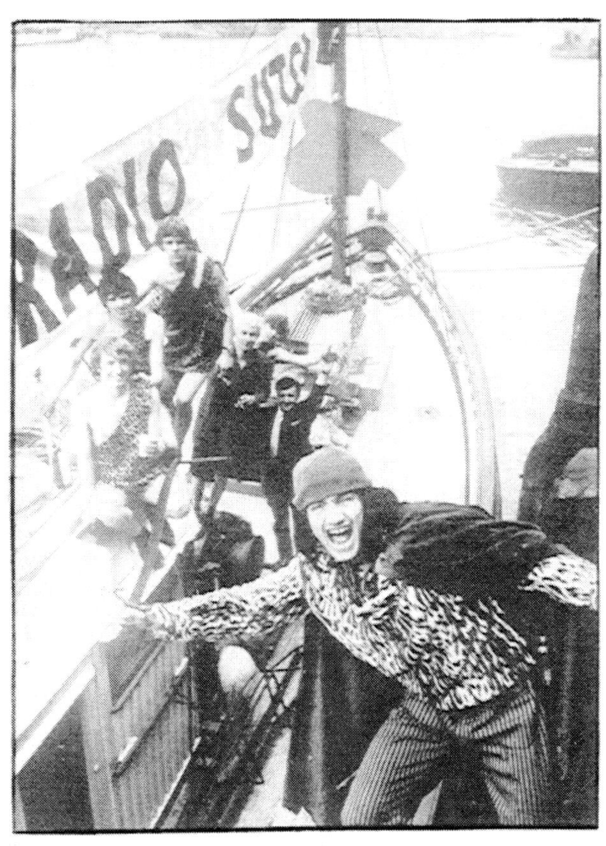


*Screaming 'Lord' Sutch and the Savages aboard the 'Cornucopia'*

## Publicity

With his manager, Reg Calvert, Sutch hired a small fishing vessel, the *Cornucopia* on which they placed a low power (500 watt) transmitter, some very basic studio equipment and then strung a wire between the ship's two masts to form an aerial.

The *Cornucopia* left the Pool of London following a press conference and photo session on 24th May 1964 supposedly to anchor outside territorial waters and begin broadcasting. Calvert assured sceptical pressmen that this was not a publicity hoax for

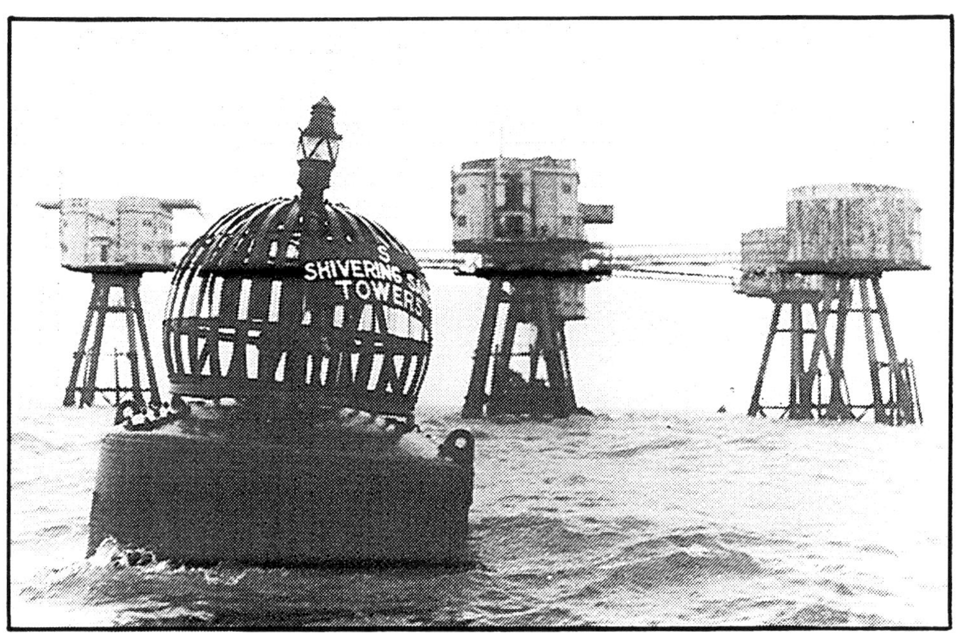


Shivering Sands Fort in the Thames Estuary

Sutch and his group, "The Savages", and that the station had in fact cost £4,000 to set up, with estimated running costs of £300 per week.

The announced plan was for the station to transmit music daily between 12 noon and 2.00pm and 5.00pm and 8.00pm. There was also talk of late night transmissions being planned between 12.15am and 2.15am, with readings from what were then considered to be risque books such as *Fanny Hill* and *Lady Chatterley's Lover*.

Two versions of how Radio Sutch actually started have been reported over the years. The generally accepted version is that within a day or two of the ship's much publicised sailing from the Pool of London the radio equipment was transferred from the *Cornucopia* to the abandoned World War Two fort at Shivering Sands in the Thames Estuary with test transmissions for the new station starting on 27th May 1964.

## Wartime Sea Forts

Shivering Sands Fort was a complex of Towers rising from the sea bed which had been built as part of the nation's coastal defence system during World War Two. The forts, of which there were originally eight in the Thames Estuary, had been maintained by the Ministry of Defence for some time after the end of the War and were finally abandoned in 1956. One fort at The Nore (similar in construction to Shivering Sands) had been demolished in 1958 as it was considered a hazard to shipping.

The War Office issued a statement on 27th May 1964 saying that Sutch and his crew were trespassing on Government property and indicated that officials, with police support, would go out to the Shivering Sands and instruct them to leave. A 'boarding party', consisting of an Army Department land agent and a Kent police officer, was subsequently sent out to Shivering Sands on 28th May 1964, but was recalled to Gravesend before reaching the Fort.

In an explanation of the apparent change of policy the Army Department later issued a statement saying that it had originally intended to serve a notice on the occupants that they were trespassing and to carry out an inspection for any damage to the Fort and the navigational lights housed there. In the meantime, however, the Port of London Authority advised that there had been no damage and accordingly the Army Department representative was recalled.

### Radio Free Yorkshire

*On 5th July 1964 John McCallum, Liberal candidate for Bridlington and John Crawford, Liberal candidate for Howden used a ship anchored in Bridlington Bay off the Yorkshire coast to broadcast as Radio Free Yorkshire.*

*John McCallum was quoted later as saying that the broadcast had been made to "demonstrate the dangers of pirate radio and to protest against the conditions which allow pirate radio to exist."*

On 5th June 1964 a question was asked in Parliament by Shadow Postmaster General, Roy Mason (Labour) as to why no action had been taken by the Ministry of Defence to remove the occupants of the Shivering Sands Fort and whether a licence had been granted to them to operate a radio station. Mr. Arthur Ramsden (Con.),Minister of State for the Army,stated in a written reply :-

*Although the Fort is no longer required for defence purposes and has remained unmanned for some years it still belongs to the Crown and the persons who took up residence in it last week were, and so far as I know, still are, trespassing.*

*I understand that they have caused no damage to the Fort, and I concluded last week that immediate action to remove them from what must be a rather uncomfortable spot would not be worth the time and effort involved.*

*No permission has been given for these people to enter the Fort or to use it for any purpose. The grant of a licence to operate a radio station from a place lying within territorial jurisdiction, as this Fort does, is a matter for the Postmaster General, with whom I am in touch.*

This evidence from the Ministry of Defence records and Parliamentary statements seems to confirm that the Shivering Sands Fort was indeed occupied and being used as a base for a radio station by Sutch and his team at the end of May 1964. The Minister's statement also clearly indicates that from the outset the Government accepted that Shivering Sands was within British territorial waters - a factor which was to become the cause of confusion and controversy some two years later.

However, another version of the sequence of events (contained in an interview given by David Sutch himself many years later) states that Radio Sutch did in fact broadcast from the *Cornucopia* for about two weeks at the beginning of May 1964 during the afternoon hours when the boat was not being used for its primary purpose - fishing. According to this interview the transfer of equipment to Shivering Sands was not made until after the fishing boat's owner encountered problems with his insurers for allowing the vessel to be used as a radio station. After failing to find any other boat owners willing to hire their vessels to the station, Sutch and his team made some preliminary enquiries about the disused wartime forts in the Thames Estuary. Discovering that they had been abandoned for some years by the Government, Sutch simply decided to occupy them, claiming squatter's rights.

The true sequence of events surrounding the start of Radio Sutch is probably a mixture of both these versions. Although there have never been any documented reception reports or recordings it is possible that broadcasts from Radio Sutch did take place from the *Cornucopia* in the weeks prior to her appearance for the press at the Pool of London. Equipment then being transferred to the Shivering Sands Fort after adequate publicity had been generated for the 'new' station.

## Britain's First Teenage Station

Whichever version is correct, test transmissions were heard from Radio Sutch on 1542kHz (194m) on 27th May 1964. The broadcast which started, not surprisingly, with a record by Screaming Lord Sutch himself -"Jack the Ripper" - was on very low power and was only audible within a close radius of the Fort. However, within a few days the transmitter power had been increased and the station was heard 10-15 miles inland in Essex and North Kent. The wavelength was also now being announced on air as 200m.

To begin with there were just three on-air staff - 'Lord' Sutch himself, his manager Reg Calvert, and one of Sutch's personal friends and road manager Brian Paul (real name Poole). Radio Sutch use Calvert's music agency offices at 7 Denmark Street, London as its land-based headquarters and as a mailing address and point of contact for advertisers or anyone wishing to work for the station.

Promoted as "Britain's First Teenage Radio Station" broadcasting hours for Radio Sutch, although advertised as 12 noon - 2.00pm and 5.00pm - 11.00pm, were erratic, with DJs oversleeping and consequently sometimes opening transmissions up to an hour late. Another reason for the sporadic broadcasts was that, initially at least, the station's transmitter was battery powered and had to be turned off while new batteries were connected or flat ones recharged. Eventually however, the Fort's original wartime generator was repaired and put into working order, but none of the equipment used by the station was of professional broadcast standard and the poor sound quality and weak transmission signal reflected these deficiencies.

The station was off the air for over three days at the beginning of June 1964 because of a generator breakdown and rough seas had prevented an engineer reaching the Fort to carry out repairs. During those few days the station had to broadcast an emergency message, on low power, for its tender supply boat to come from Whitstable with medical aid for a DJ who was ill. The tender was unable to leave port because of the rough seas, but an RAF helicopter from Manston was scrambled and air lifted the relief DJ, Colin Dale, (real name Mills) to Margate General Hospital where he was diagnosed as suffering from food poisoning.

Shortly after this incident an appeal over the air by "Lord" Sutch for any passing fishing boats to deliver water to the Fort led to what was to become a permanent tendering arrangement for Radio Sutch and its successor station on Shivering Sands. Eric Martin, owner of a record shop - The Record Centre - in Oxford Street, Whitstable heard the appeal by David Sutch and arranged with a local boat owner to deliver supplies to the Fort. Before he knew it this one-off gesture of assistance quickly developed into a regular tendering service.

Musically Radio Sutch's output favoured rock and roll, rhythm and blues and country and western artists. During the daytime singles and EP (extended play) records predominated, but quite often during the evenings, whole sides of LPs (long playing, now more generally referred to as albums) were played without interruption from a DJ. In this respect Radio Sutch could have claimed to be Britain's first album station!

Reg Calvert used Radio Sutch to extensively promote the various artists and pop groups he managed through a partnership with Terry King and the King Agency. As well as Screaming 'Lord' Sutch and The Savages these included artists such as The Fortunes, Johnny Kidd and the Pirates, Cliff Bennett and the Rebel Rousers, The Rocking Berries, The Hulabaloos and The Outlaws. Recordings by these groups - often only demos or poor quality tapes which had been recorded live at clubs and dance halls - received a disproportionate amount of airtime on the station compared to the established, chart-listed artists of the day.

### Radio Albatros

*Reports appeared in June 1964 that another offshore radio station, Radio Albatros, was to begin broadcasting from an ex-trawler anchored in the Wash.*

*The station was intended to be local in appeal with news and events listings aimed at the target area of East Anglia*

*However despite repeated reports throughout the summer of 1964 the station never actually came on the air.*

It has been estimated that in its early weeks Radio Sutch's broadcasts only reached an area of about 50 miles radius from the Shivering Sands - the lucrative target of London was well outside its transmitter range. Reg Calvert later managed to acquire a more reliable and stronger diesel powered transmitter which he installed on the Fort and as a consequence the station's signal improved sufficiently for it to reach parts of outer London.

Radio Sutch employed no sales staff, but in order to generate some advertising revenue DJ Brian Paul obtained a tape recorder and a copy of the local Whitstable newspaper. He read out aloud and recorded all advertisements appearing in the newspaper and arranged to play them on the air, but not before he had contacted each advertiser telling them about their free 'plug' and the approximate time of broadcast.

A number of businesses were impressed with the response they received to these free commercials and bought further airtime on the station, giving it a little much needed revenue. However, over the four months life of the station there were only ever two really regular advertisers - Andy's of Whitstable (a record shop whose proprietor had connections with Calvert's music publishing business) and Cliff Davies Cars of Shepherds Bush, London who provided transport for Sutch's personal appearance tours.

Regular audience figures for Radio Sutch were never reliably obtained, but they were generally accepted to be only a few thousand compared to the millions attracted to the station's contemporary offshore competitors, Radio Caroline and Radio Atlanta.

Because of the poor quality of its transmissions and the general lack of organisation Radio Sutch never became an established or professional radio station, nor did it seriously try to do so. It was a 'fun' station run as much for the benefit of those taking part in the broadcasts as for any listeners who may have tuned in and it certainly never posed a competitive commercial threat to either Radio Caroline or Radio Atlanta, both of whom were in an entirely different league.

However, although relatively insignificant as a radio station, the importance of Radio Sutch in the history of offshore broadcasting should not be underestimated for two reasons:-

- Radio Sutch established the principle that the disused and abandoned wartime forts in the Thames Estuary made readily available and suitable bases for offshore radio stations and it was not long before other, more professionally organised, broadcasters took up this pioneering example.
- Although at first posing no competitive threat during the summer of 1964, Radio Sutch later developed into a station which did become a serious rival for Radio Caroline and the other shipborne broadcasters, driving two of those stations into a tragic conflict and eventually jeopardising the whole future of British offshore radio.

## Radio Invicta

Another broadcaster to follow Screaming 'Lord' Sutch's example and occupy a disused fort in the Thames Estuary was Radio Invicta. This station was launched by a consortium of three men - Tom Pepper (real name Harry Featherbee) (a Kent fisherman), Charles Evans (landlord of the "Oddfellows Arms" at Folkestone) and John Thompson (a journalist who had been involved in the unsuccessful Voice of Slough/GBLN project in 1962 )(see Chapter 5). However, quite soon in the life of the station Tom Pepper tried to exclude his partners from the business and this resulted in some ugly incidents involving threats of violence and damage to property.

### Radio Sutch Dance Nights

*Using Reg Calvert's promotional expertise Radio Sutch held a series of Dance Nights, first at the King's Hall, Herne Bay and later at Dreamland in Margate. At these Dance Nights many of Reg Calvert's groups performed and Radio Sutch DJs made personal appearances. Being staged at venues within Radio Sutch's limited reception area the Dance Nights attracted a good attendance from local people interested in seeing live on stage the presenters they heard on the station. Attendances were also boosted at the Margate venue by holiday makers from there and the nearby resort of Ramsgate.*

RADIO INVICTA
FOLKESTONE
KENT, ENGLAND

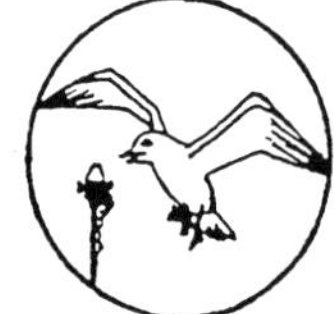

TECHNICAL
ENGINEERING
DEPARTMENT

The good Music Station on 306 metres Medium Wave.

Radio Invicta based itself on the Red Sands Fort off Whitstable in the Thames Estuary, a fort similar in construction to the one at Shivering Sands already being used by Radio Sutch. The station's broadcasts were aimed at Kent, Essex and London and test transmissions were first reported to have taken place on 3rd June 1964, just a week after Radio Sutch began its fort-based broadcasts. For the next few weeks these tests continued using various frequencies in the medium waveband and by the time regular programmes started on 17th July 1964 the station had settled on a frequency of 985kHz (306m), but the transmitter power was always low, only about 750 watts.

**Radio Invicta advertising rates**

| | |
|---|---|
| *Midnight-2.00am* | *-24* |
| *2.00-7.00am* | *-18* |
| *7.00-9.00am* | *-27* |
| *9.00-10.00am* | *-18* |
| *10.00-11.00am* | *-27* |
| *11.00-11.30am* | *-15* |
| *11.30-1.00pm* | *-27* |
| *1.00-2.00pm* | *-24* |
| *2.00-3.00pm* | *-30* |
| *3.00-5.00pm* | *-18* |
| *5.00-6.00pm* | *-27* |

*Prices were in Guineas (£1.05) and included background noises and sound effects where needed.*

Broadcast times to begin with were from 7.00am-7.00pm, but this was amended to 12midnight - 6.00pm and finally became a 13 hour schedule from 5.00am - 6.00pm. Radio Invicta's format had a bias towards middle of the road, easy listening music and proved popular with a dedicated audience in the station's small reception area, because it provided a musical alternative to the other pop based offshore stations on the air at that time.

The station, which established land-based offices at 35 Bouverie Square, Folkestone Kent, was promoted in publicity material as "The Good Music Station". Programmes carried titles such as "Date with Romance", "Memory Lane" (largely using old 78rpm records) and "Pot Luck" - a record request programme in which the listener asked for a specific record number to be played. The number supposedly corresponded to a number in the station's record library, but in fact the on-air DJ played whatever he wanted, whilst keeping up the pretence of the 'lucky number' system.

Radio Invicta had difficulty attracting advertisers and carried very few commercials, mainly ones for Houchin Electronics (whose proprietor had backed the station financially) and Nestledown Mattresses. Ironically it was Tom Pepper's desire to obtain more advertising revenue that led to tragedy for him and ultimately spelt the end of the station altogether.

**Radio Invicta Programme Schedule - August 1964**

| | |
|---|---|
| **5.00am** | **Early Morning Spin** |
| **7.00am** | **Breakfast Show** |
| **9.00am** | **Top Sticks** |
| **10.00am** | **Mail Call** |
| **11.00am** | **Strictly for Highbrows** |
| **11.30am** | **Pot Luck** |
| **12.55pm** | **Information Desk** |
| **1.00pm** | **Lunch Box** |
| **2.00pm** | **Date With Romance** *(Mon-Fri)* |
| | **A Seat in the Stalls** *(Sat and Sun)* |
| **3.00pm** | **Memory Lane** |
| **4.00pm** | **Afternoon Session** |
| **4.30pm** | **Kiddies Corner** |
| **5.00pm** | **Music for the Evening** |

## The Tower of Power - Radio City

By September 1964 Screaming 'Lord' Sutch, having been offered a concert tour in Australia and New Zealand, was no longer interested in further involvement with the radio station he had founded some four months earlier. His manager, Reg Calvert, who had been the driving force behind the project anyway, acquired Sutch's interest for £5,000 and took over complete responsibility for operating the station. Record shop owner Eric Martin, who had arranged tendering services and supplies for Sutch, became Station Controller and Manager of the new station - Radio City.

Reg Calvert had been in the pop music business since the late 1950's after a varied career which included printing, jam making and playing in dance bands. He opened a record shop, The Band Box, in Southampton in 1957 and also started promoting rock and roll shows at local venues along the south coast. This eventually led to him becoming manager for a large number of pop artists and groups and, after encountering unwelcome attention from a rival management group in Southampton, Reg Calvert moved his operation to a former stately home, Clifton Hall, in Rugby, Warwickshire.

During the first few weeks of September 1964 Reg Calvert's new station changed frequencies three times - from the former Radio Sutch frequency of 1542kHz (194m) first to 1535kHz (195m), then to 1524kHz (197m) and finally back to 1535kHz (195m), but reception of the signal was far from satisfactory.

## Radio Red Rose

*Many other businessmen explored the possibility of establishing offshore radio stations having witnessed the success of Radio Caroline. One such venture was planned by three Liverpool club owners, James Ireland, Alan Williams and Mr S Roberts, in July 1964. They hired a ship, Red Rose, and were reported to have made test transmissions for an hour and a half from a position twenty miles off Liverpool on 12th July 1964. After this broadcast the ship reportedly headed back to Amsterdam for the installation of additional equipment and an increase in its aerial height. However, although the backers announced that their station would start broadcasting 24 hours a day from the beginning of September 1964 nothing more was heard of this venture or of Radio Red Rose.*

In order to improve signal quality Calvert obtained and installed some Navy surplus transmitting equipment and on 30th September 1964 Radio City programmes started again this time on 1262kHz (238m). The station was on the air for 12 hours a day from 7.00am-7.00pm and music policy differed slightly from Radio Sutch in that more pop and chart material was broadcast, but always heavily promoting artists managed by Reg Calvert.

The station also achieved a greater degree of on-air reliability than its predecessor, with a pre-determined and advertised schedule of programmes throughout the day. The signal was of improved quality too thanks to the new transmitter and the station's broadcasts even managed to reach significant parts of London. Unfortunately, advertisers were still not attracted to Radio City as they were to the more successful Radio Caroline and the only way Calvert could find to generate income for the station was to broadcast taped American religious programmes such as "The Revival Hour", "The Voice of Prophecy" and "The Wings of Healing". The payments received for transmitting these programmes accounted for about 80% of the station's income at this time and enabled it to stay on the air despite the lack of more conventional commercial advertising.

## Radio City's first rate card, November 1964

*7 seconds -£2*
*15 seconds -£3*
*30 seconds -£5*
*45 seconds -£7*
*60 seconds -£10*

Tendering arrangements for Radio City were often haphazard - deals were made with local fishermen to deliver staff and supplies to the Shivering Sands Fort. DJs leaving the Fort often then had to accompany the fishermen on their regular fishing expeditions, lasting twelve hours or more, before arriving back on land for shore leave. Once on shore DJs had to report to a public house in Whitstable, the Wall Tavern, where Reg Calvert arranged to hand them their pay.

RADIO CITY

LONDON

7 DENMARK STREET W.C.2 · TEL. TEMPLE BAR 6303/4 & 6332/3

KENT & SUSSEX SALES DIRECTOR

OXFORD STREET · WHITSTABLE TEL. WHITSTABLE 4060

In mid-December 1964 another ex-Royal Navy transmitter was acquired by Radio City and music broadcasts were switched to 1034kHz (290m) (but announced as 299m), while the original transmitter was used to air the sponsored religious programmes on a separate frequency of 1605kHz (187m). In this way the station was able to broadcast the financially important sponsored religious programmes without interrupting the normal music output which appealed to most listeners.

## Radio London

By late November 1964 the situation off the British coast was that there were four offshore radio stations on the air ( Radio Caroline North, Radio Caroline South, Radio City and Radio Invicta) while two others (Radio Atlanta and Radio Sutch) had opened and closed during the preceding six months. With such intensive activity it might be thought no more developments would take place before the years' end, but two significant events did happen in those final weeks of 1964 involving the opening of a major new offshore station and the tragic end of another.

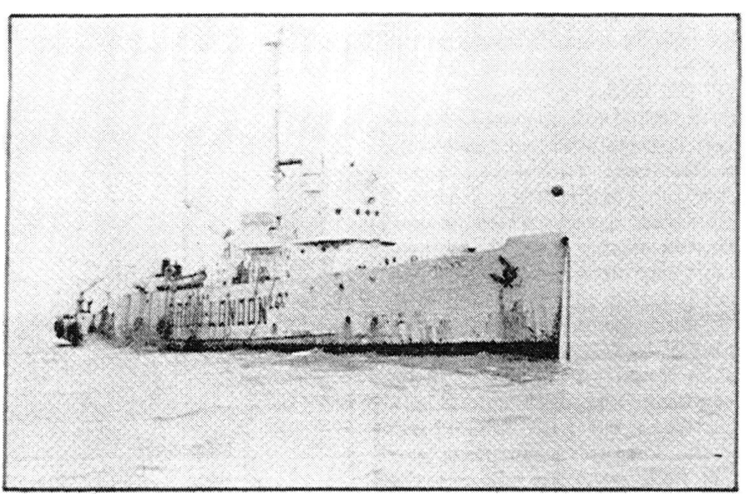

The 'Galaxy' anchored off Essex

On 19th November 1964 the former US Navy minesweeper *Galaxy* dropped anchor within sight of the Shivering Sands Fort (home of Radio City) and started test broadcasts on 725kHz (412m) and later on 926kHz (324m) using the call sign Radio London.

The ship had been fitted out as an offshore radio station in Miami, from where she sailed on 22nd October 1964. In wartime service the *Galaxy* (then known as *Density)* had rescued 500 men from a sinking ship and dealt with almost as many mines planted in vital shipping lanes. Following this service she had been converted into a cargo vessel, before going to Miami to be transformed into her new role as an offshore radio station.

### Groundings

*Although offshore radio operators tried to anchor their ships in relatively sheltered positions the vessels were always vulnerable to the forces of nature. Inevitably they (and their crews) suffered at the mercies of gales and rough seas, with countless occurrences of driftings, aerials being damaged and stations temporarily put off the air.*

*Sometimes the storms were so severe that the ships were driven ashore. There are 16 recorded occasions when offshore radio ships were grounded. Most were re-floated and returned to their position in international waters, some had to be scrapped after sustaining irreparable damage, but incredibly only one offshore radio ship sank during a storm - the Mi Amigo on 20th March 1980.*

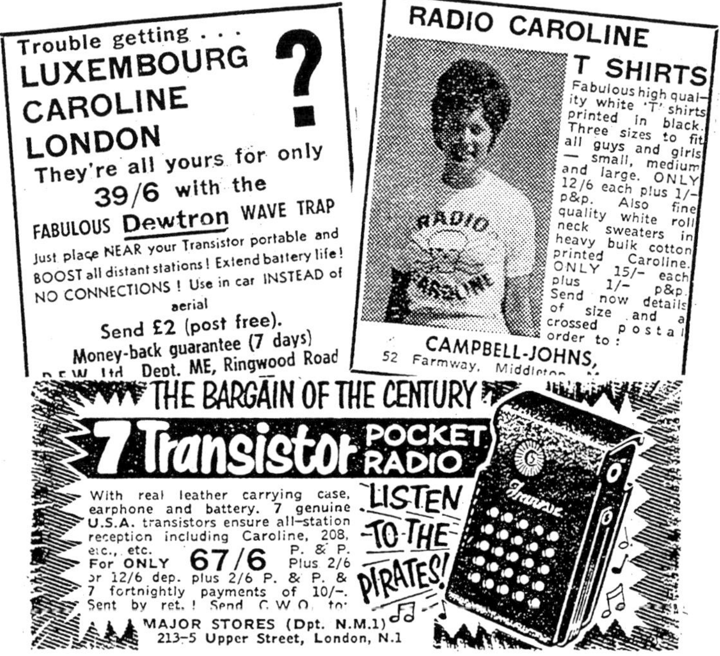

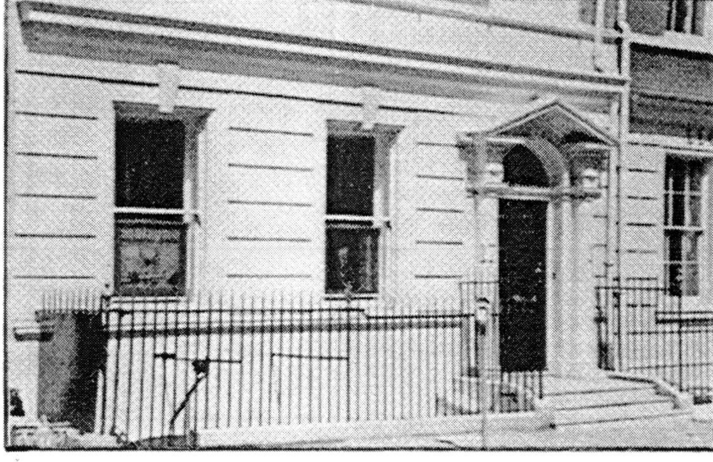

Radio London headquarters, 17 Curzon Street, London W1

The station broadcasting from the *Galaxy* was the brainchild of Don Pierson, a Texas businessman who in April 1964 had heard about the launch of Radio Caroline, paid a fact finding visit to Britain to see what offshore radio was all about and returned to the USA to develop his own project.

Radio London was run by a highly professional and well organised team and from the outset it threatened to become a serious challenger to Radio Caroline. The *Galaxy* boasted a 212' aerial mast and a powerful 50Kw transmitter enabling the station to reach most of southern England and the Midlands. Additionally, Radio London's programming and advertising sales teams were far better organised than those of its rivals and the station sounded professional and successful from the start.

Radio London's initial investors included:-

- Don Pierson, a Dallas car dealer (Dodge and Chrysler), owner of the Abeline National Bank and Mayor of Eastland, Texas
- Tom Dannaher, owner of Wichta Falls Airport
- Mal McIlwan another car agency dealer (Cadilac and Ford) and
- Jack McGlothlin, a Texas oil millionaire.

Pierson was manager of the project, McIlwan dealt with sales, McGlothlin was responsible for legal and financial arrangements while Dannaher supervised the fitting out of the ship.

Initial capital of $500,000 (£300,000) was raised by these four businessmen who between them held a controlling interest in the project, but shares were also sold to 13 other smaller investors with business backgrounds in construction, car dealing and banking.

A trust fund, Marine Investment Co. Inc. registered in Grand Bahama leased the ship from another company, Panavess Inc. of Panama for £28,000 and purchased £90,000 worth of broadcasting equipment which was later installed on the vessel in Miami. Advertising sales for Radio London were handled by a British-registered company, Radlon (Sales) Ltd. which operated from offices at 17 Curzon Street, London W1. Altogether total initial investment in the station was estimated to have been over £1.5million.

Gordon McLendon (owner of Dallas station KLIF and ex-partner in the Swedish offshore station Radio Nord) (see Chapter 3) acted as programme consultant to the new station while Mal McIlwan hired ex-advertising man Philip Birch as Radio London's Managing Director in England. These two men had known eachother from the days when Birch worked in America as an

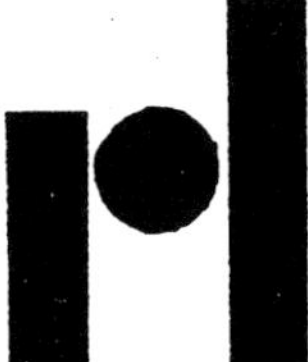

RADLON (SALES) LTD 17 CURZON STREET LONDON W1 MAYfair 5361

Directors: P. T. Birch (Managing). G. J. W. Bean T.D., F.C.A.

**Radio London's first ratecard, December 1964**

*7.00am-1.00pm £76*

*1.00pm-6.00pm £64*

*All other times £56*

*Rates for 30 second spots. 7 and 15 second spots were available pro rata.*

*Sponsored programmes were in 15 minute segments with 90 seconds of commercial time.*

account executive (mainly on the Ford Motors account) with J Walter Thompson, then the world's largest advertising agency.

Head of Sales at Radio London was Alan Keen who left Fleetway Publications, where he was Assistant Advertising Manager with *Woman's Mirror*, to join the new radio station. Another advertising professional, Dennis Maitland also joined the sales department of Radio London from book and newspaper publishers Odhams Press, where he was Advertising Manager for *Woman's Weekly* and *Housewife* magazines. He had also previously worked in advertising sales at the *Daily Mail*.

Because of the contacts Radio London had been able to establish through its experienced sales staff the station was able to go on the air with a number of 'blue chip' advertising contracts from day one, adding considerably to the station's instantly professional sound. The early successes of the sales team continued and during its first year on the air Radio London broadcast commercials for over 250 nationally known brands or products including Beechams medicines, Shell petrol, Players Richmond cigarettes, Carreras Guards cigarettes, various washing powder brands produced by Unilever and various IPC magazines including *Reveille* and *Bride*. Sponsored programmes also came from CEMA Bingo, Currys Electrical shops, Peter Stuyvesant cigarettes, Vernons Pools, Brooke Bond Tea and S and H Pink Trading Stamps.

## Radio London News

Before its launch Radio London had planned to do something no other British offshore station had attempted - provide a regular and comprehensive news service. This plan revealed the influence of the station's American programme consultant Gordon McLendon who had developed the concept at his station in Dallas and successfully introduced a similar service on the former Swedish offshore station, Radio Nord.

A number of news agencies were approached to provide the service but Reuters and Associated Press made it clear from the outset that they were not willing to provide a feed of news to Radio London. Another agency, United Press International did, however, make an offer to provide Radio London with a news service, but the cost was prohibitive and the offshore station declined to accept the proposal.

A tentative agreement was then reached with the *Sun* newspaper, which in 1964 was published by Odhams Press and was generally considered to be the mouthpiece of the British Labour Party, a very different publication from its present day descendent. However, having made an initial agreement to supply Radio London with news Odhams's solicitors then advised that, because of legal uncertainties about the status of offshore radio stations, the *Sun* should withdraw its offer. So, having failed to secure a regular supply of news from any of the recognised means Radio London had to resort to the professionally unsatisfactory, but convenient and inexpensive arrangement later adopted by all other offshore stations and pirated news from the bulletins of established broadcasters, mainly the BBC and Voice of America.

Stories of the professionalism and technical superiority of Radio London worried those managing Radio Caroline long before the MV *Galaxy* arrived off the British coast. It is now known that during the weeks before Radio London came on the air Ronan O'Rahilly, aware of the new station's superior sales expertise, approached Philip Birch suggesting a merger of the two advertising sales organisations - Caroline Sales and Radlon (Sales). From Radio London's point of view this was never taken as a serious proposition, and a response containing a series of demands which were inappropriate and unacceptable to Radio Caroline, quickly put an end to the suggestion.

However, had O'Rahilly's approach succeeded it would have been Radio Caroline which benefited most from the deal because the sale of commercial airtime was one of that station's biggest weaknesses and that defect was destined to cause the organisation some fundamental problems during the following 12 months.

## Big L sails in

Ronan O'Rahilly continued to monitor preparations being made by Radio London for a launch at the end of 1964. When the *Galaxy* arrived in the Thames Estuary and Radio London started broadcasting from the original anchorage near the Shivering Sands Fort he quickly realised it could be liable to prosecution as it was within British territorial limits. O'Rahilly advised the rival management about possible consequences for all offshore broadcasters if the new station continued broadcasting from inside territorial waters. This friendly warning was heeded and the *Galaxy* moved to an anchorage off Frinton-on-Sea, Essex, near to the *Mi Amigo,* home of Radio Caroline South, and certainly outside British territorial limits.

Test transmissions from this new position started on 5th December 1964 on 1125kHz (266m) but stopped abruptly the following day because problems were being caused by structural features within the MV *Galaxy.* The vessel, being a former minesweeper, was fitted with miles of copper wiring to help in thedetection of mines and this was having an adverse effect on the radio transmissions. Engineers had to set about fully insulating the studios and transmitters to prevent further interference to the signal and no broadcasts were heard from Radio London until 18th December 1964, this time on 1137kHz (265m).

Apparently now satisfied with the performance of all technical equipment and the strength of its signal Radio London commenced regular transmissions on 1124kHz(266m) at 6.00am on 23rd December 1964. The opening announcement was made by Pete Brady:-

*Radio London is now on the air with regular broadcasting. The station will bring to Britain the very best from Radio London's Top 40, along with the up-to-date coverage of news and weather, Radio London promises you the very best in modern radio.*

"I Could Easily Fall in Love" by Cliff Richard was the first record played on Radio London. The station, which broadcast at this time from 6.00am-9.00pm was only using about 17Kw of its potential 50Kw transmitter power. A fifth

*Radio London's first DJ team, 1964*

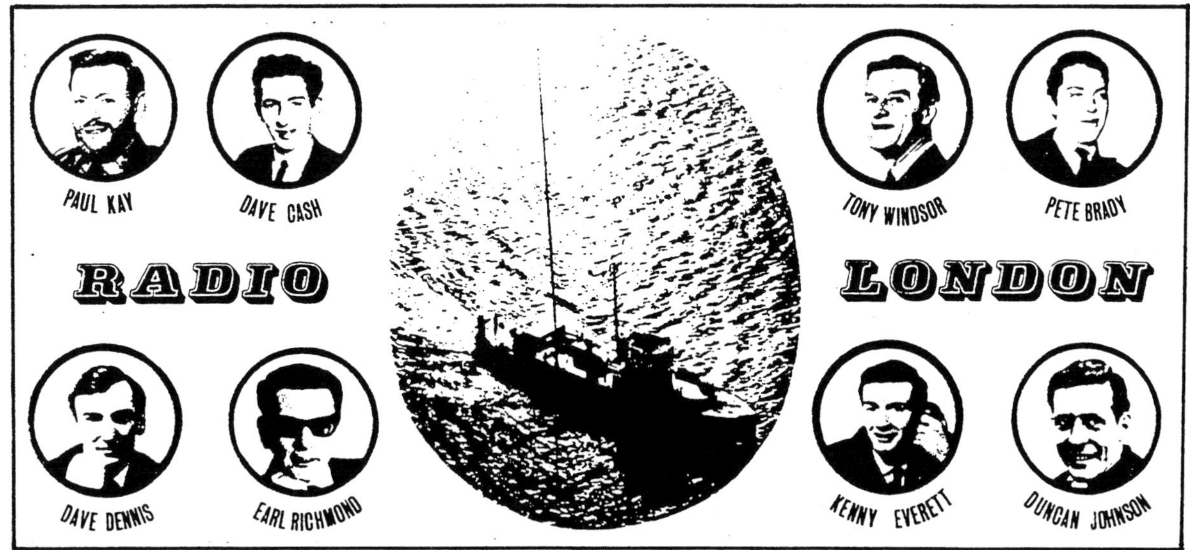

**Radio London's First Programme Schedule December 1964**

6.00am Pete Brady Breakfast Show
9.00am Earl Richmond Show
12 noo Dave Dennis Show
3.00pm Tony Windsor Show
6.00pm Kenny Everett Show
7.00pm The World Tomorrow *(sponsored religious programme)*
7.30pm Kenny Everett Show
9.00pm Closedown

*News bulletins prepared and read by Paul Kaye were broadcast each hour on the half hour, with weather on the hour.*

British offshore radio station was now on the air, less than nine months since the first ship, MV *Caroline* had dropped anchor off the Essex coast.

Radio London's format was quite strictly based on the Top 40 (known on the station as the Fab 40) with records being allocated to one of three categories which were played on a rotation basis each hour. Category A were the top ten records of the week, Category B were the remainder of the Top 40 and Category C were new releases. There were also slots in the format rotation for LP tracks and Flashbacks (old Fab 40 hits).

Initially the American backers had wanted to name the station Radio KLIF (London), the Big K, (after McLendon's station in Dallas) with tapes of the Dallas programmes being rebroadcast in an undiluted American style to an unsuspecting British audience. However, they eventually settled for a change of name to Radio London (Big L), with a watered down version of the highly Americanised Top 40 format, which it was thought would be more acceptable to British listeners.

This fundamental disagreement over format, although patched up at the time of the station's launch in 1964, was to lead quite soon to Don Pierson and some of the other initial backers withdrawing from the Radio London project to set up their own all-American format offshore radio station.

## Offshore tragedy

While Radio London was successfully launching itself as Britain's newest offshore broadcaster another station was experiencing some traumatic and dramatic times.

Early in December 1964 Radio Invicta's owner, Tom Pepper, approached the *News of the World*, which at that time was advertising quite extensively on Radio Caroline, asking the newspaper to consider buying airtime on his station. The *News of the World* agreed to one trial commercial being broadcast on 19th December 1964 and indicated that if found to be satisfactory then there was a possibility that it would purchase further airtime on Radio Invicta.

Tom Pepper considered this offer from the country's biggest circulation newspaper to be a major breakthrough for his struggling little station and wanted his Senior Announcer and Programme Director, Ed Moreno, to voice the live commercial. Moreno was off the station on shore leave at the time, but Pepper persuaded him to return to the Red Sands Fort to prepare for the commercial's transmission.

The two men left Faversham harbour in the station's 'tender', the 36' long *David*, early in the morning of 16th December 1964 after experiencing great difficulty starting the small ship's engine. After Ed Moreno, together with some fresh food supplies, had been transferred to the Fort, DJs Simon Ashley (real name Barry Hoy) and engineer Martin Shaw joined Pepper in the *David* for the return journey and some welcome Christmas shore leave. They departed from Red Sands shortly after 11.00am and those left behind on the Fort noticed that the *David's* engine again appeared to be spluttering as she disappeared into the mist.

At about 6.00pm the same day a police launch came to the Red Sands Fort and reported that Tom Pepper's body had been found near Reeves Beach, Whitstable, tied to a small wooden life raft. Ed Moreno was asked by the police to leave the Fort and formally identify Pepper's body, but before doing so he hurriedly recorded a tribute to his former boss which was aired on the station the following day. More wreckage and oil drums were later found floating in the sea near the Street Buoy, but of the three men on board the *David* that day only one other body was ever found. Even then it was several months later and had become so badly decomposed that it was only identified from a tape recording of a Radio Invicta programme found in a pocket of the clothing.

A coroner's inquest into the death of Tom Pepper (Harry Featherbee) was held on 22nd December 1964 , when an open verdict was recorded. The East Kent Coroner said he was not satisfied about the sea worthiness of the *David* and advised that there should be some sort of direct radio communication be established between the Fort and the station's landbase.

For months after this incident much rumour and speculation surrounded the circumstances of the death of the three men on board the *David* and there were even suggestions that the incident had not been just an unfortunate accident. In the immediate aftermath of the tragedy Pepper's widow and his former partners Charles Evans and John Thompson continued to operate Radio Invicta, but there were many disagreements about ownership and station policy. There was speculation in the press at the end of 1964 that The Batchelors pop group, whose records were extensively promoted on Radio Invicta, were interested in buying the station, but nothing definite ever came of this story and in February 1965 Radio Invicta quietly closed.

Altogether 1964 had been a very eventful year for British offshore radio. The first station, Radio Caroline had come on the air at the end of March, closely followed by its rival, Radio Atlanta in May. By the beginning of July these two stations had merged and with two ships Radio Caroline was able to provide a service covering large parts of England, Scotland, Wales and Ireland.

Also in May 1964 Screaming 'Lord' Sutch had taken over the ex-wartime Shivering Sands Fort in the Thames Estuary and a few months later, in September, had sold out to his manager Reg Calvert - who immediately re-launched the station as Radio City.

Another Thames Estuary Fort, Red Sands, had been taken over in June 1964 and used by Radio Invicta for a localised service to south east England, but the station suffered a tragedy in December that year when its owner and two staff were drowned.

Finally, a few days before Christmas 1964 the most powerful and professionally organised offshore station yet, Radio London, came on the air.

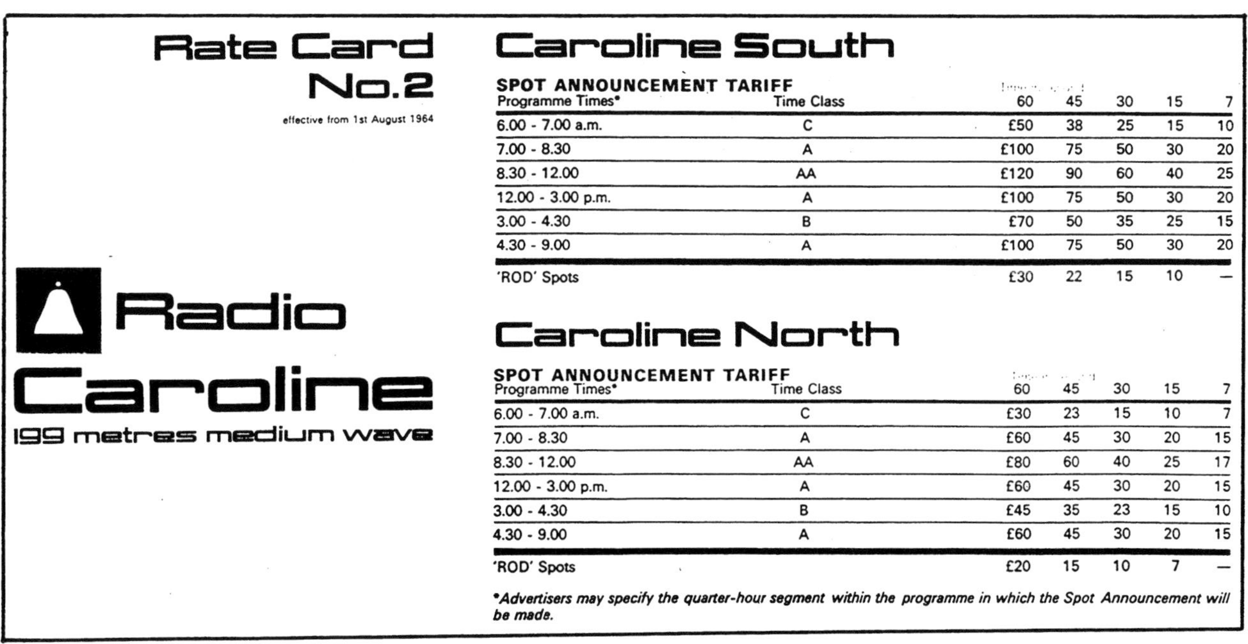

Rate Card No.2

effective from 1st August 1964

Radio Caroline

199 metres medium wave

Caroline South

SPOT ANNOUNCEMENT TARIFF

| Programme Times* | Time Class | 60 | 45 | 30 | 15 | 7 |
|---|---|---|---|---|---|---|
| 6.00 - 7.00 a.m. | C | £50 | 38 | 25 | 15 | 10 |
| 7.00 - 8.30 | A | £100 | 75 | 50 | 30 | 20 |
| 8.30 - 12.00 | AA | £120 | 90 | 60 | 40 | 25 |
| 12.00 - 3.00 p.m. | A | £100 | 75 | 50 | 30 | 20 |
| 3.00 - 4.30 | B | £70 | 50 | 35 | 25 | 15 |
| 4.30 - 9.00 | A | £100 | 75 | 50 | 30 | 20 |
| 'ROD' Spots | | £30 | 22 | 15 | 10 | — |

Caroline North

SPOT ANNOUNCEMENT TARIFF

| Programme Times* | Time Class | 60 | 45 | 30 | 15 | 7 |
|---|---|---|---|---|---|---|
| 6.00 - 7.00 a.m. | C | £30 | 23 | 15 | 10 | 7 |
| 7.00 - 8.30 | A | £60 | 45 | 30 | 20 | 15 |
| 8.30 - 12.00 | AA | £80 | 60 | 40 | 25 | 17 |
| 12.00 - 3.00 p.m. | A | £60 | 45 | 30 | 20 | 15 |
| 3.00 - 4.30 | B | £45 | 35 | 23 | 15 | 10 |
| 4.30 - 9.00 | A | £60 | 45 | 30 | 20 | 15 |
| 'ROD' Spots | | £20 | 15 | 10 | 7 | — |

**Advertisers may specify the quarter-hour segment within the programme in which the Spot Announcement will be made.*

# Chapter 9

# TV Island

While all this activity had been taking place off the British coast events connected with offshore radio in continental Europe had not remained static. When four Scandinavian Governments passed legislation outlawing offshore radio stations in 1962, Radio Syd off Sweden had defiantly continued broadcasting. Off the coast of Holland Radio Veronica had established itself as a very popular station and the politically fragmented Dutch Government was hesitant about taking any positive action to ban it.

In the early hours of 9th January 1963 the Radio Syd ship, *Cheeta,* broke her anchor chain and began drifting through pack ice towards the island of Saltholm. At 6.30am Radio Syd stopped transmissions because the crew feared that by then the ship had drifted inside Swedish territorial waters. In fact the radio ship drifted through the ice for about five hours before a tug from Limhamn was able to reach her, but by that time the *Cheeta* was moving towards the port under her own power. Nevertheless the tug assisted *Cheeta* into the Malmo Yacht Club harbour at Limhamn where she was met later that afternoon by a crowd of supporters who had gathered on the quayside.

During the severe winter of 1963 The Oresund froze solid and although no one knew it at the time it was to be four months before Radio Syd was able to return to the air because it was impossible for the *Cheeta* to leave port.

Weather conditions did eventually improve and by 1st April 1963 the *Cheeta* was able to sail again to her anchorage and resume transmissions for Radio Syd. However, the *Cheeta's* journey back to The Oresund was not without incident. As the radio ship was leaving harbour she collided with a passenger ferry, but luckily damage was minimal and the accident did not prevent her sailing to international waters off Malmo.

*Britt Wadner*

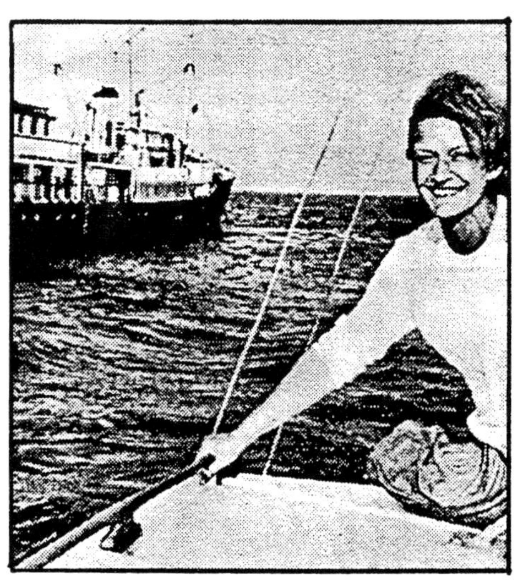

With Radio Syd continuing to broadcast it attracted large numbers of listeners and advertisers who were prepared to break the law to support the offshore station. This support was not without penalty, however. In May 1963 eleven Swedish advertisers were convicted and fined for buying airtime on Radio Syd and in October the same year Mrs. Britt Wadner, the station's owner was once again fined for allowing broadcasts to continue in defiance of the 1962 legislation.

Britt Wadner was involved in further court appearances in March and August 1964 and on the latter occasion was sentenced to one month in jail for allowing Radio Syd to continue broadcasting. Under Swedish law a prisoner is permitted to continue with his or her professional occupation while serving their jail sentence and this resulted in the bizarre circumstances of Mrs. Wadner recording programmes in her cell at Hinseberg Prison, for later transmission on Radio Syd! Despite the authorities' continued action against the station and its advertisers Radio Syd was still immensely popular in southern Sweden and the announcement of Mrs. Wadner's jail sentence in August 1964 produced a large public demonstration of support in Malmo.

## Radio Syd grounded

However, it was not the law, but the natural elements which were to silence Radio Syd for a while at the end of 1964. A storm blew up in The Oresund on 17th September 1964 during which the Radio Syd ship *Cheeta* went adrift and eventually ran aground near Malmo. The radio ship had been damaged below the waterline, but after some temporary repairs she was re-floated on the noon tide two days later and towed into Malmo where it was planned to fully repair the storm damage. She was temporarily berthed at the Kockums Mekaniska Verkstads Aktiebolag shipyard while arrangements were made for the repairs to be carried out, but during the evening of 7th October 1964 the temporary repair to her hull failed and the *Cheeta* sank at the quayside. Damage to equipment on board the radio ship was extensive and the cost of salvage would have been prohibitive, so the decision was made to scrap *Cheeta* and replace her with another vessel.

Fortunately Britt Wadner had already purchased the other former Radio Mercur vessel, *Cheeta 2,* shortly after that station had closed in August 1962. This enable Radio Syd to return to the air within a very short time - less than two weeks - of its original vessel sinking in Malmo.

## Dutch offshore competition

Meanwhile, off the Dutch coast Radio Veronica continued to flourish throughout 1963, attracting larger audiences and increasing numbers of advertisers who were willing to commit large sums from their budgets to mount campaigns on the station, in the apparent absence of any Government action being taken to silence it. In 1964 the Veronica Top 40 chart was introduced, as were some live programmes from the *Borkum Riff,* all of which added considerably to the vibrant sound of the station in contrast to the state broadcasting network and further increased its popularity in Holland.

Towards the end of 1963 elaborate plans were being made for a new radio and television station based, not on a ship this time, but on a man-made structure similar to a small scale oil drilling platform. At the time there was considerable public dissatisfaction with the programme output of the Dutch state television system, NTS, and a group of Dutch businessmen decided to establish their own station to provide a more exciting and entertaining service for viewers.

Businessman I. P. Heerema and Rotterdam shipbuilder Cornelius (Cor) Verolme, together with business colleagues Joseph Brandel and M Minderop formed a company - Reklame Exploitatie Maatschappij - more usually known as REM, which was to own and operate the twin broadcasting stations. Further capital for the project was raised from a share issue to the public handled by the Teixeira de Mattos Bank, on behalf of an organisation named Volksaandelen Trust (People's Share Trust). This public share issue was thirty times oversubscribed.

The company's main objective was to provide an offshore commercial television service for a large area of Holland, hence the need for a stable structure from which to operate. Their oil platform style structure, which became

### Dutch Television in 1964

*The Dutch state television service, Nederlandse Televisie Stichting (NTS) was owned by the Government who provided the studio and transmitter facilities. These facilities were then contracted out to six organisations, formed and financed by mainly religious groups in Holland who then provided the actual programme material broadcast by the service. These programme contractors received income from Government grants and subscriptions raised by members of the various groups or societies.*

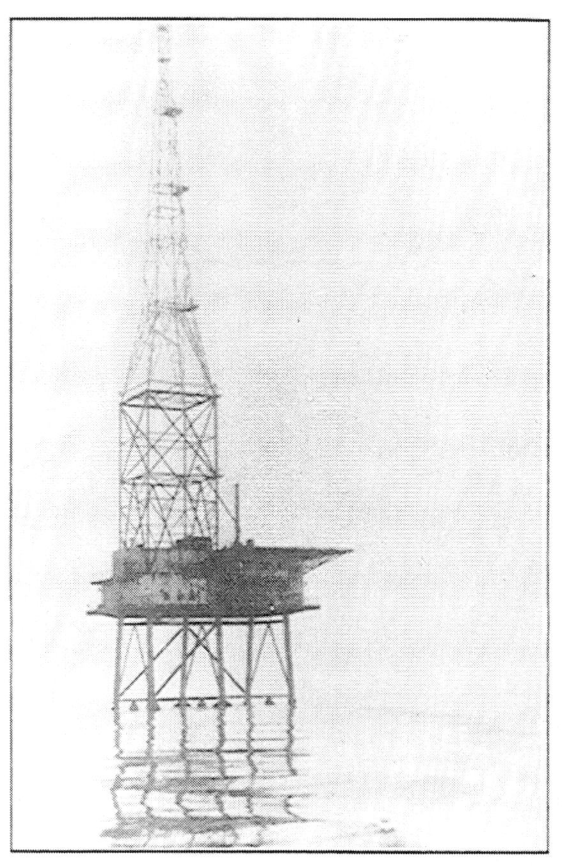

REM Island off Noordwijk

known as the REM Island, was unique in offshore broadcasting history, being purpose designed and built in prefabricated sections, using the shipbuilding experience and facilities of a yard in Cork, Ireland owned by Cor Verlome.

The prefabricated sections were transported from Ireland on the MV *Global Adventurer* in May 1964, but the project nearly faced an early disaster when a dockside crane collapsed across the ship as it was being loaded in Cork harbour. The *Global Adventurer* had to sail from Ireland with the wreckage of the crane across her decks, calling in at Southampton to have it removed before continuing her voyage to a position in international waters six miles off Noordwijk on the Dutch coast where the artificial Island was to be erected.

Similar in appearance to a North Sea oil rig, the legs of the REM Island were sunk through a 60' depth of water into the sea-bed and then filled with concrete. The main platform containing the living accommodation and studios was 40' above sea level, with the huge transmitter mast towering over 360' above sea level. The whole 'Island' measured about 40' x 80' with a helipad situated on top of the accommodation building so that supplies and programme tapes could be brought out to the station even during rough sea conditions.

Accommodation on the 'Island' consisted of a dormitory, kitchen, dining room, control room , generator room, crew cabins and a radio studio as well as a small television presentation suite comprising a studio used for broadcasting continuity announcements, on screen captions and station identifications a telecine equipment room and a control room. The 'Island' was staffed by a crew of seven maintenance engineers, mostly Belgians, and seven radio/television engineers (on contract from a British based company, Sicra Ltd.) who worked on a two week on , one week off rota.

## Radio and TV Noordzee

Construction of the 'Island' was completed during the night of 4/5th June 1964 and the broadcasting equipment was installed by communications giants RCA, after Pye the first company approached to equip the station, had refused the contract because they considered the offshore television and radio project to be unfeasible.

Test transmissions for the radio station on board REM Island started on 19th July 1964 on 1071kHz (280m) moving after a few days to 1485kHz (202m). On 23rd July the frequency was changed yet again to 1400kHz (214m) which proved to be more satisfactory and so on 29th July 1964, following an opening announcement in English, regular broadcasts under the call sign Radio Noordzee started in Dutch. The English announcement said:-

*Hello listeners in Holland. This is Radio Noordzee. This is the voice of the REM Island direct from Radio Noordzee. This is Radio Noordzee.*

Radio Noordzee then broadcast daily between 9.00am and 6.15pm with programmes of popular and chart music.

Having achieved the launch of their radio station and in the process generating a considerable amount of interest and press publicity the backers set about

## TV Noordzee

*Broadcasts from TV Noordzee were confined to the evening and late night hours, usually 6.30pm-8.00pm and 10.00pm- 11.30pm, with a one hour transmission on Sunday mornings. Programme content included many syndicated English and American series:- "The Saint", "Robin Hood", "William Tell", "Ben Casey" and "Rin Tin Tin", "The Invisible Man", "Supercar", "Wagon Train", "Mr. Ed", "The Bob Cummings Show", "My Three Sons", "Leave it to Beaver", "Victory at Sea", "87th Precinct", and "The New Breed", all with Dutch subtitles.*

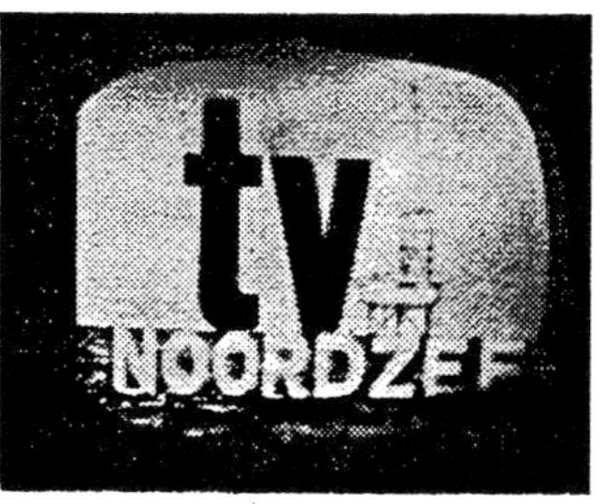


fulfilling their main objective, the opening of an offshore commercial television service. Television test transmissions, under the call sign TV Noordzee, started on 15th August 1964 at 6.30pm on channel E11, directed at a primary reception area which contained an estimated 750,000 television sets. Reception reports were received from over 100 miles inland and a public opinion poll carried out at the end of August 1964 showed that one third of all Dutch households owning a television set within the reception area had tuned into TV Noordzee at some time during the first week of test transmissions.

Regular television broadcasts started officially on 1st September 1964 at 6.30pm. The first commercial broadcast was for Johnson's Pledge furniture polish and other advertisers on that first night including Macleans toothpaste, Brylcreem hairdressing cream and Dubonnet wine, as well as some products from major Dutch-based companies.

Joe Brandel, who had experience working on television in America was the station's General Manager and Lloyd Williams Associates, a London based agency advised on programme buying.

Commercials were recorded on 16mm cine film and spliced into the programmes which were also obtained from distributors on cine film in the land-based studios before being sent out to the station, generally a week in advance of transmission. Although video tape was still in its development stages in 1964 the station planned to eventually install facilities to handle this new means of recording programmes and even had plans to construct a presentation studio in Amsterdam with video facilities.

As an incentive to buy airtime on the new, unfamiliar commercial television station advertisers were given an introductory 33% discount on the published ratecard rates which varied between £600 and £900 per minute. Even with these discounts advertising revenue for TV Noordzee was said to have been in excess of £100,000 during the first full month of broadcasting. Although such discounts were available on airtime booked until May 1965, it was estimated from the response received to the initial broadcasts that the operation would be profitable within a year - recouping £1.5million of capital investment

## Government Action

The Dutch Government, which since 1960 had been remarkably tolerant of Radio Veronica's broadcasts, took an entirely different view about the new, more powerful television and radio station located on the REM Island. They were furious that such a powerful broadcaster could establish what appeared to be a permanent base off the coast and beam programmes to millions of Dutch homes. Although Radio and TV Noordzee programmes were confined to entertainment the Government really feared that the REM Island transmitter, or another similar operation, could be used for political propaganda purposes.

## Radio and TV Noordzee staff

*Only six people (in addition to secretaries and typists) operated Radio and TV Noordzee from its landbased headquarters:-*

*Joe Brandel, General Manager of REM who was under contract to launch the stations*

*Dick Harris, Programme Director*

*Almer Tjepkema, Production Controller*

*Andre Gottmer, Public Relations*

*Willy Hougenbirk, Advertising Controller*

*Guy Bloomer, Programme Adviser representing London based Lloyd Williams Associates*

The main argument was not over the existence of a commercial television service - some members of parliament wanted advertising on television - but they wanted to exert control over who provided the service. This was largely because the broadcasting organisations on the state system at the time had strong connections with the political parties and did not want to lose control to an independent, commercial organisation such as REM.

On 16th September 1964 the Lower House of the Dutch Parliament, the Second Chamber began to discuss the situation and the following day it was decided by 114 votes to 19 to introduce legislation which would bring the artificial island within Dutch territorial limits.

In order to achieve this objective the Government proposed to rely on the 1958 United Nations Geneva Convention, which defined the limits of a 'continental shelf' over which coastal states could exercise sovereignty. Under this Convention a country could extend its boundaries out to sea for a distance of up to 200 miles, relying on the extent to which the submerged landmass ('continental shelf") adjoining the coast projected seawards. Any physical structure supported by part of the sea-bed which formed this 'continental shelf', whether inside or outside the limits of territorial waters, would then come under the jurisdiction of that country.

By first ratifying the 1958 Geneva Convention (to which Holland was not even an original signatory) and then enacting its own legislation - the North Sea Equipment Act 1964, the Dutch Government was thus able to bring the REM Island within its jurisdiction. Many other European countries had invoked the provisions of the Geneva Convention to claim sovereignty over oil and gas deposits found beneath the North Sea, but it had not previously been invoked with the specific intention of silencing an offshore broadcasting station.

The Dutch Minister of Justice, Dr. Scholten, said he hoped the REM organisation would voluntarily cease broadcasting once the Bill became law. Speaking in the same debate the Minister of Education, Arts and Sciences, Dr. T Bot, promised a radical alteration of the Dutch radio and television services, possibly involving the introduction of advertising and allowing private companies to establish stations.

## Radio and TV Noordzee become TROS

About six weeks before the new legislation was expected to come into effect the assets of TV Noordzee were transferred to a British company, High Seas Television Ltd., of London. This holding company, owned by Eric Bent, director of a London based printing company, had a nominal share capital of £100 and was authorised by REM to operate the television station and determine its daily programme schedule. At the same time ownership of the REM Island itself was transferred to a Panamanian registered company - Expoitatacion De Construcciones Martitima Excomarsa.

Having transferred, on paper at least, ownership of both the structure and the broadcasting operation Radio and TV Noordzee's owners argued that, although the artificial Island was built on the 'continental shelf' the companies owning the structure and the stations broadcasting from it were both foreign and therefore Dutch broadcasting laws could not be enforced against them. As a precaution, however, they took out an insurance policy for 9 million Dutch Guilders (£900,000) through Lloyds of London against the risk of any physical seizure of the 'Island' by the Dutch authorities.

At about the same time that the assets of REM were transferred to new owners a new organisation - Televisie en Radio Omreop Stichting (TROS) was formed by some of the people behind the REM Project with the objective of applying for a temporary licence to transmit from the artificial Island. In the six weeks between its formation and the passing of the new Dutch legislation TROS enrolled over 200,000 members, which qualified it as an organisation able to apply for such a licence under the Dutch broadcasting system.

In the run-up to the introduction of legislation the REM organisation had insisted that if it were forced to close transmissions it would take the Dutch Government to the International Court. However, the length of time it would have taken to haer this case,and the promised introduction of commercial television and radio in Holland (which in fact did not happen for many more years) would have meant the reason for Radio and Television Noordzee's existence had disappeared hence the formation of TROS to try and claim a foothold in the legal broadcasting system.

The hope was that TROS, broadcasting with a temporary licence from the REM Island would be in a position to benefit from the grant of a permanent licence when the promised review of Dutch broadcasting took place. An alternative strategy was also devised - AVRO, the oldest broadcasting organisation in the Dutch system offered REM three hours a week of airtime on its NTS allocation to transmit TV Noordzee programmes.

The television station from the REM Island was extremely popular with the public - 80% of the population was shown in a Gallup poll to be against banning the station and two other public opinion organisations also confirmed that the audience for TV Noordzee was rapidly expanding.

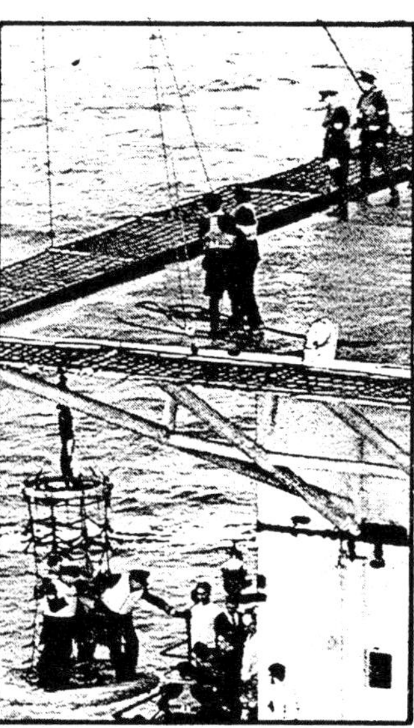

Police board the REM Island

Nevertheless the Dutch Government vigorously pursued its opposition to the offshore television (and radio) station housed on the REM Island and legislation giving effect to an extension of sovereignty over the continental shelf and any structures built on it was passed in the Dutch Senate, by 57 votes to 9, on 1st December 1964, becoming law twelve days later. The new law had been designed specifically to close Radio and TV Noordzee and did not apply to Radio Veronica, which by December 1964 had been on the air for four and a half years, because that was a ship-based station and not permanently attached to the continental shelf.

In compliance with the new legislation TV Noordzee in fact ceased transmissions on 12th December 1964, after only three and a half months on the air - such was the speed with which the Dutch Government had acted to silence it. However, Radio Noordzee did continue to broadcast in defiance of the law and Cor Verolme instructed crew on board the REM Island not to physically repel any official boarders who may be sent to close the station as this could jeopardise the insurance cover which had been taken out for such an eventuality.

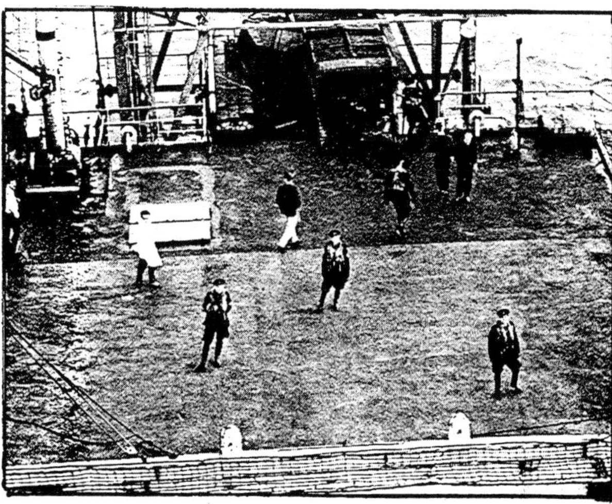

## Raid

After five days of Radio Noordzee broadcasting in defiance of the new law the Dutch authorities decided to act.They had delayed action the day after the new law came into effect because of bad weather and then information was received that the REM Island now belonged to a Panamanian company. The broadcasting rights were also held by the British company, High Seas Television Ltd who at that stage were threatening legal action against the Dutch authorities.

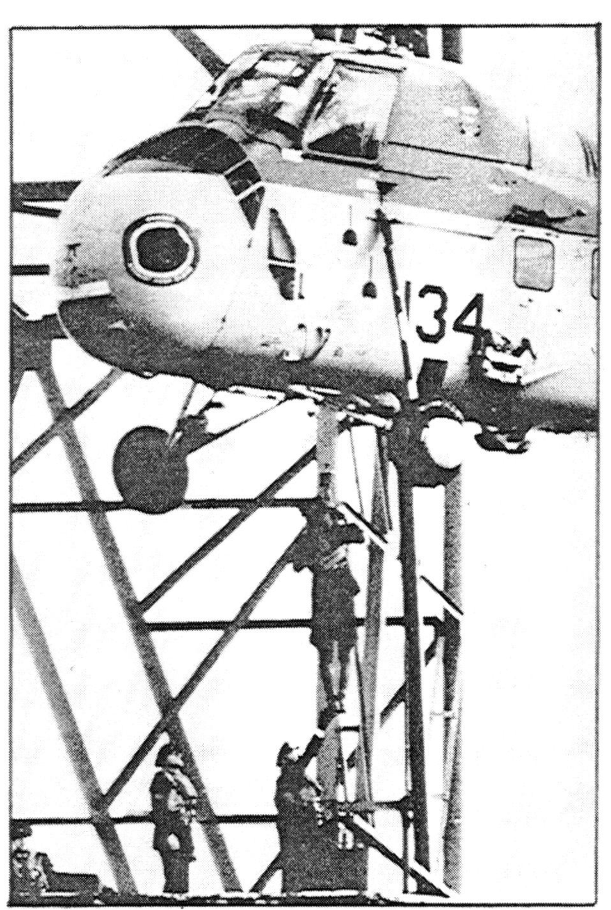

A helicopter lands police on the REM Island

The Dutch Naval vessel, *Delftshaven* took up position 200 yards from the REM Island at approximately 8.58am on Thursday, 17th December 1964. Five minutes later three helicopters appeared and hovered overhead, the first dropped a marker flare onto the rooftop helipad and at 9.03am the other two landed a force of armed police on the artificial Island. At 9.07am transmissions of Radio Noordzee were abruptly silenced by the authorities in the middle of the record "Paradiso" by Anneke Gronloh during a programme presented by Sonja van Proosdjijk .

Radio Noordzee's closure and the confiscation of its broadcasting equipment was carried out under the personal supervision of J F Hartsuijker, Amsterdam's Assistant Public Prosecutor, who had arrived on board the *Delftshaven.*

Both Radio and TV Noordzee had proved highly popular with audiences and advertisers alike and during the three and a half months the two stations were on the air advertising income exceeded £300,000 - all at the reduced introductory rates. However, an estimated £7m of investment in the People's Share Trust subsequently disappeared without explanation and the Teixeira de Mattos Bank went into liquidation shortly after the offshore stations' enforced closure. A director of the Bank was later jailed and for many years afterwards there were various rumours and accusations in Dutch financial circles about fraudulent activity in connection with the operation of the stations.

The loss of Radio, and especially TV, Noordzee was not just one felt by audiences. The Dutch film industry, which had benefitted substantially from the television station's existence, lost a large amount of work in producing commercials and continuity announcements, while the Dutch advertising industry lost the opportunity to generate income from the sale of airtime to clients as well as the investment many agencies had made in television commercial production facilities.

The REM Island itself was maintained after the closure of the broadcasting stations and was advertised for sale in October 1965. Although never used for radio or television broadcasts again it still stands today and has been used for a number of other purposes from weather monitoring to a training base for oil rig workers.

In 1965 the TROS organisation which had been founded by investors involved in the REM Project acquired the right to airtime on the legal Dutch radio and television networks, and has since become one of Holland's most respected broadcasting organisations.

# Chapter 10

# More Expansion

Off the British coast as 1965 dawned both Radio Caroline stations were undoubtedly market leaders in offshore commercial radio, but Caroline South's position was about to be seriously challenged by Radio London, which had arrived just before Christmas 1964.

Radio City was also starting to establish itself as a minor challenger to both Caroline South and Radio London, but the other fort-based station, Radio Invicta, was going through a crisis following the drowning of its owner and two staff in December 1964, and it eventually closed quietly in February 1965.

Radio Caroline North started the new year with some problems caused by rough weather on the night of 13th/14th January 1965 when the starboard anchor chain snapped. With the other anchor unable to hold in the severe storm, the MV *Caroline* began to drift, but eventually the Captain managed to manoeuvre the ship so that she remained outside territorial waters and rode out the storm. Within a week a new one and a half ton anchor and four and a half ton chain were installed on board the radio ship.

## Strasbourg Convention

A Labour Government had been returned in the October 1964 British General Election and consequently a new Postmaster General, Mr. Anthony Wedgewood Benn was now in charge of matters appertaining to offshore radio stations. For the first few months of his period in office he continued his predecessor's procrastination over dealing with the 'problem' of offshore broadcasters, always arguing that there were higher legislative priorities and that concerted action by all European Governments was the way forward.

The first step towards achieving this action came on 22nd January 1965 when member states of the Ministerial Committee of the Council of Europe signed "The European Agreement for the Prevention of Broadcasts Transmitted from Stations Outside National Territories" more commonly known as the Strasbourg Convention. Under the terms of this Convention any state which signed or later ratified it agreed to also enact domestic legislation to prohibit the establishment of offshore broadcasting stations and to prevent any collaboration with such stations by their citizens. The Strasbourg Convention applied to any ships, aircraft or other floating or airborne objects under the jurisdiction of a particular country, but importantly it did not go so far as to permit action to be taken directly by one state against ships, aircraft or citizens of another. It was, however, open to individual countries, once they had ratified the Convention, to legislate through their own parliaments to ban offshore stations broadcasting from off their coasts.

Although British legislation did not come before parliament immediately after the signing of the Strasbourg Convention the issue of offshore radio was raised

### Sir Winston Churchill's Funeral

*Britain's wartime Prime Minister, Sir Winston Churchill, died in January 1965 and in recognition of the significant contribution he had made to the destiny of the nation he was accorded a State Funeral - almost unprecedented for a person who was not a member of the Royal Family. The State Funeral took place on 24th January 1965 - a Saturday - and while the BBC Radio services carried a commentary and coverage of the service and subsequent tributes the two main offshore radio stations paid their own tribute to the former statesman. Radio London actually closed during the funeral service, then played classical music and recorded tributes for a large part of the remainder of the day. Radio Caroline also played classical music and broadcast its own documentary detailing the major events of Churchill's life, but unlike Radio London the station remained on the air all day.*

**Racing Teams**

*In association with the British Racing and Sports Car Club Radio Caroline sponsored a Clubman's Sports Car Formula Championship during 1965, presenting trophies to the first three in the championship and a cash prize to the winner. The station also exhibited a Formula III Brabham at the Racing Car Show in 1965.*

*Radio London also operated its own competitive car racing team during the year.*

in the House of Commons in March 1965. The Postmaster General was asked for details of instances where interference had been caused to legitimate broadcasters by offshore radio stations. In a written reply he detailed 19 cases where offshore stations had allegedly caused interference to maritime communications and in seven of these Radio Caroline was identified as the culprit, an allegation which was later hotly disputed by the station's management and technical experts.

Despite the moves in European parliamentary circles to start the process of outlawing offshore radio a milestone was reached at Easter 1965 when Radio Caroline celebrated its first birthday. To mark the occasion the station introduced four 'Bell Awards' which were presented to various artists for their contribution to musical entertainment during the preceding twelve months. Recipients were -

The Animals - best group record of the year ("House of the Rising Sun")

The Beatles - best and most consistent artists

Petula Clark - best female recording ("Downtown")

Tom Jones - best male recording ("It's not Unusual")

Birthday messages and greetings from over twenty artists were also recorded and included in programmes on both the North and South Caroline stations during the Easter weekend.

## Caroline 'Goodguys' revamp

At the end of its first year on the air, in March 1965, Radio Caroline had achieved advertising income of £294,000, with estimated running costs put at between £100,000 and £150,000. This was a significant achievement in a market environment largely unfamiliar with the use of radio as an advertising medium. Unfortunately for the station , much of this advertising revenue had been earned during its first nine months, prior to the arrival in late December 1964 of Radio London. The impact of this new rival can be demonstrated by advertising revenue figures for March 1965 which show that Caroline South was struggling to achieve an average income of just £1,000 per week. The growing popularity and professionalism of Radio London contrasted strongly with the weaknesses of Radio Caroline's management structure and commercial airtime sales techniques. These deficiencies were to cause further internal problems at Radio Caroline later in the year.

*A trade promotion for air-time sales by Radio Caroline, making use of early listenership survey findings*

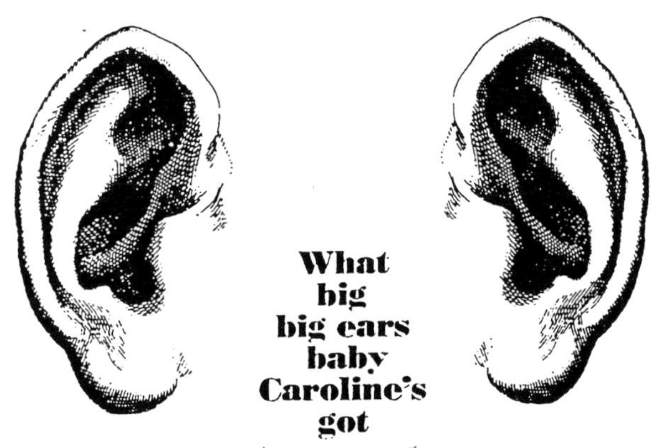


Believe it or not, Radio Caroline is only *one* year old, this Sunday. Yet Caroline's ears have grown out of all proportion to her years. Attwood currently puts her weekly audience at 12·5 million ears (pairs) per week. Why not buy some? At 5d a thousand (pairs) they're a snip. Ring Michael Parkin at HYD 9721.

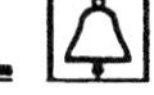


Radio Caroline's management decided to revamp the station's tired and out-dated format - something which had never been addressed before - in the face of stiff competition from newcomer Radio London. A news service, Caroline Newsbeat, was introduced in April 1965 and in May the Caroline South DJs were re-launched as personality "Caroline Goodguys", modelled on a similar successful initiative by one of New York's most popular music stations of the mid- sixties, WMCA. But most importantly programme content was changed to a format based on the "Sound 65" chart (to rival Radio London's "Fab 40") although this was later changed to the "Caroline Countdown of Sound", a Top 50 chart.

Both Caroline stations also began to broadcast an hour long programme each evening between 6.00 and 7.00pm sponsored by Roulette Records, which was pre-recorded in New York and hosted by the legendary American DJ, Jack Spector from station WMCA in New York.

The revamp of Radio Caroline's format resulted in increased interest from audiences and advertisers. An indication of the dramatic decline in Radio Caroline's advertising revenue after the arrival of Radio London in December 1964 and of a revitalisation after the format changes in April 1965 can be seen from these monthly advertising income figures:-

November/December 1964 £47,952 (before Radio London arrived)

December1964/January 1965 -£28,721} (after Radio London's initial
January/February 1965 -£32,558 }broadcasts)

March/April 1965 -£32,341} (after the revamp of Radio Caroline's
April/May 1965 - £49,259 } format and presentation style)

Unfortunately this sudden transformation in style and format - effectively an Americanisation of the station, diluted for the benefit of British listeners - did not come across to the audience in quite the way it was intended. The Caroline DJs, or "Goodguys" were uncomfortable with their new image and many of the sponsored programmes on the station at that time conflicted both in content and presentational style with the hurriedly introduced psuedo-American format.

The simple reason for this was that during late 1964, before Radio London's launch, Caroline had succeeded in selling a large number of 15 and 30 minute sponsored shows which were produced directly by advertising agencies (mainly J Walter Thompson and S H Benson) on behalf of their clients. The sponsors included significant national brands such as Player's Anchor cigarettes, Andrews Liver Salts, Princes Foods, Chappell Pianos, Fynon Liver Salts and Miners Make-up and so gave the station a deal of respectability as well as much needed income. The problem was, however, that nearly all these programmes were hosted by well known 'establishment' personalities such as Anne Shelton, Kenneth Horne, Stirling Moss and Vera Lynn, who were more likely to have been heard at the time on the staid and dated BBC Light Programme than a vibrant, youthful offshore radio station.

Many of the contracts were for daily or weekly segments to be broadcast over periods of 13 or 26 weeks - well into 1965 and after the station's format change. Radio Caroline itself had little or no direct input into either the musical content or presentation of these sponsored segments and when they were inserted into the station's own revitalised live programming the two styles inevitably clashed. Although very lucrative financially for Radio Caroline these programmes were probably responsible, in the south at least, for large numbers of listeners re-tuning their radios to a rival station and a radio audience once lost is notoriously difficult to recapture.

## Big L

Despite its perceived success everything was not immediately perfect at Radio London either. To the average listener the station sounded far more professional and, more importantly, in touch with their current musical tastes than any other offshore broadcasters. However, during the station's first few weeks on the air many of the DJs struggled with the presentation of Radio London's American style Top 40 format. Nevertheless Radio London still came across as a more listenable station, particularly in comparison to Radio Caroline South, which in the early months of 1965 was suffering from an identity crisis due to a lack of a clearly defined programme format.

On 19th April 1965 the crews of both Radio Caroline South and Radio London played a significant part in the rescue of a USAF pilot who was forced to ditch in the North Sea. The Captain of the tender was manoeuvring away from the *Mi Amigo* when he saw a parachute floating out of the sky about three quarters of a mile away from the radio ship. Flight Lieutenant John Wynn's plane, a F.101 Voodoo Tactical Jet, had developed engine trouble on the return leg of a practice flight from its base in Laon, France. The pilot was forced to eject from his plane and when he hit the sea he injured his back and was temporarily knocked unconscious. The tender diverted to the scene of the crash and recovered Flight Lieutenant Wynn from the sea before heading to the *Galaxy* to change crew and deliver supplies to Radio London. With the injured pilot still on board the tender then made its way to Harwich where an ambulance was waiting to take the airman to hospital

Radio London started to promote 'Disc Shows' at London's Marquee Club, in Wardour Street during the summer of 1965. These Shows, which were hosted by Radio London DJs, on shore leave were in fact forerunners of what would now be called discos and were staged between 2.30pm and 5.30pm each Saturday afternoon. Big L Fan Club members were entitled to a reduced admission charge on production of their Club membership card.

## DATELINE DIAMONDS

*During the summer of 1965 the Radio London ship, Galaxy, became the set for a film - "Dateline Diamonds". The film's storyline centred around a blackmailer who also became involved in diamond smuggling operations using a fictitious offshore radio station as a base.*

*The film starred William Lucas, Kenneth Cope, George Mikell, Conrad Phillips, Patsy Rowlands and Anna Carteret. Radio London DJ Kenny Everett also appeared in many scenes.*

*Dateline Diamonds was directed by Jeremy Sumners, produced by Harold Shampan and Harry Benn with screenplay by Tudor Gates. Music in the film was supplied by The Small Faces, The Chantelles and Kiki Dee.*

**MARQUEE CLUB** — **JUNE 1965 PROGRAMME**

90, WARDOUR STREET, LONDON, W.1. (GER 8923)

| Day | Date | Programme |
|---|---|---|
| Tues. | 1st | THE MOODY BLUES.<br>The Muleskinners. |
| Wed. | 2nd | THE SETTLERS.<br>The Virginians.<br>The Merrydown Folk. |
| Thur. | 3rd | LONG JOHN BALDRY<br>and the Hoochie Coochie Men.<br>ALEX HARVEY and his Soul Band. |
| Fri. | 4th | Gary Farr and the T-BONES<br>and supporting group. |
| Sat. | 5th | JOHNNY DANKWORTH<br>and his Orchestra with Bobby Breen.<br>DICK MORRISSEY Quartet<br>featuring Phil Seamen. |
| Sun. | 6th | CLOSED. |
| Mon. | 7th | THE WHO.<br>Jimmy James and THE VAGABONDS. |
| Tues. | 8th | THE YARDBIRDS.<br>Mark Leeman Five. |
| Wed. | 9th | THE SETTLERS.<br>The Dedicated Men.<br>Alan Rogers' Ragtimers. |
| Thur. | 10th | LONG JOHN BALDRY<br>and the Hoochie Coochie Men.<br>ALEX HARVEY and his Soul Band. |
| Fri. | 11th | Gary Farr and the T-BONES<br>and supporting group. |
| Sat. | 12th | DICK MORRISSEY Quartet<br>featuring Phil Seamen.<br>Special Guest: IAN HAMER.<br>RONNIE ROSS Quartet. |
| Sun. | 13th | "NEW FACES"<br>featuring a number of Britain's exciting new jazz musicians.<br>Members 5/-, Non-members 6/-. |
| Mon. | 14th | SOLOMON BURKE.<br>Jimmy James and THE VAGABONDS.<br>MIKE COTTON SOUND.<br>Members 6/-, Non-members 8/6. |
| Tues. | 15th | SPENCER DAVIS GROUP.<br>Mark Leeman Five. |
| Wed. | 16th | THE SETTLERS.<br>The Dedicated Men.<br>Alan Rogers' Ragtimers. |
| Thur. | 17th | LONG JOHN BALDRY<br>and the Hoochie Coochie Men.<br>ALEX HARVEY and his Soul Band. |
| Fri. | 18th | Gary Farr and the T-BONES<br>and supporting group. |
| Sat. | 19th | DICK MORRISSEY Quartet<br>featuring Phil Seamen.<br>TONY KINSEY QUINTET. |
| Sun. | 20th | "SUNDAY SPECTACULAR"<br>with TOMMY QUICKLY<br>and the REMO 4<br>and Special Guests.<br>Members 5/-, Non-members 7/6. |
| Mon. | 21st | Jimmy James and THE VAGABONDS.<br>RONNIE JONES and the Blue Jays. |
| Tues. | 22nd | To be announced. |
| Wed. | 23rd | THE SETTLERS.<br>The Dedicated Men.<br>Alan Rogers' Ragtimers. |
| Thur. | 24th | LONG JOHN BALDRY<br>and the Hoochie Coochie Men.<br>ALEX HARVEY and his Soul Band. |
| Fri. | 25th | Gary Farr and the T-BONES.<br>The Crow. |
| Sat. | 26th | DICK MORRISSEY Quartet<br>featuring Phil Seamen.<br>Special Guest: KEN WRAY.<br>RONNIE ROSS Quartet. |
| Sun. | 27th | By Popular Demand (7.30 and 9.30 p.m.):<br>"JAZZ ON A SUMMER'S DAY"<br>(The best film on jazz) with supporting cartoon programme.<br>Members 4/-, Non-Members 6/-.<br>Tickets available in advance. |
| Mon. | 28th | Jimmy James and THE VAGABONDS<br>and supporting group. |
| Tues. | 29th | SPENCER DAVIS GROUP.<br>Mark Leeman Five. |
| Wed. | 30th | DUTCH SWING COLLEGE BAND.<br>THE SETTLERS.<br>Members 6/-, Non-members 7/6. |

*(All programmes are subject to alteration.)*

**RADIO LONDON'S DISC SHOW**

This popular series of Saturday afternoon record shows run in conjunction with *Radio London* and compered by their own team of disc jockeys will continue throughout June with top popsters as special guests. The sessions run from 2.30 to 5.30 and have proved tremendously popular with the fans. Admission: Members 3/-, Non-members 4/-.

TUESDAYS at 8.15-8.45 p.m.

**READY, STEADY, RADIO**

Top Line Recording Artists will be featured on this *Radio Luxembourg* show introduced by Keith Fordyce and Dee Shenderry.

## Radio City expansion plans

Over on Shivering Sands Fort Radio City was fast becoming a significant rival in the battle for offshore radio audiences. Whilst not achieving the level of advertising income of either Radio Caroline or Radio London, it was nevertheless earning over £20,000 a month, mainly from sponsored American religious programmes. With running costs of only £2,500 a month Radio City claimed to be so successful financially that its owner Reg Calvert explored the possibility of opening a second fort-based service, using another of the abandoned Thames Estuary Forts -Knock John.

Equipment worth about £3,500 was landed on Knock John Fort by Radio City staff who proposed to start test broadcasts for a new station during the summer. Unfortunately for Radio City another potential offshore radio operator, Essex businessman Roy Bates, already had his sights set on the Knock John Fort and a bitter, sometimes violent, territorial dispute broke out between the two rival groups.

Reg Calvert also made an attempt to launch a second station in April 1965 when he tried to purchase an ex-supply boat from the Royal Navy. He planned to anchor this vessel in the Bristol Channel and use it as a base from which to beam radio (Radio City West) and possibly even television programmes (City TV), to the west of England, Wales and the south Midlands. However, the project did not materialise and with the loss of Knock John Fort to Roy Bates's group the idea of Radio City launching a second station faded for the time being during the summer of 1965.

Attention was turned instead to improving coverage for Radio City itself. In June 1965 professional riggers erected a new 240' aerial mast on the Shivering Sands Fort and a new 10Kw transmitter was installed to replace the previous 3.5Kw equipment. Broadcasting hours for Radio City were also extended at this time to 13 hours a day, from 6.00am-7.00pm.

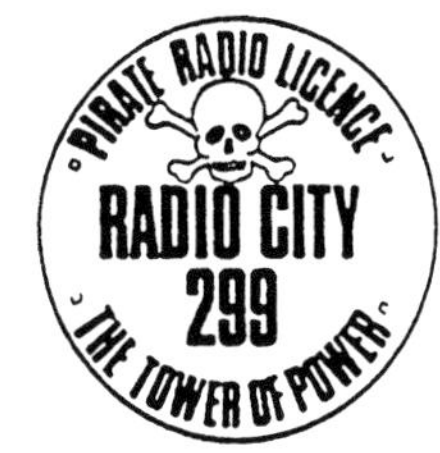


### Radex Project

*In April 1965 stories began to circulate about another planned 'offshore broadcasting project. Using the name Radex plans were announced by backer Jim de Grey to launch a 24 hours a day pop radio service and also twelve hours of television programmes to be broadcast on Channel 6. This was a reserved channel allocated to the Radio Astronomy Service at Cambridge and was not available for use by either the BBC or Independent Television companies. Professor Martin Ryle, Director of the Radio Astronomy Service at Cambridge was reported as saying "If this station comes on the air at the same time as we are working we just cannot operate. We are using two large radio telescopes and one would be put out of action. I am absolutely appalled by the incredibly feeble action being taken by western Europe against these pirate radio stations. People just do not seem to be worrying. I am very worried by all this."*

*The Radex project, which was registered in the Bahamas, planned to use a ship anchored off Whitstable, and was reported to have had American backers who put up over £1million to launch the stations and keep them on the air. However, the backers later withdrew their support and the project never materialised.*

## KING Radio

Following the demise of Radio Invicta two of Tom Pepper's previous partners, Charles Evans and John Thompson, together with DJ Mike Raven (who had had earlier dealings with Radio Invicta) and a group of other Kent businessmen decided in February 1965 to take over what was left of the station. Although John Thompson and others quite quickly withdrew from the new project DJ Mike Raven decided to go ahead with the plan and, together with two colleagues, took some studio equipment out to Red Sands Fort in March 1965.

On arrival at the Fort they were amazed to find three men - DJs Roger Gomez and Bruce Holland together with an engineer called Roy - who had been left stranded on Red Sands after the initial attempt to broadcast test transmissions for the new station had failed. All their supplies had run out and very little water was left - they had lived on dehydrated peas for ten days!

Mike Raven and the others soon put the Fort's transmitter in working order and started test transmissions for the new station, KING Radio, on 1259kHz (238m), later changing to 1267kHz (237m). For some reason which has never satisfactorily been explained these taped test transmission programmes asking for listener's reception reports erroneously referred to the station as being based on the Nore Fort, which had been demolished in 1958. After about two weeks of testing the equipment and producing a satisfactory signal regular programmes from KING Radio started on 24th March 1965 on 1267kHz (237m), but announced on air as 236m.

## KING Radio Programme Schedule

**7.00am** Rise and Shine
**8.00am** Mike and Mandy's Breakfast Show
**9.00am** Country Style
**9.30am** South of the Border *(Latin American) -weekdays*
All That Jazz *(Saturday)*
Concert Hall *(Sunday)*
**10.00am** Mailbeat *(Dedications)*
**11.00am** Music from the Shows
**11.30am** Our Kinda Folk *(Folk Music)*
**12 noon** Lunchbox
**2.00pm** Melody Hour
**3.00pm** Memory Lane
**3.30pm** Lucky Numbers
**4.30pm** Stateside 65
**5.00pm** Up and Coming *(new releases)*
**6.00pm** Raven Around *(Rhythm and Blues music, hosted by Mike Raven)*
**7.00pm** Closedown

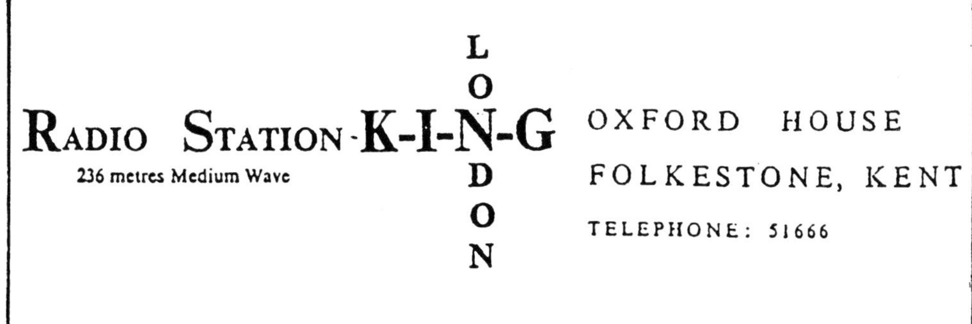


The format was deliberately designed to be different from all other offshore stations then on the air. Keeping away from the strict Top 40 format, KING Radio played middle-of-the-road, country and western, rhythm and blues and Latin American music together with a sprinkling of pop classics. DJs often read short poems or greeting card verses between records and for a time the station promoted itself with the slogan "Wonderful Words - Wonderful Artists".

After a few weeks of broadcasting Mike Raven and the other DJs started to try and secure some long-term financial backing for the KING Radio project - Roger Gomez and Bruce Holland spent a week negotiating with the Kent millionaire who had backed Tom Pepper's Radio Invicta, but he was no longer interested in any further involvement with offshore radio.

Eventually Charlie Evans (former part owner of Radio Invicta) and Folkestone camera dealer Maurice Gothing decided to continue financing the embryo KING Radio hoping that a substantial backer could be attracted to the easy listening format station.

KING Radio had its landbased offices in Oxford House, Folkestone Kent and the station's signal reached the south east coast, part of East Anglia and even outer London. Unfortunately the format of KING Radio - known colloquially as the "station on sticks" - never really caught the imagination of listeners, nor did it attract the support of many advertisers, achieving audience figures of only about 20,000 at peak listening times.

## More problems at Caroline

In August 1965 Radio Caroline South increased its hours of transmission with the introduction of the "Party Time" programme from 9.00pm-12 midnight on Fridays and Saturdays. Also about this time a new shift pattern was introduced for the DJs, giving them two weeks on the ship, but only one week ashore instead of two as had previously been the practice.

This change in shift rota coincided with the sudden departure (either because they were fired or had resigned) of a number of the early Radio Caroline DJs including Doug Kerr, Garry Kemp, Jon Sydney, Mike Allen and Roger Gale. These departures, ostensibly over the revised working arrangements, revealed a deeper problem facing Radio Caroline and in particular Caroline South at the time. An internal inquiry had criticised many of the DJs for sounding unenthusiastic about the new "Good Guys" format, perpetuating a 'square' , out of touch station image and playing too much 'inappropriate' music. In other words they lacked the commitment to compete effectively with the much more vibrant Radio London.

A Gallup poll in the autumn of 1965, the results of which were not published at the time, showed that in its primary target area Caroline South had only a 0.9% audience share compared to Radio London's 14.7% and the BBC Light Programme's 30.4%. The poll also revealed that the largest daily audience for

## Radio Pamela

*Test broadcasts from a boat anchored off Clacton,Essex were heard on 13th May 1965 under the call sign Radio Pamela.*

*The station, set up by businessman Reg Torr, only ever broadcast once again, on 19th May 1965 on 223m (1343kHz)*

Radio London was between 11.00am and 1.00pm (780,000), while for Caroline South it was between 5.00pm and 7.00pm (160,000).

As a consequence of the listening pattern revealed by these figures Radio Caroline's advertising income fell dramatically during 1965. Radio London was picking up all the lucrative commercial contracts and the bulk of the Caroline network's revenue was coming as the result of national campaigns, which included the coverage area of Caroline North. In effect Caroline North was subsidising the operation of its sister station and had Caroline South been a single operation rather than part of a national network it is doubtful whether, commercially, it would have survived after 1965.

By contrast Caroline North was highly successful at this time and in fact throughout its entire life. There are a number of reasons for this, but it must always be remembered that Radio Caroline North held a unique monopoly position and although other stations were planned to compete for northern audiences none ever materialised. Caroline North experienced some minor competition in 1966, but only on the fringe of its coverage area, from Radio Scotland (particularly while that station was anchored off the west coast of Scotland and off Northern Ireland) and Radio 270 (anchored off Yorkshire). However, neither of these smaller stations made any dramatic impact into Caroline North's primary area and the station always attracted a large and dedicated audience not only in the north of England, but in Wales, Scotland, Northern Ireland and along the east coast of Southern Ireland.

As previously mentioned the programme output from Caroline North was always far more suited to its audience than that of Caroline South. Ronan O'Rahilly maintained direct control over Caroline North after the merger with Radio Atlanta and gave DJs the freedom to play the music they knew listeners wanted to hear. Geographically, too, the station covered an area of the country which in the mid-1960's was the home of pop music - Liverpool and north west England. It is hardly surprising therefore that the DJs were able to relate closely to what their audiences wanted to hear and the station's programming reflected this close contact.

Caroline North also benefited from a talented team of DJs and in particular the first Programme Director Tom Lodge, who was responsible for deciding the station's programming style. It is no coincidence that in 1966 Tom Lodge together with another successful Caroline North DJ, Mike Ahearn, were brought south to help re-launch Caroline South and build up its audience figures.

Airtime sales - the lifeblood of any commercial radio or television station - were also more successful in the north. Although Caroline North benefited from the large national campaigns, indeed its very existence made that national advertising possible, the station also carried a huge volume of 'local' advertising. This local advertising was sold by a team based in the station's Liverpool offices, but covered the whole of the north west of England, Wales, Scotland and Ireland and many businesses in these areas soon became household names through advertising on Caroline North. By contrast direct sales for Caroline South by the stations's own staff were only bringing in a few hundred pounds a week by the autumn of 1965 and the Gallup poll report even recommended closing the Chesterfield Gardens Sales Department entirely as it was not considered cost effective.

## Caroline Continental

*During the summer of 1965 Radio Caroline South started broadcasting a programme aimed at its many thousands of listeners in Europe. "Caroline Continental" was broadcast each Sunday morning between 10.00am and 11.00am and consisted of record dedications to and from listeners in Germany, France, Holland and Belgium as well as Britain. The programme was hosted by Garry Kemp who spoke seven foreign languages.*

*A commercial opportunity was also exploited by this programme, promoted as a service to British advertisers who wanted to sell their products in Europe, which at that time was not a single market as it is now. Under the title 'Radio Caroline Export Drive' British advertisers were offered up to an 80% discount on standard rates, and commercials were produced in up to four languages.*

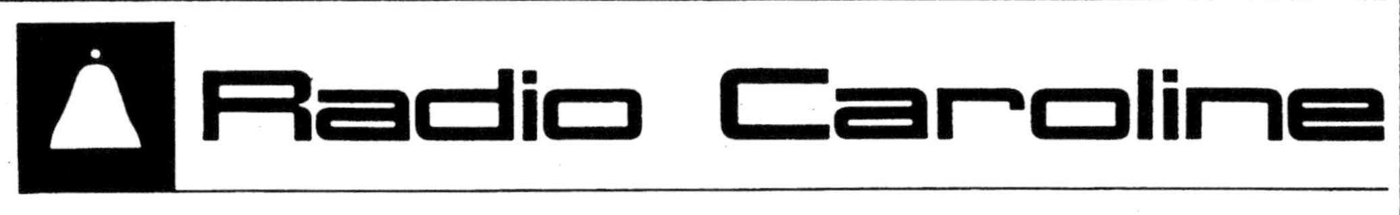

*In October 1965 Radio London organised a concert tour in association with The Beatles' Manager, Brian Epstein - Star Scene 65, featuring such artists as the Everley Brothers, Cilla Black, and Billy J Kramer. The concert, which toured various venues in the Radio London reception area between the 8th and 28th October 1965 was hosted by DJ Pete Brady. At the beginning of December 1965 the Big L Disco opened in Charing Cross Road with DJs Tony Windsor, Dave Cash, Dave Dennis, Mark Roman appearing live on stage.*

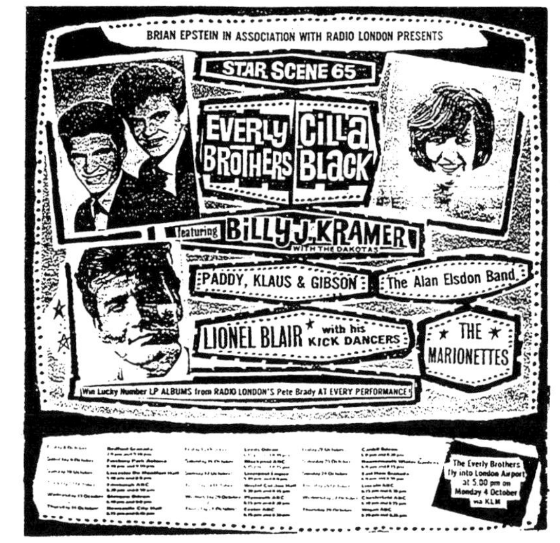


## Radio 390

After KING Radio had been on the air for a few months it became apparent to financial backers that in its existing state the station would never be commercially successful. One of these backers, David Lye, although concerned about the financial viability of KING Radio, was still convinced that a non-Top 40 format station could be successful if it were properly structured. With this view firmly in mind David Lye approached a business colleague, public relations consultant Ted Allbeury, to see if he could produce any ideas for improving the station's image and ratings.

Ted Allbeury, as well as being a public relations consultant (he was at the time senior partner in the press and public relations consultancy Allbeury Coombes and Partners) was also a farmer and later became a successful author of spy thrillers, many based on his own wartime experiences in the Intelligence Corps.

A report from Allbeury Coombes and Partners was subsequently presented to the owners of KING Radio suggesting the introduction of a radically different format for the ailing station, one which relied totally on what they referred to as 'sweet music' presented as an audio magazine targeted at a specific daytime audience sector - housewives.

As well as a general format the actual style of presentation was also considered by Allbeury's consultancy and it was recommended that the brash, psuedo-American approach adopted at the time by other offshore stations should be avoided by the proposed easy listening station.

In summary the report recommended that "the programmes should be sweet in flavour and soft in presentation". A further important recommendation was that the range of the station's transmissions should be increased to cover the most important market areas, namely the whole of the south east of England (rather than just the Kent and Essex coast and outer London), with additional fringe areas if possible as a bonus for advertisers.

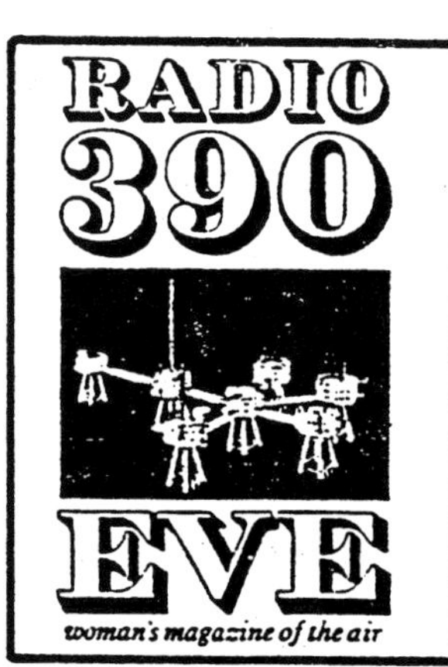


At first it was planned to rename the station Radio Eve, but Ted Allbeury quickly realised that this title reflected only the target audience and did not convey the station's wavelength to potential listeners. As the wavelength would not necessarily be published in the press or appear on radio dials, a decision was eventually made to change the proposed station's name to Radio 390. The audio women's magazine concept was retained however, under the umbrella title "Eve-The Woman's Magazine of the Air" and programme content was still to be directed mainly at the housewife audience during the day.

On adoption of these recommendations by the owners of KING Radio, it quickly became obvious that new capital would have to be injected into the station before the plans could be implemented. The business plan prepared by Allbeury Coombes and Partners was used to raise new financial backing and a new company, Estuary Radio Ltd., was formed to operate the revamped station.

Most of the fresh capital, amounting to about £20,000, was raised by three new directors - Chris Blackwell, Mike Mitcham and Jon le Trobe who joined the board of Estuary Radio Ltd. One of the former owners of KING Radio, Maurice Gothing also remained on the board of the new company and Ted Allbeury was appointed Managing Director, with full responsibility for implementing the whole scheme. Another former KING Radio backer, David Lye also joined Estuary Radio Ltd. as Company Secretary.

**RADIO 390 AIMS AT THE HOUSEWIFE**

**RADIO 390, which is to be developed as the prototype of a legitimate shore-based commercial radio station, was due to start transmissions this week.**

Previously known as Radio King, Radio 390 has an RCA transmitter with 35kw output and is located at Red Sands Fort, outside territorial waters off Whitstable. The primary signal area of 150 miles radius includes Hull, Nottingham, Birmingham, Bristol, and Bournemouth. The wave length is 390 metres, medium wave.

Radio 390 is owned by Estuary

press and press consultants.

Mr. Allbeury says that Radio 390 will not be a vehicle for continuous "pop". Its programmes will be for housewives and will be made up of the more melodius type of music. Instead of disc jockeys, announcers will present the programmes. Features of interest to women are planned. The primary signal area contains seven million housewives.

Transmission will be from 7 am

weekdays

advertising. A different field of commerce and industry will be covered each week-day evening as follows:—Monday, the building industry; Tuesday, engineering; Wednesday, agriculture; Thursday, advertising and marketing; and Friday, retailing. This programme will give manufacturers the opportunity of talking to their customers direct.

In the first six months there will be a straight rate for advertising on "Eve—the Woman's Magazine of the Air" all through

Much of the new capital was used to buy out the remaining owners of KING Radio and to purchase new technical equipment in line with the objective of substantially increasing the station's coverage area. A new 10Kw RCA transmitter was purchased for £9,000 and installed on Red Sands Fort during the summer of 1965. At the same time a new 200' aerial mast was also erected on one of the towers, giving an impressive aerial height above sea level of over 290'.

Inside the towers two air conditioned studios were custom-built, to a design used at that time by the New Zealand Broadcasting Corporation. Each studio had two turntables, a microphone, 7 channel audio console, two tape decks and cartridge players for commercials. Power for broadcasting requirements and the living quarters was developed from two of the Fort's original wartime generators which were re-commissioned and these, together with new ones installed in another of the towers, developed a combined output of 160Kw.

During the time preparations were being made for a re-launch of the easy listening station (and while KING Radio was still broadcasting) Estuary Radio Ltd. made a formal application to the Postmaster General on 10th July 1965 seeking the granting of a landbased broadcasting licence. Not unexpectedly the application was refused and work to establish the new station on Red Sands Towers continued. This was finally completed by late September 1965 at a cost of over £150,000.

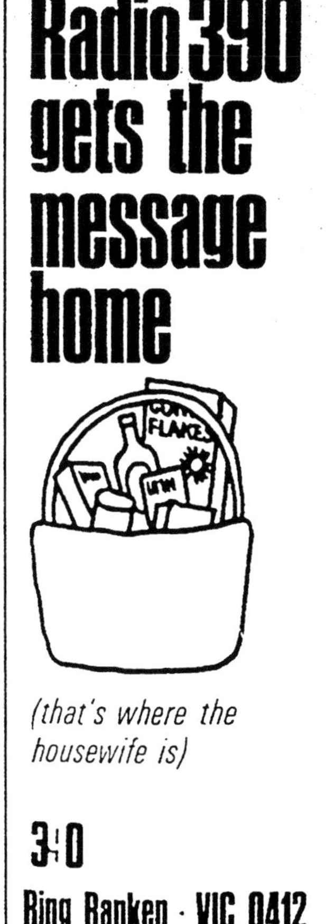


Meanwhile KING Radio had continued to broadcast while these improvement works were going on at Red Sands Fort, but that station finally closed on 22nd September 1965. Its transmitter on 1267kHz (237m) did, however, remain on the air for a further few days broadcasting a taped announcement asking listeners to re-tune to Radio 390 on 773kHz (388m).

Radio 390 made its first test transmissions at 4.00pm on 23rd September 1965 with regular programmes of easy listening or 'sweet' music, starting a few days later on 26th September 1965 from 6.30am - 12 midnight. The first record played on the new 'sweet music' station was "Moonlight Serenade" by Glenn Miller. The term 'sweet music' as interpreted by Radio 390 in fact included a wide mix of non-pop music, ranging from 'standards' of the 1930s and 1940s, through jazz, rhythm and blues, military and organ music, to contemporary light music.

There were no DJs on Radio 390, presenters were known as 'announcers' and were positively discouraged by station policy from promoting themselves as personalities, then a common practice on the Top 40 format offshore stations. In keeping with its overall policy of projecting a 'respectable and traditional' image the station also adopted the practice of closing its transmissions at the end of each day by playing the National Anthem.

## Radio 390 Programme Schedule,1965 (Weekdays)

6.30am Bright and Early
7.00am Morning Melody
7.50am Revive Your Heart
8.00am Morning Melody
9.00am Stars on Disc
9.30am Light and Bright
10.15am Masters of the Organ
10.35am Pause for Prayer
10.45am Keyboard Cavalcade
11.00am LP Special
11.15am Dr. Paul *(Australian soap)*
11.30am Music From the Shows
12 noon Lunchbreak
1.00pm From Me to You
2.00pm Playtime *(children's programme)*
2.10pm Moonmice *(children's programme)*
2.15pm Melody Fair
3.15pm Spotlight
3.30pm Intermezzo
4.00pm Memory Lane
4.30pm Tea Time Tunes
5.00pm Music Bound
6.00pm Scene at Six
6.30pm The World Tomorrow *(sponsored American religious programme)*
7.00pm Country Style
7.30pm From Me To You
8.00pm Dinner at Eight
8.30pm Continental Cabaret
9.00pm Serenade
11.55pm Thoughts at Midnight
12 midnight Closedown

*News bulletins were broadcast at 9.00am, 1.00pm, 5.00pm and 9.00pm daily*

A number of other programming innovations were also adopted by Radio 390 - a daily programme for pre-school children, "Playtime" and a five minute 'radio cartoon', "Moonmice", both of which started immediately after the BBC's "Listen With Mother" children's programme had ended at 2.00pm. Another 'first for offshore radio was the daily Radio 390 soap opera "Dr. Paul", which the station bought in from Australian commercial radio and aired at the same time each day as the BBC's soap "Mrs. Dale's Diary". Ted Allbeury also later started his own Sunday evening 'fireside chat' programme under the title "Red Sands Rendezvous" in which he talked to listeners about a wide range of issues of social concern.

Unlike its predecessors on Red Sands Fort (Radio Invicta and KING Radio) Radio 390 was an immediate success with audiences and advertisers alike. The station attracted advertising contracts from large and well known national advertisers from the outset - the first commercial it transmitted was for the national weekly magazine, *Reveille.* Ted Allbeury's imaginative concept of targeting a different audience from the other offshore stations and playing a completely different type of music proved that there was indeed a place in the market for an easy listening station.

Radio 390's success was also assisted by the strength and quality of its transmission signal. The combined aerial and Fort tower height of 290' enabled the station to use a wavelength of 388m (announced on air as 390m) which was a clear channel away from the more crowded middle and upper end of the medium waveband.

The power put into the transmitter was usually only 10Kw, but a maximum of 35Kw was sometimes achieved by the station's engineers. Ironically, a listenership survey carried out by the BBC in October 1965 estimated that Radio 390 must be using a power of at least 60Kw, such was the strength of the station's signal throughout much of the south east of England. This combination of clear wavelength and aerial height enabled the station to cover a much larger area including most of southern England, East Anglia, the Midlands and a large part of Wales, certainly far in excess of the management's initial expectations.

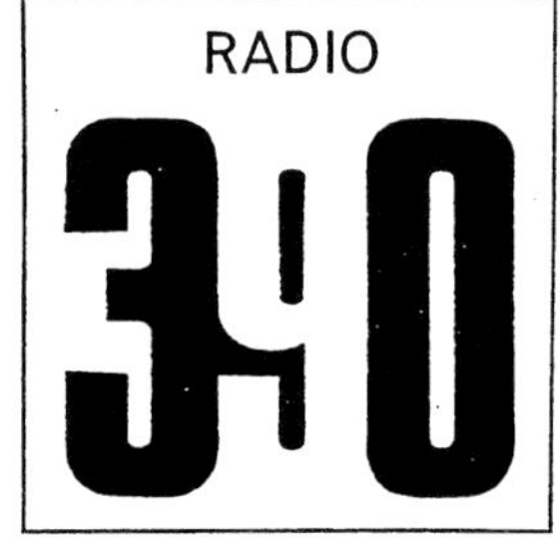


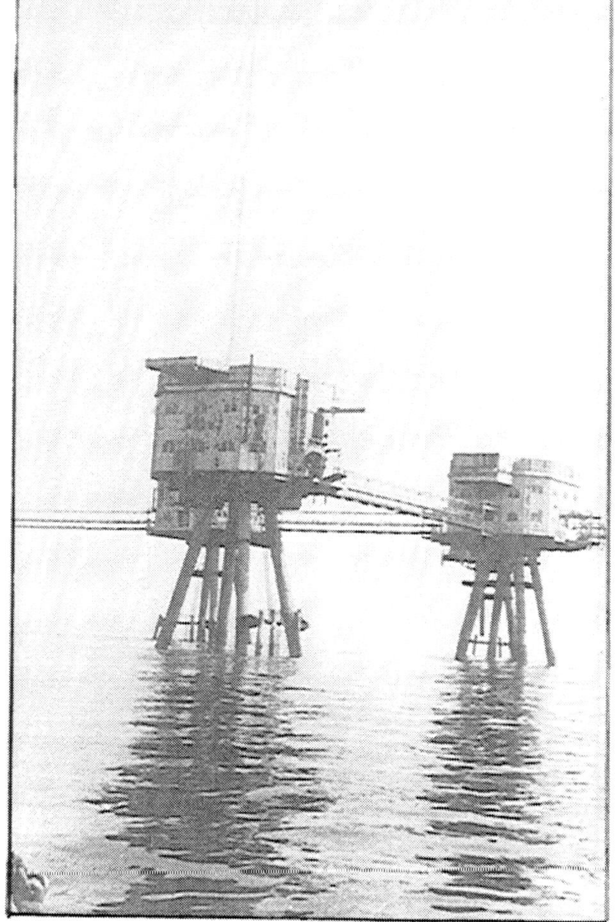

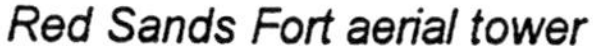
*Red Sands Fort aerial tower*

## Radio Essex

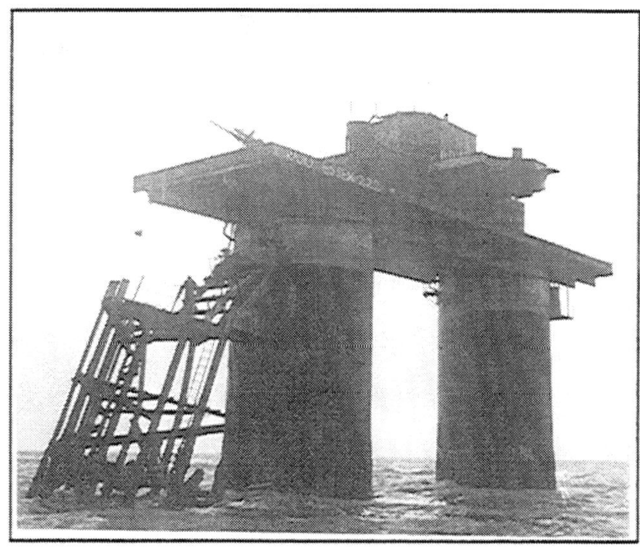
Knock John Fort used by Radio Essex

Another potential offshore radio station operator was also interested in the Thames Estuary Forts during 1965. Roy Bates an Essex fisherman and businessman decided to investigate the possibility of starting his own radio station after witnessing the early success of Radio Caroline and the initiative of Screaming 'Lord' Sutch in making use of the abandoned Thames Estuary wartime forts.

Bates, who knew the waters of the Estuary well, spent some months in late 1964 and early 1965 visiting the various forts, of which there were then six. The former Army forts at Red Sands and Shivering Sands were both already being used by offshore radio operators, but he selected an ex-Navy fort at Knock John to be the base for his planned station.

The ex-Navy Forts, of which there were then four still standing (the other three were Roughs, Sunk Head and Tongue Sands) had been built to an entirely different design from the former Army structures at Red Sands and Shivering Sands. The Navy Forts were much smaller overall and consisted of a single tower with a platform mounted on two concrete legs. Living quarters were built on top of the platform as were the anti-aircraft batteries, while the concrete legs of the Forts were hollow and provided eight storeys of storage areas for ammunition and supplies.

Having identified the Fort he wanted to use for his station, to be known as Radio Essex, Roy Bates set about raising finance, acquiring equipment and finding broadcasting and engineering staff. These arrangements took a few months to complete and during the summer of 1965 when Bates was finally ready to start installing the broadcasting equipment he returned to Knock John with colleagues Mark West and Richard Palmer to discover that Reg Calvert of Radio City -who had also identified Knock John as a suitable base for his proposed second outlet - had already landed some of his own equipment and staff on the Fort.

The Radio Essex men asserted their 'right' to use Knock John and the violent struggle which ensued between the two rival groups resulted in the Radio City staff being forcibly evicted from the Fort. After this Reg Calvert abandoned plans to launch a second station based at Knock John.

Having disposed of the rival personnel Bates and his group set about restoring two of the wartime generators to provide power for the Fort and also constructed rudimentary studios in one of the old storerooms. Broadcasting equipment was primitive and consisted of some low power domestic and government surplus items.

The transmitter, installed in a room next to the studio, was a 1Kw ex-USAF radio beacon (manufactured before the Second World War by RCA Victor) which had been converted for broadcasting use by Bates's te am. A transmitter aerial was also constructed on top of the Fort using some scaffolding poles and lengths of copper wire.

Test transmissions from Radio Essex started on 27th October 1965 on 1351kHz (222m), later moving to 1353kHz, but still being announced on air as 222m. Regular programmes, consisting of middle of the road music during the day and Top 40 at night, began officially on 7th November 1965.

### Radio Essex Programme Schedule

**6.00am Get Up and Go Type Show**

**9.00am Good Morning Show**

**12 noon Afternoon Spin**

**3.00pm The Sound of Music**

**6.00pm Big Bands**

**7.00pm Essex Goes Pop**

**8.00pm An Evening with Essex**

**11.00pm Essex Beat Club**

**3.00am Night Owl**

*News bulletins were broadcast on the even hour between 8.00am and 8.00pm except Sundays when it was on the odd hour between 9.00am and 9.00pm. Weather forecasts were aired on the half hour.*

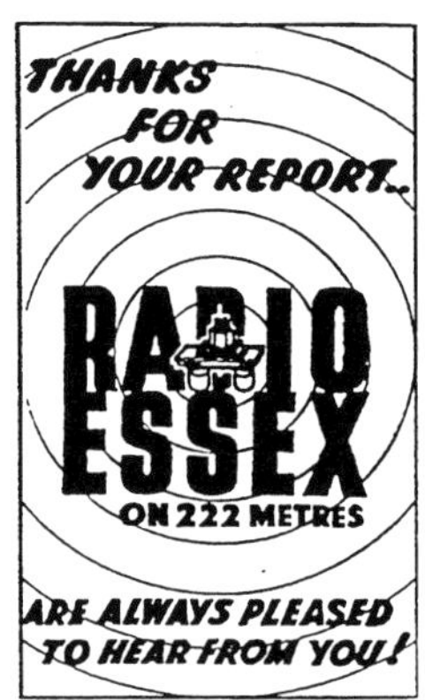


Radio Essex transmitted on a very low power and its primary coverage area was the county of Essex. It claimed to be mainland Britain's first local radio station, announcing itself as "The Voice of Essex" and to this end concentrated on securing advertising mainly from local companies and businesses.

Initially the hours of transmission were from 7.00am to 9.00pm, but Radio Essex later became Britain's first 24 hour a day radio station, with night-time transmissions attracting a small, but regular audience. The 24 hour schedule continued six days a week with a six hour closedown early on Monday mornings to enable transmitter maintenance work to be carried out.

with the compliments of **RADIO ESSEX**

**ROY BATES**
**on 222 metres**
**THE VOICE OF ESSEX**

**33 AVENUE ROAD, WESTCLIFF-ON-SEA, ESSEX Telephone: Southend 41132**

*The station used Roy Bates's home, 33 Avenue Road, Southend on Sea, Essex as its address for mail and commercial sales.*

## Tower Radio

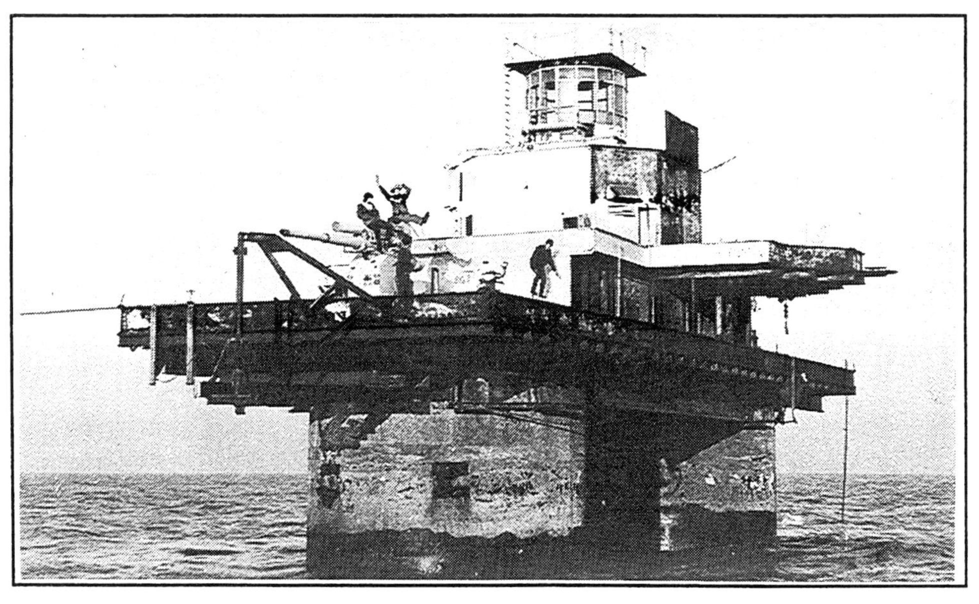

*Sunk Head Fort used by Tower Radio*

A more ambitious plan to use a Thames Estuary fort as a broadcasting base was announced in October 1965. Two Essex businessmen, Eric Sullivan (who had previously been involved with Radio Pamela, see page 108) and George Short formed Vision Productions to launch an offshore radio and television station from the ex-Navy fort at Sunk Head.

Structually Sunk Head was one of the least stable Thames Estuary Forts, having been damaged when it was hit by a ship in the 1950's, but it was taken over by Sullivan and Short in October 1965 at about the same time Roy Bates was launching Radio Essex. Test transmissions for the proposed radio station - Tower Radio - took place at the end of October 1965 at first on 1261kHz (238m) and then on numerous other frequencies until eventually 1268kHz (236m) was selected as being most satisfactory. Unfortunately, the low power of the transmitter (250 watts) and constant technical problems meant that the station's broadcasts could hardly be received on land, except along the immediate Essex coastal area.

Claims were made that test transmissions for Tower TV took place during the early hours of 9th November 1965, with a blurred picture of a test card said to have been received on Channel 5 in Essex. The television station from Sunk Head Fort was in fact a hoax although there were some photographs published which indicated that such a venture may have been planned.

Test transmissions for Tower Radio continued throughout November 1965, but on 29th November the station's aerial was damaged and the following day messages were sent out during the broadcasts informing those on land that water and lubricating oil supplies were nearly exhausted. This situation was rectified on 2nd December when the tug, *Agama* managed to deliver 300 gallons of water, food and oil supplies to Sunk Head and the following week a new 5Kw transmitter was taken out to the Fort.

Tower Radio (and Tower TV) announced plans to start regular transmissions on 1st January 1966, but test transmissions for the radio station ceased abruptly on 20th December 1965 and nothing more was heard from the Sunk Head Fort for over three months.

## Caroline/City 'merger'

In September 1965, at the same time Radio 390 was replacing KING Radio the other established fort-based station, Radio City, was negotiating with ship-based rival Radio Caroline about a possible merger.

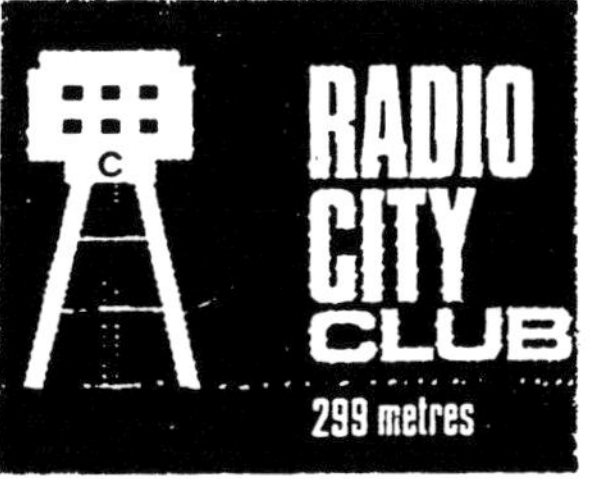


Having lost the base for his own planned second station, (Knock John) to Roy Bates's Radio Essex group Reg Calvert approached the Project Atlanta side of Radio Caroline, through Major Oliver Smedley, offering Radio City for sale. This approach was supposedly to raise capital for his latest 'scheme' - a somewhat improbable project to launch an offshore television station from a submarine on the sea-bed, but the deal did not proceed entirely as planned. Project Atlanta was not as enthusiastic as Calvert about acquiring Radio City largely because of its own financial difficulties and the serious staffing and format problems facing Radio Caroline South at that time.

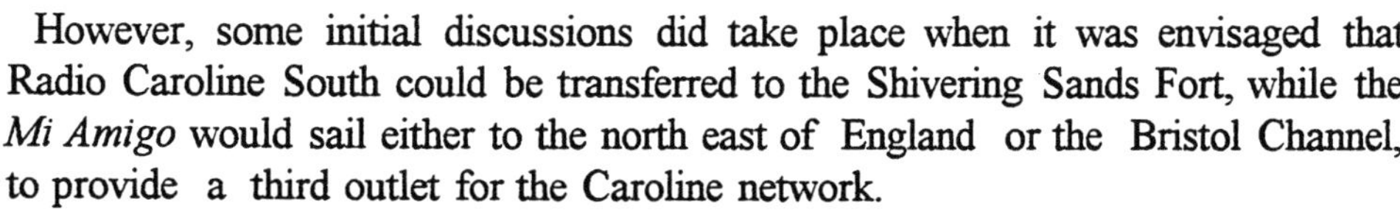

However, some initial discussions did take place when it was envisaged that Radio Caroline South could be transferred to the Shivering Sands Fort, while the *Mi Amigo* would sail either to the north east of England or the Bristol Channel, to provide a third outlet for the Caroline network.

The outcome of these negotiations was an agreement that Project Atlanta would arrange for the installation of a 10Kw RCA transmitter on Shivering Sands which could be used to provide an improved signal should Radio Caroline South transfer to the Fort. However, when the equipment was eventually delivered to the Fort by Project Atlanta/Caroline staff, it was found to be 25 years old and in such a poor condition that it failed to work properly.

This transmitter, which Oliver Smedley had obtained second hand from a radio station (KCYC) in Fort Worth Texas was later to feature significantly in the battle for control of the offshore airwaves. Because the supposedly 'new' transmitter was useless Radio City had to continue broadcasting with the equipment which Reg Calvert had installed on the Fort nearly 12 months earlier.

Despite the setback over the transmitter some other positive agreements did come of the negotiations between Radio City and Project Atlanta which, although stopping short of a full merger, brought the two stations closer together.

# RADIO CITY

Representing
Radio City's Broadcasting Stations, Great Britain.

Telephone: TEMPLE BAR 6332 and 3

7 DENMARK STREET, LONDON, W.C.2

All Advertisements must comply with the British Code of Advertising Practice.

Advertising time is limited to maximum of 6 minutes in one hour.

TAPES One complete copy of each tape must be received 10 days before the date of transmission.

SCRIPTS Two copies of each script must be received at least 14 days before the date of transmission. No charge is made for normal production or the service of Station Announcer.

SPOT ANNOUNCEMENT TARIFF
6 am - Midnight

| Time in Secs. | 6 am - 9 am | 9 am - 1 pm | 1 pm - Midnight |
|---|---|---|---|
| 60 | £30 | £60 | £40 |
| 45 | £20 | £40 | £30 |
| 30 | £15 | £30 | £20 |
| 15 | £7. 10s. | £15 | £10 |
| 7 | £4 | £8 | £5. 10s. |

These included an amalgamation of the two advertising sales teams and an agreement for Radio City to relay Caroline's "Newsbeat" news service, as well as airing promotions for some Caroline South programmes. In return Project Atlanta was to pay Radio City's tendering, fuel and other day-to-day operating costs. From Radio Caroline's point of view it was hoped that the amalgamation of the two sales teams would help relieve its desperate advertising situation brought about by the strong competition from Radio London which had been starkly highlighted in the recent, but then unpublished, Gallup poll.

The merger of the sales teams came into effect on 1st October 1965, but was not a success. Within three months the arrangement had been terminated by Radio City amidst allegations that it was owed up to £8,000 in advertising revenue and that its tendering and other operating costs had not been paid by Project Atlanta. Radio City took back responsibility for the sale of its own airtime and payment of its operating costs with effect from 1st January 1966, while legal disputes about the money owed from the joint sales operation continued for many months afterwards.

Within the Radio Caroline organisation itself Ronan O'Rahilly's Planet Productions acquired the assets of Project Atlanta in December 1965 and Allan Crawford resigned from the station's board of directors. The merger agreement between the two rivals which had been negotiated in June 1964 had in many respects been something of a sham. Although to the average listener Radio Caroline appeared to be a national network the two component stations had been run quite differently, one (Caroline South) under the control of Crawford and the other (Caroline North) under O'Rahilly's influence. This situation had now been rectified by O'Rahilly gaining complete control of both ships and the radio stations they housed. Despite the elimination of Project Atlanta from the Caroline organisation at this time the Project's Chairman and largest shareholder, Major Oliver Smedley, (who had been involved with the now failed negotiations with Radio City) retained ownership of his 60,000 shares

## Rhodesia

*On 13th December 1965, Prime Minister Harold Wilson answering questions in the House of Commons during a debate on the then major problem of Rhodesia's self declared independence from the British Commonwealth acknowledged positively for the first time the existence of Radio Caroline, hitherto only the subject of criticism or derision. Opposition Members were asking how, in view of Rhodesia's censorship laws, reliable news and information could reach those inside the country who were still loyal to Britain. In reply the Prime Minister said, "We are doing what we can to improve the audibility of the broadcasting service from outside. If we have to take expert advice from the experience of an organisation known as Radio Caroline we shall not hesitate."*

With O'Rahilly's Planet Productions having complete control of both Caroline stations plans were prepared to introduce technical improvements, particularly to Caroline South, which it was hoped would counter the stronger signal of rival Radio London. A wavelength change and substantial increase in power was planned for the *Mi Amigo,* but as so often in the history of offshore radio the forces of nature were to intervene before these ambitious plans could be put into effect and caused the Caroline organisation unexpected problems during the early months of 1966

Consideration was also given in the autumn of 1965 to ways in which reception of Radio Caroline North could be improved in its target area. One idea was to move the anchorage position of the MV *Caroline* from Ramsey Bay in the Isle of Man to a position nearer the mainland. In order to assess the most suitable location plans were made for the MV *Caroline* to set sail on 30th October 1965 on a cruise across the Irish Sea to Fleetwood in Lancashire then down the coast across Liverpool Bay and around the North Wales coast ending near Llandudno.

Listeners were invited to fill in reception log forms during the weekend cruise, stating how the quality of the station's signal had varied each hour with the change in the ship's location. Clive Singleton, spokesman for Caroline North was quoted in a press article as stating, "I have been concerned for some time about the number of our listeners who live in pockets [of poor reception]. I feel that we must be able to offer 100% reception throughout the UK. This exercise is a way of finding out if a new location close in to England is the answer. Caroline's move is obviously part of a battle with Radio London to remain Britain's number 1 station." However, the planned cruise never actually went ahead due to bad weather and shortly afterwards plans to relocate the MV *Caroline* were abandoned.

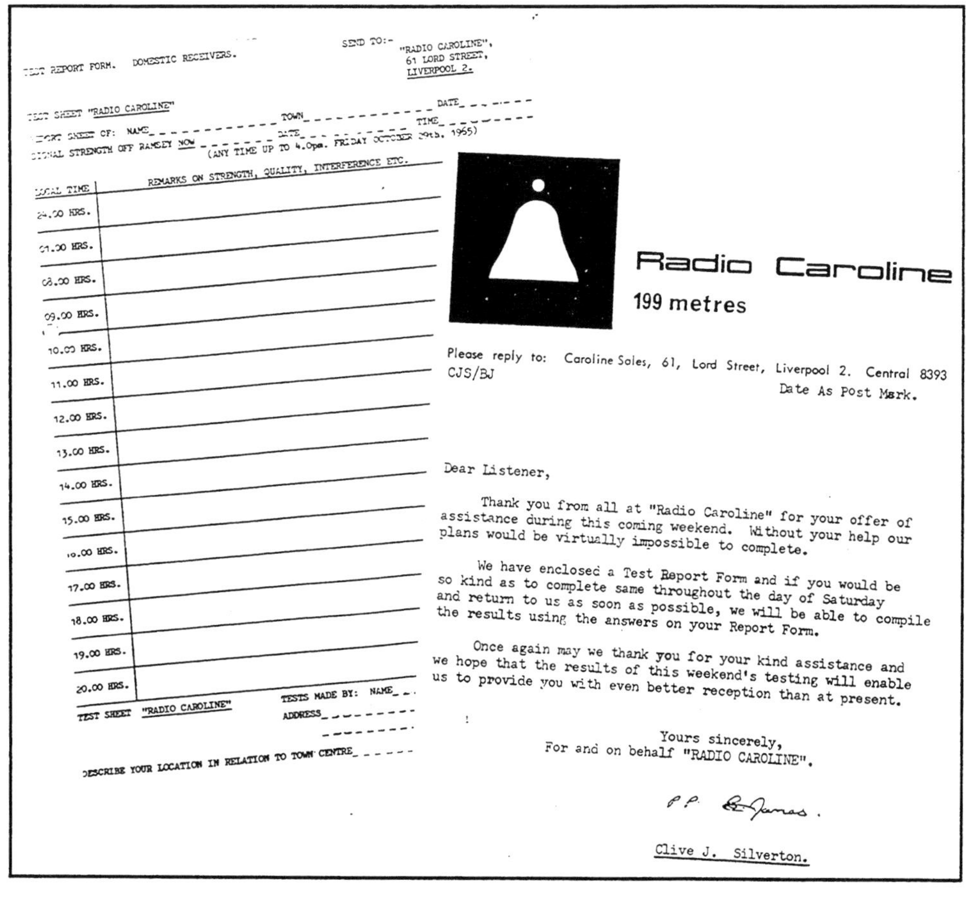

TEST REPORT FORM. DOMESTIC RECEIVERS.

SEND TO:- "RADIO CAROLINE", 61 LORD STREET, LIVERPOOL 2.

TEST SHEET "RADIO CAROLINE" TOWN________ DATE______

[illegible] SHEET OF: NAME________ DATE______ TIME______

SIGNAL STRENGTH OFF RAMSEY NOW (ANY TIME UP TO 4.0pm. FRIDAY OCTOBER 29th. 1965)

| LOCAL TIME | REMARKS ON STRENGTH, QUALITY, INTERFERENCE ETC. |
|---|---|
| 24.00 HRS. | |
| 01.00 HRS. | |
| 08.00 HRS. | |
| 09.00 HRS. | |
| 10.00 HRS. | |
| 11.00 HRS. | |
| 12.00 HRS. | |
| 13.00 HRS. | |
| 14.00 HRS. | |
| 15.00 HRS. | |
| 16.00 HRS. | |
| 17.00 HRS. | |
| 18.00 HRS. | |
| 19.00 HRS. | |
| 20.00 HRS. | |

TEST SHEET "RADIO CAROLINE" TESTS MADE BY: NAME__ ADDRESS________

DESCRIBE YOUR LOCATION IN RELATION TO TOWN CENTRE______

Radio Caroline

199 metres

Please reply to: Caroline Sales, 61, Lord Street, Liverpool 2. Central 8393

CJS/BJ

Date As Post Mark.

Dear Listener,

Thank you from all at "Radio Caroline" for your offer of assistance during this coming weekend. Without your help our plans would be virtually impossible to complete.

We have enclosed a Test Report Form and if you would be so kind as to complete same throughout the day of Saturday and return to us as soon as possible, we will be able to compile the results using the answers on your Report Form.

Once again may we thank you for your kind assistance and we hope that the results of this weekend's testing will enable us to provide you with even better reception than at present.

Yours sincerely,
For and on behalf "RADIO CAROLINE".

P.P. [signature]

Clive J. Silverton.

## Radio and TV Retailers Conference Boycott by BBC

*At a Radio and Television Retailers Association Conference held in Brighton in October 1965 Conservative MP, Mr. Eldon Griffiths told delegates "The pirate stations are providing a service the BBC has lamentably failed to provide. Millions of people, the large majority under 30, now listen regularly to these stations. Let us not have outright banning of a service which gives pleasure." Mr. Griffiths went on "Unless you can tune to one of the pirates the only choice is between various services of the same outfit - the BBC. This is simply not good enough and anyone who thinks that it satisfies the British public has only to look at the explosion of interest in Radios London, Caroline and 390." Interestingly this was the same conference which the BBC decided to boycott because representatives of offshore radio stations were present and at which Philip Birch, Managing Director of Radio London, was invited to speak.*

## Radio Channel

*Another offshore radio station announced plans to launch in the autumn of 1965. Based on a former Italian naval vessel anchored off Bexhill-on-Sea Radio Channel planned to broadcast 24 hours a day, but the station never actually came on the air.*

## Radio Scotland

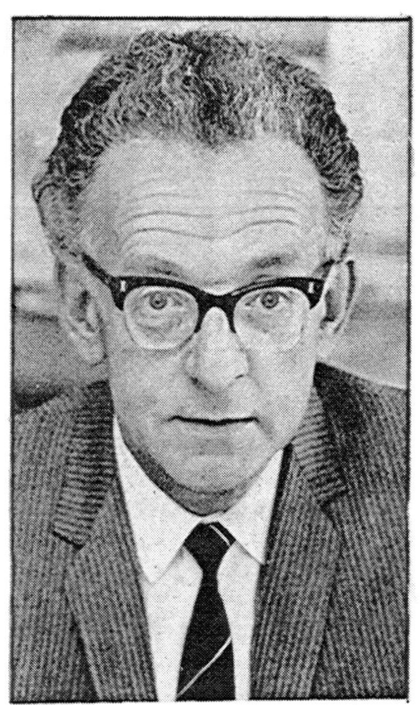
Tommy Shields

As 1965 drew to a close yet another offshore radio station was preparing to take to the air.

Back in October 1964 a company, City and County Commercial Radio (Scotland) Ltd., had been formed by a group of Scottish businessmen and registered in the Bahamas. Publicly the directors of the company declared that they wanted to apply for local radio licences in various Scottish cities including Glasgow, Edinburgh, Aberdeen and Dundee. However, the real and rather thinly disguised reason for the company's formation was to launch an offshore commercial radio station to serve the whole of Scotland.

Managing Director of City and County Commercial Radio (Scotland) Ltd. was James Donald, a theatre manager from Dundee, but the public face of the company was Tommy V Shields, an ex-employee of magazine, newspaper and comic publishers, D C Thomson. Tommy Shields had long been an advocate of commercially funded broadcasting and had first applied for a commercial radio licence in 1947, which was refused by the authorities. His close involvement with the launch of Scottish Television in the early 1960s convinced him again of the need for a commercial radio station serving Scotland. Under the title TVS Publicity he now owned and operated the advertising sales outlet for the proposed offshore station.

Other shareholders in the main company included Sir Andrew Murray (a former Edinburgh Lord Provost and Vice-Chairman of the Scottish Liberal Party) together with Andrew Lewis Carr and Stanley Jackson, both directors of the Equitable Industrial Co. Ltd. a property development and entertainment company based in Scotland.

The 'Comet'

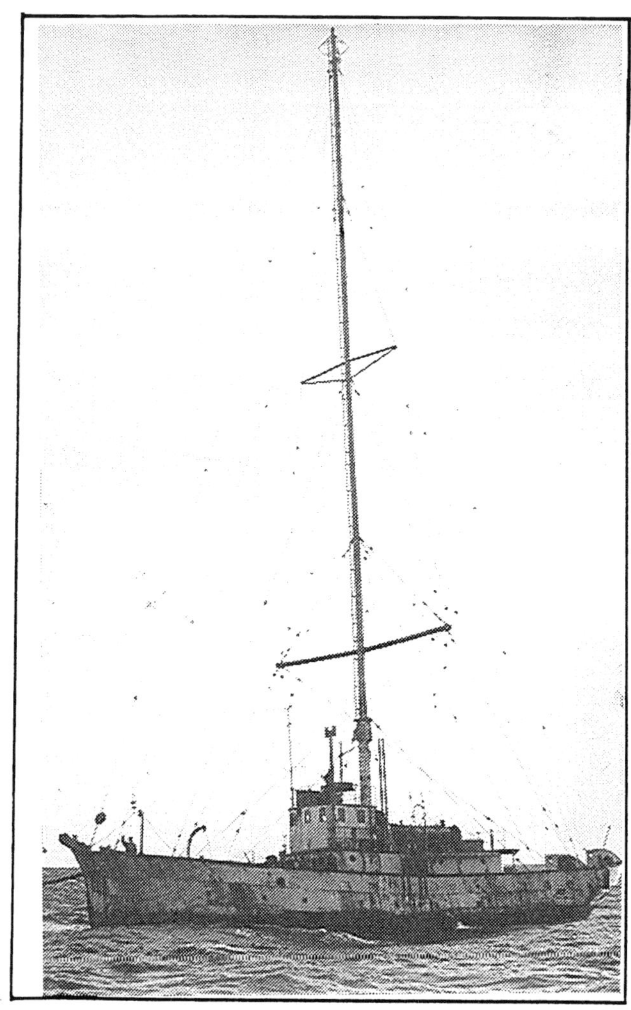

During the summer of 1965 Tommy Shields located an ex-Irish lightship, *Comet* which he considered suitable to use as a base for the new offshore station. The *Comet,* which had no engines, had to be towed from Ireland to Guernsey in the Channel Islands where she was stripped of all superstructure and fitted with a 145' aerial mast, two 10Kw transmitters and on-board studio facilities.

First news of plans for Radio Scotland appeared in the Glasgow *Evening Times* on 9th December 1965 and for a few weeks speculation was rife about the opening date for the new station.

Work on the *Comet* was only completed shortly before Christmas 1965 and the radio ship was again towed from the Channel Islands towards her proposed anchorage near Dunbar in the Firth of Forth off the East coast of Scotland. However, during the journey the tow line snapped and the problems encountered in securing a replacement line meant that the *Comet* did not finally arrive at her anchorage until the early hours of 30th December 1965, three days later than had been planned.

Consequently there was no time for proper test transmissions to take place as the planned opening date for the new Scottish station was Hogmanay,

31st December 1965, at 10.30pm. Because the ship had been delayed in arriving at her anchorage the crew had to hurriedly assemble the broadcasting equipment and the first transmission for Radio Scotland was eventually made just ten minutes before midnight on 31st December 1965 on 1241kHz (242m) but only using a reduced power of 8Kw.

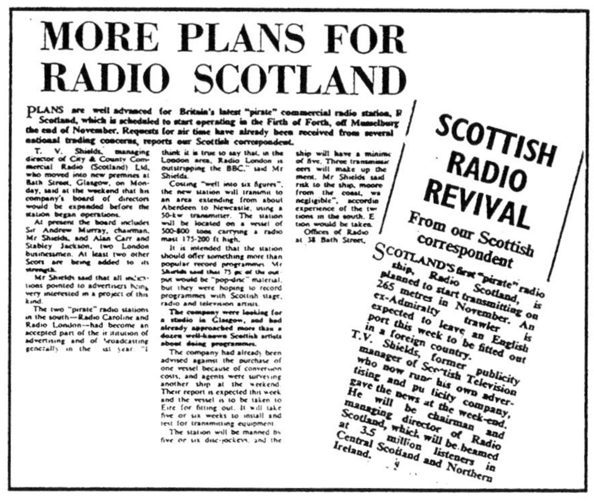

# MORE PLANS FOR RADIO SCOTLAND

PLANS are well advanced for Britain's latest "pirate" commercial radio station, R Scotland, which is scheduled to start operating in the Firth of Forth, off Musselburg the end of November. Requests for air time have already been received from several national trading concerns, reports our Scottish correspondent.

T. V. Shields, managing director of City & County Commercial Radio (Scotland) Ltd, who moved into new premises at Bath Street, Glasgow, on Monday, said at the weekend that his company's board of directors would be expanded before the station began operations.

At present the board includes Sir Andrew Murray, chairman, Mr Shields, and Alan Carr and Stabley Jackson, two London businessmen. At least two other Scots are being added to its strength.

Mr Shields said that all indications pointed to advertisers being very interested in a project of this kind.

The two "pirate" radio stations in the south—Radio Caroline and Radio London—had become an accepted part of the institution of advertising and of broadcasting generally in the last year. "I think it is true to say that, in the London area, Radio London is outstripping the BBC," said Mr Shields.

Costing "well into six figures", the new station will transmit to an area extending from about Aberdeen to Newcastle, using a 50-kw transmitter. The station will be located on a vessel of 500-800 tons carrying a radio mast 175-200 ft high.

It is intended that the station should offer something more than popular record programmes. Mr Shields said that 75 pc of the output would be "pop-disc" material, but they were hoping to record programmes with Scottish stage, radio and television artists.

**The company were looking for a studio in Glasgow, and had already approached more than a dozen well-known Scottish artists about doing programmes.**

The company had already been advised against the purchase of one vessel because of conversion costs, and agents were surveying another ship at the weekend. Their report is expected this week and the vessel is to be taken to Eire for fitting out. It will take five or six weeks to install and test for transmitting equipment.

The station will be manned by five or six disc-jockeys, and the ship will have a minimu of five. Three transmissio eers will make up the ment. Mr Shields said risk to the ship, moore from the coast, wa negligible", accordin experience of the tw tions in the south. E tion would be taken.

Offices of Radio at 38 Bath Street,

# SCOTTISH RADIO REVIVAL

From our Scottish correspondent

SCOTLAND'S first "pirate" radio ship, Radio Scotland, is planned to start transmitting on 265 metres in November. An ex-Admiralty trawler is expected to leave an English port this week to be fitted out in a foreign country.

T.V. Shields, former publicity manager of Scottish Television who now runs his own advertising and publicity company, gave the news at the week-end. He will be chairman and managing director of Radio Scotland, which will be beamed at 3.5 million listeners in Central Scotland and Northern Ireland.

The station's Managing Director, Tommy Shields officially launched Radio Scotland at 12 midnight with the following announcement:

*Good Evening. This is a proud moment for me and indeed for all of us here for after many months of trial and tribulation Radio Scotland is now a floating reality. Thanks to the skill and ingenuity of a dedicated band of radio engineers and the loyality of our team we have been able to convert a former Clyde built lightship, the Comet, into one of the most modern offshore broadcasting stations in the world. Now, our aims are simple and straightforward - to provide a new, exciting form of entertainment radio and to offer advertisers a new, simple and economic medium in which to sell to millions of homes in Scotland and northern England.*

The declared programme policy for Radio Scotland was that 60% of output would consist of pop music, with the other 40% being largely of traditional Scottish interest. Radio Scotland took advantage of the recent staff purge at Radio Caroline South by engaging some of its former DJs ( notably Roger Gale, who became Radio Scotland's first Programme Director) to help launch the new station.

Broadcasting hours for Radio Scotland were initially 6.00am - 7.30pm and 11.30pm - 2.00am, with an 8.00am commencement on Sundays. The station had also established land-based studios for pre-recording some programme material and commercials, together with offices for its sales and administration staff at 20 Cranworth Street, Glasgow, renaming the building Radio Scotland House.

Although £300,000 had been spent on equipping and launching Radio Scotland, by the time transmissions started vital items of equipment were still missing and work on fitting out some of the technical facilities had not been completed. Because of this last minute rush to put on the air early transmissions caused interference to maritime communications in Scotland, drawing accusations of irresponsibility from the Postmaster General and the Coastguard Service.

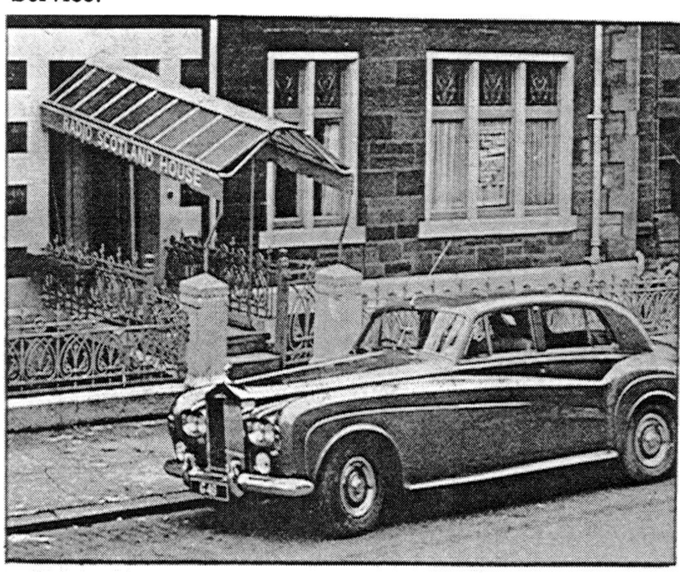


*Radio Scotland House, 17 Cranworth Street, Glasgow*

## Radio Scotland's first Programme Schedule

*31st December 1965/1st January 1966*

**11.50pm Welcome to Radio Scotland**

**11.59pm Auld Lang Syne**

**12.00 midnight Ceilidh** *with David Kinnaird*

**2.00am Beatles Show '66** *(sponsored by the station's first advertiser, the News of the World)*

**2.30am Top 50 of '65** *with Roger Gale*

**5.00am Scottish Top Twenty**

**6.00am Rooster Call**

**9.00am Hit the Deck**

**12 noon The 242 Clan**

**2.00pm Popscotch**

**3.00pm Line Up**

**4.00pm Blast Off**

**7.00pm Look Ahead**

**7.05pm Radio Church of God**

**7.35pm Interval** *(actually the station closed for a few hours because of poor night-time reception)*

**10.30pm Saturday Stampede**

**12.30am Night Owls**

**2.00am Closedown**

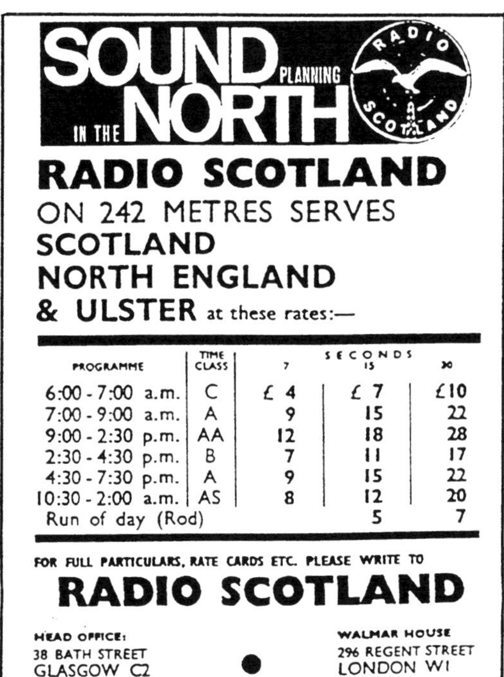

SOUND IN THE NORTH PLANNING

RADIO SCOTLAND

RADIO SCOTLAND
ON 242 METRES SERVES
SCOTLAND
NORTH ENGLAND
& ULSTER at these rates:—

| PROGRAMME | TIME CLASS | SECONDS 7 | 15 | 30 |
|---|---|---|---|---|
| 6:00 - 7:00 a.m. | C | £ 4 | £ 7 | £10 |
| 7:00 - 9:00 a.m. | A | 9 | 15 | 22 |
| 9:00 - 2:30 p.m. | AA | 12 | 18 | 28 |
| 2:30 - 4:30 p.m. | B | 7 | 11 | 17 |
| 4:30 - 7:30 p.m. | A | 9 | 15 | 22 |
| 10:30 - 2:00 a.m. | AS | 8 | 12 | 20 |
| Run of day (Rod) | | | 5 | 7 |

FOR FULL PARTICULARS, RATE CARDS ETC. PLEASE WRITE TO

RADIO SCOTLAND

HEAD OFFICE:
38 BATH STREET
GLASGOW C2
Phone DOU 5726

WALMAR HOUSE
296 REGENT STREET
LONDON W1
Phone LANgham 9401

Radio Scotland's first rate-card

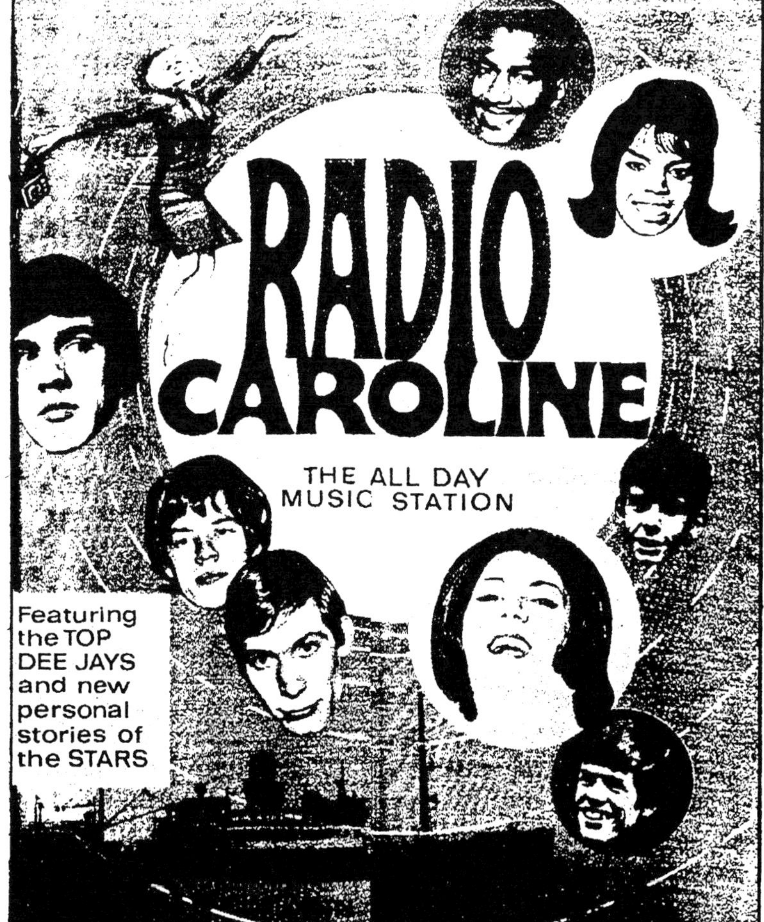


In 1965 the Radio Caroline Annual was published containing features on the station, its DJs and contemporary pop stars.

This was the front cover.

## Chapter 11

# The Bubble Bursts

With the turn of the year British offshore radio was about to enter a period of rapid expansion and fierce competition.

However, the newest station, Radio Scotland, was beset with technical problems and forced to transmit on low power until 16th January 1966 when a vital component arrived from the USA, enabling the station to increase its transmitter output to 20Kw. During the first six weeks of 1966 the station also experienced various problems with its generator and aerial mast, causing a number of breaks in transmission and frequent temporary closures.

Despite the increase in power Radio Scotland's signal, whilst good in Edinburgh and along the east coast remained poor on the western side of Scotland, particularly in the commercially important Glasgow area. Additionally, at night the signal was badly affected by a loud whistle caused by interference from Europe, so a decision was taken by the station's management to change Radio Scotland's frequency. A number of minor changes were tried and rejected but eventually 1260kHz (238m) was chosen, although the announced wavelength for Radio Scotland continued to be 242m.

Radio Scotland's first few weeks on the air with repeated breaks in transmission, a weak signal in the west of Scotland and poor quality programming, led to dissatisfaction amongst listeners and a sharp decline in advertising revenue. Tommy Shields' own admission in a *Scottish Daily Express* interview on 20th February 1966 that the station had had "a pretty ropy start" did not help the situation, but he went on to try and reassure listeners and advertisers by announcing that "we have now found our feet and have the nucleus of a first class commercial station." Few shared his optimism at the time.

The station's programme format quite soon changed substantially from what had originally been envisaged in an effort to attract larger audiences and a greater number of advertisers. Radio Scotland abandoned its promised emphasis on Scottish programming and concentrated instead on a Top 50 chart format, with only a limited amount (about 15%) of airtime being given over to Scottish programmes such as "Ceilidh" and "Larry Marshall and the One o'Clock Gang". The station also started promoting itself as 'Big S' in imitation of Radio London's 'Big L' slogan.

Despite all its technical and programming difficulties Radio Scotland's very presence off the northern coast of Britain had a tremendous immense impact on listeners, who were used to a largely London-based radio service from the BBC. For the first time here was a radio station whose output was directed specifically at a Scottish audience and not treating its listeners as an afterthought on a remotely based 'national' service.

Although for commercial reasons Radio Scotland had been forced to modify its initial pledge on the proportion of Scottish programme material, by doing so the

### *Comet* flooded

*On 10th February 1966 Radio Scotland was forced to go off the air after the Comet's chain locker shipped over five feet of water in heavy seas which were breaking across the vessel's bows. A distress message was sent out and a helicopter from RAF Leuchars was scrambled but due to the appalling weather conditions had to return to base before reaching the radio ship. The Dunbar lifeboat was then launched and after battling through heavy seas eventually reached the Comet, to deliver a heavy duty bilge pump. This equipment enabled the radio ship's crew to clear the flooded compartment, and Radio Scotland was able to return to the air.*

**Radio Scotland programme schedule, January 1966**

6.00am Rooster Call

9.00am Now Hear This

11.00am Elevenses with David Kinaird

12noon Swing Across Midday

1.00pm The One o'Clock Gang Show

1.30pm Shindig

2.30pm Laze Around

4.30pm Countdown

7.00pm Look Ahead

7.05pm Radio Church of God

7.35 pm Closedown *(for three hours)*

10.30pm Blast Off

12midnight Northern Lights

2.00am Closedown

station had in fact helped bring many aspects of the 'Swinging 60's' north of the border. This applied not just to music but the whole ethos of that era and at last young people in Scotland could keep in touch with the changing fashions, tastes and attitudes of those vibrant mid-60's years.

One of the station's most popular programmes was Jack McLaughlin's "Ceilidh", with its strong emphasis on Scottish music - to many seeming to symbolise the whole raison d'etre of the station. However, what became known only after Radio Scotland closed was that this programme began its life as a deliberate satire of all that it appeared to stand for.

In the early weeks of the station's life Jack McLaughlin, as one of the few native Scottish DJs on board the *Comet,* was asked to host a weekly programme of traditional Scottish music, using an appropriate style of presentation. McLaughlin was reticent about the wisdom of this sort of programme being featured in the schedules of what he considered should be a Top 40 pop music station so he decided to present it in a totally over- the-top way, with an exaggerated Scottish accent and an even more imaginative 'Scottish' vocabulary.

Quite soon, however, the station received some complaints from its more dour traditionalist listeners who took offence at McLaughlin's light-hearted comments and presentation style, so a management decision was made to discontinue the programme. No sooner had this been done than the station was inundated with even more complaints about the sudden absence of the programme so it was quickly re-introduced and became one of Radio Scotland's most popular features for the remainder of the station's life.

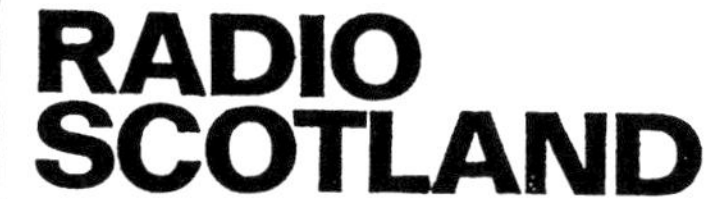


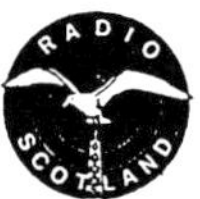


Please reply to

ROYALTY HOUSE
DEAN STREET
LONDON, W.1
Telephone: REGent 4323

PETERKIN & DUNCANS
21 GOLDEN SQUARE
ABERDEEN
Telephone: Aberdeen 28288

IRISH PUBLIC RELATIONS (Consultants) LTD.
ULSTER BRANCH HOUSE
SHAFTESBURY SQUARE
BELFAST, 2
Telephone: Belfast 30605

*Head Office:*
RADIO SCOTLAND HOUSE
CRANWORTH STREET
GLASGOW, W.2.
Tel.: WEStern 9701-2-3-4

## Stranded

The early weeks of 1966 were stormy off the whole of the east coast of Britain, as Radio Scotland had already discovered in the north and other offshore stations were soon to experience, even more dramatically, in the south.

During the evening of 11th January 1966, in a Force 8 gale, the Radio London ship *Galaxy* began to drag her anchor and drift towards the shore. At 2.45am on 12th January 1966 Walton-on-the-Naze coastguards requested the Clacton lifeboat to launch, but by that time the Radio London crew had managed to start the *Galaxy's* engines and were able to prevent the ship drifting any further towards land. When the immediate drama was over the *Galaxy* was found to have drifted some 4 miles from her anchorage and was only 2 miles from Clacton beach, clearly inside British territorial waters. Because of this transmissions did not start as usual at 6.00am that morning and it was not until the tug *Kent* together with the station's own tender assisted *Galaxy* back to her anchorage in international waters that Radio London was eventually able to resume broadcasts after seven hours of silence.

A week later, on 19th January 1966 the Essex coast was experiencing yet more bad weather with a Force 8 gale and driving snow. At 9.00pm that evening Walton-on-the-Naze coastguards noticed that the Radio Carolinc South ship, *Mi*

*Amigo,* was not at her usual position and appeared to be dragging her anchor. The swivel rope controlling the ship's three anchors had snapped and, without anyone on board realising, the *Mi Amigo* had begun to drift towards the coast.

Attempts by the coastguard and North Foreland Radio, using emergency channels and even flashing lamps, to warn the *Mi Amigo* that she was adrift were unsuccessful. Radio Caroline's agent in Harwich, Percy Scadden, also tried to alert the crew by flashing his car headlights at the radio ship, again without success. He then decided to charter the tug *Kent* from Felixstowe in an effort to reach the ship and try to prevent her drifting any further, while the regional television station, Anglia Television, was also asked to broadcast a warning message to the crew of the radio ship. Although the message was flashed on television screens during the evening's programmes it is uncertain how successful this action was as some reports have indicated that the crew were watching programmes on another television channel that night .

Walton-on-the-Naze lifeboat was launched and the Clacton lifeboat stood by ready to provide assistance if necessary, while Caroline South's own tender, *Offshore I,* left Harwich to try to reach and assist the radio ship whose crew were still oblivious to their own plight. It was only shortly before the tender reached the *Mi Amigo* that the crew realised their perilous situation. By then, however, it was too late and as repeated attempts were made to start the engines the ship drifted further and further towards land. The crew were experiencing the same difficulty in starting the *Mi Amigo's* engines that the Radio Nord crew had encountered on the same ship back in 1962 - a lack of adequate compressed air pressure (see Chapter 3).

At around midnight the *Mi Amigo* ran aground at Holland Haven, Frinton-on-Sea, narrowly missing one of the many concrete groynes which are situated all along that stretch of beach. At 12.20am on 20th January 1966 the Captain put out a Mayday call requesting assistance, but neither the lifeboat nor *Offshore I* could get close enough in the shallow water off the beach to help those on board the stranded radio ship. In freezing temperatures and heavy seas it was another hour before 25 members of the Coastguard Service, together with auxiliaries from the Walton Life-saving Apparatus Company, were able to rig up a Breeches Buoy and, in an operation illuminated only by parachute flares, five

*The 'Mi Amigo' aground on Frinton beach*

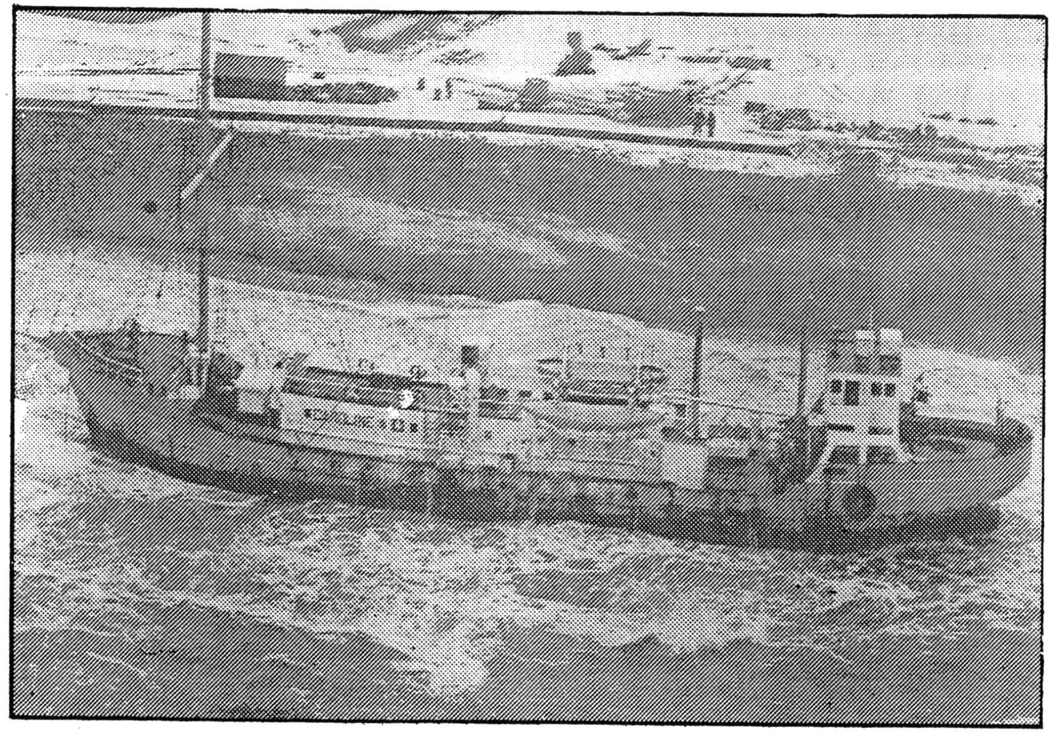

DJs, two radio engineers and a steward were taken off the ship. The Captain and six crew members stayed on board the *Mi Amigo* while coastguards and lifeboat crew stood by for what turned out to be a further 36 hours to provide assistance if required. The rescued DJs and radio crew were taken to the Portobello Hotel in Walton-on-the-Naze where they were given food and dry clothing.

When daylight broke on 20th January 1966 it became apparent just how fortunate the *Mi Amigo* had been - a few yards either side of her were those concrete groynes, which had she struck one would almost certainly have damaged the radio ship beyond repair. As it was the vessel was listing slightly and had already sunk about four feet into the soft sand on the beach.

The noon high tide that day gave the *Mi Amigo* a severe buffeting, threatening to drive her further on shore and smash the ship against the sea wall. During the afternoon the Dutch salvage tug *Titan* arrived on the scene and took up position some 500 yards offshore. An 800 yard long cable was attached to the *Mi Amigo* and on the midnight high tide numerous attempts were made by the salvage tug to drag the stricken vessel off the beach. However, the re-floating attempt had to be abandoned at 2.30am on 21st January 1966 when the five inch thick tow line snapped under the tremendous strain of trying to free the *Mi Amigo.*

By the time of the next high tide the Captain of the *Mi Amigo* had decided to try and free the vessel himself using an operation known as kedging. This involved attaching the *Mi Amigo's* anchor to a long cable and taking this out into deep water where it was dropped until it held on the sea-bed. Then, by a combination of winching on the cable and using the power of her own engines the *Mi Amigo* successfully pulled herself out of the sand and was re-floated on the incoming tide.

Once free of Frinton Beach the Captain anchored the *Mi Amigo* about a mile offshore while divers inspected her hull. Some minor damage had been sustained by the radio ship and it was decided that before returning to her anchorage she should be taken to Holland for permanent repairs to be undertaken. After temporary repairs had been completed at sea the *Mi Amigo* sailed under her own power, accompanied by the *Titan,* for Holland, arriving at the Zaanlandse Scheepsbouw Maatschappij NV shipyard in Zaandam on 23rd January 1966 where she was dry docked.

## Awards

*Later in 1966 members of the rescue and emergency services received awards for the part they played in assisting and rescuing the crew of the Mi Amigo. On 22nd June 1966 the Walton Life-saving Apparatus Company was presented with the Board of Trade Shield for the rescue of the Mi Amigo crew, the first such rescue in the Company's 60 year history, while on 23rd September 1966 the crew of the Walton-on-the-Naze lifeboat received inscribed certificates from Rear Admiral Sir Edward Irving for their part in the rescue operation.*

Caroline is back home —but still silent

**Tug Goes To Aid Of Grounded Pop Ship**

**Eight Taken Off By Breeches Buoy: Six Stay Aboard**

**Pop ship Caroline adrift**

Pirate Queen says: I'll lend my ship

## Caroline South struggles back

Radio Caroline South, beleaguered throughout 1965 by the loss of advertising revenue to Radio London, a series of on-air staff changes, an unsuccessful format change and, most significantly, a general lack of cohesive management, now found itself off the air altogether for what appeared likely to be an indefinite period while the *Mi Amigo* was undergoing repairs.

However, an unexpected helping hand came from Scandinavia, where the last remaining Swedish offshore station, Radio Syd, had itself been forced off the air on 18th January 1966 due to extensive pack ice forming in the Baltic Sea. The station's owner, Britt Wadner, had her ship *Cheeta 2* sail south for safety intending to anchor her in the comparatively warmer waters off the Dutch coast near the Radio Veronica vessel until weather conditions in the Baltic improved. After hearing of what had happened to the *Mi Amigo* she immediately offered to divert the *Cheeta 2* to England to provide a temporary base from which Radio Caroline South could recommence broadcasts. Not surprisingly Ronan O'Rahilly readily accepted the offer, which was reported at the time to be free of charge, but in fact Radio Caroline paid Britt Wadner £750 a week, in cash, for the use of *Cheeta 2*.

Under the command of Mrs. Wadner's son Carl Gustav, *Cheeta 2* arrived off Harwich on 31st January 1966, just eleven days after the *Mi Amigo* had run aground, but Radio Caroline South's broadcasts could not restart immediately because the Swedish radio ship was only equipped for FM transmissions. Bad weather conditions prevented the necessary modification works being carried out for some days and it was not until 2.00pm on 12th February 1966 that test transmissions for Radio Caroline South were able to start from the *Cheeta 2*, but they were only on a very low power.

When regular programmes eventually began transmissions had to be restricted to 10.00am-4.00pm because reception during the hours of darkness was impossible on such low power, even in nearby Essex and East Anglia. The transmitter on board *Cheeta 2* constantly caused trouble and Caroline South was off the air again from 20th to 26th February 1966 and from 28th February to 6th March 1966. Various items of technical equipment had to be brought from the *Mi Amigo* in Holland and installed on board the *Cheeta 2* to boost her power and eventually regular broadcasting hours were re-introduced.

Unfortunately for Caroline South more problems followed in late March 1966 when the *Cheeta 2* was buffeted for three days by gale force winds. On 25th March 1966, with the station again off the air, *Cheeta 2* began to take in water and the tender *Offshore I* came alongside to assist with the pumping operation. Although another tug was already on its way from Holland with stronger pumps, by 3.30pm that afternoon the *Cheeta 2* was reported to be sailing northwards under her own power, with *Offshore I* alongside, heading for port. However, engine trouble on the radio ship brought an abrupt halt to this voyage and both vessels were forced to drop anchor off Lowestoft overnight.

The following day *Offshore I* and a tug from Great Yarmouth, *Hector Reid*, towed *Cheeta 2* into Richards (Shipbuilders) Ltd at Lowestoft for repairs. The problem was traced to a cracked flange plate which had allowed sea water to seep into the engine's lubricating oil. Repair work was completed at the shipyard by the end of March and *Cheeta 2* left Lowestoft in the late evening of 1st April 1966, with broadcasts from Radio Caroline South starting once again the following morning.

### Philip Soloman

*In February 1966 Radio Caroline's management company, Planet Productions Ltd. acquired the services (and financial investment capital) of a new full time working director, Philip Soloman, who had previously worked for Decca Records and had been an agent and concert promoter, mainly for Irish groups, including The Batchelors.*

*One of Soloman's early initiatives was to launch a record label which would be used by Radio Caroline to extensively promote unknown artists. He negotiated deals for the records to be manufactured by CBS under the label Major Minor and for them to be distributed by Selecta Records, a subsidiary of Decca. Contractural problems delayed the launch of the Major Minor label until November 1966, when both Caroline stations suddenly began to heavily plug its first two releases by relatively unknown Irish groups, the O'Brien Brothers and Odin's People. The lack of success in achieving national British chart ratings for these two releases was hardly surprising, but it led to Major Minor negotiating deals with American record companies to launch already successful material by US artists such as the Isley Brothers and Kim Western on to the UK market.*

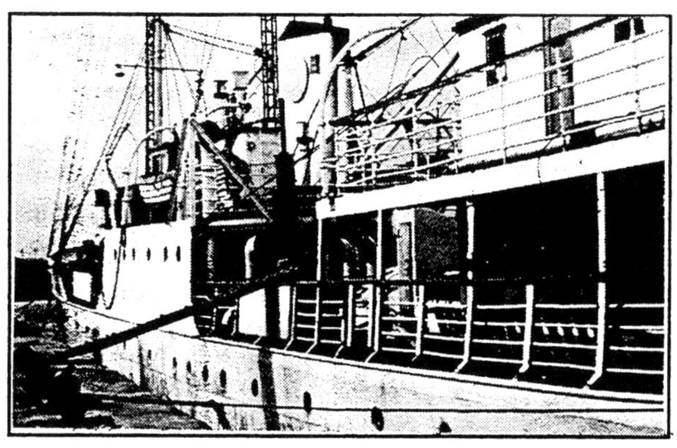

'Cheeta 2' in dock at Lowestofft

## Caroline South's new wavelength

Meanwhile, since the end of January 1966 the *Mi Amigo* had been in Holland undergoing repairs and the opportunity was taken by Radio Caroline management to install a new 50Kw transmitter, enabling the station to compete more effectively with the powerful signal of rival Radio London.

On 5th April 1966, the *Mi Amigo,* now fully repaired and with new radio equipment on board, left Holland arriving off the Essex coast two days later. Test transmissions on a new frequency of 1169kHz (256m), started from the *Mi Amigo* on 17th April 1966, but within a few hours a short in the aerial mast brought these broadcasts to an abrupt halt.

Bad weather prevented engineers repairing the aerial immediately Frustrated by yet more delays adding to the length of time Caroline South had been off the air and knowing that Radio London was about to increase its own transmitter power, Ronan O'Rahilly set out in a tender to try and deal with the problem personally. However, before he arrived one of the station's DJs, Tony Blackburn, managed to climb the *Mi Amigo's* mast and remove the rogue wire which had been causing the short circuit. Test transmissions then resumed on 25th April 1966, changing to a frequency of 1187kHz (253m, announced as 259m) the following day.

Throughout this time normal Radio Caroline South programmes were still being broadcast from the *Cheeta 2* and some DJs from Caroline North were brought south to help with the test transmissions from the *Mi Amigo.* For a few days there were two separate programmes being broadcast under the call sign of Caroline South, but at 6.00am on 27th April 1966 the *Mi Amigo* was able to resume responsibility for the station's regular programming - on the new frequency of 1187kHz (253m),, announced as 259m. *Cheeta 2* then continued to relay these transmissions and DJ Robbie Dale stayed on board to make announcements asking listeners to re-tune to the new frequency. This arrangement continued until 11.00am on 1st May 1966 when the *Cheetah 2's* role as home to Caroline South ended and she was anchored temporarily in the River Stour near Harwich.

With a new powerful transmitter and new frequency giving improved reception across southern Britain broadcasting hours for Radio Caroline South were gradually increased - at first from 6.00am-12 midnight, later to 6.00am-2.30am (on 30th June 1966) and eventually to 24 hours with effect from 6th August 1966.

### Time off air

*In the 87 days which had elapsed between the Mi Amigo running aground on Frinton Beach and returning to her anchorage Radio Caroline South, despite having been loaned another fully equipped radio ship, had been off the air for a total of 43 days - and even when the station had been broadcasting it was on reduced power or reduced transmission hours (or both). Consequently Caroline South had suffered a further serious reduction in audience levels and lost yet more advertising revenue - only the income from Caroline North was keeping the network on the air and financially stable.*

While Caroline South had been experiencing over thee months of turmoil and disrupted transmissions Radio London by contrast had provided listeners and advertisers with a continuity of service and had built an even larger audience for itself in the absence of any real competition from its main rival. In April 1966 it was announced that Radio London's advertising revenue had exceeded £600,000, 90% of which came from national advertisers.

The success of the station was reflected in the DJs rates of pay and opportunities for them to make additional earnings whilst on shore leave from the ship.

At the beginning of 1966 DJs on Radio London were paid about £50 per week compared to Radio Caroline's £25. Radio London DJs could also earn as much again in their week off the ship through personal appearances at shop openings, pop gigs and other events organised by or booked through Philip Birch's own agency operated from the station's Curzon Street headquarters. In June 1966 the Big L Discos were launched at Wimbledon Palais, with live appearances by DJs on shore leave.

Radio Caroline also started to stage a number of live appearance functions where their DJs hosted discos or introduced pop groups on stage, but although popular these never quite matched those staged by Big L.

## Radio Tower

At the beginning of March 1966 transmissions began once again from the Sunk Head Fort where attempts had been made the previous October to launch another offshore radio station (see Chapter 10). This time the station was calling itself Radio Tower and test transmissions took place between 5th and 28th March 1966 on a number of frequencies between 1270kHz (236m) and 1260kHz (238m).

Announcements were made that regular programmes for Radio Tower would begin on 21st April 1966 with broadcasting hours being from 7.00am to 7.00pm. The new station's format was to be directed at a local audience, with news and current affairs programmes as well as features for 'minority' interests. Radio Tower eventually began its programming on 29th April 1966 on 1282kHz (234m) and continued on very low power for about two weeks, the last reported transmission being on 12th May 1966.

At the beginning of June 1966 Peter Jeeves, Joint Managing Director of Vision Productions, the company behind Radio Tower, issued a statement admitting that the station had experienced repeated technical problems in putting out a good signal. Also, apart from one or two shops in Colchester and Clacton, no advertisers had been attracted to the station and as a consequence without sufficient commercial revenue the project had foundered.

### Radio Tower's advertising rates

*7.00-8.30am - £20*

*8.30-12 noon - £40*

*12 noon- 4.00pm -£20*

*These rates are for 30 second spots.*

*The Sales Executive for Radio Tower was Basil von Rensberg, who had been Radio Manager for an advertising agency in South Africa and was formerly a technical producer for SABC. He later went on to organise the Dutch Headquarters for Radio Caroline in 1967 (see Chapter 12)*

## Radio Scotland moves

Radio Scotland meanwhile was still experiencing difficulties in achieving a satisfactory signal output to the west of the country - although it was attracting a mailbag of about 1,000 letters a day from listeners in places as far away as Denmark, Sweden, Norway, Holland, Germany and south east England!

*Radio Scotland launched its own fan club, the 242 Clan, to deal with listener's enquiries about the station and its DJs. The Clan, which was similar to the Big L Club and the Caroline Club, was managed by Cathy Spence, a former beauty queen, and produced promotional items for the station such as car stickers, DJ photos and pin badges. However, Radio Scotland went further than any other British offshore station and launched its own monthly magazine - 242 - with editorial covering events surrounding the station and its personalities as well as general music and show business news, with particular emphasis on Scotland. The magazine was edited by Jim Blair, formerly a reporter on the 'Glasgow Evening Times'.*

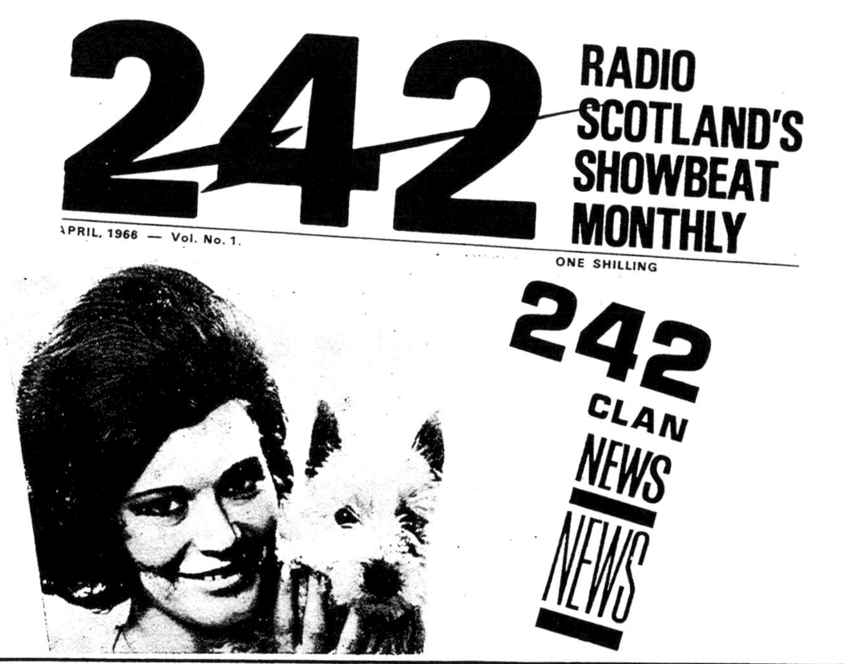

Despite this widespread popularity the station's primary target audience was in Scotland and Radio Scotland was clearly failing to reach large sectors of that potential audience.

At the end of April 1966 Radio Scotland's management decided to tow the *Comet* around the north of the country to a new anchorage on the west coast, near the holiday resort of Troon. The station had planned to continue broadcasting throughout the 1,000 mile, month long voyage, but this idea had to be dropped because of a number of problems encountered on the *Comet.* On 23rd May 1966 a fire put one of the ship's main generators out of action, while shortly afterwards the aerial mast was damaged and the ship's lifeboat was lost overboard during a storm.

The *Comet* did eventually arrive off the west coast and from its new anchorage position Radio Scotland was able to provide a much better signal to Glasgow and the west of Scotland.

## Local Yorkshire station

The spring and summer of 1966 was a particularly active period for British offshore radio. As well as Radio Caroline South being re-launched on a new frequency and Radio Scotland moving from the east to west coast another station was due on air in April 1966. Known as Radio 270, this station was to be based on a ship anchored off the North Yorkshire coast.

The idea for this 'local' offshore station had originated in November 1965 when, inspired by the success of stations in the south east of England, a group of businessmen got together to make plans for a similar operation to serve Yorkshire and the north east. A company, Ellambar Investments Ltd., was formed to raise finance for the project.

The three businessmen initially involved were Don Robinson (who had financial interests in various tourism and leisure projects including Flamingo Park Zoo in Scarborough and Morecambe Marine Land in Lancashire), Bill Pashby (a local fisherman based in Scarborough) and Roland Hill (who owned farmland on the outskirts of Scarborough). Don Robinson had instituted the project after talking with Ronan O'Rahilly about Radio Caroline and the success of that and other offshore radio stations in the south east of England.

News of the project quickly spread through Scarborough and many local businessmen expressed an interest in using the services of the proposed station to advertise their company's products. Foremost amongst these was local supermarket owner, Wilf Proudfoot, who initially approached all local advertising agencies to try and find out how he could buy airtime on the planned station to promote his stores.

Don Robinson heard of these enquiries from an agency contact and approached Wilf Proudfoot inviting him not just to advertise, but to become involved financially in funding the station. Proudfoot readily accepted the offer and produced a financial business plan as well as persuading many other investors to put their money into the project.

Another local businessman, Leonard Dale, then became the major shareholder and Chairman of Ellambar Investments Ltd. He was Managing Director of the internationally renowned Dale Group of companies, including Dale Electronics which later provided generator and electrical equipment to the project and assisted with fitting out the offshore station's ship.

Over the next few months the usual complicated web of asset ownership and company registration arrangements were put in place to protect investors once the station had come on air. The radio station itself was registered in Panama as Progressiva Compania Commercial SA, with Jack Lamont, the American film producer named as the company's principal director. An Australian, Noel Miller was appointed as the Panamanian company's British agent and he also later acted as senior DJ and Programme Director for the radio station. The holding company for the whole project, Ellambar Investments Ltd. was actually registered in Britain, but had 'loaned' its entire capital of £50,000 to Progressiva Compania Commercial S A in Panama.

The consortium purchased a former Dutch fishing vessel, the *Oceaan VII* which was registered in Honduras. The ship, which had been built in 1939, was designed for drift fishing and had a sail at her stern to help maintain a fixed position while her nets were in the water. For this reason (and the fact that she was very cheap to buy) she was considered eminently suitable as a base for a floating radio station. Conversion work was carried out in the Channel Islands where two studios, and a 154' tall aerial mast were installed, together with generators from Dale Electronics, a 10Kw RCA transmitter, a 6,000 gallon water tank, two 650 gallon diesel oil tanks, a water distillation unit, radar and radio-telephone facilities - all at a total cost of only £75,000.

A very short timescale had been allowed for fitting out and equipping the station, with an on-air date of 1st April 1966 being planned - and almost achieved. A press conference was arranged in the Grand Hotel, Scarborough on that date with the intention that at 12 noon the station would come on air, witnessed by the assembled journalists and thereby generating enormous publicity in the local and national press. However, the station did not achieve this target and because of the date the sceptical journalists treated the whole event as an elaborate April Fools hoax.

Unfortunately for the project's embarrassed backers what happened out at sea was beyond their control. The *Oceaan VII* had sailed from Grimsby, where she had called for final fitting-out, but had encountered unseasonable bad weather and suffered some storm damage. The DJs and radio crew had set out from Scarborough in another vessel the previous night for a planned rendezvous at sea with *Oceaan VII*. They had taken with them a supply of records and other programme material so that the station could open as planned at 12 noon.

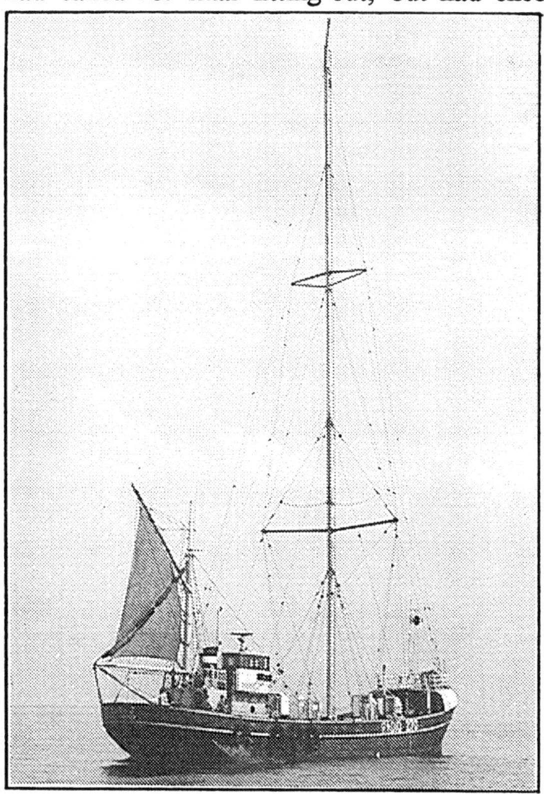
*'Oceaan VII' at anchor off the Yorkshire coast*

However, shortly after they had transferred to the *Oceaan VII* at 3.00am that morning a Force 7 gale blew up off the Yorkshire coast, and a 100' section of the aerial mast collapsed across the deck of the would-be radio ship. The *Oceaan VII's* crew risked their lives on deck during the storm to cut free the remains of the aerial mast and its rigging before any further damage could be caused to the ship.

## Wilf Proudfoot

*Wilf Proudfoot was a former RAF officer, local councillor and Conservative MP for Cleveland from 1959-64. During his period as an MP he had served as a Parliamentary Private Secretary, first to the Minister of State at the Board of Trade and then to the Minister of Housing and Local Government. As well as his political achievements Proudfoot had also built up a successful business, owning a chain of supermarkets and other shops in Scarborough and North Yorkshire.*

## Radio Freedom

*Publicity material was isued in May 1966 announcing the launch of a politically based offshore radio station, Radio Freedom, to be anchored off the Essex coast.*

*The station was to be "the first offshore station to broadcast unfettered, without fear or favour, political thought on a wide range of subjects".*

*Although a start date of early August 1966 was mentioned Radio Freedom never came on air.*

Consequently, much to the embarrassment of those waiting in the Grand Hotel in Scarborough, Radio 270 was unable to go on the air as planned at mid-day on 1st April 1966. Later that same day the *Oceaan VII's* problems were compounded by a fouled propeller and she had to be escorted into Scarborough harbour by two local fishing vessels.

Rough weather in the North Sea persisted for a few days, delaying the radio ship being towed to Grimsby for repairs which themselves took a lot longer than originally anticipated. In a newspaper interview at the end of April 1966 Leonard Dale, Chairman of Ellambar Investments, explained that the delay in putting Radio 270 on the air was because they were "taking extra time to re-check and double check every aspect of the station, where a failure seems even a remote possibility we are planning additional precautions."

## Radio 270 launched

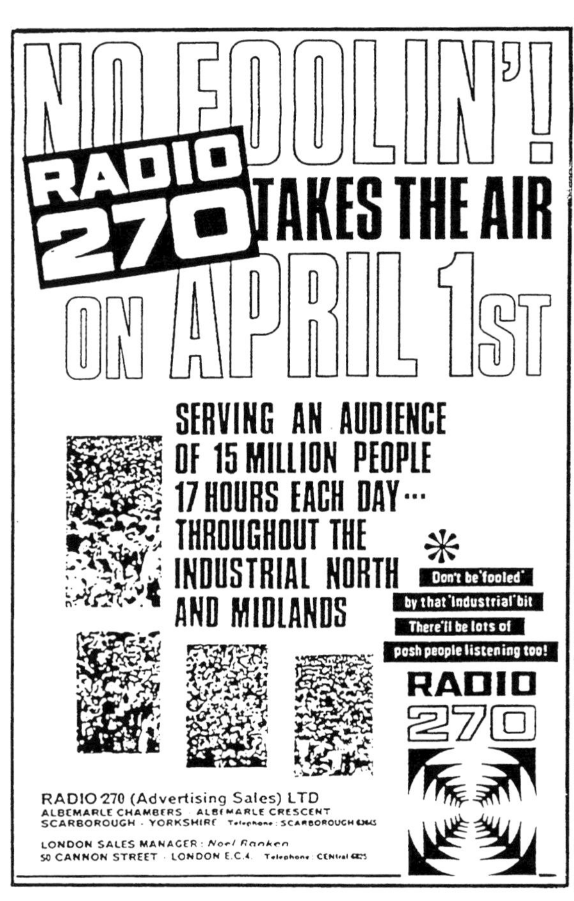


It was not until 4th June 1966 that test transmissions for Radio 270 eventually started on 1115kHz (269m) with full programming starting on 9th June 1966. The station adopted a Top 40 format and tried to base its presentation style on the successful contemporary American Top 40 stations such as WABC, WMCA and WINS in New York. Unfortunately the slick presentation style of the role models did not come easily to a team of largely English and Australian DJs who tried to effect a 'mid Atlantic' drawl in their programme presentation and from a listener's point of view the overall effect was far from successful.

The station suffered technically, too, with a faulty power supply causing record s and tapes to play at erratic speeds and there was a general lack of quality in the recording of commercials and jingles (many of the latter having been pirated off air from other offshore stations). During its first few weeks of broadcasting Radio 270 was frequently closed for 'essential maintenance', a euphemism for repeated generator failures, a problem which was to plague the station throughout its life even until its final few moments on the air 14 months later.

Before Radio 270 opened the station had announced that its programming would be aimed at a local audience and it did carry a significant amount of local advertising as well as community announcements and charity appeals. To encourage local businessmen to advertise the station introduced free introductory spots for very small advertisers with subsequent rates discounted to £3 for 15 seconds. Radio 270 also gave a lot of air time to charitable organisations such as local Rotary clubs, children's homes, the Royal National Lifeboat Institute, Oxfam, the Salvation Army, and Wireless for the Blind, for which it raised over £500 through sales of "Fight for Free Radio" car stickers at one (old) penny each.

A programme unique amongst the offshore radio stations was the "270 Swap Shop" where listeners wrote in with details of items they wanted to swap, together with their address or telephone number and this information was then broadcast free of charge.

One operational aspect, which was also unique to Radio 270, was the absence of a regular tendering vessel to deliver bulk supplies of food, fuel and water. When these were needed the *Oceaan VII* sailed into port, usually Bridlington

Harbour, loaded whatever was required and returned to her anchorage in international waters. It was not unknown for Radio 270 transmissions to continue throughout these unannounced visits to port!

A rough and ready means of audience research was undertaken by the station during its early weeks of broadcasts through the heavy promotion of listener competitions and prize offers. Address information obtained from listeners responding to these competitions and offers as well as other general enquiries for record requests, DJ photos etc. was used by the station to gauge how far its signal was reaching. From the volume of replies received Radio 270 also tried to project the estimated size of its audience.

Remarkably, given the constant technical problems which blighted the station, its signal was reasonably strong in large areas of the north and Midlands. There were even reports from Lincolnshire that listeners in that area could not pick up their preferred station, Radio London, on the adjacent 266m wavelength because of the strength of Radio 270's signal!

**Radio 270 Programme Schedule (1966)**

**Radio 270 operated alternative schedules to account for DJ's shore leave:-**

| | *Schedule A* | *Schedule B* |
|---|---|---|
| 6.30am | Leon Tippler Breakfast Show | Paul Burnett Breakfast Show |
| 9.00am | Dennis the Menace Show | Roger Keene Show |
| 12noon | The Neddy Noel Show | Boots Bowman Show |
| 2.00pm | Dennis the Menace Show | Roger Keene Show |
| 4.00pm | Neddy Noel Show | Boots Bowman Show |
| 7.00pm | Hal Yorke Show | Paul Burnett Show |
| 9.00pm | Andy Kirk Show | Alex Dee Show |
| 12midnight | The Midnight Hour | The Midnight Hour |
| 1.00am | Closedown | Closedown |

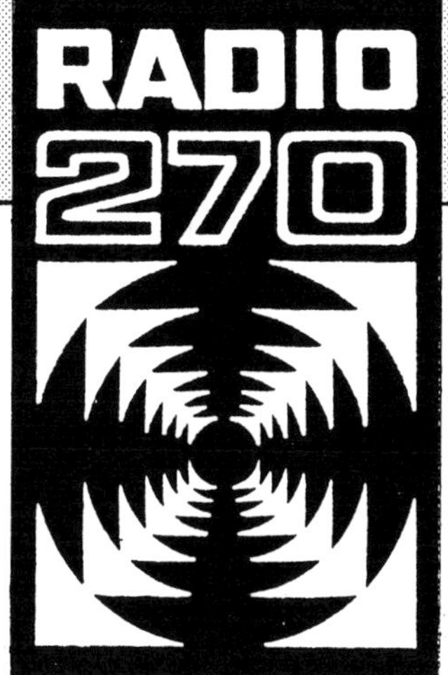


## More Springtime Activity

A lavish press conference in London on 20th April 1966 announced the launch of yet another offshore radio project - the most ambitious so far, with two separate stations based on the same ship.

It was announced at the Conference that the new project would start broadcasts from off the Essex coast by the end of April, but in fact test transmissions for the two new stations - Radio England and Britain Radio - did not take place until 3rd May 1966.

Although based on the same ship the twin stations were to be radically different from eachother and from any other offshore or landbased stations then on the air. Radio England, which planned to compete in the market area already covered by Radios Caroline, London and City, was to be a brash, all-American Top 40 format station, while Britain Radio, although still largely American in format, was to present easy listening music aimed at the same audience sector as Radio 390.

Behind this ambitious project were some of the original backers of Radio London - Don Pierson, Bill Vick and Tom Dannaher. They had broken away from Radio London early in 1965 after fundamental boardroom differences over that station's programming style and format. There was a strong body of feeling, including the three men now involved with the new project, that Radio London should adopt a more undiluted American format rather than the watered down version which had been adopted and, in fact, become an overnight success with

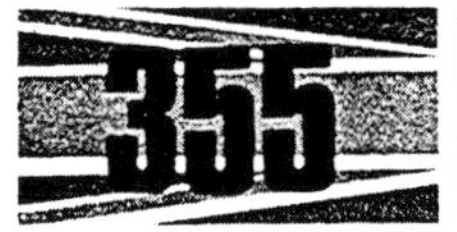

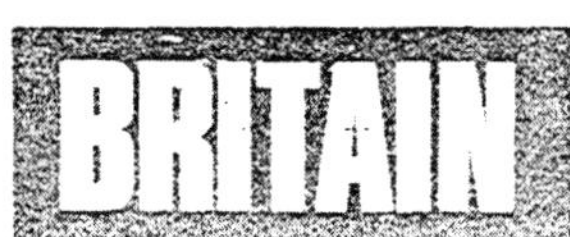

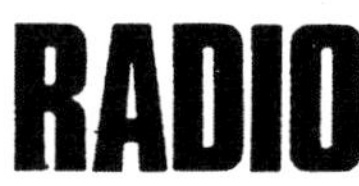

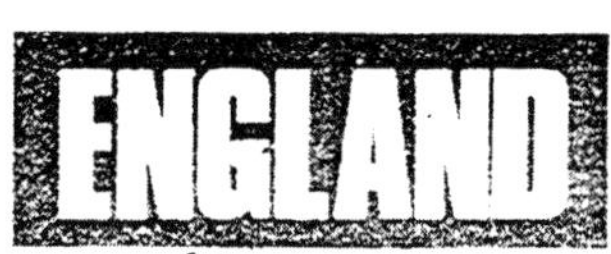

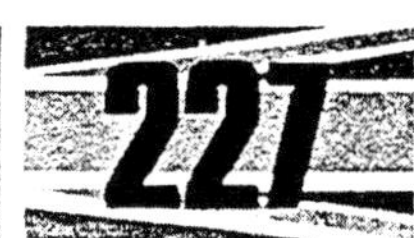

listeners. Fortunately this point of view did not predominate at Radio London, but far from convinced that they had mis-read the British market in 1965 a group led by Don Pierson set about launching another offshore station based heavily on the American Top 40 format radio of the early 60's. Money was to be no object!

A management company was formed for the new project - Pier Vick Ltd., with registered offices at 17 Berkley Street, London W1, although the station's mailing address and administrative offices were actually located at 32 Curzon Street, London W1, a short distance from Radio London's headquarters. Bill Vick became Managing Director of the company, with Don Pierson acting as Project Overseer and another American, Jack Curtis fulfilled the dual role of Project Co-ordinator and also General Manager of the easy listening station, Britain Radio. Cinema advertising agents Pearl and Dean also held an interest in the twin station venture as well as being responsible for the sale of airtime.

## Fitting out

The project's ship, *Olga Patricia,* later renamed *Laissez Faire,* had been built in New York in 1944 as a military landing craft. After the end of the Second World War she had been used as a general cargo ship, and was rumoured to have been used at one time to carry home the bodies of American GIs killed in the Korean War. However this story which has been widely circulated was apparently completely untrue.

At the beginning of 1966 the ship was taken from the Panama Canal Zone to Dodge Island Shipyard in Biscayne Bay, Miami where she was fitted out for her new role in great secrecy at a reported cost of £1,450,000. The ship's equipment included a 160' aerial mast and twin studio facilities, each costing about £70,000, for the two completely separate radio stations.

Installation of equipment on the radio ship was carried out by Continental Electronics from Dallas and completed by March 1966. When the company tried to hand over the completed vessel to the project's backers they were told by one of them, Tom Dannaher, that in his opinion the aerial mast was insufficiently guyed and likely to collapse. Dannaher spoke from experience - he had been closely involved with the installation of similar equipment on the Radio London vessel *Galaxy* in 1964. Continental Electrics insisted that the system had been computer designed, was the best available and would withstand any extreme weather conditions.

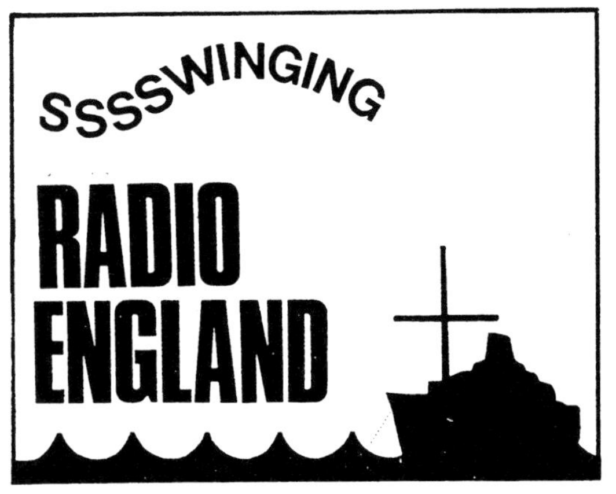


Shortly after the *Laissez Faire* sailed from Miami for Britain the aerial mast did in fact collapse and Continental Electronics in Dallas were called back to rectify the fault. The company appeared to accept responsibility at this stage, but asked that the ship sail to Puerto Rico where qualified engineers would be available to re-install the aerial system.

There then followed a series of delays and a display of gross inefficiency in dealing with the aerial mast problem. When the *Laissez Faire* arrived in Puerto Rico the Captain was told that the engineers were not available and that he should proceed to the Azores for the work to be carried out. Again when the vessel arrived in the Azores Continental electronics failed to provide the promised engineers and asked that the ship sail on to Lisbon where European representatives of the company would be able to undertake the work.

The *Laissez Faire* spent two weeks in Lisbon before anyone from Continental Electronics arrived to look at the vessel and then informed Tom Dannaher (who had flown to Portugal to try and resolve the delays personally) that the port did not have the appropriate equipment to erect the new mast and engineers would have to be brought from West Germany. Continental Electronics then suggested that the ship should sail to her proposed anchorage off the British coast and the work would be carried out on the mast at sea.

However, shortly before the *Laissez Faire* left Lisbon the local Portuguese agent from Continental Electronics arrived on board, having heard unofficially that the vessel was in port and needed work involving his company's equipment. The local agent, who had not been informed by his own company in Dallas of the situation, told Tom Dannaher that the work could have been carried out in Lisbon, but by then it was too late to change the arrangements and the vessel sailed for her anchorage off Harwich. Here she lay at anchor and silent while Continental Electronics arranged to bring equipment from Dallas and from West Germany to rebuild the aerial system.

Test broadcasts eventually started from the ship starting on 3rd May. To begin with Radio England broadcast on 845kHz (355m), while Britain Radio tested on 1320kHz (227m) although the potential transmitter power of 55Kw for each station was not achieved due to technical problems.

For most of May 1966 test broadcasts continued sporadically on these frequencies with regular interruptions and breakdowns while the Continental Electronics equipment was adjusted and modified. The cost of the delays in putting both Britain Radio and Radio England on air and in a revenue-earning position (which had originally been envisaged for March 1966) was claimed to be over $2.25million and the station's backers pursued a bitter legal dispute against Continental Electronics, claiming that the company had not satisfactorily installed the broadcasting equipment on the *Laissez Faire* and had failed to rectify the problems promptly.

On 3rd June 1966 the Italian Government complained that the transmissions from Radio England were interfering with its Roma 2 station and as a result the two offshore stations swapped frequencies while transmitter power was reduced significantly during the evenings. The Italian Government also complained to Panama about interference from stations on board the *Laissez Faire*. As a result the *Laissez Faire's* registration was withdrawn and the vessel remained a stateless ship for two months until she was re-registered in Honduras. This information was not publicised at the time for fear of possible boarding by the authorities as well as violation of the ship's insurance cover.

Regular programmes from both stations eventually started on 16th June 1966 with Radio England on a frequency of 1331kHz (225m) - announced on air as 227m - and Britain Radio on 845kHz (355m).

The 'Laissez Faire '

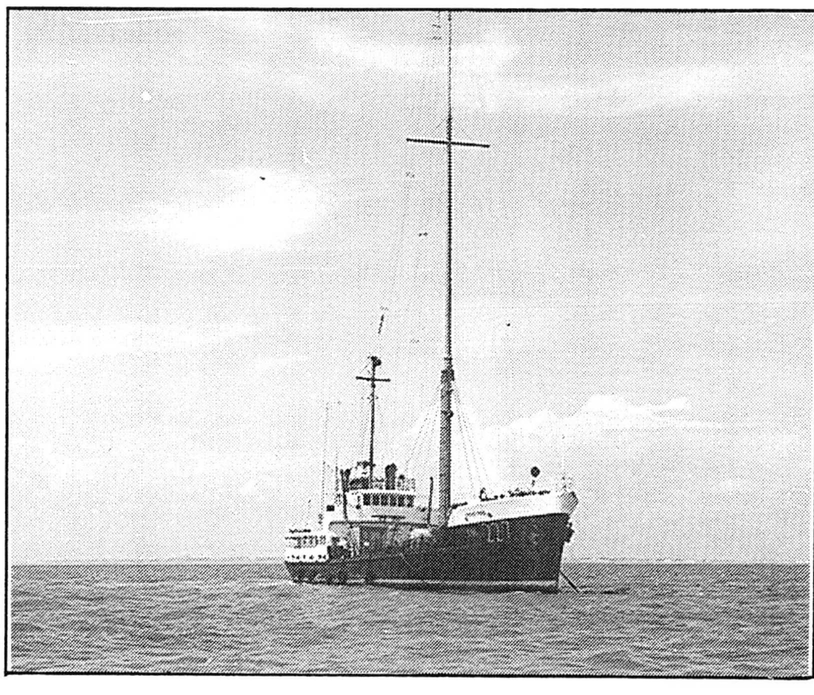

## SRE Programme Material

*Much US chart material, including some from artists unknown in Britain, was played on Radio England and a daily taped programme, hosted by DJ Gary Stevens from New York station WMCA contained American music and links which was either not understood or largely not of any interest or relevance to British audiences. By contrast one of Gary Stevens' fellow DJs at WMCA, Jack Spector, whose taped programmes had been heard daily on both Radio Caroline stations since 1965 made some effort to tailor his presentation and music content to suit British audiences.*

## Swinging Radio England

Programming on Radio England (or Swinging Radio England as it was more usually known) was something entirely new to British audiences. It was undiluted and unashamedly American in style with fast talking DJs, known as "Boss Jocks", making much use of technical gimmicks such as echo and reverberation units, as well as an automated Carousel unit - the first to be used in Europe.

This unit, similar in principle to a juke box, but working with tape cartridges instead of discs, could be used to provide either non-stop music automatically (as Radio England did at weekends with its "Golden Oldies" programme or Britain Radio did on its overnight service) or be incorporated into DJ controlled programmes. The equipment also stored commercials and station identification jingles on cartridges and had the ability, in response to a cue tone, to activate programmes recorded on reel to reel tapes. When each piece of music on the reel to reel tape ended another cue tone activated the carousel unit to insert further commercials or jingles automatically.

Before coming over to England to launch their twin offshore station project in the spring of 1966 Vick, Pierson and Curtis hired a number of DJs from American Top 40 stations, mainly in Georgia. To supplement this nucleus of American broadcasting staff they also recruited some English DJs and deliberately engaged staff who had little or no previous radio experience. The theory behind this policy was that the US DJs would be able to influence their inexperienced British colleagues in the style of presentation required on the stations, but at the same time the presence of some English voices would appeal to listeners more so than a totally American team. The adoption of this policy was later to lead to a serious conflict between the two groups, helping to undermine the success of the whole project and in particular the Top 40 station, Radio England.

Radio England also brought with it jingles which had been custom made for the station by Promotion and Marketing Services (PAMS) of Dallas, Texas, based on their Series 27 package. These jingles were intended to give the station a clear identity and help to establish it in the increasingly competitive British offshore radio market. Somewhat naively, however, Radio England played these jingles without voice over interruption from DJs during test transmissions. Most other contemporary offshore stations recorded the jingles, edited them to include their own identification and then used them during their own programmes before the new station was able to begin regular broadcasts. The effect of this was that when it did begin regular transmissions Radio England sounded as though it was using the same jingles as all the other stations and had nothing original of its own, when in fact the reverse was true. To combat this Radio England quickly acquired another jingle package from Spot Communications, one of the smaller production companies in Dallas, using the "Batman" theme, which at that time was a popular cult television series.

## Radio England programme schedule, June 1966

**6.00am Ron O'Quinn Show**

**10.00am Larry Dean Show**

**2.00pm Jerry Smithwick Show**

**6.00pm Roger Day Show**

**10.00pm Rick Randall Show**

**2.00am Graham Gill Show**

*News and weather at 15 minutes past the hour*

*Weather at 15 minutes to the hour*

Although the station's audience in July 1966, one month after coming on air, was recorded in an NOP survey as 2,274,000 Radio England's format never really caught on with audiences, advertisers or even its own English DJs. There was constant ill feeling between the English and American staff on board the *Laissez Faire* - the Americans thought the English naive and inexperienced in broadcasting matters, while the English accused the Americans of misreading British audience tastes and trying to impose undiluted American format radio.

This conflict eventually resulted in the 'resignation' of four of the original US

"Boss Jocks" in September 1966 after they became totally disillusioned with the operation of the station. Initial commercial contracts (which in the first five weeks of broadcasting had brought in £11,000) were by and large not renewed by dissatisfied advertisers and as a consequence the American backers decided the station was not generating a sufficient return on their investment.

Coupled with this slump in advertising revenue the station mounted a huge nationwide tour - "Swinging 66", with artists such as The Small Faces, Crispian St. Peters, Neil Christian, Dave Berry and (in the London venues) Wayne Fontana. The tour was hosted by Radio England DJs Larry Dean, Jerry Smithwick and Roger Day, but after two disastrous London concerts Roger Day was left to compere the rest of the venues alone.

Starting on August 12th "Swinging 66" was booked to appear at venues (mainly cinemas) in Lewisham, Finchley Park, Birmingham, Stafford, Leeds, Glasgow, Newcastle, Liverpool, Manchester, Cardiff, Exeter and Southampton. The venue selection for the Tour, which included towns and cities well outside Radio England's transmission area, highlighted yet again how the station's American backers misjudged the British market. They claimed, and probably genuinely believed, that the twin stations operating from the *Laissez Faire* gave national coverage, but in reality Radio England and Britain Radio's daytime signals hardly reached beyond the Midlands. As a consequence people turning up, by chance, at venues in the north of England or even Scotland, knew little or nothing about Radio England and any on-air promotions completely wasted because the station's signal did not reach those areas.

Overall the Tour was a massive and costly failure losing over £17,000, bringing even further financial problems for the station. Another problem left over from the Tour was how to dispose of 50,000 unsold concert programmes. It was decided to offer them for sale 'autographed' by pop starts who had participated in "Swinging 66" and they were extensively advertised on Radio England. It subsequently came to light that most of the 'autographs' were copies signed by secretarial and office staff at Pier Vick. Only about 1,000 programmes were sold in this promotion - another costly loss to the station.

## Britain Radio

In contrast to Radio England its sister station, Britain Radio catered for a quieter, older audience. This station also brought with it a set of custom-made jingles (based on PAMS "Smart Set" series) to help create its identity in the market place - "Hallmark of Quality - Britain Radio". Fortunately for Britain Radio these were not pirated by rival stations, as had happened with Radio England's original jingle package.

Although it was supposedly catering for the same audience sector as Radio 390, Britain Radio adopted an entirely different programming style. Instead of the 15 and 30 minute segments specialist music, which Radio 390 had so successfully tailored for its audience, Britain Radio adopted the same 'horizontal' format as its pop rivals using three or four hour long programmes, but with the DJ's playing easy listening music instead of Top 40 pop. Unfortunately audiences and advertisers were not won over - the July 1966 NOP survey showed Britain Radio's listenership as only 718,000 compared with Radio 390's 2,633,000.

Despite its apparent failure to appeal to British audiences and advertisers Britain Radio can lay claim to having achieved two offshore radio 'firsts'. One of its initial advertisers, Sunbake Bakeware, used the station to launch a new range of products in a series of commercials broadcast in English, French, Dutch and German. It was not the use of a multi-language approach which made these

### NOP SURVEY

*In July 1966 National Opinion Polls Ltd. carried out a survey of listenership to commercial radio stations available to British audiences. The survey results showed the following figures for all adults:-*

***Radio Caroline***
*8,818,000*

***Radio Luxembourg***
*8,818,000*

***Radio London***
*8,140,000*

***Radio 390*** *2,633,000*

***Radio England***
*2,274,000*

***Radio Scotland***
*2,195,000*

***Britain Radio***
*718,000*

***TOTAL AUDIENCE***
*39,900,000*

commercials unique (both Radio London and Radio Caroline had aired French and Dutch language commercials before), but rather it was the fact that for the first time an advertiser had chosen to use offshore radio (and a new station at that) to mount a campaign for the launch of a new product, a practice normally reserved for established and proven media outlets.

The other landmark for Britain Radio was the first political advertisement broadcast on a British offshore radio station. This happened on 29th September 1966, when Mr. M McLaren - the Ratepayer's candidate in a by-election for Harwich Town Council - bought airtime on Britain Radio. He was able to do this because the Representation of the People Act 1947, which requires that broadcasters give equal airtime to all candidates standing in an election, did not apply to Britain Radio as it operated from outside British jurisdiction. As a matter of record Mr. McLaren won the by-election by 260 votes, but it is impossible to accurately attribute his success solely to the advertisement on Britain Radio.

Even before the launch of Radio England and Britain Radio from the *Laissez Faire* Bill Vick and Don Pierson had made it clear that they wanted a licence to broadcast legally from land. On 19th July 1966 by Pier Vick Ltd. submitted a formal application to the Postmaster General requesting that Radio England and Britain Radio be granted a licence to come ashore and continue broadcasting, or as the application stated "to install and operate two radio transmitting stations within the UK for the public benefit and at no public cost". Not surprisingly the application was refused.

## Radio London expansion plans

As well as all this activity from newcomers to the offshore radio business some of the already established stations were engaging in expansionist plans in the continued absence of any action from the Government to suppress them.

An indication of the optimism with which they viewed their future at that time came in February 1966 when Radio London reached an agreement with the Performing Rights Society for the station to pay fees (on a percentage of advertising revenue basis) for an initial period of three years, to be followed after that by an agreed fixed-rate payment. Having survived the winter storms Radio London was continuing to capture listeners and advertisers from the troubled Caroline South, which during the first few months of 1966 was either off the air completely or operating on much reduced power from its temporary base, *Cheeta 2.*

In May 1966, in response to Caroline South's new stronger transmitter and wavelength change as well as the powerful broadcasts of newcomer, Swinging Radio England, Radio London spent over £50,000 on new equipment to boost its own transmitter output to 75Kw. However, the station also had plans for even greater expansion in two other directions.

The first of these was to follow Radio Caroline's example and establish a sister station serving the north of England from an anchorage in the Irish

RADIO LONDON 266

Sea, using the call sign Radio Manchester. Staff from Radio London even examined the *Cheeta 2* after Radio Caroline South had finished using her, with a view to the ship becoming the base for Radio Manchester, but the vessel was found to be in such an unseaworthy condition that this idea was pursued no further. During the summer of 1966 other events arising from negotiations to establish a second station in the south meant that Radio London's plans for a northern outlet were abandoned.

The planned second outlet in the south came about in April 1966 when Radio London's Managing Director, Philip Birch, opened negotiations with Radio City's Reg Calvert. He proposed a take over of the fort-based station to re-launch it as an easy listening service to rival Radio 390 and the recently announced Britain Radio, using the call sign UKGM - United Kingdom Good Music.

A deal was struck in May 1966 under which Radio London would manage the UKGM operation for Reg Calvert and take 55% of its advertising revenue, while the Radio City boss would retain ownership of his station and all its equipment. In addition both stations (Radio London and UKGM) would have a joint servicing and tendering arrangement as well as a combined advertising sales company. It was planned that the agreement would come into effect on 1st June 1966 and that UKGM would become fully operational on 1st July 1966.

Early in June 1966 two DJs from Radio London, Keith Skues and Duncan Johnson together with Office Manager Dennis Maitland, went to Shivering Sands Fort to assess the condition of Radio City's transmitter and studio equipment. At about the same time all City's DJs were invited to Radio London's headquarters in Curzon Street to be told of the plans for UKGM and offered jobs on the new station.

However, the merger plans did not go ahead quite as envisaged. It came to light that, as well as negotiating this deal with Radio London, Reg Calvert had secretly continued to have parallel negotiations with Major Oliver Smedley of Project Atlanta - the original organisation behind Radio Atlanta in 1964 which also had links with Radio Caroline from July 1964 until December 1965. Previous negotiations between these two men had resulted in September 1965 in the joint Radio Caroline/Radio City advertising sales fiasco and the delivery of an obsolete transmitter to the Shivering Sands Fort by a team from Project Atlanta (see Chapter 10).

In these latest negotiations Smedley offered Calvert £10,000 cash for Project Atlanta to purchase Radio City outright or, alternatively, the equivalent amount of shares in a joint operating company. Reg Calvert remained non-committal to Smedley's offer while at the same time continuing his clandestine negotiations with Radio London, which eventually culminated in the UKGM proposal.

## Radio City boarded

Plans for the launch of UKGM were first made public in a newspaper article on 16th June 1966. Oliver Smedley, reading for the first time of this agreement between Radio London and Radio City, feared that he was being double crossed by Reg Calvert and that his Project Atlanta transmitter on Shivering Sands (for which he had still not been paid by Calvert) would be put to use by the new easy-listening station.

On Saturday 18th June 1966 Smedley hurriedly arranged a boarding party to go out to Shivering Sands Fort to reclaim his transmitting equipment. The boarding party, accompanied by Smedley and Kitty Black (another of the original Project Atlanta shareholders) left Gravesend Pier in the tug *Vanquisher* just before midnight on Sunday 19th June 1966, arriving at the Fort some three hours later.

### Radio City

*Amongst the 1960s offshore pop stations Radio City must be credited with introducing some truly unique and innovative programmes.*

*As well as the usual DJ shows the station aired a daily request programme - the 5 x 4 Show with only Rolling Stones (5 members) and Beatles (4 members) records being played.*

*The Auntie Mabel Hour, devised and hosted by Ian McRae, was a satirical comedy programme lampooning just about every aspect of 60s pop culture. this included offshore radio itself when a broadcast by 'Radio 310' (based on easy listening station Radio 390) was included in one programme. The Auntie Mabel Hour also presented a special pantomime edition on Christmas Day 1966, with all DJs on board the station taking part.*

**UNIT PRODUCTIONS (U.K.)**
ISL 7178/9
*Invite you to listen to:*
**'ED MORENO PROGRAM'**
**"WHAT'S NEW"**
"RADIO CITY" (299 metres)
at 1 p.m. daily
GUESTS
*Sunday, April 17th—*
MARTHA & THE VANDELLAS
*Sunday, April 24th—*
DAVE BERRY
A Unit Production Presentation

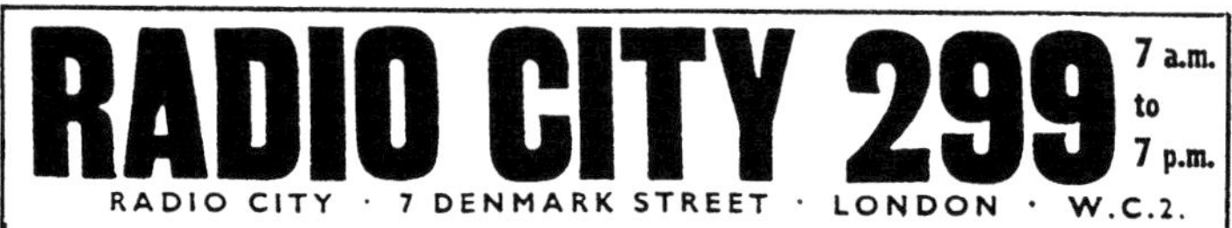


RADIO CITY 299
Britain's Most POWERFUL Commercial Voice

On Shivering Sands Fort Radio City had closed for the day and the seven broadcasting and engineering staff were all asleep as Smedley, Black and the boarding party of seventeen hired men scrambled onto the structure, successfully occupying it and meeting no resistance whatsoever. Smedley and Black then removed the transmitter crystal and returned with it to Gravesend, leaving the remainder of the boarding party in occupation of Shivering Sands and the Radio City staff locked in their quarters unable to put their station on air as usual at 6.00am on Monday 20th June 1966.

In the meantime Oliver Smedley and Kitty Black drove from Gravesend to the home of Radio London's Managing Director, Philip Birch, and confronted him outside his house when a heated conversation took place. The two men eventually agreed that they should meet again later that same day at Project Atlanta's offices in Dean Street, London. Although details of the meeting remained private at the time they were revealed later in a Court hearing which resulted from a dramatic development the following day.

## Reg Calvert shot dead

On Tuesday 21st June 1966, the day after his station had been silenced, Reg Calvert reported the raid to police at Scotland Yard. The police were uncertain whether or not they could take any action because it was thought by them that Shivering Sands was outside British territorial limits.

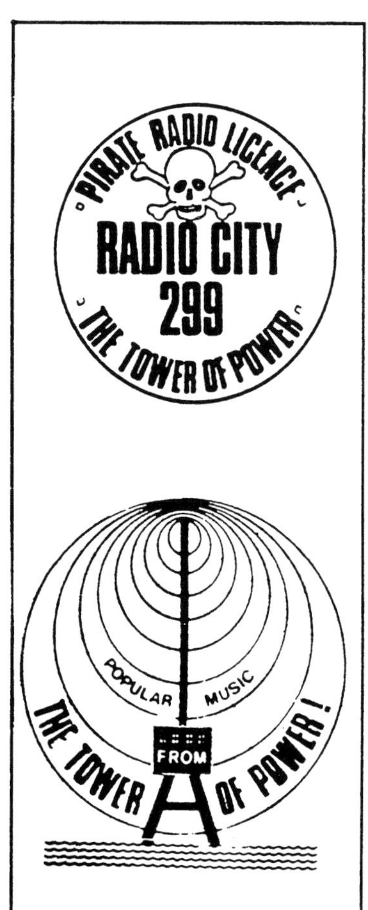


Having received no satisfaction or assistance from the police Reg Calvert drove later that same evening to Major Oliver Smedley's house in Duck Street, Wendens Ambo, near Saffron Walden, Essex, together with a radio engineer Alan Arnold. Calvert entered the house by forcing his way past Smedley's housekeeper and secretary, Pamela Thorburn and demanded to know where the Major was. A scuffle developed between the two men in the hall and the sitting room, where Calvert ripped the telephone off the wall to prevent Miss Thorburn calling for help. Calvert then picked up a marble bust with which he threatened Miss Thorburn, eventually throwing it to the ground and smashing it into fragments. Meanwhile, Alan Arnold, fearing the consequences of Calvert's rage, had gone next door to seek help. As he went outside he heard a shot and returned to find Smedley in the doorway of the dining room holding a shotgun. Seconds later Reg Calvert staggered into the hall where he collapsed and died from gunshot wounds.

While the struggle between Reg Calvert and Miss Thorburn had been going on in the sitting room Oliver Smedley had gone out the back of his cottage and asked his neighbour to telephone the police. Smedley then returned to his house, picked up a shotgun and in the struggle with Calvert fired a shot which killed him. Witnesses reported that throughout the struggle with Miss Thorburn Reg Calvert had been shouting that he was a desperate man and that he was going to get Smedley, dead or alive. A gas cartridge, the size of a ballpoint pen, was later found by police in the clothing on Calvert's body.

Police arrived at Smedley's cottage at about 11.00pm and Detective Superintendent George Brown, Deputy Head of Essex CID took charge of the inquiry into the shooting of Reg Calvert. Major Oliver Smedley was arrested at his cottage and the following morning formally charged with murdering Calvert.

Oliver Smedley appeared before a special court in Saffron Walden on Wednesday 22nd June 1966, where his solicitor told Magistrates that his client completely denied the charge of murder. After a five minute hearing the Magistrates remanded Smedley in custody for a further eight days.

The same day as Smedley's Court appearance Detective Superintendent Brown together with five other police officers went out to Shivering Sands to question the seven Radio City staff and members of the boarding party who were still occupying the Fort. They left three and a half hours later having taken statements, but without making any arrests.

Reg Calvert's Secretary, Mrs. Jill Wildman told press reporters, eager to get to the bottom of the story, that the Radio City staff on Shivering Sands had been instructed to stand-by until they could resume transmissions once again. She also said that she knew who was behind the boarding party, but refused to reveal details, which led to intense speculation in the press and elsewhere about a pirate radio 'war' taking place off the British coast.

On Thursday 23rd June 1966 Calvert's widow Dorothy appeared on television stating that she hoped to have Radio City back on the air in two or three days time. She also announced that the negotiations to sell Radio City, which had been taking place before her husband's death, were now in abeyance. Following this television appearance Mrs. Calvert received a threat from an anonymous caller warning that she should not under any circumstances attempt to visit the Shivering Sands Fort.

Just what the consequences would be if she had visited the Fort were graphically demonstrated on Friday 24th June 1966 when a boat carrying British and foreign journalists, accompanied the Radio City tender as it sailed towards Shivering Sands. Journalists witnessed the boarding party, with oxyacetylene burners, threaten to cut the catwalks, fell the transmitter mast and to repel anyone attempting to set foot on the Fort. Eventually, however, two Radio City engineers were allowed to board the Fort and two others, Paul Elvey and Phil Perkins, together with the station's young cook, Leslie Dunn were permitted to leave.

Those Radio City staff who had been released gave police a valuable insight into the attitude of mind and tactics adopted by the boarding party since it had invaded the Fort. Apparently they had been reasonable for the first few days until a barge attempted to deliver supplies to the Fort on Thursday 23rd June. After this visit the boarding party informed Radio City staff that any attempt by Dorothy Calvert or others to land on the Fort would be met by the destruction of the transmitter masts and the severing of catwalks linking the individual towers, hence the dramatic display of force for journalists the following morning.

Faced with the threatened destruction of the station Mrs. Calvert wisely resorted to instructing her solicitors to institute proceedings against the boarding party, but even this was not straight forward because of uncertainty about the territorial status of Shivering Sands. This uncertain situation continued for some time, with the police taking no action to remove the boarding party and the Ministry of Defence, which under different circumstances claimed the Thames Estuary Forts were Government property, now denying any responsibility at all for the Fort.

Without warning on Sunday 26th June 1966, exactly a week after arriving, the boarding party left Shivering Sands Fort. Using a spare transmitter crystal which had been hidden from the boarders, Radio City started test transmissions again at 9.30pm that evening and by 10.00pm the station was back on the air.

Major Oliver Smedley appeared in Court again on 18th July 1966 when a preliminary hearing was held at Saffron Walden. At this hearing full details of the dealings between Reg Calvert, Oliver Smedley and Philip Birch were revealed publicly for the first time. The catalyst to the whole affair was Smedley's fear that Calvert had double crossed him and he wished to reclaim the £10,000 Project Atlanta transmitter from Shivering Sands before it could be used by any 'rival group'.

Details of the meeting in Project Atlanta's offices in Dean Street on 20th June 1966 were also outlined to the Court. Oliver Smedley and Kitty Black, representing Project Atlanta, together with Philip Birch of Radio London were present when the meeting started at 11.30am. Reg Calvert joined them at some point later. During the meeting Smedley suggested that as owners of the transmitter equipment Project Atlanta should be included in the UKGM deal which had already been agreed between Calvert and Birch, but his proposal was turned down. Before leaving the meeting Reg Calvert made a number of threats to use a nerve gas which he claimed to have invented to remove Smedley's boarding party from 'his' Fort.

Evidence of events at Smedley's cottage on the evening of 21st June were given to the Court by various witnesses. Smedley's solicitor argued that his client had acted in self defence, protecting himself and his housekeeper against a trespasser in his home who was threatening to murder both of them.

After a 50 minute retirement the Magistrates decided to commit Oliver Smedley for trial at Chelmsford Assizes in October, but on a charge of manslaughter rather than murder. Smedley was granted bail for a sum of £500 plus two sureties of £500 each.

At the two day hearing in Chelmsford on 11th October 1966 the sequence of events on 21st June 1966 and the circumstances surrounding the boarding of Shivering Sands Fort were related to the Court. Oliver Smedley's solicitor again argued that his client had acted in self defence, protecting himself, his housekeeper and his home from a violent intruder. The jury, without retiring to consider the evidence presented to them, returned a 'not guilty ' verdict and Oliver Smedley left court a free man.

## Government response

These dramatic events at the end of June 1966, which became known as the 'Radio City Affair', did much to shatter the fun packed, 'pirate' image of the offshore radio stations, revealing a ruthless world of double-dealing, financial intrigue, physical violence and death threats. Although Project Atlanta had, for a time, been joined with Radio Caroline and merger negotiations had taken place in 1965 between Caroline and Radio City, Radio Caroline now did everything possible to disassociate and distance itself from the unsavoury events on Shivering Sands Fort. Likewise Radio London's Philip Birch, who had negotiated the UKGM deal with Radio City's owner Reg Calvert, immediately withdrew from the agreement when he saw Calvert's threatening behaviour at the Dean Street meeting on 20th June. This to a lesser extent also effectively distanced Radio London from events at Shivering Sands.

In Parliament MPs pressed the Government to take action against offshore broadcasters in the light of the boarding of Shivering Sands Fort and the subsequent shooting of Reg Calvert. Postmaster General Anthony Wedgewood Benn told the House that the Government's Bill to outlaw offshore stations was ready to be introduced, but this would not happen immediately because of possible prosecutions arising from the Radio City Affair and the death of the station's owner.

On 27th June 1966 the Minister of Defence for the Army, Mr. Gerald Reynolds, rejected a suggestion from opposition MPs that his Department should invade the Thames Estuary forts by saying in a rather bland statement: "There is no present or foreseeable defence purpose which would require me to exercise control over these forts."

The Home Secretary, Roy Jenkins, was asked to call for a report from the Chief Constable of Essex on police action taken over the boarding of Shivering Sands, while the Attorney General, Sir Elwyn Jones, was urged to introduce legislation bringing the Thames Estuary forts within British jurisdiction and to refer the boarding of Radio City to the Director of Public Prosecutions.

None of these requests were agreed to by Government Ministers, but on 1st July 1966 the Postmaster General announced that legislation to outlaw offshore radio stations would now be introduced before the summer recess. In the light of events at Radio City the Government had rearranged its parliamentary timetable to accommodate such legislation, which only weeks before it had been saying could not be dealt with in that session. The Postmaster General also indicated that the Government was contemplating a "general review of broadcasting policy" which would include "the better provision of popular music on a national basis as well as the establishment of local public service radio stations."

## Radio 390 expansion plans

Another fort-based station, Radio 390 also had expansionist plans during the spring and summer of 1966, but as might be expected these were approached in a more genteel manner than the violent wheelings and dealings taking place over on Shivering Sands Fort.

Shortly after coming on the air in late 1965 Radio 390 had commissioned a survey to establish independent evidence of its audience level and signal strength for the benefit of potential advertisers. The results had shown not only that the station's signal was strong in a surprisingly wide area of the south and Midlands, but that there was a huge demand for its style of 'sweet music', easy-listening programmes.

During May 1966 Ted Allbeury, Managing Director of Radio 390 opened negotiations with Mrs. Britt Wadner, owner of the former Scandinavian station Radio Syd, to purchase her radio ship, *Cheeta 2*, which was lying at anchor off Harwich having fulfilled her role as a temporary home for Radio Caroline South. Although others, notably Radio London, had looked at the possibility of purchasing *Cheeta 2* nothing had ever been concluded and because of tougher laws passed in Sweden at the beginning of 1966 there was now no possibility that Radio Syd could ever return to the air from its former anchorage off Malmo.

**RADIO 390**
**IS ONE YEAR OLD**

ON this happy occasion we would like to thank our millions of listeners, our advertisers, and all those people who have given us loyal support throughout our first year of broadcasting on 390 metres and we will continue to present better music for all the family and look forward to greeting you with bigger and brighter shows throughout the coming year.

**RADIO 390**
**one year old on**
**Sunday, 25th Sept., 1966**

***Radio 390 presents:***

Scene at 6—Mondays to Fridays at 6 p.m. featuring the latest releases. Morning Melody, 7.30 to 9 a.m. music to make your morning. Memory Lane, daily at 3.30 to 4 p.m. all of your old favourites. The Mike Raven show daily at 7 p.m. all that is best in R & B. Serenade, sweet music to while away your evenings daily at 9 p.m. (9.30 on Sundays). Warners request show every Sunday at 11.15 a.m. A happy reminder of your holiday.

Starting soon. Words and Music: review of all the latest paper backs with music to match.

With non-stop music from 6.30 a.m. to midnight seven days a week.

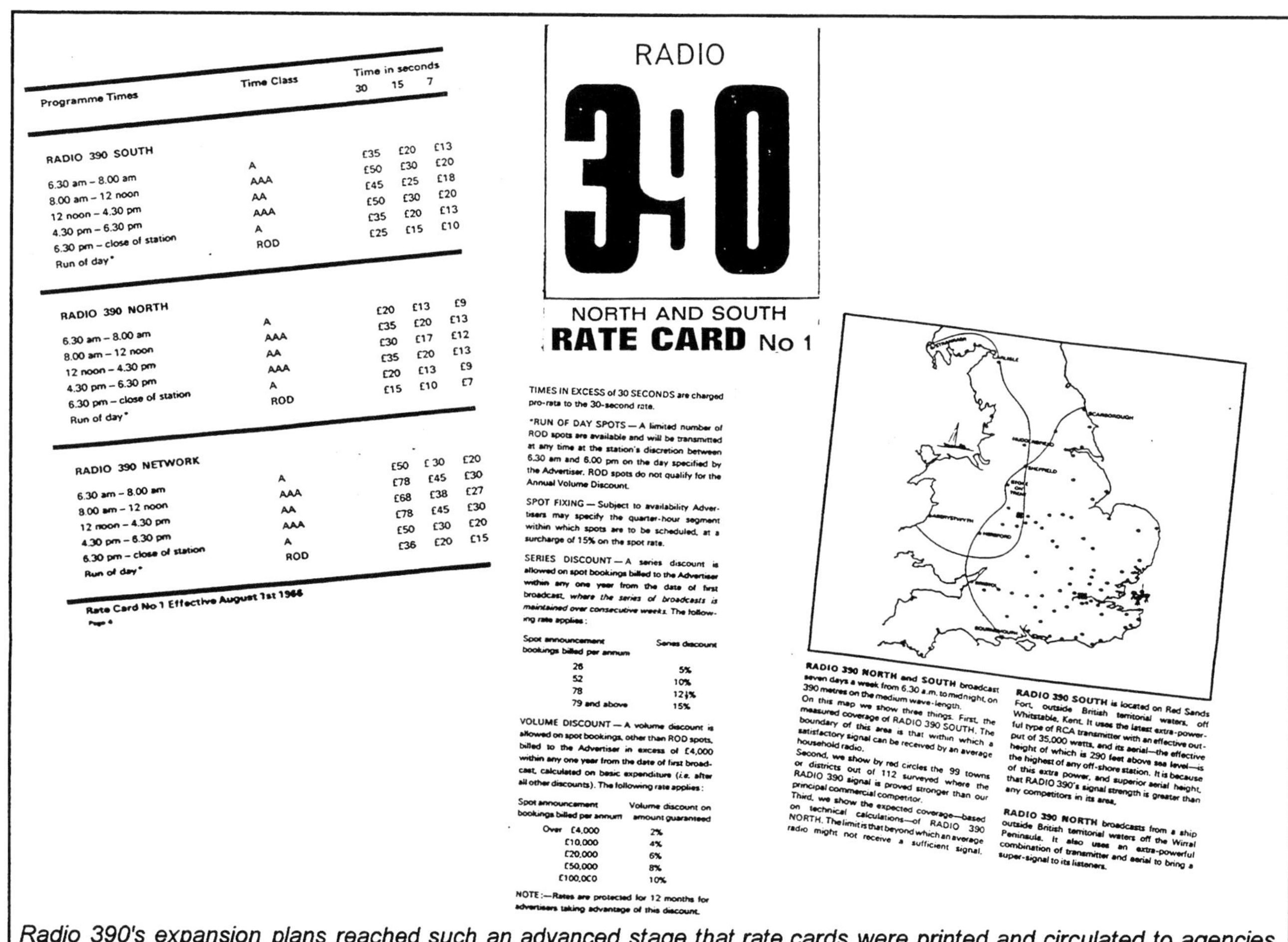

| Programme Times | Time Class | Time in seconds 30 | 15 | 7 |
|---|---|---|---|---|
| **RADIO 390 SOUTH** | | | | |
| 6.30 am – 8.00 am | A | £35 | £20 | £13 |
| 8.00 am – 12 noon | AAA | £50 | £30 | £20 |
| 12 noon – 4.30 pm | AA | £45 | £25 | £18 |
| 4.30 pm – 6.30 pm | AAA | £50 | £30 | £20 |
| 6.30 pm – close of station | A | £35 | £20 | £13 |
| Run of day* | ROD | £25 | £15 | £10 |
| **RADIO 390 NORTH** | | | | |
| 6.30 am – 8.00 am | A | £20 | £13 | £9 |
| 8.00 am – 12 noon | AAA | £35 | £20 | £13 |
| 12 noon – 4.30 pm | AA | £30 | £17 | £12 |
| 4.30 pm – 6.30 pm | AAA | £35 | £20 | £13 |
| 6.30 pm – close of station | A | £20 | £13 | £9 |
| Run of day* | ROD | £15 | £10 | £7 |
| **RADIO 390 NETWORK** | | | | |
| 6.30 am – 8.00 am | A | £50 | £30 | £20 |
| 8.00 am – 12 noon | AAA | £78 | £45 | £30 |
| 12 noon – 4.30 pm | AA | £68 | £38 | £27 |
| 4.30 pm – 6.30 pm | AAA | £78 | £45 | £30 |
| 6.30 pm – close of station | A | £50 | £30 | £20 |
| Run of day* | ROD | £36 | £20 | £15 |

Rate Card No 1 Effective August 1st 1966

Page 4

RADIO

390

NORTH AND SOUTH

**RATE CARD** No 1

TIMES IN EXCESS of 30 SECONDS are charged pro-rata to the 30-second rate.

*RUN OF DAY SPOTS — A limited number of ROD spots are available and will be transmitted at any time at the station's discretion between 6.30 am and 6.00 pm on the day specified by the Advertiser. ROD spots do not qualify for the Annual Volume Discount.

SPOT FIXING — Subject to availability Advertisers may specify the quarter-hour segment within which spots are to be scheduled, at a surcharge of 15% on the spot rate.

SERIES DISCOUNT — A series discount is allowed on spot bookings billed to the Advertiser within any one year from the date of first broadcast, *where the series of broadcasts is maintained over consecutive weeks.* The following rate applies:

| Spot announcement bookings billed per annum | Series discount |
|---|---|
| 26 | 5% |
| 52 | 10% |
| 78 | 12½% |
| 79 and above | 15% |

VOLUME DISCOUNT — A volume discount is allowed on spot bookings, other than ROD spots, billed to the Advertiser in excess of £4,000 within any one year from the date of first broadcast, calculated on basic expenditure (*i.e.* after all other discounts). The following rate applies:

| Spot announcement bookings billed per annum | Volume discount on amount guaranteed |
|---|---|
| Over £4,000 | 2% |
| £10,000 | 4% |
| £20,000 | 6% |
| £50,000 | 8% |
| £100,000 | 10% |

NOTE:—Rates are protected for 12 months for advertisers taking advantage of this discount.

**RADIO 390 NORTH and SOUTH** broadcast seven days a week from 6.30 a.m. to midnight, on 390 metres on the medium wave-length.

On this map we show three things. First, the measured coverage of RADIO 390 SOUTH. The boundary of this area is that within which a satisfactory signal can be received by an average household radio.

Second, we show by red circles the 99 towns or districts out of 112 surveyed where the RADIO 390 signal is proved stronger than our principal commercial competitor.

Third, we show the expected coverage—based on technical calculations—of RADIO 390 NORTH. The limit is that beyond which an average radio might not receive a sufficient signal.

**RADIO 390 SOUTH** is located on Red Sands Fort, outside British territorial waters, off Whitstable, Kent. It uses the latest extra-powerful type of RCA transmitter with an effective output of 35,000 watts, and its aerial—the effective height of which is 290 feet above sea level—is the highest of any off-shore station. It is because of this extra power, and superior aerial height, that RADIO 390's signal strength is greater than any competitors in its area.

**RADIO 390 NORTH** broadcasts from a ship outside British territorial waters off the Wirral Peninsula. It also uses an extra-powerful combination of transmitter and aerial to bring a super-signal to its listeners.

*Radio 390's expansion plans reached such an advanced stage that rate cards were printed and circulated to agencies and potential advertisers detailing plans for the introduction of Radio 390 North and the VHF (FM) service in the south.*

The plan was to anchor the *Cheeta 2* off the coast of the Wirral peninsular in the north west of England to broadcast 'sweet music' programmes under the call sign Radio 390 North. With the original station on Red Sands Fort renamed Radio 390 South, this would have given listeners and advertisers an easy listening station with almost national coverage and an alternative to Radio Caroline's national pop music service.

Another finding of the 1965 survey indicated that there would be a demand amongst listeners for VHF (FM) transmissions from Radio 390 to London and south east England. The station made plans to introduce such a service in the summer of 1966 on Radio 390 South in parallel with the increased national coverage.

However, differences of opinion amongst the Radio 390 board of directors and prosecutions brought against the station by the authorities combined to prevent these advanced plans being put into practice. *Cheeta 2* also suddenly became unavailable at about this time. The vessel had been moored off Harwich since ending her service with Radio Caroline South, but in mid-July 1966 she dragged her anchor in heavy seas and had to be towed into port. Here a writ of attachment was nailed to her mast by creditors and she was impounded by the Admiralty Marshall pending the outcome of an outstanding salvage claim.

On the programming side Radio 390 did introduce a number of innovative features during the summer of 1966. From 11th July 1966 the station broadcast (twice a day at 7.30pm and 12 midnight) a half hour magazine programme "The

Voice of Business" - directed each day towards a particular industrial sector-

- **Monday** Building and Construction
- **Tuesday** Manufacturing and Engineering
- **Wednesday** Advertising and Marketing
- **Thursday** Retailing
- **Friday** Agriculture ('Agri-business')

These programmes, which were designed to attract advertising from the daily target sectors, included sales success features as well as customer information on prices and distribution services. Special advertising rates were charged for this programme - £100 for a five minute interview/ promotion (including all production costs) and £50 for a two minute scripted announcement.

## The beginning of the end

The events on Radio City and the subsequent questions in the House of Commons at the end of June 1966 had brought into sharp focus the Government's failure to act on two fronts. Firstly to take some positive action against the fort-based broadcasters who, despite all their assertions to the contrary, were illegally occupying Government-owned properties, which by virtue of the provisions of an Order in Council adopted in 1964, were within territorial waters

This often overlooked fact was highlighted by the Chairman of the British Copyright Council, Sir Alan Herbert, who suggested that the Navy should be sent to Shivering Sands Fort and pointed out again to the authorities that the Forts were within territorial waters - "It has been said that the Fort is outside the territorial limits and that no court will take the case. This is a dangerous delusion. The Towers have been in territorial waters since 30th September 1964, under an Order in Council specially made for the purpose by the last Government. Moreover they are in the area of the Port of London Authority and all the criminal laws apply."

The Order in Council referred to was the Territorial Waters Order in Council which came into effect on 30th September 1964 and allowed for the extension of British territorial waters beyond the (then) three mile limit. (See Chapter 1)

Secondly the Labour Government had continued its Conservative predecessor's procrastination over taking action against offshore broadcasters in general, claiming higher legislative priorities and lack of parliamentary time. This was despite Britain having ratified the Strasbourg Convention provisions to outlaw offshore broadcasting in January 1965. As a further reason for not introducing anti-offshore radio legislation the Government relied on its vague promise to undertake a "general review" of broadcasting policy, including the creation of a legal alternative to the 'pirate' stations as well as a public service based local radio network.

### Radio 390 programme schedule, Summer 1966

*Monday - Saturday*

6.30am Bright and Early
7.00am The World Tomorrow
7.30am Morning Melody
9.00am Cover Girl
9.15am You and the Stars
10.00am South of the Border
10.15am Masters of the Organ
10.35am Pause for Prayer
10.45am Keyboard Cavalcade
11.15am Doctor Paul
11.30am Music from the Shows
12noon Lunch Break
Meet Mike and Mandy
*(Sat 12.00-12.30)*
1.00pm From Me to You
2.00pm Playtime
2.15pm Melody Hour
3.15pm Movie Melody
Spotlight *(Sat)*
3.30pm Memory Lane
4.00pm Intermezzo
4.30pm Tea Time Tunes
5.00pm Country Style
5.30pm Continental Cabaret
6.00pm Stateside
6.30pm The World Tomorrow
7.00pm Mike Raven Show
7.30pm Voice of Business *(Mon-Fri)*
8.00pm Dinner at Eight
8.30pm From Me to You
9.00pm Serenade
11.00pm *Sunday Times* Hour of Jazz *(Sat)*
12midnight Voice of Business *(Mon-Fri)*
12.30am Epilogue and Closedown
*(12 midnight Sat)*

**Danger Man**

*An episode of the 60s television drama series, Danger Man, was filmed aboard Red Sands Fort in 1966.*

*The episode, "Not So Jolly Roger" starred Patrick McGoohan as Danger Man, John Drake and had a storyline of intrigue and murder aboard a pirate radio station.*

*Series producer Sidney Cole explained some of the difficulties encountered in filming the episode: "Informal contact was made with the famous Radio 390 then operating from a wartime anti-invasion fort in the Thames Estuary.*

*Officially the pirates didn't exist . Communications between them and the shore could only take place on a hush-hush radio in emergencies. When it came to the actual filming getting cameras and equipment aboard the pirate fort was a hazard in itself. Technicians had to be hoisted aboard amid 20 feet high waves.*

*And when Patrick McGoohan is seen clambering onto the 60ft high tower in a storm, there's no stunt man involved. McGoohan did it himself."*

In this atmosphere of apparent immunity from official action the offshore stations flourished and multiplied throughout late 1965 and early 1966. However, the Radio City affair, with its graphic demonstration of anarchic and violent behaviour spelt the beginning of the end for all British offshore broadcasters - the Government could no longer be seen to delay taking action to deal with a situation which was rapidly and very probably becoming out of control.

Two days after the 1st July announcement that legislation would now be introduced before the summer recess Postmaster General Anthony Wedgewood Benn was replaced in a Cabinet reshuffle by a new Minister, Edward Short. He was to adopt a far more positive and aggressive attitude towards outlawing the offshore broadcasters and a few days after taking up his appointment Mr. Short announced that once they had been closed the offshore stations would not be replaced by local commercial stations - broadcasting in Britain was to remain firmly under public control.

On 13th July 1966 Mr. Short told the House of Commons that the planned legislation would implement the provisions of the 1965 Strasbourg Convention and follow the principles of equivalent Scandinavian laws. These laws not only made it illegal to own or work for offshore broadcasting stations but also prevented any citizen of the country, or any company registered in the country, advertising on or supporting them in any way.

## The Marine Offences Bill

The Bill to outlaw offshore broadcasting stations - the Marine etc. Broadcasting (Offences) Bill (M.O.B.) was eventually introduced into the House of Commons on 27th July 1966 and received its formal First Reading. The provisions contained in the Bill applied to all structures, floating, fixed or airborne, which could be used as bases for broadcasting and prohibited any British citizen or company from owning, operating, working for, supplying, advertising on or in any way assisting an offshore station. Penalties for contravening the Bill's provisions were £100 fines or three months imprisonment, or both on conviction in a Magistrates Court or two years in prison and an unspecified fine on conviction at Quarter Sessions or Assizes.

The initial reactions from the offshore stations to the Bill were defiant, containing general expressions of determination to fight its introduction and continue broadcasting.

**Radio Caroline** condemned the Bill as "spiteful, unimaginative and a negation of basic freedom that seeks to put an outright ban on the enjoyment of 25 million regular listeners to offshore radio, without submitting any alternative proposals for satisfying the legitimate demand." At the same time the station engaged a public relations company to help it fight the legislation when Parliament reassembled in the autumn.

**Radio City** owner Dorothy Calvert said she hoped enough MPs in Parliament would realise that the offshore stations were giving the public a service they wanted and would throw the Bill out.

Bill Vick of **Radio England/Britain Radio** said "our ship is American owned and crewed, and the DJs are American. I have already been approached by several continental businessmen about advertising." By coincidence on the day of the Bill's publication Radio England/Britain Radio held a champagne party at the Hilton Hotel in London. Attended by 600 guests, including many contemporary pop stars, and costing over £4,000 (the bill for which was never paid) it was a public relations exercise designed to demonstrate support from the world of show business for offshore radio stations in general.

**Radio Essex** owner Roy Bates said he would live abroad to escape the provisions of the planned legislation.

**Radio London's** Managing Director Philip Birch promised to move the station's headquarters abroad, to supply the ship from Spain and Holland and obtain advertising from New York and Paris. He went on to state that the Bill would discriminate against British manufacturers who would no longer be able to use Radio London to advertise their products. Radio London, he said, would still be broadcasting in 30 years time.

**Radio Scotland** claimed to have a plan to continue broadcasting by supplying the *Comet* from Ireland, moving its anchorage 70 miles out into the Atlantic, installing a more powerful transmitter and replacing the Scottish crew and DJs with foreign staff. The station organised a petition and within a month two and a half million signatures had been collected.

**Radio 270** Managing Director Wilf Proudfoot promised that his station would find ways of getting round the legislation, if it ever succeeded in progressing beyond the First Reading stage. The station launched a campaign urging listeners to write to their MPs and 'fight for free radio'.

A **Radio 390** spokesman said that the station would use the former Radio Syd ship, *Cheeta 2* as a base from which to continue its broadcasts if the Government took action against them on the Red Sands Fort. The station would, he said, meet the salvage claim outstanding on the vessel and release her from Harwich. The 'sweet music' station also exhorted its listeners to write to their MPs protesting against the proposed legislation.

In the House of Commons opposition to the Marine etc. Broadcasting (Offences) Bill was immediate. On 28th July 1966, the day after the Bill's First Reading two Conservative MPs, Mr. Iremonger and Mr. Gresham-Cooke, tabled a motion which stated that "the Bill will deprive millions of people of the sound of music they love and can at present only get from the pirate stations". Another Conservative MP, Mr. Eldon Griffiths, called on the Postmaster General to "make speedy provision for legitimate local broadcasting stations to meet the British people's evident desire for a wider range and greater variety of broadcasting than is at present available from the BBC."

Perhaps the most concise summary of the feelings of those opposed to the new Bill's provisions was contained in an article published in *The Economist* on 30th July 1966:- *The Bill to put down the pop pirates was published last Thursday. It is a ripe cartload of needless rubbish. The unlicensed commercial broadcasting stations around Britain's coast give a good deal of harmless pleasure and do very little practical harm.*

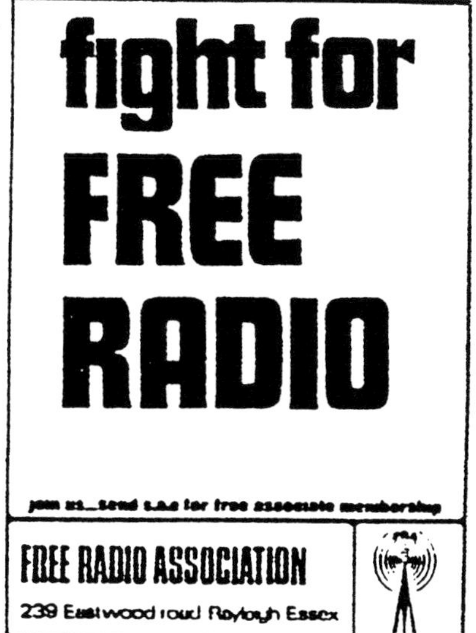


*Publicity material issued by 'Free Radio' listeners' groups*

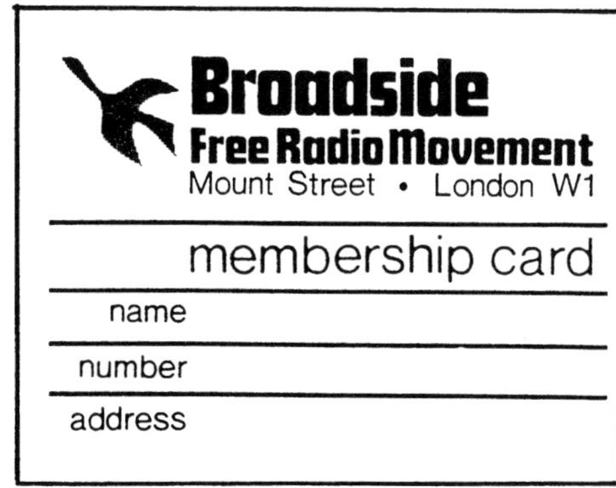

## Arguments against and in support of the offshore stations

*Despite their huge audience figures the British offshore stations were not popular with everyone, particularly Government departments and various trade organisations - perceived as a threat by the former to existing national and international agreements and by the latter to the vested interests of their own membership.*

*Many arguments were put forward for outlawing the offshore stations, but essentially they followed variations of one or more of the following themes:-*

- 1. The offshore stations 'pirated' frequencies and transmitter powers not allocated to them under international agreements, in particular the 1948 Copenhagen Convention and (occasionally) caused interference to legitimate stations using these frequencies. Britain was a signatory to various international agreements and it was therefore the Government's responsibility to uphold its obligations. As a supplementary to this the international frequency allocation argument was also used to refute any suggestion that the offshore stations should be invited on land or that a network of commercial stations could be established to compete with the BBC. "The frequencies are not available for use in Britain" was the standard reply to any proposals by 'commercial' or 'local' radio pressure groups to establish stations on land.

- 2. The offshore stations' transmissions interfered with maritime, ship-to-shore and emergency service communications, posing a possible threat to the lives of those who found themselves in distress at sea and needing assistance.

- 3. The offshore stations avoided paying copyright fees for the recorded music they broadcast and did not observe any 'needletime' restrictions on the number of hours of such music transmitted each week - as the BBC was obliged to do under a hard won agreement with Phonographic Performances Ltd.

*As a counter to these accusations the offshore stations, and their supporters, put forward the following arguments:*

- 1. At the time (the mid 1960s) over 300 of the 500 medium wave stations operating in Europe did so on frequencies not allocated under the 1948 Copenhagen Convention, including 'respectable' stations such as Vatican Radio, Voice of America and Radio Luxembourg.

- 2. Admittedly there had been some complaints of interference in the early days of offshore broadcasting, but the number of instances where offshore transmissions had caused interference with maritime and emergency communications was rare. The offshore stations had a responsibility to avoid such interference being caused by their transmissions, a responsibility which most stations acknowledged. They continually made efforts to avoid providing grounds for any such accusations being directed at them. Apart from this moral responsibility the stations also had a vested interest in avoiding disruption to the emergency service's communications network because they themselves were at some stage likely to need assistance - a fact demonstrated many times during the history of offshore broadcasting.

- 3. Some of the larger offshore stations offered to make payments for copyright and performance fees (although it must be said the majority did not). Phonographic Performances Ltd. refused to accept any such monies but the Performing Rights Society did accept payments (in particular from Radio Caroline, Radio London and Radio 390) and this fact was much publicised by the stations as evidence of their good intentions. However, what was not so widely publicised by either party was that whilst the PRS openly accepted these payments, the organisation did not feel it could fully condone or support the existence of offshore radio.

*With the possible exception of the argument about interference to maritime and emergency communications (which in reality was more of a theoretical than real possibility) the other arguments appear even more irrelevant today than they were thirty years ago. Britain now has over 150 commercial local or regional radio stations, 56 BBC local and regional stations, 5 BBC national radio networks and 3 national commercial radio stations, all of whom have been found and allocated frequencies from within Britain's quota under international agreement. Virtually all of these stations have a music based format, pouring out hundreds of hours a week of recorded music. This, it was argued at the height of the offshore stations' popularity, would destroy the music industry and with it the livelihoods of musicians everywhere. Experience has shown that if anything the reverse has proved to be the case.*

## Two fort-based stations prosecuted

Some stations, however, did not have to wait for the introduction of legislation proposed in the Marine etc. Broadcasting (Offences) Bill before action was taken against them.

On 21st September 1966 summonses were served by the Post Office on the owners of Radio 390, Estuary Radio Ltd., and its Secretary, David Lye alleging that "on 16th August 1966 at Red Sands Tower, situated eight and a half miles off the coast but within the Thames Estuary, the company did unlawfully use apparatus for wireless telegraphy, namely a transmitter, contrary to section 1 of the Wireless Telegraphy Act 1949". The station's Managing Director, Ted Allbeury was served with a similar summons the following day and the hearing of the case against all parties was subsequently fixed for 24th November at Longport Magistrates Court, Canterbury.

A week later, on 29th September 1966 Roy Bates, head of Radio Essex, was served with a similar summons to be heard at Rochford Magistrates Court alleging the illegal use of a transmitter at Knock John Fort, again contravening the Wireless Telegraphy Act of 1949. Mr. Bates then announced that he had taken over another fort at Tongue Sands, 9 miles off Margate, and would use this as a broadcasting base for a new station - to be known either as Radio Albatross or Radio Kent. Then at the beginning of October 1966 he changed the name and format of his existing station, Radio Essex to BBMS (Britain's Better Music Station), which now broadcast easy listening music during the day and pop music between 9.00pm and 6.00am.

The other fort-based station, Radio City, remained un-summonsed at this stage but surprisingly a ship-based station, Radio Scotland, was served with a summons in December 1966 alleging that it had broadcast from within territorial waters from its anchorage off Troon on the west coast of Scotland. The basis for this prosecution, which eventually came to court in March 1967, lay in a complicated legal argument about the definition of a bay, but in effect the *Comet* was allegedly anchored inside British territorial waters. The detailed arguments and result of this prosecution will be discussed in Chapter 12.

*Unfortunately for the fort based stations the Thames Estuary is a classic example of a 'Bay' defined in international law.*

## Radio 390 closure

When the Radio 390 case came to be heard at Canterbury on 24th November 1966 Ted Allbeury and David Lye both pleaded not guilty to the charges against them. The Post Office gave evidence from three of its engineers that the station had broadcast on 773 kHz (388m) on 16th August 1966 and that these transmissions had been monitored and recorded at three separate locations - Shoeburyness in Essex, Morden Point on the Isle of Sheppey and Herne Bay, Kent. Another Post Office witness confirmed that on 10th July 1965 Estuary Radio Ltd. had applied for a licence to broadcast radio programmes, but that the application had been refused.

The case against Radio 390 centred not just on the fact that the broadcasts had taken place, but whether in fact Red Sands Fort was within British territorial waters. Sir Peter Rawlinson QC, appearing on behalf of Estuary Radio Ltd. and its two officers, stated that the Fort was at least 6 miles off the Kent coast

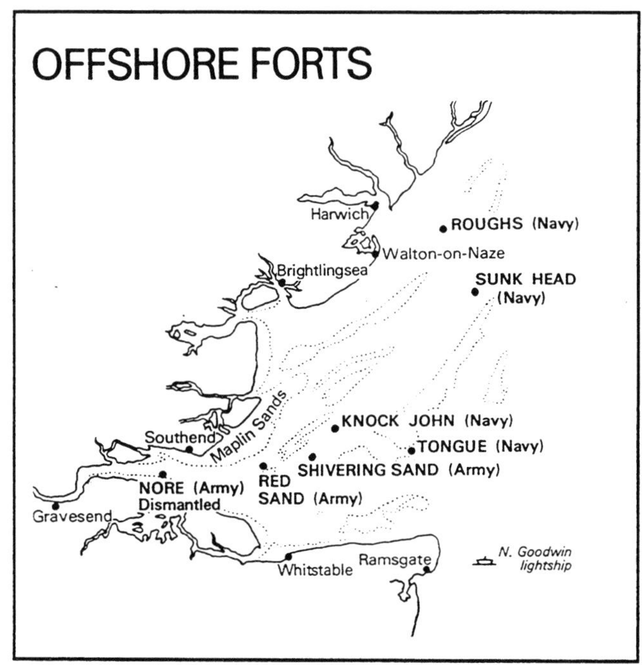

> **BBMS programme schedule**
>
> **6.00am Daybreak Programme**
>
> **Weekend Special** *(Sat/Sun)*
>
> **9.00am Morning Melody**
>
> **12noon Musical Magazine**
>
> **2.00pm Swing Session** *(Sat/Sun)*
>
> **3.00pm Music 'till Six Afternoon Spin** *(Sat/Sun)*
>
> **5.00pm Country and Western** *(Saturday)*
>
> **Jazz Along An Hour** *(Sunday)*
>
> **6.00pm Swing Session**
>
> **7.00pm Evening Inn**
>
> **9.00pm-6.00am Formula 67**

and therefore outside territorial waters. For the Post Office John Newey argued that under the terms of the Order in Council adopted in September 1964 to ratify the 1958 Geneva International Convention of the Sea, the Thames Estuary can be considered a 'bay' if the area of water within it exceeded the area of water in a semi circle drawn from a baseline across the indentation of the coast. A crucial factor in this calculation therefore is the positioning of the two points between which the artificial baseline is drawn.

A naval surveyor, Lt. Commander P B Beasley, Head of the Hydrographic Department at the Ministry of Defence told the court that he calculated the area of water in the bay to be 683 square miles, five square miles more than in the semi-circle across the indentation of the coast. To arrive at this calculation he had drawn a line from Walton-on-the-Naze to North Foreland and included tidal water in the River Thames up to Greenwich and in the River Medway up to Rochester.

A further argument by the Post Office to substantiate the claim that the Fort was inside territorial waters was based on the provision in the Geneva Convention relating to low tide elevations. This provision determines the starting point for calculating British territorial waters and includes all 'islands' uncovered at low water. The Post Office claimed that because Middle Bank, a sandbank off the Isle of Sheppey, was regularly uncovered at low tide it met this provision and, therefore, formed the baseline from which the extent of territorial waters could be calculated.

Sir Peter Rawlinson, summing up on behalf of Estuary Radio Ltd. said the prosecution had only been able to place the Fort within territorial waters by taking into its calculations stretches of the River Thames and River Medway to provide an area of water just sufficient (by only 5 out of 683 square miles) to comply with the terms of the Geneva Convention.

Despite these arguments, however, the magistrates found that the Post Office had proved its case and fined Estuary Radio Ltd. £100 for using an unlicensed transmitter inside territorial waters, while Ted Allbeury and David Lye were given unconditional discharges. A Post Office application for confiscation of £12,000 worth of transmitting equipment and the award of costs was refused by the Court.

Although immediately giving notice of appeal against the Court's decision Ted Allbeury announced that, pending the outcome of that hearing, Radio 390 would have to close. So at 11.00pm on 25th November 1966 Radio 390 played a tape recorded message from Mr. Allbeury in which he explained to listeners the reasons for the station having to go off the air:-

*Hello there, this is Ted Allbeury speaking. I am making this recording on the evening of the 23rd November, the day before I go to court in Canterbury. If the Canterbury Magistrates come down on our side it will be destroyed and you'll never hear it, but if we lose, it is almost certain we will be allowed to appeal. However, it is possible that it might be decided by the Court that we should cease broadcasting pending the appeal being heard. You know that I shall do everything possible to come back on the air as quickly as possible. I am advised that it might take three to four weeks for the appeal to be heard and if we win the appeal we should start broadcasting again immediately. However, if we lost the appeal it would mean that we should have to cease broadcasting from the Fort. I should expect to make some alternative arrangements.*

*I am of course very sad to be making this broadcast. Your newspaper will I am sure keep you informed. I have never been so happy as while I have been running Radio 390. Your kindness and warmth towards us has given me great pleasure. I can't believe that this is the end, but for now all I can say is what I always say - take care of yourself, goodnight and God Bless.*

The duty announcer then said simply "This is Radio 390 now closing down." and the station closed in the usual manner by playing the National Anthem.

**POP PIRATES ARE SUNK**

**Radio 390 goes off the air**

## Radio Essex/BBMS closure

Five days later, on 30th November 1966 Roy Bates of Radio Essex appeared at Rochford Magistrates Court to answer similar charges that he had used an unlicensed transmitter for radio broadcasting at the Knock John Fort.

Mr. Newey again appeared for the prosecution and used the same arguments he had successfully presented the previous week against Radio 390 - that the Thames Estuary was a bay under the provisions of the Geneva Convention and thus (in this case) the West Barrow sandbank gave a low tide elevation which brought the Knock John Fort inside territorial waters. The Post Office engineers gave evidence of monitoring Radio Essex transmissions on 1353kHz (221.7m) on 16th August 1966 from three locations - Herne Bay in Kent, Shoeburyness in Essex and Morden Point on the Isle of Sheppey. Another Post Office official confirmed that an application had been made by Mr. Bates for a licence to broadcast, but as with Radio 390 this had been refused.

Roy Bates, appearing on his own behalf, argued that his station was outside the jurisdiction of the Court because it was located more than 3 nautical miles off the Essex coast. However, the magistrates found that the Knock John Fort was within British territorial waters and imposed a fine of £100, but refused a Post Office request for confiscation of transmitting equipment and payment of costs. Mr. Bates immediately lodged an appeal but his station, BBMS did not cease transmissions, as Radio 390 had done after its conviction. Against the advice of his solicitor, Mr. Bates decided to keep his station on the air from the Knock John Fort.

BBMS had changed frequency slightly to 1349kHz (222.4m) by the beginning of December 1966, although still announced on air that it was broadcasting on 222m. With no money to continue operating the station and an absence of almost any advertising income since September 1966 when the summons alleging illegal transmissions had been issued, BBMS was only able to struggle on for a few more weeks.

There are two versions of when BBMS actually closed, one date is given as 4.30pm on Christmas Day 1966, while another report states that the station stayed on the air until 3rd January 1967. Which version is correct cannot be conclusively confirmed but, what is known for certain is that the transmitting equipment on Knock John Fort was dismantled and removed to Roughs Tower, another ex-Navy Fort which was clearly outside territorial waters by definition of any of the evidence produced in the recent court cases. Here Roy Bates and his family set about establishing their 'ownership' of the Tower but the expected radio transmissions did not materialise. However, the story of the Bates family and Roughs Tower was to unfold in a surprising and most unusual way over the next few years.

Radio 390's appeal against conviction was heard by the High Court on 12th December 1966 before the Lord Chief Justice, Lord Parker, sitting with Lord Justice Salmon and Mr. Justice Blain. Estuary Radio Ltd., seeking to have its conviction by Canterbury Magistrates quashed, was again represented by Sir Peter Rawlinson QC. After hearing the arguments presented by both sides the Court ruled the following day (by a majority of 2 to 1) that the provisions of the Order in Council of September 1964 did have the effect of bringing Red Sands Fort inside British territorial waters and as a consequence the station had been illegally transmitting from that location. Lord Justice Salmon disagreed with the majority view of his two colleagues and it was suggested that Estuary Radio Ltd. could take the case to the House of Lords for final determination. However, Ted Allbeury told reporters outside the Appeal Court that it would be too costly and ultimately pointless to take the appeal to the House of Lords and, therefore, Radio 390 would stay off the air.

## Caroline Cash Casino

Meanwhile, Radio Caroline, having distanced itself from the Radio City affair by issuing a press release stating that all connections with Project Atlanta and Major Oliver Smedley had been severed in 1965, continued to consolidate and improve its own programme format.

Following the refurbishment of the *Mi Amigo,* the introduction of a new wavelength (259m) and a more powerful transmitter in May 1966 the output from Caroline South improved enormously under the guidance of a new Programme Director, Tom Lodge, who had brought down from the North ship by Ronan O'Rahilly.

Tom Lodge recruited a new team of DJs, many without previous radio experience, but who displayed enthusiasm in their presentation style and an empathy for the music they were playing. Under Tom Lodge's direction Caroline North had programmed successfully since arriving off the Isle of Man in July 1964 and he introduced the same style to the South ship during 1966. As a result Caroline South started to sound a far more interesting radio station and more in touch with its audience's musical demands than had previously been the case.

### Caroline TV

*Plans were announced in May 1966 for the launch of Caroline TV from the 'Cheeta 2', which had been equipped and used for television broadcasting by Radio Syd at the end of the previous year.*

*Caroline TV planned to broadcast from 10.00am-3.00pm and from 10.00pm-3.00am, but problems with the condition and ownership of 'Cheeta 2' prevented these plans coming to fruition.*

Despite all these programming adjustments one big weakness still remained - a lack of substantial advertising income. Many big advertisers were still preferring to spend their money with Radio London while Radio Caroline (and Caroline South in particular), although attracting some major brand names, had to rely heavily on small advertisers or in-house promotions for T-shirts, fashion jewellery or Caroline Club membership to fill its commercial airtime.

In August 1966 Ronan O'Rahilly engaged two consultants to revamp the Caroline Sales organisation and generate more advertising income for the station. Terry Bates and Alan Slaight (who had both worked very successfully in Canadian commercial radio) were charged with the task of selling airtime, creating commercial opportunities, promoting in-house merchandise and generally advising on sales administration. Terry Bate, although English by birth, was Vice-President of Stephens and Townrow and of CBS Radio in Canada and joined Radio Caroline on a seven year contract.

One of the consultant's first objectives was to cut overheads and costs by drastically reducing the size of the Sales Department at Caroline House, while at the same time managing to achieve a larger volume of airtime sales. Bate was also credited with the introduction of one of the most successful sponsorship deals ever achieved by an offshore radio station - "Caroline Cash Casino".

The concept of this promotion was that large cash prizes were offered to listeners who successfully solved clues broadcast during the 'Cash Casino' slots - aired hourly from 9.00am to 1.00pm each day. Major brand names sponsored the competition including Weetabix, Findus Frozen Foods, Galaxy Chocolate, VP Wines, Nabisco Shredded Wheat, Alberto VO5 Shampoo and Libby's Canned Fruit products. Listeners were required to submit a product proof of purchase (usually a carton flap or bottle label) with their Cash Casino entries and Radio Caroline used these to demonstrate to individual sponsors the enormous success of the promotion.

The Cash Casino programme segments, hosted by Canadian DJ Bill Hearne, were taped at Caroline House and aired simultaneously on both the North and South ships. Each segment had a different sponsor and contained a new clue (in the form of a rhyming couplet) each day. Listener's answers were 'drawn' from a mail sack during each segment and £10 was added to the jackpot total for every incorrect answer drawn.

Jackpot prizes awarded in the Caroline Cash Casino promotion ranged from £460 to £4,070 and during ten separate competitions a total of £26,190 was won by listeners. At the height of the competition the basement of Caroline House was filled with mail sacks bulging with listener's entries, a demonstration in itself of the enormous popularity of the Cash Casino feature. Within the first eleven weeks of the competition over one million entries were received showing the following breakdown for each of the four original sponsors:-

Alberto VO5 Shampoo - 99,840

Findus Frozen Foods - 174,491

Libbys Canned Fruits - 424,228

Weetabix Breakfast Cereal - 394,216

Other major sponsorship deals were also arranged by Terry Bate including "Lucky Birthday Bonanza" (sponsored by Golden Wonder Peanuts), and "Partners in Profit" (sponsored by Weetabix and Ajax), all of which gave Caroline, and in particular Caroline South, a far more commercially successful sound, generated much needed income and heightened audience awareness of the station.

### Caroline Cash Casino Number 7 - Clues

*1. If you'd bring our subject Close to hand You'd do well to think Of a foreign land.*

*2. The place we mean is quite far from here, And the object sought is their native gear.*

*3. A crescent moon And stars - just two,*

*4. Would, in a certain form, Provide a lead for you.*

*5 The country which We implicate,*

*6. Is bordering on A Balkan State.*

*7. But please don't dwell Beyond the British shore,*

*8. If you'd find the thing That we're looking for.*

*9. This "foreign" object Which you seek to name,*

*10. Has, in association, Certain claim to fame.*

*11 You may think of a cap Or even hat;*

*12. But if you covet the prize You must go further than that.*

*13. This elusive object I would guess you've seen*

*14. Many a-time On your TV screen.*

*15. Innumerable times Throughout the year*

*16. Will, with its owner, On the stage appear.*

*17. Adorned it i With a tuft of cords,*

*18. While the one below Many laughs affords.*

*The prize of £2,820 was won on the day this 18th clue was broadcast (23rd March 1967), the answer being comedian Tommy Cooper's Fez.*

## Caroline North wavelength change

Radio Caroline North had continued uninterrupted broadcasting throughout early 1966 and, apart from the loan of some DJs to assist with test transmissions from the refurbished *Mi Amigo* in April, the station had remained relatively unscathed by all the troubles affecting her sister in the south. During the summer of 1966 plans were announced to increase the transmitter power of Caroline North to 50Kw and for a change in wavelength for the station to 259m, bringing it in line with Caroline South.

The practical difficulties of changing wavelength and increasing transmitter power while at the same time maintaining a normal daily programme service were tremendous. Radio Caroline North achieved both by closing its normal service on 1520kHz (197m) at 8.30pm, 9.30pm or 10.00pm (depending on the day of the week and the number of sponsored religious programmes to be transmitted) and then re-opening again an hour later with test broadcasts on

## Wedding

*Yet another offshore radio 'first' was achieved by Radio Caroline North during September 1966 when one of the station's DJs, Mick Luvzit (Brown) was married on board the MV Caroline to Janet Teret, sister of another DJ, Ray Teret. The ceremony which was conducted by the Captain of the MV 'Caroline', Martin Gips, under Panamanian law (as that was the country of registration of the radioship) was broadcast live during the afternoon of 21st September 1966.*

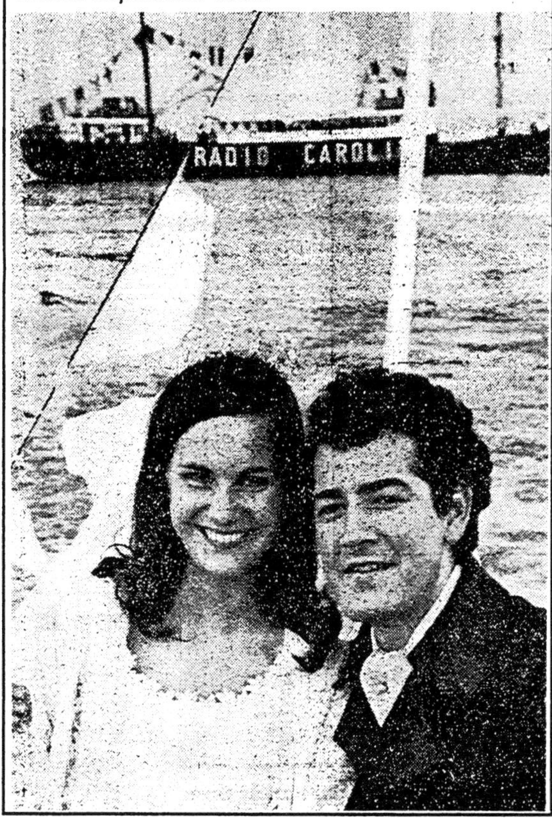


1169kHz (257m). These tests continued throughout the night under the programme titles " West of Midnight" ( an hour after normal closedown until 12 midnight) and "East of Midnight" (12 midnight until 5.55am). Normal programming then resumed at 6.00am on 1520kHz (197m).

These test transmissions started on 30th October 1966 and continued throughout November and into early December. A daytime test on the new frequency took place on 23rd November 1966 when the station's complete output from 1.10pm until 5.55am the following morning was on 1169kHz (257m), reverting to 1520kHz (197m) at 6.00am on 24th November. The permanent change to the new wavelength was eventually achieved on Sunday 18th December 1966 and Radio Caroline North then joined her sister station broadcasting under the national call sign "Caroline on 259".

## Radio 270 bomb hoax

Off the east coast of England Radio 270 continued to experience technical difficulties throughout the latter half of 1966 resulting in frequent breaks in transmission. However, a problem of a different sort arose in October 1966 when an un-stamped letter addressed to the station was opened by the Post Office in Scarborough and found to contain a note with the following message:- " There is a limpet mine attached to the ship. This is not a hoax".

The police were informed, as were the station's management, but because of a ban on direct ship-to-shore communications with the radio ship Humber Radio refused to allow a call to be made to the *Oceaan VII.* Meanwhile the crew remained unaware for some hours of the possible danger they were in .

A call was eventually put through to the radio ship but only after Managing Director, Wilf Proudfoot had contacted the Postmaster General personally, and Police had repeatedly requested Humber Radio to relax the ban. Ironically because of the communications ban the crew of *Oceaan VII* did not adopt normal maritime practice and keep a constant radio watch. As a result when the call was eventually made after strenuous efforts by management and police no response was received from the radio ship. Eventually at 4.20pm the Burmah Nort Sea Oil Rig, *Sea Quest*, managed to make contact with *Oceaan VII* and relayed the message to the crew who searced the ship, but found nothing. Largely because the crew had been unaware of the situation for most of the day Radio 270 had continued to broadcast normal programmes throughout this 'crisis'.

Radio 270 was off the air again at the beginning of November 1966 and on 3rd November the Captain of the *Oceaan VII* made an emergency call to Humber Radio saying his vessel had a seized main shaft and required urgent assistance.The radio ship was towed into Scarborough for repair by the tug *Success II* and within a few days was able to return to her anchorage, enabling Radio 270 to resume transmissions. However, the unfortunate station suffered further breaks in transmission later in November and early December 1966 due to storm damage and eventually it was decided that the *Oceaan VII* should move to a more sheltered anchorage off Bridlington.

## SRE closure

After some weeks of speculation and rumours an announcement was made in mid-October 1966 that Radio England would be closing and the station's frequency leased to a Dutch language broadcaster, Radio Dolfijn.

Radio England had not been the commercial success its American backers had hoped - the programming format was too brash for British audiences and, with a declining listenership, advertisers could not be persuaded to buy airtime on the station. In addition there had been constant professional friction between the American and British DJs on board the *Laissez Faire* and the disillusionment of those still on board when the station closed was clearly evident in the final few hours of broadcasting - quite clearly they could barely wait to finish their individual programmes slots and close the station. Radio England eventually ceased transmissions at midnight on 5th November 1966 after presenting one of the most lack-lustre final hours of broadcasting in offshore radio history.

The following day the Dutch language station, Radio Dolfijn took to the air. This station was owned by Verkoopmatschappij NV of Amsteldijt 63, Amsterdam and broadcast on the former Radio England frequency from 6.00am - 12midnight. The station's format was similar to that of Britain Radio, with a number of Dutch DJs presenting programmes live from the *Laissez Faire*. Radio Dolfijn, nicknamed 'Flipper Radio' built up a small audience in Holland but never posed a real commercial threat to the longer established and far more popular Radio Veronica (see Chapter 13).

Despite the fact that Britain Radio had been less successful in audience terms than its sister station its own transmissions were not affected by the closure of Radio England. The easy listening station continued to broadcast much as before, but now shared the *Laissez Faire* with the new station Radio Dolfijn seeking to break into the Dutch market.

About this time too Radio London briefly explored the concept of providing programmes and selling airtime for the benefit of Dutch listeners and advertisers. The plan involved producing four hours a day of bi-lingual Dutch and English programmes and advertising, but the station did not attempt to provide a complete service aimed at the Dutch market (in direct competition with Radio Veronica) in the way that Radio Dolfijn did.

At the end of November 1966 an approach from the rebel Rhodesian Government led by Ian Smith, to purchase £50,000 worth of advertising on Radio London was turned down by the station because the commercials would involve political propaganda material. It was feared, quite understandably, that the broadcasting of such material could only hasten the implementation of proposals contained in the Marine etc. Broadcasting (Offences) Bill which was then starting its passage through the Parliamentary process.

## White Paper- The Future of Broadcasting

Towards the end of 1966 the BBC began to fuel the debate about how to eliminate the British offshore radio stations. In November 1966 it published the results of a survey, carried out by its own Audience Research Department and based on a sample of only 5,000 people nationwide. This survey claimed to show that:-

- more than three quarters of the population over 15 never or hardly ever listened to the offshore stations;
- the BBC Light Programme had a daily audience four times greater than the total of the offshore stations' audience; and
- the daily audience for offshore stations amounted to only 6,250,000.

### Estimated advertising income of the offshore stations

*(September 1966)*

***Radio Scotland*** *-£30,000 per month*

***Radio 270*** *£7,000 per month*

***Radio 390*** *£14,000 profit per month*

***Radio London*** *£1 million during the first nine months of 1966*

### Caroline and Luxembourg

*Late in 1966 Jean Prouvost, owner of the French magazine Paris Match, together with a number of other businessmen had acquired a controlling interest in the French service of Radio Luxembourg. The station, then third in the French audience ratings asked Ronan O'Rahilly to advise on how their situation could be improved. He was given a two hour slot in the programme schedules and former Radio Caroline South DJ 'Emperor' Rosko was hired to present the programme - the Mini-Max Show - using the title 'President' Rosko.*

The results of this survey can be contrasted with the one carried out by NOP in July 1966 which, although concentrating on commercial radio listenership as opposed to BBC, showed a substantially higher overall audience level for the offshore stations.

The BBC produced some further anti-offfshore radio information in its Annual Report for 1965/66 which stated that the stations were spoiling reception of continental radio stations and "stealing the legal property of British musicians, gramophone companies and other copyright holders." The Report went on "Although willing to do so, the BBC has not been free to provide such a service on its legally allocated frequencies since it has to use its three networks to serve the community as a whole." This statement was a clear indication that the BBC were exploring means by which they could introduce an alternative service to the offshore stations, but they were also experiencing resistance from organisations such as the Musicians Union and even some members of the Government who reportedly were in favour of establishing a separate radio organisation to provide a continuous pop music service.

However, this option seemed to have been dismissed when on 20th December 1966 the Government published its long awaited White Paper on the Future of Broadcasting. The document proposed that the BBC would be authorised tooperate a popular music service, using the medium wave frequency which was then allocated to the Light Programme (1215kHz (247m) and also launch nine experimental local radio stations using VHF (FM) frequencies only.

This second proposal was a defeat for the local commercial radio lobby, which did not just consist of offshore radio station operators but a large number of community and business based groups who for many years had argued in favour of a commercially funded alternative to the BBC. The White Paper firmly rejected any suggestion that local radio should be operated by commercial interests, stating -"It is of first importance to maintain public service principles in the further development of the broadcasting service." At a press conference to launch the White Paper the Postmaster General, Edward Short, emphasised the point that the local radio experiment should not be commercially funded- "We have excluded this. We feel it is incompatible with the objective of a local radio station, which would be to contribute to the communal life of the town. I do not think you can reconcile this with commercial interests."

The offshore stations and other commercial radio interests reacted angrily to the White Paper proposals. Radio Caroline called it a "manifesto for monopolists" and a spokesman for the station went on to say, "It does little but perpetuate the dreariness of British broadcasting which the public has clearly rejected in its enthusiasm for the offshore stations." The Secretary of the Local Radio Association, John Gorst, said his organisation completely disagreed with the White Paper's proposals and that the limitation of the nine local stations to VHF (FM) only would mean that just 11% of the population would be able to receive their transmissions.

1966 closed on a somewhat depressed note as far as offshore radio was concerned. Two stations had been closed as the result of prosecutions, another prosecution was pending and both the Government and the BBC had revealed their own plans which clearly offered no long-term future for the offshore broadcasters.

## Chapter 12

# The end of an era

The year 1967, destined to be one of the most significant for British offshore radio, started with the return of a station which had closed the previous November. Radio 390 resumed broadcasts at midnight on 31st December 1966, claiming it had new evidence to show that its base at Red Sands Fort was at least one and a half miles outside British territorial waters.

During the prosecution of Estuary Radio Ltd. in November 1966 the Post Office had relied on the exposure, at low tide, of Middle Sands sandbank to argue that the three mile territorial limit could then be calculated from this point. Radio 390 had now taken measurements of its own and was satisfied that the Middle Sands sandbank was in fact never fully exposed at low tide.

However, the optimism amongst some Estuary Radio directors of this new evidence being successful in persuading the authorities that the station operated outside British jurisdiction was not shared by all at Radio 390. Managing Director Ted Allbeury resigned from the company on 10th February 1967 saying "I honestly believe a ship has greater potential than the Forts. The Forts are constantly being harassed by the Government. I have not been able to persuade my shareholders to take a ship and am therefore hamstrung to continue."

Two days later it was announced that he had joined Britain Radio, which he intended to re-launch with a format similar to Radio 390 and that he had taken with him a number of the fort-based station's announcers. Meanwhile David Lye, Company Secretary of Estuary Radio Ltd., took over as Acting Managing Director of Radio 390.

Following the recommencement of broadcasts new summonses were issued by the Post Office against Radio 390 once again alleging the illegal use of transmitting equipment within territorial waters. This time, however, the hearing was to be at Southend, rather than Canterbury, Magistrates Court. On 17th February 1967 Sir Peter Rawlinson QC, acting on behalf of Radio 390 applied to the High Court seeking an order to prevent the magistrates at Southend from hearing the case. He argued that the Post Office was "shopping around" to find a court that would convict his clients, but Lord Justice Winn, Mr. Justice Ashworth and Mr. Justice Widgery refused the application saying that they had no powers to prevent the prosecution being heard in any court.

On 23rd February 1967 magistrates sitting at Southend heard a total of 28 summonses against Estuary Radio Ltd. and its directors Ted Allbeury, Maurice Gething, John la Trobe, Christopher Blackwell, Michael Mitcham and David Lye. Each summons alleged that the station had broadcast from inside British territorial waters without a licence on 4th, 5th, 6th and 7th January 1967.

During the hearing representatives of the Royal Navy were called by the prosecution to give evidence that the sandbank at Middle Sands was indeed exposed at low tide. They produced a photograph to the Court showing Lt.

**Radio 390 is on the air again**

Mr Ted Allbeury, managing director of Estuary Radio which operates the pirate station, Radio 390, said yesterday that the station resumed broadcasting on Saturday and was back again from 6 30 a.m. yesterday.

"We shall stay on the air now," he added. "We have new evidence that our Red Sands tower is at least a mile and a half outside territorial waters. It is now up to the GPO to summon us again if it feels it has a case."

Radio 390 went off the air on November 25 after Canterbury magistrates found that the tower was inside territorial waters. Estuary Radio was fined the maximum of £100 for using a wireless transmitter without a licence.

Mr Allbeury and the company secretary, Mr David Lye, also found guilty, were given absolute discharges.

Commander John Mackay standing on the exposed sandbank holding a Union Jack flag which he had firmly planted in the sand.

At the end of the two day hearing all defendants were found guilty, with Estuary Radio Ltd. being fined £200 and the individual directors £40 each, but this time the station remained on the air pending the outcome of an appeal against this, its second, conviction.

Aggrieved by this apparent defiance of the magistrates' decision the Post Office applied to the Queens Bench Division of the High Court on 10th March 1967 seeking an injunction to prevent Radio 390 from continuing to broadcast. Acting Managing Director David Lye then accused the Post Office of trying to stop the station proceeding with its appeal by issuing the writ and confirmed that Radio 390 would only cease broadcasting if the High Court granted the injunction.

This case was eventually heard in May 1967 when an injunction requiring Radio 390 to cease its transmissions was granted by Mr. Justice O'Connor. However, Sir Peter Rawlinson successfully pleaded for a 19 day period of grace while leave was sought to appeal against the decision. David Lye said "we have lost today, but our fight to keep the station on the air goes on."

## Radio City closure

Meanwhile, the other remaining Thames Estuary fort-based station, Radio City, continued with its broadcasts not yet having been summonsed or prosecuted. The authorities had delayed taking action against Radio City allegedly because of the outstanding criminal charges involving Major Oliver Smedley, but these had actually been disposed of in October 1966 (see Chapter 11). The more likely reason for the delay was the public statements made by police and other official agencies of 'uncertainty' over the territorial position of Shivering Sands - an excuse they had used for not taking any decisive action at the time of the boarding of Radio City in June 1966.

However, a close watch was being kept on events surrounding the Shivering Sands Fort and in January 1967 Scotland Yard informed Radio City's owner, Dorothy Calvert, that information had been received about plans for another attempt to forcibly take over the Fort. Mrs. Calvert visited Shivering Sands on 26th January 1967 and instructed staff to be on constant alert for a possible landing attempt and to broadcast a warning at the first hint of trouble.

Eventually the authorities themselves acted and on 31st January 1967 a summons was issued against Mrs. Calvert alleging the illegal use of a radio transmitter on Shivering Sands in contravention of the Wireless Telegraphy Act 1949. At Rochford Magistrates Court on 8th February 1967 Mrs. Calvert defended her station's right to broadcast by arguing that all personnel travelling to and from the Fort were subject to clearance by HM Customs and when Radio City had been forcibly boarded the previous June police had taken no action because Shivering Sands was held to be outside their jurisdiction.

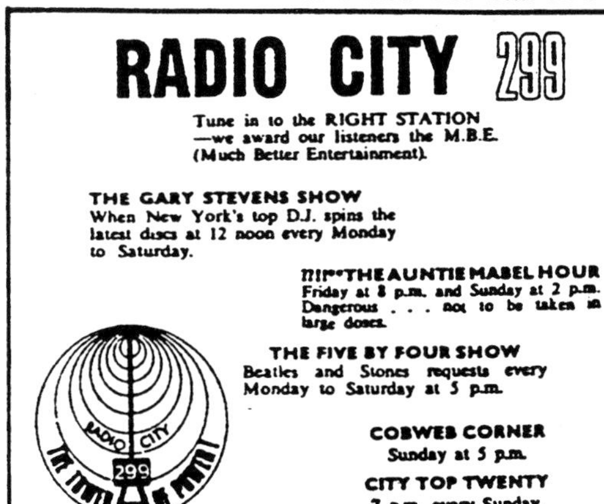


The magistrates were not persuaded by Mrs. Calvert's arguments, however, and ruled that the Fort was within British territorial waters. Mrs. Calvert was fined £100, but no order was made for costs or for the confiscation of Radio City's transmitting equipment.

After the court's decision Mrs. Calvert reluctantly

decided that the station should close without any undue delay and at 12 midnight on 8th February 1967 Radio City left the air for the last time. The final hour was filled with a nostalgic discussion amongst the Radio City DJs about life on the station and the prospects for the future of radio broadcasting in Britain.

## Caroline 'payola' scandal

In January 1967 it emerged that Radio Caroline was operating a 'payola' system for playing records outside its Top 50 chart. The station admitted that it charged £100 to play a new releases for 2 weeks and if after that time the record had not entered the Top 50 chart it was removed from the playlist. This whole practice came to light as a result of Radio Caroline's refusal to continue playing a new single by Cliff Bennett (which had been released on one of the EMI labels) after it had failed to reach a position in the station's Top 50 chart.

In contrast promotion of the station's own record label, Major Minor, which Philip Solomon had launched in November 1966, was increased from the initial one play per half hour to a point where by the middle of 1967 records released by the label's artists constituted a very significant proportion of overall programme content.

Since the arrival of Philip Soloman on Radio Caroline's board of directors in February 1966 there had been an increased emphasis on the financial aspect of running the station rather than on its musical output. As far as the listeners - and many DJs - were concerned the whole concept of paying for record plays and the constant plugging of one particular label's artists destroyed the spontaneity of programming which had been introduced, particularly on Caroline South , during the early and middle months of 1966.

Caroline's main rival, Radio London officially denied that it operated a similar payola system, but its own Fab 40 chart regularly contained many unknown artists whose material never appeared in other charts either on rival offshore stations, the BBC or in the national music press.

### Wilf Proudfoot

*Wilf Proudfoot, Radio 270's Managing Director experienced problems with his shareholders in February 1967 when a meeting was called to try and remove him from office. The shareholders of Ellambar Investments Ltd. called the meeting saying that there had been a lot of unrest and they did not like some of the things which had taken place in connection with the running of the station. Wilf Proudfoot was being blamed for the station having frequent periods off the air due to technical difficulties, with the subsequent loss of commercial income and there had also been a high turnover of staff, many of whom had complained about living conditions aboard the Oceaan VII. In the end, however, a unanimous vote of confidence was passed in Wilf Proudfoot and he remained as Managing Director of Radio 270.*

## Radio Scotland prosecution

In March 1967 yet another offshore radio station found itself in court for allegedly broadcasting within British territorial waters, but unlike previous cases involving the Thames Estuary fort-based stations this time it was the ship-based Radio Scotland. The station had moved during the previous summer to a position off Troon on the west coast of Scotland in an effort to improve its signal to the Glasgow area. It was the choice of anchorage after this move and the application of the Territorial Waters Order in Council of 1964 relating to the definition of what constitutes a bay that led to the prosecution.

The case was heard on 13th March 1967 at Ayr Sherriff's Court where the prosecution alleged that "on 14th September 1966 on a hulk moored in the Firth of Clyde, near Lady Isle, in the Parish of Dundonald, in territorial waters adjacent to the British Isles, Radio Scotland had used a transmitter for the purpose of wireless telegraphy without a licence." The prosecution case again relied on the provisions of the 1964 Order in Council (implementing the 1958 Geneva Convention ) relating to the area of water required to define a bay thus putting the *Comet* within territorial limits. This same argument had also been used successfully by the Post Office in its prosecution of the Thames Estuary fort based stations.

Procurator fiscal, Mr. R J Cruickshank, said that Post Office engineers had monitored Radio Scotland's broadcasts from three positions on the Ayrshire coast and plotted the position of its vessel, under the terms of the 1964 Order in Council, as being at least **35 miles inside** territorial waters. Defence Solicitor Mr. Hugh T McCalman stated that the owners of Radio Scotland had honestly believed that they were operating in international waters as the ship was moored six and a half miles from the nearest coastline.

City and County Commercial Radio (Scotland) Ltd., which pleaded guilty to the charge was fined £80, but a 'not guilty' plea by Managing Director Tommy Shields was accepted by the Court. Following this prosecution the station left the air while preparations were made to tow the *Comet* back to Scotland's east coast and a new anchorage off St. Abbs Head on the Firth of Forth.

Bad weather caused a cancellation of the planned five day tow and the ship was forced to lay silently at anchor off Troon for two weeks with only one DJ and a skeleton crew on board. During gales at the beginning of April 1967 the *Comet* broke from her anchor and was only saved from drifting ashore by the tug *Cruiser* which towed the radio ship up and down Kames Bay, Rothesay for two days until an emergency anchor had been lowered.

## Radio Scotland and Ireland

All this time Radio Scotland was off the air and losing an estimated £1,000 each day in advertising revenue, while the cost of keeping the silent radio ship at anchor was put at £1,500 per week. The station's board of directors decided that something had to be done urgently to put the station back on the air so on 7th April 1967 the *Comet* was towed to a position off Ballywater, Northern Ireland. From here transmissions started two days later under the call sign Radio Scotland and Ireland. The station's name was later changed to Radio 242.

However, the station's signal in Scotland was weak and problems were encountered with the Irish Customs authorities over tendering arrangements. They insisted that the station's tender should either operate from a customs port or pay a fee on each occasion it sailed in order to cover the cost of a Customs officer travelling to another port to make an inspection of goods being taken out to the radio ship. In the end it was decided to run a tender from Belfast (a Customs port) rather than pay the additional fees, but this meant that it had to travel a distance of more than 20 miles to reach the *Comet.*

Complaints were also received that Radio Scotland and Ireland/Radio 242 was causing interference to lighthouse communications in Belfast Lough and to licensed broadcasting services in Ireland. So by the end of April 1967 after just three weeks on the air from its Northern Irish anchorage transmissions from the *Comet* were terminated. Arrangements were made at the beginning of May for the tug, *Campaigner,* to tow the *Comet* back to an anchorage off Fifeness on the east coast of Scotland. However, instead of the planned five days the towing operation took over three weeks due to delays caused by gales and bad weather.

Staffing problems were encountered by Radio Scotland at the end of May 1967 shortly after the station had returned to the air from its east coast anchorage putting a further strain on the much troubled station. Co-ordination Controller Brian Holden was sacked by Tommy Shields over alleged mismanagement of the station - he was blamed for Radio Scotland's long periods off the air and its loss of advertising income. Four DJs (including Senior DJ Bob Spencer) together with Sales and Promotions Manager Eddie White then resigned in sympathy with Brian Holden.

During the Committee Stage of the Marine etc. Broadcasting (Offences) Bill Radio Scotland and its financial arrangements were attacked by Labour MP,

Hugh Jenkins. He asked a series of questions about the involvement of the Equitable Industrial Society of Scotland and one of its directors who had served a term of imprisonment. Radio Scotland's Managing Director, Tommy Shields denied that the station's finances were supplied by Equitable Industrial which, he said, only had a 'nominal' shareholding. However, he acknowledged that a brother of the person named by Hugh Jenkins served on the board of directors.

This attack on the station's financial background had in part been brought about by Radio Scotland's involvement in the Glasgow Pollock by-election, in which Tommy Shields had at one time planned to stand as an independent candidate supporting the concept of commercial radio for Scotland. In the event he decided, on advice from his fellow directors not to stand. This was because if, as seemed likely, he failed to win the seat or even attract a substantial number of votes, it would have provided political ammunition for the Government in its drive to outlaw offshore commercial radio. However, Radio Scotland did advise listeners in the run up to the by-election to vote for the Conservative Party candidate if they believed in free commercial radio.

All the time off the air between March and 8th May 1967 (when the *Comet* arrived back off the east coast) had cost Radio Scotland an estimated £15,000 in lost advertising revenue alone. On top of that the station had incurred the cost of towing the *Comet* first to Belfast Lough and then back to the east coast of Scotland. At this time financial projections by the station's accountants showed that in order to recoup initial investment and cover the annual running costs of £100,000 Radio Scotland would need to remain on the air, in a revenue earning situation, for at least another nine months. The station had resorted to broadcasting an appeal for listeners to make donations towards the cost of moving the *Comet* again after the company's prosecution in March 1967, but despite Radio Scotland's huge audience only £325 was raised.

## Liquidation

Problems of a financial nature were also affecting another offshore broadcaster early in 1967. Pier Vick Ltd., the managing company behind Britain Radio and the former Radio England was in severe financial difficulties and went into voluntary liquidation in March 1967. Creditors were told that the company, which had been formed in March 1966 with a share capital of only £2 now had debts of £111,491 with assets of only £5,004.

In November 1966 because of a lack of advertising revenue from the operation of its all-American format station, Radio England, Pier Vick Ltd. had leased the frequency to a Dutch broadcaster, Radio Dolifjn. Meanwhile, Britain Radio's easy listening format broadcasts had continued, although advertising revenue and audience levels were still declining.

Pier Vick had set out with Britain Radio to challenge 'sweet music' station Radio 390, but their American style format had not worked. A number of informal approaches were made by the American team to Ted Allbeury, Managing Director of Radio 390, suggesting either a merger of the two stations or a joint management operation. However, the other Directors of Estuary Radio Ltd. (Radio 390's owners) refused to consider these options.

Early in 1967 Ted Allbeury had found himself unable to continue as Managing Director of Radio 390, having been unsuccessful in persuading his fellow directors either to join with Britain Radio on the *Laissez Faire* or to use the former Radio Syd and Caroline South vessel, *Cheeta 2* as a base for the 'sweet music' station. The latter arrangement would have involved Radio 390 having free use of the *Cheeta 2* in return for the vessel's owner, Britt Wadner, being allowed to share in the station's operating profits.

Shortly after leaving Radio 390 Ted Allbeury was again approached by the management of the now ailing Pier Vick company inviting him to join Britain Radio as Managing Director. Ted Allbeury eventually agreed to look at the American station's financial records and Pier Vick asked for his advice on their continued operation. Based on what he had seen in the financial papers Ted Allbeury's recommendation to the Americans was not to spend any further money on the project because on anticipated performance Britain Radio would be unable to turn in a profit before the Marine etc. Broadcasting (Offences) Bill became law later in 1967. Undeterred by this recommendation the Pier Vick management then asked Ted Allbeury how much it would cost to keep Britain Radio on the air and agreed to put up whatever was required financially if he would agree to run the station.

At the beginning of February 1967 Ted Allbeury joined Britain Radio announcing in a press interview that " Britain Radio is a very professionally run outfit, they are determined to go on despite the difficulties they have been having." However, almost as soon as he had been appointed Jack Curtis, the American General Manager of Britain Radio, resigned 'for professional and personal reasons', but it was obvious that the two men had widely differing views about the future format for the easy listening station. Ted Allbeury had plans to introduce the Radio 390 concept of 15 and 30 minute programming segments to Britain Radio - a style which Jack Curtis called "Stone Age Radio, a series of segmented dirges stitched together by sterile announcements." In response Ted Allbeury referred to Britain Radio's existing format, which had been conceived and operated by Jack Curtis, as a "lucky dip".

During the third week of February 1967 the *Laissez Faire's* aerial mast was damaged after the vessel became caught in early spring tides and a Force 9 gale. At the time the *Laissez Faire* had no qualified or experienced seamen on board to ensure that the ship was positioned correctly, which would have enabled her to ride out the storm. The Captain had left the ship for a weeks shore leave and had not been replaced because of financial difficulties facing the management company, Pier Vick. To compound the problem the First Mate had jumped ship while some marine engineers failed from shore leave. Aboard the *Laissez Faire* at the time were the Dutch broadcasting crew of Radio Dolifijn, the English broadcasting crew of Britain Radio, a transmitter engineer, one marine engineer, a cook and a deck hand.

The storm damage caused the top 83' of the mast to shear off, bringing with it two cage aerials and a tangle of guy wires. The debris fell over the side of the *Laissez Faire* causing her to take on a 15 degree list. In an attempt to stabilise the vessel the inexperienced crew lashed the wreckage to the side of the *Laissez Faire* and started the engines to try and turn the ship and prevent further damage. The Coastguards, lifeboat service and Air Sea Rescue service were all alerted, but not called out to assist at that stage. Eventually the weather calmed sufficiently for the crew to secure the remaining wreckage of the aerial and prevent further damage to the radio ship.

A few days later the *Laissez Faire's* Captain returned to assess the damage which had been caused to his vessel. With both radio stations off the air most DJs from the Dutch and English stations were taken off the ship, leaving just two English DJs (Dave McKay and Alan Black) and two transmitter engineers on board.

On 7th March 1967 the Captain was instructed to raise the radio ship's anchor and take the vessel to the Wijsmuller ship yard at Zaandam, near Amsterdam for repair. On arrival in Holland the Dutch Customs authorities came aboard the *Laissez Faire* and sealed the transmitter room and studios. However, the radio crew managed to temporarily remove the seals and use the studio equipment while the ship was in harbour.

One of the station's original American backers, Tom Dannaher, visited the *Laissez Faire* in Zaandam and authorised the shipyard to carry out repairs to the mast. This authorisation to incur expenditure on repairs was given at a time when the station's management company, Pier Vick, was in severe financial difficulties. Some of the station's backers tried to persuade Don Pierson and Bill Vick to withdraw from the operation altogether, but before any such management changes could take place Pier Vick was put into voluntary receivership on 14th March 1967.

Managing Director of Britain Radio, Ted Allbeury, who together with John Withers (brother of ex-Radio Atlanta and ex-Radio London DJ Tony Windsor (Withers) had recently formed Carstead Advertising Ltd. immediately entered into negotiations with the Receiver to take over operation of the twin stations on the *Laissez Faire*. Carstead Advertising was to pay all profits from the two stations to a new company, Laissez Faire Ltd., which had been formed by new American backers.

## Radio 355 launched

After repairs had been completed to the *Laissez Faire* in Holland, now under the supervision of Ted Allbeury, the ship sailed back to the British coast. Arrangements were also made for the vessel to use the same Wijsmuller tender as Radio London and Caroline South, saving the expense of operating a separate service as the former management had done.

The new company planned to re-launch Britain Radio as Radio 355, with a format based partly on the successful Radio 390 style, still aiming at a largely housewife audience, but with a more up-tempo range of music. Radio Dolifjn was to be renamed Radio 227 and continue broadcasting to a Dutch audience.

However, the Britain Radio format change was once again to be a cause of dissent amongst the station's staff. A number of ex-Radio 390 announcers, including Chief Announcer Stephen West, whom Ted Allbeury had persuaded to join Radio 355, were sent out to the *Laissez Faire* with instructions to introduce the new format. This new arrangement did not meet with enthusiasm amongst the former Britain Radio DJs who had rejoined the *Laissez Faire* and some of the 390 staff experienced problems settling to life aboard the radio ship - they were used to presenting programmes from the relative stability of a sea fort.

After a few weeks of operating the 390 style of format Ted Allbeury realised that it was not going to be as successful as he had hoped and his co-director, John Withers, arranged for his brother, Tony Windsor (who had recently left Radio London) to join Radio 355 as Programme Director with a remit to revamp the station. Tony Windsor quickly decided that the format would have to be changed back to the three or four hour 'horizontal' programming as previously adopted on Britain Radio.

It soon became apparent that there were deep professional frictions developing over the new format between the ex-390 announcers who had joined Radio 355 with Ted Allbeury and the former Britain Radio staff who had remained with the ship-based station. Some of the ex-390 announcers, including David Allen and Stephen West, left Radio 355 shortly after this format change and returned to their former station on Red Sands Fort (which was still on the air thanks to the protracted legal appeals waiting to be heard in the courts). Meanwhile, Tony Windsor recruited a new team of DJs for Radio 355 - Tony Meehan and Jack

### Radio 355 programme schedule, March 1967

|  |  |
|---|---|
| 6.00am | Rise and Shine |
| 7.00am | Breakfast Club |
| 9.00am | Double Feature |
| 9.30am | Light and Bright |
| 10.30am | Pause for Prayer |
| 10.40am | Showcase |
| 11.00am | Elevenses |
| 11.30am | Top of the Morning |
| 12.30pm | The World Tomorrow |
| 1.00pm | Requests |
| 2.00pm | Melody Hour |
| 3.00pm | Cafe Continental |
| 3.30pm | Allegro |
| 4.00pm | For the Children |
| 4.15pm | Afternoon Star |
| 4.30pm | Mainly Instrumental |
| 5.30pm | Middle of the Road |
| 6.30pm | The World Tomorrow |
| 7.00pm | Make Mine Country Style |
| 7.30pm | Requests |
| 8.00pm | Music in the Night |

McLaughlin were enticed away from Radio Scotland, Mark Sloan, Martin Kayne and Phil Martin who had left Britain Radio when Ted Allbeury took over as Managing Director agreed to rejoin the station and the team was completed by Dave McKay and Alan Black who had remained with the station throughout all its troubles and format changes.

The change in programming style worked and despite the station's initial difficulties and its relatively short life-span estimates in mid 1967 showed that Radio 355 had built an audience in the region of 2,250,000, compared with Britain Radio's 718,000 in the NOP Survey twelve months earlier. However, the station still found difficulty in attracting substantial amounts of advertising and relied heavily on sponsored American religious programmes for much of its income.

With the successful re-launch of Radio 355 completed attention was then turned by Ted Allbeury to the re-launch of the Dutch station operating from the *Laissez Faire* under the call sign Radio 227 (see Chapter 13).

**Radio 355 programme schedule, May 1967**

6.00am Breakfast Club

7.00am The World Tomorrow

7.30am Breakfast Club

9.00am Tony Monson Show

10.30am Pause for Prayer

10.45am Tony Monson Show

12noon Mark Sloane Show

12.30pm The World Tomorrow

1.00pm Mark Sloane Show

3.00pm Dave McKaye Show

6.00pm Kayne's Kingdom, Martin Kayne

7.00pm 355 Countryfied

7.30pm John Aston Show

9.00pm Dave McKaye Music

10.30pm A B Spree

11.55pm Epilogue

12midnight Closedown

## 'Free Radio' supporters

The Marine etc. Broadcasting (Offences) Bill was due to receive its Second Reading in the House of Commons during February 1967 and in the weeks prior to this a number of listeners' pressure groups (or 'free radio supporters' as they became more generally known) were established. First of these groups was the Commercial Radio Listeners Association (CRLA) which was launched on 29th January 1967. Three weeks later, on 19th February 1967 at a meeting in London attended by representatives of many offshore stations, the Free Radio Supporters Association (FRSA) was formed. For their part the radio station's representatives at the meeting agreed that they would help the Association in any way they could, short of providing finance or being represented on its governing committee. In practice this meant broadcasting 'commercials' and announcements on behalf of the Association urging listeners to 'join the fight for free radio'.

The CRLA and the FRSA soon merged and, following notification from Ronan O'Rahilly that Radio Caroline would only carry announcements if the word 'supporters' was dropped from its title, the organisation became known as the Free Radio Association (FRA). Announcements for the FRA were broadcast on Radios 270, 390, Caroline and Scotland advertising a range of publicity material - car stickers, badges, leaflets etc. and urging listeners to write to their Member of Parliament expressing support for the continuation of the service provided by offshore radio stations.

The Free Radio Association also collected thousands of signatures from supporters for a petition which stated:-

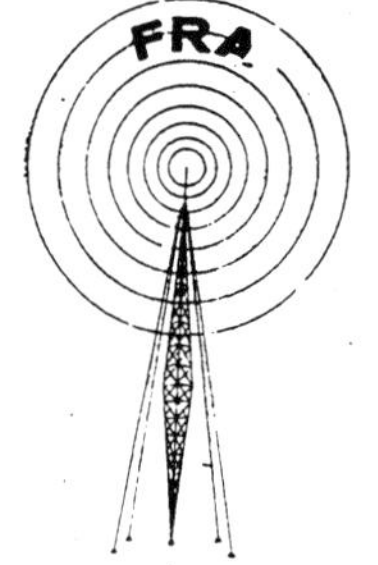


*The Free Radio Association is fighting for free speech, free enterprise and free choice. The Government is trying to crush all competition over the air by silencing the commercial stations - thereby preserving the monopoly of the BBC and depriving us of the freedom to listen to the stations of our choice. This is a step towards dictatorship. If the Marine etc. Broadcasting (Offences) Bill becomes law in its present form, free speech will be suppressed, and the Free Radio Association will be partially silenced. No doubt this would please the Government. But the Government will never silence us completely. We have pledged that we will fight and we will win.*

*This is more than a petition. It is a declaration that we, the British people will fight for freedom of the air as we have fought before when our freedom has been threatened. It is a declaration that we the undersigned support the Free Radio Association it its fight for the right of the public to listen to independent radio stations. And it is a declaration that we the undersigned will use our votes to remove this Government from power at the first opportunity and replace it with a Government which believes in free speech, free enterprise and free choice.*

Another supporters' organisation which received publicity via the offshore stations was the Broadside Free Radio Movement, which had been formed by a Cambridge University student, Peter Philipson, in April 1967, recruiting initially from the two universities of Oxford and Cambridge. In June 1967 the headquarters of the organisation was moved to London and national recruitment began following publicity on Radio Caroline. By July the Movement claimed a membership of 80,000 but by October 1967 it had collapsed totally with financial debts of £500. The Free Radio Association took over the outstanding debts and combined Broadside's membership with its own creating an organisation with a claimed membership of 100,000.

Two stations, Radio London and Radio 270, also mounted their own campaigns against the proposed legislation - Radio London DJs constantly requested listeners to 'fight for free radio' by writing to their MPs, while Radio 270 followed a similar pattern and also published, in conjunction with the Institute of Economic Affairs, a booklet entitled *Competition in Radio*, by Denis Thomas. This traced the development of commercial radio abroad as well as in Britain and concluded by supporting the introduction of a legal commercial radio system.

One further voice in support of offshore radio, came with the launch of a national publication devoted to the stations and their programmes, something which had been conspicuous by its absence for nearly three years. In mid-January 1967 the paper - *Radio News* - was published as a supplement to the *National Advertiser* (a contemporary rival to *Exchange and Mart*) and contained news and articles about the offshore stations, including detailed programme schedules. Editorially the paper argued strongly for the introduction of a legal system of land-based commercial radio in Britain. However, *Radio News* only lasted for nine issues and in March 1967 it was transferred, in a smaller format, to *Time and Tide* magazine where it was eventually phased out due to the impending introduction of legislation banning offshore radio.

Unfortunately all these campaigns, both by the listeners' organisations and the stations themselves came too late to be effective against the Government's legislative plans. The FRA had only achieved a fully paid-up membership of a few thousand by the beginning of June 1967 and as the spring and early summer months passed the stations themselves soon realised the futility of trying to prevent the introduction of legislation, although they continued to broadcast promotions against the Marine etc. Broadcasting (Offences) Bill and urged listeners to contact their MPs or a member of the House of Lords.

RADIO LONDON SAYS FIGHT FOR FREE RADIO

RADIO LONDON SAYS FIGHT FOR FREE RADIO

*'Fight for Free Radio' publicity material produced by the offshore stations*

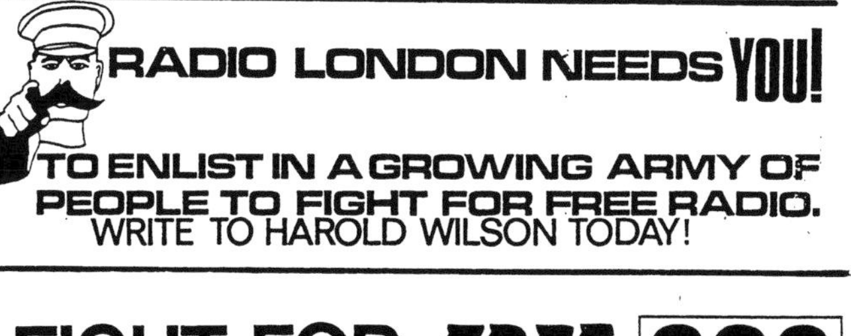


FIGHT FOR *FREE*
RADIO LONDON

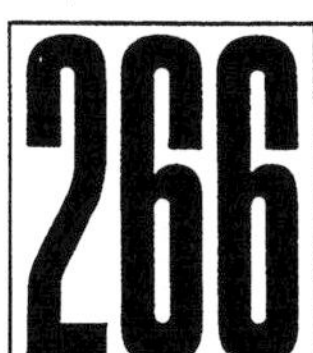


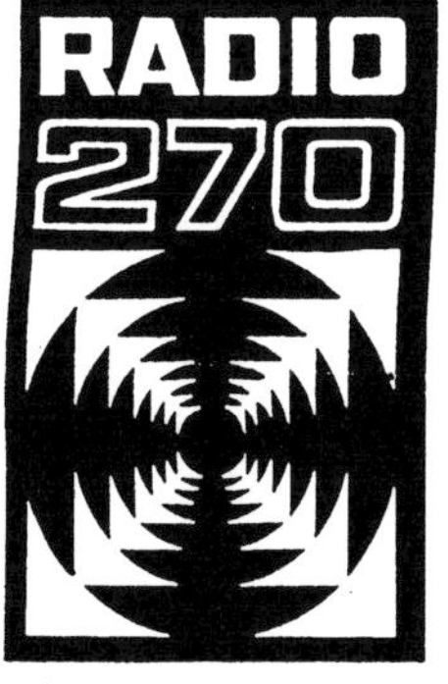


FIGHT FOR FREE RADIO

**Radio London**
**Needs You**
Radio London Needs You
To enlist in a growing army of people to fight for free radio.
Write to Harold Wilson today!

## The Marine Offences Bill debate

The House of Commons debated the Marine etc. Broadcasting (Offences) Bill on 15th February 1967 when Labour Postmaster General Edward Short moved the Second Reading. In his speech Mr. Short accused the offshore stations of pirating frequencies not allocated to them under international agreements, of allowing their transmissions to interfere with licensed stations and emergency communications and of being a hazard to shipping. The provisions of the Bill, he said, were intended to make it so difficult for offshore broadcasters to obtain supplies and advertising revenue that they would soon go out of business. If enough other countries enacted similar legislation in accordance with the 1965 Council of Europe agreement on offshore radio (the Strasbourg Convention) then, argued Mr. Short, the stations would have no sources of financial or material supply.

The Conservative (opposition) Spokesman on Broadcasting, Mr. Paul Bryan, moved an amendment declining to give the Bill a Second Reading until a comprehensive broadcasting policy had been put in place, taking into account the wishes of millions of listeners, the interests of artists and copyright holders as well as Britain's international radio frequency obligations.

The opposition argument centred not specifically on support for offshore radio, but on the need to introduce a replacement service and a wider choice for the listening public which would be commercially funded rather than provided by the BBC out of licence payer's money. A market had been identified by the offshore radio stations, but it was not intended that they should necessarily become the beneficiaries of any new landbased radio structure.

However, when it came to the vote the amendments were all defeated and the Bill received its Second Reading by 300 votes to 213 - a Government majority of 87.

The Bill then passed to the Committee Stage where opposition Conservative members proposed a number of further amendments. An attempt to exempt Scotland from the provisions of the Bill, on the grounds that some of the more remote areas could only receive Radio Scotland's transmissions, was defeated as was an amendment to exclude the clause relating to offshore television broadcasts. The opposition also suggested that implementation of the Bill should be delayed for two years after the Royal Assent (and then only with the approval of both Houses of Parliament) to give sufficient time for an alternative radio service to be established. This amendment was also defeated.

During the Committee Stage debate on the Marine etc. Broadcasting (Offences) Bill the Postmaster General accused various offshore stations of causing interference to authorised broadcasters in other European countries - Radio Scotland to Poland, Radio London to Yugoslavia and Belgium, Caroline North to Czechoslovakia and Belgium, Radio 390 to Sweden and Britain Radio to Italy.

The result of the Committee Stage deliberations were reported back to the House of Commons early in April 1967. A further attempt to exclude Scotland from the Bill's provisions was made during this Report Stage as was a proposal to exempt any offshore station which used only VHF (FM) transmissions. A new and potentially significant amendment was also proposed at the Report Stage seeking to delete the clause in the Bill which prevented newspapers publishing programme schedules of the offshore radio stations. Postmaster General Edward Short argued in favour of the clause, saying that it was a necessary provision which would be used to penalise any publications who collaborated with the stations. This amendment, along with all others proposed by the opposition, was defeated. The clause relating to the publication of programme details by newspapers, which effectively gagged the press in its freedom to publish information, was a significant departure from either the terms of the Strasbourg Convention or equivalent foreign legislation dealing with offshore broadcasting.

Having completed most of its stages in the House of Commons the Bill then passed to the House of Lords for its consideration. Here, on 1st May 1967, an opposition amendment was proposed by Lord Denham seeking to delay implementation of the Bill until alternative programmes had been provided for the 20 million listeners to the offshore radio stations. Lord Denham argued that " it is the Government's responsibility to fill the void left in the lives of their listeners by the planned demise of pirate ships with a satisfactory alternative. If they don't then someone else will do it for them." For the Government Lord Sorenson stated that the time gap between the demise of the offshore stations and the introduction of a replacement (BBC) service would only be six or seven weeks and that by supporting the amendment the Lords would be "conniving at continued illegality".

When the vote was taken, to the surprise and anger of the Government peers, the amendment was carried by 65 votes to 44, an opposition majority of 21. This opposition success was short-lived, however, because when the Bill completed its parliamentary progress during the Third (and final) Reading in the Commons on 30th June 1967 the Lord's amendment was reversed. The Bill now only required the Royal Assent to become law and this was granted on 14th July 1967.

## Stations and politics

As the Parliamentary process continued the stations themselves came to realise that arguments about freedom of expression and rights of democracy would have little impact on the Government and, despite the momentary success of the Lord's amendment, the Bill to outlaw them was almost certain to become law before the end of the summer. Consequently, feeling that they had nothing more to lose, individual radio stations gradually became involved in politics in various ways - something which they had all previously avoided.

During March and April 1967 Radio London commissioned a survey of candidates in the Greater London Council (GLC) elections to establish who supported or opposed the offshore stations. The results, which were repeatedly broadcast by Radio 270 and Radio Caroline as well as Radio London itself showed the following breakdown of candidates' views :-

| | FOR | AGAINST | DON'T KNOW |
|---|---|---|---|
| Labour | 4 | 23 | 1 |
| Liberal | 28 | 6 | 0 |
| Conservative | 38 | 0 | 0 |

An opinion poll of MPs was also conducted at the same time and this showed, not surprisingly, that the majority of (Labour) Government's MPs wanted the stations to be closed, while 65% of opposition (Conservative) MPs were in favour of the service provided by offshore radio.

**Examination of pirate radios**

The legal aspects of intervention by commercial radio stations into parliamentary and municipal elections are to be examined

**Pirates face poll probe**

## 'Radio East Anglia' hoax

*On 1st April 1967 some DJs and engineers on Radio London played an April Fool's hoax on listeners. Normal Radio London programmes were 'interrupted' by a 'new' station calling itself Radio East Anglia, between 9.30am and 11.55am. Hundreds of listeners even telephoned the Post Office to complain about the 'new' station affecting reception of Radio London.*

In Yorkshire Radio 270 agreed to accept advertisements from political parties for candidates standing in the local council elections. The Young Conservatives at York University bought time and the station planned to transmit its first political broadcast on 1st May 1967, featuring Mr. Patrick Wall MP and members of York University Conservative Association. However, because of tape recording problems the broadcast could not be made as scheduled and had to be re-recorded for later transmission. A further party political broadcast by York University Conservative Association was transmitted over Radio 270 in June 1967 again featuring Mr. Patrick Wall MP talking with Mr. John Biggs-Davidson MP about the Government's handling of foreign affairs in Rhodesia, the Middle East and Israel.

In mid-April 1967 the Postmaster General announced that his officials were examining legal aspects of the offshore station's political activities particularly in connection with rules governing the GLC and local council elections. However, no definite action appears to have been forthcoming as a result of this examination.

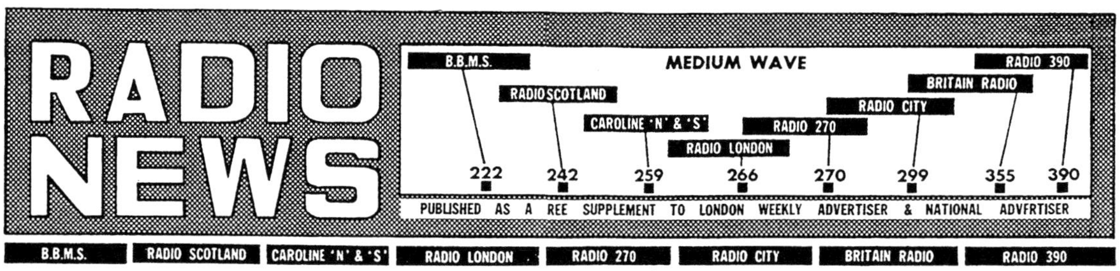


## Reply from Government

Any supporters of the offshore stations who took the time and trouble to write to their MP, the Postmaster General or even the Prime Minister received the following standard, somewhat patronising reply:-

*Many people have been very disappointed to hear that pirate broadcasting is to be stopped. It seems so harmless and is enjoyed by so many people.*

*In fact, despite the repeated claims of the pirates, their broadcasts are far from harmless. The pirates are using wavelengths which we have undertaken to leave clear for the broadcasting services in other countries. By so doing they prevent people in those countries from hearing their own domestic programmes. They also represent a danger - slight but ever present- to the radio services on which safety of life at sea depends. Moreover, broadcasting from the high seas is forbidden all over the world by international law. And the pirates make almost unlimited use of recorded material, threatening the livelihoods of the musicians and other performers whose work they use without permission or payment.*

*To date twelve European countries have complained to the Postmaster General about the pirates' interference with their broadcasting services. And communications between ships and the shore have often been seriously interfered with. If the pirate stations were allowed to continue unchecked there would soon be so much interference that broadcasting as we know it would become impossible.*

*This threat to the future of broadcasting has caused the maritime countries of the Council of Europe to agree to legislate on common lines to deal with it. The current legislation in this country carries out our obligations under the European Agreement.*

*Many people feel that an easy solution would be to 'bring the pirates ashore', that is to licence them to operate on land. This is just not possible. There are no unused wavelengths on which powerful stations like the pirate stations could operate without causing interference. In any case, if they operated within the control of the copyright laws they could not transmit the sort of programmes they have been transmitting.*

*The Government's plans for the future of sound broadcasting which have recently been announced, are designed to match our broadcasting services more closely to our needs without interfering with other people's rights.*

*But the most pressing need is to silence the pirate stations, which are flouting international regulations, earning us a bad name abroad, endangering shipping and threatening to make broadcasting end in chaos, not only in Britain but over most of Europe.*

## Battle for Roughs Tower

With the passing of the Marine etc. Broadcasting (Offences) Bill by Parliament on 30th June 1967 the offshore stations knew that they would either have to close or make elaborate alternative financial and staffing arrangements to circumvent the legislation and stay on the air.

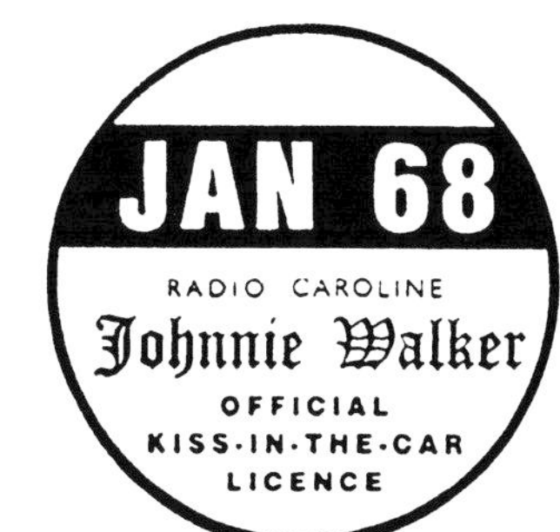


This licence is valid until January, 1968 and entitles the holder(s) to kiss-in-the-car providing the occupants are listening to the Johnnie Walker Show on Radio Caroline South

NOT TRANSFERABLE

Some stations had already begun to make alternative arrangements earlier in the year in case their efforts to defeat the legislation failed. In January 1967 Radio Caroline staff took over the Roughs Tower off Felixstowe, which was outside the then British territorial limits, even taking into account the provisions of the 1964 Order in Council for calculating territorial limits which had been used in the successful prosecutions against Radios 390, Essex, City and Scotland. Radio Caroline's personnel removed much of the wartime superstructure and created a helicopter landing pad on the Fort's platform.

French aviation consultants L'Aeronaute Ltd. were then contracted by Radio Caroline to provide, as a statement issued at the time said, ' a varied helicopter and fixed wing support for the future requirements, both exploitation and servicing, of Radio Caroline and Ronan O'Rahilly personally.' The station in fact intended using the Fort, because it was outside British territorial limits, as a supply and accommodation base for servicing the Caroline South ship, enabling food and fuel to be stockpiled there for later transfer to the radio ship without directly contravening the Marine etc. Broadcasting (Offences) Act.

However, another offshore radio station operator also had plans for Roughs Tower. After his prosecution and conviction in January 1967 Roy Bates decided to move the Radio Essex/BBMS transmitting equipment from Knock John Fort to Roughs Tower and there were a number of violent disputes between the two groups. An agreement was eventually reached that both Radio Caroline and Roy Bates would share occupation of Roughs Tower and accordingly each group landed two men on the Fort. The uneasy peace lasted for a few weeks until April 1967 when Bates's group took total possession of Roughs Tower while the Radio Caroline men had to go ashore for one of them to receive medical treatment.

The Radio Caroline organisation made a number of attempts to regain a hold on the Fort but were constantly repelled by Bates's men. This rivalry came to a violent head on 27th June 1967 when Radio Caroline sent a boarding party, on the tender *Offshore II*, led by their agent, Percy Scadden, in an attempt to finally reclaim possession of Roughs Tower.

As the Caroline party tried to climb onto the Fort Roy Bates's men opened fire on them with petrol bombs and guns. One member of the boarding party was left hanging on a rope ladder when the deck of the tender caught fire and it had to pull away from the Fort because of the danger of explosion from

### Frinton Flashing

*Listeners to Caroline South's late evening broadcasts in the mid-1960s will undoubtedly remember it, enthusiasts born too late to have listened will have heard of it, but what was 'Frinton Flashing'?*

*Anchored just three and a half miles off Frinton-on-Sea, Essex DJs on the Caroline South ship, 'Mi Amigo', could just about see land during the day, but at night any lights along the sea front were clearly visible from the ship, weather permitting.*

*Johnnie Walker, who presented the 9.00pm-12midnight programme is probably best remembered for 'Frinton Flashing', but others before him had also tried the idea - DJs on the MV 'Caroline' had asked listeners to flash car headlights at the ship as she sailed around the coast to the Isle of Man in 1964.*

*Motorists listening to Caroline South would park their cars along the seafront with their headlights directed at the radioship. At the request of the on-air DJ they would be asked to flash their headlights in response to series of questions - names, registration numbers, initials, birth dates etc. Other DJs on deck relayed information to the on-air DJ about the responses being received and by a process of elimination this would be whittled down to one, two or three vehicles.*

*In a good session the DJ could conduct a 'conversation' with the listeners in their car to the point of establishing his/her name, date of birth,boy/girlfriend's name and anything else that came to mind.*

*After Frinton Flashing sessions were over Johnnie Walker introduced a slot into his programme at 11.00pm for listeners (not just those in Frinton) to "kiss in the car" playing a long, slow romantic piece of music to create the right atmosphere! Johnnie Walker's fan club issued official "kiss in the car" licences.*

the large supply of fuel oil on board. A distress call was sent out by the Captain of *Offshore II* and Walton-on-the-Naze lifeboat was launched to provide assistance. Eventually the man who had been left on the rope ladder, John Hailes, was rescued, but only after having spent three hours dangling above the sea in a wooden crate lowered by Bates's men who had refused to allow him to climb onto the Fort itself.

Ronan O'Rahilly said he had plans for the Fort which were nothing to do with broadcasting, claiming it was to be developed as a health centre and holiday hotel. After having spent £15,000 so far on creating the helipad and associated works O'Rahilly said he intended to regain possession and expected the police to act against the occupiers within 48 hours.

Roy Bates also claimed the Fort was his and although the Radio Essex equipment was on board he did not intend to set up a radio station. "We intend to stay here against all comers" said Mr. Bates, backing up his claim by showing reporters the armoury of weapons held on the Fort, including six shotguns, a flame thrower, two air rifles and a supply of petrol bombs.

Although Essex Police met both *Offshore II* and the lifeboat when they returned to port and took statements from those on board no action was taken over the incident because Roughs Tower was outside British territorial limits and the police had no powers to act against either party.

A similar situation occurred a week later, on 3rd July 1967, when a distress call was received from the *Laissez Faire*, home of Radios 355 and 227, saying that a man on board had assaulted the Captain and was threatening murder. The incident had occurred following a visit to the *Laissez Faire* by blind guitarist Jose Felicano, who took part in a one hour live broadcast on Radio 355 that afternoon. Throughout the pop star's visit to the radio ship a tender, crewed by Dutch seamen, stood by alongside the *Laissez Faire*. As Jose Felicano was being helped on board the tender after the broadcast one of the crew members boarded the radio ship and attacked the *Laissez Faire's* Captain, Colin Lukenhurst. He subsequently held the Captain and Senior announcer Tony Windsor captive for 16 hours, threatening them with a knife. The same seaman had carried out a similar attack on Christmas Eve 1966, when he held Captain Buninga at knife-point aboard the Radio London ship, *Galaxy*.

Essex Police decided that they had no jurisdiction to act in response to the distress call because the incident had taken place on a Honduran-registered vessel anchored in international waters. Consequently they instructed the lifeboat service not to launch and referred the whole problem to the Royal Navy. The Navy in turn referred the matter to the Ministry of Defence in London who asked Coastguards to keep them informed of the situation as it developed. Out at sea the Captain of the *Laissez Faire* told all his crew to lock themselves in their cabins overnight and the following day the tender *Offshore II* set out with a boarding party and removed two Dutch crewmen from the radio ship.

Although the police had taken no action over the Roughs Tower incident in June 1967 Roy Bates later revealed that the Ministry of Defence had offered to pay him £5,000 to return the structure to the Crown. A detachment of Royal Marines and two helicopters were actually put on stand-by in case negotiations with Bates were successful, so that the Fort could be quickly reclaimed and anyone else - in particular Radio Caroline - prevented from taking possession of it again. Roy Bates, however, refused the offer from the Ministry of Defence and retained possession of Roughs Tower, eventually declaring it to be an 'independent state' - Sealand on 20th September 1967.

## SEALAND

*Roy Bates having established physical control of Roughs Tower set about creating his own sovereign territory on the Fort. He declared it to be the independent Principality of Sealand on 20th September 1967, with himself as Prince Roy and his wife as Princess Joan. A red, white and black flag was raised on the Fort to demonstrate its independent status and the new state issued its own passports, currency and postage stamps.*

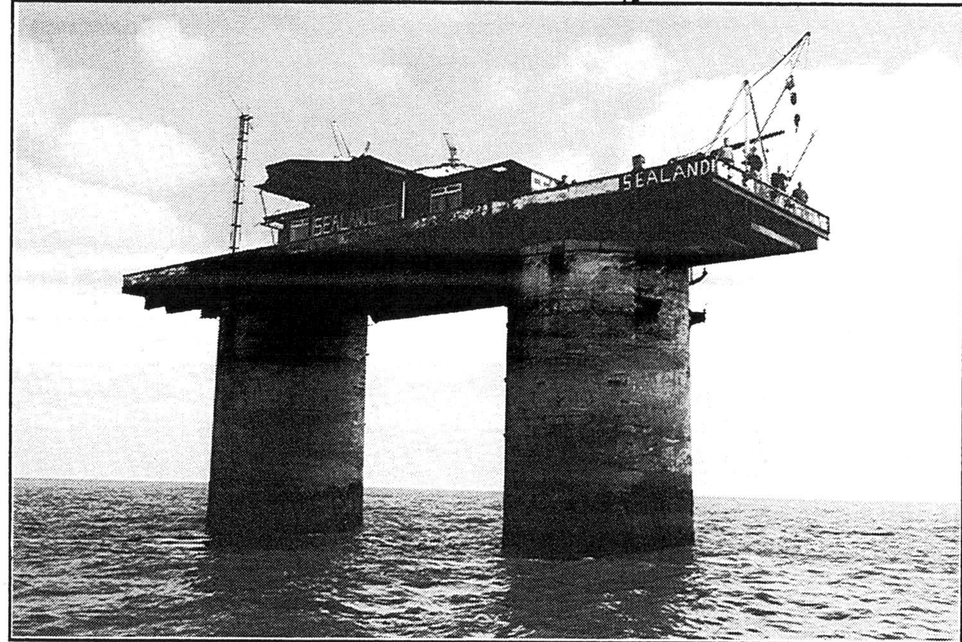


*Unfortunately for Roy Bates few of these initiatives were recognised by the international community, although the Belgian Post Office delivered letters bearing the Sealand stamps and France and Spain accepted Sealand passports as proof of identity. The coinage only remained legal tender on the Principality itself although it was of interest to collectors, as were the postage stamps.*

*The British Government refused to accept Sealand as an independent state because it did not fulfil the conditions required for statehood under international law. However, Dr. Pela Vitanyi, a professor of international law at Nijmegen University in Holland advised Roy Bates that he had effectively taken control of territory without a master and because the British authorities had not acted against him they had effectively accepted his claim to the Fort.*

*Roy Bate's claim to sovereignty seemed to be reinforced by a British court in 1968 when his son, Michael, was charged with illegal possession of firearms and firing shots at Trinity House personnel. The Court ruled that it could not hear the case because Roughs Tower (Sealand) lay outside British territorial limits. A further boost to the independent status of Sealand came in May 1979 when the Archbishop of Canterbury gave permission for a wedding to be conducted on the Fort. Gordon Wilkinson, Sealand's Security Chief, married Karen Huxtable in a ceremony conducted by the vicar of Harwich, Rev. Jim Chelton.*

*Over the years Sealand has been rumoured to be planning the launch of radio and television services - plans for three stations in the mid-1970s, and Arabic station in 1980, satellite radio relays in 1983 and Sealand TV in 1986, but all came to nothing. A group of amateur radio Operators from West Germany did, however, transmit on shortwave and FM from Sealand in September 1983 and were given special Sealand call-signs for the month long duration of their broadcasts.*

*A number of elaborate plans for the development of Sealand have been made, including the construction of floating hotels, leisure complexes and the creation of a freeport, but all have come to nothing. The introduction of the British Territorial Sea Act 1987 effectively brought Roughs Tower inside British territorial limits and all chance of independent developments taking place seemed to fade.*

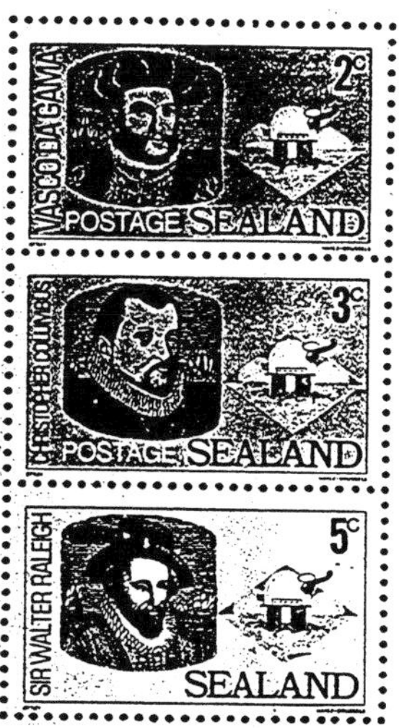


*Stamps issued by Sealand*

## Alternative plans

During the time Radio Caroline had been in partial possession of Roughs Tower, in March 1967, the station also asked 20 of its British staff to consider giving up their citizenship if they wished to remain with the station after the Marine etc. Broadcasting (Offences) Bill became law. The station also engaged seven more American and Canadian staff to enable it to continue broadcasting and made arrangements with a French public relations firm, Services et Methodes, to secure advertising from various European sources. Meanwhile Terry Bate, who had joined Radio Caroline in 1966 to improve its sales operation, used his a company in Toronto - Marich Associates - to try and secure advertising for the station from businesses in North America. An office was also opened in Holland in May 1967, managed by South African Basil van Rensberg, to act as a new headquarters for the station after the British legislation had come into effect.

The station also announced that once the British legislation was enacted it had plans to secure further income by launching a second service from the *Mi Amigo* in addition to Radio Caroline South. This service was to be staffed by Dutch DJs with programmes directed at Holland, tapping into the lucrative Dutch advertising market.

Carstead Advertising, operators of Radios 355 and 227, also opened an office in Amsterdam with the object of trying to secure foreign advertising to enable the twin stations to continue broadcasting after the new legislation became law.

At the end of May 1967 three transmitter valves were delivered to the Radio London vessel *Galaxy,* so that, from a technical point of view, the station would be able to continue broadcasting for anything up to six years. The station also set up an office in Holland under the control of one of its directors, Dennis Maitland, to act as a supply base and Managing Director Philip Birch announced that in future Radio London would rely almost entirely on American advertising income.

Tendering arrangements for the larger stations were made through the Offshore Supply Company, a subsidiary of the Dutch salvage organisation Wijsmuller. Directors of the Dutch company informed the offshore stations that their vessels, *Offshore I, II, and III* would still be available for tendering purposes after the new legislation had been introduced, but they would have to operate from bases in Holland, Spain, or Ireland rather than south east England or the Isle of Man.

Early in July 1967 Radio Caroline announced that on the first day the new legislation came into effect the station would use a British DJ, newsreader and religious broadcaster to break the law by taking part in programmes. Ronan O'Rahilly threatened to challenge any subsequent prosecution of these British staff at the Court of Human Rights in Strasbourg, although legal experts had considerable doubts as to whether such action would have been successful.

Poet, dramatist and founder of the English Stage Company, Ronald Duncan also announced in the *Daily Telegraph* on 23rd June 1967 that he had offered his services to Radio Caroline after the new legislation had become effective. He had already written a series of brief sketches pointing out the likely effects, in terms of freedom of speech and freedom of the individual, of the provisions contained in the Marine etc. Broadcasting (Offences) Bill and these had been broadcast on Radio Caroline since the spring of 1967. Ronald Duncan called on other writers to join him because, he said, "This is an issue of far greater importance than at first appears. Its implications cuts right across the freedoms of the individual. As has been proved so often in history these can be easily whittled away - and when they are it takes a formidable social upheaval to re-establish them."

### Radio London programme schedule, June 1967

5.00am Pete Drummond

9.00am Paul Kaye

11.00am Coffee Break

12noon Tony Brandon

3.00pm Mark Roman

6.00pm Pete Drummond

7.00pm The World Tomorrow

7.30pm Pete Drummond

9.00pm Willy Walker

12midnight John Peel

The Marine etc. Broadcasting (Offences) Act received the Royal Assent on 14th July 1967 and Postmaster General Edward Short announced that its provisions would come into effect one month later, on 15th August 1967. One by one the offshore stations gave their reactions to this news. With the reality of the legislation becoming law and despite earlier defiant claims to the contrary, Radios 270, Scotland, 355 and 227 all announced that they would close before the 15th August deadline.

Radio 390 was at that time still fighting its own appeal against prosecution under entirely different legislation, but the directors had already rejected transferring operations from the Red Sands Fort to a ship in international waters so the outlook for the station was not very optimistic. Only the two largest stations, Radio London and Radio Caroline, confirmed that they would definitely continue broadcasting after 15th August 1967. Philip Birch of Radio London made one final desperate plea to the Postmaster General calling on him to "allow the stations to continue supplying 25 million listeners with a popular music service which they have enjoyed for the past three years."

## Radio 390 appeal decision

Radio 390's application to be allowed to continue broadcasting on the grounds that the Red Sands Fort was outside territorial limits was finally heard in the Court of Appeal (Civil Division) before Lord Justice Sellars, Lord Justice Diplock and Lord Justice Winn in July 1967. Their decision in a judgement given on 28th July 1967 ruled that the Fort was within territorial limits and dismissed the station's appeal against its February conviction. Counsel for Estuary Radio Ltd., Mr. J P Harris, asked for a stay to enable the station to remain on the air until the Marine etc. Broadcasting (Offences) Act came into effect on 15th August 1967, but the Court refused this application. Lord Justice Sellars told the defendants "there is no reason why you should broadcast any longer, all you have to do is cease broadcasting 18 days earlier than you would have done."

After the hearing David Lye, Acting Managing Director of Estuary Radio Ltd., told reporters outside the court that the protracted legal battle had cost the station £10,000 and as a consequence the company had lost virtually all the profit it had earned over the year and ten months Radio 390 had been broadcasting.

Out on Red Sands Fort the Radio 390 staff listened to the BBC Home Service 1.00pm news bulletin to hear of the Appeal Court's decision because no direct communication between the station's land-based office and the Fort was

### Radio Caroline programme schedules, June 1967

| Caroline South | Caroline North |
|---|---|
| 6.00am Tommy Vance | Leighton Early Show, Jerry Leighton |
| 9.00am Mike Ahearn | The Big Wide Wonderful World of 'Daffy' Don Allen |
| 12noon Dave Lee Travis | Bob Stewart Show |
| 3.00pm Keith Hampshire | Mick Luvzit |
| 6.00pm Robbie Dale | Requests in Action |
| 8.30pm Christ to the Nation | (8.00) The World Tomorrow |
| 9.00pm Johnnie Walker | (8.30) Closedown |
| 12midnight Steve Young | Midnight Surf Party |
| 3.00am Night Owl Prowl | (2.00) Closedown |

permitted. Despite hearing the Appeal Court's decision staff on Red Sands Fort continued presenting Radio 390 programmes as normal throughout the afternoon of 28th July 1967 until official instructions were received from the station's management.

The management meanwhile made arrangements for the station's tender to be despatched from Whitstable for the last time carrying instructions for staff on the Fort to cease transmissions and finally close Radio 390. The tender arrived at Red Sands shortly after 5.00pm on 28th July 1967. The station's 5.00pm news had just been read, including an item about the Appeal Court's decision against Radio 390, and the next programme, "On the Scene" was started by announcer Christopher Clark. After the end of the first record senior announcer Edward Cole interrupted the programme to read the message which had been sent from the management of Estuary Radio Ltd.:-

*Due to an injunction imposed in the High Court today at the request of the Post Office Radio 390 is now required to cease broadcasting. We should like to express our immense appreciation to the millions of listeners who have always supported us during the past two years and through our many struggles to stay on the air. It is very disappointing to all of us that we are not able to continue to provide you with the programmes you enjoy, but perhaps one day we will be allowed to do so again. Until then on behalf of Mr. Lye, our London office, the relief staff and everybody here I should like to say goodbye.*

At 5.10pm the station played the National Anthem and Radio 390 closed for the final time.

Immediately following Radio 390's closure most of the announcers and radio engineers left Red Sands Tower, but four men stayed on board to guard the £40,000 worth of equipment until it could be removed. Early in the morning of 5th August 1967 a group of men persuaded the owner of a fishing boat, *Shemali,* to take them out to Red Sands where they forcibly boarded the Fort, threatening the remaining Radio 390 staff with violence if they resisted. The invaders then proceeded to strip radio equipment and central heating radiators worth about £1,000 from the towers and took it away in the *Shemali.* A Radio 390 engineer on the Fort managed to send an SOS message to his wife using a low power transmitter he had hidden in one of the Towers and she in turn contacted Estuary Radio's Acting Managing Director, David Lye. The SOS had also been also picked up by the fishing boat *Kestrel* whose skipper informed police and a helicopter from RAF Manston was despatched to the Fort with a police officer and doctor on board. However, by the time the helicopter arrived the raiders had left Red Sands Fort.

Meanwhile, David Lye, using a friend's light aircraft, conducted his own search of the Thames Estuary for the fishing boat *Shemali,* which he eventually located and photographed. When the *Shemali* arrived at Southend it was met by Port of London Authority officials who arrested those on board and towed the vessel to Canvey Island where police were waiting to question them about the theft of material from Red Sands Fort.

**MEET US ON 390 METRES**

## Impact of the Radio 390 case for British and International Law

*The extent of territorial limits at any point along a coastline - which by its very nature is uneven and contains many indentations - is measured from a baseline, commonly the low water mark as plotted on official charts. However, this very practice became the central point in the argument over the extent of territorial waters during the case involving Radio 390, in 1966/67. The judgement in the case (Post Office v Estuary Radio Ltd.) and the subsequent appeal (R v Kent Justices, ex-parte Lye) was so fundamentally important that it was subsequently embodied in the Wireless Telegraphy Act, 1967 as the definitive ruling on the starting point for measuring the extent of British territorial waters. The Act also gave a statutory basis (rather than decree by Royal Perogative as with the 1964 Order in Council) to the determination of what constituted a low tide elevation. The decision in this case was a significant legacy from the offshore radio era to the application of British and international law.*

*Bays also pose another problem for determining the base line from which territorial waters can be measured. Bays are defined as "well marked indentations of the land of such proportions as to contain landlocked waters and constitute more than just a curvature in the coast." The Geneva Convention contains a complex mathematical formula for calculating the area of water in a bay which involves drawing a semicircle from a diameter line which itself is drawn across the mouth of an indentation. If the area of water on the indentation side of the baseline is as large as, or larger than, the area of water within the semicircle then the indentation may be regarded as a 'bay' and treated as internal (as opposed to territorial) waters.*

*The determination of the natural entrance points of the Thames Estuary for the purposes of drawing the (theoretical) semicircle's diameter baseline was a crucial point of argument in the Radio 390 case. The measurements made by the authorities at that time included not only the Thames Estuary waters themselves, but waters in main rivers up to high water marks - resulting in a very narrow margin of difference for determining whether or not the area constituted internal waters - yet another decision involving offshore radio which is now embodied in British law.*

*Get the top pops from*
**LUXEMBOURG & CAROLINE ON 'RIVIERA' & 'MAJORCA'**

There are two new names on the pop-scene. Riviera and Majorca—two splendid new Philips portable radios. Stylish, powerful, really with-it, they give pin-point tuning of Luxembourg, Radio Caroline and other pop-music stations, bring in all your favourite programmes loud and clear. These are just two of the brilliant models from Philips New World range. See and hear them all at your nearest Philips dealer.

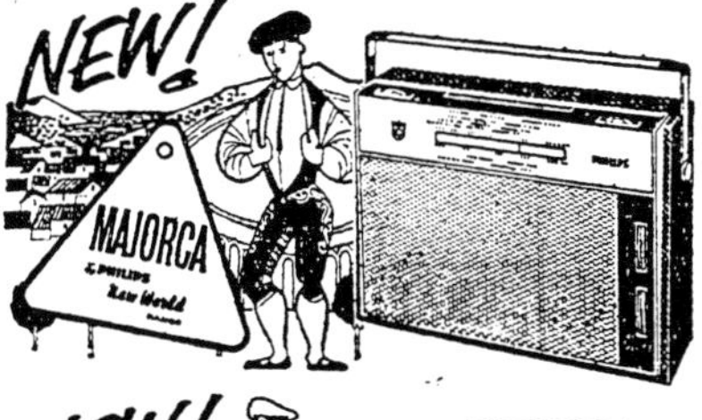


Luxury two-wave portable, model 336 16½ gns. Big sound from a 6"x4" loudspeaker housed in an attractive cabinet of luxury padded rexine.

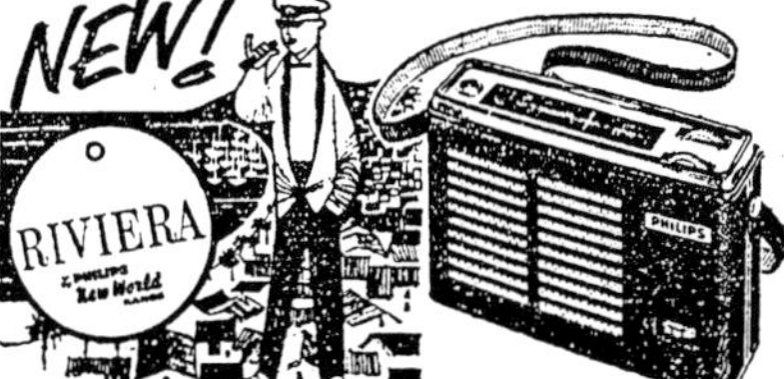


Two-wave camera-style portable, model 237 11 gns. Luxurious padded leathercloth cabinet *plus* micro-miniaturisation. Today's top two refinements in one marvellous portable.

*Radio manufacturers often used the offshore stations to promote their products*

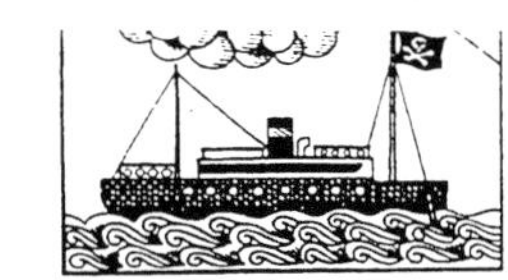

**You meet a better class of pirate on a Grundig**

Some 15-guinea radios give you the music. A Grundig makes it feel alive! There's no fuzziness or fading—you could be right out there with the pirates! Post this coupon now to Grundig (GB) Ltd., London, S.E.26, and tune in on a whole new range of Grundig radios priced from 15 gns. You'll get a free 32-page colour catalogue, plus full details of Grundig's famous tape recorders and stereograms.

NAME ..........

ADDRESS ..........

GRUNDIG

TVT2

**This coupon is legal**

**RADIO LONDON RELEASE:**

NEWS CENTRAL

RELEASED THROUGH: RADLON (SALES) LTD (REPRESENTATIVES FOR RADIO LONDON)
17 CURZON STREET LONDON W.1. MAY 5361

## Radio London's shock announcement

The same day on which Radio 390 closed, 28th July 1967, Radio London listeners were told in a dramatic announcement that, contrary to previous statements, the station would not continue broadcasting after 15th August 1967. Managing Director Philip Birch said "We have received hundreds of thousands of letters from listeners asking us to continue, but we would be getting too close to the law. As we have never yet broken the law we have decided to cease broadcasting. Our ship will be up for sale." The real reason for the station's closure was of course its inability to obtain sufficient advertising revenue from foreign sources to finance continued broadcasting.

The actual announcement broadcast to Radio London listeners said:-

*It is with deep regret that after nearly three years of broadcasting, Radio London will be closing down on August 14th. It is unfortunate that this Government's attitude towards independent radio has consistently been one of suppression as part of a determined plan to continue the Government's monopoly in radio broadcasting. Radio London has repeatedly pointed out that the British public could benefit from dozens of independent radio stations operating under licence on land, but the Government has said no. This is in spite of the fact that the Prime Minister has in his possession a study by National Opinion Polls that shows that 69% of the population are in favour of allowing the free radio stations to continue broadcasting. We understand that the new Government programme, which will be called Radio 1, is largely modelled on Radio London and will employ many Radio London DJs. We receive hundreds of thousands of letters from listeners but possibly this Government imitation is the greatest tribute of all.*

### BBC plans announced

*At the end of July 1967 the BBC unveiled its long awaited plans for the introduction of a pop radio service to replace the offshore stations. The old Home, Light and Third Programme networks were to be abolished and in their place four new stations were to be launched:-*

- *Radio One was the new pop music station.*
- *Radio Two a revamped Light Programme.*
- *Radio Three a classical music and speech channel, replacing the Third Programme.*
- *Radio Four was to carry the Home Service speech and news programmes.*

*It was claimed that 60 hours a week of extra broadcasting would result from the sweeping changes to be introduced at the end of September 1967.*

A similar problem also affected Carstead Advertising, whose Managing Director Ted Allbeury, had already announced earlier in the month that Radios 355 and 227 would also be closing before the Marine etc. Broadcasting (Offences) Act came into effect. Efforts had been made, using Radio 227's office in Holland, to obtain foreign advertising for the two stations, but as with Radio London this had proved unsuccessful. Additionally Ted Allbeury was 'warned' that he was under surveillance by the authorities and that, as a British citizen, he should not contemplate operating the stations from abroad while at the same time expect to slip in and out of the country without being stopped once the Marine etc. Broadcasting (Offences) Act was in force.

## The first closures

Dutch language Radio 227 was the first station to close in advance of the provisions of the Marine etc. Broadcasting (Offences) Act coming into effect. The station closed without ceremony following the end of normal programmes at 6.00pm on 23rd July 1967 (see Chapter 13).

Ten days later, on 2nd August it was announced that Radio 355 would be closing at midnight on Saturday 5th August 1967. The station's final two hours were hosted by Programme Director Tony Windsor and all DJs who were on board the *Laissez Faire* at the time also took part. Shortly before midnight the last commercial - for Silexene paint - was played and Managing Director Ted Allbeury made a closing speech pointing out to listeners the restrictions on personal liberty and freedom contained in the Marine etc. Broadcasting (Offences) Act:-

*This is to say goodbye. You and I have seen a lot of things happen in the last few years, the first commercial radio station serving Great Britain, and from midnight on 14th August a new set of restrictions on the people of this country. It will then be illegal for a newspaper to write about pirate radios, the only subject that it's illegal for a newspaper to write about. On 15th August for the first time since the Middle Ages, there will be such a thing as an illegal sermon.*

*I've just come back from the United States where there are over 6,000 radio stations. In San Francisco, Dallas, New York or any other city for that matter, you can have a choice of thirteen television channels and twenty radio stations. Whether you want news, pop or sweet music it's there. The choice is yours and it doesn't cost you or the government a penny. I would like to read you two paragraphs of the FCC and NAB rules which govern commercial radio and television in the United States.*

*'Any qualified citizen, firm or group may apply to the Federal Communications Commission for authority to construct a standard AM or FM or television broadcast station.' The second paragraph goes as follows:- 'We believe that radio broadcasting in the United States of America is a living symbol of democracy, a significant and necessary instrument for maintaining freedom of expression as established by the First Amendment to the Constitution of the United States.' That sounds like real democracy at work to me.*

*The reasons given for closing us down are excuses of course, not reasons - just political dogma surrounded by a tremendous element of hypocrisy. Do I believe in Socialist dogma? No, not particularly. There are many so-called Socialists who supported the pirates and many who are for commercial radio. I've been a Socialist all my life, up to now, anyway. But I believe in freedom - freedom to choose what we want, freedom to work hard with real money in our pockets, not freedom to be unemployed.*

*On one of my programmes way back I got a flood of mail because I played "Land of Hope and Glory, Mother of the Free". Are we free any more? Isn't it time to set ourselves free? Free to work hard and live well, free to be entertained as we choose and free from the thousands of petty and miserable restrictions that are being placed on us and placed on our lives day after day. We need a new slogan now "Give Us Back Our Freedom and We'll Work Hard. Set Us Free From the Bureaucrats."*

## For Sale -one radio ship!

*Radio 270's Managing Director, Wilf Proudfoot, announced that the station would close at one minute to midnight on 14th August 1967, saying "we have not broken the law up to now and we don't intend to in the future." Even before Radio 270's closure the station's vessel Oceaan VII was put up for sale through a local firm of estate agents, Tuckley and Co., with an asking price of £25,000.*

WE must be THE ONLY ESTATE AGENTS offering a PIRATE RADIO SHIP! We are instructed by the pirates (we'll act for anyone!) to offer a useful ship known as Oceaan 7. Fully equipped as radio transmission station with 10 kilowatt output. Extensive crew and disc jockey accommodation. Would make floating home with unusual intercom installation—everyone could hear your Hi Fi! £12,500 o.n.o. Many records could be included in the price.

*This country, this people have a record for inventiveness, industry, commercial success, tolerance second to none, but right now we're carrying a burden that would make the strongest falter.*

*To all of you who have written to me, my thanks. To all who tried to help us, the thanks of all of us. Everyone of us here sends you good wishes and our hope is to be back with you some day. We'll miss you and I hope you'll miss us. Love from Ann, Terry and myself and Goodnight and God bless.*

This final programme actually over-ran and Radio 355 eventually closed at 21 minutes past midnight on 6th August with "Auld Lang Syne" being played followed by the National Anthem.

Both stations operated by Carstead Advertising had closed before the effective date of the Marine etc. Broadcasting (Offences) Act because insurance for the *Laissez Faire* was due for renewal and it was not considered worthwhile extending that cover for less than two weeks.

After DJs and radio crew had left the *Laissez Faire* the ship sailed to Flushing in Holland on 18th August 1967 and then crossed the Atlantic, arriving in Miami on 21st September 1967, with her mast having been damaged during a storm.

These closures and announcements of intended closure left Radio Caroline alone saying it would defy the new law and continue broadcasting after 15th August 1967. Contingency plans for this to happen had already been put in place by the station's management. In June 1967 all British members of Radio Caroline's board of directors resigned, except Philip Solomon, who held Irish citizenship and was therefore able to continue running the station with fellow Irishman Ronan O'Rahilly. A number of American, Australian, Canadian and South African DJs were said to have been recruited and standing by to join the station after 15th August 1967. Meanwhile, on both the North and South stations many British DJs were saying during the early days of August 1967 that they would stay on with Radio Caroline and defy the new law.

## Manx support for Caroline

One demonstration of support for Radio Caroline came unexpectedly from a source that had initially been very hostile to the station - the Government of the Isle of Man. Since mid-1964 Radio Caroline North had become very popular on the Island, not just because of the entertainment it provided, but because the station gave the Island's holiday resorts an immense amount of free publicity, greatly boosting the Manx tourist trade and general economy.

In April 1967, as the British House of Commons was approving the Marine etc. Broadcasting (Offences) Bill, the Isle of Man Parliament, the House of Keys, voted by 19 to 3 to reject the same Bill being added to the Island's statute book. In doing so the Island Government offered some hope for the future existence of Caroline North. Ronan O'Rahilly even announced that he was negotiating with the Manx authorities to bring Radio Caroline ashore so that the station could operate from a base on the Island, although realistically this was unlikely to have been achieved at that time.

Throughout the summer of 1967, as the British Government proceeded with enacting its own legislation, the Manx Government stood its rebellious ground. Undeterred, Westminster announced at the beginning of August 1967 that the Marine etc. Broadcasting (Offences) Act would be applied to the Island (and also the Channel Islands) by means of Orders in Council signed by the Queen - effectively imposing the legislation against the wishes of the Island's own Parliament and its people.

### Wilson tapes

*Plans were promoted by Radio Caroline during late summer 1967 to broadcast after - 15th August 1967 - tapes allegedly exposing details of the private life of Prime Minister Harold Wilson, but in the event this was not done. Whether such tapes really existed and if so what information they contained is unknown, but undoubtedly more harm than good would have been done for Radio Caroline's cause and reputation if they had been aired.*

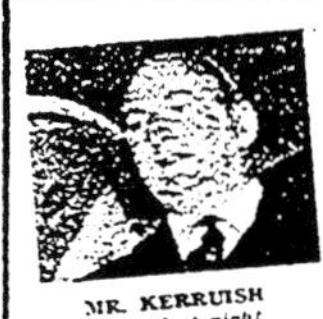


WE DON'T ACCEPT ORDER TO SHUT RADIO CAROLINE, SAYS SPEAKER

**Freedom move by Manxmen**

*They're upset— but U.D.I. idea surprises Manx*

**MANX MAY CHALLENGE BRITAIN**

The prospect of this unwanted piece of legislation being forced on the Isle of Man's statute book brought to the surface all the Manx nationalistic feelings and there was talk of the Island breaking its ties with Westminster and declaring complete independence.

An Independent Member of the House of Keys, Roy McDonald (who was also Chairman of the Manx Broadcasting Commission) proposed a resolution rejecting the imposition of legislation on the Island and demanded that the situation be considered by the United Nations Committee responsible for overseeing the interests of colonial peoples. Roy McDonald emphasised that he was not particularly supporting Radio Caroline, that just happened to have brought the real issue to light. The real issue so far as he and others were concerned was the imposition of unwanted British legislation which had already been rejected by the semi-independent Island's own Parliament. Mr. McDonald's resolution was approved by the House of Keys and the Island's Governor, Sir Peter Stallard, was forced to recall the full Island Parliament, Tynwald, from its summer recess to consider the rapidly deteriorating constitutional situation.

Support for Radio Caroline North remaining at anchor off the Island was stepped up in July 1967 when the Postmaster General rejected a request from the Manx Broadcasting Commission for an increase in transmitter power for the local (legal) commercial station, Manx Radio. If they could not have a powerful station of their own to broadcast the Island's attractions to listeners on the mainland then many Manxmen were happy to see Caroline North remain in Ramsey Bay and to let it fulfil that function for them.

On 3rd August 1967 it was announced that Tynwald's petition to the Privy Council Committee (which was responsible for extending the Marine etc. Broadcasting (Offences) Act to the Island) had been rejected and, as a consequence, the Queen would be asked to sign an Order in Council imposing the legislation on the Island. After this announcement there was speculation about the Island engaging in all sorts of rebellious activity - the issuing of Manx passports, a takeover of the Post Office service on the Island, and even the creation of a Manx national army, but all came to nothing.

Tynwald, the Manx Parliament, met on 8th August 1967 in a joint session of its two Houses - the House of Keys and the Legislative Council. During seven hours of heated debate Roy McDonald agreed to withdraw that part of his resolution referring the imposition of British legislation on the Island to the United Nations, but replaced it with a reference to the Commonwealth Secretariat.

When it came to the vote, the lower house, the House of Keys, supported Roy McDonald's amended resolution by 16 votes to 8, but the 10 member upper house, the Legislative Council, voted unanimously against it. The House of Keys immediately adjourned to its own chamber and voted to continue with its previous decision to fight the imposition of unwanted mainland legislation. Ronan O'Rahilly who had witnessed the debate from the public gallery told waiting reporters afterwards that Radio Caroline North would remain in Ramsey Bay whatever the Manx or British Governments decided, any prosecutions of staff or advertisers which arose as a consequence would, he said, be fought all the way to the European Court of Human Rights.

## Radio London closure

The first station to close on Monday 14th August 1967, the day before the Marine etc. Broadcasting (Offences) Act came into effect, was Radio London. Throughout the day farewell messages were broadcast from many pop stars who, in part, owed their success to Radio London - Beatle Ringo Starr, The Bee Gees, Cilla Black, Dave Davies, Episode Six, Chris Farlowe, David Garrick, The Hollies, Englebert Humperdink, Tom Jones, The Kinks, Lulu, Sandie Shaw, Nancy Sinatra, The Small Faces, John Walker and several American stars who recorded on the Tamla Mowtown label. During the station's final hour between 2.00pm and 3.00pm Managing Director Philip Birch told listeners:-

*Staff in Curzon Street listen to Radio London's final hour*

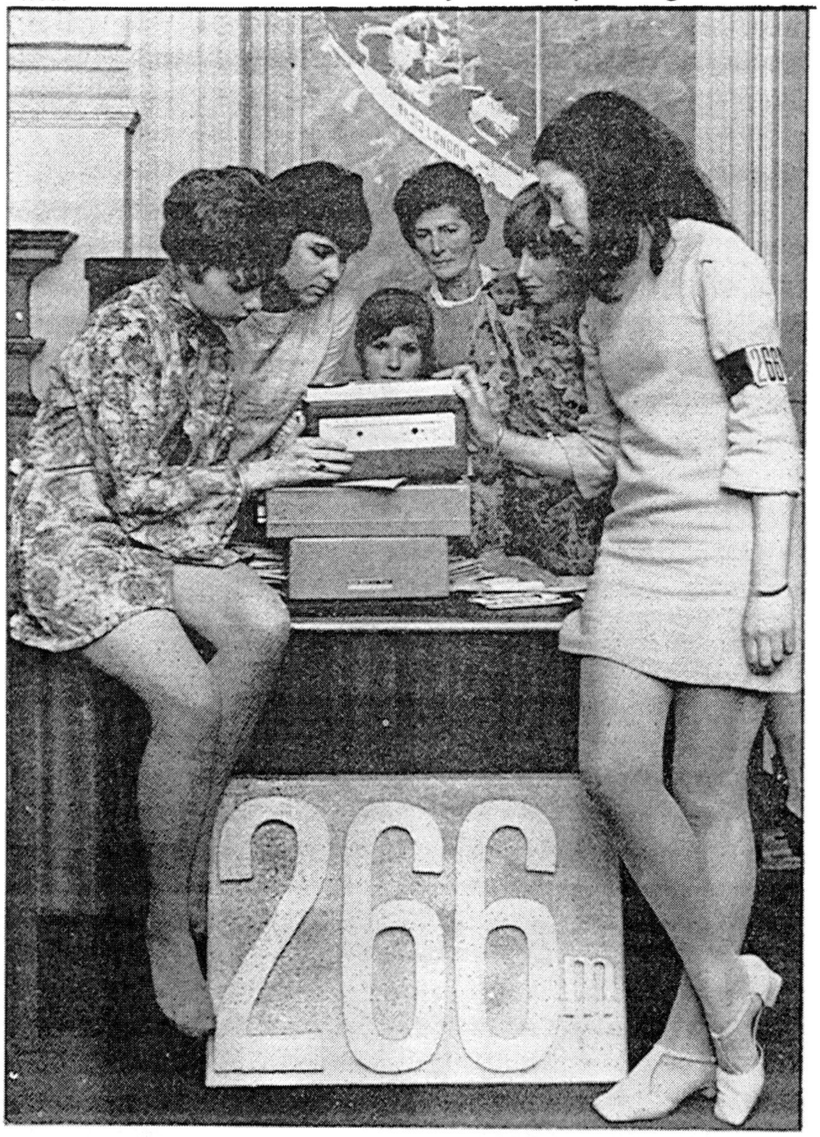

*It was just three years ago this month that the idea for Radio London was born. Four months after that time Radio London was on the air, and four months after that National Opinion Polls showed that it had millions of listeners. Now it's to end. During the last three years I feel that Radio London has done very little harm, but an awful lot of good. During those three years it has helped organisations such as the Institute for the Blind, Oxfam, the Cancer Fund and the Lifeboat Service to raise funds for their very worthwhile causes. It has saved the life of an airman who bailed out over the North Sea and was picked up by Radio London's tender.*

*In closing Radio London I would like to give very special thanks to Lord Denham who fought our case in the House of Lords and to Lord Arran for all his help; to the Shadow Postmaster General, Paul Bryan; to Ian Gilmour and the other MPs who stood up in the House of Commons and fought our case.*

*I would like to give my personal thanks to all of the staff of 17 Curzon Street; to all the disc jockeys; to Captain Buniga and his crew; to the 1,027 advertisers who supported Radio London in the last three years and used Radio London to help sell their products. But most of all I'd like to thank you, one of the 12 million listeners in the United Kingdom and one of the 4 million listeners in Holland, France, Belgium, Germany and other countries on the Continent for all the support you have given Radio London during the last three years.*

*If during that time Radio London had brought a little warmth, a little friendliness, a little happiness in your life then it's all been worthwhile. As one listener put it "The world will get by without Big L, but I'm not sure if it will be a better place." Thank you.*

The final hour on Radio London had been pre-recorded a few days earlier with the station's last news bulletin at 2.30pm being the only live input. The programme was hosted by senior DJ Paul Kaye and consisted of a brief history of the station, farewell messages from pop stars and DJs as well as some nostalgic music. Advertisers paid heavy premiums for their announcements to be included in this programme - in fact advertising time had been sold at premium rates throughout the station's last few days on the air - and the final commercial broadcast on Radio London was for Consulate cigarettes. It was estimated that during its relatively short life-span of two years and eight months Radio London had made a £100,000 profit for its investors.

Paul Kaye was the last remaining DJ from the station's original line-up and his was the first and last voice heard on Radio London. After the final record, "A Day in the Life" by the Beatles, had been played Paul Kaye said simply *Big L time is 3 o'clock and Radio London is now closing down.* The station left the air after playing its theme music (Big Lil) and one final jingle. Engineers then shut off the transmitter, removed the crystal, switched off the control panel and locked

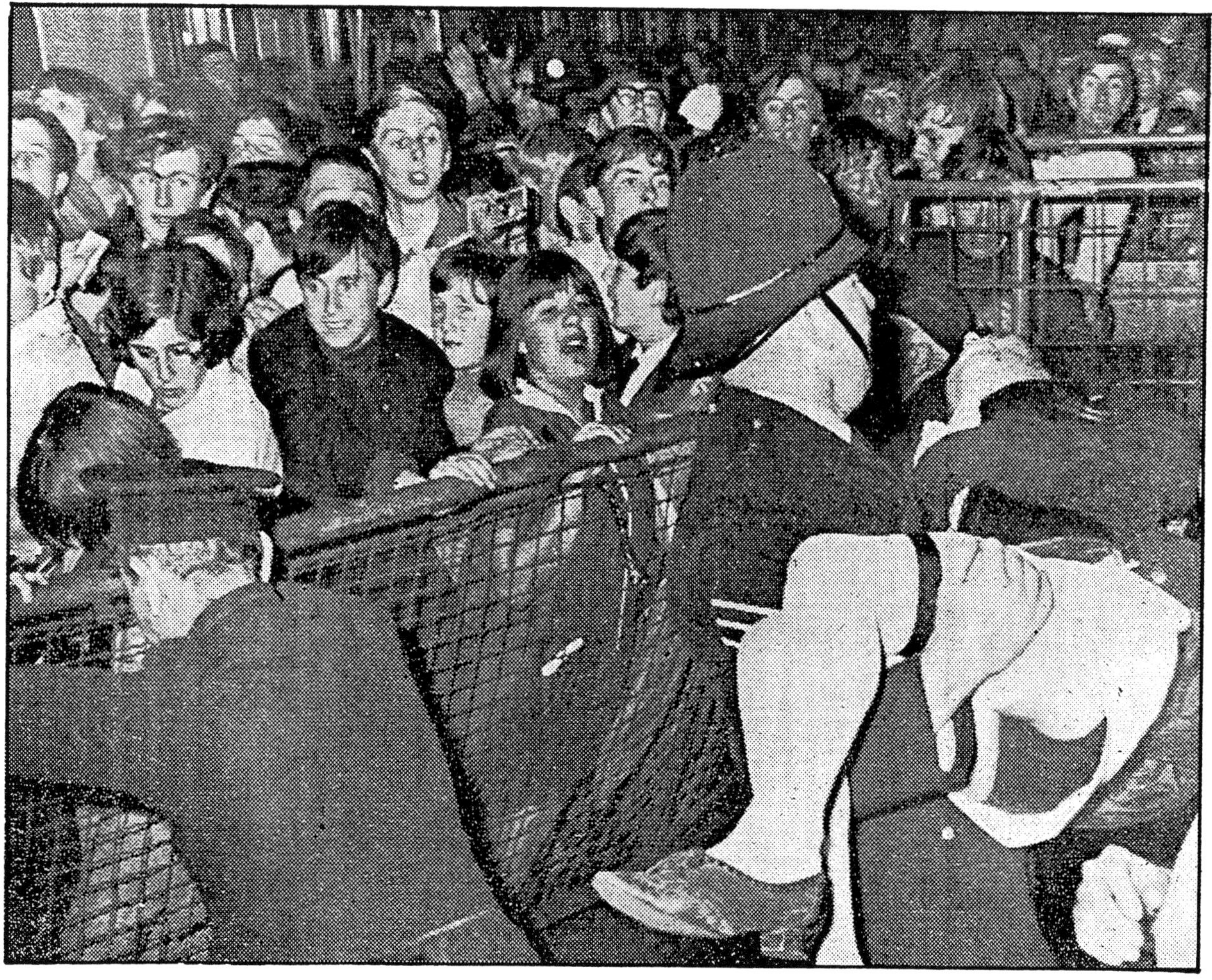

*Crowds at Liverpool Street Station mob Radio London and Radio Caroline DJs*

the studio. Just after 3.00pm Robbie Dale on Radio Caroline South paid a tribute to the rival station which had just closed. He observed a minutes silence before Radio Caroline returned to playing music - once more the lone voice of offshore radio, in the south at least.

The Big L DJs and radio engineers left the *Galaxy* later that afternoon and were taken to Felixstowe where they were greeted by fans who had gathered on the quayside. This welcome, however, was nothing compared to that which awaited them when their train arrived at Liverpool Street Station in London. Here over 1,000 supporters had gathered during the afternoon and when the train carrying the Radio London DJs arrived from Ipswich at 6.40pm the crowd surged through barriers and police lines. Hundreds of fans besieged the DJs on the train and many young people as well as the police who were trying to restrain them were knocked down and injured in the crush. When the Radio London staff eventually managed to make their escape from the train to a waiting car this too was surrounded by fans, many of whom climbed on the roof and bonnet.

Meanwhile the *Galaxy* remained silently at anchor off the Essex coast for a few days with only her Dutch Captain and crew on board. On 19th August 1967 she raised her anchor and sailed to Hamburg in West Germany, where she arrived two days later. There were many rumours and plans for the ship to be used as an offshore radio station once again, but that story unfolded very slowly over the following few years.

## Radio 270 closure

In the north two of the three remaining offshore stations also closed shortly before midnight on 14th August 1967.

On the east coast Radio 270 planned a final hour which was to have included all the station's DJs broadcasting live from on board the *Oceaan VII*. However, rough weather prevented those DJs on shore leave travelling to the ship to join their colleagues but unofficial arrangements were made for a helicopter to drop a tape containing their farewell messages onto the deck of the *Oceaan VII*. This arrangement was made by Radio 270's Deputy Programme Director, Mike Hayes who persuaded a friend at RAF Leconfield, Tony Harrison to take the tape on a helicopter 'training flight' over the North Sea. Because on the unofficial and unauthorised nature of the delivery the tape was accompanied by a message instructing those on board the *Oceaan VII* not to mention on the air how it had arrived.

Unfortunately when the tape and accompanying message were dropped from the helicopter they landed, not as planned on the deck of the *Oceaan VII* but in the sea. Those on board the radio ship, knowing nothing of the secretive nature of the mission, announced to listeners at 9.15pm that an RAF helicopter was hovering over the *Oceaan VII* and thanked "the boys at Leconfield" for coming out to see them on their final day! The RAF authorities immediately launched an official inquiry into this completely unauthorised 'training flight' and it was reported that Prime Minister Harold Wilson demanded to see a personal copy of the report on the incident.

Radio 270's final hour then went ahead with those DJs on board *Oceaan VII*, as well as the Captain and crew reminiscing about life on the station. Unfortunately studio equipment during that final programme suffered from surges in power due to the ship's continuing problem with jelly fish which were being sucked into the generator cooling system. For listeners the effect of this problem was that records were played at the wrong speeds and sounded totally distorted.

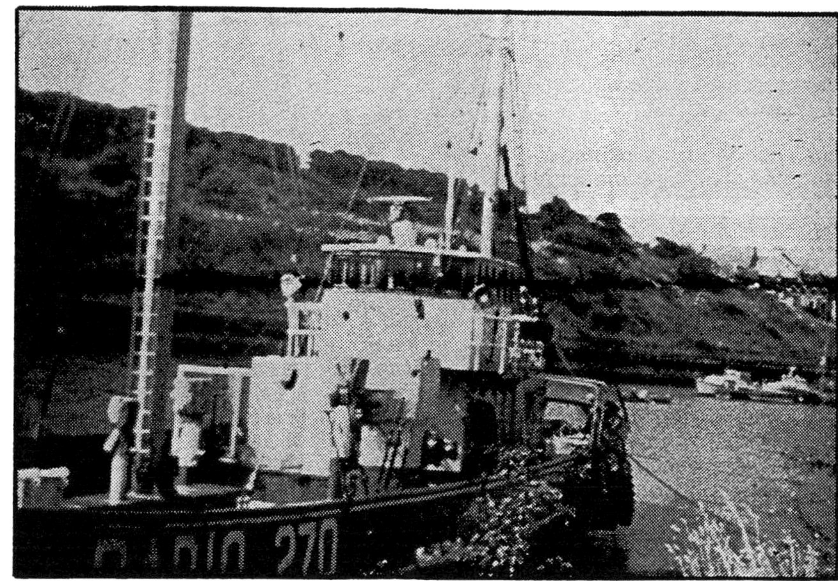


'Oceaan VII' up for sale in Whitby Harbour

The station's final programme also contained farewell messages from Leonard Dale, Chairman of Radio 270 and Managing Director Wilf Proudfoot (who sent a telegram from Spain where he was on holiday) both expressing the hope that eventually they would be able to return to the airwaves, from a land-based station. At 11.55pm the final announcement was made by Programme Director Vince 'Rusty' Allen:-

*I'm gonna miss you one hell of a lot. I hope that maybe some day soon in the not too distant future we'll meet on the air again. This is Radio 270 broadcasting on 1115 kilocycles in the medium waveband. The time is one and a half minutes before midnight and we're now closing down. On behalf of the 270 men, the radio technicians, the Captain and crew and everybody onshore concerned with Radio 270, this is Rusty Allen wishing you God bless and God speed. Goodnight and Goodbye. Radio 270 is now closing down.*

After playing the National Anthem, the station left the air for the final time at 11.59pm. From a business point of view Radio 270, which claimed an audience of four and a half million listeners, was not an outstanding success. At one point it had debts of over £50,000, but before the station closed the directors made arrangements for all staff and creditors to be paid out of their own funds. Ultimately, the original shareholders were the people who lost financially because of the station's closure.

The DJs and crew who had been on board the *Oceaan VII* left the ship immediately after the station closed and arrived in Bridlington Harbour at about 1.15am the following morning, 15th August 1967, where they were met on the quayside by a crowd of about 600 fans. The *Oceaan VII* herself, which had already been offered for sale by local estate agents Tuckley and Co., sailed to Whitby where she berthed later that same afternoon. Although nobody could have guessed it at the time the ship and her radio equipment's connections with offshore radio were not finished yet!

## Radio Scotland closure

Further north, off the Scottish coast, Radio Scotland also closed at midnight on 14th August 1967. The final day's programmes were pre-recorded in the station's Glasgow studios and most of the DJs had already left the *Comet* during the afternoon of 14th August to join 2,000 fans at a Close-down Clan Ball in Glasgow. Mark Wesley (West) and Tony Allan stayed on board the radio ship to play the taped programmes and finally close Radio Scotland. Before leaving the ship, however, the DJs threw the station's entire record collection overboard and pictures of this 'ceremony' appeared the following day in many national newspapers.

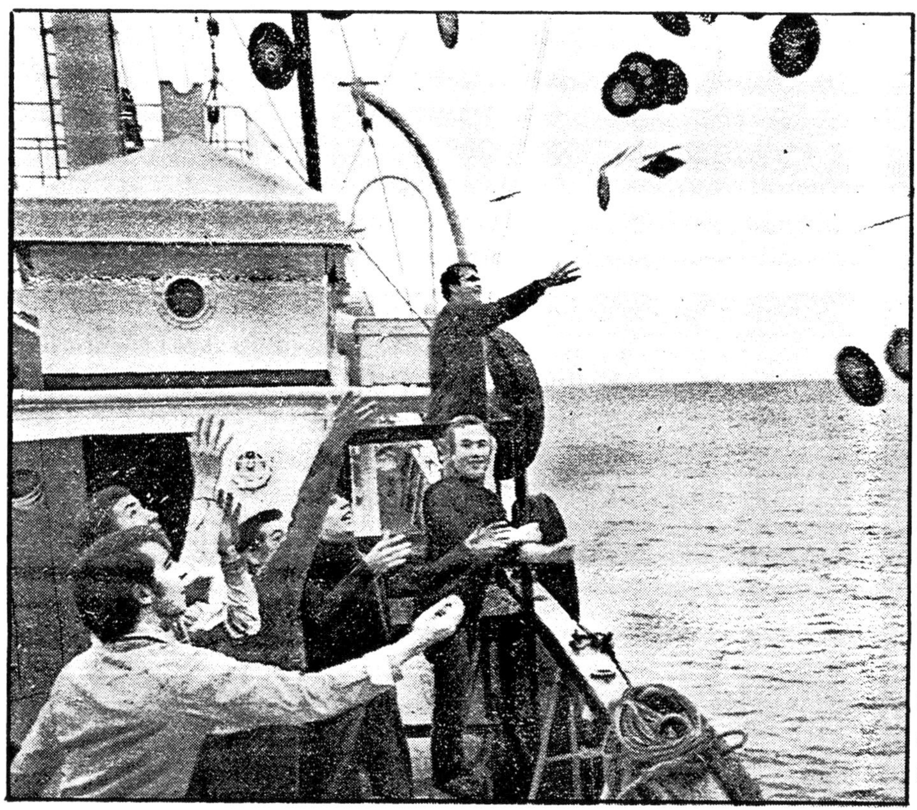

DJs on board the 'Comet' throw Radio Scotland's record collection overboard

The station's final hour contained messages and tributes from former staff and from Managing Director Tommy Shields who said it was the sadddest day of his life. Radio Scotland announced that during the nineteen months it had been on the air the station had lost £100,000, due largely to the cost of towing the *Comet* from the east to the west coast and back again, as well as the general lack of advertising revenue as a result of poor signal quality and frequent periods off the air while the ship was being repositioned.

Managing Director, Tommy Shields made the following emotional closedow announcement:-

*Soon, very soon now, the Senior DJ on the Comet will line up the National Anthem for the last time aboard our brave wee ship lying off the Fife coast. And when the signal is put over to the radio engineer 'end of transmissions' that will be the last sound ever to be heard from Radio Scotland.*

*I'm sitting all alone in the studio here and the hands on the clock are simply racing away, round and round. Oh dear, if only there was a way to stop it and go back to New Year's Eve 1965. Now while the last record was on I looked around the studio in a nostalgic mood, as it's quiet here, and I heard the voices of the many, many artists who came in to entertain us from Max Bygraves to Jimmy Logan, Julie Rogers, Willy Starr, Larry Marshall, and a host of other people. Well, they're all away now and the studio is quiet. It will never be used again for any broadcasts from Radio Scotland and that is the end, as I said, of an era.*

*I would like to take this opportunity before we go off the air forever of paying an especial tribute and thanks to a very wonderful team I've had with me on the Comet. All DJs, the crew and the Captain.*

*From all of the boys and girls at Radio Scotland House if I may I would like to say a big thank you to all the former DJs who were with us too, from Brian Holden who was Co-ordination Executive way back in the early days. Thanks for his loyalty and enthusiasm to Bob Spencer, Alan McKenzie, the comedian with the golden voice, Freddie White, the lad from Aberdeen, Roger Gale, who was our first Senior DJ, Alan Black and to all of those young men who wanted to become DJs on Radio Scotland.. To you, and all of you in fact, a very big thank you again.*

*We in Scotland have never accepted defeat lightly in the past. We have been suppressed and oppressed many times in our long illustrious history, but we have always come back to win. For we are a proud, independent people. We have demanded the retention of Radio Scotland. It has been reused us. But I don't think it will be for long, for we are Scotland the Brave!*

*Well, from all of us at Radio Scotland it's not Goodbye, merely au revoir. I wish to express my sincere thanks to all of you very wonderful people out there, people of Scotland, for your wonderful loyalty and support.*

*It only remains for me to say in the dying moments of Radio Scotland to thank you from the bottom of my heart and say Goodbye and God Bless to you all. Bye Bye.*

After spending three days at anchor following Radio Scotland's closure the *Comet* was eventually towed into the port of Methil, where the aerial mast was removed and the vessel put up for sale. About six months after the station closed Managing Director Tommy Shields died as the result of a kidney complaint, at the age of 49, reportedly never having recovered from the shock of losing his beloved Scottish radio station.

## Caroline continues

With Tuesday 15th August 1967 less than a minute old only two British offshore radio stations remained on the air in defiance of the new law - Radio Caroline North and Radio Caroline South. On board the *Mi Amigo,* home of Radio Caroline South were three Englishmen - DJs Johnnie Walker and Robbie Dale as well as newsreader Ross Brown.

At 12 midnight Johnnie Walker and Robbie Dale, sounding almost as if they were reassuring eachother as much as the listeners, announced that the station, now renamed Caroline International, would continue broadcasting:-

**Johnnie Walker** *This is your radio station. This is Radio Caroline. It is now 12 midnight. We want to say welcome to the new phase of broadcasting from Caroline. I want you to know something, that is a station that belongs to you and as a right can't ever be taken away from you. There are a lot of people along the coast tonight who are flashing their headlamps at us. Very nice to see you. You have made us more happy and I couldn't think it was possible, but you have made us more happy than we are already. Dale, what are you doing there?*

**Robbie Dale** *I'm looking out of the porthole window. It really is amazing to see all those cars out there and to know that we're not alone in this our most important moment. It's tremendous!*

**Johnnie Walker** *Let's say a couple of Thank You's now. Robbie and myself would like to say thank you to our leader, Ronan O'Rahilly, Mr. Philip Soloman and all who work for Radio Caroline to make it possible for us to sit here and speak to you now. Also to thank the many, many people who have been with Caroline since that Easter Sunday way back in 1964. We are still here because you have given us such tremendous support. This is Radio Caroline it is now 12 midnight.*

After playing the 60s civil rights anthem, "We Shall Overcome" Johnnie Walker went on to say:-

*Radio Caroline would like to extend its thanks to Mr. Harold Wilson and his Labour Government for at last, after over three and a half years of broadcasting, recognising this station's legality, its right to be here, its right to be broadcasting to Great Britain and the Continent, its right to give the music and service to the people of Europe which we have been doing since Easter Sunday 1964. We in turn recognise your right as our listener to have freedom of choice in your radio entertainment and of course that Radio Caroline belongs to you. It is your radio station even though it costs you nothing. And as we enter this new phase in our broadcasting history you naturally have our assurance that we intend to stay on the air, because we belong to you and we love you. Caroline continues!*

By continuing to broadcast the three Englishmen on board the *Mi Amigo* now each faced up to two years in prison and a £400 fine if they ever returned to Britain.

During the previous day the rest of the British staff had left the *Mi Amigo* for the final time - DJs Keith Hampshire and Tom Edwards, together with newsreader Gerry Burke, had decided to part company with the station rather than become exiled from Britain. In future the station's tender would travel not from Essex, but from Holland, making a journey to and from the *Mi Amigo* of about 20 hours and any British staff would have to live abroad rather than run the risk of being arrested on their return to the UK. In fact those who defiantly remained with the station did later return to Britain on a regular basis and although the authorities were aware of this no direct action was taken against those individuals. The Caroline North ship was to be tendered from Dundalk in the Irish Republic, a journey of about 18 hours in good weather and the same restrictions applied to British staff on board the MV *Caroline* who were obliged, in theory at least, to take up residence abroad.

Those who remained on board both Caroline ships after 15th August 1967 began to experience increasing feelings of isolation. This was particularly true for Caroline South staff who, apart from contact with their own landbased office had always had the neighbourly company of crews aboard the *Galaxy* and *Laissez Faire.* As a goodwill gesture about three days after the Marine etc. Broadcasting (Offences) Act had come into effect Ronan O'Rahilly arranged for a small boat to travel out to the *Mi Amigo*, under cover of the sea mist in the area at the time, and deliver food, newspapers and an advance wages payment. This contact with the station's management provided morale boosting reassurance for those on board the radio ship, but unfortunately it was not repeated during the long lonely months which followed.

## Caroline North's stay of execution

On 15th August 1967 Radio Caroline North was, technically, still not outlawed as were all other offshore stations. This anomaly occurred because the station's ship was anchored off the coast of the Isle of Man whose Government had refused to implement the Marine etc. Broadcasting (Offences) Act. The Order in Council imposing the British version of the Act on the Island (together with similar orders for Guernsey and Jersey) did not come into effect until 31st August 1967 so supplies and personnel could quite legitimately be transferred to and from the ship using the Island's ports. However, English staff on board the MV *Caroline* had decided, like their southern colleagues to quit the station on 14th August 1967 for fear of prosecution under the Marine etc. Broadcasting (Offences) Act. DJs Tony Prince and Dave Lee Travis, newsreader Dave Williams and Canadian DJ Jerry King left the ship late in the afternoon of 14th August and arrived in Ramsey Harbour aboard *Offshore III* in the early evening to be met by a crowd of fans and well wishers. Earlier that day a similar crowd had seen five other DJs leave for the MV *Caroline* in defiance of the new law - Englishmen Dee Harrison, Martin Kayne and Mark Sloan, together with Canadian Don Allen and Australian Jimmy Gordon all joined the ship to continue Caroline North programming after 15th August.

*Caroline North's tender leaves Ramsey Harbour on one of its last supply runs, August 1967*

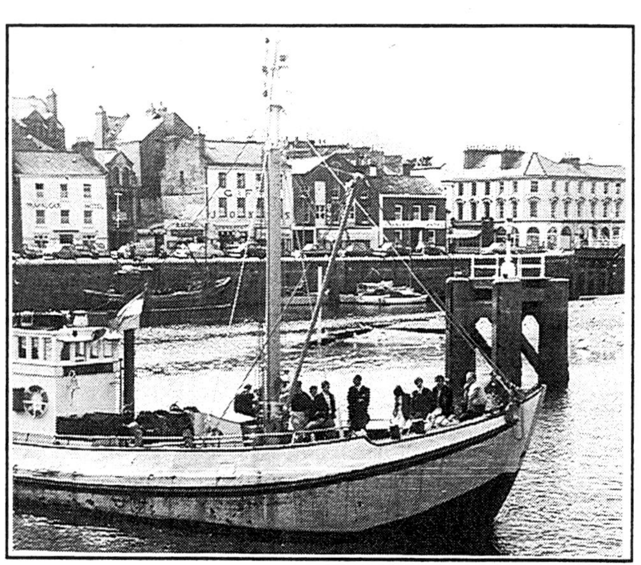

As the Marine etc. Broadcasting (Offences) Act was not actually applied to the Isle of Man until 31st August 1967 Radio Caroline North continued to be serviced from Ramsey for a further two weeks although such arrangements had now been outlawed on the British mainland. The last tender left Ramsey at 8.30pm on 31st August 1967 to make the final delivery of supplies and crew before the provisions of the British law became effective on the Isle of Man. Also during the evening of 31st August 1967 the Isle of Man Steam Packet Company's ferry, *Manxman* took over 2,000 people on a special cruise from Douglas to Ramsey Bay, circling the MV *Caroline.*

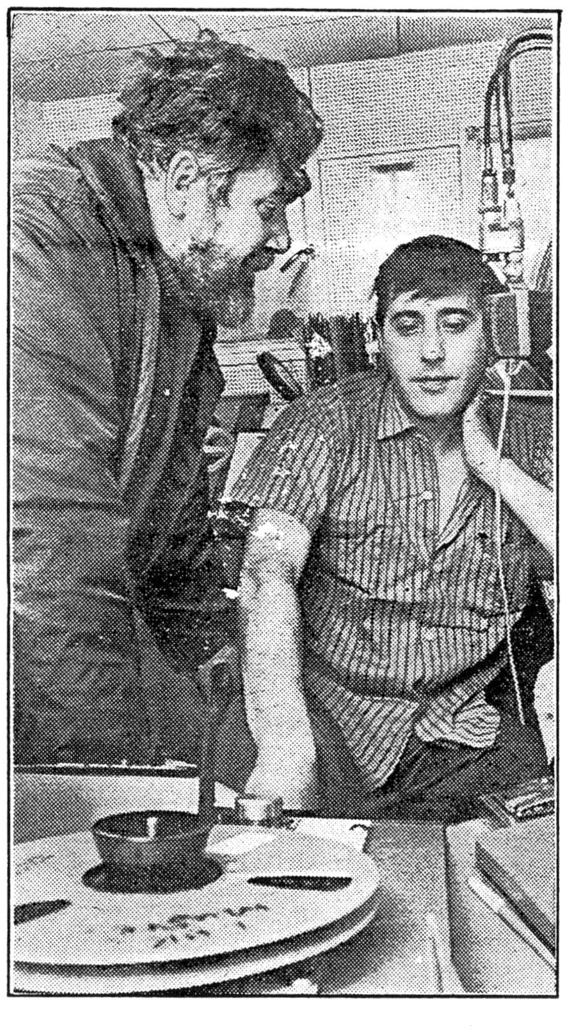

*During the two weeks 'period of grace' for Caroline North a Labour MP, James Dunn, visited the MV Caroline and talked on air with DJ Don Allen on 24th August 1967 (left). Mr. Dunn said his visit was to thank the station for supporting a charity of which he was a founder member, C.A.R.E. During the interview he apologised for the Marine etc. Broadcasting (Offences) Act saying, "I personally have my own views, but the Government has decided this and I must follow. I regret that it has happened."*

*When asked later about the possible illegality of his visit to the offshore station Mr. Dunn said, "I understand the new Act does not apply to the Isle of Man until the order is made against it by the Manx Government - if that happpens - next week. Anyway, I do not agree with the Marine etc. Broadcasting (Offences) Act in its present form."*

On 31st August, at midnight Don Allen, Senior DJ on Caroline North, played the Manx National Anthem, thanked the Isle of Man Government and people for their continued support and announced:- *This is the Northern voice of Radio Caroline International on 259m, the continuing voice of free radio for the British Isles*. After a period of two weeks grace (and regular tender runs) because of a quirk in the legislative processes, Radio Caroline North and its crew had now officially joined its southern sister station in being totally isolated from Britain. Although they didn't know it at the time, it was to be another six weeks before a tender even visited the radio ship again.

**"WE STAY" SAYS CAROLINE SPOKESMAN**

**Detectives At Ramsey Quayside**

## Isolation and hardships

Following the implementation of the Marine etc. Broadcasting (Offences) Act Radio Caroline became virtually cut off from Britain although Ronan O'Rahilly, as an Irish citizen, continued to operate quietly from an office at the former Radio Atlanta headquarters in Dean Street, London using the cover of a company named Mid-Atlantic Films. In response to any enquiries from the press or authorities O'Rahilly claimed now to only be involved in the film production business. Although this was partially true the company also acted as a secret base for recruiting Radio Caroline staff and obtaining supplies of records.

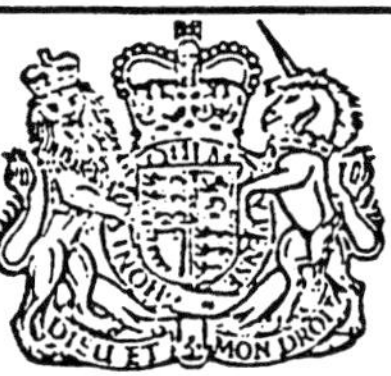

Marine, &c., Broadcasting (Offences) Act 1967

CHAPTER 41
ARRANGEMENT OF SECTIONS

Section
1. Prohibition of broadcasting from ships and aircraft.
2. Prohibition of broadcasting from marine structures
3. Prohibition of acts connected with broadcasting from certain ships and aircraft, and from marine structures outside United Kingdom.
4. Prohibition of acts facilitating broadcasting from ships, aircraft, &c.
5. Prohibition of acts relating to matter broadcast from ships, aircraft, &c.
6. Penalties and legal proceedings.
7. Special defence available in proceedings for carrying goods or persons in contravention of section 4.
8. Saving for things done under wireless telegraphy licence.
9. Interpretation.
10. Power to extend Act to Isle of Man and Channel Islands.
11. Short title and commencement.

Caroline House in London had been closed on 8th August 1967 and the station's operational headquarters transferred to the Amsterdam office which had been opened the previous April under the management of South African born Basil von Rensburg.

Radio Caroline offices were also claimed to exist in New York, Paris and Toronto, but in fact the New York office was only an accommodation address in Madison Avenue and the Toronto office was the headquarters of Marich Associates - the company run by Terry Bate, who had been brought to the Caroline organisation in 1966 to help sell the station to prospective advertisers. Neither office in North America produced any real advertising contracts for Radio Caroline, although the number of American religious programmes aired by both the North and South stations did increase to about two hours a day during the latter part of 1967. Revenue from these sponsored religious programmes undoubtedly helped keep the stations on the air in the absence of any 'mainstream' advertising income. The Paris office, too, did not succeed in generating advertising income for the station and plans to open further offices in Tokyo and Germany never came to fruition. The station's new address in Holland was not revealed to listeners for over two weeks after the Marine etc. Broadcasting (Offences) Act had come into force, a factor which added further to the feeling of isolation for DJs on the radio ships who had been used to receiving a regular supply of fan letters and record requests from their audiences.

What really did keep Radio Caroline on the air financially after 14th August 1967 was the heavy promotion of Major Minor records featuring artists such as David McWilliams, Raymond LeFevre and his Orchestra and the Roberto Mann Singers, as well as a large number of relatively unknown Irish folk singers. These 'plug' records -which numbered up to fourteen an hour at one point, were contained on a list supplied to both ships and DJs were instructed to play them to the exclusion of anything else they may have wished to include in their programmes.

Although financially necessary the directive from Philip Soloman (who was now effectively running the Caroline stations) to include these records in the station's output caused much resentment amongst DJs, particularly on Caroline South whose reception area contained hardly any audience for such material. Caroline North did at least have an audience in Ireland who appreciated the largely folk-based music, but saturation exposure of certain artists eventually became too much even for them.

A number of dummy 'announcements' and 'advertisements' from British companies were also broadcast at this time in an attempt to confuse the authorities, who were known to be monitoring the station's output. These dummy commercials also provided cover for any true advertisers who, it was claimed, had bought £300,000 worth of airtime - enought to keep the station operating for at least six months.

The fake advertisements which were broadcast included products from various large British companies such as Horlicks, Nestle and Beechams, who all strongly denied that they had bought airtime on the station in contravention of the Marine etc. Broadcasting (Offences) Act. A spokesman for Beechams said, "All our contracts with the station ended last November. All they are doing is using old commercials and putting them out without our permission." Similar denials were issued by cigarette manufacturers Du Maurier, Peter Stuyvesant and Consulate as well as Swiss watch manufacturers Bulova, whose promotion continued to be aired at the top of each hour preceding the station's news bulletins.

Although much of what these companies claimed was true - and there was a lot of bluffing by Radio Caroline about its advertising income after 14th August 1967 - there were in fact still a number of contractural agreements with advertisers which the station happily continued to fulfil. Vidor Batteries had signed a contract with Radio Caroline and Radio London for a three month campaign starting in June 1967, before the announcement of the implementation date of the Marine etc. Broadcasting (Offences) Act and, therefore, although illegal by then its products continued to be promoted on both Caroline stations until late 1967.

One advertiser, Derek Gardner Photographics of Leatherhead and Epsom, had run a campaign on the station during the early summer of 1967 which included promotional offers available until the end of September 1967. When Radio Caroline South continued to broadcast these commercials after 15th August 1967, again in fulfillment of its contract, Derek Gardner visited the Amsterdam headquarters to deliver a personal protest to the station's management.

Another company, who had hardly ever advertised on offshore radio - Rowntrees Confectionery - also found many of its products, particularly Jelly Tots, Smarties, Spangles and Kit Kat being promoted on Radio Caroline after 15th August 1967. In this instance the station had taped the soundtrack of television commercials and was re-broadcasting them as 'dummy' advertisements.

Officially Radio Caroline denied that they were transmitting any free advertisements and claimed that contracts for these international products had been entered into quite legally before the Marine etc. Broadcasting (Offences) Act became effective.

# The Marine etc Broadcasting (Offences) Act 1967

## How it may affect you

Pirate Radio Stations operating off our coasts may, of course, be said to broadcast the type of entertainment enjoyed by a large number of listeners.

On the other hand, they can, and do, cause serious interference with stations already operating on internationally agreed wavelengths, not only in this country but abroad. Protests have come from all over Europe. They may also jam ship's radio and interfere with distress signals, shipping forecasts, gale warnings and other essential messages.

### Action by Parliament

To deal with this situation Parliament passed the Marine etc Broadcasting (Offences) Act, which came into force on August 15, 1967. The full provisions of the Act may be studied by applying for further information at Her Majesty's Stationery Office. The following is a condensation.

### The Act

It is an offence under the Act to participate in any way in the activities of pirate radio stations or ships. Briefly:

Apparatus: (1) operating or assisting in the operation of the broadcast apparatus (2) carrying or agreeing to carry the broadcast apparatus in a ship, or (3) supplying, maintaining, installing or repairing the apparatus.

Supplying: Carrying people or goods to and from such stations or ships, provisioning (food, etc.), delivering any other item required or the engaging of crew.

Broadcasts: Taking part in any broadcast from pirate radio stations as an announcer or performer; or in any other capacity.

Advertising: Finally, it is illegal to *advertise by means of broadcasting from these stations, to create or supply any material (including scripts, tapes or other recordings) for such broadcasts; or to invite anyone else to do so.*

### The Penalties

The maximum penalties for all these offences are the same: TWO YEARS imprisonment or a fine to be determined by the Court, or both.

### The Popular Music Programme

None of this is to ignore the fact that there are audiences for all kinds of popular music. And the new service to be provided by the B.B.C. from 30th September, 1967, will, the Government believe, meet the needs of these audiences.

## British Government action

Despite Radio Caroline's gesture of defiance in continuing to broadcast after the implementation of the Marine etc. Broadcasting (Offences) Act the authorities in Britain were determined to enforce the legislation and prevent any further stations taking to the air.

The Post Office spent nearly £18,000 placing advertisements in over 70 newspapers and magazines warning potential advertisers and suppliers of the provisions of the Marine etc. Broadcasting (Offences) Act and the penalties which could be imposed for contravening it. The publications carrying such advertisements included *The Times, Financial Times* and *Life* Magazine as well as local newspapers, particularly those circulating in areas which had been tendering bases for the offshore stations. A full page advertisement was also taken, at a cost of £1,200, in the American magazine *Time,* in a bid to dissuade any foreign-based companies, particularly those with offices or headquarters in America, from buying airtime on Radio Caroline. Referring to the audiences left behind by the demise of the offshore stations the advertisements ended with the announcement that " The forthcoming BBC music programme will, the Government believes, meet the needs of these audiences."

Another more dramatic step taken by the authorities to prevent any more offshore stations coming on air was the demolition of the Sunk Head Tower, one of the wartime fort in the Thames Estuary. Unlike many of the other ex-Forts Sunk Head Tower, eleven miles off Felixstowe, was without doubt outside British territorial waters and therefore provided a potential base for a future radio or television station or supply facility. It had in fact been occupied by the unsuccessful Tower Radio project at the end of 1965 and early 1966, but had remained virtually abandoned since then because it was considered unstable (see Chapter 10).

On 18th August 1967 a team of 20 Royal Engineers from Maidstone landed on the Fort from the Naval tug *Collie* to begin cutting away the superstructure and lay explosive charges. By Monday 21st August 1967, just a week after the Marine etc. Broadcasting (Offences) Act had become law, the Army was ready to destroy Sunk Head Tower. Shortly after 4.00pm that day Captain Alan Cowie set the fuses to 2,220 pounds of explosive in the Fort and then leapt onto the *Collie,* which left the area rapidly. Eighteen minutes later a huge explosion enveloped the Tower spreading debris across a half mile area of the Thames Estuary. The explosion itself could be clearly seen and heard by Radio Caroline South DJs on the *Mi Amigo*, who made a number of references to the Fort's demolition during their programmes that afternoon.

When the smoke from the explosion had cleared all that remained of the Sunk Head Tower was the two concrete stumps which had once formed the legs of the Fort. Ironically the Captain of the *Collie* that day, Captain Bill Penny, had been a member of the original Navy party which had towed the wartime structure from Harwich in 1940 and positioned it in the Thames Estuary.

The initial euphoria which surrounded Radio Caroline's defiance of the Marine etc. Broadcasting (Offences) Act soon subsided as practical operating difficulties came to the fore. By September 1967 both ships were (theoretically at least) being tendered from foreign ports - the *Mi Amigo* (Caroline South) from IJmuiden in Holland and the MV *Caroline* (Caroline North) from Dundalk in Ireland. Fuel and major supplies for both ships came from Holland, but this involved a round trip which took over a week for the tender on a journey to the MV *Caroline* in Ramsey Bay. Both stations operated with just few on-air staff and radio engineers, the two week on, one week off rotas had gone and DJs had to spend many weeks on board the ships without a break. Also, to provide airtime cover, programme shifts for the DJs were extended from the previous three hours to four, and sometimes even six, hours at a time.

Programme material, and in particular new release records, also became more and more difficult to obtain and deliver to the ships so quite quickly the station had to dispense with its Top 50 chart, although it tried to maintain the illusion of a chart for some weeks after August 15th 1967.

Essential items of equipment and supplies were also in short supply and Caroline South in particular suffered from frequent transmitter breakdowns and periods off the air. Eventually, on 26th September 1967, Radio Caroline South reduced its transmission hours from 24 hours a day to a 5.30am-2.00am schedule, the first tangible sign that the station was encountering severe difficulties in providing a full programme output and maintaining regular lines of supply.

## BBC launch 'replacement'

Meanwhile, the much heralded replacement for the offshore stations, BBC Radio One was set to be launched on 30th September 1967. The station, which had been carved out of the BBC Light Programme (now itself re-named Radio Two) was to broadcast pop music from 7.00am-7.30pm each day and carry 'light entertainment' and easy listening music from 5.30am -7.00am and from 7.30pm until 2.00am the following morning.

The BBC station's Controller, Robin Scott, announced his DJ line up on 4th September 1967. Of the thirty names announced fourteen were from the offshore stations, the majority coming from Radio London. It was also revealed that the station would carry jingles, station identifications and promotions for other shows - all based on the style of the offshore stations, but without any commercial announcements.

On 30th September 1967 the old Light Programme opened as usual at 5.30am and continued until just before 7.00am when former Caroline South and Radio London DJ Tony Blackburn launched the new BBC pop station with the 'Breakfast Show'. The first record played on Radio One was "Flowers in the Rain" by The Move.

Unfortunately on the day Radio One was launched Radio Caroline South, which should have provided listeners with a real alternative, was experiencing severe technical problems and was either off the air for long periods or just playing continuous taped music.

## Caroline struggles on

Tenders visited the two Radio Caroline ships sporadically, often failing to bring essential items or sometimes even a replacement crew, a reflection of the difficulties of operating long distance supply routes. DJs spent many weeks at a time on board the two radio ships and the cumulative demoralising effect of this lifestyle came to be reflected in the station's programme output, dictated as it was largely by the Major Minor 'plug list'. Significantly neither those on board the ships, nor the station's listeners realised at this time that revenue earned from the constant playing of these 'plug list' records was not being used to pay Radio Caroline's bills.

However, despite this negative side to the continued operation of Radio Caroline some positive progress was achieved during the last two months of 1967. New DJs were clandestinely recruited to the station by Ronan O'Rahilly using his Mid-Atlantic Films operation in London and Amsterdam as a 'front'.

## Radio One's opening schedule

*Despite all the hype and promises that the new BBC station would be a replacement for the offshore stations it soon became apparent, even on that first day of broadcasting that Radio One still retained much of the programming style of the old Light Programme and it even simulcast many of the programmes which were intended primarily for Radio Two's older and less pop orientated audience. A look at the opening day's programme schedule illustrates this perfectly:*

**7.00am The Tony Blackburn Breakfast Show** *-based on Radio London's format with jingles and Top 40 hits.*

**8.30am Junior Choice** - *a new name for the old "Children's Favourites programme dating back to the early 1950s.*

**9.55am Crack the Clue** *hosted by former Radio London DJ, Duncan Johnson A poor attempt to imitate the Caroline Cash Casino type of competition and without the big money prize!*

**10.00am Saturday Club** - *from the Light Programme this programme used BBC bands to play cover versions of hits*

**12noon Midday Spin** *hosted by ex-Caroline South DJ Emperor Rosko, the second (of two) all record programmes.*

**1.00pm Jack Jackson Show** *another legacy of the Light Programme, a mixture of big band music and comedy inserts.*

**1.55pm Crack the Clue** *(repeat of the morning programme)*

**2.00pm Where It's At** *a magazine style programme, again from the old Light Programme, hosted by Chris Denning.*

**3.00pm Best of Newly Pressed** *another Light Programme show introduced by Pete Murray, playing new release records which were exempt from needle time restrictions.*

**4.00pm The Pete Brady Show** *an ex-Radio London DJ, but playing non Top 40 radio material.*

**5.30pm Country Meets Folk** *presented by Whally Whyton. A specialist music programme, not for Top 40 radio.*

**6.30pm Scene and Heard** *another topical pop magazine programme presented by Johnny Moran*

**7.30pm** *Radio One then carried Radio Two's output until its closedown at 2.00am which included "Caterina Valente Sings", "Pete's People" -Pete Murray with studio guests and live performances and "Night Ride" consisting largely of film soundtrack music, live guest performances and other non needle time music.*

## Radio Luxembourg

*The initial connections between Radios One and Two, with much duplication of output continued long after the station's launch in September 1967 and the evening schedules, particularly after 7.30pm provided listeners who wanted to hear pop music with no alternative but to tune either to Radio Caroline (if they were not listening there already) or Radio Luxembourg.*

*Faced with the changed radio market following the abolition of nearly all the British offshore stations and the launch of Radio One, Radio Luxembourg had to quickly take steps to update its own image if it was to survive. Radio Luxembourg was still formatted in 15 or 30 minute segments and nealy all its advertising revenue came from direct sponsorship of these programmes. Despite the introduction of three or four hour 'strip shows' from American radio by the offshore stations, with spot advertisements inserted between records, Radio Luxembourg had doggedly retained its traditional format.*

*From March 1968 (coincidentally just after Radio Caroline had been closed) the station's management introduced some fundamnental format changes which involved phasing out the sponsored taped programmes and replacing them with live three hour 'strip shows' presented by a team of DJs resident in Luxembourg, recreating in some small part the camerardie of an offshore ship or fort. The station also introduced for the first time in its history an hourly news service, initially presented by ex-Radio London newsman Paul Kaye and telexed out to the Grand Duchy by the Daily Mirror because the authorities still refused to grant the station a direct land-line link with London.*

*Many of these changes in Radio Luxembourg's output were introduced under the guidance and influence of former Radio Atlanta, Radio London and Radio 355 DJ Tony Windsor, who joined the station as assistant to Programme Director Tony McCarthy. At Luxembourg Tony Windsor built a team of experienced offshore radio DJs including Tony Prince and Bob Stewart (from Caroline North), Paul Burnett (from Radio 270 and later Manx Radio) and also gave inexperienced newcomers such as Noel Edmonds and David 'Kid' Jensen their break into radio. This first team was the beginning of a succession of other ex-offshore DJs and management staff who joined Radio Luxembourg during the late 1960s and early 1970s.*

The new recruits included British as well as foreign passport holders and their arrival helped relieve some of the long on-air shifts and general feeling of isolation encountered by the original August 1967 'rebels' on both the Caroline ships. Amongst the new recruits were Spangles Muldoon, Andy Archer, Stevie Merike, Carl Mitchell and Bud Ballou, while Roger Day was enticed back to offshore radio to join Caroline South.

Caroline North too had some staff changes later in 1967 because although the station had gone into isolation with a larger DJ staff than its sister station many of these soon left and had to be replaced. Ross Brown had transferred to Caroline North in October 1967, under the name 'Freddie Beare', while two other DJs, Ripley Thorne and 'Lord Charles Brown' joined in October and November 1967 respectively.

Despite these clandestine recruitments and the facade of a foreign-based operation it had become common knowledge by late 1967 that Radio Caroline staff from both ships were quietly travelling in and out of Britain in contravention of the law, but without hindrance from the authorities. The Post Office were fully aware of the operational difficulties being experienced by Radio Caroline, as well as its fragile financial situation, and seemed content to wait for the natural demise of the station rather than make folk heros out of individual DJs by prosecuting them for breaking the Marine etc. Broadcasting (Offences) Act.

As 1968 dawned both Radio Caroline stations were still on the air, each staffed by a small crew of DJs who had reluctantly become used to the hardships of an isolated life in the North Sea or Irish Sea. DJs frequently made on-air comments about the lack of supplies, equipment or records and morale generally fell to an all time low. Although they were still being paid regularly Radio Caroline's DJs were now earning much less than their predecessors had prior to 15th August 1967. At the beginning of 1968 Radio Caroline DJs rates of pay ranged from £25 a week for the senior staff to £17 a week for the new, less experienced recruits. This was roughly half the amount that 'star' DJs on Radio London or even Caroline itself were earning in late 1966 and early 1967.

In spite of the low morale one positive programming achievement at this time was the reintroduction of a US Hot 100 chart with a regular supply of records having been arranged from across the Atlantic. However on the financial side Ronan O'Rahilly admitted for the first time that Radio

## 'FIGHT FOR FREEDOM' SPEECH

*During a period of particularly deep depression in late 1967 about the prospects for offshore radio and Radio Caroline in particular Johnnie Walker broadcast this 'vision for the future' which has now become a legend in offshore radio history.*

*This is the story of man's fight for freedom. The beginning is in the past, the middle is now, the end is in the future. It is a story of sadness and triumph.*

*August 14th as disc jockeys Robbie Dale, Johnnie Walker and Ross Brown leave Liverpool Street Station spurred on towards the sea by the hundreds of cheering people. See them now as they stand on the tender. There are tears in their eyes as their families, their homes and their loved ones are left behind.*

*Three o'clock on this Monday afternoon and on 266 Big L is heard for the last time. Caroline is alone. These three men prepare for midnight, for in a few hours time they are to challenge the might and power of the British Government. They will become criminals.*

*Midnight approaches and it is August 15th. Johnnie Walker announces that Caroline belongs to you, that she loves you and she will continue. The Beatles sing "All You Need is Love". These men sound happy, but underneath they are sad, for they now know they have passed the point of no return. They are not sad for long. They are joined by other men who also gave up so much to fight for freedom. The seas are rough and cruel, life is hard but as each day passes the moment of triumph draws nearer.*

*The British people rally round. They send food, they send comfort and they send their love. All you need is Love - and Love overcomes.*

*The British Government relents. Caroline raises her anchor and heads for England. See her now, majestically and proudly sailing up the river towards the capital that has welcomed so many victors in British history. But none as victorious as these men. They stand on the deck waving to the millions of people who line the Thames. This time the tears flooding from their eyes are tears of happiness. The insurmountable odds have been surmounted. They re-unite with their families, with their friends, with their loved ones.*

*We are near the end of our story. London's sky-line has a new landmark pointed towards the heavens - Caroline's aerial - at last beaming out its love and music to a free and peaceful nation.*

*We have overcome. The battle is over. Free Radio becomes a way of life, but never taken for granted. For no man will ever forget Monday, August 14th nineteen hundred and sixty seven.*

Caroline's income was below expectations and the prospect of actually making a profit from the station's operations seemed remote - a break-even on operating costs now appeared the only possibility.

## Caroline towed away

After struggling to overcome all sorts of practical difficulties and hardships for six months to keep the Caroline stations on the air events took an unexpected and dramatic turn at the beginning of March 1968. During the afternoon of 2nd March a tug anchored a mile from the MV *Caroline* in Ramsey Bay, refusing to state its intended destination to the Isle of Man maritime authorities. The tug made no attempt to communicate either with the authorities or with the crew on board MV *Caroline,* who had themselves identified it as a Dutch vessel, but had no particular reason to suspect it was a threat to the radio ship.

Programming on both the North and South stations continued as normal that day with Radio Caroline North ending its transmissions shortly after 10.00pm following the regular Saturday night "Country and Western Jamboree", presented by Don Allen. Radio Caroline South closed at midnight following Johnnie Walker's programme, during which he had made a passing reference to the fact that the station may have to go off the air in the near future to enable the *Mi Amigo* to be dry docked for essential maintenance. The full irony of this remark, innocuous as it was at the time, became only too apparent the following morning.

In Ramsey Bay the DJs and crew of the MV *Caroline* were awoken at 2.00am on Sunday 3rd March 1968 by a loud thump as the tug *Utrecht* came alongside and Dutch seamen boarded the radio ship. They made for the Captain's cabin and summoned senior DJ Don Allen and the Chief Engineer to read a letter from the Wijsmuller Tender and Offshore Supply Co. stating that broadcasting was to cease , the studios were to be sealed and the transmitter crystal removed. Radio Caroline staff entered into a heated argument with the Dutch boarders about the legitimacy of their action, which amounted to piracy on the high seas, but with the threat of physical violence ever present they reluctantly complied with the instructions contained in the letter.

Meanwhile, staff on the *Mi Amigo*, unaware of what had happened to their sister ship during the night, opened transmissions of Radio Caroline South as usual when at 5.00am on 3rd March 1968 engineer Ray Glennister started a half hour continuous music programme, prior to Roger Day's Breakfast Show at 5.30am. However, that programme never began because at 5.20am the *Mi Amigo* was boarded by Dutch seamen from the tug *Titan* and the station was abruptly put off the air. An identical letter to that read to the Caroline North staff was then read to the Captain and crew of the *Mi Amigo* and, although the duty engineer tried to broadcast an emergency message the microphone was snatched from his hands and all broadcasting staff were locked in the ship's lounge.

**RIDDLE OF RADIO CAROLINE SHIPS**

**Last of the pop pirates vanish**

MYSTERY surrounded Radio Caroline, the outlawed pop pirate station last night when both of its ships vanished from their moorings.

The *Mi Amigo's* anchor was then raised by the Dutch crew and the silent radio ship was taken in tow by the *Titan.* In an obvious effort to confuse both those on board the *Mi Amigo* and outside observers the ship was first towed northwards to a position off East Anglia, where two more tugs joined the *Titan.* The tow then proceeded in an ever changing zig zag course across the North Sea with the ultimate destination uncertain at the time to all but the Dutch tug's crew.

In what had been a carefully planned and co-ordinated operation the tug *Utrecht* also attempted to take the MV *Caroline* in tow at 6.00am on 3rd March 1968, but difficulties were experienced in raising the radio ship's anchor. In the end a decision was made to cut the anchor chain to release the MV *Caroline* and it was some twelve hours later before the tow actually commenced.

None of the staff on either radio ship knew for certain what was happening, other than the obvious fact that they had been forcibly put off the air. At first they didn't even know of their sister ship's fate. Those on board the *Mi Amigo* speculated that they were being towed to Holland for repairs, a scenario which had been hinted at by Johnnie Walker during his programme the previous evening. The *Mi Amigo* eventually arrived in Amsterdam on Monday 4th March 1968 and was docked "for normal repairs" according to a statement issued by the Wijsmuller Tender and Offshore Supply Co., which went on to say that ultimately the vessel would be returned to her anchorage and Radio Caroline could resume broadcasts.

The tow for the Caroline North ship, MV *Caroline,* was a much longer one lasting several days and she was shadowed for part of the journey by Royal Navy vessels. At first the crew thought the ship was heading for Greenore to be fitted with a new transmitter or, when it became obvious that this was not the case, they speculated that they may be going to take over Radio Caroline South broadcasts from off the Essex coast while the *Mi Amigo* was being repaired.

Neither theory proved to be correct and the MV *Caroline* arrived in Amsterdam on 8th March 1968 where she was docked near the *Mi Amigo*. The two radio ships were later moved to the Verschure shipyard and writs were attached to their masts, effectively detaining the ships inport. It became clear that Radio Caroline would not be returning to the air from either of these vessels in the near future.

## Paid off

After their arrival in Amsterdam staff were paid off, given tickets to fly back to Britain and told to await instructions to return - instructions which never came. Some DJs decided to wait in Holland for a while to see how the situation would develop hoping that somehow the ships would be released, while others returned home to Britain immediately.

The authorities did not stop or prosecute any of the Radio Caroline DJs when they re-entered Britain. Although the Marine etc. Broadcasting (Offences) Act had been responsible for Radio Caroline's isolation it was not the provisions of the Act which finally brought about the station's demise. The real reason for the seizure of both Radio Caroline ships lay in the financial management, or lack of it, within the Radio Caroline organisation itself. Wijsmuller's Tender and Offshore Supply Co had been contracted to provide a supply and servicing facility to both ships, but had not been paid since late 1967, although the money to do so was available from within the Caroline organisation. Wijsmuller's directors were divided amongst themselves over how to recover the money owed to them, some favoured negotiation with Radio Caroline's management while others, who won the day, preferred seizure of assets in lieu of the outstanding debts.

Philip Solomon, who by that time was the real force behind Radio Caroline, insisted that Wijsmuler put the ships back to sea before any debts would be paid, but the tender company insisted on payment first and continued to hold both ships in Amsterdam as security.

Nevertheless the Post Office and the British Government had achieved what they wanted all along - the silencing of the last remaining offshore broadcaster, so it seemed unnecessarily petty to make scapegoats of individual DJs.

## Caroline's planned return

The Radio Caroline organisation put a brave face on the situation in early March 1968, promising that the station would return once repairs had been completed and insurance arrangements sorted out. However, with the contimnuing arguments over unpaid bills to the tender company there was no real chance of the station's immediate return from either the *Caroline* or the *Mi Amigo*. Ronan O'Rahilly ,who had virtually lost control of Radio Caroline to Philip Soloman in the months since the introduction of the Marine etc. Broadcasting (Offences) Act, then started to put together his own package for re-launching the station from another vessel.

Together with a group of trusted ex-Caroline DJs (Don Allen, Jim Gordon, Roger Day, Andy Archer, Ross Brown and Roger Scott) O'Rahilly devised a plan to try and relaunch the station from the former Radio 270 vessel *Oceaan VII*. This vessel was still up for sale in Whitby Harbour and O'Rahilly, using the psuedonym O'Connor, made a number of visits to the Yorkshire port to negotiate the purchase of the ship through the local estate agents, Tuckley and Co. He planned to anchor *Oceaan VII* off Frinton-on-Sea, Essex and resume broadcasts of Radio Caroline on Easter Sunday (14th April)1968.

However, press reporters obtained information about this plan and published the story of Radio Caroline's Easter return. Although at the time this advance publicity was blamed for the failure of the scheme, negotiations for the purchase of the *Oceaan VII* had in fact already fallen through. The only other ex-offshore radio ship still available, the *Galaxy,* (former home of Radio London), was briefly considered by Ronan O'Rahilly but the £60,000 price being asked for this vessel was thought to be too high.

With the last British offshore station of the 1960's now silent many listeners started tuning to the broadcasts of Radio Veronica which was still transmitting from off the Dutch coast.This station, which had withstood the arrival and demise of British offshore radio, started to receive an enormous amount of mail from British listeners who preferred tuning to a foreign language broadcast they could hardly understand, rather than BBC Radio One, the replacement for their own offshore stations. In response to this increase in its English speaking audience Radio Veronica introduced some English programming in June 1968 and even engaged former Radio Caroline South DJ Robbie Dale, to present a show four evenings a week. This was some, albeit small, consolation for a generation of English speaking offshore radio listeners, who reluctantly now had to face the fact that perhaps the Government had won after all and there would be no more offshore stations anchored off the British coast.

## Chapter 13

# The Sound of Europe

Although the centre of offshore radio activity had been focused off the British coast during the mid-1960s, there had also been some stations broadcasting to other European countries during that period.

In southern Sweden Radio Syd continued to defy the 1962 Scandinavian legislation outlawing offshore radio stations. Although the station's original vessel *Cheeta* had run aground and subsequently sunk in Malmo Harbour in October 1964, Radio Syd brought into use another vessel, *Cheeta 2* which had been purchased from the former owners of Danish Radio Mercur. Radio Syd had therefore able to return to the air within two weeks of the *Cheeta* sinking.

Britt Wadner, Radio Syd's owner, was imprisoned again for one month in May 1965 after being convicted on charges of contravening the anti-offshore radio legislation. In June 1965, twenty seven advertisers were also prosecuted by the Swedish authorities for promoting their products on the station. A public opinion poll survey at that time showed that Radio Syd was attracting 80% of listeners in southern Sweden and such immense popularity made the station's owners determined to continue broadcasting despite the frequent prosecution of both themselves and their advertisers.

During the summer of 1965 Radio Syd made plans to start television transmissions from the *Cheeta 2,* which was already partially equipped for such a service from the embryo plans made between the vessel's former owner, Radio Mercur and the now defunct Radio Nord in the spring and summer of 1962 (see Chapter 3). Over £60,000 was spent installing a 5Kw transmitter, a new 90' aerial mast and on completing the on-board television studio facilities.

Faced with this continued defiance from Radio Syd and the prospect of an offshore television station being launched from the same vessel, the Swedish Government set about drafting further legislation to strengthen the existing anti-offshore broadcasting law in mid-1965. This new, tougher legislation was designed to follow the Council of Europe recommendations to ban offshore broadcasting stations, which had been agreed at the Strasbourg Convention earlier that year (1965) and extended the authorities' powers to prosecute anyone who assisted an offshore station in any way as well as to confiscate the station's assets.

Pending the introduction of this new law the Swedish authorities continued with prosecutions against Radio Syd and its advertisers using the existing legislation. In December 1965 Mrs. Wadner was convicted and given yet another jail sentence, this time for three months and during the same month several more advertisers were prosecuted for buying airtime on the station.

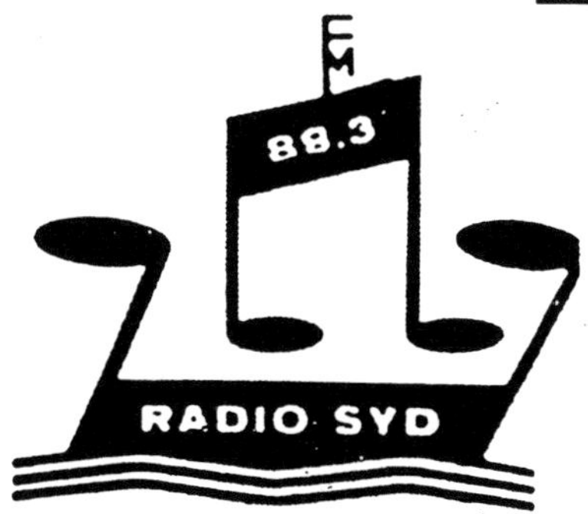


### Radio Centre

*Plans were announced in June 1965 for the launch of a new Swedish offshore radio station - despite legal proceedings which were being taken against Radio Syd's owner, Britt Wadner.*

*The station planned to have two ships, one anchored off the island of Urno (near Radio Nord's former anchorage) in the north and off Gothenburg in the south to give complete national coverage of Sweden.*

*Radio Centre planned to transmit on medium wave (unlike Radio Syd) and feature Swedish music and artists. Unfortunately the tougher legislation being planned by the Swedish Government prevented Radio Centre actually coming on air.*

## TV Syd

The television transmission equipment was fully installed on board *Cheeta 2* by early December 1965 and on 13th December the first test transmissions for TV Syd took place on UHF Channel E41. Once the equipment had been fully tested plans were made to launch a television service from the ship broadcasting programmes to the Malmo area for 12 hours a day.

However, on 18th January 1966 severe pack ice started to form in The Oresund and *Cheeta 2* was forced to leave her anchorage for fear of being trapped and crushed in the frozen seas. Consequently both Radio Syd and the fledgling TV Syd had to suspend transmissions until the weather improved and the vessel could return to her position off Malmo. The station's owners were reluctant to allow the ship to enter a Swedish port for fear that the vessel would be impounded by the authorities using their new powers of confiscation so they planned to sail *Cheeta 2* to a temporary anchorage in comparatively warmer waters off the Dutch coast, near the Radio Veronica vessel *Norderney,* until the winter ice in The Oresund had melted.

When Radio Syd had been forced to close due to extreme weather conditions the station was at the height of its popularity and there had been the exciting prospect of a regular offshore television service starting as well. Radio Syd's final ratecard, issued at the end of 1965, but never actually used by the sales team due to the station's absence from the airwaves, quoted advertising rates of 30 Swedish Kroner (SKr) for 10 seconds airtime on Radio Syd and 300SKr for 10 seconds on TV Syd.

As *Cheeta 2* was sailing to her proposed new anchorage, the *Mi Amigo,* home of Radio Caroline South, ran aground on the English coast and hearing of this catastrophe Mrs. Wadner offered the use of her vessel as a temporary home for Caroline. The offer was accepted by Radio Caroline's Ronan O'Rahilly and the *Cheeta 2* was diverted to anchor off the Essex coast, where she arrived on 31st January 1966 (see Chapter 11).

Radio Syd never in fact returned to the air off the Swedish coast, largely because of the tougher legislation introduced by the Swedish Government during the early months of 1966. Also the *Cheeta 2* became involved in the British offshore radio scene, as a temporary home for Caroline South and later as a proposed base first for Radio London's planned northern station, Radio Manchester, and then for the planned easy-listening station Radio 390 North. Unfortunately neither of these plans came to fruition and *Cheeta 2* languished in Britain for some time while ownership and financial disputes were resolved (see Chapter 12).

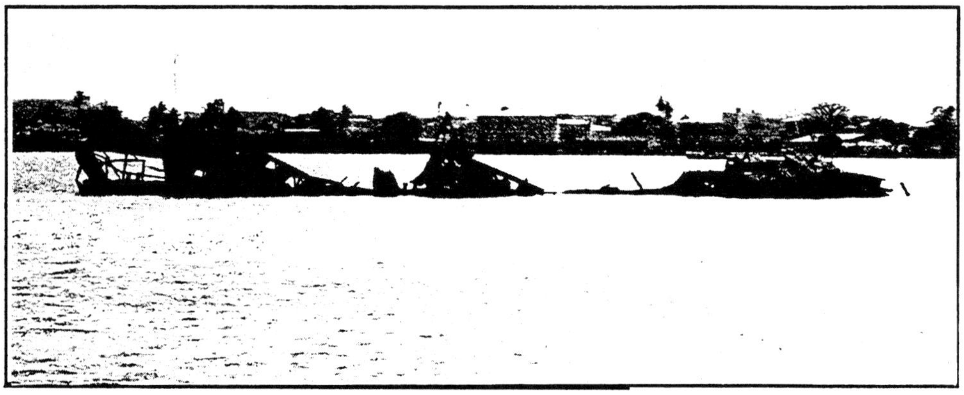

### Radio Syd in Africa

*After surviving various legal battles over ownership while off the English coast Cheeta 2 eventually sailed, first to Holland in November 1967 then via Spain to Morocco and the Canary Islands arriving in Las Palmas in December 1967.*

*Here she was rebuilt as a floating restaurant and disco and later sailed to Bathurst (now Banjul) Harbour in Gambia, West Africa. There Mrs. Wadner and her daughter Connie had been granted a licence to operate Radio Syd at first from the ship and later from a land-base. Radio Syd has continued to broadcast from this legal base to Gambia on 910kHz (329m) while the Cheeta 2 remained in Bathurst Harbour for some time as a floating restaurant.*

*The vessel, which became neglected and in a generally poor condition was torn from her moorings during a hurricane in the mid 1980s and eventually sank in the Gambia River. Mrs. Wadner took up residence in Gambia and lived there for many years supervising the operation of her radio station and floating restaurant as well as a hotel - the Wadner Beach Hotel. She retired at the beginning of the 1980s and returned to her native Sweden where she died in March 1987.*

*'Cheeta 2' sunk in the Gambia River*

## Radio Veronica expansion

Off the Dutch coast Radio Veronica continued to gain in popularity both with listeners and advertisers while remaining relatively secure in the absence of any action from the Dutch Government to outlaw offshore broadcasting. At the beginning of 1965 the Radio Veronica ship *Borkum Riff* broke her anchor chain during a storm and nearly sank.

The continued and growing success of Radio Veronica led in 1965 to the introduction of a pop music service on the Hilversum Network. Hilversum 3 started broadcasts on 13th September 1965 in the hope that it would attract young listeners in Holland, in particular from Radio Veronica and the successful British station Radio London whose broadcasts were popular in Europe.

1966 saw the introduction of some major changes for Radio Veronica. The format of the station was changed from quarter and half hour long programme segments to the 'horizontal' programme style of two or three hour shows, along the lines of the British offshore stations. Also at this time the station started broadcasting live programmes from the radio ship rather than relying on a completely taped output. All these changes were brought about as the result of a visit to the United States by the DJ/Programme Director Joost de Draayer to study the latest broadcasting and programme format techniques.

The station's operating base was also changed in August 1966. The original vessel, *Borkum Riff* was replaced by the larger and more luxurious *Nordeney,* an ex-trawler, which was completely refitted for her new role as a floating radio station. A new 10Kw transmitter and improved aerial system were installed as was a special anchoring mechanism which enabled the ship to turn in bad weather without twisting the chain. Luxurious accommodation for the crew was constructed on board as well as new broadcast studios, a news studio and transmitter room.

*'Norderney' at anchor*

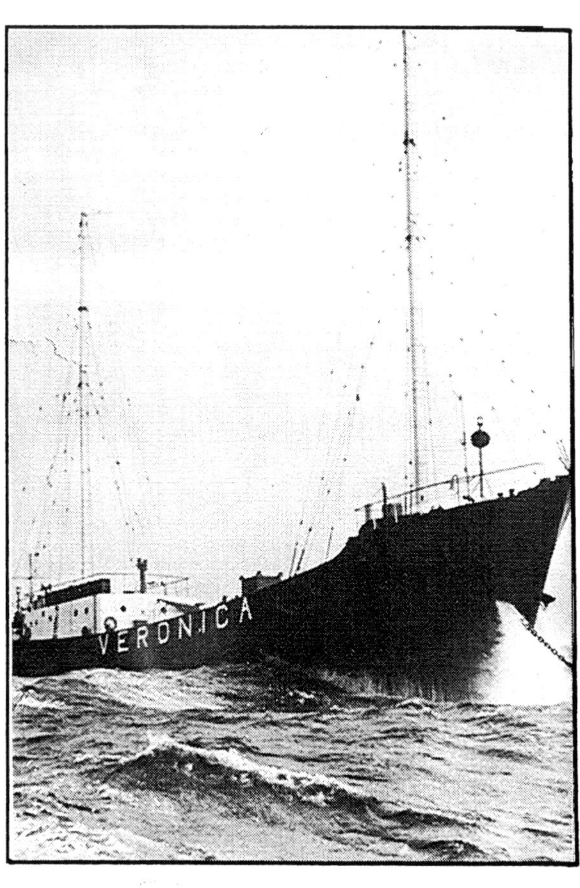


Much of this work, including the transmitter installation was carried out in Zaandam, but later the *Norderney* anchored near the *Borkum Riff* and other items of equipment were transferred to the new ship, using the station's tender *Ger Anna.* Throughout this time transmissions of Radio Veronica programmes continued from the *Borkum Riff,* but once all equipment had been installed on the *Norderney* test transmissions began from the new ship. Only when satisfactory reception reports had been received and the station's management was completely satisfied that Radio Veronica was putting out an improved signal did the station transfer to *Norderney.* Once operations had been transferred the original Veronica ship *Borkum Riff* was towed into harbour and scrapped.

Interestingly, before the *Borkum Riff* was replaced Radio Veronica received an offer from Cor Verlome, the shipbuilding magnate who had been the driving force behind the one time rival Radio/TV Noordzee from the REM Island in 1964. He proposed carrying out repairs to the *Borkum Riff* at sea, but Radio Veronica directors refused his offer and decided to proceed instead with the purchase of a new ship.

## Radio Dolfijn and Radio 227

During the latter part of 1966 and early 1967 Radio Veronica briefly encountered competition from two other Dutch language stations, Radio Dolfijn and later Radio 227. Both these would-be rivals for Dutch listeners were based on board the *Laissez Faire* anchored off the English coast and programmes were directed at Holland using a powerful 55Kw transmitter.

Radio Dolfijn had started broadcasting in November 1966, hiring transmitter and studio facilities on board the *Laissez Faire*, which had previously been used by the unsuccessful American format station, Swinging Radio England. The new Dutch language station, which broadcast from 6.00am - 12 midnight at first adopted an easy listening format (an alternative to Radio Veronica's Top 40 based programming) but later it too started to play Top 40 music during the evening hours. The station attracted a moderate audience in Holland, but was never as popular, or commercially successful, as the 'home based' and longer established Radio Veronica.

Radio Dolfijn went off the air in February 1967 when the *Laissez Faire's* aerial mast was damaged during a storm (see Chapter 12). By the time the ship returned to her anchorage off the English coast the broadcasting operation had been taken over by Ted Allbeury's Carstead Advertising Ltd. after the previous owners, Pier Vick Ltd. had gone into voluntary liquidation. The new company opened an easy-listening English language station from the radio ship, Radio 355, to replace the former Britain Radio and for a while also continued the arrangement with the Dutch language Radio Dolfijn.

However, once Radio 355 had been sucessfully launched and its format finalised attention turned to the Dutch station. Ted Allbeury and his team realised that Radio Dolfijn with its easy listening daytime format and Top 40 music at night was having very little impact on either Dutch audiences or advertisers, both generally preferring the Top 40 format of Radio Veronica. So a decision was made to re-launch the Dutch language station from the *Laissez Faire* as Radio 227, using the former Swinging Radio England format and even that station's jingles which were cannibalised and edited for the new station.

Radio 227 officially took to the air on 3rd June 1967 and within two weeks was claiming to have attracted audiences far in excess of the level which its predecessor, Radio Dolfijn, had been able to achieve. Despite this claim the station still did not come anywhere near attracting the level of commercial success in Holland which the well established Radio Veronica and advertising revenue remained low.

With the passage of the British Marine etc. Broadcasting (Offences) Bill through Parliament some tentative arrangements were made by Carstead Advertising on behalf of Radio 227 and Radio 355 to enable both stations to continue broadcasting by moving all operations to Holland and hopefully attracting sufficient foreign advertising. However, these plans proved unfruitful and it was decided that continued operation after the introduction of the new British legislation was not a viable proposition - the required volume of international advertising was simply not available.

When the insurance arrangements for the *Laissez Faire* expired early in July 1967 both Radio 227 and the English language Radio 355 were closed only a matter of weeks before the introduction of the British Marine etc. Broadcasting (Offences) Act.

Radio 227 was actually the first station off the British coast to close in advance of the new legislation coming into effect. The DJs station's DJs were told at short notice that their services would no longer be required after 1.00pm on 23rd July 1967 as the final five hours of programmes were already available on tape. Without any ceremony Radio 227 then closed after the end of normal programming at 6.00pm that day. The closure of the Dutch language broadcasts from vessels off the British coast meant once again that Radio Veronica had the Dutch market to itself, although neither of the potential rivals had made an impact into the established station's audience or advertising figures. Unfortunately for Radio Veronica that comfortable monopoly position was not to last forever.

## Radio Veronica in English

Radio Veronica itself managed to attract a substantial British audience in 1968 following the sudden closure of both Radio Caroline stations in March of that year. Response from British listeners to the station's output was significant enough for the management to introduce a limited amount of English language programming and former Caroline South DJ Robbie Dale was engaged to present these programmes four evenings a week.

Also during 1968 Radio Veronica started an 'International Service' hiring airtime on Radio Popularie de Mallorca and broadcast a series of programmes hosted by DJs from the station, including an English language one presented by Robbie Dale. The plan for this service was that airtime would be hired on a number of stations along the Spanish holiday coast and in the Balearic Islands, so that Radio Veronica programmes could be heard by Dutch holidaymakers.

Throughout the late 1960s Radio Veronica continued to broadcast, unhindered by Government action, and became accepted as almost part of the Dutch broadcasting establishment. Unfortunately in mid-1968 reception of the station's signal in Holland began to suffer, particularly at night, when a Swiss station on the same wavelength (192m) increased its transmitter power.

Radio Veronica briefly examined the possibility of introducing FM transmissions in October 1968 and even undertook test transmissions on another medium wave frequency (557kHz (538m) during the early morning hours after normal closedown. However, no firm decision was made to change the station's broadcasting frequency at that time.

In March 1969 Radio Veronica moved its land-based studios and administrative offices to larger premises - a specially converted villa

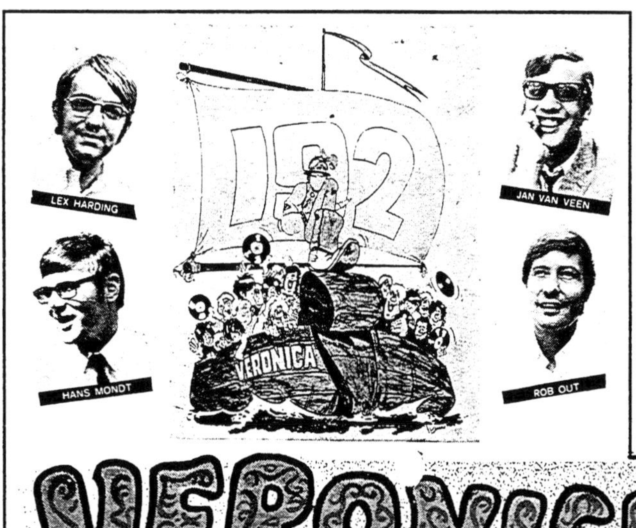




### Radio Veronica programme schedule, September 1970

*Weekdays*

**6.00am Breakfast Show** *Tom Collins*

**9.00am Music While You Work** *Hans Mondt*

**10.00am Morning Show** *Tineke and Gerard de Vries*

**12 noon Chiel Montagne Show**

**2.00pm Lex Harding Show**

**4.00pm Rob Out Show**

**6.00pm Juke Box** *(requests) Stan Haag*

**7.00pm Lex Jo**, *Lex Harding*

**8.00pm Veronica's R and B Hop** *(Monday)*

**Country and Western Show** *(Tuesday and Friday)*

**European Hits** *(Wednesday)*

**Please Walk In** *Suhandi (Thursday)*

**9.00pm Hans Mondt Show (Classical Magazine)** *(Wednesday)*

**11.00pm Radio Drama** *Klaas Vaak*

**2.00am Closedown** *(except Fridays* **2.00am-6.00am Night Time Show***)*

in Utrechtseweg on the outskirts of Holland's broadcasting capital, Hilversum. This building housed administrative and sales facilities as well as recording studios and an extensive record library. At about this time too, Radio Veronica had some tentative plans to launch two new radio ships off the coasts of two South American Dutch colonies - Dutch Guyana (Suriname) and Dutch Antillies, but the plans came to nothing.

## Caroline Revival Hour

*With both Caroline stations off the air and no immediate prospect of their return, French theatre company owner, Yves Kuhn set about planning a tribute to his favourite station in December 1968. He planned to try and broadcast a monthly hour long programme, using the title Caroline Revival Hour, over the medium wave transmitter of Radio Andorra, a small Principality in the Pyrenees between France and Spain.*

*The first programme was scheduled for the early morning of 2nd March 1969, just twelve months after the two Caroline ships had been silenced. Yves Kuhn contacted a number of ex-Caroline DJs asking if they would host the programme. Four replied saying that they would be willing, Don Allen, Stevie Merike, Bud Ballou and Martin Kayne. Eventually Don Allen, as the longest serving Caroline DJ, and one who had served on both ships, was chosen to present the Revival Hour.*

*A limited amount of advertising was obtained, mainly from free radio interest groups, which helped finance the broadcast but this, together with other donations from listeners, only covered about half the operating costs of £357 for that single hour.*

*The programme itself was broadcast on 428m between 1.00 and 2.00am on 2nd March 1968 and contained many memories, jingles and records associated with the history of Radio Caroline. Although reception was not particularly good in all parts of Britain, suffering from fading and interference in the south and Midlands, and just too weak to reach the north or Scotland over 2,000 letters were subsequently received by Yves Kuhn from people who had tuned to the broadcast.*

*Unfortunately plans to broadcast further Caroline Revival Hour programmes came to nothing because sufficient advertising could not be found to fund the project. However, Radio Andorra itself conducted some further late night test programmes aimed at Britain during April 1969 as Radio 428 and later some British businessmen hired the transmitters to launch a short-lived progressive music station - Radio Rupert.*

*In March 1970 another progressive music station, The Magnificent Flying Machine was broadcast over Radio Andorra in competition with the successful Radio Geronimo, which used the more powerful transmitters of Radio Monte Carlo.*

*As Yves Kuhn had found with the Caroline Revival Hour and the backers of Radio Rupert had also discovered, reception of broadcasts using Radio Andorra's medium wave facilities was not of sufficient quality in Britain to make such projects viable and the experiments discontinued. However, Radio Andorra's shortwave transmitter was used between 1976 and 1981 for broadcasts by Radio Scandinavia and World Music Radio.*

## German offshore radio plans

Following the closure of Radio London off the English coast in August 1967 the station's ship *Galaxy* was sold for £10,000 and the new owners sailed her to Hamburg for an overhaul. *Galaxy* arrived in the West German port on 21st August 1967 and was berthed in the Finkenwerder works of Howaldtswerke-Deutsche Werft AG.

The vessel was briefly considered by Ronan O'Rahilly as a possible base from which to re-launch Radio Caroline after that station's two ships had been seized in March 1968, but the asking price of £60,000 was thought to be too high.

Meanwhile, other more ambitious plans existed for the *Galaxy* and throughout the summer of 1968 work went ahead on refurbishing the vessel. This was scheduled to be completed by October 1968 and plans were announced to launch West Germany's first offshore station on 1st November 1968. The new station, Radio Nordsee, although to be anchored off the West German coast was officially directed at audiences in Switzerland. The project was being backed by two Swiss advertising men - Emile Luthle and Norbert Schwerd of the Gloria International Agency, based in St. Gallen. They planned to anchor the *Galaxy* in Deutscher Bucht, a position between Heligoland and Cuxhaven and the station was to broadcast from 5.00am to 1.00am with an easy-listening format during the day and pop music at night. Manager and Project Director for the station, Klaus Quirini of the German Disc Jockey Organisation, based in Aix la Chapelle, announced in October 1968 that the ship would have a crew of 28, including five DJs and that Radio Noordsee would have the following general programme schedule:-

| | |
|---|---|
| 5.00am | Instrumental music and 'happy tunes' |
| 9.00am | German Hits and items of interest to housewives |
| 1.00pm | Programmes for young children |
| 5.00pm | Drivetime |
| 7.00pm | Hot Hits music |
| 1.00am | Closedown |

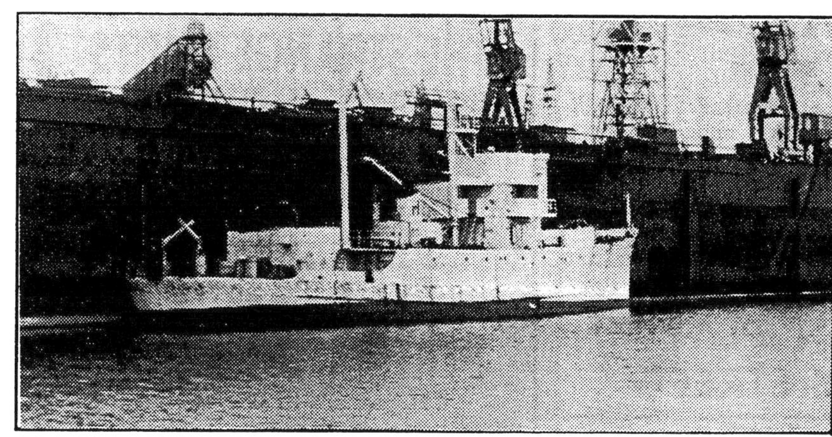
*'Galaxy' in Hamburg 1968*

In common with so many offshore projects, however, the announced starting date came and went without anything being heard on the air. In fact the *Galaxy* was still in dock at the beginning of November being overhauled and refitted. A revised on-air date of 12th December 1968 also came without any progress being made.

Meanwhile, the West German Government hurriedly introduced legislation, along the lines of the British Marine etc. Broadcasting (Offences) Act, to outlaw any offshore broadcaster which anchored off its coast and prohibit West German citizens from working for or advertising on such a station. This new legislation was scheduled to come into effect in July 1969, so the proposed station from the *Galaxy* was threatened with almost immediate closure before the ship had even left dock. The final blow for Radio Nordsee came in January 1969 when Emile Luthle decided to withdraw his financial support and the whole project collapsed.

## Mebo takes over

Two Swiss engineers who had been engaged to instal radio equipment on board the *Galaxy* for the aborted Radio Nordsee project decided later in 1969 that they would try and launch an offshore station of their own. The two engineers, Erwin Meister and Edwin Bollier, purchased another ship, the *Bjarkoy* which had been built in Norway and re-registered her in Panama under the name *Mebo* - an acronym derived from the first two letters of each of their surnames.

Not long after work had started on converting this ship it was decided that a much larger vessel would be more suitable so they acquired an ex-Norwegian coaster, *Silvretta.* She was renamed *Mebo II* and taken back to the yard in Slikkerveer, Holland - where she had been built in 1952 - to be converted into a radio ship. The original *Mebo* was retained for use as a tender to service the larger radio ship once at sea.

This conversion work took some months to complete, but the ship was transformed into the most luxurious offshore radio station ever. *Mebo II* had the most up-to-date technical and broadcasting equipment, fitted carpets, showers, cooking facilities and everything to make life for the DJ's and crew on board as comfortable as possible. Four transmitters were also installed on the ship, one 105Kw RCA medium wave (the most powerful in Europe although it never operated at that output) one 1.2Kw FM and two 10Kw short wave. All radio equipment was supplied through Meister and Bollier's Swiss electronics company Mebo Telecommunications Ltd. of Zurich. The ship, which was painted in psychedelic colours, also carried a 140' aerial mast, which with its combination of transmitters enabled the station's signal to be beamed to a world-wide as well as a European audience.

Money seemed no object to the two Swiss engineers. They had spent nearly £50,000 on acquiring and partially fitting out the original vessel, *Mebo,* before abandoning work to start again with the larger *Mebo II,* which itself cost another £90,000 to purchase and convert. These figures do not include radio and broadcasting equipment supplied through Mebo Telecommunications Ltd., who were very secretive about the sources and cost of the facilities they installed on the radio ship.

## Radio Geronimo and Radio Monte Carlo

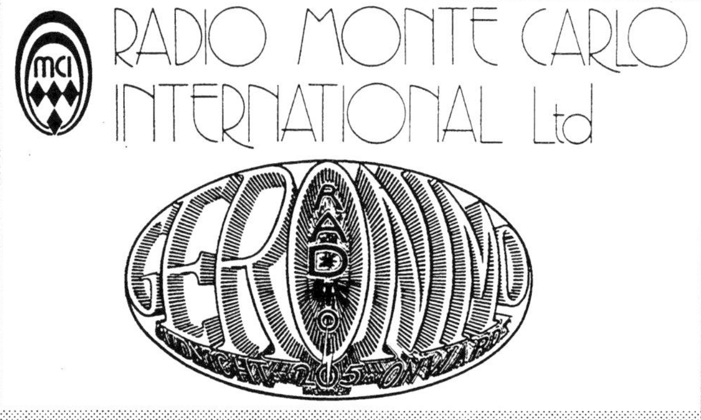


*Following their experiments in Andorra the backers of Radio Rupert, Tony Secunda and Jimmy Miller, were convinced that there was a demand in Britain for an 'alternative' music station. They re-launched their project ads Radio Geronimo over the more powerful transmitter of Radio Monte Carlo on 205m in early 1970. The format was largely rock based, but the station also played classical, jazz and other forms of minority interest music. Broadcasts were initially for three hours a week on Friday, Saturday and Sunday, but such was the demand that these transmissions were soon increased to nine hours a week. It was estimated that the station was attracting an audience of over 350,000 in Britain alone.*

*Originally it was planned to finance the station through normal advertising spots, but prospective advertisers wanted to exert too much influence over programme content. An alternative means of raising finance was then devised, utilising a mail order sale catalogue of American import records which were aired on the station.*

*Despite its comparative success Radio Geronimo's transmissions ended suddenly in October 1970 - the station was said to be in substantial debt to Radio Monte Carlo for the hire of transmitter facilities and there were also some concerns about aspects of the programme content. The concept of a 'progressive' music station was resurrected some years later on the offshore station, Radio Seagull, which at one time utilised the services of DJs involved with Radio Geronimo (see Chapter 16).*

*Radio Monte Carlo meanwhile announced plans of its own to launch a late night station directed at Britain. Radio Monte Carlo International was launched on 1st December 1970 with programmes presented by Dave Cash (ex-Radio London) and Tommy Vance (ex-Caroline South and Radio London). The three hour long early morning broadcasts were based on a Top 50 format for the first two hours, with a final hour of 'progressive' music. Unfortunately advertising support was not forthcoming for the station and in March 1971 Radio Monte Carlo International programmes were discontinued.*

Meister and Bollier, then 32 and 34 respectively, were self-made millionaires who owned a number of night clubs in Zurich as well as their telecommunications company, whose main business activity involved purchasing and supplying electronic equipment to various Third World countries. Some years later Bollier claimed that money to finance the offshore radio station had come from Cavitas (a Roman Catholic charity) which bought Japanese radio equipment from Mebo Telecommunications Ltd. in 1968 to set up a radio network in Biafra. A similar contract in Yugoslavia also provided a substantial amount of money which was used to fund the project while there are also unconfirmed reports that a Swiss bank invested five million Deutschemarks in the offshore station. The mysterious financial arrangements of the station on board the *Mebo II*, and its operation once on the air, attracted much speculation involving allegations of political interference and espionage.

## RNI launched

*Mebo II* left Rotterdam on 22nd January 1970 and sailed to an anchorage off Noordwijk on the Dutch coast. Test transmissions for the new offshore station - Radio North Sea (Nordsee) International (RNI) started the following day on 6210kHz (49m short wave band) and on 102mHz FM, with taped music and announcements in English and German. The English DJ involved in these test transmissions was Roger Day, formerly of Radio England and Caroline South, while the German announcer was Horst Reiner. Tests on the medium wave frequency of 1610kHz (186m) started on 11th February 1970, again with pre-recorded announcements in English and German.

On 24th January 1970, the day after the *Mebo II* arrived at her anchorage, the tender *Mebo I* collided with the radio ship while transferring an anchor chain. Water poured into the transmitter room through the broken porthole, but test transmissions were not significantly affected. On 26th January 1970 the Panamanian Consul in Rotterdam was reported to have removed the *Mebo II* from his country's maritime register.

Reception particularly on medium wave, was poor with interference being experienced from the Morse transmissions of a maritime station - 186m is near the ship-to-shore communication wavelengths and not really suitable for broadcast radio use.

Regular programming from RNI eventually started at 6.00pm on 28th February 1970 on 186m medium wave, 6210kHz short wave and 102mHz FM.

**Tune in & TURN ON**

**RNI**

**Radio NorthSea International**

**RNI's first programme schedule, February 1970**

| | |
|---|---|
| 6.00am | German Service |
| 8.00am | Roger Day |
| 10.00am | Johnnie Scott |
| 12noon | German Service |
| 2.00pm | Roger Day |
| 4.00pm | Johnnie Scott |
| 6.00pm | German Service |
| 8.00pm | Roger Day |
| 10.00pm | Johnnie Scott |
| 12 midnight | German Service |
| 2.00am | Closedown |

*(The two DJs on the German Service were Hannibal and Axel.)*

The immediate impact of RNI's arrival off the coast of Holland was enormous and it was to produce a fundamental change in the relationship between the Dutch authorities and offshore broadcasters. In fact the launch of RNI, although welcomed and enjoyed at the time by so many listeners throughout Europe, and particularly in Britain, was to prove a disastrous turning point in the history of European offshore radio.

Some Dutch newspapers started a campaign almost immediately for the Government to outlaw offshore radio stations, the feeling was that the arrival of RNI, even though it did not at that time broadcast any programmes in Dutch, was a threat to the broadcasting system of Holland. Radio Veronica was tolerated by the press and the authorities, but this more powerful new arrival was considered a far more serious potential threat.

The PTT reported almost as soon as transmissions started from RNI that complaints had been received about the station's broadcasts on 186m causing interference to a station in Italy and the shortwave transmissions interfering with the Norwegian Navy distress frequencies. On 4th March 1970 the Dutch Pilot Service reported that RNI medium wave transmissions were interfering with their communications on 187m and as a consequence the maritime authorities had been forced to transfer to 182m. An Editorial in a Dutch newspaper the day after this alleged interference said:-

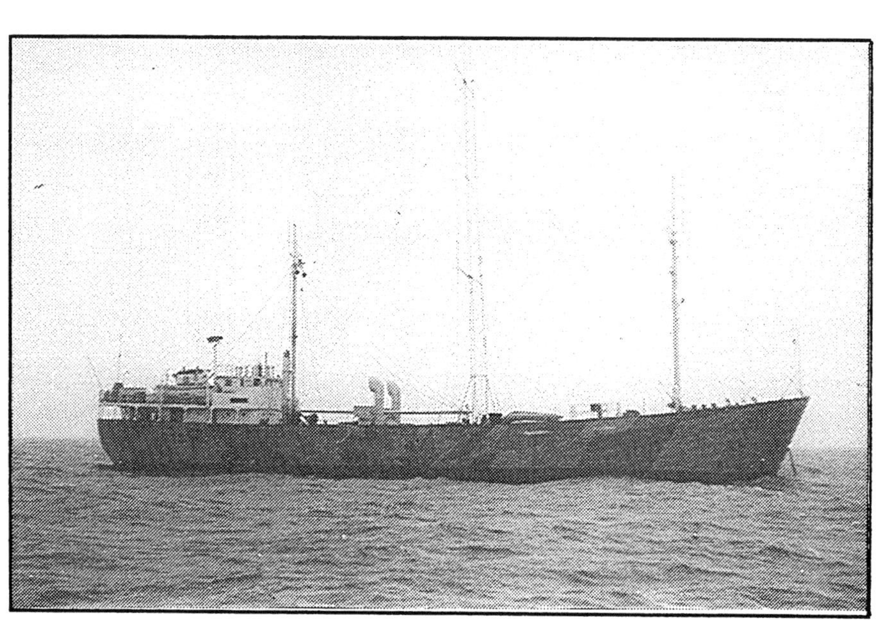
*'Mebo II ' at anchor*

*If the Dutch Parliament doesn't react very soon against the offshore radio station, by signing the Strasbourg Convention, big problems can be expected. If RNI gets a large audience other groups could think that bringing a radio ship into international waters is the way to get not only a large listenership but also a lot of profit. There is also the problem that the new radio station, Radio North Sea International, causes a lot of interference with the pilot service in Vlissingen. Contact between ships on the North Sea and Westerschelde on one side and the Pilot Service on the other is almost impossible at the moment.*

## RNI moves

Just less than a month after starting regular programmes the *Mebo II* left her anchorage off the Dutch coast on 23rd March 1970 and headed towards England, anchoring off Clacton-on-Sea, Essex the following morning. With all the allegations of interference and bad publicity in the Dutch press Meister and Bollier thought that by repositioning their station off the British coast it would have a better chance of commercial success. Unfortunately for RNI this was not the case because the British authorities were to prove even more determined their Dutch counterparts to silence the new powerful offshore station.

Broadcasting of RNI's programmes had continued throughout the voyage from Holland but severe interference was caused, again by the medium wave transmissions, to British coastguard communications. Following protests from the Coastguard Service, Trinity House (the lightship and lighthouse authority) and the Ministry of Posts and Telecommunications RNI ceased transmissions on medium wave at 1.25pm on 27th March 1970 for 'frequency adjustments'. Programmes continued on the FM and short wave frequencies for a few days until they too went off the air on 1st April 1970 due to a technical failure.

The *Mebo II* remained at anchor off the British coast and after ten days silence RNI returned to the air on 10th April 1970. The station now transmitted on 102mHz FM as well as a new medium wave frequency of 1578kHz (190m) with revised programme schedules:-

| | |
|---|---|
| 5.30am - 7.00am | German Service |
| 7.00am - 8.00pm | English Service |
| 8.00pm - 11.00pm | German Service |
| 11.00pm - 2.00am | English Service |

### Jamming

*The jamming of RNI's signal was certainly a fundamental change in policy for the British Government - in 1964 it had rejected, at Cabinet level, the jamming of earlier offshore stations as an unacceptable practice However, there were rumours that the latest decision, which had again been taken at the highest possible level- Prime Minister Harold Wilson's Cabinet - had more to do with possible political propaganda directed at Britain than interference being caused by RNI to foreign radio networks.*

*There had been persistent rumours that the whole RNI operation was part of a political plot to bring down the then British Government. One theory on this linked the Mebo organisation in Switzerland with the rebel Biafran regime in Africa - there had certainly been telecommunications and electronics trade dealings between the two organisations. It has been suggested that RNI was to be used as a base to broadcast propaganda in favour of the rebels and against the official Nigerian Government, which itself had support and backing from Harold Wilson's Labour administration.*

## British Government jamming

However, the new medium wave frequency caused interference to Norwegian radio stations and also affected the signal of Dutch offshore station Radio Veronica on 192m. In an unprecedented move the British Ministry of Posts and Telecommunications authorised the official jamming of RNI's medium wave signal on 190m on 15th April 1970, using a 800c/s tone from Beacon Hill Naval Radio Station at Rochester, Kent. The Minister concerned, John Stonehouse, announced that the jamming had been initiated at the request of the Italian and Norwegian authorities.

At 8.30pm the same evening, 15th April 1970, RNI closed its medium wave transmitter. Test transmissions on a new frequency of 1385kHz (217m) and also on a new FM frequency of 100mHz started during the evening of 30th April

1970, but once again the Government's jamming signal appeared. The 217m broadcasts were discontinued on 1st May and the medium wave transmitter remained silent for nearly two weeks until 13th May 1970 when test transmissions of RNI's programmes were heard on 1230kHz (244m), adjacent to BBC Radio One on 1215kHz (247m).

This choice of frequency was a tactical move by RNI to confirm once and for all whether the jamming was politically motivated - 244m was clear of the maritime and emergency frequencies - and any jamming could potentially affect Radio One on the adjacent 247m. The jamming did continue, however, and RNI regularly broadcast the following message:-

*RNI apologises to you, our listeners, for the interference heard on our transmissions. This illegal jamming is directed from the Labour Party and organised by the Post Office. This action is meant to discourage us from providing you with our normal service. However, RNI shall make every effort to continue programmes as usual. No free western country has ever jammed a free broadcasting station before, even in time of war.*

Listeners to RNI quickly identified the source of the jamming and in response to requests from DJs listeners attended a demonstration on 31st May 1970 outside the naval premises in Rochester used to transmit the jamming signal.

When regular programmes started on this new frequency on 16th May 1970 the signal remained clear for five days until once again, on 21st May, the British Government started its jamming signal. This time the action was allegedly being taken at the request of Czechoslovakia, but because of RNI's frequency change the jamming signal itself now caused interference to BBC Radio One transmissions in Kent and Essex. By 28th May RNI was playing a cat and mouse game with the jammers, changing frequency every 15 or 20 minutes between 1227kHz and 1232kHz. However, each time the station changed frequency the jamming signal followed and the attempt to avoid interference to its medium wave transmissions in this way was halted by RNI after only a few hours.

## 1970 General Election

The Labour Government in Britain had called a General Election for 18th June 1970 and on 1st June Edwin Bollier, announced that RNI would close the day after the election if the Labour Party were returned to power. At the same time he also announced the immediate closure of the unsuccessful German Service, which the station had tried to sustain since it came on the air earlier in the year.

Listeners tuning in to RNI's transmissions on 13th June 1970 were surprised to hear the station using the call sign Radio Caroline International. The owners of RNI had come to an agreement with Ronan O'Rahilly that they would mount an intensive anti-Labour Party campaign in the days immediately before the General Election. The use of Radio Caroline's name would, it was thought, have more impact with listeners, many of whom were voting for the first time since the qualifying age had been reduced from 21 to 18 years. Listeners in this age group would certainly remember the original Radio Caroline and, with memories rekindled by the latest transmissions from the *Mebo II*, it was hoped that they would also recall the actions of the Labour Party in bringing about the demise of British offshore stations in the mid 1960's and cast their vote for the Conservative Party.

So went the theory and key marginal constituencies in London and the south east of England were targeted while a continuous stream of anti-Labour propaganda was broadcast by the station in the run up to election day. A campaign bus, with Free Radio slogans and photographs of 'Chairman Wilson' toured London promoting the station and the fact that the Labour Government had authorised the jamming of its transmissions. Ronan O'Rahilly and one of the original Radio Caroline DJs, Simon Dee, travelled on the bus handing out printed material - in all over five and a half million leaflets were distributed during the campaign.

Communications between the landbased operation and the *Mebo II* were established through Ronan O'Rahilly enlisting the assistance of a amateur radio operator in Clacton-on-Sea, Essex. Erwin Meister then installed sophisticated ultra high frequency communications equipment in the Clacton premises, which the British Post Office was unable to detect or intercept. This equipment was used during the pre-election campaign to transmit messages and up to the minute information to the *Mebo II* for re-broadcast during programmes. An important link in rallying supporters during this campaign was the Free Radio Association (FRA), which was still operated by Geoffrey Pearl from Rayleigh in Essex. The FRA provided facilities in the form of telephone numbers and addresses through which listeners could contact the station in response to on air appeals for help distributing campaign leaflets, stickers etc.

*Leaflets/posters produced during the 1970 election campaign*

DAILY Mirrorcle **YOUR FREEDOM IS AT STAKE...**

Your television, your radio and your newspapers are being CENSORED by the Labour Government during this Election Campaign.

You can see nothing about the illegal jamming of Radio Nordsee by the Labour Government on any of the media in your home.

Your decision on JUNE 18 may be the last FREE decision you have.

THINK before you vote. ☐

**RADIO NORTH SEA ILLEGALLY JAMMED BY LABOUR GOVERNMENT**

ONCE BRITAIN WAS FREE: THINK, VOTE WISELY

VOTE ON 18th JUNE 1970

GENERAL ELECTION

**LABOUR 'JAMS' RADIO NORTH SEA**

**radio caroline international**

the ship broadcasting 6½ miles off Clacton on 244 meters has been "jammed" by the G.P.O. for the past two months.

"Jamming" is a practice only exercised so far by communist government's, dictatorships and—*in the case of R.C.I.—By the Labour Government.*

Radio Caroline International is a *legal* station operating in International waters *and therefore not under British jurisdiction.*

Therefore, the "jamming" of R.C.I. by the G.P.O. is *illegal*, according to the International Radio Regulations signed in Geneva in 1959.

This "jamming" can only be called a dictatorial action by the Labour Government.

**if you disagree**

With these tactics, if you want to be free to tune into the radio station of your choice, if you agree with us that the "jamming" of R.C.I. could be the beginning of the end of freedom in Britain then you

Vote against the illegal "jamming" of R.C.I. by the Labour Government.

*Make sure that the candidate you vote for is willing to bring*

**free radio back to britain!**

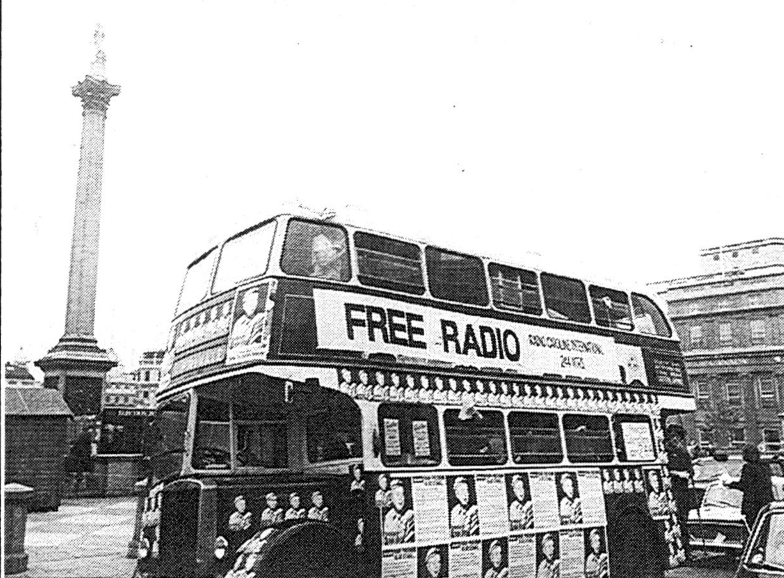


*The Free Radio bus in Trafalgar Square, June 1970*

The Campaign for Independent Broadcasting and the Free Radio Association organised an anti-jamming rally and march to Downing Street on Sunday 14th June 1970. The event was widely publicised on Radio Caroline/RNI and a special programme was broadcast during the demonstration which was relayed to supporters assembled in Hyde Park. It was estimated that up to 10,000 people joined in the demonstration and speakers at the rally included Ronan O'Rahilly, David Prewitt (Chairman of the Campaign for Independent Broadcasting). Following the rally the protest march to Whitehall and Downing Street was led by Ronan O'Rahilly, one of Caroline's first DJs, Simon Dee and James Bond actor, George Lazenby.

On 16th June 1970, just two days before the General Election, Prime Minister Harold Wilson personally authorised the use of the most powerful transmitter in Europe - a one megawatt facility kept at Droitwich for use in a national emergency - to jam RNI's signal.The transmitter was relocated to a plot of land owned by the Marconi Company in Canewdon, Essex from where it was used to continue the jamming of RNI's signal on medium wave. this jamming transmitter was so powerful that it also caused interference to television sound and other authorised radio transmissions in the south east of England.

## Disappointment for RNI

Against all opinion poll predictions the Labour Party lost the General Election on 18th June 1970, with many marginal seats in London and the south east being gained by the Conservative Party. Although almost impossible to quantify it is virtually certain, and now generally accepted by political historians, that the campaign mounted by RNI/Caroline during the run up to election day had a significant impact on the result of the 1970 General Election, particularly in those in London and south east marginal constituencies.

The day after the Election, 19th June 1970 RNI dropped the Radio Caroline call sign - its objective of putting the Labour Party out of power had been achieved, but its hope that the incoming Conservative Government would immediately stop the jamming did not materialise. the new government realised just what a powerful force the station had been and that it could conceivably be used in a similar way to broadcast propaganda against its own policies. Additionally there was continued pressure from broadcasters and governments in Switzerland, Italy, Norway and Holland for the offshore station to be silenced.

A change of frequency to 1385kHz (217m) was made on 28th June 1970, but the jamming followed shortly afterwards and the station reverted to 1230kHz(244m) on 30th June.The same day the use of the powerful jamming transmitter at Canewdon was stopped, but only to be replaced by the original jamming signal from Rochester Naval Base. Further jamming added tothe station's problems on 3rd July 1970 when the shortwave signal on 6210kHz (49m band) was jammed by the Norwegian Rogaland coastal maritime radio station.

That same day representatives of RNI met the new British Minister of Posts and Telecommunications, Christopher Chattaway, to discuss the situation but came away without any assurance that the jamming signal would be switched off. In fact on 14th July the Minister announced in Parliament that, contrary to assurances given by his party before the June General Election, the jamming of RNI's signal would now continue indefinately. It is thought by many observers that this decision had been made by the incoming Conservative administration in the light of information, now available to them for the first time in top secret Cabinet papers from the outgoing Labour Government. This information is thought to be concerned with the perceived threat to national security posed by

### WHO DO YOU THINK YOU ARE KIDDING, MR WILSON?

One feature of the Caroline/RNI Election Campaign was a song, especially written and recorded for the purpose by a group of DJs using the name 'The Opposition' which was played frequently during programmes in the days running up to the 1970 General Election. The words were sung to the signature tune of the BBC television series "Dad's Army".

*Who do you think you are kidding, Mr. Wilson*

*If you think Free Radio's down?*

*We are the boys who will stop your little game*

*We are the boys who will make you think again.*

*So, who do you think you are kidding, Mr. Wilson*

*If you think Free Radio's down?*

*Mr Stonehouse starts to jam at 5.21*

*And he goes home at 2 am, his dirty work is done.*

*So, who do you think you are kidding, Mr. Wilson*

*If you think Free Radio's down?*

*If you think you can crush us*

*We're afraid you've missed the bus.*

*So, who do you think you are kidding, Mr Wilson*

*If you think Free Radio's down?*

## Ministry letter

Listeners who took the trouble to write to the authorities to complain about the continued jamming of RNI after the General Election, and the effect of that jamming on reception of BBC Radio One, received the following standard reply from the Ministry of Posts and Telecommunications:-

*Following the recent change of Government the Minister has carefully considered the problems of pirate broadcasting and has stated that illicit broadcasting will not be tolerated and that the Government must abide by its international obligations in combating the illicit use of wavelengths.*

*In order to force a pirate radio station, Radio North Sea International, off the air a transmitter has been activated - but not before its interference potential was tested. Tests with ordinary domestic receivers show no interference to Radio 1 beyond the immediate vicinity of the transmitter.*

*Our action in opposing the pirate station has been fully accepted by the International Frequency Registration Board of the International Telecommunications Union which is the international authority on interference and the control of frequencies.*

*If in maintaining our stand in defence of law and order we have caused interference to the reception of Radio 1 to a very small number of listeners it cannot be compared with the number of listeners who are receiving interference from the pirate by his own deliberate act.*

*I am extremely sorry for any interference you are experiencing from our transmission but I am sure you would agree that it is essential to maintain law and order in the field of broadcasting and in the use of scarce radio frequencies and that is the sole aim of our action.*

RNI's presence off the British coast which had originally given rise tothe intensive jamming campaign against the station.

Perhaps those rumours about deals with rebel African Governments had some basis in truth or there was something even more sinister about RNI and those behind it which gave rise to continuing concerns. It is certain that the decision to jam the station was not undertaken lightly - it was a tactic which had not been used before RNI's arrival off the British coast, and despite the presence there of other offshore stations since 1970, it has not been used again since.

## Return to Holland

The weeks of jamming and resultant frequency changes had badly affected the commercial viability of RNI and with no assurance forthcoming from the British authorities that the jamming would stop the station's owners decided they had had enough. Transmissions were discontinued at 10.55am on 23rd July 1970 and the *Mebo II* raised her anchor and sailed back to Holland, anchoring off Scheveningen the following day. Broadcasting started once again on all frequencies at 7.00am - without any sign of a jamming signal from the British authorities. The FM transmissions were moved from 100mHz to 102mHz, but the medium wave and shortwave frequencies remained as they had been off the British coast.

On 27th July 1970 the Dutch PTT sent a telegram to RNI's head office in Zurich complaining that the medium wave transmissions on 244m were interfering with the Hilversum 3 station on 240m. Three days later complaints were received that the FM transmissions on 102mHz were interfering with the Netherlands Bus Company's communications, so on 31st July all transmissions from the *Mebo II* were stopped yet again.

The station was back on the air by 3rd August 1970 on 6205kHz in the 49m shortwave band from 6.00am and on 1385kHz (217m) medium wave from 9.00am. FM transmissions returned on 96mHz at 4.00am the following morning and a new 31m shortwave band transmission was started on 9940kHz on 5th August 1970.

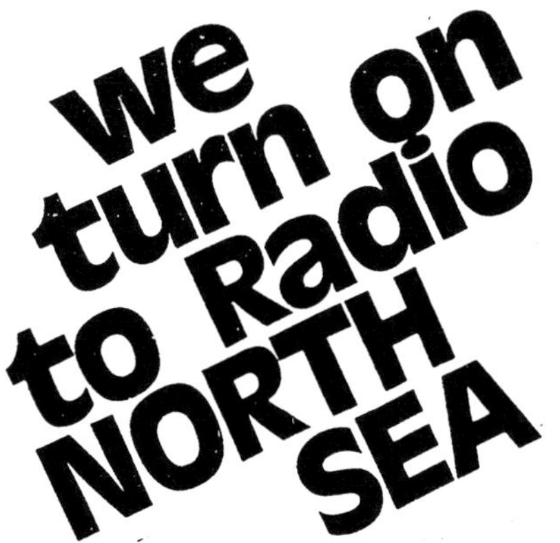


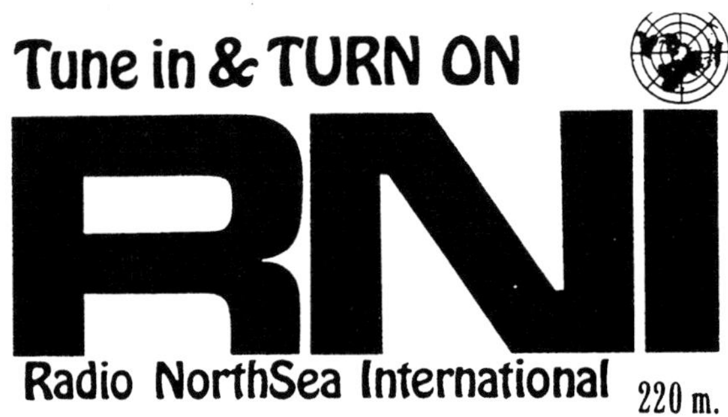

Programmes, now all in English, were presented from 6.00am - 3.00am and everything went well for about two weeks until a storm on 17th August 1970 damaged the medium wave transmitter putting it off the air for five days. A further set of frequency changes took place on 23rd August when medium wave transmissions were changed to 1367kHz (220m) and FM moved to 100mHz, while the short wave frequencies in the 31m and 49m wavebands remained unchanged.

## Dramatic attack

While all this activity was going on out at sea events involving RNI ashore were equally bizarre. In early August 1970 Amsterdam night club owner Kees Manders (who for a short time in 1959 had been involved with the embryo Radio Veronica as its 'Artistic Director' See Chapter 4) announced that he was RNI's new Commercial Director and would secure advertising for the station now that it had returned to the Dutch coast.

However, on 26th August 1970 the RNI tender, *Mebo I,* was arrested and chained up in Scheveningen Harbour as the result of court action taken by Manders who claimed he was owed £3,000 in advertising commission. Both Erwin Meister and Edwin Bollier denied ever even hiring Manders to sell airtime on RNI, but the following day, acting on 'information received' PTT officials raided the Grand Hotel in Scheveningen and removed, from a room occupied by RNI's two Swiss owners, radio equipment allegedly used for unauthorised communications with the *Mebo II.*

Matters came to a head on 29th August 1970 when, at about 1.20pm the crew on board *Mebo II* sighted two vessels heading towards the radio ship. One vessel was the tug *Huski,* the other a Panamanian registered launch, *Viking* - owned by I P Heerema who had been involved in the REM Island offshore radio and television project in 1964.

The *Viking* came alongside *Mebo II* and Kees Manders boarded the radio ship demanding to talk to the master, Captain Harteveld. Manders offered the Captain an amount of money to take the radio ship into Scheveningen Harbour, but when this was refused he threatened to cut the anchor chain and tow in the *Mebo II* himself, using the tug *Huski.* Manders then left the radio ship and the *Viking* drew away.

DJs made dramatic appeals over the air for RNI's listeners to telephone the station's head office in Zurich and its representatives staying at the Grand Hotel, Scheveningen. The response to these appeals was so large that Scheveningen telephone exchange was blocked for over an hour and the one in Zurich went out of action completely - unable to cope with the massive volume of incoming international calls.

After a short while the *Huski* and *Viking* both sailed towards the radio ship again and from the deck of the *Mebo II* the crew and DJs repelled the would-be boarders with missiles. The *Huski* then sailed to the bow of the *Mebo II* and attempts were

### Caroline TV

*Broadcasting hours were to be from 6.00pm - 12 midnight five days a week and 6.00pm-2.00am the other two days. Programme plans included a two hour daily pop show, a chat show ("Out of Your Mind"), feature films, documentaries, series, cartoons and news.*

*Each plane was to have an on-board studio for news broadcasts and live interview inserts.*

**Pop pirate TV is here!**

**SAYS CAROLINE MAN RONAN O'RAHILLY**

*Ronan O'Rahilly started to put together plans for a Caroline Television station in 1968, after the enforced closure of the two Caroline radio stations. Using two huge Constellation planes flying at 20,000 feet twelve miles off the east coast he proposed to beam television programmes to Britain every night between 6.00pm and 3.00am. The concept, however unlikely it may sound, was technically feasible - the American Forces were already successfully using such a means to broadcast television signals in Vietnam.*

*A number of press conferences were held in London to publicise the plan, but the project then faded from the media's attention. However, by mid-1970, while involved with the Caroline/RNI Election Campaign, Ronan O'Rahilly announced that Caroline TV was now scheduled to start regular transmissions from 1st July. Over £1.25 million was said to have been invested in Caroline TV and sufficient advertising promised to keep the station on the air for at least six months. Despite this extensive publicity no broadcasts were ever made by Caroline TV and Ronan O'Rahilly blamed the failure on the withdrawal of support from advertisers and backers in the face of British Government pressure.*

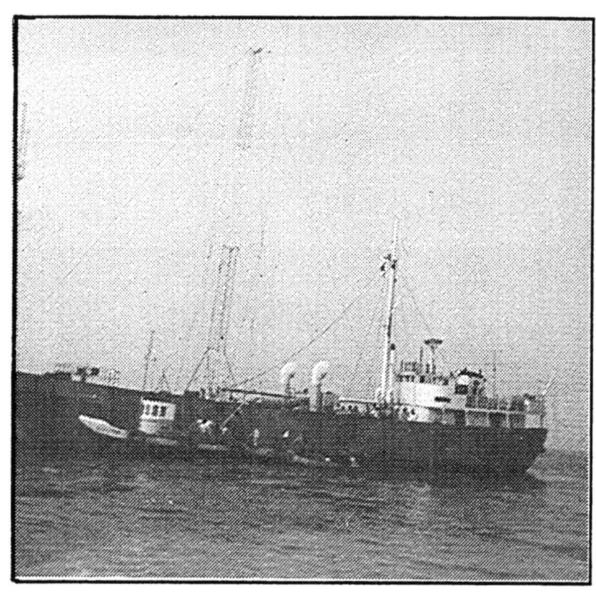

'Eurotrip' alongside the 'Mebo II' after the attempted boarding

made by those on board to cut the radio ship's anchor chain. At this point RNI staff threatened to throw petrol bombs at their attackers if they did not pull away. Throughout this drama listeners were given a running commentary of events with continuous announcements requesting assistance and stating that the ship was being attacked in an act of piracy on the high seas.

Having failed either to board the *Mebo II* or cut her anchor chain the attackers then decided to use a water cannon mounted on the *Huski* to put the radio ship's aerial mast out of action and silence the station. However, they were warned over the air by DJ Carl Mitchell that the high voltage in the area of the transmitter mast would arc back through the water jet and probably kill those on board the tug. This seemed to deter the attackers who switched off the water cannon and temporarily withdrew once again, but some water which had earlier been fired from the tug had already affected the short wave transmitter, putting it off the air for a while.

By the time the *Huski* was ready to approach the Mebo II again the station's other tender, *Eurotrip,* was heading towards the radio ship with Erwin Meister and Programme Director Larry Tremaine on board. Manders and Heerema left the scene before the tender arrived, but threatened that they would return later.

## Explanation

When the situation had calmed down Programme Director Larry Tremaine went on air to explain to listeners something of what had been happening. He stated that Manders had no contract with Mebo Ltd. to act on its behalf and he had attempted piracy on the high seas by attacking the radio ship that afternoon. Various DJs then thanked everyone who had responded to their pleas for assistance and later in the afternoon the Dutch Navy frigate *Van Nes* took up position near the *Mebo II*, staying throughout the night and the next day in case the attackers returned.

Back on land Kees Manders dismissed the whole incident, claiming he only went to have a look at the radio ship. Hereema on the other hand claimed that both he and Manders were in fact directors of RNI and had been appointed to the board by Meister and Bollier a few weeks earlier when the Swiss men had been seeking financial assistance to keep their station on the air.

The true position only became clear much later. RNI had suffered financially from the jamming of its signal, numerous frequency changes and the re-positioning of the *Mebo II* from the Dutch to the British coast and back again. Advertising income had virtually dried up and Meister and Bollier had sought a cash injection to keep the project alive. They approached Hereema, who agreed to provide £50,000 in return for which Meister and Bollier gave him a 12.5% interest in the station. At the beginning of August 1970 Hereema arranged for his colleague, Kees Manders, to be appointed Commercial Director of RNI and although a verbal agreement was made to this arrangement nothing was confirmed in writing. Meister and Bollier later resented and rejected the Dutch men's increasing influence on the operation of RNI and this in turn led to the impounding of the station's tender and ultimately the attempted towing in of the *Mebo II* by Kees Manders.

In the weeks that followed a number of claims and counter claims were made by both sides with Mebo Ltd. claiming damages from Manders for the attack on the radio ship and for the time their tender was chained up in Scheveningen Harbour.

## Sudden closure

On 22nd September 1970 the 9940kHz (31m band) shortwave transmitter started carrying a separate 'World Service' programme for eight hours a day between 10.00am-12 noon, 2.00pm-4.00pm and 6.00pm-10.00pm. However, a further turn of events immediately curtailed this new programming initiative. Late in the evening of 23rd September 1970 a small boat from Scheveningen, *De Redder,* arrived alongside the *Mebo II* and delivered a message from RNI's Swiss owners to the radio crew instructing them to close the station at 11.00am the following morning.

The station's DJs, stunned by the unexpected turn of events and the suddenness of RNI's closure continued with their programmes as normally as possible, but at regular intervals they read out the following announcement from the owners:-

*RNI is voluntarily closing down at 11.00am tomorrow morning due to the pressure in the Dutch Government to close the offshore stations.*
*Our director in Zurich feel that it would be better for the people of Holland for us to suspend broadcasting so that the Dutch Government will not attempt to close down Radio Veronica, so dearly loved by the people of Holland for the last 10 years.*

The final hour between 10.00 and 11.00am on 24th September 1970 was presented by Andy Archer and Alan West who jointly closed RNI after thanking listeners and advertisers for their support since the station had opened its transmissions at the beginning of the year.

After RNI had left the air Erwin Meister tried to explain that the ship had been sold to an African country and would shortly be broadcasting from a position in the Mediterranean. The real reason for RNI's sudden and unexpected closure only became apparent some time later when it was revealed that rival station Radio Veronica had paid its Swiss owners to cease broadcasting. Radio Veronica directors, feeling their own future threatened after 10 successful years of broadcasting, paid Mebo Ltd. one million Dutch Guilders (£100,000) to keep RNI off the air. The 'loan' was to be repaid in full if RNI recommenced broadcasting during that period, but to try and ensure that that did not happen Radio Veronica arranged to provide their own captain and crew for the *Mebo II,* which remained at anchor off Scheveningen.

At that stage Radio Veronica publicly denied any involvement in, or even knowledge of, the reason for their rival's closure. A Veronica director was quoted in a Dutch newspaper report the day after RNI's closure as saying: "We've heard that they closed down due to financial reasons. As for the rumours that we had a regular contact, or even a contract, with the Swiss owners, we can only say that these are merely rumours."

## Capital Radio

Radio Veronica had, for the time being, succeeded in eliminating one of its rivals off the Dutch coast. However, another much smaller and less powerful offshore station was still broadcasting to Holland, but this was not perceived as a direct threat to Radio Veronica's position in the radio market place.

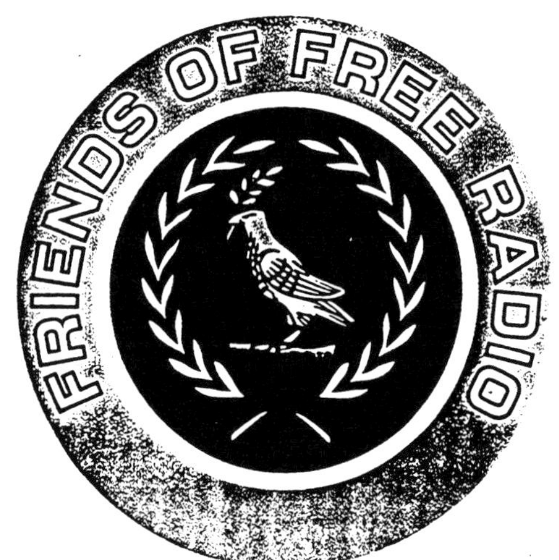


The origins of this smaller offshore station, Capital Radio, lay not in a commercially orientated organisation, but in a foundation for professional broadcasters - The International Broadcasters Society(IBS). This Society had been established in May 1964 by Tim Thomason and his wife Berthe Beydals, who was also Radio and Television Correspondent for *De Telegraaf,* one of Holland's major daily newspapers. By 1967 the Society had enrolled 2,000 members worldwide and provided them with research assistance, study projects and newsletters about all aspects of broadcasting. In addition those members who made an outstanding contribution to their profession were awarded the shield of the Society at an annual honours ceremony.

In October 1969 the IBS decided to establish its own offshore radio station to provide a ' respectable, ethical and professional radio service for European audiences in keeping with the standards proclaimed by the Society'. This was undoubtedly an idealistic objective in a very competitive and commercial world and the IBS acknowledged that the station would have to rely to some extent on commercial income, although this was to be limited to avoid having a detrimental impact on programmes. The station's policy also provided for it to carry two hours of religious programmes each day as well as time allocated for paid political broadcasts.

Tim Thomason engaged the assistance of British author and publisher Paul Harris, who had written a number of books about offshore radio, and together they set about examining the practicalities of launching the new station. By December 1969 Thomason had arranged finance through an investment of £40,000 from Dutch businessman Dirk de Groot, who lived in Switzerland and operated the Liechtenstein based Mississippi Trade and Investment Corporation.

*'King David' with the unique ring aerial*

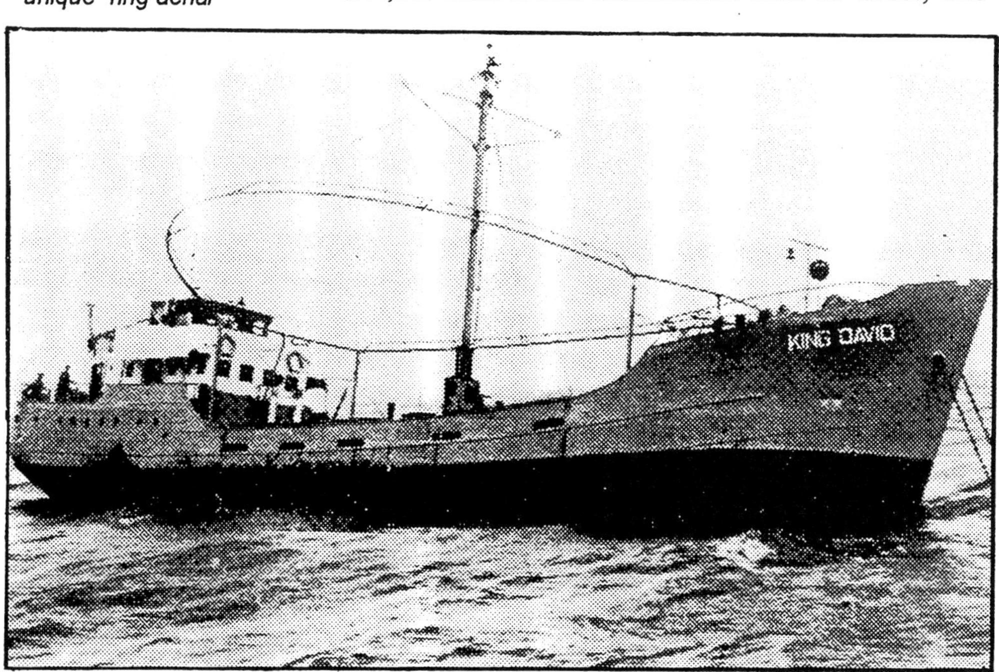


A holding company, Kangaroo Pioneering Co. Est. was established in the Liechtenstein capital Vaduz, as a joint venture between the Mississippi Trade and Investment Corporation as financiers, and the Saltwater Foundation, who were ideologically rather than commercially involved in the project.

The search then began for a ship on which to house the station, together with a smaller vessel to act as a tender. After many abortive attempts to purchase vessels in Britain and Europe at the end of January 1970 the organisation found and purchased, for £4,000, a Dutch trawler, *De Twee Gezusters*, which was to be used as the station's tender. The vessel was renamed *Kangaroo* after the project's holding company, and re-registered in Panama.

A few weeks later, in early February 1970 a former coaster, the *Zeevaart,* which was lying in Groningen Harbour in Holland was purchased by the project for use as a base to house the planned offshore station. The vessel was renamed *King David* and taken to Zaandam, near Amsterdam for conversion into a radio ship.

Meanwhile, the *Kangaroo* sailed to the British port of Scarborough in North Yorkshire to collect essential items of radio equipment. Arrangements had been made for the IBS to purchase the transmitter and studio equipment formerly used by Radio 270, which having been removed from the *Oceaan VII* before she had been scrapped was now in storage in Scarborough. Two diesel generators had also been ordered from Dale Electrics in Yorkshire, who had supplied similar equipment for the same 60's British offshore station. However, because of unexpected official interest the radio equipment and the fact that the *Kangaroo* was found to be too large to enter Scarborough Harbour, the loading operation was transferred to Middlesbrough. Here it was successfully completed without hindrance from the authorities and shipped back to Holland for installation on the *King David.*

As if to underline its fundamental difference from the other commercially orientated offshore stations Capital Radio also managed two other unique achievements.

While work progressed on converting the *King David* arrangements were made to re-register the ship and obtain a flag for her to fly, as required by international maritime law. After hearing about the aims and objectives of the IBS offshore radio project and being interested in seeing it come to fruition Prince Franz Josef II of Liechtenstein personally

Capital Radio's rate card

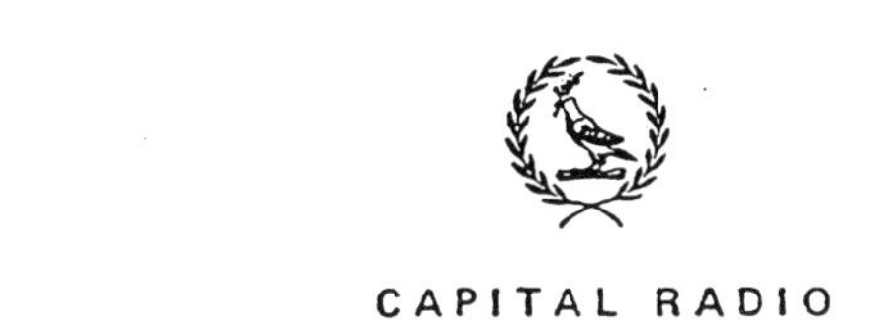

CAPITAL RADIO

1970/71 — RATE CARD — 1970/71

Prime Time : 06:00 – 24:00 Hrs — Late Night : 24:00 – 06:00 Hrs.

SPONSORED MUSIC PROGRAMMES „Guaranteed Minimum Expenditure Contracts"

A : 1/1 Hour Programme ( 6 x 1 minute spots ) per programme :

| | Prime Time | Late Night |
|---|---|---|
| 365 times within any 12 month period | f. 1000 | f. 750 |
| 260 times within any 12 month period | f. 1250 | f. 1000 |
| 52 times within any 12 month period | f. 1500 | f. 1250 |
| 26 times within any 12 month period | f. 1750 | f. 1500 |
| 12 times within any 12 month period | f. 2000 | f. 1750 |

B : 1/2 Hour Programme ( 3 x 1 minute spots ) per programme :

| | Prime Time | Late Night |
|---|---|---|
| 365 times within any 12 month period | f. 750 | f. 500 |
| 260 times within any 12 month period | f. 850 | f. 650 |
| 52 times within any 12 month period | f. 1000 | f. 750 |
| 26 times within any 12 month period | f. 1250 | f. 1000 |
| 12 times within any 12 month period | f. 1500 | f. 1250 |

INDIVIDUAL SPOTS inserted in unsponsored programmes :

| | Prime Time | Late Night |
|---|---|---|
| 500 spots ( 60 seconds each ) per spot | f. 150 | f. 125 |
| 250 spots ( 60 seconds each ) per spot | f. 200 | f. 150 |
| 100 spots ( 60 seconds each ) per spot | f. 250 | f. 200 |
| 50 spots ( 60 seconds each ) per spot | f. 350 | f. 300 |
| 1 spot ( 60 seconds ) per spot | f. 500 | f. 400 |

CONTRACTS

All sales made by, or on behalf of, CAPITAL RADIO must be confirmed on the official „Sales Contract Form" and are subject to the conditions deposited with the Chamber of Commerce (Kamer van Koophandel te Hilversum) and the Court of Justice ( griffie van de arrondissementsrechtbank te Amsterdam )

INTERNATIONAL BROADCASTERS SOCIETY
Elisabethgaarde 20/28
BUSSUM (NH) - Holland

Telephone : (02159) 10005 — Telex : 16488

approved the registration of the *King David* by his country. For the first time in its history this land-locked European Principality was to allow its flag to fly from a ship at sea and the crew on board the *King David* were given uniforms and ranks of seniority in what effectively became the Liechtenstein Navy!

The aerial system designed for the station was also unique. Nothing similar had been seen on an offshore (or landbased) station before. Acting on an American military design theory the backers of the Capital Radio Project decided to construct a circular loop aerial, suspended from a central vertical mast and hanging about 20' over each side of the ship. The overhanging segments were hinged so that they could be stored within the overall width of the *King David*, thus enabling her to travel through the North Sea canals and to enter port without causing any obstruction or hazard.

The aerial had a circumference of 67m (theoretically giving an equivalent in signal output to a vertical mast of the same height) and was mounted about twelve feet above the deck of the *King David.* According to the theory advanced for this type of construction 90% of the station's signal would be in the form of ground waves and, therefore, it would be much stronger in the primary reception area than a signal from a conventional transmitter aerial radiated in ground and sky waves, much of which is lost.

By the end of April 1970 work was completed and the *King David* left IJmuiden Harbour on 25th April to commence test broadcasts. However, as the hinged segments of the ring aerial were lowered on each side of the ship the whole structure buckled and the vessel was forced to return to port for repairs. After repair the *King David* set sail again on 1st May 1970 and this time a short test broadcast was made on 1115kHz (270m) using a tape recording of the BBC World Service to prove that the, until then, theoretical aerial system did in fact work. Further work was undertaken on the ship and her transmitting equipment during May 1970, while on land programme tapes were recorded in studios in Bussum.

During the evening of 13th June 1970 the *King David* quietly moved to an anchorage off Noordwijk, within sight of the former REM Island used by the short-lived Radio and TV Noordzee in 1964. Official test transmissions started the following day but the station was still plagued by technical problems, mostly associated with its ring aerial system. The *King David* had to put into harbour again at the end of June after the aerial system collapsed again during a storm, knocking one of the crew unconscious on the deck of the ship.

*'King David' with damaged aerial*

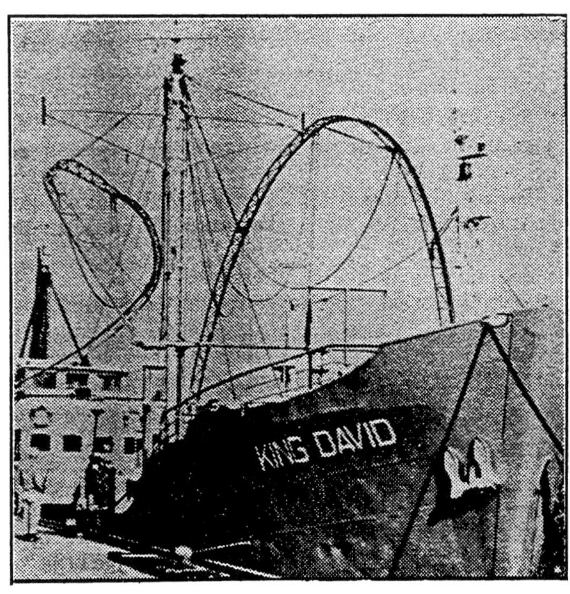


A new, stronger, double ring aerial was installed and the station resumed test transmissions on 14th July 1970, but further problems followed with the transmitter and aerial insulators. Vital spare parts then had to be ordered and obtained from America before the station could even think about commencing regular broadcasts.

Despite all these problems when Capital Radio did manage to start broadcasts it achieved a reasonable signal strength and its programmes were audible in Holland, Belgium and along the south east of England. Regular programmes started officially at 8.00am on 1st September 1970 with continuous middle-of-the-road music and station identity announcements in both Dutch and

English. The first two hours of broadcasting consisted of pre-recorded programmes of music, an address from Tim Thomason on the aims and objectives of the IBS and Capital Radio followed by a brief history of offshore radio presented by Paul Harris. This opening programme was repeated every four hours throughout the day. The hours of transmission were from 6.00am-2.00am.

Further problems plagued the new station when, just over a week later during the evening of 9th September 1970, an insulator exploded and Capital Radio was put off the air. Scheveningen Maritime Radio refused to handle a call from Capital Radio's office to the *King David* and arrangements had to be made to send out the tender, *Kangaroo,* with instructions for the radio ship to return to port for repair. However, difficulties were encountered raising the *King David's* anchor in the Force 8 gale and a crew member, Third Officer Arie van Bent, had his leg trapped by one of the chains which suddenly began to run out after a retaining wire snapped. The Dutch air-sea rescue service was then called to winch the injured crewman off the *King David* and take him to hospital where doctors decided that his injured leg must be amputated. Meanwhile in extremely hazardous conditions the *Kangaroo* managed to tow the *King David* into IJmuiden for repairs.

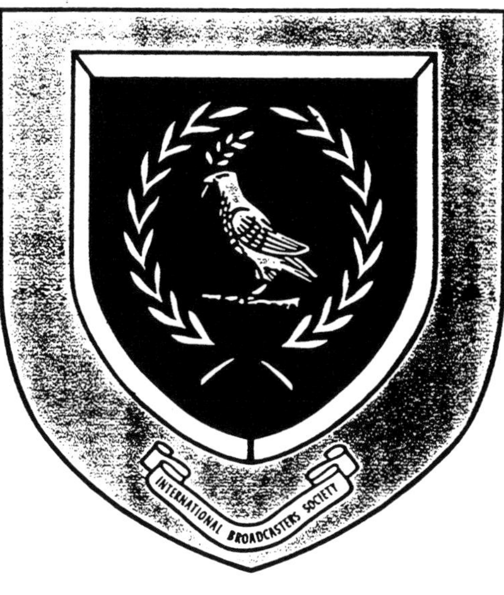


**VRIENDEN VAN VRIJE RADIO**
**Postbus 270**
**BUSSUM - Holland**

During the ship's month long stay in port the station's owners were threatened with prosecution by the PTT for having installed a transmitter without Government permission, contrary to Dutch law. Consequently repairs to the *King David* were hurriedly completed and she left harbour on 8th October 1970, but was forced to return after a few hours at sea when yet again part of the ring aerial system collapsed. Two days later the *King David* was able to return to her anchorage in international waters and transmissions of Capital Radio recommenced.

For almost a month the station was able to maintain a regular programming schedule and a good signal strength. A club was started for listeners - Vrienden van Vrije Radio - which enrolled over 5,000 members within a few weeks. Advertisers also began to purchase airtime on the station as the threat of imminent Dutch Government action against offshore stations receeded in the weeks following the unexpected closure of RNI on 24th September 1970.

## Disaster

Just as everything seemed to be going well for Capital Radio disaster struck in the early hours of 10th November 1970. At about 2.00am it was discovered that the anchor chain had snapped and the *King David* was drifting in a Force 9 gale. Attempts to lower the emergency anchor proved fruitless because it would not hold the radio ship in the stormy conditions. Shortly after 3.00am the *King David's* Captain, Leen Plug, sent a Mayday message to Scheveningen Maritime Radio who alerted the rescue services. The IJmuiden lifeboat, *Johanna Louise*, and the Noordwijk beach rescue boat *Kurt Carlsen* were both launched and headed towards the stricken *King David.* At the same time the Wijsmuller Salvage Company picked up the Mayday message and despatched one of its salvage tugs, *Hector,* to attempt to put a line on board the drifting radio ship, thereby entitling the company to claim a salvage fee.

The *King David* continued drifting towards the shore and at 5.10am the *Kurt Carlsen* took all crew except the Captain and one engineer off the radio ship. By 5.30am the *King David* had run on to the beach at Noordwijk, just 200 yards in front of the Palace Hotel. An initial inspection of the radio ship at low tide revealed that there was little damage to her hull and it was hoped to re-float her on the noon high tide, using the services of the Wijsmuller salvage tug . However, following preliminary discussions with the Wijsmuller representative at Noordwijk it became apparent that this would not be possible. Special cables needed to be brought from IJmuiden and arrangements then had to be made to secure these to the radio ship and to the tug *Hector* which, due to the shallow water off the beach, could not come close to the stranded *King David.*

Delayed by continuing bad weather and the non-arrival of various items of equipment it took three days before everything was ready for the salvage attempt. During this time the *King David* had endured a battering from the waves and wind and as a consequence had sunk deeper into the soft sand of Noordwijk beach.

The first salvage attempt was made at 2.00am on 13th November 1970, but had to be abandoned after the *King David* refused to shift from her position, embedded deep in the sand. After bulldozers removed sand surrounding the ship later that morning a further salvage attempt was made on the afternoon high tide. This time it was successful and at 2.40pm the *King David* was pulled from Noordwijk beach and towed into IJmuiden Harbour.

A week later the *King David* was towed to dry dock at Amsterdam and inspected for damage, which was found to be minimal. However, some repairs were required, most of all a new anchoring system, and arrangements were then made to transfer the radio ship to the CV Volharding shipyard in another part of Amsterdam.

As the *King David* left dry dock on 26th November 1970 she was pursued by a police launch and when the vessel arrived at the shipyard police and court officials arrested the ship and chained her up. Wijsmullers had put in a claim of £15,000 for salvaging the *King David* and through a court order sought to have her immobilised until this sum was paid. Pleas to the salvage company from the IBS for the radio ship to be allowed to return to sea, enabling Capital Radio to resume broadcasts went unheeded. Had they been allowed it would have enabled the station to earn advertising income which in turn would have provided funds to pay off the debt - a contract for £50,000 worth of airtime sales existed with an American religious sponsor and many other advertising contracts were also said to be in the pipeline.

Although there was no prospect of this revenue being earned as a result of Capital Radio returning to the air the IBS did continue to meet bills incurred by the station for running costs and staff wages, with Tim Thomason and his wife putting their personal assets into the Society's funds while at the same time trying to raise further financial capital in the USA.

By the end of 1970, however, IBS staff who had been involved with Capital Radio were working without pay in an effort to find some way of bringing the station back on the air and a number of 'rescue' operations were explored, but all came to nothing. Then in the early months of 1971 what remained of the IBS and the Capital Radio project were dramatically drawn into the ferocious pirate radio war being fought at that time off the Dutch coast.

# Chapter 14

# 'Sound from the sea'

Offshore radio was not a phenomenon exclusive to the Northern Hemisphere. On the other side of the world in New Zealand, then one of the most traditional and conservative of countries, the concept of offshore radio was used during the mid-1960s, as a means to break the state radio monopoly.

The New Zealand Broadcasting Corporation (NZBC) and its predecessor had held a monopoly right to broadcast since the early 1930s and operated both radio and television stations throughout the country. As with most other state monopoly broadcasters NZBC had become stale and insular and by the mid-1960s was clearly failing to meet the demands of listeners, particularly its young ones.

Like most European state broadcasting systems the forerunner to NZBC, New Zealand Broadcasting Service (NZBS), had been established in the 1930s to enable the government to have control over the development of radio. The NZBS too radio broadcasting out of the hands of the pioneer private developers, who if allowed to continue operating were perceived as a threat to the whole communications medium at a time of rapid technical developments. The NZBS, as a government 'department' established a national radio service serving all areas of New Zealand, but as with all such organisations it became bureaucratic and unwilling to consider change or innovation.

Then in 1961 the New Zealand government changed the status of the NZBS to that of an independent corporation, renamed it the New Zealand Broadcasting Corporation (NZBC) and gave it powers to issue licences for private radio stations to be established - effectively creating competition for its own network. Not surprisingly the NZBC consistently decided not to implement these additional powers granted to it by the government. If any person or organisation subsequently requested the NZBC to invite applications for private licences they were usually told that the particular area was already well served by its own stations and no further action was ever taken.

David Gapes, a young journalist on the *New Zealand Truth* had an idea to break this state monopoly and provide the sort of radio entertainment people of his generation wanted. When working on the *Daily Mirror* in Sydney he had witnessed the lively output of both the private and public sector Australian broadcasters and also read stories about the early European offshore stations, particularly Denmark's Radio Mercur and Britain's Radio Caroline. He was deeply impressed by the way they had taken on the established state systems and revolutionised radio broadcasting in their respective countries. He reasoned that if a similar station could be launched from a base off the coast of New Zealand it would have much the same effect on radio entertainment in that country. However, he recognised that because of the geographical nature of New Zealand, isolated as it was in the Pacific Ocean with no near neighbour which could be used as a tendering or supply base, the project would be much more

> **'Hauraki'**
>
> *A name had to be decided for the station, one which would convince potential backers and advertisers that the project was indeed a serious proposition. Eventually the name Radio Hauraki was chosen, because it was to be from a position in the Hauraki Gulf that the radio ship would make its broadcasts. Only after deciding that this was a suitable name for the station did David Gapes and Bruce Baskett consult a Maori dictionary to check the meaning of the word "Hauraki". To their astonishment the translation given was "sound from the sea", a definition they saw as a good omen for the success of the project.*

difficult to operate than those in Europe. Anyway he had no financial resources and knew nothing at all about radio broadcasting in either technical or managerial terms.

## Feasibility studies

Although seemingly impossible to launch, the idea of establishing an offshore radio station did not go away and during the early part of 1965 David Gapes discussed the proposal with fellow journalist Bruce Baskett. After much thought both men agreed to pool their savings and when they had accumulated NZ$1,000 give up their jobs in Wellington and move north to the more heavily populated city of Auckland, where a radio station would have more chance of commercial success.

Before taking this step, however, some preliminary enquiries were made about the technical and practical aspects of the project. Most important of these was the difficult problem of identifying a likely anchorage position for the proposed station's ship. The planned target area of Auckland lies at the head of a gulf, which forms a large bay at the top of New Zealand's North Island. Under international maritime law all waters within a line drawn from one headland to the other across the mouth of a bay are declared to lie inside territorial waters (see Chapter 1). At first it was thought that the ship would have to anchor three miles outside this line, effectively 50 miles out to sea, which would have been too dangerous in the exposed seas beyond Great Barrier Island.

However, a closer examination of maps revealed that there existed a small triangle of sea between Little Barrier Island, Great Barrier Island and the Coromandel Peninsular which was according to the law, technically international waters - despite the fact that it was completely surrounded by New Zealand's own territorial waters. David Gapes and his partner were satisfied that they had now found a mooring position, (identified as 36 degrees 20 minutes south and 175 degrees 15 minutes east) which, although it was 50 miles from Auckland would be safe legally and enable a satisfactory radio signal to reach their planned target area.

Neither of the men knew anything about the technical side of radio, but David Gapes had met an amateur radio enthusiast, Dennis 'Doc' O'Callaghan when he worked in Auckland some years previously. O'Callaghan was eventually tracked down and persuaded to join the offshore radio project as its technical expert. He worked out some details which showed that, technically the project seemed feasible, but Dennis O'Callaghan wanted to wait until sufficient finance had been raised before giving up his job to join the proposed station on a full time basis himself.

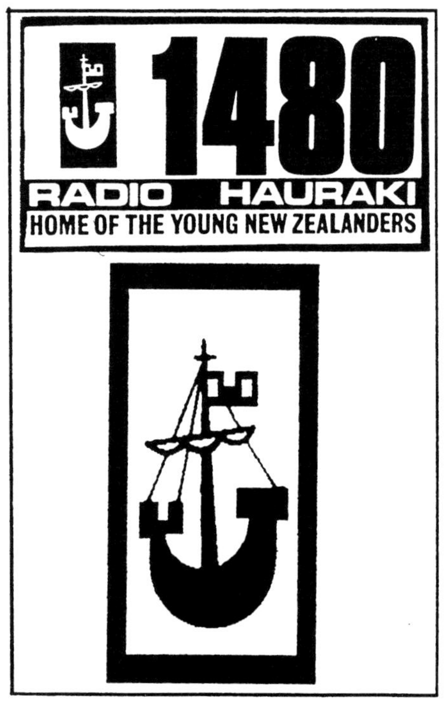


Having now satisfied themselves that both legally and technically the idea seemed feasible David Gapes and Bruce Baskett set about finding a suitable ship to use as a base for their offshore station. Here they were assisted by an old contact of David Gapes, Jim Frankham, head of A G Frankham Ltd., a coastal shipping company which happened to be selling much of its fleet to concentrate on the road haulage side of its business. Frankham was able to offer, on very reasonable financial terms, a small wooden coaster, the *Hokianga,* which was surplus to his company's requirements.

Having completed the preliminary plans by November 1965 David Gapes, his wife Wendy and Bruce Baskett left their jobs and homes in Wellington and moved north to Auckland to begin detailed work on the project. Although they still lacked any financial backing they gradually started planning in detail various other aspects necessary to launch and operate an offshore radio station.

Pirates may raid NZBC for staff

ANNOUNCERS ENTHUSIASTIC

THE NZBC could lose some of its brightest young technicians and announcers to the pop pirate station, Radio Hauraki, when it starts transmitting later this year.

Commercial airtime rates were calculated and in order to prove attractive to advertisers they were designed to fall between the expensive rates charged by Auckland's major commercial station 1ZB and the relatively new commercial competitor 1YD, (which in any case was only on the air 20 hours a week), both of which were owned by NZBC.

Obtaining financial backing for the offshore radio project proved far more difficult than expected because businessmen and private investors were unwilling to take the risk of losing money on such an unknown proposition. David Gapes decided to approach the large tobacco companies (who had boycotted the NZBC for a number of years in protest against a restriction on cigarette advertising on television before 9.00pm) thinking they would be anxious to advertise their products on a non-NZBC commercial station.

At the beginning of 1966 Rothmans gave very serious consideration to Gapes's request for the company to invest NZ$20,000, sufficient to buy a ship and transmitting equipment, but at the end of February the company finally decided not to support the project after all.

This negative decision was a major setback and almost the final straw for David Gapes and Bruce Baskett. At that point the whole project nearly foundered - their savings were nearly exhausted, financial backing was not forthcoming and they also discovered that the ship which had been promised to them, the *Hokianga,* would not now be available for up to six months. Bruce Baskett decided he had had enough and left the project at this stage, and with Dennis O'Callaghan still working abroad, this left David Gapes and his wife on their own to find the elusive funding.

## Rivals

In March 1966 word reached Gapes that another group was also making plans to put an offshore radio station on the air. Fearing that this group would be better prepared technically and financially than Radio Hauraki Gapes and O'Callaghan (who returned to New Zealand in mid-March 1966) earnestly set about furthering their own, now almost semi-dormant, project.

Detailed plans were drawn up for the station's format, the pre-recording of programmes in landbased studios and various technical aspects, including the selection of a wavelength which would not cause interference to established legal stations. However, despite all this planning that crucial financial backing was still not available to lift the ideas off the drawing board and into reality.

Using his contacts in journalism David Gapes decided to make one more bid to attract financial backing and support. He felt it was time to go public and be more positive about the plans for Radio Hauraki, while at the same time frightening off any possible opposition in the form of a rival offshore project. On April 9th 1966 (Easter Saturday) the *New Zealand Herald* carried a front page story about Radio Hauraki, generally giving the impression that the scheme was far more advanced than it really was, and even suggesting that the station would be on the air within six months.

The *Herald* article was the first definite public information that an offshore radio station was being planned for New Zealand and official reaction to the news was one of bureaucratic buck-passing. The New Zealand Post Office said it could do little to police the activities of a station operating outside the three mile territorial limit, any action in this direction, they said, would be a matter for the Government. The Government's Minister of Broadcasting, Jack Scott, said he did not think action against the station would be necessary admitting somewhat surprisingly, that he was "... not sure how far my powers in this respect would extend."

Despite making this public statement of uncertainty Jack Scott was destined to become heavily involved in the Radio Hauraki saga from two directions - as well as being the Minister responsible for Broadcasting he was also New Zealand's Minister of Marine, and as such had overall control of ship surveys and safety matters, a role he was to bring into play as the planned station looked more and more certain to become a reality.

However, not all reaction was hostile to the planned offshore radio station. The Wellington *Sunday Times* of 1st May 1966 carried an editorial welcoming the challenge posed by the planned offshore broadcaster to the state monopoly of NZBC:-

*The excitement of piracy aside, the only reason for welcoming this challenge and the only lasting effect it is likely to have are in emphasising to the Government the suffocating grip one corporation has on the two media (radio and television) in this country. The NZBC is not only the monopoly operator: it is also the authority which recommends to the Minister of Broadcasting whether new licences will be issued. Recent statements by the Minister, Mr. W J Scott, indicate that this authority is soon to be clipped back. A second curtailment should be of the corporation's monopoly on radio broadcasting. The huge capital investment on TV would seem to rule out the possibility of a second authority here at this stage. But radio, in a vacuum of programme ideas since TV grabbed the limelight, needs the spur of competition from someone with a more firmly based transmitter than the pirates have to offer.*

These seemingly definite and advanced plans for Radio Hauraki announced in the *Herald* article came as a bombshell to two ex-NZBC staff, Derek Lowe and Chris Parkinson, who had secretly been working on an offshore radio project of their own for some months. Chris Parkinson had been a staff announcer with NZBC, but had left to do freelance voice-overs for commercials and sponsored programmes. Derek Lowe had left NZBC to establish his own company producing jingles and commercials, often employing Chris Parkinson to do the voice-overs.

**Pirate Radio Station In Gulf Planned**

**A pirate radio station beaming a programme of popular music to the Auckland province from a ship beyond the three-mile limit, in the Hauraki Gulf, may begin broadcasting in about six months.**

A group of young Auckland business men say they are adding the finishing touches to their plan to break the monopoly of the New Zealand Broadcasting Corporation.

Mr D. Gapes, business manager for the enterprise, said yesterday he was confident of complete success provided neither the Government nor the Broadcasting Corporation interfered.

**Not Illegal**

"Our lawyer has assured us that there is nothing illegal about what we plan to do," he said. "Short of extending the limit of territorial waters or blacklisting companies which advertise with us I cannot see anything they can do.

"We have selected our wavelength carefully to ensure that we do not interfere with the Broadcasting Corporation, the ambulance services or any other broadcaster."

Mr Gapes said that initially the station would broadcast a morning breakfast session starting a quarter of an hour before 1ZB and ending about 10 a.m. and an afternoon-evening session ending about 7.30 p.m.

It was hoped ultimately to broadcast 24 hours a day.

Because of the difficulties of working records and turntables in a moving ship all tunes would be tape-recorded on shore.

"The programme will consist entirely of pop music," said Mr Gapes. "I am sure that pop music is what most people like to hear and we will be producing programmes to meet the majority taste.

"We are negotiating with two leading Australian disc jockeys to compere the programmes."

Mr L. R. Sceats, deputy director-general of the Broadcasting Corporation, said yesterday he had heard nothing of plans for a pirate radio station. He declined to comment.

An official of the radio division of the Post Office in Wellington said a licence for a private radio station would not be granted to an applicant unless a warrant had been obtained from the Broadcasting Corporation.

He agreed the Post Office itself could do little about a pirate station working outside the three-mile limit—"this would be a matter for the Government"—but added he thought it would be difficult for such a station to find a frequency free of interference. Most frequencies were already in use.

As with the Radio Hauraki group, Lowe and Parkinson had planned every detail of their proposed station, but they too lacked financial resources or backing to get the project any further. After reading the *Herald* article Lowe and Parkinson approached Gapes and O'Callaghan and there followed much discussion, with each side warily sounding the other out to establish the opposition's viability. Both groups eventually realised that they were each at about the same stage of planning and it was agreed that they should pool their talents and what little resources they did have to progress their individual plans as one combined project.

## Financial backing

The newly combined group established itself in a small office in Swanson Street, central Auckland and set about producing a demonstration tape to show potential backers and advertisers just how Radio Hauraki programmes would sound. Advertisers were wooed with promises of a station carrying commercials on Sunday, adverts for alcohol and tobacco and the adoption of a generally "hard sell" approach in commercial scripts - all features which at that time were not available on the NZBC stations.

However, despite all their efforts and meticulous planning the four men still could not convince any large company to back the offshore radio station project financially. A further approach was made to another company - tobacco giants W D and H O Wills, but when this eventually resulted in refusal the directors decided to adopt a policy that when Radio Hauraki did get on the air (and there was no doubt in their minds that one day they would) the station would ban tobacco advertising. All the large companies in this sector had shown considerable initial interest in the proposed offshore station, but despite raising false hopes time after time they had subsequently refused to put up any backing money.

Attention then turned to approaching other large industrial organisations for support and amongst these was New Zealand's then only independent national oil company, Europa Oil. Derek Lowe made a three hour presentation to Europa's advertising account executive and offered a tempting deal - Radio Hauraki would give Europa Oil NZ$20,000 worth of advertising when it came on the air in return for NZ$10,000 cash immediately to enable equipment to be purchased for the station.

Three weeks later, much to the surprise of David Gapes and his colleagues, who had become used to refusals, Europa Oil executives agreed to the proposal and Radio Hauraki was at last able to move forward with its plans, which up until then had been only a dream.

There were some conditions attached to the financial deal, however. Advertising for Europa Oil was to begin on a date to be agreed after 1st October 1966 (Hauraki's target on-air date), but Gapes, Lowe, Parkinson and O'Callaghan were required to give personal guarantees to refund the NZ$10,000 to the company if transmissions had not started at the latest by 15th November 1966. One other important condition - the whole project was considered so risky in legal and commercial terms that Europa Oil's involvement was to be kept top secret and all documentation and dealings had to be handled in the name of its advertising agency, Mackay King Advertising.

For its part Radio Hauraki was now able to formally establish itself as a private limited liability company - Pacific Radio Advertising Ltd., with the four partners as equal shareholders and a nominal capital of NZ$20,000. However, because of the dire financial position of the four partners it was only a paper transaction and none of the shares were actually paid up, a situation that was to continue throughout the station's life.

As plans for putting the station on the air gathered momentum Radio Hauraki moved from its small temporary offices to larger premises at Colebrook's Building in Anzac Avenue, Auckland. Here two studios were constructed, together with

### Possible criticism

*One criticism levelled at Radio Hauraki which those behind the project wished to dispel was that it had failed to try and secure a legal broadcasting licence from the authorities. With Pacific Radio Advertising Ltd. established and the partners knowing they had financial backing for their offshore project they decided, as a safety measure, to submit an application to the NZBC requesting a private broadcasting licence for the Auckland area. The application was of course refused, but at least they had tried.*

administrative and advertising sales offices. Obtaining professional quality technical equipment for the studios, and in particular parts to build a transmitter proved very difficult because of New Zealand's import restrictions on goods of that nature. Eventually an old US Navy wartime transmitter was acquired from a radio amateur and secretly moved to the basement of the station's offices where it was stripped and re-built by Denis O'Callaghan.

Other offers of financial support started to arrive now that the project appeared to be turning into a reality. Jim Frankham, (who had helped the team to find a ship for their station) guaranteed Radio Hauraki an overdraft of up to NZ$4,000 and also bought a shareholding of NZ$2,000 in Pacific Radio Advertising. Two other Auckland businessmen - Jim Haddleton and Harry Miller - also bought an interest in the station.

Anticipated capital costs for putting Radio Hauraki on the air were NZ$21,000 in July 1966, but even with the NZ$10,000 from Europa Oil the financial situation was still critical so plans were implemented to try and secure some definite promises of advertising revenue. David Gapes and Derek Lowe visited every Auckland advertising agency, talked about the station's plans and played the now much used demonstration tape to scores of account executives. The result was amazing even to those behind Radio Hauraki who believed so passionately in their own project - advertising contracts worth NZ$16,000 were secured, mainly from local Auckland-based companies.

In order to ease the project's financial difficulties Jim Frankham devised a deal whereby the station could charter the *Hokianga* from him for six months from August 1966, at a deferred rental payable the following February. After that date, by which time the station planned to be on the air and earning substantial advertising revenue, a regular monthly rental was to be introduced.

Problems with having to re-register the ship outside New Zealand, thus putting her outside the New Zealand Government's jurisdiction, were planned to be overcome by the simple expedient of removing the propeller. Technically this turned the vessel into a barge and as such deleted her from the shipping register as well as from the requirement to undergo full Marine Department surveys and be crewed to the same high level as a registered ship.

Some unexpected and unwelcome developments struck the Radio Hauraki team in July 1966, which indicated that they were not alone in planning an offshore radio station. A mysterious advert appeared in the *Auckland Star* inviting potential staff and advertisers to write to a proposed offshore station - Radio Maverick - at a Post Office Box address in Auckland. The threat of a rival project at this time worried not only the Radio Hauraki team, who feared loss of financial support and advertising revenue, but also caused concern to the Government Minister Jack Scott, who was later quoted as saying, "I thought I could perhaps cope with one, but I was going to have difficulty coping with two. Having seen what happened in England I didn't want to see the same thing happening in New Zealand."

Enquiries by the Radio Hauraki team revealed that a Canadian-Mexican, Antonio Santa Maria Fernandez, had been the person who placed the advertisement in the *Auckland Star*. He claimed to be the local representative of a group of Canadian businessmen who planned to anchor a former American Liberty ship off the New Zealand coast, equipped with a powerful transmitter and fully fitted out as a broadcasting base for a station to be called Radio Ventura. Letters sent by Fernandez to advertising agencies claimed Radio Ventura would have a 5Kw transmitter and that the project had already cost its backers NZ$100,000.

Serious doubts remained within Radio Hauraki about the true viability of the Radio Ventura scheme, but news of yet more potential offshore competitors soon began to reach them. A group in Wellington (South Island) planned to anchor a ship in the Cook Straits, serving both the North and South Islands. This project was backed by a former NZBC advertising and production executive Colin Broadley, who had unsuccessfully applied for a job with Radio Hauraki and, having been turned down, decided to launch his own station. In a determined act of self preservation the Radio Hauraki team managed to persuade Broadley's backers to withdraw their support for his planned station, but at the same time agreed, as a token gesture, to employ him after all so they could keep an eye on his activities.

Having neatly disposed of one potential rival yet another came to light at the end of July 1966. A newspaper headline announced **"PIRATE RADIO BATTLE: TWO NEW STATIONS IN FIGHT FOR AIRWAVE FORTUNE"**. The person behind this second project, Radio Southern Cross, was Keith Ashton who had also left the Radio Hauraki team following disagreements over policy. He claimed Radio Southern Cross would start its transmissions on 24th October 1966, with 24 hour a day programming.

## Government attitude hardens

Faced with all this increased speculation about planned offshore stations and the prospect of a British style 'pirate war' breaking out off the New Zealand coast the Government started to make serious noises about taking action to prevent any of the stations coming on the air. These events in New Zealand were taking place at about the same time as the shooting of Reg Calvert and the rivalry between British offshore stations (see Chapter 11).

New Zealand's Prime Minister, Keith Holyoake, revealed that his Government was studying the then draft British legislation (the Marine etc. Broadcasting (Offences) Bill) and seriously considering the introduction of a similar measure. At the same time the New Zealand Post Office and the Marine Department made public statements about their existing respective powers to deal with matters such as unauthorised transmissions, interference with legal broadcasts, the registration of shipping and requirements for satisfactory navigational and life-saving equipment on board ships.

This apparent hardening of the Government line, from turning a 'blind eye' to Radio Hauraki's initial plans to the active consideration of legislation, did not stop further announcements of further proposed stations off the New Zealand coast. Plans for an offshore television station were announced and another radio station, Radio International, was said to be ready to start broadcasts in September 1966 from a 130 ton ship then being fitted out in Fiji. While the offshore television station plan seemed to have little substance, the Radio International project was altogether a more serious proposition. It was backed by a company known as International Advertisers Ltd., which included an number of prominent Auckland businessmen amongst its backers and had a paid up share capital of NZ$50,000.

Meanwhile, Radio Hauraki pressed ahead with its own plans, still preparing to come on air by 1st October 1966 or earlier if possible. A devastating blow to these plans came in August 1966 when Radio Hauraki was informed that the ship promised by Jim Frankham, the *Hokianga,* would not now be available for another four months. The only other vessel Frankham could offer at that time was a 35 year old coaster, *Tiri,* which had been tied up in Kings Wharf for several months in a state of semi decay. Faced with mounting bills, the ever increasing threat of competition from a multitude of other offshore stations and the possibility of imminent Government legislation against them the Radio Hauraki team concluded they had no time to lose if they were to get on the air by 1st October 1966. They reluctantly accepted Jim Frankham's offer of the old coaster, feeling that they had little or no alternative.

The *Tiri* was hauled into dry dock and work started to repair and convert her for her new role, with all staff, including future broadcasters, advertising personnel and the four directors of Radio Hauraki working 15-18 hours a day preparing the ship. Once work on the hull had been completed the *Tiri* was moved from the dry dock to a less expensive berth in the Western Viaduct Lighter Basin, not far from Auckland City centre.

A request was submitted to the Marine Department for the *Tiri* to be de-registered (having had her propeller removed) and inspected to receive a certificate of completion as a barge. The first inspection took place on 18th August 1966, followed by a series of other, more detailed inspections each resulting in a requirement for additional work on the ship before inspectors could be satisfied. It soon became clear that the Marine Department was using its powers to make life as difficult as possible for Radio Hauraki in the hope that continued delays in registering the ship would finally bankrupt the proposed station before it could even get on the air. Nevertheless the dedicated Radio Hauraki team toiled day and night on their vessel and by 14th September 1966 all work stipulated by the surveyors had been completed. It now seemed the granting of a certificate would be a mere formality.

With the project's financial situation becoming daily more desperate and the continuing threat of Government action the Radio Hauraki team were anxious to put their station on the air as soon as possible so that they could start earning revenue from the promised advertising contracts. In the belief that the ship was now finally ready to be issued with a certificate by the Marine Department plans were made to tow the *Tiri* from her berth on Saturday 17th September 1966 and for the station to come on the air officially at 11.00am on 1st October. With this date firmly set the station's DJs started recording programmes in the land-based studios and the *Tiri* was loaded with supplies and equipment ready to take up position at her anchorage in international waters.

Just as they thought the dream was about to become a reality the project suffered yet another devastating set-back. At 6.00pm on Friday 16th September 1966, after the close of normal business and the day before the ship was due to be moved from her berth, the Marine Department's Auckland office informed David Gapes that the *Tiri* must be surveyed as a ship, not a barge. The Marine Department also indicated that the vessel would be detained pending a further survey as it was suspected she was unsafe. Both the survey and detention orders were signed by Jack Scott in his capacity as Minister of Marine and meant effectively that the *Tiri* was under arrest.

A secret meeting was arranged between Radio Hauraki directors and Jack Scott the following day to thrash out the latest situation and an amazing series of deals were proposed by the Minister in an attempt to dissuade the broadcasters from setting sail. During the meeting Jack Scott indicated that if his National Party were re-elected at the forthcoming General Election, independent radio stations would be established in major cities, including Auckland and hinted that in the light of this assurance the planned launch of the offshore station should be cancelled. Understandably the Radio Hauraki team were not prepared to wait either for the result of the General Election or for the vague promise to establish independent stations becoming a reality. They already had debts of NZ$8,000 and needed to put their offshore station on the air and earning revenue as soon as possible.

Jack Scott then offered to personally approach the station's creditors and try and persuade them to wait for payment pending a decision on Radio Hauraki's future. As a compromise it was eventually agreed that the Minister would also try and persuade the NZBC Board to award a contract to Radio Hauraki to provide programmes for station 1YD in Auckland. In return Radio Hauraki agreed to keep their ship in port until the NZBC Board's decision was known.

Morale at Radio Hauraki reached an all time low at this point as the various authorities continued to procrastinate on decisions relating to the survey of the *Tiri* and the supply of programme material to station 1YD. On 29th September 1966, two days before the station's original planned on-air date the Radio Hauraki team met to decide their next move. Some wanted to wait a while longer to see if the Minister could convince the NZBC Board to award them a programme supply contract, others were in favour of sailing the *Tiri* out to sea immediately and starting broadcasts. Eventually, by a narrow majority, it was decided to keep the *Tiri* in port pending a decision from the NZBC Board.

Most of the Radio Hauraki team took part time jobs to earn some money while they waited, but throughout October 1966 the signs from NZBC became less and less encouraging. After a further staff meeting on 15th October 1966 it was decided they would wait no longer and secret plans were prepared to sail the *Tiri* at midnight on Saturday 22nd October 1966. The day before the planned sailing date the NZBC Board finally issued a statement saying that an inquiry was being set up to examine the question of private radio companies supplying their stations with programme material. A real decision from the NZBC still appeared a long time away and, if it were needed, this latest statement reinforced Radio Hauraki's own decision to press ahead with their offshore plans.

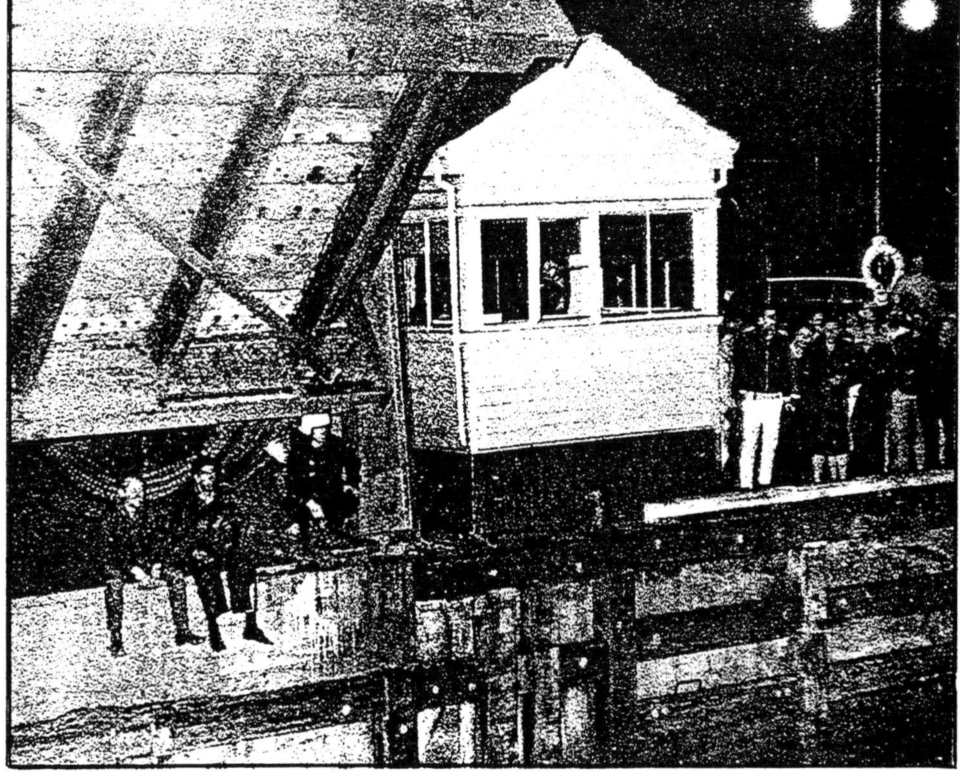

*Brian Strong, David Gapes and Peter Telling sitting in the jaws of the bridge*

## Dramatic sailing

Preparations to sail the *Tiri* from the Western Viaduct, including re-fitting the propeller, did not go unnoticed, however, and by the evening of Saturday 22nd October 1966 the *Auckland Star* was carrying a story predicting that the 'pirates' would set sail at 11.30pm that night. Shortly after this news had been published police arrived in strength at the *Tiri's* berth and warned David Gapes and Derek Lowe of the consequences for them if they violated the ship's detention order. At about the same time too, the police launch *Deodar* took up position outside the entrance to the Lighter Basin.

A surprise arrival at the Western Viaduct later that evening was Minister Jack Scott who tried to persuade the Radio Hauraki team not to set sail and to give him 24 hours to try and convince the NZBC Board to change its mind about the supply of programme material. The Hauraki men agreed to the Minister's suggestion, not because they expected a change of mind from the NZBC, but because the propeller had still not been fully re-fitted to the ship and the extra time would be valuable, indeed essential, if the *Tiri* was to leave under her own power.

On Sunday 23rd October 1966 work on refitting the propeller to the *Tiri* was completed and, watched throughout the day by an increasingly large crowd on the quayside, plans continued for the ship to set sail. Jack Scott made one last attempt to persuade the Radio Hauraki people to postpone sailing, but to no avail and by 8.00pm that evening the decision had been made to slip the *Tiri* from her berth and head for the open sea.

Throughout the evening the crowd, as well as a large contingent of police, watched and waited for signs of the *Tiri* making a move. The crew had already decided that an unexpected, sudden departure would be required if they were to evade the threat of forcible detention from the police present at the Western Viaduct Basin. Eventually one by one the mooring ropes were released and the *Tiri* slowly left the quayside, but one senior police officer, Inspector Ken Thompson, managed to leap on board before the vessel got into the centre of the Lighter Basin. Unfortunately for the Radio Hauraki team when the *Tiri* did reach the centre of the Basin there was insufficient water there and the ship became embedded in the mud.

At the same time the authorities had started to lower the road bridge across the entrance to the Basin, which would effectively block the *Tiri's* exit to the open sea. This action had been taken contrary to a promise given personally by Jack Scott that the bridge would not be lowered to prevent the ship leaving its berth. In a desperate attempt to prevent further lowering of the bridge three Radio Hauraki men, David Gapes, Peter Telling and Brian Strong positioned themselves in the jaw of the bridge, risking serious injury or even death by being crushed in the closing machinery. Warned of this danger by calls from the agitated crowd the authorities eventually switched off the power and stopped the bridge, leaving just enough space for the *Tiri* to sail through.

With help from the crowd who hauled on a rope thrown from the *Tiri*, the stranded radio ship was pulled from the mud and into a sufficient depth of water to enable her to sail once again under her own power. Just as the *Tiri* passed beneath the partially lowered road bridge the ship's mast became entangled on the tip of the structure. Two more of the Hauraki team, Colin Broadley and Ian Magan then climbed the 50 degree sloping bridge, secured a rope halfway up the mast, threw the other end of it to the crowd, and positioned themselves at the very top edge of the bridge. In a joint effort with the crowd, who took the strain of the rope, Colin Broadley used his feet to force the tip of the mast past the edge of the road bridge. However, just as this obstacle was cleared part of the *Tiri's* superstructure hit the road bridge and the impact swung the ship sideways, completely blocking the Basin entrance.

This gave police the opportunity they needed. Three officers climbed from the quayside onto the Tiri while the police launch *Deodar* came alongside and more policemen were then able to scramble aboard the radio ship. Scuffles broke out on board between the police, who were in the majority, and Radio Hauraki staff.

Meanwhile, in all this confusion Hauraki man Murray McGill climbed the mast and secured another rope for the crowd to pull. This time the *Tiri* cleared the bridge and sailed full ahead into the main harbour, with a contingent of police officers still on board.

Once clear of the quayside crowds and the lights of the television launch which had followed for a short distance, the police who were trapped on board the *Tiri* started taking tough action, forcing their way to the engine room, disconnecting the fuel line and eventually stopping the main engine. With the radio ship immobilised the police launch *Deodar* drew alongside once again and took the eleven Radio Hauraki men off to face charges of obstructing Marine Department inspectors and defying the detention order which had been placed on the *Tiri* five weeks earlier.

A special court hearing was convened at 2.00am on Monday 24th October 1966 when, despite police arguments that they should be kept in custody in case they tried once again to take the *Tiri* out to sea, all defendants were granted bail. However, with the abandoned radio ship now under armed guard at the Devonport Naval Base any action of this sort by Radio Hauraki seemed an improbability.

## Public support

Following the arrest of the *Tiri* and her crew there was a huge surge in public support for Radio Hauraki, with much criticism being levelled at Jack Scott, who was seen as being responsible for preventing the radio ship putting to sea. Given the backroom negotiations which Scott and Radio Hauraki's directors had held to try and resolve the situation and his discussions with NZBC on behalf of Hauraki, much of this criticism was not warranted, but the public at that time were unaware of all the activity which had taken place behind the scenes between the opposing sides.

Jack Scott did issue a statement blaming the NZBC for not making up its mind about commissioning programmes from private radio stations for its YD network, but at the same time he criticised Radio Hauraki for not being prepared to wait for a decision on their application for a land-based licence. He also made it clear that although the Government was aware of public demand for Radio Hauraki's service it would not condone the offshore station's 'maverick activities'.

*Supporters outside Aukland Town Hall*

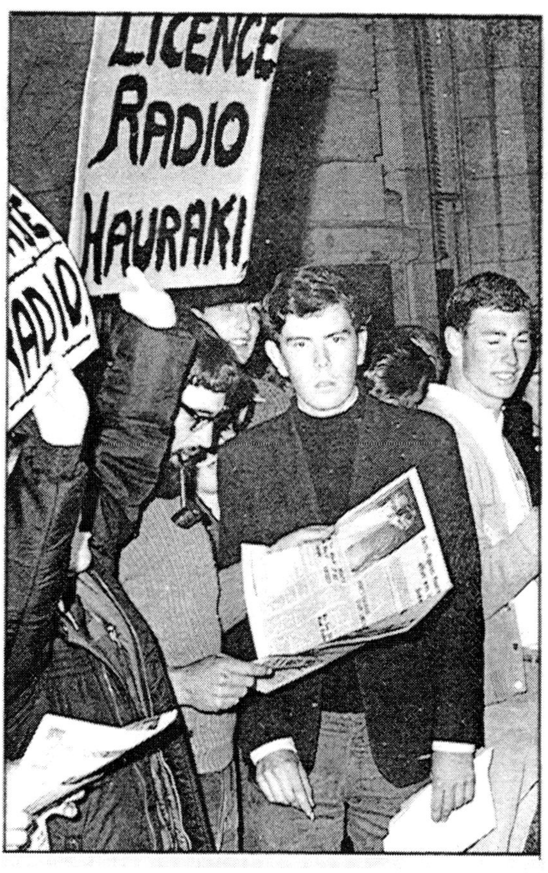


Meanwhile Radio Hauraki's directors decided to capitalise on the surge in public support following the incident at the Western Viaduct and hurriedly arranged a public meeting in Auckland Town Hall to protest at the Government's handling of the whole issue of private broadcasting.

The meeting was arranged for Wednesday 26th October 1966 and the Radio Hauraki team spent two days publicising the event throughout the City with posters and leaflets. Their efforts were rewarded when on the night crowds of supporters filled the 2,200 seats in the Town Hall, while hundreds more were locked outside the building. The audience, which seemed to represent a large cross section of the population, not just young people, heard Derek Lowe and David Gapes pledge that they would put Radio Hauraki on the air somehow, either from land or sea.

Following the meeting 1,000 people marched from the Town Hall to Freyberg Wharf where the *Tiri* (which had been returned to Radio Hauraki by the Marine Department earlier that day) was moored, but guarded by police. David Gapes appealed to the crowd to leave the Wharf and not cause any more trouble with the police, a request with which they obligingly complied. The significance of this meeting, and a similar one the following day in Hamilton, was that it demonstrated to the authorities the strength of public support for Radio Hauraki, even though the station had not yet even made a broadcast.

The Radio Hauraki team appeared at Auckland Magistrates Court on 2nd November 1966 to face the various charges against them. Roger Maclaren, solicitor for Pacific Radio Advertising, appeared on behalf of the four directors and barrister Paul Temn appeared for the other six members of the Radio Hauraki crew who had been arrested on 24th October 1966. The two Hauraki lawyers believed strongly that their clients had a good case and had subpoenaed Government Minister Jack Scott to appear at Court to testify as a witness.

Prosecuting Counsel, David Morris called Albert Wall, district surveyor at the Marine Department to testify that in mid-September 1966 the *Tiri* had been detained pending completion of a satisfactory survey. However, under cross examination Mr. Wall had to concede that he had actually been instructed by the Minister in Wellington not to complete the survey which had been arranged with the ship's owners. He also admitted that the *Tiri's* hull was not necessarily unsafe, as had earlier been suggested by his Department. Defence lawyers also managed to elicit from witnesses that Jack Scott, as Minister for Marine as well as Broadcasting, had imposed the detention order on the *Tiri* for politically motivated rather than safety reasons and had thus exceeded his powers in law. Maclaren, having established enough of a case on behalf of his clients from the cross examination of prosecution witnesses did not, in the end, call Jack Scott to give the Court his version of events.

The magistrate, Mr. L.G.H.. Sinclair, gave his verdict on 7th November 1966 and concluded that Jack Scott had indeed misused his Ministerial powers relating to marine surveys in order to prevent the *Tiri* being taken to sea and used as a base for an offshore radio station. The charges against the Radio Hauraki team were all dismissed.

ORDER HOLDS PIRATE RADIO SHIP

*Pirate radio ship stopped*

Minister Calls For Survey

'Pirates' off coast of N. Zealand

## Radio Hauraki launched

With the court case behind them jubilant Radio Hauraki directors now set about planning to secretly and quietly sail the *Tiri* from Freyberg Wharf to the open sea. Departure date was set for 10th November 1966 at 10.00pm, when the tide would be in their favour, and the Wharf virtually deserted. The decision to go to sea had been prompted by further petty harassments from the authorities, in particular the Marine Department who were still finding faults to be rectified before they would grant the *Tiri* a seaworthiness certificate.

This time the departure plan went like clockwork, with the *Tiri* sailing almost silently past the Wharf gatekeeper and into the open sea before anyone in authority realised that she had gone. On board were five Radio Hauraki crew and six journalists, who had been promised the exclusive story of the ship's sailing in return for their silence in the hours before departure. Finally at 6.30am on 11th November 1966 the *Tiri* dropped anchor at her mooring in the triangle of international waters within the Hauraki Gulf.

After having waited for so long to sail its vessel out to sea the planned timetable for launching Radio Hauraki was a tight one - test transmissions to begin at 6.00am on 12th November 1966, with station identity announcements every half hour; two hours of continuous music from 9.00am and regular programmes commencing at 11.00am with a documentary about the history of the station's fight to get on the air.

With the aerial mast still in pre-fabricated sections on the *Tiri's* deck the crew realised it would be impossible to have it erected and working in time for the planned start of transmissions, so they set about creating a temporary aerial by stringing hundreds of metres of wire between the ship's own masts. Unfortunately this work on the aerial as well as tuning the station's transmitter took much longer than had been anticipated and the planned 6.00am opening of Radio Hauraki was not achieved. It was not until 5.00pm that day, 12th November 1966, that everything was ready for the first test broadcast to start, then just as power was fed to the transmitter an output valve blew and with no spare part on board the ship Radio Hauraki was forced to remain silent.

*'Tiri' at anchor in the Hauraki Gulf*

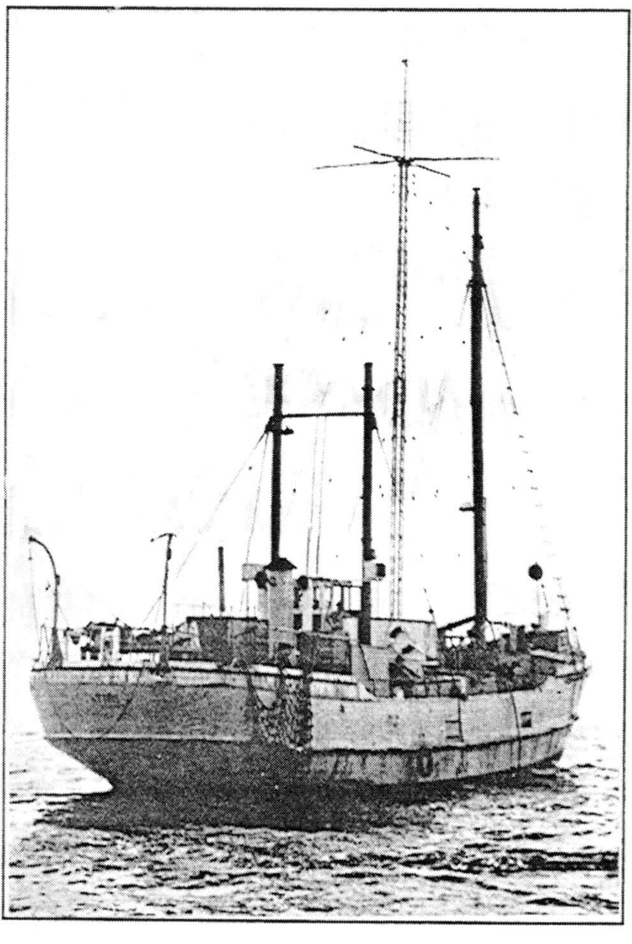

During the night and much of the following day a severe storm tossed the *Tiri* at her anchorage and the crew on board suffered their first experience of sea sickness. After about 48 hours the storm eventually receded and the Radio Hauraki crew renewed their efforts to put the station on the air. However, there were further unexpected transmitter problems and it was not until a week later - the afternoon of 21st November 1966 - that Radio Hauraki broadcast its first, weak, test signal. Although many listeners telephoned the station's Auckland offices to say they had heard the transmission it quickly became apparent that the signal was not powerful enough to reach the size of audience the station needed to be commercially successful. Further weak broadcasts would have been futile so the directors decided to stop the tests while the permanent aerial mast was erected on board the *Tiri*.

On 26th November 1966 the radio ship tied up at Port Tryphena on Great Barrier Island to enable the crew to erect the aerial mast. They built the first 50' by using the ship's on-board winch, but it was impossible for this method to be used to extend the mast any higher. An attempt at using a helicopter to hoist the upper sections into place was also unsuccessful, so in the end professional riggers had to be engaged to complete the work.

Over 100' of mast was erected, which together with a 30' telescopic aerial, was considered sufficient to produce a good signal for the station's target area. During the evening of 1st December 1966 the *Tiri* sailed back to her anchorage in the Coleville Channel and at about 8.00pm test transmissions were resumed. This time the signal was loud and clear throughout Auckland and the surrounding area. DJ Bob Leahy announced: *You're listening to Radio Hauraki, Top of the Dial, and we're broadcasting a test transmission on 1480.* He went on to ask for reception reports and as a result of this first real test broadcast over 12,500 letters were received by the station's Auckland office.

Success was short-lived, however. The next day, 2nd December 1966, another storm blew through the Coleville Channel and it was decided to sail the *Tiri* back into Port Tryphena for shelter. Before the ship reached port disaster struck when the newly erected aerial mast collapsed over the side and, for the safety of those on board, its remains had to be cut away and abandoned.

Once safely in port the crew set about erecting a replacement mast, using a spare 50' section of the original structure with a 20' whip aerial mounted at the top. With this new arrangement in place the *Tiri* once again took up her position in international waters and test broadcasts resumed at 9.00am on 4th December 1966, although the signal was not as clear as the transmissions a few days earlier with the original, taller mast.

Two hours later, at 11.00am, Radio Hauraki started regular broadcasts with a documentary programme about the history of the station and the background to the people who had been involved in bringing it on the air. So revolutionary was the concept of Radio Hauraki that this first programme included a detailed explanation of what Top 40 format radio was and how it would sound.

Throughout the week that followed Radio Hauraki steadily built up a large audience, despite frequent technical breakdowns and a sometimes faltering signal. Advertisers too seemed happy to use the station to reach a new market sector who had not previously been attracted to the NZBC stations - young people with money to spend. For its part the NZBC tried to counter the impact of Radio Hauraki's programmes by extending the broadcasting hours of its two stations in the Auckland area 1ZB and 1YD, but the young audience still preferred the offshore station, even with (or perhaps because of) all its technical and reception problems.

One of these problem was finally resolved in January 1967 when a 70' telescopic extension was placed on top of the *Tiri's* 50' lattice mast, considerably improving the station's signal and giving advertisers a larger potential audience.

Now that Radio Hauraki was on the air the station was able to earn much needed revenue from advertising, estimated to be about NZ$13,000 in the first month alone. However, the position remained precarious and the company had little financial management experience within its ranks even to produce an accurate set of accounts. The station had many creditors, some of whom were willing to bankrupt the company if necessary in order to recover their money, so professional accountants had to be brought in to sort out the mess.

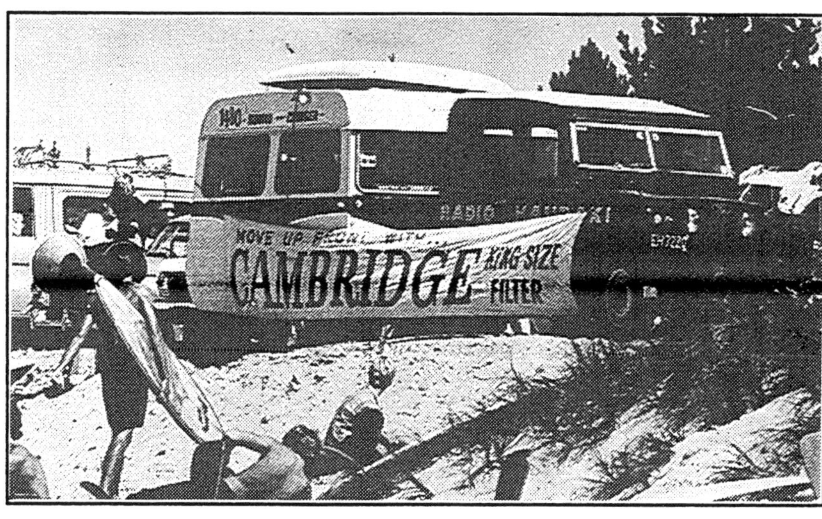


1480 Sound Cruiser

A system of instalment payments was arranged with the largest creditors to stave off the threat of bankruptcy proceedings being taken against the station and proper charging systems for collecting advertising revenue were quickly put in place.

## Expansion and popularity

A significant success was achieved in January 1967 when Coca Cola agreed to buy airtime on Radio Hauraki and a number of other major advertisers soon followed suit, providing much needed additional revenue for the station. By June 1967 Radio Hauraki employed a staff of 58 and had managed to make a trading profit during the previous three months.

A second studio was constructed in the Auckland land-based offices to cope with the increased programme and commercial production requirements of the station. The equipment from this studio was capable of also being fitted into a caravan which toured beach areas as the '1480 Sound Cruiser' promoting the station.

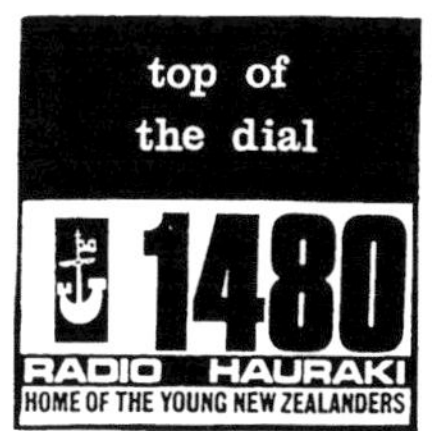


Radio Hauraki's record library was also enlarged as it now had a source of supply for material which had not yet been released by the record companies in New Zealand - many overseas visitors and contacts regularly brought records into the country and freely passed them on to the station. An Air New Zealand steward provided the station with a particularly valuable weekly supply of new American releases when returning from regular trips to Los Angeles.

The result of this sudden new influx of material was that demand from listeners for discs of the latest overseas hits grew enormously. The record companies had to respond by speeding up the release of such records in New Zealand - which traditionally had lacked behind the more dynamic British and American markets. Radio Hauraki also boosted the local music industry by adopting a policy that one in every six records played should be by a New Zealand artist and it was not long before listener demand for copies of such recordings also forced the large music companies to engage and promote more local musicians.

A similar situation to that which had occurred in Britain during the early days of offshore radio soon began to develop between Radio Hauraki and the New Zealand record industry. The New Zealand Record Federation publicly criticised the continuous playing of pop records by Radio Hauraki as a potential threat to its members' record sales, but behind the scenes representatives of the individual record companies quietly made sure, as had their counterparts in Britain, that the offshore station received pre-release copies of all new recordings.

The Record Federation also sought an injunction through the courts to prevent Radio Hauraki using its member companies' records in pre-recorded programmes. Clearly this single action, had it succeeded, would have meant the end of operations for the station as nearly all programme material was pre-recorded in the land-based studios. Radio Hauraki therefore had little choice but to very reluctantly agree to pay NZ$11,000 a year in 'copyright fees' to the Federation, which then dropped the threatened court action.

### 1480 Club

*A listeners' club - the 1480 Club - was launched soon after Radio Hauraki started and quickly gained over 2,000 members who were offered station promotional material and discount vouchers to spend at participating local shops. The 1480 Club also promoted dance nights and concerts, the revenue from which provided a further source of income for the cash-strapped station.*

Tendering the *Tiri* was, in many respects, more difficult and expensive than the equivalent operation for the European offshore stations. Because, for geographical and legal reasons, the radio ship had to be anchored over 20 miles from Auckland, crew, supplies and programme tapes were usually flown to Tryphena Harbour to Claris Airfield on Great Barrier Island and were then ferried to the ship by local fisherman Bill Gibbs using his launch *Marauder*. Gibbs voluntarily made his services available to Radio Hauraki, including the use of accommodation at his home for crew transferring to and from the *Tiri*, and without this generous facility the station would undoubtedly have encountered many more supply problems. Occasionally late programme tapes or urgent supplies were dropped from a plane in water-tight canisters, landing in the sea close to the *Tiri* from where the crew were able to retrieve them.

Water and fuel supplies were more problematic. When the station first went on the air Bill Gibbs brought water to the ship in small containers, or allowed the *Tiri* to tie up at his private jetty and draw water from his domestic supply tanks. Later Radio Hauraki purchased an old whaling station wharf at Whangaparapara Harbour and it was then possible for the *Tiri* to sail in, tie up and have her tanks filled from a permanent supply pipe on the site.

Diesel fuel, in 44 gallon drums, was at first brought to the ship on local fishing boats working in the Hauraki Gulf area, but later the radio ship took fuel supplies on board when visiting Whangaparapara, often during the hours of darkness and while still broadcasting!

Broadcasting from inside New Zealand territorial waters was not unusual for Radio Hauraki, although this fact and the story behind it was not admitted publicly for many years. One night in June 1967 the radio ship broke from her anchor and drifted through the Colville Passage, narrowly escaping shipwreck on Great Barrier Island. After this incident it was decided to lay a permanent mooring buoy secured to the sea bed to which the *Tiri* could be attached and removed without having to raise or drop her own anchor.

The mooring buoy was anchored to the sea bed at a point calculated to be three miles from Pirogue Rocks off Great Barrier Island, but on checking the ship's position some time later the crew discovered that she was in fact only 2.8 miles from land and actually inside territorial waters. However, because the mooring buoy was so secure the station remained broadcasting from that position for the rest of its time at sea. The crew and directors of Radio Hauraki were surprised, but pleased, that the authorities did not appear to have realised the ship's precise position because if they had action could legitimately have been taken to board and seize the *Tiri*. It was not until later that they discovered the true situation. After Radio Hauraki had finished broadcasting at sea David Gapes and Derek Lowe visited Jack Scott in his office at the New Zealand Parliament in Wellington. Scott produced from a locked cupboard a dossier prepared by the Post Office containing full details and information about the *Tiri's* true mooring position inside territorial waters.

Although no action was taken against the radio ship at its mooring the authorities did take a very different view about the *Tiri's* visits to refuel at the Whangaparapara Wharf while Radio Hauraki was still transmitting. The Government took action against the station over this activity after repeated reports appeared in the local press about the *Tiri's* visits to port while Radio Hauraki was on the air and opposition party pressure began to grow in Parliament for anti-offshore broadcasting legislation to be introduced.

Post Office officials were sent to Great Barrier Island to watch the *Tiri's* movements closely, but because of generally good relations with the local population the crew of Radio Hauraki were able to receive advance warnings that a raid was about to take place, giving them time to sail the radio ship back to her moorings.

In November 1967 anti-offshore broadcasting legislation, based on the British Marine etc. Broadcasting (Offences) Act, was finally introduced into the New Zealand Parliament and referred to a Select Committee for detailed consideration. Subsequently a Broadcasting Authority Bill was also introduced which provided for the establishment of a new independent body to consider and grant licences for private radio and television stations. This Bill too, was referred to a Select Committee and it was estimated that it would take nearly a year before either piece of legislation could pass onto the statute books. Radio Hauraki it seemed was secure at sea for another year at least.

## Dramatic end

After 13 successful and relatively trouble free months on the air drama came unexpectedly to Radio Hauraki in January 1968. On 28th January the *Tiri* spent most of the day sailing in the area between Great Barrier Island and Little Barrier Island searching for a seaman who had fallen overboard from the launch *Weatherley*. The summer weather was good and the sea was calm all day while the *Tiri's* crew undertook the search. The radio ship herself performed well, with newly refurbished engines showing no sign of faltering at any time throughout the day's cruise.

By 5.00pm, with daylight fading and not having found the missing man, the *Tiri's* Captain, Lloyd Griffiths, decided to return the radio ship to her mooring. However, when she reached the area it was too dark to locate the mooring buoy so the crew, DJs and technicians took it in turns to maintain a watch to ensure that the *Tiri* did not accidentally drift towards land. Unfortunately, at that point the *Tiri's* engines, which had performed so well all day, began to fail leaving the ship without a means of propulsion in addition to having no secure mooring for the night. The problem was traced to a water pump which had seized, causing the engine to overheat and all attempts to instal an auxiliary pump proved unsuccessful.

Without sufficient power to hold the vessel in position and with an increasing south west wind blowing there was a real danger that the *Tiri* would be driven onto rocks at Great Barrier Island. The crew did everything they could to prevent this happening, but despite their efforts the *Tiri* did begin to drift and at about 11.15pm she hit the rocks. DJ Paul Lineham interrupted a pre-recorded programme with live Mayday messages asking listeners to phone the emergency services and alert them to the radio ship's plight. As these announcements were being made listeners could clearly hear in the background the noise of the *Tiri* as she crashed against the rocks.

Captain Lloyd Griffiths briefly managed to get the engine started and for a while the *Tiri* was able to manoeuvre herself clear of the rocks, but after several minutes the engine cut out again and the radio ship, now beam on, drifted helplessly back towards the shore.

In a final, desperate attempt to save the ship the crew tried to drop the emergency anchor but it failed to hold and the *Tiri,* driven by strong winds and pounded by the heavy sea, struck the rocks outside Whangaparapara Harbour again and again, each crash heard clearly by anxious listeners to what seemed inevitably would be Radio Hauraki's final broadcast. What appeared to be a closing announcement was made by Derek King who, after telling listeners that the crew were abandoning ship, left the microphone open so every creak and crash could be heard as the vessel hit the rocks :-

*We have hit. We are hitting continuously now. I don't know how long I can stay with you. There, we've gone again. That was rather a bad one actually. Ahhh. We have gone aground on Whangaparapara.* In the background listeners could hear the ship's siren. *There! Abandon ship. Abandon ship. I am turning the microphone up now. Abandon ship. Abandon ship. The siren has gone we are abandoning ship. The rocks are within swimming distance, we've got to go now. I'll turn the microphone up loud now. I hope the transmitter lasts out. We are abandoning ship. Our situation is in the Whangaparapara Harbour. I love you Mum and Dad.*

A minute or two later DJ Paul Lineham returned to the studio and announced that despite everything he was going to try and present a programme. He started playing a record but 20 seconds of music later he, too, announced that they were having to abandon ship. After Paul Lineham played a couple of Radio Hauraki jingles the station's transmitter went silent.

On land listeners had jammed the rescue and emergency service's switchboards with calls for them to help the *Tiri,* but assistance reached the radio ship first in the form of Bill Gibbs and his vessel *Marauder.* This launch, together with two others which arrived shortly after, made repeated but unsuccessful attempts to pull the *Tiri* off the rocks. Having been unable to rescue the *Tiri,* her crew and radio staff abandoned the vessel for their own safety and swam ashore through the heavy seas, spending the night on a beach until daybreak revealed the full extent of the radio ship's plight.

The *Tiri* had been pounded against the rocks all night and had over five feet of water in her hull covering much of the station's studio and transmitting equipment. After a brief examination of the vessel David Gapes decided that before towing the *Tiri* off the rocks all possible efforts should be made to salvage the vital transmitter and broadcasting equipment so that the station could return to the air as soon as possible from another vessel if necessary.

Insurance assessors later advised that once re-floated the *Tiri* could be

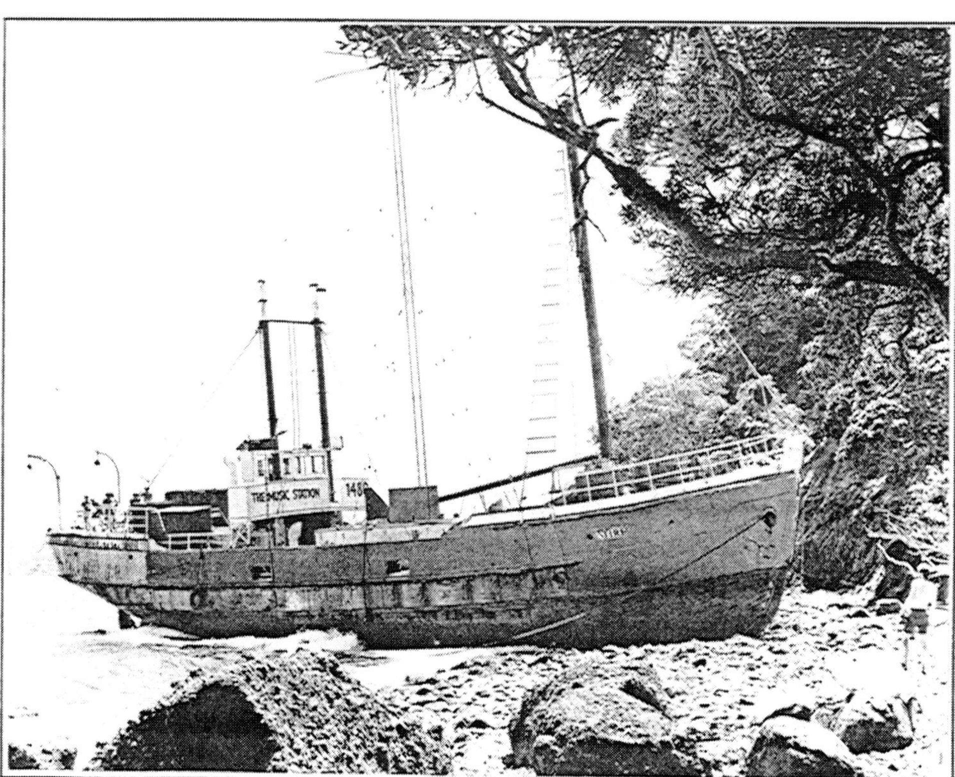

*'Tiri' shipwrecked on Whangaparapara beach*

satisfactorily repaired, - the damage to her hull was not as extensive as had at first been feared. Unfortunately it would take up to four months to complete the repair work and this was a period during which Radio Hauraki could not afford to be off the air .

On the Monday after the storm, 30th January 1968 the *Sea Toiler* pulled *Tiri* from the rocks and, after temporary patches had been welded to her hull, she was towed to Auckland, but her role as a radio ship was already finished.

## Re-launch

The directors and staff of Radio Hauraki had decided to continue operating the station, despite the financial hardship this would create both for the company and for each employee personally while no income was being generated and within days of the dramatic storm the station had received four offers of replacement ships. Quite quickly David Gapes and his team decided that the offer from their long-standing friend Jim Frankham of the vessel *Kapuni* was the best hope for the radio station's quick return.

Conversion work started almost immediately to turn the *Kapuni,* now renamed *Tiri II* into a radio ship. A 160' aerial mast was installed to provide improved reception for the station, the transmitter, which had been removed from the original *Tiri,* was steam cleaned and repaired before being installed on the *Tiri II* and a new, larger studio was also constructed on board.

Within an incredible three weeks all work had been completed and at 1.15am on 27th February 1968 the *Tiri II* left Auckland for her anchorage in international waters. Test transmissions on low power began at 5.00pm that evening and regular programmes from Radio Hauraki started once again at 7.30am on 28th February 1968. Radio Hauraki was back in business less than a month after the station's original vessel had been dashed against the rocks outside Whangaparapara Harbour.

All did not go as smoothly as planned, however, and the station was frequently off the air during March 1968 with transmitter problems. On 27th March 1968 the *Tiri II* broke from her mooring buoy and began to drift in a storm during which four insulators shattered and guy ropes holding the 160' mast in place were whipped around in the wind. As a safety precaution Radio Hauraki's transmissions were halted and the *Tiri II* made for Whangaparapara Harbour, where she eventually arrived three hours later, after a journey that in good weather would normally have taken less than an hour.

Repairs were hurriedly carried out and the station was able to return to the air on 31st March 1968, but relief was short-lived. At 6.00pm on 3rd April the new mooring chain snapped during another a storm which this time had gusts of up to 80 knots pounding the ship. Captain Lloyd Griffiths again took the ship into Whangaparapara, but experienced difficulty steering his vessel into the harbour entrance. Help arrived again from Bill Gibbs in the *Marauder,* but when an attempt to tow the radio ship failed, both vessels were forced to stay at sea overnight and ride out the storm.

The *Tiri II's* water pumps failed during the night and again the insulators were smashed, leaving the aerial mast free to swing as the ship pitched and rolled in the

*'Tiri II' takes over broadcasts for Radio Hauraki*

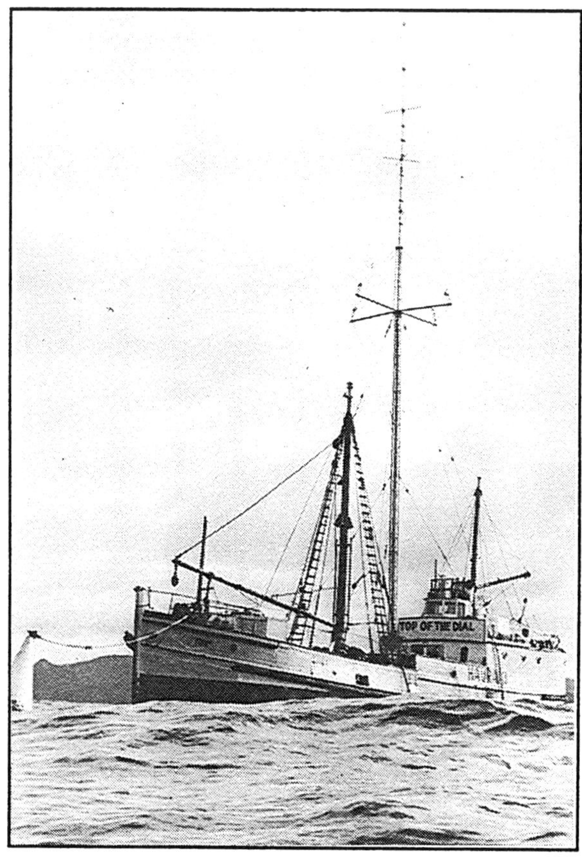

raging seas. Outriggers used to secure the mast's guy wires, which were normally about 25' above sea level, plunged below the water as the waves broke across the radio ship while the crew, wearing life jackets in case an emergency evacuation was needed, feared that the ship would sink or capsize at any moment.

Still experiencing severe problems with steering the *Tiri II* Lloyd Griffiths had to allow the radio ship to be driven by the storm on a course which would eventually take the vessel towards Auckland. The Navy minesweeper *Inverell* left Devonport at midnight to offer assistance and stood by the *Tiri II* in Whangaparapara Channel throughout the night until at first light a tug, *Otapiri,* was able to tow the radio ship into port.

On 7th April 1968, with storm damage repairs completed the *Tiri II* left once again for her anchorage, but began broadcasting only half an hour after leaving port. The Radio Hauraki staff decided that the station had already lost enough advertising revenue during the last few weeks and were determined to get back to business as quickly as they could, even if that meant broadcasting from well inside territorial waters.

Unfortunately, more than just advertising revenue had been lost during those frequent periods off the air. One of the founder partners of the station, and its technical genius, Dennis O'Callaghan decided to leave Radio Hauraki because he could no longer condone the risks staff on board *Tiri II* were being asked to take during storms such as had recently been experienced. The other two founder-directors, David Gapes and Derek Lowe, although also very much concerned about the safety of their staff, felt that if the station closed at that point there would be little of either the Radio Hauraki organisation, or strong public support left when the promised land-based licences were granted. In a desperate bid to find a middle course they requested permission from the Government for Radio Hauraki to anchor its ship in more sheltered waters within territorial limits. Pending a decision on this request the Captain of *Tiri II* was instructed to leave the mooring position and head for shelter whenever weather conditions became too rough and endangered the lives of those on board the radio ship.

This was a timely instruction because, after just 24 hours back at her mooring, the *Tiri II* was taken to Whangaparapara Wharf on 9th April 1968 and secured firmly to the wooden jetty after weather reports had forecast a severe tropical storm and 80mph winds heading towards the Hauraki Gulf area. By coincidence that same day the station heard from the new Broadcasting Minister, Lance Adams Schneider, that their request to be allowed to anchor inside territorial waters had been refused.

When the storm eventually arrived it was even more severe than had been forecast and during 100mph gusts the *Tiri II* was wrenched from the wooden jetty, taking some bollards with her. Captain Lloyd Griffiths briefly managed to turn the ship, but she was driven helplessly onto rocks, where she was pounded continuously throughout the night. The aerial mast was destroyed during the storm and when the tide receded the stranded radio ship was left high and dry, cradled between two rocks. That same ferocious storm swept southwards across New Zealand and went on to sink the inter-island ferry, *Wahine* in the entrance to Wellington Harbour, killing 54 people.

On the next high tide the tug *Otapiri* managed to pull *Tiri II* off the rocks and she was moored at Whangaparapara Wharf while repairs were carried out. Meanwhile Radio Hauraki returned to the air on reduced power by running an aerial wire from the ship, along the wharf and securing it to a tree at the top of a nearby cliff about 100' above sea level. This gave the station some sort of signal while the mast from the original *Tiri,* which had been kept on board the new ship for just such an emergency, was erected.

The temporary aerial arrangement was short-lived, however. The crew were forced to discontinue transmissions the following day (11th April 1968) when the Naval fisheries protection vessel *Ahuriri* anchored just offshore from *Tiri II's* berth, keeping the radio ship under constant surveillance. Meanwhile, erection of the replacement aerial mast was completed by 15th April 1968 (Easter Monday) and *Tiri II* was able to return to her moorings, with Radio Hauraki transmissions resuming at 6.00pm. By then of course all airtime over the important Easter holiday weekend, with its premium advertising potential, had been lost, but nevertheless the station continued to transmit pre-booked commercials in an effort to earn some much needed revenue.

An indication of just how important the ability to earn advertising revenue was to the station at that time came a few days later. On 21st April 1968, after being forced yet again to seek shelter in port during the night, Captain Lloyd Griffiths authorised Radio Hauraki's transmissions to start again at noon, with the vessel still in port. Every available hour the station was on the air meant there was an opportunity for income to be earned from the transmission of commercials and the risk of being caught broadcasting inside territorial limits seemed, financially at least, to be worthwhile.

Unfortunately for Radio Hauraki Post Office radio inspectors were monitoring the *Tiri II's* transmissions that day and, with the help of radio direction finding equipment and aerial photographs taken of the radio ship in port at the time, they managed to obtain conclusive evidence of illegal broadcasting taking place from inside New Zealand's territorial waters. Similar evidence was obtained by the Post Office on a further two occasions when the *Tiri II* was caught broadcasting inside territorial limits, having sought shelter during the worst storms in living memory.

The dilemma facing Radio Hauraki at this critical time was an unenviable one -should the station remain off the air during adverse weather conditions when its ship had been forced to seek shelter, with the consequent loss of listeners and valuable advertising income - both so vital to its future existence, or stay at sea and earn revenue by continuing to make broadcasts from sheltered waters inside territorial limits, taking a chance of being prosecuted by the authorities?

## More storms

It was a decision that had to be made again a few weeks later. On 13th June 1968 Captain Lloyd Griffiths decided to leave the mooring position in the knowledge of a weather forecast promising Force 9 gales and rough seas with waves of over 20'. However, the storm arrived much sooner than expected and when it did turned out to be even more severe than forecast - even worse than the *Wahine* storm a few months earlier - gales of 120mph and waves 30' - 40' high. With the ship unable to reach port on-air DJ Ian Ferguson described conditions for the benefit of listeners and staff in Radio Hauraki's Auckland office:-

*Conditions are still unchanged, very rough and very uncomfortable out here. All the floors of the ship are a real shambles. In the messroom it really is a messroom. There are broken cups and bits of bread and butter and beetroot juice and knives and forks. Down in the studio the place is littered with records and tapes and a radio and typewriter are lying on the floor. From the transmitter room we've lost our oscilloscope. This is the scene all over the ship. Not very good at all, not very confident, but, you know, we'll make it.*

At about 9.30pm transmissions were stopped because of the appalling weather conditions and throughout the night *Tiri II* continued to be battered by the storm.

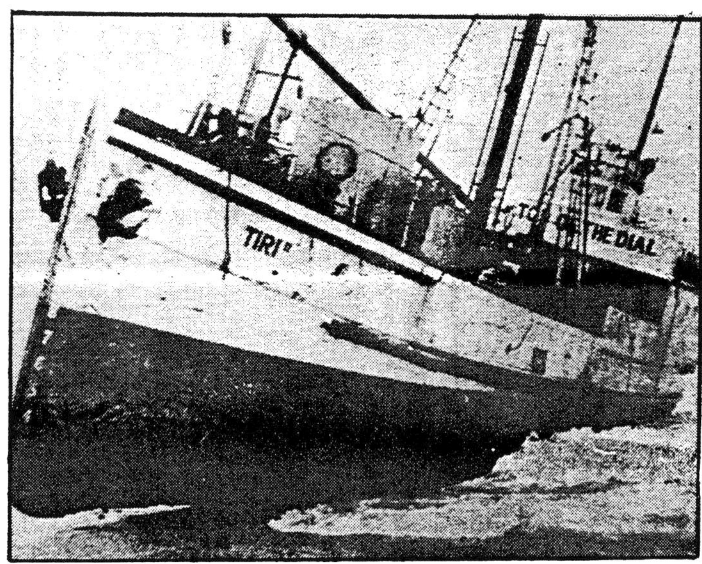

'Tiri II' on Uretiti Beach

Finally, at about 6.30am on 14th June 1968 she ran aground on Uretiti Beach, having been driven some 50 miles from her anchorage. Once again the vessel had to be rescued and towed back to Auckland for repairs, including the installation of another new 130' aerial mast. Two weeks later *Tiri II* sailed back to her mooring and Radio Hauraki began broadcasting again on 1st July 1968.

While Radio Hauraki itself had been undergoing some trying and testing times the legislative process had been continuing in the New Zealand Parliament. In September 1968 two Bills - the Broadcasting Authority Bill (designed to establish private land-based commercial radio stations) and the Post Office Amendment Bill (No 2) (designed to outlaw offshore radio stations) - came before the New Zealand House of Representatives for their second and third readings. After ten days debate the Bills were eventually passed by 37 votes to 31, but it was to be another eight months before the new Broadcasting Authority established under the legislation started to accept applications for licences from would-be private broadcasters.

Now that the legislation authorising privately owned land-based radio stations had been enacted Radio Hauraki also established a separate public company, Radio Hauraki (NZ) Ltd. This company offered 215,000 of its shares for sale to the public on 9th June 1969 and within 24 hours the issue closed, having been heavily over subscribed. Nevertheless every one of the 678 applicants was subsequently allocated a proportion of shares.

With the assistance of an Australia broadcasting consultancy Radio Hauraki (NZ) Ltd. prepared and submitted a licence application to the Broadcasting Authority before the advertised deadline at the end of July 1969. The company also took an option on a plot of land in Aukland to build its transmitter should the application be successful as well as placing provisional orders for a variety of technical equipment.

Four other groups also submitted their proposals to operate radio stations in the Auckland area at this time:-

## Tea Council to the rescue

*The frequent and repeated periods off the air during the winter of 1968 meant that Radio Hauraki had lost a lot of advertising revenue and it became harder and harder to sell airtime to potential advertisers who were sceptical about the certainty of their commercial being broadcast. Another dilemma now faced Radio Hauraki - if it was to succeed in its long term objective of obtaining a land-based licence, the offshore station had to be kept on the air, but with such a dramatic fall in advertising revenue debts to suppliers quickly mounted up and potential bankruptcy loomed. As a temporary way out of this seemingly impossible situation Radio Hauraki started offering suppliers contra-deals - free commercial airtime in payment for goods and services. Even advertisers who paid for airtime (and there were still a few) were given up to four or even six extra spots, free of charge, as a goodwill gesture to ensure their continued loyalty to the station. Although a convenient way of paying for supplies in the short term this situation clearly could not continue, so David Gapes and Derek Lowe set about trying to obtain a major advertising contract which would produce substantial income for the station.*

*Through various contacts in the advertising industry they discovered that the newly established New Zealand Tea Council was about to launch a big campaign, aimed at converting young people away from drinking coffee and into the habit of consuming tea. Radio Hauraki, whose audience was predominantly young, put a proposal to the Tea Council - NZ$50,000 worth of airtime on the station over the following 12 months in return for NZ$20,000 cash immediately. Amazingly the proposal was accepted by the Tea Council and the station soon began endlessly promoting tea, with associated events including competitions, beach parties and star interviews, all geared to convincing the Radio Hauraki audience that tea was the best liquid refreshment available.*

- Radio International (Radio i), decendants of the old adversaries who in 1966 had planned an offshore station to rival Radio Hauraki, but never went ahead with the project;
- Radio Auckland Ltd - a joint venture by the City's two daily newspapers;
- Auckland Broadcasting Co - backed by two major New Zealand industrial companies,
- Radio Haeremai Ltd, funded by the Mormon Church.

An unexpected hitch occurred in August 1969 which temporarily put an end to this wave of optimism on the part of would-be private broadcasters, Radio Hauraki included. The NZBC chalenged the procedures which had been followed by the Broadcasting Authority in inviting applications and obtained a Supreme Court order preventing the allocation of licences in the Aukland area. After much legal discussion had taken place about procedural technicalities it was decided that applications for the Auckland area would have to be re-advertised by the Broadcasting Authority in November 1969.

A preliminary hearing was held by the Broadcasting Authority on 16th December 1969 when applications from the Auckland Broadcasting Co. and Radio Haeremai were dismissed because they did not contain the detailed technical information required. However, these two applicants did later win the right to have their proposals re-considered by giving an undertaking to supply the missing information to the Broadcasting Authority's full hearing in January 1970.

That full hearing began on 27th January 1970 and lasted for 10 days, during which all applicants were closely questioned about their plans. The Broadcasting Authority's decision was made known on 24th March 1970 when it announced that Radio Hauraki had been granted one of the two licences for the Auckland area, with the other being granted to Radio International (Radio i).

This landmark decision proved, more than anything else to David Gapes and his team that all the hardship and difficulties they had endured during the previous five years had been worthwhile. They had broken the NZBC monopoly and achieved what no other offshore station up to that time had done - won a licence to come ashore and broadcast legally.

## 24 hour broadcasts

*An indication of the greater optimism felt by Radio Hauraki at this time was the introduction, just before Christmas 1968, of 24 hours a day broadcasting - the first radio station in New Zealand to do so.*

## 1111 days at sea

Attention now turned to planning in detail for Radio Hauraki to commence its broadcasts from land, something which up until that point had only ever been a dream. A decision was made to close the offshore operation at 10.00 pm on 1st June 1970, 1111 days after Radio Hauraki had started its broadcasts from the original *Tiri*.

During the last three days of broadcasting from sea all programmes were presented live from the ship and even Radio Hauraki DJs from the landbased studios went on board the *Tiri II*. Commercial airtime was sold at premium rates for those three days and 'thank you' messages were recorded by major artists, including The Beatles, Elvis Presley and The Rolling Stones for inclusion in the final programmes. After the station's final hour, which was an up-dated documentary about the history of Radio Hauraki, arrangements were made for the *Tiri II* to sail triumphantly into Auckland Harbour where a reception party was planned.

Once the offshore Radio Hauraki had closed at 10.00pm on 1st June 1970 all DJs and crew on board the *Tiri II* gathered in the studio for a champagne party and, less than an hour later, the radio ship began her final voyage into Auckland.

During the voyage, in the early hours of 2nd June, one of the station's most popular DJs, Rick Grant, was making his way along the ship's deck to his cabin when the *Tiri II* suddenly lurched in a slight sea. The incident happened as he passed a section of railings which had been crushed and never replaced following the aerial mast's collapse during the *Wahine* storm of April 1968 and Rick Grant was swept overboard. Everybody who was normally on the ship knew about the gap in the railings and took care when passing that area, but Rick Grant, who was usually based in the Auckland studios, was unaware of the dangers of the missing section.

When the crew of the *Tiri II* realised what had happened to their colleague the alarm was raised and the radio ship, together with a Danish freighter en route for Auckland, searched the area all night, but to no avail. At first light a number of small fishing boats and three Navy vessels joined the search, but by midday rough weather forced the search to be abandoned. The *Tiri II* berthed at Jellicoe Wharf in Auckland at 5.00pm on 2nd June 1970, not to a triumphant flag-flying celebration as had been planned, but somberly in a mark of respect for the drowned DJ.

With the offshore station having closed all efforts were now put into getting the land-based Radio Hauraki on the air. The holding company behind the offshore station, Pacific Radio Advertising Ltd, was wound up showing a net trading loss of just NZ $5. In a book-keeping exercise the new public company, Radio Hauraki (NZ) Ltd, paid Pacific Radio Advertising NZ$43,000 for goodwill and NZ$20,000 for radio and studio equipment removed from the *Tiri II*. Much of this money was then used by Pacific Radio Advertising to pay creditors and back wages to staff as well as payments still outstanding on the *Tiri II*. The vessel herself was eventually sold for NZ$4,500 and ended her days as a hulk on Rotoroa Island in the Hauraki Gulf.

### Change to FM

*On 11th February 1990 Radio Hauraki moved from its spot on the medium wave which it had used for nearly 20 years and began transmissions on 99mHz FM. To celebrate the move to FM a party was held for all former Radio Hauraki staff and a three hour special programme about the history of the station was also broadcast.*

Work also began on building the studios and transmitter for the new land-based station and the pressure was on all concerned to once more put Radio Hauraki on the airwaves ahead of old rivals Radio i. This challenge was met and at 6.00am on 26th September 1970 Radio Hauraki began broadcasting legally on 1476kHz (203m), from land-based studios in Auckland, beating its rival by over a month.

After many changes in both format and ownership Radio Hauraki is still broadcasting today to the Auckland area, a tribute to the work and dedication of David Gapes and those original backers who identified a need for such a station and found a way through a tangle of bureaucracy to achieve their objective.

# Chapter 15

# Stormy waters

Back to the colder and even more stormy waters of Northern Europe where at the beginning of 1971 Radio Veronica once again held the monopoly position in offshore radio off the Dutch coast.

This situation had been achieved by Radio Veronica directors paying the Swiss owners of RNI to keep their powerful radio station silent and their ship, *Mebo II* lying at anchor, but manned by Veronica personnel. The other European offshore station, Capital Radio, was also off the air at that time because its ship, the *King David,* had run aground and finances were not available to pay the salvage fee for recovery.

However, this seemingly straightforward position concealed the true situation. Beneath the surface a war was raging between the two major offshore stations, Veronica and RNI, a war which was to come to a dramatic climax later in the year, while Capital Radio the third and much smaller station, unwittingly became drawn into this tangled web.

In January 1971 Radio Veronica was due to make a further payment to keep its Swiss-backed rival silent, but the owners of RNI had plans of their own to return to the air. In December 1970 RNI's directors had attempted to repay Radio Veronica so that they could recommence transmissions from the *Mebo II.* They arrived at Veronica's offices with £100,000 cash in Deutschemarks, but Radio Veronica's management refused to accept the money.

It was at this point that the third offshore station was drawn into the feud between the two larger rivals. On 1st January 1971 one of RNI's owners, Erwin Meister, contacted the International Broadcasters Society (IBS) in Holland, owners of Capital Radio, offering to pay the salvage fee for their vessel, *King David,* if they would agree to put the station back on the air and jam Radio Veronica's transmissions. The directors of IBS wisely refused this offer, sensing that something serious was about to break out between the two larger rival stations.

They were right. On 6th January 1971 a small boat drew alongside *Mebo II* and the master of the silent radio ship, Captain Onnes ( a Radio Veronica man) was told to go ashore immediately to the shipping agents to receive an urgent message. Once Captain Onnes had left his vessel another boat carrying RNI owner Edwin Bollier, together with Swiss engineer, Bruno Brandenberger, arrived alongside the *Mebo II* and both men boarded the radio ship. The crew were told that Bollier, as owner, was taking command of the vessel and when Captain Onnes returned, having discovered that there was in fact no urgent message for him, he was physically prevented from boarding the ship by the gun-carrying Bollier and Brandenberger.

Captain Onnes was forced to return to land where he informed Radio Veronica's directors of the situation on board the *Mebo II.* Two of Radio

Veronica's directors, Bul and Jaap Verweij, together with General Manager, Norbert Jurgens, immediately went out to try and repossess the *Mebo II* , but they too were repelled by threat of gunfire from the Swiss men on board.

The following day, 7th January 1971, on instructions from Bollier the *Mebo II* was towed to a new position off Cadzand on the Dutch/Belgian border. From this anchorage it was intended to recommence broadcasts, ostensibly to Belgium rather than Holland to avoid further conflict with Radio Veronica. The transmissions for part of the day were to be under the RNI call sign while airtime during the rest of the day was to be hired by a Belgian organisation known as Radio Marina.

Belgian backers of the Radio Marina project, Valere and Cecile Broucke, had a verbal agreement with Meister and Bollier to use the *Mebo II* as a base for their station. However, although both parties spent some days discussing detailed arrangements (and some unannounced test transmissions took place from the *Mebo II* off the Belgian coast at the end of January) as is so often the case in the history of offshore radio the plans ultimately came to nothing.

At the end of January 1971 after plans for the launch of the Belgian Radio Marina had apparently failed the *Mebo II* was towed back to an anchorage off Scheveningen, within sight of the Radio Veronica ship *Norderney.* Meanwhile Meister and Bollier entered into negotiations with Dutch music publishing and record companies - Strengholt Publishing and Bassart Records (publishers of *Muziekparade* magazine and owner of the Red Bullet record label) about the re-launch of RNI, this time targeted primarily at an audience in Holland.

Negotiations were finalised by 8th February 1971 and a new company, Radio Noordsee NV, was formed to look after the programming and advertising sales on the station while ownership of the radio ship itself remained with Mebo Telecommunications Ltd. Two ex-Veronica DJs, Jan van Veen and Joost de Draaier, were engaged to oversee the Dutch language programmes between 9.00am and 4.00pm each day on the new RNI.
The remainder of the airtime was to be allocated to programmes in English, with a number of former RNI and other ex-offshore DJs joining the re-launched station.

## RNI returns

Test transmissions, in English, took place shortly after the *Mebo II* had returned to the Dutch coast at the end of January 1971, but the call sign RNI was not used until 14th February 1971, when Production Director Vic Pelli welcomed listeners to "a new era in the history of RNI". Programming continued in English all day for another three weeks, until 7th March, when the promised Dutch language daytime service commenced.

The relative positions of the Dutch and Swiss personnel in the management of RNI at this time was far from clear. Meister and Bollier maintained that the operation was being run jointly by the two groups, hence their appointment of Vic Pelli from Zurich as the station's Production Director. On the other hand Gus Jansen of Basart Records was certain that he was in control of the station and appointed former pop singer John de Mol to manage the operation. The lack of clarity in respective management roles was to be the source of further internal conflict for RNI in later months.

Meanwhile, in Belgium the Radio Marina project was still active. Having failed to secure a satisfactory agreement with RNI for the use of the *Mebo II* the people behind Radio Marina, Valere and Cecile Broucke, approached Capital Radio's owners. After some discussion they entered into an agreement with the IBS and the Kangaroo Pioneering Co. to hire their ship, the *King David,* for a period of three months at a total cost of £50,000.

However, payment of the agreed sum was delayed by the Brouckes who refused to sign to the contract pending 'consultations with their financial advisers'. In fact they were stalling Capital Radio and the IBS while at the same time engaging in a side deal which involved an attempt to extract money from Radio Veronica.

The IBS were unaware of this turn of events until Radio Veronica's lawyer contacted them two days after the Brouckes had delayed signing contracts. In the intervening 48 hours the two Belgians had approached Norbert Jurgens, General Manager of Radio Veronica, offering to stop the launch of Radio Marina from the *King David* if Veronica paid them 10 million Belgian francs (£100,000). As a result of this attempt to blackmail Radio Veronica the IBS, who until then had been unaware of the proposed deal, decided to cancel their contract with the Brouckes. In the meantime Radio Veronica directors made it clear that they were not prepared to pay the sum demanded and nothing more was heard of Valere and Cecile Broucke or the Radio Marina project.

While RNI's Dutch and English transmissions were being re-launched from the *Mebo II* the station was engaged in a fierce legal battle on land with rival offshore station, Radio Veronica. Lawyers for Radio Veronica issued a writ against Erwin Meister and Edwin Bollier requesting the courts to order *Mebo II* into port, or failing this, to authorise the Veronica organisation itself to tow in the rival radio ship. This action had been taken in the belief that the *Mebo II* was still hired to Radio Veronica as part of the September 1970 agreement between the two stations. They also argued that Meister and Bollier were in breach of that agreement by having forcibly re-taken control of the radio ship, threatening in the process to kill anyone from the Veronica organisation who tried to board her, and by starting Dutch language broadcasts in direct competition with Radio Veronica.

The court hearing took place in Rotterdam on 10th March 1971, three days after the RNI Dutch Service had gone on the air, Radio Veronica's lawyers stated that since September 1970 the station had paid RNI £100,000 to stay silent because of fears that its continued broadcasts were likely to jeopardise the future of all offshore radio stations off the Dutch coast. Radio Veronica contended that RNI had now broken that agreement by returning to the air at the end of January 1971. In response RNI's solicitors told the Court that their clients had offered to repay the money to Radio Veronica in full and in cash, but that this had been refused. When judgement was given two weeks later, on 25th March 1971, the Court ruled in favour of RNI. Judge J.G.L. Ruiter considered that having offered to return all the money RNI was then entitled to resume broadcasts from the *Mebo II* and the fact that Radio Veronica had refused to accept repayment of the 'loan' did not entitle them to pursue their interest in the rival radio ship.

## *Mebo II* attacked

Radio Veronica were, understandably, furious at the outcome of this case - elections were due for a new Dutch parliament and there were political murmurings that action would soon be taken to outlaw all offshore broadcasters. The more stations that were operating from off the Dutch coast made such Government action increasingly likely and the presence of the powerful RNI transmitters seemed to concern Radio Veronica directors most of all. As Europe's oldest surviving and most successful offshore station they did not want their

**offshore trivia**

**First 24 hour stations**

*Radio Nord (Sweden) 1962*

*Radio Essex (Britain) 1965*

*Radio Hauraki (New Zealand) 1968*

chances of being able to continue broadcasting (either at sea with the authorities continuing to turn a 'blind eye' or legally from a land-base as part of the official radio system) jeopardised by the powerful newcomer to the offshore radio scene. Some Radio Veronica directors openly referred to the need to "shut the big Dutch mouth" of RNI and secretly set about devising a scheme which, they hoped, would achieve that objective.

That scheme came to a dramatic climax in May 1971. During the evening of 15th May three men left Scheveningen beach in an inflatable boat powered by an outboard motor and sailed towards the home of RNI, *Mebo II*. On board the radio ship broadcasts were as normal for a Saturday evening while off duty DJs and radio staff were relaxing watching television. The rubber dinghy silently came alongside the radio ship and one of the three men, who was familiar with the interior layout of the Mebo II, pulled himself on board together with one of his associates.

They made their way below deck to the engine room and fixed over a pound of explosive wrapped in oil-soaked cloths on the radio ship's main fuel line. Just as they were returning to the rubber dinghy at 10.50pm the device exploded, hurling one of the boarders into the sea and immediately setting fire to the stern of the radio ship. Crew and DJs on the *Mebo II* rushed on deck to witness the rubber dinghy pulling away from the radio ship, but their main concern at the time was to prevent the fire spreading any further.

Dramatic Mayday messages were immediately broadcast on air in English by DJ Alan West and in Dutch by Captain Harteveld:

*Mayday! Mayday! This is the radio ship Mebo II, four miles off the coast of Scheveningen, Holland. We require assistance urgently due to a fire on board this vessel caused by a bomb being thrown into our engine room.*

*Mayday! Mayday! This is an SOS from Radio North Sea International.*

For over half an hour the crew desperately appealed for assistance, requesting

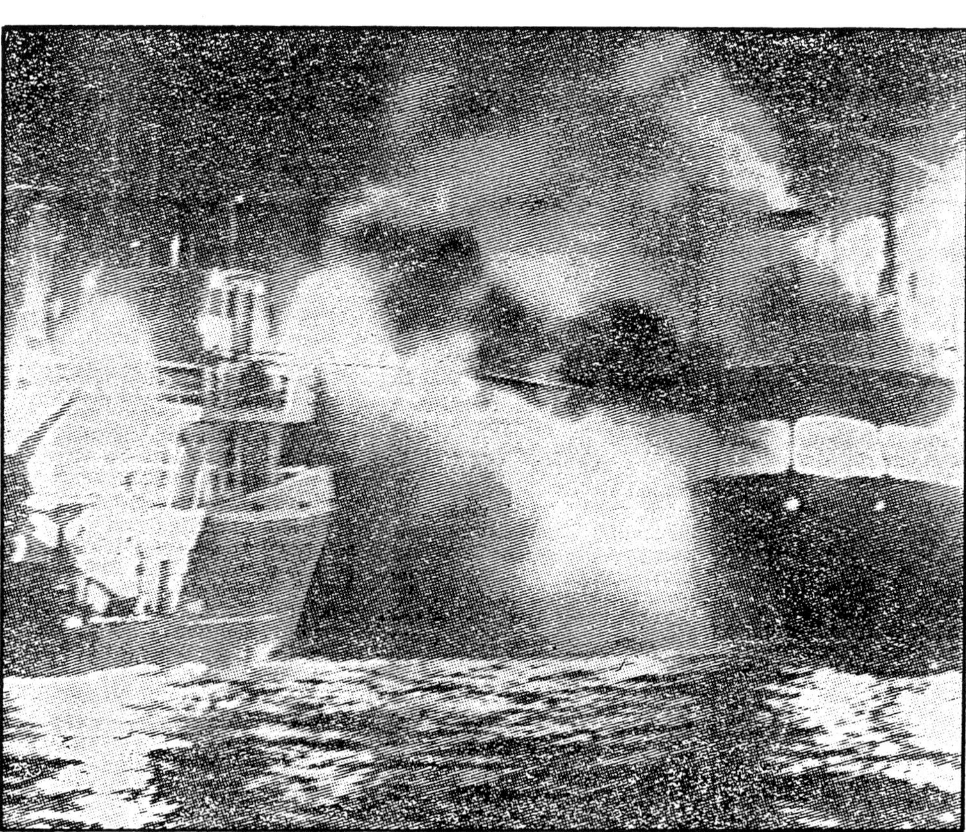

'Mebo II' on fire after the bomb attack

listeners to phone the station's Zurich offices and to alert the authorities in Holland. At one stage the fire appeared to be under control, but it suddenly flared up again, reaching the bridge and threatening to engulf the whole radioship. Forty five minutes after the explosion Captain Harteveld gave orders to abandon ship and for the benefit of the emergency services he came on air personally to announce the ship's precise position. The station's Swiss engineer reported in German for the benefit of anyone listening at the head office in Zurich and then closed transmissions on all frequencies while the DJs and remainder of the crew climbed into the lifeboats.

SOS after radio ship is bombed

Bomb SOS From Pirate Radio Ship

BOMB BLAST HITS POP PIRATE SHIP

Pop ship in 'Mayday' drama

These dramatic calls for assistance had been picked up by the Wijsmuller Salvage Control Centre at IJmuiden and the tug *Titan* was despatched to the scene. Rival salvage company, Smit-Tak in Rotterdam also despatched one of their tugs, *Smitbank* and the Scheveningen and Noordwijk lifeboats were launched as well. However, RNI's own tender, *Eurotrip* was the first vessel to arrive at the *Mebo II* and was able to take the DJs and crew on board from the radio ship's lifeboats.

The *Eurotrip,* together with the firefighting tug *Volans* then tackled the blaze on the *Mebo II* and succeeded in bringing it under control after about two hours. Throughout the drama Captain Hardeveld, together with the transmitter engineer and the ship's engineer remained on board the *Mebo II.*

With the blaze finally extinguished Captain Hardeveld allowed the DJs and radio crew to return to the *Mebo II* in the early hours of 16th May 1971 and transmissions of RNI's programmes resumed once again, continuing throughout the night as scheduled, while the Dutch Royal Navy frigate *Gelderland,* took up position and stood by alongside the radio ship.

Fortunately the blaze, although severe, had not damaged the station's studios, transmitter room or the DJ's living quarters and RNI was able to continue broadcasting virtually as normal. However, the whole of the stern end of the *Mebo II,* including the bridge, had been gutted, with the cost of damages estimated to be in the order of £28,000.

An investigation into the circumstances of this dramatic incident was immediately launched by Dutch police, the Rijkspolitie. Acting on a tip-off they arrested the leader of the boarding party, Captain Tom, in The Hague on 16th May 1971 and his two co-divers were also taken into custody later that day. The remains of the rubber dinghy and discarded frogmen's suits were subsequently found partially buried on a deserted part of Scheveningen beach.

Following detailed questioning the police decided to charge the three men with piracy on the high seas and Amsterdam police chief, Theo Nelissren, announced at a press conference that the motive behind the crime was believed to be financial, but refused to be drawn on any further details. At that stage two main question remained unanswered about the nbomb attach on the *Mebo II* -who had paid the men to carry out the attack and for what reason?

## Radio Veronica implicated

The following day, Monday 17th May 1971 police announced that they believed a wealthy Dutch businessman was the person behind the attack on the *Mebo II* and a few hours later they arrested Norbert Jurgens, General Manager of rival station Radio Veronica. The arrest surprised and shocked Holland - for some 10 years Radio Veronica had cultivated an ultra-respectable business image and, although its broadcasting vessel remained outside territorial waters, the station was generally regarded as being almost part of the Dutch media establishment. The revelation that its General Manager had paid three men to violently attack a rival radio station seemed almost unbelievable, particularly to the station's millions of loyal listeners.

A police statement soon dispelled all the images of respectability so carefully cultivated by the Radio Veronica organisation. It was revealed that Norbert Jurgens had paid the three divers £1,000 before the raid and, upon successful completion of the mission each man was to receive a further £3,000. The ultimate aim of the plot was to cripple the *Mebo II* so that she would have to enter port for repairs. Once inside Dutch territorial limits arrest orders could then be filed against the vessel by creditors, one of whom was named as Worldwide Est., a company registered in Liechtenstein which happened to be the owner of Radio Veronica's ship, *Norderney*. Norbert Jurgens was the company's Dutch representative and it was in that capacity that he had signed the contract in September 1970 with Meister and Bollier to 'hire' the *Mebo II*, forcing RNI to stay silent for over three months.

With Norbert Jurgens in custody the directors of Radio Veronica issued a statement saying that they had nothing to do with the attack on the *Mebo II*. However, in a television interview the following evening, 18th May 1971, one of Radio Veronica's directors, Bul Verweij, admitted paying Jurgens £10,000 to have the *Mebo II* brought into port, but he denied responsibility for the violent attack which had taken place in furtherance of this plan. Following his television appearance Bul Verweij was arrested by police on 19th May 1971 and charged with conspiracy in planning the attack.

Five days later the Public Prosecutor formally laid charges of piracy on the High Seas against the three divers and of complicity in the crime against Norbert Jurgens and Bul Verweij. All five men were detained in custody pending the full hearing of the charges against them.

Meanwhile, shareholders of Radio Veronica, stunned by revelations of the sinister events involving one of their own directors and their General Manager, asked Dirk Verweij (who in an earlier power struggle had been ousted from the board by his brothers Bul and Jaap) to rejoin the station.

Now that information about the unsavoury pirate war being fought off the coast of Holland had become public knowledge the Dutch Prime Minister, Piet de Jong, announced on 27th May 1971 that legislation to ratify the Strasbourg Convention of 1965 and to outlaw offshore broadcasting stations would be brought before Parliament by the end of the year. The official reason given for the threatened introduction of legislation after so many years of tolerating offshore radio stations was that interference had been caused to shipping and emergency communications. However, it was clear that (as had happened with

## Capital Radio - the end

*With the end of offshore radio now apparently in sight for the stations off Holland's coast two further events occurred at the end of May 1971 affecting the now defunct Capital Radio.*

*During enquiries into the bombing of the Mebo II the Dutch Officer of Justice, Dr. Van t'Veer, announced that the investigation into the beaching of the King David in November 1970 was to be re-opened. He said new evidence had come to light as the result of the current investigation which appeared to throw suspicion on the reason for the Capital Radio ship breaking from her anchorage. After some weeks, however, the Dutch police found that although there appeared to have been a number of incidents of foul play surrounding the King David, including the flooding of the vessel's engine room with fuel oil, there was insufficient evidence available to secure any prosecutions.*

*As the police investigation was being re-opened the IBS - owners of Capital Radio - were officially declared bankrupt in Amsterdam on 24th May 1971. The Society had tried to keep itself solvent in the hope of being able to resume Capital Radio's broadcasts from the King David, but this proved impossible and the idealistic dream of a group of professional broadcasters had come to a costly and unhappy conclusion.*

*The end for what remained of the Capital Radio venture finally came on 18th October 1971 when the station's ship, King David, was auctioned in Amsterdam. The former radio ship was sold to Rotterdam scrap dealer J Boele for £2,000 and the vessel was towed to Heerwaarden where she was left for over five years. During that time the ship was vandalised and rusted away so much that the bridge and superstructure above deck level was removed for safety reasons at the end of the 1970's. The remains of the ship were towed to a small village in central Holland in 1983 to be used as a base for a floating pier. The hulk finally sank in 1994.*

the British Government in1966 following the boarding of Radio City (see Chapter 11) the Dutch Government had now been stung into action as the result of violent disputes breaking out between the offshore stations themselves.

On RNI programming continued as normal while repairs to the *Mebo II* were carried out at sea -the ship did not enter port as had been envisaged by certain Radio Veronica directors in their plan to silence the rival station's 'Big Dutch Mouth'. Throughout the spring and summer of 1971 the newly confident RNI consolidated and expanded its services on all fronts. A news service had been introduced on 10th April 1971 and, just before the bombing, the station had extended its Dutch and English language programmes by two hours each day. At the end of June 1971 a separate 'World Service' programme was launched on the 31m and 49m shortwave transmitters between 7.00am and 3.00pm each Sunday. The financially lucrative Dutch service was again extended to 12 hours a day (6.00am-6.00pm) from 2nd August 1971 but at the expense of English language programme hours. Additionally from about this time the World Service was also extended from eight to eleven hours on Sundays, but on the 31m short waveband transmitter only.

## 'Spy ship' allegations

*Speculation about the reason for RNI's plethora of frequencies and the reason behind the various authorities' concerns, particularly in Britain, over the presence of the Mebo II off the coast was further fuelled in September 1971. At the end of that month the Dutch newspaper, 'De Telegraaf' reported that former RNI DJ, Andy Archer, had claimed that the radio ship was used to broadcast coded messages to communist countries on the shortwave bands after the end of normal daily transmissions. These claims were dismissed by the owners of the station, Edwin Meister and Erwin Bollier, but true or not they served to add something to the mystery surrounding RNI and its backers.*

**veronica blijft!**

omdat **IK** dat wil!
daarom word ik lid van de
**VERENIGING tot steun van de**
**VERONICA OMROEP STICHTING**

Naam:
Adres:
Woonplaats:
Leeftijd:
Gezinshoofd? ja / nee
(doorstrepen wat niet juist is)

Handtekening

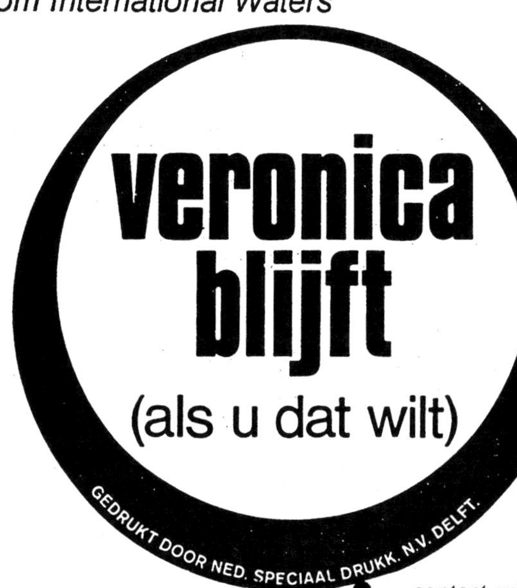


## Veronica Blijft

Radio Veronica issued a statement to its listeners when launching the Veronica Blijft campaign:-

- During the past 11 years Radio Veronica was responsible for the regrettable incident involving the *Mebo II*
- the creation of a radio station for a majority of the Dutch population
- bringing 172 hours of music per week without financial help from listeners
- an important publicity medium, helping Dutch industries
- the stimulation of Dutch record productions
- the regulation and stimulation of the sale of records
- the creation of employment for artists
- contact with the public via the Drive-in Shows - the first station to do this
- a reliable Dutch hit parade, the Veronica Top 40, as acknowledged by the international press
- the free supply of Top 40 printed sheets sent to record shops and discos
- help in the staging of pop concerts
- the payment of all recording rights, helping artists etc.
- the creation of Hilversum 3
- bringing the international pop scene to Holland
- helping human lives by organising campaigns for many worthwhile organisations, medical and others
- financial support for other organisations i.e. hospitals, schools, old people, sports clubs, musical organisations - a total of over 4 million Guilders
- the same amount in free advertising spots for charity associations and the manpower for all campaigns

During the summer of 1971 after the *Mebo II* bomb attack Radio Veronica, in a damage limitation exercise and in a bid to prove its continued popularity to a Government now actively considering legislation against offshore broadcasters, launched a campaign," Veronica blijft als u dat wilt" (Veronica stays if you wish). More than two million listeners registered their support for the station by returning signed postcards and in September 1971 the station launched its own magazine -*Veronica 192* - designed to carry positive news and information about the station and its campaign to stay on the air as well as general entertainment and pop music news.

Much of the good work created during this public relations exercise by the station received a set-back in September 1971 when extensive press coverage was given to the Court hearings against Bul Verweij, Norbert Jurgens and the three divers who had bombed the *Mebo II*. In Court the two senior Radio Veronica men admitted that they had financed the attack with the intention of forcing the rival radio ship to enter Dutch territorial waters. However, both Bul Verweij and Norbert Jurgens claimed that they thought this would be achieved by cutting the anchor chain rather than by fire-bombing the ship and endangering life in the way that had happened on the night of 15th May 1971.

The hearing was concluded on 21st September 1971 when all five men were found guilty as charged and each was sentenced to one year in prison. The piracy charges were the first to be brought in Holland since the introduction of the Dutch Penal Code in 1881. The case had raked up once again the fierce rivalry surrounding the offshore radio business in Holland during the early 1970's and had also been a second humiliation in the Dutch Courts for Radio Veronica and its dealings with rival station RNI.

## RNI continues

Drama of another kind affected RNI in November 1971. At 8.10am on 22nd November the *Mebo II* radioed that she was adrift after losing her anchor and all programmes from RNI stopped shortly afterwards as the vessel had entered Dutch territorial waters. Rescue services raced to the stricken ship and the salvage tug *Smitbank* arrived on the scene at about 11.00am. A line was put aboard the *Mebo II* and by early afternoon she had been towed back to her anchorage position in international waters. However, rough weather prevented a new anchor being fitted and the tug held the radio ship in position for nearly 24 hours until being replaced by another salvage tug *Thames*. Broadcasts of RNI's programmes were able to resume at 4.30pm on 22nd November, but the new anchor was not installed until two days later when weather conditions had calmed. Throughout this 48 hour period the radio ship was held in position in international waters by the salvage tugs.

Towards the end of December 1971 RNI's Sunday World Service was abruptly discontinued, although a programme for radio fans - DXers - continued to be broadcast once a month on the shortwave frequency. At about this time too the use of 31m shortwave band transmissions were also discontinued completely, although 49m remained to simulcast the medium wave and FM output.

It was known that the *Mebo II* had a second medium wave transmitter on board (one formerly used by British fort-based offshore station, Radio 390) and there were many rumours that a separate all day English language service would be starting at the beginning of 1972. However, it was not until the early morning of 27th March 1972 that test transmissions started on this facility on 773kHz (388m), changing later to 1115kHz (269m) and again to 845kHz (355m). Despite these test transmissions taking place no new service was launched at this time from RNI, although on the main frequencies English language programme hours were extended in May 1972.

In June 1972 the Dutch Service of RNI moved into new studios in Naarden in Holland. They occupied the same building as Strengholt publishers and Bassart Records (financial backers of the Dutch Service. The station's former studios in Hilversum had been fitted with cheap equipment while some advertising revenue could be earned to upgrade it. The new studio, which was the result of the commercial success of the Dutch language broadcasts contained extensive facilities for programme recording as well as commercial and jingle production.

## Caroline ships sold

On May 29th 1972 the two former Radio Caroline vessels, *Mi Amigo* and *Caroline,* which had lain rusting and vandalised in harbour for over four and a half years, were finally put up for sale at public auction by Wijsmullers. This had been made possible following the death of one of the Wijsmuller brothers who had always insisted on retaining the vessels in lieu of payment for his company's services to the former radio station. His brothers had not agreed with this course of action, but the impasse had prevented anything being done with the ships since they had been towed into harbour in March 1968.

### RNI programme schedule May 1971

*Weekdays*

*DUTCH SERVICE*

**6.00am Kop Op** *Peter Holland*

**6.30am Gospel Songs and Meditation** *Johann Maasbach*

**7.00am Kop Op** *Peter Holland*

**10.00am Jan en alleman** *Jan van Veen*

**12noon Joost met het weten** *Joost de Draaier*

**2.00pm Hou Maat** *Ferry Maat*

*ENGLISH SERVICE*

**4.00pm Stevie Merike**

**6.00pm Alan West**

**8.00pm Crispian St John**

**10.00pm Tony Allen**

**12midnight Dave Rogers**

**3.00am Closedown**

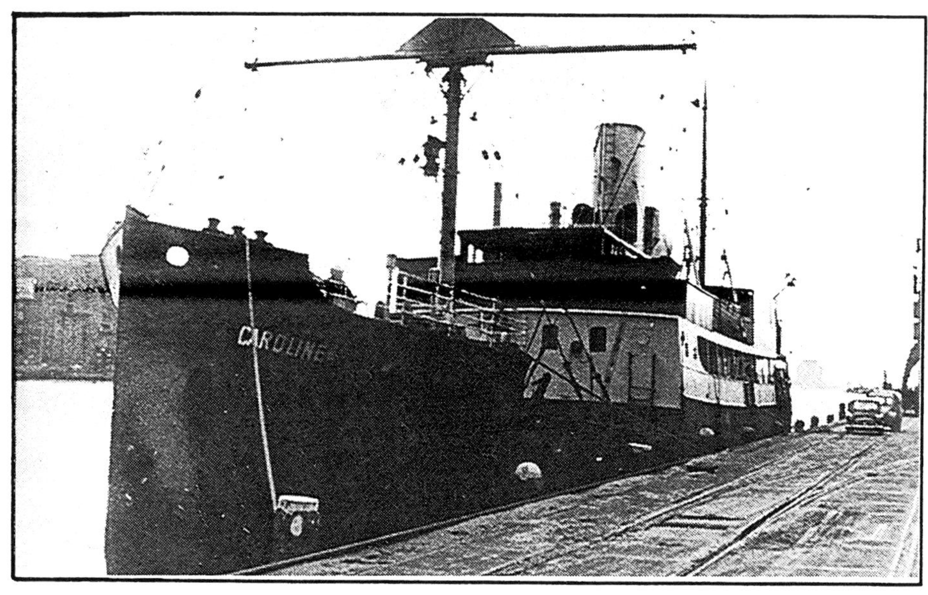


The MV 'Caroline' in Amsterdam

The auction was held by RW Bais NA and the MV *Caroline,* home to the original Radio Caroline and later to Radio Caroline North, was sold for scrap for to Frank Rijsdijk of Hendrik Ido, Ambacht £3,150 (26,270 Guilders). The former Radio Nord, Radio Atlanta and Radio Caroline South ship, *Mi Amigo*, was sold to the Hofman Shipping Agency, acting on behalf of unnamed clients for £2,400 (20,000 Guilders) and it was assumed that she too would be scrapped.

However, an announcement was made shortly after the auction that the 'unnamed clients' were in fact the Dutch Free Radio Organisation, led by Gerard van Dam himself previously an employee of the Wijsmuller Tender Company. Gerard van Dam said he planned to use the *Mi Amigo* as an offshore radio museum, restoring the vandalised studios to their former condition and creating accommodation for visitors wishing to stay on board the ship. The former radio ship was towed to a berth in Zaandam where, throughout the summer of 1972, volunteers from the Free Radio Organisation cleaned, painted and restored the vessel, removing evidence of years of neglect and vandalism.

During the time that this 'restoration' work was being carried out Radio Caroline's founder, Ronan O'Rahilly arrived in Amsterdam for a series of meetings with Gerard van Dam. O'Rahilly , who at that time was working on the production of a film, managed to convince the Free Radio Organisation that the future of the ship was not as a museum piece, but as a living radio station. He wanted to re-launch Radio Caroline and to that end he used all his natural charm and persuasiveness to regain control of the *Mi Amigo* for himself. He also saw the chance of using the re-launched station as a vehicle to promote his film production activities.

Naturally this plan was undertaken in absolute secrecy with the authorities still being led to believe that the vessel was to be converted into a floating radio museum. At the beginning of September 1972 the *Mi Amigo* quietly left her berth at Zaandam and was towed down the canal system towards the North Sea. Authorities at IJmuiden were told that the 'floating museum' was heading for England where there was a greater interest in offshore radio and where the *Mi Amigo* had spent some of her most successful broadcasting years.

## *Mi Amigo* sets sail

However, at dawn on 3rd September 1972 the *Mi Amigo* dropped anchor off Scheveningen between the *Norderney* (Radio Veronica) and the *Mebo II* (RNI). Ronan O'Rahilly then persuaded two ex-Caroline South DJs, Andy Archer and Chris Carey (Spangles Muldoon), together with radio engineer Peter Chicago - all then working on RNI - to leave their luxury radio ship and help him re-launch Radio Caroline from the battered, rusty and vandalised *Mi Amigo.*

The parts played by these RNI staff were of considerable significant importance to Radio Caroline's return to the air. Not only did they share Ronan O'Rahilly's desire to see Radio Caroline broadcasting once again, but Chris Carey and Peter Chicago actually had access to much technical equipment from both the *Mi Amigo* and the MV *Caroline.*

This had been obtained nearly two years previously when, after RNI had been paid by Radio Veronica to close in September 1970, Chris Carey, Peter Chicago and another RNI DJ, Carl Mitchell, visited the two ex-Caroline ships in Amsterdam and removed much of the studio equipment. They even gave serious consideration to removing the transmitters from the ships, but this could not easily be achieved for practical reasons. Between them they had a plan at that time to launch an offshore radio station of their own and held discussions with Dutch evangelist, Rev. Dominee Toornvliet, who at that time had a ship which could have been used as a base. (The ship did in fact find an offshore radio role later as home first to the short-lived Radio Condor and later to Radio Atlantis - see Chapter 16). However, the 1970 plan did not go ahead and when RNI returned to the air at the beginning of 1971 the three men rejoined their former station.

## Back at sea

Now that the *Mi Amigo* was free and back at sea the equipment, which many feared had been damaged or lost forever, could be returned and re-installed on the ship. Peter Chicago had also visited the two Caroline ships in Amsterdam a few weeks before they were auctioned and had managed to make an assessment of their condition and that of the transmitter equipment. He realised then that with a little hard work the transmitters could be put back into working order, although the MV *Caroline* transmitter had suffered more damage and vandalism than the *Mi Amigo* one. With this background the men deserted RNI and joined Ronan O'Rahilly in his plan to re-launch Radio Caroline.

The *Mi Amigo* remained silent at her anchorage for most of September 1972 while the transmitter and other equipment was put in working order. The ship was still a virtual wreck - the engine room was flooded and it had no functioning generators. Andy Archer and Chris Carey persuaded the former engineer and Fort Captain of 60's offshore station Radio Essex, Dick Palmer, to go out to the *Mi Amigo* off Holland and repair the vessel's engines. Dick Palmer accepted this challenge and after many weeks of hard and very dirty work he achieved the almost impossible - the *Mi Amigo's* engines and generators were stripped and rebuilt to working order.

## Disagreements

Although on the technical side work was progressing, albeit with difficulty, fundamental problems started to arise between Ronan O'Rahilly and Gerard van Dam over the actual re-launch of Radio Caroline. Ronan O'Rahilly wanted the *Mi Amigo* to anchor off the British coast where Radio Caroline had been enormously popular during the mid 1960's and he anticipated being able to easily recapture the large audience levels the station had attracted in those heady days. Gerard van Dam on the other hand felt that the commercial potential for the re-launched Radio Caroline lay in Holland where advertising on offshore radio was still not against the law. This dispute dragged on for many weeks during the late summer of 1972 and when the transmitter on board the *Mi Amigo* was finally restored to working order its switch on was delayed because of uncertainty about the final location of the ship and the target audience of the re-launched station.

Dutch offshore station Radio Veronica was planning to change frequency at the end of September 1972 and had engaged in a massive publicity campaign during the preceding weeks to ensure listeners were aware of the new frequency. Because of the likelihood that millions of listeners would be re-tuning their radios as a result of Radio Veronica's frequency change, engineers on board the *Mi Amigo* decided to switch on their own transmitter and make some test broadcasts. In the late evening of 29th September these unidentified test transmissions of continuous music were heard across Europe on 1187kHz (253m).

## A milestone day

Saturday September 30th 1972 turned out to be one of the milestone days in the history of offshore radio. During the summer of 1972 that date had been selected by Radio Veronica as the one on which the station would at last change its frequency from 192m (1562kHz) to 538m (557kHz). On the day itself the change was scheduled for 1.00pm and the final Radio Veronica programme on 192m, consisting of a brief history of the station, was broadcast from 12-12.30pm. Shortly before 1.00pm the 538m wavelength was opened with station identity jingles then regular Radio Veronica programmes recommenced on the hour. The station planned that a low power transmitter would remain broadcasting on the 192m wavelength for some days relaying a taped message asking listeners to re-tune to 538m.

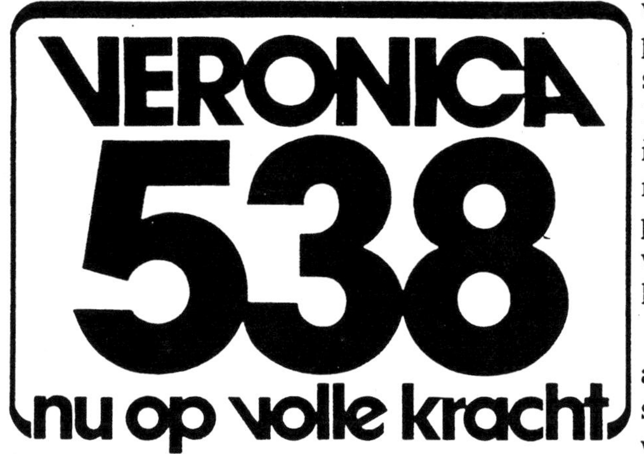


However, in an effort to steal some of Radio Veronica's audience RNI opened a second service - RNI 2 - a few seconds after 12.30pm that day on the 192m wavelength which had just been vacated by Veronica. The RNI theme tune "Man of Action" was played followed by an announcement from Tony Allan, first in Dutch then in English:-

*Good afternoon ladies and gentlemen, this is the start of test broadcasts from Radio North Sea International Two. We're transmitting on 192 metres in the medium wave band, 1562 kHz. Radio Veronica will be resuming their broadcasts at one o'clock Central European Time on 538 metres medium wave, that's 557kHz. The management and staff of the Radio North Sea network throughout Europe would like to take this opportunity to wish all our friends over at Radio Veronica the best of luck in years to come. In order not to interfere with other transmitters on this frequency we shall be closing down our test transmissions at seven o'clock in the evening.*

At 1.00pm RNI 2 relayed the opening four minutes of Radio Veronica on 538m then continued with its own programming in English, until closedown at 7.00pm:-

12.30pm Tony Allen
2.00pm Brian McKenzie
4.00pm Arnold Layne
6.00pm Terry Davies

The following day, 1st October, RNI 2 opened again at 6.00am, but the separate English language programme only lasted just over an hour then the regular RNI Dutch service was relayed in a parallel transmission. At 12noon the short-lived RNI 2 service left the air and was not heard again. Unfortunately some technical problems still needed to be resolved because the two medium wave transmitters suffered from breakthrough of signals on eachother's channel. The experiment with RNI2 had demonstrated the fact that a second medium wave transmitter was on board the *Mebo II* and it could be used to provide a separate service if enough advertising support existed.

# CAROLINE BACK ON THE AIR

Meanwhile, also at 12.30pm on 30th September 1972, just as Radio Veronica had temporarily left the air and the RNI 2 service had been launched, further test transmissions of continuous music were heard on 1187kHz (253m). These transmissions, without any announcements or station identification were heard at irregular intervals throughout the day and into the early hours of 1st October. The test broadcasts, which continued into early November 1972 came from the *Mi Amigo* and although no announcements were made at the time they heralded the imminent return of Radio Caroline, after more than four and a half years silence.

Unfortunately the dispute between Ronan O'Rahilly and Gerard van Dam continued to delay this return. Plans existed at this time to operate a Dutch language service on 1520kHz (197m) - to be known as Radio 199 - and an English language service on 1187kHz (253m) (announced as 259m), under the call sign Radio Caroline.

These plans were thwarted, however, when the *Mi Amigo* drifted during a storm on 13th November 1972 and the aerial mast collapsed. A temporary aerial was rigged and test transmissions resumed again at the end of the month on 1187kHz (253m), broadcasting a taped announcement asking for reception reports. The response to these taped announcements resulted in over 1,000 letters being received within a matter of days at the station's offices in Zeekant Holland.

At the beginning of December 1972 DJs on board the *Mi Amigo* started presenting programmes without identifying either themselves or the station. At 11.00am on 17th December the test transmissions moved to a new frequency of 1520kHzk (197m). The following day programmes, presented by on-board DJs in both English and Dutch, were aired under the call sign Radio 199. After a few days the Radio 199 identification was dropped and at 6.00am on 22nd December 1972 the station officially started to identify itself as Radio Caroline. Broadcasts continued for 24 hours a day in both English and Dutch over the Christmas holiday period. This included in the early hours of Christmas Day a link up with RNI between Andy Archer and Rob Eden.

**Radio Caroline programme schedule 22nd December 1972**

**5.00am Non-stop music**
**6.00am Crispian St John**
**9.00am Leon Keizer**
**11.00am Jeremy Bender**
**1.00pm Paul Dubois**
**3.00pm Andy Archer**
**5.00pm Gerard van der Zee**
**6.00pm Crispian St John**
**8.00pm Andy Archer**
**10.00pm Peter Chicago**
**1.00am Closedown**

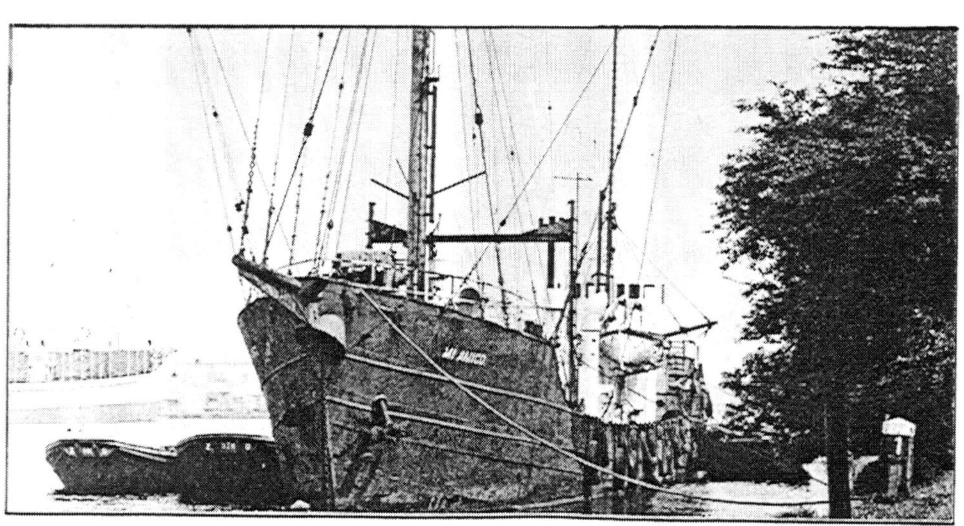

*'Mi Amigo' in 1972*

## RNI frictions

While the *Mi Amigo* was making test transmissions and Radio Veronica was settling into its new frequency over on the *Mebo II* RNI suffered a period of disruption during the autumn months of 1972 when frictions arose between the Swiss and Dutch managements of the station. On 24th October 1972 the English Service did not come on the air as usual, being replaced with non-stop music and occasional announcements in Dutch. No explanation was given to listeners for the sudden absence of regular programmes, but it soon became known that the Dutch Service Director, John de Mol had sacked all the staff and discontinued the English language programmes because they attracted so little advertising revenue. The station's Swiss owners, Erwin Meister and Edwin Bollier, had not been consulted about this change in policy and when they heard what had happened they immediately reinstated the English staff, resulting in a return of RNI's English Service at 8.00pm on 3rd November 1972, after an absence of 10 days. Just over a week later, on 12th November 1972 the English language World Service was also reintroduced on 6205kHz in the 49m shortwave band each Sunday from 10.00am - 8.00pm.

**Radio Northsea sack British disc jockeys**

**BRITISH listeners to Radio Northsea International were shocked last week when the station discontinued its English-speaking programmes.**

DJ Dave Rogers told Record Mirror this week that on Tuesday the English-speaking announcers were told by the captain of the R.N.I. ship of the decision to cease English broadcasts.

"The English disc jockeys left the ship and went to the R.N.I. headquarters in Holland," said Dave. "We were told that they had stopped the English broadcasts because they had had a lot of trouble with the English jocks and that it was not a commercially viable proposition to continue broadcasting in English.

## Caroline 'mutiny'

For Radio Caroline 1972 also ended with a dramatic turn of events. The regular transmissions, which had started on 22nd December continued uninterrupted over the Christmas holiday period, but during the early hours of 28th December the lights on the *Mi Amigo* failed. The crews of neighbouring radio ships *Norderney* and *Mebo II* witnessed rockets being fired from the Caroline ship and, fearing the vessel was in distress, they called the *Mi Amigo* only to be told that there was no problem and the rockets were being used to provide light to carry out essential repairs.

The true situation was far more serious. The Dutch crew on board the *Mi Amigo* (who had originally been engaged by Gerard van Dam) claimed they had not been paid since the vessel left harbour in September and decided to bring matters to a head by sabotaging the fuel line to the lighting generators. They hoped this would force the radio ship to return to port, but when Captain van der Kamp refused to sail in the crew then abandoned the *Mi Amigo*, leaving only him and four broadcasting staff on board. The all Dutch crew remained loyal Gerard van Dam and as well as taking this action over alleged non payment by Ronan O'Rahilly they also supported his attempts to thwart the launch of the English language Radio Caroline. the station's pre-Christmas return had been carried out by the English broadcasting staff on direct instructions from Ronan O'Rahilly who was frustrated by over three months of delays.

Transmissions of Radio Caroline programmes continued, but later that day at 3.40pm, DJ Andy Archer suddenly announced during his programme that visitors had arrived alongside the *Mi Amigo* and that he was going out on deck to investigate. The 'visitors' turned out to be the former Dutch crew of the radio ship who returned in the vessel *Seamews,* accompanied by the Royal Dutch Navy escort vessel, *Limburg.* Ten minutes later Radio Caroline left the air suddenly as the Dutchmen climbed aboard the *Mi Amigo* and fighting broke out on deck between them and the English broadcasting staff. The station was off the air for over two hours while an agreement was reached with the former crew who, having received assurances about their pay, agreed to return to duty. Transmissions from Radio Caroline then recommenced at 5.50pm, although the atmosphere on board the *Mi Amigo* remained very tense.

Two days later on 30th December 1972, Radio Caroline's transmissions closed unexpectedly at 3.00am. The *Mi Amigo's* master, Captain van der Kamp, had gone ashore, but returned shortly after the station had left the air, cut the anchor chain and towed the radio ship to IJmuiden, using the services of the RNI tender, *Eurotrip.* At first permission was refused for the *Mi Amigo* to enter port and she had to wait offshore while police boarded the radio ship demanding to see the registration papers. No papers were on board and the *Mi Amigo* was only allowed to enter port after an undertaking by the Captain of the *Eurotrip* that he would ensure all harbour costs were met.

When the radio ship did eventually arrive in Amsterdam PTT officials boarded her but did not take any action as vital parts were 'missing' from the transmitter. However, the Dutch Shipping Inspectorate, whose representatives also boarded the vessel, declared the *Mi Amigo* to be unseaworthy and issued instructions that she could only leave port after major repair work had been carried out. Despite this order the authorities clearly did not want the liability of the *Mi Amigo* in their port area, particularly as it was also the subject of a crewing dispute, and enforced the repair requirements with as much leniency and flexibility as possible.

Meanwhile in a separate action the Captain and crew had sought, and been granted, an injunction from the Haarlem District Court to impound the *Mi Amigo* until they had received their outstanding pay - estimated to total approximately £4,000. In response to this Court Order Ronan O'Rahilly announced that he had sacked the entire crew of the ship and was arranging for all repairs required by the Shipping Inspectorate to be carried out as a matter of urgency. In effect he had removed the Dutch crew originally engaged by Gerard van Dam and by doing so had gained total control of the radio ship himself.

**RADIO PUNCH-UP**

**Pop pirates mutiny**

IT WAS all sweet music on board the pirate radio ship Caroline last night after a reported mutiny earlier in the day.

Transmission from Radio Caroline ended suddenly when the disc jockey said a fight had broken out on board. He told listeners that he would go and see what was happening, but he did not return to the microphone.

The radio ship, anchored off the coast of Holland, later resumed transmission without any explanation

But the Dutch Navy Information service said the commander of the Dutch destroyer Limburg had been ordered to board Caroline after the ship had called for assistance and flares had been fired.

Dutch television showed pictures of the captain with a rifle in his hand to protect himself — according to the commentator—against the hostile attitude of three British disc jockeys.

The Dutch news agency said the captain alleged that the three Britons, dissatisfied with working conditions, had halted transmission.

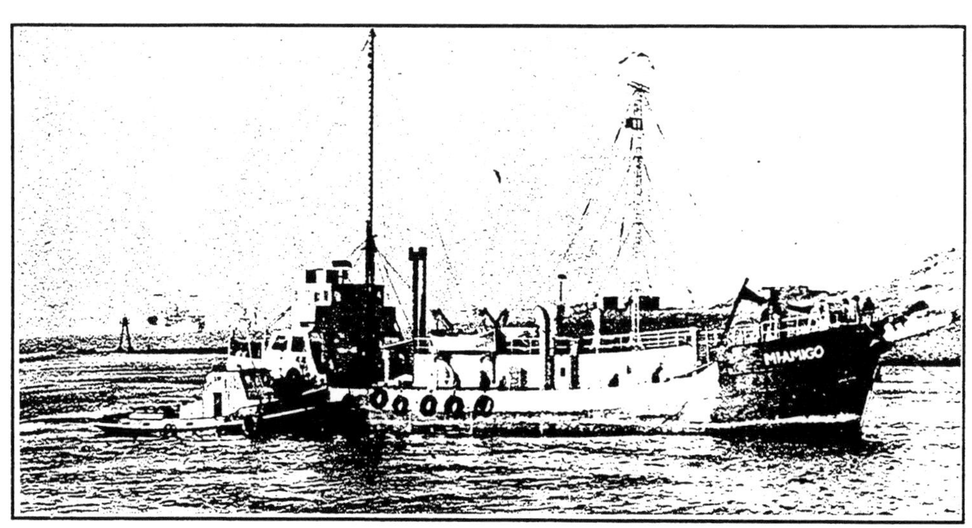


*The 'Mi Amigo' being towed into port, December 1972*

The repairs were actually completed by New Years Day 1973 and at 5.00pm the *Mi Amigo* was towed along the canal system towards the North Sea. However, the Shipping Inspectorate at IJmuiden stopped the radio ship, ordering a leak in the engine room to be repaired before she would be allowed to travel any further. With the *Mi Amigo* temporarily detained once again the former Captain and crew were granted a further Court Order at 10.00pm on 1st January 1973 Captain van der Kamp boarded and legally claimed possession of the *Mi Amigo.*

Amazingly Ronan O'Rahilly managed to raise some money from various sources and, after several hours of negotiations, the outstanding pay was handed over to Captain van der Kamp and his crew. With the Shipping Inspectorate officials off duty because of the New Year holiday superficial repairs to the *Mi Amigo* were hurriedly completed and she was towed back out to sea before any more official action could be taken to detain her. Transmissions from Radio Caroline started once again shortly after 3.00pm on 2nd January 1973, this time on 1187kHz (253m).

## 'Free Radio' Magazines

*After the closure of Radio Caroline in 1968 a large number of 'Free Radio' newsletters and magazines appeared, published by a variety of listeners' and supporters' groups in Britain and Europe.*

*Many of these were short-lived and contained unreliable news, with wild rumours of new stations and new radio ships anchoring off the coast. Others were more reliable and continued to be published regularly for a number of years.*

*Some, such as 'Monitor' and 'Offshore Echos', covered offshore radio news and issues so thoroughly and reliably that they became established as 'essential reading' for anyone interested in the subject.*

*Today 'Offshore Echos' remains as the only publication dedicated solely to the subject of offshore radio.*

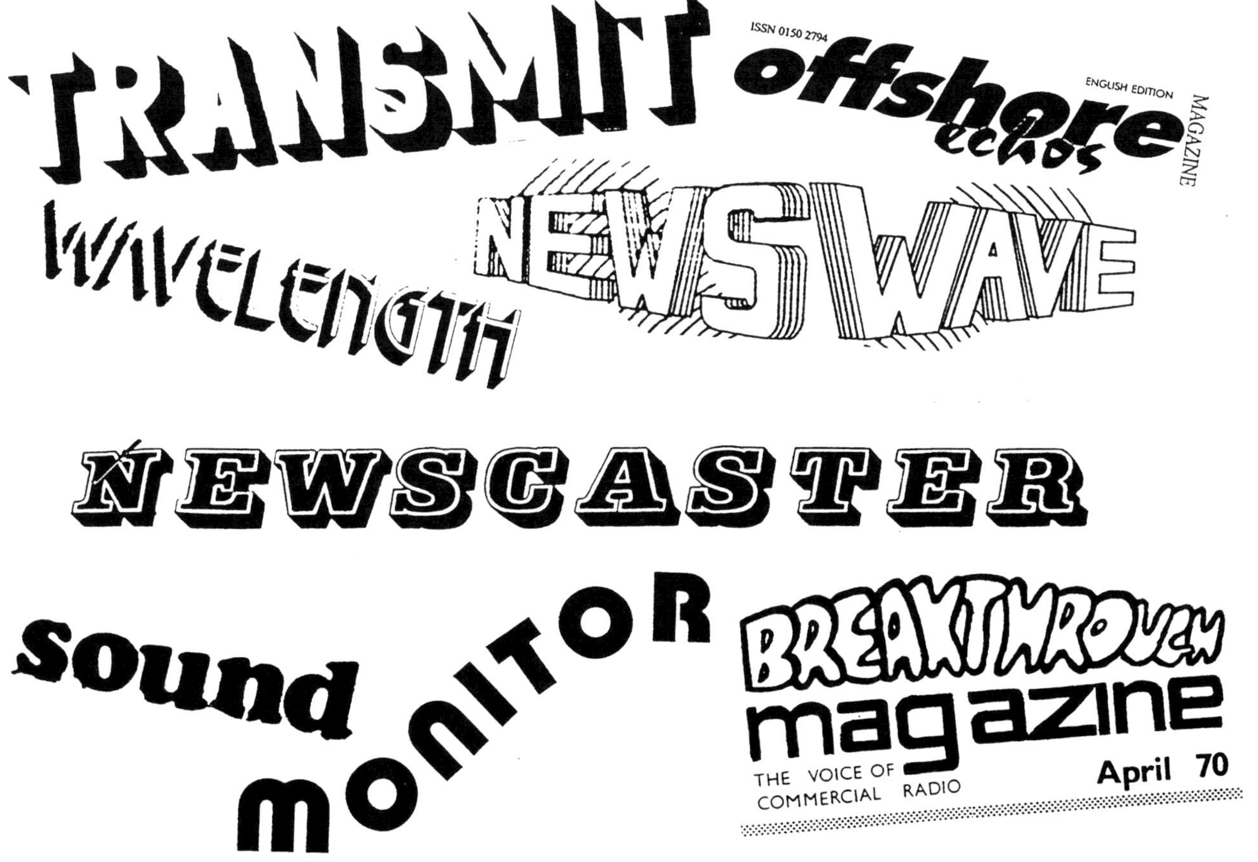

# Chapter 16

# Survival campaigns

Having successfully returned to international waters and resumed transmissions Radio Caroline settled into a regular 24 hour format during early January 1973 and the station's signal quality gradually improved. Dutch language programmes were broadcast from 6.00am-6.00pm, with an English language service in the evenings and overnight.

However, at the end of the month the station started to experience a number of technical breakdowns and went off the air completely on 21st January 1973. Regular programmes recommenced a few days later, although the transmitter was running on a very much reduced power. Further problems were experienced with the *Mi Amigo's* generators during February and March 1973 and they finally failed altogether on 26th March, forcing Radio Caroline transmissions to be discontinued. Lack of finance to replace vital parts meant that the station was likely to be off the air for some time.

**Radio Caroline programme schedule, January 1973**

**5.00am Paul Dubois**

**7.00am Mike Storm**

**9.00am Ron Dolman**

**11.00am Mike Storm**

**1.00pm Paul Dubois**

**3.00pm Ron Dolman**

**5.00pm Steve England**

**8.00pm Norman Barrington**

**11.00pm Andy Archer**

**2.00am Night Trip,** *Dick Palmer*

RNI recommenced test transmissions in the 31m shortwave band at the end of January 1973 and these continued sporadically into February. On 23rd February 1973 the *Mebo II's* anchor chain broke during a storm and transmissions on all frequencies were stopped as the radio ship had drifted inside Dutch territorial waters. Broadcasts recommenced the following day after the *Mebo II* had been towed back to her position and a new anchor chain fitted.

Adverse weather conditions caused much worse problems for three radio ships off the coast of Holland on 2nd April 1973. A gale had been blowing all day which steadily increased in intensity until it reached hurricane force, turning out to be the worst storm in living memory. At 8.45pm that evening Scheveningen Radio received a distress message from the Radio Veronica ship, *Norderney* saying that she had broken from her moorings and was drifting towards land.

## IBA test transmissions

*On 15th January 1973 the Independent Broadcasting Authority (IBA) started test transmissions in readiness for the introduction of local commercial radio in London later in the year. One of the frequencies used for the test transmissions was 557kHz (538m), the same as used by Radio Veronica off the coast of Holland.*

*The effect of these test broadcasts, which were made from a temporary aerial strung between two chimneys at the London Transport power station at Lotts Road, Battersea, was to blot out reception of Radio Veronica in London and the south east. Listeners who complained about the 'jamming' of the offshore station were told that the IBA was using a frequency allocated to Britain under international agreement and that Radio Veronica was broadcasting on the frequency without authorisation. The IBA also pointed out that it had been allocated the frequency by the Post Office before Radio Veronica had changed from 192m in September 1972.*

**RNI Programme schedule February 1973**

*Monday - Friday*

**6.00am Gerard Smit/ Mark van Amstel** *(live)*

**9.00am Branding** *(non-stop music)*

**10.00am Peter Holland, Doorsnee Noordsee**

**12noon Tony Berk in Action**

**2.00pm Ferry Maat**

**4.00pm Driemaster,** *Leo van der Groot and Alfred Lagarde (live)*

**6.00pm Nico Steenbergen**

**8.00pm Mike Ross Show** *(Mon-Wed)*

**Around Europe** *(Thursday)*

**International Top 30 Show** *(Friday)*

**10.00pm Don Allen Show** *(Mon-Fri)*

**1.00am Brian McKenzie Show**

**Friday 12midnight - 2.00am Country and Western Jamboree,** *Don Allen*

*Saturday As Monday-Friday except:-*

**10.00am Sports Programme,** *Nico Steenbergen*

**12noon Super Top 50 Show,** *Ferry Maat*

**3.00pm Dutch DJ Hitpicks,** *Tony Berk*

**4.00-6.00am Skyline Show,** *Mark Slate*

*Sunday As Monday-Friday except:-*

**12midnight Rock and Roll Show,** *Brian McKenzie*

**4.00am Skyline Show,** *Mark Slate*

**8.00-10.00pm Hitback Show,** *Mike Ross*

---

**10.00am-8.00pm RNI World Service** *on 6205kHz Shortwave (including* **10.00-11.00am Nordsee Goes DX** *with A J Beirens)*

*News and Weather on the hour between 7.00am and 2.00am*

The lifeboat *Bernard van Leer* was launched and shortly before 10.00pm it took four men off the *Norderney,* then stood by to provide further assistance if required. Half an hour later transmissions from Radio Veronica stopped suddenly, with a Dutch technician broadcasting a final message of reassurance to friends and relatives ashore. The six remaining crew members were then taken off the radio ship by the lifeboat.

Within an hour the abandoned *Norderney,* battered by wind and waves ran aground 50 yards from the entrance to Scheveningen Harbour. Meanwhile, the lifeboat with the rescued Radio Veronica crew on board was itself still at sea, unable to enter harbour until 10.00am the following morning due to the severity of the storm.

The same storm also damaged RNI's transmitter masts on board the *Mebo II* and the station's signal deteriorated so severely that by 5.00pm on 2nd April 1973 it had to leave the air. It was not until 1.15pm the following day that low power transmissions were able to start once again, but on medium wave and shortwave only. The FM aerial had been so severely damaged that transmissions in that waveband did not resume for over three weeks until a replacement aerial could be installed.

Meanwhile, the third and potentially most vulnerable radio ship, *Mi Amigo,* lost her main anchor during the storm , but the crew were able to lower the spare anchor which stopped the vessel drifting too far. She then remained largely unaffected by the severe weather, although at this time Radio Caroline itself was already off the air due to generator breakdowns and insufficient finance to carry out repairs.

## Caroline rescues Veronica

On the morning of 3rd April 1973 Caroline's owner, Ronan O'Rahilly, realised the plight of Radio Veronica whose vessel had run aground during the night and at the same time saw an opportunity to generate some much needed income. He contacted Radio Veronica's owners and offered the use of the *Mi Amigo's* studio and transmitter facilities as a temporary base for the stranded Dutch station.

From Radio Veronica's point of view it was particularly important that the station returned to the air as quickly as possible. A mass rally had been arranged in The Hague for 18th April 1973 to coincide with a Parliamentary hearing on the Dutch Government's proposed anti-offshore radio legislation. Radio Veronica had played a key role in arranging the demonstration and the station desperately needed to be on the air to publicise and report on the event.

The directors of Radio Veronica also received many other offers of help, including one from RNI for the use its second medium wave transmitter on board the *Mebo II*, but before accepting any outside assistance they decided that they would attempt to have the *Norderney* re-floated.

Salvage firm Smit-Tak worked for days trying to re-float the beached vessel, first by digging a channel in the sand to enable water to reach her and then by turning her so that the bow of the ship faced out to sea. At high tides on 7th and 8th April repeated attempts were made to re-float the *Norderney*, but she remained stubbornly embedded in the sand of Scheveningen beach. The station had by then been off the air for over five days and the directors decided they would have to accept one of the offers of assistance. They chose Ronan O'Rahilly's offer for the temporary use of the *Mi Amigo*.

A hectic 48 hours aboard the *Mi Amigo* saw the generators repaired, studio equipment overhauled and a new temporary aerial erected, all at Radio Veronica's expense. By 9.00am on 11th April 1973 test transmissions were able to commence with regular Radio Veronica programmes from the *Mi Amigo* starting at 12 noon the same day on 1187kHz (253m). Transmitter power was just less than 10Kw and, given the temporary nature of the aerial which had so hurriedly been erected on the *Mi Amigo*, a satisfactory signal was achieved enabling Radio Veronica programmes to be heard once again over a large part of Holland.

It was not until a week later, at 4.00am on 18th April 1973 that the *Norderney* was at last re-floated and towed back to her anchorage position, with test transmissions for Radio Veronica starting as soon as the vessel reached international waters. Regular Radio Veronica programmes re-commenced from the *Norderney* at 10.00am on 18th April 1973, which also happened to be the day of The Hague Parliamentary hearing and the rally in support of offshore radio.

The timely return of the *Norderney* to her anchorage and of Radio Veronica's transmissions to their usual position on the radio dial added a symbolic strength to demands from supporters outside the Dutch Parliament building for the station to be allowed to continue broadcasting. It was estimated that 150,000 people turned up at the rally and a two million signature was presented on behalf of Radio Veronica.

**Top Radio DJ Poll**

*In March 1973 the results of a "Top Radio DJ" poll, organised by the magazine 'DJ and Radio Monthly', were published and RNI English Service DJs Brian McKenzie and Mike Ross came 6th and 15th respectively.*

*Towards the end of the month both DJs ignored the possible consequences of prosecution under the Marine etc. Broadcasting (Offences) Act 1967 and returned to London to attend the award presentation ceremony held at the Inn on the Park Hotel.*

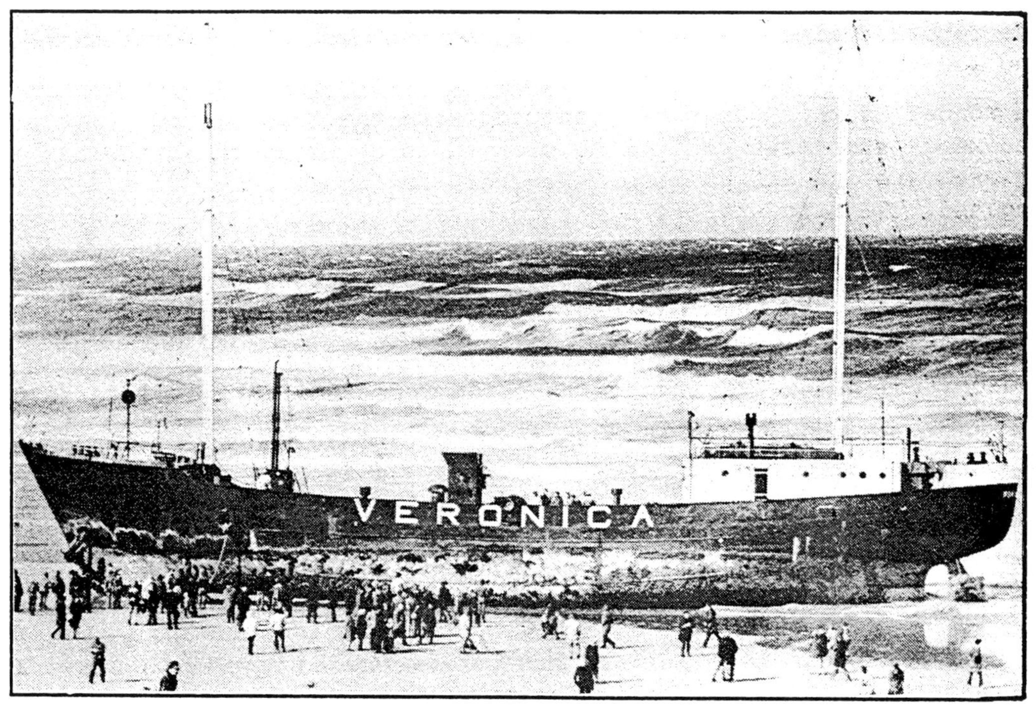


*'Norderney' stranded on Scheveningen Beach*

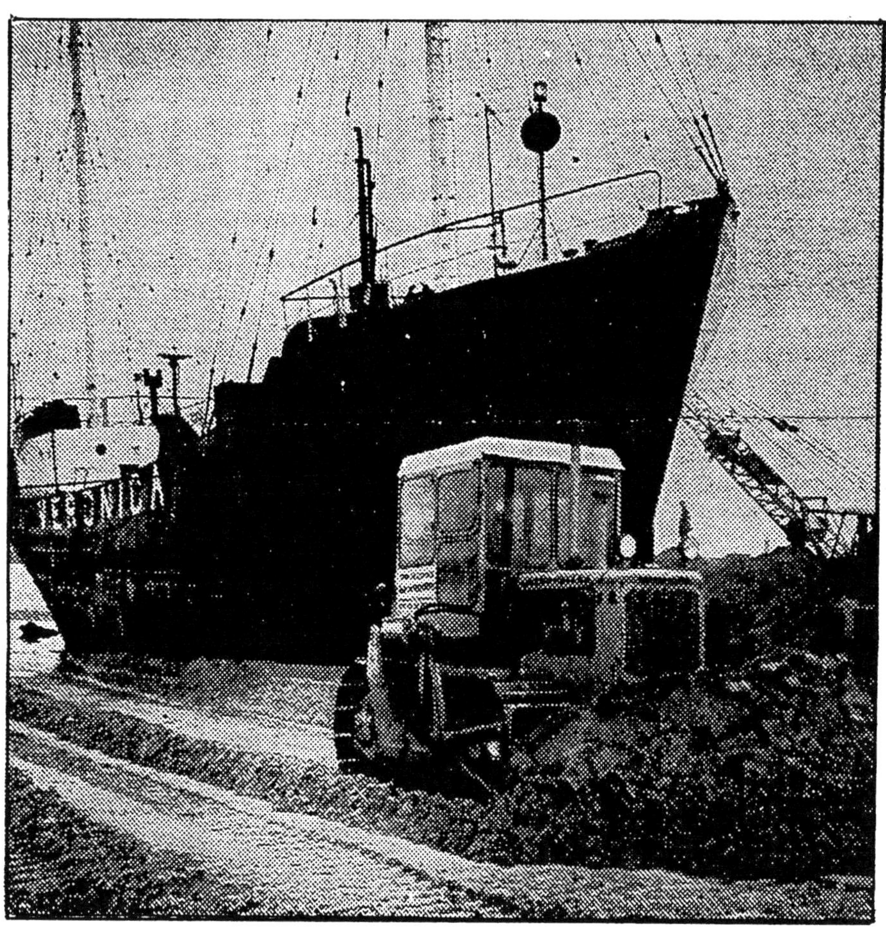


A bulldozer digs a trench around the 'Norderney' in an attempt to help refloat the radio ship

The politicians, however, were not persuaded, even by the huge demonstration of public support, the like of which had never been seen in the Dutch capital before or a public opinion poll showing that 75% of the population wanted Radio Veronica to be allowed to continue. Although nothing was decided at the 18th April hearing all the signs were that legislation would be introduced sooner rather than later to outlaw the offshore stations.

On 11th May 1973 a new, left of centre coalition Government was installed in Holland and a new Minister, Dr. Harry van Doorn, took responsibility for broadcasting matters. Despite popular public opinion, amply demonstrated outside Parliament on 18th April, he enthusiastically set about ensuring the end of offshore radio stations off the coast of Holland.

Dr. van Doorn had previously been Chairman of one of the Hilversum broadcasting companies and had virtually promised his former colleagues that, once in office, he would ensure that the offshore stations were silenced. The Dutch Cabinet decided on 20th June that it must proceed with the introduction of legislation - a decision itself brought about in part as the result of pressure from the Hilversum broadcasting companies, particularly VARA which threatened to withdraw its support for the fragile coalition government if the offshore stations were not closed.

Meanwhile, the *Mi Amigo* continued to relay Radio Veronica programmes until 6.00am on 20th April 1973, when the temporary arrangement between the two rival stations ended. Although the relay was not strictly necessary Radio Caroline planned to start its own programmes again after over a week of capturing Radio Veronica's audience with their radios tuned to 253m. Unfortunately, at the vital moment equipment on board the *Mi Amigo* failed once again and Radio Caroline was forced to close without having achieved its objective.

Nevertheless the arrangement, while it lasted, had benefited both parties - it had enabled Radio Veronica to return to the air at least a week sooner than it would otherwise have done, recapturing its audience and generating advertising income, but more importantly the station was actually broadcasting when listeners were demonstrating in its support outside the Dutch Parliament. It was a happy coincidence that these transmissions came from the *Norderney,* but had the vessel not been re-floated just hours before at least on board the *Mi Amigo* Radio Veronica had a temporary home from which to operate

## Caroline back on the air

For Radio Caroline the arrangement had enabled much needed technical repairs to be carried out on the *Mi Amigo* and the station received an all important injection of finance from the Radio Veronica organisation in the form of airtime hire fees, money which was used to purchase a completely new aerial mast. This then meant that Radio Caroline was able to return to the air during the spring and early summer of 1973, certainly a lot sooner than it would otherwise have done.

During the early part of May 1973 engineers and DJs on the *Mi Amigo* erected most of the new 165' lattice mast, constructed a second studio, refurbished another transmitter and installed a second aerial. This resulted in test broadcasts taking place on 773kHz (389m) on 13th and 14th May 1973, using a 10Kw transmitter with the original 50Kw transmitter being brought into use on 1187kHz (253m) on 15th May 1973. Within two days both transmitters and frequencies were being used to broadcast simultaneously and at the end of the month individual test transmissions using the call signs Radio Caroline One (773Khz, 389m) and Radio Caroline Two (1187kHz, 253m) were started.

By 4th June 1973 Radio Caroline was ready to start its dual service transmissions and the schedule of broadcasts from the *Mi Amigo* now looked like this:-

- Caroline International (English) 773kHz (389m) (10Kw) 6.00am-2.00am pop music
- Caroline Dutch Service 1187kHz (253m) (50Kw) 6.00am-7.00pm pop music
- Radio Caroline Overnight English Service 1187kHz (253m) (50Kw) 7.00pm-6.00am - progressive music

Unfortunately, just as everything appeared to be settling down for Radio Caroline problems were experienced with the *Mi Amigo's* generators once again and at 7.20pm on 26th June 1973 power was lost completely and both stations left the air abruptly.

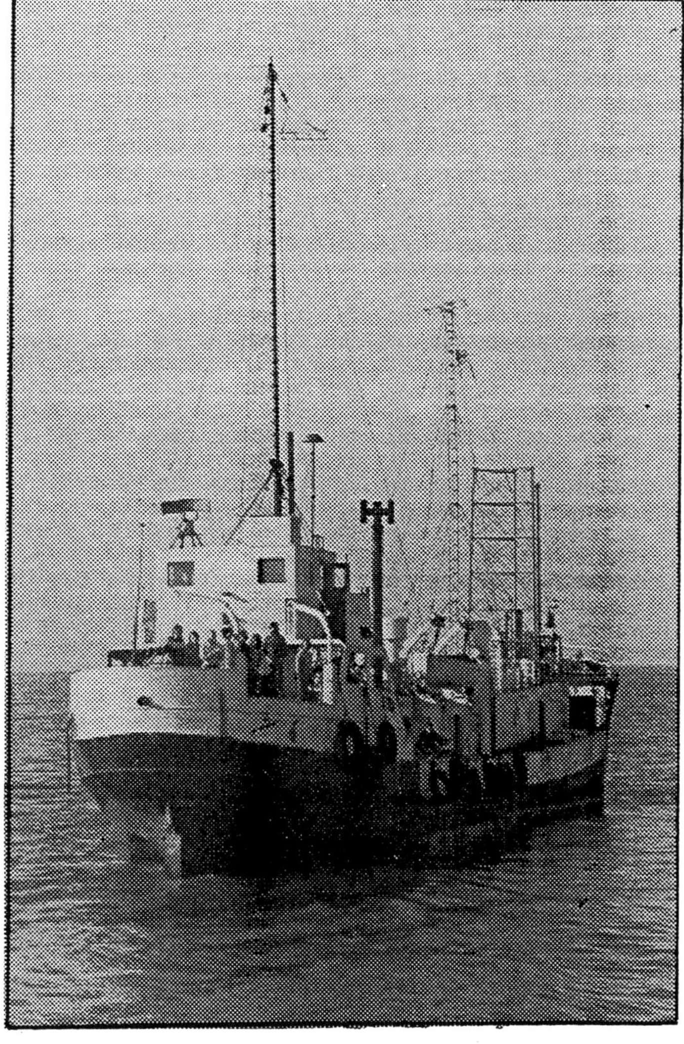

The 'Mi Amigo' with a new mast partially constructed

RNI discontinued its shortwave World Service again on 27th May 1973, although the DX programme, "Noordsee Goes DX" presented by A J Beirens, was retained every Sunday between 10.00am and 12 noon. Also at about this time the station's Zurich office was closed and the Swiss owners handed over all responsibility for radio programming to the Dutch airtime contractors, Radio Reklame Maatschappij, of Bussum. This change was partly attributed to the fact that the Swiss Government had introduced legislation against people based in that land-locked country operating offshore radio stations and partly due to the desire to demonstrate to the now hostile Dutch Government that RNI was a Dutch operation and could become eligible for airtime on the Hilversum network.

## Radio Caroline programme schedule, June 1973

*English Service (389m)*

**6.00am Non-stop music**

**7.00am Johan Maasbach** *(sponsored religious programme)*

**7.30am Paul Alexander**

**9.00am Andy Archer**

**12noon Spangles Muldoon** *(taped)*

**1.00pm Robin Adcroft**

**4.00pm Norman Barrington**

**6.00pm Paul Alexander**

**9.00pm Norman Barrington**

**12midnight Dick Palmer**

**2.00am Closedown**

*Dutch Service (259m)*

**6.00am Non-stop music**

**7.00am Joost Verhoeven** *(taped)*

**10.00am Ad Peterson** *(taped)*

**12noon Mike Storm** *(tape)*

**1.00pm Joop Verhoof** *(live)*

**4.00pm Andy Archer** *(live)*

**6.00pm Henk Meeuwis** *(live)*

**7.00pm Closedown**

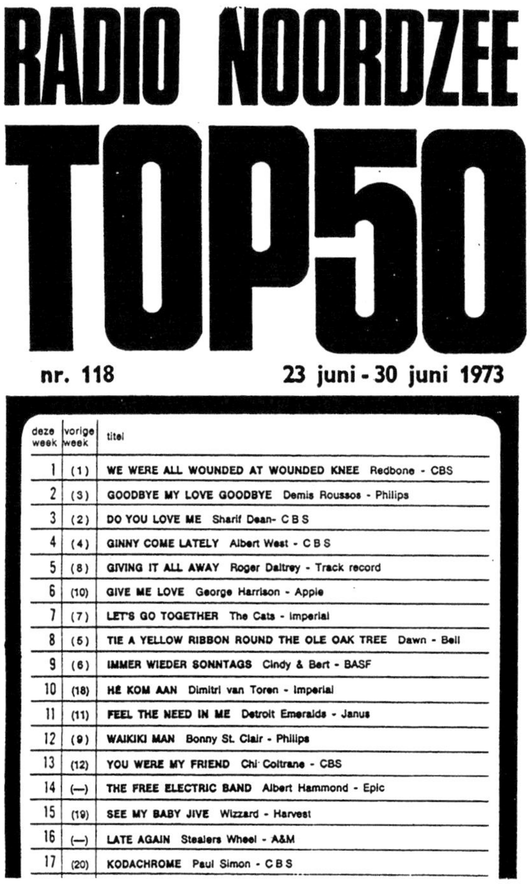

The reason for this was that in Holland at that time any organisation which set up a broadcasting society and attracted a certain number of paying members (a minimum of 15,000 each paying 5 Guilders) was entitled to an allocation of airtime on the Hilversum network.

## Campaigns launched

Early in 1973 Radio Veronica had launched the Veronica Broadcasting Society (VOS) with the aim of obtaining a broadcasting licence through the allocation of an additional wavelength on the Hilversum network and an application for that licence was submitted to the Dutch authorities.

RNI launched its own campaign, "Hou'm in de lucht" ("Keep it on the Air"), which involved heavy advertising in the press, distribution of stickers, T shirts and posters and various publicity stunts including parachute jumps, leaflet distribution from aircraft and a fleet of seven Mini cars touring the country to promote the station. An RNI caravan also toured the country signing up members and selling souvenirs. As part of the campaign RNI also sponsored a number of sports events throughout Holland.

## Dutch offshore debate

The Dutch Parliament considered the question of offshore radio again in June 1973. The delicate balance of Dutch politics was a major factor leading to the introduction of anti-offshore radio legislation at this time. It had taken five months to put together the left wing coalition government which had been in power since mid-May 1973 and various organisations who had given their support (for example some of the Hilversum broadcasting companies) now wanted some 'pay-off'.

However, the Upper House of the Dutch Parliament, the Senate, made it clear to the coalition Cabinet that they would not be rushed by Harry van Doorn and

**RADIO NOORDZEE TOP50**

**nr. 118** **23 juni - 30 juni 1973**

| deze week | vorige week | titel |
|---|---|---|
| 1 | (1) | WE WERE ALL WOUNDED AT WOUNDED KNEE Redbone - CBS |
| 2 | (3) | GOODBYE MY LOVE GOODBYE Demis Roussos - Philips |
| 3 | (2) | DO YOU LOVE ME Sharif Dean- C B S |
| 4 | (4) | GINNY COME LATELY Albert West - C B S |
| 5 | (8) | GIVING IT ALL AWAY Roger Daltrey - Track record |
| 6 | (10) | GIVE ME LOVE George Harrison - Apple |
| 7 | (7) | LET'S GO TOGETHER The Cats - Imperial |
| 8 | (5) | TIE A YELLOW RIBBON ROUND THE OLE OAK TREE Dawn - Bell |
| 9 | (6) | IMMER WIEDER SONNTAGS Cindy & Bert - BASF |
| 10 | (18) | HÈ KOM AAN Dimitri van Toren - Imperial |
| 11 | (11) | FEEL THE NEED IN ME Detroit Emeralds - Janus |
| 12 | (9) | WAIKIKI MAN Bonny St. Clair - Philips |
| 13 | (12) | YOU WERE MY FRIEND Chi Coltrane - CBS |
| 14 | (—) | THE FREE ELECTRIC BAND Albert Hammond - Epic |
| 15 | (19) | SEE MY BABY JIVE Wizzard - Harvest |
| 16 | (—) | LATE AGAIN Stealers Wheel - A&M |
| 17 | (20) | KODACHROME Paul Simon - C B S |

## RNI song

*A special song was composed as part of the RNI Campaign and played frequently during programmes on both the Dutch and English Services:-*

*RNI is here to stay*
*It's never going away,*
*We're going to rock together*

*RNI is radio,*
*The station on the go,*
*We're going to roll together.*

*So stomp your feet*
*And get set in,*
*To catch a spin,*
*We're on the ball,*
*We've got it all at RNI!*

## Dutch Broadcasting System

*In 1973 the transmission time of the three radio and two television networks in Holland, the Hilversum Network, was allocated between approximately 30 organisations, who provided programmes covering a wide spectrum of interest.*

*This system had been developed after the Second World War when the previously separate broadcasters formed the Netherlands Radio Union in 1951. The Union acted in a similar way to the British Independent Television Authority (and later the Independent Broadcasting Authority) in providing technical facilities for the broadcasters and programme makers. A similar Union was established when television broadcasting was introduced.*

*In 1967, with increasing demands from more and more organisations for airtime allocations on the Hilversum Network a revised system was introduced. This allowed groups with more than 15,000 paid-up members to be granted the status of 'prospective broadcasting society' and an allocation of one hour television airtime and three hours of radio airtime per week for two years. If the group increased its membership to 100,000 it would be recognised as an official broadcasting organisation. Church, social and political organisations were exempt from the minimum membership requirements. The 1967 Act also introduced advertising for the first time and the STER (Union for Airwave Commercials) was formed.*

*In 1969 the Netherlands Radio and Television Unions combined to form NOS (Dutch Broadcasting Society), which provided technical facilities for television transmissions was also a programme maker itself, specialising in news output. NOS was also responsible for the provision of regional 'opt out' programmes on the television network. Radio studio facilities were now provided by individual broadcasting groups and transmitters maintained by the Dutch Post Office (PTT).*

*The qualifying membership figures for airtime allocations were announced annually in July and adjustments were made in allocations to take account of changes in membership levels. All broadcasting societies have to provide balanced programming on all networks, including pop, classical music, discussions, plays etc.*

*The main broadcasting societies in Holland in 1973 were:*

| | |
|---|---|
| *VARA (Socialist Party)* | *AVRO (General Radio Union)* |
| *TROS (Successors to 1964 offshore TV and Radio Noordsee)* | *KRO (Catholic Radio)* |
| *NCRV (Dutch Christian Radio Union)* | *VPRO (Liberal Protestant Party)* |
| *EO (Gospel Radio)* | *NOS (Dutch Broadcasting Authority)* |

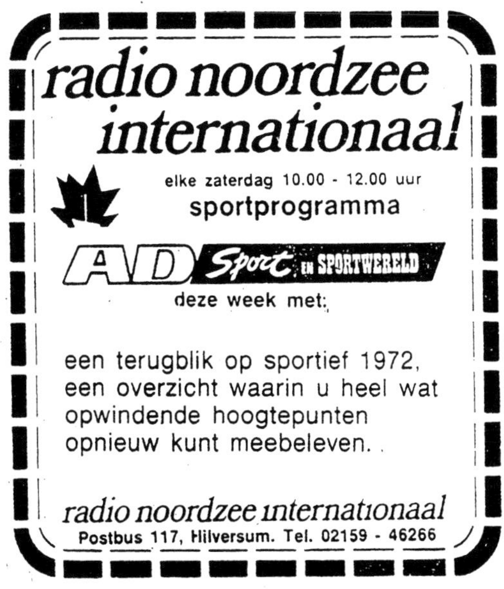


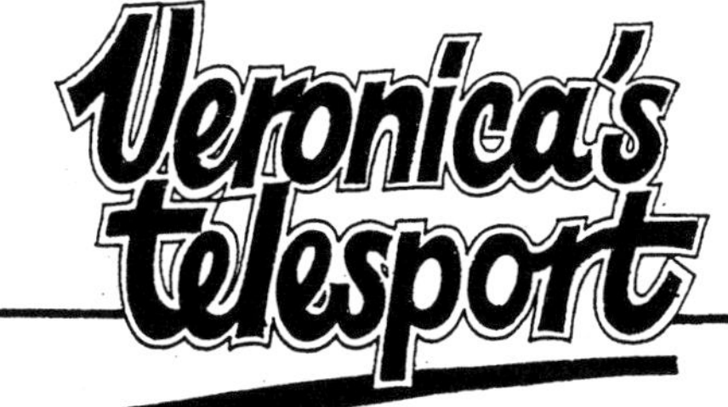


in samenwerking met de sportredactie van De Telegraaf
Luister elke zondag van 11.00-12.00 uur naar hét programma voor de sportliefhebber.
Veronica's-Telesport in samenwerking met de sportredactie van De Telegraaf
elke zondag van 11.00-12.00 uur
Radio Veronica, Postbus 218, Hilversum
Tel. 02150-51045

**luister mee naar Telesport**

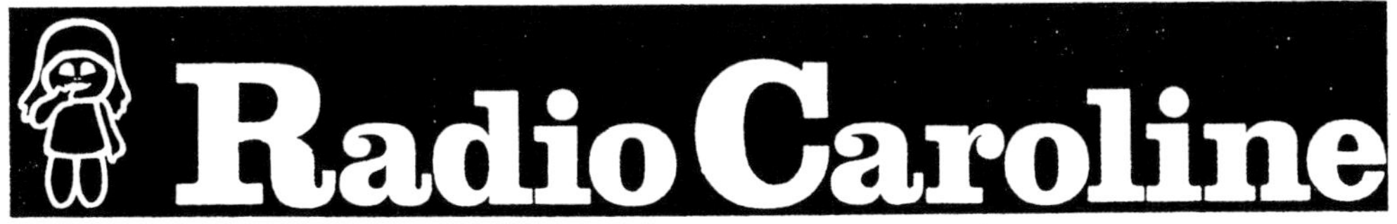

his colleagues into approving legislation against the offshore broadcasters - they wanted to examine it and its implications very carefully. This was an early indication of possible delays ahead for the Government's plans.

During the course of the debate it became clear that seven parties (holding 52 of the 150 votes) were set against the Government proposals, but another seven parties (holding a significant 98 votes) were going to support the planned legislation. The crucial factor had been the decision by one of the largest groups, the Catholics, to announce their support for the Government and this effectively meant that the legislation would be passed.

However, even amongst those who indicated support for Radio Veronica (and not necessarily the other offshore stations) some were prepared to vote for Holland to ratify the Strasbourg Convention to outlaw offshore broadcasting - their primary purpose was to secure a legal, landbased status for Veronica and the other offshore stations could still be outlawed.

The Dutch Parliament also voted against Radio Veronica's request to be allowed a separate wavelength - effectively becoming a new Hilversum 4 station. With this refusal Radio Veronica immediately announced the launch of VOO (Veronica Broadcasting Organisation), replacing the VOS (Veronica Broadcasting Society) which had been founded in expectation of the station being granted a full licence. VOO was the vehicle by which Radio Veronica now hoped to secure an allocation of airtime on the Hilversum network and it set about achieving the required number of members.

On 28th June 1973, following a three day debate, the Lower House of the Dutch Parliament voted by 95 to 37 in favour of ratifying the Strasbourg Convention and by 94 votes to 39 in favour of the Bill to outlaw offshore radio stations. The legislation still had to be passed by the Upper House which was to cause some delays for the Government.

The day after Parliament's decision RNI issued statements about the station's future. The Dutch Service would remain on the air until the new legislation came into force, but the campaign for a landbased licence (for which an application had already been made) would continue. However, the future of the International (English) Service remained uncertain and a further statement was promised later. The Hou'm in de Lucht campaign in Holland did continue and by mid July 1973 it had attracted over 30,000 members.

Radio Veronica had also attracted a considerable number of members by the end of July 1973 - over 100,000 each meeting the qualification requirements (paying the Government's radio and television licence fee, paying a subscription to the broadcasting society (VOO) and subscribing to the society's programme guide).

This number of members clearly qualified VOO to an airtime allocation, but on 8th August 1973 Minister van Doorn announced that while consideration would be given to VOO the actual number of members would have to be ratified. The Minister subsequently made various administrative changes to the qualifying rules for calculating the number of broadcasting society members and ultimately ruled that a 'member' must have registered using their full name - no abbreviations or shortened versions would be eligible.

The immediate effect of this ruling was to reduce VOO's membership level below 100,000, but the station continued its campaign to achieve legal status despite the obstacles place in its way by Minister van Doorn and eventually enrolled over 300,000 members. However, the Government now argued that, despite meeting the qualification requirements for broadcasting status, Veronica could not be allowed to join the Hilversum network because Hilversum 3 already

### RNI Dutch Service News

*RNI's Dutch Service obtained its news from a variety of sources. Casette recorders on board the Mebo II were linked to radios tuned to Hilversum 1, 2 and 3 in Holland, Belgian state radio BRT 1 and 2, the BBC World Service and Deutchlandfunk in West Germany. The station also maintained a telex link to the United Press news agency and the Dutch daily newspaper 'Algemeen Dagblad'.*

provided an adequate pop music service. Radio Veronica also made an appeal to the Government for a six month delay in the implementation of the new Dutch Marine Offences Act, but this was refused.

## Radio Atlantis launched

With continuing technical problems forcing Radio Caroline to remain silent the organisation managed to obtain two new Deutz generators which were taken out to the *Mi Amigo* and mounted on the aft deck of the ship during early July 1973. Some remaining sections of the lattice frame aerial mast were also put in place at this time giving the structure a total height of 180'. The need to achieve this installation quickly was brought about because Ronan O'Rahilly had agreed once again to hire the *Mi Amigo's* facilities to another broadcaster. This time he had arranged a deal for a new Belgian station to be launched from the *Mi Amigo* in-mid July, generating much needed income for Radio Caroline in the absence of any commercial advertising revenue of its own.

The new station, Radio Atlantis, was the brainchild of a 25 year old wealthy Belgian businessman, Adriaan van Landschoot. Because the Belgian Government had passed legislation in 1962 outlawing offshore radio stations (at the time of Radio Antwerpen's broadcasts from the *Uilenspiegel* -see Chapter 4) Landschoot had to operate his station from an address in Oostburg, Holland, where programmes were also pre-recorded in a land- based studio.

Adriaan van Landschoot had originally planned to launch the station from his own ship, but to avoid further delays he entered into an agreement with Ronan O'Rahilly to hire the *Mi Amigo's* 50Kw transmitter for 13 hours a day (at a cost of £2,000 per week) over a period of three months starting in mid-July 1973. Although the transmitter Landschoot hired was tuned to a frequency of 773kHz (388m) the new station's publicity material and on-air announcements referred to a wavelength of 385m which was what he originally planned to use had the station been based on his own vessel.

Radio Atlantis programmes were scheduled to start on 15th July 1973 and extensive publicity was given in Belgium and Holland to the new station - hence the necessity for the Caroline organisation to have all technical problems aboard the *Mi Amigo* resolved in time.

At 10.00am on 15th July 1973 test transmissions started from the *Mi Amigo* and continued for two hours with non-stop Beatles music. Radio Atlantis officially opened at 12 noon that day and programmes continued until 7.00pm in the evening. The following day a regular programme schedule was adopted from 6.00am - 7.00pm with a format of international pop music and recordings by Belgian artists.

**Radio Atlantis programme schedule, July 1973**

| | |
|---|---|
| 6.00am | Non-stop music |
| 7.00am | Luk van Kapellen |
| 9.00am | Mike Moorkens |
| 10.00am | Peter van Dam |
| 12noon | Tony Houston |
| 2.00pm | Luk van Kapellen |
| 3.00pm | Mike Moorkens |
| 4.00pm | Peter van Dam |
| 6.00pm | Tony Houston |
| 6.30pm | Mike Moorkens |
| 7.00pm | Closedown |

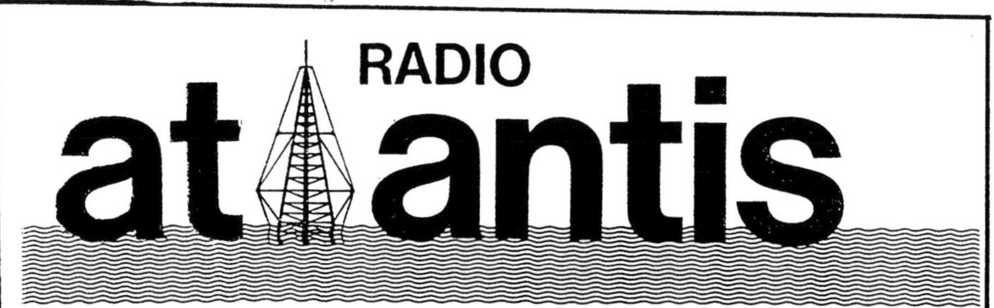

Although everything went well for a short time frequent transmitter failures during July caused the station to be off the air for various periods, and there were occasions when Radio Caroline staff on board the *Mi Amigo* had to play continuous music because the quality of the Radio Atlantis pre-recorded tapes was too poor to broadcast. Despite these difficulties, however, Radio Atlantis was an immediate success with listeners in its target area of Flemish-speaking Belgium and an estimated regular audience of 5 million was soon achieved.

## Radio Condor

Yet another offshore radio station planned to take to the air off the Dutch coast at the end of July 1973 further reinforcing the Dutch Government's view that the speedy introduction of legislation to outlaw such broadcasters was essential. During the early summer two Dutchmen Steph Willemsen and Gerrit Elferink purchased an ex-Icelandic trawler, *Emma* and started to fit her out as a radio ship at IJmuiden in Holland.

A 500 watt medium wave transmitter was built using parts from the former Capital Radio and Radio 270 10Kw RCA transmitter, which was tuned to 1115kHz (269m). Claims were also made that an FM transmitter had been installed on board the vessel, but there is no evidence that this was ever used. The proposed station, using the call sign Radio Condor, was to carry no commercials and have an easy listening music format with 'humanitarian, social and religious programmes', including airtime purchased by Dutch evangelist broadcasters Johan Maasbach and Rev. Dominee Toornvliet, who also backed the station financially.

The vessel, renamed *Zondaxonagon,* left IJmuiden on 30th July 1973 and anchored in international waters off Zandvoort. A number of test transmissions were claimed to have been made at the beginning of August, but on 10th August 1973 the ship's anchor chain broke and she was forced to return to port. After the *Zondaxonagon* had been towed into IJmuiden the Dutch Shipping Inspectorate declared her to be unseaworthy and within a few weeks she was sold for scrap.

After the sale the vessel was secretly towed out of port late in the evening of 25th September 1973, and once outside territorial waters, was re-purchased by Steph Willemse. But Radio Condor did not reappear on the airwaves because within a few weeks the *Zondaxonagon* had been acquired by yet another offshore radio station owner, Adriaan van Landschoot, who was about to transfer Radio Atlantis away from the *Mi Amigo* once the three month contract with Ronan O'Rahilly had expired.

- (POSTSCRIPT some years after the failure of the Radio Condor project Steph Willemse tried unsuccessfully to purchase the former Radio Veronica ship, *Norderney,* and also another vessel, *Maria.* Willemsen had been engaged by representatives of Suriname (formerly Dutch Guyana) to equip a radio ship for propaganda broadcasts off the South American coast. The project, however, never came to fruition.).

## Radio Seagull

Back on the *Mi Amigo* non-stop music was played on 388m after Radio Atlantis had closed on 21st July 1973. Similar continuous music programmes were broadcast for the next two evenings, but no announcements or station identities were made.

DJs from the former Radio Caroline had been pressing Ronan O'Rahilly to reintroduce an English language service from the *Mi Amigo* in addition to the Flemish output from Radio Atlantis. This eventually occurred at 8.00pm on 24th July 1973 when Andy Archer announced the start of a new English language

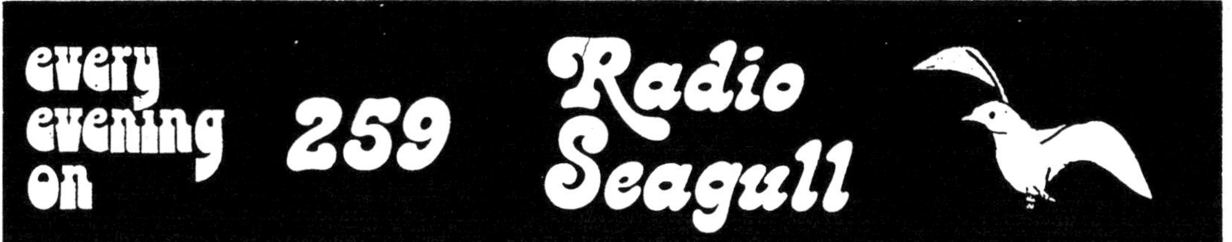


station - Radio Seagull. This new station was to broadcast 'progressive' music on 388m throughout the night until an hour before Radio Atlantis recommenced its transmissions at 6.00am the following morning. The name Radio Seagull, as well as having nautical overtones, was derived from the title of a contemporary cult book "Jonathon Livingston Seagull" about experimenting in freedom.

The introduction of an English language service was welcomed, but the format and progressive music content did not appeal to everyone - some DJs, many listeners and most potential advertisers were simply not interested in such an output. Many people still wanted a Top 40 format station, but the better established stations RNI and Radio Veronica were already catering adequately for such a market.

Of greater significance though was the likelihood that Radio Atlantis would have severed its links with the Caroline organisation sooner had an English language Top 40 station been launched at that time from the *Mi Amigo*. This after all was the format Radio Atlantis was providing during the day (although in a rather amateurish way) and any Top 40 Caroline English service, with its inevitable greater professionalism and larger audiences, would have attracted listeners and advertisers away from the Flemish station.

Radio Seagull with its 'progressive' music format was perceived by Ronan O'Rahilly as the ideal solution to these competing demands - an English language service to appease Caroline DJs and English speaking audiences, but one which was not in direct competition with Radio Atlantis, whose financial contribution was vital to keep the *Mi Amigo* at sea and operational.

Radio Seagull's service continued during the summer of 1973 although it was somewhat disorganised in presentation style and the music played was largely obscure album based material, described generically as 'progressive'. As the summer continued Radio Seagull became steadily more directionless and lacking in a definite music policy. It was only after two DJs who had been involved in the 1970 progressive music station, Radio Geronimo (see Chapter 13) joined Radio Seagull that things began to change, but not necessarily in the way originally envisaged. The DJs in question, Hugh Nolan and Barry Everett, became the dominant influence on Radio Seagull for the remainder of its time on the air during 1973, but their music choice was often very obscure, holding little interest or appeal for a mass market which the powerful *Mi Amigo* transmitter was able to reach.

It seemed that although the original concept of Radio Seagull had been devised for good reasons the actual execution of its programming style resulted in a missed commercial opportunity - not for the first or last time in Radio Caroline's history.

The influence of drugs also became a force on Radio Seagull during this period with some of the DJs regularly smoking joints of cannabis before and during their programmes. The station also started promoting the idea of love, peace and happiness - a throwback to the late 60s hippie era reflecting the cultural roots of many of the station's staff at that time. However, this was a concept which did not end after Radio Seagull closed and, under the title Loving Awareness (LA), was to play a more significant role in later Radio Caroline history.

Although audience figures were not available through any conventional research methods some small indication of the listener profile being reached by Radio Seagull at this time came from letters which were read on air by the DJs. A sizeable proportion of mail happened to come from inmates in various prisons who were serving sentences for drugs related offences and obviously felt an empathy with the output of Radio Seagull, and its DJs, during the summer of 1973!

The introduction and subsequent growth of Radio Seagull during the summer of 1973 was one factor which led to the departure of Chris Carey and his wife from the Radio Caroline organisation. Chris Carey had managed the station since its re-launch at the end of 1972 and had ensured that the *Mi Amigo* was regularly supplied with food and fuel and staffed with DJs and engineers. He was also the driving force in resolving a multitude of problems associated with returning and keeping Radio Caroline on the air during the difficult first few months.

His ambition was to try and re-create Radio Caroline as it had been in the 1960s - a successful Top 40 format station. The introduction of Radio Seagull's progressive music format, with Ronan O'Rahilly's active support, disillusioned him and, together with a number of other factors relating to the operation of the station led to him and his wife Kate leaving the organisation late in 1973. They left with a certain sense of bitterness over what they saw as a lost opportunity for Radio Caroline - to achieve greater commercial success than was being achieved at the time by either station on the *Mi Amigo* - a view which they held for sometime afterwards.

At the end of September 1973 the *Mi Amigo* was battered by severe storms and during the early morning of 1st October the recently constructed lattice frame aerial mast collapsed, leaving only a 26' section standing above the deck. Engineers hurriedly rigged up a temporary aerial by attaching wires between the remains of the original structure and the mast at the stern of the radio ship. Using only the 10Kw transmitter broadcasts of Radio Atlantis and Radio Seagull were able to start once again on 4th October, but signal strength was poor and reception for listeners was far from satisfactory.

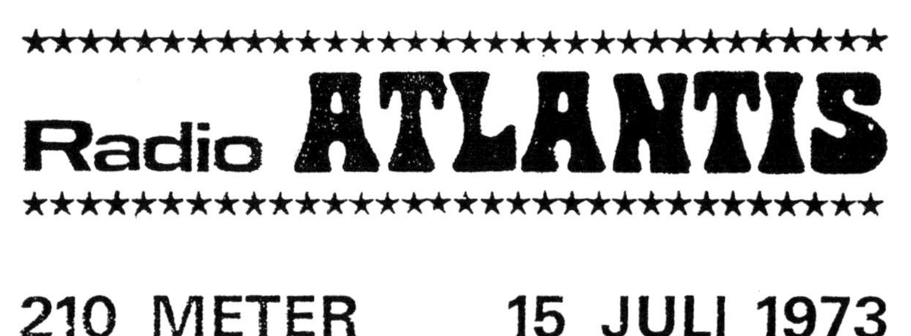


## Atlantis quits

At this time the initial three month contract between Adriaan van Landschoot and Ronan O'Rahilly was nearing its end and in addition to all the other technical difficulties, a regular supply of programme tapes for Radio Atlantis was often failing to reach the *Mi Amigo.* In an effort to provide listeners to the Flemish station with a full service old programme tapes were repeated or sometimes the English DJs, together with a Dutch crew member on board the *Mi Amigo,* presented live shows for Radio Atlantis

These on-air difficulties reflected the behind the scenes situation - Adriaan van Landschoot already had plans to re-launch Radio Atlantis from his own vessel and Ronan O'Rahilly was unwilling to renew the arrangement with him for the hire of facilities on the *Mi Amigo* because he had received a much better offer. Wealthy Belgian businessman Sylvain Tack wanted to hire the 389m transmitter on the *Mi Amigo* to launch a station of his own, using the call sign Radio Mi Amigo.

However, a further failure of the temporary aerial system, which collapsed at 9.30am on 18th October 1973, effectively put an end to all transmissions from the *Mi Amigo* for a time.

Before the aerial system collapsed, a number of test programmes had been aired after Radio Atlantis transmissions closed, first under the call sign Station 385 and then Radio Mi Amigo. These tests included a music programme called "Joepie" (named after a magazine of the same title owned by Sylvain Tack) and a taped religious programme from evangelist broadcaster Dominee Toornvliet (who had been involved in an unsuccessful attempt to launch an offshore radio station with three RNI DJs in 1970 and Radio Condor earlier in 1973).

The collapse of the temporary aerial system on 18th October 1973, which had put Radio Atlantis and Radio Seagull off the air, also delayed the planned official start of Radio Mi Amigo. In order to fulfil the lucrative contract with Radio Mi Amigo a new aerial mast was hurriedly obtained and partially erected on board the *Mi Amigo* during late October and early November 1973. Difficulties with storms and severe weather off the Dutch coast meant that only the first five of the nine section mast could be erected.

These severe storms also put the other two radio ships off the air for a short time on 13th November 1973. Radio Veronica was closed for three hours due to aerial damage and for some days afterwards the station played only non-stop music because the tender had been unable to deliver new programme tapes to the *Norderney*.

RNI also suffered breaks in transmissions due to the storms with the FM service being off the air for 10 days from 21st -31st October 1973. Other transmitter problems also plagued RNI at this time and resulted in one of the station's owners, Erwin Meister, travelling out to the *Mebo II* to carry out repairs himself. His work resulted in all three transmitters being restored to working order by mid-December 1973, but it was subsequently revealed that the RCA transmitter on board the *Mebo II* was a prototype and had been an unsuccessful design. There were inherent faults preventing it being operated at full power for any continuous period of time without overheating.

The solution would have been to strip and rebuild the transmitter, while temporarily transferring RNI's broadcasts to the 10Kw stand-by transmitter. However, the Dutch side of the operation, now more in control of the station than ever before, were unwilling to accept this solution for fear of losing their audience. They were quite happy to continue with the main transmitter operating at only 30-40Kw (out of a potential 105Kw),which still gave RNI three or four times more power than its main rival, Radio Veronica.

The English Service of RNI was extended from 11th November 1973 to run from 8.00pm to 6.00am, which together with the daytime Dutch Service put the station on a 24hour a day basis. However, there were still persistent rumours at this time that the *Mebo II* was to sail to Italy in January 1974 (when the Dutch anti-offshore legislation was expected to come into force) to provide an English, French and Italian service, Radio Nova International.

## Programmes from the *Mi Amigo* in October 1973

*Radio Atlantis*

**6.00am Non-Stop Music**

**7.00am Mike Moorkens**

**9.00am Bert Bennett**

**11.00am Joop Verhoof**

**12noon Tony Houston**

**2.00pm Top 40 Show**

**5.00pm Joop Verhoof**

**6.00pm Mike Moorkens**

*Radio Mi Amigo*

**7.00pm Peter van Dam**

**8.00-8.25pm Rev. Dominee Thoornvliet**

*Radio Seagull*

**9.00pm Johnny Jason**

**12midnight Tony Allan**

**3.00am Bob Noakes**

**5.00am Continuous music**

## *Record Mirror* poll

*'Record Mirror' on 29th September 1973 published the results of a poll to determine the most popular radio station in Britain. RNI came first with 51% of the votes, Caroline second with 15%, Radio Veronica third with 9%, while BBC Radio One received only 5%. However, the poll was not truly representative and reflected only the votes of those supporters willing to respond to the invitation to take part in the first place- RNI listeners were clearly more willing to do so than those of BBC Radio One, which in reality had a far larger audience in Britain.*

*Nevertheless 'Record Mirror' stated "Today the BBC stands condemned by Britain's pop-rock listeners who have passed a massive vote of no confidence in Radio One and the policy of government-controlled broadcasting. An overwhelming number of voters in 'Record Mirror's Radio Referendum urge the legalisation of the so called 'pirate' stations and the introduction of free radio." The introduction of local commercial radio in Britain was in fact just over a month away at the time of 'Record Mirror's poll. As a direct result of the poll's findings the paper changed its name for a few months to 'Radio and Record Mirror', and during that time carried articles and features in support of the offshore stations.*

INDEPENDENT
ILR
LOCAL RADIO

## Independent Local Radio

*Mainland Britain's first legal commercial radio stations began broadcasting in October 1973, both in London, breaking the BBC's 50 year radio monopoly.*

*First on the air was LBC a news an information station which launched on 8th October at 6.00am on 719kHz (417m) medium wave and 97.3mHz FM. A week later, on 16th October at 5.00am the music station, Capital Radio, was launched on 557kHz (539m) medium wave and 95.8 mHz FM.*

*Within twelve months of the two London based stations starting to broadcast other ILR stations were launched in Birmingham (BRMB), Glasgow (Radio Clyde), Manchester (Piccadilly Radio), Tyneside (Metro Radio), Swansea (Swansea Sound) and Sheffield (Radio Hallam) and the ILR network gradually spread throughout the country*

### RNI English (International) Service programme schedule, November 1973

7.00pm Mike Ross

9.00pm Brian McKenzie

12 midnight Don Allen

3.00am Skyline *(continuous music)*

5.00am Closedown

*A number of special programmes were included in the schedule at weekends:-*

*FRIDAY*

7.00pm International Top 30 Show

9.00pm Rock 'n' Roll Special - *Brian McKenzie*

*SATURDAY*

9.00pm Country and Western Jamboree - *Don Allen*

*SUNDAY*

7.00pm Hitback Show -*Mike Ross*

9.00pm RNI Request Show - *Graham Gill*

*MONDAY*

1.00am Contemporary Music Show -*Robb Eden*

However, the reverse was true for Radio Veronica. At the beginning of December 1973 the station was forced to suspend its 24hour weekend service and later in the month to end all weekday transmissions at midnight. This situation had been brought about because of the oil crisis facing the West in late 1973 as the result of embargoes placed on supplies by Arab oil producers.

Because of the November 1973 storms in the North Sea it was a month before any further work could be undertaken on the *Mi Amigo* to erect the four remaining sections of the new mast. this was particularly frustrating for Radio Mi Amigo which was anxious to come on the air as soon as possible before Radio Atlantis could be re-llaunched from its own vessel, stealing audiences and advertisers.

The final section of the new 165'mast was put in place by Christmas Eve and test transmissions were able to commence later that day at 3.45pm. The tests, which lasted until about 8.00pm contained no station identity announcement although the Radio Caroline theme, "Caroline" by The Fortunes, was played a number of times.

On Christmas Day 1973 DJs on board the *Mi Amigo* presented live programmes without any station identity by way of further test transmissions from 9.00am-1.00am, including a live link up with RNI from the *Mebo II.* A similar, but shorter test broadcast took place on 26th December, then further test transmissions using the call sign Radio Mi Amigo started on 28th December 1973. After these had ended at about 9.00pm that same day nothing except continuous music was heard from the MV *Mi Amigo* until New Year's Day 1974.

## Radio Atlantis returns

Meanwhile, Radio Atlantis which had left the air abruptly on the morning of 18th October 1973 when the *Mi Amigo's* temporary aerial system collapsed, had not renewed its contract with Ronan O'Rahilly. Radio Atlantis's owner, Adriaan van Landschoot , had already set about searching for his own vessel from which the station could be re-launched. There then followed a race to put Radio Atlantis back on the air before the new rival, Radio Mi Amigo, could be launched from the Caroline ship and establish itself in the Belgian radio market.

On 31st October 1973 he purchased the former Radio Condor vessel *Zondaxonagon* from its previous owner, Steph Willemse who had himself re-purchased the vessel from scrap dealers a few weeks earlier. Adriaan van Landschoot paid about 38,000 Belgian Francs for the ship, despite it having been declared unseaworthy by the authorities and the Radio Condor transmitting equipment on board being virtually useless.

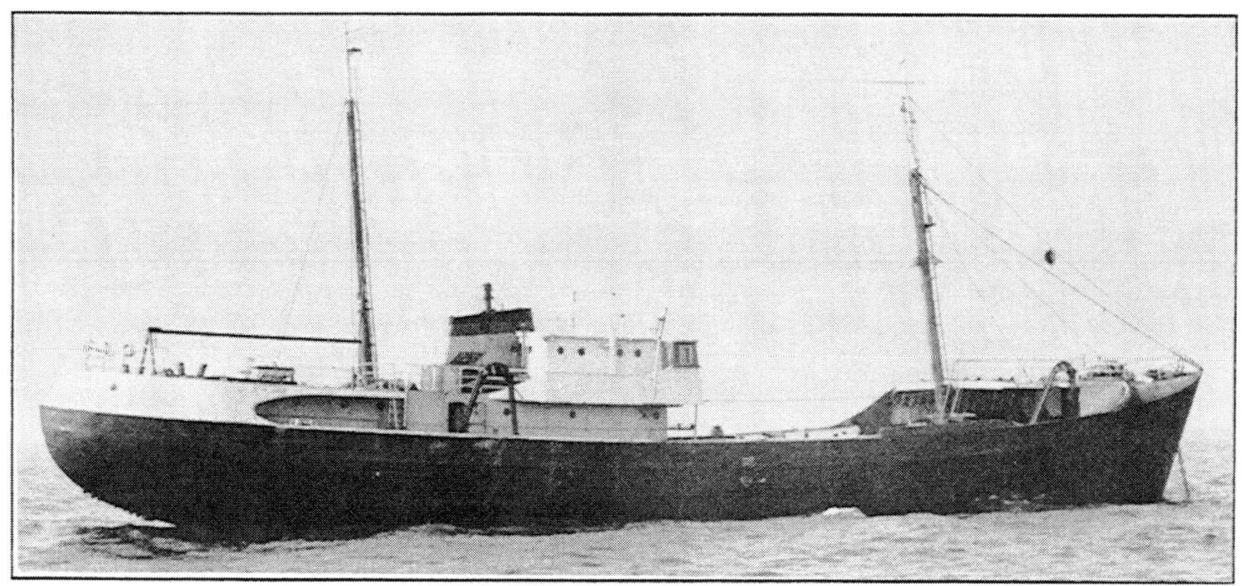

*The new Radio Atlantis ship, 'Janine'*

The ship was renamed *Janine,* after Adriaan van Landschoot's wife, and the former REM Island radio transmitter(used to broadcast programmes of Radio Noordzee in 1964- see Chapter 9) was purchased and installed on board to replace what was left of the ex-Radio 270/Capital Radio equipment with which Radio Condor had once hoped to broadcast. Test transmissions of continuous music were madeon low power from 3rd November 1973 on 656kHz (458m) and 1322kHz (227m) during which an on-air date of 15th November 1973 was given for the return of Radio Atlantis.

Unfortunately, two days after these test transmissions began the *Janine* broke from her anchor and the four crew members took to the lifeboats abandoning the drifting radio ship. Eventually the Wijsmuller salvage tug *Titan* put a line aboard the *Janine* and towed her to Cuxhaven in Germany where Adriaan van Landschoot arranged for a new anchoring system to be installed. The opportunity was also taken to carry out further improvement works while the *Janine* was in harbour and she eventually left Cuxhaven on 22nd December 1973, being towed to an anchorage in international waters off Knocke, Belgium.

On Christmas Eve 1973, the same day that unidentified test transmissions started from the *Mi Amigo's* new aerial mast, test broadcasts also took place for Radio Atlantis from the *Janine.* These transmissions on 1115kHz (269m) using very low power at first, started at 1.00pm and lasted until the early evening when reception deteriorated significantly.The test transmissions were introduced by on-board DJ Crispian St John, who had done a similar job almost exactly a year earlier on the *Mi Amigo* for Radio 199 and later Radio Caroline. English language test transmissions continued for about a week until the morning of 30th December 1973 when Flemish language programmes were introduced for the first time during daytime hours.The station then mounted an English language overnight service from 7.00pm - 6.00am, but reception during the hours of darkness continued to be particularly poor and prone to interference.

The project to put Radio Atlantis back on the air from its own vessel had been put together so hurriedly that the studio on board the *Janine* was only partially built at this time. The death of the station engineer, Chris Klinkenberg, in a freak accident on 22nd November 1973 compounded the technical problems facing the station. Klinkenberg was returning to the radio ship after a night out when the gang plank leading to the *Janine* broke and he fell into the icy waters of Cuxhaven Harbour.

During the test broadcasts DJs were forced to operate equipment which had not been fully installed and as a result frequent breakdowns were experienced, culminating within the first week of January 1974 with the station going off the air completely.

## NEWS + NEWS + NEWS + NEWS

*News bulletins featured on most offshore stations - many had regular hourly news broadcasts, while others opted for a smaller number of bulletins at peak times - breakfast, lunchtime and early evening.*

*The inclusion of news was an important element in keeping audiences tuned to the offshore stations - without such a service it was likely that many listeners would tune away to one of the 'established' stations to hear the news and probably not retune immediately to the offshore station. However, their isolated situation meant that, unlike their landbased counterparts, the offshore stations could not operate a conventional newsroom with journalists and reporters available to cover stories.*

*One station, Sweden's Radio Nord, made elaborate arrangements to gather its news (see Chapter 3), but following the withdrawal of ship-to-shore communication facilities it had to resort to doing what almost every other offshore station did - listen to the news output of landbased stations, re-write and re-broadcast it as their own news. Radio London before it even came on the air tried to obtain a legitimate source of news (see Chapter 8), but when all attempts failed that station too had to resort to 'pirating' the BBC's output.*

*This was the reason that many offshore stations broadcast their news at unusual times - 15 or 30 minutes past the hour, rather than at the top of the hour as is more usual. Newsreaders on board the ships or forts would monitor the output of 'official' stations such as the BBC Home Service, Hilversum in Holland or BRT in Belgium as well as international output from the BBC World Service, Voice of America or shortwave broadcasts from America, Canada and Europe. They then re-wrote the stories in a brief headline style and delivered their own bulletins often preceded by introductions giving the impression that the station had, for example, a 'News and Public Affairs Department', working day and night to gather information.*

*Perhaps the most theatrical news presentation came from Swinging Radio England's 'Bannerline News'. The lead story was given a big build-up -"Big news in the world today" -and bulletins consisted of headline announcements, followed by sound effects and the briefest of storylines, before the newsreader launched into the next item following the same style. Needless to say this particular presentation technique did not find favour with listeners (or presenters) and was soon modified slightly, but still retained a somewhat over dramatic style.*

*Later stations in the 1980s, in particular Radio Caroline, Radio Monique and Laser, benefited from the availability of teletext news services on television, providing a constantly up-dated source of news throughout the day, removing the necessity to monitor so closely the output of 'official' landbased radio stations. With news gathering in mind Laser even had the forethought to load two PAL system television receivers on board the Communicator before she left Britain to be fitted out in America as a radio ship - American televisions, which operate on a different system, would have been unable to receive the output of British teletext services.*

*Despite the widespread practice amongst offshore stations of pirating news sources in this way two stations regularly re-broadcast the state network's output -The Voice of Peace and Arutz Sheva. Both relayed live the hourly bulletins of Kol Israel which removed the need for on-board newsreaders and at the same time kept listeners tuned to their respective stations.*

# Chapter 17

# Closures and Defiance

Early in 1974 offshore radio activity off the Dutch and Belgian coasts was intense - four ships were riding at anchor and between them transmitting a total of seven radio services in English, Dutch and Flemish:-

- *Norderney* Radio Veronica (Dutch)
- *Mebo II* RNI (Dutch and English)
- *Mi Amigo* Radio Mi Amigo (Flemish) Radio Caroline (English)
- *Janine* Radio Atlantis (Flemish and English)

The new year started with a new station taking to the air - Radio Mi Amigo on 1187kHz (253m) from Radio Caroline's ship the MV *Mi Amigo.*

As with Radio Atlantis, this new station was aimed at a Flemish speaking audience in Belgium and, because of that country's 1962 legislation against offshore radio stations all administration and programme recording was carried out in Holland. The station established offices and three fairly basic landbased studios above a record shop in Breda, Holland and used a box number in Hilversum for listeners' requests and letters. Regular programmes started at noon on 1st January 1974, but lasted only just over an hour before a generator failed on board the *Mi Amigo* and put the station off the air completely. Radio Mi Amigo returned at 6.00am on 8th January 1974 and programmes then continued as scheduled throughout the day until 9.00pm.

Radio Mi Amigo was a far more professional station than Radio Atlantis and immediately became very popular both with listeners and advertisers. A large number of companies in Belgium, Holland and France booked airtime on the station and such was the demand from advertisers that at peak times during the day 15% of the station's programming was taken up by commercials. The station also heavily promoted three products in which owner Sylvain Tack had a business interest - Suzy Waffles, Start Records and *Joepie* music magazine.

On 22nd January 1974 the Upper Chamber of the Dutch Parliament passed the anti-offshore law -Het Verdrag van Stroatburg - by 49 votes to 12. During the

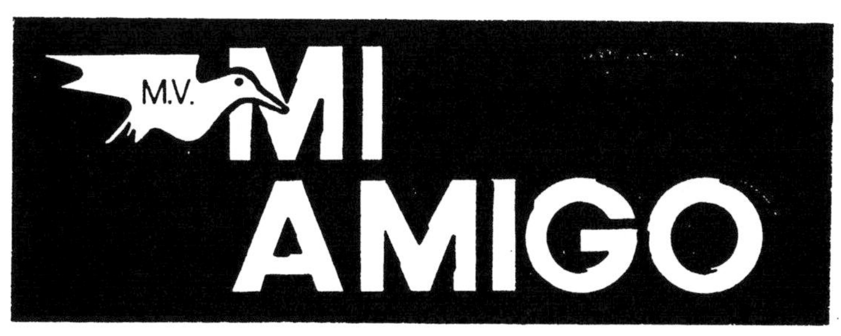


**Radio Mi Amigo's first programme schedule, January 1974**

| | |
|---|---|
| 5.00am | Non-Stop Music |
| 6.00am | Bert Bennett |
| 9.00am | Norbert |
| 11.00am | Wil van der Steen |
| 1.00pm | Joop Verhoof |
| 3.00pm | Mike Moorkens |
| 4.00pm | Bert Bennett |
| 5.00pm | Non-stop Music |
| 6.00pm | Mike Moorkens |
| 7.00pm | Secco |
| 8.00pm | Closedown |

course of the debate Minister of Culture, Harry van Doorn gave an undertaking to consider again the application from Radio Veronica to broadcast from land.

There were two options for Veronica's landbased operation. The first of these, and the one preferred by the station itself, was to broadcast on a dedicated wavelength of its own as Hilversum 4. However, this option already ruled out by Mr. van Doorn in June 1973 on the grounds of lack of finance, no frequency being available and unfairness to other broadcasting organisations who had to share airtime on the Hilversum Network.

The second option was for Veronica to be recognised as a broadcasting society and granted an allocation of airtime on the Hilversum Network, along with all the other broadcasting companies. Although the organisation established by Radio Veronica to try and obtain this status, (VOO), already had sufficient members for an allocation of airtime the Minister had been doing everything possible to thwart the offshore station joining the Hilversum Network.

A Dutch listenership survey conducted in March 1974 showed that Radio Mi Amigo, after just over two months on the air, had overtaken Radio Veronica in popularity and was a close second to the official pop music station, Hilversum 3:

| Station | % Audience Reach |
|---|---|
| Hilversum 3 | 13.3% |
| Radio Mi Amigo | 12.3% |
| Radio Veronica | 10.3% |

## Radio Seagull and Radio Caroline return

**Radio Caroline programme schedule, February 1974**

**8.00pm Andy Archer**

**10.00pm Mike Hagler**

**12midnight Norman Barrington**

**2.00am Bob Noakes**

**5.00am Closedown**

Also on board the *Mi Amigo,* Radio Seagull was reintroduced on 7th January 1974 at 9.00pm following the closure of Radio Mi Amigo's broadcasts. This English language night-time service of progressive music had originally been aired in 1973, but had been discontinued in October of that year when the *Mi Amigo's* mast collapsed. This time, however, Radio Seagull was to be differently organised. Andy Archer presented the first two hours each evening in a programme taped on land while Johnny Jason, Norman Barrington, Bob Noakes and later Brian Anderson presented their programmes live from the ship.

This re-launched, more professional Radio Seagull attracted a significant specialist audience, but without any prior announcement on 23rd February 1974, the broadcasts began as usual at 9.00pm under the call sign Radio Caroline. However, regular listeners were not too concerned about the change of name because the progressive music of Radio Seagull was continued with the format becoming more and more based on album tracks rather than singles.

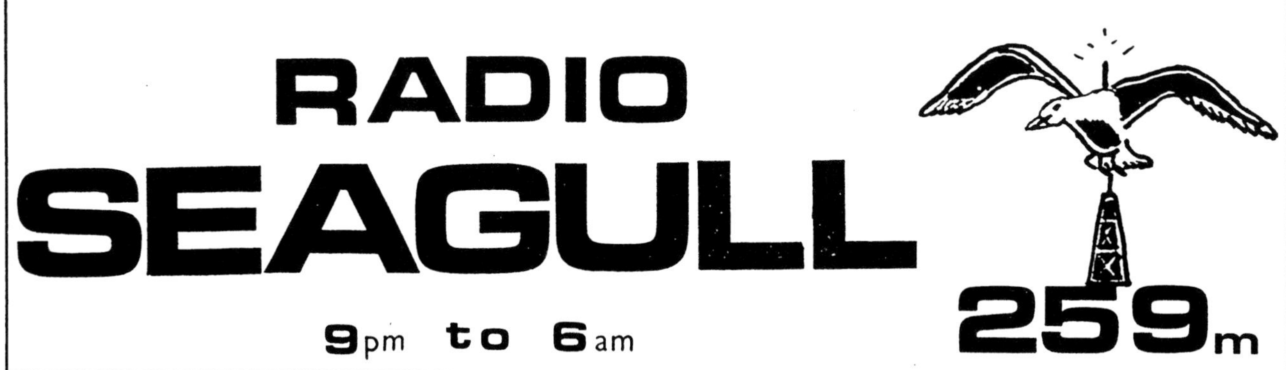

## Loving Awareness

**During the early 1970s Radio Caroline started promoting the concept of 'Loving Awareness' - basically that loving, caring, positive thoughts would conquer the selfishness and hatred prevalent in the late 20th Century world (Defensive Awareness).**

**Ronan O'Rahilly conceived and developed the philosophy out of the teachings of Mahatma Gandhi and Martin Luther King. Speaking in an interview some years later he tried to explain the thinking behind Loving Awareness:**

***Our brain has both loving energy and defensive energy. We have tapped and used the defensive one and we haven't explored in any serious way the loving one. LA is about developing a loving habit. Love is our most natural emotion, but it is the one we abuse most. Life has become a daily survival of looking after number one. Caroline is showing people that there is another way. Quite simply if you love people they will love you in return.***

**As part of its LA Campaign Radio Caroline promoted a Loving Awareness Festival at Stonehenge during the midsummer solstice in 1974. Over 3,000 people turned up, but unfortunately some acts of vandalism and damage to the ancient monument marred the occasion.**

The hour-long gap between the end of Radio Mi Amigo's Dutch daytime programming and the start of Radio Seagull's (and later Radio Caroline's) evening service was filled from 10th January by an 'International Service' of Radio Mi Amigo. This was presented by English DJs playing chart and album material with Dutch and Belgian commercials and 'plug' records, which were determined weekly by the Mi Amigo office on land.

During one of these Radio Mi Amigo International Service programmes the station linked up with Dutch national pop music station Hilversum 3, which had been established in 1965 to compete with Radio Veronica. The Hilversum service now seemingly felt threatened by the almost immediate success of offshore newcomer, Radio Mi Amigo.

The link up, made at the request of Hilversum 3, gave DJs on both stations the opportunity to discuss live on-air the state of the radio market in Holland at that time. It was achieved by an FM radio tuned to Hilversum 3 being set up in the studio on board the *Mi Amigo,* with a corresponding arrangement in the Hilversum studios, tuned to Radio Mi Amigo.

A fire broke out on board the *Mi Amigo* on 3rd March 1974 in part of the ship's heating system, injuring two crewmen, Jaap de Haan and Peter van Dyken. Requests were made over the air for listeners to telephone the Caroline office in Holland and eventually the injured men were taken ashore by Scheveningen lifeboat for hospital treatment.

## Radio Caroline's 10th Birthday

*A landmark in offshore radio history, Radio Caroline's 10th Birthday , was celebrated on 14th April 1974 (Easter Sunday) with a special four hour programme. Presented by all the English DJs on board the Mi Amigo the programme featured interviews with the station's first two DJs - Simon Dee and Chris Moore recalling their experiences of launching Britain's pioneering all day music station as well as recordings of some early programmes*

## Polish 'radio ships'

*Some reports appeared during mid-1971 indicating that up to ten radio ships were secretly being fitted out in the Polish port of Gdansk The radio ships, which were allegedly to be used off the coast of Europe and in the Middle East to broadcast Communist propaganda, were supposedly being fitted out under the technical supervision of engineers from Russia and East Germany.*

*Although the existence of these radio ships was the subject of rumour and speculation for some time during the early 1970s, they were never used to broadcast propaganda as had been feared by the Western security services.*

## Radio Atlantis technical problems

Radio Atlantis meanwhile was still experiencing technical problems with its equipment on board the *Janine.* The station had gone off the air at the end of 1973 because of equipment failures and a general lack of preparedness, but after some intensive work by the engineers test transmissions took place on 5th and 6th January 1974. Regular broadcasts for the re-launched Radio Atlantis commenced on 7th January 1974, but with continuing technical problems the station was frequently off the air and reception on 1115kHz (269m) was poor. At 2.45pm on 3rd February the station's frequency was changed to 1493kHz (201m), but the signal was worse than ever and transmissions returned to 1115kHz (269m) the following day.

Daytime Flemish programmes on Radio Atlantis were largely pre-recorded in land-based studios in Holland, although sometimes there were live programmes from on-board DJs, however, the night-time English Service, which ran from 7.00pm-7.00am was presented live from the *Janine.*

Technicians worked on the station's transmitting equipment throughout February 1974 and a significant improvement in signal strength was achieved by the end of the month. In a further effort to improve reception transmissions on 1115kHz (269m) were terminated at 4.00pm on 3rd March 1974, resuming an hour and a half later on 1331kHz (225m), but announced on air as 227m. However, this was to be only the beginning of many frequency changes for Radio Atlantis during 1974. Towards the end of March their signal was being jammed by a transmission from Italy so on 4th April the station changed to 1322kHz (227m). Unfortunately this frequency suffered through interference from an East European station and three days later Radio Atlantis returned to 1331kHz (225m), but the Italian jamming signal also returned. The station closed for a few hours during the night of 16th/17th April 1974 while the transmitter was re-tuned to 962kHz (312m), but reception on this frequency, too, was badly affected, this time by a North African station.

Despite these on-going technical problems Radio Atlantis managed to improve its output in programming terms at least. On 18th March 1974 news bulletins were introduced during the English Service on the half hour and from 4th May the English programme schedule was extended to 13 hours each day (6.00pm-7.00am).

Reception of RNI across Europe had improved significantly as the result of an increase in power early in 1974. The station also re-introduced a recorded early morning programme on the English Service, "Skyline" between 4.00 and 6.00am every day. Skyline was hosted by Louise Quirk and recorded in the studios of Manx Radio on the Isle of Man, where she worked as a daytime presenter and newsreader. The programme on RNI had been arranged by Don Allen who had come to the offshore station from Manx Radio.

Nothing is stable for long in the world of offshore radio, however. Just as Radio Atlantis seemed to have largely resolved its technical difficulties and the programming quality and content was improving, the natural elements intervened causing the station further problems at the beginning of June 1974.

During a violent storm on 6th June 1974 the *Janine's* aerial mast collapsed and by an unfortunate series of coincidences the transmitter had also started to fail at about the same time, resulting in the station going off the air completely. The following morning the crew awoke to realise that the *Janine* had broken from her anchor chain during the night and drifted 20 miles northwards, ending up on a sandbank off Westkapelle. On land the station's owner, Adriaan van

Landschoot, realised that something was wrong and immediately started to search for the stranded radio ship in his private plane. Once he had located the vessel he arranged for her to be towed back to her original position in international waters off Knokke, where a new eleven ton anchor and chain were fitted.

Broadcasts were able to recommence on 9th June 1974 and at the same time a new item of equipment, a linear amplifier - designed to increase the output strength of the station's signal - was installed and tested. However, the amplifier did not work as intended and its use resulted in insulators being blown and a small fire breaking out on the *Janine's* deck. Repeated attempts to correctly install the amplifier only resulted in further breakdowns affecting other equipment on the Jannine so eventually the idea of boosting the station's signal in this way was dropped until sufficient spare parts could be obtained.

Despite these difficulties and frequent breakdowns Radio Atlantis, while it was on the air, managed to put out a reasonable signal and became increasingly popular in its target area of Belgium and Holland as well as in the south and east of England. A 500 watt shortwave transmitter was installed and tested on 6225kHz (48.17m) on 25th July 1974, but nothing more was heard from this outlet after that date.

The Flemish Service of Radio Atlantis stopped carrying advertisements at the end of June 1974 because of fears that Belgian authorities would take action against the station's owners. Meanwhile, the English Service managed to attract some advertising, but in any event the personal financial resources of Adriaan van Landschoot met the weekly running costs of the station, estimated to be about £1,500.

Radio Atlantis celebrated its First Birthday on 15th July 1974 with a special programme presented by Steve England and Andy Anderson reminiscing about events of the previous twelve months. Three days later Adriaan van Lansdchoot and seventy guests arrived aboard the *Janine* for a Birthday Party which included more on-air celebrations.

On 1st August 1974 at 5.30pm the station's transmitter crystal was damaged beyond repair and Radio Atlantis was put off the air. The station was forced to use one of its other crystals, tuned to another frequency, to return to the air and during the early morning of 2nd August 1974 Radio Atlantis recommenced broadcasts on 1317.5kHz (228m), moving a few days later to 1313kHz (229m). However, reception on this new frequency was affected after dark by interference so on 12th August 1974 a further move was made to 1331kHz (225m), but the jamming from the Italian station, which had been experienced a few months earlier, returned and Radio Atlantis had to move back to 1313kHz (229m). For a period of four days from 11th-14th August 1974 the station broadcast an all-day English service, presented live by the on-board DJs, because storms had prevented a tender delivering new supplies of programme tapes for the scheduled Flemish Service.

Rumours of another offshore station circulated in mid-1974 - Radio Benelux was said to be planning Flemish and English language services for 22 hours a day. The owners of the pop magazine, *Hitorama,* who had previously attempted to purchase Radio Atlantis, were said to be behind the new project. DJs from Radio Mi Amigo and Radio Luxembourg were reported to have joined the station, which at one time had enquired about purchasing the MV *Peace,* then laid up in Marseilles after the closure of the Israeli offshore station, Voice of Peace in 1973 (see Chapter 18). However, despite all these seemingly definite plans nothing was ever heard of Radio Benelux.

## Programme Choice

*Despite the impending introduction of Dutch legislation against the offshore stations seven services were transmitting off the coast of Holland in June 1974. Here is an example of the programming choice which listeners had at that time.*

### RNI

*Dutch Service*

**6.00am Dick de Graaf Show**

**9.00am 'Branding',** *non-stop music*

**10.00am Ted Bouwens Show**

**12noon Tony Berk Show**

**2.00pm Ferry Maat Show**

**4.00pm 'Driemaster',** *Leo van der Groot*

**6.00pm 'Live Show',** *Marc van Amstel*

*English Service*

**8.00pm Don Allen**

**10.00pm Brian McKenzie**

**1.00am Robin Banks**

**3.00am 'Skyline',** *Louise Quirk*

*Sundays -RNI World Service*

**10.00am Northsea Goes DX**

**11.00am Our World in Action,** *A J Beirens*

### Radio Atlantis

*Flemish Service*

**7.00am 'Luc brebgt U van uw stuck',** *Luc van Kapellen*

**9.00am Ellie Prins**

**10.00am Victor van Rhijn**

**12noon 'Smakelijk eten',** *Tony Houston*

**1.00pm 'Musikale Reception',** *Theo van de Velde*

**3.00pm Van den Bos is weer los',** *Fred van den Bos*

**5.00pm Ellie Prins**

*International Service*

**6.00pm 'Blast-Off',** *Steve England*

**9.00pm 'Starshine',** *Andy Anderson*

**11.00pm 'Midnight Special',** *Dave Rogers*

**1.00am 'Apollo 312'**

**3.00am 'Yawn into Dawn'**

**5.00am 'Snap, Crackle and Pop'**

### Radio Mi Amigo

**6.00am Haike de Bois**

**7.00am 'Welkonin de Wereld der Wakkeren',** *Bert Bennett*

**9.00am 'Met Peter gaat het beter',** *Peter van Dam*

**10.00am 'De Norbert Show',** *Norbert*

**12noon 'Met Frans van der Drift op drift',** *Frans van der Drift*

**2.00pm Joop Verhoof**

**4.00pm Mike Moorkens**

**6.00pm 'Met Peter gaat het beter ',**

**7.00pm English Service, Brian Anderson**

*Radio Caroline*

**9.00pm Andy Archer**

**11.00pm Mike Haggler**

**1.00am Norman Barrington**

**3.00am Samantha du Bois/Bob Noakes**

### Radio Veronica

**6.00am 'Ook Goeie Morgen I',** *Bart van Leeuwen*

**7.00am 'Ook Goeie Morgen II',** *Hans Mondt*

**8.00am 'Ook Goeie Morgen III',** *Tom Collins*

**9.00am 'Muziek terwijl un werkt**

**10.00am 'Koffietijd',** *Tineke*

**11.00am Stan Haag Vandaag**

**12noon Will wil wel**

**1.00pm Rob Out Show**

**2.00pm Bart van Leeuwen Show**

**3.00pm Hans Mondt Show**

**4.00pm Tom Collins Show**

**5.00pm Lex Harding Show**

**6.00pm 'Jukebox,** *Stan Haag*

**7.00pm Lexjo**

**8.00pm Frans van der Beek Show**

**9.00pm Willem Keukenhof Show**

**10.00pm Tineke**

**11.00pm Chiel Montagne Show**

**12 midnight Non-Stop**

## Closures

With the progress of legislation through the Dutch Parliament during the spring and summer of 1974 to finally outlaw offshore broadcasting the individual radio stations started to make decisions about their respective futures, as had happened in Britain in 1967.

**Radio Veronica** made it clear from the outset that it would not defy the new law and would close its offshore station when the Dutch Marine Offences Act came into effect. Radio Veronica had campaigned vigorously to become part of the established broadcasting system in Holland and in order to achieve that goal it was not going to do anything illegal to jeopardise its position. The station had secured enough subscribers to entitle it to an allocation of airtime on the (non-commercial) state broadcasting system and this is where the directors saw the immediate future of the organisation in the absence of a law to grant them a separate commercial licence. There was some speculation that the station would hire airtime from Radio Luxembourg, but this plan, if it ever existed, came to nothing.

At **RNI** on the other hand there was considerable doubt about the future of the station. Rumours circulated for many weeks about the imminent closure of the Dutch Service and the repositioning of the *Mebo II* to a new anchorage from where she could continue broadcasting English language programmes. However, in the end it was decided that both the English and Dutch Services would close when the new law came into effect in Holland, but rumours still persisted about the future location of the *Mebo II* and its role as a floating radio station.

**Radio Atlantis** announced on 17th August that the station would close in the face of the Dutch Marine Offences Act and, in fact, the Flemish Service closed just over a week later at 2.00pm on 25th August 1974. For the remainder of its time on the air Radio Atlantis broadcast an all-day English language service with the on-board DJs being given a virtual free hand by Adriaan van Landschoot to programme the station as they wished.

**Radio Caroline** and **Radio Mi Amigo** announced that they would continue broadcasting after the new law came into effect. Radio Caroline again prepared to defy all official action against it and go into illegality as it had done in 1967 in the face of similar British legislation. The station closed its office in Holland on 1st June 1974 and started to use Radio Mi Amigo's Spanish postal address instead. Programme hours for Radio Caroline were gradually increased, first at the beginning of June to 8.00pm-6.00am and then in August from 7.00pm-6.00am, with frequent hints from DJs that there would soon be an all-day English Service.

It was announced on 12th August 1974 that the provisions of the Dutch Marine Offences Act were to become effective at midnight on 31st August 1974 and despite having 300,000 members the VOO (Radio Veronica) would not be granted a licence or given an airtime allocation on Hilversum. All stations located off the coast of Holland, except Radio Caroline and Radio Mi Amigo, made arrangements to cease transmissions before the law became effective.

The first to close was the Radio Atlantis Flemish Service which left the air on 25th August 1974, leaving the station operating an all day English language service for its final week on the air. During this period the English DJs did their best to re-create the atmosphere and 'sound' of the 1960's British offshore stations.

Next to close was RNI's English Service, which left the air at midnight on 30th

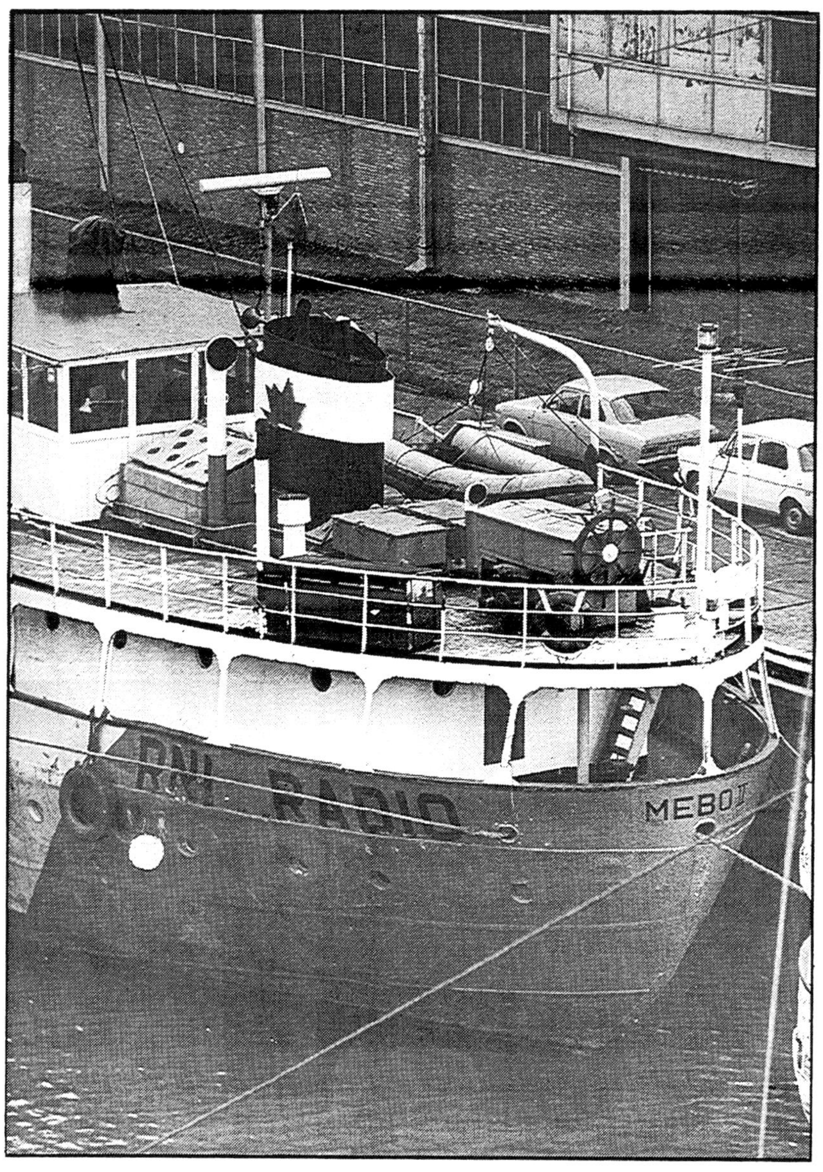


'Mebo II' in Slikkerveer being re-fitted

August 1974. During the final hour all English DJs on board the *Mebo II* took part in a farewell programme full of emotion and nostalgia, with Senior DJ, Don Allen, closing the station for the last time at midnight. The station's Dutch Service, normally on the air from 6.00am then opened immediately after the English programmes had finished at midnight, continuing throughout the night and during the following day. From 10.00am -8.00pm on 31st August 1974 RNI transmitted its final World Service programme on shortwave with shows in English, French, German and Dutch throughout the day At 8.00pm that same evening, four hours earlier than had originally been planned, the RNI Dutch Service was also terminated with all DJs on board, English and Dutch, saying their final farewells.

The *Mebo II* remained at her anchorage until 9th September 1974 when she sailed to the De Groot van Vliet shipyard in Slikkerveer. Together with the *Mebo I* she was dry docked and both vessels were scraped, painted and overhauled. On board the *Mebo II* the transmitter equipment was stripped and overhauled, while a new record library and three new studios were constructed to replace the existing two studio facility. The aerial mast was heightened by 15', a second medium wave aerial was installed and all equipment tested and tuned using a dummy load. Altogether £400,000 was spent on this refurbishment work and it was announced publicly at that time that the ship would sail to an anchorage off Genoa in Italy and commence broadcasts under the call sign Radio Nova International.

Another potential use for the refurbished radioship was as home to Radio Mi Amigo and the owner of that station, Sylvain Tack, visited the *Mebo II* while she was in Slikkerveer. However, neither of these plans came to fruition and the ship was destined to have a much different future than that planned for her in the autumn of 1974. (see Chapter 18)

Radio Veronica closed at 6.00pm on 31st August 1974 following an emotional last hour presented live from the *Norderney* by DJ Rob Out. Station Managing Director Bul Verweij (now a free man again after having completed a prison sentence for his part in firebombing RNI's ship *Mebo II*) said farewell to listeners after the final newscast at 5.30pm and at 6.00pm Rob Out closed the station with the words "With the end of Veronica dies a piece of democracy in the Netherlands and that is a pity for you, for Veronica and especially for Holland." After playing the Dutch National Anthem a Veronica jingle was aired, but cut off part way through as the transmitter on board the *Norderney* was switched off for the final time, ending over 14 years of broadcasting. All staff and visitors who had been on board then left the *Norderney* on the station's tender *Ger Anna* and on the local fishing boat, *Loekie*. When they arrived in Scheveningen about an hour and a half later they were met by a huge crowd of fans and supporters of the station which had become a Dutch national institution.

The *Norderney* remained at anchor for over a year after Radio Veronica closed. Manned by a crew of nine she stayed at sea amidst persistent rumours that the station would return to the air from its offshore base. However, on 11th August 1975 she was towed into IJmuiden and later moved to a berth in Amsterdam, near the City's Central Station. (see Chapter 19)

Radio Atlantis, having already closed its Flemish language service was operating an all-day English Service for the last six days of August 1974. On 30th August the station's land-based DJs presented their final shows on tape and throughout the following day all DJs on-board the *Janine* presented their individual final programmes. From 6.00pm all staff joined in a "Goodbye Show" which lasted until 7.05pm when the station switched off its transmitters for the last time.

Early the following morning, 1st September 1974 the station's tender, *Onrust,* raised the *Jannine's* anchor and towed the radio ship to Vlissingen where she was met by a crowd of over 1,000 fans and well wishers. However, two days later an arrest warrant was placed on the ship by Harry van de Velde, who claimed he was owed money for the transmitter equipment which the station had been using. Adriaan van Landschoot had attempted to sell the ship as a fully equipped radio station before Radio Atlantis closed, but the asking price of £40,000 was too high for the prospective purchaser and the deal fell through.

## Caroline continues - again

As the midnight deadline approached for the Dutch Marine Offences Act to come into effect most of the offshore stations had already closed, but there was a very different story from the *Mi Amigo*. During the afternoon of 29th August 1974 the ship had raised her anchor and, accompanied by a tug, sailed across the North Sea to a position off the Essex coast of England, near the Kentish Knock Lightship. The *Mi Amigo* had begun the voyage using her own engines, but it soon became apparent that they had seriously deteriorated and were not really powerful enough to take the ship across the North Sea. In the end the *Mi Amigo* was towed to her new position by the accompanying tug.

Broadcasts of both stations on board the ship - Radio Mi Amigo and Radio Caroline - had continued as normal during this voyage. The move had been made because Ronan O'Rahilly felt that the authorities in Holland were likely to forcibly board and tow the radio ship into harbour because there were Dutch nationals on board. This proved to be a wise move, with considerable foresight, because just such a scenario was to occur in 1981 with another radio ship and in 1989 Radio Caroline itself suffered an act of forcible boarding in international waters by the Dutch authorities (see Chapters 20 and 25).

At the end of normal transmissions at 7.00pm on 31st August 1974 (just as all the other Dutch offshore stations were closing) listeners to Radio Mi Amigo

**Radio Caroline programme schedule 1st September 1974**

7.00pm Brian Anderson *(taped)*

9.00pm Graham Gill *(taped)*

11.00pm Mike Hagler *(taped)*

1.00am Tony Allan *(live)*

3.00am Peter Haze *(live)*

6.00am Closedown

were invited to tune in again as usual at 6.00am the following morning. However, when the station did re-open on 1st September 1974, now in contravention of the new Dutch law, old programme tapes were aired along with a number of live shows by some of the English DJs from Radio Caroline on board the *Mi Amigo.*

The reason for this was that a few days earlier Dutch police had raided the station's offices in Breda and confiscated a supply of programme tapes which were destined to be taken out to the *Mi Amigo* for transmission from 1st September onwards.

Radio Caroline itself had continued broadcasting defiantly after midnight on 31st August 1974, becoming 'illegal' for the second time in its history. Both stations operating from the *Mi Amigo* now gave a mailing address in Playa de Aro, Spain and it was announced that in future Radio Mi Amigo programmes would be recorded in that country and the ship serviced and supplied from a Spanish port - Spain at that time was one of the few remaining European countries not to have ratified the 1965 Strasbourg Convention outlawing offshore broadcasting.

In order to avoid problems with the Dutch authorities Radio Mi Amigo programmes after the beginning of September 1974 were ostensibly targeted towards a Belgian audience, to the exclusion of most Dutch material. However, a number of commercials previously aired on Radio Veronica and RNI's Dutch Service were broadcast during this time, although the companies concerned denied booking airtime on the station. It seemed that Radio Mi Amigo was following Radio Caroline's practice in late 1967 and early 1968, broadcasting fake commercials to try and confuse the authorities and create the impression that the station was still receiving advertising income in spite of the new law.

Other commercials were broadcast and paid for in an indirect way to circumvent the Dutch and Belgian Marine Offences Acts. Advertisers placed their announcements in one of a number of magazines (*Joepie, Pop Telescoop* etc.) and the wording was read out on-air as 'information' being passed on from publications. In this way it was difficult, if not impossible, for the authorities to prove whether or not the advertisers had intended their announcements to be broadcast on the offshore station.

The authorities were not fooled by the cover story that Radio Mi Amigo programmes were being recorded in Spain. On 26th September 1974 Dutch police, suspicious that the station was still operating from Holland, raided premises previously used above a record shop in Breda, but were unable to find any evidence of programme material being recorded there. Although station owner Sylvain Tack publicly denied that he still had anything to do with the operation of Radio Mi Amigo, programmes were in fact secretly being recorded at one of his Suzy Waffles factories in Buizingem, Belgium. However, after a Dutch television programme broadcast this information during October 1974 recording was hurriedly transferred to studios in, an isolated farmhouse near Oprakel, Belgium.

The radio ship *Mi Amigo,* now anchored off the English coast, was supplied at this time with food, oil and water by fishing vessels from small Belgian and Dutch ports on journeys which took up to 48 hours to complete. A tender service had been attempted from the Spanish port of Bilbao, but it turned out to be impractical and too hazardous a journey, crossing the rough waters of the Bay of Biscay.

DJs and crew, however, were clandestinely ferried to and from the radio ship using small ports and isolated beaches on the south east coast of England, a practice which quickly caught the attention of the British authorities. On 29th October 1974 two DJs were ferried out to the *Mi Amigo* from Burnham-on-Crouch in Essex, but on the return journey their launch was boarded by police and Home Office officials and four crewmen were detained and questioned, but not charged. A month later, on 26th November 1974 a tender from Brightlingsea, Essex was photographed from a helicopter as it approached the *Mi Amigo* and on return to port those on board were questioned by police and Customs officials. Following this questioning of the vessel's crew some items of ship-to-shore communications equipment were confiscated in a police raid on premises later that same evening.

## Radio Dolphin

While Radio Caroline and Radio Mi Amigo continued to broadcast from off the English coast rumours persisted that the other former Belgian offshore station, Radio Atlantis, would return to the air. The station's ship *Janine* had been arrested shortly after arriving in port as part of a legal dispute over the ownership of transmitter equipment. However, a number of ex-Radio Atlantis DJs took over the former Gunfleet Lighthouse off Frinton-on-Sea, Essex during September 1974 and started work on refurbishing the long abandoned structure. Studios and living accommodation were constructed and a re-conditioned 10Kw Collins transmitter was acquired from the USA and installed in the lighthouse.

**PIRATE STATION SWOOP**

**POLICE and Home office officials have raided the Gunfleet Old Light House in the Thames Estuary. The disused tower was almost ready for the launching of a station, going under the name of Radio Atlantis.**

**The raid took place in the dark one night, and the officials removed a generator, tape and record decks, an aerial and the transmitter from the tower.**

Their planned station, Radio Dolphin, was scheduled to start transmissions on 1232kHz (244m) on Christmas Day 1974, but in the early hours of 19th December 1974 a party of twenty four Royal Marines, Police, Home Office and Trinity House officials arrived at the lighthouse in four boats - two police launches and two Navy patrol vessels. Two Trinity House men asked for, and were given, permission to board the lighthouse ( which although abandoned was still in the ownership of the lighthouse authority). On discovering the radio transmitting equipment which had been installed they called on the Home Office, Police and Marines to dismantle and confiscate it.

Meanwhile, in Belgium former Radio Atlantis owner Adriaan van Landschoot, together with Roger Hendricx, Tony Houston and Marc van Pelegen appeared in court on 4th September 1974 charged with offences under the Belgian Marine Offences Act of 1962. The case was referred to the Brussels High Court where it was heard on 29th November 1974 and all four men were found guilty as charged. Adriaan van Landschoot was fined £18,000 and given a three month prison sentence, suspended for five years, while the other three were each fined £3,500.

## RNI refurbished

Back in Holland the *Mebo I* and *Mebo II* left the shipyard at Slikkerveer on 9th October 1974, but were immediately detained by the authorities acting under the provisions of the Dutch Marine Offences Act. Prior to this raid an item had been broadcast by London's ILR news station, LBC, stating that the *Mebo II* was not really destined for Italy as had been announced, but in fact was to anchor off the British coast to broadcast Radio Nova International programmes.

A preliminary hearing into the right of the owners to move the vessels, one of which carried radio transmitting equipment, contrary to the new Dutch law, was held on 11th November 1974 with a full hearing taking place on 4th December. At that hearing lawyers for the owners of the vessel argued that because the ship was registered in Panama the laws of that country, which stated that the radio transmitters aboard *Mebo II* counted as cargo, should apply. The Court was not swayed by this argument, however, and when judgement was given on 10th December 1974 the owners were given permission to take the *Mebo II* out of port only after the transmitters had been removed from the vessel. An appeal was lodged by the ship's owners but this hearing did not take place for another three months.

The effect of all this legal argument about whether or not the *Mebo II* could leave port meant that the proposed Radio Nova project off the coast of Italy - if it was ever really a serious plan - never came to fruition. A land-based station of the same name, run by some former RNI DJs did, however, establish itself in northern Italy, taking advantage of the confused state of that country's broadcasting laws at the time which allowed unlimited numbers of private radio and television stations to be established.

By the end of 1974 there were only two offshore radio stations broadcasting to northern Europe. Holland, the country which hitherto had been most tolerant of offshore broadcasters had finally succeeded in closing all but one of the radio stations and effectively chased the remaining radio ship, the *Mi Amigo*, away from its coast.

Despite having the world's longest continuous offshore radio service in Radio Veronica listeners in Holland now had nothing to show for those fourteen years of commercial enterprise radio. The Hilversum Network was still in place and the authorities were doing all they could to prevent Radio Veronica joining that system through the airtime allocation to which they were undoubtedly entitled. Radio Veronica appealed through the courts against the Minister's ruling, subsequently won its battle to secure airtime and went on to become one of the biggest operators in the state radio and television system.

The other major offshore operator in Holland, RNI, failed to acquire an entitlement to airtime on the state system, but that organisation too refused to die and subsequently managed to re-emerge to provide radio programmes to Holland in another guise. In fact the former offshore rivals eventually became part of the same media conglomerate (see Chapter 29).

Surprisingly, bearing in mind its long years of tolerance towards the commercial offshore Radio Veronica, Holland was slow to introduce an independent commercial radio system, and only did so 20 years after the closure of the offshore stations because of pressure from the European Parliament. Unfortunately the offshore stations, although fondly remembered by many listeners, were not a direct influence on changes in the Dutch radio system as they had been in other European countries. The Dutch offshore stations had been outlawed without the majority of people realising how it had happened. It was a matter of political expediency on the part of a fragile Government to allow Minister Henri van Doorn to introduce and process the legislation rather than force him to resign and provoke various groups into withdrawing their support for the coalition.

# Chapter 18

# Peace and Freedom

For over 15 years most offshore broadcasting activity had taken place from the waters off northern Europe, but 1973 saw the launch of two very different ventures in more unlikely locations.

In Israel restaurant owner and former pilot Abie Nathan had long been campaigning for a peaceful solution to the recurring conflicts between Arab and Jew in the Middle East. He had made a number of unsuccessful attempts to arrange a peace settlement before and after the 1967 Six Day War between Israel and Egypt, but all this earned him was a fine and a prison sentence for having contact with the enemy.

By 1969 Abie Nathan had decided that the way forward in his peace campaign was to establish a radio station which could be used to air the views of both sides in the conflict and at the same time provide entertainment in the form of music which was of universal appeal irrespective of religious or nationalistic beliefs.

To get this project underway Abie Nathan established the Shalom Peace Foundation and travelled to Holland where he managed to raise £29,000 worth of backing. In Holland he also located a suitable ship to act as a base for his planned radio station, the *Cito,* a former freighter which had been the last vessel built by the Dutch before the Nazi invasion in 1940. The *Cito,* renamed *Peace,* sailed to America in 1969 with a Captain and volunteer crew, who received only out of pocket expenses for their services.

In America Abie Nathan set about raising further funding for his project, but despite promises American businesses and authorities were not really interested. In desperation Abie Nathan started lecturing on the theme of 'Peace', which raised some cash in the form of fees and staging concerts, with Arab and Israeli entertainers on the same bill. At one concert in New York's Carnegie Hall Abie Nathan gave away 1,000 free tickets to likely benefactors and appealed on stage for donations towards the cost of launching his Peace radio station, but only succeeded in raising $150 (less than £100).

Concerts were also staged on board the MV *Peace* in New York Harbour, including one by American folk singer Pete Segar, but with overheads and the limited audience space on the vessel it was impossible to make a profit in this way.

Abie Nathan then tried another fund raising approach. He organised an auction of his collection of paintings, from his art gallery in Israel. Although over 6,000 people were invited to the auction only twenty actually turned up and just $28 (£18) was raised.

The fund raising difficulties he was experiencing were due in part to lack of public awareness about the Peace Foundation and its aims. The American media were reluctant to publicise the Peace Foundation Project and Abie Nathan could find no other means of publicising his mailing address for enquiries and

## Abie Nathan

*Abraham Nathan was born in 1932 in Iran to Jewish parents, but brought up in India by Jesuit priests. He became an RAF pilot and a captain in the Israeli Air Force. Shortly before the outbreak of the Six Days War in 1967 he flew from Israel to Port Said in Egypt in an effort to convince the Egyptians not to start hostilities. He made a number of further attempts to talk to the Egyptians after the end of the Six Days War and was fined and jailed on his return to Israel for having made contact with the enemy.*

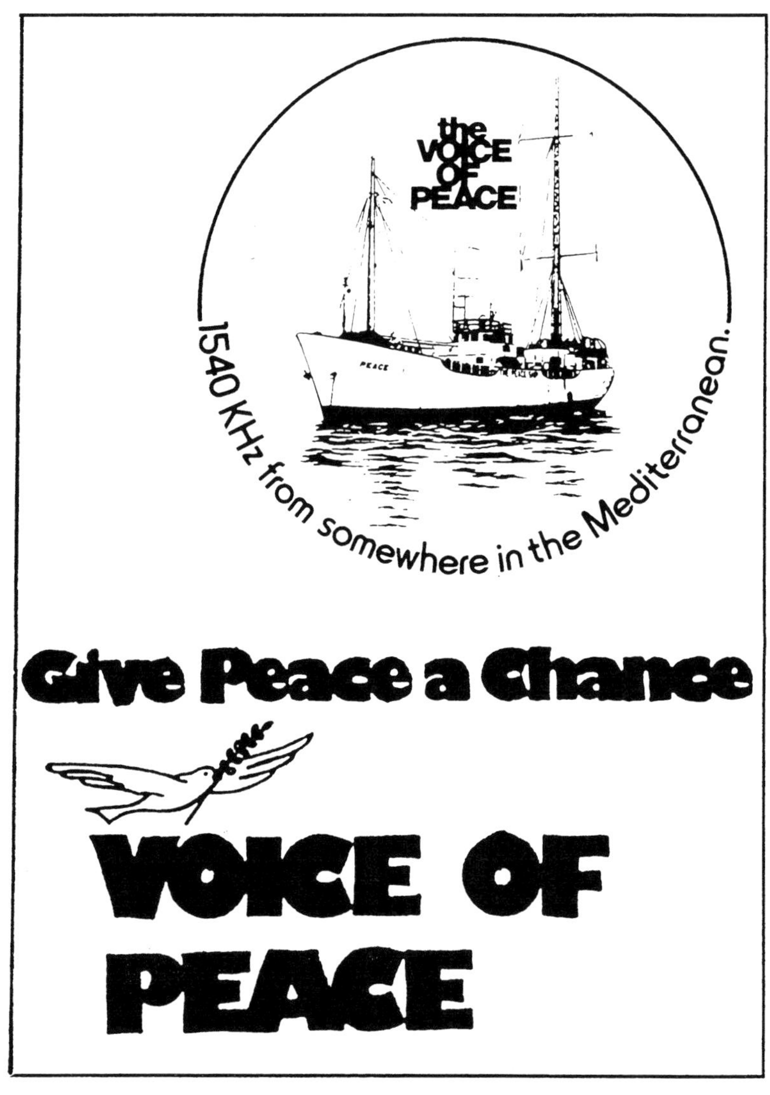


donations, although he was convinced many people would provide support for the Peace Foundation if they only knew about it. By 1972, after almost three years of tireles campaigning he had only managed to collect £33,000 worth of donations, much of which was swallowed up in harbour fees for the MV *Peace.*

Abie Nathan then decided that it was futile to continue in this way expecting donations from the American public when he had no means of reaching them through the media. He planned instead to fund the whole project himself and returned to Israel where he sold his home, restaurant and art gallery, raising some $100,000.

With this money he returned to New York and set about equipping the MV *Peace* as a floating radio station. However, because of the length of time the vessel had remained moored in harbour she had deteriorated and needed much more work than originally anticipated. Abie Nathan found himself short of about $40,000 to complete the project.

After two months of waiting and hoping that somehow the additional money could be raised he tried one, last desperate tactic. He went on an indefinite hunger strike. This single action provoked immense media interest and Abie Nathan appeared on the nationally networked "Today" breakfast television programme with Barbara Walters. Within 48 hours of his appearance over $50,000 worth of donations had been received from supporters across the USA. The media coverage also resulted in an increased awareness of the aims and objectives of the Peace Foundation. Further donations quickly started to arrive, including one from the Canadian Council of Churches specifically to purchase diesel fuel for the MV *Peace* and to cover running costs of the radio station's first three months on the air.

With sufficient funding now available to get the project started Abie Nathan was able to press ahead with converting the MV *Peace* for her new role. Studios were constructed , broadcasting equipment, including two 25Kw transmitters and a 160' aerial mast, were installed on board the vessel. This work was completed in early 1973 and on 16th March 1973 the ship left New York, making a series of test transmission on 1540Khz (195m) while at sea. After putting into Bermuda for repairs to a leak in her hull, the MV *Peace* continued her voyage across the Atlantic and through the Mediterranean, eventually arriving off Cyprus in mid-April 1973.

POP PIRATE ABIE IN PEACE CRUSADE

Further test transmissions took place from a position off the coast of Israel, but a violent storm caused some damage to the MV *Peace* and she was forced to take shelter at a calmer anchorage off Cyprus. Here it was discovered that the storm damage had resulted in water leaking into and contaminating the ship's fuel supply so the MV *Peace* sailed to the French port of Marseilles for emergency repairs, arriving there on 20th April 1973.

Once these repairs had been satisfactorily completed the vessel was able to return to her anchorage off Israel and continue with test transmissions. Official broadcasts for the new station - simply called the Voice of Peace - started at 8.00pm on 26th May 1973, initially on a 24 hour basis with programmes and announcements mainly in English, but some were also in French, Hebrew or Arabic. However, after a short time the hours of transmission were reduced to 12midnight-2.00am, Sunday to Friday and 10.00am - 2.00am on Saturdays.

## Popularity

A survey carried out in Israel shortly after the Voice of Peace started broadcasting showed that it was the most popular station amongst people under the age of 25. Programming was mainly western pop music, except for a daily hour of classical music during the early evening. The station's signal in Israel and Lebanon was strong, although in Egypt, where Abie Nathan also wanted to target his peace messages, reception was usually only possible after dark.

To begin with the Voice of Peace carried no paid advertising, but instead broadcast messages of peace and announcements in support of Israeli industry and commerce. Although laudable for a station dedicated to the cause of peace this policy unfortunately meant that no revenue was coming in to meet the day-to-day running costs and eventually the Voice of Peace had to start taking paid advertising to survive - the funds donated to the Shalom Peace Foundation were by now running very low.

*The MV 'Peace' being converted to a radio ship*

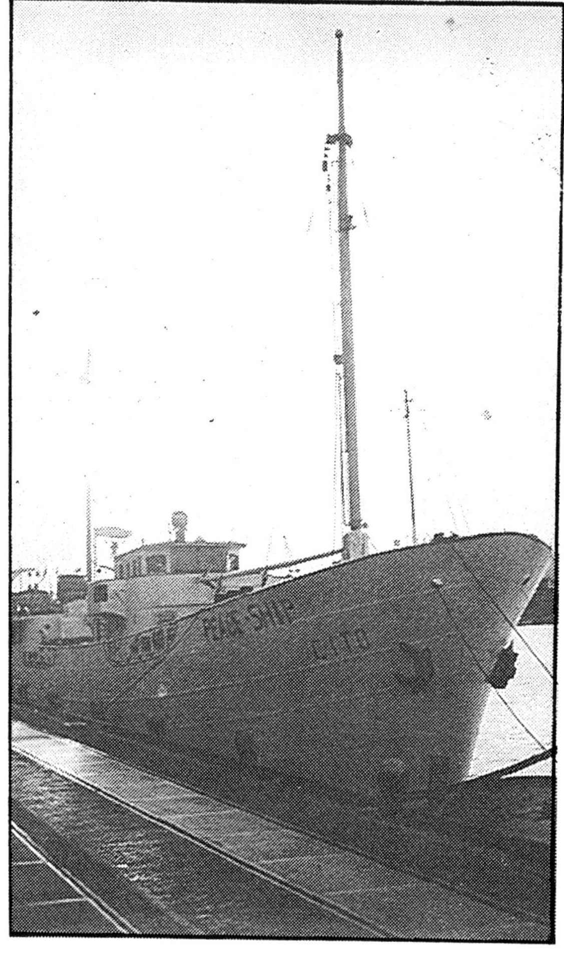

The MV *Peace* used various anchorages off Israel from which to broadcast and the station never gave its precise location over the air - it was simply announced as "The Voice of Peace from somewhere in the Mediterranean". Supplies and crew changes took place from Haifa in Israel and it was common practice for the MV *Peace* to enter harbour herself to be re-supplied with food, water and fuel oil. Transmissions were suspended while this operation took place but it was not unknown for broadcasts to continue well inside Israeli territorial waters while the ship was sailing to and from port.

During the October 1973 Six Day War (which precipitated the 1974 oil crisis in the West) the MV *Peace* anchored off the Suez Canal in Egypt, broadcasting appeals to the armies of both sides to stop fighting. On 6th October an Israeli gun boat came alongside the MV *Peace* and ordered her Captain to enter port. Abie Nathan, on board his vessel at the time, broadcast a live account of what was happening and then closed the station. When the MV *Peace* arrived in port it was immediately arrested and detained by the Israeli authorities.

## Peace statement

**Abie Nathan broadcast this statement about the aims and objectives of the Voice of Peace during one of the early test transmissions:-**

*The Jewish people know what it is to suffer, to pay the price, to drift from place to place through the generations. They know what it is to be a refugee from one place to another. Never let it be said that our neighbours, our Palestinian brothers will have to, or need to, learn of the trials and tribulations of being refugees.*

*There is much that can be done. I may not have the answers, but together as people maybe we can find them. Maybe after twenty five years we could stretch out a hand of magnanimity. We could find a way for people on both sides for just a little reason, with a little faith, a little concern, a little love. Maybe it is time for us to get together, to reason together. A way must be found before it is too late.*

*For the next few days we will drift around the Mediterranean, occasionally chat with you, give you music that you may like. We will try to give you news of some of the good things that are happening in this world. We would like to invite you, those who think they can contribute, people with different views, to write to us at Post Office Box 1010, Nicosia, Cyprus. Tell us what you think of this programme. If you would like to join, even for a few days, we would welcome you. We will try to arrange to have people from both sides,, or at least people from any side with different points of view so that we can have a dialogue about the problems that concern all of us. This platform belongs to you. We call upon you to use it. Try with these microphones to create the kind of climate that will, maybe, help our leaders to stand down from their rigid positions.*

The vessel and its crew were later released and allowed to sail back to an anchorage off Famagusta. Cyprus from where broadcasts of the Voice of Peace recommenced.

Financial difficulties were still being experienced by Abie Nathan, advertisers had largely withdrawn their support from the station and he appealed to the public for donations towards the estimated cost of £30,000 to keep the Voice of Peace on the air. This appeal resulted in only £500 being raised and due to lack of funding the Voice of Peace was forced to close at 3.00pm on 9th November 1973. The MV *Peace* sailed silently into Ashdod and most of the crew left the ship.

Disappointed and frustrated Abie Nathan vowed that somehow he would find sufficient funding to return the Voice of Peace to the airwaves. Early in December 1973 he sailed the MV *Peace* towards Europe where he planned to broadcast appeals for donations and support for his peace campaign. Just before Christmas 1973 the Peace anchored off Southern Italy, but the transmitter remained silent and early in January 1974 the vessel arrived once again in Marseilles, where she was docked while Abie Nathan set about trying to raise further financial backing. Although no one knew at the time it was to be over 12 months before any progress was made in this direction and the MV *Peace* remained berthed in Marseilles throughout this time.

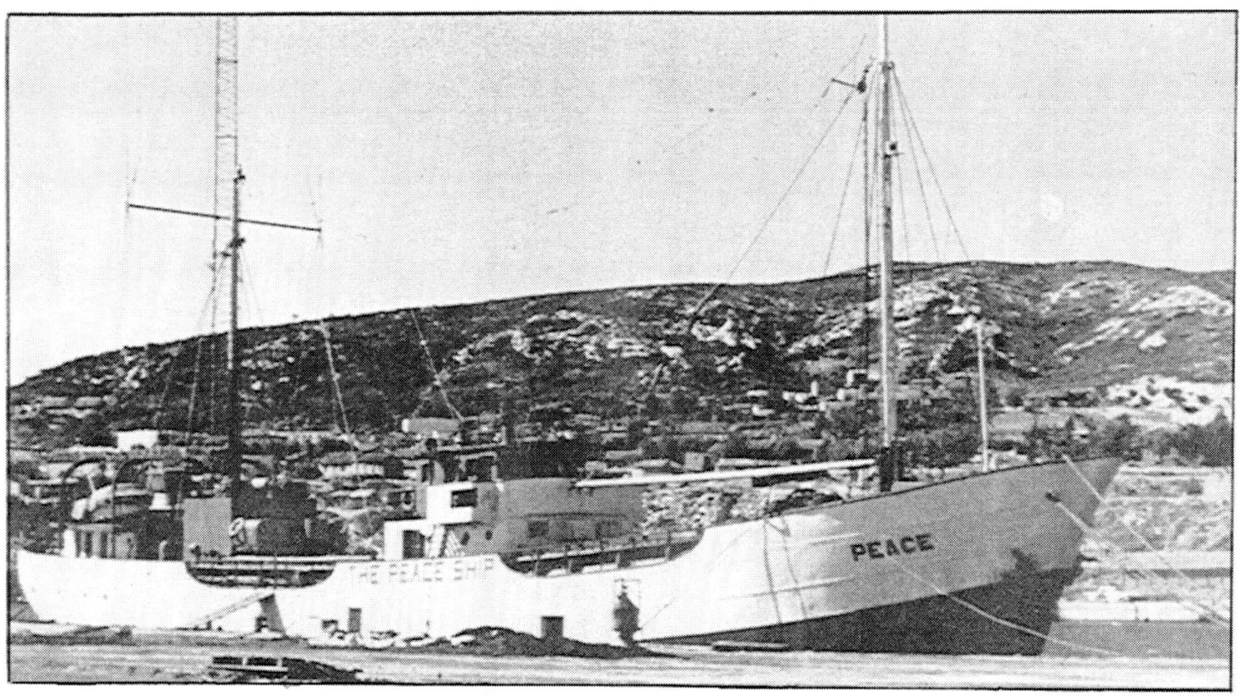


*The 'Peace' ship in Marseilles*

## Radio Free America

While the Voice of Peace had been broadcasting from "somewhere in the Mediterranean" another offshore radio station had been launched, this time 6000 miles away, off the Atlantic coast of the United States of America. The background to the arrival of this particular offshore station lay in a dispute over the complex Federal rules governing legal land-based broadcasting in America.

Rev. Carl McIntire, then 67, was pastor of the Bible Presbyterian Church of Collingwood, New Jersey and owned two stations - WXUR - AM and WXUR - FM in Media, Pennsylvania. His syndicated programme "20th Century Reformation Hour" was at one time carried by 610 radio stations across America, but because of the extreme views he often expressed during these broadcasts many stations started to cancel contracts, fearing the FCC would revoke their own licences for transmitting such material. Listeners made huge donations as a result of appeals made during these programmes and the widespread cancellation of contracts led to financial difficulties for McIntire.

He had also run into trouble with the governing body of American broadcasting - the Federal Communications Commission (FCC) about the so-called 'fairness' rule entitling all parties to have equal hearing in any broadcast debate containing controversial subject matter. The Commission alleged that McIntire had used his stations as a platform to air controversial and one-sided discussions on current events, without balanced editorial comment as required by FCC Regulations. (This rule was eventually abolished by the FCC, but not until 1987.)

The FCC, frustrated by McIntire's continued flouting of the fairness rule decided to close both WXUR outlets on 5th July 1973, ostensibly for failing to keep regular station logs. Carl McIntire announced during the final programmes on WXUR that he would find a way of returning to the airwaves with a new station, which he would call Radio Free America, and promised to do so within two weeks.

In order to stay outside FCC control McIntire planned to use a ship anchored in international waters as a base for his new radio station, but instead of the anticipated two weeks it took himsix weeks to find and equip a suitable vessel.

The ship eventually acquired by McIntire was the MV *Oceanic,* a former minesweeper which had also latterly been used as a base for scuba diving off Cape Canaveral in Florida. The vessel was leased by McIntire, using his own personal finances and re-named *Columbus.* By the end of August 1973 she had been fitted out as a floating radio station with a 10Kw RCA transmitter, an aerial array consisting of wire strung along the ship supported by the 100' central mast as well as some rudimentary studio equipment including a control panel, microphone and four reel-to-reel tape decks. The ship, which was crewed by six marine staff and two radio technicians, took up position in international waters off Cape May, New Jersey on 28th August 1973.

## First transmission

Radio Free America had its landbased headquarters in Carl McIntire's "Christian Admiral" Hotel at Cape May, New Jersey. McIntire proposed to give listeners to his new station a demonstration of free speech "as the Founding Fathers had intended it." Some broadcasts, including news bulletins, were to be transmitted live from the MV *Columbus,* with guest speakers being taken out to the radio ship, while other programmes would be pre-recorded on land. Plans were even announced to install a laser transmitter at the "Christian Admiral" Hotel to relay up-to-date news to the ship at its anchorage outside the three mile territorial limit.

### Rev. Carl McIntire

*Rev. Carl McIntire had left the United Presbyterian Church in 1936 to form his own Bible Presbyterian Church in Collingwood. Within a few years he had helped to set up the American Council of Churches and the International Council of Christian Churches with a membership of over 200 organisations in 73 countries. As well as attracting a large number of followers in his Church he acquired a lot of land and property including the four largest hotels in Cape May, New Jersey, a college in Philadelphia - The Faith Theological Seminary, a conference centre and three apartment buildings as well as 280 acres of undeveloped land near Cape Canaveral in Florida. He also owned the 'Christian Beacon' weekly newspaper which had a circulation of 145,000 in 1973. Carl McIntire held extremely right wing views, opposing any policy which hinted at socialism. In 1970 he opposed the negotiated peace settlement to America's involvement in the Vietnam War and led several groups marching through Washington in protest at the withdrawal of American troops.*

**Rev. McIntire Plans Radio Station**

PHILADELPHIA (UPI) — The Rev. Carl McIntire says he will set up a radio station in the Atlantic Ocean to broadcast his fundamentalist points of view. He plans to call it "Radio Free America."

McIntire announced his plans at an Independence Day rally on the steps of the building where the charter declaring the colonies' intent to break with England was signed.

A test carrier signal was transmitted from the *Columbus* on 1160kHz (259m) shortly before midnight (EST) on 12th September 1973. Then just after 1.30am the following morning the first music was broadcast from Radio Free America. However, this test transmission only lasted half an hour due to technical problems with equipment which ultimately resulted in a small fire breaking out in the control room and on the wooden deck of the *Columbus.*

The following day, 14th September 1973 the ship broke from her anchor and was forced to enter port for repairs and to have a new anchor installed. Some work was completed, although the new anchor could not be fitted immediately, but nevertheless the *Columbus* left port at 7.00pm on 15th September and sailed into international waters along the New Jersey coast. Radio Free America made a further four hour test broadcast while the ship was sailing up and down the coastline during the early morning of 16th September 1973. Later that same day the ship entered port to have her new anchor fitted and three days later she was back at sea again transmitting programmes for Radio Free America.

Official programmes commenced at 12.23pm on 19th September 1973 with a hymn and a taped announcement from the station's owner, Rev. Carl McIntire. The *Columbus* did not drop anchor while these broadcasts were being made, but again sailed up and down the New Jersey coast, in international waters, between Cape May and Avalon. To begin with the quality of the station's signal was weak, but power was gradually increased during the day, although an output of only 5Kw was ever achieved from the 10Kw transmitter on board the *Columbus.*

By late afternoon on 19th September 1973, a few hours after official programmes had started from Radio Free America, the FCC announced that they had received a complaint of interference from station WHLW in Lakewood, New Jersey, which broadcast with a power of 5Kw on 1170kHz (256m). In fact the interference was only marginal and at the extreme edge of WHLW's coverage area, but as he wanted to avoid any suggestion that his offshore station was causing interference to any other broadcaster Carl McIntire closed Radio Free America at 10.15pm on 19th September 1973. The FCC announced that it had

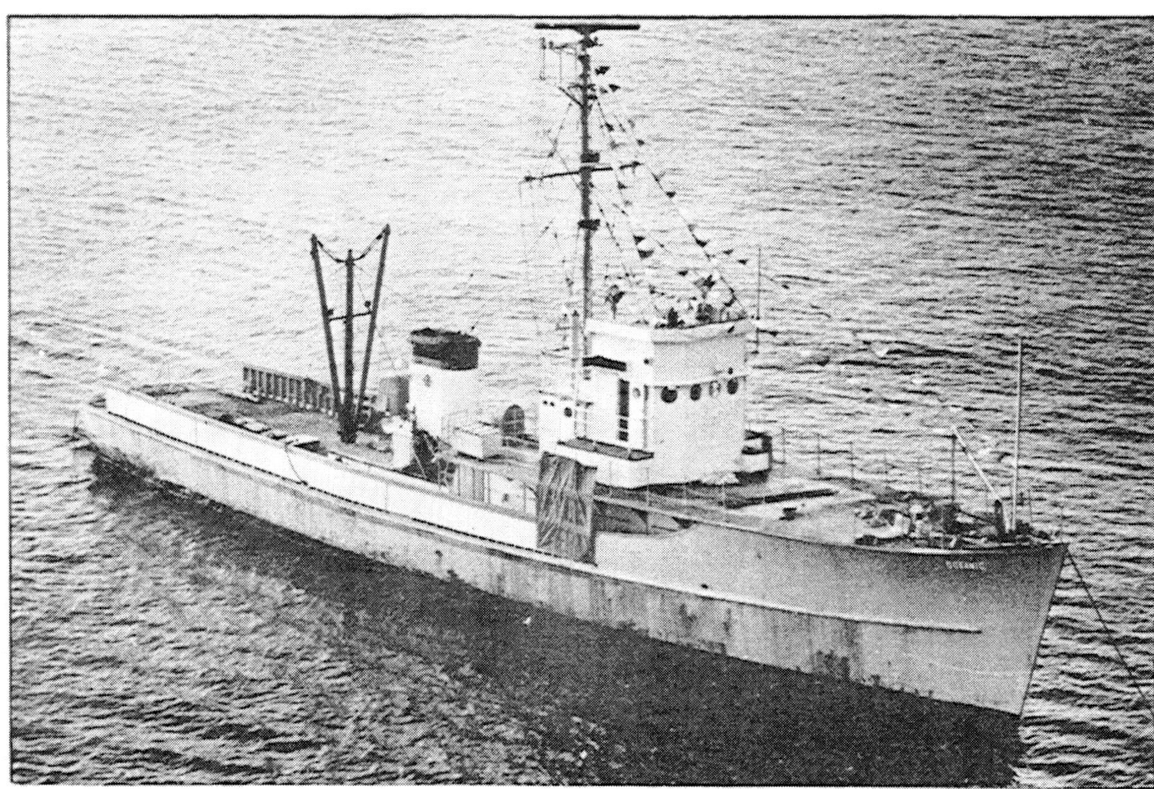

*The 'Columbus', home to Radio Free America*

agents listening to transmissions from the *Columbus* and, once evidence of broadcasts taking place or causing interference to legal stations had been collected, it would a seek a Restriction Order from a Federal Court to close Radio Free America.

Carl McIntire, however, remained defiant - he refused to call his broadcasting vessel or Radio Free America a pirate - he claimed to be a refugee from the US broadcasting system and said he actually wanted the courts to hear a test case on his right to broadcast.

On 20th September 1973, following an application by the FCC, a Federal Court in Camden, New Jersey issued a temporary Restriction Order prohibiting Radio Free America from transmitting again until at least 1st October 1973, when a decision would be taken about whether or not to make the order permanent. This Restriction Order was issued by the Court as the result of two complaints of interference having been received by the FCC - one from WHLW in Lakewood, New Jersey and one from KSL in Salt Lake City, Utah - over 2,000 miles away from Radio Free America's low power transmitter!

## Restriction Order

The New Jersey court had jurisdiction over Radio Free America, because although transmitting from international waters, the MV *Columbus* was registered in the USA. Under an amendment to the Communications Act of 1934 (passed following the demise of the world's first offshore radio station, RKXR, which had broadcast from a ship off California in 1933 -see Chapter 2) transmissions from any US registered ship or aircraft is prohibited, except in cases where a licence has been granted by the FCC. The provisions of the Act also left Carl McIntire personally liable to a fine of $10,000 or a one year jail sentence for operating his unlicensed radio station.

Carl McIntire had deliberately maintained the USA registration of the *Columbus,* claiming that in his view any requirement for him to obtain a licence to broadcast from offshore was unconstitutional having regard to the doctrine of Freedom of Speech enshrined in the American Constitution.

Whilst off the air because of the Restriction Order Carl McIntire decided that if Radio Free America ever returned it would do so on a new frequency of 1608kHz (186m) to avoid any further allegations of interference. However, despite the transmitter being tested on this frequency while the *Columbus* was still in Cape May Harbour, Radio Free America never did broadcast again. It was not until some six months later, in March 1974, that the legal position was finally resolved and the temporary Restriction Order on the station was made permanent.

The radio transmitting equipment was eventually removed from the *Columbus* and stored in a Cape May warehouse, while the vessel itself was returned to her previous owners as the lease payments had not been met by Carl McIntire once his station had been forced off the air.

The American authorities had acted firmly to silence Radio Free America and demonstrated, not for the first or last time, that unlike other Western governments at the time they were not prepared to tolerate a radio ship broadcasting off their coast.

## The Voice of Peace returns

Back in Europe the MV *Peace* was still in Marseilles Harbour in early 1975, while Abie Nathan sought more financial backing to re-launch his station in the Middle East - the Voice of Peace.

The financial side of the Voice of Peace was always precarious and there were frequent rumours that despite Abie Nathan's intention to return the station to the airwaves the ship would be taken over or sold to another broadcaster. There were rumours in 1974 that a European group had purchased the radio ship to launch a new station, Radio Benelux, but these proved to be unfounded (see Chapter 17) At one time a German religious organisation took a three month option on purchasing the ship from Abie Nathan and paid him not to sell it to anyone else during that time.

Despite these offers Abie Nathan passionately wanted to keep the Voice of Peace in the Mediterranean and hopefully use it to contribute towards a peaceful settlement of the years of conflict in the Middle East. During the summer of 1975 he conceived a plan to try and return the offshore station to the air with some financial security. In the hope of achieving, at the very least, some major publicity for the Voice of Peace and the Peace Foundation, he decided to sail the MV *Peace* to Port Said in Egypt. Here he planned to take on journalists and television crews then sail through the newly opened Suez Canal paying goodwill visits to Aquabah and Eilat before returning to the Mediterranean.

The Suez Canal had been closed and blocked since the Six Days War of 1967 and Abie Nathan's plan was for the MV *Peace* to be the first ship through after its re-opening. He also planned that the Voice of Peace should broadcast throughout the voyage, but if the authorities would not allow that to happen then Abie Nathan hoped the very fact that his vessel had been allowed to sail into Egyptian waters would break the barrier to Arab countries buying airtime on the re-launched station.

The obvious effect of this, from a commercial point of view, would be a potential surge in advertising revenue guaranteeing the future of the Voice of Peace. If he failed to achieve this Abie Nathan warned that when the three months option to purchase by the German religious organisation had expired he would have to sell the station to them or another buyer in order to pay off his outstanding debts.

The MV *Peace* left Marseilles on 28th May 1975 and once it had reached open seas the transmitters were switched on and a loop tape with the message "Give Peace a Chance" was played for about an hour. Following this a tape, prepared by Abie Nathan and French journalist Jacques Bonnier, was played in which Abie Nathan thanked the people of France for their help and support while the Peace had been in Marseilles. Once this taped programme had finished DJs presented an English/French Top 40 show, then the tape was repeated.

Unfortunately problems were experienced with the transmitter and broadcasts had to be discontinued at about 4.00pm, before the ship had even reached Italy. By 3rd June 1975 the *Peace* was about forty miles from Port Said and transmissions were started again during which announcements were made that the ship planned to sail through the Suez Canal to "Herald a new era of Peace".

These transmissions lasted until the early morning of 5th June when, at the request of the Captain , they were halted as the ship had reached the Egyptian territorial limit. However, after a furious row between Abie Nathan (representing the owners of the ship, the Shalom Peace Foundation of New York) and the Captain (Englishman Len Clements) the transmitters were re-activated on Abie Nathan's instructions and a programme of continuous music was played.

Within a short time an Egyptian gunboat started to shadow the *Peace* coming alongside just after dawn and instructing the Captain to follow it to a position three miles off Port Said and about half a mile from the Canal Buoy where it was told to drop anchor. The gunboat then took up position about 300 yards away and the crew played Egyptian music through its loudspeaker system. Throughout that day (5th June) a large flotilla of other ships assembled at the Canal Buoy and, when the waterway was officially re-opened by Egyptian President Anwar Sadat, one by one they were piloted through.

The crew of the MV *Peace* had been assured by Abie Nathan that they would be the first ship through the Canal when it was reopened, but they had to watch as all the other ships gradually made their way through, leaving only the *Peace* at the Canal Buoy, guarded by the gunboat. Attempts were made to communicate with the Egyptian warship by radio telephone and Morse code using flashing lights, but after some hours the only reply they received was to "wait for instructions". Meanwhile the gunboat continued blasting Egyptian music across to the *Peace.*

## Anchored off Suez

On 8th June more ships arrived at the Buoy to form another convoy travelling south-bound through the Suez Canal. A Pilot boat visited each one in turn to arrange their passage, but avoided and ignored the *Peace* ship. That evening, when the other ships had left the area and sailed into the Canal, the Egyptian gunboat started dropping anti-personnel bombs around the MV *Peace.*

After a further five days, during which attempts were made to contact the Pilot boat and Port Said Radio, both of whom refused to answer, Abie Nathan managed to contact some backers in America and the United Press Agency, using the facilities of Cyprus Maritime Radio. As a result of these contacts with the outside world the crew on board the radio ship learned that reports were circulating in Egypt to the effect that the MV *Peace* had sunk!

Eventually a message was relayed to the Port Said Harbour authorities and the Pilot boat came alongside the MV *Peace* on 16th June 1975. After taking details of crew nationalities, intended destination and cargo they told the Captain to wait for further instructions and left. Nothing more was heard from the authorities but after about a week the gunboat was replaced by another one which started sailing intimidatingly close to the MV *Peace,* almost ramming the radio ship.

Meanwhile, the crew on board the *Peace* were becoming more and more frustrated - food and fresh water supplies were running short and one of the generators also failed, cutting the ship's power supply and air conditioning system. After a few more days Abie Nathan was forced to contact Port Said Harbour authorities asking permission to enter port as he had two sick men on board - and English crew member and Australian DJ, Keith Ashton.

The day after he made this request a launch carrying two officials from the Suez Canal Authority, Egyptian Police officers and a doctor drew alongside the MV *Peace* and the men came aboard. After treating the sick men they left saying they would return later to collect the two crew members on board the radio ship who were Egyptian nationals. They did return and removed the two Egyptian crewmen some three days later., but with them gone it reduced what little chance remained that the MV *Peace* would be able to enter Port Said.

Abie Nathan succeeded in contacting the Egyptian Pilot boat again and this time he was informed that the ship could not enter the Suez Canal as it had no agent in Port Said. Arrangements were then made through contacts in Marseilles, for an Egyptian agent to be appointed, but the company subsequently refused to act for the *Peace* ship.

While the MV *Peace* lay at anchor, unable to move, tensions on board continued to build - the Captain and broadcasting staff wanted to sail to a position off Israel and start transmissions, marine crew members on loan to the *Peace* ship wanted to go ashore and move to their next ship. Having got so far with his plans Abie Nathan would have none of this and, despite repeated requests from his crew, was prepared to sit and wait indefinitely for the Egyptian authorities to allow the radio ship through the Suez Canal.

However, after nearly three weeks at anchor off the Canal Buoy Abie Nathan decided that the *Peace* would have to sail to a position outside Egyptian territorial waters from where he could broadcast a special appeal to President Sadat asking again for permission to enter the Suez Canal. The Egyptian authorities had never actually refused the Peace ship permission to enter the Canal, but had just kept the vessel waiting in the hope that one day Abie Nathan would give up and leave the area.

This in fact happened on 26th June 1975 and as the MV *Peace* sailed away from the Canal Buoy the gunboat circled and pursued the radio ship for a while, turning its guns threateningly towards Abie Nathan and his crew. Because of uncertainties about whether the Egyptians were operating a twenty or a fifty mile territorial limit the Captain of the MV *Peace,* without informing Abie Nathan, actually sailed the ship to a position off Israeli territorial waters. From here, and in the belief that he was in fact off Egypt, Abie Nathan broadcast his personal appeal to President Sadat, explaining the history of the Peace Foundation, the Voice of Peace radio station and his mission to enter the Suez Canal.

Nothing was heard from the Egyptian authorities - they probably had not even picked up the broadcast anyway, so Abie Nathan instructed the Captain to sail to a position off Ashdod from where they could obtain fresh supplies of food and water.

## Return to Israel and 'closure'

Almost immediately the Voice of Peace started broadcasting to Israel once again and, even with only three DJs on board, it managed to maintain a 24 hour schedule because the engineering staff took turns at playing continuous music programmes. Meanwhile, each evening Abie Nathan came on the air to talk about peace and play 'peace music'.

While these broadcasts were being made the ship sailed northwards to a position off Haifa and then Abie Nathan announced suddenly during his programme:- "This is the Voice of Peace and we're closing down now and sailing into harbour to try and raise some more money to continue with our job." He indicated that he planned to either sell the ship to the German religious organisation or if he could raise enough money from selling airtime, he was prepared to turn the station into a commercial venture once again. The Voice of Peace then closed playing the "Give Peace a Chance" loop tape.

The MV *Peace* sailed into Haifa where she was met by hundreds of fans and a flotilla of yachts and small boats. An Israeli television crew also came on board and interviewed Abie Nathan about his plans for the future. Abie Nathan made further statements saying that if he could not raise sufficient finance to continue operating the Voice of Peace as a commercial station he would have to sell the radio ship.

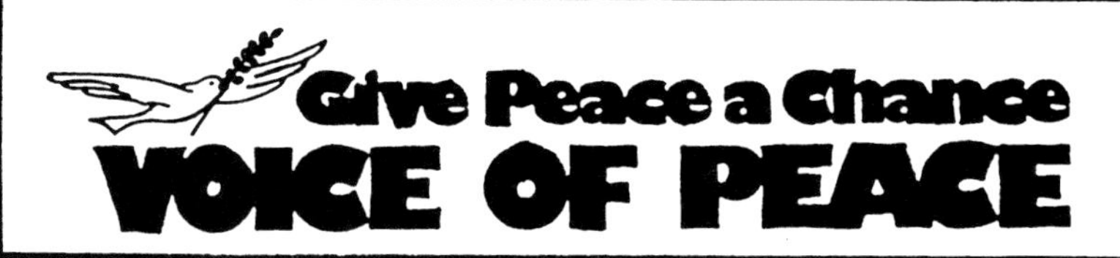

## Another attempt

However, the money was raised and at the end of July 1975 the MV *Peace* , stocked with five months fuel supplies, left Haifa with broadcasts from the Voice of Peace recommencing on 1st August.

In mid-September 1975 after about six weeks of relatively uneventful broadcasting from off the Israeli coast the *Peace* ship sailed south once again towards Egypt, hoping that this time it would be allowed through the Suez Canal. Yet again though Abie Nathan was refused permission by the Egyptian authorities who sent two warships to stand by the MV *Peace,* preventing her entering the Canal unofficially.

As a gesture of peace and goodwill Abie Nathan then decided to hire a small boat and sail into Port Said himself to deliver flowers from the people of Israel. On his arrival in Port Said he was arrested by the Egyptians, blindfolded so that he could not see any military installations, and taken to Cairo. Here he was questioned for several hours by Egyptian police and later deported to Rome.

Meanwhile, the Egyptian warships started to continuously circle the MV *Peace,* firing their machine guns across her bow and throwing grenades in the sea near the radio ship. Those on board the MV *Peace* decided to leave the area after two days of Egyptian harassment and they sailed back to anchor off Israel to resume normal broadcasts.

## Commercials rule

Throughout the months after the aborted Suez Canal trip the Voice of Peace continued to broadcast from off the coast of Israel, although never actually announcing its precise location, just "somewhere in the Mediterranean".

During the summer of 1976 the station revamped its format, largely as the result of ex-RNI and Radio Caroline DJ, Crispian St. John, taking over as Programme Director. The station began playing an all-hits format rather than records by largely unknown artists and almost immediately audience figures increased dramatically. Casey Kasem's American Top 40 Show, syndicated worldwide by Watermark Productions, based in Hollywood USA was also broadcast twice a week during the summer of 1976. This programme attracted a large audience particularly from amongst UN soldiers stationed in the Middle East and from tourists visiting Israel.

The amount of advertising carried on the Voice of Peace also increased as a direct result of the format change although at first most commercials were in Hebrew gradually more and more English language ones appeared. Amongst advertisers attracted to the newly formatted station were Austin Allegro cars, VW cars and Schweppes soft drinks. A major deal was also struck with Faberge Perfumes who bought airtime on the Voice of Peace to promote their brands of toiletries and deodorants as well as sponsoring the number one record each week in the station's Top 40.

So much commercial airtime was being booked by Israeli (and in particular Tel Aviv based) companies at this time that a planned peace mission voyage by the MV *Peace* to the Lebanese port of Beirut was abandoned - the station simply could not afford to be away from its primary target area and upset its advertisers. To some people the cancellation of a 'peace initiative' such as this seemed to destroy the whole raison de entre of the Voice of Peace - it had started out as a non-commercial radio station to campaign for peace and now its potential for disseminating those peace messages was being subordinated to commercial considerations.

**offshore trivia**

**Smallest radio ship**

***LENGTH:*** *'Uilenspiegel' (Radio Antwerpen) - 70'*

***WEIGHT:*** *'Cheeta' (Radio Mercur) - 107 tons*

*(Discounting 'Cornucopia' and 'Galexy' which were only used for short-term broadcasts.)*

## Entebbe

*On 27th June 1976 an Air France air bus, flight A300B, was hijacked on a flight from Athens to Paris and flown to Entebbe Airport in Uganda, where it remained on the tarmac for some days. Abie Nathan decided that he would do all he could to secure the release of the passengers being held hostage and during a two hour broadcast on the Voice of Peace he announced that he would personally travel to Uganda to help. He subsequently flew to Entebbe in his private plane to negotiate with the hijackers. His talks with them and his observations of the situation on board the Air France plane assisted the subsequent Israeli-backed commando operation which overpowered the hijackers and secured the release of the hostages.*

In defence of this situation and, perhaps slightly embarrassed by the commercial success of the Voice of Peace, Abie Nathan declared that large donations from the substantial advertising revenue (estimated to be worth over £88,000 at that time) would be made to deserving causes. After meeting running expenses for the station profits from advertising income were then used to support charities and organisations involved in work of a humanitarian nature as well as for victims of war. As an example contributions were made to various childrens' hospitals (both Arab and Jewish) as well as donations to refugees of the Guatemalan earthquake.

The station was hugely popular with listeners and the Voice of Peace came top in a public opinion poll organised by the state radio network, Kol Israel, in late 1976, receiving over 40% of listeners votes. In response the state network introduced its own pop music based service - Programme C, Reshet Gimel - to compete with the popularity of the Voice of Peace.

Although largely responsible for the station's success the Voice of Peace format at this time was very tight and made little or no allowance for DJs personal preferences. This and the rule that individual DJs were not allowed to promote themselves as personalities led to dissatisfaction and disillusionment amongst some of the radio crew on the Voice of Peace. This feeling was compounded by the fact that they received very little feedback from listeners and what small amount of mail that did get through was often written in Arabic or Hebrew, which the largely English speaking crew could not understand.

A London based company, Broadcast Placement Services, operated by Maggie Stevenson, was appointed as British advertising representative for the Voice of Peace in July 1976. In addition to trying to sell airtime to large international advertisers BPS also recruited DJs for the Voice of Peace and made jingle packages for the station. Advertising rates of £30 for a thirty second spot were being quoted to prospective advertisers. Early successes included advertising campaigns place through British agencies for Leyland cars, Fiat cars, and Revlon and Max Factor cosmetics.

With the enormous success of the Voice of Peace plans were formulated in the autumn of 1976 for the launch of an offshore television station from the MV *Peace*. These were later abandoned, however, for fear that the Israeli Government would take action to close both the radio and television services. As with many other governments, particularly in Europe, the Israelis appeared willing to tolerate an offshore radio station, but felt very differently about the prospect of an offshore television station. The issue of offshore television was to come to the fore again in Israel later, but Abie Nathan and the Voice of Peace were not involved in any way.

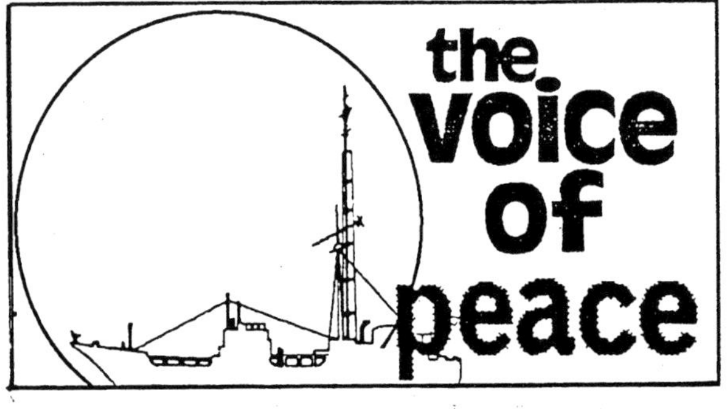


## Through Suez at last

Just as the Voice of Peace appeared to be enjoying commercial and programming success things began to change in late October 1976. Many advertising contracts, mostly from Israeli based companies, were either cancelled or simply not renewed. This development, coming as it did in a period of success and popularity for the station remained a mystery to DJs and listeners alike for over two months.

Towards the end of December 1976, however, the reason became clear to all. The MV *Peace* had entered Haifa on 5th December where she was refuelled and restocked with supplies. She sailed from port two weeks later, heading southwards towards Egypt because Abie Nathan had at last been given permission to sail the M V *Peace* down the Suez Canal.

He had been in discussion with the authorities in Egypt for some time to secure their permission and one condition of this had been that to demonstrate its impartiality to all sides the station should not continue to carry a high volume of Israeli advertising. Permission was only finally received once Abie Nathan had agreed to this condition and been able to prove that the MV *Peace* was not an Israeli vessel, but was in fact registered in Panama. A further stipulation imposed by the Egyptian authorities was that the Voice of Peace did not transmit during the voyage.

Flying the Panamanian flag MV *Peace* arrived off Port Said on 31st December 1976 and was immediately put under guard by the Egyptian Navy. In the early hours of the following morning, January 1st 1977 the *Peace* ship was escorted as part of a convoy to the mouth of the Suez Canal.

The MV *Peace* sailed along the Canal on 2nd/3rd January 1977 arriving at the Red Sea port of Eilat on the 4th to be greeted by local residents and the Mayor of the town. From here it was planned to sail the *Peace* to Aqaba in Jordan before returning through the Suez Canal to the Mediterranean, and the Mayor of Eilat gave Abie Nathan a gift to present to his opposite number in the Jordanian city as a gesture of goodwill. Unfortunately the Jordanian authorities later refused to allow the *Peace* ship to enter Aqaba to present the gift.

Meanwhile, in Egypt the news media largely ignored the voyage by the *Peace* ship through the Suez Canal and the authorities also prevented Abie Nathan distributing toys and sweets to Egyptian children. After being unable to complete large parts of his mission Abie Nathan sailed the *Peace* back through the Suez Canal, arriving in the Mediterranean and recommencing broadcasts from the Voice of Peace on 10th January 1977.

## Voice of Peace programme schedule, mid-1977

**6.00am Breakfast Show,** *Carl Kingston*

**9.00am Morning Programme,** *Crispian St. John*

**12 noon Showcase,** *Rick Dennis spotlighting different kinds of music soul, country and western, progressive etc.*

**2.00pm Afternoon Programme,** *Tony Mandell*

**4.00pm Drive Time,** *Kas Collins*

**6.00pm Peace Programme,** *Abie Nathan*

**7.30pm Classical Music**

**9.00pm Rick Dennis**

**12 midnight Steve Williams**

**3.00am Arabic Music Programme** *Egeal, an Arabic speaking DJ*

VOICE OF PEACE LTD. קול השלום בע"מ

13, FRUG St. P.O.Box 4399, TEL-AVIV רחוב פרוג 13, ת.ד. 4399, ת"א

## News

*For its first few years on the air the Voice of Peace did not carry news bulletins. Although the DJs would have liked to introduce such a service they could never persuade Abie Nathan to agree. He argued that because most of the broadcasting staff were British or 'western' they did not fully understand the Middle East problems and they could unwittingly compile biased news bulletins which, in a volatile situation, could prove dangerous. From time to time Abie Nathan himself would go on air, often from his home or the station's landbased offices via the Motorola mobile telephone, to talk about various news stories and give his views and opinions on current issues. He also presented a regular "Peace Programme" each evening between 6.00 and 7.30pm during which he covered topics relating to current affairs in the Middle East.*

*A regular news service was, however, introduced on the Voice of Peace in April 1977. This was presented on the top of each hour - on the even hour the BBC World Service news was relayed and on the odd hour bulletins from the Israel state radio, Kol Israel were transmitted. Later in the year the BBC bulletins were dropped in favour of those from Kol Israel.*

*The news service was introduced because the Voice of Peace realised that it was losing 60% of its audience in Israel at the top of each hour as listeners tuned to the state radio to hear the latest news and then either did not, or were slow to, re-tune back to the Voice of Peace.*

## *Mebo II* move to Libya

Legal action involving former the RNI ship *Mebo II* continued in Holland throughout 1975. Mebo Ltd. were pursuing a claim in the Dutch courts for repayment of harbour fees incurred while their two ships, *Mebo I* and *Mebo II* had been forcibly detained during 1974/75.

By the end of January 1976 the ships were free to leave Holland and had reportedly been sold by Mebo Ltd. to an un-named African country. It was estimated that Mebo Ltd. had lost 3 million Dutch Guilders (£600,000) as a result of the ships being detained in Holland and 100,000 Guilders (£20,000) in legal expenses for the various court cases - money which Edwin Bollier wanted to reclaim from the Dutch Government. Although former RNI engineers Bob Noakes and Robin Adcroft (Banks) had been retained by Mebo Ltd. to accompany the two ships on their expected voyage to the Mediterranean this claim through the courts further delayed the departure of the ships, which had originally been planned for 15th August 1976.

In November 1976 both ships were dry docked once again to be cleaned and re-painted. During this time two 10Kw transmitters from the former Radio Veronica ship, *Norderney,* (now in Amsterdam) were installed on the *Mebo I* (re-named *Angela*), prompting an investigation by the Dutch Post Office (PTT) with a consequent further delay to the ship's departure.

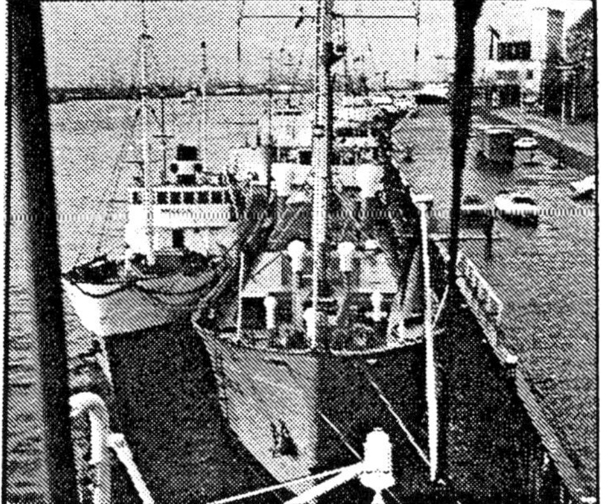

Right *'MeboII' and 'Angela' in Rotterdam, January 1977*

Finally in January 1977 the Dutch authorities issued a statement saying:- "The Attorney General at the Court of Justice in The Hague declares that the confiscation of the *Mebo II* has been cancelled and that the *Mebo II* and the *Angela,* with existing transmitting apparatus therein, can leave the Netherlands with due observation of the Customs control."

Following this announcement both ships were given engine trials in harbour and on 14th January, after inspections by Customs officials they left the de Groot van Vliet shipyard and sailed into Rotterdam to take on supplies.

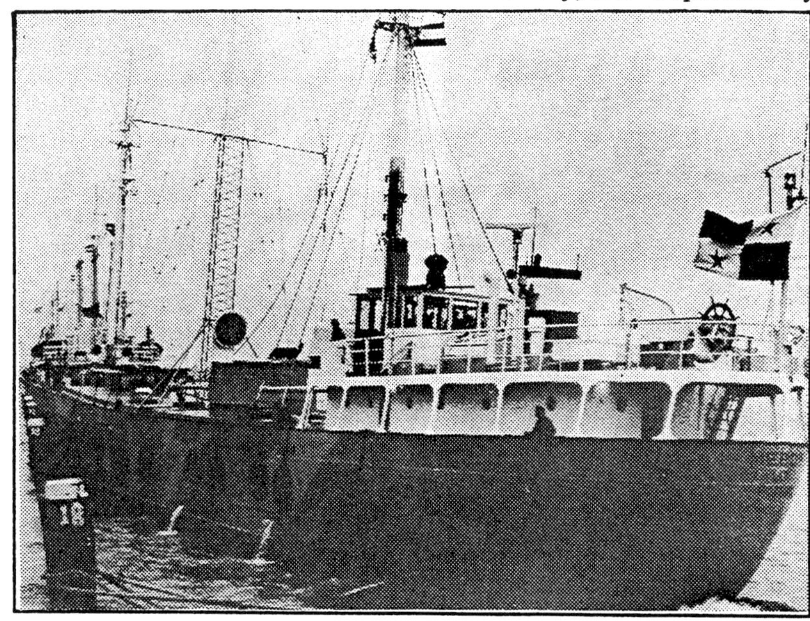

*'Mebo II' preparing to leave Holland*

While docking in Rotterdam the *Mebo II* collided with another ship causing over £3,000 worth of damage. The authorities immediately placed a detention order on the radio ship, fearing she would leave port without paying for the damage, but the costs were met by Mebo Ltd. and on 16th January 1977 both vessels left Holland, sailing south towards a new destination and a new role in the Mediterranean which was to be unlike anything ever experienced by an offshore radio station before or since.

## Mebo ships leave Holland

Both ships had Dutch Captains and engineers on board, but the marine crew were mainly from the Cape Verde Islands. Also on board the *Mebo II* was ex-RNI engineer and DJ Robin Adcroft (Robin Banks).

After the two vessels had sailed under the bridges of Rotterdam they were tied to the Parkkade Pier to have supplies loaded for their forthcoming voyage to a destination which at that time remained a mystery. Whilst tied up the *Mebo II* struck another ship, the West German vessel *Estebrugge,* which in turn shunted into two other ships causing £3,000 worth of damage. The owners of the *Estebrugge* insisted that the *Mebo II* be detained until repair work had been completed and paid for.

Once repairs to the damaged ships had either been completed or covered by insurance guarantees both the *Mebo II* and the *Angela* sailed from Parkkade on 16th January 1977. The two ships dropped anchor in international waters for the night before setting off on their voyage to Tripoli, Libya. Bad weather slowed the journey and after calling at Ceuta, a Spanish harbour in Morocco on 1st February 1977 to take on fresh supplies of food, fuel and water both ships eventually arrived off Tripoli on 9th February. However, it was not until five days later that they were allowed to enter Tripoli Harbour when the Libyan authorities had satisfied themselves that the vessel's registration documents were in order. At this time, too, the crew were all paid off, although radio engineer Robin Adcroft remained on board the *Mebo II.*

During February and March 1977 a number of test transmissions were made by Robin Adcroft from Tripoli Harbour. These transmissions, on 1232kHz (243m) using a power of about 40Kw, took place generally between 8.00 and 11.00pm, local time and consisted of records and announcements by Robin Adcroft, but there were no station identifications. Later some tests were also made on 773kHz (388m) using the old Radio Veronica 10Kw transmitter which had been installed on the *Mebo II,* the other ex-Radio Veronica transmitter was at that time stored as cargo on the *Angela.*

These test transmissions had to be halted after a few weeks because it was discovered that they were causing interference to local communications facilities in the Tripoli area. A further series of test transmissions from the *Mebo II* began on 2nd May 1977 on 6205kHz in the 49m shortwave band as well as 773kHz (388m) and 90mHz FM. Again the tests were presented by Robin Adcroft and consisted largely of music and announcements, but this time knowing that some

**offshore trivia**

**Radio ship to house most stations**

*'Mi Amigo' - Nine (Radio Nord, Radio Atlanta, Radio Caroline South, Radio 199, Radio Caroline (post 1972), Radio Atlantis, Radio Mi Amigo, Radio Seagull, Radio Veronica)*

**offshore trivia**

**First and last advert on Radio Caroline offshore**

***FIRST:*** *Woburn Abbey (1st May 1964)*

***LAST:*** *West German State Lottery (4th November 1990)*

**offshore trivia**

**Longest running offshore Top 40 programme**

*Radio Veronica - every week for 8 years 8 months (first broadcast 3rd January 1965, last offshore edition 31st August 1974).*

European offshore radio enthusiasts would probably be listening on shortwave, the occasional RNI jingle was inserted between records. At the top of each hour the former RNI theme, "Man of Action" was also played.

On 19th May 1977 test transmissions also started in the 31m shortwave band on 9810kHz, making a total of four transmitters broadcasting simultaneously from the *Mebo II* - the first time that had happened in over three years. Unfortunately because of interference from a powerful Russian station the use of the 31m shortwave band frequency had to be abandoned in mid-June.

## Libyan broadcasts

By 29th June 1977 the transmitters on the *Mebo II* were being used to relay the English language programmes of the Socialist People's Libyan Arab Jamahiriyah Broadcasting Corporation (SPLAJBC), itself transmitting from Tripoli on 1406kHz (213.9m). These relays, which were arranged by Robin Adcroft on instructions from Mebo Director Edwin Bollier in Switzerland, were thought to have been for the benefit of Libyan Embassies throughout the world. However, no feedback was received from this potential audience and the broadcasts from *Mebo II* stopped after about two weeks.

On 8th August both the *Mebo II* and the *Angela* raised their anchors and sailed from Tripoli Harbour arriving three days later, first at Benghazi and finally at Derna Harbour - 600 miles from Tripoli and close to the Egyptian border.

Transmissions under the call sign LBJ - Libyan Post-Revolution Broadcasting were made on 773kHz (388m) using the 10Kw former Radio Veronica transmitter. The main 100Kw transmitter on the *Mebo II* was ready to be used on 1232kHz (243.5m) but at the last moment the Libyan authorities instructed the radio engineers that it must not be used.

At this stage programmes consisted of music, with no propaganda or information, and continued for about five hours each night, half of that time being live programmes presented by Robin Adcroft and the remainder pre-recorded taped programmes. Gradually the FM and shortwave transmitters on board the *Mebo II* were also brought into use during the test broadcasts, but towards the end of October 1977 a problem developed in the medium wave aerial. The *Mebo II* then left Derna on 30th October 1977 for a new anchorage off Benghazi.

After arriving off Benghazi test transmissions were resumed on all three wavebands, but after two days engineers were instructed to turn off the medium and shortwave outlets, leaving only FM to carry the five hours of nightly broadcasts. After about ten days the *Mebo II* and the *Angela* entered Benghazi Harbour and engineers were told to keep the transmitters silent until arrangements had been made for Libyan frequencies to be allocated to them.

Despite this instruction a number of relays of the FM test transmissions were broadcast on 6205kHz shortwave in December 1977 and early January 1988, announced simply as "a programme of international music on 90mHz FM."

On 15th January 1978 the, by now regular, programme did not start as usual at 7.00pm local time and announcement broadcast later in the evening indicated that the *Mebo II* was actually sailing away from Benghazi Harbour. The radio ship eventually arrived off Tripoli once again on 19th January and broadcasts, consisting of a relay of the Socialist People's Libyan Arab Jamahiriyah Broadcasting Corporation (SPLAJBC) in English, were made until 8.30pm local time. These programmes were mainly news bulletins, music and talks about international affairs.

On some occasions once the domestic relay had finished western pop music was played until another relay, this time in Arabic, commenced later in the evening. Broadcasts settled into a regular pattern of relays of the land-based domestic service in Libya with transmissions all simulcast on 6206kHz (48.35m shortwave), 1402 kHz (213.9m medium wave) and 92mHz FM.

On 5th April 1978 the *Mebo II* and the *Angela* became the official property of the Libyan Government and were re-named *El Fatah* and *Almasira* respectively. The two ships were dry docked in Tripoli and repainted, the former *Mebo II* in red and cream and the former *Angela,* in blue, white and black. Whilst in dry dock both vessels were manned by between six and twelve armed guards at all times.

A Libyan Navy spokesman said that when they had finished with the ships it was planned to take them out into the Mediterranean and sink them to prevent anybody else using the radio transmitting facilities. The vessels were not to be sold again because the Libyans stated they did not want them to fall into the hands of any "undesirable people", probably a reference to the Israelis.

A foreign language service of the Libyan Broadcasting service SPLAJBC started from *El Fatah* on 11th June 1978. Each day six Arab announcers, three French speaking and three English speaking, travelled out to the ship in Tripoli Harbour to present live programmes. The announcers relied on radio engineers Robin Adcroft and 'Printz' to operate the technical equipment for them and they were the only two Europeans allowed on board the radio ship - even announcers broadcasting on the European Service of SPLAJBC were required to pre-record their programmes in landbased studios. The *El Fatah* was treated as a classified military vessel and no one was officially allowed to talk about its existence.

This broadcasting arrangement lasted only until the end of June 1978 when plans were announced for a new daily service, consisting of readings from the Holy Koran, to be broadcast using the 100 kW medium wave transmitter on 1232kHz (243.5m) between 6.00am and 6.00pm (GMT).

## Final English programme

*On 14th August 1978 Robin Adcroft and 'Printz' decided to make a clandestine broadcast on shortwave to commemorate the eleventh anniversary of the introduction of the British Marine etc. Broadcasting (Offences) Act. This transmission took place between 5.00 and 6.00am (GMT) before the broadcasts of Holy Koran readings started and were the last English language programmes made from the 'Mebo II'.*

## Destroyed

With the two ships becoming classified military establishments very little information is available about their use after late 1978 when the two remaining European radio engineers had been replaced. It is known that the *El Fatah* was dry docked in Malta during June 1979 being overhauled and re-painted. She returned to Libya in September 1979, having been repainted in the Libyan national colour, green, and recommenced transmissions of SPLAJBC shortly afterwards.

There were a number of reports of sightings of the *El Fatah* after that date. She was reported variously to have run aground on rocks off Malta and also been sighted in Portugal during 1981 and 1982 in connection with a possible use by a breakaway group from the Radio Caroline organisation anxious to return that station to the air.

However, all these reports were inaccurate and the *El Fatah* continued to be used to relay programmes of the SPLAJBC until sometime in 1980 after which she was, as predicted by the Libyan authorities some years earlier, towed into the Mediterranean and sunk as the result of being used as target practice by the Libyan Air Force. It is believed that the former *Mebo I* (*Angela*) also suffered the same fate.

## Voice of Peace

Meanwhile, the MV *Peace,* having arrived back off Israel from its voyage through the Suez Canal in January 1977, continued to broadcast Voice of Peace programmes and the station built on its previous popularity with listeners and advertisers.

In May 1977 Abie Nathan was prevented from leaving Israel after Government Treasury officials claimed the Voice of Peace owed millions of Israeli pounds in income taxes. The order preventing him leaving the country was issued after Treasury officials had informed a Court that they considered the Voice of Peace to be a commercial enterprise and therefore liable to pay taxes. The Treasury were claiming tax payments for the period 1974-1976, including the time during which the MV *Peace* was in Marseilles and the Voice of Peace was not even on the air.

Abie Nathan's response to the Treasury was that he did not owe any money because the Voice of Peace was a non-profit making organisation. He had reluctantly started broadcasting commercials in 1975 to help meet running costs of the Voice of Peace, but had donated all his profits since then to Arab and Jewish charities.

A survey conducted in August 1977 claimed that the Voice of Peace had an estimated audience of 23 million - a quarter of all radio listeners in the Middle East. The area covered by the survey was bounded by Saudia Arabia in the south, Egypt in the west, Cyprus in the north and Iraq in the east. Surprisingly the survey results, published in the British trade magazine *Broadcast,* revealed that the largest audience for the Voice of Peace was in Egypt were an estimated 11 million people claimed to listen regularly.

However, despite these figures a similar and probably more accurate survey in Israel revealed that the Voice of Peace was only the third most popular station, behind the state pop music service of Reshet Gimel and the Army station, Galei Zahal. Reshet Gimel's success was attributed to the fact that it played more commercial music and golden hits than the Voice of Peace, but the popularity of the Army station was surprising because its format was not completely music based - they often broadcast comedy, talk and discussion programmes. However, unlike Reshet Gimel and the Voice of Peace the Army station did not carry commercials and this in itself may have appealed to a proportion of listeners who preferred not to have advertisements interrupting their radio programmes.

## Shortwave tests

On 12th August 1977 the Voice of Peace started test broadcasts on 6245kHz in the shortwave band. Further test transmissions were also reported to have been made on 6240kHz in September and October 1977 with reception reports being received from many countries particularly in western Europe. At the beginning of September 1977 the medium wave transmitter increased its power to 75Kw and changed frequency very slightly from 1540kHz to 1538kHz, although the station continued to be announced on air as the 'Voice of Peace on 195m.'

In late 1977 the Voice of Peace's London representatives, Broadcast Placement Services, ceased operations. This organisation had been heavily involved in the recruitment of English speaking broadcasting and engineering staff as well as the sale of commercial airtime on the Voice of Peace to non-Israeli companies.

At about the same time Abie Nathan decided to dispense with the services of the Tel Aviv advertising agency which sold airtime on the Voice of Peace to Israeli-based companies and to sell all airtime himself. However, this did not

### VOP Tourism Promotion

*The Israeli Ministry of Tourism started promoting the Voice of Peace in May 1977 when it included the station's programme schedules in its weekly information sheet - an indication of the reasonable degree of tolerance shown towards the offshore station by the authorities.*

work out as successfully as he planned and this change of policy marked the start of a period of considerable problems for the Voice of Peace. Advertising revenue declined quite sharply and money was no longer available to maintain or repair vital equipment which in turn led to the station suffering frequent technical breakdowns and periods off the air.

## Closure threat

This unsettled situation continued throughout the remainder of 1977 and into early 1978, then on 17th February 1978 the *Jerusalem Post* announced some shock news **VOICE OF PEACE MAY CLOSE - NO ADS.** The accompanying article went on to explain that the station may have to close at the end of the month because money was running out. Abie Nathan was quoted as saying that the Israeli state network (which was offering discounted rates to advertisers who did not use the Voice of Peace) and "hostile advertising agents" had all but squeezed his station out of the commercial market. In addition storm damage to the ship and its broadcasting equipment had cost nearly half a million Israeli pounds to repair.

Amongst advertisers who had withdrawn support from the station at this time was Coca Cola and Abie Nathan promised to start a retaliatory advertising campaign on the Voice of Peace urging listeners to drink water. For some time after this the station did in fact carry promotions pointing out the benefits of water as a healthy and refreshing drink.

Later in the article Abie Nathan stated that despite the *Broadcast* survey of August 1977, which showed the station having an audience of 23 million listeners in the Middle East, some of the big advertising agencies had spread rumours that the station had hardly any audience. With hindsight the truth was probably somewhere in between - an audience of 23 million in the Middle East seems improbably high and it was always tacitly acknowledged that the station's main audience, and indeed the bulk of its advertising income, came from Tel Aviv. Despite having boosted the signal power in September 1977 the station's reception area was mainly confined to the Tel Aviv coastal strip, although it did undoubtedly have some dedicated listeners in other areas and countries as well.

### 'Voice of Peace' may close: No ads

**By ZE'EV SCHUL**
**Jerusalem Post Reporter**

TEL AVIV. — Able Nathan's "Voice of Peace" may have to close down for good at the end of this month — almost five years since the floating radio station started broadcasts off the southern Mediterranean coast of Israel — because his money is running out.

Nathan told *The Jerusalem Post* yesterday that Israel Radio's Second and Third Programmes and hostile ad agents have all but squeezed his Peace Ship out of the advertising market. And the storms of early winter caused more than IL500,000 in damage to the ship and its equipment.

"I don't want to ask for charity," he said. "What we were earning (from advertising) — about IL200,000 a month — was just enough to keep us afloat. But now some of the big advertising people have spread rumours that we have no listening audience. Which is untrue. The reputable 'British Broadcast Magazine' rated our audience at 23 million people, all the way from Kuwait to the African shoreline.

"I really thought we were doing something worthwhile — apart from stimulating local competition, which never hurts. Israel Radio makes about IL4m. a month from advertising. I can't see how our modest revenue could have hurt the national broadcasting service," Nathan said.

He said he had offered one advertising agent double his normal 20 per cent commission, and the man had returned in short order with IL500,000 worth of advertising. "I tore the contract up in his face. I deliberately led him on just to prove that it wasn't the station audience at fault, or the lack of advertisers either."

Among those Nathan said have stopped advertising on the "Voice of Peace" is a major soft-drink producer. "I'm going to ask all listeners who want to keep this station open to drink water — no soft drinks — for a couple of days as a token of their solidarity with us," he added.

Nathan, who once owned a flourishing restaurant just off Dizengoff in Tel Aviv, says he has no assets left to sell to keep the station going. He said the ship is worth about $500,000. But it can be used only as a broadcasting station, so its potential buyers are limited.

"I had an offer from the Lebanese Phalangists, but I didn't want to become involved in politics. So unless there are new developments — and I'm not going to give in easily — the 'Voice of Peace' will go silent 11 days from today.

"If we do have to strike our colours," he added, "we'll do it with a farewell cruise, just a few hundred metres off the shore, so that everyone can see us. That will be Tuesday, the 28th."

Nathan disclosed that he had filed for permission to set up a land-based broadcasting station. "It's much cheaper. But I know that several of the agents who have stopped advertising with us have also filed for permits to set up radio and TV stations of their own."

Nathan, who in the past has flown his own plane to Egypt as a gesture of peace, said yesterday, "We may not have achieved our aim of bringing peace (to the Middle East). But I do believe we have contributed to that end. And when we made money — IL2m. in 1976/77 — we shared it with charitable institutions."

Abie Nathan threatened in the *Jerusalem Post* article that "unless there are some new developments the Voice of Peace will go silent eleven days from today."

As no new developments did take place Abie Nathan began to announce on air that because advertising contracts had been withdrawn the station would have to close on 28th February 1978. He asked listeners to join him in Tel Aviv for a farewell rally on 25th February and over 60,000 people turned up. This event received widespread publicity in Israel and went some way to convincing advertisers that the station did have a large listenership after all. On the day before the planned closure Abie Nathan decided that because so many companies, including many large Israeli firms who had not previously advertised on the Voice of Peace, had enquired about advertising, the station should stay on the air after all.

**Voice of Peace programme schedule, May 1978**

**6.00am Vince Mould**

**9.00am Guy Starkey**

**11.00am Steve Foster**

**1.00pm Kenny Page**

**3.00pm Guy Starkey - The Beatles Hour**

**4.00pm Drive Time,** *Crispian St. John*

**5.00pm Music from a featured artist,** *sponsored by the Discount Bank of Israel*

**6.00pm Twilight Time,** *easy listening music and talk by Abie Nathan*

**7.30pm Classical Music,** *Vince Mould*

**9.00pm Fifteen Forty Disco,** *Malcolm Barry*

**12midnight Kenny Page**

**3.00am Roger Swann**

*In addition throughout the week there were a number of special programmes:-*

**Tuesdays 4.00 - 6.00pm The International Top 40,** *presented by Crispian St. John*

**Fridays 9.00 -11.00pm, Hebrew music followed until 3.00am by Party Night** *disco music with Malcolm Barry.*

**Saturdays 6.00 -8.00am Arabic music**

## Kol Israel strike

By a fortunate coincidence (for Abie Nathan) the Israeli state network, Kol Israel, was forced off the air by a strike at the beginning of April 1978, a few weeks after the threatened closure of the Voice of Peace. Advertisers, now aware of the Voice of Peace's likely audience size following the rally in Tel Aviv, flocked to the offshore station and many entered into long term contracts which continued after the state network strike had ended.

During the strike, which lasted twelve days, only the Voice of Peace and the Army station, Galei Zahal continued broadcasting. The Voice of Peace benefited from increased advertising revenue because the Army station carried no commercials, but the military station did attract a larger audience at many times of the day. It did so because it still provided a news service - something the Voice of Peace was unable to do as it relied on re-broadcasting bulletins from Kol Israel. However, when Galei Zahal transmitted speech based programmes large numbers of listeners re-tuned to the offshore station's music output.

A programming initiative which was first undertaken by the Voice of Peace in 1977 was repeated again in 1978. The Eurovision Song Contest was relayed by the station in place of its normal Saturday evening programme by intercepting and using a relay intended for the Army station, Galei Zaha. The state radio service, Kol Israel in Jerusalem, was providing the Army station in Tel Aviv with a feed of the signal from Paris on FM, without a Hebrew commentary. Because the signal was directed at Tel Aviv it was received on the *Peace* ship which re-broadcast it adding a bi-lingual commentary and description of the contest by DJ Kenny Page who was watching it on Israeli television.

A public opinion survey published at the beginning of May 1978 showed listenership patterns in Israel at the end of April and indicated that 24% of 18-24 year olds tuned in to the Voice of Peace on a regular daily basis.

## Abie Nathan's 'Fast for Peace'

On 16th May 1978 Abie Nathan started a fast for peace. He said that he would not eat and was prepared to fast until death on a diet of prune juice and water until Israeli Prime Minister Menachen Begin made some move towards creating a peace settlement. He also announced that the Voice of Peace would close on 24th June 1978 - 40 days into his fast -if the Prime Minister had done nothing by then to indicate a commitment to a peace settlement. An appeal was also made to the Israeli Government to pass a resolution to the effect that no new settlements should be created until peace talks had taken place with Egypt.

The Israeli Government, however, did nothing towards meeting Abie Nathan's peace objectives so at 6.30pm on 24th June 1978, he closed the Voice of Peace and the MV *Peace* sailed into Ashdod. During the journey a continuous tape was played saying simply "We say give peace a chance".

Asked during an interview broadcast on Kol Israel what he thought the Voice of Peace had achieved during its time on the air Abie Nathan replied:-

*I think the biggest accomplishment is the realisation of the project, the very fact that we were able to create such a station in international waters and stay that long and survive. This in itself was an accomplishment.*

*Second, we could see, I think, a lot of sadness will come, I'm sure, throughout the whole region once we stop broadcasting We had a very important audience; we had more than half a million people listening to us all the time and I think we have tried to reach out to a lot of people. In the realm of human understanding and communication man hasn't really even begun. So what we try to communicate between one another. It's a long road - I think we have just started it in whatever we have done up to this date.*

A few days later, on 28th June 1978 Abie Nathan, thin, weak and in a wheelchair, visited the Israeli Parliament, the Knesset, and spoke with Government ministers. He later announced that in response to an unprecedented appeal from all 120 members of the Knesset he had decided to end his hunger strike.

Following this decision by Abie Nathan the Voice of Peace returned to the air at 8.00pm on 30th June 1978, although little if anything appeared to have been achieved by the whole incident, except that the Roll Royce generator, which had been ashore for four months for repair, had been reinstalled on the MV *Peace* during its period in Ashdod.

## Children of Lebanon

Early in July 1978 the Voice of Peace broadcast an hourly appeal for the "Children of Lebanon Appeal" which Abie Nathan had set up to provide medicines, toys and an ambulance for children suffering in the war-torn city of Beirut. Once collected he planned to take the supplies to Beirut on board the *Peace* ship, but was thwarted, at first by warnings from the authorities not to enter the dangerous war area and then by the realisation that he had no insurance cover for the ship to sail from her usual anchorage, or even a captain who could navigate the vessel on such a journey. He then tried to organise distribution of the supplies through the International Red Cross, but when this proved unsuccessful he decided to revert to his original plan and, despite warnings to the contrary, take the *Peace* ship into Lebanese waters.

### Mediterranean storms

*Storms and bad weather affecting offshore broadcasters are normally associated with the inhospitable conditions of northern waters and the Mediterranean is the last place most people expect to experience such conditions. However, at the end of March 1978 the Voice of Peace experienced some of the worst storms in the Mediterranean for many years. The MV 'Peace' kept her main engines running and steered into the storm, but despite this the radio ship was driven from her anchorage to within one mile of the shore.*

### Voice of Peace Rules for DJs and the Format in mid-1978

*The exact position of the MV 'Peace' must never be broadcast, simply refer to as "somewhere in the Mediterranean"*

*For security reasons the arrival or departure of a tender must not be mentioned on air.*

*To unify the sound of the station there are to be no spoken links before or after commercials and no jingle to be played after a commercial.*

*Time checks to be repeated on air*

*A maximum of 12 seconds is permitted for links between music.*

*There should never be any 'dead air' -silent gaps between links and music or between two consecutive pieces of music.*

*DJs are only allowed one name check per hour - to discourage the growth of personalities.*

*Requests and dedications for listeners are strictly forbidden unless approval has been given by Abie Nathan beforehand.*

*The station's format at this time was oldies orientated. Three records were played each hour from the Top 40 with the remainder (up to 13 others) being oldies, ranging from 25 years to just three months out of the charts, chosen by the DJ on air at the time. Later the format was tightened even further with DJs being required to play, in strict rotation during each hour, four Top 40 records, two new releases, one Hebrew record, one album track, one oldie, four recent hits and two tracks from compilation albums.*

The MV *Peace* raised her anchor at 3.00am on Monday 7th August 1978 an hour after transmissions of the Voice of Peace had closed and sailed towards the Israeli port of Ashdod where the supplies were loaded on board. Early on 8th August 1978 the radio ship left port heading towards Beirut with a team of DJs and an Israeli Television crew on board. Transmissions from The Voice of Peace resumed once the ship was clear of the port area, although still inside Israeli territorial waters, and continued throughout the day as the MV *Peace* sailed up the Israeli coast. At midnight on 8th August 1978 normal programmes were changed to tapes of Arabic music, with station identification announcements and messages to the people of Lebanon saying they had essential supplies on board and wanted to deliver them to Beirut.

At 8.00am on 9th August 1978 the *Peace* anchored just over half a mile from the seafront in Beirut Bay. The *Peace* ship's journey had been much publicised in the local media and shortly after her arrival off Beirut a team of international journalists came out to interview Abie Nathan. Later in the afternoon a Syrian peace-keeping gun boat arrived alongside and advised the *Peace* ship that she was in danger and should move out to international waters while attempts were made to arrange a ceasefire. The Syrians confirmed that if ceasefire arrangements were successful then the vessel could return safely to Beirut and deliver the supplies.

Anxious to complete his mission successfully Abie Nathan agreed to the Syrian request, but while the *Peace* ship was anchored in international waters they had another visit, this time from members of the Christian Phalangist forces who said they wanted to take the supplies. Abie Nathan agreed to their request, saying he didn't mind which side got them because the supplies were intended for any children irrespective of the religious or political faction to which they or their families belonged. An arrangement was made to unload the MV *Peace* at a small port, Djunieh, to the north of Beirut. However, nothing more was heard from the Christian Phalangists and, after waiting in international waters all day, Abie Nathan decided to return to Beirut, anchoring the MV *Peace* once again a few hundred yards from the shore.

## Failed mission

The ship lay at anchor for nearly two days, ignored by everyone - the authorities, all factions involved in the fighting and by the International Red Cross, who had been approached once again by Abie Nathan to help organise distribution of the supplies.

Disappointed at the apparent failure of his mission Abie Nathan announced on 12th August 1978 that the *Peace* would leave the area the following day. As she sailed away from Beirut on 13th August Abie Nathan went on the air to condemn the authorities for refusing his aid, announcing that he would now take the supplies to a refugee camp in Cyprus.

By 7.00am the following morning the *Peace* ship was within sight of Cyprus and broadcasting Voice of Peace programmes as she sailed along the Island's coast. The ship arrived in the port of Larnica during the afternoon of 14th August 1978 when supplies were unloaded and taken to the refugee camp. It was a depressed Abie Nathan who returned with the ship to her Tel Aviv anchorage on 17th August 1978 - he had put weeks of work, time and effort into the Beirut appeal only to have his initiative rejected by all sides.

The *Peace* ship encountered a crisis with the weather at the end of 1979 when, on 28th November she dragged her anchor in a storm and drifted to within a mile of the coast before the crew, which included only one qualified seaman, managed to bring the ship under control and prevent her beaching. Transmissions of the

Voice of Peace were suspended for three days while some minor damage was repaired and the ship relocated to her anchorage outside territorial waters.

In March 1980 the Voice of Peace was off the air for a while because the ship was in dry dock in Haifa undergoing an insurance examination for her Lloyds Insurance Certificate to be renewed. The opportunity was also taken to carry out some storm damage repairs and to load equipment for the planned FM stereo service. After seven weeks of silence the station eventually returned to the air on 18th April 1980 on both 1539kHz (195m) medium wave and 100mHz FM stereo, broadcasting 24 hours a day.

The Voice of Peace was once again a successful station and plans were in hand for further improvement and expansion. During visits to America and Switzerland in the summer of 1980 Abie Nathan purchased $2,000 worth of new equipment for the station including a Gates stereo mixer and plans were put in hand to build a new aerial to re-start the shortwave service, which had been discontinued at the request of the Army in 1977.

**Voice of Peace programme schedule, February 1980**

**6.00am Breakfast Show,** *Tony Mandell or Keith York*

**9.00am Morning Show,** *Kenny Page*

**12noon Afternoon Delight,** *Malcolm Barry*

**3.00pm Best Disco in Town,** *Dave Richards*

**4.00pm Drive Time,** *Kenny Page*

**5.00pm Sponsored Programme,** *Israel Discount Bank*

**6.00pm Twilight Time,** *Graham Cooke*

**7.30pm Classical Music Programme,** *Dave Richards*

**9.00pm Arabic Music**

**11.00pm Best Disco in Town,** *Dave Richards*

***12midnight Midnight Show,*** *Graham Cooke*

***3.00am Early Show,*** *Nigel Roberts*

By late 1980 tentative plans were reactivated for Voice of Peace TV to start transmissions from the MV *Peace* on 1st January 1981. Abie Nathan optimistically announced that once the television station had opened the Shalom Peace Foundation would be in a position (from increased advertising revenue) to donate 40 million Israeli pounds to charitable causes.

Weekday rates for the television station were to be £23 for 60 seconds, £11.50 for 30 seconds, while on Saturdays (Shabbat, the Jewish Sabbath) rates would be £32.50 for 60 seconds and £16.25 for 30 seconds. Advertisers who bought airtime on Saturdays only would be charged a premium rate of £24.50 for 30 seconds. However, nothing ever came of the planned television service which seemed to flounder for technical and financial reasons as well as the ever present threat of government legislation being introduced to outlaw offshore broadcasting.

As well as Israel the Voice of Peace's transmissions were also heard in Cyprus, and the Gulf of Suez in Egypt, although reception on FM was poor in Cairo itself due to interference from another station on the same frequency. A problem unique to the Voice of Peace ,and one not experienced by offshore broadcasters elsewhere, was the effect of large amounts of sand on its signal quality.

The offshore stations of northern Europe and elsewhere benefited from the conductivity of huge areas of water surrounding their transmitter bases and consequently their signals frequently reached listeners hundreds of miles outside normal reception areas. However, the existence of large desert areas in the Middle East tended to stop the Voice of Peace's medium wave signal carrying as far as would normally be expected for a ship-based station using the same transmitter power. To overcome this problem official medium wave stations in such desert areas use transmitters with a power of over 500Kw.

On 27th January 1981 storms again caused damage to the *Peace* ship, including the collapse of the aerial mast putting the Voice of Peace off the air. The *Peace* sailed into Ashdod the following day and the station was silent for a total of seventeen days during this period while repairs were carried out, losing listeners and valuable advertising income. Test transmissions started again at 8.00pm on 13th February 1981 with normal programmes resuming from 9.45pm. These transmissions took place while the ship was still in port - she did not leave until midnight - such was the financial urgency to return the station to the air.

Unfortunately the new mast only lasted ten days before it too snapped in exactly the same place as the previous structure again putting the Voice of Peace off the air. After a further few days in port it was decided to rig up a wire aerial using the ship's own masts enabling the Voice of Peace to return to the air, on medium wave only, on 27th February 1981. It was not until mid-April 1981 that a new aerial mast was erected on board the ship, but difficulties were still being experienced in returning the FM transmitter to the air.

### VOP format

*In August 1980 the Voice of Peace's format consisted of a playlist of 12 hit singles - the Dynamic Dozen - each of which was aired twice a day, with another 12-record list each of which was played once a day. Both lists contained singles selected from the UK and USA charts as well as DJs own choices. While there was also a separate playlist of 50 albums, from which up to three tracks an hour were aired. In between these specified playlist records new releases, recent hits and flashbacks were featured at the DJ's discretion. News on the hour was taken directly from the official Kol Israel station and re-broadcast live by the Voice of Peace.*

## *Odelia* television

Press reports appeared in Israel on 6th April 1981 announcing that the *Odelia,* a Liberian registered ship flying the Honduran flag, had arrived off Ashdod the previous afternoon from Greece. At first she had been refused permission to enter port on suspicion that it was a floating television station, but when the *Odelia* did enter Ashdod she was immediately inspected by the authorities. Their suspicions, based on information passed to them by the Israeli ambassador in Athens, were confirmed when they discovered the transmitting equipment in the hold.

There was no reason for the authorities to detain the *Odelia* at that time but the crew were warned of penalties they faced fro broadcasting without a licence inside Israeli territorial waters. After a few days the *Odelia* left Ashdod and anchored in a position off Tel Aviv, near the MV *Peace.*

A Tel Aviv solicitor, Yosef Seger, acting on behalf of the *Odelia's* owners indicated that his clients had invested $2million in the project and that the ship would be used to broadcast Hebrew-captioned films from outside territorial limits to the Dan region of central Israel Transmissions would be in colour on UHF Channel 59. Seger stated that the ship was stocked with sufficient supplies to last several months an arrangements had been made to service the vessel from Cyprus in case the Israeli authorities denied them access to port facilities. In contrast Abie Nathan's Voice of Peace had always been tolerated by the Israeli authorities and the MV *Peace* regularly visited port to take on supplies of fuel and water, while the Israeli Navy also kept a watchful eye on the safety of the vessel.

Floating TV station
anchors off Ashdod

Government threatens
to jam ship telecasts

'Pirate' TV ship arrives
and angers Minister

Speculation continued about who was really behind the offshore television project and what its true purpose was. This was fuelled by a story in an Athens newspaper, *Kathimerini,* that the publisher of a left-wing rival paper, *Avriani,* George Kouris, was the *Odelia's* main backer. The Israeli authorities were concerned, if this was the case, that the television station could be used to broadcast left-wing propaganda during the forthcoming General election, due in June 1981. Later in 1981 elections were also to be held in Cyprus and Greece so speculation arose that the *Odelia* could be moved to various locations and used as a powerful propaganda base.

It subsequently transpired that the original story in *Kathimierini* was incorrect and George Kouris was not involved with the *Odelia* ship or television project. Nevertheless the propaganda potential remained a cause of concern to many people, especially the Israeli authorities who made their position clear from the start. Israeli Finance and Communications Minister, Yoram Aridor, announced on 7th April 1981 that the Government would "employ all means at its disposal to disrupt television broadcasts from the ship, including jamming, and, if necessary, introduce legislation against broadcasts from beyond Israel's territorial waters."

This latter proposal would have also meant the Voice of Peace being outlawed and put an end to its 'accommodation' arrangement with the authorities, a factor which had deterred Abie Nathan in launching his own Peace TV station on two previous occasions.

The person actually behind the *Odelia* was Paul Greenwald, a Rumanian national who had lived in Israel for sixteen years, working with his father in the textile industry. He had been involved in a number of official enquiries into fraudulent activities and although never convicted Greenwald had also appeared before a number of Courts Martial for alleged desertion from the Israeli Army.

Since 1976 Paul Greenwald had nurtured the idea of starting an offshore television station, encouraged by the success of Abie Nathan's Voice of Peace radio station. He spent a long time trying to raise financial backing, find the right technical equipment and personnel and a suitable ship to act as a base for his planned station.

In 1979 he placed an advertisement in an Israel newspaper for "staff to work for a private television station which broadcasts in colour." Although he claimed to have received several hundred replies no staff were actually recruited at that time.

## Financial backing

It was not until 1980 that Paul Greenwald succeeded in finding a financial backer for his offshore television project and spent some time in Greece looking for a suitable vessel. Whilst in Greece he met shipowner, Nestar Pierrakios and told him of his plans. Pierrakios agreed to invest in the offshore television project and provide a ship which could be used as a floating base. He was quoted as saying:-

*I'm agreeing to an investment in a good subject and making the attempt to discover a market which is new and free...... I don't believe that this is a pirate ship. A pirate is someone who takes something that does not belong to him, whereas with us everything is legal. Even if the venture does not succeed I won't look on it as a loss. We are looking for new markets and I believe in free initiative, so long as it is within the bounds of the law.*

The ship provided by Pierrakios was re-named *Odelia,* after Greenwald's daughter and re-registered in Puerto Cortez, Honduras. She was converted for her new role in the Greek port of Piraeus during the winter months of 1980/81.

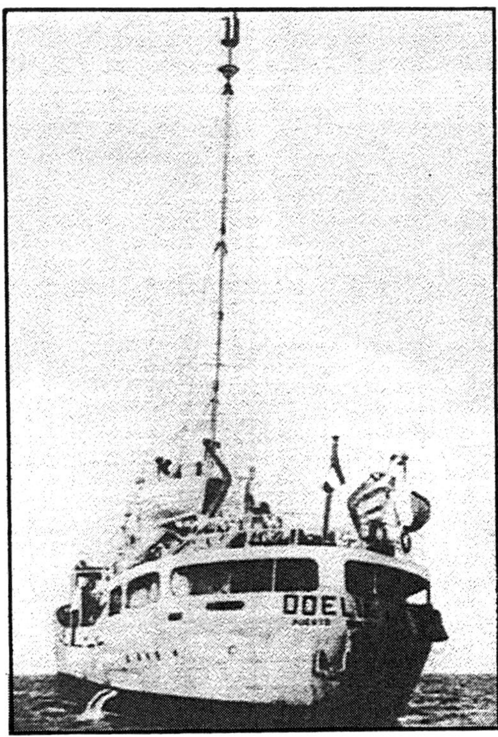

The 'Odelia'

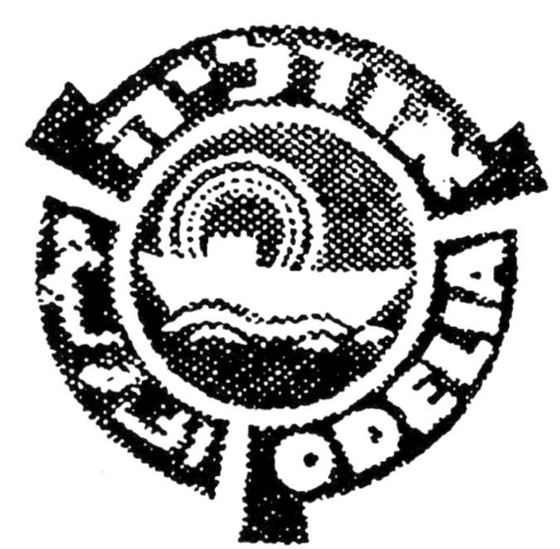

*The test card picture broadcast by Odelia TV*

Test broadcast on Channel 59 began shortly after the *Odelia* had anchored off Tel Aviv and reception reports were received from along the coastal region of Israel. Special aerials were offered for sale in Tel Aviv providing reception of the new station up to 25 miles inland. The test transmissions consisted of a test card with a drawing of the ship and the word "Odelia" printed in English, Hebrew and Arabic. Occasionally short transmissions of Italian football matches or cartoons were broadcast, but the Israelis, as they had threatened, jammed the signal with a tone on the sound and a chequered pattern effect on the vision.

## Official response

Official reaction to the offshore television station was swift and threatening. An Israeli Ministry of Communications spokesman said:-

*The Government of Israel has a definite policy as regards private television broadcasters and the Communications Ministry implements this policy. The Ministry is planning to broadcast the [official] Israeli TV programme from its own transmitter on the channel which the Odelia is using.*

The relaying of Israeli State Television programmes on Channel 59 began on 15th April 1981 to, in the words of a Ministry spokesman, "check out a transmitter."

This action seemed unnecessary because after detailed inspection of the ship the Transport Ministry declared the *Odelia* unseaworthy due to the fact that she was lacking in various essential items of equipment, had no radio-telephone operator and only one qualified deck officer - all contrary to international maritime regulations.

Following this declaration Yosef Seger, solicitor for the Odelia TV project's backers said his clients may reassess their position in the light of what he described as "Transport Ministry tricks" and the fear of the proposed station's signal being jammed.

A week later the International Transport Worker's Federation (ITF) declared crew conditions on board the *Odelia* "intolerable" and asked the Ashdod Port Authority to prevent the ship leaving until proper conditions could be provided for the crew. Within two days the ship's anonymous owners had agreed in principle to pay the crew ITF wage rates and improve the living and working conditions on board.

With the ship now back at sea and despite all official efforts to prevent the launch of the offshore television service the *Odelia* began regular transmissions on 24th June 1981.

**TV ship still held in port**

**'Intolerable' conditions found on TV ship**

**TV ship's owners to raise crew's wages**

**War of the wavelengths against Odelia**

At the end of June a resident of Rama Hasharon, Mosh Ankelvitz, petitioned the High Court of Justice in Israel to protect his right to receive broadcasts from the *Odelia* on his television set. Ankelvitz was quoted as saying:-

*I am for free initiative.*

*.... I cannot approve of interference with broadcasts coming in from an area outside Israel's territorial waters and for which Israeli laws are not valid. It is not clear to me why Abie Nathan can broadcast, but not Paul Greenwald. It is equally mysterious to me why one can get good reception in Israel of the broadcasts from Jordan, which is hostile, whereas the coloured broadcasts from the 'Odelia' are interfered with.*

After hearing the petition the Supreme Court Judge, Meir Shamgar, issued an injunction on 25th June 1981, requesting the Ministry of Communications to give reasons within fourteen days for its jamming of the *Odelia's* transmissions and ordering it to refrain from continuing this practice until the Court had made its final decision.

In reply to the Court in mid-July 1981, Gideon K Lev for the Communications Ministry warned that the *Odelia's* presence off the coast of Israel could lead to the establishment of many more offshore stations and a situation of chaos of the airwaves could arise in Israel as it had in Italy where there was at that time no restriction on the establishment of private (landbased) television and radio stations. He also warned that "The last free frequencies that are available would be taken away from the State." The Ministry also claimed that, far from being just a resident wishing to watch the offshore television station, Moshe Ankelevitz actually represented the project's backers

The *Odelia* made a few further test transmissions in mid-July 1981, including pirated copies of films. When two major film companies warned the project's backers that they would take proceedings against them for using copyright material without permission the ship was ordered back to port where she stayed until August 1981.

## New law proposed

The Order imposed on the Communications Ministry by the Court led to the submission of a proposed new law to the Economic Committee of the Knesset in July 1981. This law would prohibit Israeli citizens or Israeli owned ships from becoming involved in, or assisting, broadcasting at sea. This 'assistance' included all commercial involvement with the project, the provision of news, advertising and other services. Israeli citizens were also to be forbidden to travel to the offshore station, or give goods, including food, to the crews or finance their activities in any way. The only exception was to be in circumstances where there was a life-threatening emergency at sea.

There was, however, one major difference between this proposed law and other anti-offshore broadcasting legislation passed in Europe. The Israeli Government was to be given powers to grant special permission to individual offshore broadcasters to continue with their activities. His clause was specifically aimed at offering Abie Nathan's Voice of Peace the opportunity to continue broadcasting even after the new law had been passed.

The proposals contained in the new draft law were supported by the Israeli Association of Newspaper Publishers, worried about the possible loss of advertising revenue to the new television station, and by film distributors who were concerned about the use of their copyright material by the offshore television station.

## More tests

Test transmissions were started again in early August, but reception was poor even in Tel Aviv - which was within sight of the ship's anchorage position and close to the MV Peace. It is thought that transmitter power at the time was only about 5Kw, but the station continued to broadcast. Crew on board the *Peace* ship at this time reported watching the offshore television station's output - reception was tolerable due to the proximity of the two ships, although it is doubtful whether the station had much, if any, of an audience on land.

Programmes by this time consisted of pirated video tapes of British television stations (BBC and ITV) including all commercials and continuity announcements, but sometimes one or two Israeli commercials were inserted as well, indicating perhaps that the station was selling some airtime.

In September 1981 the Israeli Communications Minister, Mordechai Zipponi finally presented the proposed new law to the Economics Committee. The law was eventually passed by the Committee on 3rd November 1981 and approved by the Knesset some three weeks later.

Paul Greenwald said that the law could only come into force when it had been officially published and the conditions for the Government to grant individual offshore stations the right to broadcast had become known. In the meantime, he stated, Odelia TV would continue to broadcast.

However, action against the offshore television station came not from the Government but from the Marine Officers Union who announced a boycott of the *Odelia* because the crew were not being paid in accordance with trade union agreements. At about the same time the Chief Engineer of the *Odelia,* Efrat Doron, complained that Paul Greenwald had paid him $2000 per month, out of which he had to pay all other technicians. He had distributed their pay at the beginning of each month until October 1981 when Greenwald failed to make the money available until the middle of the month. After that payment Greenwald had made no further money available for him to pay the crew's wages. As a result of these complaints the Israeli authorities placed a travel ban on Greenwald, preventing him leaving the country.

The new law came into effect on 30th November 1981, one week after being passed by the Knesset. The day before, 29th November, the *Odelia* ceased transmissions, but after two days silence Paul Greenwald informed Communications Minister, Zipori that the *Odelia* would recommence broadcasting, not in Hebrew and not specifically directed towards Israel.

Broadcasts resumed again in English and Arabic, ostensibly for a Jordanian or pan-Middle East audience and a Communications Ministry spokesman commented:-

*Our investigations show that they are transmitting to Israel. The assertion that they are transmitting to Jordan is their interpretation. So long as the broadcasts can be received here they are subject to our laws.*

Within a couple of days of transmissions starting again Paul Greenwald was arrested on charges of desertion and ordered to appear before a Military Court in Jaffa on 10th December. Meanwhile, the Government started to exercise some of their new powers. On 7th December the Communications Ministry sent reports on the Captain and owner of the *Odelia* to the police for violations of the new legislation, all ship-to-shore communications with the *Odelia* were discontinued (except for emergencies) and harbour authorities in Israel were instructed to refuse entry to the offshore television ship.

The same day the *Odelia* discontinued broadcasts, according to Greenwald's wife Miri, "Until an arrangement with the Communications Ministry has been achieved." Police and Communications Ministry officials sailed around the *Odelia* in international waters on 9th December, photographing the vessel and any people on board. Some reports state that the authorities in fact boarded the *Odelia,* sealing the transmitters and removing all broadcasting crew.

This intensive action by the authorities proved too much for the *Odelia* and on 27th December 1981 the ship raised her anchor and sailed to Cyprus to take on fuel supplies. Paul Greenwald boldly announced that the vessel would return in June 1982, broadcasting to the whole of the Middle East, without advertising from Israel to avoid contravening the provision in the new law relating to Hebrew language broadcasts. There was also some speculation that the *Odelia* would return with a radio station on board as well as the television service.

A Communications Ministry spokesman said that if transmissions did resume from the *Odelia,* and were received in Israel, then they would be subject to the new law and be jammed by the authorities. Any individual or company in Israel who assisted the station would also face prosecution he confirmed. However, nothing more was heard of the ship or the *Odelia* project for some time. It is probable that the vessel was detained by authorities in Cyprus in connection with unpaid harbour fees.

## Abie Nathan hopes for licence

During August 1981 Abie Nathan spoke publicly about trying to obtain a land-based licence for the Voice of Peace, taking advantage of the clause in the proposed legislation drafted to outlaw offshore television broadcasting, but giving the Government the option to licence certain offshore stations. His plans at that stage involved beaching the MV *Peace* and relaying the station's broadcasts to various land-based transmitters around Israel. At the beginning of December 1981 he started to appear on-air regularly threatening to close the Voice of Peace at the end of the month if he did not get his licence, pointing out that his many peace initiatives would also come to an end if the station closed. Abie Nathan also told listeners (not for the first or last time ) that he felt it was unfair to keep DJs and crew on the *Peace* ship at sea because she was then 42 years old and had suffered storm damage- the offshore arrangement could not go on forever, he said.

Announcements were broadcast daily throughout December saying that the Voice of Peace would close at the end of the month if no licence was granted by the authorities. When 31st December 1981 came Abie Nathan made an hour long broadcast from the deck of the *Peace* ship between 6.00 and 7.00pm. Then after two hours of classical music there was a three hour programme of "love and peace music" until midnight when the station closed, as threatened, because no land-based licence had been granted.

The silent MV *Peace* sailed close to the shore off Tel Aviv on 1st January 1982 and the following day DJs set up loudspeakers on deck and 'broadcast' their programmes to an audience on the beach. After a week the ship sailed to Ashdod for some minor repair works and later tied up to mooring buoys in the bay, where she remained for some weeks while the argument raged in Israel about Abie Nathan's application for a land-based licence.

## Jingles and station IDs

Apart from commercials one of the most memorable programming elements of offshore radio was the use of jingles and frequent station Identity (ID) announcements.

Before the arrival of offshore radio state systems usually confined their ID announcement to a formal statement, often just before a major news bulletin. During the Second World War the BBC introduced more frequent ID announcements to reassure listeners that they were tuned to an 'official' broadcast, but this practice was largely dropped after the end of hostilities.

Even the more liberal Radio Luxembourg during the 1950s and early 1960s broadcast a very staid station ID (using the slogan "The Station of the Stars") preceeded by the famous gong.

Jingles originated in America where they had been used since the 1930s, generally for commercials, and were often performed live, particularly during sponsored programme segments. The concept of using them for station IDs and promotions came in the late 1940s.

Offshore radio brought to Europe the American approach to programming - frequent station IDs, time checks and jingles between records. The jingles either promoted the station itself, a particular category of record (flashback, hit prediction, chart climber etc.) or just the whole concept of listening to radio.

Scandinavian offshore stations were the first to use jingles - in particular Radio Nord with its American backing and programming influence. Off the British coast Radio Caroline and the other early stations were slow to use jingles, although Caroline adopted the 'bell' ID early in its life.

It was the arrival of American backed Radio London in December 1964 that brought intensive use of jingles to British radio and soon nearly all the offshore stations were using them. In Holland Radio Veronica, after hardly using any jingles during its first few years, soon jumped on the bandwagon after the British offshore stations had shown the way. Other later Dutch stations as well as offshore broadcasters in New Zealand, and Israel also made extensive use of jingles and station IDs. When state radio systems were updated to provide 'replacement' services for the offshore stations they too included the use of jingles as part of their image re-vamp.

Although extensive use of jingles is now somewhat out of fashion in radio production they are still used - a programming element taken for granted, but developed and spread due to the influence of the offshore stations.

## Chapter 19

# Live from the North Sea

Back to the North Sea where the lone offshore radio ship, *Mi Amigo*, home of Radio Caroline and Radio Mi Amigo, was still anchored off the Essex coast.

Since the Dutch Marine Offences Act had come into effect at the beginning of September 1974 Radio Mi Amigo had directed its programmes more and more towards Belgium where its programmes were extremely popular and could usually be heard in shops, bars and other public places. However, by February 1975 with no action having been taken against the station by either the Belgian or Dutch authorities more Dutch programming was gradually reintroduced (Radio Mi Amigo was still taping its programmes in an isolated farmhouse in Oprakel in Belgium at this time). This apparent lack of action by the authorities ended on 17th February 1975 when the farmhouse at Oprakel was raided by police in a carefully planned operation. Three people, including two of the station's DJs, Peter van Dam and Bart van der Laar, were arrested and over £60,000 worth of equipment was confiscated and removed from the farmhouse.

Station owner Sylvain Tack hurriedly left Belgium for the comparative safety of Spain where he admitted, for the first time since September 1974, that he was still the person behind Radio Mi Amigo. Tack set about arranging new programme recording facilities for his station in Spain, first at his villa in Playa de Aro, later moving operations to premises in the centre of this popular holiday resort. Radio Mi Amigo also hired airtime on local Spanish commercial radio stations ostensibly so that Dutch holidaymakers could listen to programmes in their own language. The theory behind this move being that it would give Radio Mi Amigo a certain legitimacy - potential advertisers could buy airtime on the programmes which were broadcast by the legal Spanish stations and it was just a 'happy coincidence' that these same programmes broadcast from a ship in the North Sea whose transmissions were received in Holland and Belgium!

### Prosecution

*In England Peter Jackson from Holland-on-Sea, Essex appeared in Clacton Magistrates Court on 7th April 1975, charged under the Wireless Telegraphy Act 1949 with the illegal operation of a radio telephone link to the 'Mi Amigo'. In November 1974 Post Office officials had raided Jackson's house and found radio transmitting equipment in the loft. He was fined £75 with £25 costs and had his radio transmitting equipment confiscated.*

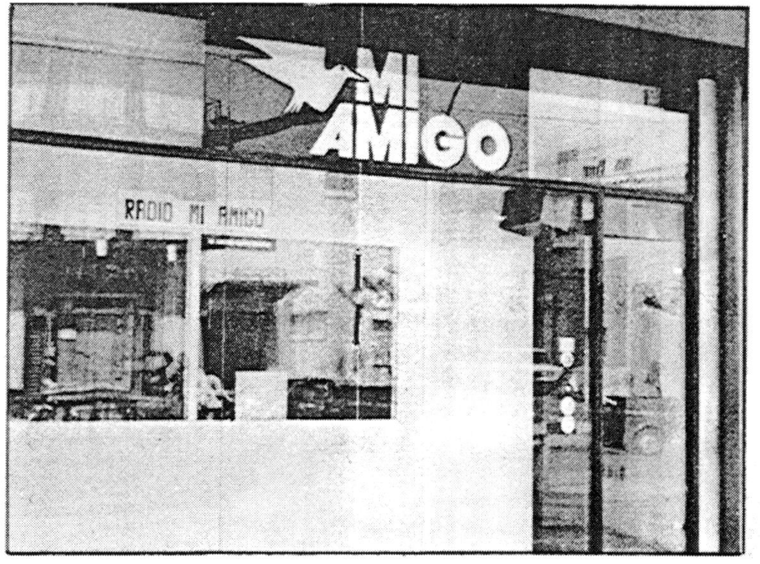


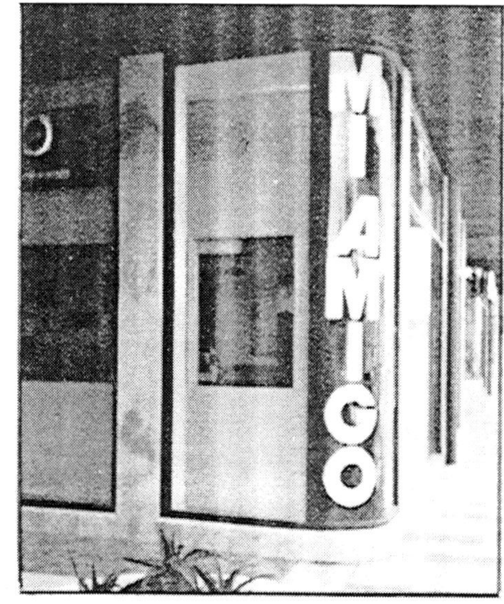


*Radio Mi Amigo's studios in Spain*

### *Mi Amigo* broadcasts January 1975

*Weekdays*

**5.00am Will de Zwijger**

**6.00am Burt Bennett**

**7.00am Mike Moorkens**

**9.00am Norbert**

**11.00am Joop Verhoof**

**1.00pm Frans van der Drift**

**3.00pm Burt Bennett**

**4.00pm Peter van Dam**

**6.00pm-5.00am Radio Caroline**

*Saturday*

**5.00am as Weekdays**

**9.00am Weekend Showtrain,** *Norbert*

**11.00am Flashback Show,** *Joop Verhoof*

**1.00pm Dutch Top 40,** *Frans van der Drift*

**3.00pm Tipparade,** *Frans van der Drift*

**5.00pm Patric Dubateau**

**6.00pm-5.00am Radio Caroline**

*Sunday*

**5.00am Will de Zwijger**

**6.00am Burt Bennett**

**7.00am Patric Dubateau**

**9.00am Weekend Showtrain,** *Norbert*

**10.00am Dutch Top 15**

**11.00am Religious Programme**

**11.30am Joepie Top 50**

**2.00pm Soul Show,** *Frans van der Drift*

**3.00pm LP Top 10**

**4.00pm Patric Dubateau**

**5.00pm Peter van Dam**

**6.00pm-5.00am Radio Caroline**

A number of Spanish commercial stations were used to hire airtime for Radio Mi Amigo's programmes including Radio Gerona and Radio Barcelona. However, some companies in Holland who took advantage of this apparent loophole in legislation and advertised on Radio Mi Amigo's 'tourist' programmes were subsequently investigated by the Dutch Fiscal Information Service.

## Tendering arrangements

With the arrival of Radio Mi Amigo on board the MV *Mi Amigo* there had come a sharing of responsibility for actually running the radio ship- the Dutch/Belgian station did not just provide financial income for the Caroline organisation through the hire of airtime, but also made a practical contribution to the operation of the radio ship. The British (Caroline) side were responsible for the actual operation and maintenance of the transmission facilities, the supply of records and programme material and radio crew for the English Service. The Dutch/Belgian side, as well as providing DJs and programme tapes for Radio Mi Amigo, were also responsible for the actual tendering of the ship and the delivery of supplies, food, fuel and water. Belgians Patrick Valain (who also ran the Mi Amigo Drive-In Show, and Germain Boy had taken over tendering of the *Mi Amigo* from the original Dutch operation, mainly because they claimed they could do it less expensively.

As well as arranging supply tenders from various European ports, including Boulogne (where they used the fishing vessel *Saint Andre Flanders*) and Zeebrugge (using the *Hosannah*), for a time between 1975 and 1978 they organised a regular delivery of programme tapes and mail to the *Mi Amigo* using a small private plane from an airfield in Ostend. To assist this particular operation DJs would announce agreed codes over the air during live programmes to advise those at the airfield of weather conditions in the vicinity of the *Mi Amigo*. If conditions were favourable tapes and mail were wrapped and sealed in plastic bags and attached to lifebelts which were thrown from the plane into the sea near the radio ship. Crew members from the *Mi Amigo* would then retrieve the lifebelts and their contents using an inflatable dinghy. Sometimes these drops had to be aborted at the last minute because weather conditions near the radio ship, favourable at the time of the coded announcement, had deteriorated significantly before the plane arrived from Belgium.

## 'New station'

Early in 1975. Gerard van Dam (who had helped secure the re-launch of Radio Caroline in 1972 ) together with Fred Bolland and Ben Bode acquired a vessel - the *Aegir* - and announced that it would be used to re-launch Radio Veronica - then still silent after closing in August 1974 when the Dutch Marine Offences Act came into force, but still fighting for permission to broadcast over the Hilversum network.

Improbable as it may seem (because the Radio Veronica ship *Norderney* was still anchored in international waters in case that station did not succeed in its fight to become legal and decided to resume offshore transmissions) Bolland, van Dam and Bode claimed to have secured a deal with ex-Radio Veronica DJ Lex Harding to re-launch the station from the *Aegir*. However, the whole fiasco came to nothing, not merely because Radio Veronica were unlikely to be involved at that delicate stage in their own battle to become legal, but there was no substantial funding behind the project, although Ben Bode claimed to have lost a considerable amount of his personal assets in trying to launch the idea.

That was not the end of the story, however, as the same three men and the same vessel were to feature again a few years later in a number of other offshore radio projects (see Chapter 20).

Meanwhile, the former owners of RNI, Mebo Ltd., were still engaged in a legal battle to regain control of their two ships, which had been seized by the authorities in September 1974 while trying to leave port following extensive refurbishment work.

A preliminary hearing in December 1974 had decided that the *Mebo II* could leave harbour once her transmitters had been removed, but the owners argued that as the ship was registered in Panama she was, under the laws of that country, entitled to carry such equipment as cargo.

**Court case ends**

**Mebo settles up and casts off**

A series of further court hearings was held during 1975 following an appeal by Mebo Ltd. against the original decision - the High Court in the Hague referred the matter to the Supreme Court, who in turn referred it back to the High Court and it was not until 2nd January 1976 that the final decision was made. The vessels could leave port, the court ruled, once the owners had paid a £1,000 fine for maintaining a radio ship inside Dutch territory after 31st August 1974 and a (returnable) deposit of £43,500 to guarantee that the ship would not be used to broadcast to Europe for a period of two years. The ships (with transmitter and radio equipment) were also ordered to leave Dutch territory within three months, but further legal arguments, claims and counter claims ensued when Mebo Ltd. sought compensation for the harbour charges they had been obliged to pay during the *Mebo II's* detention in port.

During late August 1975 a number of test transmissions took place from the *Mi Amigo* on 773kHz (388m) and for a time Radio Mi Amigo programmes on 1187kHz (253m) were also relayed on this frequency. On 27th August 1975 regular test broadcasts of non-stop music started on 773kHz with an identity announcement every 15 minutes.

## More prosecutions

By mid September 1975 four Radio Caroline staff had been on the *Mi Amigo* for over nine weeks without a break and were anxious to come ashore for some leave. Although tenders normally came from France, Belgium or Holland a tender from Brightlingsea in Essex was eventually sent out to the radio ship to collect the long-serving crew and DJs. Shortly before this tender arrived alongside the *Mi Amigo* a small fishing boat had anchored nearby, but those on board the radio ship thought nothing unusual of it at the time. As the DJs and crew transferred from the radio ship people on board the fishing boat began taking pictures of them and, thinking they were Radio Caroline fans, the DJs waved back as they climbed on board the tender. However, just inside the British territorial limit a police launch started to pursue the tender and eventually met up with the 'fishing boat' which had been anchored near the *Mi Amigo*. It was only then that the Radio Caroline staff realised they had been photographed, not by the station's fans as they had initially assumed, but by Home Office officials on a surveillance exercise. All on board the tender were subsequently arrested when it arrived back in Essex and were summonsed to appear at Southend Magistrates Court on charges under the Marine etc. Broadcasting (Offences) Act 1967.

On 18th September 1975 six people appeared at Southend Magistrates Court on charges connected with supplying or working for Radio Caroline - the first such prosecutions brought under the Marine etc. Broadcasting (Offences) Act. The Court was told that all defendants had been arrested after police had watched a small boat leave the River Crouch in Essex, visit the *Mi Amigo,* and return to Essex. DJs Andrew Dawson (Andy Archer) and John B Mair pleaded guilty to charges of broadcasting from the radio ship, contrary to the provisions of the Marine etc. Broadcasting (Offences) Act 1967, and each were fined £100 plus £50 costs. Michael Baker pleaded guilty to supplying the radio station with records and was fined £100 with £50 costs and ordered to pay a further £50 towards legal aid. Boat owner Walter Ord pleaded guilty to a charge of carrying persons from the *Mi Amigo* and was fined £25 with £10 costs, while his plea of not guilty to a charge of carrying goods was accepted by the court. Similar charges against Vincent Ferguson and Rudigar von Etzdorf (DJ Johnny Jason) were adjourned for three weeks.

At the subsequent hearing on 9th October 1975 at Southend Magistrates Court Vincent Ferguson pleaded guilty to a charge of carrying people from Wallasea Island to the *Mi Amigo* and was fined £50 with £50 costs. However, Rudigar von Etzdorf elected to go for trial by jury at the Crown Court and the case against him was adjourned to that Court.

Meanwhile, in Holland on 7th October 1975 a fishing boat, *Lovika,* was stopped and boarded by officials as she entered the small harbour of Stellendam, twenty miles from Rotterdam. The vessel was found to be carrying programme tapes and items of equipment from the *Mi Amigo* including a faulty generator which had been removed from the radio ship for repair on land. The father and son owners of the *Lovika* were later arrested and charged with offences under the Dutch Marine Offences Act. They were sent for trial in May 1976.

## *Mi Amigo* adrift

Although no one on board the *Mi Amigo* could have foreseen it at the time a crisis of far reaching proportions started to unfold on 8th November 1975. The radio ship had been buffeted for nearly 24 hours by Force 6-7 winds and, because she was low on fuel and water, she had rolled and pitched heavily throughout the day. At about 4.30pm on that dark winter afternoon the DJs and crew began to suspect that the *Mi Amigo* had broken from her anchor and was adrift, but because they had no functioning navigational equipment on board

### Radio Caroline's Berlin Service

*After a short spell on the 'Mi Amigo' in 1973, Dennis King became Advertising Manager for Radio Caroline in the station's then headquarters at van Hogendorpstraat. After Ronan O'Rahilly brought Terry Bates to Holland to try and organise advertising for the station on a more professional basis (as he had done in 1966 See Chapter 11) Dennis King worked for Radio Veronica for a while before re-joining Radio Caroline. He then stayed with the station until Radio Mi Amigo started in 1974 when he left again and entered the antiques business.*

*During a sales trip to Berlin he met Jurgen Kauer, a member of FRC Germany and together they formulated the idea of starting a German Service on Radio Caroline. Dennis King contacted Jack O'Brien, who worked for the American Forces Network (AFN) in Berlin and he arranged to record the first three Berlin Service programmes in the AFN studios.*

*These programmes were broadcast by Radio Caroline on the 1st, 9th and 16th August 1975, the first two being presented by Jack O'Brien and the third by Dennis King himself.*

*The success of the first three pilot programmes prompted Dennis King to arrange for studios to be constructed in a private house in Berlin and he had high hopes of attracting a substantial amount of advertising on the German Service.*

*Three Berlin Service programmes were transmitted each week until the end of December 1975 when they were suddenly discontinued without explanation and the station's experimental German Service never returned.*

and, in the absence of any fixed navigation points in the vicinity of the ship, they could not be certain of their actual position.

For nearly two hours they struggled to try and lower an emergency anchor and stop the ship drifting, but without success. At 6.20pm DJ Simon Barrett interrupted his programme to announce that the radio ship was adrift and asked listeners to contact the station's office to inform them that the anchor chain had broken. This message was broadcast repeatedly for about 50 minutes, together with messages to friends and relatives reassuring them that the radio ship was in no immediate danger. The Coastguard Service was then swamped with calls from listeners advising them of the *Mi Amigo's* distress, but the crew on board the radio ship had already contacted the Service over the emergency channel.

## Grounded

At 7.06pm on 8th November 1975 the *Mi Amigo* grounded on the southern end of Long Head Sands, although the crew, uncertain of the ship's position or direction of drift were convinced that they had grounded at the northern end of the sandbank. The *Mi Amigo* had dragged with her the remains of her anchor chain when she started to drift and it was decided this would have to be cut away before the engines could be started so the ship could safely manoeuvre off the sandbank.

With the chain cut and the engines eventually started the Captain set a northerly course, still thinking that his vessel was at the northern end of the Long Head Sands. However, because her true position was at the southern end this course meant that the *Mi Amigo* was actually sailing further on to the sandbank. It was half an hour before the crew realised their mistake and the Captain tried unsuccessfully to contact Coastguards on the emergency channel.

Engineer Peter Chicago and DJ Simon Barrett then interrupted normal programmes and asked over the air for Coastguards to contact the radio ship. When they eventually did make contact the Coastguard Service was able to advise the Captain of the *Mi Amigo's* exact location from information on their radar screens. At the same time a request was broadcast asking listeners to stop phoning the various emergency services because the volume of incoming calls was jamming switchboards.

By 7.53pm the ship had re-floated herself, but began to drift while the crew once again made attempts to lower the emergency anchor. Shortly after 10.00pm station engineer, Peter Chicago came on the air to announce:-

*As most of the listeners have now realised we have got problems at the moment. We broke our anchor chain this evening and since then we've been drifting in a south or south -westerly direction and we're approaching the point where we're going to enter British territorial waters. So for that reason we are now going off the air. Our current position is latitude 51 degrees 31 minutes north and longitude 1 degree 22 minutes east.*

*We are in no immediate danger. We've no real problems except the fact that we are drifting and we're unable to correct the drift of the ship. We've also got difficulties in lowering our stand-by anchors. So if anybody in the office is listening you'll realise that the situation has got quite desperate and I'm sure you're doing all you can. We are in touch with the Coastguard authorities, who've been a great assistance to us in establishing our position and if the people there are listening we'd like to ask our listeners once again not to telephone the Coastguard authorities as they are already helping us a great deal and you'll only block up their telephone lines.So thanks again.*

At 10.06pm Radio Caroline's transmitters were turned off.

## Emergency anchorage

By 1.00am the following morning, 9th November 1975, the crew had managed to lower the emergency anchor which successfully held the ship until a second anchor was put down at about 4.00pm that afternoon. However, the radio ship was now near the South Edinburgh No 3 Buoy marking one of the main shipping lanes and during the evening the Trinity House vessel, *Mermaid,* advised the *Mi Amigo* that she was a danger to other shipping in the area if she remained in that position.

Minutes after this warning was issued a tug, MS *Sauria,* owned by Gaseley and Son of Felixstowe dropped anchor near the *Mi Amigo* and stood by throughout the night. Those on board the radio ship were led to believe that the tug had been chartered by the station's office in Spain, but because it was a British registered vessel there was considerable uncertainty in the minds of Caroline staff about whether or not it would be able to tow the radio ship back to her anchorage, in possible contravention of the Marine etc. Broadcasting (Offences) Act. There was also a strong suspicion that the tug may be used by the authorities to tow the *Mi Amigo* into a British port where she would be detained, so the Captain decided that the radio ship should remain at her anchorage until the situation had been clarified.

Shortly before midday on 10th November 1975 the *Sauria* was replaced by a larger tug, *Sun XXII*, which at one stage actually tied up alongside the *Mi Amigo* and some crew members came aboard the radio ship. It was not long before serious suspicions began to grow amongst Radio Caroline staff about the inquisitiveness of the tug's crew, particularly over technical details regarding the operation of the two radio stations. In view of these suspicions the Captain decided it would be best if the tug's crew left the *Mi Amigo* and the *Sun XXII* pulled away from the radio ship. The tug's crew complied with the Captain's instructions and anchored their vessel a short distance away from the *Mi Amigo*, but close enough to provide assistance if required.

Early the same afternoon the *Mi Amigo's* Captain received a call from the station's office in Spain, via North Foreland Radio, (which during the original drifting drama on 8th November had been 'unable' to transmit telephone calls to and from the radio ship), giving instructions that Radio Caroline and Radio Mi Amigo were to stay off the air until the ship could be moved back to her anchorage in Knock Deep. They were also told that a tender from Spain was heading towards the *Mi Amigo* carrying a new heavy duty anchor and chain.

The suspicions of the *Mi Amigo's* crew about the intentions of the British tug were confirmed the following day when they heard a news broadcast on Ipswich ILR station, Radio Orwell, stating that the Captain of the *Sun XXII* had orders not to tow the radio ship back out to sea, but only to tow her into a British port. The Captain of the *Mi Amigo* then finally decided that whatever happened he would wait at the South Edinburgh No 3 Buoy until the station's own tender arrived from Spain with the new anchor.

By 12th November 1975 the Port of London Authority was anxious to know when the *Mi Amigo* would be moved clear of the shipping lanes and sent its vessel, *Maplin,* to assess the situation. Permission was sought by the Captain of the *Maplin* to come aboard the *Mi Amigo*, but this was refused so the Port of London Authority vessel drew away and circled the radio ship for 15 minutes, eventually anchoring astern for about two hours before leaving the area altogether. The tug *Sun XXII* was replaced for a short while by another Gaseley

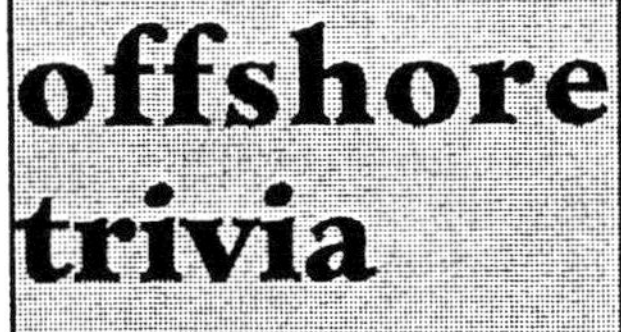


**Most frequencies used**

***SIMULTANEOUSLY:***

*RNI - Four (2 shortwave, 1 medium wave, 1 FM)*

***DURING LIFETIME:***

*(1) RNI - 11 (3 shortwave, 3 FM, 5 medium wave)*

*(2) Radio Caroline - 9 medium wave and 1 shortwave*

*(3) Radio Atlantis - 8 medium wave*

tug, *Egerton,* which remained with the *Mi Amigo* until the evening of 12th November 1975, when the Captain decided that in view of the calm conditions there was no longer any need to stay in the vicinity of the radio ship.

## *Mi Amigo* relocated

In the early hours of the following day the tender from Spain eventually arrived at the *Mi Amigo* and a new heavy duty anchor was installed on the radio ship. After food and supplies had been loaded the tender then made a number of unsuccessful attempts to tow the *Mi Amigo* from her temporary anchorage position, during which extensive damage was caused to the radio ship's railing. This half-hearted effort only succeeded in eventually pulling the radio ship to a new position half a mile north of the South Edinburgh No 3 Buoy. A representative of Radio Mi Amigo on board the tender then told the crew that the radio ship would be left at this position and they could now resume broadcasts. At about 8.00am the tender hurriedly left the *Mi Amigo* because its Captain did not want to be caught by the authorities in the act of assisting the radio ship. By 9.30am broadcasts of non-stop music had recommenced on 1187kHz (253m) with Radio Mi Amigo programmes starting again half an hour later. Radio Caroline resumed its programmes at 6.00pm that evening.

At 4.00pm that same afternoon the tug *Sauria,* together with another small fishing vessel, returned and once again anchored near the *Mi Amigo*, ostensibly to check on her safety. The crew of the radio ship subsequently monitored a ship-to-shore conversation between the fishing vessel and North Foreland Radio instructing the latter not to accept any more calls from the *Mi Amigo,* the person issuing this instruction identified himself as being a representative from the Home Office. This conversation was final confirmation for the *Mi Amigo's* Captain and crew that their initial, instinctive suspicions about the motives of the British tug sent to 'assist' them had been well founded.

The two ships stayed at anchor about 100 yards from the *Mi Amigo* until late that evening while the DJs on board decided to keep Radio Caroline's transmissions on the air all night, fearing a possible boarding by the Home Office after the station's normal early morning closedown at 2.00am.

## Raided

Transmissions from both stations continued but shortly before 3.00pm on 14th November 1975 police and Home Office officials arrived in a boat alongside the *Mi Amigo.* They informed the Captain that his vessel was anchored inside British territorial waters and requested permission to come aboard. Although he strongly disputed the claim that the *Mi Amigo* was anchored inside territorial waters the Captain had little choice but to grant permission for the police and government officials to board the radio ship.

*The route of the 'Mi Amigo's drifting around the Thames Estuary*

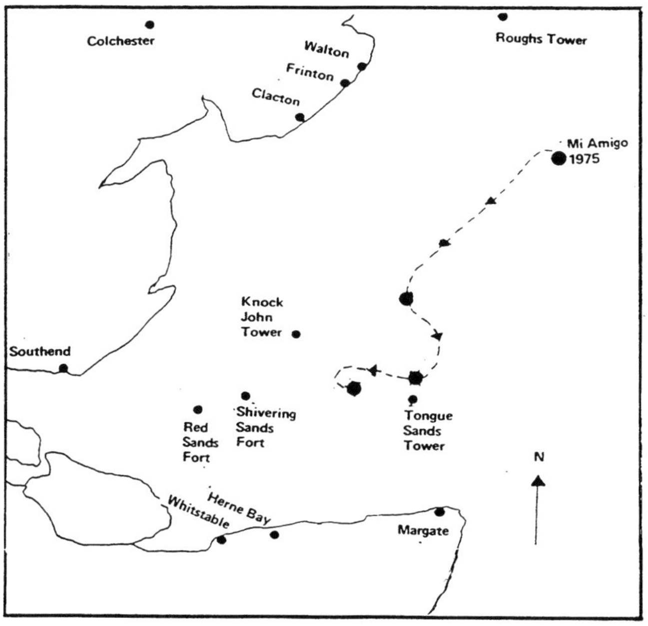

As they were climbing on board the station's engineer managed to switch off Radio Mi Amigo's taped programmes and activate a microphone in the Radio Caroline studio. Startled listeners then heard police enter the studio and a heated argument taking place during which the engineer was repeatedly told to turn the microphone off. He resisted for a short time, trying to convince police that a tape was being played, however, at 3.01pm the microphone was abruptly cut off by the boarders. Police and officials from the Home Office Radio Regulatory Department then systematically searched the *Mi Amigo* and confiscated a number of papers and programme tapes.

*Mi Amigo* Captain (Werner de Zwart) together with DJs Glen Schiller (Mike Lloyd) Simon Burnett (Simon Barrett) and engineer Peter Murtha (Peter Chicago) were taken from the radio ship shortly after 4.00pm, arriving in Southend two and a half hours later where they were subjected to passport control and Customs inspections. Dutch Captain de Zwart and American DJ, Mike Lloyd, as foreign nationals, had their passports confiscated before being allowed to 'enter' the country, while the other two, being British nationals were allowed to retain their passports. The four men were then taken to Southend Police Station where they were questioned and charged with offences under the Marine etc. Broadcasting (Offences) Act 1967.

All four men appeared before Southend Magistrates on 15th November 1975 and were remanded on bail of £1,000 each until 11th December 1975. In addition all four now had their passports confiscated but, after numerous appeals, Captain de Zwart's was returned by the Magistrates at the end of November so that he could travel home to Spain until he was required to attend the resumed hearing on 11th December.

Two days later, at 2.30am on 17th November 1975 the *Mi Amigo* lost its anchor yet again but the remaining crew on the radio ship managed to lower the spare anchor and contacted North Foreland Radio requesting a lifeboat and tug to stand by. The Margate lifeboat arrived about six hours later and took two visitors, Kelvin O'Shea and Ronald Doyle, off the *Mi Amigo,* but the Acting Captain was informed that this time there was no tug available to stand by the radio ship.

An offer from the lifeboat coxswain to take off the Acting Captain and two remaining crew members was refused and the lifeboat then headed to Ramsgate because weather conditions had deteriorated so much that it was impossible to land at Margate.

The two men rescued from the *Mi Amigo* that day were both to feature again in offshore radio history - Kelvin O'Shea became known to millions of Radio Caroline listeners under the name James Ross when he joined the station's broadcasting staff a few months later, while in 1976 Ronald Doyle became involved in a spectacularly bizarre prosecution in Liverpool for alleged infringements of the Marine etc. Broadcasting (Offences) Act.

## Further relocation

After this raid the two stations aboard the *Mi Amigo* remained silent until nearly a week later, when on 23rd November 1975 the radio ship left the South Edinburgh Channel and anchored at a position back in the Knock Deep Channel, 17 miles off Margate. After a further three days test transmissions, using the 10Kw transmitter, started at 1.30pm with Radio Mi Amigo's regular programmes returning at 3.00pm the same day. On 1st December 1975 the 50Kw transmitter was brought back into service but that evening the top of the aerial mast collapsed and the following day the station was again forced to use the 10Kw transmitter.

At Southend Magistrates Court on 11th December 1975 charges were heard against the four men taken from the *Mi Amigo* when she had been anchored inside British territorial waters on 14th November. The prosecutor, David Knight, told the court that shortly after 9.00am on 13th November 1975 radio transmissions had started from the *Mi Amigo*, then anchored just less than one mile inside British territorial waters. At 2.55pm the following day police and Home Office officials had boarded the vessel and found the defendants, with others, assisting or taking part in making radio transmissions. Evidence in the form of photographs of the radio ship and its two studios were shown to the magistrates. The Court was told that when questioned by police the Captain of the *Mi Amigo* had thought his ship was anchored in international waters.

Captain de Zwart pleaded guilty to being in charge of a ship used for radio transmissions contrary to the Marine etc. Broadcasting (Offences) Act 1967 and was fined £100 with £50 costs. Simon Burnett and Glenn Schiller pleaded guilty to charges of taking part in unauthorised broadcasts from a ship inside territorial waters and were fined £200 with £50 costs and £50 with £25 costs respectively. Engineer Peter Murtha pleaded not guilty to a charge against him of 'repairing and maintaining radio equipment knowing that it would be used for an unlawful purpose', and was further remanded on bail until 23rd February 1976, but his passport was returned by the Court. Additionally and most significantly, the Magistrates made an order giving the authorities power to seize the MV *Mi Amigo* should she ever enter British territorial waters again and authorised the confiscation of items of equipment, papers and a transmitter crystal which had been removed from the ship by police during the boarding on 14th November 1975.

## Hilversum airtime for Veronica

In Holland the former offshore broadcaster Radio Veronica, now known as Veronica Omroep Organisatie (VOO), was still fighting a battle to obtain the right to broadcast over the Hilversum network. In an effort to slightly distance itself from the offshore operation the VOO established its own offices away from the former Radio Veronica headquarters building which, although still owned by the Verweij brothers was now used by another company- Stichting Gooi en Vechtstreek.

VOO shared its new offices with the Dutch Top 40 Foundation which compiled a Top 40 Chart each week and produced an information news cassette for circulation to record shops giving up-to-date news about the pop world and new record releases. The Dutch Association of Record Retailers regarded this Top 40 as the nation's official chart, rather than the Top 30 one produced by the state pop radio network, Hilversum 3.

Also in the VOO building was a company called De Beukderin (Action) which published souvenir albums and books about the offshore Radio Veronica. All these activities were designed to keep the name of Radio Veronica in the public eye, even if its programmes could not be heard at that time despite the fact that VOO had two million members and qualified for a broadcasting licence.

That situation changed at the end of 1975 when, on 28th December, VOO finally began broadcasts on the Hilversum network - one hour a week of classical music on Hilversum 4 from 8.00am on Sundays, one hour on Hilversum 1 on Mondays (the Paul Meirer Show) and one hour on Hilversum 3 on Fridays when Lex Harding played new releases and LP tracks.

VOO also obtained airtime on the Hilversum Television Network from 21st April 1976 - three hours every third week. The first programme - broadcast from the *Norderney* - was used to celebrate offshore Radio Veronica's 16th

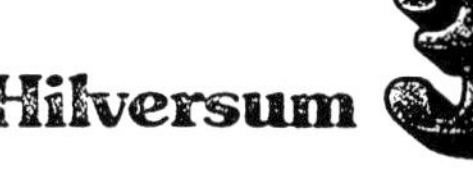


*Ieder heel uur nieuws*

**7.02 Gospelsound** *EO*
**8.03 Tijdsein**
Actualiteiten en muziek
**9.03 De muzikale fruitmand**
**10.03 Te elfder ure**

*TROS*
**11.03 Drie draait op verzoek**
Gerard de Vries
**12.03 De Hugo van Gelderen-show**
Met de Nederlandstalige Top 10 en Kwiswijs

**13.30 Pop-contact** *NCRV*
Peter Blom met de Nationale Tip 30

*NOS*
**16.03 De Nationale hitparade**
Felix Meurders
**18.03 De Vacaturebank**
Een greep uit de vrije banen bij de Gewestelijke Arbeids Bureaus
**18.10 NOS-Maal**
met Joost den Draayer

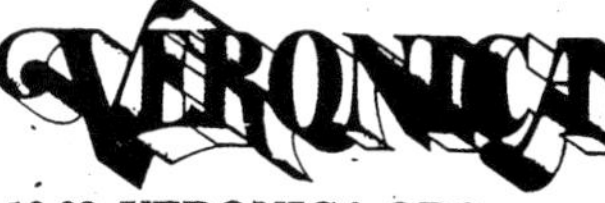


**19.02 VERONICA OP 3**
Lex Harding geeft een overzicht van het Nederlandse hitgebeuren en presenteert de twintig best verkochte schijven van de afgelopen week. Een nieuwe nationale vrijdagavondgebeurtenis
Produktie: Ad Bouman

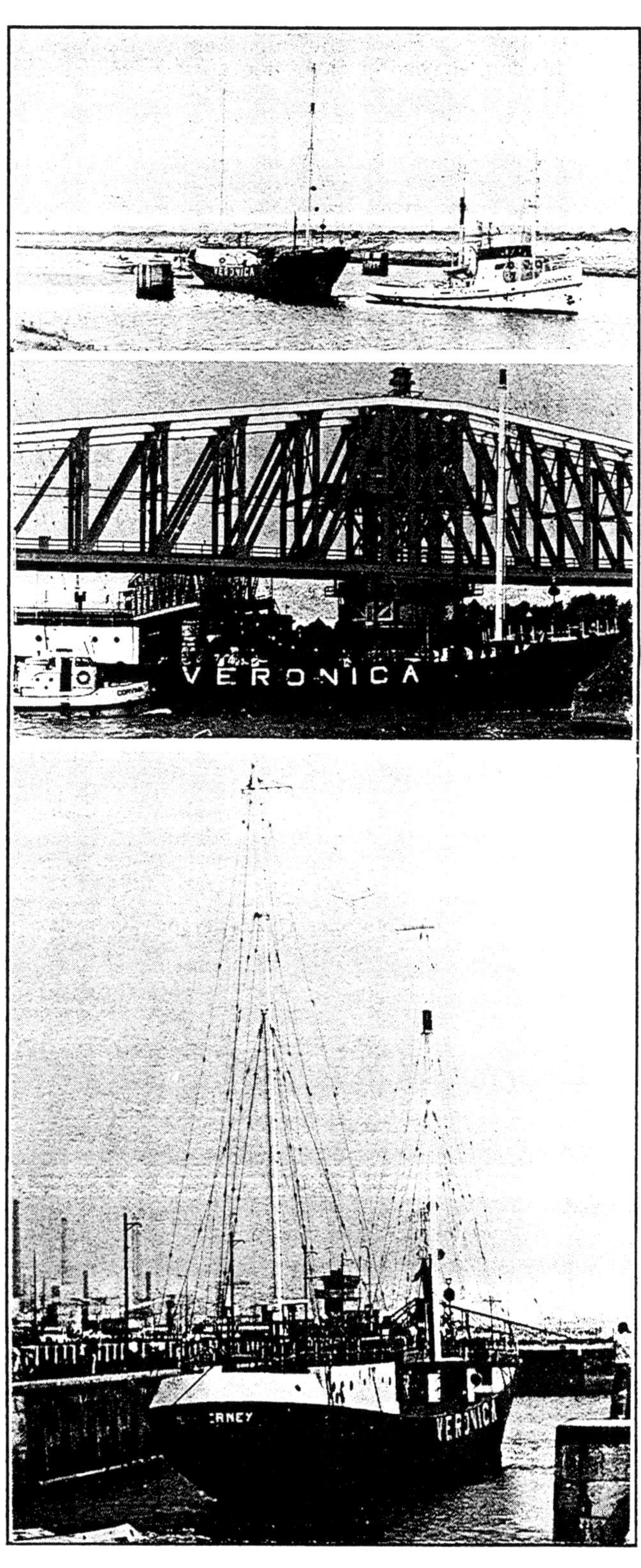


The 'Norderney' being towed into Ijmuiden, 1975

Birthday as well as including an hour and a half of topical information items and a light drama serial. These programmes had a certain amount of interactivity with audiences because at the beginning of each Veronica session viewers were offered a choice of films and the one receiving the highest number of votes in a telephone poll was subsequently aired.

The head of VOO was Rob Out, a DJ from the offshore station while a number of other ex-offshore presenters also joined the landbased station - Tineke, Lex Harding (Programme Director, Radio) while John de Mol (ex Dutch RNI Managing Director) became Programme Director, Television.

Each broadcasting organisation in Holland has its own radio/TV guide and for this purpose VOO was able to use the *Veronica* Magazine (formerly *Veronica 192* and *Veronica 538*) which had continued to be published as a general pop music magazine since the demise of the offshore radio station in August 1974.

A foundation for the preservation of the ex-Radio Veronica ship, *Norderney,* was also launched towards the end of 1975. The ship had been tied up at a quay behind Amsterdam Central Station since August 1975 when she had been towed in from the open sea after spending a year silent at her anchorage off Scheveningen. On 28th November 1975 she was towed once again, this time to Zaandam to await a decision on her future -at first plans were announced for an offshore radio museum and recording studio, but lack of finance prevented this plan going ahead. However, the VOO soon found that they could no longer afford to maintain the former radio ship so in mid-1976 they accepted an offer from a Dordrecht businessman to purchase the vessel for 60,000 Guilders (£12,000), and transform her into a floating restaurant/disco.

## Prosecutions

Back in Britain a further hearing was held at Southend Magistrates Court on 23rd February 1976 when Caroline Engineer, Peter Murtha changed his plea to 'guilty' and was fined £100 with £50 costs for maintaining radio equipment on board the *Mi Amigo*. Murtha had decided to change his plea when he discovered that the Home Office had confiscated the ship's log in which he had signed entries at least twice a day, conclusively proving that he was aware of radio transmissions taking place from the ship. Another eleven transmitter crystals seized by police during the boarding of the *Mi Amigo* in November 1975 were also confiscated by order of the Court.

With love and music

RADIO CAROLINE

Two further, but unrelated, cases alleging involvement with Radio Caroline had briefly come before the courts early in 1976. On 22nd January the case against Rudigar von Etzdorf (Johnny Jason), who in October 1975 had elected for trial by jury on charges under the Marine etc. Broadcasting (Offences) Act, was committed by Southend Magistrates to the Crown Court, and remanded on £200 bail until April 1976.

On 17th February 1976 Liverpool Magistrates held a preliminary hearing into charges against three men, John Jackson Hunter, James Monks and Ronald Doyle (one of the 'visitors' removed from the *Mi Amigo* in November 1975) who were all accused of publicising Radio Caroline's transmissions contrary to the provisions of the Marine etc. Broadcasting (Offences) Act. This case was also adjourned, coincidentally, until April 1976.

At Southend Crown Court on 26th April 1976 Judge Martyn Ward stopped the case against Rudigar von Etzdorf and ordered the jury to return a verdict of 'not guilty'. The trial had begun with counsel for the prosecution, David Knight, informing the Court that with the agreement of the defendant and his counsel, James Comyn, QC, von Etzdorf would admit a number of offences. These included charges that (using the name 'Johnny Jason') he had been on board the *Mi Amigo*, but the case for the prosecution then depended on whether the alleged broadcasts had been live or pre-recorded. Von Etzdorf had been charged under Section 5(3)(d) of the Marine etc. Broadcasting (Offences) Act 1967, which required the prosecution to prove conclusively that he had actually made the broadcasts live from the radio ship. Transcripts of two tapes were produced as prosecution evidence - one tape found in the possession of von Etzdorf and the other a recording of a broadcast made by 'Johnny Jason', but the two tapes differed in content.

Almost from the outset the trial judge had misgivings about the prosecution case and at one stage sent the jury from the Court while he held private discussions with both counsel. During these discussions Mr. Comyn asked for the case against his client to be dismissed, but Mr. Knight argued successfully for the proceedings to continue, convincing the Judge that prosecution evidence would show that von Etzdorf had confessed to the alleged offence. The jury was then recalled and the case continued.

However, when the first prosecution witnesses, Detective Sergeants Burden and Hargreaves were cross examined by Mr. Comyn it became clear that the alleged admission by von Etzdorf may never have been made - it did not appear in either officers' notebook recording their original interviews with the defendant in April 1975 and supposedly had only been 'recalled' by Sergeant Burden some nine months later, in January 1976.

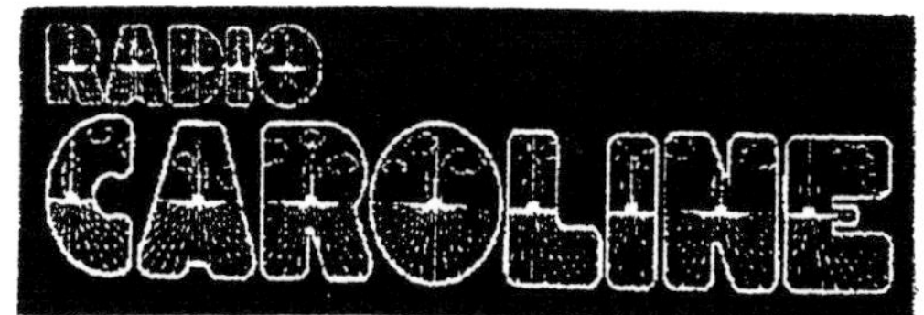

After some further discussions the Judge decided to stop the case because he was unhappy about asking a jury to decide on the issue particularly as the main prosecution evidence was not substantiated by entries in the detectives' notebooks and only came into statements made some nine months later. The Judge, after explaining that von Etzdorf had escaped through a technicality largely because the Marine etc. Broadcasting (Offences) Act had been so loosely drafted, instructed the jury to return a verdict of 'not guilty'.

## Liverpool 'stickers' case

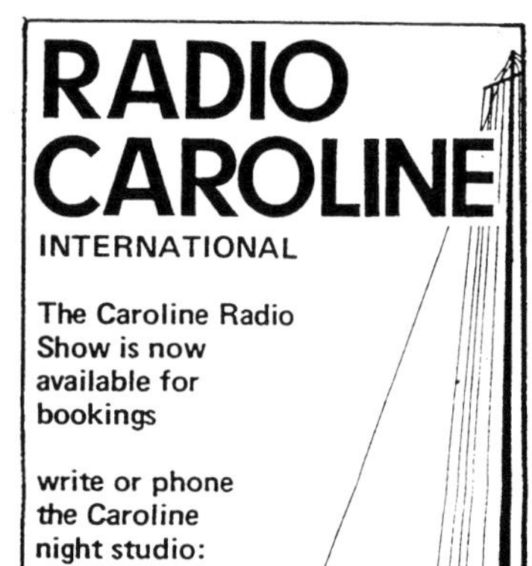


Meanwhile in Liverpool, Magistrates sat for a week in the case against the men accused of promoting and publicising Radio Caroline, and heard the prosecution call 25 witnesses to testify that the radio station was actually broadcasting at the time the alleged offences took place. Ronald Doyle was charged on five separate counts and John Jackson Hunter on one count under Section 5 (3)(f) of the Marine etc. Broadcasting (Offences) Act 1967 (which prohibits the publication of details (i.e. times and frequencies) of offshore radio broadcasts). James Monks had one charge against him, that of booking the Radio Caroline Roadshow and displaying a poster "intentionally promoting the illegal station." All three men pleaded 'not guilty'.

One prosecution witness, Home Office official, Derek Spencer German, told the Court that on 14th June 1975 he had visited Doyle's premises at 4a Prescot Street, Liverpool with two other witnesses and taken photographs of the window display which contained posters and offshore radi information. They also watched vehicles at the back of the building load up with disco equipment then followed them to the Fleece Hotel in St. Helens. Other witnesses testified to the fact that Radio Caroline and Radio Mi Amigo were at that tim broadcasting from the MV *Mi Amigo* anchored in a position in international waters near the Thames Estuary.

**Radio Caroline on tape, city court is told**

**Frequency claim at Caroline hearing**

**Night the law tuned in to the 'radio pirates'**

At the end of the hearing all three defendants were found guilty -James Monks, Manager of the Fleece Hotel, St. Helens, was fined £25 with £50 costs, while sentences against the other two defendants - John Jackson Hunter (charged with displaying a Radio Caroline sticker in his car) and Ronald Doyle (charged with running the mobile disco under the name 'Radio Caroline Roadshow') were deferred for social reports. A month later, on 21st May 1976 Doyle and Jackson-Hunter were each given a 90 day prison sentence, suspended for two years, and ordered to pay £500 costs. Not surprisingly both men decided to lodge appeals against their sentences.

Southend Magistrates were also kept busy at this time with cases involving people charged under the Marine etc. Broadcasting (Offences) Act. On 5th April 1976 those involved in the 1974 unsuccessful Radio Dolphin project on the Gunfleet Lighthouse appeared before the court. Four defendants (Andy

Anderson, Les Livermore, Ian Hurrian and Printz Holman) were originally charged with conspiring to break the Marine etc. Broadcasting (Offences) Act, but the prosecution agreed to reduce the charges to ones of supplying equipment for an offshore radio station and the cases were heard on that basis. In court the case against Hurrian was dismissed and the other three men were given conditional discharges for two years and ordered to pay £50 costs each.

This case finally ended the story of an attempt by some of the English staff of Radio Atlantis to bring that station, albeit under a different name (Radio Dolphin), back to the airwaves from a structure off the British coast. By coincidence a few weeks later, on 28th April 1976, the ex-Radio Atlantis vessel, *Janine,* was sold for scrap to Arie Rijsdijk, Bos and Son, who paid 25,000 Guilders (£5,000) for the former radio ship. After 9,000 Guilders (£1,800) had been handed over to the Vlissingen Harbour Authority in payment for outstanding dues the former owner of the ship received the remainder of the money from the sale.

## Radio Caroline 192m programmes, May 1976

6.00am Mark Lawrence

9.00am Tony Allan

12.00noon Jonathan Day

3.00pm Mark Lawrence

6.00pm Stuart Russell

9.00pm Tony Allan

12midnight Jonathan Day

3.00am Stuart Russell

## Caroline on 192m

Out on the MV *Mi Amigo,* Radio Mi Amigo programmes continued to be broadcast on 1187kHz (253m) since the ship had once again been safely anchored in international waters, in early December 1975, but test transmissions on 1520kHz (197m) and 1562kHz (192m) also took place at irregular intervals during March and April 1976. On 8th May 1976 non-stop music was broadcast on 1562kHz (192m), with a parallel transmission of the Radio Caroline output from 1187kHz (253m) at other times after Radio Mi Amigo had closed.

These tests were in preparation for an all-day English language service which eventually began at 6.00am on 15th May 1976. The broadcasting schedule from the *Mi Amigo* now looked like this:-

**Radio Mi Amigo** (1187kHz) 253m

6.00am - 7.00pm Dutch/Flemish

**Radio Caroline** (1562kHz) 192m

6.00am - 7.00pm English

**Radio Caroline** (1187kHz, 253m and 1562kHz, 192m) 7.00pm - 6.00am English

## Home Office letter

Listeners who wrote to the Home Office at the end of 1975 or early in 1976 to complain about the actions being taken against Radio Caroline and its staff received the following reply from the Aeronautical and Maritime Branch:-

*Radio Caroline is an illicit broadcasting station operating from the vessel 'Mi Amigo' moored in the Thames Estuary. Broadcasts from this station are made in contravention of the International Telecommunications Convention to which the United Kingdom is a signatory. The regulations annexed to the Convention specifically prohibit the establishment of broadcasting stations on board ships outside national territories and consequently the United Kingdom is under an obligation to do what it can to prevent such broadcasting.*

*Because radio frequencies generally are in short supply - and this is particularly true of the medium waveband - it is necessary to regulate and plan the use of frequencies nationally and internationally. Without such planning radio communication which includes safety services at sea and in the air, and television and radio broadcasting would be difficult if not impossible.*

*In the past offshore broadcasting stations have appropriated frequencies for their own use without regard to the needs of others and consequently have caused interference to vital services. For this reason member countries of the Council of Europe agreed to introduce legislation against such stations and the Marine etc. Broadcasting (Offences) Act 1967 is the United Kingdom's contribution.*

*I hope you will find information contained above will help you understand why pirate broadcasting stations cannot be allowed to operate and you will appreciate that actions must be taken to preserve the orderly use of the radio frequency spectrum.*

I LISTEN TO **RADIO CAROLINE**

ON 192 & 259

Within two weeks Radio Caroline's parallel transmissions on both frequencies during the evening and overnight had ended. The daytime Caroline English language service on 192m continued, but a separate Caroline Service was introduced after Radio Mi Amigo's closedown on 1187kHz (253m). Advertisements from some major international companies such as Walls Meat Products, K-Tel Records, Levis Jeans, Coca Cola and Wrigleys chewing gum appeared on the new daytime Caroline 192 service, but these were not all genuine paid commercials.

At about the same time Radio Mi Amigo introduced a summertime schedule, but there were initial supply difficulties and for a few weeks taped programmes failed to arrive from Spain. DJs, and news readers on board the *Mi Amigo* (including some from Radio Caroline) had to fill in these gaps with live programmes. The station also started carrying the Dutch (Veronica) Top 40 from 9th July 1976 while another innovation was the introduction of a phone-in quiz programme - listeners phoned the studios in Spain with their answers and stood to win cash prizes which accumulated (Cash Casino style) with every wrong answer. A new regular live programme "Baken 16" (Buoy 16) was introduced on 23rd July 1976 from 2.00pm-4.00pm which as well as music included news, traffic and weather reports. The title of the programme came from a (mistaken) understanding by the Dutch crew that there were 15 marker buoys in the Barrow Deep Channel which identified the position of sandbanks and the radio ship *Mi Amigo* was, in effect, the 16th buoy.

## European prosecutions

Authorities in Britain, Holland and Belgium seemed determined at this time to prosecute, sometimes on a very petty level, anyone remotely connected with either of the radio stations aboard the *Mi Amigo,* making life as difficult as possible for these individuals and the station operators in the hope that eventually the transmissions would cease.

In May 1976 the Dutch Public Prosecutor, J H C Pieters announced his Department's policy towards any Dutch companies advertising on Radio Mi Amigo. Once a commercial had been broadcast the company concerned would receive a visit from the police warning of the consequences of buying further advertising time on the station in contravention of the Dutch Marine Offences Act. If the firm concerned continued to advertise then it was liable to prosecution without further warning. As a result of this policy announcement the Dutch press reported on 12th May 1976 that some twenty companies in Holland had cancelled their advertising contracts with the offshore station.

The first case in Holland under the Dutch Marine Offences Act was heard on 11th May 1976 when two Dutch seamen - Captain Jacob Taal and Koos van Laar appeared before a court in Amsterdam charged with assisting the *Mi Amigo.* They admitted, under questioning by the Public Prosecutor and with undeniable photographic evidence presented to the court, that they had taken their boat, MV *Dolfijn,* to the *Mi Amigo* and tied up alongside the radio ship. Captain Taal had in fact worked on the *Mi Amigo* since 1972 and had sailed the vessel back out to sea after she had been taken into port by her previous master (Captain van der Kamp) following the crew 'mutiny' in December 1972 (see Chapter 15). Taal told the court that he was not the radio ship's permanent Captain, he only went aboard when the vessel needed repairing or had to be re-located, as had been the case after the drifting in November 1975. It was because he assisted the vessel at that time that Taal was now in Court.

Van Laar, who owned the *Dolfijn,* had taken Captain Taal and a new anchor chain out to the *Mi Amigo*, towed the radio ship back to her anchorage and had been paid 15,000 Guilders (£3,000) for the job - £2,000 for the new anchor chain and the remaining £1,000 for himself. He told the Court that he had done this job because he understood the *Mi Amigo* was no longer a radio ship within the meaning of the Dutch Marine Offences Act - the transmitter crystals having been removed by British police and Home Office officials when they boarded the vessel.

The Public Prosecutor asked the Court to pass suspended prison sentences on the two men as well as fines and confiscation of the *Dolfijn* - estimated to be worth 30,000 Guilders (£6,000).

Counsel for van Laar, Mr. J Tange, argued that the Public Prosecutor's call for confiscation of his client's vessel was absurdly harsh and asked Judge J A van Waarden to acquit his client. He told the Court, "There was no question of intention. The salvage operation that my client undertook was aimed purely at saving the ship and not the radio station on board. At the time my client assisted the ship the *Mi Amigo* was not a radio ship. The photograph (produced by the prosecution) merely shows a ship with a mast that is a bit out of proportion. That is no reason to call it a radio ship!"

The Court's decision was made known two weeks later when both men were found guilty. Captain Taal was fined 1,000 Guilders (£200) and given a six weeks suspended prison sentence while Koos van Laar was fined 2,000 Guilders (£400) and given an eight week suspended sentence. Judge van Waarden did not order the confiscation of the *Dolfijn* as requested by the Public Prosecutor, but he had imposed even longer prison sentences than those demanded by the Prosecutor during the trial. He did this, he said, because "it is the boldness of the people that supply the ship and who transport people and goods to and from the radio ship that enables the people who run the radio station to continue their activities."

At the end of June 1976 seven more people were prosecuted in Amsterdam for assisting Radio Mi Amigo in various ways. Four of the defendants, including two of the station's newsreaders, Bart van Leeuwen and Jan van der Meer, did not turn up at Court. One of the three who did appear admitted to having worked

## LA Band Launch

*Radio Caroline, which for some years had promoted the concept of Loving Awareness (LA), was behind the launch of a new album by a group of that name at the end of June 1976. The first airplay for the album took place on the Tony Allen Show on 23rd June 1976, when it was featured as 'Album of the Morning'. Within a few weeks the BBC, Radio Mi Amigo and (the now landbased) Radio Veronica were also playing tracks from the album.*

*The album and the LA Band were launched at a press conference in the Amsterdam Hilton - the proceedings being relayed by satellite to New York where a suite in the World Trade Centre had also been hired. One of Radio Caroline's original DJs, Simon Dee, introduced the group in Amsterdam by reading an open letter to the Beatles asking either that they re-form and start promoting love and peace again or, alternatively, allow the new band to use their name. In fact a sign behind the group on stage in Amsterdam read "Meet the Beatles".*

*This strategy backfired in both Holland and America when journalists took the view that this pretentious, unknown band had no right to consider calling themselves 'The Beatles' while the original members of that group were still performing, albeit now in their own individual roles. At the outset Radio Caroline DJs introduced the band on air as 'The Beatles', but when the hostile reaction from the Amsterdam and New York press conference became known this idea was quickly dropped and they were simply referred to as the Loving Awareness Band.*

*The members of the Loving Awareness Band were Mickey Gallagher, Charlie Charles, Norman Watt-Ray and Johnny Turnbull. They later became Ian Drury's backing group - The Blockheads.*

on the *Mi Amigo* in November 1975 (when the station was off the air) because at that time he considered it was not a radio ship as the British police had raided the vessel and removed the transmitter crystals. He claimed to have brought a new anchor chain "to save the ship and its crew", adding that the only difference from other ships was that the *Mi Amigo's* mast was a bit taller!

Another defendant was accused of repairing the transmitter on board the ship, while a third crew member was also accused of working on the *Mi Amigo* in November 1975. The three men were found guilty and fined, with two also receiving suspended prison sentences and one a term of probation.

On 1st August 1976 police questioned people aboard a fishing boat in Brightlingsea Harbour after a visit to the *Mi Amigo* and both the boat owner and the organiser of the visit were later charged and summonsed to appear before Southend Magistrates in January 1977.

Seven people appeared in court in Amsterdam on 14th September 1976 accused of various offences in connection with the *Mi Amigo* - one man found guilty on five charges of taking people to the radio ship was fined £900 with a six week suspended prison sentence, four others (three cooks and a seaman) were each fined £100 with two weeks suspended, another engineer was fined £200 with four weeks suspended and one of Radio Mi Amigo's newsreaders (who did not attend court) was fined £400 with six weeks suspended.

## Radio Mi Amigo prosecutions

In Belgium on 29th September 1976 forty one people appeared before the Correctional Court of Justice in Brussels accused of various offences in connection with Radio Mi Amigo. Thirty seven of those accused were in Court before Judge Anna de Molina, but Radio Mi Amigo's owner, Sylvain Tack, DJ Peter van Dam, technician Maurice Bokkenbroek and one other defendant were all absent.

The charges laid against Sylvain Tack in his absence were :-

(a) Operating a 'pirate' commercial radio station contrary to a law passed in May 1930, and amended by the Belgian Marine Offences Act in December 1962 prohibiting any Belgian citizen from operating a radio station without Government permission.

(b) Threatening a Dutch Television crew (AVRO TV) in 1974 when they were filming at Tack's Suzy Waffles factory

(c) Extortion demands made against Marty Products.

The Court was told that, since Tack had moved to Spain in 1975, ex-Radio Mi Amigo DJ Christian Hendrickx (known as Patrick du Bateau and in fact Sylvain Tack's brother in law) had been the brains behind the station in Belgium.

Two weeks later, on 15th October 1976 the defence case was presented. It was claimed that as some of the advertisers had not signed contracts with Radio Mi Amigo and they had no knowledge that their commercials were being broadcast. The Court was also told that only small advertisers had been prosecuted and not the large international companies whose products were frequently promoted by the station. On behalf of Sylvain Tack it was argued that other stations in Europe, including Radio-Tele Luxembourg and Vatican Radio, broadcast on frequencies and transmitter powers not authorised by the Geneva Convention and that a recent poll had shown that more than half of the people in Belgium thought it was time the law was changed to remove BRT's monopoly and introduce commercial radio.

Verdicts of 'guilty' against all defendants and individual sentences were announced by the Court on 12th November 1976:-

Sylvain Tack -One year imprisonment for the first charge, and seven months for the other two plus four million Belgian Francs (£65,000) fine.

Christian Hendrickx -Seven months imprisonment and 2 million Belgian Francs (£32,700) fine.

18 other people received prison sentences of three months and fines of 80,000 Belgian Francs (£1,300).

14 advertisers received one months suspended prison sentences and 60,000 Belgian Francs (£980) fines

Five people were each given three months probation and fined 80,000 Belgian Francs (£1,300).

Two people were each given one months probation and fined 60,000 Belgian Francs £982).

**Dutch and Belgian Marine Offences Acts.**

*Under the Belgian Act Belgian nationals are not permitted to assist an offshore radio station anywhere in the world (as is the case under Britain's Marine etc. Broadcasting (Offences) Act 1967, but the Dutch law contains a loophole which allows Dutch nationals to assist an offshore station, while living abroad.*

When asked to comment on the sentences Sylvain Tack (in Spain) said he had never been told the Court hearing was taking place and had not been officially informed of the verdict. Commenting on the blackmail charge he said Marty Products had only paid for one month out of a three months advertising contract. He had demanded the other two months payments and now claimed that the company had reported this information to the authorities alleging extortion to avoid having to make payment to him. The case involving AVRO TV had been brought about, said Tack, because they had spied on him, followed him around for eight days and then claimed that he had broken their equipment. In fact, despite the alleged 'damage' to the company's camera the film about Tack was subsequently shown on Dutch television.

At that time there was no extradition treaty between Spain and Belgium so the Belgian authorities could not insist on Sylvain Tack being sent home to serve his sentence - it could only be enforced if he returned to Belgium of his own accord.

## *Mi Amigo* flooded

Weather once again played its part in causing problems for those aboard the *Mi Amigo* in September 1976. The first indication that the crew were experiencing difficulties came in a coded message to the landbased office, broadcast during Radio Mi Amigo's programmes at 8.15am on 10th September. Although a severe storm was buffeting the radio ship the only damage sustained at that stage had been caused by a wave breaking a porthole and flooding the Radio Mi Amigo studio. This forced operations to be transferred to the Radio Caroline studio and Radio Mi Amigo programmes were then transmitted simultaneously on both frequencies - the 192m Caroline English Service being temporarily suspended to enable the revenue-earning Dutch station to broadcast as normal.

However, there was no live "Baken 16" programme that day, just continuous taped music, itself an indication that those on board the radio ship were fully occupied with other more urgent tasks. Part way through the taped music Dutch DJ Marc Jacobs interrupted the programme to announce that the Radio Mi Amigo studio had been flooded and the station was operating temporarily from the Radio Caroline studio. Normal (pre-recorded) Radio Mi Amigo programmes were broadcast again later in the afternoon and the station continued apparently as normal until its 7.00pm closedown time.

## Helicopter visit

*On 18th September 1976, just as this latest drama had apparently passed, a helicopter was spotted hovering over the 'Mi Amigo', causing some concern to those on board the radio ship, concern which deepened when the aircraft was identified as being from the Dutch Post Office (PTT) Headquarters in Rotterdam. The helicopter dropped a package into the sea near the radio ship, which the crew managed to retrieve and open only to find the following message -"Will you please ask your listeners to dial more slowly when ringing your studios in Spain as last week they blocked nearly all the telephone exchanges in Holland and some in Belgium too."*

Radio Caroline then started its programmes and apart from a reference to the Radio Mi Amigo studio having been flooded earlier that day, DJ Ed Foster did not tell listeners of the greater drama going on at the time. The first mention of this over the air came an hour and a half later when he interrupted a record to broadcast this message:-

*This is Radio Caroline broadcasting on 259m in the medium wave band from the radio ship Mi Amigo. We are on a sandbank and in distress and require assistance from shore.*

Ed Foster was instructed by the radio ship's Captain to broadcast this message as the *Mi Amigo's* anchor chain had snapped, but programming did continue as normal throughout the rest of the evening until the transmitter went silent during the early hours of the following morning. This breakdown was caused by a feeder cable snapping during the gales and this could not be repaired until welding gear had been brought out to the ship.

With Radio Caroline off the air and the *Mi Amigo* stuck on a sandbank a small boat came alongside to offer assistance. Instead of asking the crew to tow the *Mi Amigo* free of the sandbank the Captain and his Dutch crew, together with Radio Mi Amigo newsreaders Marc Jacobs and Jan van der Mer all abandoned the radio ship, leaving only four Englishmen on board - DJs Ed Foster, Mark Lawrence and Tom Anderson and engineer Peter Chicago.

These four spent some hours pumping out several feet of water from the *Mi Amigo* while they waited for welders to arrive and repair a hole which had pierced the ship's hull, as well as the broken transmitter cable. A tender eventually arrived beside the silent radio ship and, when the weather had calmed sufficiently, the necessary repairs were carried out and a new anchor and chain installed.

However, the radio ship remained stuck on the sandbank for a total of five days until another tender with a relief crew arrived and managed to tow the *Mi Amigo* back to her anchorage on 16th September 1976. Radio Caroline programmes then re-commenced at 6.00pm that evening while Radio Mi Amigo returned to the air at 7.00am the following morning with taped music and programmes presented by the four English crew left on board. Because the 192m transmitter had been damaged by flooding it was not possible to reintroduce Radio Caroline's daytime service until 22nd September 1976.

## Liverpool 'stickers' case concludes

In Liverpool the appeal hearing against the sentences passed on Ronald Doyle and John Jackson Hunter were eventually heard on 25th and 26th October 1976. The court upheld the sentence passed on John Jackson Hunter (2 years suspended prison sentence and £500 costs for displaying a Radio Caroline car sticker) but reduced Doyle's suspended prison sentence to a £100 fine, with £500 costs (for running the Caroline Roadshow Disco).

(A postscript to this story is that John Jackson Hunter refused to pay his fine and subsequently served a jail sentence for non-payment. A warrant for his arrest was issued by Liverpool Magistrates and he spent the period from 25th November 1977 to 3rd January 1978 in jail.)

This case, having now reached its conclusion, had earned a particular significance, even notoriety, in offshore radio history. The vast majority of prosecutions in Britain and elsewhere were for breaches of the Marine etc. Broadcasting (Offences) Act 1967 (or equivalent legislation) in connection with working on or supplying offshore radio stations or the ships used to house them. These Liverpool prosecutions, however, referred only to incidents connected with the publicising and promotion of an offshore station and none of those found guilty had any direct involvement with the day-to-day operation of either the *Mi Amigo* or the radio stations operating on board the vessel.

The mobile disco involved in this case was in fact established many months before Radio Caroline even returned to the air in September 1972 and operated under the name 'Radio Caroline Roadshow' quite legally during that time. The return of Radio Caroline in late 1972, although at the time welcomed by those operating the disco, also had the effect of making the use of that name illegal overnight because it contravened Section 5(3)(f) of the Marine etc. Broadcasting (Offences) Act 1967. The fact that the disco continued to operate using the name "Radio Caroline Roadshow", and by so doing was effectively promoting the offshore radio station, led the authorities to take action against those involved, petty though the charges were.

It was estimated that the case had cost £4,000 to bring to Court.

RADIO CAROLINE

INTERNATIONAL

LIVERPOOL STUDIO
4a PRESCOT STREET
LIVERPOOL 7

Complete Radio Music Programmes
D.J.'s - Jingles - Ads - News Items Etc.
Available to Clubs, Halls,
Weddings, Social Functions

## Wavelength swap

As 1976 came to a close a number of technical changes took place on board the *Mi Amigo*. The 259m transmitter went off the air for 'routine maintenance' at 2.00am on 9th November 1976 and a few days later on 17th November both the 259m Radio Mi Amigo transmissions and Radio Caroline's daytime English Service on 192m were suspended between 1.00 and 2.30pm. During these periods off the air engineers made short test transmissions on 962kHz (312m) playing continuous music and Radio Caroline jingles.

Despite using the 50Kw transmitter Radio Mi Amigo's signal on 259m was not satisfactory during the daytime in its primary target area of Holland and Belgium because of interference from a station in Budapest. The station's owners, who held a considerable control over what happened on board the *Mi Amigo*, made it clear to those behind Radio Caroline that something must be done to improve the signal. Many rumours started to circulate at this time that Radio Mi Amigo may part company with Caroline and set up its own vessel, but although nothing definite ever happened the possibility remained and Caroline's engineers realised something must be done. It was decided therefore that both stations on the *Mi Amigo* should swap wavelengths and at 12 noon on 10th December 1976 both 259m and 192m closed so that the crystals could be exchanged.

The following morning at 8.45am test transmissions, using the 50Kw transmitter, were heard on 1562kHz (192m) and regular Radio Mi Amigo programmes were broadcast on this frequency from 11.00am, just 24 hours after the temporary closure. The first programme, presented by Bart van Leeuwen, included denials of rumours that Radio Mi Amigo was planning to transfer its operations to the *Mebo II* (which was then still in Holland).

Radio Caroline did not return to the air until the early hours of 12th December 1976, now using the 10 Kw transmitter tuned to 1187kHz (253m announced as 259m) with continuous music until regular programmes started at 6.00am. Radio Caroline was now on the air on a reduced power on 259m 24 hours a day and Radio Mi Amigo on significantly increased power on 192m for 13 hours a day.

It was quickly discovered that reception of Radio Caroline on 259m was unsatisfactory in many areas and a change to 312m was contemplated. The change of Radio Mi Amigo's wavelength to 192m was not a success either - listeners in Brussels reported the signal to be much weaker and in Amsterdam it was said to be inaudible for most of the day. This problem was caused by two unexpected factors - interference from a Swiss transmitter in Beromunster and the fact that the transmitter used by Radio Mi Amigo, although supposedly capable of 50Kw was often only running at 15Kw at this time.

Transmissions from the *Mi Amigo* were also causing problems closer to home. The IBA announced that from 22nd December 1976 the ILR station Radio Orwell (whose service area included Ipswich, Felixstowe, Harwich, Woodbridge and adjoining coastal areas of south Suffolk) would begin transmissions on 212m (1412kHz) in addition to its normal medium wave frequency of 1169kHz (257m). The allocation of this additional temporary frequency followed complaints from within the Radio Orwell service area of interference (on 257m) from, as an IBA Press Release put it "Unauthorised offshore transmissions". The Press Release went on: "The new Home Office approved channel for Radio Orwell is not a permanent authorisation and may be discontinued should severe interference on 257m from unauthorised transmissions cease to be a problem within the service area."

As it happened the introduction of this additional frequency for Radio Orwell almost coincided with the swap in transmitters and frequency for the two stations on board the *Mi Amigo* - the 50Kw transmitter now used 192m for Radio Mi Amigo while the 259 wavelength used by Radio Caroline was on a power of just 10Kw, considerably reducing any chance of interference to adjacent frequencies and other stations such as Radio Orwell.

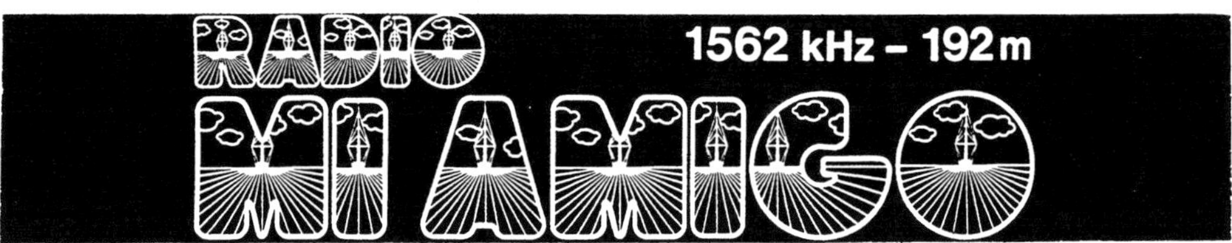


The year 1977 started with yet more prosecutions in Britain and Holland of people alleged to have been involved with activities surrounding the *Mi Amigo*. On 12th January 1977 Radio Caroline's female DJ, Samantha Dubois (real name Ellen Kraal), was found guilty by a Court in Amsterdam of broadcasting from the *Mi Amigo* and fined £200 with a three week prison sentence, suspended for two years.

Two weeks later, on 27th January 1977 at Southend Magistrates Court two men, David Hutson and Walter Ord both pleaded guilty to charges of supplying letters and newspapers to the *Mi Amigo*, while Hutson also faced a charge of promoting the station by publishing an advert and a badge. The charges related to a sightseeing boat trip arranged by Hutson on 1st August 1976. The fishing boat used for the trip, owned by Ord, had been stopped, boarded and searched by Police, Customs and Home Office officials. Unknown to the operators a police officer posing as a free radio fan was actually on board the fishing boat that day - Detective Constable Gary Skull of the Drugs Intelligence Unit.

In Court Miss Jeraine Roberts for the Director of Public Prosecutions stated that, following an advertisement for sightseeing boat trips to view the *Mi Amigo*, Detective Constable Skull had posed as a free radio fan on board Ord's trawler, using the name Simon Martin. Skull told the Court that he witnessed each of the twelve passengers purchasing a 15p Radio Caroline badge being offered for sale by David Hutson. While alongside the *Mi Amigo* Hutson threw on board record requests from passengers on the boat trip as well as mail and newspapers for the crew of the radio ship.

David Hutson was found guilty and fined £125 with £20 costs, while the owner of the fishing boat, Walter Ord, was fined £200 with £20 costs for allowing his vessel to be used to supply mail and newspapers to the *Mi Amigo.* Ord had previously been convicted under the Marine etc. Broadcasting (Offences) Act in September 1975 for taking people off the *Mi Amigo* and bringing them back to Britain.

## French connections

On 22nd January 1977 Radio Mi Amigo started transmitting French language programmes between 8.00am and 12 noon on Saturdays. Programmes included an hour of English and French records followed by a French Top 30 with flashbacks and new releases. Advertising during the programmes, such as it was consisted mostly of promotions for French artists and their albums. However, this service was discontinued after only two weeks because of the number of complaints from regular Dutch and Flemish speaking listeners in Belgium and Holland - these programmes in particular were blamed for a huge drop in Radio Mi Amigo's popularity in Belgium at that time. Reception of the station's broadcasts in France was also reported to be poor with the signal repeatedly fading, so there seemed little prospect of attracting regular advertisers from that country.

Another French connection with the station came to light at the end of February 1977 when a Court in Boulogne found five French businessmen guilty of supplying goods and carrying people to the *Mi Amigo.*

Frederic Douchedame and Patrick Ringart, both managers of a company in Boulogne; Paul Balogh, chairman of a company in Calais; Jean-Marie Talleux, manager of a fishery and Jean Pierre Delva, a draughtsman from Paris all appeared in the High Court in Boulogne on 25th February 1977 on charges of infringing the French Posts and Telecommunications Law and of carrying passengers to an offshore radio ship.

Prosecuting Counsel, Mr. Lamoine told the Court that in 1965 an international agreement had been entered into by France forbidding the operation of offshore radio stations (the Strasbourg Convention) and a domestic law had been passed by the National Assembly on 29th December 1969 giving the authorities powers to act against any French citizen involved in assisting the radio ships or stations broadcasting from them.

At the request of the British authorities the French had started investigations in 1976 into the hiring of boats in Boulogne and Calais suspected of supplying the *Mi Amigo*. The Prosecutor asked the Court to impose large fines on the defendants to demonstrate that France respects international agreements to which it is a party and commitments entered into with other countries.

Counsel for the defence, Pierre Faucquez, said his clients did not contest the facts and admitted carrying passengers to the *Mi Amigo*, however, Police and Customs officials were fully aware of the journeys they made and had not raised any objections. The Court, after a short adjournment found all defendants guilty and imposed fines ranging from 1,000 Francs (£110) to 5,000 Francs (£550).

Reports appeared in the French press at the beginning of March 1977 that another trawler, *Saint Andre des Flanders*, had been intercepted at Calais by French Maritime Police and the Frontier Air Police (PAF). On board the trawler were Andre Fauchet, Michael Delpierre and Francis Bigand who were arrested and later released on bail by the Boulogne Public Prosecutor. Calais and Boulogne Police later searched an apartment belonging to Mrs. Oonagh Huggard (also known as Oonagh Karanjia), an ex-employee of Radio Caroline and now secretary of a Liechtenstein registered company. During the search documentation relating to the supplying of Radio Caroline was discovered and it was claimed by the authorities that Mrs. Huggard was the head of Caroline's French supply network, responsible for chartering boats to transport goods and people to and from the radio ship. Mrs. Huggard was arrested, charged with arranging to supply the *Mi Amigo* and bailed to appear in court in June 1977.

The hearing on 1st June 1977 took place in the Palais de Justice in Haute Ville, Boulogne. The Court was told that the *Saint Andres des Flanders* had been intercepted by Coastguards and Calais Frontier Air Police in March 1977 when the Captain and two crewmen had been arrested. Police discovered that the trawler was carrying too much food for a normal 24 hour journey and that the quantity of fuel which was stored on board in specially made tanks was far more than the vessel itself would need.

Police enquiries established that the food and fuel were being carried to the *Mi Amigo* and further investigations led to Mrs. Oonagh Huggard who, claimed the prosecution, was now in charge of tendering arrangements for the radio ship. The Court was also told that Mrs. Huggard received payments from the owners of the

## Annan Committee Report

*The report of the Committee on the Future of Broadcasting, chaired by Lord Annan (the Annan Committee) was published on 24th March 1977. The sixteen members of the Committee had spent two and a half years considering options for the future of broadcasting in Britain. Their 500 page report was based on what Lord Annan described as four fundamental and vital principles:*

- flexibility of structure
- accountability through Parliament to a public which must be given more chance to make its voice heard
- diversity of services
- editorial independence

*The Report recommended that*

- the BBC should continue to provide two national television services, four national radio services and external services, but not local radio stations. All BBC revenue should still come from the Television Licence fee and not advertising.
- The Independent Broadcasting Authority should be re-named the Regional Television Authority and be responsible for a single service of regionally based television stations, provided by companies under contract to the Authority.
- A new body, the Local Broadcasting Authority should be established to take over responsibility for all local radio broadcasting, the development of local cable television stations and licensing hospital and university broadcasting services and local education cable services. The programmes would be provided by organisations (including non-profit making trusts) under contract to the Authority and advertising revenue was to provide their main source of income.
- Another new body, the Open Broadcasting Authority should be established to take responsibility for the fourth national television channel, to be used for educational programmes, Open University broadcasts and programmes from ITV companies as well as other independent producers. Finance for this service was to come from commercially sponsored programmes and educational grants. It was proposed that the OBA should also become responsible for an FM radio service carrying a similar mix of programmes to the fourth television channel.

*The Report also contained recommendations about the establishment of a separate fourth television service for Wales, the introduction of teletext services, a fifth national television service and a broadcast traffic information system.*

## The Pop Pirates

*A board game for offshore radio enthusiasts was launched by Music Radio Promotions in 1978. Called "The Pop Pirates" the game had two objectives for players:*

> ***to equip a radio ship for life at sea by purchasing transmitters, aerials and anchors and finding a Captain, crew and team of DJs***
>
> ***to complete the course and win a licence to broadcast from land.***

*There were many hazards on the way such as seasickness, transmitter faults, breakdowns, sabotage and shipwreck. In addition players had to battle with rival ships for advertising contracts and audience ratings. The game came complete with board, dice, tokens, pirate money, advertising contracts, audience rating cards, problem cards and all necessary components to equip the radio ship.*

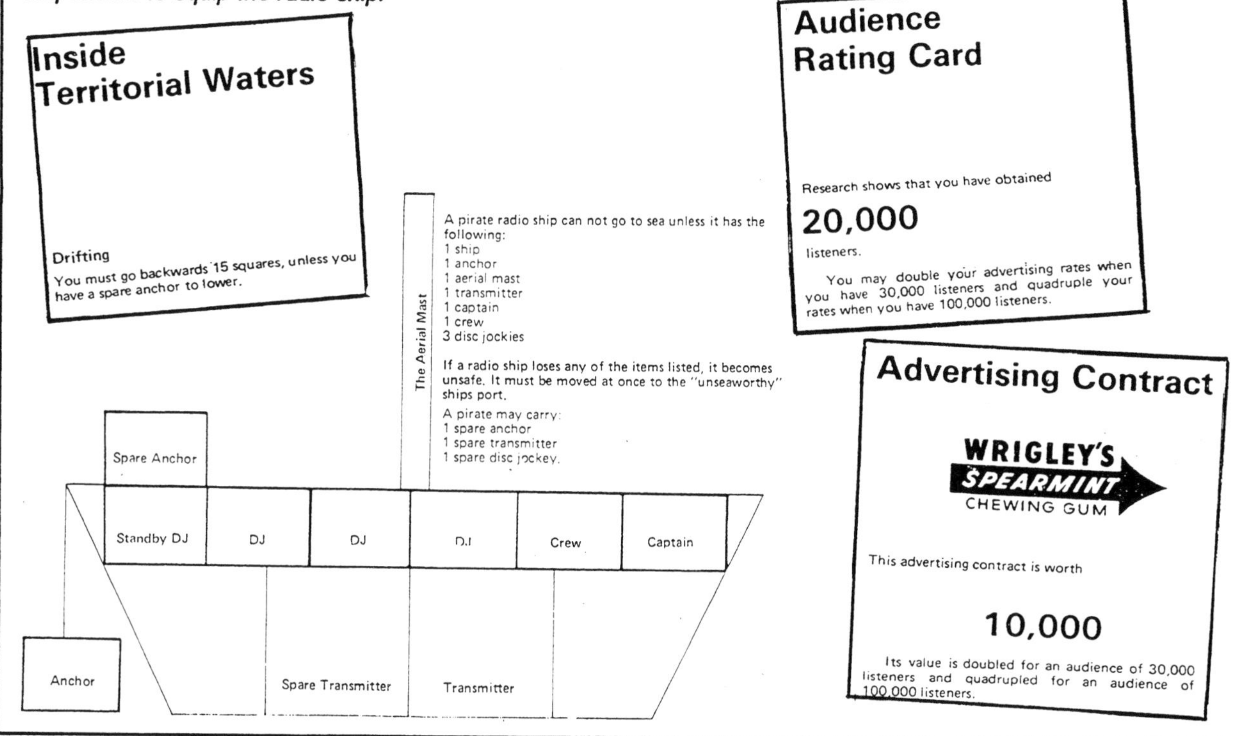


offshore station to supply the radio ship and she was responsible for arranging a tender to convey the goods. Bank documents seized at her home were produced in evidence to prove these allegations.

It was revealed that the authorities had been investigating and monitoring the supply lines from France to the *Mi Amigo* for four months before mounting the raid on the *Saint Andre des Flanders* in March 1977.

In Court all defendants admitted the charges of supplying the radio ship. Andre Fauchet, Captain of the *Saint Andre des Flanders*, said he received 1,500 francs (£190) for each tendering journey. Pierre Faucquez, representing the three seamen said Fauchet had been contracted to deliver fuel supplies to a ship 60 miles out at sea from Boulogne, but they never considered that it was illegal to do so. Counsel for Mrs. Huggard said that all his client had done was help people who found themselves in difficulties at sea.

When the Court's decision was made known on 22nd June 1977 Mrs. Huggard was fined 4,000 Francs (£500), Fauchet 5,000 Francs (£625) and the tender's mate, Francis Bigand, 2,000 Francs (£250). The crewman on the *Saint Andre des Flanders,* Michael Delpierre, was acquitted.

## Goodbye to 259m

Yet more technical changes took place on board the *Mi Amigo* early in March 1977. On the 3rd of that month Radio Caroline broadcast for the last time on 1187kHz (253m) and the station closed at 6.00pm following a three hour programme which included a tour of the ship presented live on deck by James Ross. The station's signal on this frequency now that it was only using the 10Kw transmitter had become almost intolerable for listeners so a decision was made to change to a clearer channel. A week later, at 12.23am on 9th March 1977, the station started test transmissions on 953kHz (314.6m, but announced as 319m), with regular programmes commencing on that frequency at 6.00am the same day.

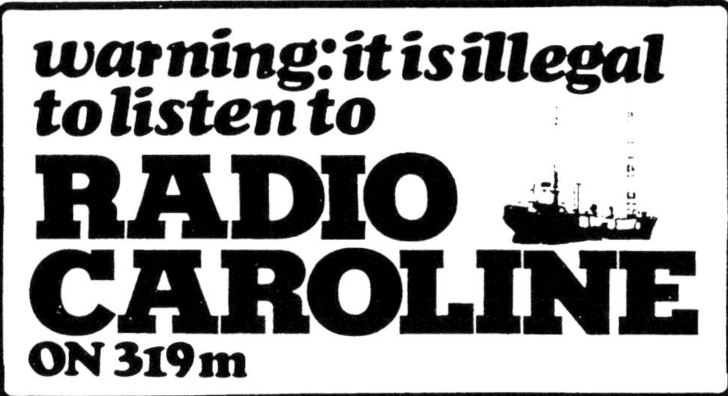


ILR station Radio Orwell, which had been allocated temporary use of 212m since December 1976 closed this frequency with the following announcement during the last week of April 1977:-

*At midnight on Saturday April 30th Radio Orwell will cease to broadcast on 212m medium wave. This is because interference on our normal wavelength of 257m ended some weeks ago and there is no longer any reason for using this additional frequency. Listeners now using 212m are therefore advised to re-tune to 257m.*

Radio Orwell had regained the use of 257m, now free of interference from the *Mi Amigo*, but it was not long before the 212m temporary wavelength was acquired for use by those on board the radio ship.

## Radio Mi Amigo on 212m

Despite the frequency and transmitter changes made in December 1976 reception of Radio Mi Amigo in its target area of Belgium and Holland also continued to be unsatisfactory and prone to interference. With pressure from the station's owners the Caroline organisation on board the *Mi Amigo* decided in July 1977 to introduce yet more changes in an attempt to improve the signal.

Radio Mi Amigo closed as normal at 7.00pm on 23rd July 1977 and no further broadcasts were made until 25th July when regular programmes commenced at 12 noon on the new wavelength, 212m (1412kHz). During the first of these programmes ("Twee-een-Twee - Een Beter Idee", "212 a Better Idea"), which was presented live from on board the *Mi Amigo* by Frank van der Mast and Hugo Meulenhoff, station engineer Peter Chicago was interviewed and explained about the changes:-

*There's a few reasons why we're changing. One of the reasons is that we've had complaints from Switzerland, from Beromunster, and we've had to reduce power slightly to avoid interference with the Swiss radio station. And there is another problem as well. Capital Radio in London is very close to the frequency which Mi Amigo has been using and that's another reason why we've had to reduce the power a little bit. .........I hope it's going to be a big improvement. I think it should make a big difference and the frequency that we are going to use is quite a clear channel.*

Reception on 212m was initially reported to be much improved in Belgium and Holland, the station's primary target area.

### Rescue

*Rescue services had to be called to the 'Mi Amigo' on 17th March 1977 when two crewmen working in an inflatable dingy alongside the ship were swept away after their securing line snapped. A rescue helicopter from RAF Manston in Kent plucked the two men from the sea and winched them back on board the 'Mi Amigo'. Transmissions from both Radio Caroline and Radio Mi Amigo were temporarily suspended during this operation to enable the helicopter to hover above the radio ship without danger of the crew being electrocuted.*

## 'Flooding' drama

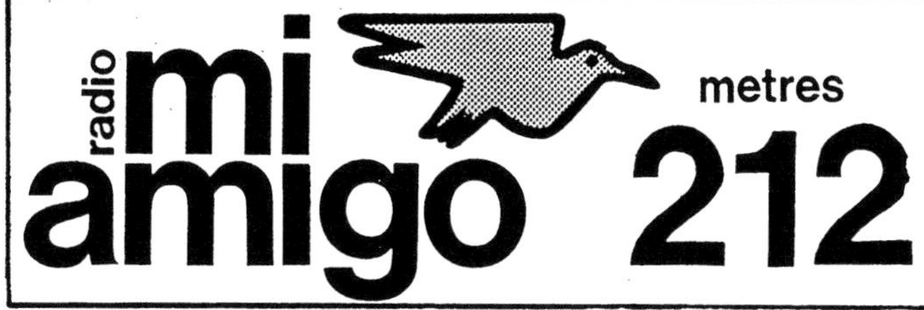


Normal programming on Caroline 319 was suspended without explanation at 9.30am on 4th August 1977 to be replaced by continuous music and station identity announcements at the top of each hour. By 3.50pm both transmitters on the *Mi Amigo* had gone off the air and remained silent until just after 8.00pm that evening when Radio Caroline returned to 319m.

The crew, having discovered severe flooding in the engine room, some of the cabins and the record library on board the radio ship had spent most of the day trying to trace the cause and pump the water out. The crew informed North Foreland Radio of their plight, but did not request assistance from the emergency services, although a Kent Police boat did come alongside to make sure that the people on board the *Mi Amigo* were alright and coping with the situation. As a precaution the life rafts were launched and inflated beside the *Mi Amigo* in case it became necessary to abandon ship.

The ship was starting to list to starboard and at first it was feared the *Mi Amigo* may be starting to sink as water appeared to be coming in through a hole in the hull. After many hours spent removing metal plates and floorboards the water was eventually discovered to be pouring from one of the generator cooling pipes in the engine room and there was actually no danger of the vessel sinking.

In the early hours of the following day, 5th August 1977, three men came ashore from a Belgian trawler at the small East Anglian port of Gorleston-on-Sea and were pursued by police. Two escaped, but one, Peter Murtha (Chicago) was arrested and appeared in Court at Norwich later the same day charged with "maintaining wireless apparatus for illegal broadcasts on the high seas between 7th July and 5th August 1977." Murtha was remanded on bail of £1,500 to appear in Court again in September.

At Norwich Magistrates Court on 9th September 1977 Peter Pearson, for the Director of Public Prosecutions, explained that the *Mi Amigo* was anchored in the Thames Estuary and from it broadcasts were made by a station known as Radio Caroline. Murtha, he alleged, was involved in the maintenance of radio equipment on the ship. On 5th August 1977 a Belgian trawler, *Vita Nova*, had entered Gorleston Harbour and from it three men leapt ashore and took a taxi which was later stopped by police. The men were initially suspected of entering the country illegally.

Murtha admitted in Court that he was responsible for maintaining radio equipment on the *Mi Amigo,* but explained; "There has been a reference to the ship broadcasting illegally on the high seas, but it is not illegal to operate. It is just that the British Government made it illegal for a Briton to work on the ship. Under international law what I am doing is not wrong. It is wrong because I was born British." The Magistrates, however, found Peter Murtha guilty and fined him £150 with £20 costs.

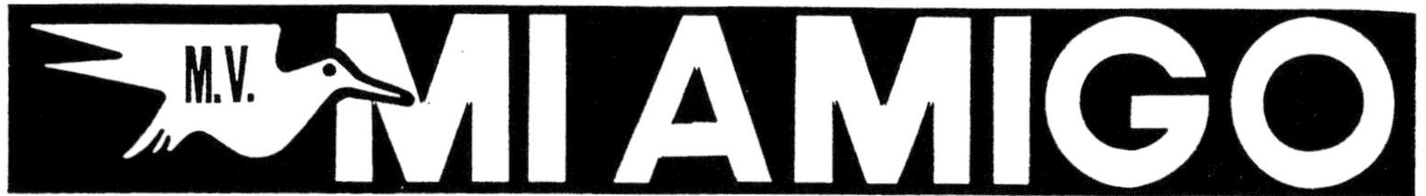


### Money appeal

In June 1977 Radio Caroline's DJs started appealing during their programmes for listeners to send £1 donations to the station:-

*Radio Caroline, Britain's first all day music station, 1964; Radio Caroline, Europe's first album station 1973; and the future is up to YOU. For the first time in fourteen years we're asking you to contribute to our continued existence. An idea which has worked successfully for some time in the USA, and an alternative source of financing suggested in the recent Annan Committee Report into the future of broadcasting. Another first for Caroline - Britain's only round-the-clock public subscription album station. YOU can help Caroline get a stronger signal. Our address for all contributions is Caroline, A 321, Rosas, Gerona, in Spain. You can give Caroline a stronger signal.*

Radio Caroline had never before asked its listeners to contribute towards the running of the station, but embarrassed DJs explained that funds were now so low that continuing the station at all was very difficult and it desperately needed a higher power transmitter. It had therefore been decided to introduce a listener subscription system, but the appeals were halted after a few weeks when only £400 was raised.

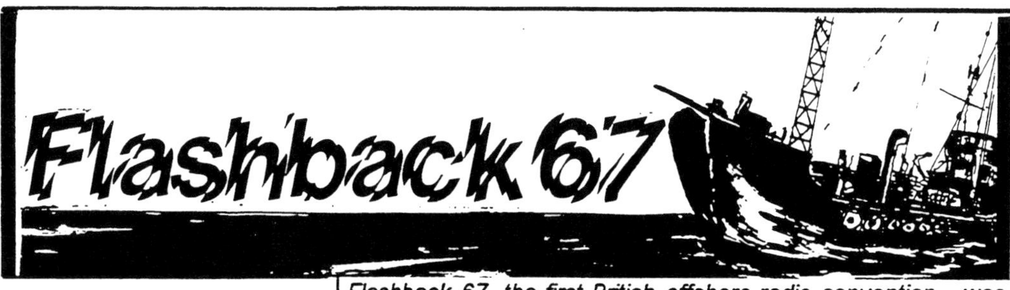


*Flashback 67- the first British offshore radio convention - was held at the Centre Hotel, Heathrow Airport over the weekend of '13/14th August 1967. The event, organised by Music Radio Promotions, included appearances by offshore radio personalities, talks, discussions, films and recordings of the offshore stations. There was also an extensive trade exhibition featuring stands from various organisations selling souvenirs and memorabilia. A Convention Dinner and Disco was held on the evening of 13th August while on Sunday 14th August Radio Caroline broadcast a live three hour link-up with Radio Mi Amigo - the programme being simulcast on 212m and 319m. The programme included interviews recorded by Robbie Dale at the Dinner the previous evening (which had been delivered overnight to the 'Mi Amigo') giving the impression to listeners that somehow the station had created a live link-up with the Convention Hotel.*

## The strain begins to tell

The strain of trying to operate a 24 hour a day offshore radio station in the late 1970s began to show during the autumn of 1977. In late August Radio Caroline had only two English speaking DJs on board the *Mi Amigo* - Stuart Russell and Roger Matthews, who between them tried to keep the station on the air for over two weeks.

As well as presenting live programmes they also used some old tapes made by former DJs, which were repeated a number of times. In addition various album and tape documentaries - "The Tamla Mowtown Story", "The Beatles Story" and a Neil Diamond Special, were each broadcast two or three times during this period. Two Radio Mi Amigo DJs who were also on the ship presented some live programmes for Radio Caroline as well as their own programmes on Radio Mi Amigo using both English and Dutch so that they could be simulcast on 319m as well as 212m.

This arrangement lasted as long as humanly possible - until 13th September 1977 when Radio Caroline started to close at 8.00 or 9.00pm, but by 17th September five new DJs had reached the ship, enabling normal 24hour programming to resume once again. Radio Caroline's troubles were not over, however, frequent breaks in transmission occurred during September, October and November 1977 and major problems with the generator ultimately resulted in a ten day silence from both stations on the *Mi Amigo* in November. This silence, together with severe storms in the North Sea and inaccurate press reports led to speculation that the *Mi Amigo* had lost its transmitting mast and Radio Caroline would be silenced forever. However, both stations on the *Mi Amigo* returned to the air on 21st November 1977, although there were a number of other minor breakdowns caused by the still faulty generator.

Radio Mi Amigo was also experiencing other problems at this time - programme tapes were prevented from reaching the radio ship in September when Dutch police detained a tender (*Z592, Hosanna*) in Zeebrugge. Three men on board, two DJs and an engineer from Radio Mi Amigo were arrested, but later released.

*Hosanna* was owned by Germain Ackx of the Pax Shipping Co. in Zeebrugge, which had previously been caught by Belgian authorities using another of its vessels( *Z588 Vita Nova* ) to tender the *Mi Amigo*. (The *Vita Nova* was the

### Evening Mi Amigo

*From 22nd August 1977 test programmes started on 212m after Radio Mi Amigo's normal broadcasts had ended at 7.00pm. These programmes lasted for two hours under the title "Mi Amigo in the Evening" and consisted of music and DJ announcements, but no commercial advertising. The tests continued throughout the remainder of August and September and on occasions were also broadcast live on the Radio Caroline wavelength (319m) because of that station's acute staff shortage.*

vessel from which three men had jumped at Gorleston-on-Sea in August 1977, leading to the arrest and prosecution of Peter Murtha). Previously, in April 1977, the same vessel had been intercepted by Belgian police while on a journey to the *Mi Amigo* with provisions, water and replacement DJ staff.

After being detained in Zeebrugge on this latest occasion the *Hosanna* was towed to Brugge where she was chained up in the harbour because the authorities alleged her documentation was not in order. In October 1977 the other Pax vessel, *Vita Nova*, was also chained up by police on suspicion of being used to tender the *Mi Amigo*. However, during the night of 18/19th November 1977 the trawler left Breskins harbour without permission and almost immediately the authorities issued a detention order for the vessel. About six weeks later the *Vita Nova* was spotted entering Calais Harbour by a police launch and Germain Ackx, together with sailor Dirck Boi were arrested, but later released. Police searching the trawler found bed linen and two electric motors which the men admitted were from the *Mi Amigo*. Consequently the *Vita Nova* was detained indefinitely pending further investigations and as a consequence causing further supply problems for the radio ship.

## Wavelength swap

Further changes in the broadcasting arrangements for both stations on board the *Mi Amigo* took place on 1st December 1977. Although Radio Mi Amigo had the use of the 50Kw transmitter tuned to 212m reception was still poor in the station's target area of Belgium and Holland, while Radio Caroline on 319m with only 10Kw of power had a much better signal reach. Therefore it was decided to swap transmitters and wavelengths.

Radio Mi Amigo was re-launched on 319m at 12 noon on 1st December 1977, using the call sign Radio Mi Amigo International and a brand new jingle package. Meanwhile Radio Mi Amigo programmes continued to be simulcast on 212m until 4th December 1977, but with a loop tape announcement superimposed advising listeners to re-tune to the new wavelength.

During December 1977 press reports appeared in Holland saying that four DJs had left Radio Mi Amigo very suddenly - two from the ship and two from the Spanish landbased studios. Reportedly DJs Marc Jacobs and Frank van der Mast had left the radio ship because they considered the *Mi Amigo* to be unsafe. The landbased DJs, Stan Haag and his wife Michelle had then supposedly left in sympathy with them and because making programmes for Radio Mi Amigo "now entailed sticking one's neck out." These disputes were a clear indication that the constant official watch on the activities of those involved with the offshore station, and action taken against some individuals in the courts, was beginning to worry others who had definite career aspirations in the legal broadcasting system, particularly in Holland.

### More French

*Yet another attempt was made to introduce a French language programme on Radio Mi Amigo in September 1977. The new service was introduced between 7.00 and 8.00pm on 28th September 1977 and although it was supposed to be a weekly programme in fact it was aired on only five more occasions before being discontinued on 26th November 1977. Listeners to the station it seemed did not like French language programming and, despite this and previous attempts to introduce such a service, advertisers could not be persuaded to buy airtime in sufficient quantity to make it a viable operation.*

## Music Radio Promotions prosecuted

Two directors of Music Radio Promotions, Mike Baron (Bridgen) and Nic Oakley, appeared before Marlborough Street Magistrates Court in London on 15th November 1977 and 6th January 1978 charged on twenty four counts of advertising Radio Caroline in their publications, *Wavelength, Radio Guide* and *MRP News*. On both occasions the case was adjourned, first to allow the prosecution more time to assemble evidence and the second on an application from defence solicitors for the hearing to be referred to the Crown Court.

The defendants were determined to fight what they considered to be an important test case - the freedom of the press to publish information - an issue which had been debated at length ten years previously when the then Marine etc. Broadcasting (Offences) Bill had been on its passage through Parliament. Now for the first time that particular clause, Section 5(3)(f), was to be tested in a Court of law.

To fund the action a 'Wavelength Legal Aid Appeal Fund' was launched and a number of offshore radio discos were held in London and south east England with guest appearances by the L A Band and offshore DJs including Simon Dee, Robbie Dale, Alan West, Mark Roman, Mark Stuart and Spangles Muldoon (Chris Carey).

On 31st March 1978 Magistrates decided to allow the case to be heard by a jury at Knightsbridge Crown Court and on legal advice Music Radio Promoions ceased trading pending that hearing. All their business activities were immediately taken over by Flashback Promotions which operated from the same address. It was over another year, however, before the case finally came before the Crown Court.

## Withdrawal of P.O. Boxes

In March 1978 a number of 'Free Radio' supporters groups received the following letter from the Post Office:-

*I am directed to inform you that the Post Office is no longer able to provide private box facilities for the organisation using the address P O Box ........ However, to enable you to inform your correspondents of the withdrawal of the facility the private box will be allowed to continue until 31st March 1978. After that date items addressed to PO Box ........will need to be treated as undeliverable. A proportionate refund of fees you have paid will be made on termination of the service.*

This letter was sent to the Free Radio Service, (using PO Box 123, Reading), Caroline Newsletter (using PO Box 35, Crawley) and Music Radio Promotions (using PO Box 400, Kings Langley). Reaction to the letter differed - the Caroline Newsletter, edited at that time by Steve Francis a British author living in Spain, was distributed by Mrs. Jean Sutton from her home in Crawley using the PO Box number. The national and local press reported the withdrawal of the Newsletter's PO box facility and a spokesman for the Post Office admitted that although the people behind the Newsletter were looking at their legal position the Post Office had a duty to protect itself against a possible contravention of the Marine etc. Broadcasting (Offences) Act.

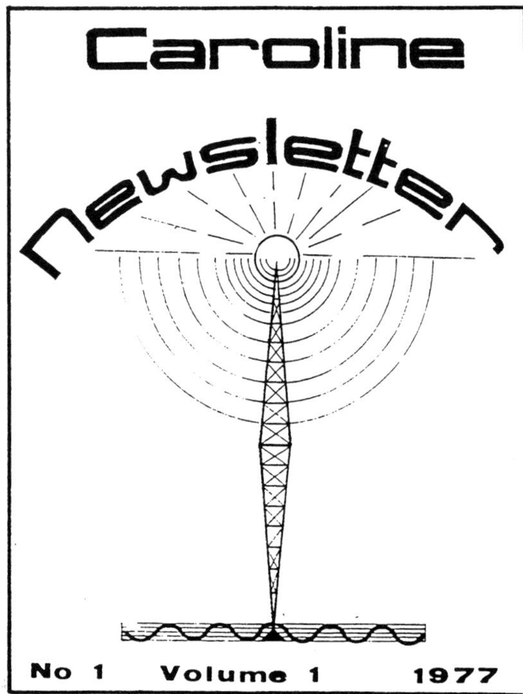


Solicitors acting for Music Radio Promotions - already involved in a legal test case under the Marine etc. Broadcasting (Offences) Act - challenged the termination of service threat with the result that the Post Office agreed to withdraw the notice on condition that MRP gave a written assurance that no more advertisements quoting the PO Box number would be aired on Radio Caroline. MRP claimed that the advertisements had been broadcast without Radio Caroline being asked or paid to do so and they had no control over what went out on air. The Free Radio Service, meanwhile, simply transferred to a private mailing organisation in London.

## Sealand

*Early in 1978 plans were announced in West Germany for the expansion of Sealand, the independent 'Principality' run by Roy Bates on the Roughs Tower off the coast of Essex. Plans included the construction of a complex of duty free shops, restaurants, hotel, entertainment centre and a radio station. Sealand Holdings Ltd. established an office in Berlin at Kurfurstendamm 90, D-100, Berlin 31, under the management of Mr. J Henkel.*

*A document issued through this office to prospective investors explained:*

*"**Location** Sealand is situated in the southern part of the North Sea, latitude 51.53 North, 01.28 East. **History** Sealand was founded as a Sovereign Principality in 1967 in what had been international waters.*

***Constitution** The Principality of Sealand is a sovereign state. The Senate will decide every issue by free vote. Sealand is pledged to recognise the right of all men to speak their mind freely and to respect the rights, beliefs and liberties of all men. Sealand is pledged to further the communication, understanding and tolerance between men of all nations, races and religions.*

***Legal System** The law of Sealand is based on the British Common Law and the British Law of contract. **Passports and Citizenship** The Sealand passport is black with a silver insignia on the face. Corps Diplomatique passports are the same except for being clearly marked as such on the face and above the insignia. The standard passport is valid for five years. **Flag** The Sealand flag is red, white and black.*

***National Emblem** The Sealand national emblem is the sea. **Language** The official language of Sealand is English."*

*To celebrate the tenth anniversary of the declaration of the world's smallest country the 'State Bank of Sealand' issued its commemorative currency in the form of Sealand Dollars, gold and silver coins bearing the image of 'Prince Roy' and 'Princess Joan'*

*Roy Bates planned to build phase one of the expansion project in West Germany and float it across the North Sea to Sealand where it would be attached to the existing fort structure. He claimed to have secured £20 million worth of backing for this first phase, mostly from industrialists in West Germany. Bates was certain that the British Government were powerless to prevent the development going ahead because, although still maintaining that Roughs Tower was in the ownership of the Crown, they had accepted that the structure was outside British territorial waters. As was often the case with Sealand, however, nothing more was heard of these ambitious expansion plans for some months.*

## Invasion

*When it happened the news was dramatic. On 8th August 1978 the 'Principality' was taken over by 'invaders' - two Dutchmen and one German. Roy Bates, 'Prince Roy' of Sealand mounted a dramatic helicopter raid on 16th August 1978 to retake the Fort and the 'invaders' surrendered after fierce hand to hand fighting. They were then held hostage by Bates and his family and made to clear up the damage caused to the Fort. The takeover had happened while Bates and his wife were on mainland Europe and their son, 'Prince' Michael, who was alone on Sealand, was overpowered, tied up without food and water for four days and then sent to Holland. He made his own way back to Britain to rejoin his parents in Essex where the re-occupation assault was planned. An Essex Police spokesman was quoted in the local press as saying " Roughs Tower is in international waters and we have no plans to take any action or become involved at all."*

*By the end of August 1978 the two Dutchmen had been released by Roy Bates and returned to Holland, but the third 'invader', German lawyer Gernot Puetz, who held a Sealand passport, was still detained on a charge of treason. A diplomat from the West German Embassy in London, Dr. Christoph Niemoller, Head of Legal and Consular Affairs, subsequently visited Sealand to try and negotiate Puetz's release.*

*Roy Bates had imposed a £20,000 fine on Puetz, but his wife in Dusseldorf could not raise the money and was quoted in 'The Times' on 6th September 1978 as saying that she was afraid to visit her husband on the Fort for fear of her own personal safety.*

*Puetz's explanation for the 'invasion' was that other former business associates of Bates - with whom he had been negotiating deals to develop Sealand - had decided to take over the Fort for their own purposes. They enrolled Puetz (as a Sealand passport holder) to assist them by leading him to believe that they had a contract to operate the 'Island'.*

*Although Bates insisted Puetz would not be released until the £20,000 fine had been paid he later relented and on 28th September the West German was finally set free. Roy Bates's wife 'Princess' Joan said; "I think he has been there long enough as a punishment. He was misguided and he now realises what he did was wrong. He's very sorry." Satisfied that Gernot Puetz had unwittingly become involved in the conspiracy Bates appointed him Sealand's Consul in Dusseldorf and paid for his journey home. However, Roy Bates was adamant that although the German had been released the £20,000 fine had not been waived - it was to be deducted from fees he earned in his new role as Consul and Legal Adviser to the Principality!*

## Radio Mi Amigo programme schedule, January 1978

*Monday - Friday*

**6.00am Ook Goie Morgen, Ferry Eden** *(live)*

**9.00am Schijven voor Bedrijven-** *factory request show with Haike de Bois*

**10.00am Op de Koffie,** *Haike de Bois*

**11.00am Keukenprets (Kitchen Fun)** *Ton Schipper*

**12noon Baken Zestien (Buoy 16),** *Herman de Graaf (live)*

**2.00pm Tussen Wal en Schip (Shore to Ship),** *Ton Schipper*

**3.00pm Persoonlijke Top 10,** *Haike de Bois*

**4.00pm Stuurboord,** *Herman de Graaf and Ferry Eden (live)*

**6.00pm Jukebox** *-request show with Ton Schipper*

**7.00pm Flashback Show,** *Ferry Eden*

*Saturdays*

**6.00am Ook Goie Morgen,** *Ferry Eden*

**9.00am Vlaams op z'n Bes,** *Haike de Bois*

**10.00am Keukenprets,** *Ton Schipper*

**11.00am Mi Amigo Top 50** *(live)*

**3.00pm Flashback show,** *Maurice Bokkebroek*

**4.00pm Nederlandstalige Toptien - Dutch Top Ten**

**5.00pm Alles Nieuw- new releases** *(live)*

**6.00pm Jukebox**

**7.00pm Flashback Show**

*Sundays*

**6.00am Ook Goie Morgen**

**7.00am Zachtjes Aan (Gently On),** *Ton Schipper*

**8.00am Cabaret-***Maurice Bokkebroek*

**9.00am Non-stop music**

**9.30am Rev Dominee Toornvliet** *-religious programme*

**10.00am Belgische Topvijftien -Belgian Top 15** *(live)*

**11.00am Koffie op Zondag** *-MOR music ,Haike de Bois*

**12noon De Nederlandse Topveertig** *(formerly Veronica Top 40)*

**3.00pm 33 Toeren op z'n Best LP tracks**

**4.00pm Radio Mi Amigo Francais** *-French language programme with Robert Longuard*

**5.00pm Discoshow** *(live)*

**6.00pm Jukebox**

**7.00pm Flashback Show**

Hurricane force winds caused extensive damage in the North Sea and the Kent and Essex coastal area of Britain on 11th January 1978, completely wrecking Margate Pier - only 15 miles from the *Mi Amigo's* anchorage, and ripping the North Hinder Lightship (30 miles from the *Mi Amigo)* from her moorings. Although both stations on board the *Mi Amigo* were already off the air because of generator problems the radio ship survived what turned out to be the worst storms in the area since 1953. Both Radio Caroline and Radio Mi Amigo eventually returned to the air on 15th January 1978.

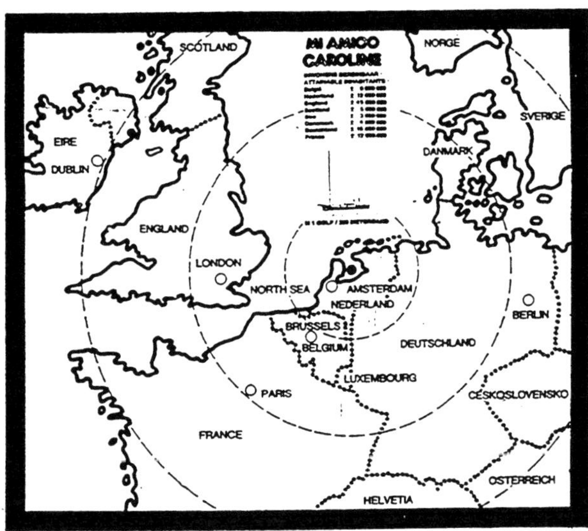


Radio Caroline's 14th Birthday was celebrated on 26th March 1978 with a special programme of listener's Top 50 Album Tracks presented between 7.30pm and 1.30am. On 31st March 1978 Miss Caroline '78 was chosen by DJs on board the *Mi Amigo* from photograph entries in a competition which the station had been promoting for some weeks. The winner, Caroline Simmons of Canterbury, subsequently appeared with DJ Rob Day at a disco at Southend Football Club where she was presented with a number of albums. Miss Caroline '78 was scheduled to appear at various Caroline Roadshow Disco venues, special events and charity football matches throughout the year.

The Caroline Fun Bus toured various seaside resorts in East Anglia and south east England during the first week of August 1978. A former London Transport double decker, it provided a base for the Caroline Roadshow Disco as well as an outlet for souvenir sales. Miss Caroline '78 accompanied the Fun Bus which called at Great Yarmouth, Lowestoft, Clacton, Southend, Herne Bay, Margate, Ramsgate, Folkestone, Hastings, Eastborne and Brighton during the week.

## Radio Delmare

Rumours of a new offshore station being launched off the coast of Holland began to appear during the summer of 1978. On 23rd June Dutch Police and PTT officials seized transmitters, 10,000 records, 225 tapes and equipment for two complete studios from on board a coaster, *Aegir,* moored in Scheveningen Harbour. The equipment which they confiscated included three ex-Belgian army transmitters tuned to medium wave, short wave and FM frequencies. The Captain of the ship and two engineers installing equipment on board were detained for questioning, but later released by police.

However, the secret was now out. The proposed new offshore radio station, Radio Delmare, was being planned by a group of free radio enthusiasts in Holland under the leadership of Gerard van Dam, who had been instrumental in returning the *Mi Amigo* to sea in 1972 and had worked as a DJ on RNI and Radio Atlantis under the name Gerard van der Zee. Both Gerard van Dam and the *Aegir* had previously featured in an abortive offshore radio project in 1975 when plans had been announced to use the vessel as a base to re-launch Radio Veronica. After the police raid on the *Aegir* Gerard van Dam announced that, despite the setback he would continue with his plans and have the new station on the air soon.

The idea for Radio Delmare had grown out of a landbased pirate project which had been running in several Dutch cities (Haarlem, The Hague, Amsterdam and Alkmaar) since early 1977 under the call sign Weekend Music Radio. The whole project reportedly cost only 2 million Belgian Francs (£33,000) to put together, which was cheap for an offshore radio station, and the financial backers (of which there were 20 in all) came mostly from Holland although originally there had been some Belgians, but they later left the project. The driving force behind Radio Delmare was Gerard van Dam, but because he had previously been declared bankrupt he was unable to enter into any financial or business transactions on behalf of the project.

Although all the radio broadcasting equipment was confiscated in the raid on 23rd June the *Aegir* herself had not been detained and at 4.30am on 26th June 1978 she slipped out of Scheveningen Harbour, anchoring at sea near the former REM Island (home of Radio/TV Noordzee in 1964). Two days later the vessel entered the port of Maassluis near Rotterdam, and over the next few weeks she was moved to various locations where more broadcasting equipment was installed without the authorities apparently realising what was happening. The ship's name was changed to confuse the authorities - at various times during this period she was known as *Ellie* and *Flip* and also used shortened versions of her registered name (*Panicopania*) -*Panic, Panico*, as well as the full version. Some fitting out was done at sea when the ship was taken out of the various ports on 'fishing trips', but in reality each time she anchored in a position near the REM Island while engineers undertook the necessary work.

### *Waverley* cruise

*On 8th May 1978 the paddle steamer 'Waverley' was used to take 600 fans on a cruise to the 'Mi Amigo' and past the various sea forts in the Thames Estuary used in the 1960s by stations such as Radio City, Radio 390, Radio Invicta, Radio Sutch and KING Radio. However, the trip was a major disappointment for fans and for those on board the radio ship. The 'Waverley 'did not circle the 'Mi Amigo' as had been planned, she just sailed past rather quickly giving fans little chance to see and photograph the radio ship.*

*This last minute change of plan was caused largely because all fans had congregated on the port side of the vessel as she approached the 'Mi Amigo', which had the effect of raising the starboard paddle out of the water and submerging the port side below axle level. The result was that the whole ship listed 10 degrees beyond its safety limit, causing an estimated £600 worth of damage. The paddle steamer's Captain decided for the safety of his ship and those on board that he should not linger in the vicinity of the 'Mi Amigo' and the trip was curtailed.*

During late August 1978 the *Aegir* anchored near the Dutch/Belgian border off Cadzand. Much work had been secretly carried out on the vessel since the police raid in June and she was now once again equipped as a radio ship. A wire aerial had been slung between the *Aegir's* two masts and the vessel was reported to be stocked with six months supply of food and provisions.

Once safely anchored in international waters test broadcasts started under the call sign Radio Delmare at midday on 21st August 1978 on 1570kHz (191.1m). These broadcasts consisted of non-stop music tapes and some live programmes presented by the station's instigator, Gerard van Dam, using his DJ name Gerard

**Radio Delmare programme schedule, weekend 9/10th September 1978**

*Saturday*

**6.00am Jan Romer** *(live)*

**7.00am Gerard van der Zee** *(taped)*

**8.00am Country Roads,** *Rob van der Meer (taped)*

**9.00am Rene de Leeuw**

***11.00am Jan Romer*** *(live)*

**1.00pm Nederlandse Top 40,** *Rene de Leeuw*

**3.00pm Tipparade**

**4.00pm Rob van der Meer** *(taped)*

*Sunday*

**6.00am Jan Romer** *(live)*

**7.00am Verzoekjes uit Marbella,** *request programme with Gerard van der Zee*

**9.00am Rene de Leeuw**

**11.00am Tweemaster,** *Jan Romer*

**1.00pm Non-stop music**

**2.00pm Rene de Leeuw**

**4.00pm Rob van der Meer** *(taped)*

van der Zee. Transmitter power at this time was less than 500 watts and a mailing address in Spain was given out regularly for reception reports. Intermittent tests continued over the next few days with slight changes in frequencies and variations in signal strength.

Official programmes from Radio Delmare began at 7.00am on 7th September 1978 , but after only a few days on air disaster struck Radio Delmare. A Force 9 gale had been blowing throughout the night of 10/11th September and at 8.00am the *Aegir* was reported to be out of control and drifting in a north easterly direction. Her two anchor chains had snapped and the ship's engines failed. Distress calls were broadcast in place of normal programmes on the medium wave frequency and startled listeners that morning heard the following announcement:-

*It won't be long before we smash on the rocks - SOS - call the Coastguards so they can come and pick us up. We are drifting and we'll soon reach the rocks. It's an SOS -SOS-MAYDAY - MAYDAY -MAYDAY - SOS - SOS from Radio Delmare. MAYDAY - MAYDAY - we are drifting. If you are listening call the Coastguards as soon as possible because we are very near the rocks. Radio Delmare lost its anchor and is now sailing at high speed towards the rocks. Help us- help us - call the Coastguards, and tell them the ship Aegir is drifting towards the Zeeland coast and is about to run aground near the Nuclear Centre. This is an SOS. This is an SOS from Radio Delmare. We broadcast from the radio ship Aegir and we are drifting - MAYDAY - MAYDAY - MAYDAY.*

On land an immediate rescue operation got underway - the tug *Smitbank* and the salvage vessel *Zeeleuw* as well as lifeboats *Zeemanspot* and *Koningen Juliana* headed for the drifting radio ship, which was now within 400 yards of a breakwater at the Hook of Holland. By 10.00am the *Smitbank* had put a tow line aboard the *Aegir* and taken the radio ship to Maasluis near Rotterdam where the four men on board were arrested and questioned for six hours by Rotterdam River Police and the PTT Radio Monitoring Service, before being released.

While the *Aegir* had been adrift there had in fact only been three men on board, but as she was being towed into Maasluis Harbour a fourth man associated with the land-based side of the station, jumped on board and he was also arrested when the ship eventually tied up.

On the orders of Public Prosecutor, Mr. Pieters, the *Aegir* was chained up in Maasluis and PTT officials seized the transmitting equipment, although the crew had managed to throw the valves overboard during the towing operation. Mr. Pieters eventually agreed to the four men being released saying that he thought it was a pity the authorities had not seized the real operators behind the station.

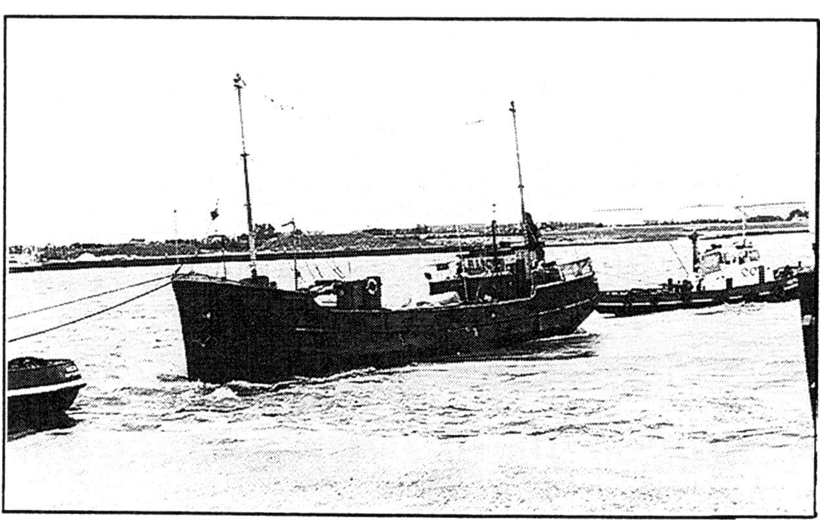

*'Aegir' under tow after running aground*

## Radio Mi Amigo split rumours

Towards the end of July and beginning of August 1978 rumours started to appear about the future of Radio Mi Amigo. A generator breakdown (not an uncommon occurrence anyway) put Radio Mi Amigo and Radio Caroline off the air between 28th and 30th July 1978 - the weekend of the Zeezenders 20 Offshore Radio Convention in Holland. At that event rumours began to spread that both stations had closed for good. When Radio Caroline did eventually return to the air on 30th July 1978 an announcement by Radio Mi Amigo DJs was carried during its programmes denying rumours of the closure which had been spread at the Zeezenders Convention.

At the beginning of August stories also appeared in the Belgian and Dutch press saying variously that a radio technician from Groningen, Ton Rabbeljee, was to buy Radio Mi Amigo from Sylvain Tack; the station was about to close because of dwindling advertising, pending court cases and the departure of a number of DJs; an American religious sect, Plain Truth, were to buy the *Mi Amigo,* have her overhauled in Spain and return to the air in 1979; or that former Radio Veronica DJ, Joost de Draayer was planning to take over the station. The Belgian paper *Het Laatste Nieuws* on 7th August 1978 even reported that the Spanish Tourist Office was about to provide financial aid to Radio Mi Amigo.

Sylvain Tack denied all these rumours, which circulated well into September 1978 and despite all the confusion the station did continue broadcasting from the *Mi Amigo* with a mixture of live and taped programmes. Behind the scenes though Radio Mi Amigo did have some real problems. One of the main difficulties in operating the station were the distances between Spain, where most programmes were pre-recorded, the ship at anchor in the North Sea and Belgium, where much of the tendering, advertising and administrative arrangements were made. Sylvain Tack, in 'exile' in Spain was widely considered to have lost control over the running of the operation.

Co-incidentally at about this time Radio Veronica was not enjoying the success it had hoped for on the Hilversum network and made some tentative enquiries about merging with Radio Mi Amigo to resume operations from an offshore base. Five Radio Veronica DJs went to Playa de Aro to hold preliminary discussions with Sylvain Tack about the possibility of this happening, but nothing definite ever came of the proposal.

## Scan Radio

Ex Caroline, RNI and Voice of Peace DJ, Crispian St. John with a number of other offshore radio DJs planned to launch a new station off the Danish coast in the autumn of 1978. The planned station, Scan Radio International, was to broadcast programmes of pop music to Britain and Europe 24 hours a day. Although extensive financial backing and advertising contracts were claimed to have been secured the planned station never materialised.

One of the principal backers of SCAN Radio was Herr Leiswader, former owner of the Star Club in Hamburg, where The Beatles played in the early 1960s.

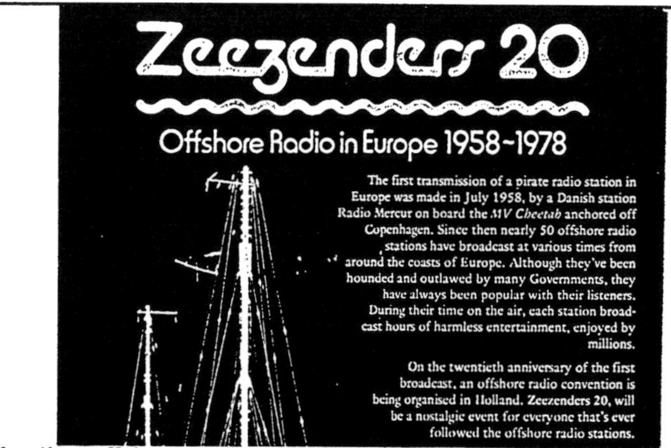


*Another offshore radio convention, held this time in Holland over the weekend of 29/30th July 1978, marking the 20th anniversary of the start of Radio Mercur in July 1958.*

*Zeezenders 20 followed a similar format to Flashback 67, featuring offshore radio personalities speaking about their experiences, films, videos and recordings of the offshore stations as well as an exhibition, sales stands and a disco.*

## Radio Hollandia programmes

*Some Radio Hollandia taped programmes had been made, using the former Radio Veronica studios in Hilversum, which Jan van Veen had purchased from Bul Verweij (his father in law). De Hoge Noot delivered tapes to some shopping centres and similar outlets for a few weeks in the autumn of 1978, with advertisers such as Camel cigarettes, K-tel records, and Muziek Express paying 15 Guilders a second for airtime. However, once the Dutch authorities became aware of the real purpose to which the tapes were to be put, warned advertisers that legal action would be taken against them if their commercials were transmitted from the 'Mi Amigo'. Events on board the 'Mi Amigo' had overtaken them and the radio ship had been silenced by generator failure.*

*De Hoge Noot was dissolved in 1979, but some of the people behind Radio Hollandia went on to become involved in other offshore radio stations in 1981 - Radio Hollandia from the Radio Paradijs ship 'Lieve' in 1981 and Radio Monique from the 'Ross Revenge' in 1984 (see Chapter 22)*

## Radio Hollandia

Sylvain Tack, however, had alternative plans of his own. Tack, who also had a financial interest in the MV *Mi Amigo* had already warned Ronan O'Rahilly that he wanted to relinquish this and purchase his own vessel for Radio Mi Amigo. Another potential offshore radio operator, Willem van Kooten became aware of Tack's desire to leave the *Mi Amigo* and approached Ronan O'Rahilly to take over the airtime rented by Radio Mi Amigo for his own project, Radio Hollandia.

News about Radio Hollandia appeared in the Dutch newspaper, *De Telegraaf,* on 18th September 1978 stating that the new station would shortly be on the air with many well known DJs from the former offshore Veronica and RNI days.

The station's programmes were to be made principally for use as background music in shopping centres, restaurants etc., but the tapes would also 'find their way' to the *Mi Amigo,* from where they would be broadcast to larger audiences in Holland and Belgium. Plans were also said to exist to offer the taped programmes to hospitals and foreign radio stations as well as pubs and discos in Spain. A company, De Hoge Noot, BV (The High Note) was formed to produce the taped programmes.

By mid-October plans seemed to be in place for Radio Hollandia and two DJs working for Radio Mi Amigo at the time, Rob Hudson and Marc Jacobs, were approached to work for Hollandia as newsreaders, tape operators and to present live programmes from the ship. De Hoge Noot was reported to have entered into a verbal agreement with Ronan O'Rahilly to broadcast the tapes from the *Mi Amigo,* but this initial fee was never paid.

Sylvain Tack, angered by the reported introduction of Radio Hollandia from the *Mi Amigo* decided in mid-October 1978 to review the plan to withdraw his station from the Caroline ship. Confusion and insecurity prevailed amongst the Radio Mi Amigo DJs on land and by mid October only one DJ - Ton Schipper remained in Spain to tape programmes. He eventually returned to Belgium, and a plan was formulated for Radio Mi Amigo to present an all live format by DJs on board the *Mi Amigo.*

However, on 20th October 1978, two days before Radio Hollandia programmes were reportedly due to start from the *Mi Amigo*, problems started to occur with the generators and just before 12noon Marc Jacobs interrupted Ton Schipper's taped programme and announced:- *This is Radio Mi Amigo. Because of generator problems we are forced to leave the air.*

The transmitter was re-activated shortly before 8.00pm that same evening, when after playing the "Caroline" theme the following coded message was read out:- "19, 40 times 2, 41 delete first two words" and the brief broadcast then ended. Although no one knew at the time this was to be the start of a long period of silence from the radio ship and led to further intense speculation about the future of both Radio Caroline and Radio Mi Amigo.

Allegations were made at the time that Radio Mi Amigo crew on board the radio ship had sabotaged the generator, making it impossible for Willem van Kooten's new station to start broadcasting from the vessel.

Meanwhile, Patrick Valain, a partner in Radio Mi Amigo with Sylvain Tack, who was also responsible, with Germain Boy for the station's tendering arrangements realised just what a bad state of repair the *Mi Amigo* was in. He approached Ronan O'Rahilly to put together a deal to replace the ship, but these discussion came to nothing.

Completely disillusioned with the operation on board the *Mi Amigo* and the lack of enthusiasm (or finance) for a change Valain and Boy, together with a group of Flemish backers - including some independent record companies - decided to go it alone without Sylvain Tack and take Radio Mi Amigo away from the MV *Mi Amigo* in the autumn of 1978.

During September 1978 Belgian police mounted a series of operations against people thought to be involved with Radio Mi Amigo. On 12th September they confiscated the tickets of 40 people about to depart for a "Week of Mi Amigo Festival" in Playa de Aro, Spain, including show business guests who were to appear at the event.

At about the same time police also raided the premises of every Belgian company which had advertised on Radio Mi Amigo, the Belgian Mi Amigo Drive In Show had its equipment seized (although it was later returned) and the office of the Belgian/Dutch magazine *Radio Visie* was raided and searched. No arrests were made as a result of all this police activity, but it demonstrated that the authorities knew who was connected with or involved in the operation of the offshore station and led to a general feeling of unease and uncertainty amongst those concerned.

## Offshore Radio Mi Amigo closes

At the end of October 1978 Sylvain Tack announced that Radio Mi Amigo would continue as a legal operation in Spain providing a daily programme for tourists "Las Sonrisas de Mi Amigo" - "The Smile of Mi Amigo". The first of these programmes was actually broadcast over a network of five Spanish local FM stations on 23rd October 1978 (three days after the offshore station had closed so suddenly) and the intention was to increase the output to a daily three hour slot from 1st January 1979.

About a month after the halt in transmissions from the MV *Mi Amigo* Sylvain Tack, received a communication from the Spanish Ministry of Culture warning that as Spain was increasing its ties with the EEC (of which it was not then a member) it was now under a moral obligation to enforce various European-wide agreements. This included the 1965 Strasbourg Convention to outlaw broadcasts from offshore radio stations and accordingly the following notice was served on Tack:-

*It is communicated to Mr. Sylvain Tack, (Belgian subject, said to be responsible for the broadcasting of Radio Mi Amigo and Radio Caroline) that the technical installations at his home and offices and the company ADOC, SA, situated in the Banco de Madrid building, Santa Cristina at Playa de Aro must cease immediately and activities which, directly or indirectly, relate to the Channel broadcasting stations Radio Mi Amigo and Radio Caroline. Assurances must be received in writing from Mr. Tack that he is ceasing such activities forthwith in order to avoid measures which would be adopted by the Spanish judicial and government authorities....."*

On 6th November 1978 a number of fishermen and radio technicians appeared in court in Bruges, Belgium on a series of charges of assisting Radio Mi Amigo following raids on the station's tenders in Ostend and Zeebrugge during September 1977. The owners of the two ships used to tender the *Mi Amigo* (*Vita Nova* and *Hosanna*) as well as the skipper, Hector Snauwaert, each received fines of 69,000 Belgian Francs (£1,200) and three months suspended prison sentences. Fisherman August Gheys, radio technician Robet Veramme and

### Wavelength re-allocation

*A new frequency allocation plan for the medium and longwave bands came into effect on 23rd November 1978. The main impact of the new plan was to require a slight change in frequency for all medium wave stations to achieve a 9kHz spacing across the band stretching from 531kHz (564m) to 1602kHz (187m), although as far as listeners were concerned this was hardly noticeable. The new plan allowed for a total of 120 channels 9kHz apart in the medium waveband which had to be shared by thousands of stations throughout the world.*

Jan de Hoop (Frank van der Mast on air) and Jan de Boer (Hugo Meulenhoff on air) - were each fined 12,000 Belgian Francs (£200). Gheys was also given one months suspended prison sentence.

The sudden closure of Radio Caroline and Radio Mi Amigo at the end of October 1978 and the length of their unexplained silence led to speculation in Britain about the future of the stations. On 14th November 1978 the *Daily Telegraph* carried the headline **SHORTAGES HELP TO SINK PIRATE RADIO** and went on to quote 'a source close to the staff of DJs' as saying:-" It could be a generator breakdown but on top of that there have been money problems. It is highly possible that Caroline will not be heard again in Britain." The article speculated further about the dwindling advertising support Radio Caroline had received in recent times and the cash crisis this had caused the station. Surprisingly, for a quality paper such as the *Telegraph,* whose readership would not normally include Radio Caroline listeners, that same issue also carried an editorial comment supportive of Caroline's stand against the authorities:-

*In what will surely be, if the decline of our defences continues at its present rate, Britain's last recorded act of power on the High Seas, the Government has finally sunk Radio Caroline. It seems that the country's first pirate pop music station, menacing the British people from an anchorage 20 miles off Frinton, has been finally forced off the air by various shortages besetting it as the result of the legislation brought in by the previous Labour Government to protect these islands from invasion by round-the-clock pop. In the process of defeating the enemy it was of course felt necessary more or less to introduce round-the-clock pop on the BBC and on new commercial stations. But, in this hour of victory, why quibble about detail? The fact is that the heroic action in defence of the BBC monopoly has now ended after a mere 11 years....What an idiotic policy it was: to try to shut our ears to the flow of pop, in turns amiable and daft, which has become the Muzak of our entire civilisation. The asses in Whitehall, the Labour Party and Broadcasting House who launched the persecution conceded as much by unleashing Radio One's pop service in the same year as the Marine Offences Act. So even the most staunch upholder of the rule of law - and we would count ourselves one such - must permit himself a private cheer that the pirates got away with it for so long...*

This story and Editorial, although supportive of Radio Caroline's defiance since the 1960s, was of course premature in the assumption that the lengthy silence from the *Mi Amigo* was permanent. The cause of the station's present problems was indeed a generator breakdown as well as a chronic shortage of diesel fuel and the radio ship was to remain silent for some months yet, apart from a few short tuning tones broadcast in early November 1978.

## Delmare return rumours

On 16th December 1978 the ship *Scheveningen 54* (being fitted out by Radio Delmare as a replacement for the now confiscated *Aegir*) made a break for the open sea to escape a Dutch police raid and headed towards the MV *Mi Amigo*, which was still anchored, but silent in the North Sea. While tied up alongside the *Mi Amigo* the *Scheveningen 54* transferred a reconditioned generator which, when connected, provided a limited source of power for those still on board the radio ship. This transfer of equipment also led to intense speculation that Radio Delmare were now about to hire from the Caroline organisation airtime vacated by Radio Mi Amigo since the main generator on the *Mi Amigo* had failed in October 1978, but as with so many rumours in offshore radio history this also proved to be unfounded.

# Chapter 20

# Adios Amigo

Fuel supplies on the *Mi Amigo* were so low by mid January 1979 that the crew had to run the generators for just three hours a day while they cooked a meal. They then remained without power for the rest of the day and as a result had no heating, lighting, television, cooking or deep freeze facilities.

The Chief Engineer left the ship in mid-January 1979 to try and organise a supply tender, leaving three English DJs and two Dutchmen on board. On 17th January 1979 the *Mi Amigo* began taking in water and at about the same time the small generator, which had been supplying what little power was available, had to be brought into full time use to operate the bilge pumps. This overworked generator failed on the night of 16th January 1979 and a larger Henschel generator had to be brought into use, consuming valuable fuel. However, that too failed after a few hours and the *Mi Amigo* was left without power and the electrically driven bilge pumps became inoperable. Meanwhile the ship continued taking in water with no means available to pump it out.

By the afternoon of 17th January 1979, with rough seas and a Force 7 gale blowing, the level of water in the radio ship began to rise alarmingly. The crew decided to call the emergency services at 3.10pm and Thames Coastguard sent a helicopter from RAF Manston to the radio ship, while the dredger, *Cambrae,* was also requested to stand by to provide assistance if required. Two other vessels in the area at the time, another dredger *Sand Serin* and the *May Crest,* diverted towards the *Mi Amigo,* while the Harwich Lifeboat, *Margaret Graham*, was also launched.

Although the helicopter offered to winch the radio ship's crew off while there was still some daylight, the DJs decided to stay on board. Shortly before 6.30pm the Harwich Lifeboat arrived alongside the *Mi Amigo* and took off all those on board -Frank (Eamon) Brooks, Brian Johnson, Tony Allen, Marcel Aykman and Bernard Gratz as well as Wilson the canary. The lifeboat crew later described the *Mi Amigo* as having her stem almost under water and her bows in the air - the estimated life of the radio ship at that time was put at less than 24 hours.

By the following morning, 18th January 1979, the weather in the North Sea had improved and during the afternoon a salvage team arrived alongside the radio ship to find her floating upright. Despite her apparent stability the vessel was full of water and engineer Peter Chicago decided to stay alone on the radio ship overnight to prevent any salvage attempts being made by third parties. Single-handedly he managed to get one of the pumps working to remove water from the engine room while another was used to pump out the studio, record library and living quarters. Fortunately the transmitter compartment remained undamaged by the sea water which had been up to a foot deep in some places.

On 19th January 1979 some of the DJs who had been removed two days earlier returned to the ship, together with other engineers and a new petrol generator enabling the *Mi Amigo* to have a regular power supply once again.

### *Mi Amigo* 'repairs'

*By 1979 the hull of the 'Mi Amigo' had started to wear very thin largely due to the age of the vessel (then nearly sixty years old) and the years of general neglect and lack of maintenance. A technique was developed by the crew for dealing with the problem of small holes which frequently appeared in the hull plates letting in water. They constructed a wooden frame between the ribs of the ship in the area surrounding the hole and then poured large amounts of concrete into the frame. Sometimes the holes themselves were first blocked with a wooden wedge, but this was a particularly hazardous operation in case the wedge went right through the thin hull plates, causing an even larger hole and the consequent risk of severe flooding.*

## Radio Caroline programme schedules, April 1979

*DUTCH SERVICE*

*Monday-Friday*

**6.00am Johan Maasbach** *(sponsored religious programme)*

**6.30am Wekkerradio (Waking Radio),** *Rene van Helst*
**8.00am Scheepsplaat (Ship's record),** *non-stop music, Tom van der Wal*

**9.00am Tussen Keuken en Combuis (Between Kitchen and Caboose)** *Ad Roberts*

**11.00am Schoon Schip (Clear Ship),** *Herman de Graaf*

**1.00pm De 19-tig Show (The Nineteeny Show),** *Paul de Wit*

**3.00pm Gangboord (Gangway),** *Rob Hudson*

**4.30pm Rev Dominee Toornvliet** *(sponsored religious programme)*

**5.00pm Closedown**

*Saturday As weekdays except:-*

**12noon De Caroline Top 50,** *Paul de Wit*

**3.00pm De Gangboord Discotheek (The Gangway Discotheque),**

**4.30pm Rev Dominee Toornvliet**

**5.00pm Closedown**

*Sunday*

**6.00-8.30am As weekdays**

**8.30am Rev Dominee Toornvliet**

**9.00am Tussen Keuken en Combuis,** *Ad Roberts*

**11.00am Schoon Schip,** *Herman de Graaf*

**12noon De 19-toen Show (The Nineteen -Then Show),** *oldies presented by Johan Visser*

**1.00pm Zondagmiddagmatinee (Sunday Afternoon Matinee,** *Paul de Wit*

**3.00pm Flessenpost (Bottle-post),** *a request show with Rob Hudson*

**4.30pm Rev Dominee Toornvliet** *(sponsored religious programme)*

**5.00pm Closedown**

*ENGLISH SERVICE*

| *Weekdays* | *Saturday/Sunday* |
|---|---|
| **5.00pm Tom Hardy** | **Tom Anderson** |
| **8.00pm Tom Anderson** | **Steven Bishop** |
| **10.00pm Tony Allen** | **Tony Allen***(Sat)* |
| | **Tom Hardy** *(Sun)* |
| **12midnight Closedown** | **Closedown** |

## Caroline returns

After five months of silence Radio Caroline managed to return to the air shortly after 9.30am on Sunday 15th April 1979 with test transmissions and regular programmes commencing at 11.00am. After half an hour of music presented in English by Tony Allen Radio Caroline's own Dutch language service started with an new team of DJs- Rob Hudson, Herman de Graaf, Paul de Wit, Ad Roberts, Johan Visser and Rene van Hebst.

Dutch programming continued throughout the day and ended with a half hour sponsored religious broadcast from the Rev. Dominee Toornvliet between 4.30 and 5.00pm when the English service of Radio Caroline commenced.

The launch of this new Dutch language service finally confirmed to listeners the rumours which had been circulating for some months that Radio Mi Amigo had broken its ties with the Radio Caroline organisation and the MV *Mi Amigo.*

Deviod of almost any real advertising the English service of Radio Caroline started to air sponsored (largely American) religious programmes from mid June 1979.

The rates for these programmes ranged from $60 for 15 minutes to $175 for an hour and contracts were negotiated by an agent in America. The inflow of cash which resulted from the sponsored religious broadcasts meant that within two months the 50Kw transmitter on board the *Mi Amigo* was brought back into service because regular fuel supplies were obtainable once again.

By contrast the Dutch Service of Radio Caroline was proving to be very successful commercially. Advertising was sold by Danny Vuylsteke, who with Ben Bode and Fred Bolland eventually took over the complete running of the station from studios Which were located at first above a bank in The Hague, but later moved to a secret address in Belgium. Fred Bolland and Ben Bode had previously been involved with Gerard van Dam in plans to launch an offshore radio station, rumoured at the time to be Radio Veronica, from the *Aegir* early in 1975 (see chapter 19). Danny Vuylsteke had also previously been involved in running the Oostburg studios of the Belgian station Radio Atlantis in 1973/74.

The Dutch Service cost between £4,000 and £5,000 a month to operate, but within quite a short time was earning between £6,500 and £9,000 a month, all from spot advertisements or sponsored programmes, with very few 'plug' records being broadcast.

## RADIO CAROLINE SPONSORED RELIGIOUS PROGRAMMES - JUNE 1979

**The Abundant Life Program** -*The Oral Roberts Evangelistic Association, Tulsa, Oklahoma*

**Prophesy for Today** - *The People's Gospel Hour, Nova Scotia, Canada*

**The International Gospel Hour** -*Churches of Christ, Fort Worth, Texas*

**The Arnold Bonk Programme** - *Christian Messianic Fellowship, Vancouver, Canada*

**How Your Mind Can Keep You Well in a Moment of Truth** - *Roy Masters, Foundation of Human Understanding, Los Angeles.*

**Wings Of Healing** - *Gloal Frontiers, Los Angeles*

**The Divine Plan Program** - *The Divine Plan, Fort Worth, Texas*

**The Power of the Word** - *The Power of the Word Broadcast, Covina, California*

**The Camp Meeting Hour**-*Louisiana*

**Monday Morning Meditations** - *All Nations Bible Broadcasts, Grand rapids, Michigan*

**Garner Ted Armstrong** - *Tyler, Texas*

**Independent Baptist Hour** - *Calvary Baptist Church, Ashland, Kentucky*

**Words of Hope** - *All Nations Bible Broadcasting, Grand Rapids, Michigan*

**The Perfect Way Program,** *The Perfect Way, Highwood, Illinois*

**The Mount Paran Worship Hour,** *Atlanta, Georgia*

**The Victory Hour,** *Macon, Georgia*

**The Hour of New Life,** *Republic of South Africa*

**Eric Butterworth Speaks,** - *London*

**The Old Country Church** - *Sarcoxie, Missouri*

## Return of Radio Mi Amigo

Former Radio Mi Amigo owner Sylvain Tack and tender operator Patrick Valain purchased a vessel of their own to re-launch the station during the early part of 1979. During the months before the station went off the air in October 1978 they had experienced problems tendering the *Mi Amigo* and considered that she was in a dangerous state of repair. It was reported that many tendering trips carried more concrete to repair holes in the radio vessel than they did fuel to supply the generators. Attempts by Sylvain Tack to persuade Ronan O'Rahilly to purchase a new vessel had also come to nothing (see Chapter 19)

An approach was made initially to Abie Nathan to purchase from him the MV *Peace,* home of the Voice of Peace in the Mediterranean, as a fully fitted and equipped radio ship. However, this came to nothing because the price asked by Abie Nathan (16 million Belgian Francs) was considered too high, a decision Valain was later to regret.

They then went to Cyprus where a ship, the *Centricity,* was purchased for conversion into a floating radio station and, in what turned out to be a ten month operation, the vessel was secretly converted and equipped in the port of Patros, Athens. The radio and transmitting equipment was purchased from the USA, secretly shipped to Greece and installed on board without attracting any attention from the authorities. The ship was renamed *Magdalena,* after Patrick Valain's wife, Magda.

## Greenpeace

*The Greenpeace vessel 'Rainbow Warrior' visited the 'Mi Amigo' a number of times during the summer of 1979 clandestinely delivering much needed supplies to the radio ship. In return Radio Caroline gave the Greenpeace Organisation free promotions on air, tying this in with the station's Loving Awareness campaign and a shared concern about the quality of the Earth's environment. On one occasion a representatives of Greenpeace, Peter Wilkinson, was interviewed by Tony Allen and a recording of the interview was broadcast on Radio Caroline on 1st August 1979.*

*Greenpeace was founded in Vancouver, in 1971 after a group of Canadians sailed to the Aleutian Islands to try and prevent an American nuclear test taking place. The organisation, whose objective was to secure a greater environmental awareness and preservation of the Earth's resources, established an outlet in Britain in 1977.*

*Using monies from the World Wildlife Fund and supporters in Holland Greenpeace purchased a former trawler to undertake many of their campaigns, including those against whaling off Iceland, the grey seal cull off the Orkneys and the dumping of nuclear waste in the Atlantic. The vessel was renamed 'Rainbow Warrior' -derived from an American Indian legend - "when the Earth is sick and the animals disappear the Warriors of the Rainbow will come to protect the wildlife and to heal the Earth."*

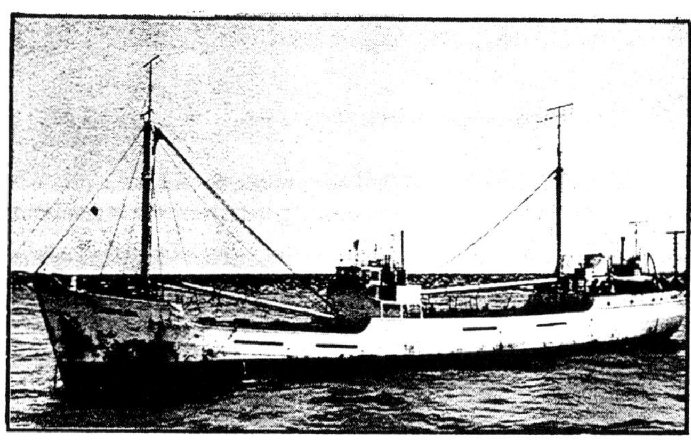

'Magdelana' home to Radio Mi Amigo 272

Unfortunately everything took a lot longer than originally expected, but the *Magdalena* left Greece in the early summer of 1979. However, she soon experienced engine failure and had to be towed through the Corinth Canal back to Patros, where repairs were carried out - adding a further one million Belgian Francs to the cost of the project. Altogether it was estimated that the re-launch of Radio Mi Amigo had cost 18 million Belgian Francs - nearly two million more than Abie Nathan had originally asked for his full equipped radio ship.

After months of rumours since Radio Mi Amigo had closed in October 1978 after the failure of the MV *Mi Amigo's* generator, the new ship finally appeared on the North Sea anchoring in various locations in mid-June 1979 and finally ending up in a position near the Thornton Bank, off the coast of Belgium.

Test broadcasts started on 25th June 1979 using a 10Kw transmitter on 1100kHz (272.72m -a non- EBU channel). These tests of continuous music, with occasional announcements to the effect that it was Radio Mi Amigo 272, continued for three days and, after a further two days silence, resumed again on 1st July 1979. The station officially opened at 12 noon that day staffed by two Belgian DJs, Ton Schipper and Ben van Praag and four Dutchmen, Wim de Groot, Daniel Bolan, Johan Vermeer and Jerry Hoogland.

The planned 24 hour a day programming lasted less than a week and then the station began to close at various times during the evening ranging from 7.00pm to 12 midnight. Radio Mi Amigo 272 adopted a much stricter format than its predecessor, with specific percentages of airtime being allocated to records from the Hit Parade (33%), records from the Tipparade (new releases) (25%), Flashbacks (12%) and Album tracks (4%).

Additionally one record in ten were a listener request and one in twenty had to be in the Flemish language. The re-launched station, which was aimed primarily at a Flemish speaking audience, also had its own magazine, *Mi Amigo Fanblad*, published in Belgium by the Mi Amigo Fan Club.

### 'Wavelength' case

*The case against two Directors of Music Radio Promotions, Mike Baron and Nic Oakley finally came to Court, after almost two years, in mid-1979. Judge Justice Gordon Friend instructed the jury to study twelve advertisements in 'Wavelength' and decide if any of them implied that Radio Caroline was still broadcasting. The jury decided that four of the advertisements did promote the station and the two defendants were fined £50 for each offence, but costs were not awarded. Both Mike Baron and Nic Oakley announced their intention to appeal against their convictions.*

## Problems continue

Rumours about the ownership of the re-launched Radio Mi Amigo began to circulate almost as soon as the station returned to the air. Some Belgian newspapers claimed that Sylvain Tack, if he had ever owned the *Magdalena*, had sold her before broadcasts began, possibly to Adriaan van Landschoot (ex-owner of Radio Atlantis) and that the use of the name 'Mi Amigo' had resulted in Tack's villa in Spain being searched by the authorities. In fact the *Magdalena* was owned by Patrick Valain, who purchased it using the Honduran registered company, Magdalena Shipping and Commercial Enterprises.

Radio Mi Amigo 272 was off the air frequently during the late summer of 1979 as the result of transmitter and generator failures. However, on 9th September 1979 when the station returned to the air after one of these breaks engineers had managed to tune the transmitter to an EBU frequency of 1098kHz (273.5m), which considerably improved reception, particularly during the hours of darkness, although it continued to be announced as 'Radio Mi Amigo 272'.

The *Magdalena* lost her anchor on 2nd August 1979 and for seven days she sailed around the Thornton Bank. In the absence of any proper equipment the crew eventually tried to anchor the vessel by throwing overboard an old motor which was attached by chains to both sides of the ship.

Not surprisingly this temporary arrangement did not work and on 14th September 1979 the *Magdalena* dragged her 'anchor' yet again, this time drifting in a north easterly direction off the Belgian coast. For two days she managed to hold a position ten miles from her normal anchorage, but on 17th September the vessel drifted onto Middle Deep Sandbank eight miles off the coast of Walcheren Island. Changing wind directions during the night sent the ship drifting once again, this time northwards towards the Belgian coast, while the crew and DJs battled to try and start the ship's engines. They did not succeed because there was no one on board who could operate the compressor mechanism.

By the morning of 18th September 1979 the radio ship had drifted 28 miles from her usual anchorage position. Radio Mi Amigo 272 opened transmissions half an hour earlier than usual at 6.00am, but stopped after only 10 minutes because the ship was being forced further and further towards shore.

No one was available to continue radio broadcasts because all DJs and crew on board were needed to try and start the engines. A desperate attempt to do this was made using a DC generator to run the compressor, but this failed when the generator cut out completely. Meanwhile, the *Magdalena* continued drifting and during the morning of 19th September 1979, in a Force 8 gale, she entered Dutch territorial waters. Shortly before nightfall that same day the radio ship finally ran aground on the Aardappelenbult Sandbank, between the islands of Goeree and Overflakkee.

The Stellendam lifeboat was launched and came alongside the *Magdalena,* but the Radio Mi Amigo 272 staff - three engineers and five DJs- decided to stay on board the stranded radio ship even though during the night she became more firmly embedded on the sandbank.

The *Magdalena* remained lodged on the sandbank for two days until, on the morning of 21st September 1979, the police launch *Delfshaven* went out and officially arrested the radio ship. The eight man crew on board was informed that the ship was to be towed into Maasluis before they themselves were removed from the vessel. Two Belgian nationals were handed over to the Belgian authorities, while the Dutchmen were arrested and held in custody for two days.

An unsuccessful attempt was made by the salvage tug *Dolfijn* to pull the *Magdalena* from the sandbank on 22nd September 1979 but it was not until mid-afternoon the following day that the police launch *RP9* managed to free the radio ship.

## Radio Mi Amigo 272 programme schedule, July 1979

*Monday-Friday*

**12 midnight** Hits na Twaalf (Hits After Twelve)

**1.00am** Lichte Non-Stop Muziek (Non-stop Light Music)

**4.00am** Welkon in de Wereld der Wakkeren (Welcome to the Wake-up World)

**6.00am** Ook Goeie Morgen (Good Morning to You, Too)

**8.00am** Schijven voor Bedrijven (Slices for Industry)

**9.00am** Keukenpret (Kitchen Fun)

**11.00am** Lunch op Zee (Lunch on the Sea)

**1.00pm** Middagpauze (Afternoon Pause)

**3.00pm** Stuurboord (Starboard)

**5.00pm** Muziekdoos (Music Box) - Request Show

**6.00pm** Varia (A Musical Miscellany)

**7.00pm** Zestig Gouden Minuten (Sixty Golden Minutes) - Oldies

**8.00pm** Geef ze een kans (Give them a Chance) - New Releases

**9.00pm** Op Wacht tot Middernacht (On Watch till Midnight)

**12 midnight** Closedown

*Saturday*

**8.00am** Muziektrien (Music Train)

**9.00am** Keukenpret

**11.00am** Belgische Nationale Hitparade

**2.00pm** Nationale Tipparade

**4.00pm** Weekend Action

**5.00pm** onwards- As weekdays

*Sunday*

**8.00am** Dixieland

**9.00am** Theater

**10.00am** Belgische Top 15

**11.00am** Puzzeluur (Puzzle Hour)

**12noon** Metamorfose

**1.00pm** All Around Hits

**2.00pm** Soul Party

**4.00pm** Club 33 (Album Tracks)

**5.00pm** onwards -As weekdays

Once re-floated the listing *Magdalena* was towed by the salvage tug *Furie II* to the small harbour of Stellendam while a temporary repair was made to her leaking hull. She was then taken on to Willemstad where she arrived on 24th September 1979 and, after a short time in this port, the radio ship was moved yet again to the van der Marel scrapyard at Zierlkzee, south of Utrecht, where police ordered that she should be scrapped as unseaworthy.

The scrapyard owner (who had previously bought and scrapped the Radio Caroline North ship, MV *Caroline,* and the Radio Scotland ship, *Comet*) purchased the *Magdalena* for 14,000 Dutch Guilders and she was broken up in October 1979.

Meanwhile, Radio Mi Amigo 272 DJ Ferry Eden put a brave face on the situation: -"We'll be back" he announced, "whatever happens to the ship." The Mi Amigo organisation and the Honduran consul in Holland both made formal complaints to the Dutch Government about the way in which the police had impounded the *Magdalena* and ordered her scrapping, but to no avail.

## Radio Delmare

On 5th January 1979 the Dutch police towed a ship, the 500 ton *Epivan* (also known as *Scheveningen 54, Helena* and originally *Oceaan IX,* a sister ship to *Oceaan VII*, home of the 1960s British offshore station Radio 270) into Scheveningen Harbour on suspicion that she was being fitted out as a radio ship. The vessel had left port hurriedly in December 1978 fearing a raid by the authorities and had spent some time alongside the *Mi Amigo* at anchor in the North Sea (see Chapter 19). When the vessel was searched, however, no transmitting equipment was found as it had already been removed and abandoned before the ship was towed into port.

In the spring of 1979 Gerard van Dam visited Italy, where at that time there were many private landbased stations operating because there was no strong Government in power to take action against them. He also went to Ireland where a similar situation existed with landbased pirates operating without little action taken against them by the authorities.

While in Italy van Dam bought a small station in Monte Marcello, Telealto Adriatico, which he renamed Radio Delmare Italia. Links were also established with landbased pirate Radio Dublin in Ireland and a system was then devised for broadcasting Radio Delmare programmes. They were aired first on the Italian station for the benefit of Dutch holidaymakers; tapes were also sent to Radio Dublin and, by a 'mysterious coincidence', would then appear on a radio ship from where they would be broadcast to the main target audience in Holland and Belgium. To cover this complicated situation Radio Delmare gave out two addresses on air for listeners' requests one in Italy and one in Holland.

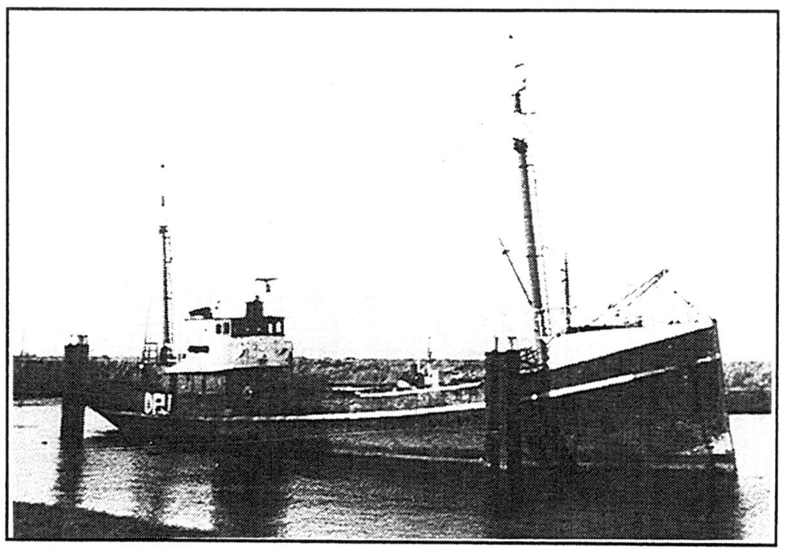

'Martina' ('Aegir II') in May 1979

In April 1979 Gerard van Dam leased the *Martina* for use as his radio ship. The Dutch authorities, suspicious of what was going on, boarded the ship in the port of Jacobshaven the same month, but were unable to take any action because there was no transmitting equipment on board at that time. On 29th April 1979 the *Martina* (now known unofficially as *Aegir II*) sailed quietly out of

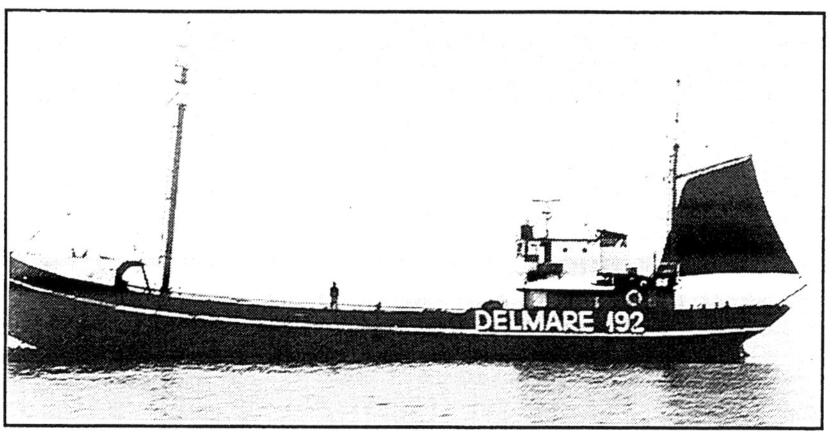


'Martina' ('Aegir II') at sea

Jacobshaven and anchored off the coast of Goeree in the same position as the former Radio Delmare ship *Aegir* in August 1978 and remained there awaiting the installation of radio equipment.

The planned re-launch of Radio Delmare received a setback in May 1979, when after some landbased transmissions had been conducted to test equipment, the authorities raided Gerard van Dam's premises near Antwerp and confiscated a van, speedboat, two cars and two US medium wave transmitters which were being modified for use on the radio ship.

However, van Dam quickly managed to acquire more transmitters and this time they were successfully installed on the *Martina.* On 2nd June 1979 non-stop music and Radio Delmare jingles were broadcast on 192m (1562kHz). These tests continued for about 10 days and by the middle of June 1979 a regular programme schedule had developed.

## Delmare's demise

Broadcasts from Radio Delmare continued almost without interruption until Sunday 12th August 1979 when each hour during the morning announcements were made in Dutch to the effect that the DJs had 'taken over' the station because they were dissatisfied with the way Gerard van Dam was running the operation and because he had failed to keep the vessel regularly supplied.

Radio Delmare's output generally deteriorated after this date and many of the taped programmes from the station's landbased studios were no longer aired. On 12th September 1979 an International Service was introduced from 6.00pm-10.00 or 11.00pm on 1610kHz (186m) after the usual 1562kHz (192m) transmissions had ended. By the third week of September 1979 only one person remained on board the *Martina* - Johan Rood the engineer and he was running the station single-handedly including presentation of all programmes! Unfortunately during the early evening of 28th September 1979 the station's signal faded out and Radio Delmare was never heard again. During its short life Radio Delmare, despite all its transmission difficulties, had received over 8,000 letters and reception reports from listeners.

### Radio Delmare programme schedule, June 1979

*Monday-Friday*

**5.00am Non-Stop Music**

**6.00am Wakker met de Bakker (Awake with the Bakker),** *Ronald Bakker*

**8.00am Musiekfabriek (Non-Stop Music)**

**9.00am Tussen Wal en Schip (Between Shore and Ship),** *Astrid de Jager*

**10.00am Peter van der Holst/ Jon Anderson**

**11.00am Kaasschaaf (Cheeseslicer),** *Kees "Kaas" Mulder*

**1.00pm Holster de Spijker,** *Peter van der Holst*

**3.00pm In het Hol van de Leeuw (In the Den of the Lion),** *Rene de Leeuw*

**5.00pm Verzoeking, record requests**

**6.00pm Sponsored programme**

**7.00pm Closedown**

*Saturday*

**5.00am Non Stop Music**

**7.00am Jan Olienoot**

**9.00am Ronald Bakker**

**10.00am Gerald van der Zee**

**11.00am Kees "Kaas" Mulder**

**1.00pm Delmare Top 30,**

**3.00pm Disco Power,** *Ronald van der Vlugt*

**5.00pm Verzoeking,** *Gerard van der Zee*

**6.00pm Sponsored Programme**

**7.00pm Closedown**

*Sunday*

**5.00am As Saturday**

**10.00am De Ab Surd Show**

**10.30am Gerard van der Zee**

**11.00am Sunday Special, live with all on-board DJs**

**4.00pm Disco Power**

**5.00-7.00pm As Saturday**

On 8th October 1979 five people were arrested in Stellendam Harbour for trying to take supplies to the Radio Delmare ship, *Martina*. They had apparently set out but were unable to find the radio ship and returned to the harbour still carrying the supplies.

By the beginning of October 1979, with Radio Delmare now silent, Johan Rood had been replaced on the *Martina* by the ship's owner Mr. Keers. When supplies failed to reach the ship because of the arrests in Stellendam Harbour Keers decided to raise the anchor himself and sail for port. Before doing so, however, he tried to disguise the ship by changing her name to *Deli* and obscuring the radio station's name and wavelength which had been painted along the vessel's side.

He had single-handedly achieved this 'disguise' by the end of the month and on 31st October 1979 set sail for Stellendam, but the ship's engines failed just as she was entering harbour and she had to be taken in tow by a local fishing trawler. Police and PTT officials were waiting at the quayside for the former radio ship and an arrest notice was attached to her mast. The following day she was towed by police launch to a berth at Willemstad.

Meanwhile, despite the lack of success with re-launching Radio Delmare Gerard van Dam was not prepared to give up the idea of operating an offshore radio station. He acquired another ship, MV *Poolster,* and started converting her in Scheveningen Harbour as the base for another proposed offshore station, Radio Capri. However, hearing of a raid being planned by police the ship hurriedly sailed on 24th October 1979 amidst rumours that she was heading for Spain to be fitted out as a new ship for Radio Mi Amigo 272, now that their vessel *Magdalena* had been scrapped. Nothing more was heard of Radio Capri or the *Poolster* in connection with offshore radio, but Gerard van Dam continued with a number of other offshore radio schemes.

Johan Rood, appeared before Antwerp Magistrates Court on 4th January 1980, charged with working for an offshore radio station. The case was adjourned until 18th January when he was found guilty of the charges, fined 800 Belgian Francs (£13) and given an 8 months suspended prison sentence.

After this case Rood was conscripted for National Service in the Belgian Army, but nevertheless he maintained contacts with members of the Delmare Clan (the station's fan club) through a newsletter and plans were announced to re-launch the station again from a landbase in Italy. Profits from advertising on this station, together with contributions from Delmare Clan members and income from a roadshow disco touring the Dutch coast, with guest appearances from Radio Delmare DJs, were to be used to equip a new radio ship, possibly anchored off the British coast broadcasting an English language service.

After Johan Rood had completed his National service he again became involved in plans to re-launch an offshore version of Radio Delmare from the *Morgenster.* However, in May 1981 this vessel, which at one time had been a tender for Radio Caroline, was impounded in Amsterdam by Dutch police, who found studio equipment, but no radio transmitter, on board. After this incident there do not appear to have been any further attempts to re-launch Radio Delmare from an offshore base.

Radio Delmare subsequently split into two distinct groups in Belgium and Holland. The Belgian group, under the control of Johan Rood, transmitted as a landbased pirate on FM and shortwave from Antwerp each Sunday. This group was supported in Britain by the Delmare Roadshow which was operated for some time by Colin Ward. Meanwhile, the Dutch group (Delmare Omroep Organisatie), under the control of Gerard van Dam, tried to obtain legal status on the Hilversum network.

On 29th April 1980 five people appeared in court in Amsterdam charged under the Dutch Marine Offences Act with equipping a ship for use as a radio station. The charges related to the original Radio Delmare vessel, *Aegir,* which had been raided in Scheveningen in September 1978, before the radio station had even commenced transmissions for the first time. In Court were Gerard van Dam, Astrid Bos, Freek van Dijk, Jan de Kat and Steph Willemse (who had previously been involved with Radio Condor in 1973). Nine others also had charges against them pending, including five crew from the *Aegir,* three others who had been arrested on board the *Scheveningen 54* (*Epivan*) when she was impounded in January 1979 (on suspicion of being fitted out as a new ship for Radio Delmare) and the ninth who was accused of tendering the *Aegir.* The court hearing was adjourned until September 1980.

## Radio Caroline

The Dutch Service of Radio Caroline experienced severe staff shortages in October 1979 and English DJs had to sit in and present many live programmes, while tapes of previously broadcast programmes were also repeated, sometimes more than once.

This situation of staff and supply shortages came to a head on 11th October 1979, when instead of starting the usual American religious programme tapes Radio Caroline closed its transmitter after an announcement by DJ Stephen Bishop. The English staff on board the *Mi Amigo* were disgruntled about the continuing staff shortages on the Dutch side of the operation and this, coupled with the shortage of fuel supplies, for which the Dutch were specifically responsible, also meant that it was impossible for Radio Caroline to maintain a 24 hour service.

Radio Caroline remained off the air throughout the following day, but returned at 7.00am on 13th October 1979 with the sponsored Dutch religious programme from Johan Maasbach, followed by continuous music for most of the remainder of the day. Fresh supplies of fuel had reached the radio ship during the hours the station had been off the air, but there were still no new programme tapes or replacement Dutch Service DJs.

From 14th October 1979 all programmes for the Dutch Service were presented by the English DJs, while the last remaining Dutch DJ, Ad Roberts, left the *Mi Amigo* to try and find out what was happening with the station's organisation in Holland. A few days later, on 17th October 1979, the situation was made worse for those left on board the *Mi Amigo* when Belgian police raided a trawler in Zeebrugge Harbour. The trawler, known simply as Z69, was carrying food and supplies to the *Mi Amigo* as well as new programme tapes for the Dutch Service of Radio Caroline.

With the Belgian tendering route now cut, four men set out in a small boat from the Kent coast during the early hours of 28th October 1979 in a desperate attempt to get more supplies to the *Mi Amigo*. However, the boat's engines failed just 600 yards from the radio ship and the crew had to be rescued by the dredger *Sandgull,* which happened to be in the area at the time. The dredger transferred the four men to a lifeboat, which in turn took them back to Margate where they were met by police. The four, two English and two Dutch were questioned, but not detained, although a number of programme tapes they were carrying were confiscated. Eventually some Dutch DJs (including the two who had been questioned by British police) reached the *Mi Amigo* and on 31st October the normal Dutch Service was able to resume.

**offshore trivia**

**Longest continuous period at sea by a radio ship**

*(1) 'Norderney' 9 years 6 months as a broadcasting radio ship (February 1965-August 1974); 10 years 6 months including a year from August 1974-August 1975 silent at anchor)*

*(2) 'Ross Revenge' 7 years 3 months as a broadcasting ship (August 1983-November 1990); 8 years 3 months including a year from November 1990-November 1991 silent at anchor)*

*(3) MV 'Peace' 18 years 4 months from June 1975-October 1993, but including frequent visits to port for repair and inspections).*

Storms hit the *Mi Amigo* in late November 1979 and from 26th November until 5th December only taped programmes were aired on the Dutch Service, with the news service being suspended altogether. As the result of improved tendering arrangements regular fuel supplies were now reaching the *Mi Amigo* and Radio Caroline was able to achieve 24 hours a day programming again from 14th December 1979 with the English Service taking up the additional three hours after 2.00am.

## New Year 'stability'

Both Dutch and English Services of Radio Caroline continued virtually as scheduled throughout the first three months of 1980, although an increasing number of taped (rather than live) Dutch language programmes appeared after the beginning of March. Also the weekly hour-long French language programme, which had been instigated in October 1979, was discontinued after the middle of January 1980.

Throughout this period too the number of taped American religious programmes broadcast by Radio Caroline continued to increase steadily with a total of thirty one different organisations buying airtime, providing the station with its only real source of revenue. Whilst essential financially the increased airtime allocated to these broadcasts undoubtedly had a detrimental effect on the station's audience levels - claimed to be 3.9 million in early 1980, although in reality it was thought to be nearer 750,000.

A further problem with tendering the *Mi Amigo* came in February 1980 when a Belgian fishing boat, *Hosanna,* disappeared in the English Channel. Although mystery surrounded the disappearance it was assumed that the boat had been hit by another vessel, possibly a supertanker, and sunk almost without trace.

Despite an extensive search the only evidence ever recovered of the Hosanna was a liferaft bearing her official number, Z592. A funeral service was held in Zeebrugge for the crew, three Belgians and two Dutchmen, including skipper Germain Ackx and his son Piet.

Gales and heavy seas returned to the North Sea on 19th March 1980, but Radio Caroline's Dutch Service, now containing mostly pre-recorded programmes, continued as normal with listeners unaware of the drama unfolding that day on board the *Mi Amigo*. The first hint of a problem came at 3.28pm when Dutch programmes were interrupted for an announcement in English. The message "number 59, 60 and code 7 within three hours" was read out "for the office" and repeated again an hour later. Then, every hour from 5.00pm onwards code numbers 59, 60 and 25 were broadcast at the top of the hour.

The code numbers were, of course, meaningless to the majority of listeners but for those actually involved with the operation of the station they indicated something was seriously wrong on board the radio ship.

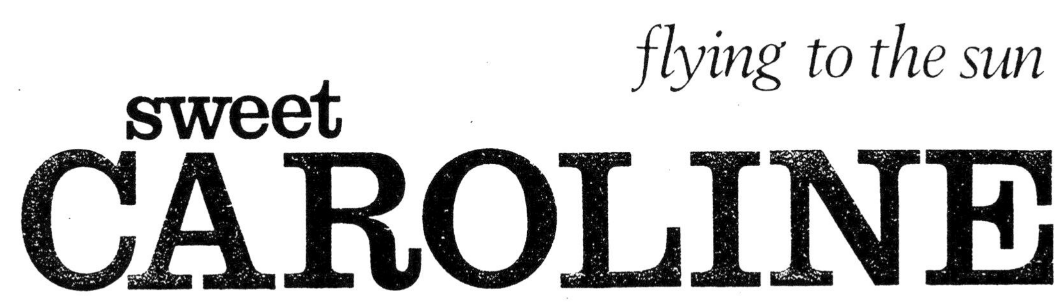

## Communications and Codes

*With true irony the offshore stations - whose business was communication - had to operate without any direct radio or telephone contact with their landbased offices.*

*Except for emergency situations ship-to-shore radio communications were usually cut off by the authorities and the cellular mobile telephone was an invention which only came late in the history of offshore radio. There were some exceptions, most notably the Voice of Peace with Abie Nathan's famous (or infamous) Motorola, but for the most part stations had to devise alternative means of relaying urgent messages to their offices.*

*They quickly learnt that on-air messages during programmes were unprofessional and, although used many times during emergency situations, often resulted in listeners jamming emergency services switchboards with calls. The raid on the 'Mebo II' in 1970 and the fire-bomb attack on the same radio ship in 1971 are prime examples of this problem.*

*A number of alternative methods were devised:-*

- *Records with a message in the title or lyric played during normal programmes to signify that assistance was needed (for example Radio City used "You Got Your Troubles" by the Fortunes while Radio Caroline relied on "Caroline" by the Fortunes, and in later years "Lady in Red" by Chris de Burgh, or a combination of these and others as during the raid on the 'Ross Revenge' in 1989.*
- *Live or pre-recorded messages often relayed during early morning hours when audience levels were small. The taped messages were sometimes transmitted at high speed, or even backwards, to appear inexplicable to the average listener. Radio Nord used this method regularly after its ship-to-shore communications had been cut.*
- *A system of code numbers which were read out by the on-air DJ, often at the top of the hour or just before a station closedown. Each number had a specific meaning - low fuel, anchor chain broken, ship adrift or just mundane supply requests such as specific foodstuffs or items of equipment which needed restocking. The code numbers, and their meanings, were changed regularly to avoid the possibility of being 'cracked' by the authorities. The code number system was used extensively by stations on board the 'Mi Amigo' in the 1970s and later on the 'Ross Revenge' to call for assistance in times of distress*
- *Perhaps the most sophisticated system was that aboard the Laser 558 ship, 'Communicator', which used satellite facilities to transmit messages between the ship and the land based contacts in Britain and America. Although for much of the station's life the satellite system was not functioning it was used on occasions, but proved very expensive and was never used for its primary purpose - to relay advertising copy direct from the New York airtime sales agents to the ship for same day broadcast.*
- *A number of stations also engaged in unauthorised or unlicensed two-way communications systems and there are a number of recorded incidents where people employing this type of communication on a beach or sea front location were apprehended by the authorities. Perhaps the most elaborate example of this type of communication system was that employed by RNI from the Grand Hotel in Scheveningen, where a bedroom was taken over and used to house radio telephone equipment linked to the 'Mebo II'.*

## *Mi Amigo* sinks

When the English Service of Radio Caroline started at 7.00pm none of the regular programmes were aired, just continuous music and the hourly coded messages for the office. The enormity of the problems being experienced by the crew on board the *Mi Amigo* only became fully apparent at midnight when Steve Gordon and Tom Anderson came on the air to make this announcement :-

*We're sorry to tell you that due to severe weather conditions and also to the fact that we're shipping quite a lot of water, we're closing down and the crew are at this stage leaving the ship. Obviously we hope to be back with you as soon as possible, but we'd just like to assure you all on land that there's nothing to worry about. We're all quite safe. Just for the moment we'd like to say goodbye. Tom?*

*Yes it's not a very good occasion really. I have to hurry this because the lifeboat is standing by. We're not leaving and disappearing, we're going into the lifeboat hoping that the pumps can take it. If they can we'll be back; if not, well I don't like to say it.*

*I think we'll be back one way or another, Tom.*

*Yes I think so.*

*From all of us, for the moment, goodbye and God-bless.*

What had been happening earlier in the day was that the radio ship's anchor chain had broken at about 1.30pm and she began to drift. The crew worked for two hours to lower the emergency anchor, which they succeeded in doing at about 4.30pm, but the *Mi Amigo* had by then hit the edge of the Long Sand sandbank. Apart from the coded messages no announcements or pleas for assistance were broadcast to listeners and anyway the situation at that time seemed stable enough with the ship having settled firmly on the sandbank at low water, a scenario which had been experienced many times before by the *Mi Amigo* and her crews.

The Coastguard Service had been advised of the problem over the emergency channel and they arranged for a lifeboat to be placed on stand-by. A short while later, at 6.15pm, with weather conditions deteriorating, the Sheerness lifeboat, *Helen Turnbull,* was launched and waited about a mile from the radio ship until it could get closer once the tide started to rise. For about two hours the crew of the lifeboat, now only 50 yards from the *Mi Amigo*, tried to persuade the four men on board to leave.

However, by about 9.30pm, with the tide rising, the *Mi Amigo* was being repeatedly pounded on the sandbank in the heavy seas and Force 9 easterly gales. Without warning she started to take in a huge volume of water and for a while the crew still refused to leave the vessel, preferring instead to try and sit out the storm and hope the emergency pumps would be able to cope until a tender arrived to tow them back to their normal anchorage.

Although during her 18 years as a home to so many radio stations the *Mi Amigo* had experienced countless such dramas, the situation this time deteriorated so quickly that the pumps could not cope with the volume of water cascading in through holes in her hull.

In the end the crew had to abandon ship in such a hurry that they did not even have time to pack their personal belongings. The station's master tapes, which had been packed in a waterproof bag also had to be left behind. It took the lifeboat nearly an hour to get the four men (DJs Tom Anderson, Steve Gordon, Dutch DJ/crew member Hans van der Laan -real name Ton Lathouwers) and Wilson II, the ship's canary, off the sinking radio ship. The crew of the lifeboat repeatedly risked their lives in mountainous seas to successfully achieve this rescue operation.

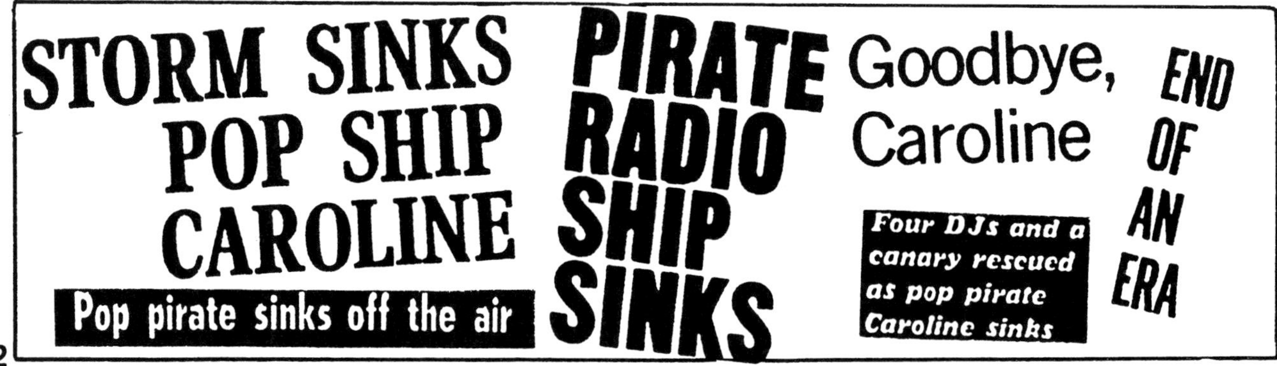

The *Mi Amigo's* generator had been left running to provide power for the abandoned vessel's navigation lights, but as they headed for land the crew of the lifeboat reported seeing the radio ship's lights go out. Three hours later the rescued crew were landed at Sheerness and interviewed by police, acting on instructions from the Home Office. Police later announced that the DJs rescued from the *Mi Amigo* would not face prosecution.

At first light on 20th March 1980 an RAF helicopter flew over the area and reported that the *Mi Amigo* had sunk, with only some superstructure and the 134' aerial mast remaining above water. Within a few days Trinity House had marked the wreck with buoys and issued an official warning to shipping in the area. On 25th March 1980 a Notice to Mariners was published stating the position of the sunken vessel and warning that under the provisions of Sections 530 and 531 of the Merchant Shipping Act 1894 the Corporation of Trinity House had taken possession of the wreck and its contents and that nothing could be removed from the sunken vessel without permission.

On the morning of Thursday 20th March 1980, for the first time in nearly 22 years, there was no offshore radio ship broadcasting off the coast of Europe.

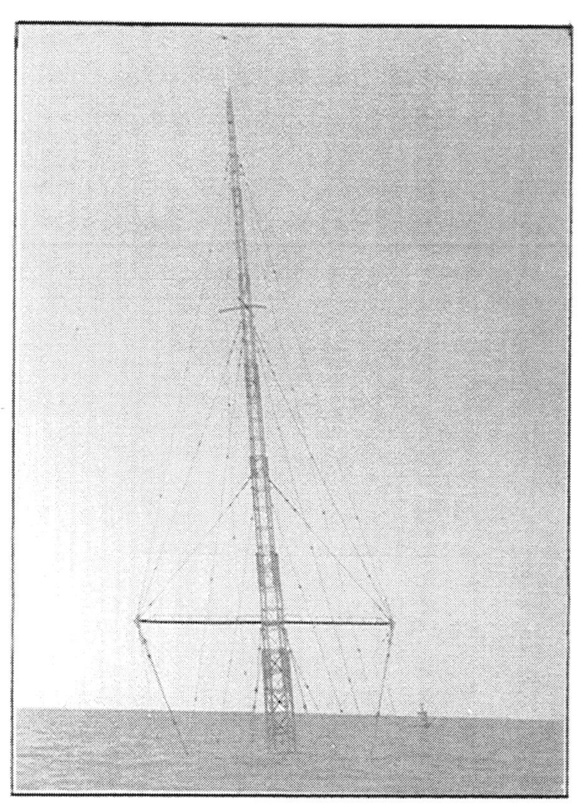

*Only the 'Mi Amigo's' aerial mast remained above water after the radio ship sank in March 1980. The mast survived for six years before itself collapsing beneath the waves.*

The end came very quickly for the *Mi Amigo* and although the ship was old and in a very poor condition, the reason for her sinking was generally regarded as dating back to the occasion in September 1976 when she had gone adrift. At that time the anchor chain had become trapped under the ship and caused damage to some of the hull plates as the *Mi Amigo* was constantly bounced on the sandbank by the rising tide. This action resulted in a total of twenty seven small holes later appearing in the hull which the crew had 'repaired' by inserting a wooden bung to seal the leak, then concreting over the surrounding area. It was the cracking of these concrete repairs as the *Mi Amigo* landed on the Long Sand, which caused leaks of such magnitude that normal pumping operations could not cope.

## Plans to re-float the *Mi Amigo*

Almost immediately after the sinking plans were announced to try and re-float the *Mi Amigo* using giant air filled bags and a floating collar. A number of personnel connected with Radio Caroline also talked positively in press interviews about the station returning "within a matter of weeks".

The Caroline Roadshow Disco, which had been touring the south east of England for several months as an operation connected with, but separate from the radio station, continued after the *Mi Amigo* had sunk, providing a focal point for many of Radio Caroline's supporters and former listeners. Ex-Radio Caroline DJ Robb Eden operated the Roadshow and he fronted plans to raise funds for re-floating the *Mi Amigo*. There were some press reports that Thanet District Council were willing to help fund the re-floating of the *Mi Amigo* with the objective of turning her into a museum and tourist attraction berthed somewhere in Kent.

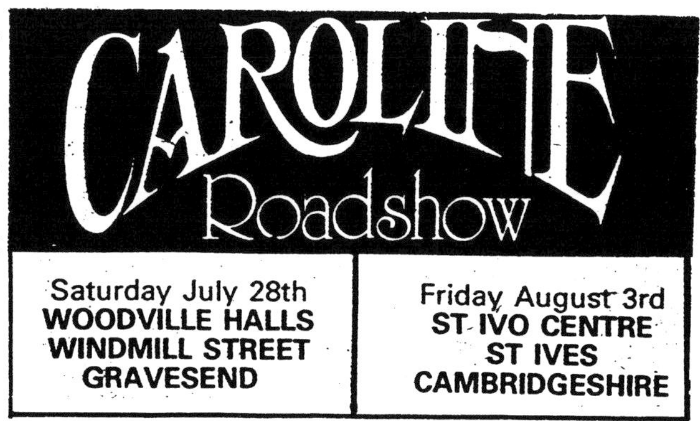


In fact representatives of the Caroline Roadshow visited various sites in Kent and held informal discussions with officers of Thanet Council about a site

## Lifeboat Rescue

For the crew of the *Helen Turnbull* the rescue from the *Mi Amigo* had been the most hazardous they had ever dealt with. The Lifeboat itself had to contend with mountainous seas on its journey out to Long Sands, had waited for over two hours while the *Mi Amigo* re-floated on the rising tide and then had to come alongside the radio ship in a number of extremely dangerous manoeuvres to rescue the crew. The following extract from an article in the RNLI journal *The Lifeboat* gives a flavour of just what the crew had to endure that night:-

*".......At 8.20pm the lifeboat was off NE Shingles Buoy and speed was further reduced to confirm position before starting to cross into Black Deep at half speed. A quarter of an hour later the lifeboat was off No 12 Black Deep Buoy and the casualty could be seen on Long Sand shoal; VHF contact was made with 'Mi Amigo' on Channel 6.*

*'Mi Amigo' was between two and three cables north north west of NW Long Sands Beacon, her anchor streamed to the north east and her bow also north east. She reported to the lifeboat that she was aground and was trying to get some pumps working; there were four people on board, all wearing lifejackets.*

*Seas were breaking right over the ship and Coxswain Bowry estimated that she was in about two feet of water; Thames Coastguard further estimated that she would be afloat at about 11.15pm and Coxswain Bowry decided to maintain position in Black Deep between No. 10 and 12 Buoys; minimum revolutions were kept on the engines to reduce the rolling and violent pounding of the lifeboat in the very heavy seas. The easterly gale was still Force 9, gusting to storm Force 10, and very rough. Short breaking seas were building up, they could be seen peaking and becoming confused as they met the edge of Long Sand Bank.*

*At 10.36pm 'Mi Amigo' called to say that she was now afloat but could still not start her pumps. Coxswain Bowry decided to close and began to crab in from the north west trying to keep head to sea, with Second Coxswain Arthur Lukey calling out depths from the echo sounder and another crew member on the radar giving distances off so that the Coxswain could concentrate on handling his boat in the breaking seas.*

*At 11.05pm the lifeboat was about two lengths astern of 'Mi Amigo's' port quarter and the radio ship could be seen to be pitching and rolling heavily and shipping seas overall. The lifeboat herself was rolling heavily in the confused seas and putting her side decks under. Coxswain Bowry urged the casualty's crew to abandon before their ship either sank or parted her anchor cable, but they did not realise the danger. It was only when they asked for their gear to be taken off and the lifeboat approached, so that she could be seen at one moment 20 feet below them on deck and then as much above them, that the danger was appreciated. They asked to be taken off at 11.50pm.*

*The lifeboat dropped back to 100 feet off 'Mi Amigo's' starboard quarter and as the confused seas gave no lee on either side Coxswain Bowry decided to try to come in on her starboard side where some rubber tyres would act as fenders. He told the four men to gather just aft of midships.*

*Second Coxswain Lukey and three other crew members lashed themselves inside the foreward guardrails with their safety lines while the last crew member stood between the wheelhouse and the rails on the port side to hand the survivors aft. Coxswain Bowry then tried to approach so that the lifeboat would come alongside between the peaks; three attempts were made and had to be abandoned as the lifeboat was in danger of being landed on the casualty's decks, but a fourth attempt was successful. One of the survivors was plucked off, then full helm and engines had to be used to take the lifeboat clear before the casualty's counter stern slammed down on her.*

*Another four unsuccessful attempts were made before the lifeboat again managed to close 'Mi Amigo' and a second of her crew could be pulled aboard. Then a third member of her crew ran down the deck with a canary in a cage and jumped aboard. His action caught everyone unprepared and the lifeboat could not get clear in time; she was caught by the next sea and flung against the ship's side. Luckily the crew member by the wheelhouse managed to jump clear and avoid injury. Three more attempts were made to take off the last survivor who could be seen clinging to a stanchion as waves swept the vessel, but without success. Then at the fourth run in at 12.25am he was safely pulled aboard the lifeboat.*

*The lifeboat was quickly taken into deep water and time spent re-tuning the radar and obtaining an exact position before course was set for Sheerness at 12.40am. Passage was made as fast as possible in the prevailing weather and the lifeboat arrived at 3.00am. She was refuelled and once again ready for service at 3.40am........"*

The crew of the *Helen Turnbull* that night were - Charles Bowry (Coxswain), Ian Mc Court, William Edwards, Arthur Lukely (Second Coxswain), Malcolm Keen and Roderick Underhill. The Coxswain and his crew were subsequently presented with bravery awards by the RNLI.

for the ship to berth and be transformed into a museum, but these plans met with some local opposition and were taken no further, either by the Council or the Caroline Roadshow.

NOTICE TO MARINERS

(No.48 of 1980)

EAST COAST OF ENGLAND

THAMES ESTUARY

WRECK

"MI AMIGO"

Latitude 51° 35' 00" N., Longitude 01° 17' 20" E.

The Wreck "MI AMIGO", which lies sunk in the position defined above, has been marked by means of a Lighted Buoy, as follows:-

MI AMIGO LIGHTED BUOY :

*Position* : 320° about 450 feet from the Wreck

*Description* : Can: Red: Exhibiting a Very Quick Flashing Red Light.

Notice is hereby given to all concerned in the Ship and Cargo that the Corporation of Trinity House has taken possession of the Wreck under Sections 530 and 531 of the Merchant Shipping Act, 1894, and that nothing may be taken therefrom without permission.

By Order,

L.N.POTTER

*Secretary*

TRINITY HOUSE,
LONDON, EC3N 4DH.

*25th March, 1980.*

560/13/7

Plans to attempt a salvage operation were soon shelved, however, when divers inspected the wreck of the *Mi Amigo* only a matter of weeks after the sinking. It was discovered that the ship had settled firmly on the bottom of the sea-bed and, reportedly, was in danger of breaking up. Further inspections were made by divers during the early summer months of 1980, but with salvage costs estimated to be in the region of £32,000 and donations of only £5,000 having been raised the re-floating plan was finally dropped altogether.

## Plans to re-launch Radio Caroline

Almost as soon as the *Mi Amigo* had sunk representatives of Radio Caroline were stating publicly that the station would return to the air from another vessel and it was reported that the station's backers had been looking for a new ship anyway, even before the *Mi Amigo* had gone down.

Plans to purchase a new ship to replace the ageing *Mi Amigo* had been mooted for some time. Ronan O'Rahilly, Peter Chicago and Sylvain Tack (owner of Radio Mi Amigo and also part owner of the radio ship) even met in Paris to discuss the various possibilities because they realised that the *Mi Amigo* was in a bad state. However, the money to purchase a replacement vessel was not available, or forthcoming, and the plans were shelved, although some enquiries about potential vessels were tentatively followed up. In the meantime of course Radio Mi Amigo had left the Caroline organisation, acquired its own vessel (*Magdalena*) and been re-launched briefly as Radio Mi Amigo 272 during June

First press reports speculating on the return of Radio Caroline appeared at the beginning of August 1980 when the *Kent Evening Post* announced that the station would be back on the air, on FM stereo as well as medium wave, before the end of the year. According to this report a new ship, a former Norwegian coaster was being fitted out in northern Spain and would be ready to anchor near to the former position of the *Mi Amigo* by the end of December 1980.

The source of this news item was attributed to "Caroline spokesman Dave Harriott". However, a month later, on September 8th 1980 the same source was again quoted in the *Kent Evening Post* saying that plans to re-launch the station had been halted by "money troubles and a strike." Supposedly the Norwegian coaster had been gutted and studios installed when the conversion was halted by a dock workers' strike and, in the meantime, the Spanish authorities had also impounded transmitting equipment brought over from America.

Other speculative reports in September 1980 spoke of Radio Caroline's return "later in the year " from a new ship, broadcasting 24 hours a day using shortwave as well as medium wave and one report even suggested that there would be a 24 hour television station showing feature films. Needless to say nothing definite ever came of these stories, but later it will be seen that each contained some

> **Tribute to Radio Caroline**
>
> *London ILR station, Capital Radio, broadcast a two hour tribute to Radio Caroline on 15th August 1980 (the 13th anniversary of the Marine etc. Broadcasting (Offences) Act coming into force). The programme, presented by Nicky Horne, contained an hour long documentary covering the 16 year history of Caroline and included interviews with Ronan O'Rahilly, and former Caroline DJs Tony Blackburn, Robbie Dale, Johnnie Walker and Chris Carey (Spangles Muldoon).*
>
> *The second hour was devoted to listeners requests for their favourite records from Caroline in the 60s and 70s. Other ex-Caroline DJs Mark Lawrence, James Ross and Steve Kent talked about life on board the 'Mi Amigo' in the 70s while Johnny Jason related his experience of being prosecuted under the Marine etc. Broadcasting (Offences) Act.*
>
> *The tribute ended with Steve Gordon relating the story of the final night of the 'Mi Amigo' and the dramatic lifeboat rescue of the crew. Nicky Horne then closed the programme on an optimistic note with "Fool if You Think it's Over".*

elements of truth about what was really happening behind the scenes to bring back Radio Caroline.

Apart from the search for a suitable ship other activities had been taking place during the summer of 1980. Radio Caroline engineers had located and purchased, through Besco International in Dallas, three second-hand transmitters from radio stations in Canada and the USA which, together with various items of studio equipment were packed for transportation across the Atlantic.

The reference in the September 1980 press reports to the use of shortwave transmissions greatly surprised those close to planning Radio Caroline's return. The idea of using shortwave had been discussed secretly between Ronan O'Rahilly and Caroline's agent in America, Roy C Lindau (Vice-President of Marketing at Major Market Radio (MMR), as a possible means of attracting major USA and international advertisers. It was thought that transmissions on shortwave would open up a worldwide market and be an attractive proposition to such advertisers. The plan had supposedly been a closely guarded secret and suspicions began to be aroused as to the source feeding such information to the press, an early indication of some dissent within the Caroline organisation.

By early December 1980 stories started to appear in trade newspapers and on Thames Television in London that Radio Caroline was set to come back on the air in January 1981. This time reports spoke of Caroline operating from an office in New York's Madison Avenue and named two men behind the new organisation - known as Caroline Sales International - businessman Anthony Kramer and Vincent Monsey, a London property dealer and wine importer, who as Paul Vincent had been a DJ on Swinging Radio England in the mid 1960's. Ronan O'Rahilly was also still reported to be involved with the project "behind the scenes".

One report in the trade newspaper *Broadcast* on 1st December 1980 stated that when Radio Caroline did return it would broadcast from a new ship anchored 12 miles off Frinton-on-Sea, Essex and transmit an Adult (Album) Orientated Rock (AOR) format 24 hours a day. According to the report transmission quality on a medium wave frequency would be much improved by the use of an 'Optimod' unit, which compressed the signal, making it so clear it would be comparable to FM output.

## Conflicts and rivalry

Caroline Sales International claimed in the report to have sold $12million worth of advertising time - the equivalent of up to six minutes an hour, 14 hours a day for three months. This was mostly for international consumer products, apart from cigarettes, which at that time the station refused to consider an acceptable product to promote. Advertising rates were reported to be £130 for 30 seconds during the peak period between 6.30am and 9.30am with the station having an anticipated initial potential audience of eight million listeners in the 16-45 age group. A new ship, reported to be a converted freighter twice the size of the *Mi Amigo*, carrying a 240' mast and a 50Kw transmitter was said to have been acquired by the station.

Although containing much speculative information the *Broadcast* article revealed, for the first time, that after the *Mi Amigo* had sunk, Ronan O'Rahilly was approached by Vincent Monsey and Anthony Kramer who were planning an offshore radio station of their own - to be called Radio Amanda. Monsey and Kramer, who had established many advertising and financial contacts through their Madison Avenue operation subsequently joined with O'Rahilly in planning the return of Radio Caroline and abandoned plans for their own separate station.

Ronan O'Rahilly left Vincent Monsey in America to progress arrangements for financial backing as well as programming and advertising deals using his network of contacts. As events turned out , however, this 'arms length' arrangement was to delay Radio Caroline's return more than Ronan O'Rahilly could possibly have envisaged at the time. Anthony Kramer, an adviser rather than a financial investor, later withdrew from the merged Caroline/Amanda project.

An early indication of the serious problems which lay ahead came in a report which appeared in the advertising trade magazine, *Campaign,* at the end of November 1980. This stated that Major Market Radio (MMR) in New York, a leading American radio sales house, was claiming through its Vice-President, Roy Lindau, to have exclusive rights to sell airtime on the new Radio Caroline. However, a Radio Caroline spokesman, named in the article as Paul Collins, was also quoted as saying that MMR was just one of three companies briefed to sell airtime on the station. It later transpired that the mysterious 'Paul Collins' was in fact Vincent Monsey, Ronan O'Rahilly's 'right hand man' in America. Clearly there were already rival interests at work within the organisation planning Radio Caroline's return and, not for the first or last time in the station's history, the lack of any central, cohesive control was to almost scupper the whole project.

### Optimod units

*'Optimod' is the brand name of a sound processing unit for am radio transmissions. The unit, which is linked to the transmitter, includes a compressor, program equaliser, multi-band limiter, clipper and transmitter equaliser. It supplies a very high average modulation (loudness), clarity and freedom from processing interference to produce a near FM clarity of signal.*

NEWS

## Radio Caroline in comeback row

by David Longman

Radio Caroline, the pirate station which heralded the start of commercial radio in the UK, is set to return to the airwaves in the New Year. But already there is a dispute over which company is selling the airtime.

Major Market Radio in New York, one of America's leading radio sales houses, is claiming exclusive sales rights throughout the world. But MMR's claim has been challenged by Ronan O'Rahilly, the former owner of the station, who is involved in the new venture.

O'Rahilly said: "There is definitely no way that any contract has been signed. The intention is to end up with an affiliation with one of the major sales houses in New York, but nothing has been decided."

Paul Collins, senior sales executive at Caroline, said: "We have a new ship and will be working from an office in Madison Avenue to control the sales side of the company. O'Rahilly will be taking his usual role with the station."

Airtime rates for the new station are starting on the low side. Roy Lindau, vice-president of marketing with MMR, claimed: "We have structured the ratecard along ILR lines — not the way we usually do things in the States. Because of the law, payment will probably be made by the New York offices of the British agencies."

Collins claims the quoted ratecard is his own and MMR is one of three sales companies briefed to come up with proposals.

The ratecard sells peak airtime at £130 for 30 seconds. Broadcasting around the clock, Caroline promises research within three months of going on the air, with JICRAR-style data every six months. The former Caroline ship, the *Mi Amigo*, sank on 19 March this year.

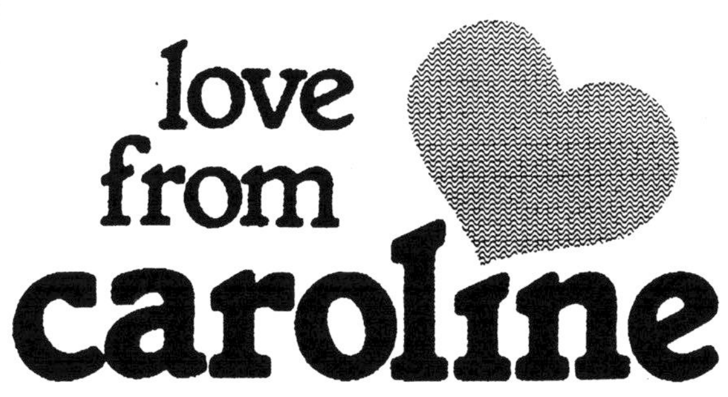


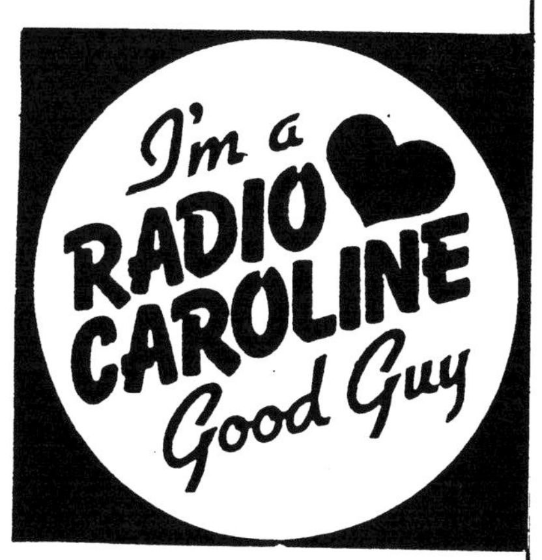


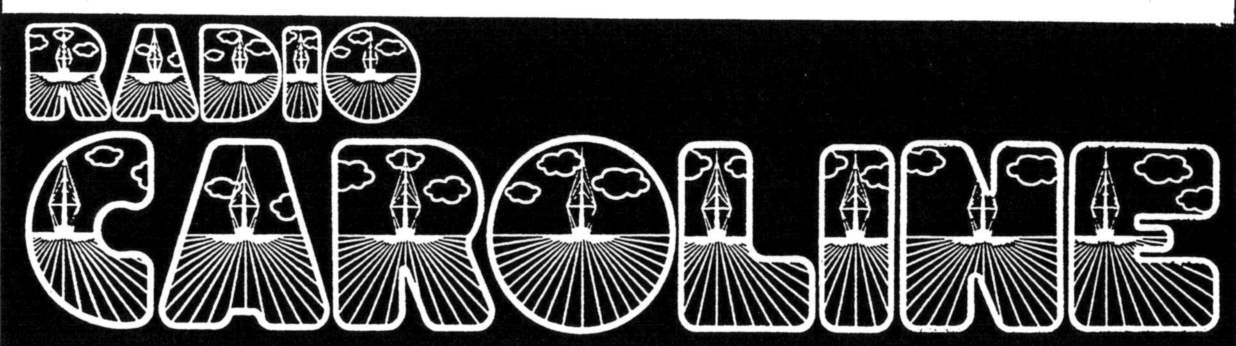

## 'Radio Phoenix' project

Plans were made by three men from Britain in 1980 to launch a new offshore radio station, Radio Phoenix. The driving force behind this project was Paul Graham (an engineer who had conducted English Service test broadcasts for Radio Delmare from the *Martina* (*Aegir II*) and had planned a Radio Mi Amigo 272 International Service from the *Magdalena*). He, together with Chris Cortez and Barrie Lancaster, planned to use the Shivering Sands Fort (home of 1960s offshore stations Radio Sutch and Radio City) as a base for the new station. Although transmitting and broadcasting equipment was available the Fort itself was found to be in a very dilapidated condition and plans to use it were quickly abandoned.

Shortly after this a number of ex-Radio Caroline DJs, including Roger Matthews, Stuart Russell and Richard Thompson, frustrated at the delays in bringing Caroline back revived the Radio Phoenix project. This time they planned to use a ship which had been located in Aberdeen - the *Birchlea.*

Dutch pop singer, Fred Bolland, who had plans to launch an offshore radio station of his own (Radio Monique), with backing from record companies and various religious groups, became interested in the Radio Phoenix project. An agreement was eventually drawn up between the two groups for the Dutch station to hire airtime during the day, while Radio Phoenix was to broadcast in English at night.

As soon as conversion work started on the *Birchlea* it was discovered that the vessel was in a much worse condition than previously realised, with no functioning engine or generators. Eventually, however, a working generator was acquired by the group and installed on the ship in Aberdeen.

Despite this work it was apparent that the *Birchlea* would never be suitable for use as an offshore radio station so another vessel was acquired, the *Cedarlea* (sister ship to the *Birchlea*). This vessel, which was also lying idle in Aberdeen, was in a much sounder condition and the project members transferred their equipment from the *Birchlea.*

Because the harbour authorities started paying increased attention to activities on board the vessel the *Cedarlea* was towed from Aberdeen in January 1981, heading for Sheerness. Here it was planned to pick up a telescopic aerial mast and then sail to a position in international waters where it would be erected and transmitters brought from Holland would be installed. Unfortunately during the tow the *Cedarlea* sustained damage to her steering gear and had to enter Middlesbrough for emergency repairs.

Later, off the Suffolk coast, the *Cedarlea* became fogbound and had to accept an offer from the Harwich and Ipswich Pilot Boats to guide her into port. She was taken to Ipswich where she docked at William Browns Quay, but shortly after this the project received some major setbacks.

The *Cedarlea's* owner started to demand more money before he would agree to take the ship back out to sea and the telescopic aerial mast failed to arrive as had been promised by its supplier.

Additionally, shortly after the *Cedarlea* had left Aberdeen a crew from Thames Television in London arrived in Scotland. The television crew managed to trace the movement of the vessel along the east coast, possibly alerted by other members of the Radio Caroline organisation, fearful of the planned rival station making it on air before their own return. With subsequent publicity given to the Radio Phoenix project financial backers, including the key Dutch Radio Monique group, withdrew their support. The ship became the subject of enquiries and visits by various authorities and by March 1981 the Radio Phoenix project had fallen apart and was abandoned.

The *Cedarlea,* after lying idle in Ipswich for some time, was herself eventually purchased later that year by the Greenpeace Organisation.

## Rumours of Radio Caroline's return

Throughout early 1981 rumours of various plans for the return of Radio Caroline continued to be published in newspapers and magazines. Mostly they were wildly inaccurate and raised false hopes in the minds of the station's supporters and potential employees, but some grains of truth were starting to filter through. A report at the end of February 1981 in the London *Evening Standard,* indicated that the station would return on Easter Sunday from a new vessel, *Imagine,* (named in tribute to the recently murdered ex-Beatle John Lennon). According to this article the ship was being fitted out at a secret European port and a $10million deal was said to have been negotiated with an American advertising and broadcasting organisation. The article went on to quote Paul Collins (alias Vincent Monsey), Marketing Director of Major Market Radio, as saying that Radio Caroline would return "with a lot of new faces and dramatic new sound".

This story, although inaccurate in many respects did have some basis in truth because in preparation for an anticipated return at Easter 1981 some famous name DJs had been clandestinely recruited by Radio Caroline's American backers. Johnnie Walker (who had taken Caroline South into a new era in August 1967 after the introduction of the Marine etc. Broadcasting (Offences) Act) was working on station KSAN in San Francisco early in 1981 when he was approached by Vincent Monsey and offered a job as Programme Director/DJ with the new Radio Caroline. Other DJs who had been with the station on board the *Mi Amigo* in 1979/1980, including Tom Hardy, Stevie Gordon, Stephen Bishop and Mike Stevens had also agreed to join the new Radio Caroline. They were all then working on Irish landbased pirate Sunshine Radio, which itself was operated by another ex-Caroline South DJ Robbie Dale. In addition Johnny Jason gave up his job with Liverpool's ILR station Radio City and made himself available to join the re-launched Radio Caroline as did two American DJs, Mitch Parker (from Washington) and Vincenta - a female colleague of Johnnie Walker from KSAN.

More, seemingly definite, information appeared in the advertising trade papers *Adweek* (2nd March 1981) and *Campaign* (20th March 1981), both quoting 19th April 1981 (Easter Sunday) as the return date for Radio Caroline. Once again the same names, Vincent Monsey, Roy Lindau and Anthony Kramer were quoted as being the people behind the station's imminent return. Also said to be involved was Warner Rush, President of Major Market Radio (MMR) in New York and the reports indicated that MMR had been contracted to sell air time on Radio Caroline. They were targeting international advertisers, particularly companies who were heavy users of radio in the USA, but had not yet advertised their products on radio in Britain. Warner Rush said, "They [Radio Caroline] required a US agent, looked at a few and chose us. We had our lawyers thoroughly investigate the set up and they deemed it proper."

Potential international advertisers received a rate card from Roy Lindau at the beginning of April 1981 claiming that Radio Caroline would "return on 19th April, with a new ship, new management, new equipment, new dial position, increased power and a new mass-appeal music format." In the document Roy Lindau described himself as Vice-President of Sales at Major Market Radio, a division of Golden West Broadcasters, who represented stations in 32 markets with offices in New York and eleven other major US cities and that the company was Radio Caroline's "exclusive worldwide sales representative."

### 'Pirate Vicar'

*Rev Dominee Gerrit Toornvliet, known affectionately as the 'Pirate Vicar' died on 18th February 1981, aged 73. He was the first evangelist to broadcast on the re-launched Radio Caroline in 1973, and his programmes were heard regularly on the station until the 'Mi Amigo' sank in March 1980. He was also a backer of other offshore stations, Radio Condor and Capital Radio, in the early 1970s. His evangelistic programme Radiogemeente Toornvliet" continued to be broadcast on radio stations, including later offshore ones after his death.*

### *Mi Amigo* wreck

*With all the speculation at the end of 1980 about the return of Radio Caroline the station's former home, the 'Mi Amigo' had her wreck buoy removed by Trinity House officials on 18th December 1980. The buoy had been placed near the vessel shortly after she sank on 20th March 1980. A Notice to Mariners (No 76) issued on 21st November stated:-*

*"Having regard to the fact that the wreck of the 'Mi Amigo' in the position Latitude 51 degrees, 35 minutes 0 seconds north, Longitude 1 degree 17 minutes 20 seconds east is indicated by a conspicuous lattice mast and the existence of the wreck has been widely promulgated and is shown on the relevant Admiralty Charts of the area, it is intended on or about 18th December 1980 to remove the buoy marking the wreck and to discontinue the station permanently."*

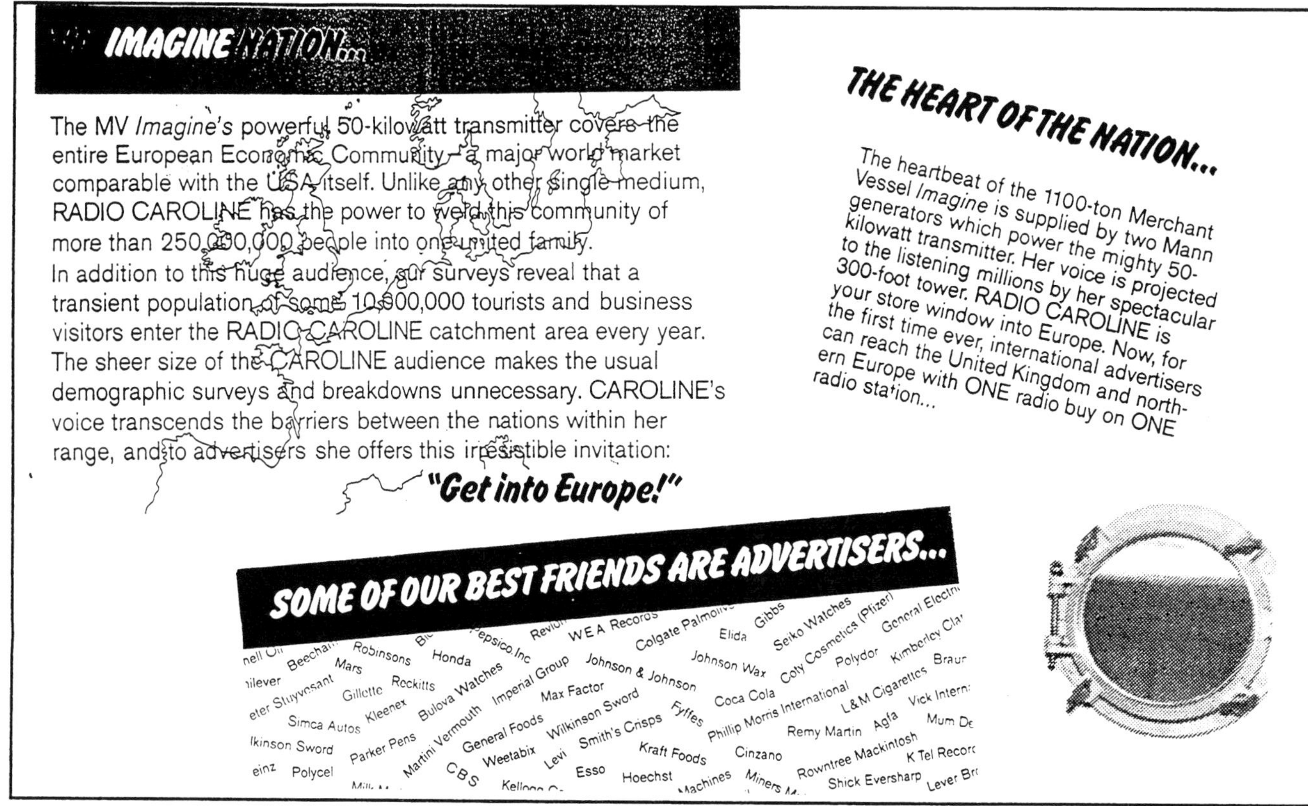


*Pages from the 'Imagine' Ratecard distributed to advertisers and agencies to promote Radio Caroline's return in 1981.*

The thrust of the sales pitch was that advertisers could "efficiently cover the entire UK and Western Europe with one radio buy on one station" and great play was made of the fact that, at the time, Britain did not have a national commercial station or even a fully developed network of ILR stations which would attract large international advertisers.

However, Easter Sunday 1981 came and went without Radio Caroline returning to the airwaves - excuses about financial problems, technical problems and a lack of advertising were all put forward to explain the continued silence of the station.

## Radio Paradijs

Shortly after the *Mi Amigo* sank in March 1980 plans for a new offshore radio station were put together by some people who had been involved in the Dutch side of Radio Caroline. These included Ben Bode and Danny Vuylsteke who joined forces with A J Beirens, formerly a presenter on RNI's World Service in the early 1970s and who since then had been involved in various Italian land-based radio stations. Danny Vuylsteke and A J Beirens had also jointly operated the Mi Amigo Drive-in Disco in Belgium and Holland and together with Patrick Valain they also subsequently became responsible for selling advertising on the Dutch Service of Radio Caroline and for tendering the *Mi Amigo*.

The proposed station - Radio Paradijs - had Belgian and Dutch backers, including Dutch pop singer Vader Abraham, Rob Aartse (owner of Fleet Records) Bart van Leer (ex- Radio Mi Amigo DJ) and Willem van Kooten (Radio Veronica DJ Joost de Draayer) (owners of the Red Bullet record company). Between them these backers reportedly invested 70m Belgian Francs (£1,200,000) in the project while Danny Vuylsteke also claimed to have personally invested a further 10m Belgian Francs (£170,000 ) to help launch the station.

Through a broker who had previously done some work for Radio Caroline, they purchased a ship, the West German coaster, *Hoheweg*. The vessel at that time was moored in Krausand, but later moved to Cuxhaven, where she was berthed and re-registered in Panama under the name *Lieve*. However, it was not long before police and harbour authorities at Cuxhaven began to take an interest in the ship and the activity surrounding it.

This was later attributed to a fundamental error on the part of one of the backers who had tried to engage a captain to sail the ship to a quiet yard where she was to be fitted out. He told the prospective captain that the ship was to be used to re-launch Radio Veronica, but it later transpired that the person he had spoken to was in fact captain of a police launch. As a result not only was the ship itself watched closely, but people involved in the Paradijs project were photographed, followed and had their telephone lines tapped.

Because of this intense interest it was decided that the *Lieve* should sail from Cuxhaven and she headed for Ireland to be finally fitted out as a floating radio station. Unfortunately, during the voyage from West Germany she sustained some damage and, after putting out an SOS message, was towed into Southampton where she remained for two weeks while repairs were carried out. The *Lieve* eventually arrived in Dublin on 11th March 1981 and the services of an ex-Radio Veronica engineer were used to instal studio and transmitting equipment on board.

It was intended that the ship should be used to broadcast three separate programmes -Radio Europa, an easy listening service on FM; Radio Paradijs - a Belgian progressive hit format station on medium wave and a second medium wave service the a Dutch language Radio Monique, operated by Fred Bolland.

## Hurried departure

Three transmitters eventually arrived from the USA at the beginning of July 1981, and were installed on board the *Lieve,* but by then there was increasing press interest in what was going on with the mysterious ship in Dublin Harbour. Because of this interest arrangements were hurriedly made to finish equipping the *Lieve* and get her out of port before the Irish authorities had an opportunity to act.

These panic-stricken arrangements included the engagement of a firm of domestic television aerial contractors (to erect the project's £40,000 aerial system. However, such was the pressure to leave port, they only achieved rigging half of the 264' mast before the *Lieve* had to sail from Dublin.

The ship left Ireland hurriedly during the evening of 15th July 1981 because press reports were about to be published revealing her location and true purpose. The Dublin *Sunday World*, under the headline, **CUSTOMS FOOLED AS RADIO PIRATES GET SHIPSHAPE**, quoted Ben Bode, in his capacity as Captain of the *Lieve,* as having told Irish Customs that the equipment on board was for the survey of fish life on the sea bed in the Persian Gulf. He was also reported to have informed Dublin shipping agents, Dublin Maritime Ltd., that computers were being installed on board the ship and the vessel was to be used as a floating sales outlet for such equipment. However. With three transmitters and £900,000 worth of other broadcasting equipment on board the ship, she clearly could not remain in Dublin now that her 'cover' had been blown.

Only five hours into the voyage from Ireland the ship encountered storms and the top 120' of the hastily erected aerial mast, which had not been fully stayed, came down. The *Lieve* battled on through the English Channel into the North Sea, but was eventually forced to anchor temporarily five miles from the former REM Island (home of Radio and TV Noordzee in 1964) off the Dutch coast.

After repairs had been carried out to the damaged aerial mast at sea some night-time test transmissions took place during late July 1981. Official tests were first heard on 24th July 1981 on 1107kHz (270m), but the station was being identified as Radio Nova on 88mHz FM stereo! This confusion was caused

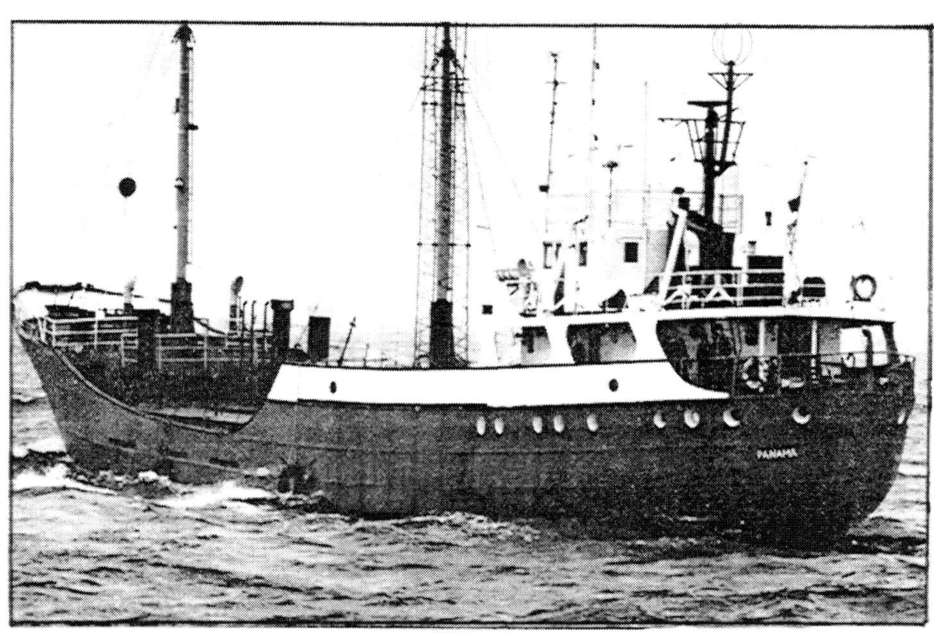

'Magda Maria' ('Lieve')

because engineers aboard the radio ship were using tapes from the Irish landbased pirate station which they had recorded while the ship was still in Dublin.

Test transmissions continued until late evening of the next day, again using tapes of Radio Nova programmes, but on 26th July 1981 a Dutch language music programme was presented throughout the day.

An aerial photograph of the new radio ship published in the Dutch daily newspaper *De Telegraaf* on 29th July 1981 concerned and disturbed the authorities because it appeared to show the vessel was carrying a satellite dish. In fact the so-called satellite dish was a cable drum mounted on the deck but questions were raised in the Dutch Parliament and the Minister of Telecommunications ordered a police and Navy raid on the radio station's vessel. This action was supposedly justified on the grounds that there were Dutch nationals on board the ship notwithstanding the fact that she was a foreign-registered vessel anchored in international waters.

## Paradijs ship seized in international waters

The Radio Paradijs ship, by now known as the *Magda Maria*, was raided at 5.30am on 1st August 1981 by police and marines from the Netherlands Naval frigate *Jaguar* and three crew members were arrested. Although the radio station was not broadcasting at the time of the raid the authorities discovered two irregularities with the ship herself - there was no qualified Captain on board at the time and the name on the bow of the vessel (*Magda Maria*) did not correspond with that on the ship's registration documents (*Lieve*) -the name had been changed during the voyage from Ireland.

On instructions from the Dutch Public Prosecutor the *Magda Maria* was then towed into port and searched by the Navy who later moved her to Amsterdam, where the radio equipment was removed and put into storage.

This unprecedented action by the authorities in seizing a legitimately registered ship in international waters caused an immediate storm of protest. Two members of the Dutch Parliament demanded that the Justice Minister, Mr. de Ruiter, explain precisely under what legal provisions the *Magda Maria* had been seized. The Panamanian company which owned the transmitting equipment on board the radio ship also instituted legal proceedings against the Dutch Government.

An Amsterdam Court was asked on 24th August 1981 to decide whether the owners of the *Magda Maria* could have the radio ship returned to them. This was something of a test case because, with the ship having being seized whilst in international waters, the Dutch Navy and Public Prosecutor were being accused of piracy by the vessel's owners.

Compania Naviera Panlieve SA, through their Dutch lawyer Reinier de Jonge, asked the Court to allow the ship to be returned to its position in international waters within 48 hours. They asserted that the Panamanian registration documents were in order and, although the registration of the vessel had ended on 15th August 1981 (while the ship was impounded) it would have been automatically renewed had the ship been allowed to remain at sea.

Although judgement was supposed to be given on 3rd September 1981, the Court had decided that the matter would have to be referred on to the High Court. A hearing before the High Court some two weeks later resulted in the Dutch Government accepting that they had been wrong to seize the ship and agreeing that the *Magda Maria* was free to leave port with all her equipment still on board, except for the transmitter crystals.

The vessel's owners decided, on legal advice, not to move the ship but to seek a further Court hearing for repossession of the transmitter crystals. It was not until December 1982, some 15 months later, that this issue was finally resolved when the Courts ruled that no operating transmitter equipment could be aboard the ship when she left Holland.

Meanwhile, far from capitulating as the authorities had hoped once the ship had been seized the backers of Radio Paradijs also instructed lawyers to take action against the Dutch Government for the alleged act of piracy. Unfortunately for the proposed radio station the complex legal argument over the release of the *Magda Maria* was to drag on for many years, until 1986, while the ship herself remained neglected in Amsterdam.

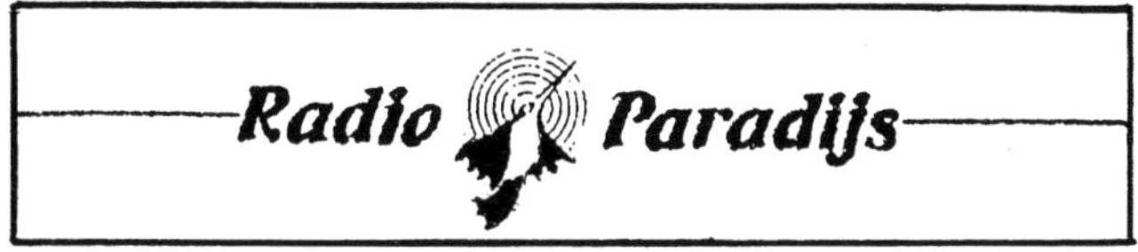


## More Caroline rumours

Further planned dates for the return of Radio Caroline in August and November 1981 were rumoured but once again nothing happened on air although a lot was going on behind the scenes. A ship was briefly considered for use by the Caroline organisation in 1980, but was found to be incapable of carrying the planned tall aerial mast. Enquiries had also been made about the possible use of the former RNI ship, *Mebo II* while Ronan O'Rahilly had contacted Abie Nathan to establish the possibility of buying the MV *Peace* when the Voice of Peace closed in December 1981. (see Chapter 18).

Radio Caroline eventually found its new ship in 1981, the former Icelandic trawler *Ross Revenge*, which was fitted out in great secrecy in the small port of Solores, near Santander, northern Spain. The delayed on-air date of August 1981 was attributed to the seizure of the Radio Paradijs ship *Magda Maria* by the Dutch authorities. Ronan O'Rahilly was reportedly not prepared to let the new Radio Caroline ship set sail until the legal wrangle over the boarding of the Radio Paradijs vessel had been resolved, although he could never have foreseen how long drawn out that particular episode would be.

On the programming side during the summer of 1981 Vincent Monsey entered an agreement with an American syndication company, Al Ham Productions, to provide programmes 24 hours a day under the call sign Radio Life, on a second transmitter from the new Caroline ship. This station's name was derived from the format "music of your life" which had been developed by Al Ham, a former bass player with the Glenn Miller Orchestra and many other American bands. Ham's then unique format, similar to that since adopted by many British ILR 'Gold' stations, consisted of hits from the 60's and 70's and was targeted at audiences in the over 35 age group.

### Radio Mi Amigo 272 court cases

*In June 1981 a number of people appeared in court in Belgium charged with being involved in the operation of Radio Mi Amigo 272 from the 'Magdalena' during 1979. On 28th June 1981 station owner, Sylvain Tack (who by then was living in Haiti) was sentenced in his absence to 12 months imprisonment and fined 4 million Belgian Francs (£65,500). 118 other people were also prosecuted either in connection with the operation of Radio Mi Amigo 272 or with advertising on the station.*

*Appeals against 49 of these sentences reached the Appeal Court in Ghent eighteen months later, in December 1982. Thirty were acquitted, half because the statute of limitations had expired, but 14 others had fines reduced from 60,000 Belgian Francs (£750) to 20,000 Belgian Francs (£250) and all jail sentences were quashed and replaced by fines.*

*By the time of these appeals Sylvain Tack (who had not appealed against his sentence) was himself in jail in France after being caught smuggling drugs into that country from South America.*

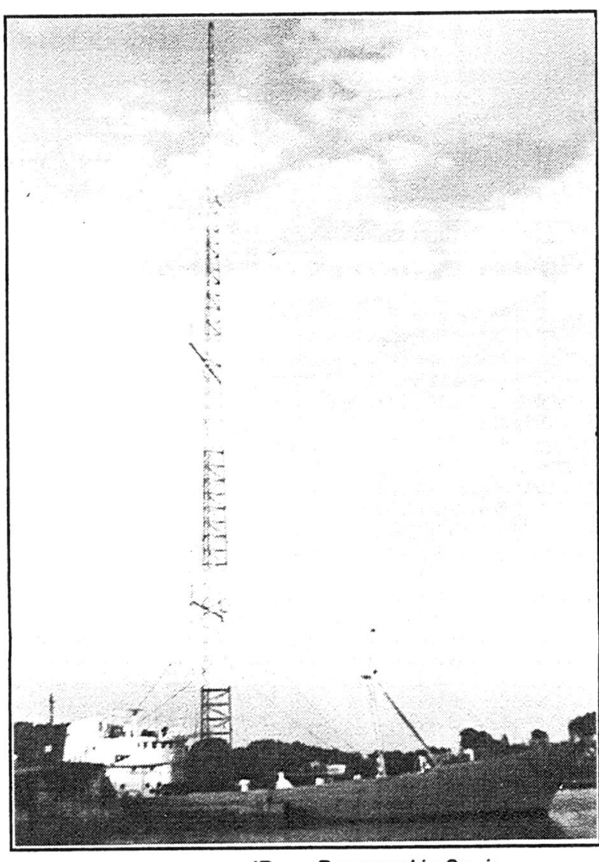
'Ross Revenge' in Spain

As part of the deal Al Ham arranged to purchase a 50Kw transmitter from Besco International in Dallas for installation on the *Ross Revenge*. This transmitter, together with the others already acquired the previous summer by Radio Caroline engineer Peter Chicago, was crated and despatched to Holland in August 1981, but on arrival they were confiscated by Dutch Customs authorities. It was a further three months before the Dutch authorities agreed to release the equipment and in December 1981 the transmitters were eventually transported in great secrecy from Holland to the Spanish port where the new ship was being fitted out.

In September 1981 legendary American DJ, Wolfman Jack, signed a contract with Vincent Monsey to present a taped drive-time show and a Saturday oldies programme, "American Graffiti", on Radio Caroline when it returned. In the belief that the station would be on the air by November 1981 Wolfman Jack actually recorded a number of these programmes, but due to some dramatic changes in Radio Caroline's financial backing arrangements, they were never actually broadcast.

### *Mi Amigo* dive

*The wreck of the former Radio Caroline ship, 'Mi Amigo' was examined by members of an Essex diving club during the late summer of 1981. Diver Jane Thornhill described the scene of the wreck more than 45 feet below the North Sea:- "...with visibility around three metres we entered the drowned wheelhouse. We saw a crab scuttle over what looked like an open-plan apartment block. Each pigeon hole in a large wall unit [the record library] had become the home of a sea creature and was festooned with seaweed decorations. It was an amazing sight which the DJs who once lived aboard could never have imagined. The sides of the ship are already covered with sea-life, but the decks are relatively clean with just a fine covering of sand."*

## Financial rift

Despite these financial difficulties within the organisation strong rumours of Radio Caroline's return continued to circulate, this time suggesting that now the transmitters had been released by the Dutch authorities and safely transported to Spain, the station would be on the air again for Easter 1982. The new radio ship, *Ross Revenge*, even sailed from port in Spain, anchoring temporarily outside the harbour - the cost of keeping her in port had by then proved prohibitive. On 27th/28th March 1982 carrier signals were heard on a number of former Radio Caroline frequencies and when a continuous test tone was received over large parts of Europe on 963kHz (319m) many listeners thought that at last the station was about to return.

The Radio Caroline organisation officially denied at the time that they had made these test broadcasts and amongst offshore radio supporters they were generally assumed to be yet another hoax, probably transmitted from a landbased pirate station. However, it has since been established that these broadcasts did indeed come from the *Ross Revenge* in Spain and, despite the risk of being caught transmitting inside Spanish territorial waters, they had been made to prove to certain financial backers and prospective advertisers that the station was serious about returning to the air and that it had a ship and equipment ready to do so.

The first public hint of what had really been going on behind the scenes was given in the trade paper *Marketing Week* on 4th June 1982. As well as containing a photograph of the new Radio Caroline ship in Spain the article made claims that $500,000 of backer's money had been lost in trying to re-launch the station.

It turned out, however, that the original American backers were unhappy about not having full control of the radio station. Disagreements had arisen early in 1982 between them and Ronan O'Rahilly over the proposed format of the station.

The Americans wanted to broadcast largely pop music to a British and European audience, while Ronan O'Rahilly had very definite views that there was a place in the market for an album based station, providing an alternative to the growing number of Top 40 stations, particularly in Britain's ILR network.

Problems had also been encountered with the original American backers over funding for the return of Radio Caroline. American businessman Jim Ryan, representing a group of 20 investors in the project, had made an agreement relating to the timing of the funding operation. This took the form of a two stage payment - an initial one enabling conversion work to take place on the ship, to be followed by a second instalment to cover the installation of radio equipment and enable the station to actually begin broadcasting.

The backers had been promised an on-air date of November 1981, which was consistent with some of the stories circulating in the press during the summer of that year. However, in September 1981 the transmitters, en-route from America, had been impounded by Dutch Customs authorities thus delaying their installation on the *Ross Revenge* and preventing the station making the November on-air date.

Unfortunately this vital information was withheld from the backers in America and instead a number of false rumours were spread about the Radio Caroline organisation, including claims of financial losses due to the project's bad management.

Shortly before the dispute over station format and control had broken out the second instalment of the funding was paid to Caroline's New York solicitor and transferred to a secret bank account in Liectenstein, enabling work on fitting out the *Ross Revenge* to continue.

Jim Ryan, hearing that the money had been transferred to the Liechtenstein account and realising they had no firm evidence at that stage that a ship was being converted, instructed lawyers to take legal action against Radio Caroline's New York solicitor accusing him of fraud and breach of contract.

A breakaway group then proposed taking control of the *Ross Revenge,* assuring the American consortium that they would be able to finish the conversion work and have the station ready to start transmissions in June 1982. To appease to the American backers, who basically wanted greater control over the whole project anyway, two possible locations were suggested for the station - in the Caribbean or off the coast of South America. Meanwhile, MMR's Vincent Monsey also contacted Jim Ryan and the American consortium offering his services to provide programmes and jingles for the offshore station provided they gained full control of the operation.

## Legal wrangle

In the meantime the *Ross Revenge* had been impounded by Spanish harbour authorities and the steering gear had been dismantled. A violent attempt was made to take over the ship in Spain, but this failed so agents for the American consortium then contacted the Panamanian Embassy in London in an attempt to change the owners' name on the vessel's registration documents, claiming to have a Court Order to this effect from the Justice Department in New York. However, the Panamanian Embassy refused to co-operate and a similar attempt to persuade the Spanish authorities by using this dubious New York Court Order also failed.

The *Ross Revenge* then became the subject of what was to be protracted legal action between the consortium of American backers and Ronan O'Rahilly's group, who themselves were now seeking potential new backers and advertisers, primarily in Canada, to re-launch the station without any further delays. James

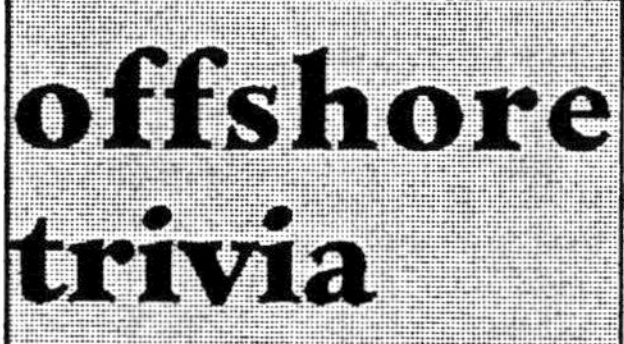


**First stereo transmissions**

*Radio Mercur (1961)*

Ryan was eventually charged and convicted on counts of fraudulent activity in connection with the management of monies associated with the planned re-launch of Radio Caroline.

## United Nations Convention on the Law of the Sea (UNCLOS)

*At the end of 1982 a significant agreement was drawn up by the United Nations covering the international use of the sea. Although concerned primarily with mining and exploration rights of the sea-bed and international fishing rights the agreement - the United Nations Convention on the Law of the Sea (UNCLOS) contained an article (Article 109) relating specifically to unauthorised broadcasting from the High Seas.*

*Article 109 states:-*

*1. All States shall co-operate in the suppression of unauthorised broadcasting from the High seas.*

*2. For the purpose of this Convention 'unauthorised broadcasting' means the transmission of sound radio or television broadcasts from a ship or installation on the High Seas intended for reception by the general public contrary to international regulations, but excluding the transmission of distress calls.*

*3. Any person engaged in unauthorised broadcasting may be prosecuted before the courts of:-*

*(a) the Flag State of the ship;*

*(b) the State of registry of the installation;*

*(c) the State of which the person is a national;*

*(d) any State where the transmission can be received;*

*(e) any State where authorised radio communication is suffering interference.*

*4. On the High Seas a state having jurisdiction in accordance with paragraph 3 may, in conformity with Article 110, arrest any person or ship engaged in unauthorised broadcasting and seize the broadcasting apparatus.*

*(Article 110 sets out the procedure military or civilian personnel must follow when carrying out such a boarding and seizure)*

*The effect of this Article meant an end to the use of 'flags of convenience' as a legal means of maintaining an offshore radio ship in international waters. Under Article 109 any State which has ratified UNCLOS agrees that a ship registered with it which is used for unauthorised broadcasting purposes can be legally boarded in international waters by the authorities of other countries which have also ratified the agreement. It may also be possible for a country which has not ratified the agreement to take such action. UNCLOS therefore introduced a major change in international law and potentially had a direct and devastating impact on any unauthorised offshore broadcasting operations.*

*The UNCLOS agreement was opened for ratification by member States on 10th December 1982 and would only come into force twelve months after the date of ratification by the 60th State.*

# Chapter 21

# 'From Somewhere in the Mediterranean'

In Israel Abie Nathan had temporarily closed the Voice of Peace on 31st December 1981 because he had not been granted a licence to operate the station from a land base. He had hoped to be allowed to do so by virtue of provisions contained in the new Israeli law against offshore television broadcasting, which gave the Government the option to licence certain offshore stations if it so wished.

It was not until 12th January 1982 that the Knesset's Economic Committee discussed Abie Nathan's licence application. The Committee was told by Communications Minister, Mordecai Zipponi that there should be a general revision of broadcasting arrangements in Israel and that there was no point in enacting a special law to effectively grant Abie Nathan a virtual monopoly in commercial radio. However, the Minister also said that if the Committee decided to recommend allowing Abie Nathan to come inshore and broadcast from an Israeli port while the general review of broadcasting law was carried out, then the Government would have no strong objections to such a temporary arrangement.

For his part Abie Nathan explained to press reporters that the Voice of Peace had lost a lot of money from cancelled advertising contracts and, as it was costing 2 million Israeli pounds just to keep the silent ship in harbour, he would have to close the station for good within a week or so.

On 26th January 1982 the Knesset Economic Committee gave its approval to a Bill allowing Abie Nathan's radio station to broadcast from shore. The licence granted under the Bill was a temporary one for three months to avoid the necessity for keeping the *Peace* at sea during the winter and it had a number of conditions:-

THE VOICE OF PEACE קול השלום

- Transmissions were to be directed at Israel only.
- Commercials were to be permitted, but the Voice of Peace would be under Government direction and its licence could be revoked at any time if the station violated various regulations.

The battle was not over because on 1st February 1982 the Israeli opposition parties warned that when the Bill came before the Knesset for its first reading they would combine to defeat it. Even the Minister of Communications, Mordecai Zipponi, was not happy with the Bill as agreed by the Economic Committee, fearing Abie Nathan would be given too much opportunity to make a vast profit out of running the station.

The Bill was subsequently discussed by the Knesset on 9th February 1982 and, despite the opposition parties' threats, passed its first reading by 32 to 11 with 1 abstention. However, less than a week later the ultra-orthadox religious party, Agudat Israel, lodged an objection to Abie Nathan's licence application on the grounds that he intended to allow his station to broadcast on Shabbat. The leader of Agudat Israel, Avraham Shapira, said that the Voice of Peace broadcasts had "nothing Israeli or Jewish in them, they disseminate the worst that foreign culture has to offer and, apart from some commercials, they are not in Hebrew. The State certainly cannot allow a private individual the licence to cause the mass desecration of Shabbat in this way." Mr. Shapira also indicated that if the coalition Government under Prime Minister Menachen Begin enacted the legislation granting the Voice of Peace a licence his party would link with the opposition Labour group on a range of other issues to bring down the Government.

Clearly Abie Nathan and the Voice of Peace were being drawn into the delicate balance of Israeli party politics affecting a much wider range of issues than just the granting of a commercial radio station licence.

On 16th February 1982 Abie Nathan addressed the Knesset and told them that in view of the strength of opposition he no longer had the mental or financial strength to fight for his licence and that he was withdrawing his application. He told a news conference afterwards that he "could no longer risk the lives of his crew in winter storms at sea" and recounted some of the peace initiatives undertaken by the Voice of Peace since it had been launched in 1973:-

The MV *Peace* had:-

- sailed to within 20Km of Port Said, Egypt and tried to tell people to stop killing each other during the Six Day War.
- sailed to Beirut when fighting was at its fiercest and broadcast appeals for the hostilities to stop.
- taken flowers to the Egyptians to express a desire from the people of Israel for peace
- sailed through the Suez Canal to Eilat and back, before President Sadat had even considered visiting Israel.
- carried medical supplies to the wounded in Lebanon.

Abie Nathan was bitter about the way he had been treated by the Communications Minister Mordecai Zipponi and Israeli Prime Minister Menachen Begin. In August 1981 Nathan had appealed to Zipponi to be given permission, because of the dangers to the lives of his crew, to broadcast from shore during the winter or until a law was passed to grant him a licence to broadcast from land. Abie Nathan alleged that Minister Zipponi had assured him that, if the Prime Minister agreed, he would give favourable consideration to his request. However, when the matter reached the Knesset Mordecai Zipponi let him down and actually spoke against the proposed law, saying that Abie Nathan should not be given a licence to make large profits out of radio broadcasting.

## Move to Ireland?

Having pulled back from seeking a land-based licence Abie Nathan took the *Peace* ship back to sea on 19th February 1982 and at 11.30am that day the Voice of Peace went back on the air. At 5.00pm Abie Nathan announced his ideas for the future of the *Peace* ship:-

**Israeli radio pirate to take 'peace' ship to Ireland**

*On Sunday morning I shall fly to London and then to Belfast to another troubled region and try to offer our help. We will go there only if we are wanted, only if we can find enough people on both sides who believe that by reason and understanding we might try to replace violence as being the only means of getting together among people. Or will we sell the ship? If we cannot then I will come back. We will have to strip the ship of everything she has, maybe sell it for charity. And then since this good old ship has been here for so long, we will not sink her, we will bury her, majestically, in the same place where she has been anchored for so many years, right here in the Mediterranean. She will be part, permanently, of this region. I shall miss you all. Goodnight. We loved you then, we love you now and we'll always love you.*

He closed his broadcast by urging listeners to go to the Square of the Kings of Israel in Tel Aviv to join a silent demonstration against the failure of the Knesset to grant him a licence.

After transmissions ended at 9.00pm the MV *Peace* sailed to Ashdod the following morning and tied up in the harbour. Over 3,000 people turned up at the demonstration in the Square of the Kings of Israel on 20th February 1982, indicating the extent of the Voice of Peace's popularity at that time. Abie Nathan was subsequently reprimanded by the authorities for not warning them in advance that such a large crowd would be gathering in the Square!

Abie Nathan then flew to Ireland for talks with Catholic and Protestant peace campaigners about the idea of the MV *Peace* anchoring off the Irish coast, but while he was away it was announced that the Bill to grant him a licence in Israel would receive another hearing in the Knesset in March 1982. It appeared after all that he had some supporters within Parliament who wanted his station to remain in Israel.

Although Abie Nathan pressed ahead with plans for broadcasting to Ireland he decided to put the Voice of Peace back on the air off Israel as a temporary measure while the Knesset gave further consideration to his land-based licence application. The ship left Ashdod on 7th March 1982, anchoring off Jaffa and two days later the Voice of Peace returned to the air with 24 hour programming. Unfortunately after only a few days of broadcasting generator problems forced the station to close and the ship returned to Ashdod for repairs and the Voice of Peace remained off the air for ten days.

After many weeks of delay the land-based licence debate eventually took place in the Knesset on 14th June 1982, but when the vote came the proposal to allow Abie Nathan's Voice of Peace to come ashore was turned down. What had seemed at one time to be a real possibility - official recognition for the Voice of Peace and Abie Nathan's peace campaign - now seemed further away than ever and the MV *Peace* stayed at sea off the Israel coast.

## Rumours of Odelia Television return

Following several months of uneventful broadcasting, during which the *Peace* ship moved to a position off Tel Aviv, concerns arose in October 1982 when rumours began to circulate about the return of the MV *Odelia* - with a radio station on board this time as well as the television station which had broadcast to Israel the previous year (see Chapter 18). The return of the *Odelia* raised worries about the introduction of an Israeli version of European style anti-offshore legislation with no theoretical provision for the Government to licence specific broadcasters if it so wished. This renewed threat to the future of the Voice of Peace prompted Abie Nathan to apply once again for a land-based licence. At about this time too, in an attempt to broaden audience appeal, the Voice of Peace's format was changed to middle of the road music with a mixture of

### VOP advertising

*The Voice of Peace carried advertising on Shabbat, the Jewish Sabbath (Saturday) while the state network, Kol Israel, was not permitted to do so. Saturday was therefore a very important day in terms of revenue earning and efforts were always made to ensure that the station was on the air and transmissions were not interrupted by technical breakdowns or routine maintenance schedules.*

*Kol Israel, the Government run commercial network had three services - Programme A Reshet Aleph (classical music), Programme B -Reshet Bet (easy listening music and news), Programme C - Reshet Gimel (a pop station, which was launched specifically to compete with the Voice of Peace). The network also had a World Service and all four services carried advertising except on Shabbat. In a bid to win advertisers away from the Voice of Peace Kol Israel at one stage offered discounted rates to any company which advertised exclusively with them.*

## Abie Nathan

*Abie Nathan was well known to be sincere in his aims for peace in the Middle East and his dogged determination to carry through his plans, although he could be awkward and unreasonable with staff. Although not a professional broadcaster he had very definite personal views about how the Voice of Peace should sound and often used to call DJs during the middle of their programme, using his Motorola portable phone, to admonish them for playing a certain record or instruct them to abandon pop music and play classical or what he called "music of love, peace and human understanding" - usually material by Joan Baez, Bob Dylan or James Taylor. Sometimes he insisted on being put on air himself, via the Motorola, so that he could let off steam about a particular issue.*

Country and Western, easy listening and Top 40 being played during the daytime.

In December 1982 problems were encountered with the official registration of the MV *Peace*. Rumours circulated that its Panamanian registration and flag had not been valid for four years, with a consequent effect on the vessel's insurance arrangements. Abie Nathan immediately flew to New York to sort the problem out with the Shalom Peace Foundation and the Panamanian authorities.

Also in relation to insurance cover during 1982 the MV *Peace* was observed to be anchored inside Israeli territorial waters, but this was officially denied by both the station and the authorities who chose to turn a blind eye to the situation. However, the insurers had stipulated that because of the ship's condition it must not be anchored out in the open sea but within reasonable distance of a port with appropriate emergency and rescue facilities available should the need arise.

The *Peace* had originally been tendered by small Arab-owned fishing boats from Jaffa, but in mid-1982 alternative arrangements were made for a tender service from Tel Aviv Marina. This particular tender also serviced an oil tanker delivering to a power station a few miles up the coast from Tel Aviv. This weekly service was sometimes augmented when a special boat was chartered to bring out urgent supplies of records, taped programmes or commercials. The MV *Peace* herself sailed into Ashdod once every six-eight weeks to be refuelled and take on supplies of water.

## Voice of Peace 10th Anniversary

On 28th May 1983 the Voice of Peace celebrated its 10th Anniversary with a full day of Beatles music, as it had played on its opening day in 1973. The MV *Peace* sailed to within a mile of Tel Aviv and was visited by dozens of yachts and windsurfers as well as Israeli and foreign television crews and journalists.

At about this time too a new generator was installed on the *Peace* and the medium wave aerial was rebuilt to its full height - the station had been operating on a slung wire antenna for some time after the original aerial mast had been damaged in storms. This temporary aerial system had badly affected the Voice of Peace's signal penetration beyond the immediate Tel Aviv area.

The first listenership survey for the Voice of Peace was undertaken in June 1983, and showed that in Tel Aviv, where reception of the station was at its best, it had a 23% audience reach. On 27th July 1983 shortwave transmissions began once again on 6240kHz (48.10m), using a power of 400 watts. These broadcasts were made possible after a centre fold dipole aerial had been rigged between the radio ship's foremast and midships mast. Reception of the shortwave transmissions were reported from Britain and Europe.

*MV 'Peace'*

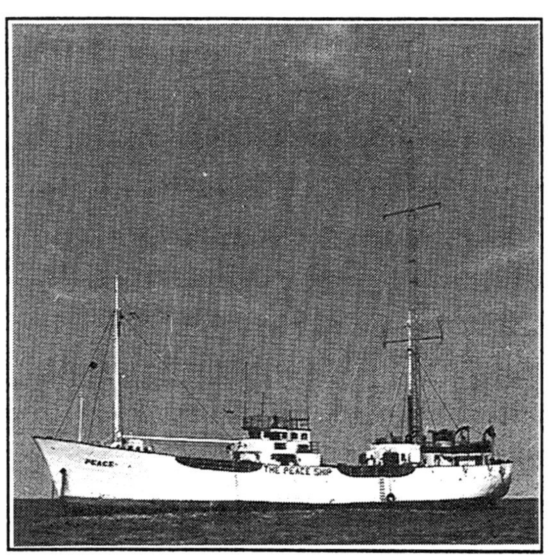


A number of rumours started to circulate in Israel during the late summer of 1983 that yet again the MV *Odelia* may return, broadcasting television and radio programmes. However, despite these persistent stories, which had surfaced a number of times during the previous 18 months and had their origin in the Israeli advertising world, nothing more was heard of this particular potential rival to the Voice of Peace. Meanwhile in November 1983 Abie Nathan was elected a Councillor on Tel Aviv City Council, a position which he proposed to use to further his peace campaigning activities.

## Technical problems

The shortwave service had closed in March 1984 on instructions from the Israeli Ministry of Communications because a complaint had been received, via the International Telecommunications Union, that the station was causing interference to Swedish Embassy communications. Abie Nathan complied with the instruction because he did not want to cause bad relations with any government.

In September 1984 the Voice of Peace returned to a 24hour programme schedule on both medium wave and FM stereo. However, there were some major generator problems aboard the MV *Peace* towards the end of the year which were largely neglected because Abie Nathan had left Israel to campaign for starving refugees in Ethiopia. Despite the technical problems and the lack of any input, financial or otherwise, from Abie Nathan the Voice of Peace did manage to continue broadcasting, but by spring 1985 the situation became desperate once again. Eventually after transmitter engineer John Burnhill left the organisation there were so many technical problems that the Voice of Peace went off the air altogether.

Abie Nathan, having returned from Ethiopia, managed to persuade a friend in the Israeli Army to make some temporary repairs to the transmitting equipment which enabled the Voice of Peace to return to the air. Shortly after this he also persuaded two former DJs, Keith York and Don Stevens, to return to the station and help keep it on the air. The station gradually began to recover from these problems and by mid-June 1985 the Voice of Peace was beginning to attract listeners and advertisers once again.

This whole episode demonstrated how dependant the Voice of Peace was on Abie Nathan. He would not allow anyone else to make major decisions about the station, but when he was absent or pre-occupied with other peace campaigns, problems remained un-addressed until eventually a crisis point being reached.

A split AM/FM service was introduced on the Voice of Peace in June 1985. The services split at 9.00pm with specialist programmes on FM -one hour of Russian music then, depending on the day of the week, either French, Italian, Greek or Romanian music and international pop music on AM. The services then rejoined after four hours for parallel transmissions of international music. Although this experiment was discontinued after four months the Russian music hour was retained in the normal programme schedule.

The revival of the station's fortunes was short-lived however. In July 1985 more problems were encountered with generators on board the MV *Peace* and this, together with staff shortages and the fact that the price of oil had doubled due to the state of the Israeli economy, led to Abie Nathan announcing yet again that he would close the station. Lack of advertising revenue, which had dwindled to virtually nothing, also played an important part in this decision. Not for the first or last time this 'closure' was Abie Nathan's way of bringing his problems to the attention of a large number of people in the hope that, somehow, both moral and financial support would be forthcoming.

A new Perkins generator was installed on the MV *Peace* in July 1986. The FM transmitter was still working but both medium wave transmitters were virtually beyond repair.

On 11th/12th May 1987 a new medium wave transmitter was installed on the MV *Peace* in Ashdod and the aerial mast, which had been damaged during the previous winter, was repaired. At the same time the FM transmitter power was returned to 20kW output after new spare parts had been delivered to the ship.

### Voice of Peace programme schedule, June 1984

**6.00am Breakfast Show,** *Robb Scott (Alan West)*

**9.00am Morning Show,** *Dave Thomas*

**12noon Afternoon Delight,** *Kevin van Gelden*

**3.00pm Russian Music Programme,** *John Fortune*

**4.00pm Drive Time,** *Quentin Martin*

**6.00pm Twilight Time,** *Dave Thomas*

**7.30pm Peace Classics,** *Robb Scott*

**9.00pm Arabic Programme**

**10.00pm Kevin van Gelden**

**12midnight Night Beat,** *John Dwyer*

**3.00am Closedown**

### Peace silence

*At sunset each day the Voice of Peace played an appeal from Abie Nathan asking listeners to pray with him for all the victims of violence in the Middle East and throughout the world. The station then went silent for 30 seconds, re-opening with "We Wish You Peace" by the Eagles.*

> **VOP news**
>
> *The Voice of Peace took its hourly news direct from the state network, Kol Israel and relayed the bulletins live. DJs on the Voice of Peace had to listen carefully for 'out cues' in the news bulletins - there were two or three in each bulletin -to recommence their own programmes. The bulletins and of course the out cues were all in Hebrew, whilst most of the DJs were only English speaking so they had to learn the cue words or phrases to know when to begin the music again. Occasionally the Kol Israel newsreaders would play tricks on the Voice of Peace DJs by reading the news faster than usual, making it more difficult to identify the cue words or sometimes after the time signal pips allowed a few seconds of dead air before starting to read the news. This particular trick left the Voice of Peace DJ in a dilemma - should he start the music or wait and see if there was any more news?*

The *Peace* left port in the early morning of 14th May 1987 and Voice of Peace test transmissions on FM started that evening at 7.30pm. Unfortunately problems were being encountered with the new medium wave transmitter which would not feed its signal into the aerial system properly and a new tuning unit had to be ordered from America. This was eventually delivered on 5th June 1987 and an engineer from the transmitter's manufacturers, Nautel, went out to the ship to install it and make sure everything was working properly.

Tests on medium wave then started during the evening of 9th June 1987 and the full medium wave service began again the following evening. A split frequency service was briefly re-introduced by the Voice of Peace on 14th June 1987 when FM carried classical music while on medium wave (AM) a live sports commentary was broadcast from Greece via a Cellnet mobile phone!

By the end of June 1987 both FM and AM transmitters were running at full power, but the station suffered problems with staff shortages throughout the summer. In general the Voice of Peace seemed to have lost its sense of purpose and lacked any real direction by mid-1987. Abie Nathan considered the Voice of Peace to be a pan-Middle East station, but although its signal was audible on FM and medium wave throughout large parts of Israel, and on medium wave only in Lebanon, Egypt and Cyprus no real peace messages were being broadcast.

In September 1987, following a visit by Abie Nathan to London to recruit more staff and stock up on CDs and records, yet another new format was introduced on the Voice of Peace. With the slogan (and jingle package) "latest hits, greatest memories" the format determined that every record played was to be an instantly recognisable current or recent hit. This revised, livelier programming resulted in a renewed interest from advertisers and quite soon the station was broadcasting up to 10 different commercials each hour.

## Kol Israel strike

In early October 1987 the Government state network, Kol Israel, was closed by a strike. The Voice of Peace normally relayed Kol Israel's hourly news bulletins from 7.00am -1.00am, so attempts had to be made to provide an alternative service using the signal from the BBC's World Service transmitter in Cyprus. However, it proved impossible to obtain a signal of satisfactory quality which could be re-broadcast by the Voice of Peace's transmitters and it was decided that staff on board the *Peace* ship should compile and read their own news bulletins.

From 10th October 1987 the station broadcast two news bulletins each day, at noon and at 7.00pm, both of which were prepared on board, using the BBC World Service as the main source of information However, following pressure on Abie Nathan from the Kol Israel journalists' trade union the on-board news service was discontinued after just over a month. The trade union argued that by providing a source of news for Israeli listeners the Voice of Peace was undermining the effect of their members' strike action at Kol Israel.

One positive side effect of the Kol Israel strike for the Voice of Peace was that the station was able to substantially increase its advertising revenue. Being the only commercial radio station broadcasting at the time advertisers vied with each other to purchase airtime and at one stage the Voice of Peace was transmitting up to 26 spots per hour. This increased income enabled Abie Nathan to purchase and install a fax machine and radar system on board the MV *Peace* and consideration was also given to the purchase of new FM and shortwave transmitters.

The strike at Kol Israel was settled early in December 1987, and almost immediately this resulted in an end to the Voice of Peace's advertising bonanza.

Transmitter problems were encountered later in the month when the offshore station was put off the air on medium wave from 21st-30th December 1987 as a result of storm damage to the aerial system. The same problem occurred again at the end of January 1988 and although the FM transmitter stayed on the air during these periods it also suffered frequent short breaks in transmission. The Voice of Peace's brief domination of the Israel radio market seemed to have come to an end.

The MV *Peace* was damaged while in port at the end of January 1988 - a two foot long gash was cut in the hull after the vessel had been swept against the dock wall. This was soon repaired, however, and the ship returned to sea to resume broadcasts on 3rd February 1988. An Optimod unit was installed on the medium wave transmitter later that month, considerably improving signal quality, but the FM service continued to suffer a number of breakdowns and ran on only about 5Kw output during this time.

COMMERCIAL INVOICE

CM591 — #5142 — April 22,1987
Mar.17,1987 — Apr.22,1987 — 1 of 1

THE BANK OF NOVA SCOTIA
P.O.Box 216
BEDFORD, N.S. B4A 2X2

ISAAC SREDNI
ADAM ROBERT INC.
3049 N.E. 163rd.
N. MIAMI BEACH, FLORIDA U.S.A.
33160

PREPAID
CANADA — ISRAEL
Sanborn's to New York - IN BOND
FOB NEW YORK - EL AL AIRLINES -TO TEL AVIV

SANBORN'S EXPRESS — HACKETTS COVE, N.S.
SANBORNS/EL AL AIR — NEW YORK
TEL AVIV — TEL AVIV, ISRAEL — U.S.FUNDS

EL AL CARGO
JOHN F. KENNEDY AIRPORT
TURN SHIP TO:
PEACE SHIP
CARE OF ABIE NATHAN
BEN GURION AIRPORT, ISRAEL

10 CRATES CONTAINING:
1 - AMPFET 10, 10KW AM BROADCAST TRANSMITTER, SPARE MODULES & ACCESSORIES. S/N 220 Freq.1539kHz
FCC: B3W8GAAMPFET10
698Kg 2.53m3

AMPFET 10 - Totally Solid State AM Broadcast Transmitter including:
1 Kit Semiconductors,lamps & fuses.
1 NAPC7 System Monitor Plug-In Module
1 NAX34 Lightning/Surge Arrestor Kit.
1 — 58,000.00 — 58,000.00

TOTAL VALUE OF GOODS US$58,000.00

$58,000.00 INVOICE TOTAL
-58,000.00 PAYMENT RECEIVED IN ADVANCE
0 BALANCE OWING

IN BOND — TRANSPORTATION & EXPORTATION BY SANBORN'S

TOTAL INVOICE VALUE PAY THIS AMOUNT US$58,000.00
April 15,1987
Hackett's Cove, Hfx. Co.,N.S.

## Voice of Peace format and audience

The Voice of Peace's format at this time still included a Russian hour and programmes of Greek or Arabic music. This policy led to growing numbers of the station's audience re-tuning to Kol Israel's pop service or the Army pop music station and not returning to the Voice of Peace. Abie Nathan used the Voice of Peace to broadcast his own views and opinions on a wide variety of subjects and frequently came on air to talk about some issue which was important to him at the time. There was no official publicity material produced for the station - the Voice of Peace relied solely on its reputation and self-generated publicity, largely due to Abie Nathan's peace and humanitarian initiatives. Apart from a number of unofficial T-shirt designs which were produced and sold in Tel Aviv shops the only other publicity came from a contra-deal with a teenage magazine - the Voice of Peace broadcast commercials for the magazine while the publication devoted half a page each week to print the station's programme schedules.

No conventional research was undertaken to determine the station's listening figures or audience profile, but from letters received by DJs at the time it was possible to crudely gauge the size of the Voice of Peace's potential audience. During the day the station appeared to be popular with girls between the ages of 15/17, while older people listened during the evenings - the classical hour being particularly popular with this audience sector. Most shops, restaurants and taxis in Tel Aviv tuned their radios to the Voice of Peace during business hours and a substantial number of the station's advertisers came from this market sector, making it in commercial terms at least, a Tel Aviv local station, although Abie Nathan certainly perceived it as having a much wider appeal.

## Peace campaigning returns

The concept of peace promotion returned at the beginning of 1988 after Abie Nathan apparently realised that the Voice of Peace seemed to be lacking any purposeful direction. He declared 26th February 1988 to be a Peace Day and to mark the visit to Israel of US Secretary of State George Schultz the Voice of Peace played only peace music in all its programmes. At about the same time the

**Abie Nathan's restaurant re-opens**

*Abie Nathan re-opened his restaurant in Tel Aviv in May 1988 - he had closed and sold the original in 1972 to raise money to establish the Voice of Peace. In a reversal of previous station policy he then started to phone the ship during the evenings from his restaurant, allowing guests to make a record request to be played on air for a particular celebration.*

station started a new programme each day (except Friday and Saturday), called "What Would We Do?" which Abie Nathan presented himself. It took the form of a phone-in discussion about problems between Jew and Arab. On Fridays at this time a chat show, in which well known people such as pop stars, show business personalities and politicians took part, was broadcast live via a telephone link with the *Peace* ship. The same time slot on Saturday was filled by a sports programme.

The Voice of Peace suffered frequent breaks in transmission during April 1988 on both medium wave and FM. A new 25Kw FM transmitter was ordered from the USA and plans were made to install it when the ship was next dry docked in Haifa for overhaul.

On 19th April 1988 the station broadcast 24 hours of classical music in memory of Israeli soldiers who had died in various wars. Also during that month the station took to relaying the soundtrack of programmes broadcast on Israel's state television network and the Educational Television Service on a regular basis. One particular television programme, "Forty State Independence", was re-broadcast each afternoon with Abie Nathan then talking on a phone-in with listeners about issues raised during the programme. On 30th April 1988 the soundtrack of the Eurovision Song Contest was re-broadcast by the Voice of Peace, while on 11th May 1988 the European Soccer Cup Final was relayed by the station.

The MV *Peace* entered Haifa on 1st May 1988 for overhaul, repair and painting and consequently the station was off the air for six days. During this period the new FM transmitter was also installed by engineers from the United States and late on 6th May 1988 the Voice of Peace returned on both medium wave and FM with test transmissions.

On 13th September 1988 Abie Nathan met PLO leader Yasser Arafat in Tunis to talk about the possibility of arriving at a peace settlement. When he returned to Israel on 16th September Nathan was arrested and interviewed by police about his visit. Later that day, after he had been released, he went on air on the Voice of Peace to tell listeners what had happened both at his meeting with Yasser Arafat and with the police following his arrest.

## Arutz Sheva

Towards the middle of March 1988 a Jewish religious organisation, Gush Emunim had approached Abie Nathan about the possibility of hiring the Voice of Peace's transmitters to broadcast an hour of programmes every week. After being refused airtime by Nathan the group then offered to buy the entire *Peace* ship from him. When this request was also refused they went on to purchase a ship of their own and set about planning the launch of their offshore station later in the year.

The station's owners Yakopv Kats and Ze'ev Hever, represented the West Bank Settlers and the policy of the station was declared to be "to advance the ideas of Settlement and Eretz Yisrael Hashlema (Greater Israel)". The new station was to be established because the Gush Emunim organisation believed Israeli state radio was biased against their right wing ideology.

At 3.00am on 21st October 1988 the new radio ship, *Eretz Hatzvi* (*Land of the Gazelle*) arrived off Tel Aviv, anchoring three miles further out to sea than the *Peace* ship and just outside Israel's six mile territorial limit (for insurance purposes the *Peace* ship was actually anchored inside the limit, but the Israeli Government had for some time turned a blind eye to this arrangement).

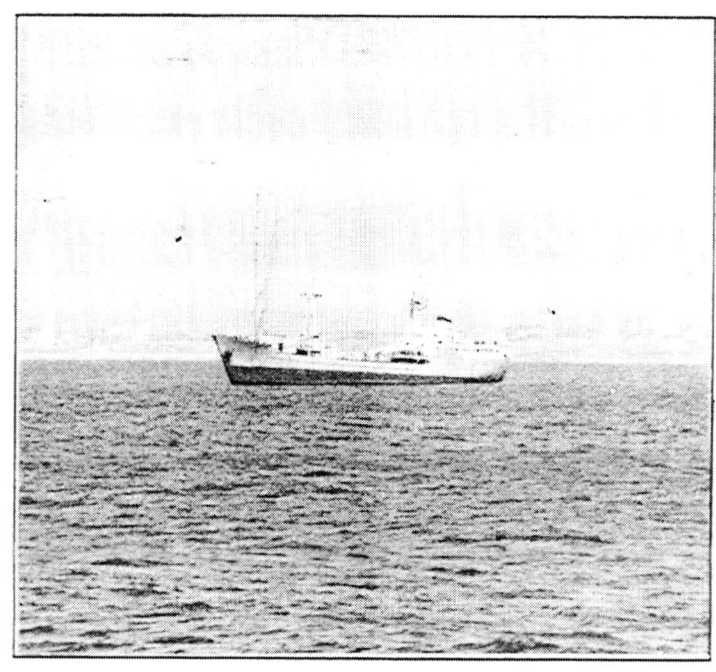

MV 'Hatzvi' at anchor off Israel

Test transmissions under the call sign Arutz Sheva (Channel Seven) started at 8.00am the same day on 918kHz (327m) using a 10KW transmitter. The tests consisted of non-stop Hebrew/Hassidic music, with occasional announcements and, as with the Voice of Peace, relays of the Kol Israel news at the top of the hour. These test transmissions continued daily from 7.00am - 10.00pm until the end of October 1988 when the ship raised her anchor and entered Haifa to have some adjustments made to the transmitter.

No more broadcasts were heard from Arutz Sheva until 18th November 1988 when the *Hatzvi* returned to her original anchorage and resumed test transmissions. Regular broadcasts then started shortly after 2.00pm on 20th November 1988. A Ministry of Communications spokesman, commenting on Israel's second offshore radio station said:-

*The law forbids transmissions from inside Israel that are not licenced by the Communications Ministry, but the Gush Emunim ship is outside our territorial waters. Although this is contrary to international law, there is nothing we can do.*

New radio station broadcasts in 'spirit of religious tradition and Jewish settlement'

**Government powerless to stop illegal Gush radio broadcasts**

Lack of cash delays Gush radio

Unlike the MV *Peace* the *Hatzvi* did not go into port to refuel, she received supplies from up to twelve small tenders each day. The station had two on-board DJs and the remaining programmes were taped in land-based studios. Arutz Sheva's managers and DJs were all practising ultra-orthodox Jews and programmes initially consisted largely of Hebrew music and material with a religious and nationalistic (Israeli) bias. Broadcasting hours at this time were Sunday-Thursday 5.00am-7.00pm, Friday 5.00am-1.00pm and Saturday 5.00pm-10.00pm - being an ultra-religious backed station transmissions closed on Shabbat (Friday afternoon to Saturday evening).

Meanwhile, by the beginning of December 1988 the Voice of Peace was down to just two DJs and Gil Katzir from the station's Tel Aviv office often went out to the ship to present programmes. Lack of advertising income was again causing financial problems and Abie Nathan claimed to be losing $50,000 a month - most commercials which were broadcast at this time were contra-deals for suppliers. Once again the station's viability had become precarious - the Voice of Peace was only managing to survive as a result of the large profits made during the lucrative days of the Kol Israel strike the previous year.

The programming situation was relieved somewhat at the turn of the year when an Israeli DJ and two new English and American presenters came on board the MV *Peace,* while two more Israeli DJs joined the station in early January 1989.

# RADIO

## PERMANENT PROGRAMS

### RADIO 1

*FREQUENCIES: 576, 1170, 1458 Khz (MW)*

Morning Exercise 0606; Hasidic Songs 0616; Mishna Page 0630; Gemara Page 0640; Bible Reading 0650; News in English 0700; News in French 0715; Golden Oldies 0730; Compass 0805; Teleradio – Listeners Info. Service 0905; Morning Pearls 1005; Hebrew Songs 1105; Mediterranean Medley 1205; News in English 1300; News in French 1330; Youth Magazine 1406; Open University 1530; News in English and French 1700; Religious Customs 1806; Programs for Olim 1900.

### RADIO 2

Hebrew Songs 0606; Morning News Highlights 0630; Driver's Corner 0652; A Moment of Hebrew 0657; This Morning: News Magazine 0700; Safe Driving 0805; House Call with Rivka Michaeli 0905; Network Magazine 1005; OK on Two 1210; Midday Current Affairs Program 1305; Art and Culture 1406; Humor 1430; Songs & Homework 1505; Hebrew Songs 1605; Magic Moments 1705; Books 1755; Free Period: Education Magazine 1806; Today: News Magazine 1900; Hebrew Songs 1935; Direct News Broadcast from ITV 2100; Midnight News Magazine 0005; Goals & Songs: Nat'l League Soccer Sat 1530-1730; Pulse:Weekly health magazine Tue 1806.

### RADIO 3

Back to Happiness 0605; Early Morning Music 0705; What, It's Nine Already? 0905; Good Things 1006; On Line 1105; Daily Love 1205; Only on Weekdays 1305; For Me and You: Songs and greetings 1406; Latest Hits 1506; Pop '89 1605; Night Songs 2305; Int'l Hit Parade Sun 1806; Israeli Hit Parade Tue 1806.

### ARMY

Morning Songs 0500; Literally Speaking 0555; Eye Opener: First news of the day 0630; 007: With Alex Ansky 0707; Good Morning Israel 0800; In The Morning 0905; Hebrew Songs 1005; As Of Now 1105; Do-Re Daily: With Dubi Lentz and Dani Karpel 1305; Daily Meeting with people from all walks of life 1405; Holiday Songs:With Erez Tal 1505; Four In The Afternoon 1605; Good Evening Israel 1700; Music Magazine with Orly Yaniv 1905 (2); Announcements for Soldiers 1957 (1); 2157 (2); News Direct from ITV 2100; Oriental Songs 2205 (1); 10 O'clock Break 2205 (2); Day In Review 2305 (1); All That Jazz 2305 (2); Night Birds 0005; Don't Wanna Sleep 0200; Nine hours of Hebrew Songs Sat 0900-1800 (2); Weekend Magazine Sat 1800-2000; Broadcast University 0605, rpt 2130; Morning Supplement: The weekend papers Fri 0707; Good Times: With Oded Kotler Fri 0905; Sandals: Two worn-out hours with Dori Ben Zeev Fri 1205.

### VOICE OF PEACE

The Breakfast Show Sun-Fri 0600; Morning Music Sun-Fri 0900; Kasach Hour: Oriental Songs Daily 1200; Afternoon Delight Sun-Thur 1300; Ma La'asot:Listeners talk to Abie Nathan Sun-Thur 1500; '50s and '60s songs Sun-Thur 1700; Twilight Time Daily 1800; Classical Music Daily 19:30; Volga Hour: Russian songs Sun-Thur, Sat 2100; Night Beat Sun-Thur, Sat 0000; Late Night Affair Daily 0300; New Israeli songs Fri 1300; Before Shabbat:With interviewer Eitan Danzig Fri 1400; Hebrew Hit Parade Fri 1500; Int'l Hit Parade Fri 1600; Singalong Fri 2100; Dance Party Fri 2300; Arabic Songs Sat 0600; Greatest Hits Sat 0800; Shabbat Sport Sat 1300; Soul Music Sat 1400; South American Music Sat 1500; Weekend Special: Int'l Singer Sat 1600; Weekend Special: Israeli Singer Sat 1700; Jazz Show Sat 2200.

### VOICE OF AMERICA

*FREQUENCIES: 1260 kHz (MW) 0500-0530; 0800-0900; 1700-1730; 1800-1830; 1100-1200. 6040 kHz (LW) 0500-0900. 9700 kHz (LW) 1700-1200*

News Hourly on the hour; Newsline Mon-Fri 0610, 0710, 0810, 1710, 1910, 2110; VOA Morning Mon-Fri 0530, 0630, 0730, 0830; Sat & Sun 0510, 0610, 0710, 0810; Music USA Mon-Fri 1930, 2210; Sat 2210; Sun 2110; Focus Mon-Fri 1810, 2010; Special English News & Features Daily 1830, 2030; Magazine Show Mon-Fri 1730, 2130; Editorial Daily 2255; World Report Mon-Fri 2310; Closeup Sat 1710, 2010; Press Conference, USA Sat 1730, 2130; American Viewpoints Sat 1810, 2110; Communications World Sat 1910, 2310; New Horizons Sun 1710, 2310; Studio One Sun 1730, 2330; Encounter Sun 1810, 2010; Critic's Choice Sun 1910; Issues in the News Sun 1930; Sunday Report Sun 2110; The Concert Hall Sun

THE NATION MAGAZINE / NOVEMBER 18, 1988

*The Voice of Peace programme schedule was published alongside those of 'official' Israeli radio stations and the Voice of America*

# Chapter 22

# Album Rock -v- Chart Hits

Legal arguments over the ownership of the *Ross Revenge* and searching for new sources of finance delayed the re-launch of Radio Caroline considerably during 1982. This situation continued into the early months of 1983.

The claims and counter claims to the radio ship took many months to be heard in the Spanish courts and the *Ross Revenge* only became available to Ronan O'Rahilly's group again in mid-May 1983 after they had regained legal possession of the vessel. Had the decision of the courts gone in favour of the former American backers at that stage Ronan O'Rahilly could have lost ownership and control of the vessel completely. Fortunately for Caroline the Americans did not appeal against the decision to release the *Ross Revenge* to Ronan O'Rahilly - had they done so the case could have dragged on for many more months further delaying the return of Radio Caroline.

New financial backers were found by Ronan O'Rahilly mainly in Canada and work was able to recommence on completing the fitting out of the *Ross Revenge*. All work was carried out in great secrecy and in late June 1983 the *Ross Revenge* was moved to dry dock where she was sandblasted and her hull was treated with protective paint to withstand long periods at sea. At this stage it was still hoped to have Radio Caroline back on the air by 14th August , the 16th anniversary of the British Marine etc. Broadcasting (Offences) Act coming into effect.

## Unwelcome publicity

On 28th July 1983 the first press reports appeared in the Dublin *Evening Herald* hinting at the imminent return of Radio Caroline. The reports were also carried by a number of Irish land-based pirate radio stations and within a few days the British national press, in particular *The Guardian*, and the *Daily Mail* were reporting the story. Official reaction to the news that Radio Caroline was about to reappear off the British coast was predictable and ill considered -the Department of Trade announced that it would consider jamming the station's signal once broadcasts commenced.

This unwelcome publicity led to the Caroline organisation deciding that the *Ross Revenge* must leave port if any threat of official action was to be avoided, so plans were rapidly advanced for the ship to sail. The *Ross Revenge* did not sail from Santander until mid-afternoon on 4th August 1983 - the harbour authorities refused to release her because there was no qualified Captain on board and there were also problems with the vessel's lifeboat. The lifeboat problem was quickly rectified and an Englishman, former salvage tug skipper and Falklands War veteran, Captain Martin Eve of Ipswich, was engaged by Radio Caroline to take command of the *Ross Revenge*. He stayed with the radio ship until she was safely at anchor off the British coast.

Four days after leaving Spain, at about 6.30am on 8th August 1983 the *Ross Revenge* was sighted off Britain's south coast under tow by the Spanish tug *Aznar Jose Luis*. Although the *Ross Revenge* could have sailed under her own power it was decided to have her towed by the foreign registered tug to prevent any intervention or boarding attempts by the British authorities. The initial sighting of the *Ross Revenge,* by a NATO fighter plane, also caused a mini security alert until the vessel identified herself as the new Radio Caroline ship.

Twelve hours later the *Ross Revenge* arrived at a position in the Kentish Knock, where she stayed overnight, moving the next day to an anchorage in the Knock Deep near where the *Mi Amigo* had sunk three years previously. The tug left the radio ship to lower her own anchor - capable of holding a quarter million ton supertanker - in an operation which took about six hours to complete.

At half past midnight on 9th August 1983 the transmitter was switched on for about 30 minutes with a carrier signal on 963kHz (319m) and further carrier signals were transmitted during the following few days in preparation for the commencement of regular broadcasts. However, by Saturday 13th August 1983 the transmitter had to be switched off because in was causing interference along the medium wave band, due to one of the deck insulators having been damaged. Without a spare insulator on board engineers had to wait until a replacement could be brought from Spain.

Three DJs joined the radio ship on 12th August 1983 - Andy Archer, who had just resigned from Centre Radio in Leicester at a few hours notice, together with Tony Gareth and Dixie Peach. They left a quiet Suffolk port shortly before dawn and travelled out to the *Ross Revenge* to join the crew who had sailed with the ship from Spain - DJs Tom Anderson, Robin Ross and Dave Simmons, together with engineer Peter Chicago. Another Captain, Irishman Joe Woods, also joined the radio ship at this time.

Despite the arrival of this full compliment of broadcasting staff there was still one main problem to resolve before full programming could commence - the on-board studios were not yet fully operational. This was due to the haste in which the *Ross Revenge* had left Spain and also to a last minute change of plan. Originally a Portakabin had been mounted on the after deck to house the broadcasting studios, but it was then decided that such a structure was unlikely to survive very long during the severe winter weather on the North Sea. The Portakabin was removed before the *Ross Revenge* sailed for Britain and, during the voyage from Spain work started on fitting out two on-board studios. This work was still continuing as the ship lay at anchor off the British coast and partly delayed the planned re-launch of the station.

*The 'Ross Revenge' in Spain, with Portakibin studios*

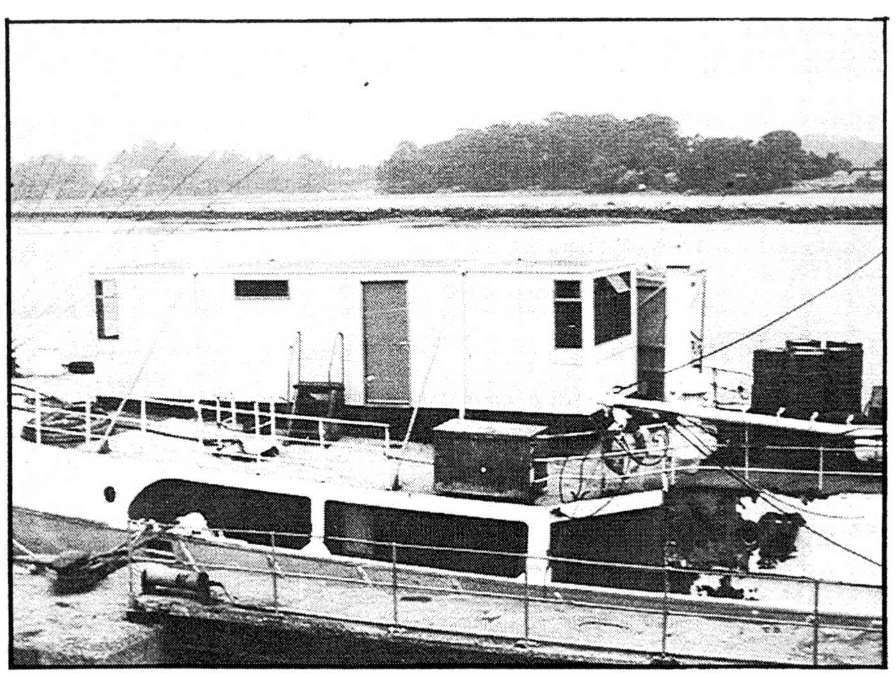

## Aerial mast

The most striking feature of the *Ross Revenge* was its aerial mast towering 300' above deck level, the tallest structure ever built on a ship. The mast had been computer designed to withstand the worst weather conditions that were likely to be encountered in the North Sea, and actually went through the main deck into the ship's hold, where it was secured in 300 tons of concrete.

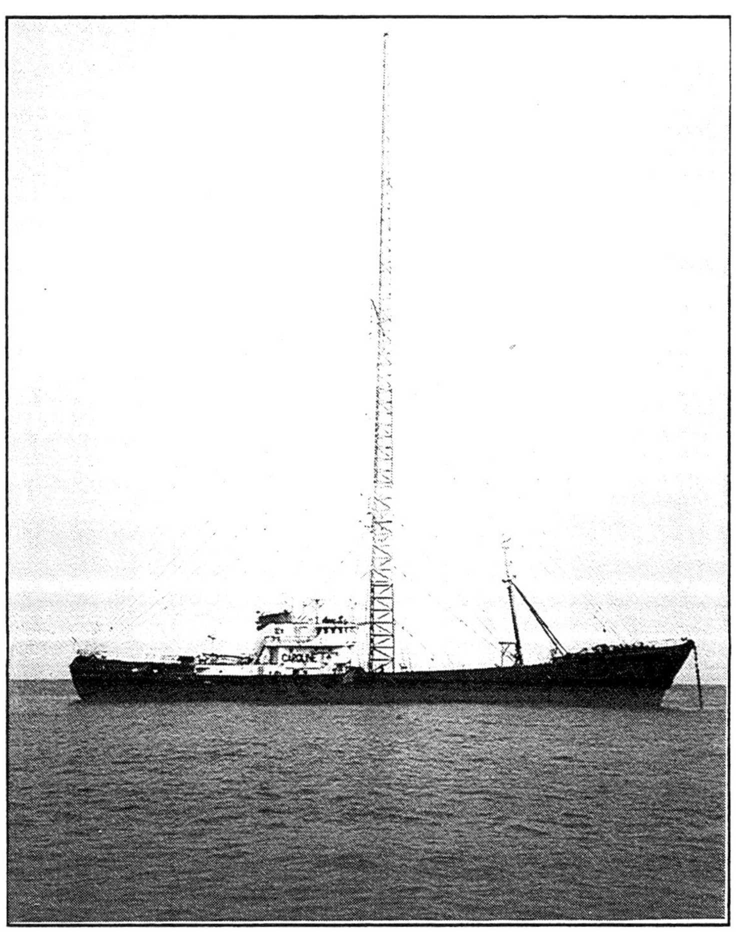

The 'Ross Revenge' at anchor off Britain

On board the ship were three transmitters - one Canadian 50Kw RCA Ampliphase and two American 5Kw RCAs, although one of the latter had been stripped for parts and was not operational. There was also an Orban Optimod AM unit to process the transmitter's signal, giving near FM quality. Two MAN generators on board each delivered a power of 136Kw and all navigational aids from the *Ross Revenge's* days as a trawler were still on the bridge. Some confusion remained about the name of the ship - many press reports insisted that the vessel was called *Imagine,* but plans to use that name had long since been dropped by the Radio Caroline organisation and she was still known and registered as the *Ross Revenge.*

Ronan O'Rahilly, interviewed on ITN's Channel 4 News on 15th August 1983 dismissed claims that the station was an illegal operation saying: "We supply from Spain and we have international advertising, our offices are in Los Angeles and New York. The station is run in strict compliance with all of the local legislation in the various European countries."

## Caroline 60's Revival Night

*A 60s Revival Night Disco was held at the Lyceum Ballroom in London on 18th August 1983 to celebrate the return of Radio Caroline, but unfortunately for various technical reasons the station's broadcasts still had not started by that date. Nevertheless the event did serve to generate further press publicity for the imminent return of Radio Caroline.*

*The event was organised by Robb Eden through his Contemporary Music Consultants business and was attended by between 400 and 500 people, including radio personalities from the 60s and 70s offshore days. Amongst celebrities present were Crispian St John, Mike Barrington, Dave Gilbee, Tommy Vance (compere), Robb Eden, Tony Blackburn, Ronan O'Rahilly and three people from behind the scenes at Caroline House in the 60s - Dick Moorcroft, Ken Evans and Colin Nicol - also the first DJ on Radio Atlanta in 1964). Artists who performed at the event included the Nashville Teens, the Carl Denver Trio, Polly Brown and Ricky Valence. The proceedings were filmed by British breakfast television station TVAM and Holland's Veronica TV.*

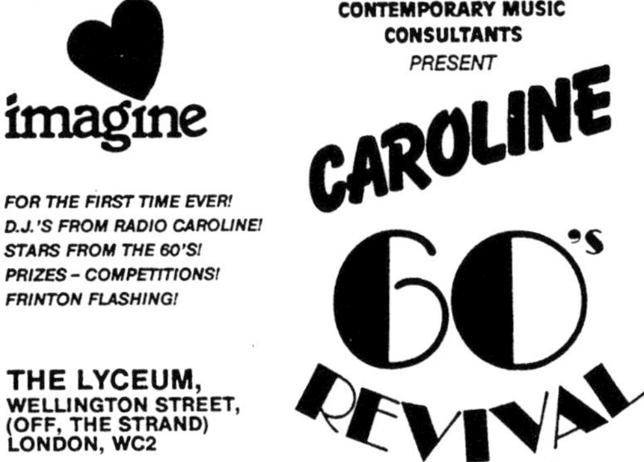

## First broadcasts

19th August 1983 saw the first actual test broadcast from the *Ross Revenge* for the re-launch of Radio Caroline. It started at 5.30am with continuous music and then at 7.30am listeners heard the first announcement - "You are listening to a test transmission from Radio Caroline on 319m, 963kHz. Our programmes commence at 12 noon tomorrow."

The following day test transmissions of continuous music resumed at 7.30am. Then at 12 noon official broadcasts started when the station's theme, "Caroline" by The Fortunes, was played followed immediately by John Lennon's "Imagine" and "Existence" by the Loving Awareness Band. It was not until 12.17pm that the opening announcement was made by DJ Tom Anderson, *Good Afternoon ladies and gentlemen and welcome to Radio Caroline on 319m, 963kHz. I'm Tom and for the next hour I'd like to take you on a couple of musical journeys through the past two decades.*

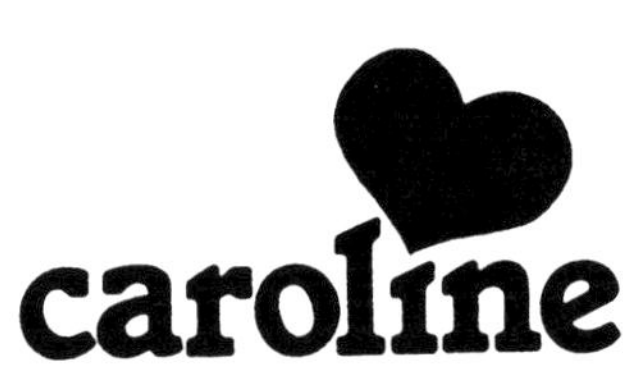


## New format

This initial opening heralded a new format concept for the station - not only was it to be album-based but the music content would take precedence over the spoken word, with two or usually three tracks being played consecutively without any interruption for DJ announcements or commercials. However, over the next few days this format was gradually watered down as various DJs began to inject more and more speech content into their programmes.

Some disappointment was expressed by listeners at the format and overall sound of the new Radio Caroline. The general explanation offered for the change from the previous Top 40 format was that the station was now directed at a new audience - 18-40 years old with an Album (Adult) Orientated Rock (AOR) format. Additionally the station was suffering some technical teething problems with equipment and lack of proper production facilities. This was attributed to the last minute reconstruction of the main studio during the voyage from Spain and meant that many promotions and inserts could only be produced after the station had closed each day.

## Dive to the wreck of the *Mi Amigo*

As the new Radio Caroline ship was arriving off the Essex coast in August 1983 members of the Canvey Branch of the British Sub-Aqua Club were busy exploring the wreck of the former Caroline ship, *Mi Amigo* on the edge of the Long Head Sand sandbank.

Underwater visibility at that time was particularly good and a team of three divers, Peter Ellegard, Clive Rowe and Phil Despy spent 35 minutes exploring the wreck of the radio ship. Peter described the dive in an article published in the Southend *Evening Echo: -*

*The remarkably good visibility of about 15ft allowed me to see everything clearly. Already the wreck has become a sanctuary and home for a myriad of sea creatures. Brightly coloured sponges and anemones clothe the hull and superstructure. Fish of all colours, shapes and sizes dart in and out of the deck fittings and cabins, or hover almost motionless alongside. While crabs, large and small have made homes for themselves in every available nook and cranny. Exotic looking jellyfish were trapped by the current, their trailing tentacles wrapped helplessly round the deck railings. And, no doubt, in the darker recesses of the ship lurked a few conga eels, common on wrecks, though I didn't see any on this dive.*

*The ship is still as it was when it throbbed to the latest pop and rock sounds. But the only sound we heard was the eerie underwater silence broken only by the bubbles from our breathing apparatus. No ghostly melodies haunt this wreck. The 'Caroline' name still proudly adorns the two bow studios. But despite inviting open hatchways and the chance to pick up a souvenir record I did not venture inside. Shining my torch into the yawning blackness all I could see was a thick layer of sand and silt, putting everything beyond recognition. The unkind name of a floating old tub that the 'Mi Amigo' earned before it sank can easily be understood. Even allowing for the ravages of the sea in places the hull and superstructure is rusted and battered.*

LIVE FROM THE NORTH SEA ON 319 Metres (963khz)

Europe's first and only album station

RADIO CAROLINE

FOR THE BEST IN MUSIC; THE TIME OF YOUR LIFE

Initially Radio Caroline's broadcasting hours were from 7.00am - 2.00am, but by the third week in September the station was opening each day at 6.00am. A rudimentary news service, consisting of headlines on the half hour at peak listening times, was started on 12th September 1983, while the famous Caroline Bell was re-introduced on 16th September. However, full station identity jingles for the new Radio Caroline were not aired until 10th October 1983. The delay in introducing these features was attributed to the fact that construction of the production studio had not been completed when the station went on the air in August - first priority having been given to building the main studio.

The station gave out a mailing address in Los Angeles, which was the office of DJ Wolfman Jack's agent, Dan Kelly. Although it was not a particularly convenient arrangement to have a mailing address 6,000 miles away from the station the system obviously worked because within three weeks of Radio Caroline's transmissions starting the first listeners' letters were being read on air by the DJs. Plans were announced in early September 1983 for the station to also open an office in Monte Carlo to handle more day-to-day matters, leaving the Los Angeles and New York agents to book and sell commercial airtime.

**Radio Caroline programme schedule, September 1983**

6.00am Peter Clark
10.00am Andy Archer
2.00pm Robin Ross
6.00pm Simon Barrett
10.00pm Carl Kingston
2.00am Closedown

## Confrontation

Radio Caroline's return in August 1983 caused an immediate confrontation with the British authorities. The frequency of 963kHz used by the offshore station had already been allocated by the Department of Trade to the organisers of a Christian Pop Festival at Knebworth Park, Hertfordshire at which pop star and evangelist Cliff Richard was billed to appear the following weekend. Although at that time Radio Caroline was only using about 17Kw of the possible 50Kw available from its transmitter, the Department of Trade was forced to allocate the pop festival another frequency to ensure that there were no complaints of interference by the event's organisers.

A similar problem also affected about twenty campus radio stations at colleges and universities throughout central and southern England, again forcing the authorities to allocate new frequencies before the start of term in September and October. Despite this reallocation by the authorities formal protests about Radio Caroline's transmissions were received from University Radio Nottingham, and similar student stations at Colchester, Sussex, Hull, Southampton and Bath.

Throughout September and October 1983 Radio Caroline's broadcasts steadily built up a large audience. A Gallup Poll survey, published at the end of October 1983, showed that in the UK an average of 7% of the adult population (around 4 million people) had listened to the station in its first few weeks on the air, with regional figures showing an audience reach of 19% in East Anglia and 12% in London and the south east. Another survey in Holland at about the same time showed that half a million people listened regularly to the station while another half a million claimed to tune in occasionally. Encouraged by these significant

**ILR station closes**

*On 6th October 1983 ILR station Centre Radio in Leicester (from which Andy Archer had left suddenly in August to rejoin Radio Caroline) went into receivership and closed. This was the first ILR station to fail financially and cease broadcasting since the commercial radio network had been introduced to Britain in 1973.*

audience figures and the success of its Album Rock Format, Radio Caroline extended its broadcasting to 24 hours a day from 12th November 1983.

The record library on board the *Ross Revenge* was said to have contained only about 1,500 albums at the time Radio Caroline came back on the air, but evidence that Radio Caroline was once more able to receive a regular supply of new records (possibly in contravention of the Marine etc. Broadcasting (Offences) Act 1967) came at the end of October 1983 with the introduction of a weekly Top 30 Album Chart.

## Arrests

Despite the encouraging audience reaction to the return of Radio Caroline the authorities were, not surprisingly, unhappy about the re-launch of the offshore station and on 19th November 1983 seven people, including DJ Andy Archer and three other Radio Caroline personnel, were arrested by police. This followed a chase of the station's tender by a police launch along the River Deben to the small harbour of Melton, near Woodbridge in Suffolk. Boat owner Mick East told press reporters later that police were waiting at the quayside when his vessel docked and everyone on board was arrested and taken to Ipswich police station for questioning while the boat itself was searched by police sniffer dogs.

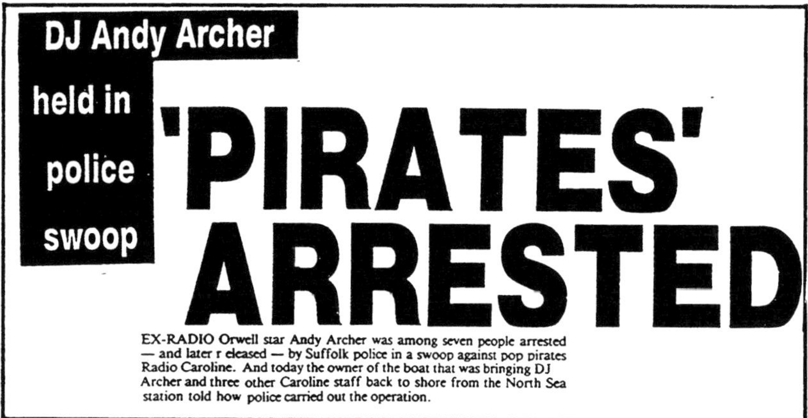

DJ Andy Archer held in police swoop

'PIRATES' ARRESTED

EX-RADIO Orwell star Andy Archer was among seven people arrested — and later r eleased — by Suffolk police in a swoop against pop pirates Radio Caroline. And today the owner of the boat that was bringing DJ Archer and three other Caroline staff back to shore from the North Sea station told how police carried out the operation.

Further action from the authorities followed on 8th December 1983 when British Telecom Maritime Services withdrew the ship-to-shore telephone facility to the *Ross Revenge*. The Department of Trade advised British Telecom that providing such a service would "amount to aiding and abetting a criminal offence contrary to the Marine etc. Broadcasting (Offences) Act 1967". However, British Telecom were still able to provide such facilities in an emergency situation where the safety of those on board the radio ship was endangered.

Although there had been occasional transmitter breakdowns and short periods off the air for routine maintenance purposes the station successfully maintained a 24 hour service throughout late November and most of December 1983.

The format of the new Radio Caroline came in for some sharp criticism from the weekly music paper *Melody Maker* at the end of December 1983 :- *The music largely played on the station is now unexpectedly conservative - a safe, predictable mixture of AOR Rock and old classics, with a smattering of soul and selected current chart material between. Caroline rarely play anything on an independent label and the only thing even vaguely revolutionary about their format is how little emphasis they put on the jocks themselves.*

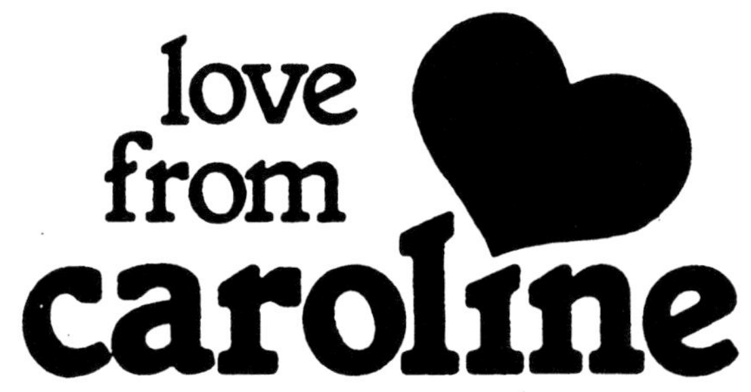

## New offshore project

As the return of Radio Caroline stole the headlines in August 1983 another offshore radio project was secretly being put together in Britain, Ireland and the USA.

This project had its origins in February 1983, when it had seemed uncertain that Radio Caroline would be able to return in the foreseeable future. John Kenning, who had been involved in and witnessed the growth and success of the Irish landbased pirate stations, claimed to have access to sufficient financial backing to launch an offshore radio station. He initially wanted to base his station off the Irish coast inside territorial waters on the basis that the Irish Government, having tolerated the increasing number of landbased stations were unlikely to hinder the launch of one from an offshore base, but in case they did the vessel could quickly be moved to international waters.

John Kenning made contact with ex-Radio Caroline DJ and engineer Paul Rusling and together they visited New York where they spoke to media salesman Roy Lindau of Music Media Radio. Lindau had previously been involved with the early plans to re-launch Radio Caroline in 1981, but until persuaded otherwise by Kenning and Rusling he at first wanted nothing to do with another British offshore radio project.

Nothing much happened for a while after these exploratory talks and in the intervening weeks John Kenning became increasingly involved with a London landbased pirate station, Radio Sovereign, which he operated with former offshore DJ Crispian St John (later Jay Jackson on Radio Caroline). Paul Rusling, who had made tentative enquiries about the availability of a suitable ship and transmitting equipment, also withdrew from the project at this time because he had serious doubts that the claimed financial resources really existed.

Meanwhile, in New York the initially sceptical Roy Lindau was still pursuing the idea of launching another offshore radio station off the coast of Britain. He joined forces with Paul Hodge (who had also been involved in the early attempts to bring back Radio Caroline in 1981/82) and together they persuaded the mysterious financial backer (Irish businessman Philip Smyth) that they could sell enough commercial airtime to international advertisers for an offshore radio station to become a viable proposition. Paul Rusling was also persuaded to re-join the project on the assurance that financial backing did really exist.

At this stage the American team planned to launch twin stations from a ship off the British coast - Radio Star, playing pop music with hits by established artists and Radio Waves, with a gold hits format. The Radio Star name was later changed to Laser because it was felt that that projected a more up to date and dynamic image.

### Radio Ursula

*In November 1983 reports appeared in the British press about another possible offshore radio station planning to start broadcasts off the coast of Britain.*

*A group of American backers were proposing to operate Radio Ursula on three medium wave frequencies, and on shortwave from a ship (reported to be a former Norwegian coaster, 'Nordlys'). the consortium planned to offer ten million shares in a company - Global Media Inc. - to finance the station. James Ryan, who had been involved with the original consortium to bring back Radio Caroline in 1980/81 and whose financial dealings had delayed and nearly killed the whole re-launch, was reportedly acting as financial agent for the new project.*

*Nothing more was heard of Radio Ursula or Global Media Inc.*

## Ship sets sail

On 27th August 1983, just a week after Radio Caroline's return to the air an ex-trawler, *Gardline Seeker*, slipped out of Lowestoft, Suffolk and headed across the Atlantic towards Florida. By the time the vessel arrived at the Tractor Marine Shipyard in Port Everglade, on 28th September 1983, she had been renamed MV *Communicator* and re-registered in Panama. The *Communicator,* which was owned by a company known as Deka Overseas, was dry docked for three weeks while work was carried out on her hull, after which she was moved to a remote part of the shipyard to be fitted out as a radio ship.

Paul Rusling supervised the installation of the transmitting and studio equipment on board the *Communicator,* but he was unable to convince the Americans that the twin stations should broadcast from a tower aerial installed on the ship. Instead they wanted, and insisted on using, a helium balloon system which had been successfully used in broadcasting Voice of America programmes in the Mediterranean and off Florida. Another unusual feature of the station's technical organisation was that all music was to be re-recorded from discs onto cartridges before being played on air. This was the system conventionally used for commercials and jingles, but had the advantage of being able to continue in use during stormy weather at sea when it was impossible to use conventional discs.

While the *Communicator* was being fitted out in Florida the backers of the second station (Radio Waves) withdrew their support and that part of the project folded. However, despite everything on board the ship having been designed to accommodate a twin operation, it was decided to amend the design and continue fitting out the vessel for the proposed Laser part of the project.

## *Communicator* sails for Britain

After fitting out works had been completed the *Communicator* left Florida on 17th November 1983 and sailed for Ireland, calling at Sao Miguel Island in the Azores for a few days at the beginning of December 1983. A full team of American DJs sailed across the Atlantic with the *Communicator,* but one of the American management team, Paul Hodge, withdrew from the project before the radio ship reached Europe. About this time too there were a number of other staff disputes and resignations causing the project to almost founder before it had properly begun.

The *Communicator* eventually docked in New Ross, County Wexford on 8th December 1983, to have some work undertaken on her anchoring system, but her presence attracted unwelcome enquiries from news reporters forcing her to put to sea again for a few days until the interest had died down. The vessel quietly slipped back into the Irish port late on 16th December and, with a temporary wire aerial slung between her masts, a test transmission was carried out in New Ross Harbour during the early hours of 17th December 1983.

Finally, in the early hours of 20th December 1983, the *Communicator* left New Ross and sailed towards the Thames Estuary where she arrived and dropped anchor, one mile off Margate, two days later. Almost immediately the *Communicator* had to ride out a violent storm and was forced to run her main engines for some hours just to maintain a stationary position at this 'sheltered' anchorage. Reports of a planned new offshore radio station appeared in the local media just before Christmas 1983, while the *Communicator* was still at anchor off Margate, although no transmissions were made from the ship during this period.

### Secrecy

Quite understandably the project's backers were anxious to maintain total secrecy about the Communicator's new role and this article in a local newspaper (the *Munster Express*) on 16th December 1983 showed just how successfully the cover story had been put across:-

*An American owned communications vessel containing millions of pounds worth of the most advanced satellite linked computer equipment slipped quietly into New Ross port for servicing last weekend. The 1,050 gross ton 'Communicator' will be engaged in vital oil-related seismic surveys off the south Irish coast during the next week or so. The 'Communicator' is fitted with a Comsat terminal near her stern and by using the Marisat or Marecs satellites, which are 22,500 miles up in space, the ship's personnel can be in constant touch with their home base, other ships or any place else in the world. It is possible that the ship could be using the NASA Landsat 4 satellite. This facility is 500 miles up in space and used to be called the Earth Resources Satellite. The 'Communicator' may also have access to the Transit Navigational Satellite System which is mainly used by the Navy and Military. Using that particular system the ship could accurately pinpoint its position to a matter of a few yards. The Master of the 'Communicator' is Captain Peter Boucher, a native of Waterford City. 47 year old Captain Boucher received his training with Irish Shipping Ltd. and is now based in America.*

After five days at anchor during the Christmas holiday period the *Communicator* sailed northwards on 29th December 1983. She circled the Radio Caroline ship, *Ross Revenge,* and at 4.00pm the same day dropped anchor in her new position, in international waters, two and a half miles south of Caroline's vessel. The project's backers had been forced to move the radio ship hurriedly because of fears that the British authorities, whose interest had been aroused by press reports and through the (illegal) interception of radio communications between the *Communicator* and land- based staff, were about to mount a raid on the vessel.

**Laser takes to the air**

## Balloon test transmissions

The first test transmission from the *Communicator* was planned to take place on 19th January 1984 using, as the American management had always insisted, an aerial held aloft by a helium balloon tethered to the ship. The helium balloon was inflated and launched at the stern of the ship with the aerial wire running up the nylon tethering rope, ending just 12' short of the balloon itself. Unfortunately, when the powerful transmitter was switched on high voltages at the end of the aerial wire melted through the nylon rope and the balloon floated away towards Europe, reportedly ending up tangled around a church steeple in Belgium.

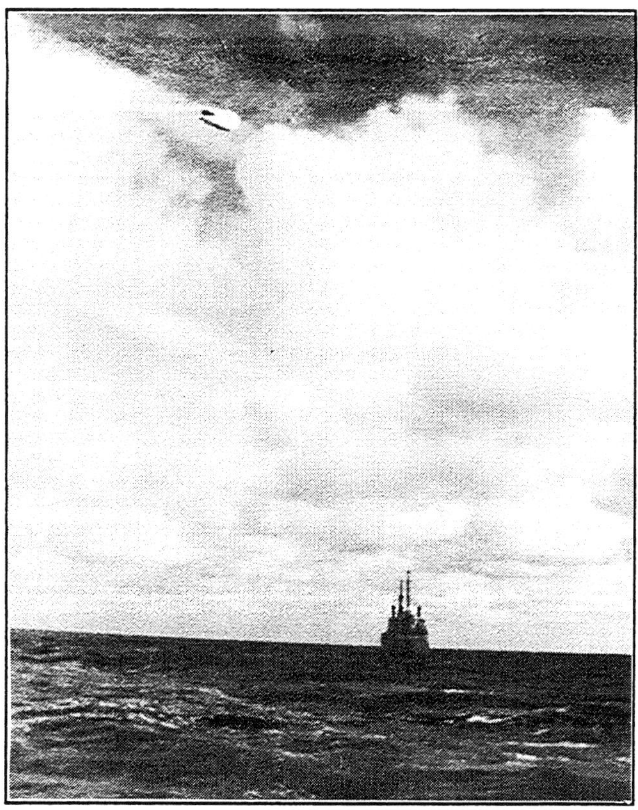

*The 'Communicator's' balloon aerial*

A second attempt was made two days later with the reserve balloon, raised to a height of 350 feet. This time test transmissions were successfully broadcast and reception reports were later received from Britain, France, Germany and Ireland. This new offshore station, using the call sign Laser 730, transmitted on a frequency of 729kHz (411m) with a power at that time of just 5Kw.

After half an hour of intermittent carrier signals the first record played on the new station was "Back to the USSR" by the Beatles, aired at 10.15am on 21st January 1984. Apart from one 45 minute break test transmissions of continuous Beatles music took place throughout the rest of that day and into the early hours of 22nd January 1983. But suddenly at 2.15am the second helium balloon broke from its tethering rope and floated away, this time reportedly ending up on a roundabout in Colchester.

An examination of the tethering rope later showed that it had been gradually cut through by the action of the Force 9 gales which had caused the rope to tighten and rub against a metal securing hook. When the tethering rope eventually snapped the balloon floated away freely, allowing the aerial wire to fall into the sea and putting the station off the air once again.

The balloons, which had been manufactured by Raven Industries of Sioux Falls, South Dakota, cost $11,000 (£6,000) each so the station's American operators conceded that they could not continue using this aerial system to broadcast. Although the theory was sound and balloon aerials had worked successfully in the Mediterranean and off the Florida coast such a system was clearly unsuitable for the severe weather conditions experienced in the North Sea.

## Caroline's "new neighbours"

The arrival of the *Communicator* was treated with some caution by Radio Caroline whose DJs made some cryptic remarks on air about "new neighbours". A spokeswoman for Radio Caroline's Los Angeles office was quoted in the press as saying that they welcomed the new rival radio station, but stressed that they were aiming at a different market "Caroline specialises in album tracks while Radio Laser will be playing Top 50 singles." This bland dismissal of the new competition betrayed a certain lack of understanding of the British radio market at the time and was to have some fundamental consequences during the following twelve months for Radio Caroline and its strictly album-based format.

The same spokeswoman was quoted again in the London *Evening Standard* on 6th January 1984 saying that commercial advertising on Radio Caroline would begin in 10 days time, an element of the programming which had been markedly absent since Radio Caroline's return four months earlier. For an offshore radio station to survive it needs a regular and steady flow of commercial revenue and clearly Radio Caroline had been experiencing difficulties selling airtime.

A New York radio sales organisation, Radio Sales International Inc. eventually managed to secure some advertising from a consortium of US companies. At about the same time too the station started publicising a new mailing address in New York, although, confusingly, the original Los Angeles address also remained in operation.

Radio Sales International was partly owned by DJ Wolfman Jack, (who was to have been one of the station's star DJs when Radio Caroline first planned to return in 1981) and was fronted by Vincent Monsey (also known as Paul Collins) who had himself been involved with the original plans to return Radio Caroline in 1981/82. Wolfman Jack's agent, Dan Kelly, was also involved - he had worked before to try and sell airtime on Radio Caroline, but without much success.

## *Ross Revenge* adrift

The *Ross Revenge* survived many storms in the North Sea at the end of 1983 and the beginning of 1984, but the elements finally won on 20th January 1984 when the radio ship lost her anchor and drifted onto a sandbank. Radio Caroline's transmissions were stopped at 9.20pm because the ship had started to list dangerously as the tide receded and she remained in this precarious position overnight. However, the following day when the tide rose again, the *Ross Revenge* was able to free herself from the sandbank and sail under her own power to a position in international waters about five miles from the Sunk Head Lightship. Broadcasts recommenced at 6.00am that morning after a temporary anchor had been dropped, while code numbers 35 and 36 were given out during early morning programmes to alert those on shore that the vessel had lost her main anchor.

Within a few days a replacement anchor was acquired and delivered to the *Ross Revenge,* enabling her to leave the temporary anchorage on 25th January 1984 and sail back to the normal Falls Head position. Broadcasts from Radio Caroline continued uninterrupted during the four hour voyage.

It was extremely important that Radio Caroline had returned to the air as quickly as possible at that time because the first paid commercials were due to be broadcast during that week. From 23rd January 1984 references were made at the end of newscasts to *Newsweek* magazine, which now sponsored Radio Caroline's news service as well as having bought promotional spots for broadcast during normal programming. Other commercial spots appeared from 27th January 1984, the first being for Jordache Jeans, with others following from Priority Air Freight, Wifa Skating Boots and the Christian Children's Fund.

Radio Caroline had survived since in August 1983 on the promotion of records from UK and international record companies and the station obviously had many contacts in the music business. Up to the end of 1983 a consortium of Canadian businessmen had also been financing the station to the tune of £4,000 per week, but this 'subsidy' had been reduced at the end of the year and the sudden loss of revenue caused many problems including the non-payment of staff wages.

## Caroline's 20th Birthday

A milestone in offshore radio history was reached over the Easter weekend of 1984 when Radio Caroline celebrated its 20th Birthday. Broadcasting continued non stop 24 hours a day over the four day weekend and the Top 500 'Classic Tracks' chart (which had been compiled from listeners' votes) was played twice during that period.

Radio Caroline's 20th Anniversary also received widespread media publicity including a half hour programme on Anglia Television, a contribution from Johnnie Walker on BBC 2's "Old Grey Whistle Test" programme, and a tribute on the BBC World Service. A number of Independent Local Radio stations in Britain also presented special programmes in tribute to Radio Caroline as did the former Dutch offshore station Radio Veronica, now broadcasting on the Hilversum network.

### Top 10 of the 'Top 500 Classic Tracks' Chart

1 ***Imagine***, John Lennon

2 ***Stairway to Heaven***, Led Zepplin

3 ***All You Need is Love***, The Beatles

4 ***Caroline***, The Fortunes

5 ***Riders on the Storm***, The Doors

6 ***Layla***, Derek and the Dominoes

7 ***Nights in White Satin***, Moody Blues

8 ***All Along the Watchtower***, Jimi Hendrix

9 ***Radar Love***, Golden Earring

10 ***Freebird***, Lynyrd Skynyrd

## WRLI

*In mid-March 1984 plans were announced by John England, a Briton who had emigrated to the USA, to re-launch Radio London. John England had made contact with former Radio London and Radio England/Britain Radio backer, Don Pierson, now General Manager of KVMX FM97 in Eastland, Texas. As well as some of the other people originally behind the same 60s offshore stations. Amongst these was Ben Tomy, formerly station Manager and Programme Director of Radio London who became President of a new project Wonderful Radio London International (WRLI).*

*The plan announced in March 1984 was to launch twin offshore stations from a ship off the British coast, capitalising on the renewed interest in offshore radio generated by Radio Caroline and the arrival of Laser. One of the twin stations, The Voice of the Free Gospel, was to feature programmes emanating from American evangelists and provide the bulk of the income for the whole venture. The second station would be WRLI, with an oldies format and carrying spot advertising. At that stage it was planned to launch WRLI on 15th August 1984, at 3.01pm - exactly 17 years since the original Big L had closed.*

*A company was formed by John England -Atlantic Charter Broadcasting Corporation and although at that stage no ship had been acquired it was announced that the project's vessel (when a suitable one was found) would be called Four Freedoms, after a keynote speech by US President, Franklin D Roosevelt in 1941 which contained references to Freedom of Speech, Freedom of Religion, Freedom from Want and Freedom from Fear. Nothing more happened with this ambitious project and by early 1985 its failure was blamed on the fact that the religious station's backers had withdrawn their support. However ,on 13th August 1984 WRLI did begin broadcasting a 15 minute programme, aired five days a week, over the transmitters of station XERF, based just across the Texas border in Del Rio, Mexico.*

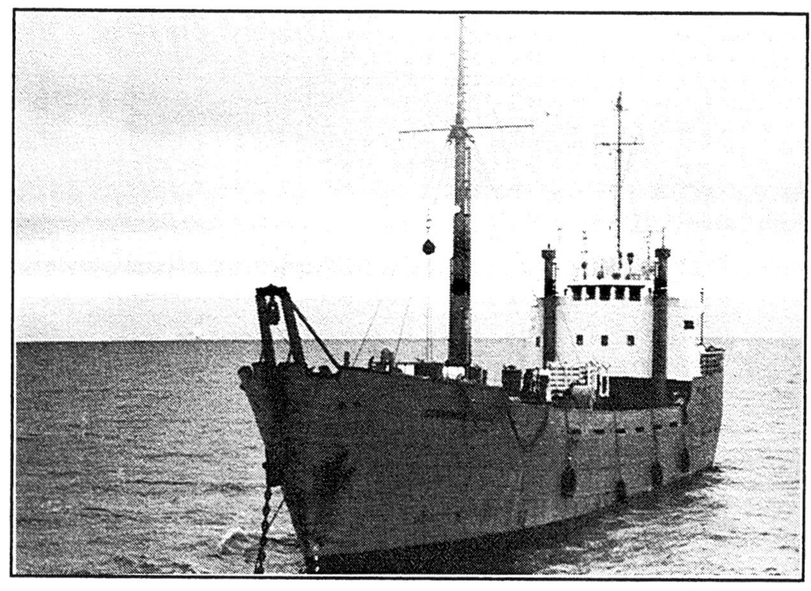

The 'Communicator' with the 'T' aerial system

## Laser tries again

Following the failure of the helium balloon aerial system on the *Communicator* the station's backer, Philip Smyth, refused to put any more money into the scheme. Roy Lindau was left in charge of the project, but with no more capital available he closed the New York office and told the crew of the *Communicator* to "salvage what they could." This almost led to the skeleton crew taking the vessel into port to sell what fuel remained on board and raise enough money to pay their fares home. However, Paul Rusling was not to be defeated and he instigated a plan, as he had originally recommended, to construct a more conventional aerial system on the radio ship.

A new temporary 'T' aerial, consisting of six strands of wire strung between the *Communicator's* front and aft masts, was completed by mid-February 1984. Weak test signals were transmitted intermittently for about two hours on 12th February and shortly before 1.00pm on 14th February 1984 test transmissions started once again on 729kHz (411m). After about twenty minutes continuous Beatles music was played with announcements in English, Dutch and German giving the ship's name and location as well as a mailing address for reception reports - Music Media International (MMI) in Madison Avenue, New York.

These test transmissions, using the 'T' aerial continued for five days until the late afternoon of 19th February 1984 when it was decided to cease broadcasts and erect an improved aerial system on board the *Communicator.* Throughout the test transmissions only one mention was made of the station's call sign -Laser 730. Listeners were informed by DJs Blake Williams and Johnny Lewis that the station would return in about 10-14 days time, but not necessarily on 729kHz, and advised them to "tune around the same area of the medium wave band."

## Permanent aerial system

These few days of tests had been broadcast to prove to Philip Smyth as well as potential advertisers that the station could transmit a reasonable signal and that the music format would be popular with listeners. As proof of this over 2,000 letters and reception reports were received at MMI's New York office following the five days of test broadcasts. After the success of the test broadcasts Philip Smyth, agreed to fund the construction of a permanent aerial system on board the *Communicator* which would enable Laser to return to the air permanently.

American engineer David Irvine, who had previously worked for the US Navy and US Coastguard, was contracted to design and build the new aerial system, which he decided to do on land despite advice about contravening the British Marine etc. Broadcasting (Offences) Act. A telescopic mast structure was acquired and partially assembled at a boat yard in Chalk Wharf, Queensborough, Essex ready for transportation to the *Communicator.* However, police and Department of Trade officials had become aware of what was going on and mounted a raid on the yard on 16th March 1984, arresting several men working on the mast construction, including yard owner Nicholas Murray, American engineer David Irvine and welder Clive Payne.

The raid and subsequent confiscation of the telescopic aerial was a major set back to Laser, further delaying its planned official launch. Following the raid the landbased side of the operation placed a number of orders with different suppliers for the necessary replacement aerial system - a device designed to try an fool the authorities and prevent any further surveillance operation as had happened at Chalk Wharf.

'Communicator' with new aerial masts, May 1984

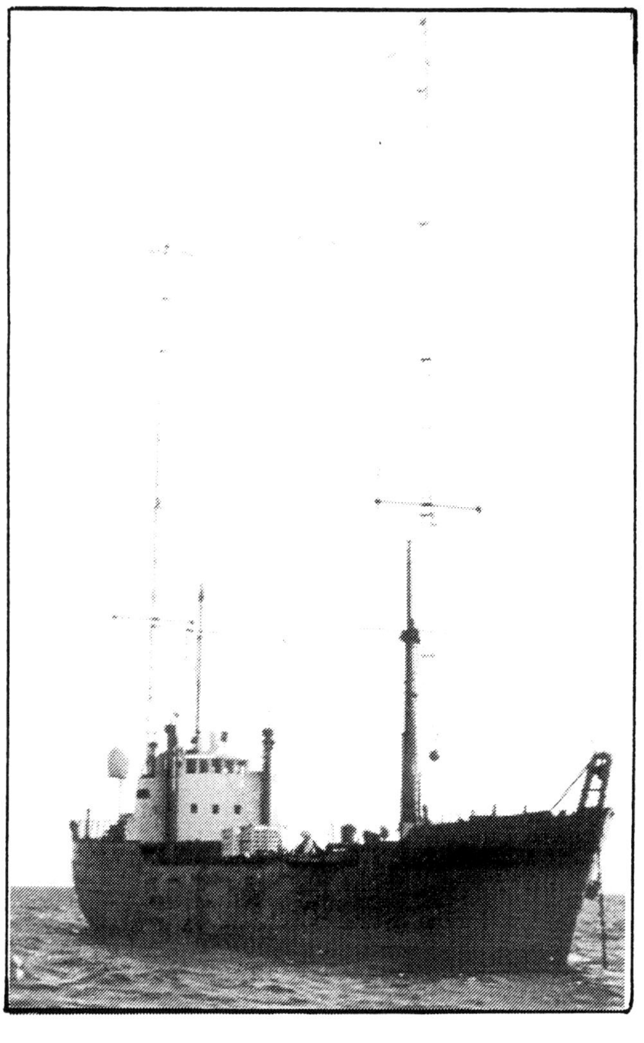

Meanwhile, the three men arrested at the boatyard were summonsed to appear before Sheerness Magistrates Court on 13th April 1984, but in the event Nicholas Murray did not attend and the charges against him were heard in his absence. Gregory Treverton-Jones, defending the accused told the Court that Irvine had been assured by the American management and understood that as long as the radio ship was outside British territorial limits there was nothing illegal in what he was doing. This of course was a weak argument and clearly demonstrated that both he and Laser's American management were not fully conversant with the provisions of the Marine etc. Broadcasting (Offences) Act and the restrictions it imposes on work in connection with an offshore radio station.

David Irvine was found guilty and fined £500, with £50 costs, welder Clive Payne was discharged by the Court due to insufficient prosecution evidence, while the case against Nicholas Murray was adjourned to a later date to give him a chance to attend Court.

Eventually, a set of mast sections were delivered to the *Communicator* by the third week in April and erected on board the ship during the Easter weekend of 1984. Once both the masts had been constructed the aerial system was wired up and after about two weeks continuous work the station was now ready to re-commence test transmissions. The promised test broadcasts started again at 12 noon on 6th May 1984, this time on 558kHz (558m).

## Laser 558 launched

Further test broadcasts continued for various periods throughout May 1984 and then, without any prior announcement, official programming for the new offshore radio station - Laser 558 - started at 5.00am on 24th May with a full programme schedule, including news bulletins at the top of each hour.

The new station quickly started advertising its own promotional items, including T- shirts, a wall poster, a video cassette, pin badges etc. but confusingly, two addresses were given out over the air at this time - MMI, in Madison Avenue, New York for the promotional items, and a PO Box in Grand Central Station, New York, for requests and dedications.

As if to underline its perceived legal status Laser 558 ended its transmissions each day with the following announcement :-

*This is All Europe Radio Laser 558 broadcasting live from the MV 'Communicator' in international waters. Laser 558 is owned and operated by Eurad SA and broadcasts in a totally free environment. At all times this station endeavours to maintain standards of good taste and responsible technical*

### Laser 558's first programme schedule, May 1984

**5.00am** Rick Harris

**10.00am** David Lee Stone

**3.00pm** Jessie Brandon

**8.00pm** Steve Masters

**1.00am** Closedown

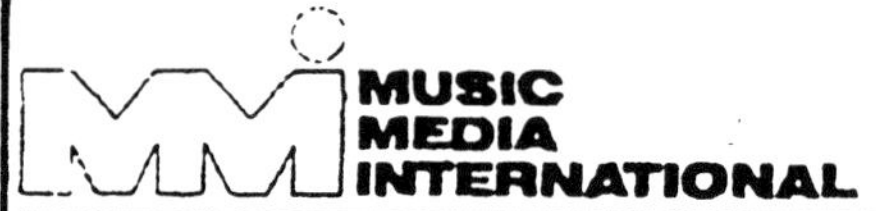


341 Madison Avenue • New York, N.Y. 10017 U.S.A.

A press release issued through MMI in New York a few days after Laser 558 opened was designed to attract potential advertisers to the station:-

**NEW PAN-EUROPEAN RADIO STATION LAUNCHED**

*The launch of Laser 558, All Europe Radio earlier this week brings another pan-European broadcast medium within reach of multi-national companies with global brand strategies. American DJs are playing hit music to listeners in nine countries from aboard a radio ship in the North Sea, making it possible for world brands to talk to millions at a fraction of the cost of local media.*

*'Pan European advertising has been a hot concept in advertising circles lately, but there's much more talk than action', says Roy Lindau, President of Music Media International Inc. the exclusive world-wide representatives of the station. 'Heavy governmental control of media has made it difficult to advertise from nation to nation or even city to city! Until now the concept has been stymied by lack of advertiser supported media with significant penetration of European households.'*

*'We play records from charts all over Europe,' says Joe Young one of the DJs and Operations Manager of the station. 'Most European hits are in English, so that is the primary language of the station, but you'll hear occasional records, promotions and commercial spots in other languages. We want to be perceived to be a true pan-European station. Over 164 million people live in nine countries in our reception area and we want to attract as many listeners as we can.'*

*Laser 558 can be a strategic medium for a pan-European umbrella campaign or a quick low cost tactical medium. Orders booked through the computer in New York at their Madison Avenue offices can be broadcast later the same day. Time rates change from $40 to $250 for thirty second spots. 'We offer complete flexibility' Lindau says. Advertisers can select fixed minutes, use live copy in DJ shows, experiment with bi-lingual copy and sponsor special programmes all within an ideal commercial environment.' Laser 558 promises listeners they're never more than a minute away from music, so minute commercial stand alone between records.*

*'Unlike pirate stations of the past Laser 558 is a legal offshore radio station,' Lindau says. 'It's a complete non-European organisation operating in international waters, so the station is, in the opinion of counsel, entirely legal.'*

**offshore trivia**

**Youngest radio ship**

*'Droit de Parole' (Radio Brod) - built 1986, used as a radio ship in 1994 - 8 years old.*

**offshore trivia**

**Least powerful transmitter**

*Radio Delmare (50 watts)*

**offshore trivia**

**Most powerful transmitter**

*RNI - 100Kw (potential)*

*operation. We will resume our transmissions of hit music in a few hours at 5.00 am in the Greenwich time zone, 6.00am in the Central European time zone. Thank you for listening today and have a good night.*

The announcement was followed by Abba's "Thank You For The Music".

Laser 558's non-stop pop music format was an immediate success with listeners and the station quickly became very popular in Britain and northern Europe. The slick presentation style and 'more music, less talk' policy appealed to a whole generation of listeners in Britain who were dissatisfied with the stale ILR and BBC Radio One programming output as well as to older listeners who remembered the similarly vibrant offshore stations of the 1960s.

Throughout the summer of 1984 Laser 558 continued to grow in popularity. Audience figures of 5 million listeners were claimed for the station, whose music policy was summarised by the slogan "You're never more than a minute away from music." Certainly in Britain it was acknowledged that the station had taken vast numbers of listeners from Capital Radio in London, other local ILR stations particularly in Kent and Essex and, most significantly, from BBC Radio One.

A presenter on one BBC local radio station was impressed by Laser's performance and in particular by one of its DJs, Jessie Brandon. That presenter was ex-Caroline and London DJ Tony Blackburn, then working on BBC Radio London, and he invited Jessie Brandon to sit in on his programme while he was on holiday during the summer of 1984. Tony Blackburn and his producer held discussions with Laser management and with Jessie Brandon about the proposal, but the BBC hierarchy refused to allow the deal to go ahead.

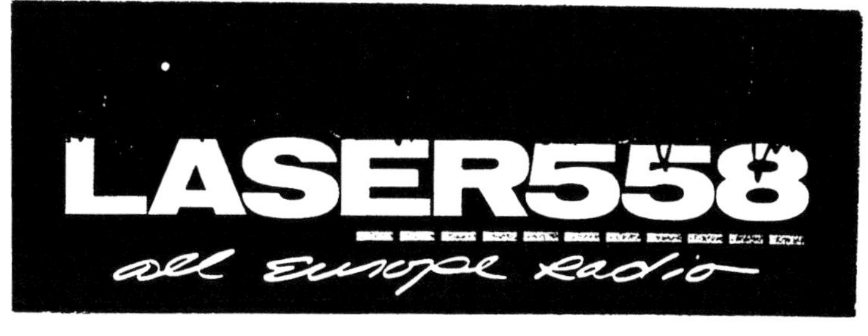


## Complaints

Complaints were received during the summer of 1984 about interference to broadcasts from Radio Telefis Eireann (RTE) from Laser 558's transmitter. However, the interference was not being experienced by listeners in the Irish Republic (RTE's target audience) but by those living in England, mainly London, who wished to tune in to the Irish station's transmissions, well outside its authorised reception area. RTE's London Representative, John O'Callaghan, complained to Laser 558's lawyer, Glenn Kolk, and to the sales representative from MMI, Roy Lindau, about interference from the offshore station. The Irish broadcaster received little sympathy from the Laser 558 men - they maintained that RTE was not a British station, it operated with a transmitter power of 500Kw, compared to Laser's 25Kw and its broadcasts were not intended to be received in London anyway. This dispute continued for some time, although Laser did offer to install filters to the sound processing equipment on board the *Communicator* to cut off their sideband 4.5kHz beyond 558kHz.

Another potential frequency conflict loomed with the announcement at the end of August 1984 that the new BBC local station, Radio Essex based in Chelmsford (planned to open in 1985) had been allocated the 558kHz frequency by the Home Office.

## Caroline's reaction

Meanwhile, the other offshore radio station, Radio Caroline continued with its AOR album format and as a consequence attracted much smaller audiences than the new Laser 558. Ronan O'Rahilly, interviewed on Channel 4 Television in June 1984, was asked what effect the success of the new rival offshore station would have on Caroline's format. "Absolutely no effect at all." He replied, "We are an album station they're, as I understand it, a Top 40 station. I find the hard-sell American thing is not totally sincere, I don't know how to define it but it's sort of a hard, brash, knock 'em over the head and you'll win style."

Not only was Radio Caroline failing to attract large audiences by maintaining its album format, but the station also suffered from broadcasting on a frequency (963kHz) which did not penetrate into the heart of south east England.

While much audience and media attention was focused on Laser 558 Radio Caroline made some efforts to try and rectify this problem and started test transmissions on 594kHz (505m) on 12th July 1984. These tests continued for over two weeks with regular requests for reception reports to be sent to Caroline's New York address. From 27th July 1984 Radio Caroline's programmes were broadcast for a few days simultaneously on 963kHz (319m) and 594kHz (505m). The announced purpose of dual frequency transmissions was to improve the station's signal into central London, which it did during the day, but 594kHz was blocked out by a West German station in Frankfurt during the hours of darkness. Consequently on 5th August 1984 transmissions on 594kHz were discontinued and the station tried the frequency of 576kHz (521m), which successfully provided an improvement in night time reception. At about this time too reports appeared in the London *Evening Standard* hinting that Radio Caroline would be changing its format to a Top 40 station to compete with Laser 558's immense popularity.

**Radio Caroline programme schedule, July 1984**

6.00am Dave Richards

10.00am Stuart Russell

2.00pm Blake Williams

6.00pm Tom Anderson

10.00pm Stuart Vincent

12midnight Closedown

## Prosecutions

The first case against Radio Caroline personnel, who had been arrested when their tender arrived in England in November 1983, finally came to court in July 1984. Disc Jockey Andy Archer appeared at Woodbridge Magistrates Court on 19th July 1984 charged with broadcasting from the *Ross Revenge* in contravention of the Marine etc. Broadcasting (Offences) Act 1967. The Court was told that an off duty police officer had witnessed provisions being loaded onto a launch at Melton and suspected it was planning to visit Radio Caroline's ship. Later Police and Home Office officials watched crates being landed on the *Ross Revenge* from the launch and personnel transferring to it from the radio ship. The launch was boarded when it docked at Melton and some Radio Caroline staff were found to be on board. Andy Archer, charged under his real name, Terence Dawson, pleaded guilty and was fined £500 with £100 costs.

Other defendants, who had been arrested at the same time appeared in Court at Woodbridge on 13th September 1984. Michael Victor East, Richard Jonathon Mitchell and David Eric Stanley all pleaded 'guilty' to taking supplies to Radio Caroline in contravention of the Marine etc. Broadcasting (Offences) Act 1967. East, owner of the boat involved was fined £60 while the other two crewmen were fined £40 each.

## Laser 558's commercial failure

Despite Laser 558's runaway success with listeners the station, through Roy Lindau and MMI in New York, had failed to sell any commercial airtime during its first three months on air. Without such revenue it was estimated at that time to be costing the station's backers £15,000 a week to keep Laser 558 on the air.

The absence of commercials was explained in an MMI press release issued on 14th August:-

*All Europe Radio Laser 558 broadcasts from aboard the MV 'Communicator' anchored in international waters in the North Sea. Laser listeners are never more than a minute away from music, a slogan the station has been using since they signed on air on May 24 1984 with six United States DJs and an international hit music playlist. This has been a very special summer for Laser listeners because it has been completely commercial free. The decision to run a summer of commercial free programming was made by Music Media International President Roy Lindau, who markets Laser advertising in New York. Lindau commented 'We had to establish credibility and build a large audience in the European market quickly and the audience really responds to limited commercial announcements.'.......... The station plans to conduct an omnibus survey in early September to verify the audience estimates and find out exactly how many people are listening. The survey will poll audiences in the United Kingdom and two other European countries with the final results becoming available at the end of September. According to Lindau the 'one minute to music' policy will still be maintained in the Fall when advertising meets the Laser airwaves. He commented, 'we have had enquiries from advertisers as far away as Australia who are interested in placing ads on Laser.' MMI expects multinational firms to be the first advertisers on the air, since the station reaches nine countries in north western Europe, namely the United Kingdom, the Netherlands, Belgium, Denmark, France, Germany, Norway, Sweden and West Germany. Commercial prices range from $40 to $250 for a 30 second spot. Sponsors can have their commercial booked in New York and transmitted by satellite for broadcast later the same day.*

## Mystery backer

The significant audience pulling power of Laser 558, its impact on other pop music stations and the continued absence of commercials fuelled the mystery of who was actually behind the station and where the seemingly endless supplies of money were coming from.

In late August 1984 reports in the London *Evening Standard* linked BBC journalist Roger Parry with Laser 558, hinting that he acted as co-ordinator for the station in Britain and subsequently Scotland Yard, together with DTI officials were asked to look into the matter. For the first time, too, speculation began to appear in the press about who the financial backers of the whole Laser project really were. All the station's publicity material had referred to money coming from US backers, but the press had now uncovered information about the involvement of Irish businessman Philip Smyth in launching the project. In response to these reports Roger Parry said he had simply been researching the station's activities for the BBC2 "In Business" programme and admitted that he had met Laser 558's 'Marketing Chief' Roy Lindau on a number of occasions.

The *Evening Standard*, however, pursued its investigations vigorously, believing it had uncovered something of the mystery behind the successful offshore station. A further report appeared on 30th August 1984 naming Philip Smyth, owner of the Sachs Hotel in Dublin as the key backer behind Laser 558.

Philip Smyth's connection with Laser had only come to light when the *Communicator's* American Station Engineer, David Irvine had been arrested in April 1984 whilst constructing the new telescopic aerial. Police found a letter from Smyth amongst Irvine's possessions.

Another of those arrested in the raid on the shipyard where Laser's aerial mast was being assembled had his case heard at Maidstone Crown Court on 24th

September 1984. Nicholas Murray, who had failed to attend Court in April, pleaded 'not guilty' to a charge of "conspiring to supply antennae masts to the MV *Communicator* " and the prosecution offered no evidence against him. The Judge directed that a verdict of 'Not Guilty' be recorded.

## First commercials

Commercials eventually started to be aired on Laser 558 from 1st October 1984 - including spots for *Ski Magazine*, Ashwin Fire Extinguishers, *USA Today*, and Marlboro cigarettes. At about the same time a listeners club - the Communicator Club - was also launched as was a weekly Lucky Numbers Competition. DJs broadcast Communicator Club membership numbers during their programmes and the holders of those numbers were asked to write to the station's New York address giving the date and time they had heard the announcement. Each winner received an album as their prize. Another listener competition was launched in November 1984 - the Laser/Contiki America Getaway Giveaway - listeners had to answer two questions and the winners received holidays in the USA, arranged by Contiki.

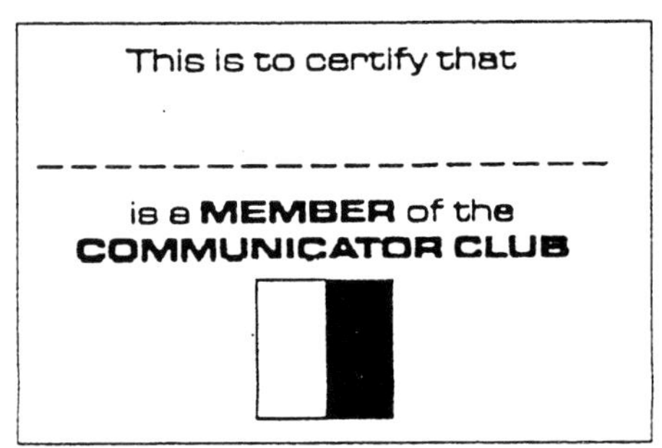


**Laser 558 programme schedule, October 1984**

5.00am Ric Harris
9.00am Dave Chaney
1.00pm Dave Lee Stone
5.00pm Jessie Brandon
9.00pm Charlie Wolf
1.00am Closedown

*(Sometimes closedown on Fridays and Saturdays was extended with a programme called "Mariners Hour' during which all members of the 'Communicator's crew appeared on air)*

An embarrassing situation for one major British company, as well as the BBC, occurred at the beginning of November 1984 when Laser 558 started advertising the TSB Rock School Competition - a venture jointly promoted by the Trustee Savings Bank (TSB) and the BBC. Laser had received a general press release about the competition and devised the commercial itself, to the embarrassment of both sponsors. The TSB made it clear that, as a British company, they were not paying for the advertisement and asked Laser 558 to stop airing it.

An audience survey carried out during October 1984 by MRIB and published at the beginning of December 1984 showed Laser 558 having an audience of five million listeners in the UK - 11% of people over the age of 15, while regional breakdowns revealed an audience reach of 23% in East Anglia and 14% in London. Unfortunately shortly before the results of this survey were published and after a very successful four months of broadcasting Laser 558 started to experience technical problems culminating in the station being off the air for two days from 23rd - 25th November after the aerial mast had been damaged. This was the first tangible sign that all was not well within the Laser organisation, with persistent rumours starting to circulate about its financial security, but the real problems for the station started to manifest themselves early in 1985.

## Caroline split frequency transmissions

Radio Caroline returned to a 24 hour schedule officially on 23rd October 1984 although night-time test transmissions had been carried out for a week prior to this on both Caroline frequencies (963kHz and 576kHz). Throughout the autumn of 1984 Radio Caroline continued to broadcast the same programmes 24 hours a day on both frequencies, but in the early hours of 11th December 1984 a split service was started between 2.00am and 6.00am each morning under the individual call signs Caroline 576 and Caroline International (on 963kHz).

Both Caroline transmitters were off the air for various periods during late November and early December 1984 for maintenance work and also at times due to severe staff and equipment shortages. Nevertheless the split frequency service continued and it soon became public knowledge that this was in preparation for the launch of another new offshore radio station. Yet again Radio Caroline had hired its facilities to a Dutch language broadcaster.

## Radio Monique

Plans had existed in 1981 to put more than one station on the air from the radio ship *Magda Maria,* - Radio Paradijs and possibly two others, but the illegal seizure of the vessel by Dutch authorities had prevented these projects coming to fruition (see chapter 20).

One of the proposed stations on the *Magda Maria* was to have been Radio Monique, with a programming format geared to promoting Dutch artists and with backing from some large record companies in Holland. Protracted legal argument between the owners of the *Magda Maria* and the Dutch authorities led to the backers of Radio Monique looking elsewhere for a base. In the autumn of 1984 they approached Ronan O'Rahilly to hire studio and transmitter facilities on the *Ross Revenge*, and this resulted in a contract with the Caroline organisation allowing Radio Monique to provide a Dutch language service from the ship which was originally planned to start on 1st December 1984.

A team of Dutch personnel came on board the *Ross Revenge* and started to rebuild the second studio, then only used by Radio Caroline for production purposes, for their own station. They also installed their own equipment, much of which had come from the Amsterdam landbased pirate Radio Uniek, which had been raided and closed by the Dutch authorities earlier in 1984.

Radio Monique was backed by a number of Dutch and Belgian businessmen, prominent amongst whom was Luc van Driessche, a director of Flemish language *Topic* magazine, owned by the Heerema Company, which itself once had connections with offshore broadcasting through the REM Island project in 1964 (see Chapter 9). A substantial financial input also came from the Canadian Lotto 6/49 organisation which had previously invested in the re-launch of Radio Caroline.

The operating company behind the station was Music Media International run by ex-record shop owner Fred Bolland (previously involved with Radio Delmare and the Dutch service of Radio Caroline in the 1970s and the Dutch sales outlet of Laser 558) and ex-Radio Veronica DJs Tony Berk and Willem van Kooten (Joost den Draayer). MMI operated quite legally in Holland selling syndicated radio programmes to legal, landbased stations in Belgium and Spain. Willem van Kooten had planned to operate a similar system in 1978 with the Radio Hollandia project (see Chapter 19).

The delay in actually putting the station on the air was due to problems encountered in late November and early December 1984 with the *Ross Revenge's* transmitter, aerial mast and generators. Only after vital spare parts had arrived on board the radio ship from the USA could the necessary repairs be carried out, enabling the split frequency broadcasts to start.

Reports of the forthcoming launch of Radio Monique from the *Ross Revenge* appeared in the Dutch newspaper *Algemeen Dagblad* on 23rd November 1984. According to these reports programme tapes used by the new station would be made by MMI primarily for legal land-based stations in Belgium and Spain, but copies would 'find their way' to the *Ross Revenge* and Radio Monique jingles would be inserted during transmission. It was also hinted that the station's presenters would include many DJs from former Dutch offshore stations, Radio Veronica, Radio Mi Amigo and RNI.

### Radio Caroline programme schedule, October 1984

6.00am Johnny Lewis

9.00am Grant Benson

12noon Alton Andrews

3.00pm Paul McKenna

6.00pm Dave Richards

10.00pm Tom Anderson

2.00am Stewart Vincent

### Radio Monique format

*Radio Monique's format was to be largely Top 40 chart material with some middle-of-the-road music as well. A news service with regular bulletins each hour and headlines on the half hour was also planned for the station. Emphasis was to be placed on new releases by Dutch artists, but the station was also to play international hits and flashbacks, with records played two or three at a time without interruption by DJs or commercial breaks. Also every three hours a Satellietschijf (powerplay) record would be aired at the top of the hour, this was to be a paid 'plug' record and would be changed on a weekly basis.*

### Ross Revenge broadcasts

*With the arrival of Radio Monique the broadcasting schedule from the 'Ross Revenge' now looked like this:-*

***963kHz (319m)*** *4.00am-7.00pm Radio Monique (Dutch)*

*7.00pm-4.00am Radio Caroline (English)*

***576kHz (519m)*** *24 hours Radio Caroline (English)*

Despite weeks of rumours the first definite indications on-air of the new station's arrival did not come until 15th December 1984. When the two Radio Caroline frequencies began carrying different programmes - Caroline on 576kHz and Dutch language test transmissions on 963kHz. The following morning Radio Monique tests began again and included a programme from Dutch evangelist Johan Maasbach, whose preachings had been featured on some previous offshore radio stations directed at Holland.

The official opening of Radio Monique took place on 16th December 1984 at 11.00am (12 noon in Europe) when a number of programmes were presented live from the ship. Opening day broadcasts included a link with the ex-offshore station Radio Veronica, now part of the Hilversum network and a tour of the *Ross Revenge*.

## Early commercials

Hoor:
Evangelist JOHAN MAASBACH
**RADIO MONIQUE**
319m A.M./963 KHz
iedere morgen van 6.30-7.00 uur
iedere zondagmorgen van 8.00-9.00 uur

Radio Monique started earning revenue from its opening day with the transmission of two sponsored religious programmes - Johan Maasbach's programme (aired daily) and Radio Gemeenschap Bloemendaal, an organisation which had been established by the late Rev. Dominee Toornvliet (the 'Pirate Vicar'). Both these broadcasters had previously bought airtime on Dutch offshore stations during the 1970s.

On 31st December 1984 Radio Monique started including commercial spots during its regular programmes, including promotions for Phonogram, CNR Records and Sport Life Chewing Gum (which later transpired to be fake). There were also a large amount of record promotions during programmes, indicating that record companies backing Radio Monique had paid for such airplay.

### Radio Monique programme schedule, January 1985

**5.00am Ron West** *(including a 30 minute religious programme from Johan Maasbach)*

**7.00am Ad Roberts**

**9.00am Maarten de Jong**

**10.00am Johan Visser**

**12noon Frits Koning**

**2.00pm Ad Roberts**

**4.00pm Johan Visser**

**6.00pm Avondblad** *(Summary of the days news, with editorial comment and details of the evening television programme listings provided by 'Tros Kompas' magazine)*

**7.00pm Closedown**

Another early advertiser on the new Dutch station was the official broadcasting organisation TROS, which promoted its *TROS Kompas* magazine. This situation had occurred because a new regulation introduced in Holland at the end of 1984 limited each broadcasting organisation to thirty seconds advertising time for themselves for programmes they produced on the Hilversum network. Cees den Daas, head of TROS Television, said that although the Belgian Marine Offences Act contained a specific clause forbidding advertising on an offshore station he believed that was not the same in the Dutch law.

Questions were asked in the Dutch Parliament following the opening of Radio Monique. Broadcasting Minister, Eelco Brinkman, stated that no direct action would be taken against the new station in view of the Court decision in the Radio Paradijs case declaring that the Dutch authorities had acted illegally in seizing the *Magda Maria* while she was in international waters. Nevertheless he promised to urge his British colleagues to watch for any signs of illegal tendering activities associated with the *Ross Revenge*.

Repeated transmitter and generator breakdowns as well as storm damage to the aerial system caused both stations on the *Ross Revenge* to leave the air for various periods during December 1984 and January 1985. On 6th January 1985, in Force 10 gales, the *Ross Revenge* dragged her anchor for about two miles and transmissions had to be terminated while emergency services were alerted. However, they were already engaged in assisting the British Rail Ferry *Speedlink Vanguard*, which had lost engine power off Harwich, so it was over three hours before the Walton-on-the-Naze lifeboat was available to stand by the *Ross Revenge*. During the early hours of the following morning the *Ross Revenge* was able to sail back to her normal anchorage position, accompanied by the lifeboat.

The *Ross Revenge's* return was assisted by the crew of the *Communicator* (who had experienced problems of their own that night) using their satellite navigational equipment to direct the Caroline vessel.

Broadcasts from the *Ross Revenge* were not able to resume until 8th January 1985, but even then both transmitters just carried continuous music for an hour and a half. Regular programmes on both stations were eventually resumed on 11th January 1985 with Radio Caroline returning (on576kHz) at 9.00am and Radio Monique (on 963kHz) at 11.00am. All this time the *Ross Revenge* was holding her position on a temporary anchor, an arrangement which lasted for ten days until a new, stronger permanent anchor was installed on board the radio ship.

## Monique success

After three months of operating Radio Monique from the *Ross Revenge* the station renewed talks with those behind Radio Paradijs (whose vessel, *Magda Maria*, they had originally planned to share in 1981). It was agreed that when the Paradijs ship had been released by the Dutch authorities they would relocate Radio Monique to that vessel, but this could not happen for some time because the hearing of the latest case involving the *Magda Maria* had recently been postponed to 12th September 1985.

In the meantime, however, Radio Monique on board the *Ross Revenge* became commercially very successful with some large advertisers purchasing airtime during the summer of 1985. The station's programme format was also proving popular with listeners and it attracted a substantial audience in its target area. During this time Radio Monique also mounted a huge promotional campaign using banner towing aircraft flying above Dutch beaches and holiday resorts. The campaign was linked to a competition in which listeners had to read the airborne messages and post them off to the station's Spanish address where they were entered in a prize draw.

## Campaign against Laser 558

The first hint of a campaign to put Laser 558 off the air was reported in the press on 17th December 1984 when it was revealed that an executive of an ILR station in Essex had discussed with a former Laser engineer ways in which the offshore station could be silenced - a recognition indeed of the popularity of Laser 558 and the threat felt by landbased stations for the loss of their audiences.

The plan, if executed, would have involved sabotaging the *Communicator,* putting Laser 558 off the air and possibly necessitating the radio ship entering port for repairs. Fortunately for all concerned this plan was not executed, but the ILR station management continued to make representations to various Government departments, trade associations as well as the IBA about the continued existence of Laser 558 and the apparent lack of official action being taken against it.

Meanwhile, on the *Communicator* further generator and fuel shortage problems affected Laser 558 during December 1984 and early January 1985 resulting in various periods off the air. Heavy snow lying on the aerial also forced a four day closure in mid-January 1985 while the crew rigged a temporary array enabling the station to resume broadcasts on low power.

These frequent breakdowns and prolonged periods off the air - coupled with a continuing lack of real advertising revenue and consequent shortages of supplies and equipment - indicated that all was not well with the Laser organisation. Confirmation of the seriousness of the situation came in an article in the trade paper, *Broadcast* on 18th January 1985 when it was revealed that Eurad SA had offered the *Communicator* for sale. A number of parties interested in acquiring the radio ship were said to have approached Philip Smyth in Ireland, including Richard Branson of Virgin (who 18 months previously had sought to 'buy in' to the re-launch of Radio Caroline; Chris Carey (ex-Caroline/ RNI/Luxembourg DJ and now owner of the highly successful Irish landbased pirate Radio Nova) and a group described as being based in East Anglia and said to include a number of ex-offshore radio broadcasters.

The same day as the *Broadcast* article appeared Roy Lindau resigned as President of MMI, the New York marketing and airtime sales agency which represented Laser 558. He was succeeded by Vice-President John Moss who immediately issued a denial that the station was up for sale, but confirmed that some discussions had taken place with Branson and Carey.

Running costs of $3,000 a day were not being covered by advertising income, but promises of $100,000 worth of airtime sales during February 1985 now depended on the station maintaining a reliability of transmission, something which it had failed to achieve during the previous two months. In fact repeated breakdowns had occurred during January and when the station was broadcasting the transmitter power was very low, resulting in a poor signal output.

Meanwhile, MMI in New York, now under the control of John Moss, continued to deny the persistent stories that Laser 558 was about to close and that the *Communicator* was up for sale. Some new American DJs were engaged by the station during February 1985 (including three girls, Chris Carson, Liz West and Erin Kelly, who became known collectively as the 'Laserettes'. There was even a story circulating at this time about the introduction of a second Laser service, playing AOR music, to compete more directly with Radio Caroline's style of programming.

Hopes that Laser 558 would now be able to sustain a more reliable and regular service were dashed once again by violent storms in the North Sea at the beginning of February 1985 which resulted in the *Communicator* losing one of her masts completely. Laser 558 had closed, earlier than usual, at midnight on 9th February 1985 due to the Force 8 gales and heavy seas which were pounding the ship at the time. The following morning transmissions from the *Communicator* did not start at the usual time and it was not until mid-afternoon on 14th February that Laser 558 was able to return to the air, using a temporary aerial arrangement and on very much reduced power. The *Communicator* had also lost her main anchor and been forced to drop a reserve anchor to maintain a position in international waters. Radio Caroline DJs broadcast information about the state of the *Communicator* after the crew of the *Ross Revenge* had contacted the rival radio ship on the emergency channel to make sure they were alright and not in need of assistance.

## Allegations of interference

Allegations of interference to the Coastguard Service's communications by Laser 558 were made at the end of February 1985. Coastguards tried without success to contact the *Communicator* to warn the station about the interference it was alleged to be accusing. Having failed to make direct contact with the *Communicator* they then asked the *Ross Revenge* to use Radio Caroline's transmitter to make an on-air appeal to her neighbour. This was eventually achieved and the Coastguard's message conveyed to the crew of the *Communicator* by Caroline DJ, Dave Richards. Laser 558 then closed its transmitter for a few minutes to enable Coastguards to determine whether the station was in fact causing the interference, but after having established that the problem was not due to Laser 558's broadcasts the station returned to the air. It later transpired that the interference problem had been caused by Essex transmitters of the BBC World Service and Radio One!

## Official dissatisfaction

On land official dissatisfaction with the operation of the two offshore radio ships continued. The British authorities intercepted what they thought was a tender from the *Ross Revenge* in March 1985. Police and Customs officials, in the Essex Police boat *Alert,* boarded and searched the vessel after it arrived in Wallasea Island and questioned those on board. Most were sightseers and offshore radio fans on one of the sightseeing boat trips to the *Ross Revenge* and *Communicator,* but police and other authorities were clearly keeping a close watch on anyone travelling in the vicinity of the radio ships.

In April 1985 the Association of Independent Radio Contractors (AIRC) sent an internal memo to all their members requesting information about people working for the two offshore radio stations, in particular Radio Caroline. At about the same time letters were also issued by the DTI to all companies who advertised on Laser 558 and Radio Caroline warning them that they faced prosecution under the Marine etc. Broadcasting (Offences) Act 1967 if their commercials continued to be broadcast.

In conjunction with the IBA, the D.T.I. has been checking on the personnel of the two off-shore pirate stations.

While it seems fairly certain that all personnel of Laser are Americans, the D.T.I. is less clear about Caroline.

The voices on Caroline appear generally to be British: do you recognise any of these voices? If you do, and can put genuine names, and any background, to them, please let me know.

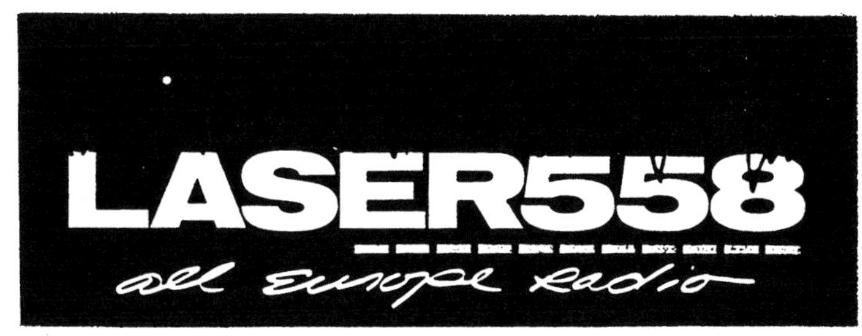


Radio Caroline, which like BBC Radio One and many landbased ILR stations, had suffered in terms of audience loss from the runaway success of Laser 558 during the summer months of 1984 appointed American radio format specialist Lee Abrams in March 1985 as a consultant to advise on future programming style and on the sale of airtime. Abrams was quoted in the American trade paper *Billboard* as saying "Caroline is getting by financially now, but they could be getting a lot more advertising than they are. We're going to help them crack the American market." Potential sectors considered suitable to buy airtime on the station included film production companies, breweries, record

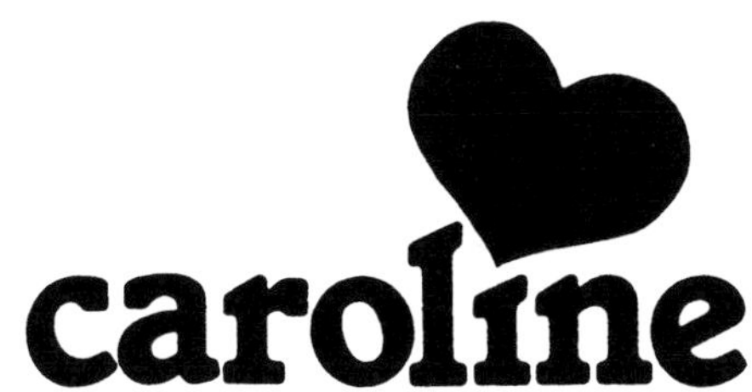

### Radio Caroline's 21st Birthday

*Radio Caroline celebrated its 21st Birthday over the Easter weekend of 1985 with an on-air party and a Top 200 album chart compiled from votes submitted by DJs who had worked on the station during the previous two decades. A recording of the original opening of the station in 1964 was played at 12 noon on Easter Saturday and throughout the weekend extracts from the 1967 official station history, "Radio Caroline" by John Venmore Rowland, were read on air.*

companies and cigarette manufacturers. As a result of this new format advice Radio Caroline's programming changed gradually during late 1984 and early 1985, becoming more inclined towards the Top 40 chart and going some way to meeting the intense challenge from Laser 558. In an attempt to appeal to multi-national advertisers the station also announced itself for a time under the call sign 'Radio Caroline International'.

## Laser 558 in difficulty

Unfortunately Laser 558's success of the previous summer had waned and the station was in severe financial and technical difficulties. In a desperate attempt to attract potential advertisers in mid-April 1985 the station started to broadcast recordings of commercials which had won the coveted Cleo Awards (the advertising industry's equivalent of an Oscar). At the conclusion of the commercial a Laser DJ congratulated the advertiser on their effective use of radio advertising, and then gave MMI's New York telephone number, blatantly suggesting that the company should buy airtime on the offshore station. It is improbable that this ploy achieved any airtime sales, but to the casual listener it gave the impression that Laser 558 was a commercially successful station.

Laser 558 was off the air again for two weeks after the *Communicator's* front mast collapsed during the afternoon of 23rd April 1985. A completely new aerial mast had to be constructed and erected on board the *Communicator* enabling Laser 558 programmes to recommence on 7th May 1985.

It was important that Laser 558 was on the air at this time because the station was planning to stage a First Birthday Party at the end of May 1985. Promotions for the event, to be held at the Hippodrome Club in London, were played on the station for a few days after its return to the air, but then were suddenly discontinued. At the instigation of the DTI, police had visited the Hippodrome's owner, Peter Stringfellow, and warned him not to stage the event because by doing so he could be in breach of the Marine etc. Broadcasting (Offences) Act. Stringfellow decided after the police visit to cancel the booking and the planned celebration of Laser 558's First Birthday never took place.

Further reports of Richard Branson's connections with Laser 558 appeared in the press on 10th May 1985, when it was stated that Virgin Atlantic Airlines was supplying Laser 558 DJs and crew with free first class tickets to and from America, in return for frequent references to the airline during the station's programmes. Branson, who had at one time been interested in buying into Radio Caroline and had previously examined ways of taking over Laser 558, claimed that he was not aware of the detail of every Virgin marketing package, but was quoted as saying "If my airline looks after Laser's DJs, and as long as it is not breaking any laws, it sounds an admirable arrangement. Laser has been kind to the airline on the airwaves." Also at about this time British events listing magazine, *Time Out* was supplying its weekly "Gig Guide" to Laser 558 in return for frequent mentions on the air. A *Time Out* spokesman was quoted as saying "We are totally sympathetic with the liberation of the airwaves and 100% behind Laser."

## 'Jamming 963' launched

On 1st May 1985 Radio Caroline's overnight programmes did not start on 963kHz immediately after Radio Monique's transmissions had ended. Instead an hour of non-stop music was played followed by an hour long taped programme from American evangelist Roy Masters of the Foundation for Human Understanding in Los Angeles, California. This became a regular daily feature of the 963kHz evening broadcasts and a large number of other sponsored religious programmes such as "The Jewish Voice", "The Tree of Life", and "The

Faith Way Baptist Hour" soon joined the station's output, providing a valuable source of revenue.

Any unsold airtime between the closure of Radio Monique at 6.00pm and the link-up with the main Radio Caroline 576 service at 9.00pm was filled with non stop music of all kinds, including classical, jazz, gospel and even old 78s. By mid-June 1985 this segment of output on 963kHz had become officially known as 'Jamming 963' and was presented by two DJs from Radio Caroline, although any connection with either Radio Caroline or Radio Monique was never referred to on air. The musical content of these sessions (which could last for up to three hours on days when there were no sponsored religious programmes) gradually became more formalised with an emphasis on jazz and Afro music.

## Caroline's Canadian connections

On 5th June 1985 the *Vancouver Sun* newspaper carried an article explaining the Expo 86 promotions on Radio Caroline and also gave the first real insight into Canadian financial backing for the station. The investment package which led to the re-launch of Radio Caroline in 1983 (following the legal wrangle with the original American investors consortium) had been put together by Canadian Businessman Nelson Skalbania.

A former employee of Skalbania, John Chambers, was now selling airtime in Canada on behalf of Radio Caroline and he approached the Expo organisation. Expo obtained approval to use Radio Caroline from their board of directors, who were aware that the offshore station operated outside British and most European law. However, it was not illegal for a Canadian company or organisation to purchase airtime on the station. Vancouver advertising agency Baker Lovick produced the commercials and Barbara Jako of Expo's Advertising Department reported that a number of enquiries had been received from Europe in response to the commercials broadcast by Radio Caroline.

## Laser 558 faces more problems

A new address for Laser 558 was introduced from mid-June 1985 - a PO Box number in Grand Central Station, New York, indicating that all was not well with the previously high profile Madison Avenue based management. John Moss and MMI had managed to keep Laser 558 on the air by various contra-deals and limited advertising income, but now a real financial crisis had been revealed.

A report in the London *Evening Standard* the following week stated that the station was facing further financial difficulties, had been forced to leave its Madison Avenue offices and had difficulty meeting bills including those of public relations consultant, Jane Norris. Also during that week DJ Ric Harris left the station suddenly without explanation and other Laser 558 DJs were reportedly looking for new jobs. The article went on to hint that while £3.5million had already been spent on launching and operating Laser 558, the continued absence of advertising from American based multi-national companies meant that the station's financial backer, Irish businessman Philip Smyth, was reluctant to invest any more cash.

With the departure of some DJs a number of programming changes took place on Laser 558 towards the end of June 1985, including the introduction of a three hour sponsored American chart show "Rockin America Top 30 Countdown", presented by Scott Shannon and syndicated by Westwood One Radio Network. Further syndicated programmes appeared during July 1985 including "Off the Record", presented by Mary Turner and featuring interviews with pop stars and "Dr. Demento", a programme consisting largely of comedy records.

More details about a financial crisis facing Laser 558 appeared in the trade magazine *Broadcast* at the beginning of July 1985. It was reported that DJs were having to wait four to six weeks for their pay and a cashflow crisis had resulted from the station's temporary closedown in May of that year when the new aerial mast was being constructed. John Moss, President of MMI denied that the office move from Madison Avenue was due to financial stringency, but did admit that there had been delays in paying some staff, although this situation was said to have been resolved and there were "enough orders on the books" for the station to continue.

## Radio Monique

Questions were asked again in the Dutch Parliament on 13th June 1985 about Radio Monique. A member of one of the right wing parties (CDA) asked the Broadcasting Minister why the Government and the law enforcement agencies were taking no action over the station and suggested that both the *Ross Revenge* and *Communicator* should be forcibly towed inside territorial waters to bring them within official jurisdiction. However, a spokesman for the Dutch Office of Justice said later that the subject of offshore broadcasting was not high on their list of priorities and until the Radio Paradijs case had been finally resolved no action would be taken against other offshore radio stations or their ships.

The results of a Dutch public opinion poll conducted during June 1985 showed that 25% of people had heard of Radio Monique while 11% - about one and a quarter million people - claimed to listen to the station regularly. Listenership was at its highest in the coastal areas of western Holland (16%), with the south attracting 8% and the north and east only managing 4% At particular times during the day certain Radio Monique programmes even attracted larger audiences than those of the national pop station Hilversum 3. It must be borne in mind, however, that these audience figures only relate to Holland and the station also attracted listeners in Belgium, West Germany, France and Britain.

On 16th July 1985 the newspaper *Algemeen Dagblad* carried an interview with co-owner of Radio Monique, Tony Berk, in which he denied working for the offshore station, saying he worked only for a Belgian land-based station.

### Radio Monique programme schedule, Spring/Summer 1985

**4.00am Drie om Drie in de Ochtend (3 for 3 in the morning)**
*Otto de Winter*

**5.30am Johan Maasbach** *(gospel songs and preachings) (taped)*

**6.00am Opstaan met Monique (Wake up with Monique)**

**8.00am Drie om Drie Benelux** *(Dutch/Belgian records)*

**9.00am Frits Koning Show or Walter Simons show**

**11.00am Berk in Uitvoering (This is Berk),** *Tony Berk (taped)*

**12noon Ron West Show**

**2.00pm Drie om Drie in de Mittag (3 for 3 in the afternoon)**

**3.00pm Maarten de Jong Show or Nico Stevens Show**

**5.00pm Radio Avondblad (Radio Evening Magazine)** *-music and information, Walter Simons*

**6.00pm Closedown**

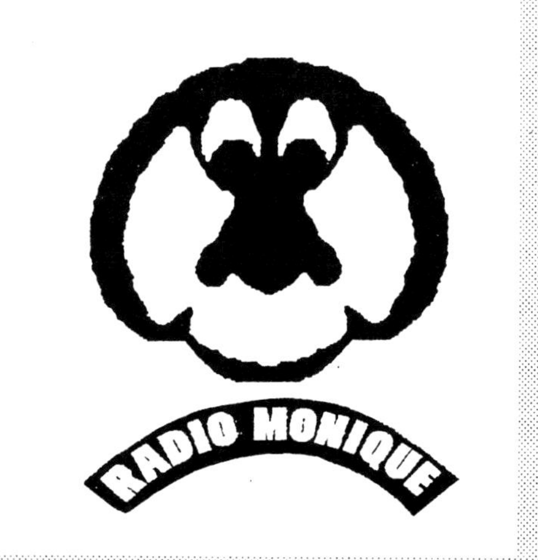

## A sinister turn of events

A sinister turn of events took place at the beginning of august 1985 affecting both radio ships anchored in the North Sea.

During the evening of 8th August 1985 a helicopter circled over the *Communicator* with its searchlight trained on the radio ship. Although no one knew at the time this was the start of what became known as "Eurosiege 85", a surveillance operation mounted by the British Department of Trade and Industry (DTI).

Laser 558 DJ Charlie Wolf announced during his show that evening that the helicopter was circling the *Communicator.* Radio Caroline listeners the following day also heard DJ David Andrews refer to an "official vessel" which had anchored 150 yards off the port bow of the *Ross Revenge.*

The "official vessel" was actually the ocean going launch *Dioptric Surveyor*, which had been chartered by the DTI to keep watch on comings and goings in the vicinity of the *Ross Revenge* and the *Communicator.* The purpose of this exercise was to photograph and identify any supply vessels which visited the two radio ships so that they could then be investigated by police when they returned to port. Helicopters were also used during the operation and the *Dioptric Surveyor* was equipped with powerful searchlights which enabled its crew to keep watch at night and monitor supplies arriving under cover of darkness.

A DTI spokesman was quoted as saying "We will keep the *Dioptric Surveyor* on station in the Thames Estuary for the foreseeable future. We want Laser and Caroline off the air." The estimated cost of the operation was rumoured to be £50,000 a month, but this later transpired to be a somewhat exaggerated figure and later was officially confirmed to be £25,000 a month, nevertheless still a substantial amount of public money. A Radio Caroline spokesman condemned the blockade as " a massive waste of public money when all we do is provide a legal music service which is enjoyed by millions." A spokesman for Laser 558 said: " they are trying to starve us out at enormous expense to the British taxpayer, but we will not give in. We will tender the ship from Spain, which is not against the law." (At that time Spain was not an EC member nor had it ratified the 1965 Strasbourg Convention to outlaw offshore broadcasting stations).

The surveillance operation was part of a campaign against the popularity of Caroline, Monique and Laser as much as against their so-called illegality. All three stations had built up huge audiences, drawing listeners away from legal music stations in England (ILR and BBC Radio One) and in Holland (Hilversum 3), as well as the pan-European Radio Luxembourg.

The DTI action in hiring the *Dioptric Surveyor* was generally accepted to have been taken as the result of pressure from the Independent Broadcasting Authority (IBA) and ILR commercial radio stations in Kent and Essex. These stations, particularly the ILR ones, felt that they had to compete on unequal terms with the offshore broadcasters who did not pay royalties and did not have to comply with the strict IBA rules and regulations which at that time included a requirement to schedule a specific number of hours of talk-based programmes.

## Voice of Hope

*Details of a planned offshore radio and television station to broadcast Christian messages and programmes to China were published in mid 1985. High Adventure Ministries, which already broadcast in the Middle East from land-based transmitters under the call sigh the Voice of Hope, announced the plans to anchor a ship in the South China Sea. George Otis, spokesman for High Adventure Ministries said: Out of the South China Seas shall soon arise Christ's message of love, salvation, healing and hope. I have just returned from Singapore where we finalised plans to anchor a 340' freighter out in international waters, just four miles off the coast of Singapore at Jahor Shoal. From the deck of this ship will rise an antenna field allowing us to broadcast at 50,000 watts power on the AM dial, 1,500,000 watts on the shortwave bands and a brand new Christian TV station. This mighty gospel ship will reach the sorely neglected two and a half billion people in Asia with Jesus' love.*

*Nothing more was heard of the Voice of Hope station, although High Adventure Ministries were rumoured to be involved in later religious based offshore broadcasting projects.*

## Dioptric Surveyor

*This vessel which became notorious in offshore radio history during the second half of 1985 was owned by Dioptric Ltd., a subsidiary of Trinity House and was on indefinite lease to the Department of Trade and Industry. The vessel was previously owned by the City of London Polytechnic's School of Navigation as a radar training vessel and was then known as the 'Sir John Cass'. In 1986 the vessel was re-named 'Surveyor' and sold to a Yorkshire businessman, who sailed her to the Bahamas.*

The DTI defended the cost of the operation by saying it had received complaints that the offshore stations had interfered with radio distress frequencies at sea and claimed this could put people's lives at risk. The stations were also alleged to have interfered with navigational aids used by helicopters serving the North Sea oil and gas rigs.

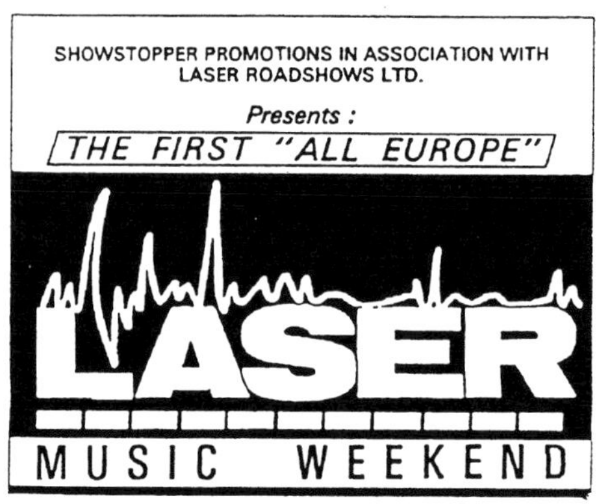


Spokesmen for both Radio Caroline and Laser 558 strongly denied that their respective transmissions were causing such interference and stated that they would continue to receive supplies, quite legally, from countries other than Britain. However, the Director of the DTI's Radio Investigation Service, Dilys Gane, said: " It is our intention that they know we really mean business this time, and we certainly would prefer that they didn't starve, we'd prefer that they came in and gave up."

In an exercise to test the effectiveness of the blockade and establish whether public money was being wasted the *Daily Star* sent a reporter to deliver supplies, T-shirts, champagne and copies of the newspaper to both the *Ross Revenge* and the *Communicator* on 14th August 1985. Their fishing vessel sailed at dawn and arrived in the vicinity of the radio ships to find that the *Dioptric Surveyor* had returned to Harwich the previous night. Nevertheless DJs on both ships were presented with supplies and photographs of them wearing *Daily Star* T-shirts and drinking champagne were published in the newspaper the following day. As the *Daily Star* boat left the radio ships the *Dioptric Surveyor* returned to her anchorage but did not pursue the reporter and his team. However, the DTI later informed the *Daily Star* that the newspaper and the journalist involved, Neil Wallis, were being reported to the Director of Public Prosecutions for contravention of the Marine etc. Broadcasting (Offences) Act 1967.

*In September 1985 a record entitled "I Spy for the DTI" by the Moronic Surveyors was released and heavily promoted on Laser 558. The record featured the voices of Laser DJs Liz West and Erin Kelly and reached no 103 in the UK singles chart.*

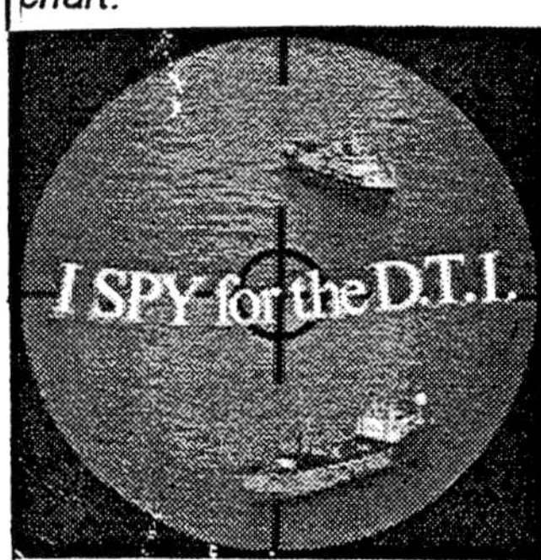


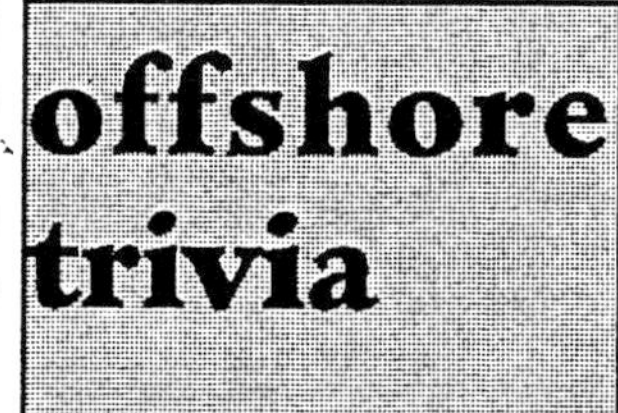


**Tallest aerial mast**

*'Ross Revenge' - 300' tallest ever mast on a ship.*

### 'Moronic Surveyor'

During their programmes DJs on Laser 558 reported on the movements of the *Dioptric Surveyor*, which earned the nickname "Moronic Surveyor". Laser 558 DJ Charlie Wolf made a particular point of reporting regularly on activities taking place on board the surveillance ship and it was he who gave the whole operation the title "Eurosiege 85". By contrast Radio Caroline DJs made far fewer references on-air to the presence and activities of the *Dioptric Surveyor* for fear of allowing the authorities to think that the surveillance was causing the station a real problem.

On 18th August 1985 an article in the *Sunday Times* stated that the surveillance operation by the *Dioptric Surveyor,* then only ten days old, had already resulted in six vessels being reported for allegedly supplying the two radio ships. Four had been reported to British Police for possible offences under the Marine etc. Broadcasting (Offences) Act, one from Holland had been reported to Dutch Police and the fifth, the *Daily Star* vessel, had been reported to the Director of Public Prosecutions.

The authorities also started to pursue firms who advertised on both offshore stations to establish whether any offence had been committed under the Marine etc. Broadcasting (Offences) Act. The Director of Public Prosecutions asked police to interview such companies, many of whom had offices in Britain, to establish how their advertising had been arranged and paid for.

## Dutch actions

In contrast to the high profile British action the Dutch authorities chose to pursue the offshore stations, particularly Radio Monique, behind the scenes. A spokesman for the Dutch Department of Justice in Amsterdam, Henk Wooldrik said:- "It's impossible to take direct action against the two ships in the Thames Estuary. We'll have to do it indirectly through possible suppliers and advertisers, but these people are very hard to trace."

On 20th August 1985 the Dutch daily newspaper, *Algemeen Dagblad* carried a report on the British surveillance operation. Dutch Minister of Justice, Korthals Altes, was reportedly trying to identify people involved with the two offshore stations on the *Ross Revenge*. The Minister indicated that the British authorities were co-operating with these inquiries and that they had also contacted the Panamanian Government to ascertain if the registration of the *Ross Revenge* was still valid and, if so, whether it could be rescinded.

There was some concern in Holland that, because of the presence of Radio Monique's Dutch staff on board the *Ross Revenge,* the *Dioptric Surveyor's* surveillance might lead to another towing-in situation as had happened with the Radio Paradijs vessel *Magda Maria* in 1979. However, Justice Minister, Korthals Altes, stated that the Dutch authorities could only investigate any alleged illegal activities on the part of Radio Monique staff if they took place in Holland.

To begin with the surveillance operation (the DTI refused to admit it was a blockade) had the effect of generating widespread publicity for the offshore stations and undoubtedly made many more people aware of their continued existence. This in turn, according to John Catlett of Laser 558, led to increased interest from potential advertisers and, at that early stage, the situation certainly seemed to be benefiting the stations more than it was hindering their operation.

However, signs of difficulties in supplying the *Ross Revenge* became apparent to listeners later in August 1985. The half-hourly Dutch news headlines were discontinued because only three Radio Monique staff were on board the ship and towards the end of the month those DJs had to extended their live programmes due to the fact that no new taped shows had been delivered through the 'blockade'. In addition supplies of fuel, food, water and oil had also started to run seriously low although this was not referred to on air for fear of giving away vital information to the authorities. By the beginning of September, however, tenders were obviously getting through once more as new or replacement DJs appeared on the station as well as a fresh batch of commercials and a new supply of taped programmes.

Similar problems seemed to afflict Laser 558 which, with continuing staff and supply shortages, reduced its programme hours at the beginning of September 1985.

### 'Anoraks DTI'

As well as reporting on the activities of the *Dioptric Surveyor* Laser 558 DJs also made a number of spoof commercials under the 'brand name' Anoraks DTI. Here is just one example:-

*Wednesday August 21st, Knock Deep, North Sea. The MV 'Communicator' goes under steam to a new location and in the process comes within a quarter mile of the 'Ross Revenge' - the closest the ships have ever been, a moment in Free Radio history. And only one Free Radio organisation is there to capture it on film! Anoraks DTI.*

*Anoraks DTI with the exclusive Laser and Caroline Together Forever poster, a large full-colour poster on heavy stock paper, a stunning photo of the 'Communicator' and the 'Ross Revenge' together, from anoraks DTI.*

*Order your posters today and check out all the other items from Anoraks DTI. They have the largest collection of photos of your favourite offshore DJs including Tommy 'What a Guy' Rivers, Fergie McNeil, Liz West, Johnny Lewis, Jonell, Peter Philips and the ships' cats, Raffles and Seawolf. Anoraks DTI - Hey everyone's an anorak at heart and at fifty thousand quid a month we have to pay for this somehow!*

## Laser 558 programme schedule, September 1985

6.00am Jonell

10.30am Tommy Rivers

3.00pm Chris Carson

7.30pm Charlie Wolf

12 midnight Closedown

## *Communicator* sets sail

Late in the afternoon of 21st August 1985 the *Communicator* raised her anchor and sailed to a new position about 10 miles away from the *Ross Revenge*, which meant that DTI officials could no longer observe both radio ships at the same time. The *Dioptric Surveyor* followed the *Communicator*, but could not anchor in the open sea, so was forced to continuously sail around the radio ship in near her new position.

The *Communicator* herself did not remain in this position for long, however, and two days later returned to her Knock Deep anchorage with the *Dioptric Surveyor* once again following closely behind. As the *Communicator* sailed to within a quarter of a mile of the *Ross Revenge* the *Dioptric Surveyor* tried to manoeuvre between the two radio ships, but was caught by a freak wave and nearly overturned. For some time after that near accident the crews of both radio ships reported that those on board the *Dioptric Surveyor* were permanently wearing life jackets!

This temporary move of position by the *Communicator* indicated quite clearly that, while the DTI could conveniently watch both ships when they were anchored in the Knock Deep, the one they really wanted to pursue was the *Communicator* to put Laser 558 off the air. For whatever reason it appeared that Laser 558 was considered more of a nuisance (threat?) than Radio Caroline and hence the *Dioptric Surveyor* closely followed the *Communicator* on her journey to and from the new anchorage position. Meanwhile, during those two days the *Communicator* was away the *Ross Revenge* remained in the Knock Deep, unobserved by the authorities and able to receive tendering visits at any time.

*The DTI campaign was intensified in September 1985 when notices were displayed at ports and harbours warning boat owners of the consequences of supplying the radio ships and the penalties for doing so which were contained in the Marine etc. Broadcasting (Offences) Act 1967.*

## Ian West

One of the more poignant events in offshore radio history occurred on 15th September 1985 - the scattering of the ashes of a lifelong Radio Caroline supporter from the deck of the *Ross Revenge*. Ian West, who had supported the station for many years died just before Christmas 1984, ironically shortly before he was due to join Radio Caroline's crew as an engineer. His family arranged with the station for a ceremony to take place on board the *Ross Revenge* during which Caroline DJ/Engineer Mike Barrington, a personal friend of Ian, said a few words before scattering the ashes on to the sea. Some flowers were then thrown into the sea and Radio Caroline observed a minutes silence in Ian's memory.

A ship's bell was presented to the crew of the *Ross Revenge* by Ian's family who had travelled out to the radio ship. The bell was simply inscribed "In loving memory of Ian West 1960-1984". The DT surveillance vessel *Dioptric Surveyor*, in the area at the time, was informed about what was happening and did not attempt to prevent Ian's family boarding the *Ross Revenge* or interfere with the ceremony on board the radio ship.

**offshore trivia**

### Most ships used by a station

***SIMULTANEOUSLY:*** *Three by Radio Mercur (1961) - 'Lucky Star', 'Cheeta' and 'Cheeta 2'*

***DURING LIFETIME OF STATION:*** *Five by Radio Caroline - 'Caroline', 'Mi Amigo', 'Cheeta 2', 'Mebo II', 'Ross Revenge'*

**offshore trivia**

### Longest surviving station

*(1) Radio Veronica (April 1960-August 1974 - 14 years continuous broadcasting from sea)*

*(2) Radio Caroline (March 1964-November 1990 - 26 years with breaks)*

*(3) Voice of Peace May 1973-October 1993 - 20 years with breaks)*

## Laser 558's financial problems

By mid-September 1985 further reports started appearing in the press about Laser 558's financial difficulties, quoting DJs who had recently left the *Communicator* who claimed they had not been paid and the ship had not received supplies of fresh water for five weeks. By 19th September 1985 there were only three DJs left on the *Communicator,* each presenting six hour programmes to fill the station's 18 hour broadcasting schedule. Some extra DJs were recruited during October, but others left so the programme schedules varied between four and six hours for most of the month - when the station was actually on the air. In fact Laser 558 was off the air for more than half of October 1985, due either to generator problems or aerial damage.

Laser "Spotlight Records" were introduced to try and generate some income for the station with record companies being offered a package - 14 plays per week of the featured record as well as twenty one 30 second commercials for £2,000.

In mid-October 1985 the DTI announced that it had no immediate plans to discontinue the surveillance operation and that the *Dioptric Surveyor* would remain on station until all those who supplied the radio ships had been identified and traced.

## DTI 'Roadshow'

In an effort to counter adverse publicity surrounding the surveillance operation (in particular criticisms of the enormous cost to taxpayers) and to explain why they wanted the offshore stations closed the DTI held a number of 'roadshow' meetings for representatives of the media during October 1985. The first meeting, at Maidstone on 16th October 1985, was chaired by Peter Anderson of the DTI's Press Office, also present were the DTI's Radio Investigation Service Director, Dilys Gane and Maurice Ricketts, Head of the Radio Investigation Services Technical Section.

Dilys Gane was reported as saying: *The pirate radio stations are putting out such power that they are jamming out both the frequencies they are using, obviously, and surrounding frequencies. We've had numerous complaints from helicopter pilots trying to land on oil rigs in the North Sea because their directional beacons are being jammed by the pirate ships and instead of getting the signals to help them land in those very dangerous conditions they're getting pop music.*

Maurice Ricketts presented the following technical reasons why, in the opinion of the DTI, the offshore broadcasters should be closed, saying they were only interested in the medium wave activities of the stations:-

- Laser's frequency - 558kHz - had been allocated to BBC Radio Essex and 963kHz - used by Radio Monique during the day and Radio Caroline at night - was allocated to university and college campus stations.

- the offshore stations *could* generate harmonic frequencies if their transmitters malfunctioned, causing interference to broadcasters using adjacent channels.

- there was a *possible* generation of what are known as inter-modulation products between the frequencies. This was illustrated by the following example: - 963kHz -576kHz =387kHz, creating a potential source of interference to North Sea Oil rigs using 386kHz and Heathrow Airport beacons using 389.5kHz.

### Radio Paradijs case

*The next hearing in the Radio Paradijs case had been set for 12th September 1985 and at that time plans still existed for the station to return to the air. In anticipation of a favourable judgement the 'Magda Maria' was taken from the Europort Harbour in Amsterdam at the end of August 1985 for refurbishment work. However, on September 12th the High Court in The Hague adjourned the case relating to the release of the vessel to 23rd January 1986 as it was claimed the Dutch Government needed more time to obtain information about the registration of the 'Magda Maria' when she was seized by the Dutch Navy in 1981.*

- the offshore station's transmissions *may* cause overloading to radios used by yachtsmen in the Thames Estuary who relied on direction finding signals from the Sunk Light Vessel on 312.6kHz. This overloading could occur because of the mixing of Radio Caroline's 963kHz broadcasts with the two megawatt BBC World Service transmissions at Orford Ness using 648kHz.

- transmissions from the offshore stations *could* cause interference to North Sea oil and gas platforms using direction finding beacons on 553.5kHz and 569.5kHz.

(author's italics)

However, despite all these theoretical technical scenarios the only specific example of interference which could be quoted by the DTI was one which occurred on 20th September 1985. The 500kHz frequency had been blocked in an area extending from the Humber to the Isle of Wight , but Mr. Anderson admitted he was not sure which station had caused this, although he suspected it was Radio Caroline who were using a temporary aerial at the time.

Mention was made during the DTI presentation of Laser 558 allegedly causing interference to Radio Telefis Eirrean's transmissions preventing listeners in London and south east England hearing the station. The DTI failed to mention that the Irish station's signal is weak anyway in the south east of England because it is a domestic service for Ireland and not aimed at an audience in Britain.

The DTI representatives then stressed the importance of all broadcasters being accountable and under their control so that if any interference occurred the situation could be rectified or the offending station closed. It was also claimed that the continued presence of the offshore radio stations could result in delays for the opening of a new BBC local station in Chelmsford (Radio Essex) because it had been allocated 558kHz, the frequency used by Laser.

A similar 'Roadshow' meeting was held in Chelmsford, Essex a few days later. During both meetings it was reported that 14 boats from Kent, Essex and Suffolk had been sighted and identified while supplying the radio ships and their details had been sent to the Director of Public Prosecutions. It was also revealed that the decision to charter the *Dioptric Surveyor* had been made, not by Civil Servants, but at ministerial level and that the widely reported cost of the surveillance operation had been exaggerated and was in the region of £25,000 a month, not £50,000 as frequently quoted in the press.

Despite all these claims and statements at the 'Roadshow' conferences the DTI had singularly failed to produce any firm evidence that interference was being caused by the offshore radio stations. Far from supporting the DTI's stance against offshore radio, which had been the object of the exercise, most press reports following the conferences were generally sceptical of the Government's approach and highly critical of the surveillance operation's cost and lack of direct results.

In a change of emphasis on 29th October 1985 the Foreign Office announced that, if requested by the DTI, they would approach the Panamanian Government and try to persuade it to withdraw official registration of the two radio ships. Without the protection of that, or another country's flag and registration documents the ships would be in breach of international maritime law and liable to boarding by the British authorities. However, the Panamanian Government had already instructed its Bureau of Shipping in London not to discuss any questions relating to the two radio ships with the British authorities.

An indication that 'Euroseige' was set to continue throughout the rough winter weather in the North Sea came on 1st November 1985 when the *Dioptric Surveyor* was replaced by a larger surveillance vessel, the 443 ton *Gardline Tracker.* Ironically this vessel was a sister ship to the *Communicator* (previously known as *Gardline Seeker*), home of Laser 558 and was still owned by Gardline Surveys Ltd. of Great Yarmouth.

On 4th November 1985 a Honduran registered fishing boat, *Windy,* which was used to tender the *Ross Revenge*, broke down after a rope fouled its propeller. The boat called for assistance and was towed into Harwich by Walton-on-the-Naze lifeboat where she was searched and the crew of four were interviewed by police. The boat owner, Howard Beer, was later prosecuted under the Marine etc. Broadcasting (Offences) Act for supplying the *Ross Revenge* (see Chapter 23).

## More financial problems for Laser 558

By late autumn 1985 yet more reports that Laser 558 was in serious financial difficulties were appearing in the press. The station's only income in recent months was said to have come from the "Spotlight" (featured plug) records and commercials placed through an organisation known as Overseas Media Incorporated, (OMI) based in London. This company, which was effectively operating as Laser 558's London office, was American owned and managed by John Catlett, President of the station's New York sales organisation, MMI. Clients who engaged the company's services were told that advertisements for their products would be placed in the "best outlets", which nearly always turned out to be Laser 558.

A number of meetings had also taken place with the giant Philip Morris Industrial Group in the expectation that Marlboro cigarettes and 7-Up soft drinks would be advertised on Laser 558, but the deal fell through. However, Laser did broadcast a number of spots for Marlboro cigarettes, but the company denied having paid for the airtime, saying the commercials had been transmitted without its authority. Overall the station's financial position seemed precarious.

During the night of 4th/5th November 1985, with deteriorating weather conditions the crew on board the *Communicator* tried to contact their landbased representatives on a CB radio channel seeking urgent assistance because of problems with the ship's generator. On the morning of 5th November 1985 programming on Laser 558 began as normal, but at 8.30am some coded messages were broadcast by DJ, Craig Novak asking the station's landbased representatives to contact the ship on emergency channel 16: *All Yankee Three are zero. Uniform, repeat uniform. November, repeat, November. Romeo two, repeat Romeo two. Channel 16 listening.*

Programmes continued normally throughout the morning although the DJs were heard less and less frequently between records. Then at 12.21pm, in the middle of the record "O Sheila", the music stopped and one minute later the transmitter was switched off.

The following day, 6th November 1985 the *Communicator* raised her anchor, with the assistance of sister ship the *Gardline Tracker,* which the DTI had used to continue the 'Euroseige' surveillance operation. The *Communicator* sailed, under her own power into Harwich, but was escorted by the *Gardline Tracker* and an Essex police launch. She arrived in the River Stour at dusk and tied up at Parkstone Quay.

The *Communicator's* Captain had sent a distress message on channel 16 saying the vessel had suffered a major power failure. An offer of help from the *Gardline Tracker* was refused at first, but assistance was later provided to raise the

*Communicator's* anchor. However, an offer from the *Gardline Tracker* to actually tow the radio ship into port was refused - the DTI could have claimed salvage fees if this had been accepted.

With the *Communicator* heading for harbour two creditors immediately announced that they would seek to have the ship impounded until they had received the money owed to them by the Laser organisation. One creditor, claiming to be owed £7,000, was Paul Rusling who had been involved in 1983 and early 1984 initially equipping the *Communicator* for her role as a radio ship. The other creditor was Gardline Surveys Ltd. who claimed they were still owed £5,000 from the original sale of the *Communicator* (under her former name *Gardline Seeker*) in 1983.

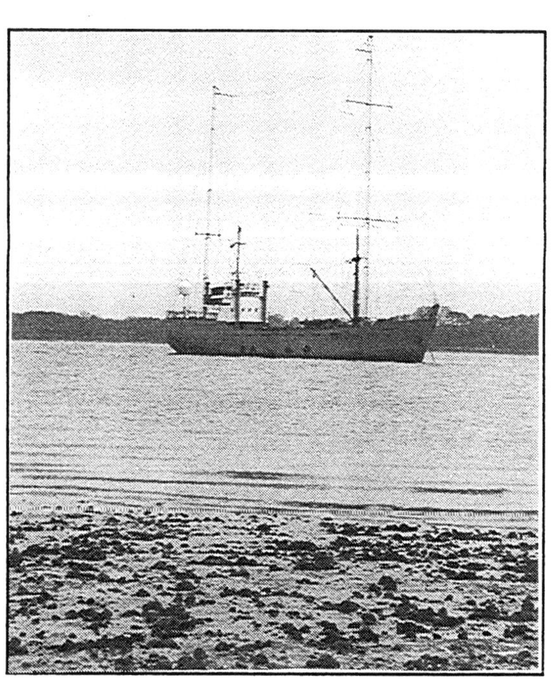

*The 'Communicator' in Harwich*

When the ship arrived in Harwich all crew and DJs (seven American and four British) remained on board and were questioned by Police, Customs, Immigration, DTI and Department of Transport officials. Later all Americans were allowed to leave the ship and were given one month visas to stay in Britain, but the Captain, Patrick Paternoster, from Ipswich, stayed on board the *Communicator.*

After the *Communicator* arrived in Harwich a DTI spokesman was quoted as saying: "One down, one to go." - a clear indication that they considered the capitulation of Laser 558 had been a direct result of its surveillance operation and it now intended to continue pursuing the *Ross Revenge* and the two stations housed aboard her.

With Laser 558 off the air some preliminary discussions were held between the station's London representatives, OMI and the Radio Caroline organisation about the possibility of hiring airtime for an overnight service from the *Ross Revenge* until the *Communicator* was available again. The planned service would have used all American staff and been funded by advertising sold through OMI, but in the absence of any definite financial commitment by OMI the proposal never materialised. Meanwhile on land the Laser Roadshow continued to operate and DJs Tommy Rivers and Charlie Wolf made guest appearances at some venues.

## *Communicator* impounded

After the *Communicator* arrived in Harwich a temporary Prohibition Order was served by the Department of Transport because of doubts about her seaworthiness and the writ issued by Paul Rusling was also served by Colchester County Court officials, acting on behalf of the Admiralty Marshal. Effectively these actions meant that the *Communicator* could not leave Harwich until repairs had been completed to make her seaworthy and all outstanding debts had been paid. The company which operated Laser now had eight days to either pay off or contest the debts, or reach a compromise settlement out of Court. If nothing was done within that time the creditors could then apply to the Admiralty Court in London for the vessel to be sold and any monies raised used to pay the outstanding debts.

On 8th November 1985, the Department of Transport confirmed the temporary Prohibition Order and formally declared the *Communicator* to be unsafe .The Department also joined the list of creditors demanding payment from Laser's backers. Their claim was for the assistance provided by *Gardline Tracker* in raising the *Communicator's* anchor before she entered Harwich on 5th November 1985.

A 'keeper' was put on board the *Communicator* by the Admiralty Marshal to ensure that she did not leave port until all outstanding matters had been resolved. However, it was not at all certain that Eurad SA, nominal owners of Laser 558, would spend money on the works specified by the Department of Transport in order to make the *Communicator* seaworthy.

The ship's generators, which had all failed while the vessel was at sea, were in fact repaired and working again within half an hour of her arrival in Harwich. Captain Patrick Paternoster explained in a press interview on 15th November 1985 why he had decided to sail the *Communicator* into port. With the atrocious weather conditions at the time, lack of power on board and the vessel dragging her anchor he felt it was the best course of action. As the only qualified seaman on board he had spent over 48 hours awake trying to keep the ship in position. During that time he had contacted the crew of the *Ross Revenge*, who had urged him to hold out for as long as possible and also suggested that he unload the Laser broadcasting equipment on to the *Ross Revenge* before entering port, but Captain Paternoster refused. In conclusion he said "I am Captain of the ship and the safety of everyone on board is my responsibility."

## DTI surveillance ends

The *Gardline Tracker* returned to sea shortly after the *Communicator* had arrived in Harwich and once again took up position near the *Ross Revenge*. From here the DTI mounted a number of surveillance and chase operations on pleasure boats carrying Radio Caroline fans out to see the *Ross Revenge*. Organiser of the trips, Albert Hood of Clacton, complained to the DTI after officials allegedly tried to board his ship and the Captain of the *Ross Revenge* also complained that the DTI dinghy was circling dangerously close to his vessel- within the 30' limit defined by international maritime law. The DTI denied both accusations, saying that their men were only there to observe and monitor boats visiting the radio ship, but a spokesman went on to claim that his staff had had bottles thrown at them from the Radio Caroline ship.

On 13th December 1985, the DTI suddenly announced that "surveillance of the pirate radio stations in the North Sea is to end." Minister for Industry and Information Technology, Mr. Geoffrey Pattice stated:- *We have achieved our objective which is to find out who was supplying the ships. The fact that Radio Laser 558 has ceased broadcasting is an added bonus and I hope that Radio Caroline will follow their example.* The cost of the operation, which lasted in total for 126 days, was estimated to have exceeded £100,000.

## Laser 558 closure explanation

Allegations in some newspapers that the *Communicator* was without food and water supplies in her last days at sea and that the crew had lived in disgusting conditions , some supposedly suffering from scurvy, were dismissed when a local newspaper reporter managed to visit the ship as she lay at anchor in the River Stour. Under the headline **WE FOUND LASER SHIPSHAPE**, Andrew Young reported in the Ipswich *Evening Star* on 16th November 1985 that the ship's galley was both clean and functional and that there was plenty of food for the crew members on board. Captain Paternoster also dismissed reports about awful conditions on his ship, but said he was fighting to be paid £2,000 in back wages while waiting at home in Ipswich to hear what action, if any, the authorities would take against him.

Explaining why Laser 558 had closed and the *Communicator* sailed into port John Catlett, President of MMI in New York and 'Manager' of OMI in London, was quoted as saying: *We had a period about ten days ago of some very bad weather, with the bad luck to have one of our major generators actually blow up at the same time as we were low on water and low on fuel, which meant that the ship moved quite easily in a storm. It was dragging anchor and the generator that's used to raise the anchor was inoperative. So the Captain decided, with the agreement of the crew and the disc jockeys on board that for the safety of those people it would be necessary to come into port.*



He also claimed to have held talks with a potential new American backer in an effort to raise the estimated £120,000 needed to free the ship from her detention in the River Stour. These talks were obviously unsuccessful because on 6th December 1985 an advertisement appeared in *Broadcast* magazine, placed by Catlett through Overseas Media Inc. in London, offering the MV *Communicator* for sale or lease for "legal re-launch by new investors."

This attempted sale was all too late because the following week the Admiralty Court in London heard an application from Paul Rusling for the *Communicator* to be sold in order that he could recover the £7,012 owed to him in respect of goods and services he had provided while the ship was originally being fitted out in Florida in 1983.

Counsel for the station's owners, Eurad SA, said the vessel was worth £1million and they did not want a forced sale, but the Admiralty Marshal informed the Court that the 30 year old ship, if sold for scrap, would be worth a tiny fraction of the figure put on it by its owners. However, Mr. Justice B C Sheen found in favour of Paul Rusling and ordered the vessel to be advertised for sale as soon as possible, unless in the meantime the company behind Laser managed to meet the claim.

## Caroline 558

After the Laser 558 vessel *Communicator* had sailed into Harwich on 6th November 1985 Radio Caroline news at 12 noon carried the story of the rival station's demise:-

*The offshore radio ship MV 'Communicator', home of Laser 558, sailed from the Knock Deep Channel today escorted by the British Government's surveillance vessel 'Gardline Tracker'. The 'Communicator' had been plagued by generator problems since yesterday and after a night of heavy storms on the North Sea the Government vessel took up position alongside the ship earlier today. It isn't yet known if the 'Communicator' had asked for assistance or if the authorities boarded the vessel. Both ships are now believed to be heading for Harwich on the east coast of England. The crew of the 'Gardline Tracker' would not comment on whether or not the action they had taken was on the authorisation of landbased officials.*

Radio Caroline closed transmissions on both 963kHz and 576kHz just after 10.00pm that same day, returning about four hours later with the 50Kw transmitter on 963kHz, but the 10Kw transmitter was now tuned to 558kHz - Laser's former frequency. This was not only an attempt, now that Laser was silent, to prevent the BBC local station in Essex claiming 558kHz, which it had been allocated by the DTI, but also an apparent move by Radio Caroline to attract Laser's former audience. The broadcasting schedule from the *Ross Revenge* at the beginning of November 1985 was now:-

558kHz Radio Caroline 558 (24 hours)
963kHz Radio Monique 4.00am - 6.00pm
Jamming 963 (including sponsored religious programmes)
6.00pm-9.00pm Radio Caroline simulcast of
Caroline 558 9.00pm-4.00am.

A format change for Radio Caroline took place on 15th November 1985 when classics from the 60s and 70s, as well as more Top 40 material, began to be featured in programmes at the expense of reggae, rock music and album tracks. The only album tracks now heard were 'featured' ones with the introduction of promotions for one particular album during each programme. After a few days this attempt to imitate Laser 558's format was relaxed and more of the traditional Caroline style of rock music again began to be included in programming. However, the Jamming 963 service was discontinued altogether and from 16th November continuous Country and Western music was played between the religious tapes during the evening until the link up of both transmitters at 9.00pm.

Programme timings were also changed from the (generally) three hour shows which Radio Caroline listeners were familiar with, to the Laser 558 style of four hour programmes, while the hours of transmission now also followed those of Laser - 5.00am - 1.00am, but a 24hour schedule was maintained at weekends.

### Caroline on shortwave

*30th November 1985 saw the first shortwave test transmission take place from the 'Ross Revenge' on a frequency of 6273kHz, relaying Caroline 963 programmes. A marine transmitter (part of the 'Ross Revenge's original communications equipment) was used for the broadcast with a power of only 500 watts and reception was generally poor. Vincent Monsey from Caroline's New York office confirmed that the tests had been official and that the station planned to transmit on short wave from about the beginning of February 1986, with a power of 5Kw to provide a World Service of Radio Caroline's programmes.*

## Radio Monique

During the summer of 1985 Radio Monique had built a large audience and attracted a number of substantial advertising contracts, but both of these success indicators began to fall by the end of November.

The problems can be traced to difficulties with tendering the *Ross Revenge* following the start of the DTI surveillance operation in August 1985. Previously the station had received a tender twice weekly, providing a vital delivery of new programme material, commercials and technical supplies. This tendering service had slipped to once every two weeks by the late summer of 1985 and after the start of 'Euroseige' a tender only visited the *Ross Revenge* perhaps every six weeks.

This disruption in supplies affected the technical operation of the station as well as the programming side-if spares were not readily available engineers experienced difficulties in maintaining equipment and lack of adequate fuel supplies also often forced early closure of the transmitter.

As a consequence of these disruptions to its regular service Radio Monique quickly lost listeners and many advertisers failed to renew or enter into new contracts. They were worried not only by the station's falling audience figures and also by increased attention from the Dutch authorities as the result of the British Government's surveillance operation.

However, despite all these difficulties Radio Monique, like Radio Caroline, managed to continue broadcasting throughout and beyond the period of the DTI surveillance operation and with its curtailment by the British Government in December 1985 the supply problems eased somewhat during the early part of 1986.

## Roland C Pearson

*One of the most prominent supporters of offshore radio in Britain died on 23rd December 1985. Roland C Pearson - 'Buster' to all who knew him was an outstanding friend to the offshore stations and those who worked on them.*

*Buster Pearson suffered all his life from haemophilia and was largely confined to a wheelchair. He first acquired an interest in radio during the Second World War when he listened to the American Forces Network because its programmes were so radically different from the BBC output. His interest in radio led to him monitoring and recording, in great detail, air traffic control broadcasts and from this information he plotted the location and destinations of aircraft flying in the vicinity of his home.*

*This in turn led to him being one of the first people in Britain to tune to the output of Dutch offshore station Radio Veronica in 1960 and in particular its English language outlet, CNBC. From this beginning grew a lifelong association with all the offshore radio stations off the British and European coast.*

*In the late 1960s he started to produce news sheets for the Southend branch of the Free Radio Association and this ultimately led to the launch of his own magazine 'Monitor' which ran to 38 issues over eighteen years. The magazine contained incredibly detailed logs of all that happened on board the various radio ships and the stations which broadcast from them and Buster was known to be an almost continuous listener to their output. This was so much the case that, on many occasions in times of distress, those on board the radio ships could confidently pass on messages in the knowledge that Buster Pearson was listening and he knew who to contact for assistance.*

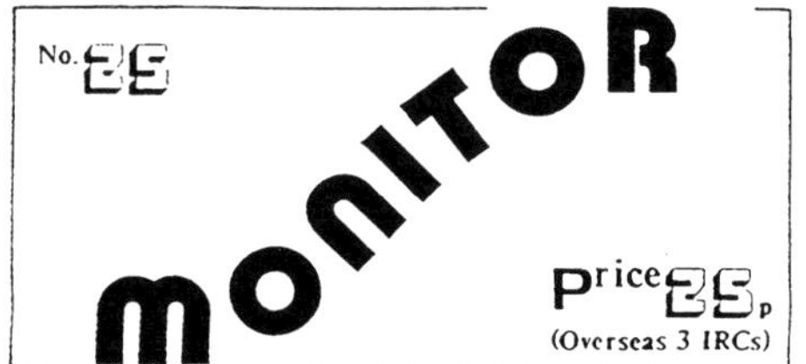


*Buster Pearson was a well respected and much liked person who, although he never actually worked for an offshore radio station, did more than most to assist and support their operation. His funeral in January 1986 was attended by many offshore DJs and personalities including Radio Caroline's founder, Ronan O'Rahilly.*

## Raffles

*Raffles was the ship's dog on board the 'Ross Revenge'. The dog had been rescued by station engineer Peter Chicago after being kicked into the Spanish harbour where the 'Ross Revenge' was being fitted out in 1982. Raffles remained on board the radio ship from that date until being taken off in August 1987 to receive treatment for a skin disease. After serving a period in quarantine Raffles went to live with Peter Chicago at his home in Kent.*

*In late 1985, with the DTI surveillance still in force, the listeners' supporters group, the Caroline Movement, launched an appeal which they felt did not contravene the Marine etc. Broadcasting (Offences) Act 1967. This involved delivering supplies to the 'Ross Revenge' specifically for the ship's dog, Raffles. The project, under the title 'Raffles DTI (Dog Treats Incorporated)' ensured that donations of food and all sorts of supplies addressed to the dog reached the 'Ross Revenge' in time for Christmas 1985.*

*Had any prosecution been brought it is doubtful whether the defence argument that the supplies were intended solely for the dog would have carried much weight, but the DTI never provided the opportunity to test this theory in practice!*

# RAFFLES THE DOG HELPS POP PIRATES

I UNDERSTAND that the disc jockeys and crew aboard pop ship Radio Caroline did not go short of festive goodies over the Christmas period.

And this was partly due to their four-legged friend, and affectionate hound called Raffles.

Being a foreign creature of the canine variety, Raffles is not covered by the Marine Offences (Broadcasting, etc) Act of 1967.

It is therefore not illegal to supply Raffles with goodies from the UK mainland — although of course, one must not deliver any items to his human crewmates out on the North Sea.

This loophole in the law led to Raffles receiving a huge amount of Christmas fare and gifts of an edible and drinkable variety.

# Chapter 23

# Beginning of the end

New Year's Day 1986 saw a further change in Radio Caroline's format with the introduction of separate services throughout the night. Instead of the two frequencies linking after the sponsored religious programmes had finished a new "Caroline Overdrive" service was introduced on 963kHz with the traditional Caroline rock and album music, while Caroline 558 continued with its pop-orientated service. Caroline Overdrive was the inspiration of DJ Tom Anderson who had returned to the *Ross Revenge* shortly before Christmas 1985 and set about implementing the various format changes - including this reintroduction of overnight programming which had been discontinued the previous November.

Early January 1986 also brought rumours of increasing financial problems for Radio Monique and suggestions that many of the station's commercials were being aired on a 'meal ticket' basis. The lack of a tender during the first three weeks of 1986 also meant the station had no new commercials, records or up-to-date Top 50 programmes and was forced to fill its broadcasting hours with repeats of old taped shows. However, a tender did manage to arrive on 21st January 1986 bringing some relief DJs as well as new programme material.

### Communicator drama

*Drama involving the former Laser 558 ship 'Communicator' occurred on 16th January 1986 when a fire broke out on board as she lay at anchor in the River Stour. The Harwich inshore lifeboat took two watchmen from the ship while four fire crews from Harwich and Colchester went on board wearing breathing apparatus to discover the cause of the fire was a faulty boiler.*

## AM Stereo station

On 5th January 1986 the *Mail on Sunday* newspaper carried a report suggesting that a new offshore station - which had been widely rumoured since early 1985 - was to be launched off the British coast. The station, to be known as Stereo 531, was said to have been a Dutch backed venture and planned to introduce medium wave stereo radio to Britain. Former Caroline DJ and Laser technician Paul Rusling was reportedly involved in the project, which also claimed to have secured American advertising contracts.

The *Mail on Sunday* report also indicated that the new station would be based on a 450,000 ton former oil tanker, *Burmah Endeavour,* which was then laid up in Southampton. However this report was strongly and quite rightly denied by the Burmah Oil Company.

In fact the journalist who wrote the story was close to the truth because the project's actual vessel, the MV *Nannell,* was also laid up in Southampton at that time, being secretly refurbished for her new role. The *Nannell's* cover story was that she had been purchased by a scrap metal company, but had subsequently been found to need extensive repair work in order that a marine safety certificate could be issued.

The new station planned to anchor its vessel near the South Knock Buoy (the original position planned for the *Communicator* in 1984). It is interesting to speculate how less effective the DTI surveillance operation (Euroseige) would have been had this plan been achieved during 1985 as originally intended.

*Stern view of the 'Nannell'*

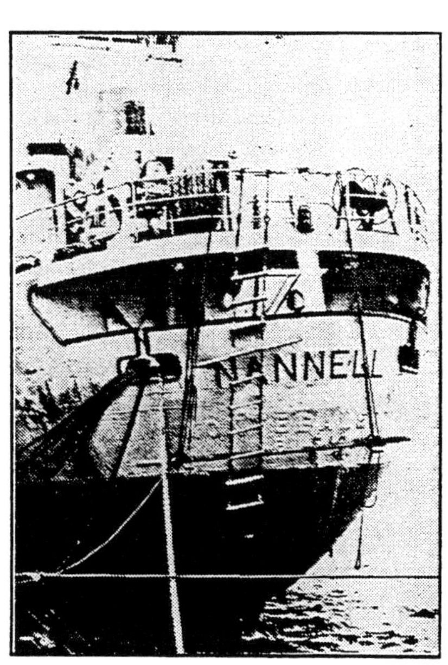

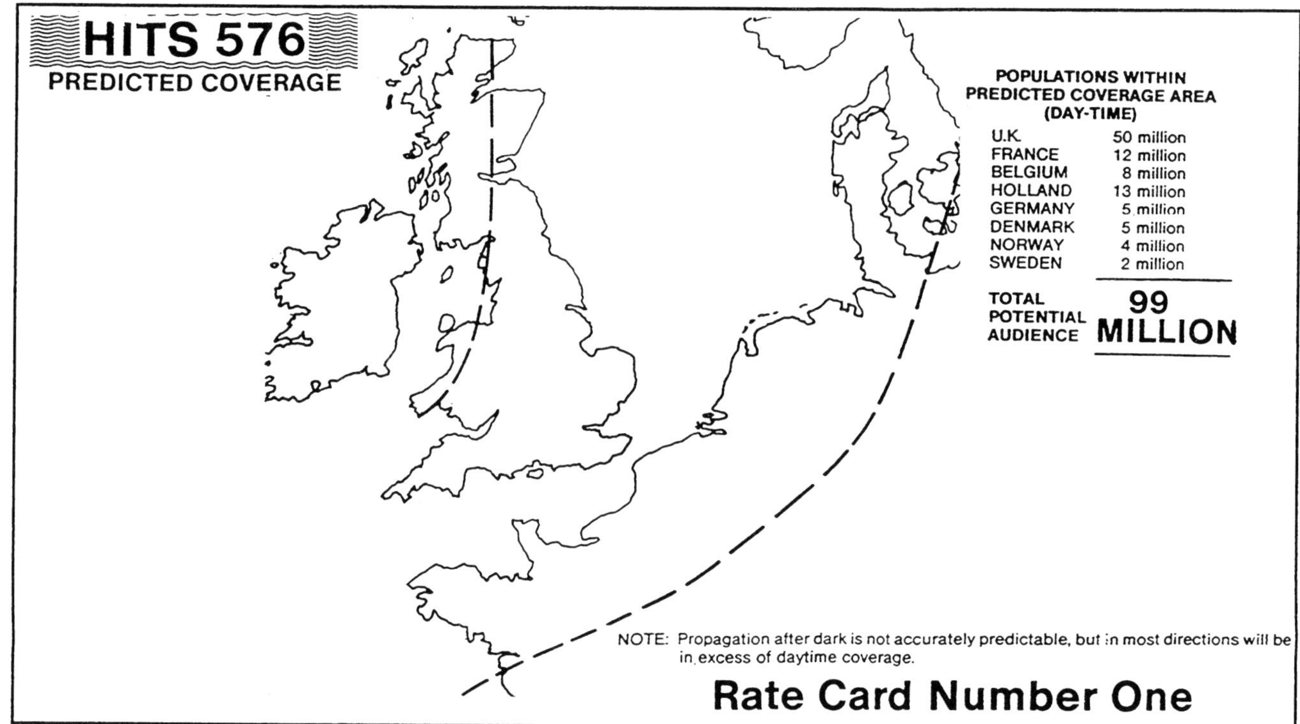


*The ambitious project to bring a stereo AM radio station off the British coast really existed and rate cards with technical information about the station and its planned coverage area were prepared.*

It was not long before press reporters linked the *Nannell* to the proposed offshore station and it became imperative to relocate the ship before any official action was take against her. A local newspaper in Southampton, the *Evening Echo*, broke the story on 1st February 1986 when it revealed that the *Nannell* was to be the home for the new offshore station Stereo 531. The DTI were quoted in the article as admitting that they knew of plans for another offshore station and that they were aware of the *Nannell's* possible involvement.

Another vessel adjacent to the *Nannell* in Southampton, the *Silver Sea,* also came under suspicion and was used by those involved with the offshore radio project to divert journalists and others expressing an interest away from their own ship.

Following publication of these press reports an attempt was made in mid February 1986 to sail the *Nannell* from Southampton. After being delayed by engine trouble the *Nannell* eventually left port on 14th February giving her intended destination as Pasajes san Juan, near San Sebastian in northern Spain. Once again the *Silver Sea* was used to divert attention from the *Nannell.* She had already been used to transport some items of equipment to Spain for the offshore radio project but when she also set sail two days after the *Nannell* she encountered storms and had to enter Brest. Here she was boarded and detained by the French authorities because she was reportedly carrying goods destined for the overthrow of the Sierra Leone government.

Meanwhile the *Nannell,* which had also suffered engine problems requiring a visit to Plymouth for repairs eventually arrived in the northern Spanish port of Santander (where the *Ross Revenge* had been fitted out in the early 1980's) and here it was intended that transmitting, studio and broadcasting equipment would be installed.

In mid March 1986 reports appeared in the trade press that two stations would now be launched from the *Nannell* - Stereo Hits 576 (the real frequency which up until then had been a closely guarded secret, using the 'Stereo 531' name as a cover) and WSOL 801. The publication of this accurate information meant that the authorities were now aware of the real plans for the proposed stations.

The British DTI approached the Spanish authorities putting pressure on them to prevent any further work being carried out on the *Nannell.* When the Spanish Ministry of the Interior instructed that work should cease on the *Nannell* (on spurious grounds that she was registered in Honduras and therefore required a Honduran broadcast licence) the project's backers thought it prudent to move their vessel. On 31st March the *Nannell* left Santander, supposedly heading for Oran in Algeria, but in fact she quietly slipped into a small port in southern France where she remained undiscovered for some time.

The unexpected need to move port and the consequent setback in fitting out the *Nannell* added to the already long delays incurred on the project and some of the initial financial backing was lost as a direct result. A further consequence was that the DJs and engineering crew who had been assembled in Spain had to be paid off and sent home while new sources of financial backing were sought.

Surprisingly this was achieved by mid May 1986 and the *Nannell* (now re-registered in Greece) sailed back to Santander where further work was undertaken without hindrance from the Spanish authorities. An aerial mast and two transmitters were installed on board the vessel, but throughout the summer of 1986 the promised financial backing did not materialise and the whole project faltered amidst internal disagreements and arguments. Meanwhile the ship languished in Santander staffed only by a small caretaker crew, but with no further conversion work being undertaken.

## *Ross Revenge* adrift

Weather once again played its part in the fortunes of the *Ross Revenge* during January 1986. Code numbers were read out on Caroline Overdrive during the late evening of 30th January 1986 and at 2.00am the following morning the 963kHz transmitter was closed. Caroline 558 continued broadcasting a little longer and the emergency code numbers were read out repeatedly for another half hour until that transmitter too left the air abruptly.

The *Ross Revenge* had broken from her anchor and was adrift in the Force 8 gale. Lifeboats from Margate (*Silver Jubilee*) and Sheerness (*Helen Turnbull*) were launched to assist the twelve people on board the radio ship, but by the time they arrived the crew of the *Ross Revenge* had managed to start the engines (which had overheated) and the radio ship was able to head back towards the Knock Deep. During the storm the *Ross Revenge* had drifted some nine miles from her anchorage to a point inside territorial waters near the Tongue Lightship and she was escorted to the Knock Deep by the Sheerness lifeboat which stood by until the early hours of the following morning when the radio ship's own emergency anchor was lowered.

Transmissions on 558kHz resumed briefly for 35 minutes with non-stop music and an announcement that regular Radio Caroline broadcasts would recommence at the earliest possible opportunity.The 963kHz transmitter was not put on the air and Radio Monique remained silent.

Department of Trade officials, who had monitored the emergency call made from the *Ross Revenge* on a Citizens Band frequency, later warned tug owners along the east coast that they would be prosecuted if they assisted the radio ship back to her anchorage and broadcasts resumed. Just how effective such prosecutions would have been is debatable because the Marine etc. Broadcasting (Offences) Act 1967 permits other vessels to assist a radio ship, or any person aboard her, in times of distress but does not make this assistance conditional on the radio station remaining silent afterwards.

Transmissions from the *Ross Revenge* were made sporadically over the next two days until normal Radio Monique programmes recommenced at 9.00am on

2nd February and Caroline 558 returned the following day. However, the crew aboard the *Ross Revenge* were obviously still experiencing difficulties because there was no news service at all and from 6.00pm Caroline 558 played only non-stop music until 9.00pm, while the 963kHz transmitter was switched off as soon as Radio Monique and the sponsored religious programmes had ended at 7.00pm. Gradually, however, transmission hours were increased during the week, including the return of the nightime Overdrive Service, and by 7th February 1986 everything appeared to be back to normal.

However, at 6.45pm that same evening, 7th February, two code numbers were read out and almost immediately both transmitters left the air abruptly.Although no reason was given at the time this break in transmission had been made because the *Ross Revenge* had drifted once again to a point just half a mile outside British territorial waters. Within two days a new anchor chain had been installed and the *Ross Revenge* moved to a position nearer her original anchorage than she had been when the Sheerness lifeboat escorted her the previous week. Shortly after this move a normal programme schedule resumed on both frequencies, including a news service, 963 religious programmes and Caroline Overdrive.

This complete service from the *Ross Revenge* was short-lived because frequent transmitter breakdowns and periods off the air for 'essential maintenance' meant Radio Caroline was unable to maintain 24 hour programming, closing between 1.00am and 5.00am on both frequencies during February 1986. On Caroline 558 in particular a shortage of DJs during the early months of 1986 meant those on board were presenting double programme shifts each of four hours duration. At other times continuous music was played with just the occassional announcement, often from a DJ not actually on board the ship but inserted between records from a pre-recorded cartridge to create the impression that the station had more staff available than in reality it did.

This period of uninspired programming, reflecting the enormous practical difficulties of maintaining an offshore radio station's broadcasting schedule in the mid-1980s, earned the station the unfortuante nickname 'Robot Radio'.

Throughout most of this period, however, the station's news service did continue and from 19th May 1986 half hourly headlines were introduced during the Breakfast Show in addition to the normal top of the hour bulletins.

## Caroline shortwave delay

The expected Radio Caroline shortwave service, promised for the end of February 1986 by US Sales Representative, Vincent Monsey, did not materialise. Monsey explained that although a 1Kw shortwave transmitter was on board the *Ross Revenge* and had been tested in November1985, they wanted to install another 5Kw transmitter before starting the service, but bad weather had prevented it being taken out to the radio ship. Two transmitters were needed, he said, because Radio Caroline wanted to offer a 24hour worldwide shortwave service. Since the November 1985 tests a new shortwave aerial system had been constructed on the *Ross Revenge* and it was now planned that the 'World Service' should start in April 1986.Much of the work on this shortwave equipment was undertaken by American radio enthusiast Al Weiner, who just over 12 months later was to feature prominantly with his own offshore station on the other side of the Atlantic (see Chapter 24).

There was some speculation about this time too that Radio Caroline may start FM transmisions. There was a difference of views about the viability of such a service - some engineers thought that the service area which could be covered would be too small and not be worth the cost of installing and operating the

**offshore trivia**

**Oldest radio ship**

*(1) 'Comet' (Radio Scotland) - built 1904 , used as a radio ship until 1967 - 63 years old.*

*(2) 'Tiri II' (Radio Hauraki) built 1909, used as a radio ship until 1970 - 61 years old.*

*(3) 'Mi Amigo' (Radio Nord, Radio Atlanta, Radio Caroline South, Radio 199, Radio Caroline, Radio Veronica, Radio Atlantis, Radio Seagull, Radio Mi Amigo) built 1921, used as a radio ship until 1980 - 59 years old.*

necessary equipment. However, Caroline's New York sales office commissioned a survey of south east England from transmitter manufacturers Harris. They subsequently reported, somewhat optimisticly in many people's view, that with a 25-30kw FM transmitter on board the *Ross Revenge* coverage of up to 85% of the London and south east area would be possible.

Although nothing came of the suggested FM transmissions there was an argument in favour of Radio Caroline providing a 'localised' FM service to the Kent and Essex coastal area to rival the ILR FM stations. It is worth remembering that RNI provided such a 'local' service on FM while anchored off both the Dutch and British coasts in the early 1970s. (see Chapters 13 and 15)

## Sylvain Tack pardoned

Sylvain Tack was granted a pardon by the King of Belgium which enabled him to return to live in his home country in April 1986.Tack, the former owner of Suzy Waffels, *Joepie* magazine and Radio Mi Amigo had been released from a French prison at the end of February 1986 and deported to his native Belgium from where he had originally fled in 1975 to avoid prosecution over his involvement with the offshore radio station. He later moved to Haiti, where he ran a hotel and at one stage was said to have become involved with the relaunch of Radio Mi Amigo 272 on board the *Magdalena* - an involvement he often denied. From there he went to live in Bolivia, where he agreed to smuggle cocain into France for his girlfriend using a false plaster cast on his leg. He had been caught by the French authorities and subsequently sentenced to eight and a half years imprisonment, reduced on appeal to five and a half years.

### Viewpoint 963

A further development in February 1986 was the rationalisation of the sponsored religious programmes into a service of their own under the umbrella title 'Viewpoint 963'. This started on 19th February 1986 and was promoted with jingles and announcements on Caroline 558.

***Viewpoint 963 programme schedule, Spring 1986***

**Gospel Songs and Meditations, Johan Maasbach** *(Daily 6.00-6.15pm)*

**Campus Church, Ernest O'Neill** *(Mon-Fri 6.45-7.00pm)*

**How Your Mind Can Keep You Well, Roy Masters** *(Mon-Fri 7.00-8.00pm)*

**World Missionary Evangelism, John Douglas** *(Mon-Fri 8.00-8.15pm)*

**Seek Me Early, Melba Frosburg** *(Sat 7.00-7.15pm)*

**Glory Clouds, Kenneth William Ricahrdson** *(Sat 7.15-7.30pm)*

**Words of Life, Robert Boyd** *(Sat 7.30-8.00pm)*

**The Sacred Name Broadcast, Jacob O Myer** *(Sat 8.00-8.30pm)*

**Harvest Time Tabernacle, Lawrence C Irish** *(Sat 8.30-8.45pm)*

**The Perfect Way Broadcast, Charles B Bernardi** *(Sat 8.45-9.00pm)*

**Bells of the Evening, Clement Victor Barnard** *(Sun 6.45-7.00pm)*

**Wings of Healing, Evelyn Wyatt** *(Sun 7.00-7.30pm)*

**The Voice of Bethel, Pastor Boyd** *(Sun 7.30-7.45pm)*

**Faithway Baptist Hour, James Broom** *(Sun 7.45-8.00pm)*

**The Jewish Voice Broadcast, Louis Caplin** *(Sun 8.00-8.15pm)*

**Word of Faith Broadcast, Pastor R P House** *(Sun 8.15-8.45pm)*

**Christian Messianic Fellowship, Albert Bonk** *(Sun 8.45-9.00pm)*

**The Greater Bibleway Temple, Bishop Smallwood E Williams** *(Mon 8.30-9.00pm)*

**Strength for Today, Laine Brown** *(Tues 8.30-8.45pm)*

**The Bible Answers, Ed and Russell** *(Tues 8.45-9.00pm)*

**The Climate of Faith, Hall of Deliverance Foundation** *(Wed 8.30-8.45pm)*

**Youthtime, Art Larson** *(Wed 8.45-9.00pm)*

**The Tree of Life, Velma Jaggers** *(Thurs 8.15-8.45pm)*

**Harvest Gleaner Hour** *(Thurs 8.45-9.00pm)*

**American Christian Countdown - Christian music, Keith Clark** *(Variable)*

## *Communicator* sold

Further drama affected the *Communicator* towards the end of March 1986 when storm force winds gusting up to 70mph caused the ship to break from her moorings at Erwarton in Harwich Harbour and she ended up running aground on the other side of the River Stour at Shotley. After spending two days embedded in the sand, because tugs could not get close enough in the shallow water to put a tow line on board, the *Communicator* was eventually refloated on 26th March 1986 and taken back to her moorings.

Meanwhile on the instructions of the High Court the former radio ship had been put up for sale by shipbrokers C W Kellock and Co Ltd of London, acting on behalf of the Admiralty Marshal. The vessel was eventually sold in early April 1986 and, despite rumours that the ship would be purchased by scrap dealers, she was actually bought by Ray Anderson of East Anglian Productions, based in Frinton-on-Sea. East Anglian Productions, a television and radio commercial production company, are also well known as producers of offshore radio documentrary albums and videos. Ray Anderson, who submitted the highest of 13 tenders, issued the following press release on 21st April 1986:-

*Frinton-on-Sea based East Anglian Productions has purchased the ex-Radio Laser radio ship the MV 'Communicator' for £35,000 from the Admiralty Marshal following the collapse of the Radio Laser Company last November. The vessel had been under arrest in the Essex port of Harwich.*

*East Anglian Productions are a Frinton based communications company producing many regional TV and radio commercials, corporate video productions and broadcast equipment sales. Ironically the company produced a documentary on Radio Laser, filmed on board last September. The Company's Managing Director Mr. Ray Anderson said that the £35,000 paid for the vessel represents a fraction of the ship's true worth. The vessel is equipped with two powerful 25 kilowatt AM transmitters, studios, generating plant and a sophisticated satellite communications system. As a working unit Ray Anderson said the true worth was closer to £250,000.*

*East Anglian Productions are now considering a number of legal options for the future use of the vessel. One includes an outright sale to a consortium for possible use in the Mediterranean Sea as a 'summer only' English speaking radio station for tourists. Also, an international film company is producing a 'rock music' film centred around the former offshore radio station and have expressed an interest in using the vessel on a hire basis. We are also expecting some interest from the various free radio organisations who may wish to see the vessel turned into a museum. However, it is more likely that the vessel will be taken to another part of the world where it could very easily be used as a commercial radio station and operate quite legally.*

During the months after her purchase by East Anglian Productions work was undertaken to refurbish and repair the *Communicator*, with the objective of satisfying the DTI safety regulations and being permitted to take the vessel out of port. Meanwhile, stories circulated widely that, as stated in the press release, the ship was to be used in the Mediterranean to provide a base for an English language offshore station for British tourists in Spain.

## *Daily Star* journalist prosecuted

At the end of June 1986 *Daily Star* reporter Neil Wallis appeared before Felixstowe Magistrates Court charged under the Marine etc. Broadcasting (Offences) Act with 'giving sustinence and comfort' in August 1985 to the crew of the *Communicator*, then home of Laser 558.

Defence Solicitor, Mr Frank Burns, told the Court:- " A conscious decision was made on the part of the Editor and Mr Wallis to expose an absurd state of affairs. It has for some time been the editorial policy of the *Star* to get involved in investigative journalism, that is no longer the domain of the so-called quality newspapers....If those investigations mean that one has to tread on the toes of the establishment then that is the risk one has to take."

Neil Wallis stated in his evidence that "..this was a serious subject, but we decided to treat it in a lighthearted way. We wanted to see whether taxpayers money was being used effectively and judiciously. When we got out there it was anything but."

Summing up Mr Burns said: "The moral of our story was to show that public money was not being spent efficiently and that the ships were still being supplied. Do two bottles of champagne, one T-shirt and a few copies of the *Star* add one jot to the sustenation and comfort of that station? I say they do not. The dignity and common sense of this Court has been reduced to an absurdity. I say the *Star* struck a blow for freedom. The press depends on the good sense of the courts to protect it in the kind of situation we find ourselves in."

Despite all this rhetoric Mr Wallis pleaded 'guilty' to the charges. He was conditionally discharged for six months, and ordered to pay £50 costs.

## Radio Monique popularity

Radio Monique, which had been experiencing financial difficulties of one sort or another for some months was in the process of negotiating a further cash injection during the early months of 1986. However, by mid-April it was reported that the potential new financial backers had withdrawn from negotiations with Radio Monique because of their inability to come to a satisfactory business arrangement.

*The 'Principality' of Sealand, which had been established on Roughs Tower by Roy Bates and his family in 1967, and was entered in the Guinness Book of Records as the world's smallest independent territory, advertised three radio licences July 1986. The licences were for a Top 40 station, an oldies station and a country music station. Licencees were to be provided with studio facilities on the Fort, with each individual station installing its own broadcasting equipment. The licence applications were handled by Hal Shaper, a Florida based music publisher and within a few weeks forty five applications were reported to have been received. However, despite the promising prospect of this 'independent state' being used as a broadcasting base nothing ever came of the project.*

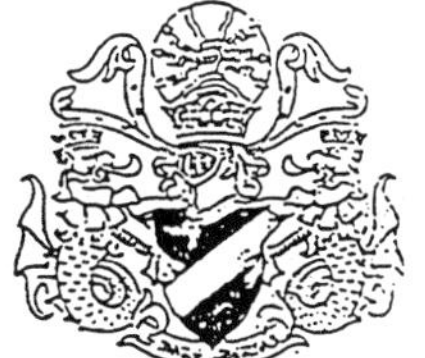

Sealand State Corporation

SEALAND
PO BOX 3
FELIXSTOWE
SUFFOLK
ENGLAND

NOT FOR RELEASE
UNTIL 00.30 THURSDAY,
JULY 31

Contact: PRINCE ROY OF SEALAND
Tel. No: 0702 338653

SEALAND STATE CORPORATION

The Sealand State Corporation of the Principality of Sealand, an independent state in international waters, some six miles off the coast of Essex, announced today (Wednesday, July 30) that it will accept tenders for broadcasting licences.

Each of the three broadcasting stations will have a potential English-speaking audience of up to 200 million listeners in the UK, France, Belgium, Holland, Germany, Denmark, Norway and Sweden.

The granting of broadcasting licences is part of the Sealand State Corporation's plan to develop the island's commercial interests. The availability of the three licences is announced now as a result of mounting international interest and commercial pressures from recording companies and the business community at large.

The station's fortunes changed somewhat in June 1986 when Radio Monique programmes were being transmitted on three Spanish legal land-based stations for several hours each day, ostensibly for the benefit of Dutch holidaymakers. Two new major advertising contracts were also entered into at about this time, one with Citizen Watches was for spots to be played every hour the station was on the air until 31st December 1986. At ratecard values then current this contract was worth 4 million Guilders, but Radio Monique agreed to accept just 6,000 Guilders for an immediate cash payment. The second contract was with Marlboro for Texas cigarettes, with a spot every hour. Again a deal was struck whereby Marlboro agreed, instead of buying the airtime outright, to pay the bill for replacement transmitter and generator parts.

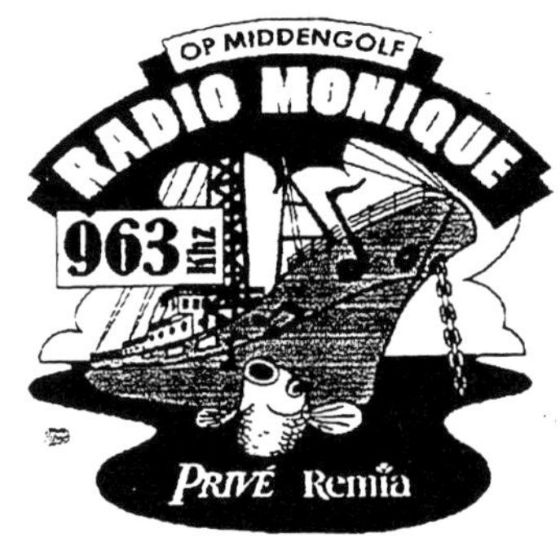


Radio Monique's format was based on pop rather than (Caroline style) rock music. The station's playlist included records from British, American and Dutch artists as well as a sprinkling of performers from other European countries. The station was fairly strictly formatted - at the top of each hour there was a Satelitschijf (Powerplay), effectively a 'plug' record. There were two of these records one for the odd hour and one for the even and they were always announced live from the *Ross Revenge*, even prior to a pre-recorded programme. At least four records each hour were flashbacks or oldies and although the DJs who taped their programmes on land made announcements after each record, those which were broadcast live from the ship often had two records played together without any announcement. The format also demanded that at least two records each hour were Dutch productions or artists - these were sometimes specified because they were 'plug' records, but at other times the choice was up to the DJ. Commercial breaks were aired about every ten minutes with a number of different adverts grouped in each break.

On 23rd August 1986 a poll was published in Holland by Music Media showing that 25% of the Dutch population listened to Radio Monique at some time, while 13% listened a few times a week, giving the station a potential audience of 1.44 million listeners in Holland alone. In big cities 41% of the population listened to the station regularly, the most popular programme being "Prijsbewust"- a prize quiz, which attracted 298,000 listeners daily. However, the station was not so popular in Belgium - one possible explanation offered for these low audience ratings was that it was virtually unknown in that country. The Belgian press gave little or no publicity to Radio Monique and this, coupled with an explosion in the number of FM landbased pirate stations, meant that listeners hardly ever tuned into the medium waveband.

NOTICE
TO MARINERS
EAST COAST OF ENGLAND

THAMES ESTUARY

WRECK

"MI AMIGO"

Latitude 51° 34'.95N., Longitude 01° 17'.35E.

The Wreck "MI AMIGO", which lies sunk in the position defined above, has been marked by means of a Buoy, as follows:-

MI AMIGO BUOY :

Position : 320° about 450 feet from the Wreck.

Description : Can: Red.

Mariners are warned to give the Wreck and Buoy a wide berth.

Mariners should note that the lattice mast of the Wreck is no longer visible.

By Order,

J.R. BACKHOUSE,

Secretary.

*The 'Mi Amigo', which had sunk in March 1980, lost her aerial mast during the late summer of 1986. The mast had stood visible and defiant for over six years but the ravages of the sea finally took their toll in mid 1986, causing the Admiralty to issue a new Notice to Mariners (no 68 of 1986) on 14th August 1986 - ironically the eve of the nineteenth anniversary of the introduction of the Marine etc. Broadcasting (Offences) Act 1967.*

Despite these apparently encouraging poll results, in Holland at least, reports appeared in the Dutch press and on television throughout the late summer of 1986 to the effect that Radio Monique was again in financial difficulties. It was even hinted that some DJs were planning to obtain an injunction against the station until they had received outstanding wages, although such legal action was likely to be difficult to put into practical effect against the offshore station.

By mid-July 1986 24 hour programming had been reintroduced on Radio Caroline, but within six weeks both channels had again returned to some 2.00am closedowns with only Caroline 558 staying on the air 24 hours at weekends and Caroline Overdrive providing a full overnight service on just three or four days a week. After further aerial maintenance work during September and early October 1986 both channels resumed full 24 hour broadcasting on 9th October and this arrangement lasted for nearly a month. November and December 1986 were punctuated by frequent transmitter and generator breakdowns causing Caroline 558, 963 and Radio Monique to go off the air for various periods.

## Technical problems

While it may be frustrating for listeners to have their favourite offshore station silent like this for a few hours due to 'technical problems' the crew on board the radio ship often faced considerable danger while they tried to repair a fault. In 1986 DJ Johnny Lewis described to *Monitor* Magazine what had happened to him while helping to fix a broken stay on the aerial tower aboard the *Ross Revenge*:-

*... We went on deck and there it was, the front stay on the mast had come adrift and the mast was doing this that and the other. We went downstairs and turned the transmitters off right away because it was catching on the feed wires and causing a lot of sparking. Of course we couldn't leave the mast doing that because it would probably have come down so we picked straws!...Three of us went up the mast. I went about sixty feet, which is high enough for me, and we managed to secure a new stay......I have bruises on my legs because where we put the new stay up, to fix it to the forward point where the anchor is, we had to grab hold of it. Now the Chief Engineer and myself grabbed hold of it and unfortunately the wind caught it. Now I'm sixteen stone , but the wind actually lifted me and the stay off the deck, pulled the stay right round the side of the ship with me hanging on to it and thrashed against the side of the ship. Anyway we managed to save the aerial and the station is still on the air. People think that broadcasting from a ship is good fun, but there's other things to do - it's not just a case that you're on the air from five till nine in the morning.*

The format changes introduced by Radio Caroline in late 1985 led to the station becoming increasingly popular, claiming over 5 million listeners by the autumn of 1986, and also attracting interest from advertisers. According to a 1986 audience survey Radio Caroline out performed all the ILR stations in East Anglia while in the general south east area it was more popular than London's Capital Radio.

## Laser 558 prosecutions

On 4th September 1986 the former Captain of the *Communicator*, Patrick Paternoster, appeared before Ipswich Magistrates to face charges under the Marine etc. Broadcasting (Offences) Act. At an earlier hearing he had denied agreeing to carry wireless equipment on the *Communicator* knowing, or having reasonable cause to believe, that it would be used for broadcasting purposes.

Before the hearing got underway counsel for Patrick Paternoster, Mr Michael Lane, argued that his client as a British subject had been charged under the Marine etc. Broadcastinhg (Offences) Act with assisting an offshore radio station. However, Mr Lane contended, the 1967 Act had been superseded by European law which prohibited discrimination on the grounds of nationality. In this case, he claimed, "English courts must give precedence and primacy to EEC law where there is a conflict between it and the UK law."

However, the magistrates supported the prosecution's view and ruled that the EEC law was intended only to prevent member states discriminating against foreigners, not to prevent action being taken against their own nationals. Therefore there was a case for Patrick Paternoster to answer under the British Marine etc Broadcasting (Offences) Act, 1967.

After this ruling the case continued but no defence evidence was offered on behalf of Paternoster. His counsel told the Court that he had taken the job because he was unemployed at the time and it was not clear to him that he was operating illegally. He had not been paid the full wages owed to him by the company behind Laser 558 and he was now unemployed again. The Court found him guilty of the offence and he was fined £150.

**Radio Monique programme schedule, December 1986**

**5.00am** **Herbert Visser** *(live)*

**6.30am** **Johan Maasbach** *(taped sponsored religious programme)*

**7.00am** **Peter de Groot** *(live)*

**9.00am** **Erwin van der Bliek** *(live)*

**10.00am** **Joost de Draayer** *(taped)*

**12noon** **Tony Berk** *(taped)*

**2.00pm** **Maarten de Jong** *(taped)*

**4.00pm** **Jan Veldkamp** *(live)*

**6.00pm** **Ronald van der Meiden** *(taped)*

**7.00pm Closedown**

## Radio Monique DJs 'strike'

For about ten days in November 1986 Radio Monique played non-stop music with hardly any announcements or commercials. DJs on board the *Ross Revenge* were disillusioned about having been left aboard the ship for weeks without a break and no sign of a tender bringing replacement staff or a fresh supply of taped programmes.

On 21st November 1986 the Radio Monique organisation, who had experienced some difficulties tendering the *Ross Revenge* and delivering a regular supply of programme material to the ship, signed an agreement with the same tender company used by the new owners of the *Communicator* (which was now back at sea) so that both ships could be supplied on the one trip from Europe. A tender eventually managed to reach the *Ross Revenge* on 27th November 1986 and a change-over of staff took place as well as a delivery of new taped matcrial so that by 29th November Radio Monique's programme schedule appeared to be back to normal

## BBC local radio in Essex

A new BBC local station, Radio Essex, had been due to come on air in November 1986 on 558kHz - one of the frequencies used by Radio Caroline since Laser 558 closed in November 1985. Trade Secretary Paul Channon, who was also MP for Southend West, announced that his Department would take all possible action to help BBC Radio Essex, saying "It is quite unthinkable that a BBC station should be pirated out of its properly allocated wavelength."

However, Radio Caroline was not about to change its frequency just to suit a local BBC station, so the problem was eventually solved by BBC Radio Essex being granted the use of 729kHz (the original Laser frequency). Station Manager Richard Lucas denied that BBC Radio Essex had suffered an major setback as the result of Radio Caroline broadcasting on its allocated frequency. "All that had been needed," he said, "was the construction of an additional transmitter at Maningtree to serve the north of the county." What he did not say though was that this additional outlet had cost licencepayers £10,000.

## *Communicator* sold again

At the beginning of September 1986 it was announced that the *Communicator* was about to be sold by East Anglian Productions to ' a buyer from Europe'. Ray Anderson denied that the ship would again start broadcasting from off the Essex coast saying, "I think the new owner will probably use the vessel somewhere in the Mediterranean in an attempt to capture business in the French and Spanish areas."

By the end of the month, however, just as it was expected the *Communicator* would be granted a seaworthiness certificate enabling the sale to new owners to be completed, Customs officials acting on behalf of the Department of Transport, immobilised the ship by removing her drive shaft bearing. Ray Anderson immediately lodged a protest with H.M.Customs and Excise about the manner in which the operation had been carried out and threatened legal action if the part was not returned within seven days.

The Department of Transport said the vessel had been immobilised because necessary safety work had not been carried out. This action was taken despite the fact that there had been no official inspectionof the extensive repairs which had been carried out since the ship's purchase by East Anglian Productions five months earlier.

Ray Anderson also revealed that Department of Trade officials had visited Felixarc Tug Co., the company who supplied fuel to the *Communicator* to enable her generator, navigational equipment and deep freeze facility to be run while the ship was in port. The company directors had been 'advised' by officials that they should not deliver any further fuel supplies to the *Communicator*.

This visit was confirmed by Mr Tim Gray, Felixarc's Managing Director who said:-"The Department of Trade has advised us that if we supply fuel or any services to the Communicator knowing it might be used as a pirate radio station we could be left open to the risk of prosecution. Although I do not suspect it would be [used as a pirate radio station], I was not prepared to take the risk and we have stopped supplying fuel to the *Communicator*."

On 20th October 1986 the *Communicator* dragged from her moorings in Harwich Harbour during gale force winds and, with her steering gear now immobilised had to be brought under control by a tug. Unfortunately this was not achieved before she had collided with the Sealink Ferry *Cambridge Ferry*, which was also moored in the River Stour. Although no structural damage was caused to either vessel, and only the ferry's paintwork was scratched, a potentially more serious danger had been the possibility of the *Communicator* colliding with an oil tanker loading fuel nearby. Ray Anderson again hit out at the 'stupidity' of the authorities in immobilising the vessel, effectively rendering the three man crew powerless to control the ship in such emergency circumstances.Harwich Harbourmaster also contacted HM Customs and Excise to request that some action be taken to prevent such a situation developing again.

The potential danger of having an immobilised ship in the harbour seemed to register quickly with Customs and Excise this time because on 24th October 1986 officials unexpectedly returned to the *Communicator* and replaced the vessel's drive shaft bearings.

## Advertising loophole

*Under the provisions of the Marine etc Broadcasting (Offences) Act 1967 it was illegal for British, but not foreign companies, to advertise on offshore radio stations. During 1986 P.D. Brown Autosales of Ipswich found a neat way around this legislation which enabled the company to advertise its services quite legally by using its car sales outlet in Australia to book advertising spots on Radio Caroline. Mr Peter Brown, owner of the garage said he had tried advertising on land-based commercial radio stations but found them 'amateurish' and felt they did not appeal to the type of customers he wanted to attract. He said he was 'very pleased ' with the response to the Radio Caroline advertisements.*

On 10th November 1986 a Panamanian surveyor went on board the *Communicator* to inspect the ship and issue the necessary certificate of registration. It then only remained for the Department of Transport to inspect the vessel and confirm that the required safety works had been carried out to enable the detention order, which had kept her in port for nearly twelve months, to be lifted.Once this had happened the *Communicator* was reportedly sailing to a secret rendesvouz with her new owner, although at this stage her future role remained shrouded in mystery. The DTI Radio Regulatory Department sent representatives to keep watch on the ship while she was being refuelled at Parkstone Quay in Harwich.

The detention order was finally lifted by the Department of Transport on 14th November 1986 and early on Sunday 16th November the *Communicator* sailed to the Cork Anchorage, off Felixstowe. She still had her two masts in position but the aerial array, which would normally have been strung between them, was lowered to deck level.

## Speculation about the *Communicator*

In the days following her departure from Harwich there was some confusion about the ship's precise location and her ultimate destination. Ray Anderson told press reporters that he understood the ship was going to Gibraltar to broadcat to the Mediterranean, but as of 16th November 1986 he had nothing to do with ownership of the vessel. The *Communicator* at that time was in fact owned by a Panamanian regiesered company, Kabo SA, which had been formed by East Anglian Productions and sold to the new owners with its major asset, the radio ship. Meanwhile Harwich Harbour officials monitored the ship heading north before she eventually left the range of their radar area. The Department of Transport were said to be 'keeping a close eye on the situation'.

Laser beams back
All-out war on pop pirate
Pop ship set for return to the air
DRIFTING SHIP AIDED BY TUG
Pop pirate Laser goes to sea again
Ex-pop pirate ship mystery
Pop ship could be heading for Med
Pirate ship leaves quay

On 20th November 1986 Department of Transport officials established that the *Communicator* was in fact still off the Essex coast, close to her former anchorage about 10 miles from Walton-on-the-Naze. Whilst the vessel had been at this anchorage the crew had rebuilt the aerial array which the British authorities had insisted be dismantled before the *Communicator* left Harwich.

Once her position had been established and confirmed speculation began to intensify about whether the *Communicator* would be used as a base to resume broadcasts to Britain once again. The IBA, acting on behalf of ILR stations, issued a statement criticising the Government for allowing the ship to set sail while still fully equipped as a radio station. The Department of Transport explained that they had no powers to detain the ship any longer on safety or seaworthiness grounds, but said it would 'swiftly and effectively' deal with the situation if a radio station attempted to broadcast from the *Communicator* once again.

On 6th December 1986 this actually happened. At 5.40pm a carrier signal appeared on 576kHz (522m) for a few minutes, returning again at 7.20pm, with music and announcements. These test transmissions, which were for a new offshore radio station - Laser Hot Hits, continued until midnight and resumed again at 6.00am the following morning. Laser Hot Hits announced that it only intended to occupy 576kHz as a temporary frequency and planned to change later, probably to 531Khz. Transmitter power was about 12Kw at this time and although there were frequent breaks for equipment modification during the day one American DJ on board the *Communicator,* John Anthony, attempted to present a number of live programmes.

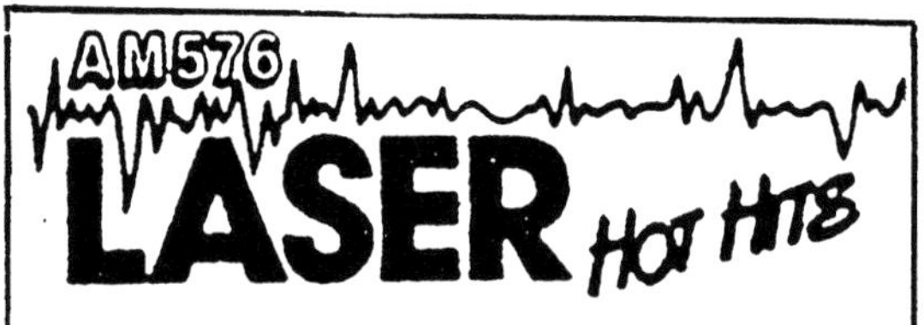


A press release issued from a Madison Avenue, New York address announced that Laser Hot Hits, would broadcast for 20 hours a day and be staffed by American DJs presenting a Contemporary Hit Radio (CHR) format, a programme style which had been created in the USA by Mike Josephs. This had the concept of playing nothing but current hits and records which had previously been chart hits, hence the station name 'Hot Hits'. Four records a week were sold as Power Plays - one featured every hour in rotation, while spot advertising was restricted to a maximum of six minutes each hour.

## Laser Hot Hits

A Dallas based sales company, Radio Waves Inc., represented in Europe by Rob Day (who also operated the Laser Roadshow Disco) claimed to have secured contracts for $250,000 (£100,000) worth of advertising during the station's first three months of operation. These contracts came mainly from major US film and entertainment corporations, international holiday companies and a leading Japanese car manufacturer. The station also had plans to promote its own anti-drugs, Aids and Christmas drink/drive campaigns.

The way in which commercials were to be featured in programmes on the new station differed from Laser 558. Laser Hot Hits proposed to air three two minute commercial breaks each hour (as opposed to Laser 558's six one minute breaks) to give listeners an opportunity to hear longer segments of uninterrupted music. However, both of these commercial formatting styles remained largely theoretical as far as the Laser stations were concerned because little real advertising was attracted by either station. Laser Hot Hits also planned to sell particular shows (a Mowtown Sounds Show or an Elvis Presley Show for example) to sponsors, guaranteeing the station income for up to a year ahead.

According to the press release all supplies for the new station would come from 'legal European sources' and, as the vessel was in international waters and staffed wholly by American DJs, Laser Hot Hits was claimed to be a perfectly legal operation.

**Laser Hot Hits first programme schedule, December 1986**

5.00am KC

9.00am Paul Dean

1.00pm John Anthony

5.00pm- Andrew Turner

10.00pm Closedown

The return of Laser, albeit under a slightly different title, was a major embarrassment to the British authorities who, twelve months previously, thought they had silenced the station for good - at a cost to the taxpayer estimated to be well in excess of £100,000. The Department of Trade announced that they would be starting a blockade to prevent supplies reaching the *Communicator* from Britain, while Coastguards and HM Customs and Excise also planned to monitor all vessels visiting the radio ship.

The IBA, representing Britain's local commercial radio stations, expressed their displeasure at Laser's return, Deputy Director of Radio, Peter Baldwin declaring the situation "very unsatisfactory" and saying: "For many years we pressed the Government to take a more positive stance and in the end they did. We were very pleased with the action they took against Laser originally and we trust they will do the same in the future."

Regular transmissions from Laser Hot Hits started on 7th December 1986, with programmes presented by American DJs, including some from the former station on board the *Communicator*, Laser 558. There was also a full schedule of commercials with news bulletins presented at the top of each hour by ex-BBC Radio One "Newsbeat" presenter, Andrew Turner.

Laser Hot Hits continued broadcasting for just over two weeks until the early hours of 15th December 1986 when the station closed because damage had been caused to the aerial during a Force 10 storm. It was ten days before Laser Hot Hits reappeared with programmes of non-stop music being played at various times until early on 31st December when the station once again went off the air without warning.

While Laser Hot Hits was silent the *Communicator* was battered by severe storms on 5th January 1987, resulting in the front mast partially collapsing and the rear mast bending in half, causing the aerial rigging to fall in a tangle on the deck.

# Former offshore stations

## Radio Paradijs - *Magda Maria*

*Although the impounded Radio Paradijs ship 'Magda Maria' was still in Amsterdam Harbour in November 1986, the Dutch courts had ruled on 29th May 1986 that the ship could be released, complete with studios and transmitting equipment, but this decision was not formally conveyed to the owners, the Pan Lieve organisation, until September, some four months later.*

*The 'Magda Maria' had been towed into port after being seized in international waters by the Dutch authorities in 1981. It had taken five years of legal argument for the vessel's owners to secure her release, but it transpired that the ship had not been maintained or protected in any way whilst in the custody of the authorities and she had been extensively vandalised.*

*Following the release order by the court two companies reportedly made contact with the Pan Lieve organisation expressing an interest in acquiring the 'Magda Maria'. However, nothing came of these negotiations and the 'Magda Maria' was still in Amsterdam in early 1987.*

## Radio London - *Galaxy*

*Since January 1974 the former Radio London vessel, MV 'Galaxy' had been abandoned in Kiel Harbour and used as a training vessel for divers. During these training sessions holes had been cut in her hull and she eventually sank at the quayside on 20th April 1979. The wreck had been an eyesore and embarrasment to the Kiel Harbour authorities and bacause of the danger of oil spilling into the dock (there were still nearly thirty tons of fuel in the 'Galaxy's tanks) a salvage operation was launched in August 1986. A plastic containment ring was placed around the vessel and she was raised by a floating crane onto dry land where she was eventually cut up for scrap.*

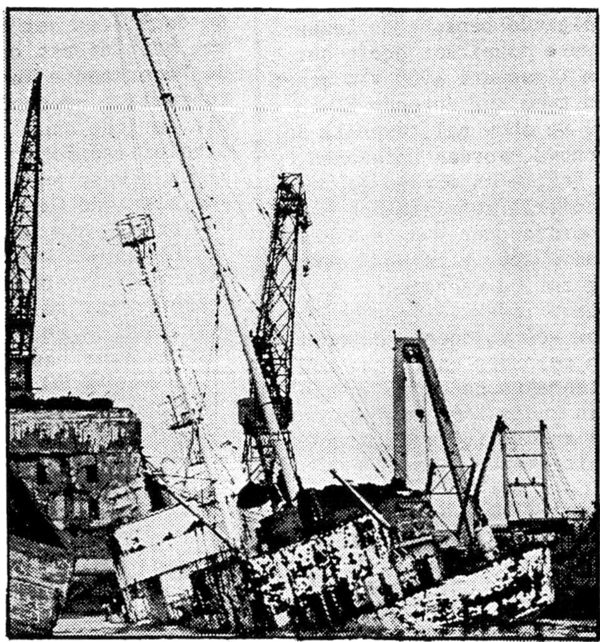

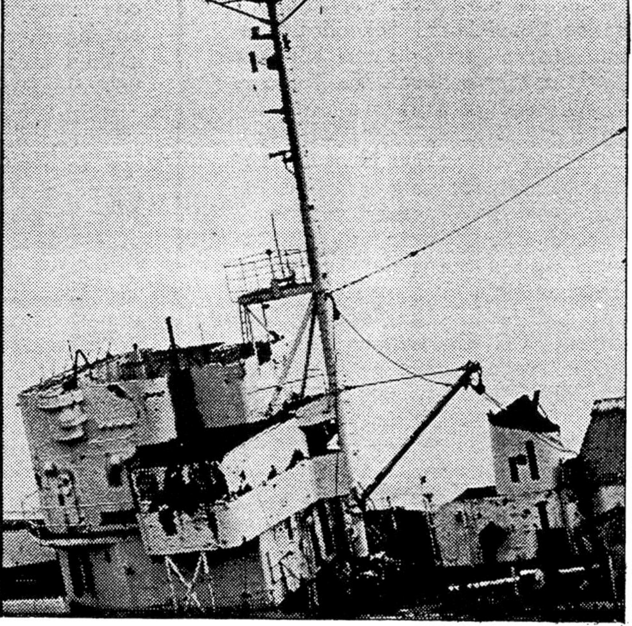

## Radio/TV Noordzee - REM Island

*Another home of a 1960s offshore station, REM Island was requestioned for a new use in August 1986. It was announced by the Dutch authorities that the artificial 'island', which had been built to house Radio and TV Noordzee in 1964, was to be used as a training base for oil rig workers learning escape and emergency procedures. The 'island' was already being used as a weather station by the Rijkswaterstaat, an authority similar to the British Trinity House.*

## Laser Hot Hits re-launched

Temporary repairs were carried out and a new 80' aerial tower was constructed using some spare sections of the old lattice mast, which were still stored on board the ship from Laser 558 days. A 'T' aerial was then rigged from this tower to the remains of the original front mast, enabling weak test transmissions to start again on 22nd January 1987.

These tests continued for over a week with various breaks each day for maintenance, although it was not until 30th January 1987 that the signal strength improved significantly. On 1st February 1987 announcements were made about the station's imminent re-launch and a number of new American DJs were heard during the course of the test broadcasts.

Laser Hot Hits was officially re-launched at 6.00am on 2nd February 1987, with a new team of DJs and new commercials, including in-house promotions for T-shirts, sweat shirts, car stickers as well as a book about Elvis Presley, a Mowtown Chartbusters album, Ski Plan Holidays and the *Sunday Sport* newspaper. News bulletins were broadcast every hour on the hour. A Laser spokesman in New York announced shortly after the station's return that one of the "Power Play" spots had been sold to a particular record company for 12 months and that these plug records alone would pay for the running costs of the station.

**Laser Hot Hits programme schedule, February 1987**

**6.00am Brandy Lee**

**10.00am D L Bogart**

**2.00pm Brandy Lee**

**6.00pm John Anthony**

**12midnight Closedown**

*News bulletins were broadcast every hour during the day*

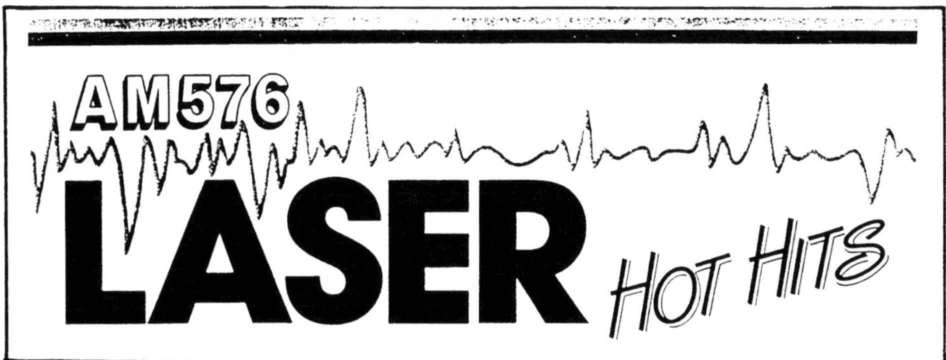


Following Laser's official re-launch the DTI announced that they would "put an end to the station for good", but did not explain exactly how that was to be achieved, except to hint that there would be someone in every British port employed specifically to look out for illegal tendering operations.

Throughout February and March 1987 there were many further breaks in transmissions from the *Communicator.* These were due mainly to the bad weather causing arcing of the temporary aerial array and, in order to avoid damage from feedback, the transmitter was usually shut down immediately. This unsatisfactory technical situation culminated in the station going off the air completely on 26th March and it remained silent until 5th April 1987 while engineers tried to solve the aerial problem. Laser Hot Hits then programmed fairly normally for two further weeks, but at the end of transmissions on Easter Monday, 20th April 1987, reference was made to the lack of diesel fuel on board the *Communicator* as well as a shortage of DJs. The station then closed for the day, but did not re-open as scheduled the following morning.

In the meantime rumours about a financial crisis affecting the station appeared in the press but the US management denied these stories, saying that Laser Hot Hits would return 'within ten days' thanks to a fresh cash injection from new backers. A station spokesman acknowledged, however, that Laser Hot Hits had suffered from a succession of technical problems since its return in December 1986, resulting in frequent periods off the air, and that there had been a cash-flow crisis due to lack of advertising revenue. This in turn had led to staff not being paid on time and the ship running low on fuel supplies.

Despite all these confident and reassuring words about new backers and massive cash injections Laser Hot Hits stayed silent for many weeks after the Easter 1987 closedown and all but one of the broadcasting staff left the ship during this time.

## Radio Monique revamps format

A new schedule from Radio Monique was introduced on 1st April 1987 when it was announced that MMI would take over almost total responsibility for programming the station.

### Radio Monique programme schedules

*Before re-vamp -22nd March 1987*

**5.00am International Breakfast,** *Erwin van der Bliek*

**8.00am Drie on Drie** *non stop music*

**9.00am Radio Gemeente Bloemendaal** *(sponsored religious programme)*

**10.00am Vader Abraham**

**12noon Rick van Houten**

**2.00pm Erwin van der Bliek**

**4.00pm Jan Veldkamp**

**6.00pm Erwin van der Bliek**

**7.00pm Closedown**

*New Programme Schedule from 1st April 1987*

**5.00am Paul Witte** *(taped)*

**6.30am Johan Maasbach** *(taped religious programme)*

**7.00am Opstaan met Monique (Get up with Monique)** *Nico Stevens (live)*

**9.00am Driesprong Gouwe Ouwe** *(oldies requests)*

**10.00am Joost de Draayer** *(taped)*

**12noon Mark de Mast**

**12.45pm Uitzendbureau Top Three,** *(sponsored by Keser employment bureau) (taped)*

**1.00pm Tony Berk** *(taped)*

**2.00pm Poptiek, Maarten de Jong** *(taped)*

**4.00pm Windkracht 4 tot 6**

**6.00pm Meidenwerk**

**7.00pm Closedown**

During the summer of 1987 there were increasingly frequent on-air complaints from some DJs about MMI's running of Radio Monique programmes and advertising and in late August it was announced that, with effect from 5th October, Radio Monique would have new owners, but the station would remain on the *Ross Revenge.*

The MMI programme supply difficulties continued in the period after this announcement and early in September 1987 there were no deliveries of new tapes. Those on board the *Ross Revenge* were forced to repeat many old programmes just to fill the station's airtime throughout the month. Programmes were still being recorded in the Hilversum studios, but because of tendering difficulties they were not reaching the ship for transmission. By early October 1987 all Radio Monique programming was either live or consisted of non-stop music without any presentation by DJs, with commercials and jingles being inserted between records. The situation was relieved somewhat by mid October 1987 after a tender managed to arrive at the *Ross Revenge*, delivering new taped programmes and replacement DJs.

On 29th May 1987, in what appeared to be an ominous sign for the future, Radio Yleis, a Finnish State service (which since 18th March had been testing on low power on 963kHz) wrote to Radio Monique in Spain advising the Dutch station that full power transmissions to Finland would be commencing later in the year on this frequency which had been allocated to it by the International Telecommunications Union) .

## Prosecutions

Meanwhile on 15th May 1987 eight people appeared before Sittingbourne Magistrates Court charged under the Marine etc. Broadcasting (Offences) Act with a large number of offences relating to the *Communicator* (in her days as home to Laser 558) and the *Ross Revenge*. All the offences were said to have occurred between 1st January 1984 and 7th November 1985. Five were charged with conveying goods to the *Communicator*, two of the five were also accused of conspiring "to secure the making of broadcasts from a ship" and a further defendant was charged with "inviting persons to advertise from a ship on the high seas". Three were also accused of conspiring to supply records to the *Communicator* while two were charged with allegedly promoting the Laser 558 Disco in October 1984 and August 1985. Additionally one person was charged with publicising the times, wavelength and contents of broadcasts made by Radio Caroline in *Time Out* magazine on 28th February 1985 and 23rd April 1985.

The hearing was adjourned a number of times during the summer of 1987 and eventually seven of the nine cases were transferred to the Crown Court and set for hearing on 15th November 1988. (see Chapter 25).

## Territorial Sea Act

A significant piece of British legislation affecting offshore radio stations came into effect on 1st October 1987. The Territorial Sea Act extended the then three mile British territorial limit to twelve miles and, as a consequence, the two radio ships positioned off the coast (*Ross Revenge* and *Communicator*) were forced to find new anchorages further out to sea.

The legislation was not primarily directed at the offshore radio stations, it was enacted to bring Britain in line with most other European countries and to assist HM Customs and Excise in their battle against smuggling, particularly in the area of drugs enforcement.

In order to determine the actual extent of the new twelve mile limit the provisions of the 1964 Territorial Waters Order in Council were invoked. This stated that any sandbank exposed at low tide - even for only one day a year - should count as the starting point for the calculation of the extent of territorial limits. It was this principle which had been successfully used to establish that the Thames Estuary Forts were inside British territorial waters during the prosecutions of Radios 390, City and Essex in 1966/67. (See Chapters 11 and 12 for more detailed explanations).

The Territorial Sea Act 1987 now gave a statutory basis to the provisions of the Order in Council (which had been made by the Queen under her unique power of Royal Perogative, i.e. without recourse to Parliament) and contained a consequential amendment to Section 9(2) of the Marine etc. Broadcasting (Offences) Act 1967. This amendment redefined the area over which the 1967 Act could be enforced to take account of the new limits. In practice, because of the use of drying sandbanks as the starting point for determining territorial limits this meant that territorial waters in most of the Thames Estuary area were now extended for over twenty miles from the coastline.

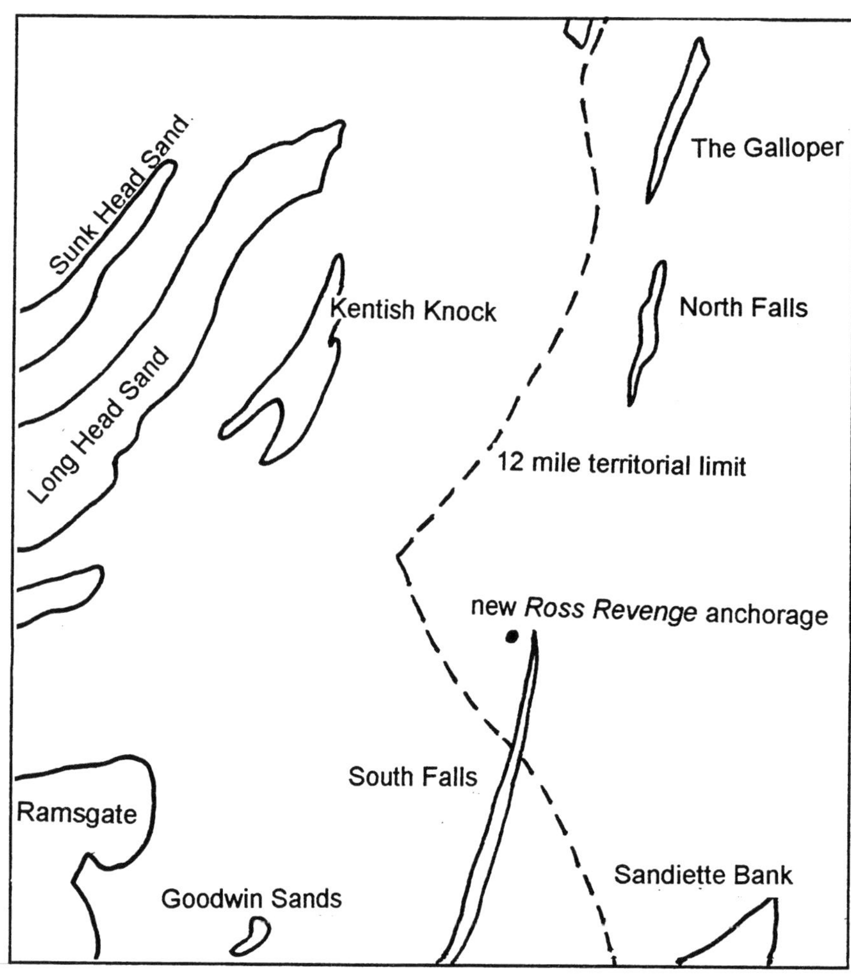


*The 'Ross Revenge' and 'Communicator' had to move from the sheltered Knock Deep Channel to the more exposed waters outside the new 12 mile limit*

The effect for the 1980s offshore stations was that the sandbanks in the Knock Deep Channel, which provided a sheltered anchorage for the radio ships, would now actually count as the starting point for the new twelve mile limit. By this definition, therefore, the *Ross Revenge* and *Communicator*, had they remained at their Knock Deep anchorages would clearly both have been well inside the new British territorial limit. The new Act also had the effect of conclusively placing all Thames Estuary Forts within British territorial waters, including the hitherto 'untouchable Principality of Sealand based on Roughs Tower off Harwich which was now fifteen miles inside the new limits. The wreck of the *Mi Amigo* at Long Head Sands was also now brought inside British territorial waters.

A statement from the Department of Trade and Industry shortly after the new Act was introduced stated that Sealand "will now be within the criminal jurisdiction of the United Kingdom Courts" and went on to indicate that action would be taken if broadcasting of any kind were to start from the Fort. On the other hand 'Prince' Roy Bates said: *Sealand has fulfilled the condition of sovereignty by title of occupation over a territory without a master.....the British authorities have tacitly taken cognisance of the existence of the Principality of Sealand by not acting against Sealand's claims.*

## Sealand TV plans

Despite the provisions of the Territorial Sea Act placing Sealand inside British territorial limits plans were announced in June 1987 for the establishment of an offshore television station on the 'Principality'. American businessman Walter Kemper planned to build a 1,000' transmitter mast on the Fort and broadcast films and music videos for eight hours a day between 5.00pm and 2.00am. Model and pin-up girl Suzanne Mizzy was introduced to the press as the main presenter of the proposed station, Sealand TV, which was scheduled to begin transmissions on 2nd September 1987, exactly 20 years after the Fort had been proclaimed an independent state by Roy Bates. Kemper announced that although $600,000 would need to be spent on equipment and with running costs of $250,000 a month, he had enough backing to operate the television station for two months without needing to attract any paid advertising.

Spokesman in Britain for the project, Ken Hanlon, indicated that the project would use recording facilities in Ireland for programme and commercial production. A variation on this story was that the studio facilities in Ireland would be linked by satellite to Sealand, and at one stage the project even considered the possibility of anchoring a former oil rig, *Trans Ocean 1*, next to

Roughs Tower to house the transmission tower. Advertising rates of £3,500 for 10 seconds and £10,000 for 30 seconds were quoted in a glossy brochure produced for circulation to prospective advertisers.

Sealand TV was to broadcast under the call sign Channel 5, on UHF channel 28 using a 7 megawatt transmitter to reach an estimated audience of 10 million in the London and south east area. However, potential viewers to this new offshore television station would have had to invest between £50 and £100 to install a new aerial because the signal would come from the opposite direction to the existing BBC and ITV transmitters at Crystal Palace in London.

As with the previous much publicised plans to grant three radio licences or to start radio stations from Sealand nothing definite ever became of the Sealand TV proposal.

## Radio ships move

The *Communicator* was the first radio ship to move once the new legislation had been enacted, although the provisions did not fully come into effect until 1st October 1987. Although Laser Hot Hits was off the air at the time the *Communicator* moved from the Knock Deep on 23rd May 1987 to a position at Fairy Bank 20 miles off Dunkirk. On 10th June 1987 Radio Caroline and Radio Monique closed without warning at 7.00am and transmissions did not resume for over six hours. When they did start again normal programmes continued for about 90 minutes before it was announced that the *Ross Revenge* had moved and was at an anchorage in the South Falls Head, a position two miles outside the new territorial limit but in much more exposed waters as well as nearer to the main shipping lanes.

In fact the *Ross Revenge's* new anchorage placed her near the route taken by the Olau Ferry Line's vessels sailing from Harwich to Holland. The radio ship became a point of interest for ferry passengers (not just offshore radio enthusiasts) and the Captains often used to sail as close as they could to the *Ross Revenge* to give them a close up view of the Radio Caroline vessel. This association built steadily over the time the *Ross Revenge* was at the South Falls Head and was to prove very useful to the station and its supporters on more than one occasion.

However, the new position in the South Falls meant that the *Ross Revenge* was full exposed to the elements, she no longer had the shelter of sandbanks which existed in the former Knock Deep anchorage. This exposure to even rougher seas considerably increase the chance of the radio ship dragging or breaking from her anchor and drifting. The danger of collision also now existed, because of her proximity to the shipping lanes whereas formerly the Knock Deep sandbanks had provided a natural safety area around the *Ross Revenge.*

Broadcasts from the *Ross Revenge* had been relatively stable since the beginning of 1987 - Caroline 558 was on the air 24 hours a day at weekends and 20 hours a day (5.00am-1.00am) during the week. The station did, however, stay on the air for 24 hours on Thursday/Friday 11th /12th June 1987 to report on the results of the British General Election.

Over on 963kHz broadcasting hours at this time were:-

4.00am-6.00pm Radio Monique

6.00pm-9.00pm (9.30pm at weekends) Viewpoint 963

9.00 (9.30pm weekends) - 4.00am Caroline Overdrive

The Caroline Overdrive service was dependent on DJ availability and engineering work.

In August 1987 a new jingle package was introduced on Caroline 558 reviving the Loving Awareness theme, and at about the same time an advertising campaign in support of the World Wildlife Fund was launched.

As well as difficulties brought about by the need to relocate due to the Territorial Sea Act Radio Caroline was also dealt another blow in mid 1987 when Panama's Directorate of Consular and Maritime Affairs announced that it was increasing maritime safety standards for ships registered in Panama and all ships over 20 years old wishing to remain so registered would have to meet the higher safety standards and be re-inspected. If they failed to comply with these new requirements they would be refused entry to the register of shipping. Also the then limited random safety checks were to be increased and any vessels which did not comply with safety regulations would be removed, making them stateless. This clearly affected the *Ross Revenge*, although those involved with the operation of the ship refused to accept that the vessel could be so easily removed from the Panamanian register and within two years this was to have very serious repercussions for the station.

## *Communicator* silent

Meanwhile throughout the summer of 1987 the *Communicator* remained at anchor and silent off the Sandettie sandbank, 18 miles from the north west coast of France. Then at the end of August 1987 she was moved, first to a position seven miles from Harwich and eventually back to the original Knock Deep anchorage (shortly to become within British territorial waters). These moves were made to enable potential new owners to inspect the vessel for use as a base to housc two new offshore radio stations - Harmony 981 -an automated station broadcasting a middle-of-the-road format of all pre-recorded programmes and Starforce 576 with an all American pop music format, similar to Laser 558. Both stations were also to carry sponsored religious programmes.

While at the Knock Deep the *Communicator* was refuelled, stocked with supplies and some former Laser engineers went on board to repair the engines and generators. At this stage it was planned to take the vessel to the Mediterranean and fit her out properly for her new role. However, the new owners decided instead that they wanted the twin radio stations on the air as soon as possible so engineering work was carried out at sea.

Two 112' aerial towers were welded together ready to be erected on the ship during September 1987 and much of the studio and living accommodation on board the *Communicator* was refurbished. With the Territorial Sea Act coming into force on 1st October 1987 the *Communicator* was moved on 30th September 1987 from the Knock Deep to the southern part of Inner Gabbard, 20 miles off Felixstowe. However, after about ten days a storm blew up and it became apparent that this exposed anchorage would be too rough for the vessel during the severe weather conditions likely to be experienced throughout the winter months. So, unable to raise her anchor because of the storm, the chain was hurriedly cut through and the *Communicator* sailed to a more sheltered position near Felixstowe, later moving back again to the Knock Deep, where she remained for some time. Here all material which had broken loose during the earlier storm was removed - just before the hurricane of 15/16th October 1987.

**offshore trivia**

**Largest number of simultaneous broadcasts from one ship**

***SEPARATE STATIONS:*** *'Ross Revenge' 1989- three stations (Radio Caroline, Radio 558, World Mission Radio).*

***PARALLEL TRANSMISSIONS:*** *'Mebo II' (RNI - four frequencies - FM, medium wave and two short-wave).*

## Hurricane

Throughout the summer of 1987 transmissions on both Radio Caroline and Radio Monique continued to become more and more reliable, in technical terms, and there were fewer breakdowns. After initial periods of uncertainty both stations appeared to have achieved a reliability of service - a situation which had not been evident on offshore radio for many years. Unfortunately this was not to last because just as everything was going so well Radio Monique experienced the programme supply difficulties with MMI and a few weeks later a major disaster struck the *Ross Revenge.*

During the night of 15/16th October 1987 a hurricane swept across south east England, causing major destruction and loss of power supplies throughout a huge area. As a result many land-based radio and television stations were put off the air or operated a much reduced service. On the *Ross Revenge* Radio Caroline and Radio Monique were programming normally until 7.30am on 16th October when they too were both forced to close for about an hour due to problems with the aerial mast arcing. Both stations returned later and broadcasts continued throughout the day, although the arcing problem persisted repeatedly tripping the transmitter, so at 3.00pm it was decided to close both stations. Transmissions on 558kHz resumed just after 11.00pm that evening for about an hour when listeners were informed that the aerial feeder wires leading to the *Ross Revenge's* huge mast had been slightly damaged and emergency repairs were being carried out.

During the night of the hurricane the other radio ship, the silent *Communicator,* kept her anchor down and although the crew realised the vessel must be dragging, they had no idea of their precise location because her radar equipment had been put out of action. As a safety precaution the main engine was started and run at full ahead throughout the night and much of the next day until the worst of the hurricane had subsided.

By midday on 16th October 1987 the crew finally managed to establish their position and realised to their horror that, even with the engine running full ahead and the anchor down, the *Communicator* had dragged 25 miles north west to a position just ten miles off Aldeburg, Suffolk.

## *Communicator* plans abandoned

All storm damage on the *Communicator* had been repaired and broadcasting equipment was functioning again by the end of October 1987. The 576kHz transmitter was run on a dummy load with a test transmission during which DJs Blake Williams and Johnny Lewis presented a programme using the call sign Radio Sunk on 31st October 1987 - the ship was by this time anchored near the Sunk Head Lightship.

Unfortunately although all the engineering work had been completed plans for the twin stations - Starforce and Harmony - from the *Communicator* had come to nothing due to financial problems. In mid-November 1987 with only two crew on board and reports of more severe storms on the way it was decided to take the radio ship to a more sheltered anchorage at Shipwash, but after 24 hours she was again moored at the Cork Anchorage two miles off Felixstowe, waiting to enter Harwich.

## Monique frequency change

The *Ross Revenge* had, amazingly, been relatively unaffected by the mid-October hurricane and both Radio Caroline and Radio Monique continued broadcasting virtually as normal, with some minor breaks in transmission, until the end of November 1987.

### Monique Basketball Team

*Plans were announced in October 1987 for the Orcas Basketball Team to be sponsored by Radio Monique from 1st January 1988. The contract had been signed by Music Service SA a Spanish based company which also organised the religious programmes transmitted from the 'Ross Revenge'.*

In mid-November 1987 there was a change in frequency for Radio Monique which had been brought about following the increase in power during September of the Finnish station, Radio Yleis. From that date reception of Radio Monique and Radio Caroline's 963kHz service (including the Viewpoint religious programmes) during the hours of darkness had become significantly affected by interference. Radio Monique was almost blotted out completely in Scandinavia and much of Northern Europe, while the station's primary target area in Belgium and Holland suffered from interference early in the morning as well. As a consequence some religious sponsors had withdrawn their programming when reception on 963kHz became badly affected by the Finnish station's transmissions.

Radio Monique's change in frequency was made with hardly any prior notice. The station closed at 6.00pm on 13th November 1987 and the usual Viewpoint religious programmes commenced but were discontinued an hour later. A brief announcement was broadcast saying that there would soon be a frequency change for both Radio Monique and Viewpoint, with full details being announced in due course on Caroline 558. Transmissions from the *Ross Revenge* on 963kHz then closed for the last time.

At 1.00am the following morning Caroline 558 also closed and both stations were off the air for over 24 hours. Caroline 558 returned shortly after 6.00am on 15th November 1987 and within half an hour Radio Monique had also recommenced transmissions on a new frequency of 819kHz (366m). Viewpoint also changed to 819kHz on 15th November 1987.

**Radio Monique's final programme schedule, 24th November 1987**

**5.00am Wim van Egmond** *(live)*

**6.30am Johaan Masbach** *(taped religious programme)*

**7.00am Poplepel, Peter de Groot** *(taped, repeat)*

**9.00am Wim van Egmond** *(live)*

**11.00am Joost de Draayer** *(taped)*

**12noon Tony Berk** *(taped, repeat)*

**2.00pm Popclub, Ad Roberts** *(taped, repeat)*

**4.00pm Edwin van der Bliek** *(taped)*

**6.00pm Wim de Valk** *(live)*

**7.00pm Closedown**

At about this time too there were further rumours that a new shortwave service would be started from the *Ross Revenge* to carry the Viewpoint programmes. Some tests were carried out on a number of shortwave frequencies during September 1987 and on 28th October the programmes of Caroline 558 were relayed on 6220kHz, later transferring to 5955kHz. Reception reports were requested during these broadcasts but dramatic developments affecting the radio ship were to prevent any further shortwave experiments taking place for a few months.

## 300' tower crashes overboard

On 24th November 1987 programming continued as normal throughout the day on both Caroline 558 and Radio Monique, despite a strong north easterly gale starting to buffet the *Ross Revenge* during the afternoon. The storm continued throughout the evening and night, increasing in intensity and whipping up heavy seas which caused the radio ship to pitch and roll.

Radio Monique closed as normal at 7.00pm with the usual announcement that the station would return at 5.00am the following morning. After Viewpoint programmes had finished that evening the 819kHz transmitter was switched off while Caroline 558 continued to broadcast, but left the air suddenly at 2.51am the following morning, 25th November, when aerial feeder cables split.

About an hour and a half later DJs and crew on the *Ross Revenge* heard a huge crash and went on deck to discover to their horror that the ship's massive 300' aerial tower had broken away at deck level and fallen into the sea. Luckily the tower had collapsed over the starboard side of the ship and not fallen forwards or backwards onto the vessel where it would have caused major damage and possible injuries.

The Captain of the *Ross Revenge* informed the Coastguards at North Foreland Radio of what had happened and they offered to arrange for a helicopter to

## Viewpoint Programmes

*The importance of the revenue to Radio Caroline from sponsored religious programmes can be seen from the extent of the Viewpoint programme schedule for November 1987.*

**Gospel Songs and Meditation Johan Maasbach** *(Sunday 6.00-6.30pm other days 6.00-6.15pm)*

**Garner Ted Armstrong** *(Daily 6.30-6.45pm)*

**Campus Church, Ernest O'Neill** *(Weekdays 6.45-7.00pm)*

**Roy Masters** *(Weekdays 7.00-8.00pm)*

**Word for Today, Chuck Smith** *(Weekdays9.00-9.30pm)*

**Sister Polly** *(Monday 6.15-6.30pm)*

**Christian Messianic Fellowship, Albert Bonk** *(Sunday 8.45-9.00pm and Monday 8.15-8.10pm)*

**Bibleway, Smallwood E Williams** *(Monday 8.30-9.00pm)*

**New Testament Studies, Joseph E Sorrell** *(Monday 9.30-10.00pm)*

**Strength for Today, Layne Brown** *(Tuesday 8.30-8.45pm)*

**Bible Answers, Ed and Russell** *(Tuesday 8.45-9.00pm)*

**Jewish Voice, Mark Epstein** *(Tues, Wed, Thurs. 9.30-9.45pm)*

**Jacob's Ladder, Elder Emerson** *(Tuesday 9.45-10.15pm)*

**Climate of Faith, Franklin Hall** *(Wednesday 8.30-8.45pm)*

**Youth Time, Art Larson** *(Wednesday 8.45-9.00pm)*

**Gospel Blessings, Glyn A McAdden** *(Wednesday 9.45-10.00pm)*

**Sar Shalom, Irene Hanley** *(Thursday 8.15-8.30pm)*

**Scripture for England, Pete Peters** *(Thursday 8.30-8.45pm)*

**Harvest Gleaner, E Harold Henderson** *(Thursday 8.45-9.00pm)*

**Keith Slough Commentary** *(Thursday 9.45-10.00pm)*

**Digging In, Joanne Bunoe** *(Friday 8.15-8.30pm)*

**Ordinary People, Lloyd and Kathy Perkins** *(Friday 8.30-9.00pm)*

**Narrow Way, Knox Johnson** *(Saturday 6.15-6.30pm)*

**The King's Business, James Lee** *(Saturday 6.45-7.00pm)*

**Seek Me Early , Melba Fosburg** *(Saturday 7.00-7.15pm)*

**Faith Ministries, Hobarth Freeman** *(Saturday 7.15-7.30pm)*

**Words of Life, Paul Kitzmiller** *(Saturday 7.30-8.00pm)*

**Sacred Name Broadcast, Jacob O Meyer** *(Saturday 8.00-8.30pm)*

**Perfect Way, Charles B Bernardi** *(Saturday 8.45-9.00pm)*

**The Divine Plan** *(Saturday 9.00-9.15pm)*

**Love Walk With Jesus, Wes Daughenburgh** *(Saturday 9.15-9.45pm)*

**Sunshine, Lloyd E Meyer** *(Sunday 6.45-7.00pm)*

**Wings of Healing, Evelyn Wyatt** *(Sunday 7.00-7.30pm)*

**Voice of Bethel, Pastor Boyd** *(Sunday 7.30-7.45pm)*

**Faithway Baptist Hour, James Broom** *(Sunday 7.45-8.00pm)*

**Moments of Inspiration, H L Gibson** *(Sunday 8.00-8.15pm)*

**Word of Faith, R P House** *(Sunday 8.15-8.45pm)*

**Old Country Church, Paul Smith** *(Sunday 9.00-9.15pm)*

**Family Bible Hour, Ben F Palmer** *(Sunday 9.15-9.30pm)*

**Hal Lindsay** *(Sunday 9.30-10.00pm)*

**Revival of America, Leroy Jenkins** *(Sunday 10.00-11.00pm)*

winch the crew off the radio ship, now that there was no aerial mast in the way! However, the crew decided to stay on board although the rescue services remained on stand-by in case conditions deteriorated.

At first light on 25th November 1987 the remains of the mast hanging over the side of the *Ross Revenge,* which were causing the vessel to list slightly, were cut away and the crew informed North Foreland Radio that they were no longer worried about the stability of the ship and the rescue helicopter was taken off stand-by.

The full extent of other damage caused by the falling mast was revealed when the crew set about cleaning up the rest of the ship. It was discovered that the falling tower had shattered the main insulator at deck level, this in turn had forced a copper rod through the deck, striking and damaging the diplexer unit, a device which enabled the two station's to broadcast from the same aerial.

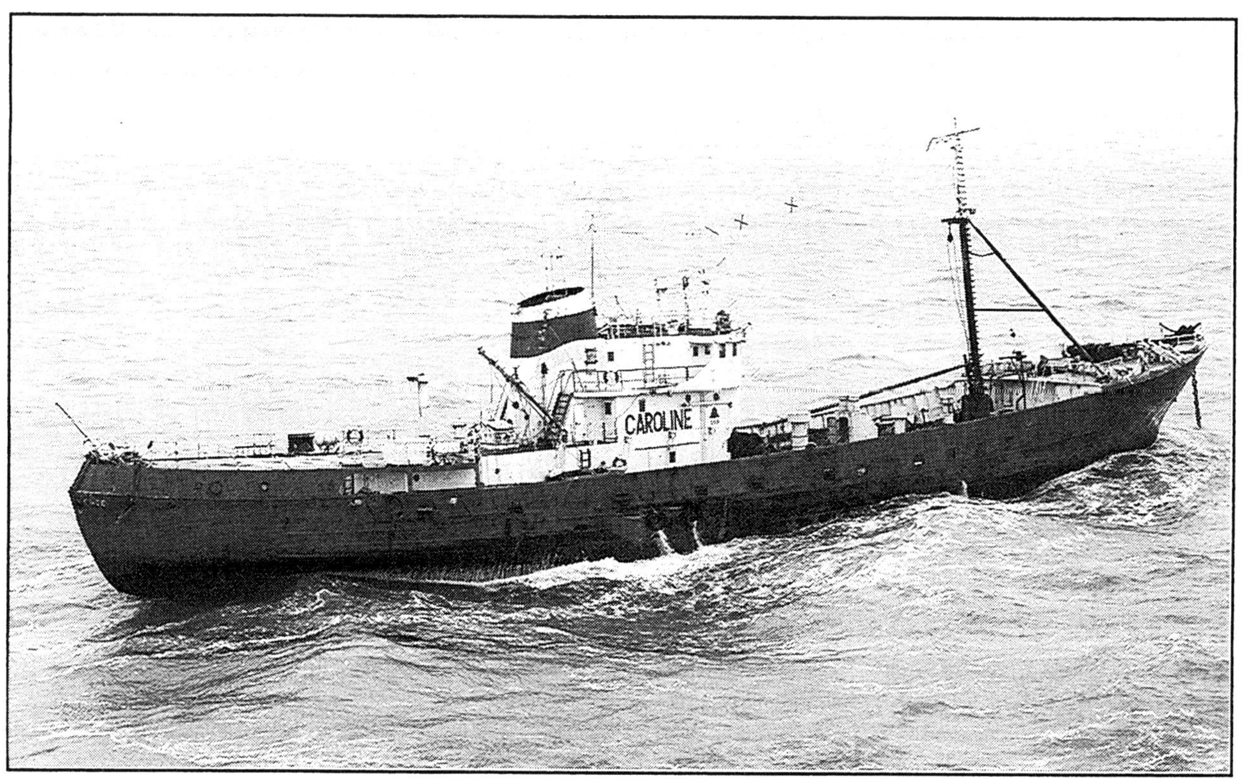


*The 'Ross Revenge' after the collapse of the 300' aerial tower*

Some damage had also been caused by sea water entering the studio through a leaking porthole and various items of equipment in the galley, messroom and living quarters had been dislodged and strewn about. The records in the library had been spilled from the wall racks and the Radio Monique studio had sustained damage caused by heavy items of equipment being flung around during the storm.

On land there was considerable disbelief that the massive aerial mast could have succumbed so totally to the elements, having been purpose designed and built to withstand the worst North Sea weather and survived the recent hurricane. The seas were still too rough for a tender to visit the radio ship to inspect the damage, so a member of the Caroline organisation on land was sent on an Olau Line ferry trip to Holland to assess the situation as the ferry routinely sailed close to the *Ross Revenge*. After making contact with the *Ross Revenge* crew using a two way radio from the ferry he was able to confirm once and for all that only a few inches of the 300' tower remained above deck level.

## Emergency aerial system

With both stations on the *Ross Revenge* now off the air the Caroline organisation desperately needed to find a way of earning revenue - from the Dutch broadcaster hiring airtime, the sponsored religious programmes and the Canadian Lotto 6/49 promotions. It was clear that an emergency replacement aerial system would have to be constructed at sea to enable some sort of signal to be transmitted from the Ross Revenge.

Incredibly this was achieved in appalling weather conditions before the end of November 1987 when station engineer Peter Chicago constructed a temporary wire aerial array, strung between the ship's original fore mast and the funnel. Using this array Caroline 558 was able to return to the air by 3rd December 1987, but at first only with a very weak signal and the occasional record being played between transmitter tuning tones. A more reliable service was provided from about 1.15pm the following day when DJs attempted to present normal programming until midnight, although the station's weak signal was badly affected by night-time interference.

Broadcasts gradually increased over the following week with three or four hour shows from on board DJs, providing a 5.00am - midnight (and sometimes even overnight) service, although news broadcasts were not reintroduced at this time, just weather and traffic reports.

By 11th December 1987 there were only two DJs left on board the *Ross Revenge*, brothers Steve Conway and Chris Kennedy who between them managed to provide a 12 hour service between 6.00am-6.00pm, even re-introducing news bulletins from 21st December 1987. When a new relief of DJs arrived on Christmas Day individual programme hours were reduced from six or more to four, while transmissions were extended once again until midnight. Over the final week of 1987 hours of transmission and length of individual programmes varied enormously, but the station managed to stay on the air for 36 consecutive hours from 7.00am on New Year's Eve to 8.00pm on New Year's Day to welcome in 1988.

## Boatman jailed

On 27th November 1987 a Shoeburyness boatman, Howard Beer, who had been fined £500 in September 1985 for delivering diesel fuel to the *Ross Revenge*, appeared in Court again, charged under the Marine etc. Broadcasting (Offences) Act 1967 with ferrying sightseers to the *Ross Revenge*. He had been apprehended when his vessel, *Windy*, was towed into Harwich in November 1985 after a rope became entangled in its propeller. (see Chapter 22). The delay in hearing the charges was because Howard Beer had asked for them to be heard before a jury at the Crown Court.

At the Southend Crown Court hearing in November 1987 he pleaded guilty to three charges of allegedly supplying the *Ross Revenge* and was given a nine months jail sentence. Not surprisingly Beer lodged an appeal against his absurdly severe sentence. On 13th January 1988 the Court of Appeal in London ruled that the sentence imposed on him was too long and ordered his immediate release. Nevertheless, by then Howard Beer had already spent seven weeks in jail - the only person in Britain (so far) to have received a custodial sentence for contravening the provisions of the Marine etc. Broadcasting (Offences) Act 1967.

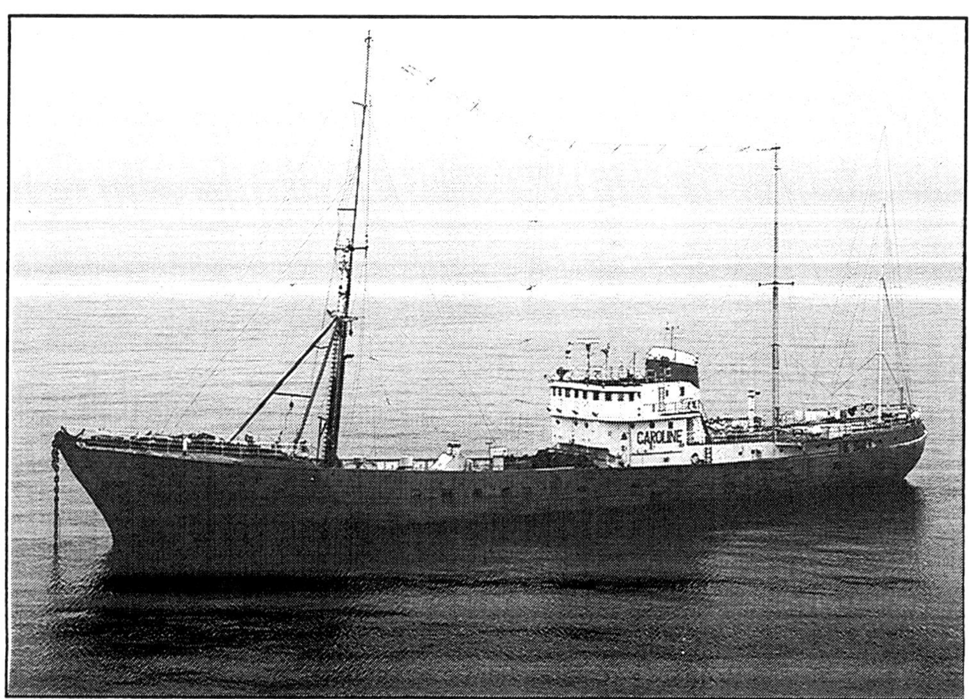


*The 'Ross Revenge' with a temporary aerial array*

## Lotto 6/49

*Long before Britain introduced a National Lottery many countries in other parts of the world operated such game. One of these countries was Canada where twice weekly draws were held each Wednesday and Saturday.*

*The principle was the same as the British National Lottery - select 6 out of 49 numbers to win a possible jackpot prize, hence the trade name Lotto 6/49. In 1986 the Canadian Lottery was estimated to sell $2 billion worth of tickets, producing revenue of $740 million for the national and provincial governments to spend on community, sports and cultural organisations.*

*A number of organisations, not directly connected with the Canadian Lottery authorities, set up operations to sell tickets abroad, a practice which was not illegal under Canadian law, hence the promotion of Lotto 6/49 over the airwaves of Radio Caroline and Radio Monique via a company called Bet Canada (registered in British Colombia as International Betcan Ltd.). The Dutch authorities soon put pressure on the Canadians to withdraw the Lotto 6/49 commercials from Radio Monique fearing that this would have a detrimental effect on their own state lottery, but the promotion continued via Radio Caroline and provided much needed financial income for that station.*

# Chapter 24

# Land of the Free

In 1987 a group of people were actively planning to establish an offshore radio station off the eastern coast of the United States of America. This somewhat improbable project (in a country which, unlike the more restrictive state broadcasting systems in Europe, had thousands of legal commercial radio stations catering for every conceivable listening taste) had its roots in 1971 when two New York radio enthusiasts became involved in unauthorised landbased broadcasting operations.

Al Weiner and Joe P Ferraro both constructed transmitters in their homes in Yonkers, New York and operated unauthorised radio stations under the call signs WXMN and WSEX, dedicated to love and peace. Their broadcasts did not last long, though as the Federal Communications Commission (FCC) raided both stations in August 1971 and the two men were charged with violating the Communications Act of 1934. When the cases came to court Weiner and Ferraro were found guilty and each given sentences of 12 months probation. However, they never lost their enthusiasm and desire to operate radio stations.

Some time later Al Weiner moved to Maine where he acquired and operated two small legal stations in Presque Isle, under the call sign WOZI. His real desire though was to operate a legal station in his home town of Yonkers, New York, an area he felt was under served by existing radio broadcasters. For fifteen years he repeatedly applied to the FCC for a licence to establish a station in Yonkers, but each time he was turned down on the grounds that there was no frequency available to allocate to him.

During the course of making these repeated applications Al Weiner discovered a little known provision in the FCC Regulations which allowed an existing broadcaster to establish a small, low power (100watt) auxiliary station on a frequency of 1622kHz (185m) to relay programming back to the main studios. In 1983 Weiner applied to the FCC for a licence to establish such an auxiliary outlet in Yonkers for his station WOZI in Maine. After a few months his application received approval and he was licenced to build station KPF941, which eventually went on the air in 1984.

When the FCC realised what Al Weiner had cunningly, but quite legally, achieved it threatened to revoke all licences previously granted to him, forcing him to sell both WOZI stations at an estimated loss of $100,000 on his original investment.

After so many years of trying to obtain a legal licence for Yonkers and ending up with nothing at all Al Weiner and Joe Ferraro decided that the only alternative left open to them was to establish an offshore radio station in international waters, which, they thought, would be outside the FCC's regulation and control.

Later in 1984, after the forced sale of WOZI, the two men started searching for a suitable ship on which to house their planned offshore radio station. Al Weiner contacted Radio Caroline anchored off the British coast and spent some time on board the *Ross Revenge* assisting with the shortwave transmitter experiments in November 1985. At the same time he received much useful advice and encouragement for his own planned offshore station from Ronan O'Rahilly and Radio Caroline staff on the *Ross Revenge*.

By the end of 1985 a suitable ship, the *Litchfield*, had been discovered for sale in Boston. The vessel had originally been used by a Japanese fishing fleet as a refrigerated cargo ship and had later been seized by US Coastguards after she was found to be involved in a drug trafficking operation. Weiner bought her at a US Marshals auction for about $100,000 using a company called International Ship Owners of Yonkers, New York which he had registered to disguise the true purpose to which the vessel would be put. He re-named her *Sarah*, after his wife.

The vessel, although considered suitable for her planned new role, needed much work to make her seaworthy and functional as a floating radio station. Her conversion started in the spring of 1986 and there followed months of work installing new generators, plumbing and heating systems, restoring living accommodation, building studios and general cleaning and painting. Two studios were planned for the station - a main on-air studio and a production facility, but only the main one was ever actually constructed.

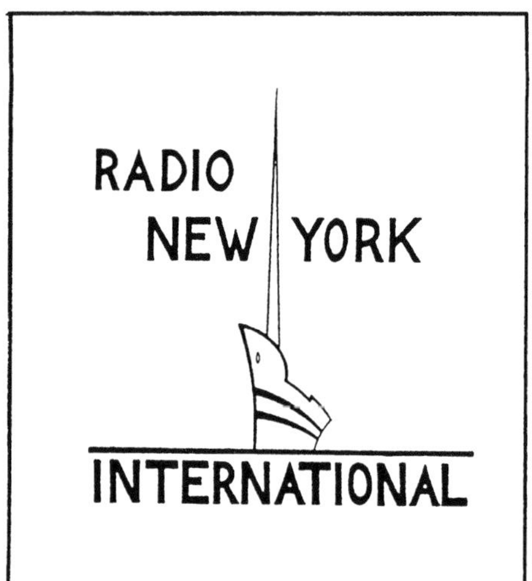


Five transmitters were installed on the *Sarah* - a 5Kw medium wave, tuned to 1620kHz (185m), a back-up 1Kw, medium wave, a 10Kw FM, tuned to 103.1mHz, a 300 watt military surplus shortwave transmitter, which was tuned to 6240kHz and a Government surplus long wave transmitter tuned to 190kHz (1579m).

The 103' aerial mast was erected in September 1986 - a solid steel tower welded to the *Sarah's* main deck. From this the medium wave 'T' aerial was strung to the ship's rear light tower, the FM transmitter was positioned at the top of the tower, the shortwave aerial was a simple dipole strung between the main tower and the conning tower while, for long wave, a 15' whip aerial was fixed to the deck.

Throughout the winter of 1986/87 internal work was carried out on the ship, mainly involving wiring of the studios and transmitters and reconditioning the power supply generator. Much of this was undertaken almost single-handedly by Al Weiner.

## Radio New York International launched

By the spring of 1987 final preparations were made to take the *Sarah* out to sea, but at that time the ship did not have a suitable anchor and chain which would hold her in position. Eventually a Navy surplus chain and battleship anchor were obtained and installed on the radio ship in the expectation that they would be suitable to cope with stormy weather conditions likely to be encountered off the eastern seaboard of the United States. The *Sarah* was also re-registered in Honduras and by early July 1987 she was stocked with supplies of food, water and 10,000 gallons of diesel fuel.

On 20th July 1987 the *Sarah* was towed out of Boston Harbour and in the early hours of 22nd July 1987 she arrived at her anchorage four and a half miles off Long Island, New York. Here the radio ship, with the supply vessel which had towed her from Boston, waited until daylight the following morning before the crew lowered the massive anchor.

With the *Sarah* now in position and ready to broadcast all but two of the station's staff left the vessel to prepare programme tapes on shore, while the remaining project members, Al Weiner and Ivan Jeffries (Rothstein), stayed on board to tune equipment and start test transmissions. The first of these tests took place on 23rd July 1987 with taped music interrupted by live announcements from Weiner and Jeffries announcing the name of the station - Radio New York International (RNYI).

The format was described as being "free form rock'n' roll - current hits and hits of the 60s, 70s and 80s." Radio New York International also had an underlying philosophy of "Love Peace and Understanding", which its organisers hoped would "raise the awareness and consciousness of listeners regarding themselves, their brothers and sisters and the planet Earth."

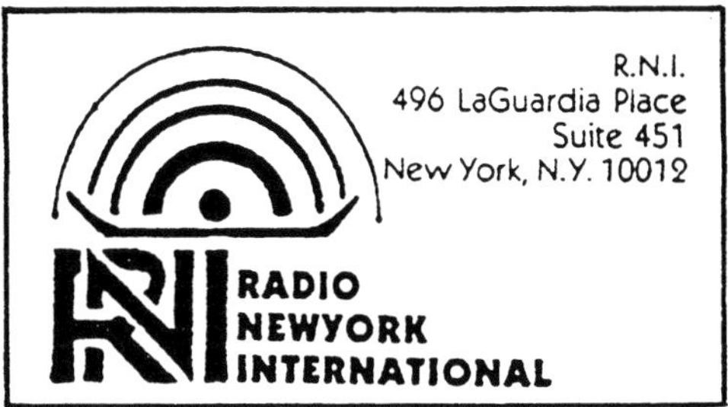


Test transmissions continued throughout the night and again during the evening of 24th July 1987. Some problems were experienced with the medium wave transmitter, although reception on other frequencies was good with reception reports even coming from listeners to the long wave transmission, a band not normally used for broadcast radio in the USA.

After the demise of Radio Free America in 1973 (see Chapter 18) the FCC had threatened that it would closedown any other offshore station which attempted to broadcast to the USA, prosecute the operators and confiscate all equipment. Until RNYI went on the air in 1987 nobody had attempted to challenge the FCC in this way, fearing the enormous court costs which would be involved, let alone any fine or penalty which may be imposed.

## Authorities take action

On 25th July 1987 at about 5.30pm a US Coastguard cutter, with machine guns uncovered, came alongside the *Sarah* and the crew announced that they intended to board the radio ship. Al Weiner and Ivan Jeffries, the only people on board the *Sarah* refused at first, but relented after being advised that the ship would be forcibly boarded if they did not agree. The Coastguards claimed they only wanted to inspect the ship's papers, registration documents and safety equipment, but when they eventually came on board they also brought with them two officials from the FCC.

Despite Al Weiner's objections that they had no right to board a foreign registered vessel in international waters, the FCC men insisted that they had authority to come aboard the *Sarah,* although they were not specific about the grounds for their presence at that time. As well as the FCC officials representatives of US Immigration and the Drug Enforcement Agency also boarded and searched the ship. The FCC officers informed Al Weiner that radio transmissions from the ship must cease, despite his assertion that they had no power to make such a demand because the Communications Act of 1934 did not apply outside US territorial limits.

The Coastguards and various agency officials eventually left the *Sarah* after about two and a half hours, but Weiner and Jefferies, shaken by the experience did not resume test transmissions that evening.

After carefully considering their situation overnight both men concluded that what they were doing was not illegal, simply outside the parameters of US law, and that the Coastguards and FCC had no right to harass them in such a way, positioned as they were in the freedom of international waters. Having reached this conclusion the two men decided to resume test transmissions again on all four frequencies during the evening of 26th July 1987, and these broadcasts continued for six hours without interruption.

In New York media interest in the new offshore radio station had been aroused following the authorities' visit and on 27th July 1987 many boats with reporters and television crews visited the *Sarah.* Amongst these was a reporter from the *Greenwich Village Voice,* R J Smith, who asked to stay on board for a few days to experience life on a floating radio station. Al Weiner and Ivan Jefferies agreed to allow him to stay on the *Sarah* - the extra pair of hands on board would be helpful and any subsequent publicity could only benefit RNYI.

Further test transmissions for RNYI started at 6.00pm on 27th July 1987 and, because everything was going so well with the equipment and a third person was now on board the *Sarah,* to help with operations it was decided to continue broadcasting until 2.00am the following morning.

Only one real problem had been encountered during the various test broadcasts and that was with the medium wave transmitter which was burning out its capacitors as the result of feedback. By 27th July this problem had been solved and new capacitors were fitted to the transmitter. Except for that minor difficulty the four days of test transmissions had proved so successful that the project members planned to start regular broadcasts from Radio New York International from 1st August 1987.

## *Sarah* boarded

The authorities, however, had other ideas. At 5.30am on 28th July 1987, a few hours after test transmissions had finished, the three men on board the *Sarah* were awoken by a loud hailer from the US Coastguard cutter, *Cape Horn.* Officials on the cutter warned that they intended to seize the radio ship and claimed to have permission from the Honduran Government to board the vessel, forcibly if necessary. Fearing for the safety of his ship and his 'crew' ( associate Ivan Jeffries and the visiting journalist R J Smith) Al Weiner, as 'Captain' of the *Sarah,* decided to offer no resistance.

Armed officials then boarded the *Sarah* and announced that they were seizing the radio ship and arresting those on board for violating international law, although they were not specific about which law had been violated. Weiner, Jefferies and Smith were handcuffed and detained on deck while FCC officials dismantled equipment in the studio and used wire cutters and hacksaws to sever the cables feeding the transmitter.

While this act of official vandalism was going on the three men remained handcuffed to the deck of the *Sarah* for four and a half hours before being transferred to the Cape Horn where they were again told that the radio ship was to be towed in and all broadcasting equipment would be removed by the FCC. Requests from Al Weiner and the other two men to be allowed to contact their lawyers as well as protests about violation of their civil and constitutional rights were ignored by the various officials who had boarded the *Sarah.*

The Coastguards were experiencing difficulties in raising the *Sarah's* huge battleship anchor and after a further three hours they decided to transfer the men to land using another launch while the *Cape Horn* remained alongside the radio ship. When they arrived in Brooklyn, New York Al Weiner and his colleagues were met by a huge crowd of supporters and journalists who had followed the drama all day on television news reports. Two lawyers from a New York practice volunteered their services to the men from the radio ship and advised them throughout the formal procedures following their arrest.

It subsequently transpired that when Al Weiner and his colleagues were arrested and taken from the *Sarah* the authorities had produced no search, seizure or arrest warrants, nor was there any documentation from Honduras authorising the forcible boarding of the vessel - as had originally been claimed by the Coastguards when they arrived alongside the radio ship.

Weiner, Jeffries and Smith were eventually charged with "conspiracy to impede the functioning of the United States Government" (i.e. challenging the FCC's authority) and violating an international agreement - the 1984 International Telecommunications Union (ITU) agreement to prohibit broadcasts from offshore stations. These charges were spurious and ill-conceived because neither Honduras nor the United States, amongst many other countries worldwide, had enacted domestic legislation to enforce the ITU agreement. Interestingly there were no specific charges against the three men of violating FCC rules governing broadcasting to or within the United States.

At the subsequent Court hearing the magistrate raised some questions about the powers of the FCC (which is largely a regulatory body) to arrest the men and seize their equipment, issues which remained unanswered at the time. Weiner, Jefferies and Smith were released without bail on condition that they reappeared at Court again 30 days later and in the meantime did not engage in broadcasting of any kind.

## Charges dropped

A month later, on 27th August 1987, just minutes before the three men were to re-appear in Court they were informed that the prosecution was dropping all charges against them. The authorities had decided that the case against the operators of Radio New York International - and doubts about the procedural legality of their arrest - was too weak to stand up to scrutiny in Court.

Free from the threat of prosecution Al Weiner and his associates now made plans to obtain re-possession of their ship and equipment while at the same time filing claims against the US Government for illegal arrest and $50,000 worth of property damage. They also appealed to the many people who had supported them at the time of their Court appearance for financial donations and practical help, so that Radio New York International could be put back on the air as quickly as possible.

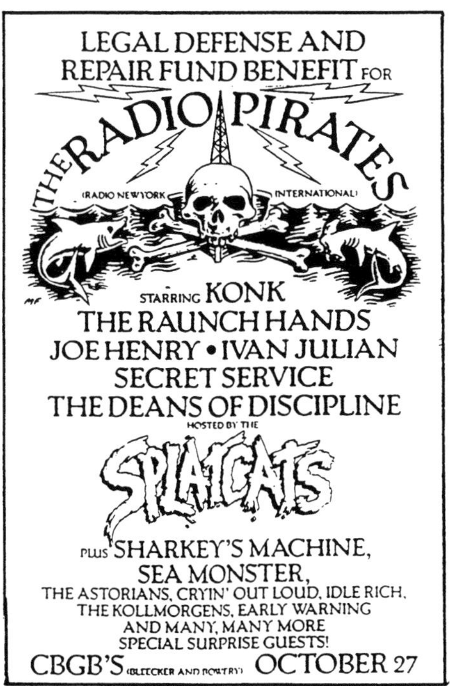


## *Sarah* re-fitted

After Al Weiner had successfully repossessed the MV *Sarah* she was taken back to Boston Harbour for repair. A new generator and $70,000 worth of broadcasting equipment was installed in a programme of work which took almost a year to complete. However, when the *Sarah* left harbour again on 17th July 1988, towed by the tug *Munzer,* the US Coastguards gave chase and boarded the ship demanding to inspect her registration papers and sailing orders. Finding only an expired Honduran registration document the Coastguards decided that the ship was violating an order which had been imposed on her the previous year to remain in port. The Captain of the *Munzer* was instructed by Coastguards to tow the *Sarah* back to her berth in Boston Harbour or face a fine of $25,000 a day.

Coastguards and harbour officials strenuously denied that the FCC had requested them to detain the radio ship in port, although Al Weiner claimed that this was the motive behind their actions.

On 10th September 1988 the *Sarah* finally managed to leave Boston Harbour and anchored early the following morning at a position four and a half miles off Point Lookout, Long Beach, Long Island. The ship lay at anchor in this position for over a month without any sign of broadcasts being made -Operations Manager Randi Steele said: " We don't intend to go on the air until we've established a legal right to do so." He also claimed that the ship's new registration was being finalised so that when Radio New York International did return it could legally stay on the air, hopefully without interference from the FCC. In fact the ship, which was said to have been sold to a British company, was being registered with Roy Bates's Principality of Sealand, sited on Roughs Tower off the Essex coast of England. However, Sealand was not recognised for ship registration (or any other) purposes by the US Government although those behind RNYI were either unsure of this fact or chose to ignore it.

*STATIONARY*

*Music ship's bid to sail is thwarted*

## RNYI starts transmissions ......

The return of Radio New York International just after 8.00pm on 15th October 1988 was heralded by a test signal on 1620kHz (185m). A RNYI station identification announcement was made at 9.00pm and then continuous music played throughout the night until the early morning hours of 16th October 1988.

The FCC were swift to take action against the offshore station's return to the airwaves and on 17th October 1988 it applied to the US District Court seeking a temporary Restraining Order forbidding the station to broadcast. Once the Order had been granted by Judge John J McNought FCC officials arrived aboard a US Coastguard cutter alongside the *Sarah* at 10.00pm that same evening. They attempted to serve the Restraining Order, but the crew of the radio ship refused to allow the officials on board the *Sarah* arguing that they were a legally registered vessel anchored in international waters and not bound either by the Court Order or the rules of the FCC.

The Coastguards then asked whether a member of the *Sarah's* crew would come on deck and take the Restraining Order from them, but again the radio ship's crew refused because they did not want the officials getting close enough to forcibly board the vessel as had happened the previous year.

## .....and is silenced again

Having failed to physically deliver the Court Order the Coastguards then read its provisions to the crew of the *Sarah* over the maritime radio, after which they formally asked the Captain of the radio ship, Josh Hayle, whether he was going to comply by ceasing RNYI's transmissions. After taking about ten minutes to consider their position Josh Hayle informed the Coastguards that those on board the Sarah would comply with the Restraining Order. They feared that if they did not agree to comply the *Sarah* would once again be forcibly boarded at gunpoint by the authorities and all radio equipment damaged or destroyed.

Throughout these discussions with the Coastguards RNYI's test broadcasts of non-stop music had continued, but shortly after the crew had reluctantly decided to comply with the Restraining Order the station went off the air.

Shortly before Christmas 1988 Judge McNought made the temporary Restraining Order against RNYI a permanent one and advised the people behind the station to apply for a legal, landbased broadcasting licence when the waveband above 1610kHz (186m) became available the following year.

The Court also ruled that as well as internal broadcasts the FCC does have jurisdiction over all broadcasts into the United States from whatever source. This was a significant, if somewhat curious decision which, because if taken to its logical conclusion, would give the FCC powers over any foreign broadcaster including, for example, the BBC World Service or Radio Moscow's shortwave service.

After the Court decision RNYI owner, Al Weiner, remained defiant, saying that he would put the offshore station back on the air "one way or another, hopefully within the next two months." He maintained that a radio station based on a ship anchored in international waters was outside the jurisdiction and control of the FCC and that his station had operated on a frequency which caused no interference to any legal stations.

The US authorities also remained equally determined to prevent the Sarah, or any other ship for that matter, being used as a base for an offshore radio station. This policy was assisted greatly at the beginning of January 1989 when, coincidentally, the USA extended its territorial waters limit to 12 miles from the shoreline, putting the *Sarah* at her Long Island anchorage well within the jurisdiction of all official bodies.

Al Weiner decided to appeal against the December 1988 Court decision and, pending hearing of that case, the *Sarah* was moved back to Boston. The appeal hearing eventually took place in the Federal Court on 3rd August 1989 and, in a decision made known early in September 1989, the ruling that the FCC did have powers to control broadcasts into the USA from outside territorial limits as well as those emanating from within the country itself was confirmed. This Court ruling finally gave legal status to the hitherto untested theoretical extent of the FCC's powers outside the USA. These powers had originally been incorporated within the FCC's constitution when it was established following the anarchic activities of the first commercial offshore radio station, RKXR, operating off the California coast in 1934 (see Chapter 2).

## Shortwave outlets

When the FCC eventually extended the medium wave frequencies available to broadcasters on 1st July 1990 Al Weiner was offered a licence for his station, Radio New York International. However, the offer was refused because he wanted the station to be "free and outside of FCC control."

Weiner also had plans to operate RNYI on shortwave where it could reach a world-wide audience and, although now prevented from using its offshore base, RNYI did reappear in September 1990 on the frequency of shortwave station World Wide Christian Radio (WWCR) in Nashville, Tennessee. These broadcasts initially took place for four hours on Monday evenings from 17th September 1990. Gradually various other shortwave outlets were introduced leading to a 7 days a week service from RNYI. A daily programme was also broadcast from 18th March 1991 on short wave station WRNO on 7355kHz.

Later in 1991 RNYI used these shortwave facilities to offer Radio Caroline airtime following the grounding and subsequent detention in port of the *Ross Revenge* (see Chapter 26). Tapes of Radio Caroline programmes were also broadcast, courtesy of RNYI, over a second shortwave outlet in Costa Rica - Radio for Peace International, a station jointly owned by World Peace University and the University of Peace, both United Nations affiliated organisations.

Meanwhile, following the failure of the second attempt to launch RNYI in 1988

### FCC duplicity

*In the light of the Federal Court ruling about the extent of the FCC's powers it is interesting to note that during 1989, while assembling their own case in preparation for Al Weiner's appeal hearing the Commission received a request for assistance from the French Government.*

*This request was to investigate interference being caused on 6215kHz from World Mission Radio (WMR), broadcasting at that time from the 'Ross Revenge' anchored off the British coast. The French authorities were pursuing a case against the operators of a vessel tendering the 'Ross Revenge' because WMR was allegedly causing interference to maritime communications in Brest. WMR had an office in New York, hence the reason for the French Government's request to the US authorities. However, the FCC refused to assist in the enquiry, claiming that they could not exercise control over foreign radio station broadcasts.*

the MV *Sarah* remained in Boston Harbour. There were stories in September 1991 that she had been sold to a new consortium, MPLX, in which John England (who had earlier planned to re-launch Radio London from an offshore base - see Chapter 22) was involved with an associate, Gene Baskir. They had plans with groups in China to establish an offshore station, Radio Tianamin, and for this purpose the *Sarah* was to be renamed *Liberty*. There were also some stories that the ship may have been used to broadcast programmes to North America using the Radio Caroline call sign, but nothing definite came from any of these plans.

## The *Fury* Project

Voyager Broadcast Services

"Your Lighthouse of the Air"

Al Weiner's interest and involvement in offshore radio did not end with the apparently fatal 1989 Court ruling against RNYI. While continuing to operate his station over hired shortwave outlets he became involved in planning another offshore operation, this time determined to ensure that legally and financially he would not be vulnerable to action from the various regulatory authorities.

During the early months of 1993 Al Weiner was invited to join this new offshore project as Technical Adviser. The project in question was an ambitious one - although offshore based it was designed to be licensed and perfectly legal and the radio ship was to house four stations broadcasting to a world-wide audience on shortwave.

Voyager Broadcast Services, set up jointly by Al Weiner and his partner in the project, Scott Becker, issued a press release on 20th September 1993 announcing that the new offshore station would be based on the MV *Fury*, which the two men had jointly purchased. Voyager planned to rent airtime on two of the four transmitters to any individuals or organisations who wished to broadcast, at a charge of $75 an hour. Al Weiner made it known that such airtime would be available to Radio Caroline if it wished to take advantage of the facility as a means of putting that station back on the air.

The third transmitter was to be reserved exclusively for the use of the registration/licensing country, Belieze, while the fourth was to be used by the project's main backer, the Overcomer Ministry based in South Carolina.

The founder of the Overcomer Ministry, Brother R Stair, had provided most of the funding for the project, estimated to be in excess of $500,000. Brother Stair was already an accomplished radio evangelist whose doomsday predictions were aired over WWCR and WRNO shortwave stations as well as many other stations across the USA. One of his programmes had even been relayed from the MV *Fury* on 12th July 1993 whilst she was in Boston Harbour being fitted out as a radio ship. During this broadcast Brother Stair explained about plans for his new world-wide radio station and asked for donations from listeners.

The original plans were for some programmes to be fed to the ship via satellite from studios in New

### Brother Stair

*Brother Stair was a preacher and evangelist in the true American tradition. In 1987 he had forecast that the United States would be destroyed within two years and that Ronald Reagan would not complete his term as President. He also claimed that by the end of 1988 the US economy would collapse and the country would be involved in a nuclear war with Soviet Russia. His predictions were generally made during broadcasts on over 100 radio stations throughout America.*

*In 1988 about 40 of his followers joined him in establishing a commune in a former motel and surrounding farmland in Walterboro, South Carolina. Brother Stair claimed that this was the first of what he called 'cities of refuge' which he proposed to establish where strict rules were imposed - no drinking, smoking, swearing or watching television and followers of his Overcomer Ministry were not allowed to engage in credit purchases or even seek medical help from doctors.*

*Despite this unusual lifestyle Brother Stair denied he was a cult leader, although in 1988 forty parents in Pennsylvania claimed he had induced their children to sell their belongings, leave their families and sign over all their funds to the Overcomer Ministry.*

*After his predictions of the late 1980s failed to come true Stair stopped putting dates to his doomsday prophesies, but never gave up his mission to spread his message across the world - hence the Fury Project.*

York and then re-broadcast from the *Fury*. Other programmes were to be taped or broadcast live from the ship. The satellite facilities came about through Scott Becker, who operated a satellite airtime brokerage company - Becker Satellite Network in New York.

There were stories circulating that the *Fury* would also be equipped with medium wave and FM radio transmitters as well as a UHF television transmitter, but no definite proposals for the use of these facilities were made public.

Both the ship and the radio stations were to be properly licensed - by the Central American country of Belieze - and broadcasts would take place from within its territorial waters. Despite many stories and rumours circulating at the time there were never any plans for the vessel to anchor off either the USA or Britain for fear that she would be forcibly boarded by their respective authorities. Al Weiner's experience with the RNYI ship *Sarah* in 1989 and the boarding the same year of the *Ross Revenge* by the British and Dutch authorities made him determined that the project should be fully licensed and legal from the outset.

The MV *Fury* was partially fitted out in Boston Harbour - where Al Weiner's former offshore vessel, MV *Sarah,* was still located. In fact some of the broadcasting equipment from the *Sarah* was transferred to the *Fury* whilst both vessels were in Boston.

Originally it was planned that the stations would be on the air by the autumn of 1993, a date later postponed to Christmas. In fact there were so many delays with engine problems and general fitting out that the *Fury* did not set sail from Boston until 5th November 1993 and even then it was only to head for South Carolina where she was to be re-painted.

Towards the end of November 1993 a Washington radio station broadcast details of the plans for what had by then become known as the '*Fury* Project' and the story was soon picked up by other media outlets across the USA. The FCC had also become aware of the existence of the *Fury* and the plans for her to be used as an offshore radio station. In late December 1993 one of their monitoring stations reported picking up transmissions on a shortwave frequency often used by landbased pirates and they were traced to South Carolina. In early January 1994 FCC officials headed to Charleston, South Carolina, where they spent two weeks tracking unauthorised radio broadcasts.

## FCC raid

In the early hours of 14th January FCC monitors picked up some test tone transmissions which their direction finding equipment identified as coming from the MV *Fury,* anchored on the Wando River in Charleston.

On 19th January 1994 US Coastguard and FCC officials boarded and seized the *Fury,* which by then was in the Halsey and Cannon Shipyard, Charleston. After ordering the crew to leave the radio ship additional FCC officials arrived with cutting equipment and a barge crane and, during a 36 hour operation, they removed and seized every piece of radio equipment on the grounds that the ship was an un-licensed pirate station - the very situation Al Weiner had all along sought to avoid. Assistant US Attorney Joseph P Griffith Jr. said that it was the Government's intention merely to seize the radio equipment and not pursue criminal charges against individuals.

As justification for its actions the FCC claimed that the previous Friday, 14th January 1994, they had identified the *Fury* as the source of illegal broadcasts on 7415kHz shortwave. Before boarding the vessel and seizing radio equipment they had obtained a Court Order from the District Court of South Carolina, which had been granted on 18th January.

## "Blown Away"

*In 1993 the former RNYI ship, 'Sarah' was sold to a film company and used in a scene involving an explosion on board ship. The Film "Blown Away", directed by Stephen Hawkins and starring Jeff Bridges as Jimmy Dare of the Boston Bomb Squad centres on his pursuit of an Irish terrorist, played by Tommy Lee Jones.*

*The 'Sarah' was sold by Al Weiner to MGM studios in June 1993 and she was converted for her role in the film - a new plywood deck was constructed on the ship, 5,000 feet of fuse wire was laid beneath this false deck leading to 30 pounds of explosives and 500 gallons of petrol. The explosion, which was carried out by members of the Boston Police Explosive Ordinance Unit, was watched by a large crowd which had gathered in the Boston Harbour area.*

*Two stuntmen leapt from the deck into the Harbour just seconds before the explosion (which were actually four separate explosions triggered at five second intervals) sending a 300 foot fireball into the air. Hundreds of windows in buildings were blown out by the explosion and later the film company was inundated with damage claims for cracked walls and ceilings. Fortunately the producers had taken out large insurance policies to cover such claims - one building near the film set on the quayside was insured for $20 million.*

*After the 30 second scene had been shot the charred hull of the 'Sarah' was towed to a pier in Charlestown Naval Base where a salvage company began dismantling the vessel's upper deck. It was reported that two enquiries had been received to purchase what was left of the 'Sarah', but the salvage company, New England Marine Salvage, planned to completely scrap the former radio ship if the sales fell through.*

## *Fury* Project dead

Al Weiner, despondent at losing yet another potential offshore radio station, initially claimed that he had only ever tested the transmitter equipment on board the *Fury* into a dummy load and that someone else on board the vessel had, without his knowledge, engaged in unauthorised broadcasts. Later, however, he issued a statement saying that on the dates quoted by the FCC it would have been impossible for the *Fury* to have made any transmissions because the equipment on board was at that stage inoperative and had no power supply. This later statement was subsequently reaffirmed by Al Weiner in a declaration to the US Federal Court in February 1994.

The MV *Fury* had been gutted of all radio equipment by the FCC, although the vessel herself was left intact she was of no further use as an operational offshore radio station. After the raid Brother Stair said he would have nothing more to do with the offshore radio project, having already spent some $300,000, but it was reported that the Overcomer Ministry would be suing for $40 million damages arising from the raid on what they considered to be a legally registered and licensed radio station. In the event this legal action was not pursued as Brother Stair felt it would prove too expensive. He did, however, continue to maintain his point of view that the raid on the *Fury* was a deliberate attempt by the US authorities to silence his 'preachings' and stop his views being broadcast worldwide.

There was another, more straightforward, theory that the raid had been prompted by an ownership dispute involving radio equipment removed from the former RNYI ship, *Sarah.* A Washington company, which claimed ownership of the *Sarah* and all the radio equipment left on board her, claimed that Al Weiner had removed the equipment without authorisation and installed it on the *Fury.*

Whatever the reason for the raid the action by the FCC effectively put an end to the whole '*Fury* Project' before it had had the opportunity to transmit a single programme. There is no doubt that the concept of the plan was sound - a legal, licensed offshore station broadcasting from within the registry state's territorial waters. This, in part at least, was one approach the Radio Caroline organisation had examined as a means of circumventing Britain's 1990 Broadcasting Act.

However, once again the American authorities had exercised their extensive powers to prevent the station ever being able to commence transmissions and, despite optimistic statements that Voyager Broadcasting Services would purchase and equip another ship this incident brought to an end attempts by American citizens and organisations to become directly involved in American-based offshore radio broadcasting.

# Chapter 25

# Raided !

Bad weather persisted in the North Sea throughout the early days of 1988. On Radio Caroline (which had returned to the air in December 1987 using a temporary aerial following the collapse of its 300' mast) broadcasting hours were somewhat erratic until after 7th January when a regular 6.00am-8.00pm schedule was established. However, after a week of apparent stability Caroline 558 went off the air for nine days and did not return until 24th January.

During those nine days silence four 15' sections of telescopic mast had been erected at the stern of the *Ross Revenge* and the front mast had been extended to 90' by welding sections of copper pipe on top of the existing structure. This was obtained from the former cod liver oil storage piping used in the vessel's days as a fishing trawler, but unfortunately, the additional rigging which was really essential for the mast extensions could not be installed due to the appalling winter weather conditions.

Using this new telescopic aerial Caroline 558 was able to return to the air with a stronger signal than was possible with the temporary array, but it was not a permanent solution and did not provide a facility for a separate Dutch language station to broadcast simultaneously. The reinstitution of a revenue earning Dutch language service was of utmost importance to Caroline, but in the absence of

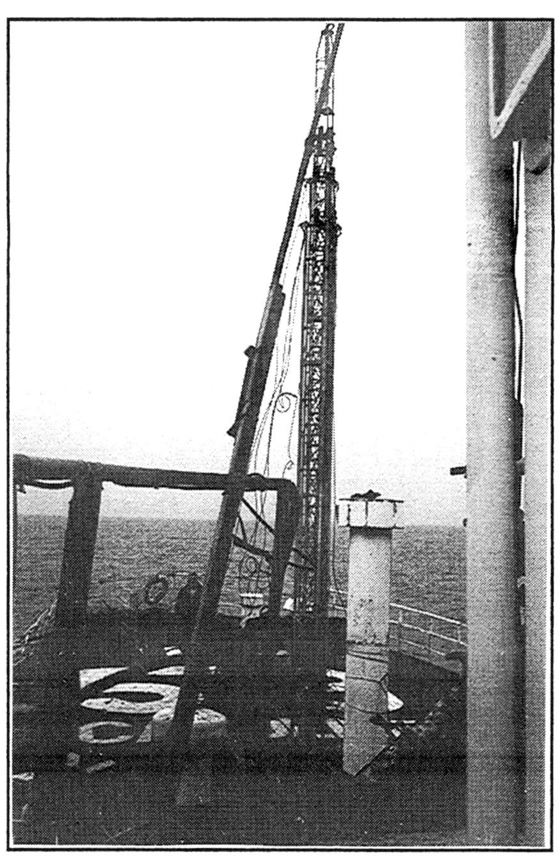

*The telescopic aerial being erected on the 'Ross Revenge'*

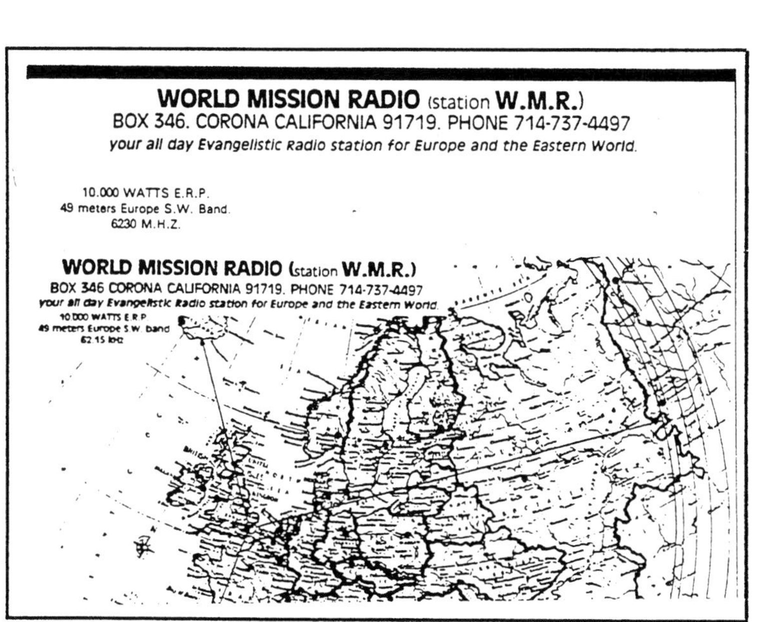


*WMR ratecard indicating the likely coverage of the station's shortwave signal*

adequate technical facilities another approach was tried. This involved the concept of broadcasting the financially lucrative sponsored religious programmes on shortwave to a, theoretical, world-wide audience.

Some shortwave tests had been made in November 1985 and further shortwave broadcasts from the *Ross Revenge* took place on 22nd February 1988 when Caroline 558 was relayed in parallel on 6210kHz. Two weeks later, on 6th March 1988 more shortwave test transmissions were made, but this time a separate programme was broadcast with station identifications in English, French and Italian. The transmissions were halted for two short periods to enable engineers on board the *Ross Revenge* to receive reception reports from other stations and radio amateurs on the same and adjacent frequencies. During this time reports were received from Ireland, Holland, Denmark, Scotland, France, Italy and West Germany, while other reception reports obtained later showed that Radio Caroline's shortwave broadcasts had been heard in Wisconsin USA, Australia, New Zealand and Poland. Further test transmissions on shortwave were made throughout March and April 1988 on a number of frequencies including 6210,6215 and 6205 kHz, but all generally relayed the normal Caroline 558 programmes.

## World Mission Radio

Following successful completion of these tests a new station was launched from the *Ross Revenge* on 1st May 1988 on the shortwave frequency of 6215kHz. Using the call sign World Mission Radio (WMR) the station broadcast a range of sponsored (largely American) religious programmes as well as tapes from Dutch evangelist Johaan Maasbach which were also broadcast four times each day in Dutch and English.

### Communicator sails in again

*The 'Communicator' finally sailed into Harwich again on 3rd February 1988. The former Laser 558 and Laser Hot Hits vessel had lost her anchor in a storm and with only two crew members on board and a shortage of fuel the decision was made to enter port. The ship sailed into West Parkstone Quay and almost immediately was declared unseaworthy by the authorities. The DTI also boarded the vessel and cut all cables and wires leading to and from the transmitter and aerial. Finally the 'Communicator' was taken to a scrapyard at Shotley where she was beached in the mud, having no anchor of her own to enable her to remain in the River Stour itself.*

On medium wave, although all immediate efforts in late 1987 had been put into returning the 558kHz transmitter to the air after the mast collapse, the Radio Caroline organisation was also anxious to reinstate the 819kHz transmitter, but this could not be achieved from the temporary 'T' aerial on the *Ross Revenge.* A new mast had to be obtained to facilitate the higher frequency transmissions and Caroline's management thought it had found the answer with a revolutionary new carbon fibre mast from Canada, known as a 'Valcon' aerial. This aerial was claimed by its manufacturers to produce a suitable medium wave signal from a much shorter length of mast than a conventional arrangement and therefore did not need to be guyed.

A new generator was delivered to the *Ross Revenge* in mid-March 1988 and installed just under a month later, increasing the ship's power output to 500kva. The new Valcon mast had also arrived from Canadian late February 1988 and after a tuning unit had been installed and feeder cables connected from the transmitter room the 135' structure was erected on the *Ross Revenge* in mid-May 1988. However, almost as soon as it had been erected the Valcon mast cracked at its base and it proved necessary, after all, to attach guy wires to hold it in place.

The new generator and aerial mast on the *Ross Revenge* was in preparation for the launch of a Dutch language service on 819kHz. In readiness for this new service some Dutch DJs arrived on board the *Ross Revenge* during April 1988 and presented a few live programmes, in English, on Caroline 558.

From late evening on 21st May 1988 Caroline 558 programmes were simulcast on 819kHz as test transmissions and this arrangement continued for three days, with a three day break, resuming again on 28th May. By 30th May 1988 everything seemed ready for the new service and at 10.00am a separate Dutch language programme began on 819kHz with some live shows and some recorded material announcing that it was a test transmission for a new station, Radio 819. Listeners were asked to send reception reports to PO Box 146, Playa de Aro, Gerona, Spain - an address formerly used by Radio Mi Amigo and Radio Monique.

Commercials were broadcast during these test programmes including ones for Dino Records, Singapore Airlines, Sprite, Atari computers, Bose loudspeakers, Tokai lighters, Texas cigarettes and Sunrise Travel Agency. The organisation providing programme material to the station was KMMI - Kroon Music Media International, based in Hilversum. An associated advertising agency in Luxembourg, Kroon Advertising, sold airtime and obtained commercials for the new station.

The Dutch language tests continued throughout 30th May 1988 until shortly before 8.00pm and resumed again the following morning, but then ended abruptly at 9.15am. The reason for this was that the carbon fibre Valcon mast had melted, and split in half with the top section crashing to the deck of the *Ross Revenge*. Attempts were made to rig up a temporary system using a 'sausage aerial' strung from the remaining half of the Valcon mast to the 558 aerial mast, but this caught fire within minutes of the transmitter being switched on. With the Valcon mast having failed miserably arrangements had to be made to obtain a more conventional mast structure so that Radio 819 could return to the air.

## Lattice-work mast

A number of lattice-work mast sections were acquired and, in a series of clandestine tendering trips, they were transported out to the *Ross Revenge*. The original plan was to build a single 160' tower, but this was later amended to a two tower construction with the aerial array strung between them. Also the first 40' of each tower was now to be of dual construction for added stability and as a consequence further mast sections had to be acquired and shipped out to the *Ross Revenge*.

This all contributed to the delay in actually starting construction work, much to the annoyance of the Dutch who, having hired the airtime and technical facilities on board the *Ross Revenge*, naturally wanted to put their programmes back on the air quickly. Equally from Caroline's point of view the delay was frustrating because it was vital to have the Dutch station broadcasting as the hire of airtime and associated tendering arrangements were financially lucrative to the organisation.

This double pressure led to a dramatic change of schedules on 9th July 1988 when Caroline 558 gave up its frequency during the daytime to the Dutch language station. The following announcement was broadcast every fifteen minutes on Caroline 558 during the previous day:-

*You're listening to Caroline 558, your 24 hour music station. In order to carry out essential engineering and technical reorganisation to bring you a better service on 558 and a new station on 819kHz it is necessary for Caroline to suspend daytime transmissions from Saturday for a period of about a month. After this time Caroline will return on 558 twenty four hours a day with a better service than ever before. During the next month a Dutch language music station will be heard on 558 during the day, with Caroline continuing unaltered throughout the night. So stay tuned to 558 for the best in twenty four hour music.*

### Offshore history

*With the start of Dutch language test transmissions offshore radio history was made on the 'Ross Revenge'. On 30th May 1988, the ship became home to three radio stations broadcasting separate programmes simultaneously - Caroline 558 (on 558kHz), World Mission Radio (on 6215kHz short wave) and Radio 819 test transmissions (on 819kHz).*

## Radio 558 Opening Day programme schedule

9.00am Erwin van der Bliek

12noon Fred van Amstel

3.00pm Lex van Zandvoort

5.00pm Erwin van der Bliek

7.00pm Closedown

## Radio 558

The Dutch service, now known as Radio 558, then began its broadcasts at 8.00am on 9th July 1988 with live programmes from the on-board Dutch DJs immediately after Caroline's early morning programme had finished. DJ Erwin van der Bliek opened the new station by saying:-

*Europe, Good Morning it is 9 o'clock exactly (8 o'clock in Britain). This is live from the North Sea, a Dutch language test transmission on 558 kilohertz AM. With you until 7 o'clock this evening with only the best music.*

Radio 558 transmissions then settled into a twelve hour schedule from 6.00am - 6.00pm, and an international news service, in English, was introduced from 11th July 1988 with two bulletins daily at 8.30am and 3.30pm. After the station had been on the air for about two weeks an hourly Dutch news service was also introduced with headlines on the half hour.

From 15th July 1988 a half hour programme from Dutch evangelist Johaan Maasbach was introduced twice daily at 6.30am and 6.30pm. Radio 558's format was virtually the same as Radio Caroline's, but to begin with the station's output was directed mainly at Holland with hardly any programme material designed for Belgian listeners.

## Spain

*After many years as one of the few remaining European countries from which offshore radio stations could legally be supplied and serviced Spain finally ratified the 1965 Strasbourg Convention outlawing offshore broadcasting on 5th March 1988. Spain had joined the then EEC in 1986 and was bringing itself into line with other member states on a wide range of international legislation and treaty agreements. Having ratified the Strasbourg Treaty the next step was for Spain to enact domestic legislation making it an offence for its nationals to work for, supply or advertise on an offshore broadcasting station.*

Some programmes were sponsored - both the American Top 40 and the Drive In Show being backed by Texas cigarettes and other advertisers on the new station included Aqua Sun Travel agency, Sunrise Travel Agency, Ducados cigars, Tokai lighters, *Top Ten Pop* Magazine, Irex slimming aids, Atari computers, Dino records and the Canadian Lotto 6/49.

The news service in Dutch was discontinued from 22nd September 1988 because interference from the *Ross Revenge's* shortwave transmitter was affecting the on-board telex facility. The English news service was not affected because this was obtained from the British television teletext services Ceefax and Oracle. Although irregular attempts were made to re-introduce the Dutch news bulletins later in the month a full service was not resumed until mid-October 1988 after a new telex receiver had been installed aboard the *Ross Revenge.*

## Radio 819

During the morning of 22nd October 1988 tuning tones were heard on 819kHz. Radio 558 itself did not come on the air until shortly before 2.00pm that day and when it did the programmes were relayed in parallel on both 558 kHz and 819kHz. An announcement was made that after three months on its temporary frequency Radio 558 had now become Radio 819 once again.

RADIO 558 heet nu:
RADIO 819
op de middengolf
muziek voor
iedereen

From midday on 5th November 1988 Radio 819 was heard only on 819kHz, while Radio Caroline was able to resume 24 hour programming on 558kHz. The Dutch station's broadcasting hours were extended from 17th December 1988 when Radio 819 returned to the air and programmed overnight on Saturdays and Sundays after 'Viewpoint' religious programmes had finished. Unfortunately power on 819kHz was only about 5Kw and reception of the Dutch station's signal in its primary target areas of Holland and Belgium was not very satisfactory.

The Caroline Overnight Alternative Service was reintroduced on 819kHz in January 1989, but during February Radio 819, along with Radio Caroline was off the air for various periods while a team of specialist aerial riggers constructed new aerial masts on board the *Ross Revenge.*

During mid and late February 1989 shortages amongst the Dutch staff on board the *Ross Revenge* once again led to many old Radio 819 taped programmes being repeated two, three or even four times, just to fill airtime hours and there were also many periods of continuous music without any announcements or news. This situation continued until the first week of March 1989 when a tender managed to deliver some more DJs and fresh supplies of programme material to the *Ross Revenge* and the news service was reintroduced from 6th March 1989.

**Caroline 558 programme schedule, December 1988**

*5.00am Ian Mack*

*9.00am Nigel Harris*

*1.00pm Dave Asher*

*4.00pm Steve Richards*

*7.00pm Neil Gates*

*9.00pm Tony Kirk*

*11.00pm Kevin Nelson*

*12midnight Closedown*

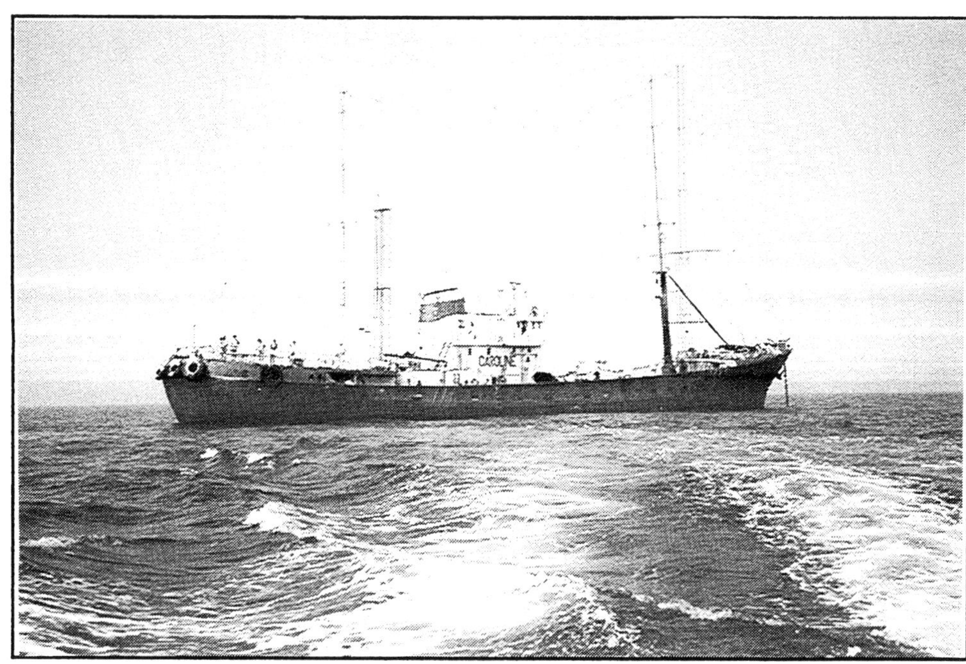

*New aerial masts on the 'Ross Revenge'*

## 'Euroseige' prosecutions

On 18th November 1988 seven people, including two DJs, appeared before Canterbury Crown Court charged with assisting the running of offshore stations Radio Caroline and Laser 558 in 1985, during what had become known as the 'Euroseige' operation. Five were charged under the Marine etc. Broadcasting (Offences) Act of "conspiring to supply food, drink, medical aid and equipment" to the radio stations while two other people were accused of "conspiring to procure the making of broadcasts from the ships and of supplying records to" DJs. Other charges levelled against some of the defendants were of "inviting a holiday company to advertise on one of the stations" and "illegally promoting the Laser 558 Roadshow." However, before the case proceeded the Director of Public Prosecutions dropped the charges against one defendant because of a procedural technicality and deferred the case involving the Laser 558 Roadshow. The trial itself lasted several days and all defendants were ultimately found guilty as charged and fined £1,000 with £1,500 costs. They were given four months to pay their fines and warned that failure to do so would result in terms of imprisonment being imposed.

The case which was dropped by the Director of Public Prosecutions was against Anthony Elliot, Editor of *Time Out* magazine, who was accused of publishing details of Radio Caroline's programmes. Anthony Elliot said: *The case calls into question the legality of any media examination where such examination includes the report of truthful information about station operators or programmes. Apparently the Government wishes the public to believe that pirate radio stations do not really exist. So the media must not, on pain of heavy fines, report any evidence to the contrary.*

### Cuban offshore station plans

*During early August 1988 reports appeared about the establishment of an offshore radio and television station off the Cuban coast. The station, to be known as La Voz del Cuba Independiente (the Voice of Cuban Independence) was to be established by a group which had operated a landbased pirate station for over six years campaigning for democratic government in Cuba.*

*The offshore project was expected to be based on a 120' fishing boat anchored in international waters off Key West, Florida some 75 miles from the coast of Cuba. However, the project never came to fruition partly because the American Federal communications Commission (FCC) threatened to stop the station broadcasting on the grounds that such an operation was against international treaties. The FCC also threatened to seize any US registered ship used to house the planned radio and television stations.*

All convicted defendants appealed against their sentences and the appeal hearing took place on 19th March 1990 before Lord Justice Watkins and Justices Waite and Nolan. The appeal centred on a ruling given by the Crown Court judge and, it was argued by the defence, if that ruling was found to be flawed then the charges could not stand. Those accused believed that they were not breaking the law as Laser 558 was staffed entirely by American citizens. Therefore it was not covered by Section 3 of the Marine etc. Broadcasting (Offences) Act 1967 (which deals with the use of broadcasting equipment by British citizens on a foreign registered ship). The defence case was that in bringing the charges under Section 3 the prosecution had misinterpreted the provisions of the Act.

Despite these arguments the three Appeal Judges decided that the prosecution's interpretation of Section 3, and that of the Crown Court Judge, had been correct and dismissed the appeal. Lord Justice Watkins said he thought it was Parliament's intention in passing the Marine etc. Broadcasting (Offences) Act "to prevent as far as possible broadcasts from ships lying in the sea outside territorial limits."

## Caroline's Silver Jubilee

Radio Caroline celebrated its 25th Birthday over the Easter weekend of 1989. The station started to broadcast the Top 1001 at 7.00am on Good Friday, 24th March and continued the countdown throughout the weekend.

On Easter Sunday, 26th March a group of over 500 Caroline supporters took part in a trip organised by the Caroline Movement on the *Olau Britannia* ferry between Britain and Holland, sailing close to the *Ross Revenge* on the outward and return journeys. Radio Caroline's founder, Ronan O'Rahilly, joined the supporters on the voyage.

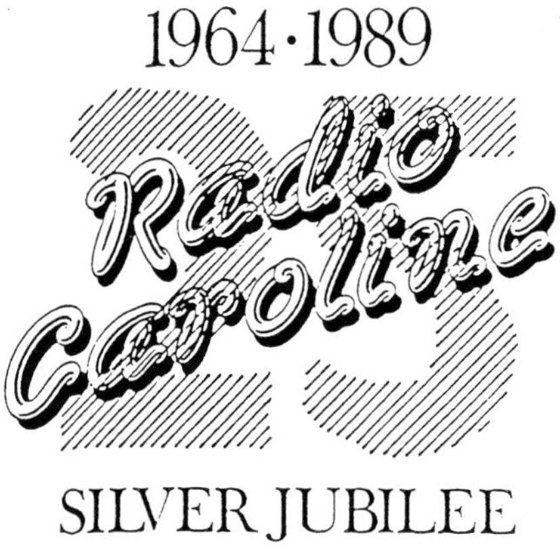

1964·1989
Radio Caroline
SILVER JUBILEE

DJs on the *Ross Revenge* had planned to speak to fans on the ferry from the deck of the radio ship as she passed by on the return journey. Unfortunately, this had to be abandoned because foggy conditions meant that the Olau vessel could not sail as close to the *Ross Revenge* as had been hoped.

At 11.55am on Easter Sunday the Top 1001 was interrupted and a five minute segment of old jingles and announcements from the station's 25 years broadcasting were played. At 12 noon after the Caroline Bell DJ Steve Conway said:-

*This is Caroline 558, your all day music station, 25 years old. Thank you to all the listeners, thank you to all the people who've been involved especially Peter Chicago and especially the Silver Fox. We're going to play you three songs which explain what Caroline is all about, three songs in a row. Nothing but good music from the Lady.*

The three songs played were "All You Need is Love", by the Beatles, "Voice of Love", by Loving Awareness and "Fool if You Think it's Over" by Chris Rea. After a fourth record of special significance for Caroline and her fans, "On My Way Back Home" by the New Riders of the Purple Sage, the Top 1001 countdown was resumed.

As part of the Birthday celebrations Caroline 558's programmes were simulcast by Radio 819 up until 2.00pm on Easter Sunday.

The 25th Anniversary of the start of British offshore radio was also widely featured in the national press and on television. BBC Television's "Daytime Live" programme on 20th March carried a nine minute feature about Radio Caroline including interviews with Ronan O'Rahilly, Steve Conway, Dave Asher and Johnnie Walker. ITN News also reported the celebration cruise organised by the Caroline Movement.

A few days after the Easter weekend Johnnie Walker broadcast a further tribute to Radio Caroline when the whole of his lunchtime programme on BBC GLR in London came from the *Tattershall Castle,* anchored in the River Thames. Guests on the programme were ex-Caroline DJs Tommy Vance, Mike Ahearn and Gerry Burke.

er komt nog steeds
muziek uit zee

RADIO 819

middengolf (am)

wenst U een zalig
Nieuwjaar bij het luisteren
naar de programma's op
819

ZEEZENDERS BESTAAN! EN HOE!
DUS OOK IN 1989 MIDDENGOLF
LUISTEREN

## Radio 819 format re-vamp

A public opinion poll published at the end of April 1989 showed that the much troubled Radio 819 was not very popular in Holland, having a daily audience of only 25,000 listeners. In an effort to boost audience figures a new format was introduced from 5th June 1989 under the title "Holiday Radio 819".

Part of the reason for such low audience figures was the poor signal being put out on 819kHz from the *Ross Revenge*. Throughout the summer of 1989 Radio 819 was threatening to leave the *Ross Revenge* or even have the radio ship moved to a position off the Dutch/Belgian coast to improve signal quality until the new mast was completed. Other options reportedly considered by Radio 819 were to use the *Nannell* or the *Communicator,* because twenty advertising contracts were reported to have been secured but could not be confirmed because of the poor signal. To try and improve this situation Radio Caroline engineers built and installed a completely new aerial system aboard the radio ship, although this work itself resulted in both stations frequently having to go off the air for short periods adding further to the loss of audience loyalty.

### Radio 819 programme schedule, June 1989

**5.00am Get Up with 819** *(live)*

**6.30am Johaan Maasbach** *(sponsored religious programme)*

**7.00am De Morgenstand heeft Muziek in de Mond** *(live)*

*9.00am From Breakfast 'till Coffee Time, Ellie van Amstel (taped)*

**11.00am Coffee Time,** *Krijn Torringa (taped)*

**12noon Ria Valk** *(sponsored)*

**12.20pm A Slice of Bread and Ross** *(live)*

**2.00pm The Sound Barrier,** *Erwin van der Bliek (taped)*

**4.00pm Midday Express,** *Jan Veldkamp (taped)*

**5.00pm Heading into the Wind** *(live)*

**7.00pm Closedown**

## *Communicator* back at sea

One of the other two radio ships considered by Radio 819, the *Communicator,* had left Harwich early in April 1989, but nothing connected with her former role as home to Laser 558 and Laser Hot Hits was left on board, except for the transmitters and aerial masts. HM Customs visited the vessel shortly before she left Harwich and were informed by the caretaker crew that she was destined for the scrapyard.

A tug towed thc *Communicator* back to sea and she anchored for over a month near the Sandettie sandbank off northern France. By mid June 1989 the *Communicator* set sail for Lisbon where she was to be refitted for use as a propaganda station broadcasting evangelical programmes to the people of Romania as well as Dutch and English language music programmes.

# IRISH LANDBASED PIRATES

*Landbased pirate radio stations were established in Ireland, as in many other countries, in the late 1960s in the wake of the closure of the offshore stations, although the concept of illegal landbased was well known long before that date. However, due to far less stringent laws governing unlicensed broadcasting stations pirates in Ireland flourished and grew in strength and numbers.*

*In Ireland although the stations were raided by Post and Telegraph staff a loophole was discovered in the legislation which required the authorities to return, in a complete state, and confiscated equipment within seven days of a raid. Operators, who at that time were generally enthusiasts and radio hobbyists, simply waited for the return of their equipment and put their stations back on the air. It therefore became futile for the authorities to try enforcing the law once the loophole had been discovered and become widely known.*

*In the late 1970s bigger, professional operators started to exploit the loophole in Irish law and considerable sums of money were both invested and recouped by means of profits from some of the larger landbased pirate stations.*

*A number of ex-offshore DJs were leading this explosion in Irish landbased pirate radio, including Brian McKenzie (RNI), Chris Carey (Spangles Muldoon of Caroline and RNI), Tony Allen (Radio Scotland, RNI, Caroline and the Voice of Peace) and Robbie Dale (Caroline and Radio Veronica).*

*The first so-called 'super pirate' in Ireland opened on 29th September 1980 - Sunshine Radio on 539m was based in the Sands Hotel, Portmarnock, Dublin. It was owned by Chris Carey and Robbie Dale with financial backing from ex-Radio Caroline Director Philip Soloman. Sunshine Radio featured a number of ex-offshore radio DJs amongst its presenters and was run on a professional business basis as if it were a legitimate station.*

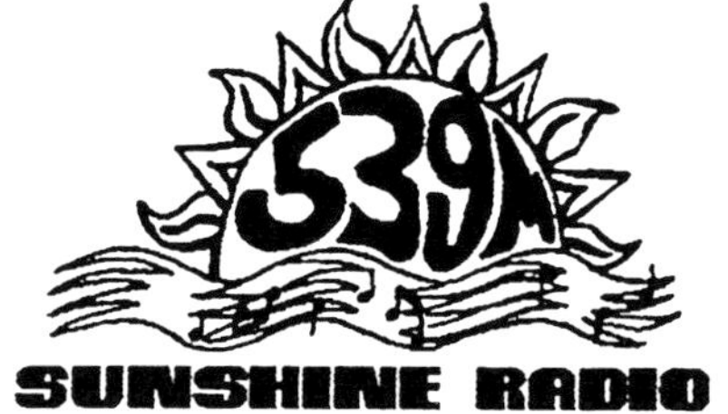


*However, other smaller landbased pirates resented the competition from the powerful Sunshine Radio transmitter and destroyed its mast in a sabotage attack. This was a foretaste of similar rivalries and sabotage attacks which were to emerge amongst landbased pirate radio operators in Ireland over the next few years. After this unfortunate incident Philip Solomon withdrew his financial backing, but Chris Carey and Robbie Dale continued to operate the station. Eventually after eight months Robbie Dale took over completely while Chris Carey went on to launch a second powerful landbased pirate station - Radio Nova - also based in Dublin, in June 1981.*

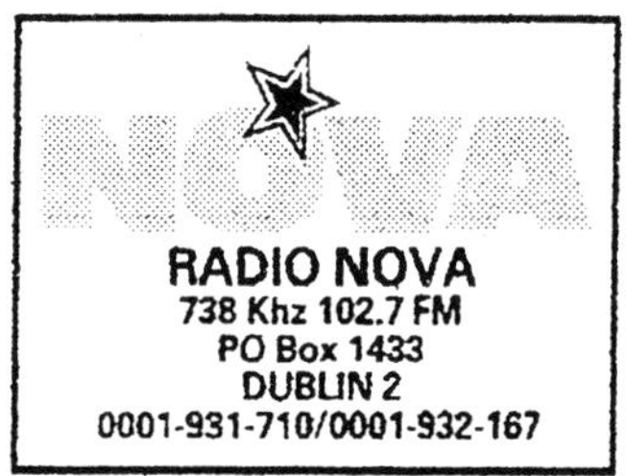


*Radio Nova operated on FM at first, with a powerful 10Kw AM transmitter being introduced from September 1981. This gave Radio Nova a large catchment area, spreading over to the west costa of Britain where a sales office was established in Liverpool and posters advertising the station appeared on buses and hoardings.*

*A further super pirate came on the air in March 1982, based in Cork, using the call sign South Coast Radio and from then on the number of landbased pirates stations exploded - Chris Carey at one time owned and operated three separate stations. Dozens of ex-offshore radio DJs went to Ireland to take part in the huge boom in unlicensed radio and regularly moved between stations which were soon located in every town and city all over the country.*

*Many of the larger stations were very profitable (particularly Nova, Sunshine and South Coast) and for a time they became accepted as part of the Irish media scene. Many stations promoted 'community causes' such as raising funds for local hospitals or the promotion of youth employment in their areas - devices generally designed to secure further respectability.*

*Meanwhile the Irish Government, which had many more serious problems to deal with, not least its own political survival, delayed taking any action to silence the landbased pirate stations.*

*Finally the Government decided to act in 1988 and passed the Broadcasting and Wireless Telegraphy Act outlawing the landbased pirate stations prior to the introduction of a local commercial radio network. The pirates were required to close down by 30th December 1988, a day before the legislation came into effect, in order that they could be eligible to apply for legal licenses when they were advertised.*

This project had been put together with an organisation, De Ondergandse Kerk (The Underground Church), which had offices in Holland, Germany and Switzerland. Former Radio Caroline, Radio Mi Amigo and Radio 819 backer, Fred Bolland became responsible for supervising the refitting of the *Communicator* for her new role.

By coincidence this project was being put together at the time the Dutch authorities were investigating the whole question of offshore radio and contemplating some drastic action against those involved with such operations. In the knowledge that some of their nationals were involved in the new project for the *Communicator* and that it was to be used as a propaganda station the Dutch requested the Portuguese authorities to mount a raid on the vessel, fearing that it may be used as part of a conspiracy against the Dutch Government. The Portuguese police subsequently raided the ship and confiscated studio equipment and transmitter parts.

After this raid some questions arose as to the financial security of the project and various accusations were made about misappropriation of funds. Nevertheless some equipment from the former Radio Paradijs ship *Magda Maria* were purchased and shipped to Lisbon to replace that confiscated by the Portuguese authorities.

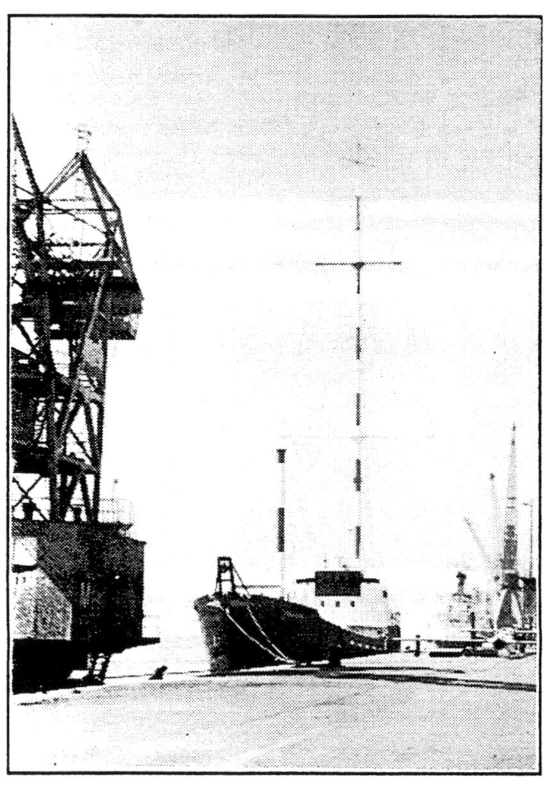

*The 'Communicator' in Portugal with new aerial masts*

The whole Romanian broadcasting project came to an end with the revolution at Christmas 1989, which removed the dictator Nicolai Chauchesqu and led to the abandonment of many of his repressive laws and institutions. However, the *Communicator* was still the subject of contested ownership rights and she remained in Portugal, with little or no work being done aboard her for some time.

## *Nannell* re-named *Mi Amigo*

The other vessel briefly considered as an alternative home for Radio 819 was the MV *Nannell,* which had been planned to be the base for Stereo 531. The *Nannell* was forced to leave Santander in northern Spain rather hurriedly on 10th June 1989 after the Spanish authorities started showing an unusual amount of interest in the vessel, which by now had been re-named *Mi Amigo.*

It later became clear that the increased level of interest in the *Nannell* was, as with the *Communicator* in Lisbon, part of the preliminary investigations into the planned launch of new offshore stations which ultimately led to the Dutch/British raid on the *Ross Revenge* in August 1989.

On the voyage north to Blankenberge off the Belgian coast the *Nannell/Mi Amigo* lost part of her newly erected aerial tower and one of the transmitters on board was also damaged. Reports circulating at this time suggested that some of the people formerly involved with Radio Mi Amigo now controlled the ship (hence her renaming) and plans were in hand to re-launch that station.

## Surveillance suspicions again

From early July 1989 DJs and crew on board the *Ross Revenge* began to suspect that the radio ship was under surveillance by the authorities once again. Although nothing was said over the air on either Radio Caroline or Radio 819 the *Ross Revenge* crew monitored a small patrol boat anchoring near the radio ship for periods of three or four days at a time throughout July and early August. A French Navy patrol vessel also paid frequent visits, circling the *Ross Revenge* and then disappearing for a few days before returning to the area once again. It was thought that the purpose of these visits by the French was to observe how high out of the water the radio ship was lying- an indication of roughly the amount of fuel remaining in her tanks. From this information a reasonable calculation could be made of the time within which a tender was likely to visit the *Ross Revenge* to deliver fuel.

On one occasion when a Dutch fuel tender did arrive at the *Ross Revenge* and tied up to transfer its cargo two British police boats together with a DTI vessel drew alongside and warned the crew of the Dutch ship that they were breaking international law. Meanwhile officials on board the police and DTI launches photographed and videoed the radio ship and anybody who appeared on deck.

Further filming of activities on board the *Ross Revenge* took place during the following weeks from a light aircraft and a helicopter, which hovered low and close to the radio ship in an attempt to obtain shots of the on-air DJ through the Radio Caroline studio porthole. The French Navy patrol vessel also continued to pay the radio ship regular visits, but throughout all of these events DJs said nothing on air to indicate to listeners that they were experiencing problems from the authorities.

At the beginning of August 1989 there were rumours that some sort of direct action was being planned against the *Ross Revenge,* although on 16th August the Dutch authorities denied these stories, quoting the Court decision following the seizure of the Radio Paradijs ship, *Magda Maria*, eight years previously (see Chapter 20).

Despite this categoric statement by the Dutch authorities, the very next day police raided twenty premises in Holland and seven in Belgium, all owned or occupied by people suspected of being associated with the three offshore radio stations based on the *Ross Revenge.* Police in Spain also interviewed ex-Radio Mi Amigo DJ Maurice Bokkenbroek, who operated the PO Box number in Playa de Aro on behalf of both Radio 819 and Caroline 558. A number of other people who worked for the offshore stations or Kroon Music Media in Holland were also interviewed and various documents and programme tapes were seized. Advertisers and sponsor's premises were visited by the authorities - Texas products, the main backer of Radio 819, had its office raided as did evangelist Johaan Maasbach's World Mission Radio, whose programmes were transmitted on the shortwave service from the *Ross Revenge.*

Raids were also mounted on the premises of various people thought to be involved in planning a re-launch of Radio Mi Amigo from the *Nannell.* Although no arrests were made at the time police claimed to have gathered enough evidence from the raids to detain four people "in the near future." Local Dutch and Belgian radio stations who carried Kroon Music Media syndicated programmes, (some of which were included in Radio 819's programme schedules) were also visited, but all denied having anything to do with the offshore station. However, at one of these stations, Europoort Radio in Rotterdam, police actually confiscated some of the programme tapes.

## *Ross Revenge* visited by authorities

Meanwhile, in the North Sea on Thursday 17th August 1989 a British Coastguard vessel, *Landward,* circled the *Ross Revenge* a few times and then took up position close to the radio ship. Later a member of the crew asked permission to board the *Ross Revenge*, but this was refused. A Dutch official on the *Landward* then informed crew members on the radio ship that the Radio 819 organisation on land had been raided and all people associated with the station arrested, including DJs and advertisers. He also asked the crew of the *Ross Revenge* to close down their transmitters.

The crew, confused and uncertain about what had really taken place on land, said they would discuss the request amongst themselves and give the *Landward* a decision later. Ultimately the crew decided that the Dutch nationals on board the *Ross Revenge* should leave the ship to try and find out what had really happened to the landbased side of the organisation. The English and American nationals would remain on board the radio ship.

Later in the afternoon the *Landward* returned to hear the crew's answer and were told that only Dutch personnel were prepared to leave the radio ship. Officials on the *Landward* then said the plan had changed and everyone must leave the *Ross Revenge* irrespective of nationality. The crew obviously would not agree to this and advised those on board the *Landward* that there was no point in discussing the matter further.

Suspecting that something dramatic was about to happen Radio Caroline's engineer, Peter Chicago, who was on shore leave, made his way back to the *Ross Revenge* later that night in a small dinghy. He took command of the ship and spent some hours hiding equipment and spare parts in various places on the *Ross Revenge*. He also decided that there should be no further contact with those on board the *Landward.*

## Distress indicators

During the morning of Friday 18th August 1989 programmes on both Caroline 558 and Radio 819 continued as normal, but at 10.30am the pre-recorded "Coffee Time" programme on Radio 819 was interrupted and the record "Ring Ring" by Abba was played continuously for thirty minutes. This was a desperate coded message for the station's land-based office to contact the *Ross Revenge*, using the mobile telephone.

The first indication listeners to Caroline 558 had that all was not well came twenty minutes later at 10.50am when three records, "Imagine", "Lady in Red", and a Loving Awareness track were played continuously as a coded indication to the station's land-based representatives that something was seriously wrong aboard or near the *Ross Revenge*. Throughout the morning DJ Neil Gates started announcing the station as "Radio Caroline" rather than "Caroline 558" and indicated that after midday Radio Caroline programmes would also be broadcast on 819kHz.

On Radio 819 the normal taped programme started at 11.00am and continued for an hour and twenty minutes then, without warning, the 819kHz transmitter went silent. After ten minutes Caroline 558 programmes were relayed on 819kHz and this simulcast arrangement continued for the remainder of the day. The programmes of WMR on the shortwave transmitter were discontinued shortly after midday.

At 1.00pm Caroline News informed listeners to both frequencies what had been happening that morning:-

*The Radio Caroline ship, 'Ross Revenge', anchored in the international waters of the North Sea was approached at 9.15am this morning by a vessel from Britain and the crew identified themselves as officials of the Department of Trade and Industry. Also on board was a representative of the Dutch radio authorities. They stated that international action was being taken to silence the broadcasts emanating from the 'Ross Revenge'. Permission to board the radio ship for discussions on the future of the ship and its crew was refused by the Captain. However, talks took place and negotiations are continuing.*

Later that evening Radio Caroline announced that the DTI vessel, *Landward,* had been joined by a Dutch ship, the *Volans,* (a Dutch Ministry of Works tug used in 1971 to tackle the fire on the RNI ship, *Mebo II*) (see Chapter 15) which had on board Dutch police, Dutch Radio Regulatory Department (Opsporings Controle Dienst - OCD) officials as well as some hired 'heavies'.

## *Ross Revenge* boarded in international waters

Separate programmes commenced again on Radio 819 the following morning, Saturday 19th August 1989, but consisted largely of continuous music, although one or two of the scheduled taped programmes were broadcast. Programmes on Caroline 558 continued as normal with Tony Kirk's breakfast show from 5.00-9.00am, then Caroline Martin started her programme at 9.00am, but left the air early to be replaced by Chris Kennedy.

The *Landward* again tried to make contact with those on board the *Ross Revenge* but received no response from the radio ship. They then advised over the ship-to-shore radio that a final decision must be made by the crew to leave the *Ross Revenge* by 12 noon.

The crew on board the *Ross Revenge* took no action at this stage to comply, but when the *Volans* was spotted coming out of the mist toward the radio ship Peter Chicago contacted North Foreland Radio asking for assistance from the Coastguards. His call was not acknowledged.

The *Volans* then drew alongside the *Ross Revenge* and an officer from the Dutch Water Police asked permission to come aboard and inspect the ship's registration papers. Both requests were repeatedly refused, but the police insisted that they had powers to ask for the ship's papers and that the Captain was obliged to produce them. Peter Chicago eventually told them the *Ross Revenge* was registered in Panama, but again refused to produce the registration documents.

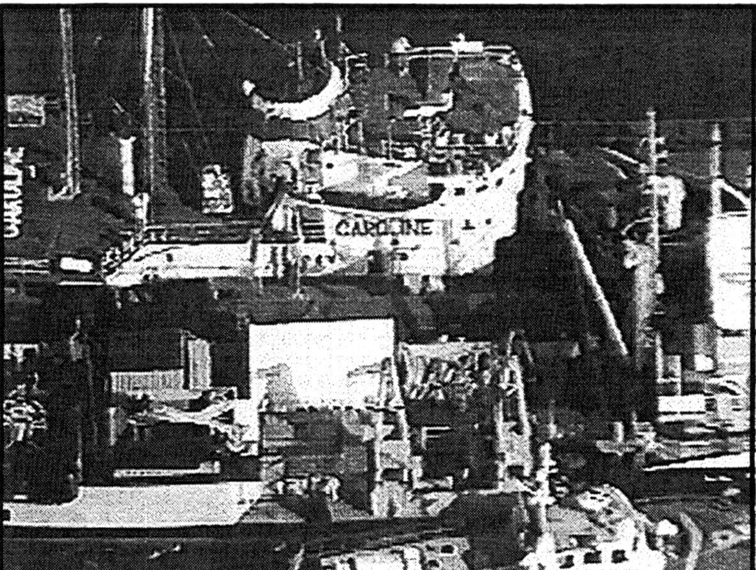


*'Volans' and 'Landward' alongside the 'Ross Revenge', 19th August 1989*

After his fourth refusal the police attempted to climb aboard the radio ship. One officer was initially pushed back but others forced their way on board, in the process punching and knocking Peter Chicago to the deck. Once on board they again asked three more times to see the ship's registration papers and eventually, in the face of overwhelming force, Peter Chicago produced them. The police then stated that they had come to dismantle the transmitters and studios on board the *Ross Revenge* and asked for his co-operation to prevent unnecessary damage. Eight named people were supposedly authorised to remove the equipment, which was to be recorded and registered but when the enormity of the task became apparent others on the *Volans* were asked to come aboard the *Ross Revenge.*

The crew of the *Ross Revenge* were in no position to repel the 30-strong armed boarding party from the *Volans,* which itself was almost as large as the radio ship. Station Engineer and ship's 'Captain', Peter Chicago, did try to prevent some men boarding the *Ross Revenge,* but he was threatened with a gun and punched as was DJ Caroline Martin when she tried to bar the door of the transmitter room. The Dutch were accompanied by DTI officials from Britain, but they took no active part in seizing or damaging the station's equipment.

While all this was going on listeners to both stations were kept informed by way of special announcements. At 12noon on Radio 819 a repeat of the "Texas American Top 40" programme from the previous week started, but was interrupted forty minutes later when the 819kHz transmitter was linked to 558kHz to broadcast a dramatic message by Caroline's Engineer, Peter Chicago:-

*This is a special announcement from the Radio Caroline ship 'Ross Revenge'. At the moment we have a large Dutch tug, the Volans, whose intentions are not clear, but which seem to be... they seem to have the intention of taking this ship from the High Seas. I'm speaking on behalf of the crew and the broadcasters on the vessel 'Ross Revenge'. We've had previous warnings, earlier on, that some kind of action was contemplated. At the moment on our starboard side we have the Dutch tug 'Volans', which seems to have the intention of taking this ship, the 'Ross Revenge', from her moorings in the international waters of the South Falls Head. We'll try and let you know what's going on as the programme continues, but I have an idea that events will move very quickly. Anybody hearing this broadcast perhaps could help us by telephoning the Coastguard to register a complaint, possibly by contacting anybody in authority that you think could help us. This is the radio ship 'Ross Revenge' broadcasting in the international waters of the North Sea and for the momment, anyway, we'll return to our regular programmes. Thank you.*

## Five services silenced

*There were five services broadcasting from the Ross Revenge at the time of the raid in August 1989:-*

- **Caroline 558** (558kHz) - English 24 hours
- **Radio 819** (819kHz) - Dutch 4.00am-7.00pm
- **World Mission Radio** (6215kHz shortwave) 4.30am-11.00pm
- **Viewpoint** (religious programmes) (819kHz) 7.00pm-various
- **Overnight Alternative** (819kHz) end of Viewpoint - 4.00am

## Radio 819 and Caroline cut off the air

After the end of the announcement the taped programme started again on Radio 819, but only two minutes later it was interrupted once more for another urgent message in English from Peter Chicago:-

*I'm interrupting this programme to give you a message from the crew on board the vessel 'Ross Revenge'. We're at anchor in the international waters of the North Sea. At the moment there is a Dutch tug, the 'Volans', which is alongside. They seem to have the intention to take this vessel from the High Seas. Anybody who is hearing this message could they please try to summon some kind of assistance for the vessel? In the meantime we continue with the programme.*

The taped "Texas American Top 40 Show" then continued until 12.52pm when it suddenly ended and there was silence on 819kHz until 1.01pm, when Caroline 558 was simulcast for what turned out to be the last seven minutes of the Dutch station's life.

At 1.08 pm both medium wave transmitters on the *Ross Revenge* fell silent and once again Radio Caroline had gone off the airwaves.

# The Drama Unfolds

From 12.45pm, a few minutes after Peter Chicago's dramatic announcement there followed almost twenty minutes of further announcements keeping listeners to Radio Caroline and Radio 819 informed about the dramatic events taking place on board the *Ross Revenge.*

***12.45 Chris Kennedy*** *This is the radio ship 'Ross Revenge', Radio Caroline, broadcasting from the international waters of the North Sea. It appears that we are now being boarded by a Dutch tug. We are being boarded by a Dutch tug. We hope to continue broadcasting as long as humanly possible.*

The station's theme, "Caroline" by The Fortunes, was played continuously in the background to these announcements.

***12.47 Bruce Munroe*** *Representatives of the Dutch Government have just boarded the 'Ross Revenge'. At the moment one of the people that's come aboard has been violent towards our engineer. We haven't a clue what's going on at the moment.*

***Chris Kennedy*** *All we can say is these guys are definitely not here to take photographs!*

***Bruce Munroe*** *No. And at the moment we have the DTI standing by at the rear of the ship. They are not at this stage appearing to do anything. We're going to make enquiries whether or not they are going to allow this behaviour. As I say there's been some violence and its on behalf of the ..er.. it's the Dutch people that have been doing it. We'll get back to you.*

***Chris Kennedy*** *Right. In the meantime lets send these people a message from us. Here are the Beatles on Caroline and "All You Need is Love".*

***12.50 Chris Kennedy*** (at the end of the Beatles record) *This is the radio ship 'Ross Revenge'. We appear to be in quite a dangerous predicament at tho moment, Bruce?*

***Bruce Munroe*** *Yes. At the moment we have a ship alongside us. It's a Dutch vessel, the 'Volans', I believe. and it's endangering everybody on board. With shouting in the background he continued; One more message please Chris. I've just spoken to the Dover Coastguard, for anybody listening, would they please stop now calling the Coastguard. Once again anybody who's listening, please stop calling Dover Coastguard. Dover Coastguard are apparently now fully aware of the situation.*

"All You Need is Love" was again played until at

***12.52 Chris Kennedy*** *Love is all you need. We've got Nigel Harris with us. Nigel?*

***Nigel Harris*** *Yes. We have now been boarded by the Dutch authorities. We are in desperate need of help and they are trying to shut the station down and take us all off ...but we are in international waters. This is a breach of this vessel's right to be here and I desperately plead for help. We need help now.*

***Chris Kennedy*** *So please anybody who's listening, anybody who's in authority, anybody who thinks they can do anything at all, please help us. This is Radio Caroline anchored in the international waters of the North Sea. We are currently being boarded.*

After a short piece of music, the record was faded out and Chris Kennedy returned to say

*The latest piece of news we have on board the 'Ross Revenge' is apparently, whether we can believe it or not, but according to our sources this particular vessel, this Dutch vessel, this hostile Dutch vessel, is acting on behalf of the British Government.*

***Neil Gates*** *Please call your local MP, councillors, local radio stations. local newspapers, anybody, please help, quick!*

***Chris Kennedy*** (with "Caroline " playing in the background) *Thank you Neil Gates. We've got just about, well not quite, everybody in the studio at the moment. We've got a fine crew here.*

After a few more bars of "Caroline" had been played Chris Kennedy asked Nigel Harris for another update.

***12.53 Nigel Harris** The authorities are on board and making their way to the studio.*

***Chris Kennedy** Right. This could be the end. We wish you .....*

**Nigel Harris** interrupted *We'll stay as long as we can.*

***Chris Kennedy** We wish you a lot of love. We've been here since 1964, Easter Sunday 1964 and hopefully someday Radio Caroline will be back. In fact I feel sure that we will. Please keep listening.* The station's theme tune, "Caroline", played continuously in the background.

***12.55 Neil Gates** This is Radio Caroline. The radio ship 'Ross Revenge', anchored in the international waters of the North Sea. This is a Panamanian vessel being boarded illegally on behalf of the Dutch and British Governments. There's a Dutch tug alongside and they are already on board the ship. They have already used violence against certain crew members here on board the 'Ross Revenge'. If you can help us please call your local radio station, local media, anything, anyone you think can help us. Call, please now before Caroline goes.*

***12.56*** (with "All You Need is Love" playing in the background) ***Chris Kennedy** This is Radio Caroline broadcasting from the international waters of the North Sea, the voice of Loving Awareness. It's four minutes before one o'clock and this radio ship is currently being boarded. In fact we have on board us, I understand, that various officials from various countries are crawling all over this radio ship. There seems little we can do.*

***12.58 Chris Kennedy** continued A very good afternoon to you on this black day. It is Saturday 19th August 1989, the radio ship Ross Revenge, home of Radio Caroline for many many years. We have been boarded by officials, and indeed one might even go so far as to say a couple of thugs, from a Dutch vessel which is alongside. Several members of the crew have been manhandled and it appears that it is their intention to tow this ship away. This is of course a flagrant breach of international regulations*

***Nigel Harris** It was exactly six years today since our broadcasts started from this boat, this is a fine anniversary present.*

***Chris Kennedy** One wonders about the timing of this event.*

***Nigel Harris** Twenty five years on the air, six years on this boat and they have now illegally boarded us in international waters, with every intention of towing this vessel away.*

**Chris Kennedy** (with "All you Need is Love" playing in the background) *So if there is anybody, anybody at all out there who can perhaps offer us some assistance, whatever that might be, please, please, please please try. It's coming up to one minute before one o'clock. We've had just about everybody associated with the radio station in the studio. We have Caroline Martin who's beside me, not looking too well.....*

***12.59 Bruce Munroe*** interrupted, *Discussions are going on now downstairs.....*

***Chris Kennedy** Apparently discussions are going on in the messroom , we shall keep you posted. In the meantime just to reiterate that message. This is the radio ship 'Ross Revenge' anchored in the international waters of the North Sea. We have been boarded by a Dutch vessel. Once again we have been boarded illegally by a Dutch vessel.*

*At **13.01** Radio 819 began to simulcast the broadcast on 558kHz. And after playing "Caroline" and some Loving Awareness jingles, the record "Love You to Know", by Loving Awareness, was started.*

***13.04 Chris Kennedy** Do you know what it's like to be free? Over the years since Easter Sunday 1964 we have known what it's like to be free. And the only trouble about freedom is that it scares a lot of people, particularly the people who themselves are not free. And when they see freedom the only thing they can think to do is that they have to try and stamp it out. And Radio Caroline refuses to be stamped out!*

***13.05 Nigel Harris*** interrupted *Caroline 558. We will be leaving the air at any moment now, the boarding party are finding their way to the transmitter room and they are going to dismantle all our broadcasting gear, take the studios to pieces, dismember the... dismantle the generators and then incapacitate the ship totally. They'll also be taking staff with them, but I'm not too sure how that one works at the moment. But they are now* *making their way downstairs. We will be going off the air anytime.*

**Chris Kennedy** *Nigel, this is the saddest day of my life and I think it's going to be a sad day for a lot of people.*

**Nigel Harris** *Yes, I know, but we just can't fight them, there's too many of them they have a tug the size of the Ross and it's not the end I'm sure, although it's easy to say that.*

**Neil Gates** *The 'Ross Revenge' is not the only ship in the world we will be back we can assure you of that. Caroline will return The 19th August 1989 is the day the UK, Great Britain, became a totalitarian state.*

**Chris Kennedy** *Radio Caroline. We love you too much to leave you forever. Please keep tuned over the weeks and months to come to our frequencies and I feel sure that you will hear something in the not too distant future.*

The "Caroline" theme continued playing

***13.06 Chris Kennedy*** *We've got a further news update for you. Here is Dave Richards.*

**Dave Richards** *Yes. The situation is that representatives from the Dutch Government and Coastguard are on board; their intention is in fact to take various broadcast equipment. We're not sure whether that includes our AC generator supply, but surely it does include our shortwave frequency, the 819 frequency and vital components or the whole transmitter for the 558 frequency, also our studio equipment. While they intend us as people no harm the basic problem is that they basically just want the ship off the air. They're leaving the ship, and they're leaving the people on board it.*

**Nigel Harris** *We have the option to go ashore, apparently, if we want to. Right Do you know what's happening? Bruce Munroe, come and explain things.*

**Bruce Munroe** *Right. As it stands the gentlemen are going to remove the transmitter from the ship and take a few other things as well. What they have just told us is that we are free to go back to Holland with them where there will be no more charges pressed. We will also be able to go back to England and there will be no charges pressed there. Alternatively, we can stay on the 'Ross Revenge'. Now....*(to someone who had entered the studio) *would you like to say anything sir, before we go off?*

***13.08*** At that point the 558kHz transmitter was cut off. On 819kHz Bruce Munroe continued *...Alright. Don't bother. It's gone.*

With "Caroline" still playing in the background the 819kHz transmitterthen too fell silent.

**Pop pirates silenced**

**CAROLINE IS SCUPPERED**

RADIO Caroline, Britain's first pirate pop station, was forced off the air yesterday after 25 years.

Dutch police boarded the ship, Ross Revenge, at noon, allegedly smashing transmitting gear and manhandling the Dutch skipper and British DJ Caroline Martin.

**Dutch police raid pirate radio ship**

**Caroline knocked off the airwaves**

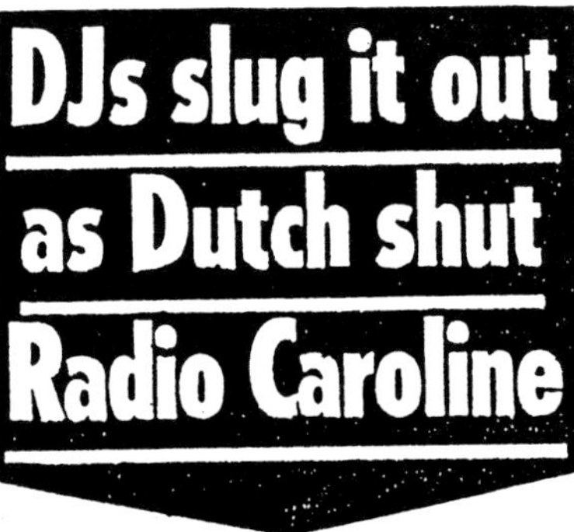


**Pirate Radio Caroline is silenced in sea raid**

PIRATE radio station Radio Caroline was silenced yesterday in a raid by Dutch officials.

The station ship Ross Revenge was in international waters in the southern North Sea when it was boarded in a joint operation involving Dutch coastguards, police and trade inspectors.

British Department of Trade and Industry officials had been keeping the ship under surveillance for a week.

But a spokesman denied reports that British officials took part in the raid — and he would not comment on claims that crew members were hurt in the operation.

He said DTI officials were busy trying to persuade British crew members to accept passage to Ramsgate for questioning.

The boarding party dismantled the station's transmitting equipment and Dutch crew members were taken off and returned to Holland.

The spokesman said: "The ship has been causing a great deal of interference to authorised broadcasts, not only in Holland but throughout Europe. It has also been causing problems with emergency services."

Howard Rose, editor of the journal Now Radio, said Radio Caroline staff told him the ship's captain and chief engineer were "severely beaten" in the raid.

They claimed the 30-strong boarding party manhandled other staff, including disc jockey Caroline Martin.

Last night the ship's Canadian directors were considering legal action over the raid.

The raiders objective was to dismantle and seize everything on board the *Ross Revenge* which could be used by Radio 819, and this included items from the Radio Caroline operation as well - transmitters, aerial systems, studio equipment, records and tapes. However, the hired Dutchmen who were brought along to do the job by OCD and police were drinking heavily and as the day wore on they resorted to vandalising and smashing equipment. Some items which were transferred to the *Volans,* including the fragile ceramic insulators and studio equipment, were smashed as they were thrown from the deck of the radio ship. The *Ross Revenge's* aerial array was cut from the masts and loaded on to the *Volans,* but the masts themselves, so painstakingly built by the crew of the radio ship, were left relatively undamaged.

The transmitters on board the *Ross Revenge* were too large to move so it was decided to dismantle them, but this was achieved by smashing the equipment with sledgehammers rather than simply cutting wires or pulling plugs. A similar fate befell the generators except one which the boarders were persuaded to leave intact as it was needed to provide navigational lights for the *Ross Revenge,* as required by international maritime law.

During the late afternoon the raiders left the *Ross Revenge* to take some refreshment on the *Volans.* This 'tea break' had been partly negotiated by Peter Chicago and afforded the opportunity for him and other crew members on board the radio ship to retrieve and conceal further items of equipment before they could be transferred to the Dutch tug.

When the *Volans* left the *Ross Revenge* later that day two Dutchmen from Radio 819, DJ Arie Swets and ship's cook Eddie Altenbergh, were on board, having voluntarily agreed to leave the radio ship following reassurances by the authorities that they would not be arrested when they returned to Holland. All British staff remained on board the radio ship.

## 'Justification'

In an attempt to justify their incredible actions against the *Ross Revenge* the Dutch Office of Justice stated that for over 12 months there had been complaints from several countries about interference to maritime transmissions from Radio 819's broadcasts. Amongst countries alleged to have complained were Sweden, France, Britain, and even Hungary - which is landlocked and has no maritime communications system. The Dutch Minister of Justice, Mr. Mijnsen, said that rumours of planned new offshore stations joining Radio Caroline and Radio 819 at sea had been an important factor in their decision to mount the raid when they did.

The prospect of further offshore radio stations coming on the air in the latter half of 1989 had brought matters to a head and the Dutch then felt that they had no option but to silence the broadcasts from the radio ship anchored off the British coast.

At that time there were three possible additional offshore radio projects preparing to come on the air:-

- a Flemish language station from the *Nannell* (now renamed *Mi Amigo*) which had hurriedly left port in June and anchored off Blakenberge;
- a station from the *Communicator* which was then being refitted in Portugal;
- Power 531, a station backed by an organisation known as the Sound of Europe, using the MV *Mercury 2.*

## International Maritime rules

*International Maritime rules require ships at sea to have a qualified Captain, senior engineer, generator engineer, cook and three deckhands.*

*Radio Caroline after its return in 1972 and after the initial period following the re-launch from the 'Ross Revenge' in 1983 did not always follow these rules. Some other offshore stations also relied on the on-board radio staff to double up in undertaking maritime duties and responsibilities.*

The Radio 819 organisation was alleged to have told the Dutch authorities that they planned to close the station anyway at the end of August because advertising income had not been sufficient to cover their operating costs.

The *Volans* arrived in Scheveningen early in the morning of 20th August 1989 and the equipment seized from the *Ross Revenge* was transferred to a warehouse in the port. It later became known that the raid had been some eighteen months in the planning. The Dutch authorities had initially requested the British to arrest Ronan O'Rahilly, but this was refused while the French and Belgians had been requested to exert tighter controls in their ports on tendering activities associated with the *Ross Revenge.* This Dutch request had also been refused by both countries on cost grounds.

## Reaction to the raid

There was some speculation about the validity of the registration of the *Ross Revenge* at the time of the boarding and questions were raised about whether the Dutch authorities had again, as with Radio Paradijs in 1981, committed an act of piracy on the high seas. However, the people behind Radio Caroline were confident enough of their legal position to instruct London maritime solicitors, Richards Butler, to institute proceedings against the Dutch authorities and the DTI on behalf of the owners of the *Ross Revenge*, Grothan Steamship Lines, alleging piracy, assault and criminal damage - estimated to be in the region of half a million pounds.

At first the British DTI denied that it had taken part in the boarding of the *Ross Revenge,* claiming that their officials had remained on the *Landward* observing the operation. However, DTI officials did board the *Ross Revenge* and journalists who visited the radio ship during the raid were able to identify and photograph at least one of them. The Department later admitted its involvement and a spokesman said, "the Dutch authorities asked for our (technical) officers to render assistance to make equipment safe, and this was given."

A press release issued by Peter Moore on behalf of Radio Caroline the day after the raid stated:-

*The Canadian directors of Radio Caroline said they were 'shocked and horrified at this act of piracy'. They said that having taken urgent legal advice they would be bringing charges of piracy, assault and criminal damage against the authorities and against the individuals concerned. ... It seems that both the British and Dutch Governments are now involved in a 'deniability exercise'. The British Department of Trade and Industry issued a statement claiming that no British officials were involved in the boarding, and that the UK officials were in another vessel keeping surveillance. Journalists who went to the scene yesterday spoke to a DTI official, who identified himself as Mr. Jim Murphy. He identified himself while he was actually on board the 'Ross Revenge' and was interrogating the crew. Photographic and video evidence exists of the wholesale damage created during the raid. The Dutch raiders were also drinking heavily and left behind a large number of bottles which have now been removed from the ship. The Radio Caroline legal advisers are having these bottles tested for fingerprints, for use in the forthcoming legal actions to be taken against both the Dutch and British authorities and the individuals involved.*

## Emergency supply arrangements

As a result of the raid there were immediate problems for Caroline in arranging supplies of fuel and food for the people still on board the *Ross Revenge* - in the past tendering had been undertaken by the Dutch. Temporary permission was received from the DTI in Britain for supplies to be taken from a British port so long as a radio station was not broadcasting from the *Ross Revenge.*

A month after the raid, on 17th September 1989, the Caroline Movement listeners' group organised a demonstration in London to show support for the station itself and for those members of the crew who had remained on board the *Ross Revenge*. Caroline Movement members were asked to donate records and food parcels which were later taken to the *Ross Revenge* for the benefit and comfort of those still on board.

About 600 people attended the demonstration in London, marching from outside the DTI offices in Waterloo Bridge Road , across Westminster Bridge, past the Houses of Parliament and ending up at Lambeth Pier. Here it had been planned to rendezvous with the Caroline Movement's own vessel, *Galexy,* but due to tidal problems it had not possible to bring her up the Thames, so another boat (the *Sidney Hall*) was hired as a replacement. A number of Radio Caroline DJs and crew arrived on this vessel to meet the demonstration and collect donations - over a ton of food and thousands of vital replacement records for the station's library. The Caroline Movement also launched a 'Caroline Legal Fund' to help raise finance towards the legal action being taken against the Dutch Government and their hired raiding party.

Meanwhile, the station's solicitors, Richards Butler, had written to the DTI on behalf of their clients, asking for an explanation of its involvement in the raid on the *Ross Revenge* in August 1989 and pointing out the illegality of this action under international law.

## Caroline Legal Fund

*This was established shortly after the August 1989 raid on the 'Ross Revenge' and was managed by the listeners' supporters group, the Caroline Movement. Its primary purpose was to fund legal action on behalf of Radio Caroline against the various authorities and individuals who had been party to the raid. However, as the position surrounding the status of the 'Ross Revenge's registration became clear legal action was not pursued as vigorously as at first envisaged. The initial costs incurred by Richards Butler in exploring the legal position and advising on the best course of action accounted for approximately half of the £25,000 raised by the Fund. Once these fees had been paid the remainder of the Fund was then used to provide supplies for the crew on board the 'Ross Revenge'.*

## Atlantic 252

*A new radio station was preparing to launch to Britain during the summer of 1989. It was not an offshore station, but it did have connections with some people formerly involved with Laser 558 and Laser Hot Hits.*

*The new station, a joint venture between Radio Luxembourg and Radio Telefis Eirrean was to be based in Ireland, broadcasting, quite legally, on the longwave frequency of 252kHz allocated to Ireland under international agreements.*

*The project had been in the planning stage for some time under the code name Radio Tara and it was planned to target 15-34 year olds with a Hot Hits format. Studios for the new station were in premises located in Trim, twenty five miles north west of Dublin, with the transmitter site being some six miles away. The station was to use two 300Kw Continental transmitters linked to provide over 500Kw output enabling its signal to cover much of Britain.*

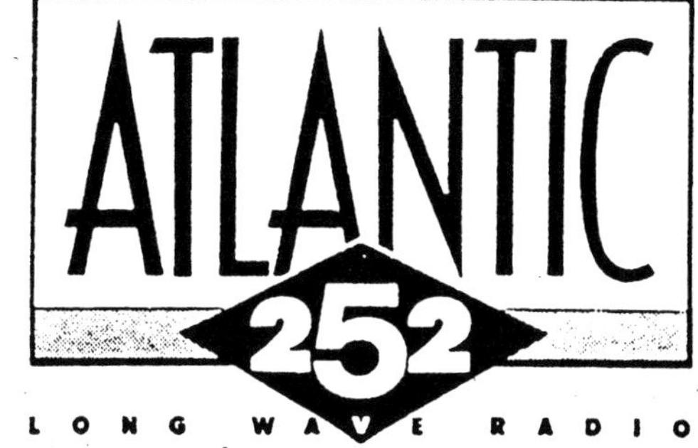


*Test transmissions for Atlantic 252 started (initially on 254kHz) on 31st July 1989 and the station opened officially on 1st September 1989 at 8.00am. Consultant to the new station was ex- Laser Manager, John Catlett, while two other former Laser personnel joined the broadcasting staff, DJ Charlie Wolf and newsreader Andrew Turner.*

*The British Foreign Office complained to the Irish Government that the establishment of Atlantic 252 was a misuse of a frequency allocated under international agreement for Irish domestic use. The Irish Department of Communications replied that Atlantic 252 was a national station within Ireland, but admitted that it did have an 'overspill' reception area.*

*Despite all official protestations Atlantic 252 quickly established itself with listeners and advertisers as a very popular national station, providing a genuine alternative to BBC Radio One and the ILR network, with its slick presentation, tight playlist of the most popular current hits and the slogan "never more than 90 seconds away from the music."*

## Caroline returns

Meanwhile on board the silent *Ross Revenge* engineer Peter Chicago, almost single handedly, managed to rebuild a medium wave transmitter from spare parts he had hidden away before the raid and from the wreckage of the short wave transmitter. This remarkable feat enabled Radio Caroline to return to the air within six weeks of having had virtually all its equipment smashed and taken away by the Dutch and British authorities.

The first test transmission, on 558kHz, took place on 30th September 1989 with a weak tuning tone appearing in mid-afternoon, increasing considerably in strength by late evening. Shortly before 9.00pm the station theme, "Caroline" by The Fortunes, was played followed by continuous music. This initial transmission closed shortly after midnight with an announcement that the station would re-open at noon the following day. Further tuning tones were heard during the morning of 1st October 1989 and shortly after 12 noon Caroline 558 returned as promised, with two DJs, Caroline Martin and Dave Asher sharing the programme hours until close at 6.00pm.

For the next few days the station managed to keep up a 12 hour schedule from 6.00am-6.00pm with Caroline Martin, Dave Asher and later Peter Chicago presenting the programmes. Transmissions continued regularly on this basis for the rest of October 1989 with more DJs gradually re-joining the *Ross Revenge*. Throughout this period there were a number of breaks in transmission and early closedowns, but yet again Radio Caroline had managed to defiantly provide a service for its listeners, despite all the efforts of the authorities to silence the station for good.

When Radio Caroline returned to the air on 1st October 1989 the Dutch OCD announced that there would be no further action taken against the station as its weak transmissions were not audible in Holland. In fact despite the very temporary nature of the rebuilt transmitting equipment the station's broadcasts were received by listeners in a large part of Holland, particularly the coastal areas.

OCD inquiries into the involvement of various people in offshore radio continued throughout September and October 1989 and on 7th November many people who had worked for Radio 819 were called in for interview by officials. These interviews were not confined to activities involving Radio 819, older associations with the former Radio Monique and even Radio Delmare, which had been on the air ten years previously, were also pursued during the OCD investigation.

## Caroline's frequency allocated to ILR station

Having failed to close Radio Caroline by force another tactic to try and silence the station was adopted by the authorities at the end of October 1989 when it was announced that the new London ILR station, Spectrum Radio, would be allocated the 558kHz frequency. Spectrum Radio itself, which had some connections with landbased pirate radio operations and a definite empathy for Radio Caroline, were not at all happy about being used by the authorities as a means to silence the offshore station's transmissions. The DTI remained adamant, however, that Radio Caroline must be closed and issued a statement saying -"An unlicensed broadcaster on a frequency allocated to an authorised station would present us with a priority case for clearing the airwaves."

## 'Normal' service

After successfully completing a month back on the air Radio Caroline tried to introduce as many regular features as possible during November 1989 to give the impression that everything had returned to normal, or as near normal as possible on an offshore radio station. The sponsored religious programmes, lifeblood financially for Radio Caroline, returned under the umbrella title "Viewpoint" on 1st November 1989 from 7.00pm-10.15pm. A commercial was aired every hour on the hour from 13th November for Dawn Valley convenience health foods, while there were also promotions for the Caroline Roadshow and a 'Welcome Back Caroline' event at Burley's Nightclub in London. Transmission hours were also extended to 24hours a day from 14th November 1989 and at the same time a regular news and weather service was re-introduced.

From this attempt at apparently normal programming, the average listener could be forgiven for assuming that the station had got over its 'difficulties' following the August raid, but behind the scenes Radio Caroline's landbased support organisation had virtually collapsed. Nobody, except a small group of the most dedicated of workers, wanted to be associated with the station in the weeks after the raid and the supply of programme material - new records and tapes - almost completely dried up, forcing DJs on board the *Ross Revenge* to record the latest hits from local ILR stations in Kent and Essex for re-broadcast during Radio Caroline's programmes. Even those dedicated few who continued working to keep the station on the air came under surveillance by the authorities and their private and business telephones were being tapped. For this reason much of the organisational communication at that time was undertaken from a variety of public telephone boxes and in public houses.

On board the *Ross Revenge* work was undertaken to thwart any further boarding attempts - the transmitter hold was sealed from the main deck area with access being restricted to a route via the engine room bulkhead. The outer doors were also fitted with security locks, making it more difficult for any future raiders to gain direct access to the broadcasting studios.

Broadcasting equipment at this time - most of it items which had been hidden from the raiders - was basic and DJs improvised as best they could to keep the station on the air. The station also had difficulty in obtaining regular supplies of fresh food and basic necessities such as cleaning materials, toiletries and clean bedding although these problems were eventually overcome by support from listeners' groups and local boatmen prepared to make clandestine trips to the *Ross Revenge* in defiance of the authorities.

Meanwhile, the station's solicitors, Richards Butler, had written to the DTI on behalf of their clients asking for an explanation of its involvement in the raid on the *Ross Revenge* in August 1989 and pointing out the illegality of this action under international law.

## Format adapted

Despite all these practical difficulties Radio Caroline managed to continue transmissions with a remarkable degree of reliability throughout December 1989, even mounting special programmes over the Christmas and the New Year holiday period. Following the loss of the record library in the August raid Radio Caroline had to adapt its format to AOR, relying less and less on the Top 40 material which it was virtually impossible for the station to obtain on a regular basis.

**offshore trivia**

**Largest radio ship**

***LENGTH:*** *'Odelia' (Odelia TV) - 264' (second largest 'Ross Revenge' (Radio Caroline, Radio Monique) - 210')*

***WEIGHT:*** *'Odelia' - 1219 tons (second largest 'Ross Revenge' - 978 tons)*

Since the station had returned at the beginning of October 1989 its transmissions had been on very low power, less than 1Kw, achieving a signal range of less than 100 miles from the *Ross Revenge.* However, when transmissions resumed on 9th January 1990, after a three day silence for engineering work, there was a significant increase in power to 4Kw, giving the station a much improved signal range of about 300 miles. This increase had been a critical factor in trying to persuade the evangelistic organisations to continue buying airtime on the station - its only source of income at that time.

## Lockerbie Bombing

*Unlikely as it may at first seem the Lockerbie disaster, in which a Pan Am airliner was blown out of the sky by a terrorist bomb above the Scottish village in December 1989, has a connection with offshore radio history.*

*The official inquiry report into the disaster published two years later revealed that a MST-13 microchip in the bomb circuitry had been found embedded in a shirt traced to a shop in Malta. The microchip was part of a timer device manufactured by Mebo Inc. of Zurich, which had been the company behind Radio North Sea International (RNI) in the early 1970s and had later sold its ships, 'Mebo' ('Angela') and 'Mebo II' to the Libyan Government.*

*Although a Director of Mebo Inc., Edwin Bollier, maintained that the microchip was from a circuit board made for household appliances sold throughout the Middle East it was subsequently revealed that only twenty of the timers were manufactured by Mebo and all were sold to the Libyan Government in the mid 1980s. A similar timer had been used in the destruction of a French UTA jet in 1989 when it was blown up over the Tenere Desert in Nigeria.*

*The Toshiba radio which contained the Lockerbie bomb was in a suitcase smuggled onto the plane using stolen luggage tags. The suitcase also contained clothing, including a shirt, which had been purchased in a shop in Malta. One of the two terrorists wanted for the bombing, Lamen Khalifa Fhimah, worked as an employee of Libyan Arab Airlines in Malta.*

# Chapter 26

# Drifting along

In Holland the ODC stated publicly in January 1990 that if the Rechtskamer (the Dutch equivalent of the British Director of Public Prosecutions) decided that the action taken in boarding the *Ross Revenge* was considered illegal then all equipment seized would have to be returned. Encouraging as this at first appeared that statement was then qualified when an ODC spokesman went on to explain that this only related to Radio Caroline's equipment and not that used by Radio 819 and WMR, both of which were directed at Holland and therefore considered by the ODC as legitimate targets for suppression.

For some time, and particularly since the August 1989 raid, there had been a divergence of views amongst those involved with Radio Caroline about the station's future - should it remain at sea despite all the practical difficulties and constant harassment from the authorities, or should some alternative legal land-based arrangement be explored?

The signs of a real rift in the organisation behind Radio Caroline began to appear in public for the first time in January 1990. A group of former staff announced plans to bring Radio Caroline ashore and operate it as a satellite radio station, using the sub-carrier facilities of satellite television stations. However, Radio Caroline's owners, and Ronan O'Rahilly in particular, refused to have anything to do with this project emphatically stating that the station would remain at sea where it had legally operated for nearly 26 years.

## Sealand shooting

On 23rd February 1990 the Royal Marine Auxiliary vessel, *Golden Eye* sailed close to the 'Principality' of Sealand housed on Roughs Tower, off Harwich. Fearing a raid on the 'Principality' similar to the one on the *Ross Revenge* the previous August security men on Sealand, including ex-Caroline engineer Mike Barrington fired shots at the Navy vessel, which called the Coastguard Service for assistance.

The matter came to a head some months later when Mike Barrington appeared in Court on 29th November 1990 on charges in connection with the incident, including the possession of a shotgun without a licence, assault occasioning actual bodily harm and common assault. Barrington said he had been concerned about the proximity of the *Golden Eye* (150 yards) to Sealand and when the Ministry of Defence vessel moved to within 50 yards of the Fort he had fired a warning shot. He had not intended to injure anyone on the Navy vessel. After a two day hearing the Court acquitted Barrington on all charges.

It is interesting to note that the prosecution was actually brought before the British Courts as a result of the extension of territorial sea limits in 1987, bringing Sealand inside British jurisdiction, and that no immunity was claimed because of Sealand's supposed 'independent' status.

**Typical Radio Caroline programme schedule, February/March 1990**

6.00am Gavin Ford

9.00am Nigel Harris

12noon Caroline Martin

2.00pm- Neil Gates

4.00pm Dave Taylor

6.00pm Viewpoint

9.15pm Neil Gates

11.00pm Paul Shelton

2.00am Closedown

## Frustrations begin to show

Severe weather in the North Sea during the first three months of 1990 caused a number of breaks in transmission for Radio Caroline, but generally the station managed to maintain a reasonably regular programme schedule and the increased signal strength in January was successful in attracting additional sponsored religious programmes into the "Viewpoint" service during February 1990.

In Holland the Dutch authorities decided in February 1990 that, despite assurances to the contrary given at the time of the raid on the *Ross Revenge* in August 1989, the two Dutchmen who voluntarily left the radio ship and returned on the *Volans* - Arie Swets and Eddie Altenbergh, would now be charged for their involvement with Radio 819 and in addition the land-based backers and tendering organisation behind Radio 819 would also face prosecution.

Frustration with the difficulties of operating Radio Caroline in the months after the August 1989 raid spilled over on to the airwaves in March 1990 when some DJs started making comments about the station's management, or apparent lack of it. The station's land-based supporters were in fact working very hard to keep the whole organisation together and the station on the air, but isolated out on the *Ross Revenge* for weeks at a time the DJ's perception of the situation was somewhat different. This culminated on 16th March 1990 when DJ Neil Gates referred to the station as "Radio Clapped Out" and at the close of his programme that day, after again complaining bitterly about the management's "couldn't care less attitude" and lack of new record supplies said, "I hope you enjoy listening to Caroline, it probably won't be here much longer."

*LADY IN RED CRUISE*
*on "Old London"*

*Easter Sunday*
*from Lambeth Pier at 12.30 p.m.*

*ADMIT ONE*

Fortunately that pessimistic prediction proved untrue and Radio Caroline was able to celebrate its 26th Birthday on Easter Sunday 15th April 1990, by playing classic album tracks from the previous two and a half decades. A number of Radio Caroline personalities also joined fans on a "Lady in Red" cruise on the River Thames the same day to celebrate the station's birthday. In mid-April 1990 Radio Caroline started publicising a new mailing address in Fort Lauderdale, Florida - they had not given one since the raid in August 1989. At the same time the London address for "Viewpoint" was closed and a new one was given in San Jose, California, USA.

### *Goddess of Democracy*

An offshore project of a different kind materialised in March 1990 when a French based group - Federation for Democracy in China - fitted out a ship as an offshore radio station with the intention that it would sail to a position off the Chinese coast. From here they planned to broadcast twelve hours a day of uncensored news, information and music to the population of mainland China in response to the repression of opposition groups after the Tiananmen Square Massacre of 1989. One of the station's founders, Wu'er Kaixi said, "On the waves of the first free Chinese radio everyone will speak." The station's ship had been re-named *Goddess of Democracy* in tribute to the statue of the same name which had been erected by pro-democracy supporters in Tiananmen Square in 1989.

The project had been sponsored by the Chinese business community around the world (including substantial amounts from Hong Kong) together with the French magazine *Actuel*, and the British magazine *The Face*. Wu'er Kaixi was one of the

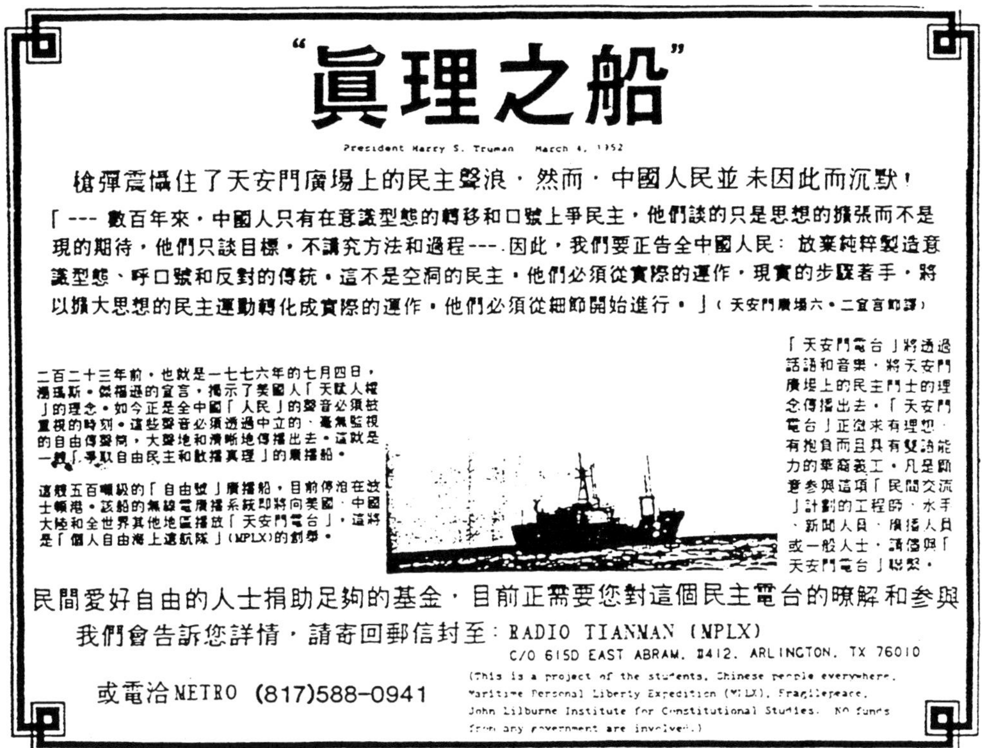


student leaders in Tiananmen Square during the anti- communist demonstrations the previous year and had fled in exile to Paris where he met with *Actuel* reporter Christophe Nick. Together they devised a plan for launching an offshore radio station to broadcast freely to mainland China.

It was planned that, after a six week voyage from La Rochelle in France, the station would begin transmitting music, interviews and anti-communist propaganda on 25th April 1990 possibly using a balloon aerial system. In order to avoid jamming which had been threatened by the Chinese Government, the station proposed to change frequencies at regular intervals. As well as jamming the Chinese Government also threatened to use force to stop the planned offshore radio station's broadcasts and said it would not tolerate any country or organisation supporting the station or its ship.

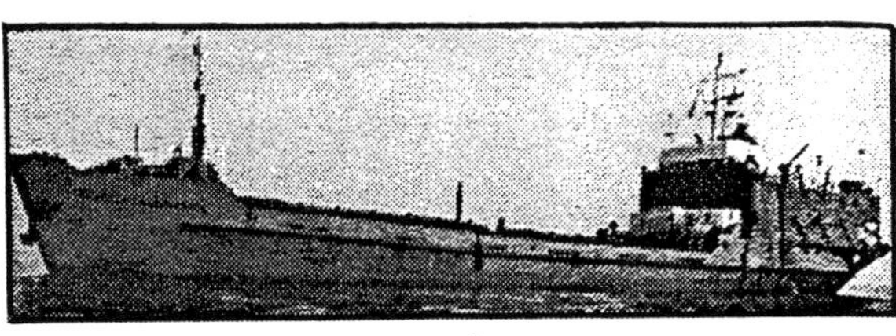
*The 'Goddess of Democracy'*

However, transmissions did not begin as scheduled on 25th April 1990. After being unable to successfully star broadcasting from the East China Sea, because it could not find a regular port for the vessel was reported at one stage to be heading towards Singapore. Later the Taiwanese Government granted the *Goddess of Democracy* permission to broadcast from a port on the breakaway non-communist Chinese island. However, authorities in mainland China warned Taiwan of serious consequences if it allowed the ship to begin transmissions from within its territory and the whole project faltered at this point.

The *Goddess of Democracy* was subsequently purchased by a local businessman, Wu Meng-wu, in April 1991 and it has since been docked in the port of Anping. Wu Meng-uu tried to sell the ship to the Chinese government as a museum dedicated to the history of the pro-democracy movement in China, but this offer was refused.

## Other offshore stations in the South China Sea

*There have been a number of offshore stations reportedly operating in the South China Sea, mainly for political purposes. Amongst those known to have broadcast are-*

- Voice of the People's Liberation Army
- Radio Flash
- The October Storm
- Redifussion Central
- Popular of Peking

## Radio Veronica's 30 Birthday

*The veteran Dutch offshore station Radio Veronica, now part of the state Hilversum system, celebrated its 30th Birthday on 18th April 1990. Broadcasting via the Hilversum 2 network the station broadcast between 7.00am and 5.00pm that day live from a ship which sailed from Scheveningen to Katwijk and back. The day of celebrations ended with a pop concert on Scheveningen Beach which was relayed live between 3.00 and 5.00pm.*

*Many ex-Veronica DJs presented or took part in the programmes that day and the signal from the 'radio ship' was relayed to Hilversum's landbased transmitters via a light aircraft. At various times while the plane had to land for refueling the ship sailed close to shore so that the signal could be relayed direct to the landbased transmitter.*

*The same day Dutch television - Nederland 2 - also broadcast a two hour documentary about the history of Radio Veronica.*

## ILR station begins tests

Spectrum Radio in North London, which had been officially allocated the 558kHz frequency used by Radio Caroline, announced the start of its test transmissions in May 1990.

In the face of these test transmissions starting on the same frequency as Radio Caroline carried the following announcement on 16th May 1990 :-

*Radio Caroline regrets that many listeners will soon be experiencing severe interference to our signal on 558kHz, a channel that we have been using for the last five years. The source of this interference will be a new London based station which, in a move calculated to force a confrontation between ourselves and the British authorities, has been forced to transmit on the same frequency as this radio station. Caroline suggest that listeners might like to offer their sympathy to the new station by calling them immediately on 081-905 5000 or 905 5151 or 905 5555. Similarly listeners to both stations might like to register protests by calling the IBA on 0345 078787 or the DTI, who are responsible for this situation on 071-215 7877.*

*Caroline hopes that this problem, which is not of our making and which is beyond our control, will shortly be resolved. We know that our loyal listeners will support us at this difficult time.*

*Caroline seeks no dispute with any organisation on land and simply wishes to continue providing the musical entertainment which has been enjoyed by generations of British and European listeners since Easter Saturday 1964.*

Within a day or so, however, the request for listeners to phone Spectrum to complain was dropped, Caroline accepted that it was not the London station's fault that it had been allocated this frequency - it was being used by the authorities as part of a larger operation to try and force Radio Caroline off the air by blotting out its signal.

This latest campaign to silence Radio Caroline was believed to have had its roots with the Association of Independent Radio Contractors, who had been highly critical of offshore radio in the past and were instrumental in persuading the DTI to mount the "Eurosiege" operation in 1985.

Spectrum 558 tests eventually started on 19th May 1990 from a temporary transmitter at Lots Road Power Station in Chelsea, the same site as had been used in 1973 by Britain's first two ILR stations, LBC and Capital Radio. A further statement was broadcast by Radio Caroline to explain to listeners the possible cause of interference to its signal:-

*Listeners to Radio Caroline may be experiencing severe interference to our signal on 558kHz. The source of this interference is a transmitter at Lots Road, Chelsea which is operated by the Independent Broadcasting Authority who, in a most unsportsmanlike and provocative move, have chosen to broadcast on the frequency that we have been using for the last five years. The inevitable consequence of this action is that listeners to Caroline and the new London station will not be able to hear their programmes.*

Reception for listeners to both stations was affected by the mutual interference, although this situation varied from location to location. In particular the signal within the Spectrum target area (inside the M25) was unsatisfactory and the station's Managing Director, Keith Belcher, was quoted in the London *Evening Standard* as saying "We are deeply unhappy. Our signal is very unsatisfactory and this is making the difficult job of attracting advertisers even harder."

On 29th May 1990 Spectrum 558 announced that its planned opening on 1st June had been postponed and that it was taking legal action against the IBA for breach of contract and loss of advertising revenue. Spectrum were angry at being used by the IBA as part of their operation to close Radio Caroline. Two days later the IBA announced "measures have been taken to remove the interference" and that it had agreed to allocate Spectrum a new frequency. In return, Spectrum agreed to drop the breach of contract action, but pursued its claim for compensation in respect of the £750,000 which had been spent in publicity and promoting the 558kHz frequency.

Spectrum Radio was allocated an additional frequency of 990kHz (303m) with a new site for its transmitter - Fulham Football Club's ground at Craven Cottage. It later transpired that both the transmitter and its associated Portakabin had been erected at the football ground without planning permission from the local council. Test transmissions for Spectrum on 990kHz eventually started in mid-June 1990, but the station also continued to broadcast on its original frequency of 558kHz.

## Broadcasting Bill debate

Meanwhile, another serious even potentially fatal, threat to the future of Radio Caroline and in fact any offshore broadcasting station off the British coast was being assembled in the British Parliament where the Broadcasting Bill was passing through its various legislative stages. One particular clause, Clause 159, had been added to the Bill at a comparatively late stage in the procedure, on 9th May 1990, significantly amending the Marine etc. Broadcasting (Offences) Act 1967

This amendment was to allow the Royal Navy and the Army to board offshore radio ships and use "reasonable force" to make arrests and seize equipment. These provisions could be exercised beyond territorial limits and allowed the British Government to exercise its powers on a foreign registered ship in international waters - a hitherto unacceptable and illegal practice. Additionally those taking part in, or authorising, such a boarding were to be immune from prosecution or claims for damages.

Speaking in the House of Lords debate on the Second Reading of the Bill on 5th June 1990 Lord Annan (who had chaired a committee in 1976 on the Future of British Broadcasting -see Chapter 19) said:-

*I particularly dislike the extraordinary amendments to the Marine Broadcasting Act 1967 which are aimed at Radio Caroline. The amendments proposed will make it unlawful for any foreign ship on the high seas to broadcast to the United Kingdom. It will enable the police, the Army, Customs officers and anyone who is authorised by the Secretary of State to board and seize these foreign ships and to seize their documents..... I realise that the Home Office regards Radio Caroline as a maddening wasp and is infuriated that its attempts over the years to swat it have failed. However, surely this station is not a wasp but a common or garden cabbage white. Why break a butterfly upon the wheel? Why run the risk of an embarrassing diplomatic confrontation? That could perfectly well happen if the vessel turned out to be under an American flag.*

Replying in the debate for the Government Home Office Minister Earl Ferrers said :-

*... Lord Annan said they [pirate radios] were not wasps that should be swatted but just harmless butterflies. He said it was absurd to send the Navy, the Customs and Uncle Tom Cobley and all after these radio stations. The provisions on pirate radio are justified and necessary. The radio spectrum is a valuable resource and has to be carefully planned. Unauthorised transmissions have put the safety of life channels at risk and at times of emergency could cost lives. Moreover by interfering with the wider variety of channels they could also reduce listener choice.*

*The provisions of the Bill are in accordance with international law. The United Nations Law of the Sea Convention allows states to act against ships on the high seas of any nationality, or none, if broadcasts from them can be received in their territory or cause interference. Of course the powers will be exercised with moderation and restraint in the case of foreign-flag flying vessels to avoid the diplomatic controversy which the noble Lord fears.*

## International reaction

The fact that the United Nations Convention on the Law of the Sea was not yet in force and that, in common with most other European countries, Britain was not even a signatory to it was not disclosed by Earl Ferrers during his speech.

The International Chamber of Shipping wrote to the Home Office on 18th July 1990 expressing its concern over the proposed change to British law regarding the boarding of foreign registered ships in international waters, saying " May we ask that Her Majesty's Government look again at the international implications of this extension of UK law to include foreign flag ships operating on the high seas, particularly in relation to article 22 of the Geneva Convention on the High Seas 1958 and suggest that, in the circumstances, more restricted powers of search and arrest might be considered appropriate."

Lord Monson spoke in the House of Lords on 25th July 1990 about the proposed amendment to the Marine etc. Broadcasting (Offences) Act 1967:-

*Clause 159 and its associated Schedule 14 were introduced into the Bill at a late stage in the other place (i.e. the House of Commons). Honourable members had little time to absorb or debate its full and alarming implications.*

*It is an open secret that the purpose of Clause 159 is to smash Radio Caroline. This is a so called pirate radio station which has been harmlessly operating for 26 years. The material it broadcasts may not be my cup of tea or that of most members of this Committee. However, it is perfectly innocuous and gives enormous pleasure to a large number of people in London and south east England. They are mainly respectable, middle aged people who tend to have listened to the station since it opened in the mid 1960s.*

*Clause 159 has alarming implications for international law - in particular maritime law - and for civil liberties. The powers which Her Majesty's Government are seeking against Radio Caroline are very much greater than the powers which they have, in the past, sought and obtained against hijackers, smugglers and drug traffickers.*

Speaking in the same debate Lord Annan picked up on the boarding powers being sought in the Bill:-

*Section 7A goes far beyond any other statute such as the Drug Trafficking Offences Act 1986 in infringing the principle of extraterritoriality. However, there is much more to it than that. Section 7A empowers servants of the Crown to seize property and detain persons, to require the crew to produce documents and - this is the most extraordinary and reprehensible - to grant officials immunity who are engaged in search and seizure.*

After questioning the assertion made by Earl Ferrers in an earlier debate that these provisions were in accordance with international law and pointing out that it was impossible for the Government to rely on the provisions of the United Nations Convention on the Law of the Sea, because Britain was not a signatory to that document, Lord Annan went on:-

*...I am not pleading for an illegal radio station. Like the noble Lord, Lord Monson, from the voluminous mail I receive I am in no doubt that there are many people who listen to and enjoy that radio station. No doubt it is popular, but that is not my purpose. My purpose is to bring home to the Government and to the public that the Government are about to pass a clause which is illegal in international law and an affront to those who care about the principles of justice.*

Replying for the Government Earl Ferrers refuted the points raised by Lords Monson and Annan:-

*Lord Monson said that what pirate stations do is innocuous. I totally disagree. I do not think it is innocuous. The reality is quite different. The radio spectrum is a valuable natural resource. Its use has to be carefully planned and regulated, especially with the explosive growth in the use of radio for communications and for broadcasting.*

*Lord Annan said that this provision will offend against international comity. I say to the noble Lord that pirate radio stations often offend against and infringe the law of the country. Why do they position themselves just outside territorial waters and use British frequencies if it is not to avoid British law?*

The debate continued with Earl Ferrers rehearsing again the arguments about interference allegedly caused by offshore stations to other communications and restated the Government's view that the proposed clauses in the Bill were in accordance with international law, notwithstanding the fact that the United Nations Convention on the Law of the Sea had not been ratified by Britain.

After an adjournment for two days the House of Lords Committee returned to the Broadcasting Bill to consider some amendments proposed by Lord Monson which would have had the effect of diluting the Government's "draconian" proposals. However, Lord Monson's amendments were defeated by 93 votes to 29.

## Registration of the *Ross Revenge*

In June 1990 solicitors Richards Butler, acting for Radio Caroline, wrote to the Department of Trade, the owners of the *Landward* and the Dutch Embassy in London advising that their clients were seeking compensation for actions taken against the *Ross Revenge* in August 1989. The Dutch Embassy was informed that its nationals had committed acts of assault (including indecent assault), battery and false imprisonment against individuals on board the *Ross Revenge* and acts of trespass and removal of goods against the vessel's owners, Grothan Steamship Co. Inc.

However, in July 1990 information came to light which cast doubt about the validity of the registration of the *Ross Revenge* in Panama. The solicitors, Richards Butler, preparing legal action on behalf of Radio Caroline and certain crew members following the August 1989 raid undertook to investigate and try to establish the true position.

By the end of October 1990 Richards Butler had informed the Caroline Legal Fund (which had been formed to meet legal costs on behalf of Radio Caroline

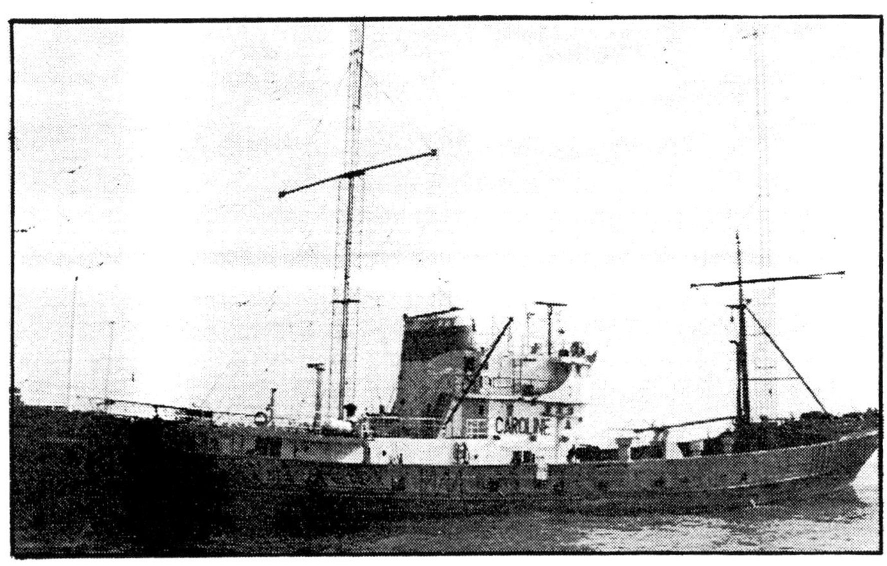


The 'Ross Revenge' in June 1990

after the raid) that having met with representatives of the Panamanian Government they felt that any allegations that the *Ross Revenge* was not registered could be defended, but at considerable cost.

At the same time Richards Butler had agrees to take on, as a test case, a claim for damages by a crew member, Neil Gates, using Legal aid funding. The Caroline Legal Fund decided in view of the high cost of any other legal action to let this individual test case proceed and paid all outstanding costs incurred to date by Richards Butler.

Meanwhile various supporters of Radio Caroline had been making their own enquiries into the registration status of the *Ross Revenge* with representatives of the Panamanian Government in Britain, the USA and in Panama itself. These enquiries produced the astonishing response that the *Ross Revenge* was not registered and that any certificate indicating that she was had not been issued correctly. Furthermore the Panamanian Government indicated that if broadcasting resumed from the *Ross Revenge* it would as the British Government to take measures to ensure that the radio ship was silenced for good.

The various enquiries made of Panamanian Government Departments then triggered an internal investigation in Panama into the circumstances surrounding the registration of the *Ross Revenge*. Because of the complicated way in which the vessel's registration had been organised in 1982 some doubt was cast on its authenticity. The 'President' of Grothan Steamship Lines Inc. (the registered owner of the *Ross Revenge*), Zosimo Guardia Varela, even offered to sell information to the inquiry team because the Panamanian investigation was spreading to other affairs with which he was involved.

The results of the Panamanian investigation became known at the beginning of January 1991, confirming all that had previously been gleaned by various means during the preceding months. The *Ross Revenge* had been deleted from the Panamanian Shipping Register by Resolution 603-04-04-ALCN dated 12th January 1987. This was in compliance with Article 30, No. 2665 of the Radio Communication Regulations which had been introduced prohibiting unauthorised broadcasting from the high seas by Panamanian registered vessels.

Confirmation that the *Ross Revenge* was not correctly registered in Panama now meant that with the provisions of the Broadcasting Act having come into force on 1st January 1991, Radio Caroline had no choice but to stay off the air.

Although silent the *Ross Revenge* remained at sea, but supplying the ship became a major problem in view of the legal uncertainties. Ultimately for the safety and comfort of those on board an agreement was entered into with the DTI about supplying the *Ross Revenge* from British ports, the so-called 'Section 7 Truce'.

In order to achieve this a support organisation - known as the *Ross Revenge* Support Group (RRSG) - was established in January 1991 initially as an arm of the Caroline Movement. Before it could start delivering supplies to the *Ross Revenge* however, legal advice was obtained on such an undertaking. That advice indicated that a written undertaking should be supplied by the owners of the *Ross Revenge* to the DTI that although at sea the ship would not be involved in broadcasting in contravention of the British law. The situation would of course change if the *Ross Revenge* and Radio Caroline were granted registration and licences to broadcast legally by any (Third World) country.

On 12th February 1991 Richards Butler wrote to the DTI on behalf of Grothan Steamship Lines Inc. giving an assurance that the *Ross Revenge* would not be used for illegal broadcasting and on that basis the RRSG was able to officially arrange tendering and supply facilities for the ship.

Meanwhile, in April 1991 Richards Butler advised that in view of the information now available to them about the registration of the *Ross Revenge* they felt that the test case involving Neil Gates should be pursued through the Dutch legal system, but the cost was likely to be considerable as no legal aid facilities would be available. Neither the Caroline Legal Fund or Neil Gates had any prospect of being able to provide finance for such an action in Holland and therefore the prospect of any legal action on behalf of either Radio Caroline, the crew or owners of the *Ross Revenge* arising from the August 1989 raid appeared to be at an end.

## Radio Caroline Ltd.

*A plan was announced at the beginning of August 1990 by a group calling itself Radio Caroline Ltd. to apply to the new Radio Authority (being created under the Broadcasting Bill to replace the IBA) for a national radio licence. A press release issued by the group made it clear that they had no involvement with the offshore Radio Caroline.*

*Radio Caroline Ltd. which had been formed three years earlier by a group of community radio enthusiasts proposed a rock/AOR format. A unique concept put forward by the group, under the leadership of Richard Hilton, was to use profits from the national station to other fund local radio stations through a charitable trust.*

RADIO 558
CAROLINE
MUSIC THROUGH THE 90's

## Spectrum Radio begins transmissions

Spectrum Radio eventually started official transmissions on both 990kHz and 558kHz on 25th June 1990 and at 2.00pm that afternoon Radio Caroline's signal began to be badly affected by a loud buzzing noise. Shortly afterwards Radio Caroline announced that it would be going off the air for transmitter and aerial work to be carried out and the station then closed at 2.30pm.

Radio Caroline was off the air for some ten days until test transmissions were heard on 558kHz in the early hours of 6th July 1990 and again on 8th July, with reception reports being requested to the Fort Lauderdale address. A carrier signal was also heard on 576kHz on 11th July 1990, but no further test transmissions were heard from the *Ross Revenge* until the end of July 1990 when some short broadcasts of non-stop music were made. Radio Caroline was experiencing enormous operational difficulties at this time anyway and the blotting out of its signal by Spectrum Radio transmissions meant that it was unable to provide any semblance of a regular service either for its listeners or the religious programme sponsors who contributed the bulk of the station's financial income.

## "Remember the Raid"

Apart from these occasional test broadcasts Radio Caroline's transmitters remained virtually silent after 25th June 1990, but at 3.00pm on 19th August the station opened again on 558kHz, for an hour and a half long special programme, "Remember the Raid", dedicated to everyone who was on board the *Ross Revenge* on that date in 1989 when the radio ship had been raided and silenced by the Dutch and British authorities. The station played some album tracks from its Top 500 list and shortly after 4.00pm paid tribute to those who had been on board in 1989:-

*The current broadcasting crew of the MV 'Ross Revenge', Rico, Chris Adams, Tony Palmer, Chris Frisco, Louise Roberts and myself, Nick Jackson, would like to dedicate this 'Remember the Raid' broadcast to those who were on board on Saturday the 19th August 1989, to Dave Asher, Caroline Martin, Dave Richards, Tony Kirk, Nigel Harris, Neil Gates, Melanie McArthur, Bruce Munroe, Chris Kennedy, Andy Bradgate, Arie and Eddie and last but by no means least, Peter Chicago.*

After playing a few more album tracks the special broadcast ended at 4.30pm and the transmitters on board the *Ross Revenge* remained silent for another three weeks. Then, quite suddenly, at 6.00pm on 10th September 1990 regular transmissions recommenced from Radio Caroline on 558kHz, although the signal still suffered interference from Spectrum Radio's broadcasts. For a few days Radio Caroline just operated a twelve hour overnight service, but on the afternoon of 14th September the transmitter was switched on at 2.00pm for DJ Ricky Jones to announce that the *Ross Revenge* was being circled by a vessel, the *Landward*, and DTI officials on board were taking photographs of the radio ship. After about four and a half hours in the vicinity of the *Ross Revenge* the *Landward* sailed away, but anxious DJs, fearing another possible raid on the radio ship, kept Radio Caroline's transmitter on air throughout that night in case they needed to make emergency announcements for assistance.

Nothing happened as a result of the *Landward's* visit that day, but on 16th September 1990 during the overnight transmissions a message was broadcast every half hour saying that Radio Caroline would be voluntarily closing down at midnight to enable 'positive steps' to be taken for the station to continue in the long term.

The return to 558kHz had caused a further rift within the Caroline organisation. Many had expected the station to return on a different frequency (possibly 576kHz) and some staff even refused to return to the *Ross Revenge* until such a change took place. From the listener's point of view reception on 558 was not possible in many areas due to Spectrum Radio's transmissions, but Caroline management felt that there was a principle at stake and they did not want the offshore station to be effectively driven off its frequency by the authorities.

## New frequency

Radio Caroline remained silent for nearly three weeks before returning to the air on 4th October 1990, this time on 819kHz, with intermittent carrier signals and test transmissions containing station identity announcements. In the end the deciding factor to change frequencies had been the need to return to the air the "Viewpoint" sponsored religious programmes, now the station's only source of revenue. This recommenced at 6.00pm that same evening and a full service of Radio Caroline programming started at 6.15am on 6th October 1990. Virtually normal programming continued for ten days, but there were a number of early closedowns and by 16th October transmissions were ending at 6.00pm each evening for technical work to be carried out to try and improve signal strength. The news service was suspended altogether on 20th October because of the extreme difficulties of maintaining a full programme schedule due to the shortage of staff and resources on board the *Ross Revenge.*

## Last broadcast from Caroline in international waters

These severe difficulties in supplying the *Ross Revenge* meant that towards late October and early November 1990 Radio Caroline started to experience more frequent periods off the air due to lack of programme material, spare parts and most importantly fuel for the generators. Even when broadcasts did recommence there was an increased use of continuous music due to problems in staffing the station. However, those DJs who were on board did their best to try and maintain as normal a service as possible given the inhospitable weather and grim working conditions.

Neil Gates, who despite his earlier misgivings about Radio Caroline's management, had returned to the *Ross Revenge* during October 1990 presented his programme from 9.35pm on 4th November 1990, after "Viewpoint" had finished. The station closed as usual just after 1.00am on 5th November 1990 and although no one knew it at the time that was to be the final programme broadcast by Radio Caroline from its offshore base in international waters.

At 6.15am on 6th November 1990 a carrier signal was heard on 819kHz, but no broadcasts from Radio Caroline took place and the transmitter was finally switched off at 8.47am. A severe shortage of fuel on board the *Ross Revenge* meant that literally every available drop was needed to keep the generator functioning just to provide lighting on board the ship - none could be spared to run the transmitter or other broadcasting equipment.

## Broadcasting Bill becomes law

The Broadcasting Bill was debated further in the House of Lords in October 1990 when Lord Monson again made some attempts to dilute the provisions relating to the boarding and searching of ships in international waters. He eventually elicited the following assurance from Earl Ferrers on behalf of the Government:-

*The powers will be exercised with moderation and restraint. We intend to consult the flag state, where there is one, to ensure that it does not object before we act against a foreign flag vessel. Stateless vessels of course are not under the diplomatic protection of any government when on the high seas. Any force used will be kept to a minimum.*

*The powers are modelled on articles 109 and 110 of the United Nations Convention on the Law of the Sea. The noble Lord is perfectly right that the United Kingdom has not yet become a party to that Convention. However, that is for reasons totally unconnected with radio. The exercise of the powers will be totally in accordance with international law. That does not depend on the Convention coming into force or the United Kingdom becoming a party to it.*

After the debate the Lords passed the Broadcasting Bill and returned it to the House of Commons where its received its Final Reading. The Bill received the Royal Assent on 1st November 1990 and its provisions, including the infamous amendment to the Marine etc. Broadcasting (Offences) Act, came into effect on 1st January 1991.

Almost immediately protests were made in the European Parliament against the Broadcasting Act's provisions giving British authorities extensive powers to board foreign ships in international waters.

On 29th November 1990 a question was tabled in the European Parliament by Mme Elmalan, of the French left wing Groupe Coalition des Gauches, questioning British authority to stop and search foreign ships in international waters. A further attempt was made in the European Parliament just before

Christmas 1990 to challenge the validity of the Broadcasting Act's amendment to the Marine etc. Broadcasting (Offences) Act, involving the boarding of foreign registered ships in international waters. This time the request was placed by the French Green Party which stated; "we may not want to listen to Radio Caroline, but everyone has a right to listen to Radio Caroline."

## *Ross Revenge* abandoned

With Radio Caroline now off the air and the supply of fuel dangerously low the *Ross Revenge* suffered a major power failure at the end of November 1990 which left the vessel without the facility to illuminate navigation lights at night- a strict requirement under international maritime regulations. There were no cooking or heating facilities on the ship either and, with the main generator having failed, a small deck-mounted petrol engine had to be brought into use. This was to provide navigational lights as well as some limited internal lighting and power because the Trinity House authorities had warned the crew of the *Ross Revenge* that the vessel must be lit at night.

However, on 10th December 1990 this petrol generator was damaged during a Force 10 storm and despite the efforts of the crew to relocate it from the open deck to a more sheltered position on the bridge it repeatedly failed again. An added problem was that barrels of petrol stored on deck to fuel the generator had been washed overboard during the storm, so once again the *Ross Revenge* was left without any source of lighting or power.

Faced with this desperate situation the crew called Radio Caroline's landbased organisers who alerted Dover Coastguard to the *Ross Revenge's* plight. The Coastguards madc contact with the radio ship on the emergency channel and at 10.30pm on 10th December 1990 were informed by the crew that the *Ross Revenge* had only three hours of fuel supply left. Ramsgate lifeboat was alerted by the Coastguards, but advised that because of the Force 9/10 gales and the number of sandbanks in the vicinity of the South Falls Head they would be unable to reach the radio ship.

**Dramatic airlift from ship in Force 10 gale**

Rescue ends in disaster for Caroline

**Caroline trio are winched to safety**

At 11.00pm the Air Sea Rescue Service sent a Sea King helicopter to the *Ross Revenge* and by 11.45pm it had succeeded in rescuing the three crew members from the radio ship - Richard Marks (Rico), Christopher James Masson (Chris Andrews) and Caroline Cooke (Caroline Martin). They were flown to RAF Manston in Kent and briefly questioned by police before being allowed home.

Meanwhile, with the radio ship abandoned and having no navigation lights a DTI vessel came alongside and shone its searchlights on the *Ross Revenge* to make it visible to passing shipping. The following morning, 11th December 1990, a Trinity House vessel, *Partician,* visited the *Ross Revenge* and her crew boarded the un-manned radio ship to check its condition.

That same day Dover Coastguard issued a general report to shipping in the area that the *Ross Revenge* was abandoned, but at anchor, in a position 15 miles off Margate. North Foreland Radio and other coastal radio stations also issued hourly warnings to local shipping advising of the *Ross Revenge's* position and the fact that she was unlit and un-manned.

## Re-claimed

With their radio ship abandoned on the high seas and the danger increasing by the hour that she would be seized by the authorities, Radio Caroline's land-based staff made strenuous efforts to reclaim the *Ross Revenge*. A tender was chartered on 11th December 1990, but after two hours of attempting to transfer people aboard the radio ship it was forced to abandon the operation due to the mountainous seas and the effects of exposure being experienced by the exhausted crew.

These stormy conditions lasted for a few days preventing any further boarding attempts either by the authorities or by Radio Caroline staff themselves and the *Ross Revenge* had to be left to the mercy of the elements. Sea conditions had improved marginally by 14th December 1990 and at about 11.00am station engineer Peter Chicago, and DJ Richard Marks (Rico) successfully reclaimed the *Ross Revenge* for Radio Caroline, just hours ahead of two foreign tugs which were on their way to take the abandoned ship for salvage. This exercise had been extremely perilous and on more than one occasion nearly resulted in the two men capsizing their rubber dinghy. Had this happened, given the atrocious weather conditions, it would almost certainly have resulted in them drowning.

## Truce

A condition of Radio Caroline staff being allowed to re-board the *Ross Revenge* and for the ship to be openly supplied from Ramsgate was an extraordinary undertaking to the authorities that no attempt would be made to recommence broadcasts from the vessel. This unprecedented agreement was entered into against a background of firm information that the British authorities intended to use their new powers under the Broadcasting Act (which was due to come into effect on 1st January 1991) to forcibly board the ship using military personnel and prevent it transmitting radio programmes. A Radio Caroline spokesman claimed that they even had knowledge of a date for the proposed raid - 5th January 1991 and therefore the truce with the DTI had been agreed to forestall such hostile action.

Having reclaimed the ship and entered into this agreement with the authorities, Peter Chicago and other crew members set about clearing up the *Ross Revenge,* repairing the main generator and providing lighting once again both inside and on various positions outside for navigational purposes.

The near devastating loss of the *Ross Revenge* and the truce with the authorities to keep the transmitter silent meant that there was no money coming in to the Radio Caroline organisation from either advertising or sponsorship. In February 1991 new group was established to provide support for the skeleton crew on board the radio ship and to raise finance for essential maintenance works, including the purchase of a new, reliable generator. The group, known as the *Ross Revenge* Support Group, managed to raise sufficient funding from donations and the sale of memorabilia to purchase a 10kva Petter generator, which was delivered to the radio ship at the end of April 1991.

### *ROSS REVENGE* SUPPORT GROUP (RRSG)

*The aims of the RRSG on its formation in February 1991 were:*

- To keep the *Ross Revenge* at sea and to render her safe and sound
- To ensure that her volunteer crew live in a safe and comfortable environment
- To improve the condition of the ship after the last three years of unavoidable neglect. These improvements are to the ship's marine capability and not to her ability to broadcast
- To keep the name of Caroline in the public eye and to widely state her case for being allowed to continue
- To counter any threat by appropriate legal action
- To research ways that Caroline might return to the air without breaking any law, nor kow-towing to the authorities

## Exploratory talks

On 1st October 1990 a meeting took place between representatives of the Caroline Movement listeners' supporters group and official of the Department of Trade and Industry to explore the views of the authorities about the possibility of Radio Caroline being granted a licence to broadcast. The management of Radio Caroline were not represented at the meeting nor did they wish to indicate to the authorities that the station wished to become part of the British landbased radio system. However, the supporter's group felt they should at least explore that possibility to see what was and was not feasible in the light of the new powers contained in the Broadcasting Act which made it virtually impossible for Radio Caroline to continue broadcasting from its offshore base.

From its perspective the DTI indicated that the meeting was able to take place only because Radio Caroline was off the air at that time. The DTI could see no problem with Radio Caroline applying for a landbased licence, but stresses that it would have to compete with other groups. A number of national radio licences were to be advertised in the near future by the IBA or its successor body, the Radio Authority (which had been established under the Broadcasting Act) , but the initiative would have to come from Radio Caroline - the station could not expect to be 'granted' a licence simply because it had been operating offshore for twenty six years.

The meeting also tentatively explored Radio Caroline's position regarding the granting of short-term special events licences (or Restricted Service Licences as they became known) and was told again in principle that there would be no fundamental objection from the authorities to the station making such an application.

Following this meeting a number of those present representing the Caroline Movement decided that they needed to "safeguard the situation" so that if necessary Radio Caroline could be in a position to apply for a landbased licence. This action was taken without agreement from those involved with operating the offshore station at the time. The organisation, calling itself Radio Caroline (UK) Ltd., announced in December 1990 that it would submit an application for a licence to establish a local landbased station in Kent or Essex and, if successful, would employ many staff from the offshore station.

As part of their plans they also announced that a trust would be established to refit the *Ross Revenge* and use her as the local station's broadcasting base. Radio Caroline's founder and owner, Ronan O'Rahilly dismissed the plan, however, stating that the *Ross Revenge* would be kept at sea and as "the only free station on earth" he was not prepared to sell out to the breakaway group.

During 1989 and 1990 Radio Caroline had faced an onslaught of tactics by various authorities to silence the station - the raid on the *Ross Revenge* by the Dutch and British authorities, the blotting out of its signal by the deliberate allocation of the same frequency to a new ILR station in London, constant harassment from the authorities to thwart its tendering and supply lines and, most significant of all, the measures added at a late stage to the Broadcasting Bill which were specifically aimed against the station.

## Loophole in Broadcasting Act

Meanwhile, Radio Caroline was exploring an apparent loophole in the 1990 Broadcasting Act, which seemed to provide the only means by which an offshore radio station could now exist without fear of the Act's draconian powers of boarding and seizure being implemented.

This loophole theoretically allowed for a foreign country to licence both the ship and a radio station broadcasting from it, then both could be considered as part of that nation's broadcasting system and therefore a legal operation. Radio Caroline set about approaching many Third World countries offering its ship and her radio transmitting facilities as the base from which they could establish an external broadcasting service. Quite why any country should want to do this off the coast of Britain remained unclear, but the theoretical possibility of finding yet another loophole in legislation designed to stop the station broadcasting remained an exciting challenge for those behind Radio Caroline.

Exploratory talks were in fact held between consultants acting for Radio Caroline and the Government of Liberia, which was prepared to grant the *Ross Revenge* registration and a broadcasting licence, enabling it to operate quite legally under the provisions of the Broadcasting Act.

The Liberian Government was reported to be asking £100,000 per annum, for the licence, but wanted firm evidence that any radio station on board the *Ross Revenge* would be able to broadcast to a consistent technical standard and be a commercially viable operation. This would have involved the installation of a new transmitter and aerial mast on the ship, renewing the navigational and marine equipment such as the anchor and fuel supply tanks, and establishing a London based office with a full marketing staff to sell airtime on the station.

Although legal advice was taken by the Caroline management and the proposal appeared to be within the new law, the asking price for the licence and the cost of meeting the technical and marketing conditions attaching to it were thought to be too high and the proposal was not pursued.

## Harp Larger Award

On 21st February 1991 brewers Harp Larger awarded their "Harp Beat Rock Gazetteer" to Walton-on-the-Naze Lifeboat to commemorate the work of the lifeboat station in connection with various emergencies involving the 60's offshore stations. The presentation to RNLI Secretary Philip Oxley was made on behalf of Harp Larger by ex- Radio England and Caroline South DJ Johnnie Walker and ex-Radio London DJ John Peel. Also present were Radio Caroline's founder, Ronan O'Rahilly, DJ Tom Anderson and ex-Caroline staff from local ILR station Mellow Radio.

A former Coxswain of the Walton Lifeboat, Frank Bloom was interviewed on local television after the presentation and refuted some of the arguments against the offshore stations which had been put forward at the time by various authorities:-

*They used to say that while we were looking after them other ships would be in trouble, but I don't believe that. I think it was purely officialdom.....The lifeboat station should be very honoured, that's what it's for. The [lifeboat] station did a lot of work, now it is recognised, but at the time we were the baddies helping the radio ships.*

## Radio Monique Court Case

At the beginning of March 1991 a number of people appeared in court in Belgium charged with misappropriation of funds belonging to a magazine, *Topics*. This magazine, which had been launched in 1983 was published by a company called Editop, who had invested more than three million Belgian Francs into the project.

The driving force and main investor behind the magazine was Dutchman Edward Heerema, son of one of the original investors in the Radio/TV Noordzee

## BBC2 documentary

*BBC2 carried a special documentary programme in its "Arena" series on 1st March 1991. The documentary was produced by Bob Geldof's Planet Pictures Company and featured interviews with people involved in the launch of Radio Caroline in 1964 - Ronan O'Rahilly, Ian Ross, Jocelyn Stevens and Chris Moore. Allan Crawford also spoke about Radio Atlanta and the rivalry with Caroline while Philip Soloman was interviewed about his involvement with Radio Caroline in the last few years of its time on the air in the 1960's*

*The later history of Radio Caroline from its return in 1972 to the boarding in 1989 was covered very briefly - contrary to what was originally planned by the production company. The BBC had ordered last minute cuts to this later history after a warning from the DTI about possible offences under the Marine etc. Broadcasting (Offences) Act 1967 if contemporary information about Radio Caroline was broadcast.*

project in 1964 (see Chapter 9). *Topics* magazine's editorial policy was to put forward right wing views, strongly defending such concepts as the free market economy.

In 1987 the publishing company, Editop had gone bankrupt and this court case was the result of investigations arising from that incident. Nine people including the managing Editor and Chief Editor of *Topics* magazine were charged with misappropriating the company's funds. It transpired that over 17 million Belgian Francs belonging to Editop had been diverted to finance Radio Monique, from its offshore base on the *Ross Revenge* and later as a landbased pirate.

When judgement in the case was given at the end of April 1991 five of the defendants were found guilty. The Managing Editor of *Topics* was given an eighteen month suspended prison sentence, the Chief Editor a two year sentence (with a requirement that he must serve nine months), and two other directors were given sentences of three years, with requirements that they must each serve one year in prison. Another defendant was given a six month sentence and fined 30,000 Belgian Francs (£500), but Edward Hereema was acquitted on all charges.

## Caroline on satellite

With its ship lying silent and negotiations for a 'Third World' licence proving unfruitful it was essential that the Radio Caroline Organisation found some alternative way of keeping the station alive. To the rescue in March 1991 came a former Radio Caroline and RNI DJ of the 60's and 70's - Chris Carey ( known in his offshore days as Spangles Muldoon), now a highly successful businessman had also been heavily involved with the Irish landbased pirate Radio Nova and its satellite successor. Radio Nova's broadcasts via the Astra satellite had closed a few weeks earlier, but Carey's contract with the satellite company was still in force and airtime had been paid for in advance until the end of May 1991. Radio Caroline was offered free use of this available airtime by Chris Carey as well as studio facilities at his Radio Nova premises in Camberley, Surrey.

The Caroline Organisation accepted Chris Carey's offer and continuous music, with the occasional Radio Caroline jingle, was aired as a test broadcast from 26th March 1991. Full programming on this satellite service started on Easter Sunday, 31st March 1991 between 10.00am and 6.00pm - Radio Caroline's official 27th Birthday. Most programmes were taped in a temporary studio by a team of Radio Caroline DJs, but some were presented live from the former Radio Nova premises at Camberley. Gradually over the following few days transmission hours increased to 7.00am-12 midnight, but some of this airtime was taken up by Chris Carey's other satellite station - Club Music - an evening service for night clubs and discos. The financially lucrative religious programmes formerly heard on "Viewpoint" from the *Ross Revenge* were also transmitted on the new satellite service under the umbrella title "Insight 738".

An innovation for Radio Caroline, not possible in its offshore days, was the introduction of a phone-in programme, "Forum", during which listeners could telephone the station and talk live on air about programming and other issues.

Radio Caroline's programmes continued to be broadcast in this way for just less than two weeks, but on 12th April 1991 announcements were carried throughout the day to the effect that the satellite based service would close at midnight and the final "Forum" phone-in programme turned into a major, sometimes acrimonious, debate about the station's future.

Chris Carey phoned from his yacht in Spain to say that Radio Caroline no longer needed to operate from its traditional offshore base because this means of broadcasting had outlived its original objective - breaking the monopoly of the BBC and Radio Luxembourg. Carey then informed listeners of the reason behind the sudden closure of the satellite service. The authorities, he said, had told him that unless the *Ross Revenge* was brought in from its anchorage, Radio Caroline programmes could not continue to be broadcast via satellite. He went on to say "We decided that the best thing to do was to close down tonight while you could say goodnight properly. If you don't, the plug will be pulled in the middle of your programme."

Radio Caroline's long serving engineer, Peter Chicago, then phoned the programme to explain his, and Radio Caroline's position:-

*I am saying in a very clear way that the Radio Caroline Management wants to keep the Radio Caroline station on the air. No we're exploring various different possibilities that would enable us to do that and we're looking for a way which is legal. We're not looking to break the law and go back on air if we can find a legal way of broadcasting from the high seas at the position where the 'Ross Revenge' is anchored at the moment. If we can find a legal way of doing that we will.*

*Obviously with that in mind we don't want to move the ship from its present position, not without a clear and successful alternative available...........To me the key point in a lot of these discussions is why did we keep the boat out at sea and why do we insist on keeping it out there? I think very clearly that the reason that we want to keep the boat out at sea is because it is the only particular symbol that identifies Caroline.*

*Any studio anywhere in England could assemble a group of ex-Caroline DJs and it could call itself Radio Caroline, but it wouldn't really be the heart of what the radio station's been about. Radio Invicta at one point was staffed entirely by ex-Caroline DJs, but Radio Invicta was never Radio Caroline. Contact Radio in France where again every disc jockey is an ex-Caroline DJ, but if you listen to Contact it is not Caroline.*

*I am just saying to the listeners that if you want a radio station that comes from Camberley, that comes from Innovation House, then call it anything else, but it is not Caroline and it hasn't sounded like Caroline..... I believe its carrying the name of Caroline under false pretences and as somebody that's very much part of Caroline, I don't want to see this pretence continue.....Although I thank Chris (Carey) for the offer and I am sure that the offer was well meant I quite frankly wish that the project had never gone ahead in the first place.*

After this heated debate Radio Caroline programmes on the Astra satellite service closed at midnight, but controversy continued about the real reason why the service had ceased so abruptly. Radio Caroline claimed that Chris Carey was attempting to take over the station, replacing Caroline taped programmes with his own ex-Radio Nova DJs, while the DTI denied that there had been any discussions with Chris Carey or pressure from them for the *Ross Revenge* to be brought into port.

## How Satellite Radio Works

*On satellite broadcast services more bandwidth is available than on conventional, terrestrial services. By employing advanced digital technology up to nine sound channels can be transmitted with every television picture channel, giving scope for dozens of radio stations to broadcast. The major drawback at present is that receiving equipment is generally confined to the television set linked to the satellite decoder or to a hi-fi system in turn itself linked to that set. In other words it is not portable, although manufacturers are working on solving this problem.*

*The channels used for satellite radio services are known as 'sub-carriers' and each is broadcast on a different frequency, usually grouped in pairs for stereo transmission purposes. The primary sub-carrier and the first pair of secondary sub-carriers are generally used to carry the television sound in mono and stereo respectively, but this leaves six sub-carriers per television channel for radio services. It is therefore possible to have six mono or three stereo radio stations (or a combination of either) for each satellite television channel.*

## Meeting with Radio Authority

A further meeting was held in June 1991 between the DTI, the new Radio Authority and this time representatives of Radio Caroline (including solicitors Richards Butler) as well as the Caroline Movement supporters group. The Director of the Radio Communications Agency at the DTI, Barry Maxwell, confirmed to those present that the Agency had no objection to Radio Caroline broadcasting, under licence, from the *Ross Revenge*. David Vick, Head of Development at the Radio Authority, confirmed that Radio Caroline could apply for an advertised licence, as could any organisation, the only restriction being that no one involved in such application had been prosecuted under the Wireless Telegraphy Act 1949, or the Marine etc. Broadcasting (Offences) Act 1967 within the last five years.

Any application would need to demonstrate a need for the type of service they proposed to provide and also produce a business plan with evidence of the investment of funds for the project. The Radio Authority expressed satisfaction with Caroline's format and the use of the *Ross Revenge* as a base from which to transmit, subject to its equipment meeting the required technical specifications. They also indicated that a licence was expected to be advertised by Spring 1992 for a London station using the 990kHz frequency and also outlined the arrangements for the station applying for 28 day Restricted Service Licences (RSL).

## Shortwave outlets

Another outlet for Radio Caroline's programmes was found in July 1991, via Al Weiner's Radio New York International shortwave service. A series of half hour taped programmes outlining the history of Radio Caroline were presented during RNYI's output over the powerful 100Kw transmitter of shortwave station World Wide Christian Radio. These programmes were aired on the first, second and fourth Monday of each month.

Further possibilities of utilising shortwave broadcasting facilities were also explored by Radio Caroline in late 1991, using the services of Radio Fax, based in Ireland.

Radio Fax had been founded by a group who had applied for a licence to broadcast from Britain on a shortwave frequency in 1986 and again in 1988. Having been refused such a licence they decided to set up transmitting facilities in Ireland, where the laws were more relaxed and a number of test broadcasts were made in July and August 1988. When the Irish Government passed the Broadcasting and Wireless Telegraphy Act in 1988, effectively outlawing landbased pirate stations, Radio Fax along with most others closed. However a loophole was discovered in the legislation which seemed to permit shortwave transmissions to continue unlicensed and Radio Fax resumed its broadcasts again in April 1991. An offer was made to relay tapes of Radio Caroline programmes from its transmitter base in Ireland, but legal difficulties ultimately prevented this happening as planned. Radio Caroline did, however, arrange for some programmes to be transmitted on shortwave from Ireland later ( see Chapter 29)

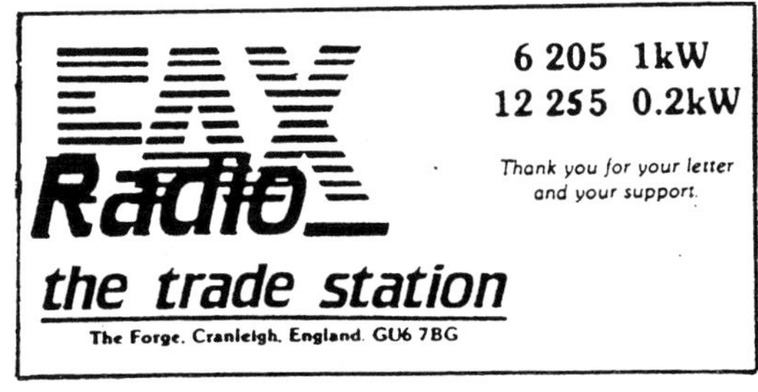


## European concern over Broadcasting Act

Following questions and representations which had been submitted by certain members the European Parliament decided to set up a Commission to examine the legality of the section of Britain's new Broadcasting Act giving powers to the authorities to board foreign registered ships in international waters. A large number of Euro MEPs, particularly French members, also indicated their support for the right of Radio Caroline and the *Ross Revenge* to operate from international waters. Frederic Sevriere, a member of the French Green Party, even spent three weeks aboard the radio ship in August 1991 to learn about the station and prepare a first hand report for his colleagues to assist in their campaign on behalf of Radio Caroline in the European Parliament.

Ronan O' Rahilly commented about Radio Caroline being switched off at a press conference in Calais on 19th October 1991, which had been arranged in connection with the campaign on behalf of the station in the European Parliament:-

*The law they brought in was the result of an action they took in 1989, which you are all aware of, with British and Dutch boarding the ship and basically committing an act of piracy.......The European Members of Parliament are being asked to change that law..........We decided to switch off on January 1st due to the fact that we didn't want them to come over the side a second time and smash up what was left. In the meantime we are negotiating with a third world country and that country will give us a licence to broadcast.*

The campaign, mounted by supporters groups *Offshore Echo's Magazine* and France Radio Club, paid off in an unexpected way at the end of October 1991 when the Municipality of Calais formally gave its support to Radio Caroline "for supporting the right of free expression".

## Helicopter visit

Meanwhile, a caretaker crew of three or four people continued to look after the *Ross Revenge* which remained anchored at sea, but silent, pending a decision on the future of Radio Caroline. While this caretaker crew busied themselves keeping the *Ross Revenge* at sea an unusual incident happened on 6th October 1991. A Sea King helicopter from RAF Manston's Air Sea Rescue Unit arrived and hovered over the bow of the radio ship. Permission was sought, over channel 16, for the helicopter crew to carry out an air sea rescue exercise using the *Ross Revenge*, which would involve landing a man on the deck of the radio ship. Captain of the ship at the time, Steve Conway, gave permission on the clear understanding that it was for rescue training purposes only.

The helicopter pilot then asked if it was safe for them to approach closer to the *Ross Revenge* while the transmitter was on. He was informed that the station was not broadcasting and the transmitter had not been used for many months, but the pilot claimed he was receiving transmissions on 558kHz which he believed were coming from the *Ross Revenge*. The radio ship's crew informed him again that the *Ross Revenge's* transmitters were not broadcasting; that in any event they could not be used because vital parts were missing; that only a caretaker crew was on board and that the transmissions were in fact coming from London's Spectrum Radio. Shortly after receiving this

### Radio Plus

*Radio Plus was a local radio station, based on a ship anchored half a mile off the Dutch coast, which broadcast for two days on 30th and 31st August 1991 (the anniversary of the introduction in 1974 of the Dutch Marine Offences act), in tribute to the offshore stations of the past.*

*The station was housed on the MV 'Dolfijn' (which had been used in 1975 to carry a new anchor to the 'Mi Amigo' after that vessel had drifted inside British territorial waters (see Chapter 19)*

*The first days programme schedule from Radio Plus was:-*

**6.00am Dick de Graaf** *(ex RNI and Mi Amigo)*

**9.00am Joost Verhueven** *(ex RNI and Caroline)*

**12noon Erik Beekman** *(ex Radio 819)*

**2.00pm Arie Swets** *(ex Radio 819) and Hans Knot (Dutch offshore radio supporter, writer and broadcaster)*

**4.00pm Driemaaster** *(recreated from the famous RNI programme of the same name with Dick de Graaf)*

*From 6.00pm a live beach party was broadcast by Radio Plus as well as extracts from the last hours of Radio Veronica and RNI.*

information the helicopter pilot stated that he was aborting the exercise as it was "too dangerous", and the helicopter left the area.

Whether this was really an aborted training exercise as claimed, with the pilot genuinely but mistakenly thinking that the radio station was broadcasting at the time, or possibly a fact finding mission for a future boarding raid it is impossible to say, but the radio ship's caretaker crew remained highly suspicious about their visitors that day.

## *Ross Revenge* grounded

Throughout Tuesday 19th November 1991 there were fierce storms raging in the North Sea with Force 10 winds and heavy seas. Early on the morning of 20th November 1991 Dover Coastguards reported tracking on their radar screens an unidentified ship, drifting southwards. Attempts to contact the ship on the emergency channel had been unsuccessful, but a helicopter in the area at the time eventually located and identified the vessel as the *Ross Revenge*. However, the helicopter pilot was also unable to make radio contact with the silent radio ship.

At 3.50am on 20th November 1991 the *Ross Revenge* hit a sandbank and for the first time the skeleton crew aboard the vessel became aware that the ship had drifted about 15 miles from her anchorage. They immediately contacted Dover Coastguard and were informed that the radio ship had grounded on the notorious Goodwin Sands, graveyard to hundreds of unfortunate ships over the years. A Sea King helicopter from RAF Manston was scrambled and arrived at the stranded radio ship shortly after 4.00am. However, at that time the skeleton crew refused assistance and decided to stay on board the *Ross Revenge,* leaving the helicopter to return to base.

Three quarters of an hour later the Dover Harbour Board tug *Dextrous* was despatched to the Goodwin Sands to take the *Ross Revenge* in tow and at about the same time the Ramsgate lifeboat, *Kenneth Thelwell II*, was launched, making contact with the crew of the radio ship shortly after 5.30am.

The *Ross Revenge* crew were still very reluctant to abandon their vessel and after checking the ship for damage decided to remain on board. The crew ascertained during this inspection that only a small amount of water had entered the vessel through a broken porthole and apart from that the radio ship appeared to be in a satisfactory condition. However, within an hour of that inspection taking place the crew became more and more concerned for their own safety when the *Ross Revenge* suddenly started to list dangerously to starboard as the tide receded.

At 6.25am they reluctantly decided there was no alternative but to abandon ship. Ramsgate lifeboat arrived on the scene shortly afterwards, but itself ran aground on the treacherous sands and Dover lifeboat then had to be launched to assist both stranded ships. Shell supertanker, *Shell Marketer,* which was in the vicinity at the time also stood by to provide assistance if required.

POP PIRATES PLUCKED FROM STRICKEN SHIP

Caroline pirates on rocks

Crew saved from Caroline ship in storm

Caroline crew rescued as ship runs aground

Wrecked pirates rock on

Dramatic rescue as radio ship founders

By 6.57am the RAF helicopter had returned and landed on the stern deck of the *Ross Revenge.* In a ten minute operation the helicopter airlifted the six crew members off in pairs and took them to RAF Manston where they were met by Margate Marine Rescue Unit.

Meanwhile, Ramsgate lifeboat had been re-floated and returned to base and, with the life-saving rescue complete, Dover lifeboat also stood down. The Dover Harbour Board tug *Dextrous* remained on stand-by near the abandoned radio ship, which at that time was reported to be in serious danger of capsizing.

Station Manager Peter Moore, in various press and television interviews throughout the day tried to be as positive as possible about Radio Caroline's future:-

*Whether or not we can get the ship back there is a future. We're currently negotiating with some foreign governments and if we can persuade one of them to give us a broadcasting licence we can go back to sea and broadcast as legally as Radio Luxembourg or stations such as Atlantic 252.*

The *Ross Revenge* managed against all odds to remain upright on the Goodwin Sands, but first attempts to get a line aboard the stranded radio ship later on 20th November 1991 were unsuccessful. It was not until 10.00am the following day that the *Dextrous* managed to land a salvage crew on the *Ross Revenge* and secure tow lines to her. Even with these lines in place it proved difficult to remove the radio ship from her position on the sandbank - an attempt on the evening high tide failed and it was not until the morning tide on 22nd November 1991 that she was eventually pulled free and re-floated.

The *Ross Revenge,* one of only a handful of vessels ever to have been rescued intact from the Goodwin Sands, was then towed to Dover where she arrived late in the afternoon of 22nd November 1991 and was berthed first at the Eastern

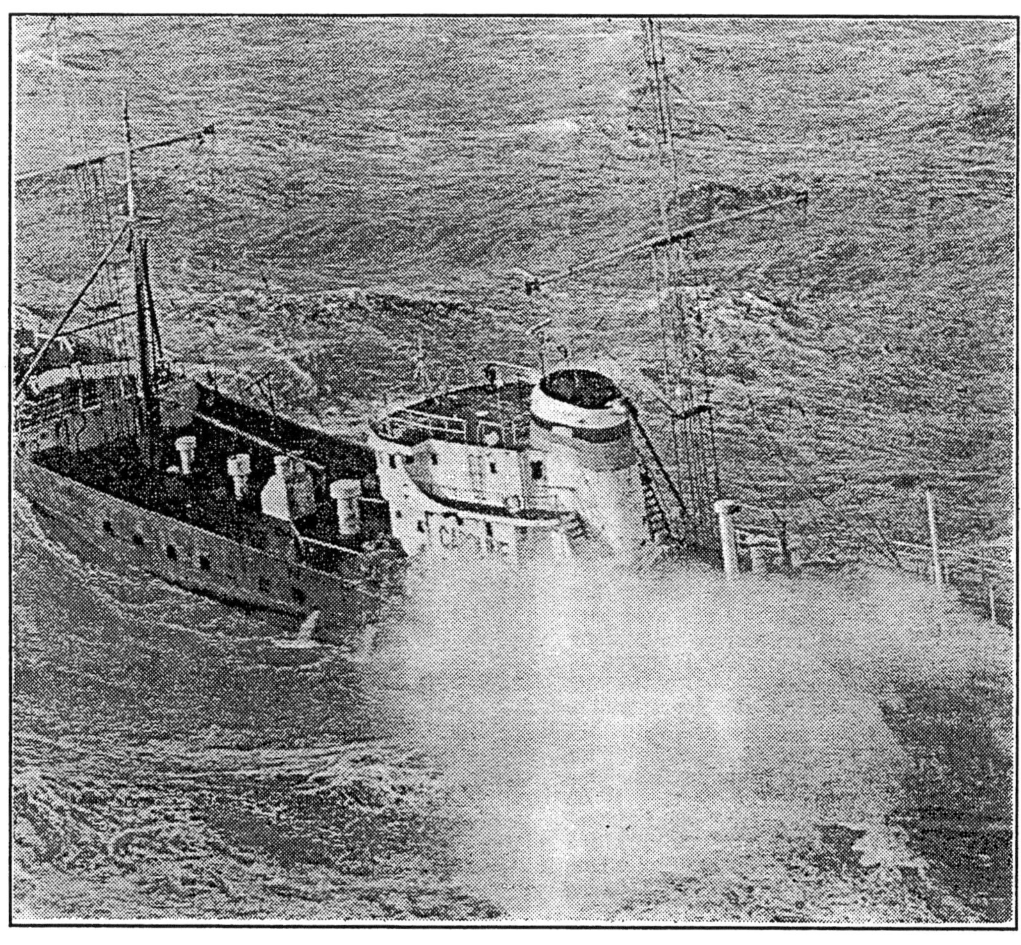

*The 'Ross Revenge' being lashed by heavy seas on the Goodwin Sands*

Docks, later moving to the quieter Western Granville Dock. The ship was immediately impounded by the authorities and, following an inspection by marine surveyors, was declared unseaworthy by the Department of Transport who identified a long list of repairs which would have to be completed before the ship could be released.

Radio Caroline management and the *Ross Revenge* Support Group immediately entered into negotiations with Dover Harbour Board over the salvage costs for recovering the *Ross Revenge*, but with the vessel now in port and under official control it seemed at the time that the life of the most famous station in British offshore radio history had come to an end. A caretaker crew of Caroline personnel were later allowed on board the ship by Dover Harbour authorities.

Irrepressible as ever Radio Caroline did manage to bounce back, although not from an offshore base and not to serve as large an audience as most people would have liked but nevertheless the station's programmes were being broadcast again.

This was achieved less than a week after the *Ross Revenge* had run aground. On 27th November 1991 Radio Caroline's broadcasts returned on satellite using some free air time donated by a Dutch station. This radio station, RNI was operated by Henk de Jong and some other people who had been involved with the original offshore station of that name in the 1970s, using the facilities of the Intel satellite. Radio Caroline programmes were carried on this facility from Monday to Thursday between 9.00 and 10.00pm, with an overnight service on Friday night/Saturday morning.

Another outlet for Radio Caroline was found at Radio 6 in Calais when on 1st December 1991 the local French FM station presented a three hour "Caroline Special", including contributions from some Caroline DJs recorded on board the *Ross Revenge* in Dover Harbour.

Potential audiences which could be attracted by both these outlets were small - satellite radio was in its infancy and attracted relatively few listeners compared to terrestrial stations while the Radio 6 local station was only available in the Calais area, although determined listeners in coastal areas of Kent could also receive the transmissions. However, the importance of these broadcasts at that particular time for Radio Caroline was psychological - the station was still maintaining a presence on the airwaves despite all official attempts over more than twenty seven years to silence it.

## Closure of Radio Luxembourg on 208

Radio Luxembourg finally closed its English language broadcasts on 208m in the medium waveband on 30th December 1991. In a three hour final programme many of the stations former DJs reminisced about the station, which had broadcast to Britain since the mid-1930s (see Chapter 1). The closing announcement was made by Stephen Williams who, as a young announcer, had opened Radio Luxembourg's English Service in 1933. The English Service of Radio Luxembourg did however continue to be broadcast on the Astra Satellite as well as 15350 kHz in the shortwave band.

Radio Luxembourg's English Service had been home to many former offshore radio DJs over the years including:-

*Norman St. John (Radio London), Tommy Vance (Radio London), Paul Burnett (Radio 270), Tony Prince (Caroline North), Paul Kaye (Radio London), Roger Day (Radio England, Caroline South, RNI), Bob Stewart (Caroline North), Duncan Johnson (Radio London), Mark Wesley (Radio Essex, Radio Scotland, RNI), Tony Windsor (Programme Director)( Radio London, Radio 355), Stuart Henry (Radio Scotland), Colin Nicol (Radio Atlanta, Radio Caroline South, Radio England), Alton Andrews (Caroline South), David Lee Stone (Laser 558), Jessie Brandon (Laser 558), Simon Dee (Caroline South), Dave Cash (Radio London), Pete Brady (Radio London), Emperor Rosko (Caroline South), Tony Blackburn (Caroline South, Radio London), John Peel (Radio London), Kenny Everett (Radio London), and Johnnie Walker (Radio England, Caroline South). In addition ex-Radio London Programme Director, Alan Keen, was General Manager of the station for many years.*

# Chapter 27

# Activity off Israel

Returning once again to the Middle East, despite the influx of new DJs to the Voice of Peace at the end of 1988 many did not stay long and the station continued to suffer from a shortage of staff and advertising revenue during much of 1989. A novel programming idea to attract more advertisers to the station was tried in August 1989 when a number of "Anniversary Specials" were aired marking events such as the 12th anniversary of the death of Elvis Presley on 16th August and the 31st birthday of Michael Jackson on 29th August.

By contrast the new Israeli offshore station, Arutz Sheva grew from strength to strength. The station had rapidly established a large audience with its mix of traditional Israeli music and 'positive' talk programmes, equalling Kol Israel's Radio Two service in terms of audience level at many times of the day. Station Manager Shulamit Melamed said: "The message we wish to impart is love for the land, people and faith of Israel. We are consciously gearing our message not only to the religious listener. We are following a middle road, one on which everyone in this nation can feel at ease". Despite its background Shulamit Melamid claimed not to be a mouthpiece for Gush Emunin, saying: "We are not formally or financially linked to the Gush. We are private people. Many of us are Judea and Samaria residents and true we have friends in Gush Emunim, but we are not its voice."

A survey by Telseker in late 1989, after Arutz Sheva had been on the air for just over a year, showed that only 30% of its listeners identified themselves as 'religious', 25% secular and the remaining 45% claimed to be 'traditional'.

To begin with the station had only attracted small, largely religious based advertisers, but once the significant audience levels had been established Arutz Sheva quickly became a recognised advertising medium.

In June 1989 Arutz Sheva, brought its ship, *Hatzvi,* closer to shore, anchoring near the MV *Peace.* Three months later it acquired a new FM transmitter and increased its broadcasting time to 17 hours a day. However, being a station owned and operated by a strongly religious organisation Arutz Sheva did not broadcast at all on Shabbat (dusk on Friday evening until dusk on Saturday) or on religious holidays. In order to ensure that no unauthorised broadcasts were made during these periods engineers cut all power to the transmitter at the start of Shabbat and it was not restored until the following night.

Conditions and rates of pay for those working on the two Israeli offshore stations also contrasted sharply. Each Arutz Sheva DJ was required to stay on board for 10 days a month, not necessarily consecutive days, and received pay ranging from £366 for new recruits, rising to £566 after three months service and reaching £716 after six months with the station. By comparison DJs on the

Voice of Peace received their air fare out to Israel, just a few hundred pounds for a six months tour of duty and, provided they stayed for the whole of that six month period, their return fare back to Britain.

It must be remembered, however, that the Voice of Peace was unlike any other offshore radio station - it existed not primarily to make a profit for its owner, but to be a vehicle for broadcasting his peace messages. In this context it relied heavily on volunteer workers who although professional broadcasters, were prepared to accept low rates of pay because they shared an empathy for the station and its 'peace' objectives.

## Abie Nathan jailed

The Voice of Peace's owner, Abie Nathan, appeared in court on 27th September 1989 on charges arising from his meetings with the PLO Leader, Yasser Arafat. The two men had met on a number of occasions, most recently in Tunis earlier in September 1989. The prosecution was brought because Abie Nathan had contravened a 1986 law prohibiting Israeli citizens from having contact with organisations such as the PLO. Nathan admitted in Court that he had met Arafat and made plans for peace between Israel and the PLO, however, he refused to accept an offer from the Public Prosecutor to reduce the maximum penalty from three years imprisonment to six months of community service in return for a confession of guilt. Abie Nathan told the Court that he undertook community service all year round and "preferred to go to jail protesting against an illegal, barbarous, anti-democratic and imbecile law."

On 2nd October, following a five day Court hearing, Abie Nathan talked on the Voice of Peace about his meetings with Yasser Arafat. The next day he was found guilty of "making forbidden relations with members of a terrorist organisation" and given a fine and a six months term of imprisonment. With some considerable publicity Abie Nathan reported to start his jail sentence on 10th October 1989 and throughout that day the Voice of Peace played music of 'peace and understanding' .

In the absence of Abie Nathan's day-to-day involvement with the offshore station and his frequent appearances on-air to talk about peace, a new programme was launched on 23rd October 1989. "Ma La'asat - Shalom" ("What Shall We Do? - Peace") in which journalists in the Voice of Peace office took part in phone-in discussions with listeners. The programme was relayed from the makeshift landbased studio in Tel Aviv via the mobile telephone link to the MV *Peace* from where it was actually transmitted.

On 8th December 1989 Abie Nathan was visited in prison by a member of the Knesset, Jossi Sarid, offering him an amnesty from his sentence if he confessed on television that his talks with the PLO Leader were a 'mistake'. Abie Nathan refused, saying he had deliberately and consciously entered into discussions with Yasser Arafat to try and bring about a settlement for peace in the Middle East and was prepared to continue his jail sentence rather than rebut what he had done.

Abie Nathan was eventually freed from jail (due to good behaviour) on 9th February 1990, after serving four of his six months' sentence. He told journalists that he would continue working for peace and was even prepared to talk with the PLO leader again - something he did within three months of his release. As a consequence Abie Nathan was arrested again on 15th May 1990 when he returned to Israel and although he was bailed to appear in Court later in the year he said defiantly: "I will go on with the talks with Arafat until there is real peace in the Middle East."

### 'Festivals'

*Throughout the summer of 1990 a series of 'Festivals' were broadcast by the commercially ailing Voice of Peace in another attempt to encourage advertisers to buy airtime on the station. Each day had a different theme - Monday - Twilight Music, Tuesday - 60s and 70s music, Wednesdays - Hebrew comedy, Thursdays - Peace songs, Fridays - Hebrew songs, Saturdays - all hit songs. There were also a number of other specials themed around particular artists such as The Beatles, Abba and the Bee Gees. Additionally there were some programmes relayed live from the beach at Tel Aviv, with competitions for listeners to find bottles buried in the sand. Each bottle contained a prize, usually a voucher to be redeemed at Abie Nathan's restaurant in Tel Aviv!*

Persistent technical problems aboard the MV *Peace* which had hindered the Voice of Peace's transmissions for some time were largely solved by a new engineer, Al Muick, during August/September 1990. The shortwave transmitter was also rebuilt and, with tentative plans to return it to the air in time for Christmas 1990, some test transmissions were reported to have taken place on 6265kHz (47.9m) on 21st November 1990. Plans were also announced for the installation of a longwave transmitter on 171kHz (1754m) to enable the Voice of Peace's signal to reach further into the Middle East, but this development did not ultimately take place.

**Voice of Peace programme schedule, October 1990**

6.00am Chris Richardson

8.00am Eli Landau

9.00am Kenny Page

12noon Non-stop Music

2.00pm John McDonald

6.00pm McLelland Hackney

7.30pm Chris Phelan

9.00pm Non-stop Music

11.00pm Kenny Page

12 midnight John McDonald

3.00am McLelland Hackney

## The Gulf War

Ironically in view of its peace mission, the Voice of Peace once again found itself broadcasting from an area adjacent to a war zone in January 1991. It had been in a similar situation in 1973 (see Chapter 18), but this time the conflict was on an even greater scale and involved some of the world's major powers.

Ever since the Iraqi invasion of Kuwait in August 1990 tension in the area had been building steadily. The situation reached a climax in mid-January 1991 when the United Nations gave Iraq's Saddam Hussain an ultimatum to withdraw his forces or face the consequences of Western allied military action. Israel was regarded by Hussain as a legitimate target in any resulting conflict because it was willing to provide support and operational bases for American military personnel and equipment. It seemed inevitable therefore that Israel would be affected in some way if a war started in the Gulf.

By mid-January 1991 there were only two DJs and three crew members left on board the *Peace* ship, most had left because of the volatile situation developing in Israel during the build-up to the Gulf War. On 15th January 1991, the day before the UN deadline expired , large quantities of supplies were taken on board the MV *Peace* in case of problems during the now seemingly inevitable war.

On 16th January 1991, after the UN deadline for Iraq to withdraw from Kuwait had passed without compliance, the *Peace* ship was moved to a safer position ten miles off Tel Aviv, but she later came to a position just six miles out, because the Motorola communications could not be maintained beyond that distance. The Arutz Sheva ship, *Hatzvi,* also moved to a position six miles from the coast and the Israeli Navy promised to keep watch on both ships during the conflict.

1540 KCS

...somewhere in the Mediteranean.

the voice of peace

P.O.B. 4399, TEL-AVIV, Israel P.O.B. 2374, NICOSIA, Cyprus

peace through communication

The day after the Gulf War actually started the Voice of Peace played peace music all day, but closed its transmissions early at 7.30pm due to the emergency situation and a desperate shortage of on-board broadcasting staff. During this period the crew which had remained with the station kept watch 24 hours a day to ensure the safety of the MV *Peace* which was considered to be in a vulnerable position anchored off Tel Aviv, a city likely to be attacked by enemy action.

This fear proved to be correct in the early hours of 18th January 1991 when two Iraqi missiles fell in the sea off Herzliya, just a few miles north of the *Peace* ship and later Iraqi Scud missiles landed on Tel Aviv itself.

## Storms

*As if the Gulf War was not enough for the crew to contend with the MV 'Peace' was buffeted by unusually bad storms at the end of January 1991 and on 1st February the medium wave aerial broke. The station managed to continue transmissions on FM only, while emergency repairs were carried out to the medium wave aerial and the following day the station returned to the air on both frequencies.*

Undeterred by this danger the Voice of Peace continued to broadcast throughout that day, but shortly before the station closed at 9.00pm air raid warnings were sounded in Tel Aviv once again. As another missile attack on Israel was expected Abie Nathan announced that if necessary he would make the Voice of Peace's transmitters available to the civil and military authorities to broadcast emergency information to the population of Tel Aviv.

At 6.00pm on 25th January 1991 another air raid alert was sounded just as Voice of Peace DJ, John McDonald was in the middle of reading the evening news. He asked listeners to re-tune to Kol Israel because the Voice of Peace was about to close until the alert was over. Shortly afterwards, in what must rank as the most amazing scene witnessed from an offshore radio ship, the crew on board the MV *Peace* watched as a US Patriot missile intercepted an incoming Iraqi Scud near Tel Aviv, while two other Patriots, which had missed their targets, actually fell on the city. Abie Nathan instructed the crew, via the Motorola, not to re-open the station until the all-clear was given. A similar incident occurred six days later when Patriot missiles again intercepted Scuds over Tel Aviv, but this time the Voice of Peace was only off the air for just over an hour.

On 11th February 1991 a further Iraqui missile attack was directed at Tel Aviv, but this time the Voice of Peace remained on the air relaying broadcasts of the Army station Galee Zahal as well as Kol Israel until what had by then become its normal closedown time of 7.30pm.

Throughout the duration of the Gulf War various members of the Knesset took part in special programmes on the Voice of Peace and talked about the developing situation and how it was affecting Israel.

Remarkably both Arutz Sheva and the Voice of Peace had managed to maintain their services throughout the Gulf War despite, particularly in the case of the Voice of Peace, severe staff shortages. Towards the end of February 1991 more DJs were recruited and the Voice of Peace's hitherto limited broadcasting hours were gradually extended to 19 a day. By the end of April 1991 with a few more new DJs having joined the Voice of Peace , including two from the now silent Radio Caroline, the station was able to return once more to a 24 hour schedule.

## Third offshore station launched

Just as the Gulf War broke out in mid-January 1991 a third offshore radio station was launched off the coast of Israel, much to the displeasure of the Communications Ministry.

The new station - Radio One - was directed at the Haifa area, a northern city and centre of population felt my many to have been neglected by the state broadcasting services and even the two existing offshore stations whose transmissions were directed largely at Tel Aviv and the surrounding area.

Radio One was the brainchild of Ghiora Izsak, who had been Marketing Manager for Aruts Sheva until he left to set up his own offshore station in November 1990. He established an operating company - Broadcasting Authority Ltd. - with $1million of financial support from German Jewish investors and leased a ship, MV *Air* (known officially as MV *Polaris*) from a Greek shipping agency.

The new station was to be a 24 hour music and information station, with local news and traffic reports directed specifically at the Haifa area. Unlike the other two Israeli offshore radio stations Radio One had no ideological or religious agenda, it was simply a local entertainment based station.

Radio One also had a strong policy of featuring local musicians and artists in its programmes and all employees were Haifa residents - to further underline its commitment to the concept of being a truly local station.

The outbreak of the Gulf War, which coincided with Radio One's launch date, meant that the station started broadcasting a full schedule of news and information programmes from the outset rather than, as had been planned, spending the first month operating test transmissions of continuous music.

Within three months of its launch Radio One was claiming an audience of 80-120,000 and was enthusiastically embraced by the Mayor and Council of Haifa. This local official support led to a situation whereby Radio One was allowed to produce its programmes in landbased studios and relay them by microwave link to the radio ship, which itself came inshore and anchored within territorial waters just outside Haifa Harbour.

A spokesman for Haifa Council said that the local authority saw the establishment of the offshore station as a positive development and challenged the Communications Ministry to prove otherwise. For its part the Communications Ministry said the Government were in the process of preparing a law to regulate the creation of local radio (and television) stations and that any station operating unofficially (i.e. without a licence from the Ministry) should be opposed.

## Second Radio One?

*At one time Broadcasting Authority Ltd. was rumoured to have a second offshore radio station off Eilat on Israel's southern coast which had to close because the ship kept drifting into Egyptian territorial waters. There were apparently plans to relocate the vessel to a position off Tel Aviv near the Voice of Peace and Arutz Sheva, from where 60% of Israel's population could be reached, but this idea never came to fruition. The company was also said to be involved in negotiations with two religious parties in the Knesset, Israel's Federation of Trade Unions (Histadrut) and a daily newspaper to operate various other offshore radio stations on their behalf.*

## More meetings with PLO

Abie Nathan began another of his 'Fasts for Peace' on 27th April 1991 to promote talks between Israel and the Palestinians, saying he would fast until the law preventing Israelis talking to the PLO had been revoked. Every hour on the hour the Voice of Peace announced the day number of Abie Nathan's fast and twice a day at 11.00am and 5.00pm he talked on air himself about how he was feeling and what he hoped to achieve by taking this action. By 14th May 1991 Abie Nathan had been admitted to hospital with heart problems and celebrations for the Voice of Peace's 18th Birthday, which had been planned for the following day, were cancelled. Only after a personal request from the President of Israel did he eventually end his fast on 17th June 1991, after 40 days without food.

The determined and unstopable Abie Nathan again met Yasser Arafat at the end of June, this time in Tunis. When he returned to Tel Aviv Airport two weeks later he was arrested by the equally determined and unstopable Israeli authorities. Later in the year, following a short trial at the beginning of October he was sentenced to a further 18 months in prison for having made repeated contact with the PLO. He said he would study the Arabic language while he was in prison this time and continue his campaign until the Israeli authorities realised that this was not a personal protest, but one for the total population of the Holy Land.

After his trial had ended Abie Nathan went on air for seven hours talking with listeners to the to the Voice of Peace about his years of effort to bring about peace in the Middle East. The following day he reported to jail to start his sentence, but despite earlier threats to close the station because of its acute financial problems the Voice of Peace continued broadcasting.

The Voice of Peace's format was changed twice during 1991 to try and attract listeners and advertisers. At the beginning of July 1991 the station adopted a contemporary music format and the 'Festival' programmes, first heard during the summer of 1990, were re-introduced to try and entice advertisers to buy airtime on the station. Then in November 1991, while Abie Nathan was in jail, a further

### Hebrew language news bulletins

*During mid-1992 the Voice of Peace introduced an hourly Hebrew language news service to rival the service provided by Arutz Sheva. Supplied by local newspaper 'Hezi Carmel' and 'Globs' Financial Magazine, these bulletins were broadcast on the half hour while news from Kol Israel was still carried at the top of the hour. Also, in what became and increasingly regular operational practice, live broadcasts were relayed by cellular telephone from the Voice of Peace's landbased studios with music inserted into the programmes by DJs on board the 'Peace' ship.*

format change was introduced involving more up-beat music during the day, the dropping of the Russian music programme altogether and the transfer of the Hebrew music programme, "Kassach", to the 9.00pm-midnight slot. From 24th November 1991 the soundtrack of the evening television news programme "Erev Hadash" ("A New Evening") was also re-broadcast by the offshore station.

## A new Government - a new approach

Abie Nathan was freed from jail on 30th March 1992 after serving only six of his eighteen months sentence. A new Labour Government had been elected in Israel and shortly after taking power it repealed the law forbidding talks between Israelis and the PLO. Abie Nathan had served two prison sentences for violating that law, now at least he could continue his quest for peace without fear of having to serve a third term.

The election of the new Government also brought hopes that legislation would be introduced to allow the establishment of privately owned commercial radio stations. The acceptance of the concept privately owned and operated broadcasting coupled with the Government's stated commitment to introduce local commercial radio stations, signalled the start of a new era in Israeli media circles.

However, political and administrative delays in introducing the new local radio network led to many potential operators growing impatient and taking matters into their own hands. This in turn led to an explosion in the number of landbased pirate stations operating in Israel, many of whom were run on a very professional basis and supported by significant advertisers.

Many of these stations became very popular and commercially successful, and although the authorities conducted frequent raids to silence them they were often able to return to the air very quickly thanks to the extent of their financial and operational support.

As an elaborate 'cover' some landbased pirates claimed to be operating from offshore bases while others did establish transmitters on board ships, openly relaying their programmes from landbased studios. A few stations, tired of the repeated raids on their landbased premises did actually move away and broadcast from an offshore base in the generally accepted manner.

From the point of view of offshore radio history this situation in Israel has made it increasingly difficult to distinguish between what are true offshore stations and what are simply cover operations for landbased pirates. However, it has been possible to identify a number of stations which have broadcast to Israel from ship-based facilities, although not all appear to have been from international waters. Some ship-based stations, which have not been located outside territorial limits and openly relayed their programmes from landbased studios, have blurred the once clear distinction between true offshore broadcasters and landbased pirates. Although having an element of offshore broadcasting relevance these stations were in essence landbased pirates, albeit that their transmitters were based on board ships.

## Legislation drafted

During 1992 a Bill had was introduced into the Knesset to establish up to twenty private local radio stations, but proposed operating restrictions meant that they were unlikely to be commercially profitable.

The Bill provided for regional stations under the control of local councils who were to decide on programme content and govern advertising regulations - the same system as the state-run Kol Israel radio network, but at a local level. Additionally the new stations would have to operate under trade union regulations and pay fees to the Bezek (Israel's communications monopoly), the local council, Ministry of Communications, Israeli Songwriter's Union and local record producers.

A spokesman for Radio One, Yoram Halper, said of the Government's new plans for private radio stations:-

*Despite the Government's contention this law will not lead to private radio broadcasting. With the burdensome regulations and required allotments of airtime for local matters the public will find the new stations as boring as Israel Radio. Listeners will continue to tune into the offshore stations and advertisers will not support a station that cannot boast a sizeable audience. It is unlikely that the stations will be profitable.*

## Arutz Sheva

Against this background the Israeli offshore stations, of which there were then three, continued to broadcast. By 1992 Arutz Sheva had widened its programme content to include a mix of traditional Middle East and Jewish music with some 'western' easy listening material (mainly from musicals and stage shows), the only criteria for inclusion being that the music should be "happy and optimistic". On the information side of its output the station claimed to only broadcast reports which looked at Israel through positive, healthy eyes."

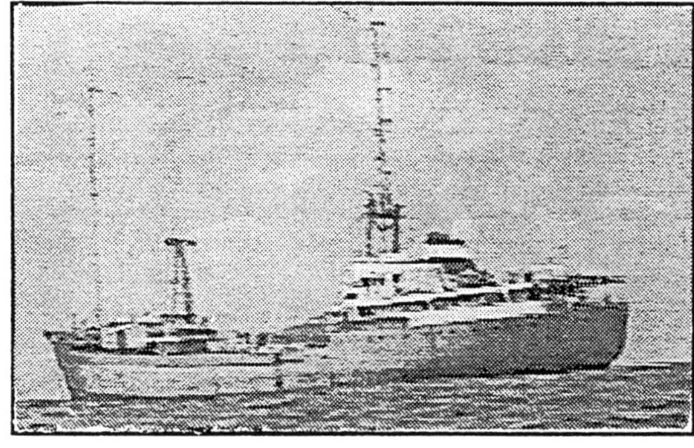

MV 'Hatzvi'

In June 1993 the Arutz Sheva ship, *Hatzvi* was given permission to anchor a mile offshore, near to Tel Aviv Marina. The station now broadcast on two medium wave as well two FM stereo frequencies and a public opinion poll in mid-1993 showed that it had a listenership of over 300,000.

A second service, Arutz Sheva Bet, was also started about this time directed specifically at 'religious listeners'. This second service included items on Jewish philosophy and history as well as public information programmes interspersed with what was officially described as "genuine Israeli music". Plans were also in existence to establish a third separate service from Arutz Sheva broadcasting in Russian and directed at the 600,000 Russian immigrants living in Israel.

Programmes were broadcast either live from the ship or sometimes (as had become the practice with other Israeli offshore stations) beamed to the radio ship from landbased studios via a telephone link. An example of this method of production was the nightly English language programme, the Ben Israel Show, which was transmitted live from studios in Jerusalem. The music and commercials included in the programme were inserted from on board the *Hatzvi*, but all talk, including live phone calls from listeners, was relayed from Jerusalem. The station also relayed Kol Israel news live at the top of each hour.

Arutz Sheva was a very professionally organised offshore station and had an office in Tel Aviv with full time staff selling airtime to a wide range of advertisers. The station did limit its commercial spots to a maximum of eight per hour, but had little or no trouble selling this volume of airtime.

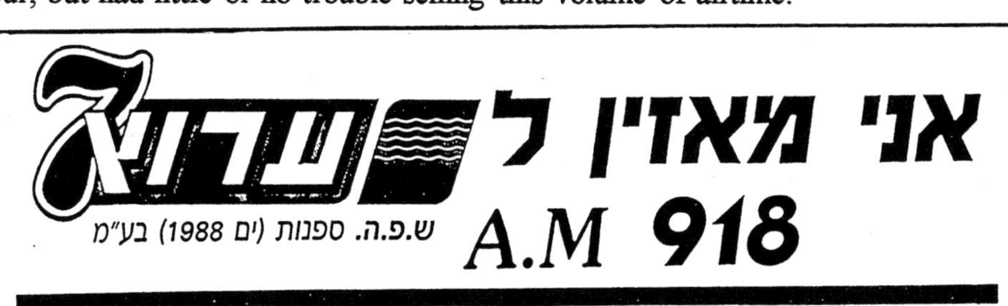

## Voice of Peace

In September 1992 the Voice of Peace changed its format yet again to 'mellow music' with a new station slogan - 'Peaceful Easy Listening'. The change had partly been brought about as the result of difficulties experienced in obtaining new records after Abie Nathan cancelled the station's subscription to *Billboard* magazine and a US based new release service. Unfortunately for the Voice of Peace by this time even local Israeli based record companies had stopped supplying the station with much new material because of its diminishing audience ratings.

The studio and broadcasting equipment on board the *Peace* ship had also been allowed to deteriorate and had not been updated or replaced for some time. By the beginning of 1993 the production studio was virtually out of commission and the main on-air studio was operated with considerable difficulty by the DJs. There was no longer a resident engineer on board the MV *Peace,* Abie Nathan relied instead on the technical expertise of one of the DJs, Kenny Page, to patch and repair the broadcasting equipment.

The 'mellow music' format was unpopular with listeners and as a consequence few commercial spots were sold because advertisers and agencies perceived that the Voice of Peace now had a very small audience. They were probably correct. The station had undergone so many format changes, suffered from technical breakdowns and competition from the more professional Arutz Sheva meant that the Voice of Peace had lost its market leader position.

Early in 1993 Abie Nathan explored the possibility of selling the Voice of Peace to millionaire Israeli media tycoon Yaacov Nimrodim, whose business interests included *Maariv,* a daily Hebrew language newspaper, a record company and a cable television outlet. Contracts were due to be signed on 1st March 1993, but the deal fell through at the last minute.

## Radio One closed

On 31st January 1993 a severe storm in the eastern Mediterranean drove the Radio One ship, MV *Air* (also known as *Polaris),* aground outside Haifa Harbour. The station, which was operated from landbased studios in Haifa, feeding its programmes by microwave link to the ship-based transmitter inside territorial waters, continued with this arrangement for some time while the ship was aground. Enquiries were made by the station's owners about the possibility of purchasing the former Laser 558/Hot Hits ship, *Communicator* (then in Portugal) as a replacement, but this plan did not go ahead.

The *Air* was eventually re-floated on 23rd March 1993 and she was berthed in Haifa port. Broadcasts of Radio One continued from this base inside Haifa Harbour with the full approval of the local Council and the Mayor who had always been very supportive towards the station. However, following elections at the beginning of April 1993, which resulted in a change of Mayor and Council in Haifa, the authorities raided the *Air* and forced Radio One to close, although it did re-emerge and operated as one of Israel's growing number of landbased pirates.

***Footnote*** *Towards the end of 1994, shortly before contracts for local commercial radio were about to be advertised, Radio One closed voluntarily because to have continued as a landbased pirate would have prevented the station tendering for a licence. This proved successful because Radio One was awarded the licence for the Haifa area and began legal broadcasts on 18th October 1995.*

**offshore trivia**

**Shortest surviving station**

*(Excluding stations which never broadcast more than test transmissions)*

*Radio 199 - 4 days (17th -21st December 1972)*

*Radio Delmare - 4 days (7th-11th September 1978)*

## Voice of Peace uncertainty

In March 1993, shortly after the proposed sale of the Voice of Peace had fallen through, the MV *Peace* was temporarily impounded by the authorities while on a regular refuelling visit to Ashdod. The ship's Panamanian registration had expired and although Abie Nathan was in America at the time arranging a renewal of the registration the Israeli authorities refused to let the ship return to her anchorage off Tel Aviv until the paperwork was sorted out. However, as a demonstration of the easy going relationship between the authorities and the offshore stations at the time (in contrast to the contemporary European and American official attitudes - see Chapters 24 and 25) the MV *Peace* was allowed to anchor just outside the harbour walls and resume broadcasting until the registration documents had been received from Panama.

By contrast to Arutz Sheva's professionalism and commercial success the Voice of Peace was now in serious financial difficulties. Rumours continued to circulate during the summer of 1993 that the Israeli Government would grant both it and Arutz Sheva, licences to operate from landbased facilities. These licences were to be in addition to the planned new network of local private stations to be launched in Israel. Earlier in the year both stations had been asked to provide applications detailing their current transmission arrangements, programming, transmitter power and area covered by their broadcasts. However, the plan came to nothing, partly because the state network, Kol Israel, mounted a vociferous campaign against the proposed granting of landbased licences to the two main offshore broadcasters.

### Voice of Peace programme schedule, Mid-1993

**6.00am** Good Morning Friends, *Kenny Page*

**9.00am** Morning Music Show, *Mike Melbourne*

**12noon** Kassach *-Hebrew music, Arik Lev*

**1.00pm** Afternoon Music Show, *Bill Sheldrake*

**2.00pm** Nathan Morley

**4.00pm** Drive Time, *Mike Melbourne*

**6.00pm** Twilight Time, *Matthew French*

**7.30pm** Classical Music, *Kenny Page*

**9.00pm** Bill Sheldrake

**12midnight** Late Night Affair, *Nathan Morley*

**3.00am** Nightwatch, *Matthew French*

By mid-1993 the Voice of Peace was said to be up for sale again. Meanwhile, in an effort to cover operating costs, Abie Nathan explored another possible use of the *Peace* ship's facilities - he tried to rent the station's transmitters to organisations operating telephone chat lines. The idea was that they would use the Voice of Peace's transmitters overnight to broadcast their service on air, but as with so many proposals affecting the station the plan came to nothing.

The failure to obtain a landbased licence had been a devastating blow to the Voice of Peace which now faced serious technical and financial problems. The station's FM transmitter had failed at the end of June 1993 and although broadcasts continued on medium wave many listeners and advertisers assumed that the Voice of Peace was off the air altogether.

Although some temporary repairs were carried out to the FM transmitter it broke down again after only a few days on the air and by 7th July 1993 the medium wave transmitter had also failed putting the Voice of Peace off the air completely. Emergency repairs were carried out when the ship entered Ashdod and within 48 hours the Voice of Peace was back on the air. However, because of these frequent periods off the air one of the few remaining large advertisers, Coca Cola, cancelled its contract with the Voice of Peace for a planned campaign promoting Sprite and Coke. By mid-July 1993 the Voice of Peace was left with only six small regular advertisers.

## Voice of Peace closure

During the late summer of 1993 more rumours began to circulate about the impending closure of the Voice of Peace. Abie Nathan had threatened, and indeed carried out (temporarily at least) such closures before, but this time the situation seemed more certain and likely to be permanent.

At the beginning of September 1993 Abie Nathan informed the crew on board the MV *Peace* that the Voice of Peace would cease transmissions at the end of that month and the station began broadcasting a daily countdown at the top of each hour. At first it was not obvious to listeners what this meant, but it soon became clear that the Voice of Peace was finally to close on 1st October 1993.

The format of the station was changed once more for the final few weeks of broadcasting from mellow music to contemporary hits and during the last few days there were a number of special themed programmes -

28th September - Elvis Day

29th September - Twilight Day

30th September - Beatles Day

## Peace accord

Abie Nathan said in an interview on 27th September 1993 that his decision to close the Voice of Peace had been partly because of debts (said to be about $250,000) which the station had accumulated and which he attributed to "an organised boycott by advertisers" and partly because he was too busy working with other projects, in particular helping victims of the recent Indian earthquake.

The main reason for closure, however, was that Israel's Prime Minister, Yitzhak Rabin, had signed an historic peace accord with PLO leader Yasser Arafat in Washington on 13th September 1993 and consequently Abie Nathan felt that his mission and that of the Voice of Peace, which he had set out to achieve in 1969, had been completed.

On 1st October 1993 Abie Nathan came on board the MV *Peace* to broadcast for the last time. Most of the remaining DJ crew (Nathan Morley, Bill Sheldrake and Clive Roper) left the ship, while Matthew French remained on board with Abie Nathan to help close the station.

Just after 9.00am Abie Nathan started a programme during which he talked at considerable length about the history of the Voice of Peace, problems he had encountered with operating an offshore radio station, the alleged 'boycott' by advertisers and his reasons for closing the station. He also thanked everyone who had worked to keep the Voice of Peace on the air for more than 20 years and explained that he planned to scupper the MV *Peace* once the station had closed.

At 1.00pm the Mayor of Tel Aviv, Shlomo Lahat, and Environment Minister, Josse Sared, came on board the *Peace* ship to plead with Abie Nathan not to sink the vessel. During an on-air discussion Mayor Lahat promised to make available a mooring for the vessel in Tel Aviv Harbour and described how he thought the ship could be converted into a Peace Museum. Abie Nathan was persuaded by this offer from the authorities and announced the address of a new Foundation which he hoped to launch to operate the Peace Museum.

After playing the last record, "We Shall Overcome" by Pete Segar, Abie Nathan said simply: "Thank you all. Shalom. Love. Peace to everyone." And at 1.57pm on 1st October 1993 broadcasts from the Voice of Peace finally ended.

After the station closed the *Peace* sailed into Tel Aviv accompanied by thirty or forty small boats full of supporters and well wishers. Abie Nathan stood on the deck of the ship wearing, for the first time in twelve years, a white shirt. He explained why in a magazine interview some weeks later:-

*For more than 12 years I have been wearing black in protest against the unwillingness of the PLO to recognise Israel and the unwillingness of my Government to talk to the PLO. Now that both sides are talking peace I can, at last, change my clothes!*

## Peace Museum plan fails

The MV *Peace* remained in Tel Aviv awaiting arrangements for her conversion into a Peace Museum as had been agreed on-air during the final broadcast. Unfortunately, due to a change in the Mayoralty of Tel Aviv and political manoeuvring which went on in the weeks after the Voice of Peace had closed the Peace Museum plan never came to fruition. Abie Nathan became frustrated by the continuing delays and ordered the MV *Peace* to enter Ashdod where all broadcasting equipment was to be removed from the radio ship. He then intended to revert to his original plan and scupper the former radio ship in international waters.

Another last minute attempt to make Abie Nathan change his mind came shortly before the MV *Peace* left harbour for the last time. He was approached by a Rabbi who offered him £14,000 to recommence the Voice of Peace broadcasts, but the offer had come too late and was refused.

The MV *Peace* sailed from Ashdod for the last time on 28th November 1993 and was taken to a position in international waters fifteen miles offshore. Once in location holes were made in the hull of the Peace and water pumped into the vessel. However, all did not happen according to plan and it was not until early the following morning, some seven and a half hours later, that the radio ship finally sank beneath the waves of the Mediterranean. By that time the vessel had drifted over four miles from its originally intended scuttling position, which had been carefully chosen because of the depth of the water. This unintended change of position later proved to be a disaster for local fishermen who claimed that oil pollution from the sunken radio ship was killing fish in the area and consequently threatening their livelihoods.

## Radio Hof

In August 1993, shortly before the Voice of Peace announced its closure, a new offshore station appeared off the coast of Israel - Radio Hof (Radio Beach or Coastal Radio). The new station, based on the MV *David,* (also known as MV *Hof*) anchored off Tel Aviv, slightly further south than the Voice of Peace or Arutz Sheva and started broadcasts of music and talk shows on medium wave and FM.

*MV 'David' ('Hof'), home to Radio Hof*

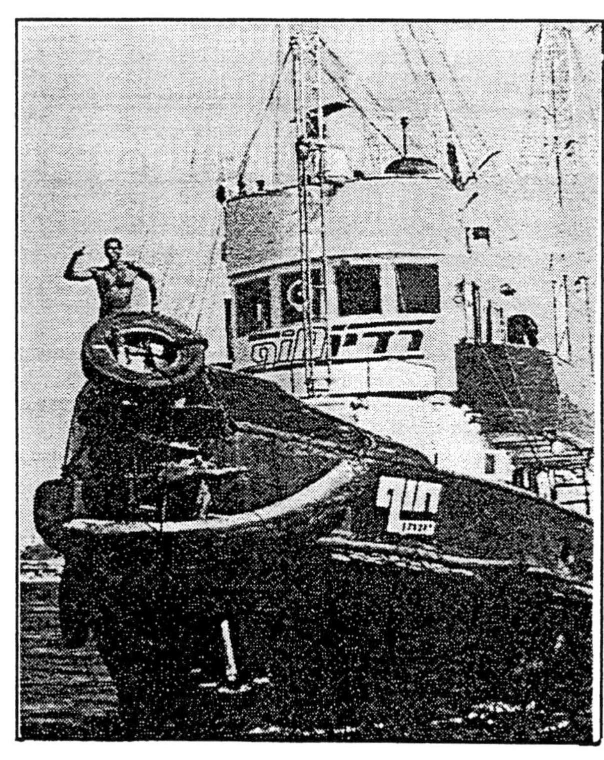

While they were searching for a vessel to house their new station Radio Hof's backers had visited and inspected the Radio Caroline ship, *Ross Revenge,* in Dover. Notwithstanding the fact that the Detention Order on the *Ross Revenge* at the time would have prevented her use anyway, they decided not to take over the Radio Caroline vessel because she did not have an air conditioning system fitted - essential for a station operating in the heat of the eastern Mediterranean!

Although Radio Hof used American trained advertising sales staff to sell airtime to advertisers the station's programming output, and its broadcasting equipment were not of a very high professional standard. Radio Hof tried to attract some broadcasters from the Voice of Peace after that station closed in October 1993, but all the DJs who were approached refused to join the new offshore station.

On 8th March 1994 the Radio Hof ship, MV *David,* broke her anchor chain during storms in the Mediterranean and drifted to a position off Herzelia. At about the same time too most of the DJ crew left after a disagreement over non-payment of wages and later the station's General Manager, Baruch Ben David was sacked. Unable to continue operating from its offshore base the station moved ashore early in April 1994 and became one of the many landbased pirates then operating in Israel. Shortly afterwards, however, Radio Hof was raided and closed by the authorities.

## Radio Gal

Within a matter of weeks of Radio Hof's enforced closure in spring 1994 a new station with the same DJs and programming format took to the airwaves. This station used the call sign Radio Gal (Radio Waves) and again operated for over a year as a landbased pirate.

However, by September 1995 Radio Gal had moved to an offshore base, using two FM frequencies to broadcast separate programmes to the Tel Aviv area. In February 1996 Radio Gal began to broadcast on a frequency used by rival offshore station, Arutz Sheva when that station was off the air for Shabbat or other religious holiday observance. In order to counter this pirating of one of its frequencies by another offshore station Aruts Sheva then responded by transmitting a continuous tone at times when its programmes were not being broadcast.

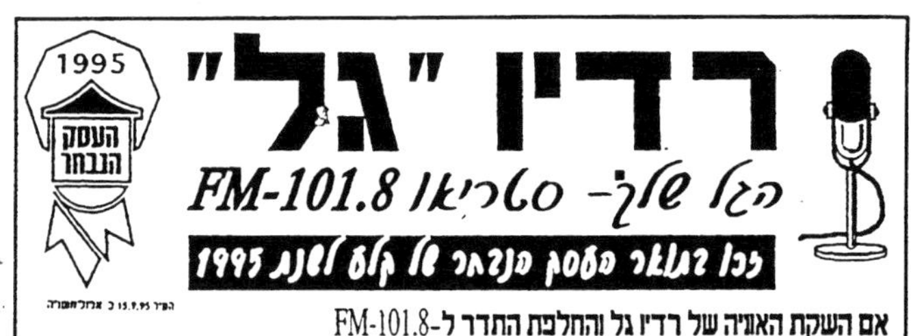


## Arutz Sheva raided

The group behind Arutz Sheva, as representatives of the settler movement was fundamentally opposed to the Washington peace accord between Israel and the PLO and the station had been critical of Israeli Prime Minister Yitzhak Rabin after his signing of the peace agreement in 1993.

In response Israeli Ministers had made several attempts to force the closure of Arutz Sheva as a voice critical of its policies, claiming that the station was "inciting certain sections of the Israeli population to rebel against the Israeli Government."

Reports began to circulate in spring 1995 that the Israeli Government was putting pressure on the Maltese authorities not to renew the registration licence of Arutz Sheva's ship, *Hatzvi.* This latest attempt to terminate the station's operations by trying to prevent the ship's renewal of registration would, had it succeeded, have rendered the vessel stateless and liable to boarding even when anchored in international waters. Claims were made by supporters of Arutz Sheva that the Israeli Foreign Ministry had officially approached the Maltese requesting them not to grant the renewal of the *Hatzvi's* registration, but this was publicly denied by the Ministry.

Whatever happened about the ships registration the *Hatzvi* remained at sea and broadcasting the increasingly popular programmes of Arutz Sheva. However, in August 1995 Israeli police, acting on a complaint from the Communications Ministry, raided the *Hatzvi* while the vessel was in Ashdod taking on supplies. The transmitters and other broadcasting equipment were removed and seized by the police.

Shortly before this raid the Knesset had approved a new law outlawing any unlicensed radio stations, mainly an attempt to deal with the growing number of landbased pirates. As justification for invoking these powers under the new law to raid the *Hatzvi* the authorities claimed that the radio ship had been transmitting inside Israeli territorial waters before she entered Ashdod.

A Government spokesman claimed that the action taken against Arutz Sheva was not directly because of its stance in opposing the peace accord with the PLO, but was merely because it was an unlicensed broadcaster.

In normal circumstances such a raid would have been a devastating, if not fatal, blow but not in the case of Arutz Sheva. The station received tremendous support from all over Israel and on 7th August 1995, just three days after the raid, it was able to return to the air , as a result of sufficient donations being made to enable new AM and FM transmitters. Having experienced this direct hostile action from the authorities the station management decided to keep the *Hatzvi* anchored in international waters in future and deliver supplies by tender.

Having failed to close Arutz Sheva by force or by making its ship stateless the Israeli authorities turned their attention to the station's operation on land. Prime Minister Yitzhak Rabin personally instructed the Israeli Air Force Museum to discontinue an advertising campaign on the station, Arutz Sheva news reporters were barred from the Knesset and Government departments were instructed not to supply the station with press releases or other information.

## Opposition party protests

These attempt to close Arutz Sheva caused protests in the Knesset where opposition members claimed that the Government was "threatening the democratic fabric of Israeli society." Claims were made that the Communications Ministry had deliberately misled the police about the station broadcasting inside territorial waters before instructing them to raid the radio ship in Ashdod. Binyamin Netanyahu, Chairman of Likud, the main opposition party in the Knesset, said: "Arutz Sheva is the only station in Israel that expresses the view of the nationalist camp, and for that reason alone Communications Minister Shulamit Aloni decided to close it down." Some members of the Likud Party went on board the *Hatzvi* to assist with the resumption of broadcasts after the raid and Binyamin Netanyahu took part in a broadcast saying that the return of Arutz Sheva was "a blessed day for Israel's democracy."

A Communications Ministry spokesman denied any such claims, reiterating the official line that Arutz Sheva was being treated in the same way as any other unlicensed radio station and the Ministry was enforcing the law "in preparation for the regional radio stations due to start transmissions in October." It was further claimed that the frequencies used by Arutz Sheva would cause interference to the broadcasts of the new regional stations.

More allegations were made against Arutz Sheva by Dedi Zucker, Chairman of the Law and Constitution Committee, who alleged that the offshore station was using two frequencies allocated to the Defence Forces to relay programmes from land based studios to the *Hatzvi,* which then transmitted them back to Israel. He also claimed that four additional landbased transmitters in Jerusalem, Safed and in the Negev Desert were being used to relay Arutz Sheva programmes and boost reception of the station for listeners in those areas.

The assassination of Israeli Prime Minister Yitzhak Rabin in November 1995 resulted in the authorities taking swift action against right wing opposition factions throughout Israel. As part of this crackdown action was taken against several people involved with Arutz Sheva and two of the station's staff were arrested after drugs and guns were found in their premises.

Tensions built in Israel during the months following this assassination and an escalation of street violence seemed likely to thwart the success of the peace accord with the PLO. This atmosphere was not conducive to a comfortable relationship between the Israeli Government and an offshore radio station so diametrically opposed to its policy on peaceful co-existence with the Palestinians. The narrow victory of Binyamin Netanyahu's Likud Party in the May 1996 Israeli General Election may serve to alter this relationship with Arutz Sheva.

## Galei Hayam Hatichon

Yet another offshore radio station began broadcasting off the Israeli coast at the end of October 1995. Galei Hayam Hatichon (Mediterranean Waves) began transmissions from the MV *Kajun* on 27th October 1995. Broadcasts of continuous music under the call sign Radio Dan also appear to have emanated from the *Kajun*, although this was never confirmed on-air by either station.

Galei Hayam Hatichon had been a long established and popular landbased pirate station, broadcasting to the Tel Aviv area 24 hours a day. However, as with many other such operations it was frequently raided by the authorities and in June 1995 the station ceased landbased broadcasts while a ship was fitted out in readiness for its transfer to an offshore base.

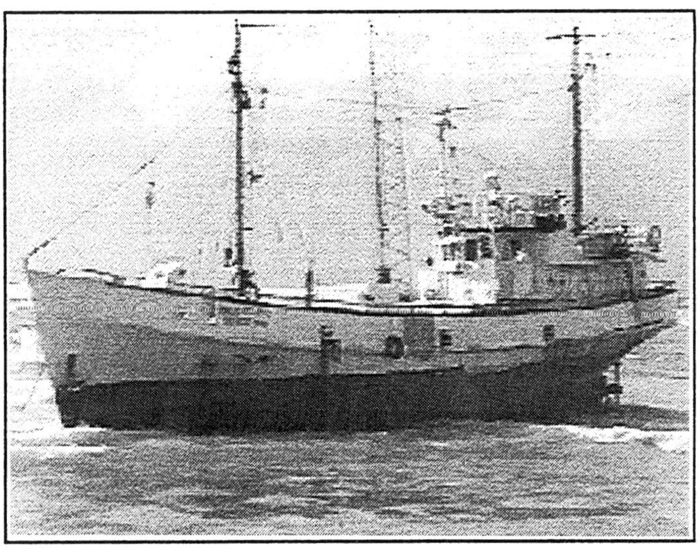

MV 'Kajun' aground off Tel Aviv

Offshore transmissions from Galei Hayam Haitchon only lasted a matter of weeks, however. In mid-November 1995, in action similar to that taken against Arutz Sheva three months earlier, the Israeli Ministry of Communications boarded the *Kajun* and confiscated all broadcasting equipment. This raid was carried out on the basis that the vessel had been broadcasting inside territorial waters after she had come into port for repairs.

The backers of Galei Hayam Haitchon took the *Kajun* back to sea while they commenced legal proceedings to recover the confiscated broadcasting equipment. Unfortunately on 23rd November, just over a week after the station had been closed, the *Kajun* ran aground sustaining extensive damage and was subsequently scrapped after being declared unseaworthy.

## Arutz 2000

During the early summer of 1995 interest in offshore radio circles in Britain began to centre on a former Trinity House lightship moored in Portsmouth.

Various rumours circulated that the ship would be converted to become a new offshore radio station broadcasting to Europe. In fact the former Towers Lightship (known as Light Vessel Number 3) had been purchased in May 1995 by an Israeli group which paid £30,000 in cash for the vessel. The same group also purchased a former inshore tug, *Tamar*, to tow the engine-less lightship to her eventual location off Israel.

Worldwide Broadcast Consultants (operated by former Caroline and Laser 558 DJ/engineer Paul Rusling) were engaged to advise the Israeli group on the conversion of Light Vessel Number 3 - now re-named *King David* - to a floating radio station. However, the consultancy subsequently withdrew from the project.

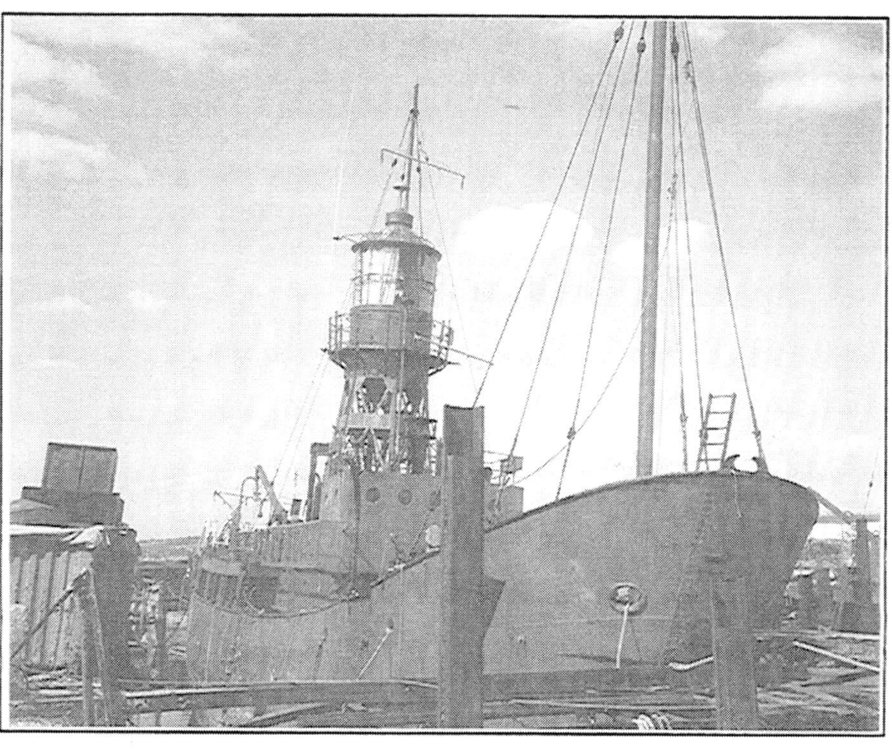

Light Vessel Number 3 in Portsmouth

Nevertheless conversion work continued throughout the summer of 1995, but came to a halt towards the end of the year when resources apparently ran short. The unusual activity on board the ship had come to the attention of the British Department of Trade and Industry (DTI) who mounted a surveillance operation in Portsmouth Harbour. Once satisfied that the conversion work meant the ship was intended for use as an offshore radio station they decided to raid the vessel.

The raid, allegedly at the request of the Israeli Embassy in London (although this connection was strongly denied) was carried out on Friday 12th January 1996 just after sundown when the orthodox Jewish backers and workers were observing Shabbat. DTI officials claimed that the timing of the raid was not deliberate, but the practical effect was that because of religious observance by the crew they met with no resistance from those on board the *King David*. Vital equipment and sections of aerial mast which had been stored on the deck awaiting erection were removed and confiscated by the authorities.

Following the raid, and fearing that the ship herself may soon be impounded, the owners arranged for the *King David* to be towed away from Britain immediately by the tug *Tamar*. However, after crossing the Bay of Biscay problems were experienced with the towing cable and both ships had to enter port in Lisbon for repairs.

No firm information had been available about the group behind the conversion of Light Vessel Number 3, but shortly after the ship was towed out of Portsmouth Arutz 2000, a landbased pirate which had been operating as an ultra-religious station in Tel Aviv for some time started making references on-air about the impending arrival of its new radio ship en-route from Britain. By 27th January 1996, however, the station was making emergency appeals for financial donations to 'rescue and salvage' its ship which had got into difficulties at sea, somewhere near Gibraltar. Reports in the early spring of 1996 indicated that the *King David* had reached Cyprus and by May she was reportedly anchored some 15 miles off the coast of Israel.

Although Arutz 2000 was claiming to be broadcasting from its offshore base at this time in reality the station was still relaying its programmes from landbased studios. During these broadcasts further appeals were made on air for listeners to make donations to the station and announcers frequently referred to the *King David* and plans to start offshore transmissions. There were unconfirmed reports circulating at the end of August 1996 that Arutz 2000 had in fact started broadcasting from an offshore base.

## Internet Pages

*Arutz Sheva became the first offshore station to make use of the Internet.*

*The station's home page contains information about Aruts Sheva (including pictures of the 'Hatzvi') and some general news. The page is also used to disseminate news and information about issues affecting the station.*

*The Internet address for Arutz Sheva is:-*

*http://www.jer1.co.il/media/arutz7/index.html*

## Government reprisals

Matters came to a head for offshore broadcasters off Israel in mid-May 1996. On 20th May Ben Gurion Airport in Tel Aviv was forced to close for two hours because of interference being caused to air traffic control communications by landbased pirate radio stations. One station was traced and raided by police and and others, including Arutz 2000 voluntarily closed to avoid similar raids.

As a direct result of the problems caused at Ben Gurion Airport the Israeli authorities took strong action against all 'unauthorised' stations, including offshore based Arutz Sheva, which received information that if its ship, *Hatzvi,* entered port it would be raided again.

Arutz Sheva sent messages via its Internet pages warning of the planned raid on the *Hatzvi* and asking readers to support the station's right to broadcast by contacting government agencies and Israeli Consulates and Embassies worldwide to lodge protests.

It had been intended, and announced on air, that the *Hatzvi* would enter Ashdod over the two day Shavuot holiday weekend at the end of May 1996. Although the Director General of Communications in Israel admitted that Arutz Sheva had not been responsible for interference at the Airport the planned raid was perceived as yet another attempt by the Israeli authorities to silence the station, which had voiced critical comments about the Government. It was probably no coincidence that this threat of action occurred within a week of the Israeli General Election.

To avoid the possible repetition of a raid and confiscation of broadcasting equipment, as had happened the previous year, the *Hatzvi* remained at sea over the Shavuot holiday weekend. Arutz Sheva has been able to continue broadcasting virtually unhindered since the victory of Binyamin Netanyahu in the May 1996 Israeli General Election.

# Chapter 28

# Official Backing

In 1991 the former communist state of Yugoslavia began to break up, with separate religious and ethnic factions each laying claim to large areas of territory and population groups. These claims were made despite over 40 years of apparent integration within and between communities and individual families and resulted in a ferocious three-sided civil war.

Serbs, Croats and Muslim forces fought each other for dominance over territory and population, in the process destroying whole towns, villages and thousands of individual lives. Any normal daily way of life ended - food, fuel and clothing supplies dried up. Although there were attempts at providing aid through the United Nations, these came too late and were prone to disruption by rival factions.

Countless attempts were made to negotiate ceasefires and agree a long term peace solution by re-defining and re-drawing territorial boundaries. Each time, however, ceasefires were broken almost as soon as they were declared and communities continued to be split, while vast numbers of people became homeless and those who were not killed in the fighting often starved to death in the ruins of their towns and villages. Those who managed to retain their homes did so by enduring the greatest of hardships - what little food and fuel there was available was in short supply and some areas had none at all. All this in a country which, although at one time under communist rule, had enjoyed a relatively high and sophisticated 'westernised' standard of living.

In a situation like this readily accepted lines of communication were destroyed along with every other semblance of a 'normal' society and many people felt that news and information was being manipulated to provide biased and unbalanced coverage of what was really happening inside the country.

Against this background a number of journalists from former state radio and television services, as well as newspapers which were no longer able to publish, fled the country and settled in Paris during 1992. One of these, former Montenegran newspaper editor, Dragica Ponorac, set about finding a way of providing his homeland with an impartial source of news and information.

The journalists made contact with a number of French humanitarian and libertarian groups, amongst whom were some people who had been involved with the 'Goddess of Democracy' offshore radio project, which was planned to broadcast to China in 1990 (see Chapter 26).

After discussions between these various groups it was decided that the best means to provide an impartial news and information service was to establish a radio station broadcasting from outside Yugoslavia. The organisation, Droit de Parole (The Right to Speak), was formed in August 1992 and initially negotiated an option to use a land-based transmitter in Hungary, powerful enough to allow broadcasts to cover all the former Yugoslav territories. However, it was later decided to use a ship-based transmitter instead mainly for safety reasons because it was feared that the land-based transmitter could be vulnerable to sabotage.

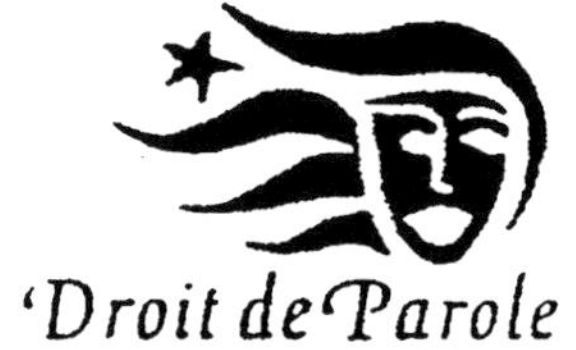

Contact was made with Radio Caroline to see if it would be possible to hire the *Ross Revenge* to use as a base for the proposed station. However, the British authorities who, in November 1990 had impounded the *Ross Revenge* in Dover (see Chapter 26), were unwilling to lift the Detention Order on the vessel so the group was forced to look elsewhere for a base.

By early 1993 they had chartered a former Antarctic research vessel, the *Cariboo,* from the Compagnie Nationale de Navigation and Compagnie Marseillaise de Reparations in France. The ship was re-named *Droit de Parole*. Using the experience of other offshore radio stations, as well as an extensive network of contacts to which the journalists had access, it was planned to start transmissions in March 1993 for an initial three month period, broadcasting objective and pacifist news to the former Yugoslavia from a position in the Adriatic Sea off Italy.

Programmes were to carry news on the war in Yugoslavia as well as reviews and analysis from the international press and the independent Yugoslavian newspapers which were still being published such as *Vreme, Borba, Monitor* and *Oslobodjenje.* The station, whose aim was "to broadcast objective news to all residents of the former Yugoslavia and combat the paranoia which is fuelled by suspicion and propaganda as a weapon of war", also planned to transmit sports news, family messages and of course music- a mixture of classical, rock and folk.

Mr. Tadcusz Mazowiecki, representing the UN Commission on Human Rights in the former Yugoslavia said the station was desperately needed "to promote actions aimed at freeing information and at halting incitement to hatred on the territory of the former Yugoslavia by the local media."

'Droit de Parole'

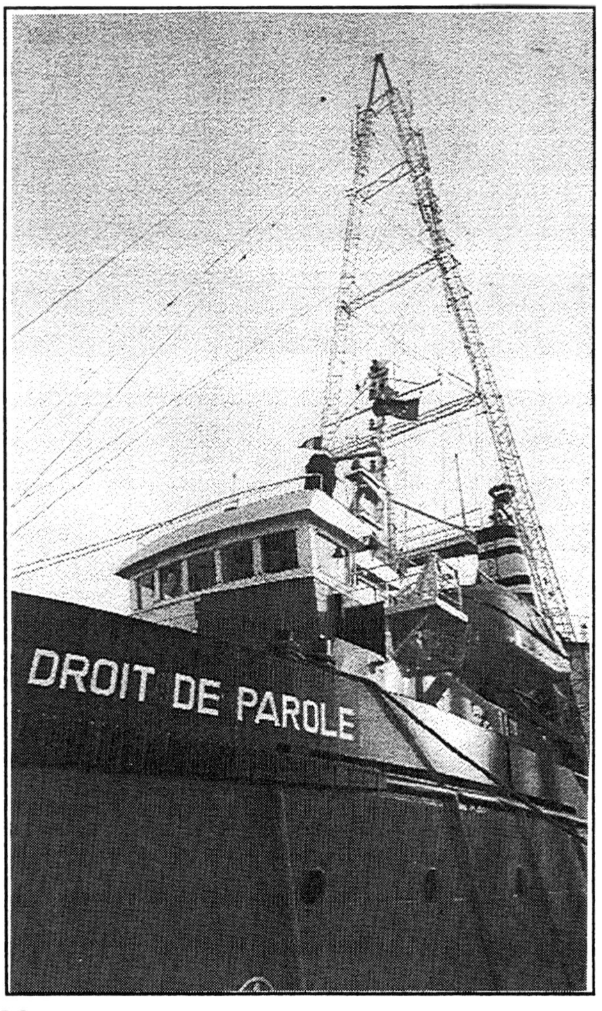


Backing for the project came from three main sources:- the European Community, which agreed to provide £875,000; an organisation known as France Libertes Association, whose president was Mrs. Danielle Mitterand (wife of the then French President); and UNESCO (a United Nations based aid organisation whose Director General, Frederica Mayor, was also a member of France Libertes). Backing was also reported to have come from an un-named British organisation as well as various press groups in the USA including the *Washington Post,* and *New York Times.*

At the outset in early 1993 the project had also been promised £240,000 by the then French Minister of Humanitarian Action, Bernard Kouchner, but after the French general elections in March 1993 brought a new administration to power that offer was withdrawn. The incoming French administration maintained that the offshore radio project was contrary to international regulations and convention agreements. Whilst this must have been disappointing for the project's organisers it at least showed a consistency of approach which their predecessors in office had lacked. The previous administration had on many occasions invoked international agreements and regulations in their opposition to Radio Caroline and other offshore radio stations operating in Europe, but apparently had been prepared to help fund the proposed offshore radio operation aimed at Yugoslavia, conveniently ignoring the international agreements.

## Radio Brod launched

After being fitted out in the French port of Marseilles the *Droit de Parole* sailed for the Adriatic on 31st March 1993, carrying a marine crew and seven journalists from all parts of the former Yugoslavia - Serbs, Croats, Slovens and Bosnians, headed by Editor-in-Chief, Dzevad Sabljakovic.

Test broadcasts, under the call sign Radio Brod (Radio Boat), started on 9th April 1993 at 11.00pm on 720kHz (416m) and regular programmes, 24 hours a day, commenced on 1st June 1993. The ship was stationed in international waters in the Adriatic Sea off Bari, but she did not anchor in a fixed position as almost all offshore radio stations in the past had done. Instead, partly for safety reasons, the vessel kept on the move sailing up and down the Adriatic broadcasting to a target area which included Serbia, Montenegro, Dalmatia and Bosnia.

Radio Brod expected its broadcasts to be jammed by the former Yugoslav states and according to radio engineer Jean Pierre Grimaldi, the ship was equipped with electronic countermeasures to deal with such an eventuality.

The *Droit de Parole* carried a 50Kw medium wave transmitter which was donated to the project by Telediffusion France (TDF) and had previously been used by Sud Radio based in Andorra. Initially some interference was caused to the station's transmissions by breakthrough from the ship's marine communications equipment and the *Droit de Parole* had to return to port after a few days to have this rectified. Some storm damage to the ship was also repaired at the same time. By 17th April 1993 the ship had returned to sea and transmissions of Radio Brod recommenced shortly afterwards this time also on 90mHz FM.

Two studios - an on-air studio and a production facility-as well as two editing suites were constructed on board the *Droit de Parole.* Communications to and from the ship by the journalists, both to their contacts in the former Yugoslavia and to other countries was made through an Inmarsat satellite facility, as well as marine telephone, cellular telephone and a direct radio link.

News was obtained by journalists working on board the radio ship via foreign press contacts, the AFP and Reuters news agencies and a network of over 40 correspondents based in Geneva, Washington, Paris and in the former Yugoslavia. Editor-in-Chief of news on Radio Brod was Dzevad Sabljakovic, a television reporter before the war, who had recruited a team of journalists from non-Government controlled media in Yugoslavia.

Short news bulletins were broadcast every hour on the hour and there were three major bulletins each day in the morning, afternoon and evening. The language used for these broadcasts sometimes depended on the nature of the news, but included Serbian, Croatian and Bosnian. Two additional news bulletins were also broadcast each day, one in English and one in French, mainly for the benefit of members of the UN forces serving in the area.

### News policy

A spokeswoman for Droit de Parole, commenting on Radio Brod's policy of providing an unbiased news service, said: *One of the factors that really had a weight on the War was 'modification' of information which gave just one side of the problem. This is the reason you've got so many prejudices. In Croatia they think whatever the Croatian Government does is OK. In Serbia it's whatever the Serbian Government does is OK. There's no critical difference in the public opinion. It is formed by the Government TV, radio and press.*

## Missing persons

A telephone number was established in Paris to enable correspondents and listeners inside and outside Yugoslavia to pass on messages to relatives and friends with whom they had lost contact during the war. The message service became a major feature of the station's broadcasts and a daily missing persons programme, "Desperately Seeking", was soon introduced. This included broadcasts of taped messages to the Paris telephone number as well as details of people living in refugee camps who wished to contact relatives from whom they had become separated. Over 3,000 messages were left at this number.

## Contrast with Radio Caroline's position

*The launch of Radio Brod and in particular its 'official' funding and support from the European Commission came at a time when Radio Caroline was wrestling with the problems imposed on it by the British Government's Broadcasting Act 1990. The powers contained in this Act relating to the suppression of offshore radio stations in international waters by official force, were based on international conventions and particularly relied on the (then inoperative) UNCLOS agreement.*

*The European Commission, in some attempt to justify its overriding of these international agreements and conventions, upon which various member states had relied so many times during the history of offshore radio, issued a statement about the funding and operation of Radio Brod. The statement said that there would be no repercussions with regard to the legality or illegality of the radio station, given the extremely unusual situation and that anyway no protests had been received from surrounding countries, with the exception of Serbia and Montenegro.*

Another major feature on the station was the hour long "Exodus" programme, broadcast three times a week, giving advice to would-be refugees on foreign visa requirements, travel facilities, contact telephone numbers and qualifications necessary for those seeking employment away from the former Yugoslav states.

## Complaints to the ITU

In June 1993, after Radio Brod had been on the air for less than two months, the International Telecommunications Union (ITU) received representations from the Serbian authorities in the former Yugoslavian capital, Belgrade. They alleged that the offshore station's use of the 720kHz frequency was illegal, because it was a frequency allocated to Yugoslavia and Radio Brod's transmissions were interfering with the Montenegran State Radio Podgorica. As well as this challenge on technical grounds Serbia also accused the offshore station of broadcasting only 'bad' news to listeners in the former Yugoslavia.

The ITU contacted neighbouring countries in the Balkans about Radio Brod's broadcasts and subsequently received a communication from the Consul of St. Vincent and the Grenadines in Monaco, who wrote explaining that a ship flying his country's flag was broadcasting from the Adriatic and asked if this was illegal in any way. The ITU informed him that under the terms of Article 422 of the 1959 Geneva Convention prohibiting offshore radio broadcasting it was illegal, but admitted that if a member country chose to ignore the Convention then there was little the ITU could do about it.

Having received this response from the ITU the St. Vincent and Grenadines Government withdrew its registration of the *Droit de Parole* on 28th June 1993 and Radio Brod was forced to close as its vessel was now technically stateless. Two days later the radio ship herself sailed to the Italian port of Bari, where the station had its offices based in a hotel, while the Droit de Parole organisation approached the ITU requesting the allocation of an official frequency to enable Radio Brod to resume its transmissions.

There then followed a month of discussions and negotiations with the various authorities in Europe and St. Vincent and the Grenadines. The Droit de Parole organisation explained in great detail to the Government of St. Vincent the nature of their offshore project and that it was supported and backed financially by the European Community and a United Nations organisation.

After Radio Brod had been off the air for nearly four weeks the authorities in St Vincent agreed to reinstate the ship's registration on a temporary basis for a period of three months, and consequently the station was able to return to the air at the beginning of August 1993.

When it returned Radio Brod continued to use 720kHz because the station's organisers had become totally frustrated with bureaucratic delays at the ITU over negotiations for the allocation of a new frequency. The station was also reportedly considering acquiring a 100Kw transmitter to achieve greater coverage of its target area in the former Yugoslavia.

## French assistance refused

Droit de Parole also asked the French authorities to request mainstream UN support for Radio Brod, but the new French Government, who had already refused to help the project financially, refused, quoting the 1982 UN Convention of the Law of the Sea (UNCLOS), under which they said the states of the former Yugoslavia would have the right to board the ship and stop Radio Brod's transmissions.

Although convenient to the French authorities this suggestion was somewhat misleading because the UNCLOS agreement had not then been ratified by the required number of states throughout the world and was not yet embodied in international law. (see Chapter 20)

During the early winter months of 1993 Radio Brod obtained further funding from the European Commission and the Emergency Humanitarian Aid Office, enabling it to continue broadcasting until February 1994. However, following this additional funding allocation some questions were raised by the Dutch Government about the financial arrangements of Radio Brod and its parent organisation, Droit de Parole.

The European Commission asked British journalist, Jim Fish, to investigate the financial management of the station both on land and on board the radio ship. The report produced after this investigation showed that there was a lack of good financial management and those working on board the *Droit de Parole* who had been promised salaries of £1,100 per month, were being paid approximately three months in arrears.

These reports of financial management difficulties were enough for the European Commission to decide not to renew funding for Radio Brod after February 1994. With the cessation of funding from its main source Radio Brod was forced to close at midnight on 28th February 1994 and organisers claimed at a press conference in Rome the following day that they had received no prior warning that backing was to cease. The station made a brief return for a few days on 7th March 1994, but closed again while new sources of funding were sought.

Ultimately this funding was not forthcoming and Radio Brod never returned to the air.

## Legality justified

*In April 1993 a spokesman for Radio Brod justified the legality of his station claiming "We are not like Radio Caroline, broadcasting a few hours of pop music and working for commercial programmes. We are fighting for the dignity of professional journalists to stop the war and re-establish the dialogue between those parts of Yugoslavia that do not communicate anymore. This gives moral legitimacy to the project"*

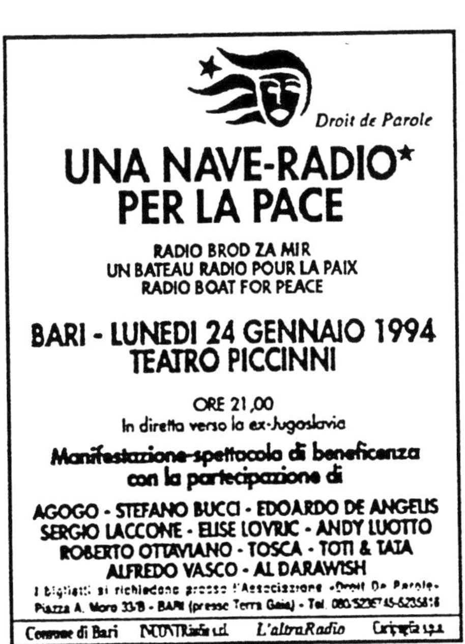

# Chapter 29

# Offshore onshore

The year 1992 opened with considerable unrest and uncertainty inside the Caroline organisation. Having secured rights of access to the impounded *Ross Revenge* in Dover at the end of 1991 a number of internal disputes then broke out between various groups over responsibility for the radio ship. This was not the first (or last) occasion such disputes came to the surface, but it was important that someone with a reasonable degree of authority should be able to deal on behalf of the Caroline organisation with the various official bodies if the *Ross Revenge* was to have any future at all with the station.

To that end Peter Moore (who since 1987 had clandestinely organised supplies of food, fuel and equipment for the *Ross Revenge* when she was at sea) became the spokesman for the station in all its dealings with the various official bodies.

Peter Moore had support and official backing from Caroline's founder Ronan O'Rahilly and despite considerable uncertainty about the true ownership of the *Ross Revenge* he was able to convince the authorities that, although title to the vessel could not be proved in the legal sense, they should deal with him if any progress was to be made with securing the repair and release of the vessel.

During the first few months of 1992 much work was put in repairing and renovating the *Ross Revenge* while at the same time those responsible for Radio Caroline tried to ensure that the station's programmes were broadcast on as many outlets as possible to maintain a presence on the airwaves.

At this time Radio Caroline could be heard on satellite via Radio Noordzee International in Norway, on shortwave via Radio Fax in Ireland and Radio New York International in America. Also from Easter 1992 a Caroline programme was broadcast on a local FM station in Calais, Radio 6, whose transmissions were audible along the Kent coast. Audience figures from these outlets were not what Radio Caroline had been used to, but the shortwave transmissions did produce reception reports from across the world.

## First Licensed broadcast - Dover

Radio Caroline again made history with its first licensed transmission from the *Ross Revenge* which began on 7th April 1992. It was also the first occasion on which Radio Caroline had broadcast using an FM frequency. The station obtained a Restricted Service Licence (RSL) from the Radio Authority for low power temporary broadcasts to a specific area, in this case Dover.

Broadcasts opened officially at 7.00am with Chris Kennedy and the event attracted considerable media coverage in the press and on local television. The programmes were presented live from the *Ross Revenge* using a microwave link to a transmitter sited on Dover Castle. Although the service was limited to the Dover area some significant advertisers bought airtime including National Coaches and English Heritage, the Government agency responsible for historic buildings including Dover Castle.

### Jocelyn Stevens

*The Chairman of English Heritage at the time of the Dover RSL broadcasts was Jocelyn Stevens who, nearly thirty years earlier, had been one of the driving forces, with Ronan O'Rahilly, behind the launch of Radio Caroline (See Chapter 6)*

The Dover RSL broadcasts covered the Easter holiday period of 1992 and marked Caroline's 28th 'official' birthday. Although Radio Caroline started transmissions on 28th March 1964 the station always considered Easter, whatever date it fell on, to be its 'official' birthday.

London ILR station, Spectrum 558 (which the authorities had sought to bring into conflict with Radio Caroline over the allocation of a frequency in 1991 (see Chapter 26) carried a special two hour programme on 24th April 1992 which included a history of the offshore station interspersed with relevant music.

When the Dover RSL finished at midnight on 4th May 1992 Radio Caroline immediately began broadcasting its programmes over satellite station QEFM. This service became a regular feature of QEFM programming between 2.00am and 6.00am each morning and the programmes were originated from Caroline's landbased studios in London.

Radio Caroline was awarded a satellite licence of its own by the Radio Authority in July 1992 and at the beginning of August started transmitting programmes via the Eutelsat satellite using a sub-carrier of the Red Hot Dutch adult television channel. At about this time too further shortwave broadcasts of Radio Caroline programmes took place from a site in Ireland. So, by various means, the station was continuing to keep a limited presence on the airwaves.

### QEFM

*Satellite broadcaster QEFM started life as a company (Radio Cheltenham Ltd.) established to bid for the ILR licence in Cheltenham in 1991. After failing to gain the Cheltenham licence the company turned to satellite and QEFM was born. After trading for a few months the station closed having failed to attract sufficient advertising to cover operating costs. Some of the people involved with the original company moved the station to Chris Carey's premises in Camberley (previously used for satellite Radio Nova and some Caroline satellite broadcasts). From here QEFM continued broadcasting until in January 1994 it was forced to close because of trading losses.*

## 25th Anniversary of the Marine etc. Broadcasting (Offences) Act

Mid-August 1992 marked the 25th Anniversary of the introduction of the British Marine etc. Broadcasting (Offences) Act 1967. In recognition of this event a number of radio stations broadcast special programmes including Capital Gold in London, which re-created the sounds of 1967 with ex-offshore DJs Tony Blackburn, Mike Ahearn and Tony Prince. The BBC local station in London, GLR, also presented some programmes based on 1967 news and music, featuring an interview with ex-Radio England and Caroline South DJ, Johnnie Walker and a 1967 Top 40 presented by another former Caroline South DJ, Tommy Vance. Various other ILR stations across the country also mounted special programmes to mark this particular anniversary in the history of offshore radio.

## First licensed offshore radio station

Another significant event to mark the 25th Anniversary of the Act's introduction was the establishment of Britain's first legal, licensed offshore radio station.

Members of the listeners' supporters group, the Caroline Movement, decided to mark the event by linking an offshore radio convention over the weekend of 14/15th August 1992 the operation of an RSL station based on a ship anchored off the Essex coast.

In April 1992 the Caroline Movement's Publicity Officer, John Burch, (who had been involved in exploratory talks in 1991 about the possibility of Radio Caroline being granted a landbased licence (see Chapter 26) renewed his contacts with the Director of the Radio Communications Agency and the Radio Authority. By the end of the month approval in principle had been given to the granting of a Restricted Service Licence to a station housed on a ship anchored within British territorial limits.

## The Caroline Movement and the *Galexy*

*The Caroline Movement had been the focal point of listeners' support for Radio Caroline during its later years from the 'Mi Amigo'.*

*When the 'Mi Amigo' sank in March 1980 the future for the Caroline Movement appeared bleak - there was no offshore radio station on the air, and it seemed certain that membership of the listeners' group would dwindle. In an effort to maintain interest and support a project was launched to try and pay for the purchase and re-floating of the former Radio London ship, 'Galaxy', then in Keil Harbour, West Germany. The long-term objective of this ambitious scheme - known as Project Galaxy - was to bring the ship back to Britain and fit her out as an offshore radio museum.*

*Unfortunately, although negotiations with the German authorities reached an advanced stage the Caroline Movement were unsuccessful in persuading them to actually release the ship. Finally in August 1986, following increasing pressure from local environmentalists the wreck of the former Radio London vessel was salvaged and scrapped (see Chapter 23) and Project Galaxy appeared to have foundered.*

*In the meantime Radio Caroline had returned from the 'Ross Revenge' and Laser 558 was transmitting from the 'Communicator' so the Caroline Movement once more had an active membership, with publications, events and a revival of its sightseeing trips for enthusiasts.*

*In 1987, when the Territorial Sea Act forced the radio ships to anchor further out to sea, the Caroline Movement had to look at the possibility of using a larger vessel to continue its sightseeing trips and they acquired the use of a former River Tyne ferry, 'Tyne Princess'. This vessel was actually purchased by Captain Alex Pluck for his own personal use, but an agreement was arrived at whereby the Caroline Movement would provide funding and volunteer labour towards renovating the ship in return for the use of her on sightseeing trips to the radio ships.*

*The former ferry was re-named 'Galexy', (an acronym of Captain Pluck's first name with that of the original Radio London ship) and she was sailed from Tyneside to Kent where many months were spent by volunteer workers renovating and restoring her.*

*In August 1987 the 'Galexy' made her first sightseeing voyage to the 'Ross Revenge' and continued to do so until May 1988 when the authorities followed and then raided her on a return trip from the radio ship. After this incident the vessel was still used clandestinely on occasions to assist and supply the radio ships. Following the raid on the 'Ross Revenge' in 1989 the 'Galexy' was one of a very small number of vessels whose owners were prepared to go near the radio ship to deliver supplies of fuel and water.*

Discussions were held with Radio Caroline's Station Manager, Peter Moore and the Euronet satellite organisation about various possible combinations of co-operative ventures to give Radio Caroline a voice at the time of this important anniversary in offshore radio history. However, Radio Caroline was already planning to have another RSL service of its own in August 1992, this time from Chatham, where it was hoped the *Ross Revenge* would then be based. In view of this it soon became clear that another vessel would have to be found as a base for any proposed 'offshore' RSL station. The Caroline Movement managed to persuade Captain Alex Pluck that his vessel, *Galexy* - which the Movement had helped renovate in the first place - should become home for Britain's first legal offshore radio station and work started on refurbishing the vessel during May 1992.

Unfortunately the Caroline Movement only had sufficient funds at its disposal to operate the RSL radio station over the Convention weekend of 14/15th August 1992 and further resources, financial and practical, had to be obtained if the station was to broadcast for the full 28 days permitted by the Licence. Fortunately operators of a former London land-based pirate agreed to invest some money and provide staff for the continued operation of the station after the Convention weekend. Income generated from admission charges to the Convention was to be used to finance copyright fees for the period of the Licence, but other running costs would have to be found from advertising income or sponsorship deals.

Work on the *Galexy* continued throughout the summer at Hoo Marina including the construction and installation of a studio and transmitting equipment. Two masts, constructed from fibreglass poles and bamboo sections, were erected on the ship with an aerial array strung between them. Conditions attached to the Restricted Service Licence prohibited an aerial being more than ten metres (33feet) above ground level, although this height limit was somewhat more difficult to define precisely on an offshore station! However, it was planned to achieve a reasonably strong signal using booster coils built into the aerial array, aided by the natural conductivity of the vast area of salt water surrounding the radio ship.

## Offshore Radio 1584

The *Galexy* left Hoo Marina in the early hours of Thursday 13th August 1992, arriving at her anchorage off Walton-on-the-Naze Pier in mid-afternoon. Test transmissions under the call sign Offshore Radio 1584 started shortly after wards and continued throughout the night. During the evening DJs on board the *Galexy* revived the 'Frinton Flashing' programme made famous in the 1960s by Johnnie Walker on Radio Caroline South.

The new offshore station received publicity on Sky Television, regional television news programmes and in the local Essex and East Anglian press. At midnight on 14/15th August 1992 Offshore Radio 1584 re-enacted what had happened exactly 25 years previously on board Radio Caroline South by broadcasting tapes of the famous Johnnie Walker/Robbie Dale "into illegality" programme and playing "All We Need is Love" by the Beatles.

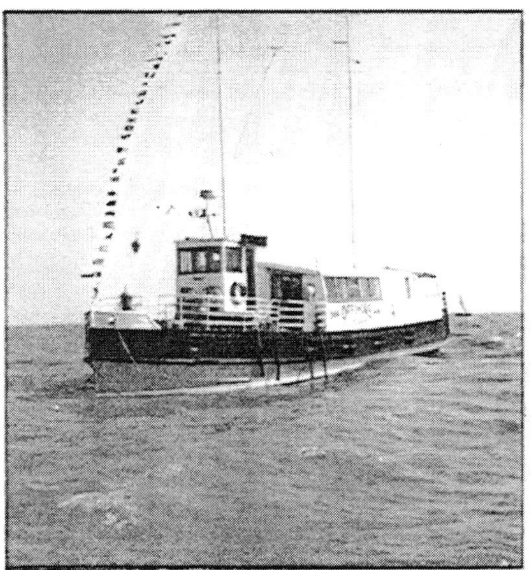

The 'Galexy' moored off Walton-on-the-Naze, August 1992

**Pop pirates to relive their early days on the waves**

POP pirate enthusiasts, including top disc jockeys from the sixties, will be in Walton to mark the 25th anniversary of the outlawing of pirate radio stations.

The radio station Offshore Radio will be moored just over a mile off Walton Pier.

It will mark the anniversary by legally broadcasting the sixties hits.

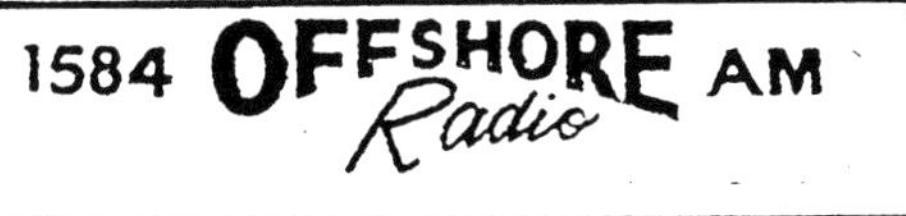


The Offshore Radio Convention itself was held on Saturday 15th August 1992 at the Naze Mariner Hotel, Walton-on-the-Naze, with appearances from many offshore radio personalities as well as DJs involved in the Offshore Radio 1584 service. Throughout the day tape recordings from the former offshore stations which had broadcast off the British or Dutch coasts were played. Some live programmes were also presented from the *Galexy* and it was hoped that personalities from the offshore radio stations of the 60s, 70s and 80s would join the crew during the day. Unfortunately although not all the personalities who were expected actually arrived at the Convention, and those who did were prevented from visiting the *Galexy* by rough weather.

The bad weather continued throughout the night of 15/16th August 1992, causing the crew on board the *Galexy* some problems and putting the station off

## Offshore Radio Memories

*A similar legal offshore station was also operating on Holland on 15/16th August 1992. Radio Plus, the local station in IJmuiden broadcast from a ship, 'Willem Beukelj', anchored off the Dutch coast for two days in August under the call sign "Offshore Radio Memories". The station's programmes covered the history of offshore radio, particularly the Dutch stations, and attracted a number of guest presenters who had worked on the offshore stations.*

the air for a few hours. Eventually it was decided to move the ship to a more sheltered location at Stone Point, but she later returned to the original anchorage off Walton-on-the-Naze Pier.

## Satellite broadcasts

The Euronet satellite service broadcast tapes of Offshore Radio 1584 programmes throughout August 1992 and on Bank Holiday Monday (31st August) changed their schedules completely to air 1584 tapes practically all day, giving the station a much wider potential audience than it could possibly achieve from its RSL transmitter.

Offshore Radio 1584 continued broadcasting throughout the week after the Convention but further practical problems began to develop and these combined with a lack of substantial advertising income seemed likely to threaten the operation of the station for the remainder of its licence period.

On 1st September 1992 a Department of Transport Marine Inspector visited the *Galexy* to inspect safety and firefighting equipment. During the inspection it was discovered that the safety certificate on the ship's life rafts had expired and the lifejackets did not carry the required markings. Additionally the ship's name, *Galexy*, did not correspond with Department of Transport records which still referred to her as the *Tyne Princess*. Because of these apparent deficiencies in complying with various regulations the Inspector would not permit the *Galexy* to return to sea and she had to remain in the safety of the Stone Point anchorage for the remainder of her time as home to Offshore Radio 1584.

A party was held on board the *Galexy* during the final day of broadcasting on 9th September 1992 and Euronet again rearranged their schedules to allow recordings of the offshore station's closing programmes to be carried a few days later. Another 'Frinton Flashing' programme was broadcast immediately before Offshore Radio 1584's final hour between 11.00pm and midnight.

Offshore Radio 1584 had been the fulfilment of a personal ambition for a group of offshore radio enthusiasts. Its concept was to recreate, as far as possible, the sort of pop music station which had existed in the heyday of offshore radio during the 1960s. By anchoring within sight of the same Essex coastal towns (Frinton on Sea and Walton-on-the-Naze) as the original stations - although much closer to the shore - it was hoped to target the large audience in the south east of England, who although now a generation older held such fond memories of listening to Radios Caroline South, London, England and all the other offshore stations of the time.

Unfortunately the reality did not fully live up to the expectation. Transmitter power for Offshore Radio 1584 was very substantially below that of even the smallest 1960s station and consequently reception was limited to the Essex coastal area. The lack of any major advertising contracts caused financial problems for Offshore Radio 1584 and it just about got through its 28 days by selling some airtime to local businesses in the Frinton and Walton-on-the-Naze areas. Staffing also proved problematic and responsibility for programming a full 28 days output fell to a small number of dedicated enthusiasts and friends who gave up all their spare time to keep the station on the air. With one or two notable exceptions big name DJs from the 60s and 70s stations, who owed their success to offshore radio in the first place, failed to show any support for Britain's first legal offshore radio station, or even to recognise the significance of the event it had been established to commemorate.

Nevertheless, the fact that Offshore Radio 1584 ever came about in the first place and that it lasted the full 28 days of its RSL licence period, is a tribute to the tenacity and dedication of those individuals behind it. Offshore Radio 1584, despite its low profile and various shortcomings, rightly deserves its place in offshore radio history for the sole reason that it was Britain's first legal offshore station.

## Radio Caroline's Chatham licence

As the Caroline Movement had been informed earlier in the year Radio Caroline itself had plans to be on the air from the *Ross Revenge* again in 1992. The station obtained a licence from the Radio Authority to broadcast to the Chatham area for 28 days from 10th August.

It had originally been intended to move the *Ross Revenge* from Dover to Chatham's Historic Naval Dockyard in time for the broadcast. However, the Department of Transport would not carry out a survey of the *Ross Revenge* (which it was hoped would lead to a lifting of the Detention Order) because of concerns over the registration and ownership of the radio ship.

Nevertheless having obtained the licence it was decided to continue with the broadcast and alternative arrangements were hurriedly put in place. At first the broadcast was made from temporary studios in Chatham, linked to the *Ross Revenge* by landline and microwave link then, after three days, live programming was introduced from the radio ship in Dover. The technical process enabling this to happen was achieved by a complicated route via a microwave link from the *Ross Revenge* to Dover Castle, a BT landline to Brighton, followed by another landline to London then to the transmitter site in Chatham. Because of delays in arranging both this link and the temporary studios in Chatham some of the 28 days of the licence period were lost and the broadcast only took place for just over two weeks from 22nd August to 7th September 1992 - resulting in lost advertising income.

### Legend

*At this difficult time in its history Radio Caroline was clearly taking every opportunity to keep its programmes on the air however limited the technical facilities or potential audience may have been. When asked in a magazine interview in September 1992 to explain why Radio Caroline managed to succeed in spite of all its difficulties Station Manager, Peter Moore said:- "You can't kill off a legend. Caroline has become something many try to copy, but they never succeed. She is the world's best known radio station - now offering high tech reception on low tech equipment. Who else can claim that ?"*

## Loss of outlets

After managing to maintan a presence on the airwaves through a variety of outlets for nearly nine months Radio Caroline's activities became somewhat curtailed after the end of the Chatham broadcast in September 1992.

Coincidentally at about that time satellite station QEFM discontinued the Caroline overnight programmes, selling the airtime to another broadcaster willing to pay a larger fee. One of the main shortwave outlets carrying Radio Caroline's programmes, Radio Fax, also closed in the autumn of 1992 following pressure from the Irish authorities, while Caroline's own shortwave transmissions became more erratic and were hardly on the air at all during September and October 1992.

However, Radio Caroline could still be heard some days each week via Scandinavian satellite station, RNI (although often these were repeats of old programme tapes) and on the audio sub-carrier of adult satellite station, Red Hot Dutch.

### Equipment to be returned

*The Dutch Ministry of Justice announced on 21st Septemmber 1992 that no charges would be brought against Dutch or British nationals arising from the raid on the 'Ross Revenge' in August 1989. The Ministry also agreed to return to Radio Caroline all broadcasting equipment and records seized during the raid, instead of disposing of the items by public auction as had been the original intention.*

*This offer was made following discussions Station Manager Peter Moore had held with Marten Roumen, (the Dutch policeman who led the raid on the 'Ross Revenge' and who was a self-confessed Caroline fan) at Euroradio 92 and was conditional on Radio Caroline signing an undertaking not to make any claims for damaged or missing items.*

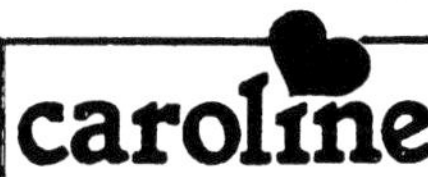

Radio Caroline can now be heard on a number of Satellite and Shortwave outlets as follows.

*SATELLITE*

**ASTRA** - Daily between 0130 and 0530 UTC/GMT on channel 16 on audio 7.38/7.56mhz. Live programming at weekends, taped during the week.

**EUTELSAT** - Weekends, Friday into Saturday and Saturday into Sunday from 2300 to 0200 on the TRT transponder on audio sub-carrier 7.38/7.56mhz.

**INTELSAT** - Mondays to Thursdays between 2100 and 2300 UTC/GMT on Intelsat VA F12 at one degree west, aimed at Scandinavia. Broadcasts are via the Norwegian TV4 11.09Ghz transponder on the mono 7.74Mhz subcarrier used by Radio Northsea International.

*SHORTWAVE*

**RADIO CAROLINE** now have their own shortwave outlet on 6305khz. Programmes from the Irish based transmitter can be heard from 1000 to 0200 every Saturday and Sunday. Moving to 6295khz and higher power soon.

**RADIO NEWYORK INTERNATIONAL** air a specially recorded Caroline news and music programme between 0400 and 0430 UTC/GMT on Monday mornings on 7435khz to North America and worldwide via a 100kw transmitter.

**RADIO FOR PEACE INTERNATIONAL** in Costa Rica repeat the Radio NewYork tapes at various times on their three shortwave frequencies of 7375, 13630 and 25945khz.

Over the Christmas holiday period of 1992 Radio Caroline programmes were broadcast via the Euronet satellite service from Christmas Eve until Boxing Day. Eighteen hours of programmes had been recorded on board the *Ross Revenge* and each one was repeated at some stage during the 36 hour broadcast.

The efforts to keep Radio Caroline on the air suffered some more setbacks at the beginning of 1993. Programmes returned on shortwave via the Radio New York International outlet on 11th January 1993, but this only lasted a few weeks because the RNYI operation was terminated in mid-February when Al Weiner became involved in another offshore project (see Chapter 24). Coincidentally at the beginning of January 1993 the Scandinavian satellite station RNI closed due to financial problems, while Caroline's own satellite service on Red Hot Dutch also came to an end 'for technical reasons'. for a while this left the shortwave service from Ireland as the only outlet carrying Caroline programmes, but even this was often off the air some weekends. Fortunately after a few weeks absence the RNI satellite service returned with new backers and once again Caroline programmes were broadcast for two hours each night.

### Radio 538

*In October 1992 former Radio Veronica DJ Lex Harding launched a new Dutch cable station, Radio 538 (named after Veronica's last wavelength in its offshore days). Many former Veronica DJs also joined the new station. On 7th November the station's DJs went on board the ex-Radio Veronica ship, 'Norderney' which was then in Maastricht and presented a day of programmes chronicling the history of the offshore station. Radio 538 went on satellite on 11th December 1992 with an opening announcement by the former Managing Director of Radio Veronica, Bul Verweij.*

## Return and release

All equipment confiscated by the Dutch during the raid on the *Ross Revenge* in 1989 was collecetd by Station Manager Peter Moore and Mike Dundee early in January 1993 following the abolition of restrictions on the free flow of goods between member states of the European Union., The studio and broadcasting equipment was eventually re-installed on the *Ross Revenge* while the thousands of records had to be re-catalogued and returned to the on-board library.

Over Easter 1993 (Caroline's 29th 'official' birthday) plans were made to link the *Ross Revenge* with Radio 6 in Calais for a series of live transmissions. Although the British Radio Communications Agency approved the plan the French authorities blocked it on the grounds that interferremnce may be caused to maritime communications. Radio 6 already broadcast regular monthly programmes presented by Caroline DJs and another French local station, WIT-FM in Bordeaux began to carry a live programme presented by Caroline DJ, Bongo, for a month from May 1993. A similar arrangement was undertaken by Johnny Reece in september 1994 when he presented Caroline programmes over Fugue FM, based outside Paris.

### Radio Luxembourg

*Radio Luxembourg (which had closed its English language service on 208m at the end of 1991) decided to terminate its satellite delivered service on 30th December 1992 due to lack of advertising revenue. A number of former Luxembourg (and offshore) DJs joined the station for the last day and at 7.00pm the German Service 'loaned' the 208m wavelength to the English Service for its final few hours.*

*During the evening a documentary history of Radio Luxembourg's 59 years on the air was broadcast and former DJs recounted their expeienceds on the station. Radio Caroline's Station Manager, Peter Moore faxed a 'thank you' message to Luxembourg which was read out on air by Jodie Scott, who as Judy Murphy had been a DJ on Radio Caroline in the late 1980s.*

*Radio Luxembourg's English Service finally closed at midnight on 30th December 1992 following a farewell message from Manager John Catlett, who, through MMI, had previously been responsible for the sales operation of offshore stations Laser 558 and Laser Hot Hits in the 1980s.*

Meanwhile work continued on refurbishing and repairing the *Ross Revenge*. The ship's engines were put in working order for the first time in many years and successfully tested over Easter 1993. Other repairs and repainting work were also undertaken in the hope that the vessel would be released from its Detention Order by the Department of Transport. However, the authorities were still stalling over carrying out another inspection of the vessel because of uncertainty about the ownership of the *Ross Revenge*.

Then after many months of negotiations with the Department of Transport agreement was finally reached in September for the vessel to be inspected. The objective was to have the Detention Order temporarily lifted so that the *Ross Revenge* could be moved away from Dover to a less expensive mooring.

In September 1993 a Department of Transport surveyor, Sam Parker, inspected the *Ross Revenge* and whilst agreeing that much repair and renovation work had been done he issued a list of final requirements which would have to be fulfilled before the Detention Order could be temporarily lifted. On 20th October another Department of Transport Inspector, Charles Curry, re-inspected the ship and was satisfied with the remedial work which had been done. A Load Line Exemption Certificate was then issued, followed a week later by an Order for Release.

Just hours after this Order had been granted the *Ross Revenge* was made ready to leave Dover. A new, cheaper mooring for the vessel had been found in the River Blackwater in Essex and the *Ross Revenge* was finally towed out of the port by the tug *Sea Challenge*. In accordance with Department of Transport requirements the *Ross Revenge* was sealed and unmanned while under tow and she reached her new mooring late in the evening of 27th October 1993.

By the beginning of 1994 rumours were circulating that Radio Caroline would return from a new ship of its own, or possibly using airtime facilities from one of the frequencies available on the new offshore station aboard the MV *Fury* (see Chapter 24). Various press reports appeared during January 1994 indicating that Radio Caroline was planning such a return from an offshore base in time for the station's 30th Birthday in March. There was even a description of a former Russian fish factory ship allegedly being converted to house the station. However as with so many previous rumours these stories came to nothing.

### Virgin 1215

*Britain's second national commercial radio station came on the air in April 1994. Virgin 1215, part of Richard Branson's Virgin Group had beaten off competition from other bidders to provide a national rock music format station.*

*Ironically the main frequency allocated to the national station, 1215kHz, was that formerly used by BBC Radio One when it was launched to 'replace' the offshore stations. In those days it was better known by its wavelength equivalent - 247m.*

*Richard Branson had long wanted to become involved in commercial radio and the format adopted by Virgin 1215 was reminiscent of Radio Caroline's pioneering album rock format. During the weeks of test transmissions preceding Virgin 1215's launch many listeners who contacted the station to convey their support for the format also drew comparisons with Radio Caroline.*

*Almost from the outset Virgin was unhappy with having to use a medium wave frequency and campaigned for the allocation of an FM channel. The station did not succeed in this campaign, but it did bid successfully for the allocation of an FM licence in London which it used largely relay the national output and provide improved reception for listeners in the capital*

## Isle of Man connection

A seemingly more hopeful scenario unfolded in February 1994 in the Isle of Man. The Island's Government considered a report on the future of its local station, Manx Radio which had been commissioned after local businessman Brian Kreisky had expressed an interest in taking over the station.

Brian Kreisksy owned the successful sports video production company, Video Vision, based on the Isle of Man and had held talks with Ronan O'Rahilly during the summer of 1993 when the idea of using one of Manx Radio's frequencies to broadcast Radio Caroline North programmes was discussed. However, after considering the 300 page report the Island's Government decided that there should be no change in the existing broadcasting arrangements or in the ownership of Manx Radio.

Nevertheless some further discussions were held with Manx Radio about the possibility of Radio Caroline hiring airtime on the local station, possibly as an overnight sustaining service. A documentary about the history of Radio Caroline and its associations with the Isle of Man was produced on board the *Ross Revenge* and Manx Radio transmitted the programme at Easter 1994. Unfortunately yet again nothing definite came of these plans to return Caroline North to the airwaves.

## Radio Caroline's 30th Birthday

The 30th Birthday of the most famous offshore station was marked at the end of March 1994 by a number of special events.

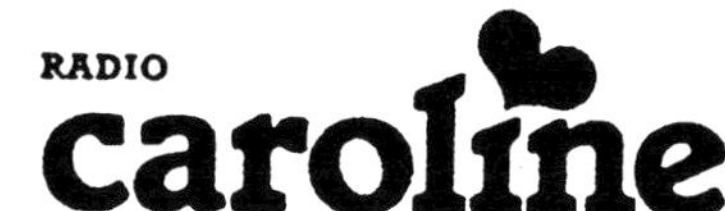


Frinton based television and radio production company East Anglian Productions arranged a '30th Birthday Bash' at the Highbells Holiday Camp, Clacton on Sea over the weekend of 26/27th March. This event included films, discussions, a dinner and a disco (hosted by ex-Caroline DJs Andy Archer and Paul Graham) as well as a special live appearance by The Fortunes, whose recording of "Caroline" had been the stations theme for much of its 30 year life.

On 27th March, 1994 Southend based ILR station, Breeze AM gave over eight hours of airtime to broadcast a special programme, "All at Sea" live from the *Ross Revenge*. The programmes, hosted by Ray Clark and Peter Phillips (both ex-Caroline DJs) featured a detailed history of Radio Caroline and included jingles and relevant musical items played between over thirty interviews with offshore personalities and the station's founder, Ronan O'Rahilly.

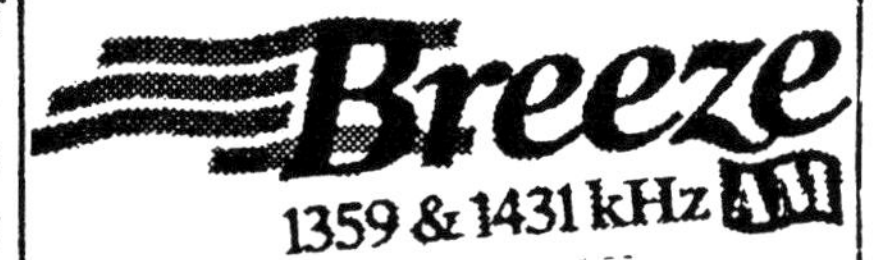


A number of other ILR and BBC local radio stations throughout the country also broadcast special tribute programmes around the time of Caroline's 30th Birthday and the occasion received coverage on Sky TV, GMTV as well as local television in the south east and East Anglia.

### London ILR Licences

*In May 1994 six licences to operate radio stations in London were advertised by the Radio Authority. A group closely associated to Radio Caroline again submitted an application (a similar application had been made in 1993 using the title Lazer FM, but had not been successful) to provide a rock music service under the title Rock City FM. The group planned to use a ship (not necessarily the 'Ross Revenge') moored in the Thames as its broadcasting base and to invite Radio Caroline to become its programme provider. Unfortunately the application was not successful.*

## South East Boatshow RSL

Plans for an RSL service by Radio Caroline itself over the 30th Birthday weekend did not come to fruition but a broadcast did take place between 16th May and 13th June 1994 in conjunction with the promotion of the South East Boatshow in Burnham on Crouch.

Because of the Detention Order which was still in force on the *Ross Revenge* as well as the prohibitive cost of relocating the vessel it was not possible to have the radio ship actually at the Boat Show in Burnham as originally planned. Nevertheless programmes were produced on board the *Ross Revenge* and broadcast via a link to a landbased transmitter site. For the final few days of the Licence period programmes were relayed live from studios at the Boat Show itself.

This particular Caroline RSL broadcast received a lot of press publicity, some of it for a number of unexpected reasons.

Veteran Caroline DJ Johnnie Walker took part in a number of programmes, including attempts to re-create the Frinton Flashing sequence from his 1960s programmes on Caroline South and this generated widespread publicity, particularly in the reception area of the broadcast.

On more than one occasion the broadcasts were deliberately jammed, prompting Station Manager Peter Moore to alert the Radio Investigation Service. The source of the jamming was traced to a device powered by a car battery and tuned to the frequency linking the ship to the landbased transmitter site. Peter Moore tried to obtain agreement from the Radio Authority for a five day extension of the licence period to compensate for the delays and breaks in transmission caused by this illegal jamming, but this request was refused.

During the broadcast Kent Police used Radio Caroline to trace and arrest a person suspected of committing burglaries in the Burnham area. The suspected person was known to be a Radio Caroline fan and crew recognised pictures of him as having been a visitor to the *Ross Revenge*. Police later arrested him as he was about to join another sightseeing trip to the radio ship.

## Rocking the Boat

*The BBC planned to use the 'Ross Revenge' during the summer of 1994 to film some scenes in a three part drama production based on Ian Ross's book "Rocking the Boat". Set in the mid 1960s the story-line dealt with the establishment of a fictional offshore radio station, but had clear and close associations with Radio Caroline. Ian Ross had been one of the people involved with Ronan O'Rahilly in launching Radio Caroline in 1964. However because of delays in raising financial backing for the production filming on board the 'Ross Revenge ' did not take place at this time.*

## Refurbishment of the *Ross Revenge*

With the *Ross Revenge* anchored in the River Blackwater volunteer groups continued working throughout 1994 on rectifying many of the outstanding faults identified by the Department of Transport.

Ernie Stephenson, who had been involved with the ship in her days as a trawler as well as during her offshore broadcasting days, supervised and carried out much of this work until he suffered a stroke in late 1994, forcing him to take a less active role. By the end of 1994 the original list of over 100 faults had been reduced to less than 20, but these still included some major items relating to the operation of the ship's steering gear.

A further RSL broadcast from Radio Caroline took place over the Christmas and New Year holiday period of 1994/95. The broadcast, on 1584kHz (189m) started on 9th December 1994 and ended on 6th January 1995 with all transmissions coming from the *Ross Revenge's* on-board transmitter - the first time this had happened since the vessel had been at sea. Revenue raised during the broadcast from advertising sales as well as souvenirs and organised trips to the *Ross Revenge* was used to pay off some of the outstanding debts to Dover Harbour Board.

The final news bulletin during this RSL broadcast contained the following statement about the future of Radio Caroline:-

*An alternative to gaining a licence is to move the ship to international waters where Radio Caroline can broadcast to the whole of Europe under a licence granted by a foreign state. Caroline management are therefore continuing to investigate a means of restoring a full time high power AM marine station to the air, in order to return Caroline to her rightful place in the European radio industry. Legal bodies working for Caroline have said that while this option will not be the most straightforward it is still possible.*

## Caroline's shortwave transmitter destroyed

*The transmitter in Ireland used for Radio Caroline's shortwave broadcasts was destroyed in the late summer of 1994. The transmitter site was also used by a group which provided unauthorised relays of British television services to Ireland and a dispute between two local groups led to the building housing the transmitter being fire bombed and all equipment inside being destroyed. This effectively put an end to Caroline's shortwave broadcasts from Ireland.*

## Dutch commercial radio licences

In the autumn of 1993 it was announced that, following a ruling by the European Court, the Dutch Government had agreed to allocate certain frequencies previously used as part of the Hilversum network for operation by private commercial radio stations. Licences were subsequently advertised and by the closing date in December 1993 twenty seven applications had been received, including ones from cable and satellite stations Radio 538, Sky Radio, Radio 10 Gold and Holland FM. Peter Moore on behalf of a group known as the Radio Caroline Partnership also submitted an application as did London based Classic FM (whose application was submitted by ex-Caroline and Laser 558 DJ Paul Rusling).

The announcement of the successful applicants in January 1994 contained some surprises. Radio 10 Gold beat off competition from Sky Radio and Radio 538 to win an AM licence, Classic FM won a licence to broadcast on FM, Radio Noordzee National (a direct descendant of the Dutch offshore RNI operation) won an FM licence, Holland FM (operated by former Radio Veronica/Dutch RNI DJ, Joost de Draayer) won a licence to operate on nine different AM frequencies. Most of these were low power relays, but one (1224kHz) had been allocated a power of 23Kw. Another AM licence was awarded to AM Nieuws to operate a news and speech based service.

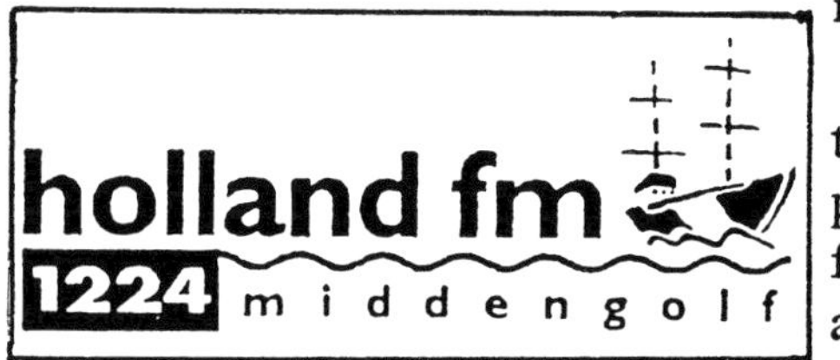


Holland FM had no sites to build transmitters, but the station solved this problem in a unique way - using a ship-based transmitter. Dutch planning regulations would have meant lengthy delays in arranging for a suitable landbased site, but a ship-based transmitter, moored on an inland sea to the north of Holland would not require planning permission.

The station at first expressed interest in acquiring the *Ross Revenge,* but with the ship still subject to a Detention Order from the British authorities attention turned to the MV *Communicator* in Portugal. Negotiations for the purchase of the *Communicator* continued throughout the spring and summer of 1994 and on 11th August th *Communicator* lef Portugal under tow by the Dutch tug *Vlieland.* The radio ship, re-painted in the Dutch national colours of red, white and blue, arrived in IJmuiden six days later with a short aerial mast in place - the remaining mast sections were stored on the deck ready to be erected to their full height of 180'. Former Radio Caroline engineer Peter Chicago was invited by Holland FM to assist with the installation of transmitting equipment on board the *Communicator.*

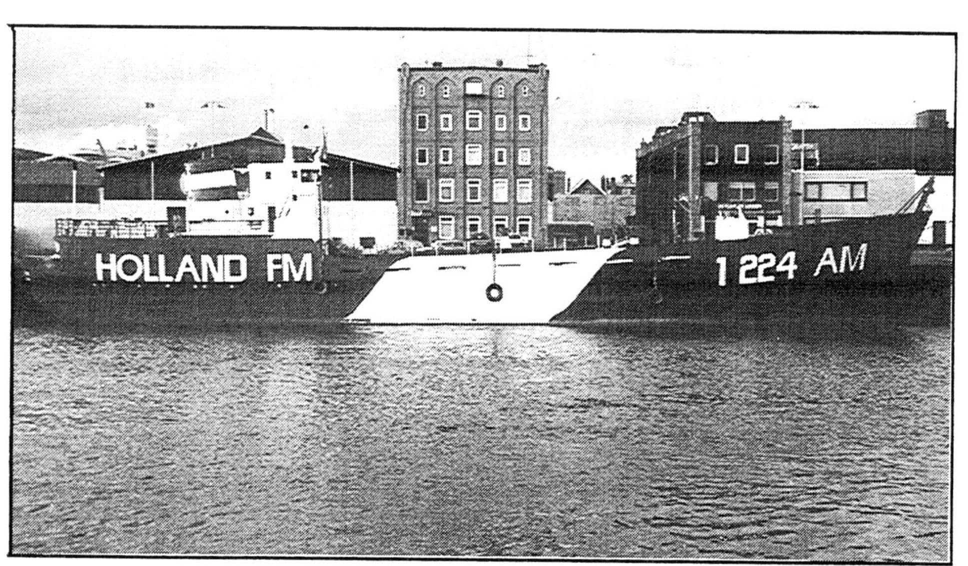


*The MV 'Communicator' ready to start broadcasts for Holland FM*

The installation of equipment took longer than anticipated and it was not until 10th October 1994 that the *Communicator* left IJmuiden for her new location in the Ijselmeer Sea. Regular transmissions of Holland Hit Radio as the station was now known, began in mid-November 1994, but although rudimentary studios had been constructed on board the *Communicator* the vessel was in fact only a relay station and not a fully operational radio ship in the normally accepted sense.

## Merger rumours

By late summer 1994, even before the *Communicator* had begun broadcasts in Holland rumours were circulating that Holland FM was seeking a merger with either RTL4 (a Dutch language satellite television and radio broadcaster backed by CTL in Luxembourg) or Radio Veronica, then part of the Hilversum public broadcasting system.

Radio Veronica had for some time been interested in leaving the public broadcasting system and becoming an independent commercial broadcaster. This would have been the station's ideal option in 1974 (see Chapter 17), but such a facility was not available then. However, by 1994 it was and the former offshore broadcaster began negotiations with one of Europe's largest independent programme makers, Endemol Entertainments. This organisation had been formed by Joop van den Ende and John de Mol Jr. (son of the ex- Programme Director of Veronica's greatest offshore rival, the Dutch RNI Service).

The terms of a proposed merger (announced co-incidentally just as the *Communicator* was being towed into IJmuiden) provided for Radio Veronica to quit the public system by September 1995 and, jointly with Endemol establish a commercial broadcasting organisation with five radio stations and one television station.

In order to create this network almost overnight Endemol was proposing to use Holland Hit Radio (over which it took complete control in October 1994) and purchase three other stations operated by the Radio 10 Group.

However, the plan to acquire these three stations fell through late in 1994 and a new arrangement was entered into by Veronica/Endemol. The combined operation, now known as the Veronica Media Group, approached CLT in Luxembourg which operated satellite television and radio station, RTL4 (to whom Endemol supplied a considerable amount of programme material). The complicated deal subsequently agreed provided for CLT to acquire 50% of the Veronica Media Group and a smaller stake in Endemol itself. Agreement on this deal was finally reached in March 1995 and the Holland Media Group was formed.

In a separate arrangement Veronica also entered into a partnership with press group Nederland Dagblad Unie (NDU) and business magazine *Quote* to set up a 24 hour news/ talk station after the original French-backed company awarded the licence for this service had backed out.

Plans were announced by the Holland Media Group for their transmissions to start on 1st September 1995 once Veronica had left the public broadcasting system and consideration was initially given to the possible re-purchase of the former Radio Veronica ship *Norderney,* to use as a transmitter base in conjunction with the *Communicator,* but this idea was dropped.

Another proposal by the Veronica news station also had an offshore connection. It initially wanted to base its transmitter on the REM Island (home of 1960s offshore Radio and TV Noordzee), but this proposal was blocked by the authorities who feared that a high power medium wave transmitter would affect the weather/ environmental monitoring equipment then installed on the artificial 'Island'. The news station also briefly flirted with the possibility of using a ship-based transmitter, but this idea was later dropped in favour of a landbased site.

Back in Britain refurbishment of the *Ross Revenge* was still in progress with volunteers working on the steering gear, firefighting equipment and removing an unservicable generator. A group of enthusiasts from the north east of England led by Peter Clayton regularly made the long journey to Essex to undertake this work.

Meanwhile Caroline broadcasts continued each month on Radio 6 in Calais until the beginning of July 1995 when a new station management discontinued the service. Programmes from Caroline were also aired for a time over a local station in Gibraltar, Solar Sound FM.

The major broadcasting event of 1995, however, was an RSL broadcast by Radio Caroline from the *Ross Revenge* anchored in a position offshore, although not actually outside territorial waters. Sponsorship for the broadcast had been obtained from the owner of Clacton Pier in Essex and the original plan was for the *Ross Revenge* to be moored alongside the Pier. However, this idea was abandoned because of doubts about the strength of the pier and also the depth of water available so close to shore. Instead it was decided to anchor the radio ship in a position approximately two miles off the coast.

Because the *Ross Revenge* was still under a Detention Order it was necessary to obtain permission from the Department of Transport to move the vessel from the River Blackwater. Department Inspector Sam Parker inspected the ship at the beginning of July 1995 and required certain safety arrangements to be put in order before permission could be granted for the move.

This work was completed and permission to move the *Ross Revenge* was granted at the beginning of August. On 4th August the radio ship was towed by the tug *Horton* from the River Blackwater to an anchorage off Clacton on Sea. Veteran offshore DJ from the 1960s, Tom Lodge, joined other DJs on board the *Ross Revenge* for the month long broadcasts. Transmissions, nostalgically using the frequency of 1503kHz (199m) began on 7th August. In addition to sponsorship from the Clacton Pier Company this particular broadcast attracted a large number of advertisers including major names such as McDonalds and Barratt Housing. A Caroline shop was established on Clacton Pier selling souvenirs of the station as well as other offshore radio memorabilia and boat trips took parties of visitors to the *Ross Revenge* (weather permitting) during the broadcasts.

**offshore trivia**

**Longest period off air**

*(1)Radio Caroline - 3 years 5 months (March 1980-August 1983)*

*(2) Voice of Peace - 1 year 6 months (November 1973-May 1975)*

*(3) Radio Delmare 7 months (September 1978-June 1979)*

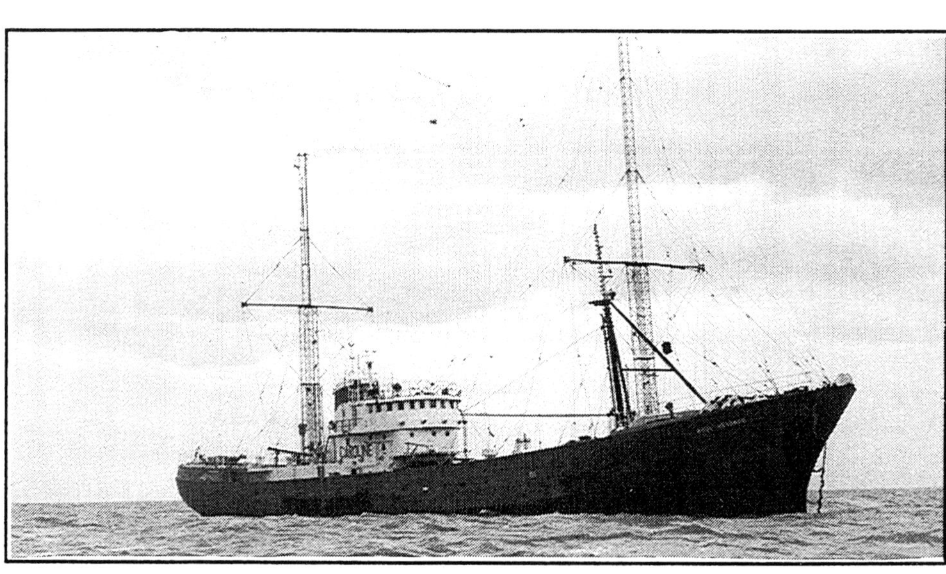

*The 'Ross Revenge' at anchor off Clacton, August 1995*

## Move to London

Immediately after the conclusion of the Clacton broadcast on 3rd September 1995 the *Ross Revenge* was towed to a sheltered position off Southend and then on 17th September she was tied up to Southend Pier. After ten days as a tourist attraction in Southend the radio ship was then towed by the tugs *Warrior* and *Horton* on a journey up the River Thames to the West India Dock where another RSL broadcast was to take place.

The towing of the Radio Caroline ship up the Thames was the fulfilment of a dream outlined by DJ Johnnie Walker in his Fight for Freedom Speech in 1967 (see Chapter 12) Although the circumstances were not entirely as he had envisaged this did not stop him and Caroline founder Ronan O'Rahilly joining the *Ross Revenge* on her journey up the River Thames.

The *Ross Revenge* took up position in the West India Dock at South Quay, ironically right outside the DTI's new offices. The London Docklands RSL broadcast had been sponsored by the organisation Charter 88, and in particular its youth section M-Power, - a pressure group established to encourage young people to register for the right to vote at local and parliamentary elections.

The arrival of the *Ross Revenge* in London received extensive media coverage and broadcasts on the opening day included programmes from ex-Caroline DJ Mike Ahearn, ex Laser 558 DJ Tommy Rivers and Tom Lodge also once again joined the station presenting programmes throughout the four week broadcast.

During her stay in London the *Ross Revenge* was visited by over 2,500 people and fees from these visits together with the sale of souvenirs and advertising time on air raised enough funds to clear debts to the Dover Harbour Board and for the River Blackwater mooring. Surplus funds were also now available to meet the cost of having the vessel dry-docked and inspected to assess her 'below the waterline' condition with a view to completing outstanding repairs required by the Department of Transport.

## Holland

In Holland Radio Veronica left the public broadcasting system and became an independent commercial broadcaster on 1st September 1995. Holland Hit Radio became Veronica Hit Radio from that date while a month later former RTL station Rock Radio became Veronica Kink FM, with an alternative rock music format. Meanwhile further competition entered the commercial arena after the Dutch Government agreed to allocate terrestrial licences to Radio 538 and Sky Radio (who had been unsuccessful in the original round of allocations and had mounted legal challenges in protest). The Government had relented to avoid the cost of prolonged legal action.

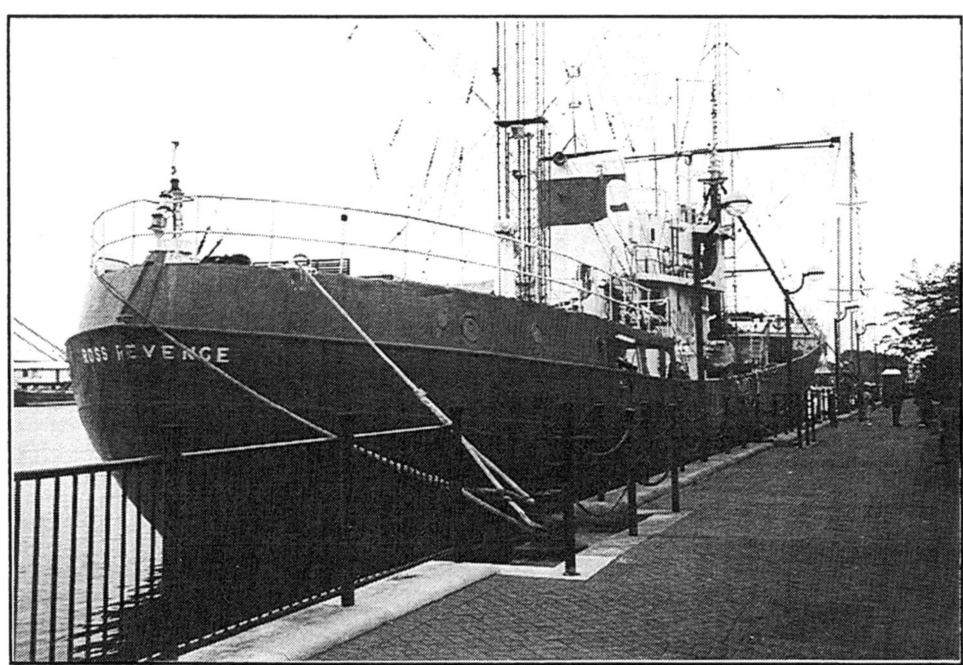


*The 'Ross Revenge' at South Quay, London Docklands, October 1995*

## Timely move

*The move from London Docklands was very timely - just four days later the IRA broke its ceasefire and renewed a mainland bombing campaign. A huge device exploded at South Quay, killing two people and badly damaging the buildings adjacent to where the 'Ross Revenge' had been moored during the Docklands RSL broadcast.*

By the spring of 1996 the Holland Media Group had decided to dispense with the *Communicator* as a transmitter base for Veronica Hit Radioand once again the vessel was put up for sale as a working radio ship. At about the same time the group's news/talk station, Veronica Nieuws Radio closed due to lack of advertising support.

## *Ross Revenge* dry docked

After the Docklands RSL broadcast finished in November 1995 the *Ross Revenge* remained in West India Dock, although she was moved slightly further along South Quay after complaints from occupiers of adjacent office buildings. During this time another internal dispute broke out within the Caroline organisation about the future of the station and the radio ship. Until this was resolved the plan to take the vessel into dry dock for inspection was delayed.

It was not until the 5th February 1996 that the *Ross Revenge* was finally towed from South Quay to the River Medway. The following day she was dry docked in Chatham Historic Naval Dockyard and the long awaited marine inspection took place.

Surprisingly because the ship had not been out of water since the early 1980s, the marine survey revealed that the *Ross Revenge* was in reasonably good condition and there had been virtually no wasting of metal on the hull. Some denting had been sustained on the starboard side, thought to have been caused by the ship bouncing on her trapped anchor chain, possibly on the Goodwin Sands. While the vessel was in dry dock her hull was re-painted and anodes were installed to prevent any deterioration of its condition.

After a few days in dry dock the *Ross Revenge* then moored in the River Medway, almost opposite the BBC Radio Kent studios, and during June 1996 another RSL service broadcast took place directed at the Chatham area.

As a result of the dry dock inspection the Marine Safety Agency (which had taken over responsibility for shipping safety matters from the Department of Transport) would not allow the *Ross Revenge* to be moved until damaged hull plates had been repaired. This effectively prevented another planned RSL broadcast taking place from Harwich in August 1996.

## Heartbeat

*An episode of the Yorkshire Television series "Heartbeat", which is set in the 1960s, featured a story-line involving an offshore radio station. The producers of the series originally approached Radio Caroline about the possibility of using the 'Ross Revenge' as a location for filming scenes in this particular episode. Unfortunately they were not able to use the vessel because the Harbour Master at Whitby refused to allow it to enter port due to its damaged steering gear. In any event the ship was still subject to Department of Transport restrictions and during the period of filming was involved in the Clacton and London Docklands RSL broadcasts. Instead the producers re-created an offshore radio ship - Radio North - using a coaster, 'Brendonian', suitably adapted with an aerial mast and rigging. East Anglian Productions produced a jingle package and provided some vintage studio equipment for use in making the episode.*

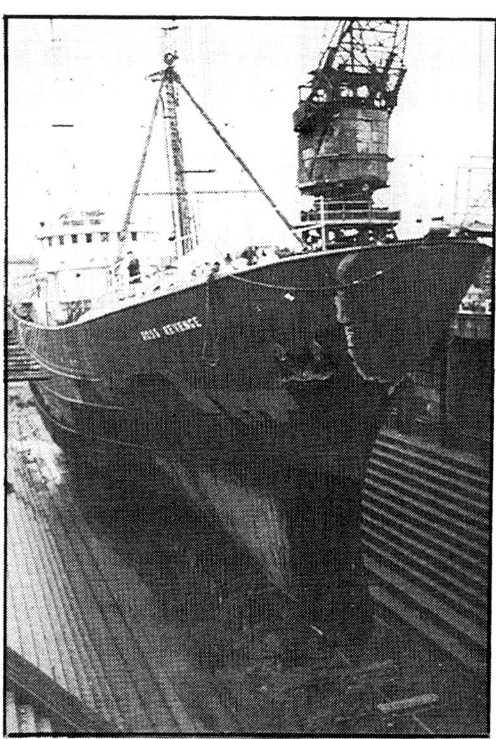

*The 'Ross Revenge' in dry dock at Chatham, February*

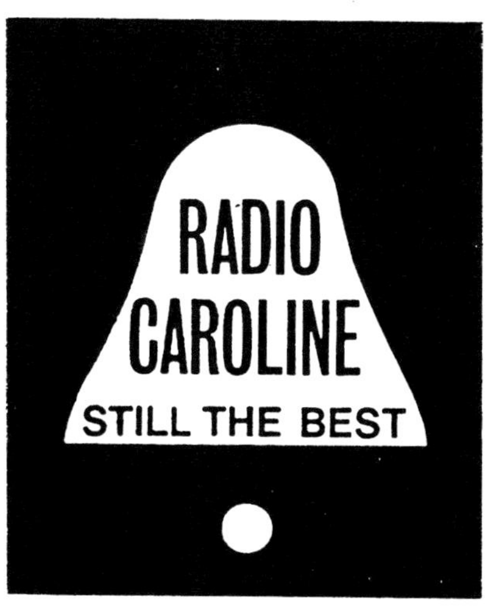

# Chapter 30

# Legacies and Future

By the mid-1990s nearly all the world's offshore radio and television stations had closed, either voluntarily or in the majority of cases as the result of legislation which made it impossible for them to continue. Only off the coast of Israel do offshore radio stations still broadcast while everywhere else the floating stations, which once attracted audiences numbered in millions, have vanished into history. So, after more than three and a half decades what had it all achieved, what impact had the phenomenon of offshore broadcasting made and what were its legacies?

The existence of offshore radio stations certainly shook up state broadcasting systems, forcing them to start providing the kind of programming listeners wanted to hear rather that what those controlling the airwaves felt they ought to hear.

Every area formerly served by offshore radio now also has a legal system of landbased commercially funded radio, but with the exception of New Zealand, this did not actually come about directly or immediately because of the offshore stations. The Scandinavian countries, Belgium, Britain and Holland all outlawed the stations off their coasts, but did not immediately introduce commercially funded replacements. Nevertheless the seeds of change had been sown by the offshore stations.

Only in New Zealand did the existence of an offshore station lead directly and simultaneously to the breaking of the state monopoly and the creation of independent, commercially funded broadcasting. Radio Hauraki was instrumental in bringing this revolution about and was rewarded with the granting of a licence to come ashore and broadcast legally - a situation many other offshore broadcasters were only able to dream about.

The New Zealand Government had sensibly parallelled its legislation to outlaw offshore broadcasting with legislation to introduce a landbased commercial radio network. This was an approach which other governments could have easily adopted, but instead they tried to preserve state monopolies for as long as possible, steadfastly refusing to accept the principle of commercially funded radio broadcasting.

Fortunately there is now a greater acceptance of commercially funded radio compared with the attitudes prevalent during the height of offshore activity in the 1960s and early 70s. Then the concept of a state monopoly was still seen as being the most appropriate, if not only, means by which radio broadcasting should be provided and, by implication, controlled.

With this change in attitude the introduction of commercial radio has eventually come about, providing a variety of choice for listeners as the offshore stations once did. It is this general acceptance of commercially funded radio, and with it the the breaking of state controlled monopolies, which is the major legacy of offshore broadcasting.

The offshore stations also exerted other, more general, influences on the world of entertainment and broadcasting, leaving behind some further significant legacies:-

- They provided a training ground and launching pad for the careers of many DJs and announcers who have since gone on to achieve further fame and popularity on landbased radio and television.
- They created a huge opportunity for launching and exposing new artists and independent record companies, many of whom have also achieved long lasting success.
- They created an awareness of radio as a successful and cost effective commercial medium for large and small advertisers.
- They drew attention to the ambiguities of the national (and international) frequency allocation system, eventually resulting in the freeing up of the broadcasting spectrum allowing a greater proliferation of local and national stations.
- They challenged the need for 'needletime' restrictions (which severely limited the amount of pre-recorded music a station could play during broadcasts). This eventually led to a complete relaxation of the restrictions, permitting stations to play virtually unlimited hours of pre-recorded music.

But perhaps the most intangible, yet significant, legacy of the offshore radio stations was - despite their relatively short individual lifespans - the enormous amount of pleasure they gave to listeners. Many people today still retain very happy memories of hours spent listening to the programmes of their favourite offshore station of twenty or thirty years ago.

## Future?

Is there any future for offshore radio and television as a means of communication?

Although as a concept offshore broadcasting has been virtually eliminated there are often stories and rumours of new stations being planned and ships being secretly fitted out in various ports. The remaining stations off the coast of Israel are tolerated at the moment, but in a volatile and highly charged political climate their life expectancy may be limited. The world's longest surviving offshore station, Radio Caroline, is still active and, although it is struggling financially and its ship is under restriction by the British authorities the station still manages to broadcast programmes over a number of, admittedly limited, outlets.

Many people associated with the station hope that somehow it may eventually resume broadcasts from its offshore base in international waters, but how practical would it be for Radio Caroline, or any other offshore station to do that?

The odds seem stacked heavily against it from a number of perspectives.

## 1. Legislative

Firstly the legislation which now exists appears to comprehensively prevent the successful long-term establishment of any offshore broadcasting station.

The concept of offshore radio and television stations pumping out their programmes and not having to comply with any of the national or international rules governing broadcasting has always irritated and worried governments worldwide.

Gradually over the years various loopholes or omissions in international and domestic legislation have been closed, making offshore broadcasting difficult if not virtually impossible. In order to achieve this some governments, notably the British, have given themselves draconian powers far beyond what was once considered generally acceptable practice in international law.

When commercial offshore stations began broadcasting in the late 1950s and early 1960s there was nothing illegal about their operation, they simply worked outside the law as it existed at that time.

They all took advantage of the (by modern comparison) small three mile territorial limit adopted by most countries. So long as their transmitters remained outside that limit, in the freedom of international waters, nothing could be done by national governments to prevent the station's broadcasts short of the sinister counter measure of jamming their signals - a practice which was only adopted on a handful of occasions.

Provided those stations on board ships complied with international maritime regulations - a country of registration for their vessel and a flag to fly in international waters - their base was immune from action by any other government. Those handful of stations which were not based on ships took steps to satisfy themselves at the outset that their bases were also in the safety of international waters, although the validity of their arguments proved to be slightly less secure.

In those early days it was also perfectly legal for stations to set up landbased offices and studios, record programmes, sell advertising, employ staff, promote goods, events and even sports teams, in fact they could do anything a legitimate business could do - so long as their transmissions did not come from within territorial limits.

Given all these loopholes through which the stations managed to operate how did officialdom react and what steps did authorities take to achieve the present-day situation?

Initially powerless to deal with the offshore broadcasters and irate that the stations (usually very successfully) were challenging their own state-run networks, governments resorted to the only approach they could within the legal framework as it then existed. They made practical operation as difficult as possible by cutting ship-to-shore telephone links and enforcing a plethora of customs and other regulations on people and goods travelling to the radio ships.

Perhaps most significantly though they tried to turn public opinion against the stations by challenging their technical operation, accusing them of endangering life by causing interference to licensed and maritime stations, or hinting that they may start broadcasting political propaganda or pornographic material.

Generally speaking stations were aware of their moral and legal obligations to avoid causing interference with other broadcasts, particularly emergency and maritime communications. Their safety and that of their crews may, and often did, rely on their own ability to contact the emergency services in times of crisis. Any allegation of such interference by the offshore broadcasters became powerful ammunition for those who opposed them and generally speaking station operators tried to prevent this by generally rectifying any technical problems if they arose.

The stations in Europe, and others later across the world, generally adopted a responsible and self-governing approach both to their technical operation and programme content, realising that irresponsibility in either was likely to result in loss of audience and the lifeblood of commercial revenue. Hence, although often unconventional and innovative in their output - usually the very reason for their establishment in the first place - nearly all stations realised the importance of maintaining basic standards in programme content and quality of transmission giving governments no excuse to outlaw them on those counts.

The stations hoped that their public popularity and support would prove insurmountable obstacles for legislators. Although this did sometimes lead to procrastination in taking action by governments who were reliant on public support ultimately all felt obliged for whatever reason, to comply with international agreements.

From quite early in the history of offshore broadcasting it was realised that concerted international action would be the only effective way to close the floating stations. The intention was that domestic legislation which resulted from the international agreements would cut the station's food and fuel supply routes, restrict staff who worked for them and, most importantly, cut their financial income through action against advertisers. Also, once in place universally, the legislation would prevent stations moving their landbased headquarters from country to country thereby continuing to operate outside the law.

The Scandinavian countries led the way with concerted action in 1962 through the Nordic Council. They legislated against stations then broadcasting off the coasts of Sweden and Denmark (the other two members of the Nordic Council, Norway and Finland, never actually had an offshore station operating off their coasts, but joined in the action as a precautionary measure).

After the expansion of stations off the Dutch and British coasts in the mid-1960s the governments of Europe (which was not a unified community as now) agreed in 1965 at a convention in Strasbourg to outlaw offshore broadcasting by the introduction of individual domestic legislation with broadly parallel provisions.

Most governments followed the lead set by the Scandinavians in 1962 and targeted legislation at their own nationals who supplied, advertised on or worked for offshore stations. Making it an offence for their own nationals to take part in any of these activities - in particular buying advertising time - would, they hoped, make it financially impossible for the commercial stations to continue. This strategy proved to be effective and stations such as Radio Caroline which defied the new laws ultimately found that without commercial income it was difficult if not impossible to sustain a broadcast service.

For many years Holland, partly because of its relatively liberal approach to such matters and mainly because of its domestic political instability procrastinated over introducing legislation. This left a large loophole in the 'concerted international approach' and enabled some stations to continue (including a return for Radio Caroline) and provided an opportunity for many more new stations to start operating.

The concerted international approach was also left wanting by Spain, which for years was not party to international agreements because of its own domestic political turmoil. It was only when the country needed to bring itself into line with the rest of Europe after joining the EC in 1986 that it belatedly started to ratify international agreements and introduced consequential domestic legislation, including laws against offshore broadcasting.

Although Spain was not ideally situated geographically, the availability of such a loophole in the concerted international action did provide a further opportunity for some offshore stations to continue long after the rest of Europe had legislated against them. However, with the move towards greater harmony and integration in Europe these loopholes have now been closed and any offshore broadcaster who remains is forced to operate even more clandestinely than usual and face constant harassment from the authorities in virtually every country.

## 2. Erosion of purpose

As well as the practical difficulties imposed by legislation offshore radio operators have also faced other, more subtle, erosions of their once dominant position, rendering the need for such a form of broadcasting virtually irrelevant if not wholly futile.

Generally when offshore radio stations were established, certainly the earlier ones, they found it easy to widen the choice of programming for listeners because they were challenging state run monopolies who tended to be stale and old fashioned in their programme output. These monopolies largely ignored the younger generation who by the 1950s and 60s were becoming a significant, radical, independent section of the population and - most importantly - they had money to spend.

That generation found a focus for their vibrant new lifestyle in the output of the offshore radio stations which in turn fed off the surge of musical innovation, particularly during the mid-1960s. The station's irrelevant challenge to the 'establishment' - fuelled by media inspired 'pirate' imagery - and huge popularity left governments bewildered as how best to tackle the problem and meet listeners' demands.

Gradually as various countries outlawed the offshore stations state systems were modified, adapted or extended. It was realised that where offshore stations operated a new market had been opened up which demanded some sort of replacement service to be provided. As a result new state channels were introduced or re-vamped to compete with or 'replace' offshore broadcasters -for example Melodi Radio in Sweden, Hilversum 3 in Holland, or BBC Radio One in Britain.

Against this background of expansion in the legal land-based radio system the number of unauthorised 'pirate' stations broadcasting from land bases also increased significantly from the late 1960s onwards as equipment became more portable and less expensive to acquire (and write-off when seized by the authorities).

Thousands of such landbased stations have come and gone (some have even integrated into the legal system) but as far as the average listener was concerned they simply added to the ever increasing choice of radio services.

The proliferation of landbased radio stations - authorised or pirate - has had the effect of making the market opportunities for an offshore broadcaster smaller and smaller. The heady days of Radio Veronica's domination of Holland's radio market, or Caroline and London's supremacy in Britain, with audiences measured in millions, will not return. The whole market is now so fragmented and the opportunity for earning a viable commercial return on an offshore operation, even without difficulties imposed by legislation, has greatly diminished.

In that respect offshore radio has become a victim of its own success. In fulfilling one of the initial primary objectives - the creation of a greater audience choice - it set in train a sequence of events which ultimately spelt the end of its own raison de entre.

Only those who have a dream (if perhaps legally and logistically impractical) of providing what is commonly known as 'free radio' still argue for the continued existence of offshore-based broadcasting. Even if all the legal and practical problems of setting up a ship-borne station in the late 1990's could be overcome the twin dilemmas still to be faced are what format should such a station adopt and which audience sector should it target?

Given that any new offshore venture would have to be financed from commercial income (assuming the legal restrictions could be overcome) the identification of a substantial and well defined target audience attractive to potential advertisers is vital. The days of a Top 40 format station attracting millions of listeners throughout a blanket coverage area have gone. Today's radio audience is far more specialist in taste and finely targeted by advertisers. Finding a new niche in the increasingly competitive market place is extremely difficult, even for a landbased operation.

## 3. Technical developments

There have also been a number of technical developments which have threatened the potential viability of offshore broadcasting.

The proliferation of legal (and illegal) landbased stations was aided by developments making studio and transmitting equipment more compact, easier to obtain and relatively less expensive. Other developments, particularly satellite and cable broadcasting have themselves provided further opportunities for many more stations to be established and even many terrestrial broadcasters now offer split frequency services.

FM is now accepted by most listeners as providing the best quality signal, generally in stereo. For a generation who have grown up listening to the crystal clear quality of CD recordings this is hardly surprising. Medium wave tends to be used by oldies, gold or speech-based stations where its quality is more acceptable both to programme content and the audience age profile. The efforts by Richard Branson's national rock music station, Virgin 1215, to negotiate a swap of its medium wave frequency for an FM outlet within months of coming on air, his success in achieving the award of an FM licence to broadcast to London and the use of satellite to deliver a quality stereo signal nationally graphically illustrate the demands placed on broadcasters from listeners and advertisers for a good quality signal.

Although some offshore stations used FM frequencies most relied on medium wave to carry their signal to the greatest possible audience. The propagation of a medium wave signal is, fortuitously, enhanced by the large amount of salt water surrounding an offshore station's base. This factor often gave offshore stations an audience well outside their primary target area - some of the Essex based stations had regular audiences in north east England and Scotland as well as large parts of Scandinavia because their signal travelled great distances across the vast expanse of the North Sea. Paradoxically these same stations sometimes failed to reach into the major market area around London because the signal 'skipped' completely over the capital.

Therefore unless a modern day offshore radio station is prepared to provide only a local service on FM (which is probably not cost effective) it is virtually obliged to remain on medium wave to achieve the greatest coverage area. However, audiences are notoriously reluctant to re-tune even within a waveband - encouraging them to move to an alternative waveband, perhaps for a reduced quality signal, is a costly exercise. Nevertheless, longwave broadcaster Atlantic 252 has demonstrated that it can be done, but substantial financial resources are required, probably far beyond the means of any fledgling offshore station.

Many people see parallels between satellite delivered radio and the offshore stations. A transmitter in space, they say, gives freedom to broadcast to a huge audience - potentially even larger than any of the offshore stations ever have achieved. However, the reality is somewhat different. It is true that a large potential audience exists, but satellite radio is in its infancy. Receiving equipment is restricted and programme output is not as yet sufficiently attractive to encourage people to invest in even more hardware.

Because satellite radio broadcasts are delivered via sub-carriers of satellite television channels their output can generally only be heard through the television set speakers or, by an extension, a stereo system. It is not portable, nor is it available to one of the largest radio listening audiences - people travelling in their cars. Technical developments in the future will undoubtedly overcome these limitations and satellite radio will be as easy to receive as terrestrial broadcasts, but for the time being that is not the case.

The delivery of radio (and television) services by cable provides a huge potential for the establishment of many more stations - targeted to quite small geographic areas or audience sectors. The proliferation of this kind of station, not dependent on the limited availability of broadcast frequencies, will further dilute the market place and remove the need for stations to be established offshore.

## Future need

Given that legally, commercially and technically the odds seem stacked against the success of any offshore station what are the chances of such an operation being established again and is there a real need for it anyway?

There will always be the 'free spirit' businessman or enthusiast who wishes to operate a station - free radio - outside of any national or international restriction and legislative requirements. To many people Radio Caroline in particular epitomises this 'freedom' concept where the offshore station is seen as the last bastion of unregulated, self-governing broadcasting. This is a concept which has been carefully nurtured and fought over for more than 30 years, to the extent that the station has become a legend in its own lifetime.

Radio Caroline has continued to defy all attempts to close it, even after a succession of potentially fatal events - the towing-in of its ships in 1968, numerous groundings, the sinking of the *Mi Amigo* in 1980, the collapse of its aerial tower in 1987, the Dutch/British government backed raid and confiscation of its equipment in 1989, the introduction of draconian British legislation in 1990 designed to prevent its continued operation and the near fatal grounding of the *Ross Revenge* in 1991. The station has always managed to recover and continue, albeit now on an extremely reduced scale,but with the theoretical possibility of becoming a regular full time broadcaster once again.

It is conceivable, given the resourcefulness of people still involved with the station that Radio Caroline will one day try, and possibly succeed for a while, to operate again from an offshore base. Quite what its target audience and format will be is a matter for conjecture as is the source of any financing which will be required to continue broadcasts for any length of time after the initial re-launch.

Realistically the concept of a commercial offshore radio station succeeding today seems very remote. There are from time to time rumours of plans for new stations to be launched serving South America or Far East 'Third World' countries who are not party to international agreements. These stations could provide a base for general entertainment, but they are more likely to be established for political or religious output - the latter financed by international evangelical organisations eager to spread their preachings worldwide. This was a concept used successfully by World Mission Radio on shortwave from the *Ross Revenge* in 1988/89 and for the stations planned from the MV *Fury* in 1993/4.

If the phenomenon of offshore radio is to continue at all the more likely scenario is for it to be the mouthpiece of a semi-official project used to provide a political or social voice to an area or country where free speech is not the norm. The initial role model for the commercial offshore radio stations - the Voice of America ship, *Courier* - was established in the 1950s to fulfil just this function, pumping western propaganda into Communist Europe.

Similarly, Radio Brod existed off Yugoslavia in 1993/4 because many international government agencies, despite their individual and collective efforts over the years to silence offshore broadcasters, deemed it worthwhile funding and tolerating such an operation. At the same time they flagrantly violated their own legislative rules with the purpose of breaking through the restrictions and censorship existing in war torn Yugoslavia at that time.

## The end of a phenomenon

With these possible exceptions - and perhaps the unexpected 'free spirit' entrepreneur - it is difficult to foresee any large scale restoration of the phenomenon of offshore broadcasting. The offshore stations challenged the established systems and attitudes of their day in a sphere of entertainment which until then had generally failed to keep pace with changing social and market demands. The service they provided ultimately led to changes in the state broadcasting systems and (although it often took some years) the eventual introduction of commercially funded radio stations. For that reason alone they deserve to be recognised and respected for the part they played in 20th Century broadcasting and social history.

However, the very multiplicity of radio services which exists today as a result of these changes also means that the need for offshore based broadcasting is no longer there. The choice, diversity and range of services now available has virtually eliminated the need for any new 'unofficial' challengers.

Despite the glamorous and fanciful 'pirate' imagery portrayed by the media the concept of offshore broadcasting was in reality dangerous, difficult and highly volatile. Most people who worked on or operated an offshore radio station would probably now agree that as a concept it was right at the time, but it never held any permanency as a long term method of broadcasting.

It could only ever have been a means to an end and not an end in itself.

# Appendix 1 -The Stations

| | Radio Antwerpen | Radio Atlantis |
|---|---|---|
| Location | *Uilenspiegel;* off Zeebrugge, Belgium | *Mi Amigo*, off Schevinengen, Holland (July-Oct 1973), *Janine*, off Knokke, Belgium (Dec 1973- 31st August 1974) |
| Frequency/Wavelength* | 201m and 7600kHz, 41m s/w | 385m from *Mi Amigo*; 227m later 312m, also 6225kHz s/w from *Janine* |
| Transmitter/Power | 10Kw | 50Kw (from *Mi Amigo*), 1kW (ex -REM Island Transmitter) from *Janine* |
| Broadcasting Hours | 7.00am-12midnight | 6.00am-7.00pm (from *Mi Amigo*) 6.00am-7.00pm (Flemish) 7.00pm-6.00am (English) from *Janine* |
| Opening Date | 15th October 1962 | 15th July 1973 (from *Mi Amigo*) 7th January 1974 from *Janine* |
| Closing Date | 16th December 1962 | 18th October 1973 from *Mi Amigo* 25th August 1974-Flemish Service, 31st August 1974-English Service (from *Janine*) |
| Format | Light music | Pop music |
| | **Arutz Sheva** | **Radio Atlanta** |
| Location | *Hatzvi* off Tel Aviv | *Mi Amigo*, off Frinton-on-Sea, Essex |
| Frequency/Wavelength* | 918kHz ( 326 m), 711kHz (421.9m), 1143kHz (262.4m), 105mHz FM | 201m |
| Transmitter/ Power | Harris 25Kw | 10Kw |
| Broadcasting Hours | 5.00am-7.00pm, closed Shabbat | 6.00am-6.00pm, later 6.00am-8.00pm |
| Opening Date | 20th November 1988 | 12th May 1964 |
| Closing Date | still broadcasting (September 1996) | 2nd July 1964 (merged with Radio Caroline) |
| Format | Orthodox Jewish Music | Light popular music |
| | **BBMS** | **Britain Radio** |
| Location | Knock John Fort in the Thames Estuary | *Laissez Faire*, off Walton-on-the-Naze,Essex |
| Frequency/Wavelength* | 222m | 355m |
| Transmitter/Power | 1Kw ex-USAF radio beacon modified for broadcasting use | 55Kw |
| Broadcasting Hours | 24hours | 24 hours, later 6.00am-12 midnight |
| Opening Date | October 1966 | 16th June 1966 |
| Closing Date | 25th Dec. 1966 or 3rd January 1967 | 21st February 1967 |
| Format | Easy Listening (day) pop (night) | Easy Listening music |
| | **Radio Brod** | **Capital Radio** |
| Location | *Droit de Parole*, in the Adriatic Sea | *King David*, off Noordwijk, Holland |
| Frequency/Wavelength* | 720kHz (416m) and 90mHz FM | 270m |
| Transmitter/Power | 50Kw | 10Kw |
| Broadcasting Hours | 24 hours | 6.00am-2.00am |
| Opening Date | 1st June 1993; August 1993 | May-Aug. 1970 (tests) 1st Sept. 1970 |
| Closing Date | 28th June 1993; 28th February 1994 | 10th November 1970 (ran aground) |
| Format | Western pop music, news about former Yugoslavia, messages for missing people | MOR music |

| | Radio Caroline | Radio Caroline South |
|---|---|---|
| Location | *Caroline*, off Felixstowe, Harwich and later Frinton-on-Sea Essex | *Mi Amigo*, off Frinton -on-Sea Essex (12th Feb-27th April 1966 on board *Cheeta 2*) |
| Frequency/Wavelength* | 199m | 199m, from April 1966 259m |
| Transmitter Power | 10Kw (potential for 20Kw) | 10Kw (from April 1966 50Kw) |
| Broadcasting Hours | 6.00am-6.00pm, later 6.00am-10.00pm and 12.05am-3.00am | 6.00am-8.00pm; 9.00pm-12midnight (August 1965);6.00am-12 midnight (April 1966); 6.00am-2.30am (June 1966); 24 hours (August 1966) 5.30am-2.00am (September 1967) |
| Opening Date | 28th March 1964 | 3rd July 1964 |
| Closing Date | 2nd July 1964 (merged with Radio Atlanta) | 3rd March 1968 (ship towed away) |
| Format | Light and popular music | Pop music; based on Top 50 from August 1965 |
| | **Radio Caroline North** | **Radio Caroline (1972-1980)** |
| Location | *Caroline*, off Ramsey, Isle of Man | *Mi Amigo* off Scheveningen, Holland (from 30th August 1974) off Essex |
| Frequency/Wavelength* | 199m; from December 1966 259m | 259m (to March 1977); also 389m (May 1973); 192m( May 1976) 319m (from 9th Mar. 1977) |
| Transmitter/Power | 20Kw (50Kw from November 1966) | 10Kw and 50Kw (potential) |
| Broadcasting Hours | 6.00am-8.00pm, 12midnight-3.00am (from Sept. 1966 6.00am-10.00pm) | 24 hours<br>192m English Service 6.00am-7.00pm |
| Opening Date | Broadcast while *Caroline* sailed around the coast from Essex 2nd-7th July 1964 | (tests) from 30th Sept. 1972, regular from Dec. 1972 various periods off air due to technical problems |
| Closing Date | 2nd March 1968 (ship towed away) | 20th March1980 (*Mi Amigo* sank) |
| Format | As Caroline South | Pop and Rock music, album based |
| | **Radio Caroline (1983-1990)** | **Radio City** |
| Location | *Ross Revenge*, off Essex, later off Kent | Shivering Sands Fort in the Thames Estuary |
| Frequency/Wavelength* | 963kHz (319m); 576kHz (from Oct. 1984); 558kHz (from November 1985) | 238m(from Sept. 1964); 299m and 187m (from December 1964) |
| Transmitter /Power | 50Kw | 3.4Kw (10Kw from June 1965) |
| Broadcasting Hours | various | 7.00am-7.00pm, later 6.00am-7.00pm, then 6.00am-12 midnight |
| Opening Date | 20th August 1983 | Sept. 1964 (replaced Radio Sutch) |
| Closing Date | 5th November 1990 | 8th February 1967 |
| Format | Album Rock, later more Top 40/chart | Top 40 (religious service on 187m) |
| | **CNBC** | **Radio Condor** |
| Location | *Borkum Riff*, off Katwijk aan Zee, Holland | *Zondaxonagon*, off Zandvoort, Holland |
| Frequency/Wavelength* | 192m | 269m |
| Transmitter/Power | 1Kw | 500w (ex-Radio 270 and Capital Radio) |
| Broadcasting Hours | 8.00am-1.00pm | Only ever broadcast test transmissions |
| Opening Date | (tests) January 1961 | (tests) early August 1973 |
| Closing Date | March 1961 - never started regular programming | 10th August 1973 after anchor chain broke and ship declared unseaworthy |
| Format | Light music | Easy listening with humanitarian, social and religious programmes |

| | **Radio Dan** | **DCR** |
|---|---|---|
| Location | *Kajun*, off Tel Aviv, Israel | *Lucky Star*, off Copenhagen, Denmark |
| Frequency/Wavelength* | 88.5mHz FM | 94mHz |
| Transmitter/Power | | 20Kw |
| Broadcasting Hours | 24 hours | 3.30pm-11.00pm (weekdays)<br>9.00am-12 midnight (weekends) |
| Opening Date | October 1995 | 15th September 1961 |
| Closing Date | November 1995 | 29th Jan.1962(merged with R. Mercur) |
| Format | Continuous pop music | Classical music, light music, plays and discussions |
| | **Radio Delmare** | **Radio Dolfijn** |
| Location | *Aegir*, off Cadzand, Belgium (1978)<br>*Martina*,(*Aegir II*) off Cadzand 1979 | *Laissez Faire*, off Walton-on-the-Naze, Essex |
| Frequency/Wavelength* | 191m(1978),192m and 186m (1979) | 227m |
| Transmitter/Power | 500watts | 55Kw |
| Broadcasting Hours | 6.00am-6.00pm | 6.00am-12midnight |
| Opening Date | 7th September 1978; 11th June 1979 | 6th November 1966 |
| Closing Date | 11th Sept.1978 (ship ran aground)<br>28th September 1979 | May 1967 |
| Format | Popular music | Easy listening , Top 40 at night |
| | **Radio England** | **Radio Essex** |
| Location | *Laissez Faire*, off Walton-on-the-Naze, Essex | Knock John Fort, in the Thames Estuary |
| Frequency/Wavelength* | 227m | 222m |
| Transmitter/Power | 55Kw | 1Kw, from ex-USAF radio beacon modified for broadcasting use |
| Broadcasting Hours | 24 hours | initially 7.00am-9.00pm, later 24 hours |
| Opening Date | 16th June 1966 | 7th November 1965 |
| Closing Date | 5th November 1966 | October 1966 (became BBMS) |
| Format | American style Top 40 | MOR during daytime, Top 40 at night |
| | **Radio Free America** | **Radio Gal** |
| Location | *Columbus*, off New Jersey, USA | off Tel Aviv, Israel |
| Frequency/Wavelength* | 259m,later 186.5m | 101.8mHz FM; later 101.1mHz FM |
| Transmitter/Power | 10Kw potential | |
| Broadcasting Hours | only ever broadcast test transmissions | |
| Opening Date | (tests) 12th Sept. regular) 19th September 1973 (12.23pm) | September 1994 |
| Closing Date | 19th September 1973 (10.15pm) | still broadcasting (September 1996) |
| Format | | Pop music |
| | **Galei Hayam Hatichon** | **Radio Hauraki** |
| Location | *Kajun*, off Tel Aviv, Israel | *Tiri*, later *Tiri II* off Hauraki Gulf, NZ |
| Frequency/Wavelength* | 95.1mHz FM | 1480kHz (203m) |
| Transmitter Power | | 1.75Kw |
| Broadcasting Hours | 24hours | 6.00am-2.00am, 24 hours (from Dec.1968) |
| Opening Date | 27th October 1995 | 4th December 1966 (from *Tiri*), 28th Feb 1968 (from *Tiri II*) |
| Closing Date | November 1995 | 1st June 1970 (off air Jan/Feb 1968 after *Tiri* shipwrecked) |
| Format | Middle Eastern Music | Top 40 |

| | Radio Hof | Radio Invicta |
|---|---|---|
| Location | *Hof* (*David*) off Tel Aviv, Israel | Red Sands Fort in the Thames Estuary |
| Frequency/Wavelength* | 102mHz FM | 306m |
| Transmitter/Power | | 750 watts |
| Broadcasting Hours | | 7.00am-7.00pm, later 12midnight - 6.00pm, then 5.00am-6.00pm |
| Opening Date | August 1993 | 17th July 1964 |
| Closing Date | March 1994 | February 1965 |
| Format | Pop music | Easy Listening |
| | **KING Radio** | **Laser 558** |
| Location | Red Sands Fort in the Thames Estuary | *Communicator* off Essex |
| Frequency/Wavelength* | 236m | 729kHz, later 558kHz |
| Transmitter/Power | 750 watts | 25Kw |
| Broadcasting Hours | 7.00am-7.00pm | 5.00am-1.00am |
| Opening Date | 24th March 1965 | 24th May 1984 |
| Closing Date | 22nd Sept. 1965 (became Radio 390) | 5th November 1985 |
| Format | Easy Listening/Jazz/Folk | Top 40 |
| | **Laser Hot Hits** | **Radio London** |
| Location | *Communicator*, off Essex,later off Kent | *Galaxy*, off Frinton-on-Sea, Essex |
| Frequency/Wavelength* | 576kHz | 266m |
| Transmitter/Power | 25Kw | 50Kw, later 75Kw |
| Broadcasting Hours | 5.00am-10.00pm | 6.00am-9.00pm, later 5.30am-2.00am |
| Opening Date | 7th December 1986 | 23rd December 1964 |
| Closing Date | 20th April 1987 | 14th August 1967 |
| Format | Hot Hits | Top 40 |
| | **Radio Mercur** | **Radio Mi Amigo** |
| Location | *Cheeta*, later *Cheeta 2* off Copenhagen, Denmark also *Cheeta* and *Lucky Star* off Funen, Denmark | *Mi Amigo*, off Schevinengen, Holland from 30th August 1974 off Essex |
| Frequency/Wavelength* | 93.12mHz FM, 89.55mHz FM (from Sept. 1958); 88mHz FM (East-from Feb. 1961) and 89.58mHz FM (West - from Nov. 1961) | 259m<br>192m (from 11th December 1976)<br>212m (from 25th July 1977) |
| Transmitter/Power | 8Kw (*Cheeta*) 20Kw (*Lucky Star*) | 50Kw potential, often less than 10Kw |
| Broadcasting Hours | 7.30-9.30am, 5.00pm-12midnight, later 6.00am-11.00am, 2.00pm-12midnight | 5.00am-8.00pm, later 5.00am-6.00pm |
| Opening Date | 2nd August 1958. 25th November 1961 (Radio Mercur West) | 1st January 1974 |
| Closing Date | 10th July 1962 (West), 31st July 1962 (East) | 20th October 1978 |
| Format | Popular music | Top 40 |
| | **Radio Mi Amigo 272** | **Radio Monique** |
| Location | *Magdalena* off Thornton Bank,Belgium | *Ross Revenge* off Essex, later Kent |
| Frequency/Wavelength* | 272m | 963kHz; 819kHz from Nov. 1987 |
| Transmitter/Power | 10Kw | 50Kw potential |
| Broadcasting Hours | 24hours, later reduced to 6.00am-7.00,8.00,9.00pm or midnight | 4.00am-6.00pm |
| Opening Date | 1st July 1979 | 16th December 1984 |
| Closing Date | 18th September 1979 | 24th November 1987 (mast collapse) |
| Format | Chart records, flashbacks, album tracks. 1 in 20 records of Dutch origin | Pop music, Top 40, Dutch artists |

| | Radio New York International | Radio Nord |
|---|---|---|
| Location | *Sarah*, off Long Island New York,USA | *Bon Jour* (*Magda Maria*) off Stockholm |
| Frequency/Wavelength* | 185m mw; 103.1mHz FM; 6240kHz (sw) and 190kHz (lw) | 495m |
| Transmitter/Power | Medium wave-5Kw, FM-10Kw, Short wave - 300w. Long wave 75w | 10Kw (potential 20Kw) |
| Broadcasting Hours | only ever broadcast test transmissions | 6.00am-6.00pm, later 24 hours |
| Opening Date | 23rd July 1987; 15th October 1988 | 8th March 1961 |
| Closing Date | 28th July 1987; 17th October 1988 | 30th June 1962 |
| Format | 'Free Form Rock and Roll' | Top 40 |
| | **Radio Noordzee** | **TV Noordzee** |
| Location | REM artificial island, off Noordwijk, Holland | REM artificial island, off Noordwijk, Holland |
| Frequency/Wavelength* | 214m | Channel E11, Band III |
| Transmitter/Power | 10Kw | 10Kw |
| Broadcasting Hours | 9.00am-6.15pm | 6.30pm-8.00pm, 10.00pm-11.30pm |
| Opening Date | 29th July 1964 | 1st September 1964 |
| Closing Date | 17th December 1964 (raided) | 12th December 1964 |
| Format | Popular music | Films and syndicated US and British programmes with Dutch sub-titles |
| | **Odelia Television** | **Offshore Radio 1584** |
| Location | *Odelia*, off Tel Aviv, Israel | *Galexy*, off Walton-on-the-Naze, Essex |
| Frequency/Wavelength* | Channel 59 | 1584kHz |
| Transmitter/Power | 5Kw | 1 watt |
| Broadcasting Hours | | 24 hours |
| Opening Date | May 1981 (tests); July 1981 | 13th August 1992 |
| Closing Date | August 1981; December 1981 | 9th September 1992 |
| Format | Films, cartoons | Pop music/offshre radio nostalgia |
| | **Radio One** | **Radio Paradijs** |
| Location | *Polaris* (*Air*), off Haifa, Israel | *Lieve* (*Magda Maria*), off Holland |
| Frequency/Wavelength* | 105.3mHz | 270m |
| Transmitter/Power | | |
| Broadcasting Hours | 24 hours | only ever broadcast test transmissions |
| Opening Date | 21st January 1991 | 24th July 1981 (tests) |
| Closing Date | March 1993 (became landbased pirate, closed end of 1994, awarded official licence October 1995) | 1st August 1991 (ship raided by Dutch authorities) |
| Format | Pop music, local news and information | Progressive Hit Radio |
| | **RKXR** | **RNI** |
| Location | *City of Panama*, off Los Angeles, California, USA | *Mebo II,* off Schevinengen, Holland, (off Clacton, Essex (March-July 1970), (off Cadzand, Belgium) 7th-31st January 1971 |
| Frequency/Wavelength* | 815kHz, 368m | MW-186m; 190m; 217m; 244m; 220m SW-6210kHHz(49m); 6205kHz(49m);9940kHz(31m) FM-102mHz,100mHz; 96mHz |
| Transmitter/Power | 5Kw | 100Kw (mw); 1Kw (FM); 10Kw (sw) |
| Broadcasting Hours | | various |
| Opening Date | May 1933 | 28th Feb. 1970; re-opened 14th Feb.1971 |
| Closing Date | August 1933 | 24th Sept. 1970; 30th Aug. 1974 (English); 31st August 1974 (Dutch) |
| Format | Popular music | Top 40 |

| | Revolutionary People's Radio | Radio Scotland |
|---|---|---|
| Location | *El Fatah* (formerly *Mebo II*) Tripoli Harbour, Libya. Also from Derna Harbour using call sign Libyan Post-Revolutionary Broadcasting | *Comet*, off Dunbar (Dec. 1965-April 1966); off Troon (May 1966-Apr.1967); off Ballywater, Northern Ireland (Apr. 1967); off Fifeness (May-Aug.1967) |
| Frequency/Wavelength* | 213m, 388m (mw); 90mHz (FM); 6205kHz (sw) | 242m |
| Transmitter Power | 10Kw ex-Radio Veronica transmitter | 20Kw |
| Broadcasting Hours | various | 6.00am-7.30pm and 11.30pm-2.00am, later 6.00am(8.00 Sundays)-2.00am |
| Opening Date | June 1977 | 31st December 1965 |
| Closing Date | early 1980 | 14th August 1967 |
| Format | news/music/takls/Koran readings | Top 40, some Scottish programming |
| | **Radio Seagull** | **Skanes Radio Mercur** |
| Location | *Mi Amigo* off Schevinengen, Holland, later off Essex | *Cheeta; Cheeta 2* (from January 1961) off Copenhagen, Denmark |
| Frequency/Wavelength* | 388m | 89.55mHz |
| Transmitter/Power | 50Kw (potential) later 10Kw | 8Kw |
| Broadcasting Hours | 9.00pm-6.00am | 11.00am-2.00pm(weekdays); 12noon-5.00pm (weekends); from Aug. 1959-11.00am-3.00pm; from Feb. 1961-7.00am-8.00pm, 11.00pm-12midnight |
| Opening Date | 24th July 1973; 7th January 1974 | September 1958 |
| Closing Date | 17th October 1973; 22nd Feb. 1974 | March 1962 |
| Format | 'Progressive' music | Popular music for Swedish audiences |
| | **Radio Sutch** | **Radio Syd** |
| Location | *Cornucopia*, later Shivering Sands Fort in Thames Estuary | *Cheeta* off Copenhagen, Denmark, later *Cheeta 2* off Malmo, Sweden |
| Frequency/Wavelength* | 200m | 89.62mHz FM, later 88.3mHz FM |
| Transmitter/Power | 500 watts | 5Kw |
| Broadcasting Hours | 12noon-2.00pm, 5.00pm-11.00pm | 6.00am-3.00am |
| Opening Date | Early May 1964, from *Cornucopia*, 27th May 1964 from Shivering Sands | 1st April 1962 |
| Closing Date | September 1964 (became Radio City) | 18th January 1966 (ship left Baltic) |
| Format | Pop music | Popular music |
| | **TV Syd** | **Radio Tower/Tower Radio** |
| Location | *Cheeta 2* off Malmo, Sweden | Sunk Head Fort, Thames Estuary |
| Frequency/Wavelength* | Channel E41 | 234m |
| Transmitter/Power | | 250 watts |
| Broadcasting Hours | 12 Hours/day (planned) | 7.00am-7.00pm |
| Opening Date | 13th December 1965 (tests) | Oct. 1965 (tests); 29th April 1966 |
| Closing Date | 18th January 1966 (ship left Baltic) | Dec. 1965 ; 12th May 1966 |
| Format | | Popular music, local news, features |
| | **Radio Veronica** | **Voice of Peace** |
| Location | *Borkum Riff*, later *Norderney* off Schevinengen, Holland. From 11th-20th April 1973 *Mi Amigo* off Holland | *Peace*, off Tel Aviv, Israel |
| Frequency/Wavelength* | 185m; later 192m. From 30th Sept. 1972: 538m.11th-20th April 1973 259m | 1540kHz, 100mHzFM and 6245kHz, later 6240kHz short wave |
| Transmitter/Power | 1Kw, later 10Kw | 25Kw , later 75Kw (mw); 20Kw (FM); 400watts (short wave) |
| Broadcasting Hours | various | various |
| Opening Date | 6th May 1960 | 26th May 1973; June 1975 |
| Closing Date | 31st August 1974 | 9th Nov. 1973; 1st October 1993 |
| Format | Popular music, later Top 40 format | Pop music /peace announcements. |

| | World Mission Radio (WMR) | Radio 199 |
|---|---|---|
| Location | *Ross Revenge*, off Kent | *Mi Amigo*, off Scheveningen, Holland |
| Frequency/Wavelength* | 6215kHz (sw) | 199m |
| Transmitter/Power | | 10Kw |
| Broadcasting Hours | 4.30am-11.00pm | 6.00am-1.00am |
| Opening Date | 1st May 1988 | 17th December 1972 |
| Closing Date | 19th August 1989 (ship raided) | 21st December 1972 |
| Format | Religious/Evangelistic programmes | Pop music |
| | **Radio 227** | **Radio 270** |
| Location | *Laissez Faire*, off Walton-on-the-Naze, Essex | *Oceaan VII*, off Scarborough, later off Bridlington, Yorkshire |
| Frequency/Wavelength* | 227m | 270m |
| Transmitter Power | 55Kw | 10Kw |
| Broadcasting Hours | 6.00am-12 midnight | 6.00am-1.00am |
| Opening Date | 3rd June 1967 | 9th June 1966 |
| Closing Date | 23rd July 1967 | 14th August 1967 |
| Format | Top 40 | Top 40 |
| | **Radio 355** | **Radio 390** |
| Location | *Laissez Faire*, off Walton-on-the-Naze, Essex | Red Sands Fort, in the Thames Estuary |
| Frequency/Wavelength* | 355m | 390m |
| Transmitter Power | 55Kw | 10Kw |
| Broadcasting Hours | 6.00am-12 midnight | 6.30am-12midnight |
| Opening Date | March 1967 | 26th Sept. 1965; 31st December 1966 |
| Closing Date | 6th August 1967 | 25th Nov. 1966; 28th July 1967 |
| Format | Easy Listening music | Easy Listening music |
| | **Radio 558** | **Radio 819** |
| Location | *Ross Revenge* off Kent | *Ross Revenge*, off Kent |
| Frequency/Wavelength* | 558kHz | 819kHz |
| Transmitter Power | 50Kw potential (often much less) | 50Kw potential (often only 5Kw) |
| Broadcasting Hours | 6.00am-6.00pm | 5.00am-7.00am, 24hours weekends |
| Opening Date | 9th July 1988 | 22nd October 1988 |
| Closing Date | 22nd Oct. 1988 (became Radio 819) | 19th August 1989 (ship raided) |
| Format | Top 40 | Top 40 |

*These are the announced frequencies/wavelengths used by each station during regular broadcasts. Many stations used frequencies/wavelengths which were not precisely the same as that announced on-air or used other frequencies/wavelengths during test transmissions.

# Appendix 2 The Ships

| | Aegir | Air (Polaris) |
|---|---|---|
| Former Name(s) | *1152Z, Express, Panicopania* | |
| Description | Deep sea Trawler | |
| Length/Tonnage | 115' /250tons | /237tons |
| Built | 1929 | 1956 |
| Flag State | Cuba | Honduras |
| Stations Housed | Radio Delmare (1978) | Radio One |
| Ultimate Fate | Detained by authorities after running aground. Sold 1981 | Driven aground off Haifa. Salvaged and sold. |
| | **Borkum Riff** | **Caroline** |
| Former Name(s) | | *Fredericia* |
| Description | German lightship | Danish passenger ferry |
| Length/Tonnage | | 200'/693tons |
| Built | 1911 | 1930 |
| Flag State | Panama; Guatemala; East Germany | Panama |
| Stations Housed | Radio Veronica, CNBC | Radio Caroline, Caroline North |
| Ultimate Fate | Scrapped 1966 | Scrapped 1980 |
| | **Cheeta** | **Cheeta 2** |
| Former Name(s) | | *Habat* |
| Description | German fishing boat | |
| Length/Tonnage | /107tons | /450tons |
| Built | | |
| Flag State | Panama (later claimed to be Honduras,but probably stateless) | |
| Stations Housed | Radio Mercur, Skanes Radio Mercur, Radio Syd | Radio Mercur, Skanes Radio Mercur, Radio Syd, TV Syd, Caroline South |
| Ultimate Fate | Damaged during storm 1964, sank at quayside before being repaired. Scrapped. | Sailed to Gambia in 1968 , sank in Gambia River |
| | **City of Panama** | **Columbus** |
| Former Name(s) | | *Oceanic* |
| Description | | Minesweeper |
| Length/Tonnage | | 135' / |
| Built | | |
| Flag State | Panama | USA |
| Stations Housed | RKXR | Radio Free America |
| Ultimate Fate | | Returned to original owner |
| | **Comet** | **Communicator** |
| Former Name(s) | | *Tananager; Charterer; Gardline Seeker* |
| Description | Irish lightship | Trawler, coaster, survey vessel |
| Length/Tonnage | 90'/500 tons | 177'/490 tons |
| Built | 1904 | 1954 |
| Flag State | | Panama |
| Stations Housed | Radio Scotland; Radio Scotland and Ireland, Radio 242 | Laser 558, Laser Hot Hits. Holland FM, Veronica Hit Radio(inland) |
| Ultimate Fate | Scrapped | Still in use by Veronica Hit Radio, but up for sale (Sept. 1996) |

| | ***Cornucopia*** | ***Courier*** |
|---|---|---|
| Former Name(s) | | *Doddridge; Coastal Messenger* |
| Description | Fishing vessel | Cargo ship |
| Length/Tonnage | 60'/25 tons | /3,805 tons |
| Built | | |
| Flag State | | USA |
| Stations Housed | Briefly used by Radio Sutch | Voice of America |
| Ultimate Fate | | |
| | ***Droit de Parole*** | ***El Fatah*** (see ***Mebo II***) |
| Former Name(s) | *Fort Reliance; Cariboo* | *Mebo II, Silvretta* |
| Description | Antartic research/supply ship | Norwegian coaster |
| Length/Tonnage | 200'/ | 186'/630 tons |
| Built | 1986 | 1948 |
| Flag State | St. Vincenet and Grenadines | Libya |
| Stations Housed | Radio Brod | SPLAJBC |
| Ultimate Fate | Returned to previous owners | Used as target practice by Libyan Air Force, sunk 1980 |
| | ***Galaxy*** | ***Galexy*** |
| Former Name(s) | *Admirable; Density* | *Tyne Princess* |
| Description | US Navy minesweeper, cargo vessel | River Tyne passenger ferry |
| Length/Tonnage | 185'/780 tons | 75'/81 tons |
| Built | 1944 | 1940 |
| Flag State | Panama; Honduras | Britain |
| Stations Housed | Radio London | Offshore Radio 1584 |
| Ultimate Fate | Lay derelict for many years in West Germany. Sank at quayside in Keil. Scrapped 1986 | Used as private houseboat |
| | ***Hatzvi*** | ***Hof (David)*** |
| Former Name(s) | *Hajduszoboszld; Mount Parnis* | |
| Description | General cargo ship | |
| Length/Tonnage | 150' / | 85' / |
| Built | 1967 | 1955 |
| Flag State | Malta | |
| Stations Housed | Aruts Sheva | Radio Hof |
| Ultimate Fate | Still used as radio ship (Sept.96) | |
| | ***Janine*** (see also ***Zondaxonagon***) | ***Kajun*** |
| Former Name(s) | *Emma; Zondaxonagon* | |
| Description | Icelandic trawler | |
| Length/Tonnage | /403 tons | |
| Built | 1957 | |
| Flag State | | |
| Stations Housed | Radio Atlantis | Galei Hayam Hatichon/Radio Dan |
| Ultimate Fate | Scrapped | Ran aground |

| | ***King David*** | ***Laissez Faire*** |
|---|---|---|
| Former Name(s) | *Zeevaart* | *FS263, Deal; Don Carlos; Olga Patricia* |
| Description | Dutch coaster | Military landing craft; general cargo ship |
| Length/Tonnage | 150'/359 tons | 117'/562 tons |
| Built | 1938 | 1944 |
| Flag State | Liechtenstein | Panama |
| Stations Housed | Capital Radio | Radio England; Britain Radio; Radio Dolfijn; Radio 355; Radio 227 |
| Ultimate Fate | Salvaged after running aground 1970.Used as houseboat/ pier support. Sank 1994 | Re-named *Earl Conrad Jnr.* (1974). Used as fishing vessel |

| | ***Lucky Star*** | ***Magda Maria (Bon Jour) see Mi Amigo*** |
|---|---|---|
| Former Name(s) | *Nijmah Al Hazz* | *Margarethe; Olga;* later *Mi Amigo* |
| Description | Freighter | see *Mi Amigo* |
| Length/Tonnage | /240 tons | 98' (*Margarethe*); 134' (*Olga*) /470 tons |
| Built | | 1921. lengthened 1927 |
| Flag State | Claimed Libya, possibly stateless | Nicaragua |
| Stations Housed | DCR; Radio Mercur | Radio Nord |
| Ultimate Fate | Towed into port and impounded 1962. Fate unknown. | Sold to Radio Atlanta as *Mi Amigo*. Sank 1980 |

| | ***Magda Maria*** (***Lieve***) | ***Magdalena*** |
|---|---|---|
| Former Name(s) | *Ursula Legenhausen; Hoheweg* | *Demi; Centricity* (later *Mi Amigo)* |
| Description | Coaster | |
| Length/Tonnage | 170'/422 tons | 204'/655 tons |
| Built | 1957 | 1955 |
| Flag State | Panama | Honduras |
| Stations Housed | Radio Paradijs | Radio Mi Amigo 272 |
| Ultimate Fate | Scrapped after prolonged legal battle | Scrapped |

| | ***Martina*** (***Aegir II***) | ***Mebo II*** |
|---|---|---|
| Former Name(s) | *Schevinengen 54* | *Silvretta* |
| Description | Trawler | Norwegian Coaster |
| Length/Tonnage | 120'/270 tons | 186'/630 tons |
| Built | 1923 | 1954 |
| Country of Registration | | Panama |
| Stations Housed | Radio Dlmare (1979) | RNI; Radio Caroline (June 1970) |
| Ultimate Fate | Scrapped | Sunk 1980 (See *El Fatah*) |

| | Mi Amigo | Norderney |
|---|---|---|
| Former Name(s) | *Margarethe; Olga; Bon Jour; Magda Maria* | |
| Description | As Margarethe -three masted Schooner; As Olga Cargo Vessel | Trawler |
| Length/Tonnage | 98' (as Margarethe) 134' (as Olga) /470tons | 150' |
| Built | 1921, lengthened 1927 | |
| Country of Registration | Nicaragua (for Radio Nord) Panama (for Radio Atlanta and Radio Caroline) | Honduras, East Germany |
| Stations Housed | Radio Nord; Radio Atlanta; Radio Caroline South; Radio 199; Radio Caroline; Radio Veronica; Radio Atlantis; Radio Seagull; Radio Mi Amigo | Radio Veronica |
| Ultimate Fate | Sank 20th March 1980 | Converted to floating disco |
| | **Oceaan VII** | **Odelia** |
| Former Name(s) | *Scheveningen 330* | *Hazan; Tina; Theofanis; Krateros; Ceros II* |
| Description | Lugger | Cargo ship |
| Length/Tonnage | 118'/179 tons | 264'/ 1219 tons |
| Built | 1939 | 1958 |
| Country of Registration | Honduras | Cyprus, but flew Honduran flag |
| Stations Housed | Radio 270 | Odelia TV |
| Ultimate Fate | Scrapped | Unknown |
| | **Peace** | **Ross Revenge** |
| Former Name(s) | *Rolf; Westpolder; Cito* | *Freyer* |
| Description | Freighter | Icelandic Trawler, Salvage vessel |
| Length/Tonnage | 170'/570 tons | 210'/978 tons |
| Built | 1940 | 1960 |
| Country of Registration | Panama | Panama (stateless from 1987) |
| Stations Housed | Voice of Peace | Radio Caroline; Radio Monique; World Mission Radio; Radio 558, Radio 819 |
| Ultimate Fate | Scuttled, 28th November 1993 | Still used as radio ship by Radio Caroline |
| | **Sarah** | **Tiri** |
| Former Name(s) | *Dolphin; Litchfield* | |
| Description | Refrigerated cargo ship | Coaster |
| Length/Tonnage | 168'/ 409 tons | 90'/169 tons |
| Built | 1960 | 1931 |
| Country of Registration | Honduras; Principality of Sealand | New Zealand |
| Stations Housed | Radio New York International | Radio Hauraki (to Jan. 1968) |
| Ultimate Fate | Scrapped after being used in film "Blown Away" in 1993 | Abandoned hulk |

| | *Tiri II* | *Uilenspiegel* |
|---|---|---|
| Former Name(s) | *Kapuni* | *Crocodile* |
| Description | Cargo Vessel | French Navy Stores Vessel |
| Length/Tonnage | 104'/190 tons | 70'/585 tons |
| Built | 1909 | |
| Flag State | New Zealand | Panama |
| Stations Housed | Radio Hauraki (from Feb. 1968) | Radio Antwerpen |
| Ultimate Fate | Abandoned hulk | Ran aground Dec. 1962, abandoned hulk, blown up 1971 |

| | ***Zondaxonagon*** (see ***Janine***) |
|---|---|
| Former Name(s) | *Emma* (later *Janine*) |
| Description | Icelandic Trawler |
| Length/Tonnage | /403tons |
| Built | 1957 |
| Flag State | |
| Stations Housed | Radio Condor |
| Ultimate Fate | Sold to Radio Atlantis (see *Janine*). Later scrapped |

# Appendix 3 The Sea Forts

In 1941 the Admiralty and the War Office decided that more anti-aircraft protection was needed for London and Merseyside. Amphibious forts were proposed as a solution and two distinctive designs were prepared by G A Maunsell, a prominent civil engineer engaged by the Government. Maunsell's designs were for four forts to be used by the Navy in the waters of the North Sea off the Essex coast and six forts for use by the Army, three in the Thames Estuary and three in Liverpool Bay.

## NAVY FORTS

The Navy forts comprised a boat shaped reinforced concrete pontoon which carried two round towers topped by a steel deck housing armament and radar equipment. There was some initial concern in the Admiralty that the structures may become unstable due to the clay and soft shingle on the seabed of the Thames Estuary. To check this a study was made of ships which had sunk in that area and it was found that where vessels had sunk end-on to the tideway they had hardly been affected by scouring or subsidence. Accordingly the sea forts were similarly positioned so that their pontoons were lying with the tidal current.

The forts were largely prefabricated and were constructed and assembled in a specially converted dry dock basin at Gravesend by Holloway Brothers Ltd. The two towers of the forts each contained seven decks housing fuel, ammunition, water, generators and crew accommodation. The main deck had officers accommodation, while the Bofors Deck had fresh and sea water tanks as well as ventilation equipment and the main gun defences. The Control Room was fitted with telephones, radio and early radar equipment linked by landline to a shore-based HQ. At the front of each tower was a lattice steel mooring platform, known as a Dolphin, fitted with a crane used for loading supplies.

When each fort had been commissioned and equipped it was towed by tugs to its grounding position with a full compliment of crew aboard. When the forts were in position the hollow pontoons were gradually flooded with seawater until they sank to the seabed, in an operation taking less than half an hour. The first tow (Roughs Tower) started in January 1942 but due to bad weather had to be postponed until early February.

During the grounding of Tongue Sands Fort enemy aircraft were spotted approaching, the fort had to be crash dived, going into action immediately. This crash diving resulted in the fort having a slight list and it proved to be less stable than the other forts. For this reason it was considered unsuitable for use as a broadcasting base by the 60s offshore stations.

The four Navy forts were credited with shooting down 22 enemy aircraft, sinking one E boat, badly damaging another and destroying 20-30 V1 flying bombs. There were also numerous rescue missions mounted from the forts for pilots who had been forced to ditch in the North Sea.

The four Navy forts and their involvement in offshore radio were:-

**Roughs Tower** Never used for broadcasting purposes, but was the subject of fierce battles between rival offshore radio groups because it was the only one outside British territorial limits. It was finally taken over by Roy Bates and declared an independent Principality - Sealand - in 1967. Various plans were announced to develop and extend the Fort for leisure purposes but these came to nothing. The Territorial Sea Act 1987 finally brought Roughs Tower inside British territorial limits.

**Sunk Head** Used briefly by Radio Tower/Tower Radio this fort was demolished by Royal Marines in August 1967 to prevent its further use by any offshore radio station either as a broadcasting or supply base.

**Knock John** Used by Radio Essex and BBMS, but abandoned in favour of Roughs Tower by Roy Bates after a court ruling in 1966 that the fort was inside British territorial waters.

**Tongue Sands** The least stable of the Navy forts it was not used by any offshore broadcaster, although it was briefly considered by Roy Bates as a possible base for his planned second station, Radio Kent/Radio Albatross. The fort finally collapsed into the sea during a Force 11 gale on 22nd February 1996.

## ARMY FORTS

The Army forts were designed to conform as far as possible to the format of a shore based battery, with emphasis on anti-aircraft defence. Each fort, which consisted of seven separate towers linked by catwalks, had four heavy and two light guns with a central Control Room and a searchlight position. The Thames Estuary forts were also built by Holloway Brothers Ltd. at Gravesend while the Mersey Forts were built at Bromborough Docks.

The fort complex as a whole comprised a central control tower surrounded by five further gun towers and a searchlight tower to the rear. Each individual tower had a base of reinforced concrete supporting four pre-cast hollow concrete legs, braced by a steel frame. The superstructure on top of the legs consisted of an octagonal building with 6mm thick steel plated walls, containing three decks. Each tower carried its own supply of fresh and seawater, while the Bofors Gun tower and the searchlight tower carried fuel supplies. All fuel and water supply tanks were linked by a network of pipes along the interconnecting catwalks.

When built each tower was towed to its grounding position between two specially constructed barges and positioned on the sea-bed by pumping compressed air into the hollow legs. The first tower to be put in position was always the central Bofors Gun tower which could then protect the others as they were lowered The whole operation, including the installation of the inter-connecting catwalks took several days to complete.

The three Thames Estuary Army forts and their involvement with offshore radio were:-

**Great Nore** (code name U5). This was demolished in 1959 as it was considered too much of a hazard in the main shipping lanes following a collision involving a Swedish ship.

**Red Sands** (code name U6). Used by Radio Invicta, KING Radio and Radio 390. This was the only one of the Thames Estuary Army forts to remain intact.

**Shivering Sands** (code name U7). Used by Radio Sutch and Radio City. One of the towers was demolished as the result of a ship colliding with it I the early 1950, killing four men.

The Army forts in the Mersey Estuary were all demolished in the early 1950s as they were considered to be a danger to shipping.

# Bibliography

There have been a number of other books published covering the subject of offshore broadcasting. The following list contains the major works, some but not all of which were consulted for reference purposes during the preparation of this book. Although many are no longer in print these titles may be of general interest as further reading on the subject.

*Offshore Radio* - Gerry Bishop, Iceni Enterprises 1975

*Radio Caroline* - John Venmore Rowland, Landmark Press 1967

*When Pirates Ruled the Waves* - Paul Harris, Impulse Publications 1968

*Broadcasting from the High Seas* - Paul Harris, Paul Harris Publishing 1977

*To Be a Pirate King* - Paul Harris, Impulse Publications ,1971

*Pop Went the Pirates* - Keith Skues, Lambs Meadow Publications, 1994 (ISBN 0 907398 03 0)

*History of Radio Nord* - Jack Kotschack,Forlags AB, Stockholm 1963 and Impulse Publications 1970

*The Shoestring Pirates* - Adrian Blackburn, Hodder and Stoughton 1974 (ISBN 0 340 19510)

*The Lid off Laser* - Paul Rusling, Pirate Publications , 1984

*Last of the Pirates* - Bob Noakes, Paul Harris Publishing 1985 (ISBN 0 86228 0923)

*Butterfly Upon the Wheel* - Peter Moore, Offshore Echo's Magazine, 1992 (ISSN 0150 2794)

*De Veronica Sage* - Gerth van Zanten, Teleboek NV, 1968

*SOS - 10 Days in the Life of a Lady* - Simon Barrett, Paul Harris Publishing 1984

*Selling the Sixties* - Robert Chapman, Routledge 1992 (ISBN 0 415 07970 5)

In addition a number of magazines have provided invaluable contemporary reference sources, in particular:-

*Monitor Magazine*

*Offshore Echo's Magazine*

*Newscaster* (Free Radio Campaign)

*Wavelength* (Music Radio Promotions)

*Script* (Music Radio Promotions)

*C M Bulletin* (Caroline Movement)

*Caroline Newsbeat* (Radio Caroline)

# Index

## D



## E



## F

## L



## M



## N

## S

## T



## U



## V